YOUNG ADULT FICTION CORE COLLECTION

CORE COLLECTION SERIES

FORMERLY
STANDARD CATALOG SERIES

MARIA HUGGER, GENERAL EDITOR

CHILDREN'S CORE COLLECTION
MIDDLE AND JUNIOR HIGH CORE COLLECTION
SENIOR HIGH CORE COLLECTION
PUBLIC LIBRARY CORE COLLECTION: NONFICTION
FICTION CORE COLLECTION
GRAPHIC NOVELS CORE COLLECTION

YOUNG ADULT FICTION CORE COLLECTION

EDITED BY

JULIE CORSARO

KENDAL SPIRES

GABRIELA TOTH

AND

CHRISTI SHOWMAN FARRAR

H. W. Wilson
A Division of EBSCO Information Services, Inc.
Ipswich, Massachusetts
2015

GREY HOUSE PUBLISHING

Cover: Three Boys on Bikes (© raymenie, iStock).

ISBN 978-1-6192-5866-2

Young Adult Fiction Core Collection, 2015, published by Grey House Publishing, Inc., Amenia, NY, under exclusive license from EBSCO Information Services, Inc.

Publisher's Cataloging-In-Publication Data
(Prepared by The Donohue Group, Inc.)

Young adult fiction core collection / edited by Julie Corsaro [and 3 others]. -- [First edition].

pages ; cm. -- (Core collection series)

Edition statement supplied by publisher.
Includes indexes.
ISBN: 978-1-61925-866-2 (hardcover)

1. Young adult fiction--Bibliography. 2. Young adults--Books and reading--United States. 3. Best books. I. Corsaro, Julie. II. Series: Core collection series.

Z1037.A1 Y68 2015
011.62/5

CONTENTS

PREFACE

YOUNG ADULT FICTION CORE COLLECTION, available in print only, is a selected list of fiction books recommended for young adults, excerpted from the Middle & Junior High and Senior High Core Collections available from Grey House Publishing. Core Collections databases are also available via EBSCOhost and updated weekly.

What's in this Edition?

A star (★) at the start of an entry indicates that a book is a "most highly recommended" title. These titles constitute a short list of the essential books in a given category or on a given subject. There are often a number of recommended titles on a single subject, such as Science Fiction, and the Short List designation helps a user who wants only one or two. Other titles included represent "core collection" titles, a longer list of core books.

Scope

All books listed are published in the United States, or published in Canada or the United Kingdom and distributed in the United States.

The Core Collection excludes non-English-language materials, with the exception of bilingual titles.

This collection also excludes most works widely known as "classic literature." This was done as an effort to both save space and to concentrate on recommending titles that are perhaps less well-known. Additionally, extensive conversations with high school librarians indicated that additions of classics to the collection were primarily based on local curricula, not on recommendations from the Core Collection. While some classics remain in the collection, the removed titles can still be found on EBSCO*host*.

Preparation

Books included in this edition were selected by experienced librarians representing public library systems and senior high libraries across the United States who also act as a committee of advisors on library policy and trends. The names of participating librarians and their affiliations are listed in the Acknowledgments.

Organization

The Core Collection is organized into two parts: the List of Fictional Works; and an Author, Title, and Subject Index.

Part 1. List of Fictional Works. This is arranged alphabetically by author, with complete bibliographical and cataloging information given for each book. This arrangement, along with the descriptive and critical annotations, provides a useful guide to book selection. Entries include such information as price and ISBN to facilitate acquisitions.

Part 2. Author, Title, and Subject Index. This is a comprehensive key to the List of Fictional Works with entries for authors, titles, and subjects.

ACKNOWLEDGMENTS

H. W. Wilson and EBSCO Information Services express special gratitude to the following librarians who both advised the company in editorial matters and assisted in the selection and weeding of titles for this Core Collection:

Advisory Board

James Bobick
Library Consultant
Pittsburgh, Pennsylvania

Angela Carstensen
Covenant of the Sacred Heart
New York, New York

Betty Carter
Library Consultant
Coppell, Texas

Gail de Vos
SLIS University of Alberta
Edmonton, Alberta, Canada

Laura Harrington
North Andover High School
North Andover, Massachusetts

Pam Spencer Holley
Library Consultant
Hallwood, Virginia

Steven Jablonski
Skokie Public Library
Skokie, Illinois

Joquetta Johnson
Randallstown High School
Randallstown, MD

Mary Rasner
Library Consultant
Melrose, Massachusetts

Angela Leeper
University of Richmond
Richmond, Virginia

John Meier
Penn State University
University Park, Pennsylvania

John Peters
Children's Literature Specialist
Bronx, New York

Heather Campbell Shock
West Virginia Library Commission
Charleston, West Virginia

Linda Ward-Callaghan
Joliet Public Library
Joliet, Illinois

DIRECTIONS FOR USE OF THE CORE COLLECTION

USES OF THE COLLECTION

YOUNG ADULT FICTION CORE COLLECTION is designed to serve a number of purposes:

As an aid in purchasing. The Core Collection is designed to assist in the selection and ordering of titles. Annotations are provided for each title along with information concerning the publisher, ISBN, price, and availability. In evaluating the suitability of a work each library will want to consider the special character of the school and/or community it serves.

As an aid to the reader's advisor. The work of the reader's advisor is furthered by the information about sequels and companion volumes and the descriptive and critical annotations in the List of Fictional Works, and by the subject access in the Index.

As an aid in verification of information. For this purpose, full bibliographical data are provided in the List of Fictional Works. Entries also include recommended subject headings based upon *Sears List of Subject Headings*. Notes describe editions available, awards, publication history, and other titles in the series.

As an aid in curriculum support. Subject indexing, grade levels, and annotations are helpful in identifying materials appropriate for lesson planning and classroom use.

As an aid in collection maintenance. Information about titles available on a subject facilitates decisions to rebind, replace, or discard items. If a book has been deleted from the Core Collection in this edition because it is no longer in print, that deletion is not intended as a sign that the book is no longer valuable or that it should necessarily be weeded from the collection.

As an instructional aid. The Core Collection is useful in courses that deal with literature and book selection for young adults.

ORGANIZATION

The Core Collection consists of two parts: a List of Fictional Works, and an Author, Title, and Subject Index.

Part 1. List of Fictional Works

The List of Fictional Works is arranged alphabetically by author. The information supplied for each book includes bibliographic description, suggested subject headings, an annotation, and frequently, an evaluation from a notable source.

Each listing consists of a full bibliographical description. Prices, which are always subject to change, have been obtained from the publisher, when available, and are as current as possible. Entries include recommended subject headings derived from the *Sears List of Subject Headings*, a brief description of the contents, and, whenever possible, an evaluation from a quoted source. The following is an example of a typical entry and a description of its components:

Chbosky, Stephen

★ The **perks** of being a wallflower; [by] Stephen Chbosky. Pocket Bks. 1999 213p pa $14

Grades: 9 10 11 12 **Fic**

1. School stories 2. Letters -- Fiction 3. Young men -- Social life and customs -- 20th century

ISBN 0-671-02734-4

LC 99-236288

This novel in letter form is narrated by Charlie, a high school freshman. "His favorite aunt passed away, and his best friend just committed suicide. The girl he loves wants him as a friend; a girl he does not love wants him as a lover. His 18-year-old sister is pregnant. The LSD he took is not sitting well. And he has a math quiz looming. . . . Young adult." (Time)

"Charlie, his friends, and family are palpably real. . . .This report on his life will engage teen readers for years to come." SLJ

The star at the start of the entry indicates this is a "most highly recommended" title. The name of the author, Stephen Chbosky, is given in conformity with *Anglo-American Cataloguing Rules*, 2nd edition, 2002 revision. The title of the book is *The perks of being a wallflower*. The book was published by Pocket Books in 1999.

The book has 213 pages and does not contain illustrations. It is published in paperback, and sells for $14.00. (Prices given were current when the Collection went to press.) The book is recommended for any of the following grade levels: 9 10 11 12.

At the end of the last line of type in the body entry is **Fic** in boldface type. The notation "Fic" implies that the book is a work of fiction.

The numbered terms "1. School stories 2. Letters -- Fiction 3. Young men -- Social life and customs -- 20th century" are recommended subject headings for this book based on *Sears List of Subject Headings*.

The ISBN (International Standard Book Number) is included to facilitate ordering. The Library of Congress control number is provided when available.

Following are three notes supplying additional information about the book. The first is a description of the book's content, in this case, an excerpt from *Time* magazine. The second is a critical note from *School Library Journal*. Such annotations are useful in evaluating books for selection and in determining which of several books on the same subject is best suited for the individual reader. The final note describes special features, such as a bibliography, if applicable. Notes are also made to describe sequels and companion volumes, editions available, awards, and publication history.

Part 2. Author, Title, and Subject Index

The Index is a single alphabetical list of all the books entered in the Core Collection. Each book is entered under author; title (if distinctive); and subject. Appropriate added entries are made for joint authors and editors. "See" references are made from forms of names or subjects that are not used as headings. "See also" references are made to related or more specific headings.

The following are examples of Index entries for the book cited above:

Author	**Chbosky, Stephen** The perks of being a wallflower
Title	The **perks** of being a wallflower. Chbosky, S.

Subject   **LETTERS -- FICTION**
Chbosky, S.   The perks of being a wallflower

Standards Used

Anglo-American Cataloguing Rules, 2nd ed., 2002 revision, 2005 update. Chicago: American Library Association, 2005.

Bristow, Barbara A. and Christi Showman Farrar, eds. *Sears List of Subject Headings.* 21st ed. Ipswich, MA: The H. W. Wilson Company, 2014.

Dewey, Melvil. *Abridged Dewey Decimal Classification and Relative Index.* 15th ed. Edited by Joan S. Mitchell, et al. Dublin, Ohio: OCLC, 2012.

YOUNG ADULT FICTION CORE COLLECTION

FIRST EDITION

50 Cent (Musician), 1975-

Playground; with Aura Moser. Razorbill 2011 314p $17.99

Grades: 7 8 9 10 **Fic**

1. Bullies -- Fiction

ISBN 978-1-59514-434-8; 1-59514-434-X

Thirteen-year-old Butterball doesn't have much going for him. He's teased about his weight. He hates the Long Island suburb his mom moved them to so she could go to nursing school and start her life over. He wishes he still lived with his dad in New York City where there's always something happening, even if his dad doesn't have much time for him. Still, that's not why he beat up Maurice on the playground.

"Readers who were ever confused about having a gay parent, or being overweight, or going through a parental breakup, or just wanting to fit in and be accepted by their peers, will relate to Butterball. 50 Cents's debut young adult novel is a quick read that will be great for discussions on a variety of important and timely topics." Voice Youth Advocates

Abbott, Ellen Jensen

Watersmeet. Marshall Cavendish 2009 341p il $16.99

Grades: 6 7 8 9 10 **Fic**

1. Fantasy fiction

ISBN 978-0-7614-5536-3; 0-7614-5536-1

LC 2008-315

Fourteen-year-old Absina escapes the escalating violence, prejudice, and religious fervor of her home town, Vranille, and sets out with a dwarf, Haret, to seek the father she has never met in a place called Watersmeet.

"The relationship between Abisina and Haret is warm and engaging, and the dialogue between them cleverly captures the slow development of their camaraderie. . . . Fans of Ursula Le Guin's character-driven fantasies will enjoy this story of Abisina's quest to unify both her divided country and her divided self." Bull Cent Child Books

Abdel-Fattah, Randa

★ **Does** my head look big in this? Orchard Books 2007 360p $16.99

Grades: 7 8 9 10 11 12 **Fic**

1. School stories 2. Muslims -- Fiction 3. Australia -- Fiction 4. Clothing and dress -- Fiction

ISBN 0-439-91947-9; 978-0-439-91947-0

LC 2006-29117

Year Eleven at an exclusive prep school in the suburbs of Melbourne, Australia, would be tough enough, but it is further complicated for Amal when she decides to wear the hijab, the Muslim head scarf, full-time as a badge of her faith—without losing her identity or sense of style. "Grades seven to ten." (Bull Cent Child Books)

"While the novel deals with a number of serious issues, it is extremely funny and entertaining." SLJ

★ **Ten** things I hate about me. Orchard Books 2009 297p $16.99

Grades: 7 8 9 10 **Fic**

1. School stories 2. Muslims -- Fiction 3. Lebanese -- Fiction 4. Australia -- Fiction 5. Prejudices -- Fiction

ISBN 978-0-5450-5055-5; 0-5450-5055-3

LC 2008-13667

This novel is set in Australia. Jamilia, known in school as Jamie, tries to hide her Muslim heritage from her classmates, until her conflicted feelings become too difficult for her to bear. "Grades six to nine." (Bull Cent Child Books)

A "message of the importance of self-disclosure to maintain loving relationships of all kinds plays itself out as Jamie learns to negotiate her roles as daughter, sister, and friend. Readers will also get an enlightening look at post-9/11 racial tensions outside the U.S. and the problems they pose for Muslim teens." Bull Cent Child Books

Abrahams, Peter

★ **Bullet** point. HarperTeen 2010 294p $16.99

Grades: 9 10 11 12 **Fic**

1. Prisoners -- Fiction 2. Criminal investigation -- Fiction 3. Father-son relationship -- Fiction

ISBN 978-0-06-122769-1; 0-06-122769-2

LC 2009-25440

The only thing seventeen-year-old Wyatt knew about his biological father was that he was serving a life sentence, but circumstances and a new girlfriend bring them together, and soon Wyatt is working to prove his father's innocence.

"Edgier and sexier than most YA novels dare, Abrahams' thriller wrenches guts with a Richard Price-like facility. Readers will be as irretrievably drawn in as Wyatt." Booklist

Reality check. HarperTeen 2009 330p $16.99; lib bdg $17.89; pa $8.99

Grades: 7 8 9 10 **Fic**

1. School stories 2. Gambling -- Fiction 3. Social classes -- Fiction 4. Missing persons -- Fiction

ISBN 978-0-06-122766-0; 0-06-122766-8; 978-0-06-122767-7 lib bdg; 0-06-122767-6 lib bdg; 978-0-06-122768-4 pa; 0-06-122768-4 pa

LC 2008-22593

After a knee injury destroys sixteen-year-old Cody's college hopes, he drops out of high school and gets a job in his small Montana town, but when his ex-girlfriend disappears from her Vermont boarding school, Cody travels cross-country to join the search.

"Abrahams writes a fine thriller that is pitched to attract everyone from reluctant readers to sports fans to romantic idealists." Voice Youth Advocates

Abrams, Amir

Hollywood High. Dafina KTeen Books 2012 310 p. (prebind) $20.80; (paperback) $9.95

Grades: 9 10 11 12 **Fic**

1. School stories 2. Teenage pregnancy -- Fiction
ISBN 0606263780; 0758263171; 9780606263788; 9780758263179

LC 2012418660

This book is told by four high school narrators, all spoiled daughters of entertainment industry elites, "including ex-New Yorker London, tabloid queen Rich and . . . Spencer. Heather . . . supports her alcoholic mother with her own acting career and struggles with an Adderall addiction. Drama escalates practically within milliseconds. . . . Much of the drama involves competition over boys." (Kirkus)

Acampora, Paul

Defining Dulcie. Dial Books 2006 168p hardcover o.p. pa $6.99

Grades: 7 8 9 10 **Fic**

1. Bereavement -- Fiction 2. Runaway teenagers -- Fiction
ISBN 0-8037-3046-2; 978-0-8037-3046-5; 0-14-241183-3 pa; 978-0-14-241183-4 pa

LC 2005-16186

When sixteen-year-old Dulcie's father dies, her mother makes a decision to move them to California, where Dulcie makes an equally radical decision to steal her dad's old truck and head back home.

"Strong and quirky characters who see life as an inextricable mix of sadness and humor, sorrow and hope, are the hallmark of this memorable first novel." SLJ

Ackley, Amy

Sign language; a novel. Viking 2011 392p $16.99

Grades: 7 8 9 10 **Fic**

1. School stories 2. Death -- Fiction 3. Fathers -- Fiction 4. Bereavement -- Fiction 5. Family life -- Fiction
ISBN 978-0-670-01318-0; 0-670-01318-8

LC 2011003001

Teenaged Abby must deal with her feelings about her father's cancer and its aftermath while simultaneously navigating the difficult problems of growing up.

"This is an amazing debut novel for readers who appreciate contemporary teen fiction. It is both moving and realistic, a result of the well-crafted family relationships. The author succeeds in creating genuine connections that manage not to feel forced or rushed, despite the pace of the story, which spans three years." Voice Youth Advocates

Acosta, Marta

Dark companion; Marta Acosta. Tom Doherty Assoc. 2012 364 p. (hardcover) $17.99

Grades: 9 10 11 12 **Fic**

1. School stories 2. Orphans -- Fiction 3. Supernatural -- Fiction 4. Private schools -- Fiction 5. Schools -- Fiction 6. Boarding schools -- Fiction
ISBN 0765329646; 9780765329646; 9781429988292

LC 2012011656

This book tells the story of Jane Williams. "Orphaned at the age of six, [she] has grown up in a series of foster homes, learning to survive in the shadows of life. . . . [S]he manages to win a scholarship to the exclusive Birch Grove Academy. There, for the first time, Jane finds herself accepted by a group of friends. She even starts tutoring the headmistress's gorgeous son, Lucien." But, the "more she learns about Birch Grove's recent past, the more Jane comes to suspect that there is something sinister going on. . . . As Jane begins to piece together the answers to the puzzle, she must find out why she was brought to Birch Grove—and what she would risk to stay there." (Publisher's note)

Ada, Alma Flor, 1938-

Yes! we are Latinos; by Alma Flor Ada and F. Isabel Campoy; illustrated by David Diaz. Charlesbridge 2013 96 p. ill. (reinforced) $18.95

Grades: 7 8 9 10 **Fic**

1. Hispanic Americans -- Fiction 2. American poetry -- Latino authors 3. Short stories 4. Immigrants -- Fiction 5. Emigration and immigration -- Fiction 6. Latin Americans -- United States -- Fiction
ISBN 158089383X; 9781580893831

LC 2012027214

In this book, the authors "shape fictional portraits of 13 young people living in the U.S., who have diverse experiences and backgrounds but share a Latino heritage. The first-person narrative poems range from reflective to free-spirited, methodical to free-association. . . . Informative nonfictional interludes . . . address relevant subjects, including immigration, the challenges migrant workers face, and Cuba-U.S. history." (Publishers Weekly)

Includes bibliographical references and index

Adams, Richard

Watership Down; Scribner classics ed.; Scribner 1996 429p $30; pa $15

Grades: 6 7 8 9 10 **Fic**

1. Allegories 2. Rabbits -- Fiction
ISBN 0-684-83605-X; 0-7432-7770-8 pa

First published 1972 in the United Kingdom; first United States edition 1974 by Macmillan

"Faced with the annihilation of its warren, a small group of male rabbits sets out across the English downs in search of a new home. Internal struggles for power surface in this intricately woven, realistically told adult adventure when the protagonists must coordinate tactics in order to defeat an enemy rabbit fortress. It is clear that the author has done research on rabbit behavior, for this tale is truly authentic." Shapiro Fic for Youth. 3d edition

Adler, Emily

Sweet 15; by Emily Adler and Alex Echevarria. Marshall Cavendish 2009 240p $16.99

Grades: 7 8 9 10 **Fic**

1. School stories 2. Family life -- Fiction 3. Puerto

Ricans -- Fiction 4. Quinceañera (Social custom) -- Fiction
ISBN 978-0-7614-5584-4; 0-7614-5584-1
LC 2008-21391

Shortly before her fifteenth birthday, Destiny Lozada's traditional Puerto Rican mother and feminist older sister hijack her quinceanera, each pushing her own agenda and ignoring the possibility that Destiny, a skateboarding tomboy, might have her own ideas about the coming-of-age ritual she is about to participate in.

"Destiny's resolution, the engaging dialogue, boys, gossip, best friends, fashion, texting, the first kiss and the city of New York all play a part in this charming, fresh and funny coming-of-age novel that will entertain teen readers, especially girls." Kirkus

Adlington, L. J.

Cherry Heaven. Greenwillow Books 2008 458p $16.99; lib bdg $17.89
Grades: 7 8 9 10 **Fic**
1. Science fiction 2. Orphans -- Fiction
ISBN 978-0-06-143180-7; 0-06-143180-X; 978-0-06-143181-4 lib bdg; 0-06-143181-8 lib bdg
LC 2007-24679

Kat and Tanka J leave the wartorn city, move with their adoptive parents to the New Frontier, and are soon settled into a home called Cherry Heaven, but Luka, an escaped factory worker, confirms their suspicion that New Frontier is not the utopia it seems to be.

"In this complex, absorbing, and sometimes disquieting novel, Adlington creates a world that is distinctly different from our own, yet chillingly familiar." Booklist

★ The **diary** of Pelly D. Greenwillow Books 2005 282p hardcover o.p. pa $8.99
Grades: 7 8 9 10 **Fic**
1. Science fiction
ISBN 0-06-076615-8; 0-06-076617-4 pa
LC 2004-52258

"On the planet Home From Home, Toni V is a brute laborer, a barely educated member of the Demolition Crew that is busy pulverizing the bombed-out remains of City Five's central plaza. Pelly D is a hip member of the swank elite who used to live in an exclusive apartment fronting the plaza. Their stories come together when Toni V uncovers Pelly D's diary in the debris. . . . Middle school, high school." (Horn Book)

"Adlington has crafted an original and disturbing dystopian fantasy told in a smart and sympathetic teen voice." Booklist

Agard, John

The **young** inferno; written by John Agard; illustrated by Satoshi Kitamura. Frances Lincoln Children's 2009 un il $19.95
Grades: 8 9 10 11 12 **Fic**
1. Novels in verse 2. Hell -- Fiction
ISBN 978-1-84507-769-3; 1-84507-769-5

"The narrative poems in this short book are accessible and have important things to say about the state of the human race. . . . The hoodie-wearing protagonist . . . awakens in a strange and frightening forest. A dark man appears and introduces himself as the tale-teller Aesop: he is to be the teen's escort through Hell. . . . As the pair travels through the Circles of Hell, they see the sins of mankind. . . . The scribbled, heavy-lined black ink and watercolor illustrations convey exactly the right mood for a book about a modern-day expedition into Hell. This will be a great book to pair with a discussion about Dante's Inferno and/or poetic structure." SLJ

Agell, Charlotte

Shift. Henry Holt and Co. 2008 230p $16.95
Grades: 7 8 9 10 **Fic**
1. Science fiction 2. Religion -- Fiction 3. Family life -- Fiction 4. Resistance to government -- Fiction 5. Environmental degradation -- Fiction
ISBN 978-0-8050-7810-7; 0-8050-7810-X
LC 2007-46942

In fifteen-year-old Adrian Havoc's world, HomeState rules every aspect of society and religious education is enforced but Adrian, refusing to believe that the Apocalypse is at hand, goes north through the Deadlands and joins a group of insurgents.

"The story is made particularly compelling by the economy and lyricism of the writing style. . . . Readers seeking contemplative and philosophical science fiction will find this a haunting exploration of government gone awry and one boy's steadfast pursuit of justice." Bull Cent Child Books

Aguirre, Ann

Enclave. Feiwel & Friends 2011 262p $16.99
Grades: 8 9 10 **Fic**
1. Horror fiction 2. Fantasy fiction 3. Dystopian fiction 4. Apocalyptic fiction 5. Zombies -- Fiction
ISBN 978-0-312-65008-7; 0-312-65008-6
LC 2010031039

In a post-apocalyptic future, fifteen-year-old Deuce, a loyal Huntress, brings back meat while avoiding the Freaks outside her enclave, but when she is partnered with the mysterious outsider, Fade, she begins to see that the strict ways of the elders may be wrong—and dangerous. "Grades six to eight." (Bull Cent Child Books)

"In this skilled though violent postapocalyptic thriller, Deuce has newly earned the rank of Huntress. . . . It's her duty to provide meat for her loveless, draconian enclave, deep beneath the streets of a ruined city, as well as to defend it against cannibalistic Freaks, who are gradually eliminating the scattered human survivors of a vaguely remembered plague. . . . Aguirre . . . has created a gritty and highly competent heroine, an equally deadly sidekick/love interest, and a fascinating if unpleasant civilization." Publ Wkly

Horde; by Ann Aguirre. Feiwel & Friends 2013 422 p. $17.99
Grades: 8 9 10 **Fic**
1. Science fiction 2. Dystopian fiction 3. Monsters -- Fiction
ISBN 1250024633; 9781250024633

This book, by Ann Aguirre, is the conclusion to the Enclave trilogy. "Salvation is surrounded, monsters at the gates, and this time, they're not going away. When Deuce, Fade, Stalker and Tegan set out, the odds are against them. But the odds have been stacked against Deuce from the moment she was born. She might not be a Huntress anymore, but she doesn't run. With her knives in hand and her companions at her side, she will not falter, whether fighting for her life or Fade's love." (Publisher's note)

"Deuce's skills from her Huntress days come in handy when a horde of mutant "Freaks" descends upon the humans of her post-apocalyptic world, but trusting some of the enemy turns out to be a worthwhile risk. Relationships, including Deuce's romance with Fade, soften a bloody tale; as in previous compelling installments, readers should suspend disbelief for Deuce's background-belying vocabulary and emotional intelligence." (Horn Book)

Outpost; by Ann Aguirre. Feiwel & Friends 2012 320 p. $17.99
Grades: 8 9 10 **Fic**

1. Monsters -- Fiction 2. Teenagers -- Fiction 3. Survival skills -- Fiction 4. Science fiction 5. Survival -- Fiction 6. Teenage girls -- Fiction
ISBN 0312650094; 9780312650094
LC 2011287957

In this book by Ann Aguirre "months have passed since Deuce and her band of survivors joined Salvation, a fortified settlement in the middle of Freak-infested land. While Tegan, Fade, and Stalker find helpful community roles, Deuce struggles to adjust to life where, as a female, she is forbidden from fighting. When the Freaks evolve into more cunning foes, however, Deuce's superior combat skills are instrumental in establishing an outpost to protect the town." (Booklist)

"When this follow-up to Enclave (2011) begins, trained Huntress Deuce and fellow travelers Fade, Stalker and Tegan have lived two months amid the town of Salvation's affluence, strict gender roles and relative freedom from the putrid, slavering, mindless Freaks who plague their world... Overall, an engaging world and forward-moving plot with a resolution that promises new settings and challenges in Book 3." (Kirkus)

Alban, Andrea

Anya's war. Feiwel and Friends 2011 188p $16.99
Grades: 7 8 9 10 **Fic**

1. Jews -- China -- Fiction 2. Jewish refugees -- Fiction 3. Abandoned children -- Fiction 4. Sino-Japanese Conflict, 1937-1945 -- Fiction
ISBN 978-0-312-37093-0; 0-312-37093-8
LC 2010-37089

In 1937, the privileged and relatively carefee life of a fourteen-year-old Jewish girl, whose family emigrated from Odessa, Ukraine, to Shanghai, China, comes to an end when she finds an abandoned baby, her hero, Amelia Earhart, goes missing, and war breaks out with Japan. Based on the author's family history.

"Most moving are the scenes with the full cast of family characters, who are irritating, irritable, funny, surprising, mean, and prejudiced. Alban also explores the complexities of Anya's Jewish community. . . . An important addition to literature about WWII refugees." Booklist

Albin, Gennifer

Crewel; Gennifer Albin. by Gennifer Albin. Farrar Straus Giroux 2012 368 p. (hardcover) $17.99
Grades: 8 9 10 11 **Fic**

1. Spiritual gifts 2. Secrecy -- Fiction 3. Psychics -- Fiction 4. Science fiction
ISBN 0374316414; 9780374316419; 9780374316440
LC 2011043930

In author Gennifer Albin's book, "sixteen year-old Adelice Lewys has a secret: she wants to fail. Gifted with the ability to weave time with matter, she's exactly what the Guild is looking for, and in the world of Arras, being chosen as a Spinster is everything a girl could want. . . . It also means the power to embroider the very fabric of life . . . [and] Adelice isn't interested. Not that her feelings matter, because she slipped and wove a moment at testing, and they're coming for her--tonight. Now she has one hour . . . to escape." (genniferalbin.com)

Alegria, Malin

Estrella's quinceanera. Simon & Schuster Books for Young Readers 2006 272p $14.95
Grades: 7 8 9 10 **Fic**

1. Mexican Americans -- Fiction 2. Quinceañera (Social custom) -- Fiction
ISBN 0-689-87809-5

Estrella's mother and aunt are planning a gaudy, traditional quinceañera for her, even though it is the last thing she wants.

"Alegria writes about Mexican American culture, first love, family, and of moving between worlds with poignant, sharp-sighted humor and authentic dialogue." Booklist

Alender, Katie

Bad girls don't die. Hyperion Books 2009 352p $15.99
Grades: 7 8 9 10 **Fic**

1. School stories 2. Sisters -- Fiction 3. Demoniac possession -- Fiction
ISBN 978-1-4231-0876-4; 1-4231-0876-0
LC 2008-46179

When fifteen-year-old Lexi's younger sister Kasey begins behaving strangely and their old Victorian house seems to take on a life of its own, Lexi investigates and discovers some frightening facts about previous occupants of the house, leading her to believe that many lives are in danger.

This "novel is both a mystery and a trip into the paranormal. . . . With just enough violence, suspense, and romance to keep readers turning pages, this . . . will be a popular addition to any YA collection." Booklist

Followed by: From bad to cursed (2011)

Alexander, Jill S.

Paradise. Feiwel and Friends 2011 246p $16.99
Grades: 7 8 9 10 **Fic**

1. Love stories 2. Drums -- Fiction 3. Family life -- Fiction 4. Bands (Music) -- Fiction 5. Country music -- Fiction
ISBN 0312605412; 9780312605414
LC 2010050900

Teenaged Paisley Tillery dreams a career as a professional drummer will take her out of her small Texas town, but when her country rock band gets a handsome new lead singer from Paradise, Texas, those dreams may change.

"Strong, rural Southern storytelling and mother-daughter conflict are integral parts of the plot. . . . Alexander's simmering plot is . . . driven by a complex story and multiple, complex characters." SLJ

The **sweetheart** of Prosper County. Feiwel and Friends 2009 212p $16.99

Grades: 7 8 9 10 **Fic**

1. Texas -- Fiction 2. Bullies -- Fiction 3. Bereavement -- Fiction 4. Mother-daughter relationship -- Fiction

ISBN 978-0-312-54856-8; 0-312-54856-7

LC 2008-34757

In a small East Texas town largely ruled by prejudices and bullies, fourteen-year-old Austin sets out to win a ride in the next parade and, in the process, grows in her understanding of friendship and helps her widowed mother through her mourning.

"This is a warm, humorous story. . . . A refreshing picture of teen angst, with realistic dialogue and memorable characters." SLJ

Alexander, Kwame

★ The **crossover**; a basketball novel. by Kwame Alexander. Houghton Mifflin Harcourt 2014 240 p. $16.99

Grades: 7 8 9 10 11 12 **Fic**

1. Rap music 2. Novels in verse 3. Twins -- Fiction 4. Brothers -- Fiction 5. Basketball -- Fiction 6. Fathers and sons -- Fiction 7. African Americans -- Fiction

ISBN 0544107713; 9780544107717

LC 2013013810

In this novel, by Kwame Alexander, "12-year old Josh Bell . . . and his twin brother Jordan are awesome on the court. But Josh has more than basketball in his blood, he's got mad beats, too, that tell his family's story in verse. . . . Josh and Jordan must come to grips with growing up on and off the court to realize breaking the rules comes at a terrible price, as their story's . . . climax proves a game-changer for the entire family." (Publisher's note)

"Twins Josh and Jordan are junior high basketball stars, thanks in large part to the coaching of their dad, a former professional baller who was forced to quit playing for health reasons, and the firm, but loving support of their assistant-principal mom...Despite his immaturity, Josh is a likable, funny, and authentic character. Underscoring the sports and the fraternal tension is a portrait of a family that truly loves and supports one another. Alexander has crafted a story that vibrates with energy and heart and begs to be read aloud. A slam dunk." (School Library Journal)

He said, she said; by Kwame Alexander. Harper, an imprint of HarperCollinsPublishers 2013 336 p. (hardcover bdg.) $17.99

Grades: 9 10 11 12 **Fic**

1. High school students -- Fiction 2. Man-woman relationship -- Fiction 3. Love -- Fiction 4. Schools -- Fiction 5. High schools -- Fiction 6. African Americans -- Fiction 7. Protest movements -- Fiction

ISBN 006211896X; 9780062118967; 9780062118974

LC 2012043496

"Claudia Clarke--sharp, opinionated, and Harvard-bound--is the only girl who isn't impressed by quarterback Omar "T-Diddy" Smalls. Omar takes a bet that he can win Claudia over, and when his usual seduction tactics fail, he applies his social clout to Claudia's cause du jour. His burgeoning social awareness and transformation from carefree jock to true campus leader are satisfying and convincing." (Horn Book)

Alexie, Sherman, 1966-

★ The **absolutely** true diary of a part-time Indian; art by Ellen Forney. Little, Brown 2007 229p il $18.99

Grades: 8 9 10 **Fic**

1. School stories 2. Friendship -- Fiction 3. Family life -- Fiction 4. Native Americans -- Fiction

ISBN 0316013684; 9780316013680

LC 2007-22799

National Book Award for Young People's Literature (2007)

Boston Globe-Horn Book Award: Fiction and Poetry (2008)

Budding cartoonist Junior leaves his troubled school on the Spokane Indian Reservation to attend an all-white farm town school where the only other Indian is the school mascot. "Grades seven to ten." (Bull Cent Child Books)

"The many characters, on and off the rez, with whom he has dealings are portrayed with compassion and verve. . . . Forney's simple pencil cartoons fit perfectly within the story and reflect the burgeoning artist within Junior." Booklist

Almond, David, 1951-

★ **Clay**. Delacorte Press 2006 247p hardcover o.p. pa $8.99

Grades: 7 8 9 10 **Fic**

1. Horror fiction 2. Supernatural -- Fiction

ISBN 0-385-73171-X; 0-440-42013-X pa

LC 2005-22681

The developing relationship between teenager Davie and a mysterious new boy in town morphs into something darker and more sinister when Davie learns firsthand of the boy's supernatural powers.

"Rooted in the ordinariness of a community and in one boy's chance to play God, this story will grab readers with its gripping action and its important ideas." Booklist

★ The **fire-**eaters. Delacorte Press 2004 218p $15.95

Grades: 7 8 9 10 **Fic**

1. Great Britain -- Fiction

ISBN 0-385-73170-1

LC 2003-55709

First published 2003 in the United Kingdom

In 1962 England, despite observing his father's illness and the suffering of the fire-eating Mr. McNulty, as well as enduring abuse at school and the stress of the Cuban Missile Crisis, Bobby Burns and his family and friends still find reasons to rejoice in their lives and to have hope for the future.

"The author's trademark themes . . . are here in full, and resonate long after the last page is turned." SLJ

★ **Kit's** wilderness; 10th-anniversary edition; Delacorte Press 2009 229p $16.99
Grades: 6 7 8 9 10 **Fic**

1. Ghost stories 2. Great Britain -- Fiction 3. Coal mines and mining -- Fiction
ISBN 978-0-385-32665-0; 0-385-32665-3
First published 1999
Michael L. Printz Award, 2001

Thirteen-year-old Kit goes to live with his grandfather in the decaying coal mining town of Stoneygate, England, and finds both the old man and the town haunted by ghosts of the past

The author "explores the power of friendship and family, the importance of memory, and the role of magic in our lives. This is a highly satisfying literary experience." SLJ

★ **Raven** summer. Delacorte Press 2009 198p $19.99
Grades: 7 8 9 10 11 12 **Fic**

1. Orphans -- Fiction 2. Great Britain -- Fiction 3. Fate and fatalism -- Fiction
ISBN 978-0-385-73806-4; 0-385-73806-4
LC 2009-1661

Led to an abandoned baby by a raven, fourteen-year-old Liam seems fated to meet two foster children who have experienced the world's violence in very different ways as he struggles to understand war, family problems, and friends who grow apart.

"The tension builds to a shocking and totally believable ending. . . . A haunting story, perfect for group discussion." Booklist

★ **Skellig**; 10th anniversary ed.; Delacorte Press 2009 182p $16.99; pa $6.99
Grades: 5 6 7 8 9 10 **Fic**

1. Fantasy fiction
ISBN 978-0-385-32653-7; 0-385-32653-X; 978-0-440-41602-9 pa; 0-440-41602-7 pa
First published 1998 in the United Kingdom; first United States edition 1999
Michael L. Printz Award honor book

Unhappy about his baby sister's illness and the chaos of moving into a dilapidated old house, Michael retreats to the garage and finds a mysterious stranger who is something like a bird and something like an angel.

"The plot is beautifully paced and the characters are drawn with a graceful, careful hand. . . . A lovingly done, thought-provoking novel." SLJ

The **true** tale of the monster Billy Dean; David Almond. Viking 2011 255 p. $17.99
Grades: 9 10 11 12 **Fic**

1. Dystopian fiction 2. Children and war -- Fiction 3. Parent-child relationship -- Fiction
ISBN 0763663093; 9780763663094
LC 2012358384

This novel, by David Almond, is "about a hidden-away child who emerges into a broken world. Billy Dean is a secret child. . . . His father fills his mind and his dreams with mysterious tales and memories and dreadful warnings. But then his father disappears, and Billy's mother brings him out into the world at last. He learns the horrifying story of what was saved and what was destroyed on the day he was born, the day the bombers came to Blinkbonny." (Publisher's note)

"The opening scenes of this postapocalyptic, psychological novel describing the protagonist's confinement in a small, locked room is strongly reminiscent of Emma Donoghue's adult title Room (Little, Brown, 2010). Billy Dean's mother was seduced by an unethical priest, and young Billy is forced to suffer the consequences of their affair by being kept hidden. The compelling story is told from Billy's point of view and with the language and phonetic spelling of a child whose development has been stunted by his lifelong imprisonment... This challenging title demands to be read more than once, and even then it will leave questions unanswered." (School Library Journal)

Alonzo, Sandra

★ **Riding** invisible; written by Sandra Alonzo; illustrated by Nathan Huang. Hyperion 2010 234p il lib bdg $15.99
Grades: 7 8 9 10 **Fic**

1. Horses -- Fiction 2. Brothers -- Fiction 3. Family life -- Fiction 4. Personality disorders -- Fiction
ISBN 978-1-4231-1898-5; 1-4231-1898-7
LC 2010-05041

After his older brother Will attacks his horse, Shy, Yancey runs away into the desert. Follow his adventures as he returns home to face life with a brother who has "conduct disorder."

"Written in a journal style and punctuated with sketches depicting Yancy's experiences, there's a lot here to engage readers." Horn Book Guide

Alpine, Rachele

Canary; by Rachele Alpine. Medallion Press 2013 400 p. $9.99
Grades: 9 10 11 12 **Fic**

1. Secrecy -- Fiction 2. Rape victims -- Fiction 3. Father-daughter relationship -- Fiction
ISBN 1605425877; 9781605425870

"In this debut novel . . . Kate Franklin's . . . . dad is hired to coach at Beacon Prep, home of one of the best basketball teams in the state. In a blog of prose and poetry, Kate chronicles her new world--dating a basketball player, being caught up in a world of idolatry and entitlement, and discovering the perks the inner circle enjoys. Then Kate's fragile life shatters once again when one of her boyfriend's teammates assaults her at a party." (Publisher's note)

"In an engrossing, carefully unfolding drama, sophomore Kate Franklin adjusts to a new school, a powerful set of friends and a family that is falling apart... Overall, a sophisticated, evocative portrait of a teen girl finding her place among peers and family." (Kirkus)

Altebrando, Tara

The **best** night of your (pathetic) life; Tara Altebrando. Dutton Books 2012 240 p. (hardcover) $16.99
Grades: 9 10 11 12 **Fic**

1. Bullies -- Fiction 2. High schools -- Fiction 3. Treasure hunt (Game) -- Fiction 4. Schools -- Fiction

5. Interpersonal relations -- Fiction
ISBN 0525423265; 9780525423263
LC 2011029964

In this book, "high-school senior Mary Gilhooley and her friends have spent . . . the last four years feeling like underdogs and also-rans. Having suffered constant ridicule from Oyster Point's resident bully . . . Jake Barbone, they are all just dying to go away to college and never come back. But with only a week until graduation, there's one last thing Mary feels they absolutely must do together: compete against Barbone in the . . .Scavenger Hunt -- and win." (Publisher's note)

"Funny and nostalgic, a highly contemporary riff on a timeless rite of passage." Kirkus

Dreamland social club. Dutton Children's Books 2011 389p $16.99
Grades: 7 8 9 10 **Fic**

1. School stories 2. Twins -- Fiction 3. Amusement parks -- Fiction 4. New York (State) -- Fiction 5. Coney Island (New York, N.Y.) -- Fiction
ISBN 978-0-525-42325-6; 0-525-42325-7
LC 2010-38070

"The distinct setting of this book, and unique teen characters such as Tattoo Boy, a Goth dwarf, a boy with no legs, and a 'giant,' will help readers connect with this delightful journey of one girl's self-discovery." Libr Media Connect

Alvarez, Julia

★ **Before** we were free. Knopf 2002 167p $15.95; lib bdg $17.99; pa $5.99
Grades: 7 8 9 10 **Fic**

1. Family life -- Fiction 2. Dominican Republic -- History -- 1930-1961
ISBN 0-375-81544-9; 0-375-91544-3 lib bdg; 0-440-23784-X pa
LC 2001-50520

In the early 1960s in the Dominican Republic, twelve-year-old Anita learns that her family is involved in the underground movement to end the bloody rule of the dictator, General Trujillo

This "is a realistic and compelling account of a girl growing up too quickly while coming to terms with the cost of freedom." Horn Book

Finding miracles; Julia Alvarez. Knopf 2004 264p $15.95; pa $6.99
Grades: 8 9 10 11 12 **Fic**

1. School stories 2. Adoption -- Fiction
ISBN 0-375-82760-9; 0-553-49406-6 pa
LC 2003-25127

Fifteen-year-old Milly Kaufman is an average American teenager until Pablo, a new student at her school, inspires her to search for her birth family in his native country

"Complex multicultural characters and skillful depiction of Latino culture raises this well-written, readable novel, which is a school story, a family story, and a love story, to far above average." Voice Youth Advocates

Amateau, Gigi

A **certain** strain of peculiar. Candlewick Press 2009 261p $16.99
Grades: 6 7 8 9 **Fic**

1. Ranch life -- Fiction 2. Grandmothers -- Fiction
ISBN 978-0-7636-3009-6; 0-7636-3009-8

Tired of the miserable life she lives, Mary Harold leaves her mother behind and moves back to Alabama and her grandmother, where she receives support and love and starts to gain confidence in herself and her abilities.

"Mary Harold is a wonderfully complex and honest character. . . . [Her] narrative is heartfelt and poignant, and the message that being 'different' is nothing to be ashamed of will resonate with readers." Voice Youth Advocates

Amato, Mary

Invisible lines; illustrations by Antonio Caparo. Egmont USA 2009 319p il $15.99; lib bdg $18.99
Grades: 6 7 8 9 **Fic**

1. School stories 2. Moving -- Fiction 3. Social classes -- Fiction 4. Single parent family -- Fiction
ISBN 978-1-60684-010-8; 1-60684-010-X; 978-1-60684-043-6 lib bdg; 1-60684-043-6 lib bdg
LC 2009-14639

Coming from a poor, single-parent family, seventh-grader Trevor must rely on his intelligence, artistic ability, quick wit, and soccer prowess to win friends at his new Washington, D.C. school, but popular and rich Xander seems determined to cause him trouble.

"The author's subtle sense of humor is at work here. . . . This fresh story is enhanced by notes and drawings from Trevor's fungi notebook. With its short chapters, snappy dialogue, and scientific extras, the novel should find a wide audience." SLJ

Anderson, Jessica Lee

Border crossing. Milkweed Editions 2009 174p $17; pa $8
Grades: 7 8 9 10 **Fic**

1. Alcoholism -- Fiction 2. Schizophrenia -- Fiction 3. Mental illness -- Fiction 4. Racially mixed people -- Fiction
ISBN 978-1-57131-689-9; 1-57131-689-2; 978-1-57131-691-2 pa; 1-57131-691-4 pa
LC 2008-49408

Manz, a troubled fifteen-year-old, ruminates over his Mexican father's death, his mother's drinking, and his stillborn stepbrother until the voices he hears in his head take over and he cannot tell reality from delusion.

"A sad and thought-provoking exploration of mental illness." Kirkus

Anderson, Jodi Lynn

★ **Tiger** Lily; Jodi Lynn Anderson. HarperTeen 2012 304 p. (trade bdg.) $17.99
Grades: 8 9 10 11 **Fic**

1. Love stories 2. Jealousy -- Fiction 3. Fairy tales 4. Peter Pan (Fictional character) 5. Love -- Fiction 6. Magic -- Fiction 7. Fairies -- Fiction
ISBN 0062003259; 9780062003256
LC 2011032659

This is the story of Tiger Lily, the girl Peter Pan spurned for Wendy. "Told from the perspective of Tinker Bell, the novel explores how Tiger Lily meets and falls in love with Peter, despite being betrothed to another villager, a man Tiger Lily despises. Tiger Lily and Peter's complicated inner conflicts emerge as they sort out their feelings about freedom, power, loyalty, and responsibility. When a girl from England arrives, Tiger Lily" feels jealous for the first time. (Publishers Weekly)

Anderson, Katie D.

Kiss & Make Up. Amazon Childrens Pub 2012 307 p. (hardcover) $16.99

Grades: 7 8 9 10 **Fic**

1. Occult fiction 2. School stories

ISBN 076146316X; 9780761463160

This book focuses on Emerson Taylor, who "has a gift—or a curse. She can read a person's mind with the lightest of kisses. When her financially strapped aunt announces that Emerson will not be attending private school the following year if her grades don't improve, Emerson initializes Operation Liplock. She will begin study sessions with the geeky Ivys—those destined to attend Ivy League colleges—where she will kiss them, allowing their knowledge to transfer to her mind." (School Library Journal)

Anderson, Laurie Halse, 1961-

★ **Chains**; seeds of America. Simon & Schuster Books for Young Readers 2008 316p $17.99

Grades: 6 7 8 9 10 **Fic**

1. Spies -- Fiction 2. Slavery -- Fiction 3. New York (N.Y.) -- Fiction 4. African Americans -- Fiction 5. United States -- History -- 1775-1783, Revolution -- Fiction

ISBN 1-4169-0585-5; 1-4169-0586-3 pa; 978-1-4169-0585-1; 978-1-4169-0586-8 pa

LC 2007-52139

After being sold to a cruel couple in New York City, a slave named Isabel spies for the rebels during the Revolutionary War. "Grades seven to ten." (Bull Cent Child Books)

"This gripping novel offers readers a startlingly provocative view of the Revolutionary War. . . . [Anderson's] solidly researched exploration of British and Patriot treatment of slaves during a war for freedom is nuanced and evenhanded, presented in service of a fast-moving, emotionally involving plot." Publ Wkly

Followed by: Forge (2010)

Fever, 1793. Simon & Schuster Bks. for Young Readers 2000 251p $17.99; pa $6.99

Grades: 5 6 7 8 9 **Fic**

1. Epidemics -- Fiction 2. Yellow fever -- Fiction 3. Philadelphia (Pa.) -- Fiction

ISBN 978-0-689-83858-3; 0-689-83858-1; 978-0-689-84891-9 pa; 0-689-84891-9 pa

LC 00-32238

In 1793 Philadelphia, sixteen-year-old Matilda Cook, separated from her sick mother, learns about perseverance and self-reliance when she is forced to cope with the horrors of a yellow fever epidemic. "Age ten and up." (N Y Times Book Rev)

"A vivid work, rich with well-drawn and believable characters. Unexpected events pepper the top-flight novel that combines accurate historical detail with a spellbinding story line." Voice Youth Advocates

Forge. Atheneum Books for Young Readers 2010 297p (Seeds of America) $16.99

Grades: 6 7 8 9 10 **Fic**

1. Slavery -- Fiction 2. Soldiers -- Fiction 3. Pennsylvania -- Fiction 4. African Americans -- Fiction 5. United States -- History -- 1775-1783, Revolution -- Fiction

ISBN 978-1-4169-6144-4; 1-4169-6144-5

LC 2010-15971

Sequel to: Chains (2008)

Separated from his friend Isabel after their daring escape from slavery, fifteen-year-old Curzon serves as a free man in the Continental Army at Valley Forge until he and Isabel are thrown together again, as slaves once more.

"Weaving a huge amount of historical detail seamlessly into the story, Anderson creates a vivid setting, believable characters both good and despicable and a clear portrayal of the moral ambiguity of the Revolutionary age. Not only can this sequel stand alone, for many readers it will be one of the best novels they have ever read." Kirkus

★ The **impossible** knife of memory; Laurie Halse Anderson. Viking, published by Penguin Group 2014 400 p. (hardback) $18.99

Grades: 9 10 11 12 **Fic**

1. Father-daughter relationship -- Fiction 2. Iraq War, 2003-2011 -- Veterans -- Fiction 3. Post-traumatic stress disorder -- Fiction 4. Veterans -- Fiction 5. Family problems -- Fiction

ISBN 0670012092; 9780670012091

LC 2013031267

In this book, by Laurie Halse Anderson, "Hayley Kincaid and her father, Andy, have been on the road, never staying long in one place as he struggles to escape the demons that have tortured him since his return from Iraq. Now they are back in the town where he grew up so Hayley can attend school. Perhaps, for the first time, Hayley can have a normal life. . . . Will being back home help Andy's PTSD, or will his terrible memories drag him to the edge of hell, and drugs push him over?" (Publisher's note)

"With powerful themes of loyalty and forgiveness, this tightly woven story is a forthright examination of the realities of war and its aftermath on soldiers and their families." SLJ

Prom; Laurie Halse Anderson. Viking 2005 215p $16.99; pa $8.99

Grades: 9 10 11 12 **Fic**

1. School stories 2. Pennsylvania -- Fiction

ISBN 0-670-05974-9; 0-14-240570-1 pa

LC 2004-14974

Eighteen-year-old Ash wants nothing to do with senior prom, but when disaster strikes and her desperate friend, Nat, needs her help to get it back on track, Ash's involvement transforms her life

"Whether or not readers have been infected by prom fever themselves, they will be enraptured and amused by

Ashley's attitude-altering, life-changing commitment to a cause." Publ Wkly

★ **Speak**; 10th anniversary ed.; Speak 2009 197p pa $11.99
Grades: 7 8 9 10 **Fic**

1. School stories 2. Rape -- Fiction
ISBN 978-0-14-241473-6
LC 2009-502164

First published 1999

A traumatic event near the end of the summer has a devastating effect on Melinda's freshman year in high school.

The novel is "keenly aware of the corrosive details of outsiderhood and the gap between home and daily life at high school; kids whose exclusion may have less concrete cause than Melinda's will nonetheless find the picture recognizable. This is a gripping account of personal wounding and recovery." Bull Cent Child Books

Twisted. Viking 2007 250p $16.99
Grades: 9 10 11 12 **Fic**

1. School stories 2. Ohio -- Fiction 3. Family life -- Fiction
ISBN 978-0-670-06101-3
LC 2006-31297

After finally getting noticed by someone other than school bullies and his ever-angry father, seventeen-year-old Tyler enjoys his tough new reputation and the attentions of a popular girl, but when life starts to go bad again, he must choose between transforming himself or giving in to his destructive thoughts.

"This is a gripping exploration of what it takes to grow up, really grow up, against the wishes of people and circumstances conspiring to keep you the victim they need you to be." Bull Cent Child Books

★ **Wintergirls**. Viking 2009 288p $17.99
Grades: 8 9 10 11 12 **Fic**

1. Death -- Fiction 2. Friendship -- Fiction 3. Self-mutilation -- Fiction 4. Anorexia nervosa -- Fiction
ISBN 0-670-01110-X; 978-0-670-01110-0
LC 2008-37452

Eighteen-year-old Lia comes to terms with her best friend's death from anorexia as she struggles with the same disorder.

"As events play out, Lia's guilt, her need to be thin, and her fight for acceptance unravel in an almost poetic stream of consciousness in this startlingly crisp and pitch-perfect first-person narrative." SLJ

Anderson, M. T., 1968-

★ The **astonishing** life of Octavian Nothing, traitor to the nation; the pox party. taken from accounts by his own hand and other sundry sources; collected by M.T. Anderson of Boston. Candlewick Press 2006 351p $17.99
Grades: 9 10 11 12 **Fic**

1. Slavery -- Fiction 2. African Americans -- Fiction 3. United States -- History -- 1775-1783, Revolution -- Fiction
ISBN 0763624020; 9780763624026
LC 2006043170

Michael L. Printz Award honor book (2007), National Book Award for Young People's Literature (2006), Boston Globe-Horn Book Awards: Fiction and Poetry (2007)

This is the first of two volumes in The astonishing life of Octavian Nothing, traitor to the nation series. Various diaries, letters, and other manuscripts chronicle the experiences of Octavian, a young African American, from birth to age sixteen, as he is brought up as part of a science experiment in the years leading up to and during the Revolutionary War.

"Teens looking for a challenge will find plenty to sink into here. The questions raised about race and freedom are well developed and leave a different perspective on the Revolutionary War than most novels." Voice Youth Advocates

Followed by: The kingdom on the waves (2008)

The **astonishing** life of Octavian Nothing, traitor to the nation; v. #2 The kingdom on the waves. taken from accounts by his own hand and other sundry sources; collected by M.T. Anderson of Boston. Candlewick Press 2008 561p 2 maps (hardcover: alk. paper) $11.99
Grades: 9 10 11 12 **Fic**

1. Freedom -- Fiction 2. African Americans -- Fiction 3. Slavery -- United States -- Fiction 4. United States -- History -- 1775-1783, Revolution -- Fiction 5. Slavery -- Fiction 6. Virginia --History -- Revolution, 1775-1783 -- Fiction 7. United States -- History -- Revolution, 1775-1783 --Naval operations, British -- Fiction
ISBN 0763646261; 9780763646264; 0763629502; 9780763629502
LC 2008929919

Sequel to: The astonishing life of Octavian Nothing, traitor to the nation: the pox party (2006)

In this book, a Michael L. Printz Honor Book of 2009, "[f]earing a death sentence, Octavian and his tutor, Dr. Trefusis, escape through rising tides and pouring rain to find shelter in British-occupied Boston. Sundered from all he knows -- the College of Lucidity, the rebel cause -- Octavian hopes to find safe harbor. Instead, he is soon to learn of Lord Dunmore's proclamation offering freedom to slaves who join the counterrevolutionary forces. . . . [Author] M. T. Anderson recounts Octavian's experiences as the Revolutionary War explodes around him, thrusting him into intense battles and tantalizing him with elusive visions of liberty." (Publisher's note)

"Elegantly crafted writing in an 18th-century voice, sensitive portrayals of primary and secondary characters and a fascinating author's note make this one of the few volumes to fully comprehend the paradoxes of the struggle for liberty in America." Kirkus

Burger Wuss; M.T. Anderson. Candlewick Press 1999 192p (pbk.) $7.99
Grades: 7 8 9 10 11 12 **Fic**

1. Teenagers -- Fiction 2. Conformity -- Fiction 3. Fast food restaurants -- Fiction
ISBN 0763606804; 9780763631789; 9781439530726
LC 99014257

In this book that is set "[i]n a world where every teenager works at one fast food chain or another and likes it, Anthony just doesn't fit in. His first real girlfriend has dumped him for a meathead named Turner who works at O'Dermott's, so

Anthony plots revenge. He gets a job at the restaurant and embarks on a complicated plot to pit the kids from Burger Queen against the kids from O'Dermott's--and thereby draw the BQ wrath down on company-man Turner's head. . . . [T]his book is a burlesque of teenage angst and conformist culture. . . . Anarchist vagabond Shunt is Anthony's partner in his anti-conformity crimes." (Publishers Weekly)

★ **Feed**. Candlewick Press 2002 237p hardcover o.p. pa $7.99
Grades: 8 9 10 11 12 **Fic**

1. Satire 2. Science fiction
ISBN 0-7636-1726-1; 0-7636-2259-1 pa
LC 2002-23738

In a future where most people have computer implants in their heads to control their environment, a boy meets an unusual girl who is in serious trouble

"An ingenious satire of corporate America and our present-day value system." Horn Book Guide

Anderson, R. J.

Spell Hunter. HarperCollinsPublishers 2009 329p (Faery rebels) $16.99
Grades: 7 8 9 10 11 12 **Fic**

1. Fantasy fiction 2. Magic -- Fiction 3. Fairies -- Fiction
ISBN 978-0-06-155474-2; 0-06-155474-X; 978-0-06-155475-9 lib bdg; 0-06-155475-8 lib bdg
LC 2008-27469

In a dying faery realm, only the brave and rebellious faery Knife persists in trying to discover how her people's magic was lost and what is needed to restore their powers and ensure their survival, but her quest is endangered by her secret friendship with a human named Paul.

"Filled with delicate, fantastical creatures; evil and dangerous crows; and a human who believes in love, this is a highly readable, sophisticated tale of romance and self-sacrifice." Booklist

Another title in this series is:
Wayfarer (2010)

Ultraviolet. Carolrhoda Lab 2011 306p $17.95
Grades: 7 8 9 10 **Fic**

1. Science fiction 2. Synesthesia -- Fiction 3. Extraterrestrial beings -- Fiction
ISBN 978-0-7613-7408-4; 0-7613-7408-6
LC 2011000882

Almost seventeen-year-old Alison, who has synesthesia, finds herself in a psychiatric facility accused of killing a classmate whose body cannot be found.

"Anderson keeps readers guessing throughout with several twists, including a very unexpected divergence in the last third of the book." Publ Wkly

Andreu, Maria E.

The **secret** side of empty; by Maria E. Andreu. Running Press Teens 2014 336p $16.95
Grades: 9 10 11 12 **Fic**

1. Emigration and immigration-- Fiction 2. High school students-- Fiction 3. Teenage girls — Fiction; 4. United States —Immigration and emigration — Fiction
ISBN: 0762451920; 9780762451920
LC 2013950819

This book asks "what's it like to be undocumented? High school senior M.T. knows all too well. . . . M.T. was born in Argentina and brought to America as a baby without any official papers. And as questions of college, work, and the future arise, M.T. will have to decide what exactly she wants for herself, knowing someone she loves will unavoidably pay the price for it." (Publisher's note)

"An illegal immigrant, Monserrat Thalia has kept her status a secret for years. Despite her achievements in high school, now that she's a senior her future is uncertain and she's fighting for survival. Andreu draws from personal experience, and M.T.'s struggles with first love, depression, an abusive father, and the constant fear of deportation feel wholly real. A compelling and timely story." Horn Book

Andrews, Jesse

Me & Earl & the dying girl; by Jesse Andrews. Amulet Books 2012 295 p. $16.95
Grades: 8 9 10 **Fic**

1. Leukemia -- Fiction 2. Friendship -- Fiction 3. Family life -- Fiction 4. Pittsburgh (Pa.) -- Fiction 5. High school students -- Fiction 6. Humorous stories 7. Schools -- Fiction 8. High schools -- Fiction 9. Jews -- United States -- Fiction 10. Family life -- Pennsylvania -- Fiction
ISBN 9781419701764
LC 2011031796

This book is a "confessional from a teen narrator who won't be able to convince readers he's as unlikable as he wants them to believe." It covers "[h]is filmmaking ambitions . . . his unlikely friendship with the . . . Earl of the title. And his unlikelier friendship with Rachel, the titular 'dying girl'. . . . He chronicles his senior year, in which his mother guilt-trips him into hanging out with Rachel, who has acute myelogenous leukemia." (Kirkus Reviews)

Anhalt, Ariela

Freefall. Harcourt 2010 250p $17
Grades: 9 10 11 12 **Fic**

1. School stories 2. Death -- Fiction 3. Friendship -- Fiction
ISBN 978-0-15-206567-6; 0-15-206567-9
LC 2009-18936

Briar Academy senior Luke prefers avoiding conflict and letting others make his decisions, but he is compelled to choose whether or not to stand by the best friend whose reckless behavior has endangered Luke and may have caused another student's death.

"The plot is straightforward, but the high stakes, complex character development, and realistic dialogue and interactions will keep readers riveted—and likely have them imagining themselves in Luke's position." Publ Wky

Anthony, Jessica

Chopsticks; Jessica Anthony, Rodrigo Corral. Penguin/Razorbill 2012 304 p.
Grades: 9 10 11 12 **Fic**

1. Mystery fiction 2. Musicians -- Fiction 3. Piano music -- Fiction 4. Mental illness -- Fiction 5. Missing

children -- Fiction
ISBN 9781595144355

This "mystery [book] reveals the events leading up to the disappearance of Glory, a teenaged piano prodigy who goes missing after her struggle with mental illness that causes her to play the children's waltz 'Chopsticks' obsessively. Photographs, ephemera, and instant-message screenshots weave together the details of a forbidden romance with Francisco, the boy next door. . . . The story requires . . . visual literacy. . . . An example of the emerging trend of transmedia storytelling, this book will also be available in a 'fully interactive electronic version.' The inclusion of links to online media requires Internet access and a willingness to type . . . URLs, but the content of the links can be gleaned from context." (School Libr J)

Anthony, Joelle

Restoring harmony. G.P. Putnam's Sons 2010 307p $17.99
Grades: 6 7 8 9 **Fic**

1. Science fiction 2. Voyages and travels -- Fiction 3. Environmental degradation -- Fiction
ISBN 978-0-399-25281-5; 0-399-25281-9
LC 2009-29501

Ten years after the Great Collapse of 2031, sixteen-year-old Molly McClure, with only her fiddle for company, leaves the safety of her family's island home to travel through a dangerous and desolate wasteland on her way to Oregon to find her grandparents and persuade them to return with her to Canada.

"Adeptly combining adventure and romance, Anthony's debut is a tense and often charming tale that never lets its use of the oh-so-trendy dystopian future trope overwhelm some great characters." Publ Wkly

Anthony, Piers

★ A **spell** for chameleon. Ballantine Books 1977 344p (Magic of Xanth) pa $7.50
Grades: 9 10 11 12 **Fic**

1. Fantasy fiction
ISBN 0-345-34753-6
LC 2004-597119

First volume in the Magic of Xanth series featuring Bink, a young man without magical powers in an enchanted world ruled entirely by magic. Unless he discovers his own magical talent, he will be exiled forever from Xanth, his homeland. Thus starts Bink's quest to learn what his talent truly is.

Other titles in the series are:
Air apparent (2007)
Castle Roogna (1979)
Centaur Isle (1981)
The color of her panties (1992)
Crewel lye (1984)
Cube route (2003)
Currant events (2004)
The Dastard (2000)
Demons don't dream (1993)
Dragon on a pedestal (1983)
Faun & games (1997)
Geis of the Gargoyle (1995)
Harpy thyme (1994)
Isle of view (1990)
Jumper cable (2009)
Knot Gneiss (2010)
Night mare (1982)
Ogre, ogre (1982)
Pet peeve (2005)
Question quest (1991)
Roc and a hard place (1995)
The source of magic (1979)
Stork naked (2006)
Swell foop (2001)
Two to the fifth (2008)
Up in a heaval (2002)
Xone of contention (1999)
Yon ill wind (1996)
Zombie lover (1998)

Antieau, Kim

Broken moon. Margaret K. McElderry Books 2007 183p $15.99
Grades: 7 8 9 10 **Fic**

1. Pakistan -- Fiction 2. Siblings -- Fiction 3. Kidnapping -- Fiction
ISBN 978-1-4169-1767-0; 1-4169-1767-5
LC 2006-03780

When her little brother is kidnapped and taken from Pakistan to race camels in the desert, eighteen-year-old Nadira overcomes her own past abuse and, dressed as a boy and armed with knowledge of the powerful storytelling of the legendary Scheherazade, is determined to find and rescue him.

The author "presents important issues without letting them overtake the narrative, and the classic plot and sympathetic characters add up to an absorbing read." Horn Book

Ruby's imagine; written by Kim Antieau. Houghton Mifflin Co. 2008 201p $16
Grades: 6 7 8 9 **Fic**

1. African Americans -- Fiction 2. Hurricane Katrina, 2005 -- Fiction
ISBN 978-0-618-99767-1; 0-618-99767-9
LC 2007047736

Tells the story of Hurricane Katrina from the point of view of Ruby, an unusually intuitive girl who lives with her grandmother in New Orleans but has powerful memories of an earlier life in the swamps.

"Antieau offers a complex, personal account of Katrina and its aftermath. . . . Ruby's atmospheric narrative is as dense and pungent as the bayou." Booklist

Applegate, Katherine

Eve & Adam; by Michael Grant and Katherine Applegate. Feiwel and Friends 2012 291p. $17.99
Grades: 7 8 9 10 **Fic**

1. Medical genetics 2. Biomedical engineering 3. Mother-daughter relationship -- Fiction
ISBN 0312583516; 9780312583514

In this book by authors Michael Grant and Katherine Applegate, "a run-in with a streetcar left Evening Spiker's body seriously mangled . . . [H]er widowed mother, Terra, insists on moving her from the hospital to . . . [the] biotech company . . . Spiker Biopharmaceuticals. . . . Eve's healing is strangely swift [and] Terra drops a project . . . in her lap: Design a virtual human being from scratch. With help from her feisty, reckless friend Aislin, Eve takes up the challenge." (Kirkus Reviews)

Arbuthnott, Gill

The **Keepers'** tattoo. Chicken House 2010 425p $17.99

Grades: 6 7 8 9 **Fic**

1. Fantasy fiction 2. Dreams -- Fiction 3. Uncles -- Fiction 4. Tattooing -- Fiction

ISBN 978-0-545-17166-3; 0-545-17166-0

LC 2009-26327

Months before her fifteenth birthday, Nyssa learns that she is a special member of a legendary clan, the Keepers of Knowledge, as she and her uncle try to escape from Alaric, the White Wolf, who wants to use lines tattooed on her to destroy the rest of her people.

Arbuthnott "writes with restraint and thoughtfulness, never condescending to her readers. Nyssa is a convincing mixture of ignorance, courage, and resourcefulness." Publ Wkly

Archer, E.

Geek: fantasy novel. Scholastic Press 2011 310p $17.99

Grades: 7 8 9 10 **Fic**

1. Fantasy fiction 2. Aunts -- Fiction 3. Wishes -- Fiction 4. Cousins -- Fiction 5. Great Britain -- Fiction

ISBN 978-0-545-16040-7; 0-545-16040-5

"Fourteen-year-old Ralph Stevens escapes his humdrum life when he's invited to spend the summer with his British cousins, ostensibly to set up their wireless network. What he discovers is a family given to eccentricity. . . . Things get seriously weird when their infamous aunt/fairy godmother Chessie of Cheshire turns up, ready to grant each child a wish." Publ Wkly

Archer, Jennifer

Through her eyes. HarperTeen 2011 377p $16.99

Grades: 7 8 9 10 **Fic**

1. School stories 2. Mystery fiction 3. Texas -- Fiction 4. Moving -- Fiction 5. Family life -- Fiction 6. Grandfathers -- Fiction 7. Supernatural -- Fiction

ISBN 978-0-06-183458-5; 0-06-183458-0

LC 2010-18440

Sixteen-year-old Tansy is used to moving every time her mother starts writing a new book, but in the small Texas town where her grandfather grew up, she is lured into the world of a troubled young man whose death sixty years earlier is shrouded in mystery.

"Archer's engrossing story gracefully weaves together the contemporary and historical into an eerie mystery, while examining relationships, reality, and the power of the mind." Publ Wkly

Arcos, Carrie

★ **Out** of reach; Carrie Arcos. Simon Pulse 2012 250 p. (alk. paper) $16.99

Grades: 9 10 11 12 **Fic**

1. Siblings -- Fiction 2. Drug abuse -- Fiction 3. Families of drug addicts -- Fiction 4. Runaways -- Fiction 5. Methamphetamine -- Fiction 6. California, Southern -- Fiction

ISBN 1442440538; 9781442440531; 9781442440555

LC 2011044501

In this book by Carrie Arcos, "Rachel's older brother Micah is using crystal meth, and he is lying, stealing, and hurting those who love him in order to feed his addiction. . . . An anonymous e-mail warns Rachel that Micah is in serious trouble. So Rachel teams up with Micah's fellow band member . . . Tyler, to find her brother. . . . But, despite the heartache of the search, Rachel begins to see that her life isn't destroyed -- and that Tyler is surprisingly kind and caring." (Booklist)

Armistead, Cal

Being Henry David; by Cal Armistead. Albert Whitman 2013 312 p. (hardcover) $16.99

Grades: 8 9 10 11 12 **Fic**

1. Mystery fiction 2. Amnesia -- Fiction 3. Guilt -- Fiction 4. Runaways -- Fiction 5. Concord (Mass.) -- Fiction 6. Family problems -- Fiction 7. New York (N.Y.) -- Fiction 8. Street children -- Fiction

ISBN 080750615X; 9780807506158

LC 2012017377

In this book, a "boy wakes up in Penn Station, remembering nothing. He guesses that he's about 17, he has a head injury, and he is carrying only 10 dollars. Near at hand is a copy of Walden, so for want of anything better he calls himself Henry David (Hank). He heads to Concord, Massachusetts, to find, he hopes, some clues at Walden Pond. As his memories slowly return, he remembers who he was; as he copes with the memories, he discovers who he is and can be." (School Library Journal)

Armstrong, Kelley

The **summoning.** HarperCollinsPublishers 2008 390p (Darkest powers) $17.99; lib bdg $18.89

Grades: 7 8 9 10 **Fic**

1. Ghost stories 2. Supernatural -- Fiction

ISBN 978-0-06-166269-0; 0-06-166269-0; 978-0-06-166272-0 lib bdg; 0-06-166272-0 lib bdg

LC 2008-14221

After fifteen-year-old Chloe starts seeing ghosts and is sent to Lyle House, a mysterious group home for mentally disturbed teenagers, she soon discovers that neither Lyle House nor its inhabitants are exactly what they seem, and that she and her new friends are in danger.

"Suspenseful, well-written, and engaging, this page-turning . . . [novel] will be a hit." Voice Youth Advocates

Other titles in this series are:

The awakening (2009)

The reckoning (2010)

Armstrong, William Howard

★ **Sounder**; [by] William H. Armstrong; illustrations by James Barkley. Harper & Row 1969 116p il $15.99; pa $5.99

Grades: 5 6 7 8 **Fic**

1. Dogs -- Fiction 2. Family life -- Fiction 3. African Americans -- Fiction

ISBN 0-06-020143-6; 0-06-440020-4 pa

Awarded the Newbery Medal, 1970

"Set in the South in the era of sharecropping and segregation, this succinctly told tale poignantly describes the courage of a father who steals a ham in order to feed his undernourished family; the determination of the eldest son, who searches for his father despite the apathy of prison authorities; and the devotion of a coon dog named Sounder." Shapiro. Fic for Youth. 3d edition

Arnett, Mindee

Avalon. Balzer + Bray. 2014 432p $17.99
Grades: 8 9 10 11 12 **Fic**

1. Science fiction 2. Mercenary troops--Fiction
ISBN: 0062235591; 9780062235596
LC 2013005155

This novel is "about a group of teenage mercenaries who stumble upon a conspiracy that threatens the entire galaxy. Jeth Seagrave and his crew have made their name stealing metatech: the devices that allow people to travel great distances faster than the speed of light. . . . When he finds himself in possession of information that both government and the crime bosses are willing to kill for, he's going to find there's no escaping his past anymore." (Publisher's note)

"Jeth has one last job to complete before he can buy back his parents' spaceship from a crime boss. But the ship he was sent to find carries a deadly cargo that everyone in the galaxy wants. The strong bond between Jeth and his humorously motley crew of teenage mercenaries outshines the predictable plot and will appeal to Firefly-esque space-opera fans." Horn Book

Arnold, Tedd

Rat life. Dial Books 2007 199p $16.99
Grades: 6 7 8 9 10 **Fic**

1. Mystery fiction 2. Authorship -- Fiction 3. Vietnam War, 1961-1975 -- Fiction
ISBN 978-0-8037-3020-5; 0-8037-3020-9
LC 2006-18429

After developing an unusual friendship with a young Vietnam War veteran in 1972, fourteen-year-old Todd discovers his writing talent and solves a murder mystery.

"This is a solid story . . . with a likable main character and a thrilling climax." SLJ

Arntson, Steven

The **wrap-up** list; by Steven Arntson. Houghton Mifflin Harcourt 2013 240 p. $15.99
Grades: 7 8 9 10 **Fic**

1. Fantasy fiction 2. Death -- Fiction 3. Conduct of life -- Fiction 4. Hispanic Americans -- Fiction
ISBN 0547824106; 9780547824109
LC 2012014035

This paranormal young adult novel, by Steven Arntson, is set in a "modern-day suburban town, [where] one percent of all fatalities come about in the most peculiar way. Deaths—eight-foot-tall, silver-gray creatures—send a letter ('Dear So-and-So, your days are numbered') to whomever is chosen . . . , telling them to wrap up their lives and do the things they always wanted to do before they have to 'depart.' When sixteen-year-old Gabriela receives her notice, she is, of course devastated. Will she kiss her crush Sylvester before it's too late?" (Publisher's note)

Aronson, Sarah

Head case. Roaring Brooks 2007 176p $16.95
Grades: 7 8 9 10 **Fic**

1. Family life -- Fiction 2. People with disabilities -- Fiction 3. Drunk driving -- Fiction
ISBN 978-1-59643-214-7
LC 2006-101509

Seventeen-year-old Frank Marder struggles to deal with the aftermath of an accident he had while driving drunk that killed two people, including his girlfriend, and left him paralyzed from the neck down.

"Daredevil readers will be made thoughtful by Frank's account, and they'll vividly imagine themselves into Frank's immobile shoes." Bull Cent Child Books

Ashby, Amanda

Fairy bad day. Speak 2011 336p pa $7.99
Grades: 7 8 9 10 11 12 **Fic**

1. School stories 2. Fantasy fiction 3. Ability -- Fiction 4. Fairies -- Fiction 5. Supernatural -- Fiction
ISBN 978-0-14-241259-6; 0-14-241259-7
LC 2010-046286

High schooler Emma is devastated to learn that she may not follow in her mother's footsteps as a dragon slayer, but with an unlikely band of allies she discovers that she may, indeed, be more adept at slaying giant killer fairies.

"The characters are nicely developed, the dialogue is fresh and engaging, the author's irreverent take on good versus evil will hook readers, and the satisfying plot twists will keep them involved till the end." SLJ

Zombie queen of Newbury High. Speak 2009 199p pa $7.99
Grades: 7 8 9 10 **Fic**

1. School stories 2. Zombies -- Fiction
ISBN 978-0-14-241256-5; 0-14-241256-5
LC 2008-41035

While trying to cast a love spell on her date on the eve of the senior prom, Mia inadvertently infects her entire high school class with a virus that will turn them all into zombies.

"Zombie Queen is light, fast-paced, and . . . will quench the thirst of the Christopher Pike and R. L. Stine set." SLJ

Asher, Jay

★ The **future** of us; [by] Jay Asher and Carolyn Mackler. Razorbill 2011 356p $18.99
Grades: 8 9 10 11 12 **Fic**

1. School stories 2. Computers -- Fiction 3. Supernatural -- Fiction
ISBN 978-1-59514-491-1; 1-59514-491-9

In this book by Jay Asher and Carolyn Mackler, "it's 1996, before Facebook's been invented. Yet Emma's first computer leads her to her Facebook page from fifteen years in the future. She tells only her friend and would-be boyfriend Josh, and they contemplate their futures with concern. Can their current actions change who they become?" (Voice of Youth Advocates)

"It's 1996, and Emma Nelson has just received her first computer. . . . When Emma powers up the computer, she discovers her own Facebook page (even though Facebook doesn't exist yet) and herself in an unhappy marriage—15 years in the future. Alternating chapters from Josh and

Emma over the course of five days propel this riveting read, as Emma discovers she can alter her future by adjusting her present actions and intentions." Booklist

Thirteen reasons why; a novel. Razorbill 2007 288p $16.99
Grades: 8 9 10 11 12 **Fic**
1. School stories 2. Suicide -- Fiction
ISBN 9781595141712
LC 2007-03097

When high school student Clay Jenkins receives a box in the mail containing thirteen cassette tapes recorded by his classmate Hannah, who committed suicide, he spends a bewildering and heartbreaking night crisscrossing their town, listening to Hannah's voice recounting the events leading up to her death.

"Clay's pain is palpable and exquisitely drawn in gripping casually poetic prose. The complex and soulful characters expose astoundingly rich and singularly teenage inner lives." SLJ

Ashton, Brodi

Everbound; an Everneath novel. Brodi Ashton. Balzer + Bray 2013 368 p. (Everneath) (hardcover bdg: alk. paper) $17.99
Grades: 7 8 9 10 **Fic**
1. Love stories 2. Occult fiction 3. Future life -- Fiction 4. Hell -- Fiction 5. Love -- Fiction 6. Supernatural -- Fiction
ISBN 0062071165; 9780062071163
LC 2012028327

This young adult paranormal story, by Brodi Ashton, is the sequel to "Everneath." "Nikki Beckett could only watch as . . . Jack . . . sacrificed himself to save her, taking her place in the Tunnels of the Everneath for eternity. . . . Desperate for answers, Nikki turns to Cole, the immortal bad boy who wants to make her his queen. . . . But his heart has been touched by everything about Nikki, and he agrees to help in the only way he can: by taking her to the Everneath himself." (Publisher's note)

Everneath; Brodi Ashton. 1st ed; Balzer + Bray 2012 370p. $17.99
Grades: 7 8 9 10 **Fic**
1. Love stories 2. Occult fiction 3. Fantasy fiction
ISBN 9780062071132 (trade bdg.)
LC 2011022892

This book tells the story of "Nikki Beckett [who] vanished, sucked into an underworld known as the Everneath. Now she's returned—to her old life, her family, her boyfriend—before she's banished back to the underworld . . . this time forever. She has six months before the Everneath comes to claim her, six months for good-byes she can't find the words for, six months to find redemption, if it exists. Nikki longs to spend these precious months forgetting the Everneath and trying to reconnect with her boyfriend, Jack, the person most devastated by her disappearance—and the one person she loves more than anything. But there's just one problem: Cole, the smoldering immortal who enticed her to the Everneath in the first place, has followed Nikki home. Cole wants to take over the throne in the underworld and is convinced Nikki is the key to making it happen." (Publisher's note)

Atkins, Catherine

Alt ed. Putnam 2003 198p $17.99; pa $6.99
Grades: 7 8 9 10 **Fic**
1. School stories
ISBN 0-399-23854-9; 0-14-240235-4 pa
LC 2002-16942

Participating in a special after-school counseling class with other troubled students, including a sensitive gay classmate, helps Susan, an overweight tenth grader, develop a better sense of herself

"Most of the characters . . . come to life in new and interesting ways, and Susan's story is strong, because she is reinventing family relationships as well as trying to communicate with her peers." Booklist

The **file** on Angelyn Stark; by Catherine Atkins. 1st ed; Alfred A. Knopf 2011 250p.
Grades: 9 10 11 12 **Fic**
1. Young women -- Fiction 2. Child sexual abuse -- Fiction 3. Teacher-student relationship -- Fiction
ISBN 9780375869068; 9780375969065 (lib. bdg.); 9780375899898 (ebook)
LC 2011016681

This book tells the story of "[f]ifteen-year-old Angelyn Stark [who] seems to relish her position as the head of a pack of bad girls, but her tough exterior covers a terrible secret. The summer she was 12, her stepfather, Danny, sexually molested her. The abuse stopped after a neighbor called police, but when her mom didn't believe her, Angelyn told investigators it never happened. . . . Angelyn's boyfriend, Steve, keeps pressuring her for sex, but she's only interested in her teacher, Mr. Rossi, the single adult in her life who encourages her. But Mr. Rossi is fighting demons of his own and rightly fears that a relationship with Angelyn will jeopardize his reputation." (Kirkus)

Atwater-Rhodes, Amelia

Persistence of memory. Delacorte Press 2008 212p $15.99; lib bdg $18.99; pa $8.99
Grades: 8 9 10 11 12 **Fic**
1. Witches -- Fiction 2. Vampires -- Fiction 3. Supernatural -- Fiction 4. Schizophrenia -- Fiction
ISBN 978-0-385-73437-0; 0-385-73437-9; 978-0-385-90443-8 lib bdg; 0-385-90443-6 lib bdg; 978-0-440-24004-4 pa; 0-440-24004-2 pa
LC 2008-16062

Diagnosed with schizophrenia as a child, sixteen-year-old Erin has spent half of her life in therapy and on drugs, but now must face the possibility of weird things in the real world, including shapeshifting friends and her "alter," a centuries-old vampire.

"What sets this novel apart . . . are the two narrators—Erin, grown used to, and even comfortable with, the idea that she is mentally ill; and Shevaun, willing to do anything to protect the family she's cobbled together. Secondary characters are equally compelling, and the world that Atwater-Rhodes has created is believable and intriguing." SLJ

Snakecharm; [by] Amelia Atwater-Rhodes. Delacorte Press 2004 167p (The Kiesha'ra) $14.95; pa $5.99
Grades: 7 8 9 10 **Fic**
1. Fantasy 2. Fantasy fiction
ISBN 0-385-73072-1; 0-385-90199-2 lib bdg; 978-0-385-73072-3; 978-0-440-23804-1 pa
LC 2003-20709

The peace forged by the love between Zane and Danica, leaders of the avian and serpiente realms that had been at war for generations, is threatened by the arrival of Syfka, an ancient falcon who claims one of her people is hidden in their midst.

"There is enough suspense to keep readers interested. This book is a must-have for libraries with fans of Hawksong." SLJ

Auch, Mary Jane

Ashes of roses. Holt & Co. 2002 250p $16.95; pa $6.50
Grades: 7 8 9 10 11 12 Adult **Fic**
1. Immigrants -- Fiction 2. Irish Americans -- Fiction
ISBN 0-8050-6686-1; 0-440-23851-X pa
LC 2001-51896

Sixteen-year-old Margaret Rose Nolan, newly arrived from Ireland, finds work at New York City's Triangle Shirtwaist Factory shortly before the 1911 fire in which 146 employees died

"Fast-paced, populated by distinctive characters, and anchored in Auch's convincing sense of time and place, this title is a good choice for readers who like historical fiction." SLJ

Guitar boy. Henry Holt 2010 260p $16.99
Grades: 6 7 8 9 **Fic**
1. Guitars -- Fiction 2. Musicians -- Fiction 3. Family life -- Fiction
ISBN 978-0-8050-9112-0; 0-8050-9112-2
LC 2009-50782

After his mother is severely injured in an accident and his father kicks him out of the house, thirteen-year-old Travis attempts to survive on his own until he meets a guitar maker and some musicians who take him in and help him regain his confidence so that he can try to patch his family back together.

"Budding musicians will be fascinated by the details, but all readers will find their heartstrings plucked by this story." Booklist

Augarde, Steve

X-Isle. David Fickling Books 2010 476p $17.99
Grades: 7 8 9 10 **Fic**
1. Science fiction 2. Islands -- Fiction
ISBN 978-0-385-75193-3; 0-385-75193-1
LC 2010-281037

Baz and Ray, survivors of an apocalyptic flood, win places on X-Isle, an island where life is rumored to be better than on the devastated mainland, but they find the island to be a violent place ruled by religious fanatic Preacher John, and they decide they must come up with a weapon to protect themselves from impending danger.

"Augarde's near-future apocalyptic world is gruesomely hardscrabble without being overly graphic. . . . A gripping tale of fighting for the slenderest chance of hope." Publ Wkly

Austen, Catherine

All good children. Orca Book Publishers 2011 300p $19.95
Grades: 7 8 9 10 11 12 **Fic**
1. Siblings -- Fiction 2. Individualism -- Fiction 3. Totalitarianism -- Fiction
ISBN 978-1-55469-824-0; 1-55469-824-3

In the not-too-distant future, Max tries to maintain his identity in a world where the only way to survive is to conform and obey.

"Action packed, terrifying, and believable, this entertaining novel will provoke important discussions about subservience, resistance, and individual freedom." Booklist

Avasthi, Swati

Chasing Shadows; by Swati Avasthi and illustrated by Craig Phillips. Random House Childrens Books 2013 320 p. $17.99
Grades: 9 10 11 12 **Fic**
1. Death -- Fiction 2. Teenage girls -- Fiction
ISBN 0375863427; 9780375863424

The book offers a "portrait of two girls teetering on the edge of grief and insanity. Two girls who will find out just how many ways there are to lose a friend . . . and how many ways to be lost. Holly and Savitri cope with the death of their friend Corey as they look for Corey's killer." (Publisher's note)

"Savitri's boyfriend Corey is killed and her best friend, Holly (Corey's sister), is injured by a seemingly senseless shooting. With the killer at large, Holly teeters on the brink of sanity. The narrative alternates among Savitri's voice; a second-person narrator; and Holly's perspective, told through first-person text and dramatic graphic novel style interludes. Avasthi delves deeply into the pysche of both girls." (Horn Book)

★ **Split**. Alfred A. Knopf 2010 282p $16.99; lib bdg $19.99
Grades: 10 11 12 **Fic**
1. Brothers -- Fiction 2. Child abuse -- Fiction
ISBN 978-0-375-86340-0; 0-375-86340-0; 978-0-375-96340-7 lib bdg; 0-375-96340-5 lib bdg
LC 2009-22615

A teenaged boy thrown out of his house by his abusive father goes to live with his older brother, who ran away from home years ago to escape the abuse.

"Readers seeking sensational violence should look elsewhere; this taut, complex family drama depicts abuse unflinchingly but focuses on healing, growth and learning to take responsibility for one's own anger." Kirkus

Avi, 1937-

★ **City** of orphans; with illustrations by Greg Ruth. Atheneum Books for Young Readers 2011 350p il $16.99
Grades: 5 6 7 8 **Fic**
1. Mystery fiction 2. Gangs -- Fiction 3. Immigrants -- Fiction 4. Family life -- Fiction 5. Homeless persons

-- Fiction
ISBN 978-1-4169-7102-3; 1-4169-7102-5
LC 2010049229

In 1893 New York, thirteen-year-old Maks, a newsboy, teams up with Willa, a homeless girl, to clear his older sister, Emma, from charges that she stole from the brand new Waldorf Hotel, where she works. Includes historical notes.

"Avi's vivid recreation of the sights and sounds of that time and place is spot on, masterfully weaving accurate historical details with Maks' experiences." Kirkus

Includes bibliographical references

★ **Crispin**: the cross of lead. Hyperion Bks. for Children 2002 $15.99; pa $6.99
Grades: 5 6 7 8 **Fic**
1. Orphans -- Fiction 2. Middle Ages -- Fiction
ISBN 0-7868-0828-4; 0-7868-1658-9 pa
LC 2001-51829

Awarded the Newbery Medal, 2001

Falsely accused of theft and murder, an orphaned peasant boy in fourteenth-century England flees his village and meets a larger-than-life juggler who holds a dangerous secret

This "book is a page-turner from beginning to end. . . . A meticulously crafted story, full of adventure, mystery, and action." SLJ

Other titles in this series are:
Crispin at the edge of the world (2006)
Crispin: the end of time (2010)

★ **Nothing** but the truth; a documentary novel. Scholastic Inc. 2010 177p pa $6.99
Grades: 6 7 8 9 **Fic**
1. School stories
ISBN 978-0-545-17415-2
First published 1991 by Orchard Bks.
A Newbery Medal honor book, 1992

A ninth-grader's suspension for singing "The Star-Spangled Banner" during homeroom becomes a national news story.

"The book is effectively set entirely in monologue or dialogue; conversations, memos, letters, diary entries, talk-radio transcripts, and newspaper articles are all interwoven to present an uninterrupted plot. The construction is nearly flawless; the characters seem painfully human and typically ordinary. . . . A powerful, explosive novel that involves the reader from start to finish." Horn Book

★ **Traitor's** gate. Atheneum Books for Young Readers 2007 351p $17.99
Grades: 5 6 7 8 **Fic**
1. Spies -- Fiction 2. Poverty -- Fiction 3. Family life -- Fiction
ISBN 0-689-85335-1

When his father is arrested as a debtor in 1849 London, fourteen-year-old John Huffman must take on unexpected responsibilities, from asking a distant relative for help to determining why people are spying on him and his family.

"With plenty of period detail, this action-packed narrative of twists, turns, and treachery is another winner from a master craftsman." SLJ

Ayarbe, Heidi

★ **Compromised**. HarperTeen 2010 452p $16.99
Grades: 8 9 10 11 12 **Fic**
1. Foster home care -- Fiction 2. Runaway teenagers -- Fiction 3. Tourette syndrome -- Fiction 4. Voyages and travels -- Fiction
ISBN 978-0-06-172849-5; 0-06-172849-7
LC 2009-23545

With her con-man father in prison, fifteen-year-old Maya sets out from Reno, Nevada, for Boise, Idaho, hoping to stay out of foster care by finding an aunt she never knew existed, but a fellow runaway complicates all of her scientifically-devised plans.

"Ayarbe offers a gut-wrenching, terrifyingly authentic story and memorably etched, courageous characters whose influence on each other is palpable." Booklist

Compulsion. Balzer + Bray 2011 297p lib bdg $16.99
Grades: 10 11 12 **Fic**
1. School stories 2. Soccer -- Fiction 3. Obsessive-compulsive disorder -- Fiction
ISBN 978-0-06-199386-2
LC 2010027826

Poised to lead his high school soccer team to its third straight state championship, seventeen-year-old star player Jake Martin struggles to keep hidden his nearly debilitating obsessive-compulsive disorder.

"Ayarbe exercises both enormous skill and restraint getting to the root of just how debilitating OCD can become, juxtaposing descriptions of the ways the mind's compulsions can trip a trap of mental and physical anguish against a complex, credibly casted portrayal of teen social dynamics, which are treacherous enough on their own. A gripping, claustrophobic read." Booklist

Ayres, Katherine

North by night; a story of the Underground Railroad. Delacorte Press 1998 176p hardcover o.p. pa $4.99
Grades: 6 7 8 9 **Fic**
1. Diaries -- Fiction 2. Slavery -- Fiction 3. Fugitive slaves -- Fiction 4. Underground railroad -- Fiction
ISBN 0-385-32564-9; 0-440-22747-x pa
LC 98-10039

Presents the journal of Lucinda, a sixteen-year-old girl whose family operates a stop on the Underground Railroad

This "is an absorbing tale. Ayres slips in a lot of evocative detail about the hard work of running a farm and a household before the Civil War, as well as some rather charming musing about kissing and its myriad effects on the psyche." Booklist

Bacigalupi, Paolo

The **doubt** factory: a novel. Little, Brown & Co. 2014 484p
Grades: 9 10 11 12 **Fic**
1. Corporations — Corrupt practices — Fiction; 2. Fathers and daughters — Fiction; 3. Whistle blowing--

Fiction 4. Adventure fiction
ISBN: 0316220752; 9780316220750
LC 2014002543

This suspense novel "explores the . . . issue of how public information is distorted for monetary gain, and how those who exploit it must be stopped. Everything Alix knows about her life is a lie. At least that's what a mysterious young man who's stalking her keeps saying. But then she begins investigating the disturbing claims he makes against her father." (Publisher's note)

"This openly didactic novel asks challenging questions about the immorality of the profit motive and capitalism, but does so within the context of a highly believable plot . . . and well-developed, multifaceted characters." Pub Wkly

★ The **drowned** cities; by Paolo Bacigalupi. Little, Brown and Company 2012 448p. paperback $11.00

Grades: 9 10 11 12 **Fic**

1. Science fiction 2. Apocalyptic fiction 3. Refugees -- Fiction 4. War -- Fiction 5. Orphans -- Fiction 6. Soldiers -- Fiction 7. Survival -- Fiction 8. Conduct of life -- Fiction 9. Genetic engineering -- Fiction
ISBN 9780316056243; 9780316056229 paperback
LC 2011031762

This book takes place "[i]n a dark future America where violence, terror, and grief touch everyone, young refugees Mahlia and Mouse have managed to leave behind the war-torn lands of the Drowned Cities by escaping into the jungle outskirts. But when they discover a wounded half-man--a bioengineered war beast named Tool--who is being hunted by a vengeful band of soldiers, their fragile existence quickly collapses." (Publisher's note)

★ **Ship** Breaker; Bacigalupi, Paolo. Little, Brown and Co. 2010 326p $17.99

Grades: 8 9 10 11 12 **Fic**

1. Science fiction 2. Recycling -- Fiction
ISBN 0316056219; 9780316056212
LC 2009-34424

Michael L. Printz Award, 2011

In a futuristic world, teenaged Nailer scavenges copper wiring from grounded oil tankers for a living, but when he finds a beached clipper ship with a girl in the wreckage, he has to decide if he should strip the ship for its wealth or rescue the girl.

"Bacigalupi's cast is ethnically and morally diverse, and the book's message never overshadows the storytelling, action-packed pacing, or intricate world-building. At its core, the novel is an exploration of Nailer's discovery of the nature of the world around him and his ability to transcend that world's expectations." Publ Wkly

Backes, M. Molly

The **princesses** of Iowa; M. Molly Backes. Candlewick Press 2012 442 p. $16.99

Grades: 9 10 11 12 **Fic**

1. Iowa -- Fiction 2. Schools -- Fiction 3. Popularity -- Fiction 4. High schools -- Fiction 5. Conduct of life -- Fiction
ISBN 0763653128; 9780763653125
LC 2011018622

This young adult novel follows "Paige Sheridan . . . she's pretty, rich, and popular, and her spot on the homecoming court is practically guaranteed. But when a night of partying ends in an it-could-have-been-so-much worse crash, everything changes. Her best friends start ignoring her, her boyfriend grows cold and distant. . . . A charismatic new teacher . . . encourages students to be true to themselves. But who is Paige, if not the homecoming princess everyone expects her to be?" (Publisher's note)

"Backes addresses guilt, deceit, homophobia, loyalty, and the burden of keeping up appearances in a brutally believable high school setting." Pub Wkly

Badoe, Adwoa

Between sisters. Groundwood Books/House of Anansi Press 2010 205p $16.95

Grades: 9 10 11 12 **Fic**

1. School stories 2. Poor -- Fiction 3. Ghana -- Fiction 4. Family life -- Fiction
ISBN 978-0-88899-996-2

"When sixteen-year-old Gloria fails thirteen out of fifteen subjects on her final exams, her future looks bleak indeed. Her family's resources are meager so the entire family is thrilled when a distant relative, Christine, offers to move Gloria north to Kumasi to look after her toddler son, Sam. In exchange, after two years, Christine will pay for Gloria to go to dressmaking school. Life in Kumasi is more grand than anything Gloria has ever experienced. . . . [But] Kumasi is also full of temptations." Publisher's note

Baer, Marianna

Frost; Marianna Baer. Balzer + Bray 2011 400p $17.99; ebook $9.99

Grades: 8 9 10 11 12 **Fic**

1. School stories 2. Houses -- Fiction 3. Supernatural -- Fiction
ISBN 978-0-06-179949-5; 978-0-06-209331-8 ebook
LC 2011019308

When Leena Thomas gets her wish to live in an old Victorian house with her two closest friends during their senior year at boarding school, the unexpected arrival of another roommate—a confrontational and eccentric classmate—seems to bring up old anxieties and fears for Leena that may or may not be in her own mind.

"This nuanced blend of psychological suspense and boarding-school drama will tingle the spines of plenty of readers." Booklist

Bailey, Em

Shift; Em Bailey. Random House Distribution Childrens 2012 304 p. (hardcover) $16.99

Grades: 7 8 9 10 11 12 **Fic**

1. Human behavior -- Fiction 2. Female friendship -- Fiction 3. High school students -- Fiction 4. Orphans -- Fiction 5. Popularity -- Fiction 6. High schools -- Fiction 7. Mental illness -- Fiction 8. Interpersonal relations -- Fiction
ISBN 1606843583; 9781606843581; 9781606843598
LC 2011034349

Author Em Bailey's character "Olive keeps it simple: take her meds, keep a low profile at school, stay away from the ocean (with its horrible memories), and try not to cause trouble since she's pretty sure her selfish, unruly behavior is what made her father take off six months ago. But then strange and mysterious Miranda Vaile shows up at her high school, and Olive's safeguards start to crumble. Miranda begins insinuating herself into the life of Olive's former best friend, Katie." (Publishers Weekly)

Bailey, Kristin

Legacy of the clockwork key; by Kristin Bailey. Simon Pulse 2013 416 p. (alk. paper) $17.99

Grades: 7 8 9 10 **Fic**

1. Inventions 2. Secret societies 3. Love -- Fiction 4. Science fiction 5. Orphans -- Fiction 6. Secret societies -- Fiction 7. London (England) -- History -- 19th century -- Fiction 8. Great Britain -- History -- Victoria, 1837-1901 -- Fiction

ISBN 1442440260; 9781442440265

LC 2011049871

In this book, "a teen girl unravels the mysteries of a secret society and their most dangerous invention. . . . When a fire consumes Meg's home, killing her parents . . . all she has left is the tarnished pocket watch she rescued from the ashes. But this is no ordinary timepiece. The clock turns out to be a mechanical key--a key that only Meg can use--which unlocks a series of deadly secrets and intricate clues that Meg has no choice but to follow." (Publisher's note)

Ballard, J. G., 1930-2009

Empire of the Sun; a novel. Simon & Schuster 1984 279p hardcover o.p. pa $13

Grades: 9 10 11 12 Adult **Fic**

1. Shanghai (China) -- Fiction 2. World War, 1939-1945 -- Fiction

ISBN 0-671-53051-8; 0-7432-6523-8 pa

LC 84-10630

"This novel is much more than the gritty story of a child's miraculous survival in the grimly familiar setting of World War II's concentration camps. There is no nostalgia for a good war here, no sentimentality for the human spirit at extremes. Mr. Ballard is more ambitious than romance usually allows. He aims to render a vision of the apocalypse, and succeeds so well that it can hurt to dwell upon his images." N Y Times Book Rev

Followed by The kindness of women (1991)

Balog, Cyn

Sleepless. Delacorte Press 2010 215p $16.99

Grades: 8 9 10 11 12 **Fic**

1. Love stories 2. Death -- Fiction 3. Dreams -- Fiction 4. Bereavement -- Fiction 5. Supernatural -- Fiction

ISBN 978-0-385-73848-4; 0-385-73848-X

LC 2010-00123

Eron, a supernatural being known as a Sandman whose purpose is to seduce humans to sleep, falls in love with a sad teenaged girl who is mourning her boyfriend's death.

"Suspense, believable characters and an imaginative twist on a ghost story/romance make for a lovely read." Kirkus

Bancks, Tristan

Mac Slater hunts the cool. Simon & Schuster Books for Young Readers 2010 203p $15.99

Grades: 6 7 8 9 **Fic**

1. School stories 2. Beaches -- Fiction 3. Weblogs -- Fiction 4. Video recording -- Fiction

ISBN 978-1-4169-8574-7; 1-4169-8574-3

LC 2009-00152

Mac, an Australian youth, has one week to prove that he can be a "coolhunter," identifying emerging trends and posting images on a website, but he is competing against a classmate on whom he has a crush and dealing with resistance from his best friend and his own confusion over what "cool" means.

"Mac is a likable character who will appeal to a wide range of readers." Booklist

Mac Slater vs. the city. Simon & Schuster Books for Young Readers 2011 184p $15.99

Grades: 6 7 8 9 **Fic**

1. Inventors -- Fiction 2. Web sites -- Fiction 3. Inventions -- Fiction

ISBN 1-4169-8576-X; 978-1-4169-8576-1

LC 2010006858

Mac and his reluctant friend Paul head from Australia to Manhattan to continue their work for the Coolhunter website, and once there they discover a group of young inventors whose work is meant to be kept top-secret.

"The story takes twists and turns that are both surprising and rewarding. . . . An easy sell to many middle graders." SLJ

Banks, Kate

Walk softly, Rachel. Farrar, Straus & Giroux 2003 149p $16

Grades: 7 8 9 10 **Fic**

1. Death -- Fiction 2. Family life -- Fiction

ISBN 0-374-38230-1

LC 2002-26503

When fourteen-year-old Rachel reads the journal of her brother, who died when she was seven, she learns secrets that help her understand her parents and herself

"While Banks's poetic prose may consist of simple words, its effect on the ear and heart is remarkable." SLJ

Baratz-Logsted, Lauren

Crazy beautiful. Houghton Mifflin Harcourt 2009 191p $16

Grades: 7 8 9 10 **Fic**

1. School stories 2. Bullies -- Fiction 3. Amputees -- Fiction 4. People with physical disabilities -- Fiction

ISBN 978-0-547-22307-0; 0-547-22307-2

LC 2008-40463

In this contemporary retelling of "Beauty and the Beast," a teenaged boy whose hands were amputated in an explosion and a gorgeous girl whose mother has recently died form an instant connection when they meet on their first day as new students.

"This romance transcends all of its potential pitfalls to create a powerful story about recovery and friendship." Kirkus

Twin's daughter. Bloomsbury 2010 390p $16.99

Grades: 7 8 9 10 **Fic**

1. Mystery fiction 2. Aunts -- Fiction 3. Twins -- Fiction 4. Homicide -- Fiction 5. London (England) -- Fiction 6. Great Britain -- History -- 19th century

-- Fiction
ISBN 978-1-59990-513-6; 1-59990-513-2
LC 2010-08234

In Victorian London, thirteen-year-old Lucy's comfortable world with her loving parents begins slowly to unravel the day that a bedraggled woman who looks exactly like her mother appears at their door.

"Baratz-Logsted's gothic murder mystery is rife with twists and moves swiftly and elegantly. . . . The ending will intrigue and delight readers." Booklist

Bardugo, Leigh

Ruin and rising; Leigh Bardugo. Henry Holt and Co. 2014 422p map (Grisha trilogy) $18.99
Grades: 8 9 10 11 12 Fic
1. Fantasy fiction; 2. Love stories; 3. Princes — Fiction
ISBN: 080509461X; 9780805094619
LC 2013049306

Concluding volume of the author's Grisha Trilogy. "Deep in an ancient network of tunnels and caverns, a weakened Alina must submit to the dubious protection of the Apparat and the zealots who worship her as a Saint. Yet her plans lie elsewhere, with the hunt for the elusive firebird and the hope that an outlaw prince still survives." (Publisher's note)

"Alina and company have only one hope: if they can kill the Firebird, its magical bones can be used to break the Darkling's chokehold on Ravka. In this concluding volume, Alina must rely on her childhood friend Mal's preternatural tracking ability. Bardugo's longstanding theme of 'power corrupts' is developed organically; the magic she invents will surprise and delight readers." Horn Book

Shadow and bone; Leigh Bardugo. Henry Holt 2012 358 p. (Grisha trilogy) (hc) $17.99
Grades: 8 9 10 11 12 **Fic**
1. Fantasy fiction 2. Magic -- Fiction 3. Folklore -- Russia 4. Monsters -- Fiction 5. Slavic mythology 6. Fantasy 7. Ability -- Fiction 8. Orphans -- Fiction
ISBN 0805094598; 9780805094596
LC 2011034012

In this young adult novel, "[Leigh] Bardugo draws inspiration from Russian and Slavic myth and culture to kick off her 'Grisha' trilogy. In the nation of Ravka, Alina Starkov is a junior cartographer's assistant in the army, while her best friend Mai is an expert tracker. When a perilous mission into the magically created Shadow Fold goes wrong, Mai is gravely wounded and Alina manifests the rare ability to summon light. Immediately recruited into the order of the magic-using Grisha, Alina is taken under the wing of its intimidating and powerful leader, the Darkling, and heralded as the potential destroyer of the Shadow Fold. As she navigates Grisha politics and uncovers well-hidden secrets, she realizes that the fate of the nation rests on her shoulders and she may be in grave danger." (Publishers Weekly)

Siege and storm; Leigh Bardugo. 1st ed. Henry Holt and Co. 2013 448 p. (Grisha trilogy) (hardcover) $17.99
Grades: 8 9 10 11 12 **Fic**
1. Fantasy fiction 2. Russia -- Fiction 3. Monsters -- Fiction 4. Fantasy 5. Magic -- Fiction 6. Orphans -- Fiction
ISBN 0805094601; 9780805094602
LC 2012046361

This fantasy novel, by Leigh Bardugo, is book 2 of the "Grisha Trilogy." "Alina must try to make a life with Mal in an unfamiliar land, all while keeping her identity as the Sun Summoner a secret. But she can't outrun her past or her destiny for long. The Darkling has emerged from the Shadow Fold with a terrifying new power and a dangerous plan that will test the very boundaries of the natural world." (Publisher's note)

Barkley, Brad

Dream factory; [by] Brad Barkley + Heather Hepler. Dutton Books 2007 250p $16.99; pa $8.99
Grades: 8 9 10 11 12 **Fic**
1. Love stories 2. Summer employment -- Fiction
ISBN 978-0-525-47802-7; 0-525-47802-7; 978-0-14-241298-5 pa; 0-14-241298-8 pa

Alternating chapters present the view points of two teenagers who find summer employment as costumed cartoon characters at Disney World and try to resist falling in love.

"Able writing moves the story along while strong characterization makes even secondary players come alive." SLJ

Jars of glass; [by] Brad Barkley & Heather Hepler. Dutton Childrens Books 2008 246p $16.99
Grades: 7 8 9 10 11 12 **Fic**
1. Adoption -- Fiction 2. Siblings -- Fiction 3. Family life -- Fiction 4. Mental illness -- Fiction
ISBN 978-0-525-47911-6; 0-525-47911-2
LC 2007-52657

Two sisters, aged fourteen and fifteen, offer their views of events that occur during the year after their mother is diagnosed with schizophrenia and their family, including a recently adopted Russian orphan, begins to disintegrate.

"Barkley and Hepler are the masters of alternating narration, with Chloe's and Shana's voices both believable, clearly different, and usefully complementary. . . . This is an affecting story about families struggling to readjust in the face of one member's affliction." Bull Cent Child Books

Scrambled eggs at midnight; by Brad Barkley, Heather Hepler. Dutton Books 2006 262p $16.99
Grades: 7 8 9 10 **Fic**
1. Love stories 2. Fairs -- Fiction
ISBN 0-525-47760-8
LC 2005029187

Calliope and Eliot, two fifteen-year-olds in Asheville, North Carolina, begin to acknowledge some unpleasant truths about their parents and form their own ideas about love.

"This coauthored love story unfolds in alternating chapters narrated in Cal and Elliot's hilarious, heart-tugging voices. . . . The authors raise a potentially routine summer romance into a refreshing, poetic, memorable story." Booklist

Barnaby, Hannah

Wonder show; by Hannah Barnaby. Houghton Mifflin Books for Children 2012 viii, 274 p.p $16.99
Grades: 7 8 9 10 11 12 **Fic**
1. Carnivals 2. Orphanages 3. Runaway children --

Fiction 4. Fathers -- Fiction 5. Runaways -- Fiction 6. Sideshows -- Fiction 7. Orphanages -- Fiction 8. Depressions -- 1929 -- United States -- Fiction
ISBN 0547599803; 9780547599809
LC 2011052426

William C. Morris Award Finalist (2013)

In this book by Hannah Barnaby, "Portia Remini, 13 . . . escapes . . . from the McGreavey Home for Wayward Girls to search for her father. . . . She joins a carnival. . . . On the lam from sinister 'Mister,' who runs McGreavey's, Portia learns the stories of some of the carnival's strange troupe. . . . But . . . when Mister's dragnet closes in, Portia decides that to find the answers she seeks she must return to the horror of The Home." (School Library Journal)

Barnes, Jennifer Lynn

The **Squad**: perfect cover. Delacorte Press 2008 275p pa $6.99

Grades: 7 8 9 10 **Fic**

1. School stories 2. Spies -- Fiction 3. Computers -- Fiction 4. Cheerleading -- Fiction
ISBN 978-0-385-73454-7 pa; 0-385-73454-9 pa
LC 2007-09352

High school sophomore Toby Klein enjoys computer hacking and wearing combat boots, so she thinks it is a joke when she is invited to join the cheerleading squad but soon learns cheering is just a cover for an elite group of government operatives known as the Squad.

"In addition to offering crafty plotting and time-honored, typical teen conflicts and rivalries, Barnes maintains a sharp sense of humor in this action-adventure series." Bull Cent Child Books

Another title in this series is:
The Squad: killer spirit (2008)

Barnes, John

Losers in space; John Barnes. Viking 2012 433 p. ill. (hardcover) $18.99

Grades: 9 10 11 12 **Fic**

1. Science fiction 2. Space vehicles -- Fiction 3. Runaway teenagers -- Fiction 4. Fame -- Fiction 5. Stowaways -- Fiction 6. Psychopaths -- Fiction 7. Interplanetary voyages -- Fiction
ISBN 0670061565; 9780670061563
LC 2011020579

This science fiction novel is "set in a celebrity-obsessed future. Susan Tervaille . . . is swept up in a crazy plot hatched by bad-boy Derlock. She and several friends stow away on a spacecraft headed to Mars, hoping they'll be broadcast . . . enough . . . on Earth to secure their status as up-and-coming superstars. What they don't realize is that Derlock is insane and hell-bent on snagging fame for himself -- even if it means lives are lost." (Publishers Weekly)

★ **Tales** of the Madman Underground; an historical romance 1973. Viking 2009 532p $18.99; pa $9.99

Grades: 10 11 12 Adult **Fic**

1. School stories 2. Ohio -- Fiction 3. Alcoholism -- Fiction 4. Friendship -- Fiction 5. Mother-son relationship -- Fiction
ISBN 978-0-670-06081-8; 0-670-06081-X; 978-0-14-241702-7 pa; 0-14-241702-5 pa
LC 2009-11072

ALA YALSA Printz Award Honor Book (2010)

In September 1973, as the school year begins in his depressed Ohio town, high school senior Kurt Shoemaker determines to be "normal," despite his chaotic home life with his volatile, alcoholic mother and the deep loyalty and affection he has for his friends in the therapy group dubbed the Madman Underground.

"Teens initially turned off by Barnes's liberal use of profanities and the book's length will be captured by the sharp, funny dialogue and crisp personalities of the Madmen. Even minor characters are distinctive. . . . [This] is an excellent selection for book clubs of older teens that like sinking their teeth into longer stories with substance." Voice Youth Advocates

Barnhouse, Rebecca

The **book** of the maidservant. Random House 2009 232p map $16.99; lib bdg $19.99

Grades: 7 8 9 10 **Fic**

1. Mystics 2. Memoirists 3. Writers on religion 4. Middle Ages -- Fiction 5. Religious life -- Fiction 6. Voyages and travels -- Fiction 7. Pilgrims and pilgrimages -- Fiction
ISBN 978-0-375-85856-7; 0-375-85856-3; 978-0-375-95856-4 lib bdg; 0-375-95856-8 lib bdg
LC 2008-28820

In 1413, a young maidservant accompanies her deeply religious mistress, Dame Margery Kempe, on a pilgrimage to Rome. Includes author's note on Kempe, writer of "The Book of Margery Kempe," considered by some to be the first autobiography in the English language

"Earthy, authentic, and engrossing, this fast-paced, easy read belongs on the shelf with Karen Cushman's The Midwife's Apprentice." Voice Youth Advocates

Includes bibliographical references

Barratt, Mark

Joe Rat. Eerdmans Books for Young Readers 2009 307p pa $9

Grades: 7 8 9 10 **Fic**

1. Crime -- Fiction 2. Orphans -- Fiction 3. Mental illness -- Fiction
ISBN 978-0-8028-5356-1; 0-8028-5356-0
LC 2008055972

First published 2008 in the United Kingdom

In the dark, dank sewers of Victorian London, a boy known as Joe Rat scrounges for valuables which he gives to "Mother," a criminal mastermind who considers him a favorite, but a chance meeting with a runaway girl and "the Madman" transforms all their lives.

"The unraveling of the Madman's identity is but one of the pleasures of Barratt's leisurely and convincing historical fiction." Booklist

The **wild** man. Eerdmans Books for Young Readers 2010 341p pa $9

Grades: 7 8 9 10 **Fic**

1. Crime -- Fiction 2. Fathers -- Fiction 3. Orphans

-- Fiction 4. Social classes -- Fiction 5. Impostors and imposture -- Fiction
ISBN 978-0-8028-5377-6 pa; 0-8028-5377-3 pa
LC 2010010937

In Victorian England, Joe Rat has escaped the clutches of the criminal mastermind, Mother, and is trying to make an honest living in a better part of London, but when a rich philanthropist tracks down a man claiming to be Joe's missing father—a British army deserter—he must determine where his loyalties lie.

"Barratt writes as if he is keeping an adjacent berth to Dickens; here's hoping scrappy Joe has a few more tricks up his ratty sleeves." Booklist

Barrett, Tracy

Dark of the moon. Harcourt 2011 310p $16.99
Grades: 7 8 9 10 **Fic**
1. Greece -- Fiction 2. Classical mythology -- Fiction 3. Theseus (Greek Mythology) -- Fiction
ISBN 978-0-547-58132-3; 0-547-58132-7
LC 2011009597

Retells the story of the minotaur through the eyes of his fifteen-year-old sister, Ariadne, a lonely girl destined to become a goddess of the moon, and her new friend, Theseus, the son of Athens' king who was sent to Crete as a sacrifice to her misshapen brother.

"This retelling of the myth of the Minotaur is deft, dark, and enthralling. Barrett spares readers none of the gore and violence of the Kretan goddess-worship, which involves both human and animal sacrifice. Ariadne's beliefs, though alien to modern readers, are given sufficient context to make them comprehensible. . . . This thoughtful, well-written reimagining of a classic myth is a welcome addition to the genre." SLJ

King of Ithaka. Henry Holt and Company 2010 261p map $16.99
Grades: 7 8 9 10 **Fic**
1. Classical mythology -- Fiction 2. Odysseus (Greek mythology) -- Fiction
ISBN 978-0-8050-8969-1; 0-8050-8969-1
LC 2009-50770

Sixteen-year-old Telemachos and his two best friends leave their life of privilege to undertake a quest to find Telemachos's father Odysseus. "Grades six to ten." (Bull Cent Child Books)

"The exotic climes and vivid descriptions . . . give the story a sense of immediacy and color." Booklist

Barron, T. A.

Merlin's dragon. Philomel Books 2008 305p (Merlin's dragon) $19.99
Grades: 6 7 8 9 **Fic**
1. Fantasy fiction 2. Magic -- Fiction 3. Dragons -- Fiction
ISBN 978-0-399-24750-7; 0-399-24750-5
LC 2008-2469

Basil, a small, flying lizard who is searching for others like himself, discovers that there is more to him than he knows, as he becomes engaged in Avalon's great war between the evil Rhita Gawr and the forces of good.

"Basil is an appealing, complex character. . . . This first book in a new series will captivate readers already familiar with the fantasist's Merlin chronicles." Booklist

Other titles in this series are:
Doomraga's revenge (2009)
Utlimate magic (2010)

★ The **lost** years of Merlin. Philomel Bks. 1996 326p $19.99; pa $7.99
Grades: 5 6 7 8 **Fic**
1. Fantasy fiction 2. Merlin (Legendary character) -- Fiction
ISBN 978-0-399-23018-1; 978-0-441-00668-7 pa
LC 96-33920

"A boy, hurled on the rocks by the sea, regains consciousness unable to remember anything—not his parents, not his own name. He is sure that the secretive Branwen is not his mother, despite her claims, and that Emrys is not his real name. The two soon find themselves feared because of Branwen's healing abilities and Emrys' growing powers. . . . Barron has created not only a magical land populated by remarkable beings but also a completely magical tale, filled with ancient Celtic and Druidic lore, that will enchant readers." Booklist

Other titles in this series are:
The seven songs of Merlin (1997)
The fires of Merlin (1998)
The mirror of Merlin (1999)
The wings of Merlin (2000)
The book of magic (2011)

Bartoletti, Susan Campbell

★ The **boy** who dared. Scholastic Press 2008 202p $16.99
Grades: 5 6 7 8 **Fic**
1. Courage -- Fiction 2. National socialism -- Fiction
ISBN 978-0-439-68013-4; 0-439-68013-1
LC 2007014166

In October, 1942, seventeen-year-old Helmuth Hübener, imprisoned for distributing anti-Nazi leaflets, recalls his past life and how he came to dedicate himself to bringing the truth about Hitler and the war to the German people.

Bartoletti "does and excellent job of conveying the political climate surrounding Hitler's ascent to power, seamlessly integrating a complex range of socioeconomic conditions into her absorbing drama." Publ Wkly

Baskin, Nora Raleigh

All we know of love. Candlewick Press 2008 201p $16.99
Grades: 6 7 8 9 10 **Fic**
1. Mothers -- Fiction 2. Loss (Psychology) -- Fiction 3. Voyages and travels -- Fiction
ISBN 978-0-7636-3623-4; 0-7636-3623-1
LC 2007-22396

Natalie, almost sixteen, sneaks away from her Connecticut home and takes the bus to Florida, looking for the mother who abandoned her father and her when she was ten years old.

"Baskin takes a familiar story line and examines it in a new and interesting way that will engage readers." Voice Youth Advocates

Bass, Karen

Graffiti knight. Orca Book Publishers 2014 272 p. $14.95

Grades: 7 8 9 10 **Fic**

1. Graffiti 2. Communist countries -- Fiction 3. Family life 4. Resistance to government

ISBN 1927485533; 9781927485538

"Just as Ruta Sepetys revealed a different perspective of the Holocaust in Between Shades of Gray (2011), Bass introduces another view of history unknown to many American readers...This eye-opening story shows that war's end is never tidy." (Booklist)

Summer of fire; [edited by Laura Peetoom] Coteau Books for Teens 2009 267p pa $10.95

Grades: 9 10 11 12 **Fic**

1. Germany -- Fiction 2. Sisters -- Fiction 3. Runaway teenagers -- Fiction 4. World War, 1939-1945 -- Fiction

ISBN 978-1-55050-415-6; 1-55050-415-0

"It is rare for a novel to offer a German civilian's viewpoint during Hitler's rise to power with such honesty. Alternating between Del's and Garda's voices, . . . the teen voices are immediate: Del's wry and self-aware; Garda's desperate and angry." Booklist

Bass, Ron

Lucid; Adrienne Stoltz, Ron Bass. Razorbill 2012 342 p. (hardback) $17.99

Grades: 9 10 11 12 **Fic**

1. Fantasy fiction 2. Dreams -- Fiction 3. Love -- Fiction 4. Schools -- Fiction 5. Friendship -- Fiction 6. High schools -- Fiction 7. Actors and actresses -- Fiction

ISBN 1595145192; 9781595145192

LC 2012014448

This young adult novel, by Adrienne Stoltz and Ron Bass, explores dreams and reality. "Sloane and Maggie have never met. . . . At night, they dream that they're each other. . . . Before long, Sloane and Maggie can no longer tell which life is real and which is just a dream. They realize that eventually they will have to choose one life to wake up to, or risk spiraling into insanity." (Publisher's note)

On thin ice. Red Deer Press 2006 348p pa $10.95

Grades: 8 9 10 11 12 **Fic**

1. Inuit -- Fiction 2. Polar bear -- Fiction 3. Greenhouse effect -- Fiction

ISBN 978-0-88995-337-6; 0-88995-337-6

"Set in the remote Arctic village of Nanurtalik, this novel follows Ashley as she journeys on the shaman path chosen for her through the Inuit line of her father. Disturbed by haunting—sometimes frightening—dreams of a gigantic polar bear that seems bent on destroying her, Ashley furiously draws her dreams onto paper, capturing the very essence of the bear within. . . . This novel is told with richness of language, culture, and emotion, but its sense of place sparkles brightest." Voice Youth Advocates

Bassoff, Leah

★ **Lost** girl found; Leah Bassoff and Laura DeLuca. Groundwood Books/House of Anansi Press 2014 212p maps

Grades: 6 7 8 9 10 Fic

1. Refugees — Fiction; 2. Sudan — History — Civil War, 1983-2005 — Fiction; 3. Mother-daughter relationship — Fiction

ISBN: 1554984165; 9781554984169

LC bl2014008921

"For Poni life in her small village in southern Sudan is simple and complicated at the same time. But then the war comes and there is only one thing for Poni to do. Run. Run for her life. Driven by the sheer will to survive and the hope that she can somehow make it to the Kakuma refugee camp in Kenya, Poni sets out on a long, dusty trek across the east African countryside with thousands of refugees. . . In Kakuma she is almost overwhelmed by the misery that surrounds her. Poni realizes that she must leave the camp at any cost. Her destination is a compound in Nairobi." (Publisher's note)

"Poni wants to finish her education, and she has a chance to do so when she escapes the refugee camp. Poni is a fully realized and sympathetic character. This fast-paced novel covers a lot of ground and incorporates a good deal of historical background." Horn Book

Bates, Marni

Awkward. Kensington 2012 259p pa $9.95

Grades: 7 8 9 10 **Fic**

1. School stories 2. Fame -- Fiction 3. Popularity -- Fiction

ISBN 978-0-7582-6937-9; 0-7582-6937-4

"A brilliant but socially inept girl finds herself starring in a YouTube video gone viral when she knocks over a football player and tries to give him CPR. . . . Mackenzie tries to keep her head down as the entire nation laughs at her for her awkward video moves. . . . But her notoriety takes a positive turn when the hottest rock group around turns her film into a music video with a new hit song, boosting her fame even further. . . . Bates keeps her prose light, always focusing on the comedy as she lampoons high-school popularity, and gives narrator Mackenzie some good one-liners. . . . Very funny. Should please lots of readers, awkward or not." Kirkus

Bauer, Joan

★ **Hope** was here. Putnam 2000 186p $16.99; pa $7.99

Grades: 7 8 9 10 **Fic**

1. Aunts -- Fiction 2. Wisconsin -- Fiction 3. Restaurants -- Fiction

ISBN 0-399-23142-0; 0-14-240424-1 pa

LC 00-38232

A Newbery Medal honor book, 2001

When sixteen-year-old Hope and the aunt who has raised her move from Brooklyn to Mulhoney, Wisconsin, to work as waitress and cook in the Welcome Stairways diner, they become involved with G.T. Stoop, the diner owner, and his political campaign to oust the town's corrupt mayor. "Age twelve and up." (N Y Times Book Rev)

"Bauer manages to fill her heartfelt novel with gentle humor, quirky but appealing characters, and an engaging plot." Book Rep

★ **Peeled.** G.P. Putnam's Sons 2008 256p $16.99

Grades: 6 7 8 9 10 **Fic**

1. Ghost stories 2. School stories 3. Farm life -- Fiction 4. Journalism -- Fiction 5. New York (State) -- Fiction

ISBN 978-0-399-23475-0; 0-399-23475-6

LC 2007-42835

In an upstate New York farming community, high school reporter Hildy Biddle investigates a series of strange occurrences at a house rumored to be haunted.

This is "a warm and funny story full of likable, offbeat characters led by a strongly voiced, independently minded female protagonist on her way to genuine, well-earned maturity." SLJ

★ **Squashed;** [by] Joan Bauer. 1st G.P. Putnam's Sons ed; Puffin Books 2001 194p hardcover o.p. pa $7.99

Grades: 6 7 8 9 **Fic**

1. Country life -- Fiction

ISBN 0-399-23750-X; 0-14-240426-8 pa

LC 2001-18595

A reissue of the title first published 1992 by Delacorte Press

As sixteen-year-old Ellie pursues her two goals—growing the biggest pumpkin in Iowa and losing twenty pounds herself—she strengthens her relationship with her father and meets a young man with interests similar to her own.

"Skillful plot development and strong characterization are real stengths here. Ellie's perseptive, intelligent, and funny narrative keeps the story lively right up to its satisfying conclusion." SLJ

Bauman, Beth Ann

Jersey Angel; Beth Ann Bauman. Wendy Lamb Books 2012 201 p.

Grades: 9 10 11 12 **Fic**

1. Love stories 2. New Jersey -- Fiction 3. Female friendship -- Fiction 4. Dating (Social customs) -- Fiction 5. Girls -- Sexual behavior -- Fiction 6. Beaches -- Fiction 7. Italian Americans -- Fiction

ISBN 0385740204; 9780375899003; 9780385740203; 9780385740210; 9780385908283

LC 2011030915

This book follows "[s]ix months in the life of a proudly sex-positive 17-year-old from the Jersey Shore . . . Angel Cassonetti's life is based on two things: her exquisite awareness of and facility at wielding her sex appeal, and her close, almost sisterly friendship with Inggy Olofsson. Pale and blond, studious and monogamous with her longtime boyfriend Cork, Inggy stands in sharp contrast to the easily tanned, curly brunette, scholastically blasé and sexually precocious Angel. When Angel's longtime on-again, off-again boyfriend Joey tells her he's done playing games . . . --she finds herself drifting through the summer before senior year. She begins a potentially explosive secret fling that she can't quite find a way out of." (Kirkus Reviews)

Rosie & Skate. Wendy Lamb Books 2009 217p $15.99; lib bdg $18.99

Grades: 9 10 11 12 **Fic**

1. Sisters -- Fiction 2. Alcoholism -- Fiction 3. New Jersey -- Fiction 4. Family life -- Fiction 5. Dating (Social customs) -- Fiction 6. Father-daughter relationship -- Fiction

ISBN 978-0-385-73735-7; 0-385-73735-1; 978-0-385-90660-9 lib bdg; 0-385-90660-9 lib bdg

LC 2009-10575

New Jersey sisters Rosie, aged fifteen, and Skate, aged sixteen, cope differently with their father's alcoholism and incarceration, but manage to stay close to one another as they strive to lead normal lives and find hope for the future.

"Bauman's prose is lovely and real. Vivid descriptions bring her characters to life, and the dialogue is both believable and funny. . . . The novel expertly captures the ever-hopeful ache of adolescents longing for love, stability and certainty." Kirkus

Beam, Cris

★ **I** am J. Little, Brown 2011 326p

Grades: 9 10 11 12 **Fic**

1. Friendship -- Fiction 2. Transgender people -- Fiction 3. Identity (Psychology) -- Fiction

ISBN 0-316-05361-9; 978-0-316-05361-7

LC 2010-08640

J, who feels like a boy mistakenly born as a girl, runs away from his best friend who has rejected him and the parents he thinks do not understand him when he finally decides that it is time to be who he really is.

"The book is a gift to transgender teens and an affecting story of self-discovery for all readers." Horn Book

Includes bibliographical references

Beard, Philip

Dear Zoe; a novel. Viking 2005 196p hardcover o.p. pa $13

Grades: 9 10 11 12 **Fic**

1. Death -- Fiction 2. Letters -- Fiction 3. Sisters -- Fiction 4. Bereavement -- Fiction

ISBN 0-670-03401-0; 0-452-28740-5 pa

LC 2004-57173

"On the morning planes hit the World Trade Center towers, Tess DeNunzio's three-year-old sister, Zoe, ran into the street and was killed by a car. Fifteen-year-old Tess, who was supposed to be watching Zoe, was consumed by guilt. This novel is written in the form of a letter from Tess to Zoe, chronicling the year after Zoe's death. . . . Beard captures the raw emotion of a 15-year-old girl with impressive dexterity, following Tess through the many stages of grief." Booklist

Beaudoin, Sean

Wise Young Fool; by Sean Beaudoin. Little, Brown and Co. 2013 448 p. $18

Grades: 10 11 12 **Fic**

1. Juvenile delinquency 2. Teenagers -- Fiction 3. Bands (Music) -- Fiction 4. Musicians -- Fiction 5. Juvenile detention homes -- Fiction

ISBN 0316203793; 9780316203791

LC 2012032472

In this book by Sean Beaudoin, protagonist "Ritchie grabs readers by the throat before (politely) inviting them along for the (max-speed) ride. A battle of the bands looms. Dad split about five minutes before Mom's girlfriend moved in. There's the matter of trying to score with the dangerously hot Ravenna Woods while avoiding the dangerously huge Spence Proffer--not to mention just trying to forget what his sister, Beth, said the week before she died." (Publisher's note)

"This coming-of-age story is told in alternating story lines, leading up to Ritchie Sudden's arrest and his time in a juvenile detention center... There are a lot of messages about the importance of safe driving and staying away from drugs and alcohol without being preachy. This is not a typical rock band story; it is actually interesting. The author does a brilliant job getting into the head of a troubled teen and does not shy away from racy topics." (School Library Journal)

★ **You** killed Wesley Payne. Little, Brown 2011 359p il $16.99
Grades: 9 10 11 12 **Fic**
1. School stories 2. Mystery fiction
ISBN 978-0-316-07742-2; 0-316-07742-9
LC 2010-08639

When hard-boiled, seventeen-year-old private investigator Dalton Rev transfers to Salt River High to solve the case of a dead student, he has his hands full trying to outwit the police, negotiate the school's social hierarchy, and get paid.

"This dark, cynical romp is full of clever references and red herrings, which will delight the adult noir fan and pique the curiosities of the observant outcast teen who's looking for a way to infiltrate the in-crowd." Kirkus

Beaufrand, Mary Jane

Primavera; by Mary Jane Beaufrand. 1st ed.; Little, Brown 2007 260p $16.99
Grades: 6 7 8 9 **Fic**
1. Artists -- Fiction 2. Renaissance -- Fiction
ISBN 978-0-316-01644-5; 0-316-01644-6
LC 2006025288

Growing up in Renaissance Italy, Flora sees her family's fortunes ebb, but encounters with the artist Botticelli and the guidance of her nurse teach her to look past the material world to the beauty already in her life.

"Political, historical, and art historical details provide a canvas on which this tale of murder, intrigue, and young romance is played out, but are painted with a broad stroke." SLJ

The **river**. Little, Brown 2010 215p il $16.99
Grades: 8 9 10 11 12 **Fic**
1. Mystery fiction 2. Moving -- Fiction 3. Oregon -- Fiction 4. Hotels and motels -- Fiction
ISBN 978-0-316-04168-3; 0-316-04168-8
LC 2008-50222

Teenager Ronnie's life is transformed by the murder of a ten-year-old neighbor for whom she babysat, and who had helped Ronnie adjust to living at a country inn on the banks of the Santiam River in Hoodoo, Oregon.

"With its blend of richly realistic character and slightly uncanny ambience, this will be a favorite with fans of mysteries that tug the heartstrings." Bull Cent Child Books

Bechard, Margaret

Hanging on to Max. Simon Pulse 2003 204p pa $6.99
Grades: 7 8 9 10 **Fic**
1. Infants -- Fiction 2. Teenage fathers -- Fiction
ISBN 0-689-86268-7
First published 2002 by Roaring Brook Press

When his girlfriend decides to give their baby away, seventeen-year-old Sam is determined to keep him and raise him alone.

"An easy read filled with practical wisdom, this book is highly recommended as an important edition for any adolescent classroom collection." ALAN

Beck, Ian

Pastworld. Bloomsbury Children's Books 2009 355p $16.99
Grades: 7 8 9 10 **Fic**
1. Science fiction 2. Homicide -- Fiction 3. Amusement parks -- Fiction 4. London (England) -- Fiction 5. Genetic engineering -- Fiction
ISBN 1-59990-040-8; 978-1-59990-040-7
LC 2009-8706

In 2050, while visiting Pastworld, a Victorian London theme park, teenaged Caleb meets seventeen-year-old Eve, a Pastworld inhabitant who has no knowledge of the modern world, and both become pawns in a murderer's diabolical plan that reveals disturbing truths about the teenagers' origins.

"Suspenseful and gripping. This spellbinding page-turner will keep readers on the edge of their seats." SLJ

Becker, Tom

Darkside; [by] Tom Becker. Orchard Books 2008 294p (Darkside) $16.99
Grades: 7 8 9 10 **Fic**
1. Horror fiction 2. Supernatural -- Fiction
ISBN 978-0-545-03739-6; 0-545-03739-5
LC 2007-23634

Jonathan Starling's father is in an asylum and his home has been attacked when, while running away from kidnappers, he stumbles upon Darkside, a terrifying and hidden part of London ruled by the descendents of Jack the Ripper, where Jonathan is in mortal danger if he cannot find the way out.

"This fast-paced, unrelentingly entertaining story has plenty of suspense and lots of scares." Booklist

Lifeblood. Orchard Books 2008 279p (Darkside) $16.99
Grades: 7 8 9 10 **Fic**
1. Horror fiction 2. Supernatural -- Fiction
ISBN 978-0-545-03742-6; 0-545-03742-5
LC 2007051180

As Jonathan searches London's Darkside for the same murderer that his mother was seeking when she disappeared twelve years earlier, it becomes clear that it is Jonathan who is being hunted.

"Horror lovers will thrill to this gleeful gothic bloodbath." Horn Book Guide

Bedford, Martyn

Flip. Wendy Lamb Books 2011 261p $16.99; lib bdg $19.99; ebook $10.99
Grades: 8 9 10 11 12 **Fic**

1. Supernatural -- Fiction 2. Great Britain -- Fiction
ISBN 978-0-385-73990-0; 0-385-73990-7; 978-0-385-90808-5 lib bdg; 0-385-90808-3 lib bdg; 978-0-375-89855-6 ebook; 0-375-89855-7 ebook
LC 2010-13158

A teenager wakes up inside another boy's body and faces a life-or-death quest to return to his true self or be trapped forever in the wrong existence.

"Bedford packs so much exhilarating action and cleanly cut characterizations into his teen debut that readers will be catapulted head-first into Alex's strange new world." Kirkus

Never ending. Wendy Lamb Books. 2014 291p $19.99
Grades: 9 10 11 12 Fic

1. Family problems — Fiction; 2. Grief — Fiction; 3. Guilt —Fiction; 4. Psychotherapy — Fiction
ISBN: 0385908091; 9780375865534; 9780385739917; 9780385908092
LC 2012047731

"In the wake of her brother Declan's death, Shiv and five other teens who feel responsible for the deaths of loved ones are inpatients in the new Korsakoff Clinic's first (unorthodox) therapy program. Shiv's activities in the clinic alternate with scenes flashing back toward revelation of what happened to Declan. Bedford writes with insight into and respect for adolescent grief and growth." Horn Book Guide

Beitia, Sara

The **last** good place of Lily Odilon. Flux 2010 301p pa $9.95
Grades: 8 9 10 **Fic**

1. Mystery fiction 2. Stepfathers -- Fiction 3. Runaway teenagers -- Fiction 4. Child sexual abuse -- Fiction
ISBN 978-0-7387-2068-5; 0-7387-2068-2
LC 2010-19112

When seventeen-year-old Albert Morales's girlfriend Lily goes missing and he is the main suspect in her disappearance, he must deflect the worries of his angry parents, the suspicions of the police, and Lily's dangerous stepfather as Albert desperately tries to find her, with her sister as his only ally.

"This noir thriller hooks readers with realistic dialogue, fully fleshed characters and plenty of twists. Terrific to the last, good page." Kirkus

Bell, Cathleen Davitt

Slipping. Bloomsbury 2008 215p $16.95
Grades: 6 7 8 9 **Fic**

1. Ghost stories 2. Death -- Fiction 3. Grandfathers -- Fiction
ISBN 978-1-59990-258-6; 1-59990-258-3
LC 2008-04420

Thirteen-year-old Michael and an unlikely group of allies journey to the river of the dead to help Michael's grandfather release his hold on a ghostly life and, in the process, heal wounds that have kept Michael's father distant.

"The balance between the supernatural and genuine human feelings creates a compelling mix." Booklist

Bell, Hilari

Fall of a kingdom; by Hilari Bell. Simon Pulse 2005 422 p. map (Farsala trilogy) (paperback) $6.99
Grades: 7 8 9 10 **Fic**

1. Fantasy fiction 2. Persian mythology -- Fiction
ISBN 0689854145; 9780689854149
LC 2005588003

This is the first book in Hilari Bell's Farsala trilogy. "Stories are told of a hero who will come to Farsala's aid when the need is greatest. But for thousands of years the prosperous land of Farsala has felt no such need. . . . Three young people are less sure of Farsala's invincibility. Jiaan, Soraya, and Kavi see Time's Wheel turning, with Farsala headed toward the Flames of Destruction. What they cannot see is how inextricably their lives are linked to Farsala's fate." (Publisher's note)

Forging the sword. Simon & Schuster Books for Young Readers 2006 494p (Farsala trilogy) $17.99
Grades: 7 8 9 10 **Fic**

1. Fantasy fiction
ISBN 978-0-689-85416-3; 0-689-85416-1
LC 2005017730

Farsalans, including Lady Soraya and her half-brother, Jiaan, Kavi, and others, work relentlessly and often secretly in their shared strategies regarding the ultimate defeat of the Hrum.

"Bell brings the Farsala Trilogy to a rousing conclusion. . . . The author maintains the complexity of her main characters and the intensity of the story line." Booklist

★ The **last** knight. Eos 2007 357p (Knight and rogue) $16.99; lib bdg $17.89
Grades: 7 8 9 10 **Fic**

1. Fantasy fiction 2. Knights and knighthood -- Fiction
ISBN 978-0-06-082503-4; 0-06-082503-0; 978-0-06-082504-1 lib bdg; 0-06-082504-9 lib bdg
LC 2006-36427

In alternate chapters, eighteen-year-old Sir Michael Sevenson, an anachronistic knight errant, and seventeen-year-old Fisk, his streetwise squire, tell of their noble quest to bring Lady Ceciel to justice while trying to solve her husband's murder.

"The novel is brimming with saved-by-a-hair escapades and fast-paced realistic action. . . . This well-created fantasy is a great read with worthwhile moral issues pertinent to its intended audience." SLJ

Other titles in this series are:
Rogue's home (2008)
Player's ruse (2010)

Rise of a hero. 2005 462p (Farsala trilogy) $16.95; pa $6.99
Grades: 7 8 9 10 **Fic**

1. Fantasy fiction
ISBN 0-689-85415-3; 0-689-85417-X pa
LC 2003-25164

Although the Hrum believe their war against Farsala is nearly over, Soraya has strategic information that will help if she can reach Jiaan and Kavi and their separate resistance movements, but discord and Time's Wheel seem destined to keep them apart.

"With a palpable sense of danger and an ending that promises much to be revealed, this is a sequel that will fly off the shelf." Booklist

Shield of stars. Simon & Schuster Books For Young Readers 2007 267p (The shield, the sword and the crown) $16.99

Grades: 6 7 8 9 **Fic**

1. Fantasy fiction

ISBN 978-1-4169-0594-3; 1-4169-0594-4

LC 2005-35571

When the Justice he works for is condemned for treason, fourteen-year-old and semi-reformed pickpocket Weasel sets out to find a notorious bandit who may be able to help save his master's life.

"Bell's trademark shades of gray help shift readers' perceptions of the characters and their motivations, adding an unusual layer of depth that moves this story beyond simple adventure. Weasel's choices are complex and believable." SLJ

Other titles in this series are:

Sword of waters (2008)

Crown of earth (2009)

Traitor's son; by Hilari Bell. Houghton 2012 250 p. (The Raven duet) $16.99

Grades: 7 8 9 10 11 12 **Fic**

1. Fantasy fiction 2. Magic -- Fiction 3. Bioterrorism -- Fiction 4. Environmental degradation -- Fiction 5. Native Americans -- Alaska -- Fiction 6. Alaska -- Fiction 7. Shapeshifting -- Fiction 8. Indians of North America -- Alaska -- Fiction

ISBN 9780547196213

LC 2011012241

In this companion to Trickster's girl terrorists "have released a bioplague that, unchecked, will destroy the world's trees and humanity along with them. . . . Raven, the shapeshifter . . . must persuade the reluctant 16-year-old Jason to accept Atalhanes' quest or doom will follow." (Booklist)

Trickster's girl. Houghton Mifflin Harcourt 2011 281p (The Raven duet) $16

Grades: 7 8 9 10 **Fic**

1. Fantasy fiction 2. Magic -- Fiction 3. Bereavement -- Fiction 4. Environmental degradation -- Fiction

ISBN 978-0-547-19620-6; 0-547-19620-2

LC 2010-06785

In the year 2098, grieving her father and angry with her mother, fifteen-year-old Kelsa joins the magical Raven on an epic journey from Utah to Alaska to heal the earth by restoring the flow of magic that humans have disrupted.

The "degree of nuance will sit especially well with readers who prefer their speculative fiction to be character-driven, and they'll appreciate the compelling exploration of the ways the hopeful can cope with uncertainty." Bull Cent Child Books

Bell, Joanne

Juggling fire. Orca Book Publishers 2009 171p pa $12.95

Grades: 7 8 9 10 **Fic**

1. Missing persons -- Fiction 2. Wilderness survival -- Fiction 3. Father-daughter relationship -- Fiction

ISBN 978-1-55469-094-7; 1-55469-094-3

"Sixteen-year-old Rachel's father disappeared years earlier from her family's home in the Yukon wilderness. . . . The teen sets off on a trek through the tundra and forest with only her dog as a companion, hoping to find clues about her father's disappearance. . . . Bell beautifully captures the natural world through descriptions of the mountainous terrain as well as nail-biting encounters with bears and wolves. Rachel is a smart, resourceful narrator." SLJ

Bennett Wealer, Sara

Rival. HarperTeen 2011 327p $16.99

Grades: 7 8 9 10 **Fic**

1. School stories 2. Singing -- Fiction 3. Contests -- Fiction 4. Friendship -- Fiction 5. Popularity -- Fiction

ISBN 978-0-06-182762-4

LC 2010-03092

Two high school rivals compete in a prestigious singing competition while reflecting on the events that turned them from close friends to enemies the year before.

"Through Kathryn and Brooke's experiences, teens will learn the important lesson that what you see is not always what you get. This is a must-have addition to school and public libraries collections alike." Voice Youth Advocates

Bennett, Holly

Shapeshifter. Orca Book Publishers 2010 244p il pa $9.95

Grades: 7 8 9 10 **Fic**

1. Fantasy fiction

ISBN 978-1-55469-158-6; 1-55469-158-3

In order to escape the sorceror who wants to control her gift of song, Sive must transform herself into a deer, leave the Otherworld and find refuge in Eire, the land of mortals.

This is a "rich, slightly revisionist retelling of an ancient Irish legend. Basic human emotions—fear, love, greed—move the tale along, and short first-person narratives that personalize the action are interspersed throughout." Booklist

Benoit, Charles

You. HarperTeen 2010 223p $16.99

Grades: 8 9 10 11 12 **Fic**

1. School stories 2. Conduct of life -- Fiction

ISBN 978-0-06-194704-9; 0-06-194704-0

LC 2009-43990

Fifteen-year-old Kyle discovers the shattering ramifications of the decisions he makes, and does not make, about school, the girl he likes, and his future.

"The rapid pace is well suited to the narrative. . . . In the end, Benoit creates a fully realized world where choices have impact and the consequences of both action and inaction can be severe." SLJ

Benway, Robin

Also known as; by Robin Benway. Walker Books For Young Readers 2013 320 p. (hardcover) $16.99

Grades: 7 8 9 10 **Fic**

1. Spy stories 2. School stories 3. Spies -- Fiction 4. High schools -- Fiction 5. New York (N.Y.) -- Fiction 6. Adventure and adventurers -- Fiction

ISBN 0802733905; 9780802733900

LC 2012026254

In this book, "Maggie is a safecracking prodigy and the only child of parents who work as spies for an organization called the Collective. When the family relocates to New York City, 16-year-old Maggie lands her first assignment: befriending Jesse, a cute private school boy, to gain access to the e-mail belonging to his magazine editor father, who is suspected to be planning a revealing story about the Collective." (Publishers Weekly)

"While the framework requires more than a little suspension of disbelief, the absolutely delightful cast of characters and snappy dialogue transform this book into a huge success." SLJ

Audrey, wait! Razorbill 2008 313p

Grades: 9 10 11 12 **Fic**

1. Rock musicians -- Fiction 2. Dating (Social customs) -- Fiction

ISBN 9781595141910; 9781595141927

LC 2007-23912

While trying to score a date with her cute coworker at the Scooper Dooper, sixteen-year-old Audrey gains unwanted fame and celebrity status when her ex-boyfriend, a rock musician, records a breakup song about her that soars to the top of the Billboard charts.

"Audrey's narration is swift, self-aware, and contemporary in its touch of ironic distance as well as in its style. . . . Current, fresh, and funny, this will rocket up the charts." Bull Cent Child Books

The **extraordinary** secrets of April, May and June. Razorbill 2010 281p $16.99

Grades: 6 7 8 9 10 **Fic**

1. School stories 2. Sisters -- Fiction 3. Parapsychology -- Fiction

ISBN 978-1-59514-286-3; 1-59514-286-X

LC 2010-22777

When they recover supernatural powers from their childhoods in the aftermath of their parents' divorce, three sisters use their foretelling, invisibility, and mind-reading abilities to tackle school and family challenges.

"The sisters take turns narrating, and their distinct personalities and extremely funny, often barbed dialogue will keep readers laughing as each sibling learns to trust another amazing power: the strength of sisterhood." Publ Wkly

Berk, Ari

Death watch. Simon & Schuster Books for Young Readers 2011 527p (The Undertaken trilogy) $17.99

Grades: 7 8 9 10 **Fic**

1. Fantasy fiction 2. Father-son relationship -- Fiction

ISBN 978-1-4169-9115-1; 1-4169-9115-8

LC 2011006332

When seventeen-year-old Silas Umber's father disappears, Silas is sure it is connected to the powerful artifact he discovers, combined with his father's hidden hometown history, which compels Silas to pursue the path leading to his destiny and ultimately, to the discovery of his father, dead or alive.

"Berk's setting is atmospheric and creepy, fleshed out with a wealth of funereal traditions and folklore." Publ Wkly

Mistle child; Ari Berk. Simon & Schuster Books for Young Readers 2013 352 p. (The Undertaken trilogy) (hardcover) $17.99

Grades: 7 8 9 10 **Fic**

1. Ghost stories 2. Occult fiction 3. Undertakers and undertaking -- Fiction 4. Fantasy ficiton 5. Ghosts -- Fiction 6. Families -- Fiction

ISBN 1416991174; 9781416991175; 9781442439160

LC 2012002977

This children's fantasy story, by Ari Berk, is book 2 of the "Understaken" series. "Silas Umber makes his way to the thoroughly haunted ancestral estate of Arvale to continue his training as a psychopomp. There he meets the specters of family going back thousands of years, becomes enmeshed in their subtle intrigues and undergoes a ritual that gives him the ability to banish the restless dead from this world forever. He also inadvertently frees a mad, ancient spirit." (Kirkus Reviews)

Berk, Josh

★ The **dark** days of Hamburger Halpin. Alfred A. Knopf 2010 250p $16.99; lib bdg $19.99

Grades: 8 9 10 11 12 **Fic**

1. School stories 2. Deaf -- Fiction

ISBN 978-0-375-85699-0; 0-375-85699-4; 978-0-375-95699-7 lib bdg; 0-375-95699-9 lib bdg

LC 2009-3118

"A coming-of-age mash-up of satire, realistic fiction, mystery, and ill-fated teen romance, The Dark Days of Hamburger Halpin is a genre-bending breakthrough that teens are going to love." SLJ

Guy Langman, crime scene procrastinator; Josh Berk. Alfred A. Knopf 2012 230 p. (lib. bdg.) $19.99

Grades: 7 8 9 10 11 12 **Fic**

1. Clubs -- Fiction 2. Teenagers -- Fiction 3. Bereavement -- Fiction 4. Forensic sciences -- Fiction 5. Father-son relationship -- Fiction 6. Death -- Fiction 7. Grief -- Fiction 8. Humorous stories 9. New Jersey -- Fiction 10. Mystery and detective stories

ISBN 037585701X; 9780375857010; 9780375897757; 9780375957017

LC 2011023864

This young adult presents "wisecracking humor, teenage insecurity, and the occasional corpse. When underachieving class clown Guy Langman joins his school's forensics club, it's both to help deal him with the death of his father and to meet girls. Unfortunately, his plan to get closer to the lovely Raquel Flores fails when she falls for his best friend, Anoop. Guy throws himself into the lesson plan, mastering the art of fingerprinting and using his knowledge to pry into the mysteries of his father's checkered past. Then, during a forensics competition, he finds a real dead body. Convinced that recent events tie into one another, Guy tries to get to the heart of the matter, with help from the rest of the club." (Publishers Weekly)

Bernard, Romily

Find me; Romily Bernard. HarperTeen, an imprint of HarperCollinsPublishers 2013 320 p. (hardback) $17.99

Grades: 7 8 9 10 11 12 **Fic**

1. Foster children -- Fiction 2. Teenagers -- Suicide -- Fiction 3. Computer hackers -- Fiction 4. Foster home care -- Fiction 5. Mystery and detective stories

ISBN 0062229036; 9780062229038

LC 2013021519

In this book, "Tessa Waye was Wicket Tate's best friend until five years ago when Wick's drug-dealing father drove them apart. When Tessa commits suicide and her diary is left on the teen's front steps, Wick suspects there might be a dark reason she jumped to her death. Wick and her sister, Lily, are now free of their criminal father, living a shiny new life on the ritzy side of town with their foster parents. But Wick . . . fears her father will come back for them." (School Library Journal)

Bernobich, Beth

Fox & Phoenix. Viking 2011 360p $17.99

Grades: 7 8 9 10 **Fic**

1. Fantasy fiction 2. Magic -- Fiction 3. Princesses -- Fiction 4. Apprentices -- Fiction 5. Kings and rulers -- Fiction

ISBN 978-0-670-01278-7; 0-670-01278-5

LC 2011009388

Sixteen-year-old Kai, a magician's apprentice and former street tough, must travel to the Phoenix Empire, where his friend Princess Lian is studying statecraft, and help her escape so she can return home before her father, the king, dies.

"The characters and creatures in this book are interesting and believable; the plot is a compelling mixture of adventure, mystery, and fantasy. The most remarkable element, however, is the world Beth Bernobich has created." Voice Youth Advocates

Berry, Julie

All the truth that's in me; by Julie Berry. Viking 2013 288 p. (hardcover: alk. paper) $17.99

Grades: 7 8 9 10 11 12 **Fic**

1. Truth -- Fiction 2. Kidnapping -- Fiction 3. Community life -- Fiction 4. War -- Fiction 5. Selective mutism -- Fiction

ISBN 0670786152; 9780670786152

LC 2012043218

In this book by Julie Berry, "sixteen-year-old Judith is still in love with Lucas, even after his father held her prisoner for two years and violently silenced her by cutting out part of her tongue. Another girl went missing at the same time and her body was found washed down a stream. Only Judith knows the truth of what happened to Lottie, but her muteness leaves her an outcast in the village, even from her own mother, and the truth stays bottled up inside her." (School Library Journal)

"Berry's novel is set in a claustrophobic village that seems to resemble an early American colonial settlement. Readers gradually learn "all the truth" from eighteen-year-old narrator Judith, who speaks directly (though only in her head) to her love, Lucas. Berry keeps readers on edge, tantalizing us with pieces of the puzzle right up until the gripping conclusion." (Horn Book)

The **Amaranth** enchantment. Bloomsbury U.S.A. Children's Books 2009 308p $16.99

Grades: 6 7 8 9 **Fic**

1. Fantasy fiction 2. Orphans -- Fiction 3. Extraterrestrial beings -- Fiction

ISBN 978-1-59990-334-7; 1-59990-334-2

LC 2008-22354

Orphaned at age five, Lucinda, now fifteen, stands with courage against the man who took everything from her, aided by a thief, a clever goat, and a mysterious woman called the Witch of Amaranth, while the prince she knew as a child prepares to marry, unaware that he, too, is in danger.

"A lively, quick, stylish, engaging first novel with some lovely, familiar fairy-tale elements." Publ Wkly

Bertagna, Julie

★ **Exodus**; [by] Julie Bertagna. Walker 2008 345p $16.95

Grades: 6 7 8 9 10 **Fic**

1. Science fiction 2. Floods -- Fiction 3. Greenhouse effect -- Fiction 4. Voyages and travels -- Fiction

ISBN 978-0-8027-9745-2; 0-8027-9745-8

LC 2007-23116

In the year 2100, as the island of Wing is about to be covered by water, fifteen-year-old Mara discovers the existence of New World sky cities that are safe from the storms and rising waters, and convinces her people to travel to one of these cities in order to save themselves.

"Astonishing in its scope and exhilarating in both its action and its philosophical inquiry." Booklist

Zenith. Walker & Co. 2009 340p $16.99

Grades: 6 7 8 9 10 **Fic**

1. Science fiction 2. Floods -- Fiction 3. Greenhouse effect -- Fiction 4. Voyages and travels -- Fiction

ISBN 978-0-8027-9803-9; 0-8027-9803-9

After finding that New Mungo is not the refuge they sought, Mara, leaving Fox behind, again sets out to sea with a ship full of refugees and, with the help of the "Gipsea" boy Tuck, tries to find land at the top of the world that will be safe from storms and rising water.

"This is mostly Mara's story—a plucky, imperfect heroine leading the way to an uncertain future in a hostile world." Booklist

Beyer, Kat

The **demon** catchers of Milan; by Kat Beyer. Egmont, USA 2012 288 p. (Demon catchers of Milan trilogy) (hardcover) $16.99

Grades: 7 8 9 10 11 **Fic**

1. Occult fiction 2. Italy -- Fiction 3. Demoniac possession -- Fiction 4. Demonology -- Fiction 5. Milan (Italy) -- Fiction 6. Americans -- Italy -- Fiction 7. Family life -- Italy -- Fiction

ISBN 1606843141; 9781606843147; 9781606843154

LC 2011034348

This book is "a tale of demonic possession and a centuries-old family trade in exorcism." Mia's life "is upended when a horrifying demon enters and nearly kills her. After Giuliano Della Torre and his grandson Emilio, long-estranged relatives from Milan, arrive and drive it out, they talk Mia's reluctant parents into letting her return to Italy with them." She shows a talent for the family business of exorcism. (Kirkus Reviews)

Bick, Ilsa J.

Ashes. Egmont USA 2011 465p $17.99; ebook $9.99

Grades: 8 9 10 11 12 **Fic**

1. Science fiction 2. Zombies -- Fiction 3. Wilderness survival -- Fiction

ISBN 978-1-60684-175-4; 978-1-60684-231-7 ebook

LC 2010-51825

Alex, a resourceful seventeen-year-old running from her incurable brain tumor, Tom, who has left the war in Afghanistan, and Ellie, an angry eight-year-old, join forces after an electromagnetic pulse sweeps through the sky and kills most of the world's population, turning some of those who remain into zombies and giving the others superhuman senses.

"Bick delivers an action-packed tale of an apocalypse unfolding. . . . [She] doesn't shy away from gore—one woman's guts 'boiled out in a dusky, desiccated tangle, like limp spaghetti'—but it doesn't derail the story's progress." Publ Wkly

Draw the dark. Carolrhoda Lab 2010 338p $16.95

Grades: 8 9 10 11 12 **Fic**

1. Jews -- Fiction 2. Crime -- Fiction 3. Artists -- Fiction 4. Wisconsin -- Fiction 5. Supernatural -- Fiction

ISBN 0-7613-5686-X; 978-0-7613-5686-8

LC 2009-51612

Seventeen-year-old Christian Cage lives with his uncle in Winter, Wisconsin, where his visions, dreams and unusual paintings draw him into a mystery involving German prisoners of war, a mysterious corpse, and Winter's last surviving Jew. "Grades eight to twelve." (Bull Cent Child Books)

"The novel brilliantly strikes a compelling balance between fantasy and contemporary fiction. Readers will be on the edge of their seats waiting to find out what happens next and will clamor for a sequel to follow Christian into the sideways place." SLJ

The **Sin** eater's confession; by Ilsa J. Bick. Carolrhoda Lab 2013 320 p. (trade hard cover: alk. paper) $17.95

Grades: 9 10 11 12 **Fic**

1. Hate crimes -- Fiction 2. Homosexuality -- Fiction 3. Conduct of life -- Fiction 4. Murder -- Fiction 5. Wisconsin -- Fiction 6. Photography -- Fiction 7. Farm life -- Wisconsin -- Fiction

ISBN 0761356878; 9780761356875

LC 2012015291

In this novel, by Isla J. Bick, "Ben . . . likes helping the stern Mr. and Mrs. Lange and their 15-year-old son, Jimmy. When Jimmy wins a national photography contest with sensual photographs of his own father and Ben . . ., rumors . . . start circulating about Ben, who then distances himself from Jimmy. When Ben witnesses a horrific crime and does nothing, his life spins out of control; he begins to doubt himself, his senses, his motives . . . even his connection to reality." (Kirkus Reviews)

Bickle, Laura

The **hallowed** ones; Laura Bickle. Graphia 2012 311 p. (paperback) $8.99

Grades: 7 8 9 10 11 12 **Fic**

1. Horror fiction 2. Amish -- Fiction 3. Terrorism -- Fiction 4. Family life -- Fiction 5. Bioterrorism -- Fiction 6. Coming of age -- Fiction 7. Christian life -- Fiction 8. Communicable diseases -- Fiction

ISBN 0547859260; 9780547859262

LC 2012014800

This book follows "Katie [who] is [about] to taste the freedom of rumspringa, [when] the elders close the gates of her small Amish community. . . . Katie daringly ventures Outside to find true horror: vampires have decimated a small nearby town and apparently much of the world's population. . . . Her situation is further complicated when she rescues Alex, a handsome Outsider who may or may not be a carrier of the contagion that seemingly caused the vampirism epidemic." (Bulletin of the Center for Children's Books)

The **outside**; Laura Bickle. Houghton Mifflin Harcourt 2013 320 p. (hardcover) $16.99

Grades: 7 8 9 10 11 12 **Fic**

1. Horror fiction 2. Occult fiction 3. Vampires -- Fiction 4. Amish -- Fiction 5. Coming of age -- Fiction

ISBN 0544000137; 9780544000131

LC 2012040065

Sequel to: The hallowed ones

This book is a sequel to Laura Bickle's "The Hallowed Ones." Katie, an exile from an Amish community, travels with "Alex and Ginger, the two outsiders she's befriended, seeking other survivors of the vampire plague that's unmade their world. . . . Discovering a group that's genetically engineered with immunity to vampires raises tension between them, pitting science against religion: Are these vampires aliens or mutants spawned in labs, rather than manifestations of demonic evil?" (Kirkus Reviews)

Biederman, Lynn

Teenage waistland; a novel. [by] Lynn Biederman & Lisa Pazer. Delacorte Press 2010 317p $17.99; lib bdg $20.99

Grades: 8 9 10 11 12 **Fic**

1. Obesity -- Fiction 2. New York (N.Y.) -- Fiction

ISBN 978-0-385-73921-4; 0-385-73921-4; 978-0-385-90776-7 lib bdg; 0-385-90776-1 lib bdg

LC 2009-49672

In their separate voices, three morbidly obese New York City teens relate their experiences participating in a clinical trial testing lap-band surgery for teenagers, which involves a year of weekly meetings and learning to live healthier lives.

"Without sidestepping the seriousness of the teens' weight or the surgery they undergo, the authors offer an important and hopeful story about a little-discussed subject that affects many." Publ Wkly

Bigelow, Lisa Jenn

Starting from here; by Lisa Jenn Bigelow. Marshall Cavendish Children 2012 282 p. (hardcover) $16.99

Grades: 8 9 10 11 12 **Fic**

1. School stories 2. Lesbians -- Fiction 3. Self-realization -- Fiction 4. Dogs -- Fiction 5. High schools -- Fiction 6. Fathers and daughters -- Fiction 7. Dating (Social customs) -- Fiction

ISBN 0761462333; 9780761462330; 9780761462347

LC 2011040129

In this book by Lisa Jenn Bigelow, "Colby is about ready to give up on people: her girlfriend Rachel dumps her and immediately moves onto Colby's opposite (a nice Jewish guy who does well in school), her mom is dead, and her dad is a frequently absent truck driver to whom she still hasn't come out. Only her best friend, Van, can bring her out of her shell. Then she adopts Mo, a friendly but wary stray dog, and life starts to move again." (Bulletin of the Center for Children's Books)

Bilen, Tracy

What she left behind; Tracy Bilen. Simon Pulse 2012 237 p. $9.99

Grades: 9 10 11 12 **Fic**

1. Fathers -- Fiction 2. Missing persons -- Fiction 3. Domestic violence -- Fiction 4. Family violence -- Fiction

ISBN 1442439513; 9781442439511

LC 2011028989

This book follows Sara, whose mother goes missing just before their planned escape from her abusive father. "Sara works to protect herself while trying to find her mother. Her one lifeline in her increasingly isolated world is her friend Zach, her brother's former best friend. Negotiating her father's abuse, her missing mother, and a burgeoning romantic relationship with a new guy, Sara's juggling act takes all of her strength and wits to survive." (School Library Journal)

"Sharp prose and an increasingly tense plot make this debut a page-turner." Pub Wkly

Billerbeck, Kristin

Perfectly dateless; a universally misunderstood novel. Revell 2010 259p pa $9.99

Grades: 8 9 10 11 12 **Fic**

1. School stories 2. Christian life -- Fiction 3. Dating (Social customs) -- Fiction

ISBN 978-0-8007-3439-8

LC 2010-6048

Entering her senior year at St. James Christian Academy, Daisy has less than 200 days to look stylish, develop social skills, find the right boy for the prom, and convince her parents to let her date.

"The title and cover alone ensure that teens will pick up this book, and parents will be pleased that there is nothing offensive inside the covers. Adults who enjoy YA fiction and are nostalgic for their high school years may also want to try this hilarious novel." Libr J

Billingsley, Franny

★ **Chime**. Dial Books for Young Readers 2011 361p $17.99

Grades: 7 8 9 10 11 12 **Fic**

1. Guilt -- Fiction 2. Twins -- Fiction 3. Sisters -- Fiction 4. Stepmothers -- Fiction 5. Supernatural -- Fiction

ISBN 0-8037-3552-9; 978-0-8037-3552-1

LC 2010-12140

Since her stepmother's recent death, 17 year old Briony Larkin know that if she can keep two secrets--that she is a witch and that she is responsible for the accident that left Rose, her identical twin, mentally compromised--and remember to hate her self alwaysalways, no other harm will befall her family in their Swampsea parsonage at the begining of the twentieth century. The arrival of Mr. Claybourne, a city engineer, and his university-dropout son, Eric, make Briony's task difficult. (Booklist)

"Filled with eccentric characters—self-hating Briony foremost—and oddly beautiful language, this is a darkly beguiling fantasy." Publ Wkly

Bingham, Kelly

Formerly shark girl; Kelly Bingham. Candlewick Press 2013 352 p. (reinforced) $16.99

Grades: 7 8 9 10 **Fic**

1. Artists -- Fiction 2. Shark attacks -- Fiction

ISBN 0763653624; 9780763653620

LC 2012952049

Sequel to Shark girl. While recovering from her injuries "Jane struggles with boyfriends and with her future: Will she become a nurse or continue as an artist even though she has lost her drawing hand? Her artwork continues to improve, but she feels obligated to give back to others what she received from the doctors and nurses who saved her life when she lost her right arm to a shark." (Kirkus)

Shark girl. Candlewick Press 2007 276p $16.99; pa $8.99

Grades: 7 8 9 10 **Fic**

1. Novels in verse 2. Artists -- Fiction 3. Amputees -- Fiction

ISBN 978-0-7636-3207-6; 0-7636-3207-4; 978-0-7636-4627-1 pa; 0-7636-4627-X pa

LC 2006049120

After a shark attack causes the amputation of her right arm, fifteen-year-old Jane, an aspiring artist, struggles to come to terms with her loss and the changes it imposes on her day-to-day life and her plans for the future.

"In carefully constructed, sparsely crafted free verse, Bingham's debut novel offers a strong view of a teenager struggling to survive and learn to live again." Booklist

Bjorkman, Lauren

Miss Fortune Cookie; Lauren Bjorkman. Henry Holt and Co. 2012 279 p. (hardcover) $16.99

Grades: 9 10 11 12 **Fic**

1. School stories 2. Female friendship -- Fiction 3. Friendship -- Fiction 4. Advice columns -- Fiction 5. Chinese Americans -- Fiction 6. San Francisco (Calif.) -- Fiction 7. Interpersonal relations -- Fiction 8. Chinatown (San Francisco, Calif.) -- Fiction

ISBN 0805089519; 9780805089516; 9780805096361

LC 2012006327

In this book, "Erin and her best friends, Linny and Mei, live in San Francisco's Chinatown and are" deciding where to go to college. Mei was accepted to Harvard, but "would rather attend Stanford in order to be near her secret boyfriend, Darren . . . . When Erin, who anonymously writes the advice blog Miss Fortune Cookie, answers a letter that she believes is from Mei and Mei seems to follow the advice by announcing her plan to elope with Darren, Erin is shocked." (School Library Journal)

My invented life. Henry Holt 2009 232p $17.99
Grades: 9 10 11 12 **Fic**
1. Poets 2. Authors 3. Dramatists 4. School stories 5. Sisters -- Fiction 6. Theater -- Fiction
ISBN 978-0-8050-8950-9; 0-8050-8950-0
LC 2008-50279

During rehearsals for Shakespeare's "As You Like It," sixteen-year-old Roz, jealous of her cheerleader sister's acting skills and heartthrob boyfriend, invents a new identity, with unexpected results.

"Narrator Roz is funny, well intentioned, and likable despite her cluelessness, and she is surrounded by a realistic cast of adult and teen characters representing a wide variety of viewpoints and sexual preferences. This is an enjoyable read that will be especially appealing to theater aficionados." SLJ

Black, Bekka

★ **IDrakula**. Sourcebooks/Fire 2010 150p pa $9.99
Grades: 7 8 9 10 **Fic**
1. Horror fiction 2. Vampires -- Fiction
ISBN 978-1-4022-4465-0 pa; 1-4022-4465-7 pa

This is a "take on Bram Stoker's Dracula—told exclusively through text messages, web browser screens, e-mails, and various photo and PDF attachments. . . . Black's storytelling instinct . . . consistently proves itself able to transcend gimmick. The format . . . actually lends the book a chilling sort of one-shock-per-page pulse. . . . Fast, inventive, creepy, and sure to be popular." Booklist

Black, Holly, 1971-

Black heart; Holly Black. Margaret K. McElderry Books 2012 296 p. (The curse workers) (hardcover) $17.99
Grades: 7 8 9 10 **Fic**
1. Love stories 2. Science fiction 3. Brothers -- Fiction 4. Organized crime -- Fiction 5. Love -- Fiction 6. Criminals -- Fiction
ISBN 9781442403468; 9781442403482
LC 2011028143

This book, the final volume of the Curse Workers trilogy, continues to follow "Cassel . . . [who has] figured out the truth about himself and signed on as a Fed-in-training, as has his charming and utterly unreliable older brother. But of course things don't go as planned; there are a lot of long cons Cassel has set in play or disrupted whose ripples are still being felt. And there's Lila, Cassel's best friend and the love of his life, who is also the rising head of a crime family" and who hates Cassel's guts." (Kirkus)

★ The **coldest** girl in Coldtown; by Holly Black. 1st ed. Little Brown & Co 2013 432 p. (hardcover) $19
Grades: 9 10 11 12 **Fic**
1. Occult fiction 2. Vampires -- Fiction 3. Love -- Fiction
ISBN 0316213101; 9780316213103
LC 2012043790

In this book by Holly Black, the vampires live in government-created ghettos called Coldtowns. "Seventeen-year-old Tana wakes up after a wild night of partying to discover that almost everyone in attendance has been killed by vampires. . . . Wandering through the carnage, she finds her infected ex-boyfriend, Aiden, and a mysterious, half-mad vampire named Gavriel chained in a bedroom. Escaping the massacre, Tana drives them to the nearest Coldtown," risking her life. (Publishers Weekly)

Red glove. Margaret K. McElderry Books 2011 325p (The curse workers) $17.99
Grades: 7 8 9 10 **Fic**
1. Science fiction 2. Magic -- Fiction 3. Brothers -- Fiction 4. Criminals -- Fiction 5. Swindlers and swindling -- Fiction
ISBN 1-4424-0339-X; 978-1-4424-0339-0
LC 2010-31884

Sequel to: White cat (2010)

When federal agents learn that seventeen-year-old Cassel Sharpe, a powerful transformation worker, may be of use to them, they offer him a deal to join them rather than the mobsters for whom his brothers work.

This offers "a sleek a stylish blend of urban fantasy and crime noir." Booklist

★ The **white** cat. Margaret K. McElderry Books 2010 310p (The curse workers) $17.99
Grades: 7 8 9 10 **Fic**
1. Science fiction 2. Memory -- Fiction 3. Brothers -- Fiction 4. Criminals -- Fiction 5. Swindlers and swindling -- Fiction
ISBN 978-1-416-96396-7; 1-416-96396-0
LC 2009-33979

When Cassel Sharpe discovers that his older brothers have used him to carry out their criminal schemes and then stolen his memories, he figures out a way to turn their evil machinations against them.

This "starts out with spine-tingling terror, and information is initially dispensed so sparingly, readers will be hooked." Booklist

Blacker, Terence

Boy2girl. Farrar, Straus and Giroux 2005 296p $16
Grades: 7 8 9 10 **Fic**
1. Cousins -- Fiction 2. Sex role -- Fiction
ISBN 0-374-30926-4
LC 2004-53268

After the death of his mother, thirteen-year-old Sam comes to live with his cousin and as a prank, he dresses up as a girl for school, but it soon gets out of hand.

"Sam's tale is told in very short chapters, each narrated by one of the many lively supporting characters who Sam meets. This unconventional technique works exceptionally well, telling the fast-paced story from different perspectives while delving into the ever-complicated world of sex roles." Booklist

Blagden, Scott

Dear Life, You Suck; Scott Blagden. Houghton Mifflin Harcourt 2013 320 p. $16.99

Grades: 9 10 11 12 **Fic**

1. Orphans -- Fiction 2. Church schools -- Fiction 3. Teenagers -- Conduct of life -- Fiction 4. Nuns -- Fiction 5. Maine -- Fiction 6. Bullies -- Fiction 7. Conduct of life -- Fiction 8. Catholic schools -- Fiction 9. Emotional problems -- Fiction

ISBN 0547904312; 9780547904313

LC 2013003903

This book portrays "a teen trying to figure out his place in the world and his sense of morality. . . . Cricket has lived in a Catholic church-run orphanage for years, and now that he's a senior, he's not sure if his future lies in being a drug dealer, a boxer, or in ending his own life. Other than sparring, Cricket is only motivated to watch old movies and watch out for the younger kids in the orphanage." (Publishers Weekly)

"With no plans for the future and an inability to comprehend a world in which he gets in trouble for standing up to bullies, delinquent orphan Cricket, almost eighteen, contemplates ending it all. However, he starts to reconsider when his longtime crush suddenly begins talking to him. Alternately comedic and tragic, Cricket's profane but inventive narration crafts a heartrending portrait of the antihero." (Horn Book)

Blair, Jamie

Leap of Faith; Jamie Blair. Simon & Schuster 2013 240 p. (hardcover) $16.99

Grades: 9 10 11 12 **Fic**

1. Kidnapping -- Fiction 2. Children of drug addicts -- Fiction 3. Runaways -- Fiction 4. Parenting -- Fiction 5. Fugitives from justice -- Fiction

ISBN 1442447133; 1442447168; 9781442447134; 9781442447165

LC 2012043125

In this book, "17-year old Faith recounts her grim life with her abusive, drug-addicted mother and the circumstances that motivate her to flee. Although inured to her mother's frequent male visitors, Faith longs to save the baby her mother is carrying (for pay) for a guy that Faith considers 'drug-dealing scum.' Kidnapping the newborn from the hospital, Faith drives from Ohio to Florida, determined to start a new life with baby Addy." (Publishers Weekly)

Blake, Kendare

★ **Anna** Dressed in Blood. Tor 2011 320p $17.99

Grades: 8 9 10 11 12 **Fic**

1. Ghost stories 2. Horror fiction 3. Cats -- Fiction 4. Witches -- Fiction

ISBN 978-0-7653-2865-6; 0-7653-2865-8

LC 2011018985

"Blake populates the story with a nice mixture of personalities, including Anna, and spices it with plenty of gallows humor, all the while keeping the suspense pounding. . . . Abundantly original, marvelously inventive and enormous fun, this can stand alongside the best horror fiction out there. We demand sequels." Kirkus

Blankman, Anne

Prisoner of night and fog; Anne Blankman. Balzer + Bray, an imprint of HarperCollinsPublishers 2014 416 p. (hardback) $17.99

Grades: 8 9 10 11 12 **Fic**

1. Love stories 2. National socialists -- Fiction 3. Germany -- History -- 1918-1933 -- Fiction 4. Love -- Fiction 5. Nazis -- Fiction 6. Nazis 7. Jews -- Germany -- Fiction 8. Munich (Germany) -- History -- 20th century -- Fiction

ISBN 0062278819; 9780062278814

LC 2013043071

This book, by Anne Blankman, is a "historical thriller set in 1930s Munich. . . . Gretchen Müller grew up in the National Socialist Party under the wing of her uncle Dolf, who has kept her family cherished and protected from the darker side of society ever since her father traded his life for Dolf's. But Uncle Dolf is none other than Adolf Hitler. And Gretchen follows his every command." (Publisher's note)

Blazanin, Jan

A & L do summer. Egmont USA 2011 273p pa $8.99

Grades: 7 8 9 10 **Fic**

1. Summer -- Fiction 2. Bullies -- Fiction 3. Friendship -- Fiction 4. Family life -- Fiction 5. Domestic animals -- Fiction

ISBN 978-1-60684-191-4 pa; 1-60684-191-2 pa; 978-1-60684-243-0 ebook

LC 2010-43616

In Iowa farm country, sixteen-year-old Aspen and her friend Laurel plan to get noticed the summer before their senior year and are unwittingly aided by pig triplets, a skunk, a chicken, bullies, a rookie policeman, and potential boyfriends.

"A series of mishaps add hilarity to the story. . . . All's well that ends well in this read perfectly suited for light refreshment on a hot summer day." Booklist

Block, Francesca Lia

Dangerous angels; the Weetzie Bat books. Revised paperback ed.; HarperTeen 2010 478p pa $9.99

Grades: 9 10 11 12 **Fic**

1. Friendship -- Fiction 2. Los Angeles (Calif.) -- Fiction

ISBN 978-0-06-200740-7

This compilation first published 1998

This is an omnibus edition of five Weetzie Bat books.

The **frenzy**. HarperTeen 2010 258p $16.99

Grades: 9 10 11 12 **Fic**

1. Love stories 2. Werewolves -- Fiction 3. Family life -- Fiction 4. Supernatural -- Fiction 5. Identity (Psychology) -- Fiction

ISBN 978-0-06-192666-2

LC 2009-53453

When she was thirteen, something terrifying and mysterious happened to Liv that she still does not understand, and now, four years later, her dark secret threatens to tear her apart from her family and her true love.

"Block does a nice job of weaving all these elements into a solid story that makes a quick but engaging read for fans of supernatural fiction. Reluctant readers will enjoy this story as well because of its pacing and manageable chapters." SLJ

★ The **island** of excess love. Francesca Lia Block. Henry Holt and Company. 2014 214p $16.99
Grades: 8 9 10 11 12 Fic

1. Friendship — Fiction; 2. Love — Fiction; 3. Science fiction; 4. Survival — Fiction; 5. Visions — Fiction; 6. Virgil. Aeneid — Fiction; 7. Los Angeles (Calif.) — Fiction; 8. Roman mythology; 9. Adventure fiction
ISBN: 0805096310; 9780805096316
LC 2014005284

Christy Ottaviano Books

In this companion to Love in the time of global warming (2013) "Pen, Hex, Ash, Ez, and Venice are living in the pink house by the sea, getting by on hard work, companionship, and dreams. Until the day a foreboding ship appears in the harbor across from their home." (Publisher's note)

"Just as Block's earlier novel was loosely based on The Odyssey, this is even more loosely based on The Aeneid. The result is a mesmerizing, magical, and mysterious tale of love and loss, stories and visions, and betrayal and redemption, all told in the author"s signature lyrical voice." Booklist

★ **Love** in the time of global warming; Francesca Lia Block. Henry Holt and Co. 2013 240 p. (hardcover) $16.99
Grades: 8 9 10 11 12 **Fic**

1. Apocalyptic fiction 2. Voyages and travels -- Fiction 3. Love -- Fiction 4. Science fiction 5. Families -- Fiction 6. Survival -- Fiction 7. Earthquakes -- Fiction 8. Los Angeles (Calif.) -- Fiction
ISBN 0805096272; 9780805096279
LC 2012047808

Rainbow List (2014)

In this book, after "an earthquake and tidal wave destroy much of Los Angeles, Penelope—now going by Pen—sets out to find her family. In the course of a journey that explicitly parallels the one described in Homer's Odyssey, Pen navigates the blighted landscape with a crew of three other searchers. . . . Eventually they arrive in Las Vegas (the contemporary stand-in for the land of the dead) where Pen confronts the evil genius behind her world's destruction." (Publishers Weekly)

"In this Odyssey-inspired story, after the devastating Earth Shaker, Penelope sets out into the brutal Los Angeles landscape in search of her family. She meets an intriguing boy named Hex who joins her on her journey. Block's imagery is remarkable in this sophisticated melding of post-apocalyptic setting, re-imagined classic, and her signature magical realism." (Horn Book)

Missing Angel Juan. HarperCollins Pubs. 1993 138p hardcover o.p. pa $5.99
Grades: 9 10 11 12 **Fic**

1. Ghost stories 2. Friendship -- Fiction
ISBN 0-06-023004-5; 0-06-447120-9 pa
LC 92-38299

Sequel to Cherokee Bat and the Goat Guys

ALA YALSA Margaret A. Edwards Award (2005)

This novel "stands alone but really packs a wallop for readers who already know these characters. . . . 'Missing Angel Juan' is imaginative, mystical, and completely engaging. Highly recommended for readers looking for something different." Voice Youth Advocates

Followed by Necklace of kisses

Necklace of kisses; a novel. HarperCollins Pubs. 2005 227p $21.95; pa $12.95
Grades: 9 10 11 12 **Fic**

1. Friendship -- Fiction
ISBN 0-06-077751-6; 0-06-077752-4 pa
LC 2004-59651

Sequel to Missing Angel Juan

Final novel in the series about Weetzie Bat and her Los Angeles friends and lovers. Now 40, Weetzie is "facing a midlife crisis, and so is her boyfriend, Secret Agent Lover Man, who, since 9/11, just sits idly reading the newspaper. She leaves, hoping to find herself, but this time, rather than meditating in the wilderness, she remains in her beloved L.A., moving into the expensive and magical Pink Hotel, where she luxuriates in room service, gets her nails and toenails done, kisses a sushi-eating mermaid, chats to her father's ghost, and gets a necklace of gifts from a diva, an angel, a faun, and more. The self-parody is as wonderful as ever—Weetzie doesn't have to save the world; she can just go shopping—and, as always, the magic is in the detail." Booklist

★ **Pretty** dead. HarperTeen 2009 195p $16.99; lib bdg $17.89
Grades: 9 10 11 12 **Fic**

1. Death -- Fiction 2. Vampires -- Fiction 3. Supernatural -- Fiction
ISBN 978-0-06-154785-0; 0-06-154785-9; 978-0-06-154786-7 lib bdg; 0-06-154786-7 lib bdg
LC 2008-45068

Beautiful vampire Charlotte finds herself slowly changing back into a human after the mysterious death of her best friend.

"Block takes what has up to now been the norm among vampire novels for teens and attempts to turn it on its head. This is a startlingly original work that drives a stake deep into the heart of typical vampire stories, revealing the deep loneliness and utter lack of romance in eternal life." SLJ

★ **Teen** spirit; Francesca Lia Block. HarperTeen, an imprint of HarperCollinsPublishers 2014 240 p. (hardcover bdg.) $17.99
Grades: 9 10 11 12 **Fic**

1. Spirits -- Fiction 2. Grandparent-grandchild relationship -- Fiction 3. Dead -- Fiction 4. Grandmothers -- Fiction 5. Supernatural -- Fiction 6. Beverly Hills (Calif.) -- Fiction 7. Single-parent

families -- Fiction 8. Dating (Social customs) -- Fiction
ISBN 0062008099; 9780062008091
LC 2013008057

In this novel, by Francesca Lia Block, when Julie's grandmother Miriam dies, "Julie's entire world is beginning to unravel. . . . [Then] she meets sweetly eccentric Clark, who is also mourning a loss. . . . One night, the two use a Ouija board . . . , believing it's a chance to reach out to her grandmother. But when they get a response, it isn't from Miriam. And Julie discovers that while she has been eager to regain her past, Clark is haunted by his." (Publisher's Note)

"Told in Block's signature, flowing prose, Teen Spirit is a layered story that's more about grief than it is about ghosts. Julie's narration is fast paced and accessible; readers won't be bogged down by intricate plots or complex ghost mythology. This is just a story about two kids learning to deal with loss. Julie realizes she cannot cling to the dead; she must hold her grandmother in her heart as she tries to live her own life. A beautiful story from a legendary young adult author." (School Library Journal)

The **waters** & the wild. HarperTeen 2009 113p $16.99; lib bdg $17.89
Grades: 7 8 9 10 **Fic**
1. School stories 2. Fairies -- Fiction
ISBN 978-0-06-145244-4; 0-06-145244-0; 978-0-06-145245-1 lib bdg; 0-06-145245-9 lib bdg
LC 2008031452

Thirteen-year-old Bee realizes that she is a fairy who has been switched at birth with another girl who now wants her life back.

"Fragments of poems by Yeats and Shelley are eerily apropos (and may provide an irresistible invitation for further reading). Haunting and thought provoking." Publ Wkly

Weetzie Bat. Harper & Row 1989 88p hardcover o.p. pa $7.99
Grades: 9 10 11 12 **Fic**
1. Friendship -- Fiction
ISBN 0-06-020534-2; 0-06-073625-9 pa
LC 88-6214

ALA YALSA Margaret A. Edwards Award (2005)

Follows the wild adventures of Weetzie Bat and her Los Angeles punk friends, Dirk, Duck-Man, and Secret-Agent-Lover-Man

"A brief, off-beat tale that has great charm, poignancy, and touches of fantasy. . . . This creates the ambiance of Hollywood with no cynicism, from the viewpoint of denizens who treasure its unique qualities." SLJ

Other titles about Weetzie Bat and her friends are:
Baby be-bop (1995)
Cherokee Bat and the Goat Guys (1992)
Pink smog (2012)
Witch baby (1991)

Bloor, Edward

London calling; 1st ed.; Alfred A. Knopf 2006 289p $16.96; lib bdg $18.99
Grades: 6 7 8 9 **Fic**
1. School stories 2. Science fiction 3. World War, 1939-1945 -- Fiction
ISBN 0-375-83635-7; 0-375-93635-1 lib bdg
LC 2005-33330

Seventh-grader Martin Conway believes that his life is monotonous and dull until the night the antique radio he uses as a night-light transports him to the bombing of London in 1940.

"Evocative descriptions and elegant phrasings make the writing most enjoyable, and because the author uses a first-person voice, the story seems very personal." SLJ

A **plague** year. Alfred A. Knopf 2011 305p $15.99; lib bdg $10.99
Grades: 6 7 8 9 10 **Fic**
1. School stories 2. Drug abuse -- Fiction 3. Pennsylvania -- Fiction 4. Supermarkets -- Fiction 5. Coal mines and mining -- Fiction
ISBN 978-0-375-85681-5; 0-375-85681-1; 978-0-375-95681-2 lib bdg; 0-375-95681-6 lib bdg
LC 2010050651

A ninth-grader who works with his father in the local supermarket describes the plague of meth addiction that consumes many people in his Pennsylvania coal mining town from 9/11 and the nearby crash of United Flight 93 in Shanksville to the Quecreek Mine disaster in Somerset the following summer.

"The plot is message-heavy but goes down easily because Bloor excels at writing vivid scenes. Tom is a thoroughly sympathetic narrator as he grows to realize there is value in 'blooming where you are planted.'" Publ Wkly

Taken. Alfred A. Knopf 2007 247p $17; pa $8.99
Grades: 6 7 8 9 10 **Fic**
1. Science fiction 2. Kidnapping -- Fiction 3. Social classes -- Fiction
ISBN 978-0-375-83636-7; 0-375-83636-5; 978-0-440-42128-3 pa; 0-440-42128-4 pa
LC 2006-35561

In 2036 kidnapping rich children has become an industry, but when thirteen-year-old Charity Meyers is taken and held for ransom, she soon discovers that this particular kidnapping is not what it seems.

"Deftly constructed, this is as riveting as it is thought-provoking." Publ Wkly

★ **Tangerine.** Harcourt Brace & Co. 1997 294p $17
Grades: 7 8 9 10 **Fic**
1. Soccer -- Fiction 2. Brothers -- Fiction
ISBN 0-15-201246-X
LC 96-34182

Twelve-year-old Paul, who lives in the shadow of his football hero brother Erik, fights for the right to play soccer despite his near blindness and slowly begins to remember the incident that damaged his eyesight

"Readers will cheer for this bright, funny, decent kid." Horn Book Guide

Bloss, Josie

Albatross. Flux 2010 229p pa $9.95

Grades: 8 9 10 11 12 **Fic**

1. School stories 2. Musicians -- Fiction 3. Friendship -- Fiction

ISBN 978-0-7387-1476-9; 0-7387-1476-3

LC 2009-27511

"Tess's parents have recently separated, and the teen and her mother have moved from Chicago to Michigan to start over. Once there, Tess finds herself inexplicably attracted to Micah, an angst-ridden boy who belittles her, contrasting her with his 'true love,' Daisy. Sprinkled throughout the story are italicized phrases—assertive responses that Tess lacks the self-esteem to voice aloud. In an epiphany, she realizes that her attraction to Micah stems from his familiarity: her father is insulting and abusive in the same way, and she begins to speak out, expressing the internal dialogue she has been having all along." SLJ

Blubaugh, Penny

Serendipity Market. HarperTeen 2009 268p $16.99; pa $8.99

Grades: 7 8 9 10 **Fic**

1. Fairy tales 2. Magic -- Fiction 3. Storytelling -- Fiction

ISBN 978-0-06-146875-9; 0-06-146875-4; 978-0-06-146877-3 pa; 0-06-146877-0 pa

LC 2008-10187

When the world begins to seem unbalanced, Mama Inez calls ten storytellers to the Serendipity Market and, through the power of their magical tales, the balance of the world is corrected once again.

"In this debut storytelling tour de force, Blubaugh repackages familiar folk and fairy-tale themes with contemporary verve and wit." Kirkus

Blume, Judy

Forever; a novel. Atheneum Books for Young Readers $17.99; pa $6.99

Grades: 9 10 11 12 **Fic**

1. Love stories 2. Sex -- Fiction 3. Families -- New Jersey -- Fiction

ISBN 0-689-84973-7; 0-671-69530-4 pa

A reissue of the title first published 1975 by Bradbury Press

ALA YALSA Margaret A. Edwards Award (1996)

The "story of a teenage senior-year love affair based primarily on physical attraction. Once Katherine Danziger and Michael Wagner meet at a party, they have eyes only for each other, and their romance progresses rapidly from kissing to heavy petting to lying together and finally to frequent sexual intercourse after Kath gets the Pill from a Planned Parenthood officer. . . . Characters—including adults and friends of the protagonists—are well developed, dialog is natural, and the story is convincing; however, the explicit sex scenes will limit this to the mature reader." Booklist

Tiger eyes; a novel. Bradbury Press 1981 206p $16.95; pa $6.99

Grades: 7 8 9 10 **Fic**

1. Death -- Fiction

ISBN 0-689-85872-8; 0-440-98469-6 pa

LC 81-6152

Resettled in the "Bomb City" with her mother and brother, Davey Wexler recovers from the shock of her father's death during a holdup of his 7-Eleven store in Atlantic City

"The plot is strong, interesting and believable. . . . The story though intense and complicated flows smoothly and easily." Voice Youth Advocates

Blume, Lesley M. M.

Tennyson. Alfred A. Knopf 2008 288p $15.99; lib bdg $18.99; pa $6.99

Grades: 6 7 8 9 10 11 12 **Fic**

1. Family life -- Fiction

ISBN 978-0-375-84703-5; 978-0-375-94703-2 lib bdg; 978-0-440-24061-7 pa

LC 2007-25983

After their mother abandons them during the Great Depression, eleven-year-old Tennyson Fontaine and her little sister Hattie are sent to live with their eccentric Aunt Henrietta in a decaying plantation house

"Many readers will respond to this novel's Southern gothic sensibility, especially Blume's beautiful, poetic writing about how the past resonates through the generations." Booklist

Blumenthal, Deborah

Mafia girl. Deborah Blumenthal. Albert Whitman & Company. 2014 256p $16.99

Grades: 8 9 10 11 Fic

1. Identity--Fiction 2. Mafia--Fiction 3. Father-daughter relationship--Fiction

ISBN: 0807549118; 9780807549117

LC 2013028440

"Seventeen-year-old Gia, the daughter of New York City's most notorious Mafia boss, leads a privileged life, but what she wants most is to have a normal existence in which her family is safe. When she and her best friend are pulled over for underage drinking and driving, Gia is immediately attracted to the arresting police officer—despite his lack of interest. Not one to be denied, Gia does everything in her power to wear down his resistance, all the while running for school president, posing for Vogue, and surviving mob hits." SLJ

Gia's voice is an entertaining, effervescent stream-of-consciousness, but the book's frantic pace muddles too many competing plot lines." Horn Book

Blundell, Judy

Strings attached. Scholastic Press 2011 310p $17.99

Grades: 7 8 9 10 **Fic**

1. Dance -- Fiction 2. Mafia -- Fiction 3. Homicide -- Fiction 4. New York (N.Y.) -- Fiction 5. Italian Americans -- Fiction

ISBN 978-0-545-22126-9; 0-545-22126-9

LC 2010-41078

Blundell "successfully constructs a complex web of intrigue that connects characters in unexpected ways. History and theater buffs will especially appreciate her attention to detail—Blundell again demonstrates she can turn out first-rate historical fiction." Publ Wkly

★ **What** I saw and how I lied. Scholastic Press 2008 284p $16.99
Grades: 8 9 10 11 12 **Fic**
1. Mystery fiction 2. Florida -- Fiction
ISBN 978-0-439-90346-2; 0-439-90346-7
LC 2008-08503

In 1947, with her jovial stepfather Joe back from the war and family life returning to normal, teenage Evie, smitten by the handsome young ex-GI who seems to have a secret hold on Joe, finds herself caught in a complicated web of lies whose devastating outcome change her life and that of her family forever.

"Using pitch-perfect dialogue and short sentences filled with meaning, Blundell has crafted a suspenseful, historical mystery." Booklist

Blythe, Carolita

Revenge of a not-so-pretty girl; Carolita Blythe. Delacorte Press 2013 336 p. (library) $19.99; (hardcover) $16.99
Grades: 7 8 9 10 11 12 **Fic**
1. African American youth -- Fiction 2. Teenagers -- Conduct of life -- Fiction 3. Old age -- Fiction 4. Schools -- Fiction 5. Conduct of life -- Fiction 6. Family problems -- Fiction 7. Catholic schools -- Fiction 8. African Americans -- Fiction 9. Mothers and daughters -- Fiction 10. Brooklyn (New York, N.Y.) -- Fiction
ISBN 037599081X; 9780307978455; 9780375990816; 9780385742863
LC 2012012735

This novel, by Carolita Blythe, follows "an African American girl living in 1980s Brooklyn. . . . Evelyn Ryder used to be a beautiful movie star--never mind that it was practically a lifetime ago. . . . So if you think I feel guilty about mugging her, think again. But for something that should have been so simple, it sure went horribly wrong. . . . That's why I'm returning to the scene of the crime. . . . To see if I might be able to turn my luck around." (Publisher's note)

Bobet, Leah

Above; by Leah Bobet. Arthur A. Levine Books 2012 363 p.
Grades: 9 10 11 12 **Fic**
1. Fantasy fiction 2. Adventure fiction 3. Storytelling -- Fiction
ISBN 0545296706; 9780545296700
LC 2011012955

In this fantasy novel, "Safe is an underground refuge for the sick, the broken, and the freaks, far from the prying eyes of Above. Narrator Matthew is the Teller, responsible for remembering and guarding the stories of his friends and surrogate family. . . . When the only person ever to be exiled from Safe returns at the head of an army of shadows. . . . the group navigates the treacherous world of Above as they seek to reclaim Safe and come to terms with long-hidden truths" (Publishers Weekly)

Bock, Caroline

LIE. St. Martin's Griffin 2011 211p pa $9.99
Grades: 8 9 10 11 12 **Fic**
1. Homicide -- Fiction 2. Violence -- Fiction 3. Immigrants -- Fiction 4. Prejudices -- Fiction
ISBN 978-0-312-66832-7; 0-312-66832-5
LC 2011019824

Seventeen-year-old Skylar Thompson is being questioned by the police. Her boyfriend, Jimmy, stands accused of brutally assaulting two young El Salvadoran immigrants from a neighboring town, and she's the prime witness.

"This effective, character-driven, episodic story examines the consequences of a hate crime on the teens involved in it. . . . Realistic and devastatingly insightful, this novel can serve as a springboard to classroom and family discussions. Unusual and important." Kirkus

Bodeen, S. A.

The **Compound**. Feiwel and Friends 2008 248p $16.95; pa $8.99
Grades: 7 8 9 10 **Fic**
1. Twins -- Fiction 2. Fathers -- Fiction 3. Survival after airplane accidents, shipwrecks, etc. -- Fiction
ISBN 0-312-37015-6; 0-312-57860-1 pa; 978-0-312-37015-2; 978-0-312-57860-2 pa
LC 2007-36148

After his parents, two sisters, and he have spent six years in a vast underground compound built by his wealthy father to protect them from a nuclear holocaust, fifteen-year-old Eli, whose twin brother and grandmother were left behind, discovers that his father has perpetrated a monstrous hoax on them all.

"The audience will feel the pressure closing in on them as they, like the characters, race through hairpin turns in the plot toward a breathless climax." Publ Wkly

The **gardener**. Feiwel and Friends 2010 233p $16.99
Grades: 7 8 9 10 **Fic**
1. Science fiction 2. Fathers -- Fiction 3. Genetic engineering -- Fiction 4. Single parent family -- Fiction
ISBN 978-0-312-37016-9; 0-312-37016-4
LC 2009-48802

When high school sophmore Mason finds a beautiful but catatonic girl in the nursing home where his mother works, the discovery leads him to revelations about a series of disturbing human experiments that have a connection to his own life.

"This is a fast-paced read that keeps readers guessing what the turn of a page will reveal." Voice Youth Advocates

The **raft**; S.A. Bodeen. Feiwel and Friends 2012 231 p. $16.99
Grades: 7 8 9 10 **Fic**
1. Survival skills -- Fiction 2. Wilderness survival -- Fiction 3. Survival after airplane accidents, shipwrecks, etc. -- Fiction
ISBN 0312650108; 9780312650100

This novel, by S. A. Bodeen, is a plane crash survival story. "All systems are go until a storm hits during the flight. The only passenger, Robie doesn't panic until the engine suddenly cuts out and Max shouts at her to put on a life jacket. . . . And then . . . she's in the water. Fighting for her life. Max pulls her onto the raft. . . . They have no water. Their only food is a bag of Skittles. There are sharks. There is an island. But there's no sign of help on the way." (Publisher's note)

Boll, Rosemarie

The **second** trial. Second Story Press 2010 319p pa $11.95

Grades: 6 7 8 9 10 **Fic**

1. Wife abuse -- Fiction 2. Family life -- Fiction 3. Domestic violence -- Fiction 4. Parent-child relationship -- Fiction

ISBN 978-1-897187-72-2 pa; 1-897187-72-6 pa

When his father's sentencing for domestic abuse isn't enough to protect them, Danny and his family are put into protective custody.

"This is a great story of upheaval and change, as well as the conflict a young person feels when his life is abruptly changed and he feels like he has lost control." Libr Media Connect

Booraem, Ellen

The **unnameables.** Harcourt 2008 317p $16

Grades: 6 7 8 9 **Fic**

1. Fantasy fiction 2. Utopias -- Fiction 3. Friendship -- Fiction

ISBN 978-0-1520-6368-9; 0-1520-6368-4

LC 2007-48844

On an island in whose strict society only useful objects are named and the unnamed are ignored or forbidden, thirteen-year-old Medford encounters an unusual and powerful creature, half-man, half-goat, and together they attempt to bring some changes to the community.

"Island, a creepy and restrictive world masquuerading as a utopia, is as memorable as the intricately developed inhabitants." Bull Cent Child Books

Booth, Coe

Bronxwood. Push 2011 328p $17.99

Grades: 10 11 12 **Fic**

1. Drug traffic -- Fiction 2. Foster home care -- Fiction 3. African Americans -- Fiction 4. Bronx (New York, N.Y.) -- Fiction

ISBN 978-0-4399-2534-1

Sequel to Tyrell (2006)

"Action scenes combine with interpersonal exchanges to keep the pace moving forward at a lightning speed, but Booth never sacrifices the street-infused dialogue and emotional authenticity that characterize her works. She has created a compelling tale of a teen still trying to make the right choices despite the painful consequences." SLJ

Kendra. PUSH 2008 292p $16.99

Grades: 8 9 10 11 12 **Fic**

1. New York (N.Y.) -- Fiction 2. Teenage mothers -- Fiction 3. African Americans -- Fiction 4. Mother-daughter relationship -- Fiction

ISBN 978-0-439-92536-5; 0-439-92536-3

LC 2008-12819

High schooler Kendra longs to live with her mother who, unprepared for motherhood at age fourteen, left Kendra in the care of her grandmother.

"The convoluted but redeeming friendship between Kendra and her best friend and aunt, Adonna, resonates with heartbreak and honesty. Teens will appreciate Kendra's internal justification monologues, especially in relation to her Nana. . . . From Bronx blocks to Harlem hangouts, Booth delivers dynamic characters and an engaging story." SLJ

★ **Tyrell.** PUSH 2006 310p hardcover o.p. pa $7.99

Grades: 9 10 11 12 **Fic**

1. Poor -- Fiction 2. Homeless persons -- Fiction 3. African Americans -- Fiction 4. Bronx (New York, N.Y.) -- Fiction

ISBN 0-439-83879-7; 978-0-439-83879-5; 0-439-83880-0 pa; 978-0-439-83880-1 pa

LC 2005-37330

Fifteen-year-old Tyrell, who is living in a Bronx homeless shelter with his spaced-out mother and his younger brother, tries to avoid temptation so he does not end up in jail like his father.

"The immediate first-person narrative is pitch perfect: fast, funny, and anguished (there's also lots of use of the n-word, though the term is employed in the colloquial sense, not as an insult). Unlike many books reflecting the contemporary street scene, this one is more than just a pat situation with a glib resolution; it's filled with surprising twists and turns that continue to the end." Booklist

Followed by Bronxwood (2011)

Borris, Albert

Crash into me. Simon Pulse 2009 257p $16.99

Grades: 8 9 10 11 12 **Fic**

1. Suicide -- Fiction 2. Automobile travel -- Fiction

ISBN 978-1-4169-7435-2; 1-4169-7435-0

LC 2008-36225

Four suicidal teenagers go on a "celebrity suicide road trip," visiting the graves of famous people who have killed themselves, with the intention of ending their lives in Death Valley, California.

This "novel gives a spot-on portrayal of depressed and suicidal teens with realistic voices." Kirkus

Bosworth, Jennifer

Struck; Jennifer Bosworth. 1st ed. Farrar Straus Giroux 2012 376 p. (paperback) $9.99; (hardcover) $17.99

Grades: 9 10 11 12 **Fic**

1. Love stories 2. Cults -- Fiction 3. Lightning -- Fiction 4. Supernatural -- Fiction 5. Thunderstorms -- Fiction 6. Brothers and sisters -- Fiction 7. Los Angeles (Calif.) -- Fiction 8. Mothers and daughters -- Fiction

ISBN 9781250027405; 0374372837; 9780374372835; 9781429954709

LC 2011018298

In this book, "[d]oomsday cults play tug-of-war over a teenage girl who loves getting struck by lightning. . . . After lightning hits a fault line and causes a terrible earthquake in Los Angeles . . . Mia attracts attention from both [a] fundamentalist sect and a secret society that opposes them. . . . But mysterious, handsome Jeremy warns her from choosing either side and offers a very sudden relationship." (Kirkus Reviews)

Bow, Erin

★ **Plain** Kate. Arthur A. Levine Books 2010 314p $17.99

Grades: 7 8 9 10 **Fic**

1. Fantasy fiction 2. Cats -- Fiction 3. Magic -- Fiction 4. Orphans -- Fiction 5. Witchcraft -- Fiction 6. Wood carving -- Fiction

ISBN 978-0-545-16664-5; 0-545-16664-0

LC 2009-32652

Plain Kate's odd appearance and expertise as a woodcarver cause some to think her a witch, but friendship with a talking cat and, later, with humans help her to survive and even thrive in a world of magic, charms, and fear.

"Despite the talking animal . . . and graceful writing . . . this is a dark and complex tale, full of violence—knives cut a lot more than wood. . . . Kate is undeniably a sympathetic character deserving of happiness." Publ Wkly

★ **Sorrow's** knot; Erin Bow. Arthur A. Levine Books 2013 368 p. (hardcover: alk. paper) $17.99

Grades: 8 9 10 11 12 **Fic**

1. Dead 2. Magic 3. Knots and splices 4. Magic -- Fiction 5. Identity -- Fiction 6. Fate and fatalism -- Fiction

ISBN 0545166667; 9780545166669; 9780545166676; 9780545578004

LC 2013007855

In this book, by Erin Bow, "the dead do not rest easy. Every patch of shadow might be home to something hungry, something deadly. Most of the people of this world live on the sunlit, treeless prairies. But a few carve out an uneasy living in the forest towns, keeping the dead at bay with wards made from magically knotted cords. The women who tie these knots are called binders. And Otter's mother, Willow, is one of the greatest binders her people have ever known." (Publisher's note)

"Sorrow's Knot is a dystopian novel that does not deal with the destruction of the broader world. Rather, it delves into the mythology of a group of people and how their prejudices and resistance to change came to be. Readers of suspense will love the dark tension of the story line, an ebb and flow that carries through to the very end." (School Library Journal)

Bowers, Laura

Beauty shop for rent; --fully equipped, inquire within. [by] Laura Bowers. 1st ed.; Harcourt 2007 328p $17; pa $6.95

Grades: 6 7 8 9 **Fic**

1. Beauty shops -- Fiction 2. Mother-daughter relationship -- Fiction

ISBN 0-15-205764-1; 978-0-15-205764-0; 978-0-15-206385-6 pa; 0-15-206385-4 pa

LC 2006016761

Raised by a great-grandmother and a bunch of beauty shop buddies, fourteen-year-old Abbey resolves to overcome her unhappy childhood and disillusionment with the mother who deserted her.

"This deceptively simple book reveals Abbey as a wonderful character who will appeal to a broad spectrum of readers." SLJ

Bowler, Tim

Blade: out of the shadows. Philomel Books 2010 232p $16.99

Grades: 7 8 9 10 **Fic**

1. Gangs -- Fiction 2. Homicide -- Fiction 3. Violence -- Fiction 4. Great Britain -- Fiction 5. Homeless persons -- Fiction

ISBN 978-0-399-25187-0; 0-399-25187-1

LC 2009-3155

Badly injured, fourteen-year-old Blade must continue to use his exceptional "street smarts" and waning strength to outsmart dangerous thugs while he considers surrendering to the police to face the consequences of a past he has tried to forget.

"Bowler combines the slow unveiling of Blade's past with short chapters and nonstop action to create tension and suspense." Kirkus

Followed by: Fighting back (2011)

Blade: playing dead. Philomel Books 2009 231p $16.99; pa $7.99

Grades: 7 8 9 10 **Fic**

1. Gangs -- Fiction 2. Violence -- Fiction 3. Great Britain -- Fiction 4. Homeless persons -- Fiction

ISBN 978-0-399-25186-3; 0-399-25186-3; 978-0-14-241600-6 pa; 0-14-241600-2 pa

LC 2008-37813

First published 2008 in the United Kingdom

A fourteen-year-old British street person with extraordinary powers of observation and self-control must face murderous thugs connected with a past he has tried to forget, when his skills with a knife earned him the nickname, Blade.

"Bowler delivers an intense, gripping novel. . . . Readers who like their thrillers brutally realistic will find much to enjoy." Publ Wkly

Other books about Blade are:

Blade: fighting back (2011)

Blade: out of the shadows (2010)

Frozen fire; [by] Tim Bowler. Philomel Books 2008 328p $17.99

Grades: 7 8 9 10 **Fic**

1. Brothers -- Fiction 2. Supernatural -- Fiction 3. Missing children -- Fiction

ISBN 978-0-399-25053-8; 0-399-25053-0

LC 2007-43880

First published 2006 in the United Kingdom

Fifteen-year-old Dusty gets a mysterious call from a boy who says he is going to kill himself, and while he claims to have called her randomly, he seems to know her intimately.

"Bowler plunges readers into a mystery of psychological, supernatural, and sociological dimensions. . . . The book's wintry setting is brittle and otherworldly, and the story never lacks for tension." Horn Book Guide

Boyd, Maria

★ **Will.** Alfred A. Knopf 2010 300p $16.99; lib bdg $19.99

Grades: 8 9 10 11 12 **Fic**

1. School stories 2. Theater -- Fiction 3. Musicals -- Fiction 4. Australia -- Fiction 5. Homosexuality -- Fiction

ISBN 978-0-375-86209-0; 0-375-86209-9; 978-0-375-96209-7 lib bdg; 0-375-96209-3 lib bdg

LC 2009-39888

Seventeen-year-old Will's behavior has been getting him in trouble at his all-boys school in Sydney, Australia, but his latest punishment, playing in the band for a musical production, gives him new insights into his fellow students and helps him cope with an incident he has tried to forget.

"Readers should find it easy to sympathize with Will's vibrant, deadpan narration and his frequent use of slang, while recognizing that his jocular exterior hides a deeper vulnerability. . . . Boyd effectively handles Will's final outpouring of repressed emotions: the personal growth achieved by her realistic, likeable protagonist is abundantly clear." Publ Wkly

Bradbury, Jennifer

Shift. Atheneum Books for Young Readers 2008 245p $16.99

Grades: 7 8 9 10 11 12 **Fic**

1. Travel -- Fiction 2. Cycling -- Fiction 3. Friendship -- Fiction 4. Missing persons -- Fiction

ISBN 978-1-4169-4732-5; 1-4169-4732-9

LC 2007-23558

When best friends Chris and Win go on a cross country bicycle trek the summer after graduating and only one returns, the FBI wants to know what happened.

"Bradbury's keen details . . . add wonderful texture to this exciting [novel.] . . . Best of all is the friendship story." Booklist

Wrapped. Atheneum Books for Young Readers 2011 309p $16.99

Grades: 7 8 9 10 **Fic**

1. Mystery fiction 2. Spies -- Fiction 3. Supernatural -- Fiction

ISBN 978-1-4169-9007-9; 1-4169-9007-0

"An 1815 parlor diversion leads to a fizzy, frothy caper. Agnes is a Regency debutante. . . . When she pockets the trinket she finds among the linens at her neighbor's mummy-wrapping party, she unwittingly sets off a series of catastrophes . . . that include burglaries, violent attacks and murder. . . . Bradbury weaves Egyptology, Napoleanic conquest and a flirtation with the supernatural into a spy thriller." Kirkus

Bradley, Alex

24 girls in 7 days. Dutton 2005 265p $15.99

Grades: 7 8 9 10 **Fic**

1. Dating (Social customs) -- Fiction

ISBN 0-525-47369-6

"When the love of his life rejects his invitation to the senior prom, Jack Grammar's so-called best friends pose as Jack and run a personal ad in the online school newspaper soliciting a date. . . . The result is a hilarious adventure as Jack tries to speed-date 24 girls in 7 days. . . . This entertaining guy's eye view on dating, friendship, and understanding one's self is one that most libraries will want to own." SLJ

Brande, Robin

Evolution, me, & other freaks of nature. Alfred A. Knopf 2007 268p hardcover o.p. pa $7.99

Grades: 7 8 9 10 **Fic**

1. School stories 2. Evolution -- Fiction 3. Christian life -- Fiction

ISBN 978-0-375-84349-5; 0-375-84349-3; 978-0-375-94349-2 lib bdg; 0-375-94349-8 lib bdg; 978-0-440-24030-3 pa; 0-440-24030-1 pa

LC 2006-34158

Following her conscience leads high school freshman Mena to clash with her parents and former friends from their conservative Christian church, but might result in better things when she stands up for a teacher who refuses to include "Intelligent Design" in lessons on evolution.

"Readers will appreciate this vulnerable but ultimately resilient protagonist who sees no conflict between science and her own deeply rooted faith." Booklist

★ **Fat** Cat. Alfred A. Knopf 2009 330p $16.99; lib bdg $19.99

Grades: 8 9 10 11 12 **Fic**

1. School stories 2. Obesity -- Fiction 3. Friendship -- Fiction 4. Science -- Experiments -- Fiction

ISBN 978-0-375-84449-2; 0-375-84449-X; 978-0-375-94449-9 lib bdg; 0-375-94449-4 lib bdg

LC 2008-50619

Overweight teenage Catherine embarks on a high school science project in which she must emulate the ways of hominins, the earliest ancestors of human beings, by eating an all-natural diet and foregoing technology.

The author "offers a fresh, funny portrait of a strong-minded young woman hurdling obstacles and fighting cravings to reach her goal." Publ Wkly

Brashares, Ann

3 willows; the sisterhood grows. Delacorte Press 2009 318p $18.99; lib bdg $21.99

Grades: 6 7 8 9 10 **Fic**

1. Friendship -- Fiction

ISBN 978-0-385-73676-3; 0-385-73676-2; 978-0-385-90628-9 lib bdg; 0-385-90628-5 lib bdg

LC 2008-34873

Ama, Jo, and Polly, three close friends from Bethesda, Maryland, spend the summer before ninth grade learning about themselves, their families, and the changing nature of their friendship.

"Brashares gets her characters' emotions and interactions just right." Publ Wkly

Forever in blue; the fourth summer of the Sisterhood. Delacorte Press 2007 384p $18.99; lib bdg $21.99

Grades: 9 10 11 **Fic**

1. Friendship -- Fiction

ISBN 978-0-385-72936-9; 0-385-72936-7; 978-0-385-90413-1 lib bdg; 0-385-90413-4 lib bdg

LC 2006-18782

Fourth volume of the Traveling Pants books; Sequel to Girls in pants (2005)

As their lives take them in different directions, Lena, Tibby, Carmen, and Bridget discover many more things about themselves and the importance of their relationship with each other.

"This light read is a great ending to the series. Sisterhood followers who are eagerly awaiting this final book will not be disappointed." Voice Youth Advocates

Girls in pants; the third summer of the Sisterhood. Delacorte Press 2005 338p $16.95; lib bdg $18.99; pa $8.95

Grades: 9 10 11 12 **Fic**

1. Friendship -- Fiction

ISBN 0-385-72935-9; 0-385-90919-5 lib bdg; 0-553-37593-8 pa

LC 2004-15296

Third volume of the Traveling Pants books, previous titles The sisterhood of the travelling pants and The second summer of the sisterhood

"It's the summer before the Septembers go to college, a summer in which old and new boyfriends appear, families grow and change, crises occur and are resolved, and the pants continue their designated rounds. Despite their diverse schedules, the four friends . . . reunite one final weekend before they go off to four different colleges. Readers of the other books won't be disappointed with these new adventures." Booklist

Followed by Forever in blue (2007)

The **here** and now. Ann Brashares. Delacorte Press. 2014 256p $18.99

Grades: 8 9 10 11 12 **Fic**

1. High school students--Fiction 2. Time travel--Fiction 3. New York (N.Y.)--Fiction

ISBN: 0385736800; 9780385736800; 9780385906296

LC 2013018683

"Prenna and her doctor mom are not your average immigrants. No, they have immigrated to New York from the 2090s, a future of climate-change extremes and mosquito-borne plagues that wipe out entire families and civilizations. The few who have survived the plagues and the journey back to 2010 have been charged with two challenges: change the course of environmental history and assimilate into the culture without disclosing their origins or becoming intimate with the natives. Prenna knows her friendship with Ethan is 'red-flag behavior.' When an elderly homeless man warns her that she and Ethan must prevent a murder on May 17, 2014—just days away—she realizes she must defy the community and its counselors for civilization's greater good. . . . The book's environmental message won't be missed by readers, but this is a cautionary tale rather than a didactic screed." Booklist

The **second** summer of the sisterhood. Delacorte Press 2003 373p $15.95; lib bdg $17.99; pa $8.95

Grades: 9 10 11 12 **Fic**

1. Friendship -- Fiction

ISBN 0-385-72934-0; 0-385-90852-0 lib bdg; 0-385-73105-1 pa

LC 2003-535308

"Brashares has done an outstanding job of showing the four teens growing up and giving readers a happy, ultimately hopeful book, easy to read and gentle in its important lessons." Booklist

Followed by Girls in pants (2005)

The **sisterhood** of the traveling pants. Delacorte Press 2001 294p $14.95; pa $8.95; pa $9.99

Grades: 8 9 10 **Fic**

1. Friendship -- Fiction

ISBN 0-385-72933-2; 0-385-73058-6 pa; 9780385730587 pa

LC 2002-282046

"Four teenagers—best friends since babyhood—have different destinations for the summer and are distressed about disbanding. When they find a pair of 'magic pants'—secondhand jeans that fit each girl perfectly, despite their different body types—they take a solemn vow that the Pants 'will travel to all the places we're going, and they will keep us together when we are apart.' . . . Middle school, high school." (Horn Book)

"Four lifelong high-school friends and a magical pair of jeans take summer journeys to discover love, disappointment, and self-realization." Booklist

Bray, Libba

★ **Beauty** queens. Scholastic Press 2011 396p $18.99

Grades: 8 9 10 11 12 **Fic**

1. Beauty contests -- Fiction 2. Survival after airplane accidents, shipwrecks, etc. -- Fiction

ISBN 978-0-439-89597-2; 0-439-89597-9

LC 2011-02321

In this book by Libba Bray, "on their way to the Miss Teen Dream competition, a planeload of beauty pageant contestants crashes on what appears to be a deserted island. While the surviving Teen Dreamers valiantly cope with the basics (finding food, water, and shelter; practicing their pageant skills), they become pawns in a massive global conspiracy involving a rogue former Miss Teen Dream winner; a megalomaniacal dictator; and a Big Brother-ish pageant sponsor, The Corporation." (Horn Book Magazine)

"A full-scale send-up of consumer culture, beauty pageants, and reality television: . . . it makes readers really examine their own values while they are laughing, and shaking their heads at the hyperbolic absurdity of those values gone seriously awry." Bull Cent Child Books

★ The **diviners**; by Libba Bray. Little, Brown 2012 608 p. (hardback) $19.99

Grades: 9 10 11 12 **Fic**

1. Mystery fiction 2. Historical fiction 3. Occultism -- Fiction 4. Murder -- Fiction 5. Uncles -- Fiction 6. Psychic ability -- Fiction 7. Mystery and detective stories 8. New York (N.Y.) -- History -- 1898-1951 -- Fiction

ISBN 031612611X; 9780316126113

LC 2012022868

In this book by Libba Bray, "Evie O'Neill has been exiled from her boring old hometown and shipped off to the bustling streets of New York City. . . . The only catch is Evie has to live with her Uncle Will, curator of The Museum of American Folklore, Superstition, and the Occult. . . . When a rash of occult-based murders comes to light, Evie and her uncle are right in the thick of the investigation." (Publisher's note)

★ **Going** bovine. Delacorte Press 2009 480p $17.99; lib bdg $20.99
Grades: 9 10 11 12 **Fic**
1. Dwarfs -- Fiction 2. Automobile travel -- Fiction 3. Creutzfeldt-Jakob disease -- Fiction
ISBN 978-0-385-73397-7; 0-385-73397-6; 978-0-385-90411-7 lib bdg; 0-385-90411-8 lib bdg
LC 2008-43774
ALA YALSA Printz Award (2010)
In an attempt to find a cure after being diagnosed with Creutzfeldt-Jakob's (aka mad cow) disease, Cameron Smith, a disaffected sixteen-year-old boy, sets off on a road trip with a death-obsessed video gaming dwarf he meets in the hospital.
"Bray's wildly imagined novel, narrated in Cameron's sardonic, believable voice, is wholly unique, ambitious, tender, thought-provoking, and often fall-off-the-chair funny, even as she writes with powerful lyricism about the nature of existence, love, and death." Booklist

★ A **great** and terrible beauty. Delacorte Press 2004 403p $16.95
Grades: 9 10 11 12 **Fic**
1. Mystery fiction 2. Great Britain -- Fiction
ISBN 0-385-73028-4
LC 2003-9472
After the suspicious death of her mother in 1895, sixteen-year-old Gemma returns to England, after many years in India, to attend a finishing school where she becomes aware of her magical powers and ability to see into the spirit world.
"The reader will race to the end to discover the mysterious and realistic challenges of an exciting teenage gothic mystery." Libr Media Connect

Rebel angels. Delacorte Press 2005 548p $16.95; pa $9.99
Grades: 9 10 11 12 **Fic**
1. Mystery fiction 2. Magic -- Fiction 3. Great Britain -- Fiction
ISBN 0-385-73029-2; 0-385-73341-0 pa
LC 2005-3805
Sequel to A great and terrible beauty (2004)
Gemma and her friends from the Spence Academy return to the realms to defeat her foe, Circe, and to bind the magic that has been released.
"The writing never falters, and the revelations (such as Felicity's childhood of abuse, discreetly revealed) only strengthen the characters. Clever foreshadowing abounds, and clues to the mystery of Circe may have readers thinking they have figured everything out; they will still be surprised." SLJ
Followed by The sweet far thing (2007)

The **sweet** far thing. Delacorte Press 2007 819p $17.99; lib bdg $20.99
Grades: 9 10 11 12 **Fic**
1. Mystery fiction 2. Magic -- Fiction 3. Great Britain -- Fiction
ISBN 978-0-385-73030-3; 978-0-385-90295-3 lib bdg
LC 2007-31302
Sequel to Rebel angels (2005)
At Spence Academy, sixteen-year-old Gemma Doyle continues preparing for her London debut while struggling to determine how best to use magic to resolve a power struggle in the enchanted world of the realms, and to protect her own world and loved ones.
"The novel's fast-paced and exciting ending and Bray's lyrical descriptions of the decaying realms are sure to enchant readers who loved Gemma's previous exploits." SLJ

Brenna, Beverly
Waiting for no one. Red Deer 2011 187p pa $12.95
Grades: 7 8 9 10 **Fic**
1. Asperger's syndrome -- Fiction
ISBN 978-0-88995-437-3; 0-88995-437-2
Sequel to Wild orchid (2006)
Taylor Jane Smith is "taking a biology class at college and applying for a job at a local bookstore. Her Asperger's syndrome gives her an advantage in the class, but it's making the job-application process torture. . . . Taylor, with her flinty, exasperated approach to the world, remains a fascinating character and narrator." Bull Cent Child Books

Brennan, Caitlin
House of the star. Tor 2010 282p $17.99
Grades: 7 8 9 10 **Fic**
1. Fantasy fiction 2. Magic -- Fiction 3. Horses -- Fiction 4. Princesses -- Fiction 5. Ranch life -- Fiction
ISBN 978-0-7653-2037-7; 0-7653-2037-1
LC 2010-36678
"Princess Elen of Ymbria has always wanted to be a rider of a worldrunner—a magical horse that can travel safely on faerie roads between worlds. She is invited to Earth to stay at the House of Star, an Arizona ranch where these animals are bred. The only catch is that someone from the royal family of Caledon has been invited as well. . . . Brennan creates a magical world based around a realistic ranch setting. The two main characters are complex and avoid the common clichés about princesses. Fans of fantasy and horses will find an intriguing premise and a galloping plot." SLJ

Brennan, Herbie
The **Doomsday** Box; a Shadow Project adventure. Balzer & Bray 2011 328p $16.99
Grades: 6 7 8 9 **Fic**
1. Spies -- Fiction 2. Plague -- Fiction 3. Cold war -- Fiction 4. Time travel -- Fiction 5. Extrasensory perception -- Fiction
ISBN 978-0-06-175647-4; 0-06-175647-4
LC 2010-15947
Working on a highly-classified espionage project, four English teenagers go back in time to the Cold War in 1962 to prevent a global outbreak of the bubonic plague in the twenty-first century.
"Readers who enjoy their action/adventure laced with weird science and real politics will enjoy this fast-paced, exciting second in the series." Bull Cent Child Books

The **Shadow** Project. Balzer & Bray 2010 355p $16.99
Grades: 6 7 8 9 **Fic**
1. Spies -- Fiction 2. Supernatural -- Fiction
ISBN 978-0-06-175642-9; 0-06-175642-3
LC 2009-14276

A young English thief stumbles on, and subsequently is recruited for, a super-secret operation that trains teenagers in remote viewing and astral projection techniques in order to engage in spying.

"The action has a ready-for-its-close-up cinematic quality, and there's a manageable blend of stock and original, fully fleshed characters to guarantee investment and relatability. This is the kind of mind candy that action/adventure junkies will gobble right up." Bull Cent Child Books

Brennan, Sarah Rees

The **demon's** lexicon. Margaret K. McElderry Books 2009 322p $17.99; pa $9.99
Grades: 9 10 11 12 **Fic**
1. Magic -- Fiction 2. Brothers -- Fiction 3. Demonology -- Fiction
ISBN 978-1-4169-6379-0; 1-4169-6379-0; 978-1-4169-6380-6 pa; 1-4169-6380-4 pa
LC 2008-39056

Sixteen-year-old Nick and his family have battled magicians and demons for most of his life, but when his brother, Alan, is marked for death while helping new friends Jamie and Mae, Nick's determination to save Alan leads him to uncover a devastating secret.

"A fresh voice dancing between wicked humor and crepuscular sumptuousness invigorates this urban fantasy. . . . The narrative peels back layers of revelation, deftly ratcheting up the tension and horror to a series of shattering climaxes." Kirkus

Other titles in this series are:
The demon's covenant (2010)
The demon's surrender (2011)

Team Human; Justine Larbalestier and Sarah Rees Brennan. HarperTeen 2012 344 p. (tr. bdg.) $17.99
Grades: 8 9 10 11 12 **Fic**
1. Love stories 2. School stories 3. Vampires -- Fiction 4. Female friendship -- Fiction 5. Maine -- Fiction 6. Schools -- Fiction 7. High schools -- Fiction
ISBN 0062089641; 9780062089649
LC 2011026149

In this book, "[h]igh school senior Mel Duan is not impressed when a 150-year old vampire (who looks like a teenager and talks like a 19th-century poet) enrolls in her school. Sure, New Whitby, Maine, is known for its large vampire population, but the vamps and humans keep to their own. Mel finds Francis merely annoying until her best friend Cathy falls for him and decides to become a vampire herself, at which point Mel shifts into full-blown protective mode." (Publishers Weekly)

Unspoken; by Sarah Rees Brennan. Random House Books for Young Readers 2012 p. cm. (The Lynburn legacy) (hardcover) $18.99
Grades: 7 8 9 10 **Fic**
1. Gothic novels 2. Fantasy fiction 3. Mystery fiction 4. Horror stories 5. Magic -- Fiction 6. England -- Fiction 7. Magicians -- Fiction
ISBN 9780375870415; 9780375970412
LC 2012001954

This juvenile gothic mystery, by Sarah Rees Brennan, starts The Lynburn Legacy series. "Kami Glass knows that she could be a great reporter. . . . The aristocratic, secretive Lynburns are coming home, . . . and Kami is determined . . . [to] get the scoop. Soon, two gorgeous, near-identical Lynburn cousins . . . join her journalistic team--not to mention Kami's imaginary best friend, . . . who turns out to be not quite so imaginary after all. And that's when the grisly murders start." (Kirkus Reviews)

Brewer, Heather

First kill. Dial Books for Young Readers 2011 309p il (The Slayer chronicles) $17.99
Grades: 6 7 8 9 **Fic**
1. Horror fiction 2. Vampires -- Fiction
ISBN 0-8037-3741-6; 978-0-8037-3741-9
LC 2011006061

The summer before ninth grade, when Joss sets off to meet his uncle and hunt down the beast that murdered his younger sister three years earlier, he learns he is destined to join the Slayer Society.

"This companion volume to Brewer's Vlad Tod series (Twelfth Grade Kills, 2010, etc.) provides a simple entry point into the opposite side of the vampire world—those tasked with killing the undead. . . . Action flows seamlessly into drama, and a betrayal comes after a series of clever misdirections." Kirkus

The **chronicles** of Vladimir Tod: eighth grade bites. Dutton Children's Books 2007 182p (The chronicles of Vladimir Tod) $16.99
Grades: 6 7 8 9 **Fic**
1. School stories 2. Orphans -- Fiction 3. Vampires -- Fiction
ISBN 978-0-525-47811-9; 0-525-47811-6
LC 2006030455

For thirteen years, Vlad, aided by his aunt and best friend, has kept secret that he is half-vampire, but when his missing teacher is replaced by a sinister substitute, he learns that there is more to being a vampire, and to his parents' deaths, than he could have guessed.

This "is an exceptional current-day vampire story. The mix of typical teen angst and dealing with growing vampiric urges make for a fast-moving, engaging story." Voice Youth Advocates

Other titles in this series are:
Ninth grade slays (2008)
Tenth grade bleeds (2009)
Eleventh grade burns (2010)

Brewster, Alicia Wright

Echo; Alicia Wright Brewster. Dragonfairy Press 2013 291 p. (paperback) $14.95

Grades: 7 8 9 10 11 12 **Fic**
1. Magic -- Fiction 2. End of the world -- Fiction
ISBN 0985023023; 9780985023027
LC 2012951596

"It's a world in trouble: Earth-Two, long settled by humans, will end in 10 days. Calling up all elemental practitioners to help, the Council elders have averted catastrophe only by repeatedly rewinding time back 10 days before the end. With each rewind, they become weakened echoes of their original selves. Now in the fifth rewind, their efforts focus on eliminating the Mages—formerly human 'ether manipulators' whose elemental energies have consumed their humanity—causing the crisis. Drafted as an Ethereal, Asha's pleased but perplexed—she's shown no powers so far. Why is Loken, the non-Ethereal guy who dumped her last year, leading her training group? . . . . Fully realized characters from Asha to the walk-ons lend their intense authenticity to the plot, which straddles the line between fantasy and science fiction." Kirkus

Brezenoff, Steve

Brooklyn, burning. Carolrhoda Lab 2011 202p $17.95
Grades: 8 9 10 11 **Fic**
1. Musicians -- Fiction 2. Runaway teenagers -- Fiction 3. Brooklyn (New York, N.Y.) -- Fiction
ISBN 978-0-7613-7526-5
LC 2010051447

"Homelessness, queerness and the rougher sides of living on the street are handled without a whiff of sensationalism, and the moments between Kid, the first-person narrator, and Scout, addressed as 'you,' are described in language so natural and vibrant that readers may not even notice that neither character's gender is ever specified. . . . Overall, the tone is as raw, down-to-earth and transcendent as the music Scout and Kid ultimately make together." Kirkus

Guy in real life. Steve Brezenoff. Balzer + Bray. 2014 386p $17.99
Grades: 9 10 11 12 **Fic**
1. Fantasy games — Fiction 2. Love — Fiction; 3. Role playing— Fiction 4. Video games — Fiction 5. Minnesota — Fiction
ISBN: 0062266837; 9780062266835
LC 2013021584

"Sulky metal head boy meets artsy gamer girl. Awkward teenage love ensues. When Lesh's and Svetlana's worlds collide literally in Saint Paul, Minn., it precipitates a time-honored culture clash wherein magic happens, but that's where predictability ends. In a first-person narration that alternates between the boy in black and the girl dungeon master, Brezenoff conjures a wry, wise and deeply sympathetic portrait of the exquisite, excruciating thrill of falling in love." Kirkus

Briant, Ed

Choppy socky blues. Flux 2010 259p pa $9.95
Grades: 7 8 9 10 **Fic**
1. Karate -- Fiction 2. Great Britain -- Fiction 3. Dating (Social customs) -- Fiction 4. Father-son relationship -- Fiction
ISBN 978-0-7387-1897-2; 0-7387-1897-1
LC 2009-30491

In the South of England, fourteen-year-old Jay resumes contact with his father, a movie stuntman and karate instructor, after two years of estrangement to impress a girl who turns out to be the girlfriend of Jay's former best friend.

"Jason's insecurities, resentment toward (and gradual peacemaking with) his father, and obsession with girls are believably rendered—he's the kind of awkward hero readers will be glad to see come into his own." Publ Wkly

I am (not) the walrus; Ed Briant. 1st ed. Flux 2012 280 p. (pbk.) $9.95
Grades: 8 9 10 11 **Fic**
1. Love stories 2. Rock music -- Fiction 3. Bands (Music) -- Fiction
ISBN 073873246X; 9780738732466
LC 2012004314

This novel, by Ed Briant, describes how "Toby and Zack's first gig could make or break their Beatles cover band, the Nowhere Men. But ever since getting dumped by his girlfriend, lead singer Toby can't quite pull off the Beatles' feel-good vibe. When Toby finds a note hidden inside his brother's bass claiming the instrument was stolen, he embarks on a quest to find the true owner--and hopes a girl named Michelle will help him recover his lost mojo along the way." (Publisher's note)

Bridges, Robin

The **gathering** storm; Robin Bridges. 1st ed. Delacorte Press 2012 387 p. (Katerina trilogy) (ebook) $29.97; (hardcover) $17.99; (library) $20.99
Grades: 7 8 9 10 11 12 **Fic**
1. Supernatural 2. Fantasy fiction 3. Russia -- History 4. Russia -- Fiction 5. Vampires -- Fiction 6. Supernatural -- Fiction 7. Good and evil -- Fiction 8. Courts and courtiers -- Fiction
ISBN 0385740220; 0385908296; 9780375899010; 9780385740227; 9780385908290
LC 2011026175

This novel, by Robin Bridges, follows "sixteen-year-old Katerina. . . . [T]he Crown Prince of Montenegro has taken an interest in Katiya; after a series of . . . encounters with dark faeries and reanimated corpses, however, Katiya realizes that the prince's attention has more to do with her . . . [being] a necromancer. . . . She soon finds herself ensnared in a political plot . . . against a legion of undead ghouls awoken by vampires." (Bulletin of the Center for Children's Books)

"The fully realized setting, a fantastical version of pre-revolutionary Russia, adds a level of believability to this [book]. . . . An atmospheric and complicated vampire tale." Kirkus

Brockenbrough, Martha

Devine intervention; Martha Brockenbrough. Arthur A. Levine Books 2012 297 p.
Grades: 7 8 9 10 11 **Fic**
1. Soul -- Fiction 2. Angels -- Fiction 3. Heaven -- Fiction 4. Future life -- Fiction 5. High school students -- Fiction 6. Dead -- Fiction 7. Guardian angels --

Fiction
ISBN 0545382130; 9780545382137; 9780545382144
LC 2011039768

This book follows "Jerome . . . A hell raiser when alive and killed by his cousin in eighth grade in an unfortunate archery accident, he has spent his afterlife in Soul Rehab assigned to Heidi in an attempt to win his way into Heaven. Not that he's very committed to the notion; he lost his "Guardian Angel's Handbook" pretty much right away, but he sort of tries. Heidi has more or less enjoyed Jerome's company, though he could sometimes be annoying. When Heidi, having experienced unendurable humiliation in a high-school talent show, ventures onto thin ice and falls through, Jerome does his best to save her soul--as much for her own sake, he's surprised to find, as for his." (Kirkus Reviews)

Brody, Jessica

My life undecided. Farrar, Straus and Giroux 2011 299p $16.99
Grades: 6 7 8 9 **Fic**
1. School stories 2. Weblogs -- Fiction 3. Decision making -- Fiction 4. Books and reading -- Fiction
ISBN 978-0-374-39905-4; 0-374-39905-0
LC 2009051277

Fifteen-year-old Brooklyn has been making bad decisions since, at age two, she became famous for falling down a mine shaft, and so she starts a blog to let others make every decision for her, while her community-service hours are devoted to a woman who insists Brooklyn read her 'Choose the Story' books.

"Brooklyn is a sympathetic protagonist with whom teens will identify. Her journey is fun to read, and decision-challenged readers will learn an important lesson about self-acceptance along the way." SLJ

Brooks, Bruce

All that remains. Atheneum Bks. for Young Readers 2001 168p $16; pa $6.99
Grades: 7 8 9 10 **Fic**
1. Short stories 2. Death -- Fiction
ISBN 0-689-83351-2; 0-689-83442-X pa
LC 00-56912

Three novellas explore the effects of death on young lives.

"All three offerings feature believable dialogue and attitudes true to the emotions of their young characters as well as intriguingly offbeat events." Horn Book Guide

The **moves** make the man; a novel. HarperCollins Pubs. 1984 280p hardcover o.p. pa $6.99
Grades: 7 8 9 10 11 12 **Fic**
1. Friendship -- Fiction 2. African Americans -- Fiction
ISBN 0-06-020679-9; 0-06-440564-8 pa
A Newbery Medal honor book, 1985

This is an "excellent novel about values and the way people relate to one another." N Y Times Book Rev

Brooks, Kevin

Being. Scholastic 2007 336p $16.99
Grades: 8 9 10 11 12 **Fic**
1. Science fiction 2. Identity (Psychology) -- Fiction
ISBN 978-0-439-89973-4; 0-439-89973-7

It was just supposed to be a routine exam. But when the doctors snake the fiber-optic tube down Robert Smith's throat, what they discover doesn't make medical sense.

"Gruesome scenes in gloomy British surroundings provide the backdrop for provocative questions about 'being' physically, emotionally, and rationally. . . . Sadness and frustration pervade this lively page-turner, and Robert's future is surely uncertain." Voice Youth Advocates

Black Rabbit summer. Scholastic 2008 488p $17.99
Grades: 9 10 11 12 **Fic**
1. Mystery fiction 2. Drug abuse -- Fiction 3. Homosexuality -- Fiction 4. Missing persons -- Fiction
ISBN 978-0-545-05752-3; 0-545-05752-3
LC 2007-035322

When two of sixteen-year-old Pete's childhood classmates disappear from a carnival the same night, he is a suspect, but his own investigation implicates other old friends he was with that evening—and a tough, knife-wielding enemy determined to keep him quiet.

"This dark and complicated mystery tackles the nature of friendships, loyalty and betrayal." KLIATT

Candy. Chicken House/Scholastic 2005 359p $16.95
Grades: 9 10 11 12 **Fic**
1. Drug abuse -- Fiction 2. London (England) -- Fiction
ISBN 0-439-68327-0

When fifteen-year-old Joe Beck gets lost in a disreputable neighborhood in London, he meets sixteen-year-old Candy, a heroin-addicted prostitute, and as he tries to help her, he experiences some unexpected consequences.

"Brooks's plotting is masterful, and the action twists and builds to a frenzied and violent climax." SLJ

Dawn. Chicken House/Scholastic 2009 250p $17.99
Grades: 7 8 9 10 **Fic**
1. Incest -- Fiction 2. Family life -- Fiction 3. Child sexual abuse -- Fiction
ISBN 978-0-545-06090-5; 0-545-06090-7
LC 2009-1643

First published 2009 in the United Kingdom with title: Killing God

Fifteen-year-old Dawn, who cares for her alcoholic mother, tries to suppress a painful childhood memory as she contemplates killing God, whom she blames for her father's disappearance.

"Provocative, bleak, compelling, and somewhat open-ended, this novel will appeal to those who admire unexpected strength in victims who push back mightily against being victimized." Voice Youth Advocates

IBoy. Chicken House 2011 288p il $17.99
Grades: 9 10 11 12 **Fic**
1. Science fiction 2. Gangs -- Fiction 3. Violence -- Fiction 4. London (England) -- Fiction 5. Cellular telephones -- Fiction
ISBN 978-0-54531-768-9
LC 2010054240

Sixteen-year-old Tom Harvey was an ordinary Londoner until an attack that caused fragments of an iPhone to be embedded in his brain, giving him incredible knowledge and power, but using that power against the gang that attacked him and a friend could have deadly consequences.

"This classic superhero plot, at once cutting-edge science fiction and moral fable, is guaranteed to keep even fiction-averse, reluctant readers on the edge of their seats." Kirkus

Kissing the rain. Scholastic 2004 320p $16.95
Grades: 9 10 11 12 **Fic**

1. Obesity -- Fiction 2. Homicide -- Fiction 3. Great Britain -- Fiction
ISBN 0-439-57742-X
LC 2003-57395

"After fat, bullied British teen Moo witnesses a murder, he finds himself the center of a conflict between two unsavory factions that threaten his working-class father and himself. In a casual narrative that spikes with increasing panic, Moo tells his own story, stopping short of answering the pivotal question at book's end." Booklist

★ **Lucas**. Chicken House/Scholastic 2003 423p hardcover o.p. pa $6.99
Grades: 7 8 9 10 **Fic**

1. Prejudices -- Fiction 2. Great Britain -- Fiction
ISBN 0-439-45698-3; 0-439-53063-6 pa
LC 2002-29189

On an isolated English island, fifteen-year-old Caitlin McCann makes the painful journey from adolescence to adulthood through her experiences with a mysterious boy, whose presence has an unsettling effect on the island's inhabitants

"This beautifully written allegorical tale . . . stays with readers long after it ends. . . . All of the characters are sharply defined. Lucas, with his mixture of real and unearthly qualities, is unique and unforgettable. This is a powerful book to be savored by all who appreciate fine writing and a gripping read." SLJ

The **road** of the dead. Chicken House 2006 339p $16.99
Grades: 9 10 11 12 **Fic**

1. Gypsies -- Fiction 2. Brothers -- Fiction 3. Homicide -- Fiction 4. Great Britain -- Fiction
ISBN 0-439-78623-1; 978-0-439-78623-2
LC 2005-14793

First published 2004 in the United Kingdom

Two brothers, sons of an incarcerated gypsy, leave London traveling to an isolated and desolate village, in search of the brutal killer of their sister.

"The sustained violence of the final events will be familiar to fans of films by Tarantino or, for those with historic tastes, Peckinpah, and the moral ambiguity of the ending ('Did any of it matter?') will appeal to lovers of noir, making this a useful title for readers seeking the literary equivalent of edgy cinema." Bull Cent Child Books

Brooks, Martha

★ **Mistik** Lake. Farrar, Straus and Giroux 2007 207p $16
Grades: 8 9 10 **Fic**

1. Mothers -- Fiction 2. Family life -- Fiction
ISBN 978-0-374-34985-1; 0-374-34985-1
LC 2006-37391

After Odella's mother leaves her, her sisters, and their father in Manitoba and moves to Iceland with another man, she then dies there, and the family finally learns some of the secrets that have haunted them for two generations. "Grades seven to ten." (Bull Cent Child Books)

"All of the characters seem distinct and real, thanks to the author's exceptional skill with details." Publ Wkly

★ **Queen** of hearts. Farrar Straus Giroux 2011 224p $16.99
Grades: 7 8 9 10 **Fic**

1. Sick -- Fiction 2. Manitoba -- Fiction 3. Hospitals -- Fiction 4. Family life -- Fiction 5. Tuberculosis -- Fiction
ISBN 978-0-374-34229-6; 0-374-34229-6
LC 2010-52661

Shortly after her first kiss but before her sixteenth birthday in December, 1941, Marie Claire and her younger brother and sister are sent to a tuberculosis sanatorium near their Manitoba farm.

"Readers will be held by the story's heartbreaking truths, right to the end." Booklist

Brothers, Meagan

Debbie Harry sings in French. Henry Holt 2008 232p $16.95
Grades: 8 9 10 11 12 **Fic**

1. Sex role -- Fiction 2. Rock music -- Fiction 3. Transvestites -- Fiction
ISBN 978-0-8050-8080-3; 0-8050-8080-5
LC 2007-27322

When Johnny completes an alcohol rehabilitation program and his mother sends him to live with his uncle in North Carolina, he meets Maria, who seems to understand his fascination with the new wave band Blondie, and he learns about his deceased father's youthful forays into "glam rock," which gives him perspective on himself, his past, and his current life.

"The brisk pace and the strong-willed, empathetic narrator will keep readers fully engaged." Publ Wkly

Supergirl mixtapes; Meagan Brothers. Henry Holt 2012 248 p. (hc) $17.99
Grades: 9 10 11 12 **Fic**

1. Drug abuse -- Fiction 2. New York (N.Y.) -- Fiction 3. Mother-daughter relationship -- Fiction 4. Artists -- Fiction 5. Family problems -- Fiction 6. Mothers and daughters -- Fiction 7. Single-parent families -- Fiction 8. Lower East Side (New York, N.Y.) -- Fiction
ISBN 0805080813; 9780805080810
LC 2011025738

In this book by Meagan Brothers, "Maria is thrilled when her father finally allows her to visit her estranged artist mother in New York City. She's ready for adventure, and she soon finds herself immersed in a world of rock music and busy streets. . . . But just like her beloved New York City, Maria's life has a darker side. Behind her mother's carefree existence are shadowy secrets, and Maria must decide just where -- and with whom -- her loyalty lies." (Publisher's note)

Brouwer, Sigmund

Devil's pass; Sigmund Brouwer. Orca Book Publishers 2012 237 p. (pbk) $9.95

Grades: 6 7 8 9 10 **Fic**

1. Grandfathers -- Fiction 2. Voyages and travels -- Fiction 3. Grandparent-grandchild relationship -- Fiction 4. Canada -- Fiction 5. Street musicians -- Fiction 6. Canol Heritage Trail (N.W.T.) -- Fiction

ISBN 155469938X; 9781554699384

LC 2012938220

In author Sigmund Brouwer's book, "seventeen-year-old Webb's abusive stepfather has made it impossible for him to live at home, so Webb survives on the streets of Toronto. . . . When Webb's grandfather dies, his will stipulates that his grandsons fulfill specific requests. Webb's task takes him to the Canol Trail in Canada's Far North. . . . With a Native guide, two German tourists and his guitar for company, Webb is forced to confront terrible events in his grandfather's past and somehow deal with the pain and confusion of his own life." (Publisher's note)

Brown, Jennifer

Bitter end. Little, Brown 2011 359p $17.99

Grades: 10 11 12 **Fic**

1. Friendship -- Fiction 2. Bereavement -- Fiction 3. Abused women -- Fiction

ISBN 978-0-316-08695-0; 0-316-08695-9

LC 2010-34258

"Gritty and disturbing, this novel should be in all collections serving teens. It could be used in programs about abuse, as well as in psychology or sociology classes." SLJ

Hate list. Little, Brown and Co. 2009 408p $16.99

Grades: 9 10 11 12 **Fic**

1. School stories 2. Family life -- Fiction 3. School violence -- Fiction

ISBN 978-0-316-04144-7; 0-316-04144-0

LC 2008-50223

Sixteen-year-old Valerie, whose boyfriend Nick committed a school shooting at the end of their junior year, struggles to cope with integrating herself back into high school life, unsure herself whether she was a hero or a villain.

"Val's complicated relationship with her family, . . . the surviving victims, as well as how she comes to terms with Nick's betrayal, are piercingly real, and the shooting scenes wrenching. Her successes are hard-won and her setbacks . . . painfully true to life." Publ Wkly

Perfect escape; by Jennifer Brown. Little, Brown 2012 364 p. $17.99

Grades: 9 10 11 12 **Fic**

1. Siblings -- Fiction 2. Voyages and travels -- Fiction 3. Cheating (Education) -- Fiction 4. Obsessive-compulsive disorder -- Fiction 5. Automobile travel -- Fiction 6. Brothers and sisters -- Fiction

ISBN 0316185574; 9780316185578

LC 2011027348

This book is a "road-trip drama" about brother and sister Grayson and Kendra. Kendra "defines herself by two things: her drive for academic and personal perfection, and her older brother Grayson's severe obsessive-compulsive disorder. . . . When a cheating scandal threatens to destroy Kendra's academic standing, she snaps, dragging Grayson on a cross-country trip from Missouri to California in an ill-defined attempt to 'fix' both their lives." (Publishers Weekly)

Brown, Pierce

Red Rising. Pierce Brown. Del Rey. 2014 382p $25.00

Grades: 10 11 12 Adult **Fic**

1. Resistance to government--Fiction 2. Dystopian fiction 3. Mars (Planet)--Fiction

ISBN: 0345539788; 9780345539786

LC 2013020634

"Darrow, living in a mining colony on Mars, sees his wife executed by the government, nearly dies himself, is rescued by the underground revolutionary group known as Sons of Ares, learns his government has been lying to him (and to everybody else), and is recruited to infiltrate the inner circle of society and help to bring it down from within." Booklist

"Brown's debut novel, the first volume in a planned trilogy, is reminiscent of both Suzanne Collins's The Hunger Games and William Goldman's The Lord of the Flies but has a dark and twisted power of its own that will captivate readers and leave them wanting more." LJ

Brown, Skila

★ **Caminar**; Skila Brown. Candlewick Press 2014 208 p. $15.99

Grades: 6 7 8 9 **Fic**

1. War stories 2. Guatemala -- Fiction

ISBN 0763665169; 9780763665166

LC 2013946611

This book, by Skila Brown, is "set in 1981 Guatemala. . . . Carlos knows that when the soldiers arrive with warnings about the Communist rebels, it is time to be a man and defend the village, keep everyone safe. But Mama tells him not yet. . . . Numb and alone, he must join a band of guerillas as they trek to the top of the mountain where Carlos's abuela lives. Will he be in time, and brave enough, to warn them about the soldiers? What will he do then?" (Publisher's note)

"Unlike many novels in verse, which can read like conventional narratives with line breaks, Caminarcontributes poetry that elevates the genre. In this story of a decimated Guatemalan village in 1981, readers will encounter a range of imagery, repetition, rhythms, and visual effects that bring to life the psychological experience of Carlos, a young boy caught in the violent clash between the government's army and the people's rebels...This is a much-needed addition to Latin American-themed middle grade fiction." (School Library Journal)

Bruchac, Joseph, 1942-

★ **Code** talker; a novel about the Navajo Marines of World War Two. Dial 2005 240p $16.99

Grades: 6 7 8 9 10 **Fic**

1. Navajo Indians -- Fiction 2. World War, 1939-1945

-- Fiction
ISBN 0-8037-2921-9

After being taught in a boarding school run by whites that Navajo is a useless language, Ned Begay and other Navajo men are recruited by the Marines to become Code Talkers, sending messages during World War II in their native tongue.

"Bruchac's gentle prose presents a clear historical picture of young men in wartime. . . . Nonsensational and accurate, Bruchac's tale is quietly inspiring." SLJ

Includes bibliographical references

Sacajawea; the story of Bird Woman and the Lewis and Clark Expedition. Silver Whistle Bks. 2000 199p $17; pa $6.99

Grades: 6 7 8 9 10 **Fic**

1. Explorers 2. Interpreters 3. Guides (Persons) 4. Territorial governors 5. Native Americans -- Fiction 6. Lewis and Clark Expedition (1804-1806) -- Fiction

ISBN 0-15-202234-1; 0-15-206455-9 pa

LC 99-47653

Sacajawea, a Shoshoni Indian interpreter, peacemaker, and guide, and William Clark alternate in describing their experiences on the Lewis and Clark Expedition to the Northwest

This is an "intelligent, elegantly written novel." SLJ

Includes bibliographical references

Wolf mark. Lee & Low/Tu Books 2011 377p $17.95

Grades: 6 7 8 9 **Fic**

1. Spies -- Fiction 2. Supernatural -- Fiction 3. Native Americans -- Fiction 4. Father-son relationship -- Fiction

ISBN 1-60060-661-X; 978-1-60060-661-8; 978-1-60060-878-0 e-book

LC 2011014252

When Lucas King's covert-ops father is kidnapped and his best friend Meena is put in danger, Luke's only chance to save them—a skin that will let him walk as a wolf—is hidden away in an abandoned mansion guarded by monsters.

"Bruchac has created a tense, readable novel. He combines Native American lore, supernatural elements, genetic engineering, romance, geopolitics, and adventure in one story. . . . The mystery and edge-of-your-seat action are enough to keep readers hooked." SLJ

Bryant, Jennifer

Pieces of Georgia; a novel. [by] Jen Bryant. Knopf 2006 166p $15.95; lib bdg $17.99

Grades: 6 7 8 9 **Fic**

1. Artists -- Fiction 2. Bereavement -- Fiction

ISBN 0-375-83259-9; 0-375-93259-3 lib bdg

LC 2005-43593

In journal entries to her mother, a gifted artist who died suddenly, thirteen-year-old Georgia McCoy reveals how her life changes after she receives an anonymous gift membership to a nearby art museum.

"This is a remarkable book. . . . [The] story is a universal one of love, friendship, and loss and will be appreciated by a wide audience." SLJ

Ringside, 1925; views from the Scopes trial, a novel. [by] Jen Bryant. Alfred A. Knopf 2008 228p $15.99; lib bdg $18.99

Grades: 8 9 10 11 12 **Fic**

1. Geologists 2. Novels in verse 3. Science teachers 4. Tennessee -- Fiction 5. Evolution -- Study and teaching -- Fiction

ISBN 978-0-375-84047-0; 0-375-84047-8; 978-0-375-94047-7 lib bdg; 0-375-94047-2 lib bdg

LC 2007-7177

Visitors, spectators, and residents of Dayton, Tennessee, in 1925 describe, in a series of free-verse poems, the Scopes 'monkey trial' and its effects on that small town and its citizens.

"Bryant offers readers a ringside seat in this compelling and well-researched novel. It is fast-paced, interesting, and relevant to many current first-amendment challenges." SLJ

Bryce, Celia

Anthem for Jackson Dawes; by Celia Bryce. Bloomsbury USA Childrens 2013 240 p. (hardback) $16.99

Grades: 7 8 9 10 **Fic**

1. Hospitals -- Fiction 2. Cancer -- Patients -- Fiction 3. Cancer -- Fiction 4. Friendship -- Fiction 5. Family life -- Fiction 6. Medical care -- Fiction

ISBN 1599909758; 9781599909752

LC 2012024989

In this book, "after 13-year-old Megan Bright is diagnosed with a cancerous brain tumor, she's . . . determined to have everything remain as normal as possible during her time in the hospital. . . . Megan gets closer to the only other teenager there . . . and begins to acknowledge the emotions she's been keeping buried. Initially, Jackson rubs her the wrong way, but his positivity and determined interest in Megan teach her about optimism and taking control of what she can." (Publishers Weekly)

"Sensitive and honest, this novel addresses meaningful questions concerning mortality and soul searching, and its content is appropriate for younger teens." SLJ

Buckhanon, Kalisha

Upstate. St. Martin's Press 2005 247p hardcover o.p. pa $11.95

Grades: 9 10 11 12 **Fic**

1. Letters -- Fiction 2. Homicide -- Fiction 3. Prisoners -- Fiction 4. African Americans -- Fiction 5. Harlem (New York, N.Y.) -- Fiction

ISBN 0-312-33268-8; 0-312-33269-6 pa

LC 2004-56651

Set in the 1990's, this...[novel] features Harlem teenagers Antonio, who has been convicted of involuntary manslaughter for killing his father, and his bright and ambitious girlfriend, Natasha. With Antonio in jail, the two maintain their intense relationship through the written correspondence that makes up the text. Libr J

"This is a moving, uplifting story of love and hope in the face of adversity." Publ Wkly

Budhos, Marina Tamar

Ask me no questions; [by] Marina Budhos. Atheneum Books for Young Readers 2006 162p $16.95; pa $8.99

Grades: 7 8 9 10 **Fic**

1. School stories 2. Family life -- Fiction 3. Asian Americans -- Fiction 4. New York (N.Y.) -- Fiction

ISBN 1-4169-0351-8; 1-4169-4920-8 pa

LC 2005-1831

Fourteen-year-old Nadira, her sister, and their parents leave Bangladesh for New York City, but the expiration of their visas and the events of September 11, 2001, bring frustration, sorrow, and terror for the whole family.

"Nadira and Aisha's strategies for surviving and succeeding in high school offer sharp insight into the narrow margins between belonging and not belonging." Horn Book Guide

Tell us we're home; [by] Marina Budhos. Atheneum 2010 297p $16.95

Grades: 6 7 8 9 10 **Fic**

1. Immigrants -- Fiction 2. New Jersey -- Fiction 3. Social classes -- Fiction 4. Household employees -- Fiction 5. Mother-daughter relationship -- Fiction

ISBN 978-1-4169-0352-9; 1-4169-0352-6

LC 2009-27386

Three immigrant girls from different parts of the world meet and become close friends in a small New Jersey town where their mothers have found domestic work, but their relationships are tested when one girl's mother is accused of stealing a precious heirloom.

"These fully realized heroines are full of heart, and their passionate struggles against systemic injustice only make them more inspiring. Keenly necessary." Kirkus

Buffie, Margaret

Winter shadows; a novel. Tundra Books 2010 327p $19.95

Grades: 7 8 9 10 **Fic**

1. Manitoba -- Fiction 2. Prejudices -- Fiction 3. Family life -- Fiction 4. Stepmothers -- Fiction 5. Racially mixed people -- Fiction

ISBN 978-0-88776-968-9; 0-88776-968-3

"Hatred for their wicked stepmothers bonds two girls living in a stone house in Manitoba, Canada, more than 150 years apart. Grieving for her dead mother, high-school senior Cass is furious that she has to share a room with the daughter of her dad's new, harsh-tempered wife. Then she finds the 1836 diary of Beatrice, who is part Cree and faces vicious racism as a 'half-breed' in her mostly white community. . . . The alternating narratives are gripping, and the characters are drawn with rich complexity." Booklist

Bullen, Alexandra

Wish; a novel. Point 2010 323p $17.99

Grades: 8 9 10 11 12 **Fic**

1. Fantasy fiction 2. Magic -- Fiction 3. Twins -- Fiction 4. Wishes -- Fiction 5. Sisters -- Fiction 6. Bereavement -- Fiction 7. San Francisco (Calif.) -- Fiction

ISBN 978-0-545-13905-2; 0-545-13905-8

LC 2009-22730

After her vivacious twin sister dies, a shy teenaged girl moves with her parents to San Francisco, where she meets a magical seamstress who grants her one wish.

"The detailed descriptions of San Francisco and above all the sisters' relationship provide solid grounding for a touching, enjoyable read." Kirkus

Followed by: Wishful thinking (2011)

Bunce, Elizabeth C.

Liar's moon. Arthur A. Levine Books 2011 356p $17.99

Grades: 8 9 10 11 12 **Fic**

1. Fantasy fiction 2. Mystery fiction 3. Magic -- Fiction 4. Thieves -- Fiction 5. Homicide -- Fiction 6. Social classes -- Fiction

ISBN 978-0-545-13608-2; 0-545-13608-3

LC 2011005071

In a quest to prove her friend, Lord Durrel Decath, innocent of the murder of his wife, pickpocket Digger stumbles into a conspiracy with far-reaching consequences for the civil war raging in Lllyvraneth, while also finding herself falling in love.

"A solid fantasy sequel embroils its irresistible heroine in mystery, intrigue and romance. . . . A darn good read." Kirkus

★ **Star** crossed. Arthur A. Levine Books 2010 359p $17.99

Grades: 8 9 10 11 12 **Fic**

1. Fantasy fiction 2. Magic -- Fiction 3. Thieves -- Fiction 4. Religion -- Fiction 5. Social classes -- Fiction 6. Kings and rulers -- Fiction

ISBN 978-0-545-13605-1; 0-545-13605-9

LC 2010-730

In a kingdom dominated by religious intolerance, sixteen-year-old Digger, a street thief, has always avoided attention, but when she learns that her friends are plotting against the throne she must decide whether to join them or turn them in.

"Couching her characters and setting in top-notch writing, Bunce . . . hooks readers into an intelligent page-turner with strong themes of growth, determination, and friendship." Publ Wkly

Followed by: Liar's moon (2011)

★ A **curse** dark as gold; [by] Elizabeth C. Bunce. Arthur A. Levine Books 2008 395p $17.99

Grades: 7 8 9 10 **Fic**

1. Magic -- Fiction 2. Uncles -- Fiction 3. Orphans -- Fiction 4. Sisters -- Fiction 5. Factories -- Fiction

ISBN 978-0-439-89576-7; 0-439-89576-6

LC 2007019759

ALA YALSA Morris Award, 2009

Upon the death of her father, seventeen-year-old Charlotte struggles to keep the family's woolen mill running in the face of an overwhelming mortgage and what the local villagers believe is a curse, but when a man capable of spinning straw into gold appears on the scene she must decide if his help is worth the price.

"This is a rich, compelling story that fleshes out the fairy tale, setting it in the nonspecific past of the Industrial Revolution. Readers unfamiliar with 'Rumplestilskin' will not be at a disadvantage here." KLIATT

Bunting, Eve

The **pirate** captain's daughter; written by Eve Bunting. Sleeping Bear Press 2011 208p $15.95; pa $8.95

Grades: 7 8 9 10 **Fic**

1. Pirates -- Fiction 2. Sex role -- Fiction 3. Seafaring life -- Fiction 4. Father-daughter relationship -- Fiction

ISBN 978-1-58536-526-5; 1-58536-526-2; 978-1-58536-525-8 pa; 1-58536-525-4 pa

LC 2010032409

Upon her mother's death, fifteen-year-old Catherine puts her courage and strength to the test by disguising herself as a boy to join her father, a pirate captain, on a ship whose crew includes men who are trying to steal a treasure from him.

"This is a gripping and entertaining novel that will have readers sucked in until the last page. Even teens who are not fond of historical fiction will enjoy." Voice Youth Advocates

Burd, Nick

★ The **vast** fields of ordinary. Dial Books 2009 309p $16.99

Grades: 10 11 12 **Fic**

1. Iowa -- Fiction 2. Homosexuality -- Fiction 3. Dating (Social customs) -- Fiction

ISBN 978-0-8037-3340-4; 0-8037-3340-2

LC 2008-46256

ALA GLBTRT Stonewall Book Award (2010)

The summer after graduating from an Iowa high school, eighteen-year-old Dade Hamilton watches his parents' marriage disintegrate, ends his long-term, secret relationship, comes out of the closet, and savors first love.

"A refreshingly honest, sometimes funny, and often tender novel." SLJ

Burg, Ann E.

★ **All** the broken pieces; a novel in verse. Scholastic Press 2009 218p $16.99

Grades: 7 8 9 10 **Fic**

1. Novels in verse 2. Adoption -- Fiction 3. Vietnamese Americans -- Fiction 4. Vietnam War, 1961-1975 -- Fiction

ISBN 978-0-545-08092-7; 0-545-08092-4

LC 2008-12381

Two years after being airlifted out of Vietnam in 1975, Matt Pin is haunted by the terrible secret he left behind and, now, in a loving adoptive home in the United States, a series of profound events forces him to confront his past.

This is written "in rapid, simple free verse. . . . The intensity of the simple words . . . will make readers want to rush to the end and then return to the beginning again to make connections between past and present, friends and enemies." Booklist

Burgess, Melvin

The **hit**; Melvin Burgess. Chicken House/Scholastic Inc. 2014 304 p. $17.99

Grades: 9 10 11 12 **Fic**

1. Death -- Fiction 2. Teenagers -- Drug use -- Fiction 3. Drugs -- Fiction 4. Death 5. Manchester (England) -- Fiction 6. Family life -- England -- Fiction

ISBN 0545556996; 9780545556996; 9780545557009

LC 2013013792

In this novel, by Melvin Burgess, "a new drug is on the street. Everyone's buzzing about it. Take the hit. Live the most intense week of your life. Then die. . . . Adam thinks it over. He's poor, and doesn't see that changing. . . . His brother Jess is missing. And Manchester is in chaos, controlled by drug dealers and besieged by a group of homegrown terrorists who call themselves the Zealots. . . . Adam downs one of the Death pills." (Publisher's note)

"Burgess' dystopian novel posits a near-future world in which the gap between rich and poor has grown to an unbridgeable chasm. In their despair, many have-nots are taking a new drug called Death that offers seven days of euphoric bliss followed by the oblivion of death...the novel is viscerally exciting and emotionally engaging. Best of all, it is sure to excite both thoughtful analysis and heated discussion among its readers. A clear winner from Burgess." (Booklist)

Nicholas Dane. Henry Holt 2010 403p $17.99

Grades: 10 11 12 **Fic**

1. Orphans -- Fiction 2. Child abuse -- Fiction 3. Great Britain -- Fiction 4. Child sexual abuse -- Fiction

ISBN 978-0-8050-9203-5; 0-8050-9203-X

LC 2009-51779

First published 2009 in the United Kingdom

When his single mother dies of a heroin overdose, fourteen-year-old Nick is sent into England's institutional care system, where he endures harsh punishment, sexual abuse, and witnesses horrors on a daily basis before emerging, emotionally scarred but still alive. Loosely based on "Oliver Twist."

"This is not a happy novel, despite Nick's strength and eventual survival. The horrors of violence, rape, and physical abuse are shown, as well as the long-term effects to Nick's psyche. It is not for the faint of heart, or for those in denial that seamy and dreadful things do happen. . . . A gritty and tragic indictment of 'the system' is shown in this well-thought-out book. The compelling story had me page turning, even as I was appalled by what was happening." Voice Youth Advocates

Smack. Holt & Co. 1997 327p hardcover o.p. pa $8.99

Grades: 9 10 11 12 **Fic**

1. Drug abuse -- Fiction 2. Great Britain -- Fiction 3. Runaway teenagers -- Fiction

ISBN 0-8050-5801-X; 0-312-60862-4 pa

LC 97-40629

First published 1996 in the United Kingdom with title: Junk

After running away from their troubled homes, two English teenagers move in with a group of squatters in the port city of Bristol and try to find ways to support their growing addiction to heroin

"Although the omnipresent British slang (most but not all of which is explained in a glossary) may put off some readers, lots of YAs will be drawn to this book because of the subject. Those who are will quickly find themselves absorbed in an honest, unpatronizing, unvarnished account of teen life on the skids." Booklist

Burns, Laura J.

Crave; [by] Laura J. Burns & Melinda Metz. Simon & Schuster BFYR 2010 278p pa $9.99

Grades: 8 9 10 **Fic**

1. Sick -- Fiction 2. Vampires -- Fiction

ISBN 978-1-4424-0816-6; 1-4424-0817-3

Seventeen-year-old Shay, having suffered from a rare blood disorder her entire life, starts receiving blood transfusions from her stepfather who is a physician, and, when she begins to see visions through the eyes of a vampire, she decides to investigate. She discovers a teenage vampire locked up in the doctor's office to whom she becomes attached and sets free, only to be kidnapped by the creature, who wants revenge.

This "is a fast-paced, action-packed vampire thriller with an original and refreshing story line. Gabriel's life is beautifully revealed through Shay's visions, and the well-written plot conveys depth and feeling while exploring important issues like friendship, loyalty, trust, love, and betrayal. A satisfying read with a shocking cliffhanger ending." SLJ

Burtenshaw, Jenna

Shadowcry. Greenwillow Books 2011 311p (The secrets of Wintercraft) $16.99

Grades: 8 9 10 11 12 **Fic**

1. Fantasy fiction 2. Dead -- Fiction

ISBN 978-0-06-202642-2; 0-06-202642-9

LC 2010025823

Pursued by two ruthless men of the High Council of Albiom, fifteen-year-old Kate Winters discovers that she is one of the Skilled, a rare person who can see through the veil between the living and the dead.

"Elegant, complex prose sweeps readers along." Horn Book

Burton, Rebecca

Leaving Jetty Road; [by] Rebecca Burton. 1st ed.; Knopf 2006 248p $15.95; lib bdg $17.99

Grades: 8 9 10 11 12 **Fic**

1. School stories 2. Friendship -- Fiction 3. Anorexia nervosa -- Fiction

ISBN 0-375-83488-5; 0-375-93488-X lib bdg

LC 2005018140

"In their final year of high school, best friends Lise, Nat, and Sofia make a New Year's resolution to become vegetarians. . . . As they prepare for the next steps in their lives, the girls become so wrapped up in themselves that they fail to see how their friends are growing, changing, and . . . hurting. Burton does an effective job of weaving the symptoms and personality characteristics of anorexia into an absorbing story about the tug and pull of old friendships as a teen's world expands." Booklist

Butcher, Kristin

Cheat; written by Kristin Butcher. Orca Book Publishers 2010 107p (Orca currents) pa $9.95

Grades: 7 8 9 10 **Fic**

1. School stories 2. Cheating (Education) -- Fiction

ISBN 978-1-55469-274-3; 1-55469-274-1

Laurel investigates a cheating scam at her high school.

"This novel is a realistic portrayal of high school students' attitudes towards cheating. . . . This is a well-written narrative that will challenge readers to make a decision about what's right and what's wrong." Libr Media Connect

Buzo, Laura

Love and other perishable items; Laura Buzo. Alfred A. Knopf 2012 243 p. (trade) $17.99

Grades: 9 10 11 12 **Fic**

1. Love -- Fiction 2. Work -- Fiction 3. Friendship -- Fiction 4. Australia -- Fiction 5. Maturation (Psychology) -- Fiction

ISBN 0375870008; 9780307929747; 9780375870002; 9780375970009; 9780375986741

LC 2011037579

Originally published as: Good oil. Crows Nest, N.S.W.: Allen & Unwin, 2010.

William C. Morris Award Finalist (2013)

In this book, Laura Buzo presents a love story centered on Amelia. "From the moment she sets eyes on Chris, she is a goner. Lost. Sunk. Head over heels infatuated with him. It's problematic, since Chris, 21, is a sophisticated university student, while Amelia, 15, is 15. . . . Working checkout together at the local supermarket, they strike up a friendship. . . . As time goes on, Amelia's crush doesn't seem so one-sided anymore." (Publisher's note)

Cabot, Meg

Airhead. Scholastic/Point 2008 340p $16.99

Grades: 7 8 9 10 **Fic**

1. Fashion models -- Fiction 2. New York (N.Y.) -- Fiction 3. Transplantation of organs, tissues, etc. -- Fiction

ISBN 978-0-545-04052-5; 0-545-04052-3

LC 2007-38269

Sixteen-year-old Emerson Watts, an advanced placement student with a disdain for fashion, is the recipient of a "whole body transplant"; and finds herself transformed into one of the world's most famous teen supermodels.

"Cabot's portrayal of Emerson is brilliant. . . . Pure fun, this first series installment will leave readers clamoring for the next." Publ Wkly

Other titles in this series are:

Being Nikki (2009)

Runaway (2010)

★ **All**-American girl. HarperCollins Pubs. 2002 247p hardcover o.p. pa $7.99

Grades: 7 8 9 10 **Fic**

1. Presidents -- Fiction

ISBN 0-06-029469-8; 0-06-029470-1 lib bdg; 0-06-147989-6 pa

LC 2002-19049

A sophomore girl stops a presidential assassination attempt, is appointed Teen Ambassador to the United Nations, and catches the eye of the very cute First Son. "Grades six to ten." (Bull Cent Child Books)

There's "surprising depth in the characters and plenty of authenticity in the cultural details and the teenage voices—particularly in Sam's poignant, laugh-out-loud narration." Booklist

★ The **princess** diaries. Avon Bks. 2000 238p $15.95; lib bdg $15.89; pa $6.99
Grades: 6 7 8 9 **Fic**

1. Fathers and daughters 5. Princesses -- Fiction
ISBN 0-380-97848-2; 0-06-029210-5 lib bdg; 0-380-81402-1 pa

LC 99-46479

Fourteen-year-old Mia, who is trying to lead a normal life as a teenage girl in New York City, is shocked to learn that her father is the Prince of Genovia, a small European principality, and that she is a princess and the heir to the throne

"Readers will relate to Mia's bubbly, chatty voice and enjoy the humor of this unlikely fairy tale." SLJ

Other titles about Princess Mia are:
Forever princess (2008)
Party princess (2006)
Princess in pink (2004)
Princess in the spotlight (2001)
Princess in training (2005)
Princess in waiting (2003)
The princess present (2004)
Sweet sixteen princess (2006)
Valentine princess (2006)

Cadnum, Michael

The **book** of the Lion. Viking 2000 204p hardcover o.p. pa $5.99
Grades: 7 8 9 10 **Fic**

1. Crusades -- Fiction 2. Middle Ages -- Fiction 3. Knights and knighthood -- Fiction
ISBN 0-670-88386-7; 0-14-230034-9 pa

LC 99-39370

In twelfth-century England, after his master, a maker of coins for the king, is brutally punished for alleged cheating, seventeen-year-old Edmund finds himself traveling to the Holy Land as squire to a knight crusader on his way to join the forces of Richard Lionheart

"Cadnum brilliantly captures both the grisly horror and the taut, sinewy excitement of hard travel and battle readiness. . . . There's bawdy and violent talk, but religion as part of the heart and bone of life is present, too." Booklist

Flash. Farrar, Straus and Giroux 2010 235p $17.99
Grades: 9 10 11 12 **Fic**

1. Blind -- Fiction 2. Thieves -- Fiction 3. San Francisco (Calif.) -- Fiction
ISBN 978-0-374-39911-5

LC 2009-14145

Relates one momentous day in the lives of five young people in the San Francisco Bay Area, including two teenaged bank robbers, a witness, and a wounded military policeman just back from Iraq.

"Superb writing, with many a fetching turn of phrase and meticulous care given to plotting and characterization, makes this an outstanding commentary on our times . . . and the unpredictable resolution that brings the cast to the end leaves room for reflection on motivation and character in hard times." Kirkus

Peril on the sea. Farrar, Straus and Giroux 2009 245p $16.95
Grades: 7 8 9 10 **Fic**

1. Adventure fiction 2. Pirates -- Fiction 3. Great Britain -- History -- 1485-1603, Tudors -- Fiction
ISBN 978-0-374-35823-5; 0-374-35823-0

LC 2008-5421

In the tense summer of 1588, eighteen-year-old Sherwin Morris, after nearly perishing in a shipwreck, finds himself aboard the privateer Vixen, captained by the notorious and enigmatic Brandon Fletcher who offers him adventure and riches if Sherwin would write and disseminate a flattering account of the captain's exploits.

"Cadnum's prose is vivid and evocative, brilliantly recreating life at sea in the Elizabethan era. . . . The tale is expertly paced, the varied threads of the tale elegantly woven. There's plenty here to appeal to a wide audience." Kirkus

Caine, Rachel

Prince of Shadows: a novel of Romeo and Juliet. Rachel Caine. NAL, New American Library. 2014 354p $17.99
Grades: 7 8 9 10 11 12 **Fic**

1. Families — Fiction 2. Love — Fiction 3. Vendetta — Fiction 4. Italy — History — 1559-1789 — Fiction 5. Verona (Italy) — History — 16th century — Fiction
ISBN: 0451414411; 9780451414410

LC 2013033482

The star-crossed tale of Romeo and Juliet, told through the eyes of Romeo's cousin, Benvolio, a thief known as the Prince of Shadows.

"Choosing Romeo and Juliet as her base, Caine expands the story from the viewpoint of Benvolio, Romeo's Montague cousin. While Shakespeare's plot clearly anchors Caine's, the novel focuses on providing context for the well-known story rather than embellishing it. . . . Most impressive is the author's simulation of Shakespeare's language in her prose. Never too obscure for modern readers, it retains the flavorof Shakespearean dialogue throughout, lending an atmosphere of verisimilitude that's reinforced by the detailed city setting. Simply superb." Kirkus

Calame, Don

Beat the band; by Don Calame. 1st ed. Candlewick Press 2010 390 p. (reinforced) $16.99
Grades: 9 10 11 12 **Fic**

1. School stories 2. Humorous fiction 3. Popularity/ Fiction
ISBN 0763646334; 9780763646332

LC 2010006607

Sequel to: Swim the fly.

This book, a sequel to "Swim the Fly," follows friends Coop, Matt, and Sean in tenth grade. "Right off the bat they are assigned partners for a semester-long health-class project. To his horror, Coop is paired with 'Hot Dog' Helen, the school outcast, and assigned to research contraceptives. Immediately dubbed 'Corn Dog Coop,' he is desperate for a way to salvage his social status. An upcoming Battle of the

Bands presents the perfect opportunity for him to" do so. (School Library Journal)

"Creative sexual slang and bathroom humor begin on page one, but Coop is mostly just talk. Messages about bullying and consequences of teen sex (included via the health project) add just the right note of gravitas to this rockin' romp." SLJ

Call the shots; Don Calame. Candlewick Press 2012 457 p. $16.99

Grades: 9 10 11 12 **Fic**

1. Teenagers -- Fiction 2. Friendship -- Fiction 3. Man-woman relationship -- Fiction

ISBN 0763655562; 9780763655563

LC 2012938812

In the book by Don Calame, protagonist "Sean isn't initially swayed by his crazy friend Coop's idea to make himself, Sean and their third amigo Matt into millionaires by shooting a low-budget horror film. But after his parents announce that they are having another baby . . . Sean decides to sign on as screenwriter to avoid moving into his mean twin sister's room . . . also finds himself embroiled in a terrifying romantic four-way with his new . . . girlfriend Evelyn, his drama crush Leyna and his sister's best friend, the enigmatic Nessa." (Kirkus)

Swim the fly; by Don Calame. 1st ed. Candlewick Press 2009 345 p. (reinforced) $16.99; (paperback) $7.99

Grades: 9 10 11 12 **Fic**

1. Swimming -- Fiction 2. Adolescence -- Fiction

ISBN 076364157X; 0763647764; 9780763641573; 9780763647766

LC 2009920818

Sequel: Beat the Band

In this book, fifteen-year-old Matt Gratton and his two best friends, Coop and Sean, have set themselves a summer goal of seeing "a real-live naked girl for the first time—quite a challenge, given that none of the guys has the nerve to even ask a girl out on a date. But catching a girl in the buff starts to look easy compared to Matt's other summertime aspiration: to swim the 100-yard butterfly . . . as a way to impress Kelly West, the sizzling new star of the swim team." (Publisher's note)

"Fifteen-year-old Matt has two summer goals: attract his crush Kelly's attention by learning to swim the fly and see a real girl naked. Matt and pals Cooper and Sean cook up several plots to catch a betty in the buff, but all attempts fail. . . . Fully realized secondary characters, realistically raunchy dialogue and the scatological subject matter assure that this boisterous and unexpectedly sweet read will be a word-of-mouth hit." Kirkus

Caletti, Deb

The **fortunes** of Indigo Skye. Simon & Schuster Books for Young Readers 2008 304p pa $9.99

Grades: 9 10 11 12 **Fic**

1. Wealth -- Fiction 2. Family life -- Fiction 3. Restaurants -- Fiction 4. Washington (State) -- Fiction 5. Single parent family -- Fiction 6. Waiters and waitresses -- Fiction

ISBN pa; 978-1-4169-1008-4 pa

LC 2007-08744

Eighteen-year-old Indigo is looking forward to becoming a full-time waitress after high school graduation, but her life is turned upside down by a $2.5 million tip given to her by a customer. "Grades nine to twelve." (Bull Cent Child Books)

The author "builds characters with so much depth that readers will be invested in her story. . . . Caletti spins a network of relationships that feels real and enriching." Publ Wkly

★ The **last** forever; Deb Caletti. Simon Pulse 2014 336 p. (hardback) $17.99

Grades: 8 9 10 11 12 **Fic**

1. Love 2. Death 3. Grief 4. Father-daughter relationship -- Fiction 5. Love -- Fiction 6. Death -- Fiction 7. Grief -- Fiction 8. Friendship -- Fiction

ISBN 1442450002; 9781442450004

LC 2013031010

This book, by Deb Caletti, is a "novel of love and loss. . . . Nothing lasts forever, and no one gets that more than Tessa. After her mother died, it's all she can do to keep her friends, her boyfriend, her happiness from slipping away. And then there's her dad. He's stuck in his own daze, and it's hard to feel like a family when their house no longer seems like a home. Her father's solution? An impromptu road trip that lands them in a small coastal town." (Publisher's note)

"After a trying bout with cancer, Tess's mother has died, but she's left behind a one-of-a-kind pixiebell plant. "My mother vowed that the last pixiebell would never die on her watch, and now that I have it, it isn't going to die on mine, either," Tess vows... Featuring sharp-witted first-person narration, some fascinating facts about plants and seeds, relatable characters, and evocative settings, Caletti's (The Story of Us) inspiring novel eloquently depicts the nature of mutability. As with her previous books, this love story reverberates with honesty and emotion." (Publishers Weekly)

The **secret** life of Prince Charming. Simon & Schuster Books for Young Readers 2009 322p $16.99; pa $9.99

Grades: 8 9 10 11 12 **Fic**

1. Divorce -- Fiction 2. Fathers -- Fiction

ISBN 978-1-4169-5940-3; 1-4169-5940-8; 978-1-4169-5941-0 pa; 1-4169-5941-6 pa

LC 2008-13014

Seventeen-year-old Quinn has heard all her life about how untrustworthy men are, so when she discovers that her charismatic but selfish father, with whom she has recently begun to have a tentative relationship, has stolen from the many women in his life, she decides she must avenge this wrong.

"This is a thoughtful, funny, and empowering spin on the classic road novel. . . . Because of its strong language and the mature themes, this is best suited to older teens, who will appreciate what it has to say about love, relationships, and getting what you need." SLJ

★ The **six** rules of maybe. Simon Pulse 2010 321p $16.99

Grades: 8 9 10 11 12 **Fic**

1. Oregon -- Fiction 2. Sisters -- Fiction 3. Pregnancy -- Fiction 4. Family life -- Fiction

ISBN 978-1-4169-7969-2; 1-4169-7969-7

LC 2009-22232

Scarlet, an introverted high school junior surrounded by outcasts who find her a good listener, learns to break old patterns and reach for hope when her pregnant sister moves home with her new husband, with whom Scarlet feels an instant connection.

"Reminiscent of the best of Sarah Dessen's work, this novel is beautifully written, deftly plotted, and movingly characterized." SLJ

Stay. Simon Pulse 2011 313p $16.99; ebook $9.99

Grades: 8 9 10 11 12 **Fic**

1. Islands -- Fiction 2. Washington (State) -- Fiction 3. Dating (Social customs) -- Fiction 4. Father-daughter relationship -- Fiction

ISBN 978-1-4424-0373-4; 1-4424-0373-X; 978-1-4424-0375-8 ebook; 1-4424-0375-6 ebook

LC 2010021804

"Fear tinges this summer romance and underscores the issue of abusive and claustrophobic relationships among teens." SLJ

Cameron, Peter

★ **Someday** this pain will be useful to you. Farrar, Straus and Giroux 2007 229p $16

Grades: 9 10 11 12 **Fic**

1. Conduct of life -- Fiction 2. New York (N.Y.) -- Fiction

ISBN 0-374-30989-2; 978-0-374-30989-3

LC 2006-43747

Eighteen-year-old James, a gay teen living in New York City with his older sister and divorced mother, struggles to find a direction for his life.

"James makes a memorable protagonist, touching in his inability to connect with the world but always entertaining in his first-person account of his New York environment, his fractured family, his disastrous trip to the nation's capital, and his ongoing bouts with psychoanalysis. In the process he dramatizes the ambivalences and uncertainties of adolescence in ways that both teen and adult readers will savor and remember." Booklist

Cameron, Sharon

The **dark** unwinding; by Sharon Cameron. Scholastic Press 2012 318 p. (jacketed hardcover) $17.99

Grades: 6 7 8 9 **Fic**

1. Alternative histories 2. Fantasy fiction 3. Eccentrics and eccentricities -- Fiction 4. Toys -- Fiction 5. Uncles -- Fiction 6. Inventions -- Fiction 7. Inheritance and succession -- Fiction 8. Great Britain -- History -- Victoria, 1837-1901 -- Fiction

ISBN 0545327865; 9780545327862

LC 2011044431

This steampunk novel, by Sharon Cameron, begins "when Katharine Tulman's inheritance is called into question by the rumor that her eccentric uncle is squandering away the family fortune. . . . But . . . Katharine discovers . . . [he is a] genius inventor with his own set of rules, who employs a village of . . . people rescued from the workhouses of London. Katharine is now torn between protecting her own inheritance and preserving the . . . community she grows to care for deeply." (Publisher's note)

Canales, Viola

The **tequila** worm. Wendy Lamb Books 2005 199p hardcover o.p. pa $7.99

Grades: 6 7 8 9 10 **Fic**

1. Texas -- Fiction 2. Mexican Americans -- Fiction

ISBN 0-375-84089-3 pa; 0-385-74674-1

LC 2004-24533

Sofia grows up in the close-knit community of the barrio in McAllen, Texas, then finds that her experiences as a scholarship student at an Episcopal boarding school in Austin only strengthen her ties to family and her "comadres."

"The explanations of cultural traditions . . . are always rooted in immediate, authentic family emotions, and in Canales' exuberant storytelling, which . . . finds both humor and absurdity in sharply observed, painful situations." Booklist

Cann, Kate

Consumed. Point 2011 325p $16.99

Grades: 10 11 12 **Fic**

1. Supernatural -- Fiction 2. Good and evil -- Fiction 3. Great Britain -- Fiction 4. Historic buildings -- Fiction 5. Household employees -- Fiction 6. Racially mixed people -- Fiction 7. Dating (Social customs) -- Fiction

ISBN 978-0-545-26388-7

LC 2010-20171

Sequel to Possessed (2010)

A new manager brings many changes to Morton's Keep, capitalizing on its gothic atmosphere and history, but Rayne sees ominous signs indicating that the one thing that has not changed is the evil presence she had thought was destroyed.

"Eccentric characters are well-matched by absorbing writing and a satisfactory ending. Cann effectively builds both romantic and dramatic tension in a captivating gothic atmosphere, as Rayne struggles to reconcile her modern sensibilities with myths and legends that refuse to be laid to rest." Publ Wkly

Possessed. Point 2010 327p $16.99

Grades: 10 11 12 **Fic**

1. Supernatural -- Fiction 2. Good and evil -- Fiction 3. Great Britain -- Fiction 4. Historic buildings -- Fiction

ISBN 978-0-545-12812-4; 0-545-12812-9

LC 2009-20977

Sixteen-year-old Rayne escapes London, her mother, and boyfriend for a job in the country at Morton's Keep, where she is drawn to a mysterious clique and its leader, St. John, but puzzles over whether the growing evil she senses is from the manor house or her new friends.

"This atmospheric and deliciously chilling British import gets off to a quick start, and readers will empathize with the very likable 16-year-old protagonist, who is clearly out of her element. . . . With a minimum of actual bloodshed, this supernatural delight can even be enjoyed by the faint of heart." Booklist

Followed by Consumed (2011)

Cantor, Jillian

The **life** of glass. HarperTeen 2010 340p $16.99

Grades: 7 8 9 10 11 12 **Fic**

1. Fathers -- Fiction 2. Bereavement -- Fiction 3. Family life -- Fiction

ISBN 978-0-06-168651-1; 0-06-168651-4

LC 2009-1758

Throughout her freshman year of high school, fourteen-year-old Melissa struggles to hold onto memories of her deceased father, cope with her mother's return to dating, get along with her sister, and sort out her feelings about her best friend, Ryan.

"Themes of memory, beauty, and secrets come together in this thoughtful, uplifting book that skillfully avoids Cinderella-tale predictability. . . . A gentle portrait of a girl growing through her grief." Booklist

The **September** sisters. HarperTeen 2009 361p $16.99

Grades: 7 8 9 10 11 12 **Fic**

1. Sisters -- Fiction 2. Family life -- Fiction 3. Missing persons -- Fiction

ISBN 978-0-06-168648-1; 0-06-168648-4

LC 2008-7120

A teenaged girl tries to keep her family and herself together after the disappearance of her younger sister.

"Cantor treats the shape of Abby's agony with poignant credibility. . . . This is a sensitive and perceptive account of the way tragedy unfolds both quickly and slowly and life reassembles itself around it." Bull Cent Child Books

Carbone, Elisa Lynn

Jump; [by] Elisa Carbone. Viking 2010 258p $16.99

Grades: 7 8 9 10 11 12 **Fic**

1. Mountaineering -- Fiction 2. Runaway teenagers -- Fiction

ISBN 0-670-01185-1; 978-0-670-01185-8

LC 2009-30175

In this book by Elisa Carbone, "P.K. rebels against her parents and runs away from home with Critter, a boy she's just met. Their shared love of climbing takes them to Nevada and California, pursued by police. As they get acquainted in exciting circumstances, . . . romantic tension builds." (Voice of Youth Advocates)

"Chapters range from a few sentences to a few pages, and the descriptions of the pair's climbs are riveting . . . The narrators' psychological explorations are as exhilarating as their physical exploits. . . . An incisive reflection on endurance, independence, belonging, self-knowledge, and love, this story should find a wide audience." Publ Wkly

Card, Orson Scott, 1951-

★ **Ender's** game. TOR Bks. 1991 xxi, 226p $24.95; pa $6.99

Grades: 7 8 9 10 11 12 Adult **Fic**

1. Science fiction 2. Interplanetary voyages -- Fiction

ISBN 0-312-93208-1; 0-8125-5070-6 pa

A reissue of the title first published 1985

ALA YALSA Margaret A. Edwards Award (2008)

"The key, of course, is Ender Wiggin himself. Mr. Card never makes the mistake of patronizing or sentimentalizing his hero. Alternately likable and insufferable, he is a convincing little Napoleon in short pants." N Y Times Book Rev

Other titles in the author's distant future series about Ender Wiggin include:

Children of the mind (1996)
Ender in exile (2008)
Ender's shadow (1999)
Shadow of the giant (2005)
Shadow of the Hegemon (2001)
Shadow of the giant (2005)
Shadow puppets (2002)
Speaker for the dead (1986)
A war of gifts (2007)
Xenocide (1991)

Pathfinder. Simon Pulse 2010 662p $18.99

Grades: 6 7 8 9 10 **Fic**

1. Science fiction 2. Time travel -- Fiction 3. Parapsychology -- Fiction 4. Space colonies -- Fiction 5. Interplanetary voyages -- Fiction

ISBN 978-1-4169-9176-2; 1-4169-9176-X

LC 2010-23243

Thirteen-year-old Rigg has a secret ability to see the paths of others' pasts, but revelations after his father's death set him on a dangerous quest that brings new threats from those who would either control his destiny or kill him.

"While Card delves deeply into his story's knotted twists and turns, readers should have no trouble following the philosophical and scientific mysteries, which the characters are parsing right along with them. An epic in the best sense, and not simply because the twin stories stretch across centuries." Publ Wkly

Ruins; Simon Pulse 2012 544p (hardback) $18.99

Grades: 7 8 9 10 11 12 **Fic**

1. Evolution -- Fiction 2. Time travel -- Fiction 3. Space colonies -- Fiction 4. Science fiction

ISBN 1416991778; 9781416991779

LC 2011052745

Sequel to: Pathfinder

In this book by Orson Scott Card, part of the Pathfinders series, "three time-shifters discover that the secrets of the past threaten their world with imminent obliteration. Rigg, his sister, Param, and best friend, Umbo, have joined their abilities to slip through time . . . circumventing the invisible Wall that divides their planet into 19 independent evolutionary experiments." (Kirkus Reviews)

Cardenas, Teresa

Letters to my mother; translated by David Unger. Groundwood Books/House of Anansi Press 2006 103p $15.95; pa $7.95

Grades: 7 8 9 10 **Fic**

1. Blacks -- Fiction 2. Race relations -- Fiction

ISBN 0-88899-720-5; 0-88899-721-3 pa

A young African-Cuban girl is sent to live with her aunt and cousins after the death of her mother and begins to write letters to her deceased mother telling of the misery, racial prejudice, and mistreatment at the hands of those around her.

"The main character's voice is authentic, and the other characters, sketched with spare lines, are believable and sympathetic. . . . Short chapters and lucid writing will appeal to reluctant readers." SLJ

Old dog; translated by David Unger. Groundwood Books/House of Anansi Press 2007 144p $16.95
Grades: 7 8 9 10 11 12 **Fic**
1. Cuba -- Fiction 2. Slavery -- Fiction
ISBN 978-0-88899-757-9; 0-88899-757-4
Perro Viejo, an elderly slave on a Cuban sugar plantation, "recalls his life and the endless acts of atrocity and inhumanity he has witnessed. . . . [This is a] slender but powerful story that will invite classroom discussion." Booklist

Cardi, Annie
The **chance** you won't return. Annie Cardi. Candlewick Press. 2014 344p $16.99
Grades: 9 10 11 12 **Fic**
1. Mentally ill — Fiction 2. Mother-daughter relationship — Fiction
ISBN: 0763662925; 9780763662929
LC 2013946619
In this book, protagonist Alex's "mother believes herself to be Amelia Earhart. As Alex's mother's delusion becomes more persistent, she is hospitalized, but Alex's father's insurance isn't enough, and the family has to take care of her at home. . . .When she realizes that her mother is working on a timeline that will eventually lead to her disappearance . . . her confession closes the distance she has been maintaining between herself and her friends." (Bulletin of the Center for Children's Books)
"The author creates nuanced characters and presents them with their flaws and strengths intact, including a character with a mental disorder who never loses her humanity or becomes a caricature.... This novel delivers something far more rare: a well-written, first-person narrative about negotiating life's curve balls that has a realistic ending. An honest, uncompromising story." - Kirkus

Carey, Edward
Heap House; written and illustrated by Edward Carey. Overlook Press 2014 c2013 404p illus (Iremonger, book 1) $16.99
Grades: 5 6 7 8 9 10 **Fic**
1. Family secrets — Fiction; 2. Orphans — Fiction; 3. Boys —Fiction; 4. London (England) — Fiction; 5. Houses — Fiction; 6. Great Britain — History — Victoria, 1837-1901 — Fiction
ISBN: 1468309536; 9781468309539
First published 2013 in the United Kingdom
Kirkus: Best Teen Books (2014)
NPR: Staff Picks (2014)
In this first book of a trilogy, "Clod is an Iremonger. He lives in the Heaps, a vast sea of lost and discarded items collected from all over London. At the centre is Heap House, a puzzle of houses, castles, homes and mysteries reclaimed from the city and built into a living maze of staircases and scurrying rats. The Iremongers are a mean and cruel family, robust and hardworking, but Clod has an illness. He can hear the objects whispering." (Publisher's note)
"Living among sentient trash heaps, Clod Iremonger has always been able to hear the voices of the objects that his family members carry, but the arrival of serving girl Lucy imbues the objects with a new and dangerous energy. Descriptive prose and black-and-white portraits create a unique cast of characters in a bleak, dilapidated home. Fans of Joan Aiken will flock to this dark mystery." Horn Book

Carey, Janet Lee
★ **Dragon's** Keep. Harcourt 2007 302p $17
Grades: 7 8 9 10 **Fic**
1. Fantasy fiction 2. Dragons -- Fiction 3. Princesses -- Fiction 4. Mother-daughter relationship -- Fiction 5. Great Britain -- History -- 1066-1154, Norman period -- Fiction
ISBN 978-0-15-205926-2; 0-15-205926-1
LC 2006-24669
In 1145 A.D., as foretold by Merlin, fourteen-year-old Rosalind, who will be the twenty-first Pendragon Queen of Wilde Island, has much to accomplish to fulfill her destiny, while hiding from her people the dragon's claw she was born with that reflects only one of her mother's dark secrets.
This is told "in stunning, lyrical prose. . . . Carey smoothly blends many traditional fantasy tropes here, but her telling is fresh as well as thoroughly compelling." Booklist

Dragons of Noor. Egmont USA 2010 421p $17.99
Grades: 6 7 8 9 **Fic**
1. Fantasy fiction 2. Dragons -- Fiction
ISBN 978-1-60684-035-1; 1-60684-035-5
LC 2010011311
Seven hundred years after the days of the dragon wars, magic again is stirring and three teenagers join forces to help bind the broken kingdoms of Noor and Otherworld.
"The world building and tone are just right, and the themes of friendship, loyalty, responsibility, and protection of the planet are never intrusive. Hanna and Miles are realistic teens. . . . Most of the secondary characters are equally compelling." SLJ

Dragonswood; by Janet Lee Carey. Dial Books 2012 403p.
Grades: 7 8 9 **Fic**
1. Love stories 2. Occult fiction 3. Fantasy fiction 4. Fantasy 5. Dragons -- Fiction 6. Fairies -- Fiction
ISBN 9780803735040
LC 2011021638
This juvenile fantasy novel tells the story of "Wilde Island [which] is not at peace. The kingdom mourns the dead Pendragon king and awaits the return of his heir; the uneasy pact between dragons, fairies, and humans is strained; and the regent is funding a bloodthirsty witch hunt, hoping to rid the island of half-fey maidens. Tess, daughter of a blacksmith, has visions of the future, but she still doesn't expect to be accused of witchcraft, forced to flee with her two best friends, or offered shelter by the handsome and enigmatic Garth Huntsman, a warden for Dragonswood. But Garth is the younger prince in disguise and Tess soon learns that her true father was fey." (Publisher's note)

★ **Stealing** death. Egmont USA 2009 354p map $16.99; lib bdg $19.99

Grades: 7 8 9 10 Fic
1. Fantasy fiction 2. Death -- Fiction 3. Siblings -- Fiction
ISBN 978-1-60684-009-2; 1-60684-009-6; 978-1-60684-045-0 lib bdg; 1-60684-045-2 lib bdg
LC 2009-16240

After losing his family, except for his younger sister Jilly, and their home in a tragic fire, seventeen-year-old Kipp Corwin, a poor farmer, must wrestle with death itself in order to save Jilly and the woman he loves.

"Carey's wonderful language weaves family, love, wise teachers, and petty villains together in a vast landscape. . . . This is quite simply fantasy at its best—original, beautiful, amazing, and deeply moving." SLJ

The **beast** of Noor. Atheneum Books for Young Readers 2006 497p $16.95
Grades: 6 7 8 9 Fic
1. Fantasy fiction
ISBN 978-0-689-87644-8; 0-689-87644-0
LC 2005-17731

Fifteen-year-old Miles Ferrell uses the rare and special gift he is given to break the curse of the Shriker, a murderous creature reportedly brought to Shalem Wood by his family's clan centuries

"Carey delivers an eerie, atmospheric tale, full of terror and courage, set in a convincingly realized magical realm." Booklist

Carleson, J. C.

The **tyrant's** daughter; J.C. Carleson. Alfred A. Knopf 2014 304 p. (trade) $17.99
Grades: 8 9 10 11 12 Fic
1. Teenagers -- Fiction 2. Middle East -- Fiction 3. Kings and rulers -- Fiction 4. Exiles -- Fiction 5. Schools -- Fiction 6. Dictators -- Fiction 7. Immigrants -- Fiction 8. High schools -- Fiction 9. Middle East -- Politics and government -- Fiction
ISBN 0449809978; 9780449809976; 9780449809983; 9780449809990
LC 2013014783

"Removed from her unnamed Middle Eastern country after her father is murdered during a coup, 15-year-old Laila is now living near Washington D. C. with her mother and brother...This is more than just Laila's story; rather, it is a story of context, beautifully written (by a former undercover CIA agent), and stirring in its questions and eloquent observations about our society and that of the Middle East." (Booklist)

Carlson, Melody

Premiere. Zondervan 2010 218p il (On the runway) pa $9.99
Grades: 7 8 9 10 Fic
1. Fashion -- Fiction 2. Sisters -- Fiction 3. Christian life -- Fiction 4. Television programs -- Fiction
ISBN 978-0-310-71786-7; 0-310-71786-8
LC 2009-48438

When two sisters get their own fashion-focused reality television show, vivacious Paige is excited, but Erin, a Christian who is more interested in being behind the camera than in front of it, has problems with some of the things they are asked to do

"This book is worth adding whether you have a demand for Christian novels or not. The fashion and reality-show fireworks are enough to keep even reluctant readers coming back for more." SLJ

Followed by Catwalk (2010)

Carriger, Gail

★ **Curtsies** & conspiracies; Gail Carriger. Little, Brown and Co. 2013 320 p. (Finishing school) $18
Grades: 7 8 9 10 11 12 Fic
1. Steampunk fiction 2. Espionage -- Fiction 3. Conspiracies -- Fiction 4. Science fiction 5. Robots -- Fiction 6. Schools -- Fiction 7. Etiquette -- Fiction 8. Boarding schools -- Fiction 9. Great Britain -- History -- George VI, 1936-1952 -- Fiction
ISBN 031619011X; 9780316190114
LC 2012048520

In this book, by Gail Carriger, "Sophronia's first year at Mademoiselle Geraldine's Finishing Academy for Young Ladies of Quality . . . is training her to be a spy. A conspiracy is afoot--one with dire implications for both supernaturals and humans. Sophronia must rely on her training to discover who is behind the dangerous plot-and survive the London Season with a full dance card." (Publisher's note)

"With the school's dirigible heading toward London for a liaison with an inventor studying aetherospheric travel, Sophronia (Etiquette & Espionage) is convinced that her professors are Up To Something. Is the academy affiliated with vampire hives, werewolf packs, the anti-supernatural Picklemen, or the Crown--all of whom would benefit from controlling aether technology? A witty and suspenseful steampunk romp." (Horn Book)

Curtsies and conspiracies

★ **Etiquette** & espionage; by Gail Carriger. Little, Brown 2013 320 p. (alk. paper) $17.99
Grades: 7 8 9 10 11 12 Fic
1. Spy stories 2. School stories 3. Assassins -- Fiction 4. Science fiction 5. Robots -- Fiction 6. Schools -- Fiction 7. Espionage -- Fiction 8. Etiquette -- Fiction 9. Boarding schools -- Fiction 10. Great Britain -- History -- George VI, 1936-1952 -- Fiction
ISBN 031619008X; 9780316190084
LC 2012005498

In this book, Sophronia's mother is "desperate for her daughter to become a proper lady. So she enrolls Sophronia in Mademoiselle Geraldine's Finishing Academy for Young Ladies of Quality. But Sophronia soon realizes the school is not quite what her mother might have hoped. At Mademoiselle Geraldine's, young ladies learn to finish . . . everything. Certainly, they learn the fine arts of dance, dress, and etiquette, but they also learn to deal out death, diversion, and espionage." (Publisher's note)

Carroll, Michael Owen, 1966-

The **ascension**; a Super human clash. Philomel Books 2011 378p (Super human) $16.99

Grades: 6 7 8 9 **Fic**

1. Superheroes -- Fiction

ISBN 978-0-399-25624-0; 0-399-25624-5

LC 2010029600

Teenagers with super powers must try to stop a villain who has travelled from the past in order to irreversibly alter reality.

"The characters are much less absolute in their morality than in their first outing, making the narrative even more engaging. . . . One of those rare sequels that exceed the first." Kirkus

Super human; Michael Carroll. Philomel Books 2010 325 p. ill. (hardcover) $16.99; (paperback) $8.99

Grades: 5 6 7 8 9 **Fic**

1. Superheroes -- Fiction 2. Good and evil -- Fiction

ISBN 9780399252976; 9780142419052; 0142419052; 0399252975

LC 2009-29965

A group of teenage superheroes tackle a powerful warrior who has been brought back from 4,000 years in the past to enslave the modern world.

"There is enough fighting in this book to appeal to middle school boys, and the telekinetic Roz, with a controlling superhero big brother, will appeal to girls. This title is a fast read with tension, suspense, and likeable characters." Libr Media Connect

Carson, Rae

★ The **bitter** kingdom; by Rae Carson. Greenwillow Books 2013 448 p. (hardcover) $17.99

Grades: 8 9 10 11 12 **Fic**

1. Fantasy fiction 2. Magic -- Fiction 3. Queens -- Fiction 4. Love -- Fiction 5. Prophecies -- Fiction 6. Kings, queens, rulers, etc. -- Fiction

ISBN 0062026542; 9780062026545

LC 2013011912

Sequel to: The crown of embers

This is the final book in Rae Carson's Girl of Fire and Thorns trilogy. Here, "young Queen Elisa and her companions trek into enemy territory to rescue the man she loves, while a traitor back home attempts to overthrow her. Elisa's journeys take her to . . . Invierne, where she hopes to destroy the source of the Inviernos' magic and bargain for peace; to the Basajuan desert, where only her most audacious plans have any chance to stop the war; and home to try to regain her throne." (Publishers Weekly)

★ The **crown** of embers; by Rae Carson. Greenwillow Books 2012 410 p. (hardcover) $17.99

Grades: 8 9 10 11 12 **Fic**

1. Magic 2. Queens 3. Fantasy fiction 4. Adventure fiction 5. Love -- Fiction 6. Magic -- Fiction 7. Prophecies -- Fiction 8. Kings, queens, rulers, etc. -- Fiction

ISBN 0062026518; 9780062026514

LC 2012014125

Sequel to the Morris, Cybils, and Andre Norton Award finalist book The Girl of Fire and Thorns. "Elisa is a hero. . . . [But] to conquer the power she bears once and for all, Elisa must follow the trail of long-forgotten--and forbidden--clues from the deep, undiscovered catacombs of her own city to the treacherous seas. With her goes a one-eyed spy, a traitor, and the man who--despite everything--she is falling in love with." (Publisher's note)

★ The **girl** of fire and thorns. Greenwillow Books 2011 423p $17.99

Grades: 8 9 10 11 12 **Fic**

1. Fantasy fiction 2. Magic -- Fiction 3. Prophecies -- Fiction 4. Kings and rulers -- Fiction

ISBN 978-0-06-202648-4; 0-06-202648-8

LC 2010042021

Morris Award Finalist (2012)

Once a century, one person is chosen for greatness. Elisa is the chosen one. But she is also the younger of two princesses. The one who has never done anything remarkable, and can't see how she ever will. Now, on her sixteenth birthday, she has become the secret wife of a handsome and worldly king...And he's not the only one who seeks her. Savage enemies, seething with dark magic, are hunting her. A daring, determined revolutionary thinks she could be his people's savior. Soon it is not just her life, but her very heart that is at stake." (Publisher's Note)

"This fast-moving and exciting novel is rife with political conspiracies and machinations." SLJ

Carter, Ally

Heist Society. Hyperion 2010 287p il map

Grades: 7 8 9 10 **Fic**

1. Thieves -- Fiction

ISBN 1-4231-1639-9; 978-1-4231-1639-4

LC 2009-40377

A group of teenagers conspire to re-steal several priceless paintings and save Kat Bishop's father from a vengeful collector who is accusing him of art theft. "Grades six to ten." (Bull Cent Child Books)

Carter "skillfully maintains suspense. . . . This is a thoroughly enjoyable, cinema-ready adventure." Booklist

Another title about Kat is:

Uncommon criminals (2011)

Perfect scoundrels; a Heist society novel. by Ally Carter. 1st ed. Disney/Hyperion Books 2013 328 p. (hardcover) $17.99

Grades: 7 8 9 10 **Fic**

1. Crime -- Fiction 2. Theft -- Fiction 3. Wealth -- Fiction 4. Detective and mystery stories 5. Dating (Social customs) -- Fiction 6. Swindlers and swindling -- Fiction 7. Inheritance and succession -- Fiction

ISBN 1423166000; 9781423166009

LC 2012032405

This book is an installment of Ally Carter's Heist Society series. "When Hale suddenly inherits his grandmother's billion-dollar company, it's pretty obvious that he and Kat can't be up to their old tricks anymore. But can Hale trust Kat not to dip her hand in the cookie jar and steal the company's fortune—even though he knows she's prepared to do the impossible?" (Dolly Magazine)

Carter, Caela

Me, him, them, and it; by Caela Carter. Bloomsbury Distributed to the trade by Macmillan 2013 320 p. (hardcover) $16.99

Grades: 9 10 11 12 **Fic**

1. Teenage pregnancy -- Fiction 2. Dysfunctional families -- Fiction 3. Pregnancy -- Fiction 4. Family problems -- Fiction 5. Emotional problems -- Fiction

ISBN 1599909588; 9781599909585

LC 2012014331

In this novel, by Caela Carter, "when Evelyn . . . [upset] her parents with a bad reputation, she wasn't planning to ruin her valedictorian status. She also wasn't planning to fall for Todd-the guy she was just using for sex. And she definitely wasn't planning on getting pregnant. When Todd turns his back on her, Evelyn's not sure where to go." (Publisher's note)

Carvell, Marlene

Sweetgrass basket. Dutton Childrens Books 2005 243p $16.99

Grades: 7 8 9 10 **Fic**

1. School stories 2. Sisters -- Fiction 3. Mohawk Indians -- Fiction

ISBN 0-525-47547-8

LC 2004-24374

In alternating passages, two Mohawk sisters describe their lives at the Carlisle Indian Industrial School, established in 1879 to educate Native Americans, as they try to assimilate into white culture and one of them is falsely accused of stealing.

"Carvell has put together a compelling, authentic, and sensitive portrayal of a part of our history that is still not made accurately available to young readers." SLJ

Who will tell my brother? Hyperion Bks. for Children 2002 150p hardcover o.p. pa $5.99

Grades: 7 8 9 10 **Fic**

1. School stories 2. Mohawk Indians -- Fiction

ISBN 0-7868-0827-6; 0-7868-1657-0 pa

LC 2001-51759

During his lonely crusade to remove offensive mascots from his high school, Evan, part-Mohawk Indian, learns more about his heritage, his ancestors, and his place in the world

"The blank verse format will be appealing, especially to reluctant readers. . . . [A] lovely, heart-wrenching and profound little book." Voice Youth Advocates

Cary, Kate

Bloodline; a novel. Razor Bill 2005 324p hardcover o.p. pa $9.99

Grades: 7 8 9 10 **Fic**

1. Horror fiction 2. Vampires -- Fiction 3. World War, 1914-1918 -- Fiction

ISBN 1-59514-012-3; 1-59514-078-6 pa

In this story told primarily through journal entries, a British soldier in World War I makes the horrifying discovery that his regiment commander is descended from Count Dracula.

"This story is an interesting blend of mystery, horror, and romance, and readers who love vampire novels will find it a refreshing twist to the classic story." SLJ

Followed by Bloodline: reckoning (2007)

Bloodline: reckoning. Razorbill 2007 311p (Bloodline) hardcover o.p. pa $9.99

Grades: 7 8 9 10 **Fic**

1. Horror fiction 2. Vampires -- Fiction 3. World War, 1914-1918 -- Fiction

ISBN 978-1-59514-013-5; 1-59514-013-1; 978-1-59514-179-8 pa; 1-59514-179-0 pa

LC 2006-101841

Sequel to Bloodline (2005)

In this story told primarily through journal entries, Quincey Harker, the heir to Dracula's bloodline, returns to England in 1918 to pursue Nurse Mary Seward, whose fiance has been transformed into a monstrous vampire.

"This novel about good, evil, and the gray areas in between will be a favorite with fans of the vampire genre." SLJ

Casanova, Mary

Frozen; Mary Casanova. University of Minnesota Press 2012 264 p. (hc/j: alk. paper) $16.95

Grades: 7 8 9 10 **Fic**

1. Voice -- Fiction 2. Conduct of life -- Fiction 3. Mother-daughter relationship -- Fiction 4. Memory -- Fiction 5. Families -- Fiction 6. Identity -- Fiction 7. Selective mutism -- Fiction 8. Minnesota -- History -- 20th century -- Fiction

ISBN 0816680566; 9780816680566; 9780816680573

LC 2012019376

Author Mary Casanova tells the story of a young girl's life after her mother dies. "Sixteen-year-old Sadie Rose hasn't spoken in eleven years—ever since she was found in a snowbank the night her mother died under strange circumstances . . . Like her voice, her memories of her mother and what happened that night were frozen . . . [The book] is a suspenseful, moving testimonial to the power of family and memory and the extraordinary strength of a young woman who has lost her voice in nearly every way, but is determined to find it again." (Publisher's note)

Casella, Jody

Thin space; Jody Casella. Simon Pulse 2014 256 p. (hardcover: alk. paper) $16.99

Grades: 9 10 11 12 **Fic**

1. Occult fiction 2. Fantasy fiction 3. Dead -- Fiction 4. Twins -- Fiction 5. Schools -- Fiction 6. Brothers -- Fiction 7. High schools -- Fiction 8. Supernatural -- Fiction 9. Conduct of life -- Fiction 10. Interpersonal relations -- Fiction

ISBN 158270435X; 9781582703923; 9781582704357

LC 2012045691

In this book, for "three months, high school junior Marsh Windsor has been refusing to wear shoes, ignoring schoolwork and friends, and getting into fights. His parents and teachers—even his former girlfriend—tolerate his bizarre behavior as an inability to cope with the car wreck that seriously injured Marsh and killed his twin, Austin. Only the new girl, Maddie, knows that Marsh is seeking a 'thin space,' a portal between the realms of the living and the dead." (Kirkus Reviews)

Cashore, Kristin

★ **Bitterblue**; Kristin Cashore. Dial Books 2012 563 p.

Grades: 9 10 11 12 **Fic**

1. Fantasy fiction 2. Queens -- Fiction 3. Brainwashing -- Fiction 4. Conspiracies -- Fiction 5. Fantasy

ISBN 0803734735; 9780803734739

LC 2011035026

"Sequel to Graceling, companion to Fire"-Jkt

This young adult fantasy novel "grapples with the messy aftermath of destroying an evil overlord. Nine years after Bitterblue took the crown, the young queen and her realm are still struggling to come to terms with the monstrous legacy of her father. . . . Bitterblue discovers that her people have not healed as much as she has been told. . . . [She] must draw upon all her courage, cleverness and ferocious compassion to reveal the truth -- and to care for those it shatters." (Kirkus Reviews)

★ **Fire**; a novel. Dial Books 2009 461p map $17.99

Grades: 9 10 11 12 **Fic**

1. Fantasy fiction

ISBN 978-0-8037-3461-6; 0-8037-3461-1

LC 2009-5187

In a kingdom called the Dells, Fire is the last human-shaped monster, with unimaginable beauty and the ability to control the minds of those around her, but even with these gifts she cannot escape the strife that overcomes her world.

"Many twists propel the action . . . [and] Cashore's conclusion satisfies, but readers will clamor for a sequel to the prequel—a book bridging the gap between this one and Graceling." Publ Wkly

★ **Graceling**. Harcourt 2008 471p map $17; pa $9.99

Grades: 8 9 10 11 12 **Fic**

1. Fantasy fiction

ISBN 978-0-15-206396-2; 0-15-206396-X; 978-0-547-25830-0 pa; 0-547-25830-5 pa

LC 2007045436

ALA YALSA Morris Award Finalist, 2009

In a world where some people are born with extreme skills called Graces, Katsa struggles for redemption from her own horrifying Grace, the Grace of killing. She teams up with another young fighter to save their land from a corrupt king. "Age fourteen and up." (N Y Times Book Rev)

"This is gorgeous storytelling: exciting, stirring, and accessible. Fantasy and romance readers will be thrilled." SLJ

Castan, Mike

Fighting for Dontae; Mike Castan. Holiday House 2012 150 p. (hardcover) $16.95

Grades: 6 7 8 9 10 11 12 **Fic**

1. Gangs -- Fiction 2. Reading -- Fiction 3. Children with disabilities -- Fiction 4. Schools -- Fiction 5. California -- Fiction 6. Middle schools -- Fiction 7. Conduct of life -- Fiction 8. Family problems -- Fiction 9. Mexican Americans -- Fiction 10. People with disabilities -- Fiction 11. People with mental disabilities -- Fiction

ISBN 0823423484; 9780823423484

LC 2011042115

This book is the story of seventh-grader Javier, who "does not really want to be in a gang," but thinks he must join the Playaz gang to be cool, which he desperately wants to be. "When he is assigned to work with the special-ed class at school, Javier knows that his days as a cool kid are officially over. He does not expect to enjoy it, but reading to Dontae, a severely disabled boy, becomes the one thing Javier looks forward to." (Children's Literature)

The **price** of loyalty. Holiday House 2011 150p $17.95

Grades: 7 8 9 10 **Fic**

1. School stories 2. Gangs -- Fiction 3. Mexican Americans -- Fiction

ISBN 978-0-8234-2268-5; 0-8234-2268-2

LC 2010024065

Mexican American middle-schooler Manny finds himself caught between going along with his friends who are set on forming a gang and cutting his ties to them and following his own inclination to stay out of trouble.

"Kids will recognize the peer pressure and how authorities contribute to it. . . . But the drama is never simplistic. . . . Readers will want to discuss it all." Booklist

Castellucci, Cecil

Beige. Candlewick Press 2007 307p $16.99; pa $8.99

Grades: 7 8 9 10 **Fic**

1. Musicians -- Fiction 2. Punk rock music -- Fiction 3. Los Angeles (Calif.) -- Fiction 4. Father-daughter relationship -- Fiction

ISBN 978-0-7636-3066-9; 0-7636-3066-7; 978-0-7636-4232-7 pa; 0-7636-4232-0 pa

LC 2006-52458

Katy, a quiet French Canadian teenager, reluctantly leaves Montréal to spend time with her estranged father, an aging Los Angeles punk rock legend.

This a "a good read and an interesting look at the world of punk and alternative rock." Kliatt

Boy proof. Candlewick Press 2005 203p $15.99; pa $7.99

Grades: 7 8 9 10 **Fic**

1. Motion pictures -- Fiction 2. Los Angeles (Calif.) -- Fiction

ISBN 0-7636-2333-4; 0-7636-2796-6 pa

LC 2004-50256

Feeling alienated from everyone around her, Los Angeles high school senior and cinephile Victoria Denton hides behind the identity of a favorite movie character until an interesting new boy arrives at school and helps her realize that there is more to life than just the movies.

This "novel's clipped, funny, first-person, present-tense narrative will grab teens . . . with its romance and the screwball special effects, and with the story of an outsider's struggle both to belong and to be true to herself." Booklist

First day on Earth. Scholastic Press 2011 150p $17.99

Grades: 7 8 9 10 **Fic**

1. Children of alcoholics -- Fiction 2. Extraterrestrial beings -- Fiction

ISBN 978-0-545-06082-0; 0-545-06082-6

"Mal's spare first-person narration is wistful and raw, reflecting the feelings of anyone who's ever felt misunderstood or abandoned. . . . Castellucci also creates vibrant secondary characters. . . . A simple, tender work that speaks to the alien in all of us." Kirkus

★ The **queen** of cool. Candlewick Press 2006 166p $15.99

Grades: 9 10 11 12 **Fic**

1. School stories 2. Zoos -- Fiction

ISBN 0-7636-2720-8

LC 2005-50174

Bored with her life, popular high school junior Libby signs up for an internship at the zoo and discovers that the "science nerds" she meets there may have a few things to teach her about friendship and life.

The author "offers a refreshingly nuanced and credible look at what lies behind the facade of cool." Bull Cent Child Books

Rose sees red. Scholastic Press 2010 197p $17.99

Grades: 7 8 9 10 **Fic**

1. School stories 2. Ballet -- Fiction 3. Russians -- Fiction 4. Friendship -- Fiction 5. New York (N.Y.) -- Fiction

ISBN 978-0-545-06079-0; 0-545-06079-6

LC 2009-36850

In the 1980s, two teenaged ballet dancers—one American, one Russian—spend an unforgettable night in New York City, forming a lasting friendship despite their cultural and political differences.

"The protagonist is a complexly layered character who suffers from crippling sensitivity, and her difficulty feeling at home in her body will resonate with teens. She is honest, funny, and completely authentic. . . . The prose is poetic and rich." SLJ

Castle, Jennifer

You look different in real life; Jennifer Castle. HarperTeen, an imprint of HarperCollinsPublishers 2013 368 p. (hardback) $17.99

Grades: 7 8 9 10 **Fic**

1. School stories 2. Documentary films -- Fiction 3. Identity -- Fiction 4. Celebrities -- Fiction 5. New York (State) -- Fiction

ISBN 0061985813; 9780061985812

LC 2012051743

This book follows five ordinary 16-year-olds who have been the subjects of two documentaries at ages 6 and 11. Now, many "changes have occurred since the last time they were filmed" so the "producers struggle to find usable footage and resort to staging some scenes, which in previous years was unnecessary." (School Library Journal)

Castor, H. M.

VIII; H.M. Castor. Simon & Schuster Books for Young Readers 2013 399 p. (hardcover) $17.99

Grades: 8 9 10 11 12 **Fic**

1. Great Britain -- History -- 1485-1603, Tudors 2. Kings, queens, rulers, etc. -- Fiction 3. Great Britain -- History -- Henry VII, 1485-1509 -- Fiction 4. Great Britain -- History -- Henry VIII, 1509-1547 -- Fiction

ISBN 1442474181; 9781442474185; 9781442474208

LC 2012021550

This book is a biography of Henry VIII of England. As a second son, Henry's youth is full of "fighting, jousting and gambling. When his elder brother, Arthur, unexpectedly dies, Hal realizes that . . . he now has a straight line to the throne. However . . . the difficulties of producing a royal heir, together with the thwarting of his overweening military ambition against the French by Spanish Catherine's family and his own . . . advisers cause Henry to become increasingly cynical and desperate." (Kirkus Reviews)

Caveney, Philip

Sebastian Darke: Prince of Fools. Delacorte Press 2008 338p $15.99; lib bdg $18.99

Grades: 7 8 9 10 **Fic**

1. Fantasy fiction 2. Princesses -- Fiction 3. Fools and jesters -- Fiction

ISBN 978-0-385-73467-7; 978-0-385-90465-0 lib bdg

LC 2006-25262

First published 2007 in the United Kingdom

Accompanied by his sardonic buffalope Max, seventeen-year-old Sebastian Darke meets a spoiled princess and a diminutive soldier who aid in his quest to become court jester to the evil King Septimus.

"In a very plot-driven book, the central characters are nonetheless well developed. Max is a particularly creative invention. . . . There are enough sword fights, treachery, and wicked creatures for any adventure reader. The sense of humor . . . makes it a fun read." Voice Youth Advocates

Other titles about Sebastian Darke are:

Sebastian Darke: Prince of Pirates (2009)

Sebastian Darke: Prince of Explorers (2010)

Cerrito, Angela

The **end** of the line. Holiday House 2011 213p $17.95

Grades: 6 7 8 9 **Fic**

1. Guilt -- Fiction 2. Uncles -- Fiction 3. Reformatories -- Fiction 4. Iraq War, 2003- -- Fiction

ISBN 978-0-8234-2287-6; 0-8234-2287-9

LC 2010-23475

"In the prison-like school that is his last chance, thirteen-year-old Robbie tries to recover from events that brought him there, including his uncle's war injuries and the death of [Ryan], a classmate." (Publisher's note)

"The author does an outstanding job of revealing compelling and complex characters through Robbie's narrative. . . . This book would work well as a class read-aloud or a literature circle title." Voice Youth Advocates

Chadda, Sarwat

The **devil's** kiss. Disney/Hyperion Books 2009 327p $17.99

Grades: 8 9 10 **Fic**

1. Templars -- Fiction 2. Supernatural -- Fiction 3. Good and evil -- Fiction 4. London (England) -- Fiction

ISBN 978-1-4231-1999-9; 1-4231-1999-1

LC 2009-8313

Fifteen-year-old Billi SanGreal has grown up knowing that being a member of the Knights Templar puts her in danger, but if she is to save London from catastrophe she must make sacrifices greater than she imagined.

"Scenes of spiritual warfare are gripping (and often gruesome), as is the undercurrent of supernatural romance. Chadda offers an original take on familiar creatures like vampires, the undead and fallen angels, but it's Billi's personality and tumult of emotions that will keep readers hooked." Publ Wkly

Followed by Dark goddess (2010)

Chaltas, Thalia

Because I am furniture. Viking Children's Books 2009 352p $16.99

Grades: 8 9 10 11 **Fic**

1. School stories 2. Novels in verse 3. Guilt -- Fiction 4. Child abuse -- Fiction 5. Child sexual abuse -- Fiction

ISBN 978-0-670-06298-0; 0-670-06298-7

LC 2008-23235

The youngest of three siblings, fourteen-year-old Anke feels both relieved and neglected that her father abuses her brother and sister but ignores her, but when she catches him with one of her friends, she finally becomes angry enough to take action.

"Incendiary, devastating, yet—in total—offering empowerment and hope, Chaltas's poems leave an indelible mark." Publ Wkly

Chambers, Aidan

★ **Dying** to know you; Aidan Chambers. Amulet Books 2012 275 p.

Grades: 9 10 11 12 **Fic**

1. Authors -- Fiction 2. Dyslexia -- Fiction 3. Friendship -- Fiction 4. Elderly men -- Fiction 5. Self-perception -- Fiction 6. Self perception -- Fiction 7. Interpersonal relations -- Fiction

ISBN 1419701657; 9781419701658

LC 2012000843

This young adult novel is "a story told in . . . first-person voice by a 75-year-old man. . . . Karl approaches the older man, an author, with a request. His new girlfriend, Fiorella, has tasked him with providing a series of written answers to questions . . . so that she can find out more about him. But Karl, an 18-year-old plumber who's no longer in school, is dyslexic. . . . The friendship . . . form[s] as Karl gradually gains knowledge of himself that isn't based on the previous failures in his life." (Kirkus)

Chambers, Veronica

Fifteen candles. Hyperion 2010 187p (Amigas) pa $7.99

Grades: 6 7 8 9 10 **Fic**

1. Friendship -- Fiction 2. Cuban Americans -- Fiction 3. Business enterprises -- Fiction 4. Quinceañera (Social custom) -- Fiction

ISBN 978-1-4231-2362-0; 1-4231-2362-X

"It's Alicia's quince años, and even though her thoroughly modern parents took her to Spain for her quinceañera, most of her friends are having elaborate parties to celebrate their entry into womanhood. When she realizes that a fellow intern in the mayor's office needs help in planning her quince, Alicia envisions a new business venture for her and her three best friends, Amigas Inc. . . . A warm celebration of Latin culture, especially the traditional quinceañera, this is the first in a series that is sure to draw a large audience." Booklist

Chan, Gillian

A **foreign** field. Kids Can Press 2002 184p $16.95; pa $5.95

Grades: 7 8 9 10 **Fic**

1. Love stories 2. World War, 1939-1945 -- Fiction

ISBN 1-55337-349-9; 1-55337-350-2 pa

"Fourteen-year-old Ellen, who lives near a Canadian air base that the Royal Air Force is using for training during WWII, has what she considers a tedious job as her war work: looking after her disobedient, airplane-mad younger brother, Colin. Colin introduces her to Stephen, a very young RAF trainee. . . . They find common ground and their friendship grows and deepens into love. . . . Chan beautifully captures the particular tensions and intensity of wartime relationships in this quiet, absorbing novel." Booklist

Chandler, Kristen

Girls don't fly. Viking 2011 300p $16.99

Grades: 7 8 9 10 **Fic**

1. Contests -- Fiction 2. Pregnancy -- Fiction 3. Family life -- Fiction 4. Dating (Social customs) -- Fiction

ISBN 978-0-670-01331-9; 0-670-01331-5

LC 2011010563

Myra, a high school senior, will do almost anything to win a contest and earn money for a study trip to the Galapagos Islands, which would mean getting away from her demanding family life in Utah and ex-boyfriend Erik, but Erik is set on winning the same contest.

"As Myra navigates from one trauma to the next, we know she is a princess in a scullery maid's disguise. Her cast of supporting characters is equally entertaining: sniveling Erik, sarcastic Melyssa, rough and tumble siblings, and, of course, Prince Charming, incognito as a graduate student. Funny, sensitive, loyal and endearing, Myra is a heroine to remember." Voice Youth Advocates

Wolves, boys, & other things that might kill me. Viking 2010 371p $17.99; pa $8.99

Grades: 7 8 9 10 11 12 **Fic**

1. Wolves -- Fiction 2. Yellowstone National Park -- Fiction

ISBN 978-0-670-01142-1; 0-670-01142-8; 978-0-14-241883-3 pa; 0-14-241883-8 pa

LC 2009-30179

Two teenagers become close as the citizens of their town fight over the packs of wolves that have been reintroduced into the nearby Yellowstone National Park.

This "is a lively drama, saturated with multifaceted characters and an environmental undercurrent. She writes persuasively about the great outdoors, smalltown dynamics and politics, and young love." Publ Wkly

Chapman, Fern Schumer

★ **Is** it night or day? Farrar, Straus, Giroux 2010 205p $17.99

Grades: 6 7 8 9 10 **Fic**

1. Jewish refugees -- Fiction 2. Jews -- Germany -- Fiction 3. Holocaust, 1933-1945 -- Fiction 4. World War, 1939-1945 -- Fiction 5. Jews -- United States -- Fiction

ISBN 0-374-17744-9; 978-0-374-17744-7

LC 2008055602

In 1938, Edith Westerfeld, a young German Jew, is sent by her parents to Chicago, Illinois, where she lives with an aunt and uncle and tries to assimilate into American culture, while worrying about her parents and mourning the loss of everything she has ever known. Based on the author's mother's experience, includes an afterword about a little-known program that brought twelve hundred Jewish children to safety during World War II.

"In Edith's bewildered, sad, angry voice, the words are eloquent and powerful." Booklist

Chapman, Lara

Flawless. Bloomsbury 2011 258 p. $16.99; pa $9.99

Grades: 7 8 9 10 **Fic**

1. Love stories 2. School stories 3. Friendship -- Fiction 4. Personal appearance -- Fiction

ISBN 1599906317; 1599905965; 9781599906317; 9781599905969

LC 2010049102

In this modern take on the Cyrano story, brilliant and witty high school student Sarah Burke, who is cursed with an enormous nose, helps her beautiful best friend try to win the heart of a handsome and smart new student, even though Sarah wants him for herself.

"This retelling of Cyrano de Bergerac is great fun. . . . The ending is predictable but satisfying. Each chapter begins with thoughtful quotes about love. This novel will attract both reluctant readers and literature lovers." SLJ

Charbonneau, Joelle

Graduation day; Joelle Charbonneau. Houghton Mifflin Harcourt 2014 304 p. (hardback) $17.99

Grades: 7 8 9 10 11 12 **Fic**

1. Dystopian fiction 2. Love -- Fiction 3. Loyalty -- Fiction 4. Survival -- Fiction 5. Adventure and adventurers -- Fiction 6. Government, Resistance to -- Fiction

ISBN 0547959214; 9780547959214

LC 2013034743

"Charbonneau concludes her dystopian Testing trilogy with this action-packed finale, which sees Cia Vale secretly tasked by the President of the United Commonwealth to remove the officials behind the lethal Testing process that has claimed so many young lives...As in the previous books, Charbonneau remains focused on philosophical worries and moral tests over spectacle and bloodshed, with multiple layers and twists to keep readers forever guessing. Enough potential threads are left dangling to leave room for future stories." (Publishers Weekly)

Independent study; by Joelle Charbonneau. Houghton Mifflin, Houghton Mifflin Harcourt 2014 320 p. (The testing) (hardback) $17.99

Grades: 7 8 9 10 11 12 **Fic**

1. Love 2. College students 3. Resistance to government 4. Adventure and adventurers 5. Love -- Fiction 6. Survival -- Fiction 7. Examinations -- Fiction 8. Government, Resistance to -- Fiction 9. Universities and colleges -- Fiction

ISBN 0547959206; 9780547959207

LC 2013004815

In this book, by Joelle Charbonneau, "sixteen-year-old Cia Vale was chosen by the United Commonwealth government as one of the best and brightest graduates of all the colonies. . . . [Now], Cia is a freshman at the University in Tosu City with her hometown sweetheart, Tomas—and though the government has tried to erase her memory of the brutal horrors of The Testing, Cia remembers. Her attempts to expose the ugly truth behind the government's murderous programs put her . . . in a world of danger." (Publisher's note)

"Fans of The Testing will be thrilled with this new installment and will be anxiously waiting for the story's conclusion." (School Library Journal)

★ The **Testing**; by Joelle Charbonneau. Houghton Mifflin Harcourt 2013 344 p. (hardcover) $17.99

Grades: 7 8 9 10 11 12 **Fic**

1. Examinations -- Fiction 2. Survival skills -- Fiction 3. Schools -- Fiction 4. Missing persons -- Fiction 5. Graduation (School) -- Fiction 6. Universities and colleges -- Fiction

ISBN 0547959109; 9780547959108

LC 2012018090

In this book by Joelle Charbonneau, "Cia Vale is one of four teens chosen to represent her small colony at the annual Testing, an intensive mental and physical examination aimed at identifying the best and brightest, who will go on to the University and help rebuild their shattered world. Forewarned not to trust anyone, Cia nonetheless forms a tentative partnership with resourceful Tomas, with whom she shares an unexpected emotional connection." (Publishers Weekly)

Charlton-Trujillo, E.

★ **Fat** Angie; E. E. Charlton-Trujillo. Candlewick Press 2013 272 p. $16.99

Grades: 9 10 11 12 **Fic**

1. School stories 2. Obesity -- Fiction 3. Lesbians -- Fiction

ISBN 0763661198; 9780763661199

LC 2012942623

Lambda Literary Awards Finalist (2014)

Stonewall Book Award-Mike Morgan and Larry Romans Children's & Young Adult Literature Award (2014)

This teenage novel, by E. E. Charlton-Trujillo, follows Angie, an overweight high school student who is bullied and dealing with grief over her sister, a presumed dead prisoner of the Iraq War. After entering into a friendship and lesbian relationship with a gothic new girl named KC Romance, Angie comes to rediscover her self confidence.

Chayil, Eishes

Hush. Walker 2010 359p $16.99

Grades: 8 9 10 11 12 **Fic**

1. Judaism -- Fiction 2. Suicide -- Fiction 3. Conduct of life -- Fiction 4. Child sexual abuse -- Fiction 5. Jews -- New York (N.Y.) -- Fiction 6. Brooklyn (New York, N.Y.) -- Fiction

ISBN 978-0-8027-2088-7; 0-8027-2088-9

LC 2010-10329

"The author balances outrage at the routine cover-up of criminal acts with genuine understanding of the community's fear of assault on their traditions by censorious gentiles. Moreover, she delivers her central message in an engaging coming-of-age story in which tragedy is only one element in a gossipy milieu of school and career decisions and arranged marriages, designer shoes and tasteful cosmetics, and sneak peaks out from a world of restraint and devotion into the world of Oprah." Bull Cent Child Books

Chbosky, Stephen

★ The **perks** of being a wallflower; [by] Stephen Chbosky. Pocket Bks. 1999 213p pa $12

Grades: 9 10 11 12 **Fic**

1. School stories 2. Letters -- Fiction 3. Young men -- Social life and customs -- 20th century

ISBN 0-671-02734-4

LC 99-236288

This novel in letter form is narrated by Charlie, a high school freshman. "His favorite aunt passed away, and his best friend just committed suicide. The girl he loves wants him as a friend; a girl he does not love wants him as a lover. His 18-year-old sister is pregnant. The LSD he took is not sitting well. And he has a math quiz looming. . . . Young adult." (Time)

"Charlie, his friends, and family are palpably real. . . . This report on his life will engage teen readers for years to come." SLJ

Chen, Justina

Return to me; by Justina Chen. Little, Brown and Co. 2013 352 p. (hardcover) $17.99

Grades: 7 8 9 10 **Fic**

1. Moving -- Fiction 2. Family life -- Fiction 3. Clairvoyance -- Fiction 4. Love -- Fiction 5. Architecture -- Fiction 6. Family problems -- Fiction 7. Moving, Household -- Fiction 8. Self-actualization (Psychology) -- Fiction

ISBN 0316102555; 9780316102551

LC 2012001549

In this book, "moving away from her Washington home seems to be a logical part of Reb's life plan; after the summer, she'll start at Columbia University, studying to be a corporate architect in the family firm, while her family moves to New Jersey for her father's new job. All that unravels upon their arrival on the East Coast, when her father announces that he's leaving the family to be with another woman, forcing Reb to question everything." (Bulletin of the Center for Children's Books)

Cheng, Andrea

Brushing Mom's hair; illustrations by Nicole Wong. Wordsong 2009 59p il $17.95

Grades: 4 5 6 7 8 **Fic**

1. Novels in verse 2. Sick -- Fiction 3. Cancer -- Fiction 4. Mother-daughter relationship -- Fiction

ISBN 978-1-59078-599-7; 1-59078-599-1

LC 2009021965

A fourteen-year-old girl, whose mother's breast cancer diagnosis and treatment have affected every aspect of their lives, finds release in ballet and art classes.

"With one or two words on each line, the poems are a fast read, but the chatty voice packs in emotion. . . . Wong's small black-and-white pencil drawings on every page extend the poetry through the characters' body language." Booklist

Cheva, Cherry

DupliKate; a novel. HarperTeen 2009 242p $16.99

Grades: 7 8 9 10 **Fic**

1. School stories 2. Computer games -- Fiction 3. Virtual reality -- Fiction

ISBN 978-0-06-128854-8; 0-06-128854-3

LC 2009-18292

When she wakes up one morning to find her double in her room, seventeen-year-old Kate, already at wit's end with college applications, finals, and extracurricular activities, decides to put her to work.

This is a "light and funny novel. . . . Though this is lightweight territory, there is a strong message here about being true to yourself and balancing fun and work in your life. . . . This is sure to fly off the shelves." SLJ

Chibbaro, Julie

Deadly. Atheneum Books for Young Readers 2011 293 p. $16.99

Grades: 6 7 8 9 10 **Fic**

1. Sick 2. Domestics 3. Diaries -- Fiction 4. Diaries -- Fiction 5. Sex role -- Fiction 6. Epidemiology -- Fiction 7. Typhoid fever -- Fiction 8. New York (N.Y.) -- Fiction 9. Interpersonal relations -- Fiction 10. New York (N.Y.) -- History -- 1898-1951 -- Fiction

ISBN 0689857381; 9780689857386; 978-0-689-85738-6; 0-689-85738-1

LC 2010002291

"A deeply personal coming-of-age story set in an era of tumultuous social change, this is topnotch historical fiction that highlights the struggle between rational science and popular opinion as shaped by a sensational, reactionary press." SLJ

Childs, Tera Lynn

Oh. My. Gods. Dutton Books 2008 224p $16.99

Grades: 7 8 9 10 **Fic**

1. School stories 2. Running -- Fiction 3. Stepfamilies -- Fiction 4. Classical mythology -- Fiction

ISBN 978-0-525-47942-0; 0-525-47942-2

LC 2007-28294

When her mother suddenly decides to marry a near-stranger, Phoebe, whose passion is running, soon finds herself living on a remote Greek island, completing her senior year at an ancient high school where the students and teachers are all descended from gods or goddesses.

"Childs does a great job of character development and creating a fast-paced plot to keep readers engaged." Voice Youth Advocates

Sweet venom. Katherine Tegen Books 2011 345p $17.99
Grades: 7 8 9 10 **Fic**

1. Sisters -- Fiction 2. Monsters -- Fiction 3. Fate and fatalism -- Fiction 4. Classical mythology -- Fiction 5. San Francisco (Calif.) -- Fiction 6. Medusa (Greek mythology) -- Fiction
ISBN 978-0-06-200181-8; 0-06-200181-7
LC 2010050525

As monsters walk the streets of San Francisco, unseen by humans, three teenaged descendants of Medusa, the once-beautiful gorgon maligned in Greek mythology, must reunite and embrace their fates.

"Childs clearly has a sequel (or more) in mind and uses this book to ably set up an appealing conflict, introduce quite likable characters, and get readers ready for intrigue in the romance and fate-of-the-world departments." Booklist

Chima, Cinda Williams

The **Crimson** Crown; a Seven Realms novel. Cinda Williams Chima. Hyperion 2012 598 p. (hardback) $18.99
Grades: 7 8 9 10 11 12 **Fic**

1. Fantasy fiction 2. Queens -- Fiction 3. Magicians -- Fiction 4. Fantasy 5. Wizards -- Fiction 6. Kings, queens, rulers, etc. -- Fiction
ISBN 1423144333; 9781423144335
LC 2011053079

In this fantasy novel by Cinda Williams Chima, book 4 of the Seven Realms series, "the Queendom of the Fells seems likely to shatter apart. For young queen Raisa . . . , maintaining peace even within her own castle walls is nearly impossible; tension between wizards and Clan has reached a fevered pitch. . . . Raisa's best hope is to unite her people against a common enemy. But that enemy might be the person with whom she's falling in love." (Publisher's note)

★ The **Demon** King; a Seven Realms novel. Disney Hyperion 2009 506p map (Seven Realms) $17.99
Grades: 7 8 9 10 11 12 **Fic**

1. Fantasy fiction 2. Princesses -- Fiction 3. Witchcraft -- Fiction
ISBN 978-1-4231-1823-7; 1-4231-1823-5
LC 2008-46178

Relates the intertwining fates of former street gang leader Han Alister and headstrong Princess Raisa, as Han takes possession of an amulet that once belonged to an evil wizard and Raisa uncovers a conspiracy in the Grey Wolf Court.

"With full-blooded, endearing heroes, a well-developed supporting cast and a detail-rich setting, Chima explores the lives of two young adults, one at the top of the world and the other at the bottom, struggling to find their place and protect those they love." Publ Wkly

Other titles in this series are:
The exiled queen (2010)
The Gray Wolf Throne (2011)

The **enchanter** heir; by Cinda Williams Chima. Hyperion Books 2013 464 p. (The heir chronicles) $18.99
Grades: 7 8 9 10 11 12 **Fic**

1. Massacres 2. Magic -- Fiction 3. Wizards -- Fiction 4. Terrorism -- Fiction 5. Conspiracies -- Fiction
ISBN 1423144341; 9781423144342
LC 2013013816

In this book, by Cinda Williams Chima, "someone is killing wizards and framing Nightshade, the secret organization whose job it is to track down undead souls. Jonah, . . . is also on the trail of wizard killers, but for a different reason: he wants to know who was behind the Thorn Hill disaster, where thousands of adult sorcerers and nearly as many children died. Emma, in search of her sorcerer father, lands directly in Jonah's path. Can he save her from those who think she knows the secret to Thorn Hill?" (Publisher's note)

"Chima adds two new players to her magical underworld, both with a connection to a mysterious massacre that upset the balance of power among the magical guilds and to a new threat: ghost-like "shades." Tangled conflict lines, secret identities, besieged protagonists, and nonstop action make this a thrilling and thought-provoking Heir Chronicles volume..." (Horn Book)

The **warrior** heir. Hyperion Books for Children 2006 426p hardcover o.p.
Grades: 7 8 9 10 11 12 **Fic**

1. Fantasy fiction 2. Magic -- Fiction
ISBN 0-7868-3916-3; 0-7868-3917-1 pa; 978-0-7868-3916-2; 978-0-7868-3917-9 pa
LC 2005-52720

After learning about his magical ancestry and his own warrior powers, sixteen-year-old Jack embarks on a training program to fight enemy wizards. "Grades seven to ten." (Bull Cent Child Books)

"Twists and turns abound in this remarkable, nearly flawless debut novel that mixes a young man's coming-of-age with fantasy and adventure. Fast paced and brilliantly plotted." Voice Youth Advocates

Other titles in this series are:
The dragon heir (2008)
The wizard heir (2007)

Choi, Sook Nyul

★ **Year** of impossible goodbyes. Houghton Mifflin 1991 171p hardcover o.p. pa $5.99
Grades: 5 6 7 8 **Fic**

1. Korea -- Fiction
ISBN 0-395-57419-6; 978-0-440-40759-1 pa
LC 91-10502

Sookan, a young Korean girl survives the oppressive Japanese and Russian occupation of North Korea during the 1940s, to later escape to freedom in South Korea

"Tragedies are not masked here, but neither are they overdramatized. . . . The observations are honest, the details authentic, the characterizations vividly developed." Bull Cent Child Books

Other titles about Sookan are:
Echoes of the white giraffe (1993)
Gathering of pearls (1994)

Chotjewitz, David

Daniel half human; and the good Nazi. translated by Doris Orgel. Atheneum Books for Young Readers 2004 298p hardcover o.p. pa $6.99

Grades: 7 8 9 10 **Fic**

1. Jews -- Fiction 2. National socialism -- Fiction
ISBN 0-689-85747-0; 0-689-85748-9 pa
LC 2003-25554

In 1933, best friends Daniel and Armin admire Hitler, but as anti-Semitism buoys Hitler to power, Daniel learns he is half Jewish, threatening the friendship even as life in their beloved Hamburg, Germany, is becoming nightmarish. Also details Daniel and Armin's reunion in 1945 in interspersed chapters.

"Orgel's translation reads smoothly and movingly. An outstanding addition to the large body of World War II/Holocaust fiction." SLJ

Chow, Cara

Bitter melon. Egmont USA 2011 309p $16.99; lib bdg $19.99

Grades: 8 9 10 **Fic**

1. School stories 2. Child abuse -- Fiction 3. Chinese Americans -- Fiction 4. Mother-daughter relationship -- Fiction
ISBN 978-1-60684-126-6; 978-1-60684-204-1 lib bdg
LC 2010-36630

"Chow skillfully describes the widening gulf between mother and daughter and the disparity between the Chinese culture's expectation of filial duty and the American virtue of independence." SLJ

Christopher, Lucy

The **killing** woods; Lucy Christopher. Chicken House/Scholastic 2014 384 p. $17.99

Grades: 9 10 11 12 **Fic**

1. Mystery fiction 2. Murder -- Fiction 3. Games -- Fiction 4. Mystery and detective stories
ISBN 0545461006; 9780545461009; 9780545461016; 9780545576710
LC 2013022566

"Ashlee Parker is dead, and Emily Shepherd's dad is accused of the crime. . . . What really happened that night? Before he's convicted, Emily must find out the truth. Mina and Joe . . . warn Emily against it, but she feels herself strongly drawn to Damon, Ashlee's charismatic boyfriend. Together they explore the dark woods." (Publisher's note)

"This taut, psychologically realistic murder mystery knits trauma, danger, tragedy and hope into one cohesive tale...Readers will be riveted by slow, potent reveals about the rough nature of the Game, Ashlee's insistence on danger and adrenaline, and what happened that night. The answers hurt, but they feel right and they make sense. A sprout of hope at the end is fragile and unforced. A gripping, heartbreaking, emotionally substantial look at war wounds and the allure of danger." (Kirkus)

Cisneros, Sandra

★ The **house** on Mango Street. Knopf 1994 134p $24

Grades: 7 8 9 10 **Fic**

1. Chicago (Ill.) -- Fiction 2. Mexican Americans -- Fiction
ISBN 0-679-43335-X
LC 93-43564

Originally published by Arte Público Press in 1984. Verso of title page

This is "a composite of evocative snapshots that manages to passionately recreate the milieu of the poor quarters of Chicago." Commonweal

Clare, Cassandra

City of ashes. Margaret K. McElderry Books 2008 453p (The mortal instruments) $17.99; pa $9.99

Grades: 9 10 11 12 **Fic**

1. Horror fiction 2. Devil -- Fiction 3. Supernatural -- Fiction 4. New York (N.Y.) -- Fiction
ISBN 978-1-4169-1429-7; 1-4169-1429-3; 978-1-4169-7224-2 pa; 1-4169-7224-2 pa
LC 2007-14714

Sequel to City of bones (2007)

"In this sequel to City of Bones, sixteen-year-old Clary is still coming to terms with her abilities as a demon killer, with her mother's comatose state, and with her horror over the discovery that her father, Valentine, is a power-hungry and evil exile in Downworld, a realm that exists outside of New York City. . . . Grades nine to twelve." (Bull Cent Child Books)

"The whole book is like watching a particularly good vampire/werewolf movie, and it leaves readers waiting for the next in the series. Watch this one fly off the shelves." SLJ

Followed by City of Glass (2009)

City of bones. Margaret K. McElderry Books 2007 485p (The mortal instruments) $17.99; pa $9.99

Grades: 9 10 11 12 **Fic**

1. Horror fiction 2. Devil -- Fiction 3. Supernatural -- Fiction 4. New York (N.Y.) -- Fiction
ISBN 1-4169-1428-5; 1-4169-5507-0 pa; 978-1-4169-1428-0; 978-1-4169-5507-8 pa
LC 2006-08108

Suddenly able to see demons and the Darkhunters who are dedicated to returning them to their own dimension, fifteen-year-old Clary Fray is drawn into this bizzare world when her mother disappears and Clary herself is almost killed by a monster.

"This version of New York, full of Buffyesque teens who are trying to save the world, is entertaining and will have fantasy readers anxiously awaiting the next book in the series." SLJ

City of fallen angels; by Cassandra Clare. 1st ed. Margaret K. McElderry Books 2011 424 p. (hardcover) $21.99

Grades: 9 10 11 12 **Fic**

1. Vampires -- Fiction 2. Supernatural -- Fiction 3. Magic -- Fiction 4. Demonology -- Fiction 5. New York (N.Y.) -- Fiction
ISBN 9781442403543; 1442403543
LC 2010041132

In this book, part of author Cassandra Clare's Mortal Instruments series, "Jace is plagued with horrifying nightmares of killing Clary as the pair investigates the source of demon babies. Simon, a rare Daylighter vampire, struggles to figure out who is trying to kill him. Camille, an ancient vampire, tempts Simon, while an ancient source of evil manipulates them all to an unthinkable end." (Booklist)

City of Glass. Margaret K. McElderry Books 2009 541p (The mortal instruments) $17.99
Grades: 9 10 11 12 **Fic**

1. Horror fiction 2. Devil -- Fiction 3. Supernatural -- Fiction 4. New York (N.Y.) -- Fiction
ISBN 978-1-4169-1430-3; 1-4169-1430-7
LC 2008-39065

Sequel to City of ashes (2008)

Still pursuing a cure for her mother's enchantment, Clary uses all her powers and ingenuity to get into Idris, the forbidden country of the secretive Shadowhunters, and to its capital, the City of Glass, where with the help of a newfound friend, Sebastian, she uncovers important truths about her family's past that will not only help save her mother but all those that she holds most dear.

"An experienced storyteller, Clare moves the plot quickly to a satisfying end." Booklist

City of lost souls; Cassandra Clare. Margaret K. McElderry Books 2012 535 p. (Mortal instruments) (hardback) $19.99
Grades: 9 10 11 12 **Fic**

1. Fantasy fiction 2. Siblings -- Fiction 3. Interpersonal relations -- Fiction 4. Horror stories 5. Magic -- Fiction 6. Vampires -- Fiction 7. Demonology -- Fiction 8. Supernatural -- Fiction 9. New York (N.Y.) -- Fiction
ISBN 9781442416864; 9781442416888
LC 2011042547

This book is the fifth in the Mortal Instruments series by Cassandra Clare. In it, "Clary's long-lost brother Sebastian, raised to be an evil overlord by their father (and Jace's foster father), has kidnapped Jace. . . . The narrative zips from one young protagonist to another, as they argue with the werewolf council, summon angels and demons, fight the 'million little paper cuts' of homophobia, and . . . negotiate sexual tension." (Kirkus)

Clockwork prince; Cassandra Clare. 1st ed. Margaret K. McElderry Books 2011 528 p. (The infernal devices) (hardcover) $19.99
Grades: 6 7 8 9 10 11 12 **Fic**

1. Orphans -- Fiction 2. Demonology -- Fiction 3. Supernatural -- Fiction 4. London (England) -- Fiction 5. Secret societies -- Fiction 6. Identity -- Fiction 7. London (England) -- History -- 19th century -- Fiction
ISBN 9781416975885; 9781442431348
LC 2011017869

In this book, a #1 New York Times Bestseller, set "[i]n the magical underworld of Victorian London, Tessa Gray has at last found safety with the Shadowhunters. But that safety proves fleeting when rogue forces in the Clave plot to see her protector, Charlotte, replaced as head of the Institute. If Charlotte loses her position, Tessa will be out on the street—and easy prey for the mysterious Magister, who wants to use Tessa's powers for his own dark ends. With the help of the handsome, self-destructive Will and the fiercely devoted Jem, Tessa discovers that the Magister's war on the Shadowhunters is deeply personal. . . . To unravel the secrets of the past, the trio journeys from mist-shrouded Yorkshire to a manor house that holds untold horrors, from the slums of London to an enchanted ballroom where Tessa discovers that the truth of her parentage is more sinister than she had imagined." (Publisher's note)

Clockwork princess; Cassandra Clare. 1st ed. Margaret K. McElderry Books 2013 592 p. (The infernal devices) (hardcover) $19.99
Grades: 6 7 8 9 10 11 12 **Fic**

1. Love stories 2. Fantasy fiction 3. Orphans -- Fiction 4. Demonology -- Fiction 5. Supernatural -- Fiction 6. Secret societies -- Fiction 7. London (England) -- History -- 19th century -- Fiction 8. Great Britain -- History -- Victoria, 1837-1901 -- Fiction
ISBN 141697590X; 9781416975908
LC 2012048910

This is the third installment of Cassandra Clare's The Infernal Devices trilogy. Here, "Tessa leads the fight against Mortmain (a.k.a. the Magister) and his army of clockwork automatons that threaten to wipe out the Shadowhunter race," automatons that are "reanimated with demon souls." Also of note are "Tessa's tangled relationships with her fiancé, Jem Carstairs, who has a terminal demon-related illness, and Jem's blood brother, Will Herondale, who's also in love with her." (Entertainment Weekly)

Clark, Kathy

Guardian angel house. Second Story Press 2009 225p il map (Holocaust remembrance book for young readers) pa $14.95
Grades: 6 7 8 9 10 **Fic**

1. Nuns -- Fiction 2. Jews -- Hungary -- Fiction 3. Holocaust, 1933-1945 -- Fiction
ISBN 978-1-89718-758-6; 1-89718-758-0

When Mama decides to send Susan and Vera to a Catholic convent to hide from the Nazi soldiers, Susan is shocked. Will the two Jewish girls be safe in a building full of strangers?

"Based on the experiences of her mother and aunt, Clark provides a compelling, fictionalized account documenting the courage and compassion of these nuns. . . . Black-and-white photographs and an afterword help to bring the story and history to life." SLJ

Clark, Kristin Elizabeth

★ **Freakboy**; by Kristin Elizabeth Clark. Farrar, Straus and Giroux 2013 448 p. (hardcover) $18.99
Grades: 8 9 10 11 12 **Fic**

1. Gender role 2. Identity (Psychology) 3. Teenagers -- Sexual behavior 4. Novels in verse 5. Schools -- Fiction 6. Wrestling -- Fiction 7. Family life -- Fiction 8. High schools -- Fiction 9. Sexual orientation -- Fiction 10. Transgender people -- Fiction
ISBN 0374324727; 9780374324728
LC 2012050407

Rainbow List (2014)

"High school wrestler Brendan likes girls "too much, / and not in / the same / way / everyone / else / does." Brendan's story weaves together with his girlfriend Vanessa's and that of transgender woman Angel in three-part verse-harmony. Each individual has a unique personality all his or her own in this sincere, profound rendering of sexuality, queerness, and identity." (Horn Book)

Clarke, Judith

One whole and perfect day. Front Street 2007 250p $16.95

Grades: 7 8 9 10 **Fic**

1. Australia -- Fiction 2. Family life -- Fiction 3. Grandfathers -- Fiction

ISBN 978-1-932425-95-6; 1-932425-95-0

LC 2006-20126

Michael L. Printz Award honor book, 2008

As her irritating family prepares to celebrate her grandfather's eightieth birthday, sixteen-year-old Lily yearns for just one whole perfect day together.

The author's "sharp, poetic prose evokes each character's inner life with rich and often amusing vibrancy." Horn Book

★ The **winds** of heaven. Henry Holt 2010 280p $16.99

Grades: 9 10 11 12 **Fic**

1. Cousins -- Fiction 2. Australia -- Fiction 3. Family life -- Fiction 4. Single parent family -- Fiction

ISBN 0-8050-9164-5; 978-0-8050-9164-9

LC 2009-51780

Growing up in Australia during the 1950s, "Clementine thinks her cousin Fan is everything that she could never be: beautiful, imaginative, wild. The girls promise to be best friends and sisters after the summer is over, but Clementine's life in the city is different from Fan's life in dusty Lake Conapaira. And Fan is looking for something, though neither she nor Clementine understands what it is." (Publisher's note) "High school." (Horn Book)

"Introspective, quiet prose, authentic coming-of-age characters and appreciation for the social values shaping Australian women in the mid-20th century make this a moving read." Kirkus

Clement-Davies, David

Fell. Amulet Books 2007 523p $19.95

Grades: 7 8 9 10 11 12 Adult **Fic**

1. Fantasy fiction 2. Wolves -- Fiction

ISBN 978-0-8109-1185-7; 0-8109-1185-X

LC 2006-33543

Sequel to The sight (2002)

In Transylvania during the Middle Ages, Fell, a lone wolf with unusual abilities, learns that his destiny is entwined with that of one human, fifteen-year-old Rasha, whose mysterious origins have villagers believing she is a changeling.

"This book will be deemed worth the trip by returning readers as well as some newcomers, who will find sufficient back story to illuminate this adventure and to pique interest in the earlier one." Booklist

The **sight.** Dutton Bks. 2002 465p hardcover o.p. pa $8.99

Grades: 7 8 9 10 11 12 Adult **Fic**

1. Fantasy fiction 2. Wolves -- Fiction

ISBN 0-525-46723-8; 0-14-240874-3 pa

LC 2002-16572

In Transylvania during the Middle Ages, a pack of wolves sets out on a perilous journey to prevent their enemy from calling upon a legendary evil one that will give her the power to control all animals.

"The narrative is rich, complex, and most importantly, credible, but it requires a thoughtful and perceptive reader." Voice Youth Advocates

Followed by Fell (2007)

Clement-Moore, Rosemary

Hell Week; a novel. Delacorte Press 2008 329p $16.99; lib bdg $19.99

Grades: 8 9 10 11 12 **Fic**

1. Horror fiction 2. School stories 3. Journalism -- Fiction

ISBN 978-0-385-73414-1; 0-385-73414-X; 978-0-385-90429-2 lib bdg; 0-385-90429-0 lib bdg

LC 2007-07438

Sequel to: Prom dates from Hell (2007)

While working undercover on a series of stories for her campus newspaper, college freshman Maggie reluctantly endures mixers, rites, and peculiar rules, but soon learns that members of the sorority to which she has pledged have strange powers and a terrible secret.

"This installment is topnotch fun and a satisfying follow-up for older teens. Great dialogue and smart, interesting relationships." Voice Youth Advocates

Followed by: Highway to Hell (2009)

Highway to hell. Delacorte Press 2009 357p $16.99; lib bdg $19.99

Grades: 8 9 10 11 12 **Fic**

1. Horror fiction 2. Texas -- Fiction 3. Monsters -- Fiction 4. Journalism -- Fiction 5. Witchcraft -- Fiction

ISBN 978-0-385-73463-9; 978-0-385-90462-9 lib bdg

LC 2008-5304

Sequel to Hell Week (2008)

On their way to spend spring break on a Texas beach, college freshmen Maggie Quinn and D&D Lisa are stranded in a town where some believe a chupacabra is killing animals, and as the girls investigate they get help from diverse and unexpected sources.

"It is difficult to imagine teens who have enjoyed Charmed, Buffy, or the Twilight books not loving this series." Voice Youth Advocates

Prom dates from Hell. Delacorte Press 2007 308p hardcover o.p. pa $8.99

Grades: 9 10 11 12 **Fic**

1. Horror fiction 2. School stories 3. Devil -- Fiction

ISBN 0-385-73412-3; 978-0-385-73412-7; 0-385-73413-1 pa; 978-0-385-73413-4 pa

LC 2006-11015

High school senior and yearbook photographer Maggie thought she would rather die than go to prom, but when a classmate summons a revenge-seeking demon, she has no choice but to buy herself a dress and prepare to face jocks, cheerleaders, and Evil Incarnate.

"YAs will have fun with this one, especially if they like rather crazy, humorous stories filled with smart (and smart-ass) characters." Kliatt

The **splendor** falls. Delacorte Press 2009 517p $17.99; lib bdg $20.99
Grades: 9 10 11 12 **Fic**
1. Alabama -- Fiction 2. Cousins -- Fiction 3. Dancers -- Fiction 4. Supernatural -- Fiction
ISBN 978-0-385-73690-9; 0-385-73690-8; 978-0-385-90635-7 lib bdg; 0-385-90635-8 lib bdg
LC 2009-7579

Dark secrets linking two Alabama families and their Welsh ancestors slowly come to light when seventeen-year-old Sylvie, whose promising ballet career has come to a sudden end, spends a month with a cousin she barely knows in her father's ancestral home.

"Sylvie's voice is sharp and articulate, and Clement-Moore . . . anchors the story in actual locations and history, offering au courant speculations about the nature of ghosts and magic. Her ear for both adolescent bitchery and sweetness remains sure, and her ability to write realistic, edgy dialogue without relying on obscenity or stereotype is a pleasure." Publ Wkly

Texas gothic. Delacorte Press 2011 406p $17.99; lib bdg $20.99
Grades: 6 7 8 9 10 **Fic**
1. Ghost stories 2. Texas -- Fiction 3. Sisters -- Fiction 4. Farm life -- Fiction 5. Witchcraft -- Fiction
ISBN 978-0-385-73693-0; 0-385-73693-2; 978-0-385-90636-4 lib bdg; 0-385-90636-6 lib bdg
LC 2010-47923

"It's hard to picture a successful merging of Texas ranching culture with psychic ghost-hunting and witchcraft, but that's what Clement-Moore has achieved in this novel laced with great characters, a healthy dose of humor, and a nod to popular culture. . . .Teens looking for a rollicking adventure filled with paranormal events, dastardly evildoers, and laugh-out-loud moments as Amy and Ben argue and snipe their way to love will adore this book." SLJ

Clements, Andrew, 1949-

Things not seen. Philomel Bks. 2002 251p $15.99; pa $5.99
Grades: 7 8 9 10 **Fic**
1. Science fiction 2. Blind -- Fiction 3. People with disabilities
ISBN 0-399-23626-0; 0-14-240076-9 pa
LC 00-69900

When fifteen-year-old Bobby wakes up and finds himself invisible, he and his parents and his new blind friend Alicia try to find out what caused his condition and how to reverse it.

"The author spins a convincing and affecting story." Publ Wkly

Other titles in this series are:
Things hoped for (2006)
Things that are (2008)

Things that are; [by] Andrew Clements. Philomel Books 2008 224p $16.99
Grades: 7 8 9 10 **Fic**
1. Science fiction 2. Blind -- Fiction
ISBN 978-0-399-24691-3; 0-399-24691-6

Still adjusting to being blind, Alicia must outwit an invisible man who is putting her family and her boyfriend, who was once invisible himself, in danger.

"Clements tells a riveting tale, made all the more intriguing by the choice of narrator, who experiences and describes the world differently because she cannot see.

Clinton, Cathryn

★ A **stone** in my hand. Candlewick Press 2002 191p hardcover o.p. pa $6.99
Grades: 8 9 10 11 **Fic**
1. Family life -- Fiction 2. Palestinian Arabs -- Fiction
ISBN 0-7636-1388-6; 0-7636-4772-1 pa
LC 2001-58423

Eleven-year-old Malaak and her family are touched by the violence in Gaza between Jews and Palestinians when first her father disappears and then her older brother is drawn to the Islamic Jihad

"With a sharp eye for nuances of culture and the political situation in the Middle East, Clinton has created a rich, colorful cast of characters and created an emotionally charged novel." SLJ

Coakley, Lena

★ **Witchlanders**. Atheneum Books for Young Readers 2011 400p $16.99
Grades: 7 8 9 10 11 12 **Fic**
1. War stories 2. Fantasy fiction 3. Witches -- Fiction
ISBN 978-1-4424-2004-5; 1-4424-2004-9
LC 2010051922

After the prediction of Ryder's mother, once a great prophet and powerful witch, comes true and their village is destroyed by a deadly assassin, Ryder embarks on a quest that takes him into the mountains in search of the destroyer.

"Plot twists unfold at a riveting pace, the boys' characters are compellingly sketched, and Coakley explores her subject matter masterfully without falling prey to safe plot choices." Publ Wkly

Coates, Jan L.

A **hare** in the elephant's trunk; [by] Jan L. Coates. Red Deer Press 2010 291p il map pa $12.95
Grades: 8 9 10 11 12 **Fic**
1. Refugees 2. Refugees -- Fiction 3. Sudan -- History -- Civil War, 1983-2005 -- Fiction
ISBN 978-0-88995-451-9

Inspired by the real life experiences of a Sudanese boy, follows Jacob Akech Deng's journey as he flees his home under the threat of war, and, guided by the memory of his mother, tries to survive in a refugee camp.

"This novel, based on the life of the real Jacob Deng, provides insight into the struggles of the Sudan as well as a strong, clear voice. Coates gives an unflinching and poetic glimpse into the life of a boy who chose hope in the face of adversity." SLJ

Coats, J. Anderson

The **wicked** and the just; by Jillian Anderson Coats. Harcourt 2012 344 p. $16.99

Grades: 7 8 9 10 11 12 **Fic**

1. Daughters -- Fiction 2. Prejudices -- Fiction 3. Middle Ages -- Fiction 4. Wales -- History -- Fiction 5. Household employees -- Fiction 6. Wales -- History -- 1284-1536 -- Fiction 7. Wales -- History -- 1284-1536
ISBN 0547688377; 9780547688374

LC 2011027315

In this young adult historical novel, "two girls of very different degree are brought together unwillingly by the English conquest of Wales. Cecily is in a pet at having to leave the home of her youth . . . and relocate to the Welsh frontier. . . . Cecily hates Caernarvon. She hates its weather, its primitive appointments and its natives, especially Gwinny, the servant girl who doesn't obey, and the young man who stares at her." (Kirkus Review)

Coben, Harlan , 1962

★ **Seconds** away; a Mickey Bolitar novel. Harlan Coben. G. P. Putnam's Sons 2012 352 p. (hardback) $18.99

Grades: 8 9 10 11 12 **Fic**

1. High schools 2. Mystery fiction 3. Adventure fiction 4. Murder -- Fiction 5. Uncles -- Fiction 6. Schools -- Fiction 7. High schools -- Fiction
ISBN 9780399256516; 0399256512

LC 2012026728

This young adult adventure novel, by Harlan Coben, is the second book in his Mickey Bolitar series. "Mickey . . . continues to hunt for clues about the Abeona Shelter and the mysterious death of his father--all while trying to navigate the challenges of a new high school. . . . Now, not only does Mickey need to keep himself and his friends safe from the Butcher of Lodz, but he needs to figure out who shot [his classmate] Rachel." (Publisher's note)

Shelter; a Mickey Bolitar novel. G. P. Putnam's Sons 2011 304p $18.99

Grades: 8 9 10 11 12 **Fic**

1. School stories 2. Mystery fiction 3. Moving -- Fiction 4. Uncles -- Fiction 5. Missing persons -- Fiction
ISBN 9780399256509

LC 2011009004

After tragic events tear Mickey Bolitar away from his parents, he is forced to live with his estranged Uncle Myron and switch high schools, where he finds both friends and enemies, but when his new girlfriend, Ashley, vanishes, he follows her trail into a seedy underworld that reveals she is not what she seems to be.

This is a "suspenseful, well-executed spin-off of [the author's] bestselling Myron Bolitar mystery series for adults. . . . Coben's semi-noir style translates well to YA, and the supporting cast is thoroughly entertaining." Publ Wkly

Cohen, Joshua C.

★ **Leverage.** Dutton Children's Books 2011 425p $17.99

Grades: 10 11 12 **Fic**

1. School stories 2. Bullies -- Fiction 3. Football -- Fiction 4. Violence -- Fiction 5. Gymnastics -- Fiction
ISBN 978-0-525-42306-5

LC 2010-13472

High school sophomore Danny excels at gymnastics but is bullied, like the rest of the gymnasts, by members of the football team, until an emotionally and physically scarred new student joins the football team and forms an unlikely friendship with Danny.

"Sports fans will love Cohen's style: direct, goal oriented, and filled with sensory detail. Characters and subplots are overly abundant yet add a deepness rarely found in comparable books. Drugs, rape, language, and violence make this book serious business, but those with experience will tell you that sports is serious business, too." Booklist

Cohen, Tish

Little black lies. Egmont USA 2009 305p $16.99; lib bdg $19.99

Grades: 7 8 9 10 **Fic**

1. School stories 2. Janitors -- Fiction 3. Popularity -- Fiction 4. Obsessive-compulsive disorder -- Fiction
ISBN 978-1-60684-033-7; 1-60684-033-9; 978-1-60684-046-7 lib bdg; 1-60684-046-0 lib bdg

LC 2009-14637

Starting her junior year at an ultra-elite Boston school, sixteen-year-old Sara, hoping to join the popular crowd, hides that her father not only is the school janitor, but also has obsessive-compulsive disorder.

"The characters are real, and readers will feel as if they are right alongside Sara for the ride. Cohen skillfully keeps her readers fully engaged. They will find themselves cringing at the predicaments Sara enters and wonder whether she will completely sell out." Voice Youth Advocates

Cohn, Rachel

Beta; Rachel Cohn. Hyperion 2012 331 p. (hardback) $17.99

Grades: 9 10 11 12 **Fic**

1. Love stories 2. Science fiction 3. Human cloning -- Fiction 4. Love -- Fiction 5. Cloning -- Fiction 6. Islands -- Fiction 7. Resorts -- Fiction 8. Family life -- Fiction
ISBN 1423157192; 9781423157199

LC 2012008663

In this book by Rachel Cohn, "soulless human clones replicated from the recently deceased serve the elite. Though told that they do not feel and despite being programmed to serve via imbedded data chips, the clones, inevitably, do experience feelings and rebel. Elysia is the first teenage clone. . . . Desperate to prove her worth . . . she represses her burgeoning feelings until she falls in love with another Beta masquerading as a human." (School Library Journal)

Cupcake. Simon & Schuster Books for Young Readers 2007 248p $15.99

Grades: 9 10 11 12 **Fic**

1. Stepfamilies -- Fiction 2. New York (N.Y.) -- Fiction
ISBN 978-1-4169-1217-0; 1-4169-1217-7

LC 2005-35934

Sequel to Shrimp (2005)

Former "bad girl" Cyd Charisse moves to New York City to live with her half-brother Danny while exploring career options and various relationships, including the one with Shrimp, who is surfing in New Zealand.

"Fans of the Cyd/Shrimp love story will not be disappointed with this thoroughly satisfying conclusion to the saga." SLJ

Dash & Lily's book of dares; by Rachel Cohn & David Levithan. Alfred A. Knopf 2010 260p
Grades: 9 10 11 12 **Fic**

1. Love stories 2. New York (N.Y.) -- Fiction
ISBN 9780375866593; 9780375966590 lib bdg
LC 2009054084

Told in the alternating voices of Dash and Lily, two sixteen-year-olds carry on a wintry scavenger hunt at Christmas-time in New York, neither knowing quite what—or who—they will find.

"Full of crisp vocabulary and diverse media and literary references, this light-hearted romance should have broad appeal." Voice Youth Advocates

Gingerbread. Simon & Schuster Bks. for Young Readers 2002 172p $15.95
Grades: 9 10 11 12 **Fic**

1. Parent-child relationship -- Fiction
ISBN 0-689-84337-2
LC 00-52225

After being expelled from a fancy boarding school, Cyd Charisse's problems with her mother escalate after Cyd falls in love with a sensitive surfer and is subsequently sent from San Francisco to New York City to spend time with her biological father.

"Cohn works wonders with snappy dialogue, up-to-the-minute language, and funny repartee. Her contemporary voice is tempered with humor and deals with problems across two generations. Funny and irreverent reading with teen appeal that's right on target." SLJ

Naomi and Ely's no kiss list; a novel. [by] Rachel Cohn and David Levithan. Alfred A. Knopf 2007 230p $16.99
Grades: 7 8 9 10 11 12 **Fic**

1. Homosexuality -- Fiction 2. New York (N.Y.) -- Fiction 3. Dating (Social customs) -- Fiction
ISBN 978-0-375-84440-9
LC 2006-39727

Although they have been friends and neighbors all their lives, straight Naomi and gay Ely find their relationship severely strained during their freshman year at New York University.

"Even readers who long for the pair's glamorous downtown lifestyle will sympathize with the vulnerable young people living it." Bull Cent Child Books

★ **Nick** & Norah's infinite playlist; [by] Rachel Cohn & David Levithan. Knopf 2006 183p $16.95
Grades: 9 10 11 12 **Fic**

1. Rock musicians -- Fiction 2. New York (N.Y.) -- Fiction
ISBN 978-0-375-83531-5; 0-375-83531-8
LC 2005-12413

High school student Nick O'Leary, member of a rock band, meets college-bound Norah Silverberg and asks her to be his girlfriend for five minutes in order to avoid his ex-sweetheart.

"The would-be lovers are funny, do stupid things, doubt themselves, and teens will adore them. F-bombs are dropped throughout the book, but it works. These characters are not 'gosh' or 'shucks' people." Voice Youth Advocates

Shrimp. Simon & Schuster Books for Young Readers 2005 288p $15.95
Grades: 9 10 11 12 **Fic**

1. School stories
ISBN 0-689-86612-7
LC 2003-23992

Sequel to Gingerbread (2002)

Back in San Francisco for her senior year in high school, seventeen-year-old Cyd attempts to reconcile with her boyfriend, Shrimp, making some girlfriends and beginning to feel more a part of her family in the process.

"Cohn's humor is right on. . . . The joy of the book can be found in the familiar characters and meeting new ones, and this title leaves open the possibility for a third installment." SLJ

Followed by Cupcake (2007)

★ **You** know where to find me. Simon & Schuster Books for Young Readers 2008 208p $15.99; pa $8.99
Grades: 8 9 10 11 12 **Fic**

1. Cousins -- Fiction 2. Obesity -- Fiction 3. Suicide -- Fiction 4. Drug abuse -- Fiction
ISBN 978-0-689-87859-6; 0-689-87859-1; 978-0-689-87860-2 pa; 0-689-87860-5 pa
LC 20070-0851

In the wake of her cousin's suicide, overweight and introverted seventeen-year-old Miles experiences significant changes in her relationships with her mother and father, her best friend Jamal and his family, and her cousin's father, while gaining insights about herself, both positive and negative.

"Cohn once again excels at crafting a multidimensional, in-the-moment teenage world. . . . Her work is heartbreaking . . . but it rings with authenticity." Publ Wkly

Cokal, Susann

★ The **Kingdom** of little wounds; Susann Cokal. Candlewick Press 2013 576 p. $22.99
Grades: 11 12 Adult **Fic**

1. Queens -- Fiction 2. Princesses -- Fiction
ISBN 0763666947; 9780763666941
LC 2013933162

Printz Honor Book (2014)

In this book, by Susann Cokal, it's "the eve of Princess Sophia's wedding [and] the Scandinavian city of Skyggehavn prepares to fete the occasion with a sumptuous display of riches. . . . Yet beneath the . . . celebration, a shiver of darkness creeps through the palace halls. . . . When [the] . . . prick of a needle sets off a series of events that will alter the course of history, the fates of seamstress Ava Bingen and mute nursemaid Midi Sorte become . . . intertwined with that of mad Queen Isabel." (Publisher's note)

"Despite the challenging content, the book's lyrical writing, enthralling characters, and compelling plot will give older readers lots to ponder." Booklist

Coker, Rachel, 1997-

Chasing Jupiter; Rachel Coker. Zondervan 2012 224 p. $15.99

Grades: 9 10 **Fic**

1. Faith -- Fiction 2. Autism -- Fiction 3. Brothers and sisters -- Fiction 4. Farm life -- Georgia -- Fiction 5. Moneymaking projects -- Fiction 6. Family life -- Georgia -- Fiction 7. Georgia -- History -- 20th century -- Fiction

ISBN 031073293X; 9780310732938

LC 2012051600

In this book, "16-year-old Scarlett Blaine . . . struggles to be the perfect family member and caregiver for her autistic younger brother, Cliff. . . . When Cliff sees Neil Armstrong's Moon walk, he wants to fly to Jupiter and enlists Scarlett and Frank, the local peach farmer's son, to help build a rocket. Scarlett loves Frank, but his crush on her free-spirited, older sister and her parents' fighting leave the teen wondering how to cope with a world turned upside down." (School Library Journal)

"In rural Georgia, in 1969, 16-year-old Scarlett Blaine is a people pleaser. She struggles to be the perfect family member and caregiver for her autistic younger brother, Cliff, and her mentally unbalanced grandfather...carlett puts her faith in God and family. This book is recommended for libraries looking to expand their Christian-fiction collections." (School Library Journal)

Colasanti, Susane

So much closer. Viking 2011 241p $17.99

Grades: 7 8 9 10 **Fic**

1. School stories 2. Moving -- Fiction 3. Divorce -- Fiction 4. New York (N.Y.) -- Fiction

ISBN 978-0-670-01224-4; 0-670-01224-6

LC 2010-31962

Seventeen-year-old Brooke has a crush on Scott so big that when he heads for New York City, she moves into her estranged father's Greenwich Village apartment, but soon she begins to focus on knowing herself and finding her future path.

"Colasanti has once again formulated a teen romance that feels realistic, which will make this novel a hit with readers." SLJ

Something like fate. Viking 2010 268p il $17.99

Grades: 7 8 9 10 **Fic**

1. Love stories 2. School stories 3. Guilt -- Fiction 4. Friendship -- Fiction

ISBN 978-0-670-01146-9; 0-670-01146-0

Lani and Jason, who is her best friend's boyfriend, fall in love, causing Lani tremendous anguish and guilt.

"Colasanti provides credible and engaging character development for each cast member and interactions that spark just the right amount of tension to make this a romantic page-turner." Booklist

Cole, Brock

The **goats**; written and illustrated by Brock Cole. Farrar, Straus & Giroux 1987 184p il hardcover o.p. pa $5.99

Grades: 7 8 9 10 **Fic**

1. Camps -- Fiction 2. Friendship -- Fiction

ISBN 0-374-32678-9; 0-374-42575-2 pa

LC 87-45362

Stripped and marooned on a small island by their fellow campers, a boy and a girl form an uneasy bond that grows into a deep friendship when they decide to run away and disappear without a trace.

"This is an unflinching book, and there is a quality of raw emotion that may score some discomfort among adults. Such a first novel restores faith in the cultivation of children's literature." Bull Cent Child Books

Cole, Kresley

Poison princess; Kresley Cole. 1st ed. Simon & Schuster Books For Young Readers 2012 369 p. (hardcover) $18.99

Grades: 9 10 11 12 **Fic**

1. Love stories 2. Occult fiction 3. Tarot -- Fiction 4. Ability -- Fiction 5. Prophecies -- Fiction 6. Supernatural -- Fiction

ISBN 9781442436640; 1442436646; 9781442436664

LC 2012000919

This paranormal romance novel, by Kresley Cole, is book one in the "Arcana Chronicles" series. "When an apocalyptic event decimates her Louisiana hometown, Evie realizes her hallucinations were actually visions of the future--and they're still happening. . . . An ancient prophesy is being played out, and Evie is not the only one with special powers. A group of twenty-two teens has been chosen to reenact the ultimate battle between good and evil." (Publisher's note)

Cole, Stephen

Thieves like us. Bloomsbury 2006 349p $16.95

Grades: 8 9 10 11 12 **Fic**

1. Adventure fiction

ISBN 978-1-58234-653-3; 1-58234-653-4

LC 2005030616

A mysterious benefactor hand-picks a group of teen geniuses to follow a set of clues leading to the secrets of everlasting life, secrets which they must steal and for which they risk being killed.

"This novel relies on fast action, cool gadgets, and clever problem solving." Booklist

Followed by Thieves till we die (2007)

Thieves till we die. Bloomsbury 2007 311p $16.95

Grades: 8 9 10 11 12 **Fic**

1. Adventure fiction

ISBN 978-1-59990-082-7; 1-59990-082-3

LC 2006-28419

Sequel to: Thieves like us (2006)

Teen geniuses Jonah, Motti, Con, Tye, and Patch, working for their mysterious benefactor, Coldhardt, are out to recover more stolen artifacts when one of their members is kidnapped, and they must add a rescue operation to the mission.

"The page-turning mystery's fun comes from the terrifying escapes, clever gadgetry and detailed Aztec lore, and, of course, the central cast of death-defying teen savants who discover that home is wherever they are, together." Booklist

Z. Raptor; [by] Steve Cole. Philomel Books 2011 265p (The hunting) $16.99
Grades: 5 6 7 8 **Fic**
1. Science fiction 2. Islands -- Fiction 3. Dinosaurs -- Fiction 4. Virtual reality -- Fiction 5. Father-son relationship -- Fiction
ISBN 978-0-399-25254-9; 0-399-25254-1
LC 2010041650

In New York City to spend Christmas with his father, thirteen-year-old Adam Adlar discovers that he and his father are still targets of sinister forces and, despite his father's objections, Adam finds himself drawn back into the struggle against hyper-evolved, deadly velociraptors determined to wreak havoc and spread terror.

"A non-stop ride from beginning to end, this installment is well constructed, larded with frequent and often violent action and reads even better than the first." Kirkus

Z. Rex; [by] Steve Cole. Philomel Books 2009 245p (The hunting) $16.99; pa $7.99
Grades: 5 6 7 8 **Fic**
1. Science fiction 2. Dinosaurs -- Fiction 3. Virtual reality -- Fiction 4. Father-son relationship -- Fiction
ISBN 978-0-399-25253-2; 0-399-25253-3; 978-0-14-241712-6 pa; 0-14-241712-2 pa
LC 2009-6637

From Santa Fe, New Mexico, to Edinburgh, Scotland, thirteen-year-old Adam Adlar must elude police while being hunted by a dinosaur come-to-life from a virtual reality game invented by his father, who has gone missing.

"Cole has created a likable character who manages to come out on top in an extraordinary situation. The science aspects offer an interesting perspective and dilemma for a discussion on genetic engineering. In addition, the adventure, video gaming, and the perilous, sometimes bloody scenes will capture reluctant readers who may not normally devour their reading materials." SLJ

Coleman, Wim

Anna's world; [by] Wim Coleman and Pat Perrin. Chiron Books 2009 280p il pa $10.95
Grades: 8 9 10 **Fic**
1. Shakers -- Fiction 2. Family life -- Fiction
ISBN 978-1-935178-06-4

First published 2000 by Discovery Enterprises with title: Sister Anna

The United States of America in the late 1840s is a national torn by the crime of slavery and a war of conquest in Mexico. Fourteen-year-old Anna Coburn doesn't want to grapple with such terrible issues. Forced to live among the Shakers, then plunged into upper-class Boston life, Anna faces troubling responsibilities to herself, her loved ones and to her country.

"This story accurately portrays life in a Shaker community and the fabric of America during the 1840s. . . . An excellent ancillary choice for social-studies classes." SLJ

Colfer, Eoin, 1965-

★ **Airman**; [by] Eoin Colfer. Hyperion Books for Children 2008 412p $17.99; pa $7.99
Grades: 5 6 7 8 9 **Fic**
1. Adventure fiction 2. Airplanes -- Fiction 3. Inventors -- Fiction 4. Prisoners -- Fiction
ISBN 978-1-4231-0750-7; 1-4231-0750-0; 978-1-4231-0751-4 pa; 1-4231-0751-9 pa
LC 2007-38415

In the late nineteenth century, when Conor Broekhart discovers a conspiracy to overthrow the king, he is branded a traitor, imprisoned, and forced to mine for diamonds under brutal conditions while he plans a daring escape from Little Saltee prison by way of a flying machine that he must design, build, and, hardest of all, trust to carry him to safety.

This is "polished, sophisticated storytelling. . . . A tour de force." Publ Wkly

Collins, Brandilyn

Always watching; by Brandilyn and Amberly Collins. Zonderkidz 2009 224p (Rayne Tour series) pa $9.99
Grades: 10 11 12 Adult **Fic**
1. Mystery fiction 2. Fame -- Fiction 3. Homicide -- Fiction 4. Rock music -- Fiction 5. Christian life -- Fiction 6. Single parent family -- Fiction
ISBN 978-0-310-71539-9; 0-310-71539-3
LC 2008-39515

When a frightening murder occurs after one of her famous mother's rock concerts, sixteen-year-old Shayley tries to help the police find the killer and to determine whether her long-lost father has some connection to the crime.

"This solid teen mystery, the initial entry in a new series, will appeal to young girls and adults who enjoy a good yarn." Libr J

Collins, P. J. Sarah

What happened to Serenity? Red Deer Press 2011 222p pa $12.95
Grades: 7 8 9 10 **Fic**
1. Science fiction 2. Missing persons -- Fiction
ISBN 978-0-88995-453-3; 0-88995-453-4

Katherine lives in a post-apocalyptic community completely cut off from the rest of the world and when her best friend's sister Serenity suddenly disappears, Katherine must break out of town to find her.

"The story is set in 2021 and paints a unique picture of what lack of freedom and free speech could look like if this reality existed. Collins moves beyond the basic mystery and explores the intricate workings of the mind, the body, and the power of basic knowledge. Her story will keep readers engaged from beginning to end." SLJ

Collins, Pat Lowery

Hidden voices; the orphan musicians of Venice. Candlewick Press 2009 345p $17.99
Grades: 8 9 10 11 12 **Fic**
1. Composers 2. Violinists 3. Orphans -- Fiction 4. Musicians -- Fiction 5. Venice (Italy) -- Fiction
ISBN 978-0-7636-3917-4; 0-7636-3917-6
LC 2008-18762

Anetta, Rosalba, and Luisa, find their lives taking unexpected paths while growing up in eighteenth century Venice at the orphanage Ospedale della Pieta, where concerts are given to support the orphanage as well as expose the girls to potential suitors.

"Collins's descriptive prose makes Venice and a unique slice of history come alive as the three connecting narrative strains create a rich story of friendship and self-realization." SLJ

Collins, Suzanne, 1962-

Catching fire. Scholastic Press 2009 391p $17.99

Grades: 7 8 9 10 **Fic**

1. Science fiction 2. Survival -- Fiction 3. Dystopian fiction

ISBN 978-0-439-02349-8; 0-439-02349-1

LC 2008-50493

Sequel to: Hunger Games (2008)

This dystopian young adult novel, volume 2 of the Hunger Games trilogy, takes place after a televised, state-sponsored duel known as the Hunger Games. "Katniss Everdeen has won . . . with fellow district tribute Peeta Mellark. But it was a victory won by defiance of the Capitol and their harsh rules. Katniss and Peeta should be happy. After all, they have just won for themselves and their families a life of safety and plenty. But there are rumors of rebellion among the subjects, and Katniss and Peeta, to their horror, are the faces of that rebellion." (Publisher's note)

"Beyond the expert world building, the acute social commentary and the large cast of fully realized characters, there's action, intrigue, romance and some amount of hope in a story readers will find completely engrossing." Kirkus

Followed by: Mockingjay (2010)

★ The **Hunger** Games. Scholastic Press 2008 374p $17.99; pa $8.99

Grades: 7 8 9 10 **Fic**

1. Science fiction 2. Survival -- Fiction 3. Dystopian fiction

ISBN 978-0-439-02348-1; 0-439-02348-3; 978-0-439-02352-8 pa; 0-439-02352-1 pa

LC 2007-39987

In this dystopian young adult novel, "in the ruins of a place once known as North America lies the nation of Panem, a shining Capitol surrounded by twelve outlaying districts. The Capitol . . . keeps the districts in line by forcing them all to send one girl and one boy between the ages of twelve and eighteen to participate in the annual Hunger Games, a fight to the death on live TV. Sixteen-year-old Katniss Everdeen . . . regards it as a death sentence when she is forced to represent her district in the Games." (Publisher's note)

"Collins's characters are completely realistic and sympathetic. . . . The plot is tense, dramatic, and engrossing." SLJ

Mockingjay. Scholastic Press 2010 390p (Hunger Games) $17.99

Grades: 7 8 9 10 **Fic**

1. Science fiction 2. Survival -- Fiction 3. Dystopian fiction

ISBN 978-0-439-02351-1; 0-439-02351-3

LC 2008-50493

Sequel to: Catching fire (2009)

This dystopian novel, volume 3 of the Hunger Games trilogy, takes place after heroine Katniss Everdeen has "survived the Hunger Games twice. But now that she's made it out of the bloody arena alive, she's still not safe. . . . The Capitol wants revenge. Who do they think should pay for the unrest? Katniss. And what's worse, President Snow has made it clear that no one else is safe either. Not Katniss's family, not her friends, not the people of District 12." (Publisher's note)

"This concluding volume in Collins's Hunger Games trilogy accomplishes a rare feat, the last installment being the best yet, a beautifully orchestrated and intelligent novel that succeeds on every level." Publ Wkly

Collins, Yvonne

Now starring Vivien Leigh Reid: Diva in training; by Yvonne Collins and Sandy Rideout. Griffin 2006 242p pa $9.95

Grades: 7 8 9 10 **Fic**

1. Actors -- Fiction 2. Mother-daughter relationship -- Fiction

ISBN 0-312-33839-2

"Leigh Reid, who first appeared in Introducing Vivien Leigh Reid, . . . spent the summer she was 15 with Annika Anderson, her estranged, actress mother who left the family when Leigh was just a toddler. . . . In this book, Leigh . . . is recommended for a soap-opera audition that she nails due to her varied accents and versatility. . . . This volume is pop-culture fun with a moral." SLJ

The **new** and improved Vivien Leigh Reid; diva in control. [by] Yvonne Collins and Sandy Rideout. 1st ed.; St. Martin's Griffin 2007 231p pa $9.95

Grades: 7 8 9 10 **Fic**

1. Actors -- Fiction 2. Remarriage -- Fiction 3. Mother-daughter relationship -- Fiction

ISBN 978-0-312-35828-0 pa; 0-312-35828-8 pa

LC 2006050570

When she arrives to spend Thanksgiving with her actress mother, sixteen-year-old Leigh is horrified to discover that her mother is planning to marry the producer who had fired Leigh the summer before and whose daughters are determined to sabotage their father's relationship as well as any hopes of reviving Leigh's budding acting career.

"Leigh is a likeable, funny, and realistic heroine" Kliatt

Collomore, Anna

The **ruining**; Anna Collomore. Razorbill 2013 272 p. $17.99

Grades: 7 8 9 10 11 12 **Fic**

1. Nannies -- Fiction 2. Mental illness -- Fiction 3. Psychopaths -- Fiction 4. Emotional problems -- Fiction 5. Marin County (Calif.) -- Fiction

ISBN 1595144706; 9781595144706

LC 2012032007

In this novel, by Anna Collomore, "Annie Phillips is thrilled to . . . begin . . . as a nanny for the picture-perfect Cohen family. In no time at all, she falls in love with the Cohens. . . . All too soon cracks appear in Annie's . . . perfect world. She's blamed for mistakes she doesn't remember making . . . and she feels like she's always being watched. . . . Annie's fear gives way to . . . hallucinations. Is she tumbling into madness, or is something sinister at play?" (Publisher's note)

Combres, Elisabeth

Broken memory; a novel of Rwanda. translated by Shelley Tanaka. Groundwood Books/House of Anansi Press 2009 139p $17.95

Grades: 6 7 8 9 10 **Fic**

1. Rwanda -- Fiction 2. Orphans -- Fiction 3. Genocide -- Fiction 4. Hutu (African people) -- Fiction 5. Tutsi (African people) -- Fiction

ISBN 978-0-88899-892-7; 0-88899-892-9

Original French edition, 2007

"This is a quiet, reflective story; neither laden with detail nor full of historical descriptions, it is simply one girl's horrific tale of personal tragedy. . . . Combres' story offers readers intimate access to this chapter of history as well as considerable potential for discussion." Bull Cent Child Books

Combs, Sarah

Breakfast served anytime. Sarah Combs. Candlewick Press. 2014 272p $16.99

Grades: 7 8 9 10 11 12 **Fic**

1. Bildungsromans; 2. Gifted children — Fiction; 3. Kentucky —Fiction; 4. Camps — Fiction

ISBN: 0763667919; 9780763667917

LC 2013944002

In this book, by Sarah Combs, "when Gloria sets out to spend the summer before her senior year at a camp for gifted and talented students, she doesn't know quite what to expect. Fresh from the heartache of losing her grandmother and missing her best friend, Gloria resolves to make the best of her new circumstances. But some things are proving to be more challenging than she expected." (Publisher's note)

"At a summer college program in Kentucky, a classroom of gifted students studying "The Secrets of the Written Word" grapples with life's big questions. Mercurial, dreamy, and verbose, protagonist Gloria narrates with intellectual enthusiasm and attention to emotional detail. Although the plot meanders, Gloria's open, genuine voice carries this debut novel to the end of a life-changing summer." Horn Book

Condie, Allyson Braithwaite.

Crossed; Ally Condie. Dutton Books 2011 367p map $17.99

Grades: 7 8 9 10 **Fic**

1. Fantasy fiction 2. Resistance to government -- Fiction

ISBN 978-0-525-42365-2; 0-525-42365-6

LC 2011016442

Sequel to: Matched (2010)

Seventeen-year-old Cassia sacrifices everything and heads to the Outer Provinces in search of Ky, where she is confronted with shocking revelations about Society and the promise of rebellion.

"Newcomers will need to read the first book for background, but vivid, poetic writing will pull fans through as Condie immerses readers in her characters' yearnings and hopes." Publ Wkly

Matched; Ally Condie. Dutton Books 2010 369p $17.99

Grades: 7 8 9 10 **Fic**

1. Fantasy fiction

ISBN 978-0-525-42364-5; 0-525-42364-8

All her life, Cassia has never had a choice. The Society dictates everything: when and how to play, where to work, where to live, what to eat and wear, when to die, and most importantly to Cassia as she turns 17, who to marry. When she is Matched with her best friend Xander, things couldn't be more perfect. But why did her neighbor Ky's face show up on her match disk as well?

"Condie's enthralling and twisty dystopian plot is well served by her intriguing characters and fine writing. While the ending is unresolved . . . , Cassia's metamorphosis is gripping and satisfying." Publ Wkly

Followed by: Crossed (2011)

Reached; Ally Condie. Dutton 2012 512 p. (Matched trilogy) (hardcover) $17.99

Grades: 7 8 9 10 **Fic**

1. Epidemics -- Fiction 2. Resistance to government -- Fiction 3. Government, Resistance to -- Fiction

ISBN 9780525423669; 0525423664

LC 2012031916

"This final story in the 'Matched' trilogy finds Cassia, Ky, and Xander all working for the Rising, but in different locations and for different reasons. The Rising has introduced a plague into the cities for which they have the cure. They are easily able to take control as they cure people. An unexpected mutation of the illness catches the Rising off guard, and the Pilot (the Rising's leader) realizes he could quickly lose all that has been gained." (Voice of Youth Advocates)

Connelly, Neil O.

★ The **miracle** stealer; [by] Neil Connelly. Arthur A. Levine Books 2010 230p $17.99

Grades: 8 9 10 11 12 **Fic**

1. Camps -- Fiction 2. Faith -- Fiction 3. Miracles -- Fiction 4. Siblings -- Fiction 5. Family life -- Fiction 6. Pennsylvania -- Fiction

ISBN 978-0-545-13195-7; 0-545-13195-2

LC 2010-727

In small-town Pennsylvania, nineteen-year-old Andi Grant will do anything to protect her six-year-old brother Daniel from those who believe he has a God-given gift as a healer—including their own mother.

"Neil Connelly has written a deeply thought provoking novel. . . . Throughout this gripping novel the climax builds from a slow burn to a tension packed conclusion." Libr Media Connect

Connor, Leslie

Dead on town line; illustrations by Gina Triplett. Dial Books 2005 131p il $15.99

Grades: 7 8 9 10 **Fic**

1. Ghost stories 2. Homicide -- Fiction

ISBN 0-8037-3021-7

LC 2004-15312

"Cassie's body lies hidden in a crevice, where she tries to figure out what happens next. She meets the ghost of Birdie, another murdered girl who was hidden in the same crevice years earlier. . . . Each verse/chapter adds a piece to the puzzle of Cassie's death until her body is found and the crime is solved. . . . This is an absorbing and moving story." SLJ

Constable, Kate

The **singer** of all songs. Arthur A. Levine Books 2004 297p hardcover o.p. pa $6.99

Grades: 7 8 9 10 **Fic**

1. Fantasy fiction 2. Magic -- Fiction

ISBN 0-439-55478-0; 0-439-55479-9 pa

LC 2003-9034

First published 2002 in Australia

Calwyn, a young priestess of ice magic, or chantment, joins with other chanters who have different magical skills to fight a sorcerer who wants to claim all powers for his own

"An impressive debut by an author who clearly has much to contribute to the fantasy genre." Booklist

Other available titles in this series are:

The waterless sea (2005)

The tenth power (2006)

Cook, Eileen

The **education** of Hailey Kendrick. Simon Pulse 2011 256p $16.99

Grades: 7 8 9 10 **Fic**

1. School stories 2. Dating (Social customs) -- Fiction

ISBN 978-1-4424-1325-2

LC 2010-25608

Dating a popular boy and adhering to every rule ever written, a high school senior at an elite Vermont boarding school begins to shed her good girl identity after an angry incident with her distant father.

"Hailey is a likable character, and the events leading up to and away from her episode of vandalism are believable. Her emotions ring true as well. . . . The plot develops quickly, and readers will be madly flipping pages to find out what happens next." SLJ

Cook, Trish

Notes from the blender; [by] Trish Cook and Brendan Halpin. Egmont USA 2011 229p $16.99

Grades: 9 10 11 12 **Fic**

1. Stepfamilies -- Fiction 2. Homosexuality -- Fiction 3. Dating (Social customs) -- Fiction

ISBN 978-1-60684-140-2

LC 2010-11315

Two teenagers—a heavy-metal-music-loving boy who is still mourning the death of his mother years earlier, and a beautiful, popular girl whose parents divorced because her father is gay—try to negotiate the complications of family and peer relationships as they get to know each other after learning that their father and mother are marrying each other.

"This well developed story gives readers an opportunity to see teens 'taking the high road' as they deal with both peers and parents in a novel teens will not want to put down." Libr Media Connect

Cooney, Caroline B., 1947-

Code orange. Delacorte 2005 200p hardcover o.p. pa $6.99

Grades: 7 8 9 10 **Fic**

1. School stories 2. Smallpox -- Fiction 3. New York (N.Y.) -- Fiction

ISBN 0-385-90277-8; 0-385-73260-0 pa

LC 2004-26422

While conducting research for a school paper on smallpox, Mitty finds an envelope containing 100-year-old smallpox scabs and fears that he has infected himself and all of New York City.

"Readers won't soon forget either the profoundly disturbing premise of this page-turner or its likable, ultimately heroic slacker protagonist." Booklist

Diamonds in the shadow. Delacorte Press 2007 228p $15.99; pa $8.99

Grades: 7 8 9 10 11 12 **Fic**

1. Refugees -- Fiction 2. Connecticut -- Fiction 3. Family life -- Fiction 4. Africans -- United States -- Fiction

ISBN 978-0-385-73261-1; 978-0-385-73262-8 pa

LC 2006-27811

The Finches, a Connecticut family, sponsor an African refugee family of four, all of whom have been scarred by the horrors of civil war, and who inadvertently put their benefactors in harm's way.

"Tension mounts in a novel that combines thrilling suspense and a story about innocence lost." Booklist

The **face** on the milk carton. Delacorte Press 2006 184p $15.95; pa $6.99

Grades: 7 8 9 10 **Fic**

1. Kidnapping -- Fiction

ISBN 978-0-385-32328-4; 0-385-32328-X; 978-0-440-22065-7 pa; 0-440-22065-3 pa

A photograph of a missing girl on a milk carton leads Janie on a search for her real identity.

Cooney "demonstrates an excellent ear for dialogue and a gift for portraying responsible middle-class teenagers trying to come to terms with very real concerns." SLJ

If the witness lied. Delacorte Press 2009 213p $16.99; lib bdg $19.99

Grades: 6 7 8 9 10 **Fic**

1. Orphans -- Fiction 2. Siblings -- Fiction 3. Bereavement -- Fiction 4. Connecticut -- Fiction

ISBN 978-0-385-73448-6; 0-385-73448-4; 978-0-385-90451-3 lib bdg; 0-385-90451-7 lib bdg

LC 2008-23959

Torn apart by tragedies and the publicity they brought, siblings Smithy, Jack, and Madison, aged fourteen to sixteen, tap into their parent's courage to pull together and protect their brother Tris, nearly three, from further media exploitation and a much more sinister threat.

"The pacing here is pure gold. Rotating through various perspectives to follow several plot strands . . . Cooney draws out the action, investing it with the slow-motion feel of an impending collision. . . . This family-drama-turned-thriller will have readers racing, heart in throat, to reach the conclusion." Horn Book

Janie face to face; Caroline B. Cooney. Delacorte Press 2013 352 p. (Janie Johnson) (ebk) $20.99; (trade hardcover) $17.99

Grades: 7 8 9 10 **Fic**

1. Love stories 2. Kidnapping -- Fiction 3. Family life -- Fiction 4. Love -- Fiction 5. Identity -- Fiction 6. Authorship -- Fiction 7. New York (N.Y.) -- Fiction 8.

Universities and colleges -- Fiction
ISBN 0385742061; 9780375979972; 9780375990397; 9780385742061
LC 2012006145

This book, by Caroline B. Cooney, is the conclusion to the "Janie Johnson" series which begun in 1990. "All will be revealed as readers find out if Janie and Reeve's love has endured, and whether or not the person who brought Janie and her family so much emotional pain and suffering is brought to justice." (Publisher's note)

Three black swans. Delacorte Press 2010 276p $17.99; lib bdg $20.99
Grades: 7 8 9 10 **Fic**
1. Cousins -- Fiction 2. Sisters -- Fiction 3. Adoption -- Fiction 4. Triplets -- Fiction 5. Impostors and imposture -- Fiction
ISBN 978-0-385-73867-5; 0-385-73867-6; 978-0-385-90741-5 lib bdg; 0-385-90741-9 lib bdg
LC 2009-41990

When sixteen-year-old Missy Vianello decides to try to convince her classmates that her cousin Claire is really her long-lost identical twin, she has no idea that the results of her prank will be so life-changing.

"Cooney's psychologically probing story darts among multiple characters, forming a complex web of mistrust, economic stress, and parental sins that will keep readers guessing." Booklist

The **voice** on the radio. Delacorte Press 1996 183p hardcover o.p. pa $6.99
Grades: 7 8 9 10 **Fic**
1. Radio programs -- Fiction
ISBN 0-385-32213-5; 0-440-21977-9 pa
LC 96-3688

"Janie is a high-school junior and in love with Reeve. She finally feels that her life is somewhat normal and begins to reconcile with her biological family, but the voice on the radio destroys her trust. Cooney plots an engaging and realistic picture of betrayal, commitment, unconditional love, and forgiveness." ALAN

What Janie found. Delacorte Press 2000 181p pa $6.99
Grades: 7 8 9 10 **Fic**
1. Kidnapping -- Fiction 2. Parent-child relationship -- Fiction
ISBN 0-385-32611-4; 0-440-22772-0 pa
LC 99-37409

While still adjusting to the reality of having two families, her birth family and the family into which she was kidnapped as a small child, seventeen-year-old Janie makes a shocking discovery about her long-gone kidnapper

"Readers of the previous books will find this a satisfying closure to the unsettling circumstances of Janie's life." Booklist

Whatever happened to Janie? Delacorte Press 1993 199p hardcover o.p. pa $6.99
Grades: 7 8 9 10 **Fic**
1. Kidnapping -- Fiction
ISBN 0-385-31035-8; 0-440-21924-8 pa
LC 92-32334

The members of two families have their lives disrupted when Jane who had been kidnapped twelve years earlier discovers that the people who raised her are not her biological parents

"However strange the events of this book, the emotions of its characters remain excruciatingly real." Publ Wkly

Cooper, Michelle

★ A **brief** history of Montmaray. Alfred A. Knopf 2009 296p $16.99; lib bdg $19.99
Grades: 7 8 9 10 **Fic**
1. Europe -- Fiction 2. Diaries -- Fiction 3. Islands -- Fiction 4. Princesses -- Fiction 5. Family life -- Fiction
ISBN 0-375-85864-4; 0-375-95864-9 lib bdg; 978-0-375-85864-2; 978-0-375-95864-9 lib bdg
LC 2008-49800

This book features "Sophie FitzOsborne [who] lives in a crumbling castle in the tiny island kingdom of Montmaray, along with her tomboy younger sister Henry, her beautiful, intellectual cousin Veronica, and Veronica's father, the completely mad King John. When Sophie receives a leather journal for her sixteenth birthday, she decides to write about her life on the island. But it is 1936 and bigger events are on the horizon." (Publisher's note)

"Cooper has crafted a sort of updated Gothic romance where sweeping adventure play equal with fluttering hearts." Booklist

Followed by: The FitzOsbornes in exile (2011)

The **FitzOsbornes** at war; Michelle Cooper. Alfred A. Knopf 2012 560 p. (hardcover) $17.99
Grades: 7 8 9 10 **Fic**
1. Exiles -- Fiction 2. Diaries -- Fiction 3. Historical fiction 4. World War, 1939-1945 -- Fiction 5. War -- Fiction 6. Family life -- England -- Fiction 7. World War, 1939-1945 -- England -- Fiction 8. Great Britain -- History -- George VI, 1936-1952 -- Fiction
ISBN 0375870504; 9780307974044; 9780375870507; 9780375970504
LC 2012009094

In this historical novel, by Michelle Cooper, "Sophie FitzOsborne and the royal family of Montmaray escaped their remote island home when the Nazis attacked. But as war breaks out in England and around the world, nowhere is safe. Sophie fills her journal with tales of a life during wartime. . . . But even as bombs rain down on London, hope springs up, and love blooms for this most endearing princess." (Publisher's note)

The **FitzOsbornes** in exile. Alfred A. Knopf 2011 457p $17.99; lib bdg $20.99
Grades: 7 8 9 10 **Fic**
1. Diaries -- Fiction 2. Princesses -- Fiction 3. Family life -- Fiction 4. Great Britain -- Fiction
ISBN 0-375-85865-2; 0-375-95865-7 lib bdg; 978-0-375-85865-9; 978-0-375-89802-0 e-book; 978-0-375-95865-6 lib bdg
LC 2010-34706

Sequel to: A brief history of Montmaray (2009)

In this second volume of the Montmaray Journals series, "forced to leave their island kingdom, Sophie FitzOsborne and her eccentric family take shelter in England. . . . Aunt Charlotte is ruthless in her quest to see Sophie and Veronica married off by the end of the Season, Toby is as charming and lazy as ever, Henry is driving her governess to the brink of madness, and the battle of wills between Simon and Veronica continues." (Publisher's note)

"Readers who enjoy their history enriched by immersion into the social milieu of the time period will find this a fascinating, utterly absorbing venture into English society of the late '30s." Bull Cent Child Books

Cooper, Susan

★ **Over** sea, under stone; illustrated by Margery Gill. Harcourt Brace Jovanovich 1966 252p il $19; pa $5.99

Grades: 5 6 7 8 **Fic**

1. Fantasy fiction 2. Good and evil -- Fiction

ISBN 0-15-259034-X; 0-689-84035-7 pa

First published 1965 in the United Kingdom

Three children on a holiday in Cornwall find an ancient manuscript which sends them on a dangerous quest for a grail that would reveal the true story of King Arthur and that entraps them in the eternal battle between the forces of the Light and the forces of the Dark.

"The air of mysticism and the allegorical quality of the continual contest between good and evil add much value to a fine plot, setting, and characterization." Horn Book

Other titles in this series are:

The dark is rising (1973)

Greenwitch (1974)

The grey king (1975)

Silver on the tree (1977)

Cooper, T.

Changers book one: Drew; by T. Cooper and Allison Glock-Cooper. Black Sheep/Akashic Books. 2014 285p il $11.95

Grades: 7 8 9 10 11 12 Fic

1. Science fiction 2. High school students --Fiction 3. Identity (Psychology) --Fiction 4. Fantasy fiction

ISBN: 1617751952; 9781617751950; 9781617752070; 9781617752117

LC 2013938807

"Ethan wakes up on his first day of high school to discover that he is no longer the same person he was when he went to sleep overnight he was transformed into a beautiful girl. His parents inform him that his father was a Changer and that this is the first of four transformations. He will experience each year of high school in a new body, and at the end of his senior year, he will get to choose which body he will live in for the rest of his life...By the end of this book, readers will be invested in this character and will want to know what Ethan's future holds and how he will physically and emotionally transform over the next installments." SLJ

Cormier, Robert

★ **After** the first death. Dell Publishing 1991 233p pa $6.50

Grades: 7 8 9 10 **Fic**

1. Terrorism -- Fiction

ISBN 0-440-20835-1

First published 1979 by Pantheon Bks.

ALA YALSA Margaret A. Edwards Award (1991)

"A busload of children is hijacked by a band of terrorists whose demands include the exposure of a military brainwashing project. The narrative line moves from the teenage terrorist Milo to Kate the bus driver and the involvement of Ben, whose father is the head of the military operation, in this confrontation. The conclusion has a shocking twist." Shapiro. Fic for Youth. 2d editionp

Beyond the chocolate war; a novel. Dell 1986 278p pa $6.99

Grades: 9 10 11 12 **Fic**

1. School stories

ISBN 0-440-90580-X

First published 1985

Dark deeds continue at Trinity High School, climaxing in a public demonstration of one student's homemade guillotine. Sequel to "The Chocolate War."

★ The **chocolate** war; a novel. Pantheon Bks. 1974 253p rpt $8.99; $19.95

Grades: 7 8 9 10 **Fic**

1. School stories

ISBN 9780375829871 rpt; 0-394-82805-4

ALA YALSA Margaret A. Edwards Award (1991)

"In the Trinity School for Boys the environment is completely dominated by an underground gang, the Vigils. During a chocolate candy sale Brother Leon, the acting headmaster of the school, defers to the Vigils, who reign with terror in the school. Jerry Renault is first a pawn for the Vigils' evil deeds and finally their victim." Shapiro. Fic for Youth. 3d edition

Followed by Beyond the chocolate war (1985)

★ **I** am the cheese; a novel. Pantheon Bks. 1977 233p hardcover o.p. pa $6.50

Grades: 7 8 9 10 11 12 **Fic**

1. Intelligence service -- Fiction

ISBN 0-394-83462-3; 0-440-94060-5 pa

LC 76-55948

ALA YALSA Margaret A. Edwards Award (1991)

Adam Farmer's mind has blanked out; his past is revealed in bits and pieces—partly by Adam himself, partly through a transcription of Adam's interviews with a government psychiatrist. Adam's father, a newspaper reporter, gave evidence at the trial of a criminal organization which had infiltrated the government itself. He and his family, marked for death, came under the protection of the super-secret Department of Re-Identification, which changed the family's name and kept them under constant surveillance. Now an adolescent, Adam is finally let in on his parents' terrible secret." SLJ

"The suspense builds relentlessly to an ending that, although shocking, is entirely plausible." Booklist

Cornered

14 stories of bullying and defiance. [edited by] Rhoda Belleza. Running Press Teens 2012 383 p. $9.95

Grades: 7 8 9 10 11 12 **Fic**

1. Short stories 2. School stories 3. Bullies -- Fiction

ISBN 9780762444281

LC 2011943133

This book is a "bully-themed anthology" of stories that focus "not only on teens who are targets of bullying, but also those who perpetrate it—and many . . . do both. Bullying [in the stories] takes many forms, including a teacher ridiculing students, a viral racist email and hazing on a soccer team. The contributors largely delve into bullies' behavior without resting on cliché . . . Most contributors also . . . observe that family dynamics can have as much impact as those at school." (Kirkus)

Cornish, D. M.

Factotum. Putnam Pub. 2010 684p (Monster blood tattoo) $19.99

Grades: 8 9 10 11 12 **Fic**

1. Fantasy fiction 2. Orphans -- Fiction 3. Monsters -- Fiction 4. Tattooing -- Fiction

ISBN 978-0-399-24640-1; 0-399-24640-1

Accused of being a monster instead of human, Rossamünd Bookchild looks to monster-hunter Branden Rose for help, but powerful forces are after them both, believing that Rossamünd holds the secret to perpetual youth.

"Along with many splendid names . . . and linguistic fancies . . . the author laces his rococo but fluent narrative with moral and ethical conundrums, twists both terrible and tongue in cheek, startling revelations about humans and 'monsters' alike and sturdy themes of loyalty, courage and self-realization. Readers new to the series should start with the first volume; fans will be more than satisfied." Kirkus

Foundling. Putnam's Sons 2006 434p il (Monster blood tattoo) hardcover o.p. pa $9.99

Grades: 8 9 10 11 12 **Fic**

1. Fantasy fiction

ISBN 0-399-24638-X; 0-14-240913-8 pa

Having grown up in a home for foundlings and possessing a girl's name, Rossamünd sets out to report to his new job as a lamplighter and has several adventures along the way as he meets people and monsters who are more complicated that he previously thought.

"This first book in a trilogy presents a fantasy world remarkably well developed. Included in the book are maps, a 102-page glossary, appendixes, and the author's own illustrations of the characters. The descriptions are vivid and fascinating." Voice Youth Advocates

Other titles in this series are:

Factotum (2010)

Lamplighter (2008)

Cornwell, Autumn

Carpe diem. Feiwel & Friends 2007 360p $16.95; pa $8.99

Grades: 7 8 9 10 **Fic**

1. Artists -- Fiction 2. Authorship -- Fiction 3. Grandmothers -- Fiction 4. Southeast Asia -- Fiction

ISBN 0-312-36792-9; 978-0-312-36792-3; 978-0-312-56129-1 pa; 0-312-56129-6 pa

LC 2006-32054

Sixteen-year-old Vassar Spore's detailed plans for the next twenty years of her life are derailed when her bohemian grandmother insists that she join her in Southeast Asia for the summer, but as she writes a novel about her experiences, Vassar discovers new possibilities.

"Suspenseful and wonderfully detailed, the well-crafted story maintains its page-turning pace while adding small doses of insight and humor." SLJ

Cornwell, Betsy

Tides; by Betsy Cornwell. Clarion Books 2013 304 p. (hardcover) $16.99

Grades: 7 8 9 10 11 12 **Fic**

1. Love stories 2. Selkies -- Fiction 3. Internship programs -- Fiction 4. Love -- Fiction 5. Isles of Shoals (Me. and N.H.) -- Fiction

ISBN 054792772X; 9780547927725

LC 2012022415

In this teen novel, by Betsy Cornwell, "high school senior Noah Gallagher and his adopted teenage sister, Lo, go to live with their grandmother in her island cottage for the summer. . . . Noah has landed a marine biology internship, and Lo wants to draw and paint, perhaps even to vanquish her struggles with bulimia. But then things take a dramatic turn for them both when Noah mistakenly tries to save a mysterious girl from drowning." (Publisher's note)

Corrigan, Eireann

Accomplice. Scholastic Press 2010 296p $17.99

Grades: 7 8 9 10 **Fic**

1. School stories 2. Fraud -- Fiction 3. Friendship -- Fiction 4. New Jersey -- Fiction

ISBN 978-0-545-05236-8; 0-545-05236-X

LC 2009-53869

High school juniors and best friends Finn and Chloe hatch a daring plot to fake Chloe's disappearance from their rural New Jersey town in order to have something compelling to put on their college applications, but unforeseen events complicate matters.

"Corrigan has crafted a complex, heart-wrenchingly plausible YA thriller. . . . A fascinating character study of individuals and an entire town, this tension-filled story will entice readers with a single booktalk." Booklist

Ordinary ghosts. Scholastic Press 2007 328p $16.99

Grades: 9 10 11 12 **Fic**

1. School stories

ISBN 978-0-439-83243-4; 0-439-83243-8

LC 2007-276078

Emil feels invisible at school and at home. When he finds a master key to his private school, he sneaks in to explore, and finds a reason to become visible.

"Corrigan is a superb storyteller, and her Salingeresque tale keenly depicts not only her troubled narrator's emotional struggles but also the emotional components to the physical landscapes he vividly inhabits: his home, foundered on the wreck of family tragedy, and his school, thick during the day with manipulatable adults and heedless kids, . . . but transformed at night into a place of possibility that both entices and disappoints." Bull Cent Child Books

Coutts, Alexandra

Tumble & fall; Alexandra Coutts. Farrar Straus & Giroux 2013 384 p. (hardback) $17.99

Grades: 8 9 10 11 12 **Fic**

1. Love stories 2. Apocalyptic fiction 3. Science fiction 4. Family life -- Fiction 5. Conduct of life -- Fiction 6. Interpersonal relations -- Fiction 7. Islands of the Atlantic -- Fiction 8. Asteroids -- Collisions with Earth -- Fiction

ISBN 0374378614; 9780374378615

LC 2013012969

In this book, as "the world faces a catastrophic collision with a giant asteroid, three teenagers spending the summer on Martha's Vineyard discover that their last week on Earth may be life-changing in good ways as well." Sienna "tries to relearn how to trust and love with help from a childhood friend; Zan wonders whether the dead boyfriend she has grieved for was faithful to her . . .; and Caden has to decide whether he can forgive two parents who have abandoned him." (Publishers Weekly)

Coventry, Susan

The **queen's** daughter. Henry Holt and Company 2010 373p map $16.99

Grades: 8 9 10 11 12 **Fic**

1. Queens 2. Princesses -- Fiction 3. Middle Ages -- Fiction 4. Sicily (Italy) -- Fiction 5. Great Britain -- History -- 1154-1399, Plantagenets -- Fiction

ISBN 978-0-8050-8992-9; 0-8050-8992-6

LC 2009-24154

A fictionalized biography of Joan of England, the youngest child of King Henry II of England and his queen consort, Eleanor of Aquitaine, chronicling her complicated relationships with her warring parents and many siblings, particularly with her favorite brother Richard the Lionheart, her years as Queen consort of Sicily, and her second marriage to Raymond VI, Count of Toulouse.

"Fans of historical fiction, and especially historical romance, will devour this volume." SLJ

Cowan, Jennifer

★ **Earthgirl.** Groundwood Books 2009 232p $17.95

Grades: 8 9 10 11 12 **Fic**

1. Weblogs -- Fiction 2. Environmental movement -- Fiction

ISBN 978-0-88899-889-7; 0-88899-889-9

Sabine Solomon undergoes a transformation when she joins the environmental movement and becomes involved with activist Vray Foret, but when his activities involve something that is potentially illegal, she begins to question her identity and values.

This "novel with enormous teen appeal will inspire readers to question Sabine's tactics and their own impact on the earth." Kirkus

Cox, Suzy

The **Dead** Girls Detective Agency; Suzy Cox. Harper 2012 355 p. (trade bdg.) $9.99

Grades: 7 8 9 10 **Fic**

1. Future life 2. Ghost stories 3. Mystery fiction 4. Dead -- Fiction 5. Murder -- Fiction 6. New York (N.Y.) -- Fiction 7. Mystery and detective stories

ISBN 0-06-202064-1; 9780062020642

LC 2012006567

This novel, by Suzy Cox, follows the ghost of a teenager seeking to solve her own murder. "Meet the Dead Girls Detective Agency: Nancy, Lorna, and Tess--not to mention Edison, the really cute if slightly hostile dead boy. Apparently, the only way out of this limbo is to figure out who killed me, or I'll have to spend eternity playing Nancy Drew. Considering I was fairly invisible in life, who could hate me enough to want me dead? And what if my murderer is someone I never would have suspected?" (Publisher's note)

Coy, John

★ **Box** out. Scholastic Press 2008 276p $16.99

Grades: 6 7 8 9 10 **Fic**

1. School stories 2. Prayer -- Fiction 3. Basketball -- Fiction

ISBN 978-0-439-87032-0; 0-439-87032-1

LC 2007-45354

High school sophomore Liam jeopardizes his new position on the varsity basketball team when he decides to take a stand against his coach who is leading prayers before games and enforcing teamwide participation.

"Plainly acquainted with teenagers and well as b-ball play and lingo, Coy adds subplots and supporting characters to give Liam's life dimension, but he weaves plenty of breathlessly compelling game action too." Booklist

★ **Crackback.** Scholastic 2005 201p $16.99

Grades: 7 8 9 10 **Fic**

1. School stories 2. Football -- Fiction 3. Drug abuse -- Fiction 4. Father-son relationship -- Fiction

ISBN 0-439-69733-6

LC 2004-30972

Miles barely recalls when football was fun after being sidelined by a new coach, constantly criticized by his father, and pressured by his best friend to take performance-enhancing drugs. "Grades seven to ten." (Bull Cent Child Books)

The author "writes a moving, nuanced portrait of a teen struggling with adults who demand, but don't always deserve, respect." Booklist

Craig, Colleen

Afrika. Tundra Books 2008 233p pa $9.95

Grades: 7 8 9 10 **Fic**

1. Fathers -- Fiction 2. Mothers -- Fiction 3. South Africa -- Fiction

ISBN 978-0-88776-807-1; 0-88776-807-5

"Growing up in Canada with her white South African mother, Kim van der Merwe does not know who her father is. Now, at 13, she goes to Cape Town for the first time, shortly after independence in the mid-1990s, because her mother, a journalist, is going to report on the Truth and Reconciliation Commission. . . . Visiting and meeting her family for the first time, she decides that her mission will be to discover her father's identity. . . . . The realities of the society are carefully and skillfully portrayed, so that Kim's story is truly the emotional heart of the book, and not a vehicle for ideas." SLJ

Crane, Caprice

Confessions of a Hater. Feiwel & Friends 2013 368 p. $17.99

Grades: 9 10 11 12 **Fic**

1. Popularity 2. High schools

ISBN 1250008468; 9781250008466

"In this funny story of pranks and mean-girl antics, Hailey Harper is on her way to becoming the Queen Bee of mean-even if she doesn't realize it. Before she and her parents moved to Hollywood for her dad's new job, she was bullied and ignored at school. But after she starts following the advice outlined in her older sister's diary (and wearing her old clothes), her social luck changes...The story of Hailey's downfall is realistically written, and all of the characters are well developed and very lifelike. The ending is sewn up a little too perfectly, and the pop-culture references could quickly date the narrative. Nonetheless, this is a solid recommendation for those who'd like a glimpse into the life of a Hollywood hater." (School Library Journal)

Crane, Dede

Poster boy. Groundwood Books 2009 214p $18.95

Grades: 8 9 10 11 **Fic**

1. Cancer -- Fiction 2. Siblings -- Fiction 3. Family life -- Fiction

ISBN 978-0-88899-855-2; 0-88899-855-4

"Cruising along on the fringes of stoner life is cool with 16-year-old Gray Fallon. . . . Life's all good until Gray's younger sister, 12-year-old Maggie, begins to complain about aches in her legs and arms. It's a rare form of terminal cancer. . . . Crane effectively shows a family unraveling, and Gray's authentic teen narration springs from the pages." Kirkus

Crane, E. M.

Skin deep; [by] E. M. Crane. Delacorte Press 2008 273p $16.99; lib bdg $19.99

Grades: 7 8 9 10 11 12 **Fic**

1. Dogs -- Fiction 2. Death -- Fiction 3. Friendship -- Fiction

ISBN 978-0-385-73479-0; 0-385-73479-4; 978-0-385-90477-3 lib bdg; 0-385-90477-0 lib bdg

When sixteen-year-old Andrea Anderson begins caring for a sick neighbor's dog, she learns a lot about life, death, pottery, friendship, hope, and love.

"Teenage girls who can empathize with Andrea's journey of self-discovery and its triumphs and losses will find a well-written story, with lyrical explorations of nature, and memorable characters." Voice Youth Advocates

Crawford, Brent

★ **Carter** finally gets it. Disney Hyperion Books 2009 300p $15.99; pa $8.99

Grades: 7 8 9 10 **Fic**

1. School stories

ISBN 978-1-4231-1246-4; 1-4231-1246-6; 978-1-4231-1247-1 pa; 1-4231-1247-4 pa

LC 2008-46541

Awkward freshman Will Carter endures many painful moments during his first year of high school before realizing that nothing good comes easily, focus is everything, and the payoff is usually incredible.

"Crawford expertly channels his inner 14-year-old for this pitch-perfect comedy. . . . His stream-consciousness, first-person narrative flails around in an excellent imitation of a freshman." Booklist

Carter's big break. Hyperion 2010 231p $15.99; pa $8.99

Grades: 8 9 10 11 12 **Fic**

1. Actors -- Fiction 2. Drug abuse -- Fiction 3. Self-perception -- Fiction 4. Motion pictures -- Production and direction -- Fiction

ISBN 978-1-4231-1243-3; 1-4231-1243-3; 978-1-4231-1244-0 pa; 1-4231-1244-X pa

LC 2010-5040

Sequel to Carter finally gets it (2009)

Fourteen-year-old Will Carter's summer gets off to a bad start when his girlfriend leaves him, but then he is cast opposite a major star, Hilary Idaho, in a small movie being filmed in his town and things start looking up.

"This fast and fun read will definitely appeal to reluctant readers who want to see the underdog succeed in life and love. A must-have, especially where the first book is popular." SLJ

Carter's unfocused, one-track mind; a novel. by Brent Crawford. Hyperion 2012 296 p. (Carter) (hardback) $16.99

Grades: 7 8 9 10 **Fic**

1. High school students -- Fiction 2. School stories 3. Dating (Social customs) 4. Schools -- Fiction 5. High schools -- Fiction 6. Self-perception -- Fiction 7. Dating (Social customs) -- Fiction 8. Interpersonal relations -- Fiction

ISBN 1423144457; 9781423144458

LC 2012001231

This young adult novel, by Brent Crawford, is the third book in the author's "Carter" series. "After an eventful freshman year and disastrous summer, fifteen-year-old Will Carter returns to Merrian High none the wiser. His sophomore year will present a host of new problems. . . . When Abby announces that she might be transferring to a New York arts school, Carter's world is turned upside down and he'll be forced to make the biggest decision of his life." (Publisher's note)

Cremer, Andrea

Invisibility; Andrea Cremer and David Levithan. Philomel Books 2013 320 p. (hardcover) $18.99

Grades: 7 8 9 10 11 12 **Fic**

1. Love -- Fiction 2. Invisibility -- Fiction 3. Magic -- Fiction 4. Charms -- Fiction 5. Friendship -- Fiction 6. Family problems -- Fiction 7. New York (N.Y.) --

Fiction
ISBN 0399257608; 9780399257605
LC 2012024514

This book by Andrea Cremer and David Levithan chronicles the "romance between a boy cursed with invisibility and the one girl who can see him. . . . Stephen is used to invisibility. He was born that way. . . . Elizabeth sometimes wishes for invisibility. . . . To Stephen's amazement, she can see him. And to Elizabeth's amazement, she wants him to be able to see her--all of her. But as the two become closer, an invisible world gets in their way." (Publisher's note)

"hough it begins as a stumbling, near–coming-out story (for Stephen), the novel deftly switches gears to a fast-paced supernatural thriller that will surely leave readers wanting more." Kirkus

Crewe, Megan

Give up the ghost. Henry Holt and Co. 2009 244p $17.99
Grades: 7 8 9 10 **Fic**
1. Ghost stories 2. School stories 3. Sisters -- Fiction 4. Bereavement -- Fiction
ISBN 978-0-8050-8930-1; 0-8050-8930-6
LC 2008-50274

Sixteen-year-old Cass's only friends are her dead sister and the school ghosts who feed her gossip that she uses to make students face up to their bad behavior, but when a popular boy asks for her help, she begins to reach out to the living again.

The story "provides page-turning action. . . . Mysterious plot elements and the budding relationship between Cass and the VP will quickly engage reluctant readers." Publ Wkly

The **lives** we lost; a way we fall novel. Megan Crewe. Hyperion 2013 288 p. (The fallen world) (alk. paper) $16.99
Grades: 7 8 9 10 11 12 **Fic**
1. Science fiction 2. Epidemics -- Fiction 3. Survival skills -- Fiction 4. Survival -- Fiction 5. Virus diseases -- Fiction
ISBN 1423146174; 9781423146179
LC 2012032510

This novel, by Megan Crewe, is book two of "The Fallen World Trilogy." "A deadly virus has destroyed Kaelyn's small island community and spread beyond the quarantine. No one is safe. But when Kaelyn finds samples of a vaccine in her father's abandoned lab, she knows there must be someone, somewhere, who can replicate it. . . . How much will Kaelyn risk for an unproven cure, when the search could either destroy those she loves or save the human race?" (Publisher's note)

The **way** we fall; Megan Crewe. Hyperion 2012 309 p.
Grades: 7 8 9 10 11 12 **Fic**
1. Science fiction 2. Epidemics -- Fiction 3. Survival skills -- Fiction 4. Islands -- Fiction 5. Diseases -- Fiction
ISBN 1423146166; 9781423146162
LC 2011006504

This novel, by Megan Crewe, follows "[s]ixteen-year-old Kaelyn . . . when an unidentified virus strikes her Canadian island town . . . Isolated, residents divide into . . . those that see survival as a joint effort, . . . [and] those of the everyman- for-himself mindset. . . . After her mother dies and her uncle is shot, Kaelyn struggles to keep her young cousin safe from both the virus and the roaming gangs, until she herself becomes ill." (Bulletin of the Center for Children's Books)

Crocker, Nancy

★ **Billie** Standish was here. Simon & Schuster Books for Young Readers 2007 281p $16.99
Grades: 7 8 9 10 **Fic**
1. Rape -- Fiction 2. Friendship -- Fiction 3. Child abuse -- Fiction
ISBN 978-1-4169-2423-4; 1-4169-2423-X
LC 2006-32688

When the river jeopardizes the levee and most of the town leaves, Miss Lydia, an elderly neighbor, and Billie form a friendship that withstands tragedy and time.

"This story is beautiful, painful, and complex, and the descriptions of people, events, and emotions are graphic and tangible. The rape scene is described but not sensationalized." SLJ

Crockett, S. D.

After the snow; S. D. Crockett. Feiwel & Friends 2012 304 p. (hardback) $22.55
Grades: 6 7 8 9 10 11 12 **Fic**
1. Science fiction 2. Adventure fiction 3. Winter -- Fiction 4. Missing persons -- Fiction 5. Children and war -- Fiction 6. Survival -- Fiction 7. Voyages and travels -- Fiction 8. Adventure and adventurers -- Fiction
ISBN 9780312641696
LC 2011036122

William C. Morris Award Finalist (2013)

In this book, "Willo's father can still remember what life was like in Great Britain before the country entered a new ice age. . . . When his father and the rest of his family mysteriously disappear, Willo leaves the scant safety of home to search for them. . . . [He] saves a . . . girl he encounters along the way, and together they find their way into the city, in which a long-dormant resistance movement is preparing for a final desperate exodus." (Bulletin of the Center for Children's Books)

One Crow Alone; by S.D. Crockett. Feiwel & Friends 2013 320 p. $16.99
Grades: 6 7 8 9 10 11 12 **Fic**
1. Evacuation of civilians 2. Mother-daughter relationship -- Fiction
ISBN 1250024250; 9781250024251

In this book, by S.D. Crockett, "living in an isolated Polish village with her grandmother, fifteen-year-old Magda Krol has no idea of the troubles sweeping across the planet. But when her village is evacuated without her, Magda must make her way alone across the frozen wilderness to Krakow, and then on to London, where she dreams of finding warmth and safety with her long-lost mother." (Publisher's note)

Croggon, Alison

Black spring; Alison Croggon. Candlewick Press 2013 288 p. $16.99

Grades: 9 10 11 12 **Fic**

1. Revenge -- Fiction 2. Witches -- Fiction 3. Social classes -- Fiction

ISBN 0763660094; 9780763660093

LC 2012950560

This book by Alison Croggon is "an homage to 'Wuthering Heights,' trading the English moors of the original for the remote northern wilds of Elbasa, a land of powerful wizards and strict rules concerning vendetta. . . . It's a fantasy setting, but Croggon maintains the north/south, high/low, and male/female class divisions Brontë explores; Lina, born a witch, takes the place of Catherine, while 'swarthy' Damek il Haran has his analogue in Heathcliff." (Publishers Weekly)

"Violet-eyed witch Lina, daughter of a powerful lord, is subject to the wrath of the wizards of the North, who seek to suppress any competing powers--especially those found in women. Seemingly cursed, Lina only finds strength once she sheds the control of domineering men, including her love, Damek. The magical slant of this poetic Wuthering Heights reimagining is compelling." (Horn Book)

The **Naming**. Candlewick Press 2005 492p map (Pellinor) $17.99

Grades: 7 8 9 10 **Fic**

1. Fantasy fiction

ISBN 0-7636-2639-2

LC 2004-45165

First published 2002 in the United Kingdom with title: The gift

In this first book in the Pellinor series, a manuscript from the lost civilization of Edil-Amarandah chronicles the experiences of sixteen-year-old Maerad, an orphan gifted in the magic and power of the Bards, as she escapes from slavery and begins to learn how to use her Gift to stave off the evil Darkness that threatens to consume her world.

"Unbelievably fine, this book represents fantasy storytelling at its best. This exemplary novel is sure to appeal to all fantasy fans." Voice Youth Advocates

Other titles in this series are:
The Crow (2007)
The Riddle (2006)
The Singing (2009)

Cronn-Mills, Kirstin

Beautiful Music for Ugly Children; Kirstin Cronn-Mills. Flux 2012 271 p. $9.99

Grades: 9 10 11 12 **Fic**

1. Transgender people 2. Disc jockeys -- Fiction 3. High schools -- Fiction 4. Schools -- Fiction 5. Transgender people -- Fiction

ISBN 1590207203; 9780738732510

LC 2012019028

Stonewall Book Award-Mike Morgan and Larry Romans Children's & Young Adult Literature Award

In author Kirstin Cronn-Mills's book, "it is only after hearing Gabe's friend and neighbor John . . . use Gabe's birth name that readers learn that Gabe is transgender. Being trans, Gabe opines, is like being a 45 record with an A side and a B side. When the story opens, only a few people know about Gabe's B side; the rest see him as a girl. When Gabe's radio show becomes an underground hit, generating a . . . cadre of fans calling themselves the Ugly Children Brigade, Gabe's B side is pushed further into public view." (Kirkus Reviews)

Cross, Gillian, 1945-

Where I belong. Holiday House 2011 245p $17.95

Grades: 7 8 9 10 **Fic**

1. Somalia -- Fiction 2. Refugees -- Fiction 3. Kidnapping -- Fiction 4. London (England) -- Fiction 5. Fashion designers -- Fiction

ISBN 978-0-8234-2332-3; 0-8234-2332-8

LC 2010-23671

Thirteen-year-old Khadija, a Somali refugee, becomes a model for a famous fashion designer to help her family back home, while the designer's daughter Freya and fourteen-year-old Abdi, whose family Khadija lives with in London, try to protect her.

This is a "fast-paced adventure. . . . The fashion element will engage readers who would otherwise not read this genre. . . . This broadly appealing title has an engaging cover and is a worthy addition to any collection." SLJ

Cross, Julie

Tempest; Julie Cross. St. Martin's Griffin 2012 339p. (hardback) $17.99

Grades: 8 9 10 11 12 **Fic**

1. Love stories 2. Science fiction 3. Suspense fiction 4. Young men -- Fiction 5. Time travel -- Fiction 6. Spies -- Fiction

ISBN 9780312568894

LC 2011032799

This novel follows "[n]ineteen-year-old Jackson Meyer . . . [who is] able to jump a couple of hours back in time . . . [and decides to] keep his . . . skill set a secret from his overprotective father and his beloved girlfriend Holly. When two armed men attempt to kidnap Jackson, shooting and most likely killing Holly in the process, Jackson time-jumps in a panic and inexplicably finds himself in 2007, where he is stuck until he can figure out how to get back to the future and save Holly. In the meantime, Jackson discovers that the man he has called Dad all these years is not in fact his father but rather a CIA agent and part of a shadowy government experiment called Tempest—an experiment that includes Jackson as one of its results." (Bulletin of the Center for Children's Books)

Cross, Sarah

Dull boy. Dutton Childrens Books 2009 308p $17.99

Grades: 7 8 9 10 **Fic**

1. Science fiction 2. Superheroes -- Fiction 3. Supernatural -- Fiction

ISBN 978-0-525-42133-7; 0-525-42133-5

LC 2008-34208

Avery, a teenaged boy with frightening super powers that he is trying to hide, discovers other teenagers who also have strange powers and who are being sought by the icy and seductive Cherchette, but they do not know what she wants with them.

"Avery's narration, generously peppered with swear words, is hip, witty, funny, and sarcastic." SLJ

Kill me softly; by Sarah Cross. Egmont USA 2012 331 p. (hardcover) $17.99

Grades: 9 10 11 12 **Fic**

1. Fairy tales 2. Young women -- Fiction 3. Runaway teenagers -- Fiction 4. Love -- Fiction 5. Blessing and cursing -- Fiction 6. Characters in literature -- Fiction

ISBN 1606843230; 9781606843239; 9781606843246

LC 2011045271

This book presents the story of Mira, a girl approaching her 16th birthday who "struggles to escape her fairy-tale fate" as she defies her godmother's orders and runs away from home "to return to the city of her birth and find her parents' graves." Author Sarah Cross describes the adventures of Mira and the other "vulnerable and rebellious teen characters," including "earnest Freddie, cynical Viv and captivating Felix," using the themes and plots of various fairy tales in this fantasy novel. (Kirkus Reviews)

Crossan, Sarah

Breathe; Sarah Crossan. Greenwillow Books 2012 373 p. (hardback) $17.99

Grades: 7 8 9 10 11 12 **Fic**

1. Friendship -- Fiction 2. Dystopian fiction 3. Science fiction 4. Science fiction 5. Survival -- Fiction 6. Insurgency -- Fiction 7. Adventure and adventurers -- Fiction 8. Environmental degradation -- Fiction

ISBN 0062118692; 9780062118691

LC 2012017496

In author Sarah Crossan's book, "Alina has been stealing for a long time . . . Quinn should be worried about Alina and a bit afraid for himself, too, but . . . it isn't every day that the girl of your dreams asks you to rescue her. Bea wants to tell him that none of this is fair; they'd planned a trip together, the two of them, and she'd hoped he'd discover her out here, not another girl. And as they walk into the Outlands with two days' worth of oxygen in their tanks, everything they believe will be shattered. Will they be able to make it back? Will they want to?" (Publisher's note)

Crossley-Holland, Kevin

★ **Crossing** to Paradise. Arthur A. Levine Books 2008 339p $17.99

Grades: 7 8 9 10 **Fic**

1. Kings 2. Singing -- Fiction 3. Literacy -- Fiction 4. Middle Ages -- Fiction 5. Christian life -- Fiction 6. Pilgrims and pilgrimages -- Fiction 7. Great Britain -- History -- 1154-1399, Plantagenets -- Fiction

ISBN 978-0-545-05866-7; 0-545-05866-X; 978-0-545-05868-1 pa; 0-545-05868-6 pa

LC 2007-51853

First published 2006 in the United Kingdom with title: Gatty's tale

Gatty, the field-girl who appeared in the author's trilogy about King Arthur, is now an orphan. When she is selected for a pilgrimage, she travels from her home on an English estate to London, Venice, and eventually Jerusalem. "Grades six to ten." (Bull Cent Child Books)

"Gatty, the irrepressible peasant girl first introduced in Crossley-Holland's 'Arthur' trilogy . . . comes into her own in this sweeping, vibrant story." SLJ

Crowe, Chris

Mississippi trial, 1955. Penguin Putnam 2002 231p pa $5.99; $17.99

Grades: 7 8 9 10 **Fic**

1. Children 2. Racism 3. Grandfathers 4. Murder victims 5. Fathers and sons 6. Racism -- Fiction 7. Grandfathers -- Fiction 8. Mississippi -- Race relations

ISBN 0-14-250192-1 pa; 0-8037-2745-3

LC 2001-40221

In Mississippi in 1955, a sixteen-year-old finds himself at odds with his grandfather over issues surrounding the kidnapping and murder of a fourteen-year-old African American from Chicago. "Grades seven to ten." (Bull Cent Child Books)

"By combining real events with their impact upon a single fictional character, Crowe makes the issues in this novel hard-hitting and personal. The characters are complex." Voice Youth Advocates

Crowley, Cath

A **little** wanting song. Knopf 2010 265p $16.99; lib bdg $19.99

Grades: 8 9 10 11 12 **Fic**

1. Shyness -- Fiction 2. Australia -- Fiction 3. Musicians -- Fiction 4. Friendship -- Fiction 5. Loneliness -- Fiction

ISBN 978-0-375-86096-6; 0-375-86096-7; 978-0-375-96096-3 lib bdg; 0-375-96096-1 lib bdg

LC 2009-20305

First published 2005 in Australia with title: Chasing Charlie Duskin

One Australian summer, two very different sixteen-year-old girls—Charlie, a talented but shy musician, and Rose, a confident student longing to escape her tiny town—are drawn into an unexpected friendship, as told in their alternating voices

"Crowley's prose is lyrical and lovely, her characters are beautifully crafted, and her portrayal of teen life in Australia is a delight. . . . Female readers especially will enjoy this upbeat tale." Voice Youth Advocates

Crowley, Suzanne

The **stolen** one. Greenwillow Books 2009 406p $17.99; lib bdg $18.89

Grades: 8 9 10 11 12 **Fic**

1. Orphans -- Fiction

ISBN 978-0-06-123200-8; 0-06-123200-9; 978-0-06-123201-5 lib bdg; 0-06-123201-7 lib bdg

LC 2008-15039

After the death of her foster mother, sixteen-year-old Kat goes to London to seek the answers to her parentage, and surprisingly finds herself invited into Queen Elizabeth's court.

"Intrigue, romance, and period details abound in this riveting story of Tudor England. . . . The sophisticated writing flows well, and the author does a terrific job of integrating historical details." SLJ

Crutcher, Chris

★ **Deadline.** Greenwillow Books 2007 316p $16.99; lib bdg $17.89; pa $8.99

Grades: 8 9 10 11 12 **Fic**

1. School stories 2. Death -- Fiction 3. Terminally ill

-- Fiction
ISBN 978-0-06-085089-0; 0-06-085089-2; 978-0-06-085090-6 lib bdg; 0-06-085090-6 lib bdg; 978-0-06-085091-3 pa; 0-06-085091-4 pa

LC 2006-31526

Given the medical diagnosis of one year to live, high school senior Ben Wolf decides to fulfill his greatest fantasies, ponders his life's purpose and legacy, and converses through dreams with a spiritual guide known as "Hey-Soos."

"Ben's sensitive voice uses self-deprecating humor, philosophical pondering, and effective dramatic irony." Voice Youth Advocates

Ironman; a novel. Greenwillow Bks. 1995 181p $16.99; pa $6.99
Grades: 8 9 10 11 12 **Fic**

1. School stories 2. Triathlon -- Fiction 3. Father-son relationship -- Fiction
ISBN 0-688-13503-X; 0-06-059840-9 pa

LC 94-1657

While training for a triathlon, seventeen-year-old Bo attends Mr. Nak's anger management group at school which leads him to examine his relationship with his father.

"Through Crutcher's masterful character development, readers will believe in Bo, empathize with the other members of the anger-management group, absorb the wisdom of Mr. Nak and despise, yet at times pity, the boy's father. This is not a light read, as many serious issues surface, though the author's trademark dark humor (and colorful use of street language) is abundant." SLJ

Period 8; by Chris Crutcher. Greenwillow Books 2013 288 p. (hardback) $17.99
Grades: 7 8 9 **Fic**

1. School stories 2. Missing persons -- Fiction 3. Clubs -- Fiction 4. Bullies -- Fiction 5. Schools -- Fiction 6. Kidnapping -- Fiction 7. High schools -- Fiction 8. Sexual abuse -- Fiction 9. Missing children -- Fiction 10. Mystery and detective stories
ISBN 0061914800; 9780061914805; 9780061914812

LC 2012046726

In this book, high school teacher "Bruce Logsdon's Period 8 session, held during the regular lunch period, is a place for Heller High School students to talk about their concerns and feelings. . . . When quiet, unassuming Mary Wells (called the 'Virgin Mary' by other students due to her outwardly prudish behavior) goes missing, Period 8 must grapple with the fact that their safe space has been compromised." (School Library Journal)

Running loose. Greenwillow Bks. 1983 190p hardcover o.p. pa $8.99; pa $6.99
Grades: 7 8 9 10 **Fic**

1. School stories
ISBN 9780060094911 pa; 0-688-02002-X; 0-06-009491-5 pa

LC 82-20935

ALA YALSA Margaret A. Edwards Award (2000)

"Louie Banks tells what happened to him in his senior year in a small town Idaho high school. Besides falling in love with Becky and losing her in a senseless accident, Louie takes a stand against the coach when he sets the team up to injure a black player on an opposing team, and learns that you can't be honorable with dishonorable men. . . . Grade seven and up." (Voice Youth Advocates)

★ **Staying** fat for Sarah Byrnes. Greenwillow Bks. 1993 216p hardcover o.p. pa $6.99
Grades: 7 8 9 10 **Fic**

1. Obesity -- Fiction 2. Swimming -- Fiction 3. Friendship -- Fiction 4. Child abuse -- Fiction
ISBN 0-688-11552-7; 0-06-009489-3 pa

LC 91-40097

ALA YALSA Margaret A. Edwards Award (2000)

"An obese boy and a disfigured girl suffer the emotional scars of years of mockery at the hands of their peers. They share a hard-boiled view of the world until events in their senior year hurl them in very different directions. A story about a friendship with staying power, written with pathos and pointed humor." SLJ

Stotan! HarperTempest 2003 261p pa $6.99
Grades: 7 8 9 10 **Fic**

1. Swimming -- Fiction
ISBN 0-06-009492-3

LC 85-12712

First published 1986

ALA YALSA Margaret A. Edwards Award (2000)

A high school coach invites members of his swimming team to a memorable week of rigorous training that tests their moral fiber as well as their physical stamina.

"A subplot involving the boys' fight against local Neo-Nazi activists provides some immediate action, while the various characters' conflicts tighten the middle and ending. The pace lags through the story's introduction; nevertheless, this is a searching sports novel, with a tone varying from macho-tough to sensitive." Bull Cent Child Books

Whale talk. Greenwillow Bks. 2001 220p $15.99; pa $8.99
Grades: 7 8 9 10 **Fic**

1. School stories 2. Swimming -- Fiction 3. Racially mixed people -- Fiction
ISBN 0-688-18019-1; 0-06-177131-7 pa

LC 00-59292

Intellectually and athletically gifted, TJ, a multiracial, adopted teenager, shuns organized sports and the gung-ho athletes at his high school until he agrees to form a swimming team and recruits some of the school's less popular students

"This remarkable novel is vintage Crutcher: heart-pounding athletic competitions, raw emotion, an insufferable high school atmosphere that allows bullying and reveres athletes, and a larger-than-life teen hero who champions the underdog while skewering both racists and abusers with his rapier-sharp wit." Book Rep

Culbertson, Kim

Instructions for a broken heart. Sourcebooks Fire 2011 295p pa $9.99
Grades: 8 9 10 11 12 **Fic**

1. Italy -- Fiction 2. Theater -- Fiction 3. Voyages and travels -- Fiction
ISBN 978-1-4022-4302-8; 1-4022-4302-2

LC 2011021860

While high school junior Jessa is on a Drama Academy trip to Italy with ex-boyfriend Sean and his new girlfriend, she opens her heart to change by following all of the outrageous instructions in her best friend's care package.

"Culbertson gives Jessa the room to be angry, mischievous, confused, and wounded without heading into overwrought angst, and she creates a well-developed character with the self-reflection and strength needed to pull herself out of a funk, with a little help from friends, of course." Booklist

Cullen, Lynn

I am Rembrandt's daughter. Bloomsbury Children's Books 2007 307p $16.95

Grades: 7 8 9 10 **Fic**

1. Artists 2. Etchers 3. Painters 4. Drafters 5. Plague -- Fiction 6. Artists -- Fiction 7. Poverty -- Fiction 8. Netherlands -- Fiction 9. Father-daughter relationship -- Fiction

ISBN 978-1-59990-046-9; 1-59990-046-7

LC 2006-28197

In Amsterdam in the mid-1600s, Cornelia's life as the illegitimate child of renowned painter Rembrandt is marked by plague, poverty, and despair at ever earning her father's love, until she sees hope for a better future in the eyes of a weathy suitor.

"Historical fiction, mystery, and romance are masterfully woven. . . . Cullen's novel is a reader's delight." Voice Youth Advocates

Cummings, Priscilla

Blindsided. Dutton Children's Books 2010 226p $16.99

Grades: 7 8 9 10 **Fic**

1. School stories 2. Blind -- Fiction 3. Maryland -- Fiction

ISBN 978-0-525-42161-0; 0-525-42161-0

LC 2009-25092

"Natalie, 14, knows that her future is becoming dimmer as the loss of her eyesight is a nightmare she can't avoid. . . . Part of going from denial to acceptance is attending a boarding school for the blind. . . . Natalie is a credible character and her fear is palpable and painful. . . . Readers will enjoy the high drama and heroics." SLJ

Red kayak; Priscilla Cummings. 1st ed; Dutton Children's Books 2004 209p $15.99; pa $6.99

Grades: 7 8 9 10 **Fic**

1. Death -- Fiction 2. Friendship -- Fiction

ISBN 0-525-47317-3; 0-14-240573-4 pa

LC 2003-63532

Living near the water on Maryland's Eastern Shore, thirteen-year-old Brady and his best friends J.T. and Digger become entangled in a tragedy which tests their friendship and their ideas about right and wrong.

"This well-crafted story will have broad appeal." SLJ

The **journey** back; Priscilla Cummings. Dutton Children's Books 2012 243 p. (hardcover) $16.99

Grades: 7 8 9 10 **Fic**

1. Camping 2. Voyages and travels 3. Fugitives from justice 4. Camping -- Fiction 5. Maryland -- Fiction 6. Coming of age -- Fiction 7. Conduct of life -- Fiction 8. Voyages and travels -- Fiction 9. Fugitives from justice -- Fiction 10. Juvenile detention homes -- Fiction

ISBN 0525423621; 9780525423621

LC 2012003818

In this novel by Priscilla Cummings Digger is "escaped and on the run. . . His bold escape from a juvenile detention facility nearly kills him, but soon an angry fourteen-year-old Digger is . . . hijacking a tractor trailer, 'borrowing' a bicycle, and stealing a canoe. When injuries stop him, Digger hides at a riverside campground . . . New friends, a job caring for rescued horses, and risking his life to save another make Digger realize that the journey back is not just about getting home." (Publisher's note)

Cypess, Leah

Death sworn. Greenwillow Books. 2014 346p. 2014 $17.99

Grades: 7 8 9 10 11 12 Fic

1. Assassins — Fiction; 2. Magic— Fiction; 3. Secrets — Fiction; 4. Fantasy fiction; 5. Love stories

ISBN: 0062221213; 9780062221216

LC 2013037379

"As seventeen-year-old Ileni's magic begins to fade, she's sent to the Black Mountain to tutor assassins in sorcery. With the help of Sorin, her student and assigned protector, she must discover who killed her predecessors before someone kills her. Ileni proves a compelling protagonist, and the blend of romance, assassins, magic, and murder-mystery consistently raises the stakes." Horn Book

Mistwood. Greenwillow Books 2010 304p $16.99

Grades: 7 8 9 10 **Fic**

1. Fantasy fiction 2. Magic -- Fiction 3. Kings and rulers -- Fiction

ISBN 978-0-06-195699-7; 0-06-195699-6

LC 2009-23051

Brought back from the Mistwood to protect the royal family, a girl who has no memory of being a shape-shifter encounters political and magical intrigue as she struggles with her growing feelings for the prince.

"A traditional premise is transformed into a graceful meditation on the ramifications of loyalty, duty and purpose. . . . Astonishing and inspiring." Kirkus

Nightspell. Greenwillow Books 2011 326p $16.99

Grades: 7 8 9 10 **Fic**

1. Ghost stories 2. Dead -- Fiction 3. Sisters -- Fiction 4. Kings and rulers -- Fiction

ISBN 978-0-06-195702-4; 0-06-195702-X

LC 2010012637

Sent by her father, the king of Raellia, who is trying to forge an empire out of warring tribes, Darri arrives in Ghostland and discovers that her sister, whom she planned to rescue, may not want to leave this land where the dead mingle freely with the living.

"Swordfights, blood, and double-dealing pack the pages as this action-filled story races to a surprising conclusion." Booklist

Dagg, Carole Estby

The **year** we were famous. Clarion Books 2011 250p $16.99

Grades: 6 7 8 9 10 **Fic**

1. Adventure fiction 2. Voyages and travels -- Fiction 3. Mother-daughter relationship -- Fiction

ISBN 978-0-618-99983-5; 0-618-99983-3

"Dagg writes a captivating story about the determination of a mother and daughter, who in 1896 walked from Washington State to New York City. . . . Clara's free-spirited but unreliable mother suggests that they walk nearly 4,000 miles to save their farm from foreclosure (a publisher offers them a 10,000 advance if they make it in seven months) and bring attention to the suffragist movement. . . . The pages go by quickly. . . . The journey in itself is amazing, but Dagg's tender portrayal of a mother and daughter who learn to appreciate and forgive each other makes it unforgettable." Publ Wkly

Damico, Gina

Croak; by Gina Damico. Houghton Mifflin Harcourt 2012 311 p. $8.99

Grades: 7 8 9 10 **Fic**

1. Mystery fiction 2. Soul -- Fiction 3. Death -- Fiction 4. Justice -- Fiction 5. Future life -- Fiction

ISBN 9780547608327

LC 2011017125

This book tells the story of "sixteen-year-old bad girl Lex Bartleby [who] is shipped off to her uncle Mort's farm, supposedly to figure out her anger issues with the help of manual labor. Instead, she learns that "farmer" Mort is a reaper of another kind entirely and that, as mayor of Croak, a small collection of Grim Reapers, he will be teaching Lex the family business. Although she initially takes to ferrying souls into the Afterlife with aplomb, Lex begins to question the roles of Reapers as silent witnesses to the world's injustices, especially when their knowledge of people's deaths would allow them to wreak karmic justice upon the murderers and rapists that otherwise get away with their crimes." (Bulletin of the Center for Children's Books)

Rogue; by Gina Damico. Graphia 2013 336 p. (paperback) $8.99

Grades: 8 9 10 **Fic**

1. Future life -- Fiction 2. Grim Reaper (Symbolic character) -- Fiction 3. Death -- Fiction 4. Humorous stories 5. Ghosts -- Fiction

ISBN 0544108841; 9780544108844

LC 2013004154

This book by Gina Damico follows a "band of surly teenage grim reapers risking everything on their mission to save the Afterlife. Uncle Mort's plan to save the Afterlife by enlisting Junior Grims to help destroy the portals that access it is full of risks, loopholes and secrets—and fiery-tempered, impulsive Lex is the plan's unstable lynchpin." (Kirkus Reviews)

Scorch; Gina Damico. Houghton Mifflin Harcourt 2012 332 p. (paperback) $8.99

Grades: 7 8 9 10 **Fic**

1. Fantasy fiction 2. Death -- Fiction 3. Humorous stories 4. Future life -- Fiction

ISBN 0547624573; 9780547624570

LC 2012014799

In this novel by Gina Damico "Lex is a full-time teenage grim reaper -- but now has the bizarre ability to Damn souls. . . . [S]he and her friends embark on a wild road trip to DeMyse. Though this sparkling desert oasis is full of luxuries and amusements, it feels like a prison to Lex. Her best chance at escape would be to stop all the senseless violence that she caused—but how can she do that from DeMyse, where the Grims seem mysteriously oblivious to the bloodshed?" (Publisher's note)

Dana, Barbara

A **voice** of her own; becoming Emily Dickinson: a novel. HarperTeen 2009 346p $16.99

Grades: 7 8 9 10 **Fic**

1. Poets 2. Authors 3. Poets -- Fiction 4. Massachusetts -- Fiction

ISBN 978-0-06-028704-7; 0-06-028704-7

LC 2008-10289

A fictionalized first-person account of revered American poet Emily Dickinson's girlhood in mid-nineteenth-century Amherst, Massachusetts.

"An obvious choice for curriculum support, this heartfelt, exhaustively detailed portrait humanizes the reclusive literary figure and offers an intimate sense of how a poet draws from small moments, gathered on scraps, to create great works." Booklist

Includes bibliographical references

Danforth, Emily M.

★ The **miseducation** of Cameron Post; emily m. danforth. 1st ed. Balzer + Bray 2012 480p

Grades: 9 10 11 12 **Fic**

1. Bildungsromans 2. Lesbians -- Fiction 3. Young adult literature 4. Christian fundamentalism -- Fiction 5. Gays -- Fiction 6. Montana -- Fiction 7. Orphans -- Fiction

ISBN 9780062020567 (trade bdg.)

LC 2011001947

William C. Morris Award Finalist (2013)

This book offers a story about "coming of age as a lesbian in Miles City, Montana, in the early '90s, and . . . [focuses on] teen life in a pray-away-the-gay camp. Adopted by her born-again aunt Ruth after her parents' deaths, Cameron finds her first sexual explorations result in a betrayal that lands her in a re-education program called God's Promise." Bulletin of the Center for Children's Books)

Dashner, James

The **kill** order; James Dashner. Delacorte Press 2012 329 p. $17.99

Grades: 7 8 9 10 11 12 **Fic**

1. Viruses -- Fiction 2. Survival skills -- Fiction 3. Natural disasters -- Fiction 4. Science fiction 5. Survival -- Fiction 6. Virus diseases -- Fiction

ISBN 9780307979117; 9780375990823; 9780385742887; 0385742886

LC 2012016790

In this book by James Dashner "sun flares hit the earth and mankind fell to disease. Mark and Trina were there when it happened, and they survived. But surviving the sun flares was easy compared to what came next. Now a disease of rage and lunacy races across the eastern United States, and there's something suspicious about its origin. Worse yet, it's mutating, and all evidence suggests that it will bring humanity to its knees." (Publisher's note)

The **maze** runner. Delacorte Press 2009 375p $16.99; lib bdg $19.99

Grades: 7 8 9 10 11 12 **Fic**

1. Science fiction 2. Amnesia -- Fiction

ISBN 0-385-73794-7; 0-385-90702-8 lib bdg; 978-0-385-73794-4; 978-0-385-90702-6 lib bdg

LC 2009-1345

Sixteen-year-old Thomas wakes up with no memory in the middle of a maze and realizes he must work with the community in which he finds himself if he is to escape.

"With a fast-paced narrative steadily answering the myriad questions that arise and an ever-increasing air of tension, Dashner's suspenseful adventure will keep readers guessing until the very end." Publ Wkly

Other titles in this series are:

The scorch trials (2010)

The death cure (2011)

Daswani, Kavita

Indie girl. Simon Pulse 2007 232p pa $8.99

Grades: 7 8 9 10 **Fic**

1. Fashion -- Fiction 2. Journalists -- Fiction 3. East Indian Americans -- Fiction

ISBN 1-4169-4892-9

"What sets this novel apart is Daswani's nuanced take on her character's Indian-American subculture, the pressure she feels to be like her more conventional cousins, her desire for independence, American-style, and her pride in her heritage. Indie is a heroine worth meeting." Publ Wkly

Daugherty, C. J.

Night School; C.J. Daugherty. Katherine Tegen Books 2013 432 p. (hardcover) $17.99

Grades: 9 10 11 12 **Fic**

1. School stories 2. Mystery fiction 3. Schools -- Fiction 4. Supernatural -- Fiction 5. Conduct of life -- Fiction 6. Boarding schools -- Fiction 7. Interpersonal relations -- Fiction

ISBN 0062193856; 9780062193858

LC 2012022151

In this book, "upset over the loss of her brother, Christopher, Allie's vandalism gets her expelled from school" and she is sent to the mysterious boarding school Cimmeria Academy. Students are "not to enter the woods after dark; computers and cellphones are forbidden. A few [students] . . . attend the mysterious Night School but refuse to discuss it. Even Allie's best friend, Jo, keeps secrets from her." (Kirkus)

Davenport, Jennifer

Anna begins. Black Heron Press 2008 148p $21.95

Grades: 9 10 11 12 **Fic**

1. Alcoholism -- Fiction 2. Authorship -- Fiction 3. Child abuse -- Fiction 4. Eating disorders -- Fiction

ISBN 978-0-930773-83-0

This book's "two thematically paired novellas portray unrelated teenagers who are dealing with a variety of realistic teen problems. In the first work, Anna Begins, Melissa has a body image problem, a mother who is self-absorbed and not really in her children's lives, and a crush—maybe—on her best friend's ex-boyfriend or her older stepbrother. Melissa relates these events by writing a story about them, and seeks criticism about her story from others. In A Million Miles Up, Scott is a high school junior who, in an attempt to overcome his depression and be popular, takes up binge drinking. He shares some thoughts with Elly who has problems of her own. Although it is not overtly discussed, the implications are that she is being abused by her father and is acting out by being promiscuous. . . . This book will be one of those that will be recommended and talked about between teen readers." Voice Youth Advocates

David, Keren

Lia's guide to winning the lottery; Keren David. Frances Lincoln Children's Books 2012 339 p. ill. $16.99

Grades: 9 10 11 12 **Fic**

1. School stories 2. Family -- Fiction 3. Friendship -- Fiction 4. Lottery winners -- Fiction

ISBN 1847803318; 9781847803313

This book follows "Lia Latimer, [who] is more than ready to take her future in her own hands when she wins eight million pounds in the lottery. She'll drop out of school, buy a flat, leave her annoying family behind. What could go wrong? Plenty, of course . . . Her father's struggling bakery needs a cash infusion; her mother would like a boob job; sister Natasha longs for singing lessons. Jack (the winning ticket was his 16th-birthday present to Lia) wants an Italian motor bike; his mother demands half Lia's winnings. . . . Her romance with mysterious, gorgeous Raf is a bright spot--unless he's just after her winnings." (Kirkus Reviews)

When I was Joe. Frances Lincoln 2010 364p $16.95; pa $8.95

Grades: 7 8 9 10 **Fic**

1. Crime -- Fiction 2. Witnesses -- Fiction

ISBN 978-1-84780-131-9; 1-84780-131-5; 978-1-84780-100-5 pa; 1-84780-100-5 pa

After he witnesses a murder by some ruthless gangsters, Ty and his mother go into hiding under police protection. Even with a new identity, the killers will stop at nothing to silence him.

"This book has an intriguing premise and a cast of likable and realistic characters." SLJ

Followed by Almost true (2011)

Davidson, Jenny

The **Explosionist.** HarperTeen 2008 453p $17.99; lib bdg $18.89

Grades: 7 8 9 10 **Fic**

1. School stories 2. Orphans -- Fiction 3. Scotland -- Fiction 4. Terrorism -- Fiction

ISBN 978-0-06-123975-5; 0-06-123975-5; 978-0-06-123976-2 lib bdg; 0-06-123976-3 lib bdg

LC 2007-41942

In Scotland in the 1930s, fifteen-year-old Sophie, her friend Mikael, and her great-aunt Tabitha are caught up in a murder mystery involving terrorists and suicide-bombers whose plans have world-shaping consequences.

"The characters come through as very human and quite believable. The book is well written and well crafted. The weaving and subtle twisting of historical characters and events is done with great skill. Students liking mysteries and alternative histories will quickly read this one cover to cover." Voice Youth Advocates

Followed by: Invisible things (2010)

Davies, Anna

Identity Theft. Point Horror 2013 250 p. $9.99
Grades: 9 10 11 12 **Fic**
1. Mystery fiction 2. Identity theft -- Fiction
ISBN 0545477123; 1480613169; 9780545477123; 9781480613164

In this book, "Hayley Westin knows exactly what she wants from life. As an overachiever who is determined to land a prestigious college scholarship, the high school senior doesn't have time for friends, sports, dating, or social media. So when she discovers that a fake Facebook account has been created in her name, she's convinced that someone is out to ruin her chances for the scholarship." But things might be even more malicious than they first appear. (School Library Journal)

Davies, Jacqueline

Lost. Marshall Cavendish 2009 242p $16.99
Grades: 7 8 9 10 **Fic**
1. Sisters -- Fiction 2. Factories -- Fiction 3. Bereavement -- Fiction 4. New York (N.Y.) -- Fiction 5. Triangle Shirtwaist Company, Inc. -- Fiction
ISBN 978-0-7614-5535-6; 0-7614-5535-3
LC 2008-40560

In 1911 New York, sixteen-year-old Essie Rosenfeld must stop taking care of her irrepressible six-year-old sister when she goes to work at the Triangle Waist Company, where she befriends a missing heiress who is in hiding from her family and who seems to understand the feelings of heartache and grief that Essie is trying desperately to escape.

The "unusual pacing adds depth and intrigue as the plot unfolds. There are many layers to this story, which will appeal to a variety of interests and age levels." SLJ

Davies, Stephen

Hacking Timbuktu. Clarion Books 2010 264p map $16.00
Grades: 7 8 9 10 **Fic**
1. Adventure fiction 2. Computers -- Fiction 3. Buried treasure -- Fiction
ISBN 0-547-39016-5; 978-0-547-39016-1
LC 2009-45352

London sixteen-year-old Danny Temple and friend Omar use their computer and parkour skills to elude pursuers as they follow clues in an Arabic manuscript to the mysterious cliffs of Bandiagara in sub-Saharan Africa seeking an ancient treasure.

"Davies delivers a satisfying mix of history, exotic locales, computer hacking, and parkour in this well-constructed adventure story." Booklist

★ **Outlaw.** Clarion Books 2011 192p $16.99
Grades: 7 8 9 10 **Fic**
1. Siblings -- Fiction 2. Terrorism -- Fiction 3. Kidnapping -- Fiction 4. Social problems -- Fiction
ISBN 978-0-547-39017-8; 0-547-39017-3
LC 2011009643

The children of Britain's ambassador to Burkina Faso, fifteen-year-old Jake, who loves technology and adventure, and thirteen-year-old Kas, a budding social activist, are abducted and spend time in the Sahara desert with Yakuuba Sor, who some call a terrorist but others consider a modern-day Robin Hood.

"Stephen Davies has crafted a novel full of intrigue, fast-paced action, and sly humor. The fast moving story will draw in many readers, including those who usually shy away from books." Voice Youth Advocates

Davis, Heather

Never cry werewolf. HarperTeen 2009 216p $16.99
Grades: 7 8 9 10 **Fic**
1. Camps -- Fiction 2. Werewolves -- Fiction
ISBN 978-0-06-134923-2; 0-06-134923-2
LC 2008-51967

Forced to attend a camp for teens with behavior problems, sixteen-year-old Shelby Locke's attempts to follow the rules go astray when she meets a handsome British werewolf.

"Davis weaves together a fast-paced action adventure story with issues of peer pressure, divorce, betrayal, friendship, acceptance, and, of course, romance." SLJ

Davis, Lane

I swear; Lane Davis. Simon & Schuster Books For Young Readers 2012 279 p. (hardcover) $16.99
Grades: 9 10 11 12 **Fic**
1. Suicide -- Fiction 2. Litigation -- Fiction 3. Cyberbullying -- Fiction 4. Bullying -- Fiction
ISBN 1442435062; 9781442435063
LC 2011046310

In this book by Lane Davis, "after years of abuse from her classmates, Leslie Gatlin decided she had no other options and took her own life. Now her abusers are dealing with the fallout. When Leslie's parents file a wrongful death lawsuit against their daughter's tormenters, the proceedings uncover the systematic cyber bullying and harassment that occurred. . . . Leslie may have taken her own life, but her bullies took everything else." (Publisher's note)

Davis, Rebecca Fjelland

Chasing AllieCat. Flux 2011 277p pa $9.95
Grades: 7 8 9 10 **Fic**
1. Violence -- Fiction 2. Bereavement -- Fiction 3. Mountain biking -- Fiction
ISBN 978-0-7387-2130-9; 0-7387-2130-1
LC 2010038217

When she is left with relatives in rural Minnesota for the summer, Sadie meets Allie, a spiky-haired off-road biker, and Joe, who team up to train for a race, but when they find a priest badly beaten and near death in the woods, Allie mysteriously disappears leaving Sadie and Joe to discover the dangerous secrets she is hiding.

Davis "constructs a succinct, compelling story that combines romance, suspense, and the theme of overcoming challenges. The strong sense of place, character development, and love triangle dynamics should engage cycling enthusiasts as well as a broader audience." Publ Wkly

Davis, Tanita S.

Happy families; by Tanita S. Davis. Alfred A. Knopf 2012 234 p. (hardcover) $16.99

Grades: 9 10 11 12 **Fic**

1. Twins -- Fiction 2. Family -- Fiction 3. Transgender parents -- Fiction 4. Fathers -- Fiction 5. Transgender people -- Fiction 6. Brothers and sisters -- Fiction
ISBN 9780375869662; 9780375969669; 9780375984570

LC 2011026546

In this book, "twins Ysabel and Justin struggle with the revelation that their father has begun living as a woman. . . . For spring break, Ysabel and Justin's parents arrange for the twins to stay with their father for the first time after the big news. Both the tension and the deep caring among Ysabel, Justin and Christine are palpable as the family . . . attends daily therapy sessions . . . and embarks on a guided rafting trip with other transgender parents and their children." (Kirkus Reviews)

A **la** carte. Alfred A. Knopf Books for Young Readers 2008 288p $15.99; lib bdg $18.99

Grades: 7 8 9 10 **Fic**

1. Cooking -- Fiction 2. African Americans -- Fiction
ISBN 978-0-375-84815-5; 0-375-84815-0; 978-0-375-94815-2 lib bdg; 0-375-94815-5 lib bdg

LC 2007-49656

Lainey, a high school senior and aspiring celebrity chef, is forced to question her priorities after her best friend (and secret crush) runs away from home.

"The relationships and characters in this book are authentic. The actions and dialogue seem true to those represented. Even though it is a quick read, the story is a meaningful one." Voice Youth Advocate

Mare's war. Alfred A. Knopf 2009 341p $16.99; lib bdg $19.99

Grades: 7 8 9 10 **Fic**

1. Alabama -- Fiction 2. Sisters -- Fiction 3. Grandmothers -- Fiction 4. African Americans -- Fiction 5. Automobile travel -- Fiction 6. World War, 1939-1945 -- Fiction 7. United States -- Army -- Women's Army Corps -- Fiction
ISBN 978-0-375-85714-0; 0-375-85714-1; 978-0-375-95714-7 lib bdg; 0-375-95714-6 lib bdg

LC 2008-33744

ALA EMIERT Coretta Scott King Author Award Honor Book (2010)

Teens Octavia and Tali learn about strength, independence, and courage when they are forced to take a car trip with their grandmother, who tells about growing up Black in 1940s Alabama and serving in Europe during World War II as a member of the Women's Army Corps.

"The parallel travel narratives are masterfully managed, with postcards from Octavia and Tali to the folks back home in San Francisco signaling the shift between 'then' and 'now.' Absolutely essential reading." Kirkus

De Goldi, Kate

The **10** p.m. question. Candlewick Press 2010 245p $15.99

Grades: 7 8 9 10 11 12 **Fic**

1. School stories 2. Worry -- Fiction 3. Agoraphobia -- Fiction 4. Family life -- Fiction 5. New Zealand -- Fiction 6. Eccentrics and eccentricities -- Fiction
ISBN 978-0-7636-4939-5; 0-7636-4939-2

LC 2009-49726

First published 2008 in New Zealand

Twelve-year-old Frankie Parsons has a quirky family, a wonderful best friend, and a head full of worrying questions that he shares with his mother each night, but when free-spirited Sydney arrives at school with questions of her own, Frankie is forced to face the ultimate ten p.m. question.

"De Goldi's novel is an achingly poignant, wryly comic story of early adolescence. . . . Nearly every character . . . is a loving, talented, unforgettable eccentric whose dialogue, much like De Goldi's richly phrased narration, combines heart-stopping tenderness with perfectly timed, deliciously zany humor." Booklist

De Gramont, Nina

Every little thing in the world. Atheneum Books for Young Readers 2010 282p $16.99

Grades: 9 10 11 12 **Fic**

1. Camps -- Fiction 2. Pregnancy -- Fiction 3. Friendship -- Fiction 4. Wilderness areas -- Fiction
ISBN 978-1-4169-8013-1; 1-4169-8013-X

LC 2009-40335

Before she can decide what do about her newly discovered pregnancy, sixteen-year-old Sydney is punished for "borrowing" a car and shipped out, along with best friend Natalia, to a wilderness camp for the next six weeks.

"De Gramont's compelling coming-of-age story, often poetic, compassionately probes the dilemma of and complex choices surrounding Sydney's pregnancy. As told from Sydney's point of view in an authentic adolescent voice, her growing self-awareness of 'what's discovered after losing your way' is both moving and hopeful." Kirkus

De la Cruz, Melissa

★ **Blue** bloods. Hyperion 2006 302p hardcover o.p. pa $8.99

Grades: 9 10 11 12 **Fic**

1. Vampires -- Fiction 2. New York (N.Y.) -- Fiction
ISBN 978-0-7868-3892-9; 0-7868-3892-2; 978-1-4231-0126-0 pa; 1-4231-0126-X pa

LC 2005-44786

Select teenagers from some of New York City's wealthiest and most socially prominent families learn a startling secret about their bloodlines.

"History, mythology, and the contemporary New York prep-school and club scene blend seamlessly in this sexy and sophisticated riff on vampire lore that never collapses into camp." Bull Cent Child Books

Other titles in this series are:

Lost in time (2011)
Masquerade (2007)
Misguided angel (2010)
Revelations (2008)
The Van Alen legacy (2009)

Gates of Paradise; a Blue Bloods novel. Melissa de la Cruz. Hyperion 2013 355 p. (hardcover) $16.99
Grades: 9 10 11 12 **Fic**
1. Occult fiction 2. Fantasy fiction 3. Angels -- Fiction 4. Wealth -- Fiction 5. Vampires -- Fiction 6. New York (N.Y.) -- Fiction
ISBN 1423157419; 9781423157410
LC 2012032358

This is the ninth entry in Melissa de la Cruz's Blue Bloods series. Here, "Schuyler Van Alen is running out of time. The Dark Prince of Hell is storming the Gates of Paradise, intent on winning the heavenly throne for good. This time he has his greatest angels by his side, Abbadon and Azrael--Jack and Mimi Force, as they are known in the Coven. Or so he thinks. Even as Lucifer assigns Jack and Mimi the tasks of killing their true loves, the Force twins secretly vow to defeat the Dark Prince." (Publisher's note)

De la Peña, Matt

Ball don't lie. Delacorte Press 2005 280p hardcover o.p. pa $7.99
Grades: 9 10 11 12 **Fic**
1. Basketball -- Fiction 2. Race relations -- Fiction 3. Foster home care -- Fiction 4. Los Angeles (Calif.) -- Fiction 5. Obsessive-compulsive disorder -- Fiction
ISBN 0-385-73232-5; 0-385-73425-5 pa
LC 2004-18057

Seventeen-year-old Sticky lives for basketball and plays at school and at the Lincoln Rec Center in Los Angeles but he is unaware of the many dangers—including his own past—that threaten his dream of playing professionally.

"The prose moves with the rhythm of a bouncing basketball and those who don't mind mixing their sports stories with some true grit may find themselves hypnotized by Sticky's grim saga." Publ Wkly

The **living**; Matt de la Peña. Delacorte Press 2013 320 p.
Grades: 8 9 10 11 12 **Fic**
1. Cruise ships -- Fiction 2. Natural disasters -- Fiction 3. Survival after airplane accidents, shipwrecks, etc. -- Fiction 4. Diseases -- Fiction 5. Survival -- Fiction 6. Mexican Americans -- Fiction
ISBN 9780375989919; 9780385741200
LC 2012050778

Pura Belpre Author Award (2014)

In this book, by Matt de la Peña, "Shy took [a] summer job to make some money. In a few months on a luxury cruise liner, he'll rake in the tips and be able to help his mom and sister out with the bills. . . . But everything changes when the Big One hits. Shy's only weeks out at sea when an earthquake more massive than ever before recorded hits California, and his life is forever changed. The earthquake is only the first disaster. Suddenly it's a fight to survive for those left living." (Publisher's note)

"Shy Espinoza's summer job on Paradise Cruise Lines is, literally, a disaster. A series of catastrophes befall the cruise and eventually threaten civilization as he knows it; Shy finds himself on a life raft in the Pacific Ocean with a racist "spoiled-ass blond chick." Readers wanting a fast-paced survival story with plenty of action won't mind the over-the-top plot." (Horn Book)

Mexican whiteboy. Delacorte Press 2008 249p $15.99; lib bdg $18.99
Grades: 8 9 10 11 12 **Fic**
1. Cousins -- Fiction 2. California -- Fiction 3. Mexican Americans -- Fiction 4. Racially mixed people -- Fiction
ISBN 978-0-385-73310-6; 0-385-73310-0; 978-0-385-90329-5 lib bdg; 0-385-90329-4 lib bdg
LC 2007-32302

Sixteen-year-old Danny searches for his identity amidst the confusion of being half-Mexican and half-white while spending a summer with his cousin and new friends on the baseball fields and back alleys of San Diego County, California.

"The author juggles his many plotlines well, and the portrayal of Danny's friends and neighborhood is rich and lively." Booklist

We were here. Delacorte Press 2009 357p $17.99; lib bdg $20.99
Grades: 7 8 9 10 11 12 **Fic**
1. Brothers -- Fiction 2. California -- Fiction 3. Friendship -- Fiction 4. Runaway teenagers -- Fiction 5. Juvenile delinquency -- Fiction
ISBN 978-0-385-73667-1; 0-385-73667-3; 978-0-385-90622-7 lib bdg; 0-385-90622-6 lib bdg
LC 2008-44568

Haunted by the event that sentences him to time in a group home, Miguel breaks out with two unlikely companions and together they begin their journey down the California coast hoping to get to Mexico and a new life.

"The contemporary survival adventure will keep readers hooked, as will the tension that builds from the story's secrets." Booklist

De Lint, Charles

The **blue** girl; Charles de Lint. Viking 2004 368p hardcover o.p. pa $7.99
Grades: 7 8 9 10 **Fic**
1. Ghost stories 2. School stories 3. Fairies -- Fiction
ISBN 0-670-05924-2; 0-14-240545-0 pa
LC 2004-19051

New at her high school, Imogene enlists the help of her introverted friend Maxine and the ghost of a boy who haunts the school after receiving warnings through her dreams that soul-eaters are threatening her life

"The book combines the turmoil of high school intertwined with rich, detailed imagery drawn from traditional folklore and complex characters with realistic relationships. . . . This book is not just another ghost story, but a novel infused with the true sense of wonder and magic that is De Lint at his best. It is strongly recommended." Voice Youth Advocates

Dingo. Firebird 2008 213p $11.99
Grades: 9 10 11 12 **Fic**
1. Twins -- Fiction 2. Sisters -- Fiction 3. Wild dogs -- Fiction 4. Supernatural -- Fiction 5. Space and time -- Fiction
ISBN 978-0-14-240816-2; 0-14-240816-6
LC 2007-31716

Seventeen-year-old Miguel Schreiber and a long-term enemy are drawn into a strange dream world when they fall in love with shapeshifting sisters from Australia—twins hiding from a cursed ancestor who can only be freed with the girls' cooperation.

"The fated love angle will certainly draw in romance readers, and while they may be perfectly content with just following Miguel and Lainey's connection through to its expected happy ending, the intriguing details about shapeshifting, dingoes, and Aboriginal traditions may also lead them to dig a bit further into Australian myths and culture." Bull Cent Child Books

Little (grrl) lost. Viking 2007 271p hardcover o.p. pa $8.99
Grades: 7 8 9 10 **Fic**
1. Fantasy fiction 2. Size -- Fiction 3. Moving -- Fiction 4. Friendship -- Fiction 5. Runaway teenagers -- Fiction
ISBN 978-0-670-06144-0; 0-670-06144-1; 978-0-14-241301-2 pa; 0-14-241301-1 pa
LC 2007-14832

Fourteen-year-old T. J. and her new friend, sixteen-year-old Elizabeth, a six-inch-high "Little" with a big chip on her shoulder, help one another as T. J. tries to adjust to her family's move from a farm to the big city and Elizabeth tries to make her own way in the world.

"De Lint mixes marvelous fantastical creatures and realities as he taps into young women's need to feel unique, understood, and valued." Booklist

De Quidt, Jeremy

★ The **toymaker**; with illustrations by Gary Blythe. David Fickling Books 2010 356p il $16.99; lib bdg $19.99
Grades: 5 6 7 8 **Fic**
1. Adventure fiction 2. Toys -- Fiction
ISBN 978-0-385-75180-3; 0-385-75180-X; 978-0-385-75181-0 lib bdg; 0-385-75181-8 lib bdg

"Mathias . . . upon the death of his conjurer grandfather, is spirited away from the decrepit carnival they called home. His unknown new guardian appears to be after the secret contained on an inherited piece of paper, which is now in Mathias' possession. . . . Moving briskly across an atmospheric Germanic setting, the characters are chased by howling wolves, a dangerous dwarf, and unforgiving cold in a bloody, mysterious, and darkly thrilling quest." Booklist\

DeVillers, Julia

Lynn Visible. Dutton Children's Books 2010 278p il $16.99
Grades: 6 7 8 9 **Fic**
1. School stories 2. Fashion -- Fiction
ISBN 978-0-525-47691-7; 0-525-47691-1
LC 2009-23058

"Lynn Vincent knows all the latest trends and isn't afraid to flaunt her funky style. The problem is, in small-town Pennsylvania, being fashion forward makes Lynn socially backward. . . . But when one of Lynn's unique creations makes it into the hands of a famous designer and onto the runway, it seems that Lynn might finally get her moment in the spotlight." Publisher's note

Deebs, Tracy

Tempest rising. Walker & Co. 2011 344p $16.99
Grades: 8 9 10 11 12 **Fic**
1. War stories 2. Mermaids and mermen -- Fiction
ISBN 978-0-8027-2231-7; 0-8027-2231-8
LC 2010-34339

On her seventeenth birthday, Tempest must decide whether to remain a human and live on land or submit to her mermaid half, like her mother before her, and enter into a long-running war under the sea.

"Tempest is a gutsy, independent heroine with more than enough agency to save herself from danger. . . . For readers wanting a solid, familiar, but slightly different paranormal romance." Booklist

Deedy, Carmen Agra

★ The **Cheshire** Cheese cat; a Dickens of a tale. Peachtree Publishers 2011 228p il $16.95
Grades: 5 6 7 8 **Fic**
1. Cats -- Fiction 2. Mice -- Fiction
ISBN 978-1-56145-595-9; 1-56145-595-4
LC 2010052275

"The vagaries of tavern life in 19th-century London come alive in this delightful tale. . . . The fast-moving plot is a masterwork of intricate detail that will keep readers enthralled, and the characters are well-rounded and believable. Language is a highlight of the novel; words both elegant and colorful fill the pages. . . . Combined with Moser's precise pencil sketches of personality-filled characters, the book is a success in every way." SLJ

Defoe, Daniel

Defy the dark; edited by Saundra Mitchell. HarperTeen 2013 496 p. (pbk bdgs) $9.99
Grades: 9 10 11 12 **Fic**
1. Short stories 2. Shades and shadows -- Fiction 3. Light -- Fiction
ISBN 006212353X; 9780062123534; 9780062123541
LC 2012029993

This short stories collection, edited by Saundra Mitchell, includes contributions from "sixteen established YA authors. . . . Each story takes place either at night or in the dark. . . . In Carrie Ryan's 'Almost Normal,' a group of teens witnesses a zombie invasion from atop a roller coaster, and in Rachel Hawkins's urban-legend-inspired 'Eyes in the Dark,' a teen couple on a romantic interlude in the woods are hunted by monsters." (School Library Journal)

"In this collection of seventeen original stories, wildly varied aspects and interpretations of "dark" are explored. The common thread is rather effective, even as the mix of stories address everything from monsters to nightmares to romance. Most thought-provoking here are the multiple understandings of the distinct quiet--and sometimes the horror--that can only be found in the dark." (Horn Book)

Dellaira, Ava

Love letters to the dead: a novel; by Ava Dellaira. Farrar Straus & Giroux. 2014 327p $17.99

Grades: 7 8 9 10 **Fic**

1. Death — Fiction; 2. Grief — Fiction; 3. Letters — Fiction; 4. Sisters — Fiction

ISBN: 0374346674; 9780374346676

LC 2013029594

This epistolary novel begins with an "assignment for English class: Write a letter to a dead person. Laurel chooses Kurt Cobain because her sister, May, loved him. And he died young, just like May did. Soon, Laurel has a notebook full of letters to people. . . . She writes about starting high school, navigating new friendships, falling in love for the first time, . . . and, finally, about the abuse she suffered while May was supposed to be looking out for her." (Publisher's note)

"Well paced and cleverly plotted, this debut uses a fresh, new voice to tell a sometimes sad, sometimes edgy, but always compelling narrative. Fans of Sarah Dessen and Jenny Han, get ready." Booklist

Delsol, Wendy

Flock; Wendy Delsol. Candlewick Press 2012 384 p. (hardback) $16.99

Grades: 7 8 9 10 **Fic**

1. Occult fiction 2. Infants -- Fiction 3. Sisters -- Fiction 4. High schools -- Fiction 5. Supernatural -- Fiction 6. Students, Foreign -- Fiction 7. Interpersonal relations -- Fiction

ISBN 0763660108; 9780763660109

LC 2011048371

Sequel to: Frost

This book is the final in the "Stork" trilogy. Protagonist Katla has returned to her high school life after saving her boyfriend Jack in Iceland. But "her hopes of dodging unfinished business are dashed by the arrival of two Icelandic exchange students: Marik . . . and Jinky . . . . It seems Katla not only enraged the Snow Queen by rescuing . . . Jack, she also was tricked into promising her frail baby sister to the water queen—and Marik has come to collect. What's worse, Katla doesn't dare confide in anyone lest she endanger them, so even her soul mate, Jack, is growing suspicious. And now Katla's stork dreams, her guide for matching babies with mothers, have become strange and menacing as well. (Amazon.com)

Frost. Candlewick Press 2011 376p $15.99

Grades: 7 8 9 10 **Fic**

1. School stories 2. Snow -- Fiction 3. Supernatural -- Fiction 4. Arctic regions -- Fiction

ISBN 978-0-7636-5386-6; 0-7636-5386-1

LC 2010047656

Sequel to Stork (2010)

After her boyfriend Jack conjures up a record-breaking snow storm, sixteen-year-old Kat LeBlanc finds herself facing an unusual rival in the form of an environmental researcher from Greenland who is drawn to their small town of Norse Falls, Minnesota, by the storm.

"Well-paced narration will keep readers interested—a superior paranormal adventure." Kirkus

Stork. Candlewick Press 2010 357p $15.99; pa $8.99

Grades: 7 8 9 10 **Fic**

1. School stories 2. Minnesota -- Fiction 3. Supernatural -- Fiction

ISBN 978-0-7636-4844-2; 0-7636-4844-2; 978-0-7636-5687-4 pa; 0-7636-5687-9 pa

LC 2009-51357

After her parents' divorce, Katla and her mother move from Los Angeles to Norse Falls, Minnesota, where Kat immediately alienates two boys at her high school and, improbably, discovers a kinship with a mysterious group of elderly women—the Icelandic Stork Society—who "deliver souls."

"This snappy, lighthearted supernatural romance blends Norse mythology and contemporary issues with an easy touch." Booklist

Followed by: Frost (2011)

Demetrios, Heather

Something real; Heather Demetrios. Henry Holt and Co. 2014 416 p. (hardback) $17.99

Grades: 9 10 11 12 **Fic**

1. Family -- Fiction 2. Reality television programs -- Fiction 3. Family life -- Fiction

ISBN 0805097945; 9780805097948

LC 2013030798

In this book, by Heather Demetrios, Bonnie "and her twelve siblings are the stars of one-time hit reality show Baker's Dozen. Since the show's cancellation, Bonnie has tried to live a normal life. But it's about to fall apart . . . because Baker's Dozen is going back on the air. Bonnie's mom and the show's producers won't let her quit and soon the life that she has so carefully built for herself, with real friends (and maybe even a real boyfriend), is in danger." (Publisher's note)

"It's been four years since the reality television show Baker's Dozen went off the air. Bonnie Baker, 17, feels lucky to have survived the tension and challenges from constantly being in the limelight with her 12 siblings... With likable protagonists and snappy dialogue, Something Real credibly zooms in on reality TV's impact on unwilling subjects-a shoo-in for teens drawn to contemporary romance and drama. It will especially attract those who liked the similarly compelling reality show fictional exposés Reality Boy by A. S. King (Little, Brown, 2013) and The Real Real by Emma McLaughlin and Nicola Kraus (HarperCollins, 2009)." (School Library Journal)

Dennard, Susan

Something strange and deadly; Susan Dennard. 1st ed. Harpercollins Childrens Books 2012 388 p. (hardback) $17.99; (paperback) $9.99

Grades: 7 8 9 10 11 12 **Fic**

1. Fairs 2. Ghost stories 3. Zombies -- Fiction 4. Horror stories 5. Dead -- Fiction 6. Magic -- fiction 7. Brothers and sisters -- Fiction 8. Philadelphia (Pa.) -- History -- 19th century -- Fiction

ISBN 0062083260; 9780062083265; 9780062083272

LC 2011042114

Author Susan Dennard's protagonist Eleanor Fitt "and her dear Mama have just about run out of funds, and she misses [her brother] Elijah terribly [while he is on a] . . . three-year odyssey abroad. So when . . . he's been detained, she is mightily distressed. The next day, the determined teen is off for some help from the Spirit-Hunters. . . . Her can-do attitude finds her at one point systematically disabling a throng of zombies by smashing their kneecaps with her parasol." (Kirkus Reviews)

Followed by A Darkness Strange and Lovely (2013)

Deriso, Christine Hurley

Then I met my sister. Flux 2011 269p pa $9.95

Grades: 8 9 10 11 12 **Fic**

1. Death -- Fiction 2. Diaries -- Fiction 3. Sisters -- Fiction

ISBN 978-0-7387-2581-9; 0-7387-2581-1

LC 2010-45239

Summer Stetson has always lived in the shadow of her dead sister, knowing she can never measure up in any way, but on her seventeenth birthday her aunt gives her Shannon's diary, which reveals painful but liberating truths about Summer's family and herself.

"The journey Summer goes on to 'meet' her sister is compelling, but equally interesting are her discoveries about herself and her relationships. . . . This is a book intriguing enough to read in one sitting." SLJ

Derting, Kimberly

The **body** finder. Harper 2009 329p $16.99

Grades: 7 8 9 10 11 12 **Fic**

1. Mystery fiction 2. Dead -- Fiction 3. Supernatural -- Fiction 4. Extrasensory perception -- Fiction

ISBN 978-0-06-177981-7; 0-06-177981-4

LC 2009-39675

"Violet Ambrose can find dead bodies. Their aura of sound, color, or even taste imprints itself on their murderers, and Violet's extrasensory perception picks up on those elements. . . . Derting has written a suspenseful mystery and sensual love story that will captivate readers who enjoy authentic high-school settings, snappy dialogue, sweet romance, and heart-stopping drama." Booklist

Followed by: Desires of the dead (2011)

Desires of the dead. HarperCollins 2011 358p $16.99

Grades: 7 8 9 10 **Fic**

1. School stories 2. Homicide -- Fiction 3. Friendship -- Fiction 4. Supernatural -- Fiction 5. Washington (State) -- Fiction 6. Extrasensory perception -- Fiction 7. United States -- Federal Bureau of Investigation -- Fiction

ISBN 978-0-06-177984-8; 0-06-177984-9

LC 2010017838

Sequel to: The body finder (2010)

Sixteen-year-old Violet Ambrose's ability to find murder victims and their killers draws the attention of the FBI just as her relationship with Jay, her best-friend-turned-boyfriend, heats up.

"The author paces the story beautifully, weaving together several story lines as she inches up to the final, desperate scene. . . . Imaginative, convincing and successful suspense." Kirkus

The **last** echo; Kimberly Derting. Harper 2012 360 p. (hbk.) $17.99

Grades: 7 8 9 10 11 12 **Fic**

1. Love stories 2. Parapsychology -- Fiction 3. Serial killers -- Fiction 4. Dead -- Fiction 5. Schools -- Fiction 6. Friendship -- Fiction 7. Best friends -- Fiction 8. High schools -- Fiction 9. Serial murders -- Fiction 10. Psychic ability -- Fiction 11. Washington (State) -- Fiction

ISBN 0062082191; 9780062082190

LC 2011044633

Sequel to: Desires of the dead (2011)

This book, "the third installment of the Body Finder series," begins with protagonist Violet "working for a secret agency that specializes in using paranormal powers to fight crime. . . . She still loves her normal boyfriend Jay, so she worries about the strong physical response she feels whenever she touches Rafe, a member of the team. Meanwhile, Violet doesn't know she's become the target of a terrifying serial killer." (Kirkus Reviews)

"As always, this author writes a gripping tale... Personalities come across quite strongly, as several of the characters tend toward the eccentric." Kirkus

The **pledge**. Margaret K. McElderry Books 2011 323p $16.99

Grades: 7 8 9 10 **Fic**

1. Fantasy fiction 2. Ability -- Fiction 3. Social classes -- Fiction 4. Language and languages -- Fiction

ISBN 978-1-4424-2201-8; 1-4424-2201-7; 978-1-4424-2202-5 e-book

LC 2010053773

In a dystopian kingdom where the classes are separated by the languages they speak, Charlaina 'Charlie' Hart has a secret gift that is revealed when she meets a mysterious young man named Max.

Derting "keeps her story consistently engaging through vivid description and brisk pacing. . . . Great suspense from a prolific new writer with a vibrant imagination." Kirkus

The **taking;** Kimberly Derting HarperTeen. 2014 357p $17.99

Grade: 9 10 11 12 **Fic**

1. Amnesia--Fiction 2. Teenage girls--Fiction 3. Suspense fiction

ISBN: 0062293605; 9780062293602

LC 2013958342

First title in a projected trilogy. The last thing Kyra Agnew remembers is a flash of bright light. She awakes to discover that five whole years have passed. Everyone in her life has moved on . . . but Kyra's still the sixteen-year-old she was when she vanished. She finds herself drawn to Tyler, her boyfriend's kid brother, despite her best efforts to ignore her growing attraction. In order to find out the truth, the two of them decide to retrace her steps from that fateful night." (Publisher's note)

"Heart-stopping action and suspense combined with a budding romance make this book appealing to a wide range of readers." Booklist

Desai Hidier, Tanuja

★ **Born** confused. Scholastic Press 2002 413p hardcover o.p. pa $7.99

Grades: 8 9 10 11 12 **Fic**

1. Friendship -- Fiction 2. East Indian Americans -- Fiction

ISBN 0-439-35762-4; 0-439-51011-2 pa

LC 2002-4515

Seventeen-year-old Dimple, whose family is from India, discovers that she is not Indian enough for the Indians and not American enough for the Americans, as she sees her hypnotically beautiful, manipulative best friend taking possession of both her heritage and the boy she likes

"This involving story . . . will reward its readers. The family background and richness in cultural information add a new level to the familiar girl-meets-boy story." SLJ

Despain, Bree

The **dark** Divine. Egmont USA 2010 372p $17.99; lib bdg $20.99

Grades: 7 8 9 10 11 **Fic**

1. School stories 2. Family life -- Fiction 3. Supernatural -- Fiction 4. Christian life -- Fiction

ISBN 978-1-60684-057-3; 1-60684-057-6; 978-1-60684-065-8 lib bdg; 1-60684-065-7 lib bdg

LC 2009-18680

Grace Divine, almost seventeen, learns a dark secret when her childhood friend—practically a brother—returns, upsetting her pastor-father and the rest of her family, around the time strange things are happening in and near their small Minnesota town.

"Despain raises complex issues of responsibility and forgiveness and offers no easy answers. Atmospheric and compelling." Booklist

Dessen, Sarah

Along for the ride; a novel. Viking 2009 383p $19.99

Grades: 7 8 9 10 **Fic**

1. Divorce -- Fiction 2. Infants -- Fiction 3. Stepfamilies -- Fiction 4. Dating (Social customs) -- Fiction

ISBN 978-0-670-01194-0; 0-670-01194-0

LC 2009-5661

When Auden impulsively goes to stay with her father, stepmother, and new baby sister the summer before she starts college, all the trauma of her parents' divorce is revived, even as she is making new friends and having new experiences such as learning to ride a bike and dating.

"Dessen explores the dynamics of an extended family headed by two opposing, flawed personalities, revealing their parental failures with wicked precision yet still managing to create real, even sympathetic characters. . . . [This book] provides the interpersonal intricacies fans expect from a Dessen plot." Horn Book

★ **Just** listen; a novel. Viking 2006 371p $17.99

Grades: 9 10 11 12 **Fic**

1. School stories 2. Friendship -- Fiction 3. Family life -- Fiction

ISBN 0-670-06105-0; 978-0-670-06105-1

LC 2006-472

Isolated from friends who believe the worst because she has not been truthful with them, sixteen-year-old Annabel finds an ally in classmate Owen, whose honesty and passion for music help her to face and share what really happened at the end-of-the-year party that changed her life.

The author "weaves a sometimes funny, mostly emotional, and very satisfying story." Voice Youth Advocates

Lock and key; a novel. Viking Children's Books 2008 422p $18.99

Grades: 7 8 9 10 **Fic**

1. Child abuse -- Fiction 2. Family life -- Fiction 3. Abandoned children -- Fiction

ISBN 978-0-670-01088-2; 0-670-01088-X

LC 2007-25370

When she is abandoned by her alcoholic mother, high school senior Ruby winds up living with Cora, the sister she has not seen for ten years, and learns about Cora's new life, what makes a family, how to allow people to help her when she needs it, and that she too has something to offer others.

"The dialogue, especially between Ruby and Cora, is crisp, layered, and natural. The slow unfolding adds to an anticipatory mood. . . . Recommend this one to patient, sophisticated readers." SLJ

The **moon** and more; by Sarah Dessen. Viking 2013 384 p. (hardcover) $19.99

Grades: 7 8 9 10 **Fic**

1. Bildungsromans 2. Dating (Social customs) -- Fiction 3. Father-daughter relationship -- Fiction 4. Beaches -- Fiction 5. Resorts -- Fiction 6. Coming of age -- Fiction 7. Fathers and daughters -- Fiction 8. Family-owned business enterprises -- Fiction 9. Documentary films -- Production and direction -- Fiction

ISBN 0670785601; 9780670785605

LC 2012035720

In this novel, by Sarah Dessen, "Luke is the perfect boyfriend. . . . But now, in the summer before college, Emaline wonders if perfect is good enough. Enter Theo, a super-ambitious outsider. . . . Emaline's . . . father, too, thinks Emaline should have a bigger life. . . . Emaline is attracted to the bright future that Theo and her father promise. But she also clings to the deep roots of her loving mother, stepfather, and sisters." (Publisher's note)

"Dessen's characters behave as deliciously unpredictably as people do in real life, and just as in real life, they sometimes have to make difficult choices with not-so-predictable outcomes... Completely engaging." Kirkus

That summer. Orchard Books 1996 198p hardcover o.p. pa $8.99

Grades: 7 8 9 10 **Fic**

1. Sisters -- Fiction 2. Weddings -- Fiction

ISBN 0-531-09538-X; 0-531-08888-X lib bdg; 978-0-14-240172-9 pa; 0-14-240172-2 pa

LC 96-7643

During the summer of her divorced father's remarriage and her sister's wedding, fifteen-year-old Haven comes into her own by letting go of the myths of the past

"Dessen adds a fresh twist to a traditional sister-of-the-bride story with her keenly observant narrative full of witty ironies. Her combination of unforgettable characters and unexpected events generates hilarity as well as warmth." Publ Wkly

The **truth** about forever. Viking 2004 382p $16.99; pa $6.50
Grades: 7 8 9 10 **Fic**
1. Death -- Fiction 2. Catering -- Fiction
ISBN 0-670-03639-0; 0-440-21928-0 pa
LC 2003-28298

The summer following her father's death, Macy plans to work at the library and wait for her brainy boyfriend to return from camp, but instead she goes to work at a catering business where she makes new friends and finally faces her grief.

"All of Dessen's characters . . . are fully and beautifully drawn. Their dialogue is natural and believable, and their care for one another is palpable. . . . Dessen charts Macy's navigation of grief in such an honest way it will touch every reader who meets her. " SLJ

What happened to goodbye. Viking 2011 402p $19.99
Grades: 8 9 10 11 12 **Fic**
1. School stories 2. Divorce -- Fiction
ISBN 978-0-670-01294-7; 0-670-01294-7
LC 2010-41041

"The novel nimbly weaves together familiar story lines of divorce, high-school happiness and angst, and teen-identity struggles with likable, authentic adult and teen characters and intriguing yet credible situations." Booklist

DeStefano, Lauren

Fever; Lauren DeStefano. Simon & Schuster 2012 341 p. (The Chemical Garden trilogy)
Grades: 9 10 11 12 **Fic**
1. Science fiction 2. Dystopian fiction 3. Escapes -- Fiction 4. Viruses -- Fiction 5. Genetic engineering -- Fiction 6. Orphans -- Fiction
ISBN 9781442409071
LC 2011016961

This young adult novel is the second installment in Lauren DeStefano's "Chemical Garden Trilogy." "Having recently escaped the compound where she was forced to marry, take on sister wives and ultimately become her evil father-in-law Vaughn's scientific experiment in the name of finding a cure for the virus that kills off men and women at a young age, Rhine, along with former servant and love interest Gabriel, finds herself in trouble again. Plotting another escape from a heartless 'First Generation' who runs a brothel out of an abandoned carnival site, continuing to evade Vaughn, picking up a malformed and mute girl and trying to find Rhine's twin brother should be adventurous. And finally being able to communicate freely should bring out the intimacy between Rhine and Gabriel." (Kirkus)

Perfect ruin; by Lauren DeStefano and illustrated by Teagan White. Simon and Schuster Books for Young Readers 2013 368 p. (The Internment chronicles) (hardcover: alk. paper) $17.99
Grades: 7 8 9 10 **Fic**
1. Utopias 2. Imaginary places 3. Criminal investigation -- Fiction 4. Science fiction 5. Utopias -- Fiction
ISBN 1442480610; 9781442480612
LC 2013014392

In this book by Lauren DeStefano "Morgan Stockhour knows getting too close to the edge of Internment, the floating city in the clouds where she lives, can lead to madness. Then a murder, the first in a generation, rocks the city. With whispers swirling and fear on the wind, Morgan can no longer stop herself from investigating, especially once she meets Judas. Betrothed to the victim, he is the boy being blamed for the murder, but Morgan is convinced of his innocence." (Publisher's note)

Sever; Lauren DeStefano. Simon & Schuster 2013 384 p. (The Chemical Garden trilogy) (hardcover: alk. paper) $17.99
Grades: 9 10 11 12 **Fic**
1. Love stories 2. Science fiction 3. Genetic engineering -- Fiction 4. Orphans -- Fiction 5. Survival -- Fiction
ISBN 1442409096; 9781442409095; 9781442409101; 9781442409132
LC 2012015702

This young adult dystopian romance novel, by Lauren DeStefano, is the "conclusion to the New York Times bestselling Chemical Garden Trilogy. . . . While Gabriel haunts Rhine's memories, Cecily is determined to be at Rhine's side, even if Linden's feelings are still caught between them. Meanwhile, Rowan's growing involvement in an underground resistance compels Rhine to reach him before he does something that cannot be undone." (Publisher's note)

Wither. Simon & Schuster Books for Young Readers 2011 358p (The Chemical Garden trilogy) $17.99
Grades: 9 10 11 12 **Fic**
1. Science fiction 2. Orphans -- Fiction 3. Marriage -- Fiction 4. Kidnapping -- Fiction 5. Genetic engineering -- Fiction
ISBN 978-1-4424-0905-7
LC 2010-21347

After modern science turns every human into a genetic time bomb with men dying at age twenty-five and women dying at age twenty, girls are kidnapped and married off in order to repopulate the world.

"This beautifully-written . . . fantasy, with its intriguing world-building, well-developed characters and intricate plot involving flashbacks as well as edge-of-the-seat suspense, will keep teens riveted to the plight of Rhine and her sister wives. . . . This thought-provoking novel will also stimulate discussion in science and ethics classes." Voice Youth Advocates

Deuker, Carl

Gym candy. Houghton Mifflin Company 2007 313p $16
Grades: 7 8 9 10 11 12 **Fic**
1. School stories 2. Football -- Fiction 3. Steroids -- Fiction 4. Washington (State) -- Fiction 5. Father-son relationship -- Fiction
ISBN 978-0-618-77713-6; 0-618-77713-X
LC 2007-12749

Groomed by his father to be a star player, football is the only thing that has ever really mattered to Mick Johnson, who works hard for a spot on the varsity team his freshman year, then tries to hold onto his edge by using steroids, despite the consequences to his health and social life.

"Deuker skillfully complements a sobering message with plenty of exciting on-field action and locker-room drama, while depicting Mick's emotional struggles with loneliness and insecurity as sensitively and realistically as his physical ones." Booklist

High heat. Houghton Mifflin 2003 277p $16; pa $6.99

Grades: 7 8 9 10 **Fic**

1. School stories 2. Fathers -- Fiction

ISBN 0-618-31117-3; 0-06-057248-5 pa

LC 2002-15324

When high school sophomore Shane Hunter's father is arrested for money laundering at his Lexus dealership, the star pitcher's life of affluence and private school begins to fall apart

This is "a story that delivers baseball action along with a rich psychological portrait, told through a compelling first-person narration." SLJ

Night hoops. Houghton Mifflin 2000 212p $15; pa $8.99

Grades: 7 8 9 10 **Fic**

1. Basketball -- Fiction 2. Friendship -- Fiction

ISBN 0-395-97936-6; 0-547-24891-1 pa

LC 99-47882

While trying to prove that he is good enough to be on his high school's varsity basketball team, Nick must also deal with his parents' divorce and erratic behavior of a troubled classmate who lives across the street

"The descriptions of the games are well written and accurate. Best of all, the complexities of basketball are contrasted with the complexities of life." SLJ

Painting the black. Avon Books 1999 248p pa $5.99

Grades: 8 9 10 11 12 **Fic**

1. School stories 2. Baseball -- Fiction

ISBN 0-380-73104-5

First published 1997 by Houghton Mifflin

"After a disastrous fall from a tree, senior Ryan Ward wrote off baseball. But he is swept back into the game when cocky, charismatic Josh Daniels—a star quarterback with the perfect spiral pass as well as a pitcher with a mean slider—moves into the neighborhood. . . . The well-written sports scenes—baseball and football—will draw reluctant readers, but it is Ryan's moral courage that will linger when the reading is done." Booklist

★ **Payback** time. Houghton Mifflin Harcourt 2010 298p $16

Grades: 7 8 9 10 **Fic**

1. School stories 2. Courage -- Fiction 3. Obesity -- Fiction 4. Football -- Fiction 5. Journalists -- Fiction

ISBN 978-0-547-27981-7; 0-547-27981-7

LC 2010-6779

Deuker "really cranks up the suspense in his newest page-turner. . . . The game action alone is riveting . . . but Deuker enriches the tale with several well-tuned subplots and memorable narrator/protagonist." Booklist

Runner. Houghton Mifflin 2005 216p $16; pa $7.99

Grades: 7 8 9 10 **Fic**

1. Smuggling -- Fiction 2. Terrorism -- Fiction 3. Alcoholism -- Fiction

ISBN 0-618-54298-1; 0-618-73505-4 pa

LC 2004-15781

Living with his alcoholic father on a broken-down sailboat on Puget Sound has been hard on seventeen-year-old Chance Taylor, but when his love of running leads to a high-paying job, he quickly learns that the money is not worth the risk

"Writing in a fast-paced, action-packed, but at the same time reflective style, Deuker . . . uses running as a hook to entice readers into a perceptive coming-of-age novel." SLJ

Swagger; Carl Deuker. Houghton Mifflin Harcourt 2013 304 p. $17.99

Grades: 7 8 9 10 11 12 **Fic**

1. Basketball -- Fiction 2. Child sexual abuse -- Fiction 3. Sexual abuse -- Fiction

ISBN 0547974590; 9780547974590

LC 2012045062

In this book, by Carl Deuker, "high school senior Jonas moves to Seattle [and] is glad to meet Levi, a nice, soft-spoken guy and fellow basketball player." Then, readers are introduced to "Ryan Hartwell, a charismatic basketball coach and sexual predator. When Levi reluctantly tells Jonas that Hartwell abused him, Jonas has to decide whether he should risk his future career to report the coach." (Publisher's note)

"When his family moves to Seattle, high school basketball star Jonas befriends new neighbor Levi, who plays power forward. Assistant coach Ryan Hartwell appreciates Jonas's fast-breaking style, but something about Hartwell feels wrong. Eventually his misdeeds lead to tragedy, and Jonas must find the courage to do what's right. Basketball fans will love the realistic hardwood action and the story's quick pacing." (Horn Book)

DiCamillo, Kate, 1964-

★ **Flora** and Ulysses; The Illuminated Adventures. by Kate DiCamillo ; illustrated by K. G. Campbell. Candlewick Press 2013 240 p. ill. (reinforced) $17.99

Grades: 5 6 7 8 **Fic**

1. Occult fiction -- fiction 2. Children of divorced parents -- fiction

ISBN 076366040X; 9780763660406

LC 2012947748

In this book by Newbury Medalist Kate DiCamillo, "bitter about her parents' divorce. Flora Buckman has withdrawn into her favorite comic book The Amazing Incandesto! and memorized the advisories in its ongoing bonus feature, Terrible Things Can Happen to You! She puts those life-saving tips into action when a squirrel is swallowed whole by a neighbor's new vacuum cleaner. . . . Flora resuscitates the squirrel," who now has superpowers. (Publishers Weekly)

Dickerson, Melanie

The **merchant's** daughter. Zondervan 2011 284p pa $9.99

Grades: 7 8 9 10 11 12 **Fic**

1. Love -- Fiction 2. Middle Ages -- Fiction 3. Christian life -- Fiction 4. Contract labor -- Fiction

ISBN 978-0-31072761-3

LC 2011034338

In 1352 England, seventeen-year-old Annabel, granddaughter of a knight and a would-be nun, eludes a lecherous bailiff but falls in love with Lord Le Wyse, the ferocious and disfigured man to whom her family owes three years of indentured servitude, in this tale loosely based on Beauty and the Beast.

Dickerson "manages a heartfelt romance that will stick with readers, not only for its morality but also for the exploration of a woman's place within fourteenth-century English Christianity." Booklist

Dickinson, Peter

Angel Isle; illustrations by Ian Andrew. Wendy Lamb Books 2007 500p il $17.99; lib bdg $20.99

Grades: 7 8 9 10 **Fic**

1. Fantasy fiction 2. Magic -- Fiction

ISBN 978-0-385-74690-8; 978-0-385-90928-0 lib bdg

LC 2007-7053

Sequel to The Ropemaker (2001)

While seeking the Ropemaker to restore the ancient magic that will protect their valley, Saranja, Maja, and Ribek must outwit twenty-four of the empire's most powerful and evil magicians.

"The characters are as well developed as those in the first book, and the complex, multilayered story includes more heady explorations of time and magic, joined here by thoughts on the meaning of true love." Booklist

★ **Eva**. Delacorte Press 1989 219p hardcover o.p. pa $6.50; pa $7.99

Grades: 7 8 9 10 **Fic**

1. Science fiction 2. Chimpanzees -- Fiction

ISBN 0-385-29702-5; 0-440-20766-5 pa; 9780440207665 pa

LC 88-29435

"Eva wakes up from a deep coma that was the result of a terrible car accident and finds herself drastically altered. The accident leaves her so badly injured that her parents consent to a radical experiment to transplant her brain and memory into the body of a research chimpanzee. With the aid of a computer for communication, Eva slowly adjusts to her new existence while scientists monitor her progress, feelings, and insight into the animal world." Voice Youth Advocates

★ The **ropemaker**. Delacorte Press 2001 375p $15.95; pa $7.95

Grades: 7 8 9 10 **Fic**

1. Fantasy fiction 2. Magic -- Fiction

ISBN 0-385-72921-9; 0-385-73063-2 pa

LC 2001-17422

Michael L. Printz Award honor book, 2002

When the magic that protects their Valley starts to fail, Tilja and her companions journey into the evil Empire to find the ancient magician Faheel, who originally cast those spells

"The suspense does not let up until the very last pages. While on one level this tale is a fantasy, it is also a wonderful coming-of-age story." SLJ

Dixon, Heather

★ **Entwined**. Greenwillow Books 2011 472p

Grades: 7 8 9 10 **Fic**

1. Fantasy fiction 2. Dance -- Fiction 3. Death -- Fiction 4. Magic -- Fiction 5. Princesses -- Fiction 6. Kings and rulers -- Fiction 7. Father-daughter relationship -- Fiction

ISBN 0-06-200103-5; 978-0-06-200103-0

LC 2010-11686

Confined to their dreary castle while mourning their mother's death, Princess Azalea and her eleven sisters join The Keeper, who is trapped in a magic passageway, in a nightly dance that soon becomes nightmarish.

"The story gracefully explores significant themes of grief and loss, mercy and love. Full of mystery, lush settings, and fully orbed characters, Dixon's debut is both suspenseful and rewarding." Booklist

Dixon, John

Phoenix Island; John Dixon. Gallery Books 2014 320 p. (hardback) $19.99

Grades: 9 10 11 12 **Fic**

1. Boxers (Sports) 2. Juvenile delinquents -- Fiction 3. Science fiction 4. Boxing -- Fiction 5. Orphans -- Fiction 6. Mercenary troops -- Fiction

ISBN 1476738637; 9781476738635; 9781476738659

LC 2013033616

"A champion boxer with a sharp hook and a short temper, sixteen-year-old Carl Freeman has been shuffled from foster home to foster home. He can't seem to stay out of trouble--using his fists to defend weaker classmates from bullies. His latest incident sends his opponent to the emergency room, and now the court is sending Carl to the worst place on earth: Phoenix Island," which "is ground zero for the future of combat intelligence." (Publisher's note)

"An unusual premise makes Dixon's thriller debut a welcome series kickoff...There are some predictable elements—Carl falls for an attractive girl with a secret—but the pacing and smooth prose will have suspense fans waiting for the next book, as well as the upcoming CBS adaptation, Intelligence." (Publishers Weekly)

Dobkin, Bonnie

Neptune's children; [by] Bonnie Dobkin. Walker & Co. 2008 262p map $16.99

Grades: 7 8 9 10 **Fic**

1. Terrorism -- Fiction 2. Amusement parks -- Fiction 3. Resistance to government -- Fiction

ISBN 978-0-8027-9734-6; 0-8027-9734-2

LC 2008-2680

When a biological terrorist attack kills all adults on Earth, children stranded at an amusement park work together to survive, led by Milo whose father was an engineer there, but when new threats arise and suspicions grow, rebellion erupts.

"This thriller has gripping writing that makes it hard to put down. The characterizations of the older children are well done. . . . Even with the large number of survival stories on the market, this is one worth adding to your collection." SLJ

Doctorow, Cory

For the win. Tor 2010 475p $17.99

Grades: 8 9 10 11 12 **Fic**

1. Science fiction 2. Internet games -- Fiction

ISBN 978-0-7653-2216-6; 0-7653-2216-1

LC 2010-18644

A group of teens from around the world find themselves drawn into an online revolution arranged by a mysterious young woman known as Big Sister Nor, who hopes to challenge the status quo and change the world using her virtual connections.

The author "has taken denigrated youth behavior (this time, gaming) and recast it into something heroic. He can't resist the occasional lecture—sometimes breaking away from the plot to do so—but thankfully his lessons are riveting. With its eye-opening humanity and revolutionary zeal, this ambitious epic is well worth the considerable challenge." Booklist

★ **Homeland**; Cory Doctorow. 1st ed. Tor Teen 2013 396 p. (hardcover) $17.99

Grades: 9 10 11 12 **Fic**

1. Adventure fiction 2. Hacktivism -- Fiction 3. Civil rights -- Fiction 4. Counterculture -- Fiction 5. Computer hackers -- Fiction 6. Politics, Practical -- Fiction 7. San Francisco (Calif.) -- Fiction 8. United States. Dept. of Homeland Security -- Fiction

ISBN 0765333694; 9780765333698

LC 2012037366

This is a follow-up to Cory Doctorow's "Little Brother." Here, California's economy collapses, but Marcus's hacktivist past lands him a job as webmaster for a crusading politician who promises reform. Soon his former nemesis Masha emerges from the political underground to gift him with a thumbdrive containing a Wikileaks-style cable-dump of hard evidence of corporate and governmental perfidy" and Marcus must choose whether to release it to the public. (Publisher's note)

★ **Little** brother. Tor Teen 2008 380p

Grades: 8 9 10 11 12 **Fic**

1. Computers -- Fiction 2. Terrorism -- Fiction 3. Civil rights -- Fiction 4. San Francisco (Calif.) -- Fiction 5. United States -- Dept. of Homeland Security -- Fiction

ISBN 0765319853; 9780765319852

LC 2008-1827

After being interrogated for days by the Department of Homeland Security in the aftermath of a terrorist attack on San Francisco, California, 17-year-old Marcus, released into what is now a police state, decides to use his expertise in computer hacking to set things right. "High school." (Horn Book)

"The author manages to explain naturally the necessary technical tools and scientific concepts in this fast-paced and well-written story. . . . The reader is privy to Marcus's gut-wrenching angst, frustration, and terror, thankfully offset by his self-awareness and humorous observations." Voice Youth Advocates

Pirate cinema; Cory Doctorow. 1st ed. Tor Teen 2012 384 p. (hardback) $19.99; (paperback) $9.99; (audiobook) $24.00

Grades: 7 8 9 10 **Fic**

1. Copyright 2. Runaway teenagers -- Fiction 3. Science fiction 4. England -- Fiction 5. Internet -- Fiction 6. Protest movements -- Fiction 7. Motion pictures -- Production and direction -- Fiction

ISBN 0765329085; 9780765329080; 9781429943185; 9780765329097; 9780307879585

LC 2012019871

In this book, author Cory Doctorow tells the story of Trent McCauley, a boy who "has an irrepressible drive to create . . . [films] through illegal downloading, and when he's caught, . . . [he] runs away to London, where he's taken under the wing of streetwise Jem Dodger. . . . He meets 26 and creates the persona Cecil B. DeVil. Pulled by 26 into the politics of copyright and the lobbyist money that purchases laws, Cecil becomes a creative figurehead for reform against escalating laws that aggressively jail kids." (Kirkus Reviews)

Dogar, Sharon

★ **Annexed.** Houghton Mifflin Harcourt 2010 333p $17

Grades: 8 9 10 11 12 **Fic**

1. Children 2. Diarists 3. Holocaust victims 4. Netherlands -- Fiction 5. Holocaust, 1933-1945 -- Fiction

ISBN 978-0-547-50195-6; 0-547-50195-1

LC 2010-282410

"On July 13, 1942, 15-year-old Peter van Pels and his parents entered the attic that became their home for two years. Peter is angry that he is hiding and not fighting Nazis. He is also not happy to be sharing cramped living quarters with the Franks, especially know-it-all Anne. In this novel, Dogar 'reimagines' what happened between the families who lived in the secret annex immortalized in Anne Frank's diary. In doing so, she creates a captivating historical novel and fully fleshes out the character of Peter, a boy whom teens will easily relate to." SLJ

Doktorski, Jennifer Salvato

Famous last words; Jennifer Salvato Doktorski. Henry Holt and Company 2013 288 p. (hardcover) $17.99

Grades: 7 8 9 10 **Fic**

1. Women journalists -- Fiction 2. Internship programs -- Fiction 3. Journalism -- Fiction 4. Newspapers -- Fiction 5. Self-perception -- Fiction 6. Dating (Social customs) -- Fiction

ISBN 0805093672; 9780805093674

LC 2012046312

In this book, "aspiring reporter Sam D'Angelo, 16, is interning at her local New Jersey paper for the summer, stuck writing obituaries with her occasionally annoying, college-age fellow intern AJ. When she's not taking phone calls about dead people, Sam writes humorous imaginary obits (including one for herself); spends time with her grandmother; lusts after the 'incredibly hot' features intern, Tony Roma; and covertly investigates the shady mayor with AJ." (Publishers Weekly)

"Something of a love note to print journalism, the story is nevertheless snappy and contemporary, furthered by Sam's wry, self-deprecating narration and convincingly colloquial dialogue. Cleverly titled, realistically written, and on the whole engaging and sympathetic, this story rings true." Kirkus

Dolamore, Jaclyn

Magic under glass. Bloomsbury Children's Books 2010 225p $16.99

Grades: 7 8 9 10 11 12 **Fic**

1. Fantasy fiction 2. Magic -- Fiction 3. Robots -- Fiction 4. Fairies -- Fiction 5. Singers -- Fiction

ISBN 978-1-59990-430-6; 1-59990-430-6

LC 2009-20944

A wealthy sorcerer's invitation to sing with his automaton leads seventeen-year-old Nimira, whose family's disgrace brought her from a palace to poverty, into political intrigue, enchantments, and a friendship with a fairy prince who needs her help.

"Delamore successfully juggles several elements that might have stymied even a more experienced writer: intriguing plot elements, sophisticated characterizations, and a subtle boost of girl power." Booklist

Dole, Mayra L.

★ **Down** to the bone; [by] Mayra Lazara Dole. HarperTeen 2008 384p $16.99; lib bdg $17.89

Grades: 8 9 10 11 12 **Fic**

1. Lesbians -- Fiction 2. Cuban Americans -- Fiction

ISBN 978-0-06-084310-6; 0-06-084310-1; 978-0-06-084311-3 lib bdg; 0-06-084311-X lib bdg

LC 2007-33270

Laura, a seventeen-year-old Cuban American girl, is thrown out of her house when her mother discovers she is a lesbian, but after trying to change her heart and hide from the truth, Laura finally comes to terms with who she is and learns to love and respect herself.

"Using Spanish colloquialisms and slang, this debut author pulls off the tricky task of dialect in a manner that feels authentic. As Dole tackles a tough and important topic, her protagonist will win over a range of teen audiences, gay and straight." Publ Wkly

Doller, Trish

Something like normal; Trish Doller. Bloomsbury Pub. Children's Books 2012 216 p. (hardback) $16.99

Grades: 9 10 11 12 **Fic**

1. Love stories 2. Military personnel -- United States -- Fiction 3. Triangles (Interpersonal relations) -- Fiction 4. Love -- Fiction 5. Brothers -- Fiction 6. Veterans -- Fiction 7. Afghanistan -- Fiction 8. Family problems -- Fiction 9. Afghan War, 2001- -- Fiction 10. United States. Marine Corps -- Fiction 11. Post-traumatic stress disorder -- Fiction

ISBN 1599908441; 9781599908441

LC 2011035511

In this book, "Travis is home in southwest Florida, on leave from Afghanistan and dealing with the death of his best friend and fellow soldier Charlie, the breakup of his parents' marriage, and his girlfriend having left him for his brother. While processing all of this, he meets Harper, a girl whose reputation he destroyed years ago, and the two slowly start to connect." (Publishers Weekly)

Dominy, Amy Fellner

OyMG. Walker & Co. 2011 247p $16.99

Grades: 6 7 8 9 **Fic**

1. Camps -- Fiction 2. Prejudices -- Fiction 3. Jews -- United States -- Fiction

ISBN 978-0-8027-2177-8; 0-8027-2177-X

LC 2010-34581

Fourteen-year-old Ellie will do almost anything to win a scholarship to the best speech school in the country, but must decide if she is willing to hide her Jewish heritage while at a Phoenix, Arizona, summer camp that could help her reach her goal.

"Readers will be pulled into the thoughtful exploration of one girl's emotional connection to her religion and family heritage, her struggle to balance ambition with honesty and self respect, and her delicate negotiation of being different when that difference isn't outwardly apparent." Bull Cent Child Books

Donaldson, Julia

Running on the cracks. Henry Holt 2009 218p $16.99

Grades: 6 7 8 9 **Fic**

1. Orphans -- Fiction 2. Runaway teenagers -- Fiction 3. Child sexual abuse -- Fiction 4. Racially mixed people -- Fiction

ISBN 978-0-8050-9054-3; 0-8050-9054-1

LC 2008-50278

After her parents are killed in an accident, English teenager Leonora Watts-Chan runs away to Glasgow, Scotland, to find her Chinese grandparents

"The characters in Donaldson's . . . YA debut are well drawn and their imperfections are authentic, particularly Mary's battle with mental illness. Despite heavy themes, the story is neither bleak nor gritty. The fast pace and short chapters should appeal to readers, who will celebrate the hopeful ending." Publ Wkly

Donnelly, Jennifer

A **northern** light. Harcourt 2003 389p $17; pa $8.95

Grades: 9 10 11 12 **Fic**

1. Farm life -- Fiction

ISBN 0-15-216705-6; 0-15-205310-7 pa

LC 2002-5098

Michael L. Printz Award honor book, 2004

In 1906, sixteen-year-old Mattie, determined to attend college and be a writer against the wishes of her father and fiance, takes a job at a summer inn where she discovers the truth about the death of a guest. Based on a true story.

"Donnelly's characters ring true to life, and the meticulously described setting forms a vivid backdrop to this finely crafted story. An outstanding choice for historical-fiction fans." SLJ

★ **Revolution.** Delacorte Press 2010 471p $18.99; lib bdg $21.99

Grades: 9 10 11 12 Fic

1. Princes 2. Diaries -- Fiction 3. Musicians -- Fiction 4. Bereavement -- Fiction 5. Family life -- Fiction 6. Paris (France) -- Fiction 7. France -- History -- 1789-1799, Revolution -- Fiction

ISBN 978-0-385-73763-0; 0-385-73763-7; 978-0-385-90678-4 lib bdg; 0-385-90678-1 lib bdg

LC 2010-08993

An angry, grieving seventeen-year-old musician facing expulsion from her prestigious Brooklyn private school travels to Paris to complete a school assignment and uncovers a diary written during the French revolution by a young actress attempting to help a tortured, imprisoned little boy—Louis Charles, the lost king of France.

"The ambitious story, narrated in Andi's grief-soaked, sardonic voice, will wholly capture patient readers with its sharply articulated, raw emotions and insights into science and art; ambition and love; history's ever-present influence; and music's immediate, astonishing power." Booklist

Includes bibliographical references

Donovan, John

I'll get there, it better be worth the trip; 40th anniversary edition; Flux 2010 228p pa $9.95

Grades: 7 8 9 10 11 Fic

1. Alcoholism -- Fiction 2. Friendship -- Fiction 3. Homosexuality -- Fiction

ISBN 978-0-7387-2134-7 pa; 0-7387-2134-4 pa

LC 2010014266

First published 1969 by Harper & Row

While trying to cope with his alcoholic mother and absent father, a lonely New York City teenager develops a confusing crush on another boy.

"Donovan's novel is startlingly outspoken and honest in its presentation of a young teen questioning his sexuality. . . . Such is the author's skill that the reader knows this young man's journey of self-discovery will get him to his 'there,' wherever it may be. This welcome fortieth-anniversary edition of a YA classic is an essential purchase for all libraries." Voice Youth Advocates

Dooley, Sarah

Body of water. Feiwel and Friends 2011 324p $16.99

Grades: 7 8 9 Fic

1. Arson -- Fiction 2. Camping -- Fiction 3. Family life -- Fiction 4. Homeless persons -- Fiction

ISBN 978-0-312-61254-2; 0-312-61254-0

LC 2011023523

After their trailer home and all their belongings are burned, twelve-year-old Ember and her Wiccan family move to a lakeside campground where Ember's anguish over losing her dog, as well as her friendship with the boy she fears started the fire, stops her from making new friends and moving on.

"Dooley puts readers directly into the center of Ember's plight with a heartfelt first-person narration. An enthralling tale that demystifies Wicca, humanizes homeless families and inspires reflection on friendship, forgiveness and moving forward." Kirkus

Livvie Owen lived here. Feiwel and Friends 2010 229p $16.99

Grades: 6 7 8 9 10 Fic

1. School stories 2. Autism -- Fiction 3. Family life -- Fiction

ISBN 978-0-312-61253-5; 0-312-61253-2

LC 2010-13009

Fourteen-year-old Livvie Owen, who has autism, and her family have been forced to move frequently because of her outbursts, but when they face eviction again, Livvie is convinced she has a way to get back to a house where they were all happy, once.

"This novel is an interesting perspective of what a teenage girl with autism might experience, but also a heartwarming story of how a family binds together during emotional and financial turmoil." Libr Media Connect

Dos Santos, Steven

The **culling**; Steven Dos Santos. Flux 2013 432 p. (The torch keeper) $9.99

Grades: 9 10 11 12 Fic

1. Dystopian fiction 2. Homosexuality -- Fiction 3. Resistance to government -- Fiction 4. Science fiction 5. Orphans -- Fiction 6. Contests -- Fiction 7. Survival -- Fiction 8. Brothers and sisters -- Fiction 9. Government, Resistance to -- Fiction

ISBN 073873537X; 9780738735375

LC 2012041699

Rainbow List (2014)

In this young adult dystopian novel, by Steven dos Santos, book one of "The Torch Keeper" series, "for Lucian . . . , Recruitment Day means the . . . totalitarian government will force him to . . . compet[e] to join the ruthless Imposer task force. Each Recruit participates in increasingly difficult and violent military training . . . , those who fail must choose . . . a family member to be brutally killed." (Publisher's note)

"The Establishment controls everyone and everything in this bleak future world. Sixteen-year-old Lucky and his four-year-old brother, Cole, live in a rundown building and have little to eat. Their parents are dead, and they have only a friendly (but sickly) neighbor to watch over them...This novel is similar to Suzanne Collins's The Hunger Games in its brutality, but it fails to provoke the same emotional attachment readers feel for the characters in Collins's blockbuster. In some ways, this dystopian vision seems even more unsettling; throughout the Trials, the Recruits' loved ones are killed in increasingly disturbing ways." (School Library Journal)

Dowd, Siobhan

★ **Bog** child. David Fickling Books 2008 321p

Grades: 8 9 10 11 12 Fic

1. Mummies -- Fiction 2. Prisoners -- Fiction 3. Terrorism -- Fiction 4. Family life -- Fiction 5. Northern Ireland -- Fiction

ISBN 0-385-75170-2 lib bdg; 978-0-385-75169-8; 0-385-75169-9; 978-0-385-75170-4 lib bdg

LC 2008-2998

This novel is set in Northern Ireland in 1981. 18-year-old Fergus is distracted from his upcoming A-level exams by the discovery of a girl's body in a peat bog, his imprisoned brother's hunger strike, and the stress of being a courier for Sinn Fein. "Grades eight to twelve." (Bull Cent Child Books)

"Dowd raises questions about moral choices within a compelling plot that is full of surprises, powerfully bringing home the impact of political conflict on innocent bystanders." Publ Wkly

★ **Solace** of the road. David Fickling Books 2009 260p $17.99; lib bdg $20.99

Grades: 9 10 11 12 **Fic**

1. Great Britain -- Fiction 2. Foster home care -- Fiction 3. Runaway teenagers -- Fiction 4. Voyages and travels -- Fiction

ISBN 978-0-375-84971-8; 0-375-84971-8; 978-0-375-94971-5 lib bdg; 0-375-94971-2 lib bdg

LC 2008-44603

While running away from a London foster home just before her fifteenth birthday, Holly has ample time to consider her years of residential care and her early life with her Irish mother, whom she is now trying to reach.

"A compelling psychological portrait of a girl's journey from denial to facing the facts that will let her move beyond her troubled past. . . . Readers will root for her to find her balance and arrive safely at the right destination." Publ Wkly

A **swift** pure cry. David Fickling Books 2007 309p hardcover o.p. pa $8.99

Grades: 9 10 11 12 **Fic**

1. Fathers -- Fiction 2. Ireland -- Fiction 3. Pregnancy -- Fiction 4. Family life -- Fiction

ISBN 978-0-385-75108-7; 0-385-75108-7; 978-0-440-42218-1 pa; 0-440-42218-1 pa

LC 2006-14562

Coolbar, Ireland, is a village of secrets and Shell, caretaker to her younger brother and sister after the death of their mother and with the absence of their father, is not about to reveal hers until suspicion falls on the wrong person.

"This book, with its serious tone and inclusion of social issues, will have appeal for American readers desiring weightier material, and teachers might find it useful in the classroom." Voice Youth Advocates

Dowell, Frances O' Roark

Ten miles past normal. Atheneum Books for Young Readers 2011 211p $16.99

Grades: 6 7 8 9 10 **Fic**

1. School stories 2. Farm life -- Fiction 3. Bands (Music) -- Fiction

ISBN 1-4169-9585-4; 978-1-4169-9585-2

LC 2010-22041

Because living with "modern-hippy" parents on a goat farm means fourteen-year-old Janie Gorman cannot have a normal high school life, she tries joining Jam Band, making friends with Monster, and spending time with elderly former civil rights workers.

"Janie narrates her first year in high school with her sure, smart, sarcastic voice. . . . Dowell gets all the details of ninth grade right." Horn Book

Downham, Jenny

★ **Before** I die. David Fickling Books 2007 326p hardcover o.p. pa $9.99

Grades: 8 9 10 11 12 **Fic**

1. Death -- Fiction 2. Terminally ill -- Fiction

ISBN 978-0-385-75155-1; 978-0-385-75183-4 pa

LC 2007-20284

A terminally ill teenaged girl makes and carries out a list of things to do before she dies.

"Downham holds nothing back in her wrenchingly and exceptionally vibrant story." Publ Wkly

★ **You** against me. David Fickling Books 2011 412p $16.99; lib bdg $19.99; ebook $10.99

Grades: 9 10 11 12 **Fic**

1. Rape -- Fiction 2. Guilt -- Fiction 3. Siblings -- Fiction 4. Great Britain -- Fiction 5. Social classes -- Fiction

ISBN 978-0-385-75160-5; 978-0-385-75161-2 lib bdg; 978-0-375-98938-4 ebook

LC 2010038226

When eighteen-year-old Mikey's younger sister claims to have been raped and he seeks to avenge the crime, he meets Ellie, the sister of the accused, and befriends her, complicating the situation considerably for all of them.

"Crisp, revealing dialogue, measured pacing and candid, unaffected prose round out this illuminating novel in which any reader can find someone to root for or relate to." Kirkus

Dowswell, Paul

The **Auslander**. Bloomsbury Children's Books 2011 295p $16.99

Grades: 7 8 9 10 **Fic**

1. Orphans -- Fiction 2. Adoption -- Fiction 3. Insurgency -- Fiction 4. Berlin (Germany) -- Fiction 5. National socialism -- Fiction 6. World War, 1939-1945 -- Fiction 7. Germany -- History -- 1933-1945 -- Fiction

ISBN 1599906333; 9781599906331

LC 2010035626

First published 2009 in the United Kingdom

German soldiers take Peter from a Warsaw orphanage, and soon he is adopted by Professor Kaltenbach, a prominent Nazi, but Peter forms his own ideas about what he sees and hears and decides to take a risk that is most dangerous in 1942 Berlin.

"The characters are rich and nuanced; . . . the action is swift and suspenseful; and the juxtaposition of wartime nobility and wartime cruelty is timeless." Horn Book

Doyle, Brian

Boy O'Boy. Douglas & McIntyre 2003 161p hardcover o.p. pa $12.95

Grades: 6 7 8 9 **Fic**

1. Child sexual abuse -- Fiction

ISBN 0-88899-588-1; 0-88899-590-3 pa

Living in Ottawa in 1945, Martin O'Boy must deal with a drunken father, an overburdened mother, a disabled twin brother, and a sexual predator at his church.

"Martin O'Boy is an expert observer and narrator. . . . Martin's world is believably real. Even the description of the sexual encounter seems like what a confused 11 or 12-year-old might say. " SLJ

Pure Spring. Groundwood Books 2007 158p $16.95; pa $8.95

Grades: 6 7 8 9 **Fic**

1. Canada -- Fiction

ISBN 978-0-88899-774-6; 978-0-88899-775-3 pa

It's spring in post-World War II Ottawa and Martin has found a true home. He's also working even though he had to lie about his age to get the job. Martin is also in love, but his boss is robbing the family of the one he loves.

"Doyle lovingly shapes his characters. . . . Doyle rounds out the grimness with comedic scenes." Horn Book

Doyle, Eugenie F.

According to Kit; [by] Eugenie Doyle. Front Street 2009 215p $17.95

Grades: 7 8 9 10 **Fic**

1. Ballet -- Fiction 2. Vermont -- Fiction 3. Farm life -- Fiction 4. Family life -- Fiction 5. Home schooling -- Fiction 6. Mother-daughter relationship -- Fiction

ISBN 978-1-59078-474-7; 1-59078-474-X

LC 2009-7032

As fifteen-year-old Kit does chores on her family's Vermont farm, she puzzles over her mother's apparent unhappiness, complains about being homeschooled after a minor incident at school, and strives to communicate just how important dance is to her.

Doyle's "characters are complicated and authentic. . . . Kit's obsession with ballet . . . will ring true for all teens equally focused on their own talents." Booklist

Doyle, Marissa

Betraying season. Henry Holt and Co. 2009 330p $16.99

Grades: 7 8 9 10 **Fic**

1. Magic -- Fiction 2. Witches -- Fiction

ISBN 978-0-8050-8252-4; 0-8050-8252-2

LC 2008-40593

In 1838, Penelope Leland goes to Ireland to study magic and prove to herself that she is as good a witch as her twin sister Persy, but when Niall Keating begins to pay her court, she cannot help being distracted.

"This is a full-bodied story that wonderfully combines elements of romance, fantasy, and history. . . . Whether Doyle is describing the Irish countryside, a magical incantation, or a lover's kiss, her writing is compelling, and it will be hard for readers not to be swept away by this invigorating story." Booklist

★ **Bewitching** season. Henry Holt 2008 346p $16.95; pa $8.99

Grades: 7 8 9 10 **Fic**

1. Magic -- Fiction 2. Twins -- Fiction 3. Sisters -- Fiction 4. Missing persons -- Fiction

ISBN 978-0-8050-8251-7; 0-8050-8251-4; 978-0-312-59695-8 pa; 0-312-59695-2 pa

In 1837, as seventeen-year-old twins, Persephone and Penelope, are starting their first London Season they find that their beloved governess, who has taught them everything they know about magic, has disappeared.

"Doyle takes as much care with characters . . . as with story details. This [is a] delightful mélange of genres." Booklist

Courtship and curses; Marissa Doyle. Henry Holt 2012 343 p. (hc) $17.99

Grades: 7 8 9 10 **Fic**

1. Regency novels 2. Mystery fiction 3. Magic -- Fiction 4. Witches -- Fiction 5. Self-acceptance -- Fiction 6. People with disabilities -- Fiction 7. Aristocracy (Social class) -- Fiction 8. Brussels (Belgium) -- History -- Fiction 9. Belgium -- History -- 1814-1830 -- Fiction 10. Great Britain -- History -- 1800-1837 -- Fiction

ISBN 0805091874; 9780805091878

LC 2011031999

This book tells the story of "Lady Sophronia Rosier (Sophie)," who is preparing "for her entrance into London society," despite a disability incurred from illness. She has help from "her new best friend, Parthenope" and "begins her procession into society." It soon becomes clear that someone is using magic to target her and her father. "Sophie and Parthenope begin to investigate while playing their roles in society, dreadfully aware that lives are at stake." (Voice of Youth Advocates)

Doyle, Roddy

A **greyhound** of a girl; Roddy Doyle. Amulet Books 2012 208 p. (hbk.) $16.95

Grades: 7 8 9 10 11 12 **Fic**

1. Dog racing -- Fiction 2. Family life -- Fiction 3. Dublin (Ireland) -- Fiction 4. Women -- Ireland -- Fiction 5. Death -- Fiction 6. Ghosts -- Fiction 7. Ireland -- Fiction 8. Grandmothers -- Fiction 9. Voyages and travels -- Fiction 10. Mother-daughter relationship -- Fiction

ISBN 9781407129334 Marion Lloyd; 1407129333 Marion Lloyd; 9781419701689 Amulet; 1419701681 Amulet

LC 2011042200

This book tells the story of "Twelve-year-old Mary O'Hara," an Irish girl who "is surrounded by good-humored women . . . her mum at home, her mum's mum, who is dying in Dublin's Sacred Heart Hospital, and her mum's mum's mum, who has just materialized as a ghost on her street. . . . [Roddy] Doyle divides up the novel by character, giving readers first-hand glimpses into the nature of each woman through time." (Kirkus)

Wilderness. Arthur A. Levine Books 2007 211p $16.99

Grades: 6 7 8 9 **Fic**

1. Mothers -- Fiction 2. Sledding -- Fiction 3. Wilderness survival -- Fiction

ISBN 978-0-439-02356-6; 0-439-02356-4

LC 2007-11688

As Irish teenager Gráinne anxiously prepares for a reunion with her mother, who abandoned the family years before, Gráinne's half-brothers and their mother take a dog-sledding vacation in Finland.

"The drama and adventure are leavened by generous helpings of Doyle's characteristic charm, laugh-out-loud humor, and wonderful way with words." SLJ

Draanen, Wendelin van

Runaway. Knopf 2006 250p $15.95; lib bdg $17.99

Grades: 6 7 8 9 **Fic**

1. Orphans -- Fiction 2. Homeless persons -- Fiction 3.

Runaway children -- Fiction
ISBN 0-375-83522-9; 0-375-93522-3 lib bdg
LC 2005-33276

After running away from her fifth foster home, Holly, a twelve-year-old orphan, travels across the country, keeping a journal of her experiences and struggle to survive.

"The ending of this taut, powerful story seems possible and deeply hopeful." Booklist

Draper, Sharon M. (Sharon Mills), 1948-

The **Battle** of Jericho. Atheneum Books for Young Readers 2003 297p $16.95; pa $6.99

Grades: 7 8 9 10 **Fic**

1. School stories 2. Clubs -- Fiction 3. Death -- Fiction 4. Cousins -- Fiction
ISBN 0-689-84232-5; 0-689-84233-3 pa
LC 2002-8612

When Jericho is invited to pledge for the Warriors of Distinction, he thinks his life can't get any better. As the most exclusive club in school, the Warriors give the best parties, go out with the hottest girls, and sail through their classes. And when Arielle, one of the finest girls in his class, starts coming on to him once the pledge announcements are made, Jericho is determined to do anything to become a member.

"This title is a compelling read that drives home important lessons about making choices." SLJ

Other titles in this series are:
Just another hero (2009)
November blues (2007)

Copper sun; [by] Sharon Draper. Atheneum Books for Young Readers 2006 302p $16.95

Grades: 8 9 10 11 12 **Fic**

1. Slavery -- Fiction 2. African Americans -- Fiction
ISBN 0-689-82181-6
LC 2005-05540

Two fifteen-year-old girls—one a slave and the other an indentured servant—escape their Carolina plantation and try to make their way to Fort Moses, Florida, a Spanish colony that gives sanctuary to slaves.

"This action-packed, multifaceted, character-rich story describes the shocking realities of the slave trade and plantation life while portraying the perseverance, resourcefulness, and triumph of the human spirit." Booklist

Double Dutch. Atheneum Bks. for Young Readers 2002 183p $16; pa $4.99

Grades: 6 7 8 9 **Fic**

1. Friendship -- Fiction 2. Rope skipping -- Fiction 3. African Americans -- Fiction
ISBN 0-689-84230-9; 0-689-84231-7 pa
LC 00-50247

Three eighth-grade friends, preparing for the International Double Dutch Championship jump rope competition in their home town of Cincinnati, Ohio, cope with Randy's missing father, Delia's inability to read, and Yo Yo's encounter with the class bullies

"Teens will like the high-spirited, authentic dialogue . . . the honest look at tough issues, and the team workout scenes that show how sports can transform young lives." Booklist

★ **Fire** from the rock. Dutton Children's Books 2007 229p $16.99

Grades: 6 7 8 9 **Fic**

1. School stories 2. Race relations -- Fiction 3. African Americans -- Fiction
ISBN 978-0-525-47720-4; 0-525-47720-9
LC 2006-102952

In 1957, Sylvia Patterson's life is disrupted by the impending integration of Little Rock's Central High when she is selected to be one of the first black students to attend the previously all white school.

"This historical fiction novel is a must have. It keeps the reader engaged with vivid depictions of a time that most young people can only imagine." Voice Youth Advocates

Panic; Sharon Draper. 1st ed. Atheneum Books for Young Readers 2013 272 p. (hardcover) $17.99

Grades: 9 10 11 12 **Fic**

1. Kidnapping -- Fiction 2. Ballet dancers -- Fiction 3. Dance -- Fiction 4. Sexual abuse -- Fiction 5. African Americans -- Fiction
ISBN 1442408960; 9781442408968; 9781442408982
LC 2012016339

In this book, "after teenage Diamond makes a disastrously foolish mistake, she is abducted and finds herself in terrible danger. Will she survive? Will her life ever be the same? Told from multiple points of view, 'Panic' is not only Diamond's story but also that of three of her friends, all of them students at the Crystal Pointe Dance Academy." (Booklist)

Tears of a tiger. Atheneum Pubs. 1994 162p $16.95; pa $5.99

Grades: 7 8 9 10 **Fic**

1. Death -- Fiction 2. Suicide -- Fiction 3. African Americans -- Fiction
ISBN 0-689-31878-2; 0-689-80698-1 pa
LC 94-10278

The death of African American high school basketball star Rob Washington in a drunk driving accident leads to the suicide of his friend Andy, who was driving the car

"The story emerges through newspaper articles, journal entries, homework assignments, letters, and conversations that give the book immediacy; the teenage conversational idiom is contemporary and well written. Andy's perceptions of the racism directed toward young black males . . . will be recognized by African American YAs." Booklist

Dray, Stephanie

Lily of the Nile; Berkley trade pbk. ed.; Berkley Books 2011 351p pa $15

Grades: 9 10 11 12 **Fic**

1. Queens 2. Emperors 3. Rome -- History -- Fiction
ISBN 978-0-425-23855-4
LC 2010-37153

This book focuses on "Cleopatra Selene, daughter of Antony and Cleopatra. The novel follows Selene's story from her parents' suicides, through the years that she and her brothers, Alexander and Philadelphus, were wards of Octavian, living in his sister's home until her betrothal to Juba II. . . . Dray imbues her work with meticulously researched details of Roman life, historical figures, and political upheaval.

Add magical realism and controversial goddess-worship, and you have a novel that will appeal to readers on many levels." Libr J

Duble, Kathleen Benner

Hearts of iron. Margaret K. McElderry Books 2006 248p $15.95

Grades: 6 7 8 9 **Fic**

1. Iron industry -- Fiction

ISBN 1-4169-0850-1

LC 2005-29258

In early 1800s Connecticut, fifteen-year-old Lucy tries to decide whether to marry her childhood friend who unhappily toils at the Mt. Riga iron furnace or the young man from Boston who has come to work in her father's store.

"Well-written historical fiction with a unique setting and a touch of mystery, Lucy's story will both inform and entertain readers." SLJ

Phantoms in the snow. Scholastic Press 2011 226p $17.99

Grades: 6 7 8 9 **Fic**

1. Uncles -- Fiction 2. Orphans -- Fiction 3. Pacifism -- Fiction 4. Soldiers -- Fiction 5. Military bases -- Fiction 6. World War, 1939-1945 -- Italy -- Fiction

ISBN 978-0-545-19770-0; 0-545-19770-8

LC 2010016898

In 1944, fifteen-year-old Noah Garrett, recently orphaned, is sent to live at Camp Hale, Colorado, with an uncle he has never met, and there he finds his pacifist views put to the test.

"Duble has created a likable character in Noah, whose struggles to find out who he is and where he belongs in a world at war are convincingly portrayed and realistically resolved." Kirkus

Quest; 1st ed.; Margaret K. McElderry Books 2008 240p $16.99

Grades: 7 8 9 10 **Fic**

1. Spies -- Fiction 2. Explorers -- Fiction 3. Seafaring life -- Fiction

ISBN 978-1-4169-3386-1; 1-4169-3386-7

LC 2006102712

Relates events of explorer Henry Hudson's final voyage in 1602 from four points of view, those of his seventeen-year-old son aboard ship, a younger son left in London, a crewmember, and a young English woman acting as a spy in Holland in hopes of restoring honor to her family's name.

"The author's skillful juxtaposition of these four narratives creates an absorbing work of historical fiction that manages to incorporate the viewpoints of explorers, investors, sailors, governments, family members, and neighbors of those who played a part in this fascinating era." SLJ

Dubosarsky, Ursula

★ The **golden** day; by Ursula Dubosarsky. Candlewick 2013 160 p. $15.99

Grades: 7 8 9 10 **Fic**

1. Mystery fiction 2. Friendship -- Fiction 3. Missing persons -- Fiction

ISBN 0763663999; 9780763663995; 9781742374710

LC 2012452201

In this novel by Ursula Dubosarsky "eleven schoolgirls embrace their own chilling history when their teacher abruptly goes missing on a field trip. Who was the mysterious poet they had met in the Garden? What actually happened in the seaside cave that day? And most important—who can they tell about it?" (Publisher's note)

"Spare and well written, this slim novel covers the days following a teacher's disappearance during a class outing. Eleven girls must make their way back to school where they are determined to keep their teacher's rendezvous with the local park's gardener a secret. The book's chilling atmosphere and mature tone are best suited for older readers." (Horn Book)

Dudley, David L.

Caleb's wars. Clarion Books 2011 263p $16.99

Grades: 7 8 9 10 **Fic**

1. Georgia -- Fiction 2. Germans -- Fiction 3. Family life -- Fiction 4. Segregation -- Fiction 5. Race relations -- Fiction 6. Prisoners of war -- Fiction 7. African Americans -- Fiction 8. World War, 1939-1945 -- Fiction

ISBN 978-0-547-23997-2; 0-547-23997-1

LC 2011009644

Fifteen-year-old Caleb's courageous commitment to justice grows as he faces a power struggle with his father, fights to keep both his temper and self-respect in dealing with whites, and puzzles over the German prisoners of war brought to his rural Georgia community during World War II.

"Caleb is compelling and believable, and Dudley's rich writing is impressive, clearly showing the various wars black Americans were fighting in the 1940s, both abroad and closer to home." SLJ

Duey, Kathleen

Sacred scars. Atheneum Books for Young Readers 2009 554p il (A resurrection of magic) $17.99

Grades: 7 8 9 10 **Fic**

1. School stories 2. Fantasy fiction 3. Magic -- Fiction

ISBN 978-0-689-84095-1; 0-689-84095-0

LC 2008-56044

In alternate chapters, Sadima works to free captive boys forced to copy documents in the caverns of Limori, and Hahp makes a pact with the remaining students of a wizards' academy in hopes that all will survive their training, as both learn valuable lessons about loyalty.

"The text so successfully portrays Hahp's experience in this grueling, cold-blooded wizard 'academy'—isolation, starvation, abuse and constant, unsolvable puzzles—that readers may absorb his strain, confusion and desolation themselves. . . . Absorbing and unwaveringly suspenseful." Kirkus

Skin hunger. Atheneum Books for Young Readers 2007 357p (Resurrection of magic) hardcover o.p. pa $9.99

Grades: 7 8 9 10 **Fic**

1. Fantasy fiction 2. Magic -- Fiction

ISBN 978-0-689-84093-7; 0-689-84093-4; 978-0-689-84094-4 pa; 0-689-84094-2 pa

LC 2006-34819

In alternate chapters, Sadima travels from her farm home to the city and becomes assistant to a heartless man who is trying to restore knowledge of magic to the world, and a group of boys fights to survive in the academy that has resulted from his efforts.

This is a "compelling new fantasy. . . . Duey sweeps readers up in the page-turning excitement." Horn Book

Followed by: Scared scars (2009)

Duncan, Lois

I know what you did last summer. Little, Brown 1973 199p hardcover o.p. pa $6.50

Grades: 7 8 9 10 11 12 **Fic**

1. Mystery fiction

ISBN 0-440-22844-1 pa

ALA YALSA Margaret A. Edwards Award (1992)

Four teen-agers who have desperately tried to conceal their responsibility for a hit-and-run accident are pursued by a mystery figure seeking revenge.

This book "has vivid characterization, good balance, and the boding sense of impending danger that adds excitement to the best mystery stories." Bull Cent Child Books

★ **Killing** Mr. Griffin. Dell 1990 223p hardcover o.p. pa $6.50

Grades: 7 8 9 10 **Fic**

1. School stories 2. Kidnapping -- Fiction

ISBN 0-440-94515-1 pa

First published 1978 by Little, Brown

ALA YALSA Margaret A. Edwards Award (1992)

A teenager casually suggests playing a cruel trick on the English teacher, but did he intend to end it with murder?

The author's "skillful plotting builds layers of tension that draws readers into the eye of the conflict. The ending is nicely handled in a manner which provides relief without removing any of the chilling implications." SLJ

Locked in time. Little, Brown 1985 210p hardcover o.p. pa $6.50

Grades: 7 8 9 10 **Fic**

1. Mystery fiction

ISBN 0-316-19555-3; 0-440-94942-4 pa

LC 85-23

This "is the story of a domineering mother, Lisette, and her two teenage children, Gabe and Josie, who have all drunk from the cup of eternal youth. Seventeen-year-old Nore Robbins goes to visit her father, Charles, and her new stepfamily, Lisette, Gabe and Josie, at Lisette's beautiful old estate deep in the Louisiana bayou country. Nore discovers her stepfamily's secret and, in an attempt to expose this knowledge, becomes Lisette's target for death. . . . Grades seven to ten." (SLJ)

"The writing style is smooth, the characters strongly developed, and the plot, which has excellent pace and momentum, is an adroit blending of fantasy and realism." Bull Cent Child Books

Stranger with my face. Little, Brown 1981 250p hardcover o.p. pa $8.95

Grades: 7 8 9 10 **Fic**

1. Twins -- Fiction 2. Supernatural -- Fiction

ISBN 0-440-98356-8

LC 81-8299

"There are small things, at first—a face in the mirror, a presence in an empty room, a beckoning figure on treacherous rocks—that portend 17-year-old Laurie's confrontation with the astral projection of her previously unknown, malevolent identical twin. . . . The jealous twin, Lia, pursues her, prodding her to explore astral projection so that Lia may enter Laurie's body." SLJ

"The ghostly Lia is deliciously evil; the idea of astral projection—Lia's method of travel—is novel; the island setting is vivid; and the relationships among the young people are realistic in the smoothly written supernatural tale." Horn Book

Dunkle, Clare B.

By these ten bones. Henry Holt 2005 229p $16.95

Grades: 7 8 9 10 **Fic**

1. Horror fiction 2. Scotland -- Fiction 3. Werewolves -- Fiction

ISBN 0-8050-7496-1

LC 2004-52359

After a mysterious young wood carver with a horrifying secret arrives in her small Scottish town, Maddie gains his trust – and his heart – and seeks a way to save both him and her townspeople from an ancient evil.

"Readers with a taste for fantasy rooted in folklore and history, and a stomach for grisly horror, will happily roam the mist-shrouded Highlands of Dunkle's latest creation." Booklist

The **house** of dead maids; illustrations by Patrick Arrasmith. Henry Holt and Co. 2010 146p il $15.99

Grades: 8 9 10 11 12 **Fic**

1. Ghost stories 2. Orphans -- Fiction 3. Great Britain -- Fiction 4. Household employees -- Fiction

ISBN 978-0-8050-9116-8; 0-8050-9116-5

LC 2009-50769

Eleven-year-old Tabby Aykroyd, who would later serve as housekeeper for thirty years to the Brontë sisters, is taken from an orphanage to a ghost-filled house, where she and a wild young boy are needed for a pagan ritual.

"The author manages to stay true to the essence of Wuthering Heights while creating a deliciously chilling ghost story that stands on its own. Readers do not have to be at all familiar with Brontë's gothic story of destructive love to be scared out of their wits by this one: cognoscenti, though, will recognize a few sly nods to the original." Bull Cent Child Books

Dunlap, Susanne Emily

In the shadow of the lamp; [by] Susanne Dunlap. Bloomsbury Children's Books 2011 293p $16.99

Grades: 7 8 9 10 **Fic**

1. Nurses -- Fiction 2. Crimean War, 1853-1856 -- Fiction

ISBN 978-1-59990-565-5; 1-59990-565-5

LC 2010-21158

Sixteen-year-old Molly Fraser works as a nurse with Florence Nightingale during the Crimean War to earn a salary to help her family survive in nineteenth-century England.

"Dunlap has written a story with roots deep in research about Florence Nightingale and the women who served as nurses during the Crimean War. . . . [She] . . . delivers another extraordinary novel that feels relevant even today." Libr Media Connect

The **musician's** daughter; [by] Susanne Dunlap. Bloomsbury 2009 322p $16.99

Grades: 8 9 10 11 12 **Fic**

1. Composers 2. Mystery fiction 3. Gypsies -- Fiction 4. Homicide -- Fiction 5. Musicians -- Fiction 6. Vienna (Austria) -- Fiction

ISBN 978-1-59990-332-3; 1-59990-332-6

LC 2008-30307

In eighteenth-century Vienna, Austria, fifteen-year-old Theresa seeks a way to help her mother and brother financially while investigating the murder of her father, a renowned violinist in Haydn's orchestra at the court of Prince Esterhazy, after his body is found near a gypsy camp.

"Dunlap skillfully builds suspense until the final page. . . . Readers will root for courageous Theresa through the exciting intrigue even as they absorb deeper messages about music and art's power to lift souls and inspire change." Booklist

Dunmore, Helen

Ingo. HarperCollins Pubs. 2005 328p $16.99; lib bdg $17.89

Grades: 6 7 8 9 **Fic**

1. Mermaids and mermen -- Fiction

ISBN 978-0-06-081852-4; 0-06-081852-2; 978-0-06-081853-1 lib bdg; 0-06-081853-0 lib bdg

LC 2005-19079

As they search for their missing father near their Cornwall home, Sapphy and her brother Conor learn about their family's connection to the domains of air and of water.

"Strong character development combines with an engaging plot and magical elements to make this a fine choice for fantasy readers, who will look forward to the next installments in this planned trilogy." SLJ

Other titles about Sapphire are:

The tide knot (2008)

The deep (2009)

Durst, Sarah Beth

Ice. Margaret K. McElderry Books 2009 308p $16.99

Grades: 7 8 9 10 **Fic**

1. Fairy tales 2. Polar bear -- Fiction 3. Scientists -- Fiction 4. Supernatural -- Fiction 5. Arctic regions -- Fiction

ISBN 978-1-4169-8643-0; 1-4169-8643-X

LC 2009-8618

A modern-day retelling of "East o' the Sun, West o' the Moon" in which eighteen-year-old Cassie learns that her grandmother's fairy tale is true when a Polar Bear King comes to claim her for his bride and she must decide whether to go with him and save her long-lost mother, or continue helping her father with his research

"Told in a descriptive style that perfectly captures the changing settings, Durst's novel is a page-turner that readers who enjoy adventure mixed with fairy-tale romance will find hard to put down." Booklist

Vessel; Sarah Beth Durst. Margaret K. McElderry Books 2012 424 p. (hardcover) $16.99

Grades: 7 8 9 10 **Fic**

1. Deserts -- Fiction 2. Fantasy fiction 3. Adventure fiction 4. Gods and goddesses 5. Fantasy 6. Survival -- Fiction 7. Goddesses -- Fiction 8. Fate and fatalism -- Fiction

ISBN 1442423765; 9781442423763; 9781442423787

LC 2011044691

In this book by Sarah Beth Durst, "Liyana has trained all her life to be the vessel for her desert tribe's goddess Bayla. . . . "Bayla never shows up, but the trickster god Korbyn appears in human form and gives Liyana some startling news: the gods have all been imprisoned in false vessels, and he and Liyana must retrieve the various tribes' unsuccessful vessels, figure out where the deities are being held, and rescue them." (Bulletin of the Center for Children's Books)

Edwards, Janet

★ **Earth** girl; by Janet Edwards. Pyr 2013 350 p. (Earth girl trilogy) $17.95

Grades: 9 10 11 12 **Fic**

1. Science fiction 2. People with disabilities -- Fiction 3. Children with disabilities -- Abuse of -- Fiction

ISBN 1616147652; 9781616147655

LC 2012044570

In this young adult novel set in the future, Jarra and other Handicapped are discriminated against by the Norms. "Jarra decides to show them that she is just as good as they are and applies to an off-world college conducting an archaeology dig on the abandoned buildings of New York. Reinventing herself as Jarra Military Kid, JMK watches vids and takes combat lessons. . . . Since she grew up on Earth and has been to the New York digs many times, her skills quickly allow her to shine." (School Library Journal)

"The future that Edwards constructs is creative and the dig descriptions are well thought out... The "person against nature" conflict with unstable dig conditions and solar flares makes a refreshing change." SLJ

★ **Earth** star; Janet Edwards. Pyr, an imprint of Prometheus Books 2014 360 p. (hardback) $17.99

Grades: 7 8 9 10 11 12 **Fic**

1. Children with disabilities -- Abuse of -- Fiction

ISBN 1616148977; 9781616148973

LC 2013040057

"This far-future science-fiction sequel skips tired genre tropes to offer a fresh and thrilling adventure about hazardous archaeological excavation, a mystery in the sky and a potential threat to all of humanity...Nitty-gritty archaeology details are vivid, and easy slang creates color ("Twoing" is dating; "amaz" means amazing). Edwards shows that speculative fiction needn't be dystopic, conspiracy-filled or love-triangled to be riveting and satisfying. Amaz—simply amaz." (Kirkus)

Edwardson, Debby Dahl

★ **Blessing's** bead. Farrar, Straus & Giroux 2009 178p $16.99

Grades: 6 7 8 9 10 **Fic**

1. Inupiat -- Fiction 2. Villages -- Fiction 3. Influenza -- Fiction 4. Alcoholism -- Fiction

ISBN 978-0-374-30805-6; 0-374-30805-5

LC 2008-26726

In 1917, Aaluk leaves for Siberia while her sister Nutaaq remains in their Alaskan village and becomes one of the few survivors of an influenza epidemic, then in 1986, Nunaaq's great-granddaughter leaves her mother due to a different kind of sickness and returns to the village where they were born

"It's the Nutaag's rhythmic, indelible voices—both as steady and elemental as the beat of a drum or a heart—that will move readers most. A unique, powerful debut." Booklist

★ **My** name is not easy. Marshall Cavendish 2011 248p $17.99; e-book $17.99

Grades: 7 8 9 10 **Fic**

1. School stories 2. Native Americans -- Fiction

ISBN 978-0-7614-5980-4; 0-7614-5980-4; 978-0-7614-6091-6 e-book

LC 2011002108

"Edwardson's skillful use of dialogue and her descriptions of rural Alaska as well as boarding-school life invoke a strong sense of empathy and compassion in readers. . . Edwardson is to be applauded for her depth of research and her ability to portray all sides of the equation in a fair and balanced manner while still creating a very enjoyable read." SLJ

Efaw, Amy

After. Viking 2009 350p $17.99

Grades: 7 8 9 10 **Fic**

1. School stories 2. Infants -- Fiction 3. Pregnancy -- Fiction 4. Abandoned children -- Fiction

ISBN 978-0-670-01183-4; 0-670-01183-5

LC 2010-275195

In complete denial that she is pregnant, straight-A student and star athlete Devon Davenport leaves her baby in the trash to die, and after the baby is discovered, Devon is accused of attempted murder.

"Authentic dialogue and pithy writing allow teens to feel every prick of panic, embarrassment and fear." Kirkus

Battle dress. HarperCollins Pubs. 2000 291p hardcover o.p. lib bdg $16.89

Grades: 7 8 9 10 **Fic**

1. Military education -- Fiction 2. Women in the armed forces -- Fiction 3. Military education -- New York (State) -- West Point

ISBN 0-06-028411-0 lib bdg; 0-06-053520-2

LC 99-34516

As a newly arrived freshman at West Point, seventeen-year-old Andi finds herself gaining both confidence and self esteem as she struggles to get through the grueling six weeks of new cadet training known as the Beast

"This book by a West Point graduate is a gripping, hard-to-put-down look at a young woman's struggle to succeed in a traditionally all-male environment." Voice Youth Advocates

Egan, Laury A.

The **Outcast** Oracle; Laury A. Egan. Humanist Press 2013 205 p. $13.46

Grades: 8 9 10 11 12 **Fic**

1. Fraud -- Fiction 2. Orphans -- Fiction 3. Grandfathers -- Fiction

ISBN 0931779367; 9780931779367

In this book, by Laury A. Egan, "14-year-old Charlene Beth Whitestone has been deserted by her parents, leaving her in the custody of her grandfather, C.B. Although he loves Charlie, he is a charming con artist. . . . When C.B. suddenly dies, Charlie . . . must use her wits and resourcefulness to . . . [continue] her grandfather's schemes. When a . . . stranger, Blake, arrives, he . . . mounts a lucrative PR campaign, touting Charlie as an 'oracle' and arranging for her to perform miracles." (Publisher's note)

"In this brilliantly written novel, a girl who lives with her con-artist grandfather after her parents have gone wandering hopes to lead a more honest life but must scheme to get by when he dies suddenly...Hoping to avoid an orphanage, Charlie hides Grandpa's body and stashes the cash...Egan tells the story in Charlie's first-person countrified style, but with True Grit–style lofty grammar and sentence structure, in keeping with Charlie's abundant talent. It's this highly literary, easily accessible writing that lifts this story to the very top of the heap. Simply delicious fun from start to finish." (Kirkus)

Egloff, Z.

Leap. Bywater Books 2013 256 p. $14.95

Grades: 9 10 11 12 **Fic**

1. Summer -- Fiction 2. Teenagers -- Fiction 3. Family secrets -- Fiction 4. Life change events -- Fiction

ISBN 1612940234; 9781612940236

This novel, by Z. Egloff, is set in "Summer 1979. Rowan Marks is done with high school. Next comes college. And in between there's a yawning gulf--he last carefree summer vacation. . . . But Rowan's older brother Ben is smoking way too much pot. Her best friend Danny is in love with her. And Catherine, the new girl in their small Ohio town, rubs her the wrong way. . . . Catherine steals her heart, Danny falls out with her, and Ben crashes the family car, ripping the family secrets bare." (Publisher's note)

Ehrenberg, Pamela

★ **Ethan,** suspended; written by Pamela Ehrenberg. Eerdmans Books for Young Readers 2007 266p $16

Grades: 7 8 9 10 **Fic**

1. Jews -- Fiction 2. Grandparents -- Fiction 3. Race relations -- Fiction

ISBN 978-0-8028-5324-0

LC 2006032697

After a school suspension and his parents' separation, Ethan is sent to live with his grandparents in Washington, D.C., which is worlds apart from his home in a Philadelphia suburb.

"Ehrenberg focuses on themes of race and class without sounding preachy. . . . Best of all are the portraits of [Ethan's] scrappy Jewish grandparents." Booklist

Tillmon County fire. Eerdmans Books for Young Readers 2009 175p pa $9
Grades: 9 10 11 12 **Fic**
1. Arson -- Fiction 2. Hate crimes -- Fiction 3. West Virginia -- Fiction 4. Community life -- Fiction
ISBN 978-0-8028-5345-5; 0-8028-5345-5
LC 2008-22102

An act of arson commited as an anti-gay hate crime affects the lives of several teenagers from a small town.

"This cleverly plotted and well-crafted story of abuse and vengeance is told in pieces from the varying perspectives of a half-dozen teens, and Ehrenberg uses intertwining chapters to explore their motives and desires. . . . The vividly drawn setting, almost a character in itself, embraces an important message all readers need to hear." SLJ

Ehrenhaft, Daniel

Friend is not a verb; a novel. HarperTeen 2010 241p $16.99
Grades: 7 8 9 10 **Fic**
1. Siblings -- Fiction 2. Rock music -- Fiction 3. Family life -- Fiction 4. Bands (Music) -- Fiction 5. New York (N.Y.) -- Fiction
ISBN 978-0-06-113106-6; 0-06-113106-7
LC 2009-44006

While sixteen-year-old Hen's family and friends try to make his supposed dreams of becoming a rock star come true, he deals with the reality of being in a band with an ex-girlfriend, a friendship that may become love, and his older sister's mysterious disappearance and reappearance.

"Offbeat characters, an intriguing mystery, and a sweet romance make Ehrenhaft's . . . coming-of-age story stand out. . . . The mystery—and romance—wrap up rather neatly, but readers should be impressed by the clever surprise ending." Publ Wkly

Elkeles, Simone

How to ruin my teenage life. Flux 2007 281p pa $8.95
Grades: 7 8 9 10 11 12 **Fic**
1. Jews -- Fiction 2. Israelis -- Fiction 3. Chicago (Ill.) -- Fiction 4. Father-daughter relationship -- Fiction
ISBN 978-0-7387-0961-1; 0-7387-1019-9
LC 2007005535

Living with her Israeli father in Chicago, seventeen-year-old Amy Nelson-Barak feels like a walking disaster, worried about her "non-boyfriend" in the Israeli army, her mother, new stepfather, and the baby they are expecting, a new boy named Nathan who has moved into her apartment building and goes to her school, and whether or not she really is the selfish snob that Nathan says she is.

"This book has laugh-out-loud moments. . . . Amy's thoughtfulness and depth raise this book above most of the chick-lit genre." Voice Youth Advocates

Other titles in this series are:
How to ruin a summer vacation (2006)
How to ruin your boyfriend's reputation (2009)

Perfect chemistry. Walker 2009 360p $16.99; pa $9.99
Grades: 9 10 11 12 **Fic**
1. School stories 2. Gangs -- Fiction 3. Social classes -- Fiction 4. Dating (Social customs) -- Fiction
ISBN 978-0-8027-9823-7; 0-8027-9823-3; 978-0-8027-9822-0 pa; 0-8027-9822-5 pa
LC 2008-13769

When wealthy, seemingly perfect Brittany and Alex Fuentes, a gang member from the other side of town, develop a relationship after Alex discovers that Brittany is not exactly who she seems to be, they must face the disapproval of their schoolmates—and others.

"Brittany's controlling parents and sister with cerebral palsy are well drawn, but it is Elkeles rendition of Alex and his life that is particularly vivid. Sprinkling his speech with Spanish, his gruff but tender interactions with his family and friends feel completely genuine. . . . This is a novel that could be embraced by male and female readers in equal measure." Booklist

Followed by Rules of attraction (2010)

Rules of attraction. Walker & Co. 2010 326p $16.99
Grades: 9 10 11 12 **Fic**
1. School stories 2. Drug traffic -- Fiction 3. Mexican Americans -- Fiction
ISBN 978-0-8027-2085-6
LC 2009-49235

Sequel to Perfect chemistry (2009)

Living on the University of Colorado-Boulder campus with his older brother Alex, a college student and ex-gang member, high school senior Carlos is not ready to give up his wild ways until he meets a shy classmate named Kiara and becomes unwillingly involved in a drug ring.

The author "delivers a steamy page-turner bound to make teens swoon." SLJ

Ellen, Laura

Blind spot; Laura Ellen. Houghton Mifflin Harcourt 2012 332 p. $16.99
Grades: 9 10 11 12 **Fic**
1. Mystery fiction 2. Homicide -- Fiction 3. Teenagers -- Fiction 4. Blind -- Fiction 5. High schools -- Fiction 6. Mystery and detective stories 7. People with disabilities -- Fiction
ISBN 0547763441; 9780547763446
LC 2012028976

Author Laura Ellen presents a murder mystery. "When AP student Roz discovers she's in a special ed class because of her visual 'disability,' she is furious. . . . Everything about Life Skills is awful, especially junkie Tricia, who, on the first day of school, somehow manages to get Roz to buy pot for her with the help of hottie Jonathan Webb. This isn't all bad, as soon Jonathan is . . . taking her to parties. Meanwhile, Roz . . . slowly comes to appreciate her fellow Life Skills classmates. And then Tricia goes missing after a calamitous party and is discovered dead months later." (Kirkus)

Elliot, Laura

Across a war-tossed sea; L.M. Elliot. Disney-Hyperion Books. 2014 247p $16.99

Grades: 7 8 9 10 **Fic**

1. British — United States — Fiction; 2. Brothers — Fiction; 3. World War, 1939-1945 — United States — Fiction; 4. Virginia — Fiction

ISBN: 1423157559; 9781423157557

LC 2013035303

"This follow-up to Under a War-Torn Sky (2001) picks up the story of British brothers Charles, 14, and Wesley, 10, as they learn to live as Yanks in Virginia following their escape from the firebombings and U-boat disasters of the UK. As the battle in Europe continues to rage, Charles struggles to understand American culture while looking out for Wesley, whose usually cheery nature is punctuated with traumatic memories. The book feels like it could have been written 50 years ago—and that's not a bad thing—as Elliott leads us through a series of misadventures and straight-up adventures as the boys go hunting, hold a haunted house, contribute to the war effort, and even conduct a few acts of outright heroism. Serious issues of intolerance (religious freedom in Europe, racism in America, cruelty to German POWs) permeate the story without overwhelming it, making this a breezy and enlightening read." Booklist

Elliott, Patricia

The **Pale** Assassin. Holiday House 2009 336p $17.95

Grades: 7 8 9 10 **Fic**

1. Adventure fiction 2. Siblings -- Fiction 3. France -- History -- 1789-1799, Revolution -- Fiction

ISBN 978-0-8234-2250-0; 0-8234-2250-X

LC 2009-7554

In early 1790s Paris, as the Revolution gains momentum, young and sheltered Eugenie de Boncoeur finds it difficult to tell friend from foe as she and the royalist brother she relies on become the focus of "le Fantome," the sinister spymaster with a long-held grudge against their family.

"The best aspect of this excellent work of historical fiction is Eugenie herself. Her gradual coming of age and growing political awareness provides resonant depth to what becomes a highly suspenseful survival tale." Booklist

Followed by: The traitor's smile (2011)

The **traitor's** smile. Holiday House 2011 304p $17.95

Grades: 7 8 9 10 **Fic**

1. Adventure fiction 2. Cousins -- Fiction 3. France -- History -- 1789-1799, Revolution -- Fiction

ISBN 978-0-8234-2361-3; 0-8234-2361-1

Sequel to: The Pale Assassin (2009)

First published 2010 in the United Kingdom

As the French Revolutin rages around her, wealthy and beautiful Eugenie de Boncoeur is no longer safe in her own country. She flees the bloody streeets of Paris for her cousin Hetta's house in England, narrowly excaping the clutches of the evil Pale Assassin, who is determined to force her to marry him.

Ellis, Ann Dee

Everything is fine. Little, Brown and Co. Books for Young Readers 2009 154p il $16.99

Grades: 6 7 8 9 10 **Fic**

1. Mothers -- Fiction 2. Bereavement -- Fiction 3. Family life -- Fiction 4. Depression (Psychology) -- Fiction

ISBN 978-0-316-01364-2; 0-316-01364-1

LC 2008-5847

When her father leaves for a job out of town, Mazzy is left at home to try to cope with her mother, who has been severely depressed since the death of Mazzy's baby sister.

"What makes [this book] so extraordinary is the narrative device that Ellis employs to searing effect. . . . [This] is a story so painful you want to read it with your eyes closed. It is a stunning novel." Voice Youth Advocates

★ **This** is what I did. Little, Brown 2007 157p $16.99

Grades: 6 7 8 9 **Fic**

1. School stories 2. Bullies -- Fiction

ISBN 978-0-316-01363-5; 0-316-01363-3

LC 2006-01388

Bullied because of an incident in his past, eighth-grader Logan is unhappy at his new school and has difficulty relating to others until he meets a quirky girl and a counselor who believe in him.

"Part staccato prose, part transcript, this haunting first novel will grip readers right from the start. . . . A particularly attractive book design incorporates small drawings between each segment of text." Publ Wkly

Ellis, Deborah

Bifocal; [by] Deborah Ellis and Eric Walters. Fitzhenry & Whiteside 2007 280p $18.95; pa $12.95

Grades: 7 8 9 10 **Fic**

1. School stories 2. Muslims -- Fiction 3. Prejudices -- Fiction

ISBN 978-1-55455-036-4; 1-55455-036-X; 978-1-55455-062-3 pa; 1-55455-062-9 pa

When a Muslim boy is arrested at a high school on suspicion of terrorist affiliations, growing racial tensions divide the student population.

"The story is told in the alternating voices of two students. . . . Their individual struggles to understand the flaring prejudice and their journeys toward self-discovery are subtle and authentic. . . . This is a story that will leave readers looking at their schools and themselves with new eyes." Booklist

My name is Parvana. Groundwood Books/House of Anansi Press 2012 201 p. $16.95

Grades: 5 6 7 8 **Fic**

1. Afghanistan -- Fiction 2. Interrogation -- Fiction 3. Women -- Afghanistan -- Fiction

ISBN 1554982979; 9781554982974

In this novel by Deborah Ellis "15-year-old Parvana is imprisoned and interrogated as a suspected terrorist in Afghanistan. . . . Parvana's captors" read "aloud the words in her notebook to decide if the angry written sentiments of a teenage girl can be evidence of guilt. . . The interrogation, the words of the notebook and the effective third-person narration combine for a . . . portrait of a girl and her country." (Kirkus Reviews)

★ **No** safe place. Groundwood Books/House of Anansi Press 2010 205p $16.95

Grades: 9 10 11 12 **Fic**

1. Iraq -- Fiction 2. France -- Fiction 3. Refugees -- Fiction 4. Great Britain -- Fiction

ISBN 978-0-88899-973-3

Fifteen-year-old Abdul, having lost everyone he loves, journeys from Baghdad to a migrant community in Calais where he sneaks aboard a boat bound for England, not knowing it carries a cargo of heroin, and when the vessel is involved in a skirmish and the pilot killed, it is up to Abdul and three other young stowaways to complete the journey.

"Ellis deftly uses flashbacks to fill in the backstories of each character, reminding readers of how they can never really know where people are coming from emotionally. Her writing is highly accessible, and yet understated. Orphans of the world and victims of human trafficking need all the press they can get, and this book does a great job of introducing the topic and allowing young people to see beyond the headlines of 'Another illegal accidentally dies in Chunnel.'" SLJ

Ellison, Kate

The **butterfly** clues; Kate Ellison. Egmont USA 2012 325p.

Grades: 9 10 11 12 **Fic**

1. Crime -- Fiction 2. Grief -- Fiction 3. Cleveland (Ohio) -- Fiction 4. Compulsive behavior -- Fiction 5. Death -- Fiction 6. Murder -- Fiction 7. Emotional problems -- Fiction 8. Mystery and detective stories 9. Obsessive-compulsive disorder -- Fiction

ISBN 9781606842638; 9781606842683

LC 2011024549

In this book "a girl is killed only steps away from where . . . [Lo is] walking, [and] she becomes obsessed with finding the culprit and motive. . . . The search leads her into Neverland. . . . Flynt, a friendly artist, is her guide through this underworld as she teases out a web of connections between the murdered girl, a shady strip club, and, ultimately, her brother, a runaway whose death is shrouded in mystery for most of the book." (Bulletin of the Center for Children's Books)

Ellsworth, Loretta

★ **Unforgettable.** Walker Books for Young Readers 2011 256p $16.99

Grades: 6 7 8 9 **Fic**

1. School stories 2. Memory -- Fiction 3. Synesthesia -- Fiction 4. Dating (Social customs) -- Fiction

ISBN 978-0-8027-2305-5; 0-8027-2305-5

LC 2010049590

When Baxter Green was three years old he developed a condition that causes him to remember absolutely everything, and now that he is fifteen, he and his mother have moved to Minnesota to escape her criminal boyfriend and, Baxter hopes, to reconnect with a girl he has been thinking about since kindergarten.

"A lot is going here—an exploration of of synesthesia and memory, a crime story, an environmental drama, family relationships and a sweet, earnest love story. . . . But everything works." Kirkus

Elston, Ashley

The **rules** for disappearing; Ashley Elston. 1st ed. Hyperion 2013 320 p. (reinforced) $16.99

Grades: 7 8 9 10 11 12 **Fic**

1. Witnesses -- Fiction 2. Friendship -- Fiction 3. Dysfunctional families -- Fiction 4. High schools -- Fiction 5. Moving, Household -- Fiction 6. Natchitoches (La.) -- Fiction 7. Witness protection programs -- Fiction

ISBN 1423168976; 9781423168973

LC 2012035122

In this book by Ashley Elston, "seventeen-year-old Meg Jones . . . and her family are in the witness protection program, and they've changed towns six times in less than a year. . . . Meg's mother is an alcoholic, her father is depressed and secretive, and her 11-year-old sister is having trouble coping with all of the change. Fed up, Meg wants out of the program and will do anything to save her family, including digging up what her father did to get them into this mess." (Publishers Weekly)

"The fresh first-person narration serves the story well, providing grounding in reality as events spin out of control. Though the plot may seem a bit far-fetched at times, the realistic setting, believable romance and spunky protagonist will make this one worth the trip for mystery and romance fans." Kirkus

Emond, Stephen

Happyface. Little, Brown and Co. 2010 307p il $16.99

Grades: 7 8 9 10 **Fic**

1. School stories 2. Diaries -- Fiction 3. Divorce -- Fiction 4. Dating (Social customs) -- Fiction

ISBN 978-0-316-04100-3; 0-316-04100-9

LC 2008-47386

After going through traumatic times, a troubled, socially awkward teenager moves to a new school where he tries to reinvent himself.

"The illustrations range from comics to more fleshed-out drawings. Just like Happyface's writing, they can be whimsical, thoughtful, boyishly sarcastic, off-the-cuff, or achingly beautiful." Publ Wkly

★ **Winter** town; Story and art by Stephen Emond. Little, Brown 2011 336p il $17.99

Grades: 7 8 9 **Fic**

1. Love stories 2. Teenagers -- Fiction 3. High school students -- Fiction 4. Cartoons and caricatures -- Fiction

ISBN 9780316133326; 978-0-316-13332-6

LC 2011012966

Evan and Lucy, childhood best friends who grew apart after years of seeing one another only during Christmas break, begin a romance at age seventeen but his choice to mindlessly follow his father's plans for an Ivy League education rather than becoming the cartoonist he longs to be, and her more destructive choices in the wake of family problems, pull them apart.

This is a "remarkable illustrated work of contemporary fiction. . . . Interspersed throughout are both realistic illustrations and drawings of a comic strip being created by Evan and Lucy; these black-and-white, almost chibi-style panels form an effective parallel with the plot and appeal mightily on their own. Compelling, honest and true—this musing about art and self-discovery, replete with pitch-perfect dialogue, will have wide appeal." Kirkus

Engdahl, Sylvia Louise

★ **Enchantress** from the stars; foreword by Lois Lowry. Firebird 2003 288p pa $6.99

Grades: 7 8 9 10 11 12 **Fic**

1. Science fiction

ISBN 0-14-250037-2

A reissue of the title first published 1970 by Atheneum Pubs.

A Newbery Medal honor book, 1971

When young Elana unexpectedly joins the team leaving the spaceship to study the planet Andrecia, she becomes an integral part of an adventure involving three very different civilizations, each one centered on the third planet from the star in its own solar system

"Emphasis is on the intricate pattern of events rather than on characterization, and readers will find fascinating symbolism—and philosophical parallels to what they may have observed or thought. The book is completely absorbing and should have a wider appeal than much science fiction." Horn Book

Engle, Margarita

★ **Firefly** letters; a suffragette's journey to Cuba. Henry Holt & Co. 2010 151p $16.99

Grades: 7 8 9 10 11 12 **Fic**

1. Authors 2. Novelists 3. Novels in verse 4. Cuba -- Fiction 5. Slavery -- Fiction 6. Sex role -- Fiction

ISBN 978-0-8050-9082-6; 0-8050-9082-7

LC 2009-23445

"This engaging title documents 50-year-old Swedish suffragette and novelist Fredrika Bremer's three-month travels around Cuba in 1851. Based in the home of a wealthy sugar planter, Bremer journeys around the country with her host's teenaged slave Cecilia, who longs for her mother and home in the Congo. Elena, the planter's privileged 12-year-old daughter, begins to accompany them on their trips into the countryside. . . . Using elegant free verse and alternating among each character's point of view, Engle offers powerful glimpses into Cuban life at that time. Along the way, she comments on slavery, the rights of women, and the stark contrast between Cuba's rich and poor." SLJ

Hurricane dancers; the first Caribbean pirate shipwreck. Henry Holt and Co. 2011 145p $16.99

Grades: 6 7 8 9 10 **Fic**

1. Novels in verse 2. Pirates -- Fiction 3. Shipwrecks -- Fiction 4. Caribbean region -- Fiction 5. Native Americans -- West Indies -- Fiction

ISBN 978-0-8050-9240-0; 0-8050-9240-4

LC 2010-11690

This is an "accomplished historical novel in verse set in the Caribbean. . . . The son of a Taíno Indian mother and a Spanish father, [Quebrado] is taken in 1510 from his village on the island that is present-day Cuba and enslaved on a pirate's ship, where a brutal conquistador . . . is held captive for ransom. When a hurricane destroys the boat, Quebrado is pulled from the water by a fisherman, Naridó, whose village welcomes him, but escape from the past proves nearly impossible. . . . Engle fictionalizes historical fact in a powerful, original story. . . . Engle distills the emotion in each episode with potent rhythms, sounds, and original, unforgettable imagery." Booklist

★ The **Lightning** Dreamer; Cuba's Greatest Abolitionist. Margarita Engle. Houghton Mifflin Harcourt 2013 192 p. $16.99

Grades: 6 7 8 9 10 **Fic**

1. Historical fiction 2. Novels in verse 3. Authors -- Fiction 4. Feminists -- Fiction 5. Abolitionists -- Fiction 6. Cuba -- History -- 1810-1899 -- Fiction

ISBN 0547807430; 9780547807430

LC 2013003913

Pura Belpre Author Honor Book (2014)

This book is a "work of historical fiction about Cuban poet, author, antislavery activist and feminist Gertrudis Gómez de Avellaneda. Written in free verse, the story tells of how Tula, which was her childhood nickname, grows up in libraries, which she calls 'a safe place to heal/ and dream . . .,' influenced by the poetry of Jose Maria Heredia." (School Library Journal)

Includes bibliographical references.

Silver people: voices from the Panama Canal; Margarita Engle. Houghton Mifflin Harcourt. 2014 272p $17.99

Grades: 5 6 7 8 **Fic**

1. Novels in verse 2. Racism — Fiction 3. Rain forests —Fiction 4. Segregation — Fiction 5. Panama Canal (Panama) — History — Fiction 6. Migrant labor — Fiction

ISBN: 0544109414; 9780544109414

LC 2013037485

Booklist (March 2014)

An "exploration of the construction of the Panama Canal. . . . Mateo, a 14-year-old Cuban lured by promises of wealth, journeys to Panama only to discover the recruiters' lies and a life of harsh labor. However, through his relationships with Anita, an 'herb girl,' Henry, a black Jamaican worker, and Augusto, a Puerto Rican geologist, Mateo is able to find a place in his new land." (Kirkus Reviews)

"In melodic verses, Engle offers the voices of the dark-skinned workers (known as the 'silver people'), whose back-breaking labor helped build the Panama Canal, along with the perspective of a local girl. Interspersed are occasional echoes from flora and fauna as well as cameo appearances by historical figures. Together, they provide an illuminating picture of the project's ecological sacrifices and human costs." Horn Book

★ **Tropical** secrets; Holocaust refugees in Cuba. Henry Holt 2009 199p $16.95

Grades: 7 8 9 10 11 **Fic**

1. Novels in verse 2. Jews -- Fiction 3. Refugees -- Fiction 4. Holocaust, 1933-1945 -- Fiction

ISBN 978-0-8050-8936-3; 0-8050-8936-5

LC 2008-36782

Escaping from Nazi Germany to Cuba in 1939, a young Jewish refugee dreams of finding his parents again, befriends a local girl with painful secrets of her own, and discovers that the Nazi darkness is never far away.

"Readers who think they might not like a novel in verse will be pleasantly surprised at how quickly and smoothly the story flows. . . . The book will provide great fodder for discussion of the Holocaust, self-reliance, ethnic and religious bias, and more." Voice Youth Advocates

Ephron, Delia

Frannie in pieces; drawings by Chad W. Beckerman. HarperTeen 2007 374p il $16.99; pa $8.99

Grades: 7 8 9 10 **Fic**

1. Puzzles -- Fiction 2. Bereavement -- Fiction 3. Father-daughter relationship -- Fiction

ISBN 978-0-06-074716-9; 0-06-074716-1; 978-0-06-074718-3 pa; 0-06-074718-8 pa

LC 2007-10909

When fifteen-year-old Frannie's father dies, only a mysterious jigsaw puzzle that he leaves behind can help her come to terms with his death.

"This is a tender, moving story dealing with grief and growing up and the power of art to heal." SLJ

The **girl** with the mermaid hair. HarperTeen 2010 312p $16.99

Grades: 7 8 9 10 **Fic**

1. Family life -- Fiction 2. Personal appearance -- Fiction 3. Perfectionism (Personality trait) -- Fiction

ISBN 978-0-06-154260-2; 0-06-154260-1

LC 2009-03061

A vain teenaged girl is obsessed with beauty and perfection until she uncovers a devastating family secret.

"A solid and perceptive realistic drama, this will particularly satisfy readers beginning to reconsider their own familial assumptions." Bull Cent Child Books

Epstein, Robin

God is in the pancakes. Dial Books 2010 265p $16.99

Grades: 7 8 9 10 **Fic**

1. Old age -- Fiction 2. Sisters -- Fiction 3. Religion -- Fiction 4. Euthanasia -- Fiction 5. Dating (Social customs) -- Fiction

ISBN 978-0-8037-3382-4; 0-8037-3382-8

Fifteen-year-old Grace, having turned her back on religion when her father left, now finds herself praying for help with her home and love life, and especially with whether she should help a beloved elderly friend die with dignity.

"Everything comes together in an authentic, breezy read that asks difficult questions and doesn't shy away from direct answers, or the reality that answers may not exist. With well-developed adults and a teen seeking help from God and anyone she perceives as wise, this memorable novel offers food for thought and sustenance for the soul." Booklist

Erdrich, Louise, 1954-

The **last** report on the miracles at Little No Horse; a novel. HarperCollins Pubs. 2001 361p hardcover o.p. pa $14.95

Grades: 9 10 11 12 **Fic**

1. North Dakota -- Fiction 2. Ojibwa Indians -- Fiction 3. Native Americans -- Fiction 4. Catholic Church -- Clergy -- Fiction

ISBN 0-06-018727-1; 0-06-157762-6 pa

LC 00-47198

"Even the small incidents in this novel are moments of tremendous power, stripped of sentimentality or pretension. Erdrich has developed a style that can sound as serious as death or ring with the haunting simplicity of ancient legend." Christ Sci Monit

Erskine, Kathryn

Quaking. Philomel Books 2007 236p $16.99

Grades: 7 8 9 10 **Fic**

1. School stories 2. Patriotism -- Fiction 3. Toleration -- Fiction 4. Family life -- Fiction 5. Society of Friends -- Fiction

ISBN 978-0-399-24774-3; 0-399-24774-2

LC 2006-34563

In a Pennsylvania town where antiwar sentiments are treated with contempt and violence, Matt, a fourteen-year-old girl living with a Quaker family, deals with the demons of her past as she battles bullies of the present, eventually learning to trust in others as well as herself.

"This is a compelling story, which enfolds the political issues into a deeper focus on the characters' personal stories." Booklist

Esckilsen, Erik E.

The **last** mall rat. Houghton Mifflin 2003 182p $15; pa $5.95

Grades: 7 8 9 10 **Fic**

1. Shopping centers and malls -- Fiction

ISBN 0-618-23417-9; 0-618-60896-6 pa

LC 2002-14436

Too young to get a job at the Onion River Mall, fifteen-year-old Mitch earns money from salesclerks to harrass rude shoppers

"Realistic dialogue and a keen sense of what matters to teens will draw them to this quick read." Booklist

Eulberg, Elizabeth

Revenge of the Girl With the Great Personality; Elizabeth Eulberg. Scholastic 2013 272 p. (hardcover) $17.99

Grades: 7 8 9 10 **Fic**

1. Sisters -- Fiction 2. Beauty contests -- Fiction

ISBN 9780545476997; 0545476992

In this novel, by Elizabeth Eulberg, "Everybody loves Lexi. She's popular, smart, funny . . . but she's never been one of . . . the pretty ones who get all the attention from guys. And on top of that, her seven-year-old sister, Mackenzie, is a terror in a tiara. . . . Lexi's sick of it. . . . The time has come for Lexi to step out from the sidelines. Girls without great personalities aren't going to know what hit them. Because Lexi's going to play the beauty game." (Publisher's note)

Fahy, Thomas Richard

The **unspoken**; [by] Tom Fahy. Simon & Schuster Books for Young Readers 2008 166p $15.99

Grades: 8 9 10 11 12 **Fic**

1. Horror fiction 2. Cults -- Fiction

ISBN 978-1-4169-4007-4; 1-4169-4007-3

LC 2007-00850

Six teens are drawn back to the small, North Carolina town where they once lived and, one by one, begin to die of their worst fears, as prophesied by the cult leader they killed five years earlier, and who they believe poisoned their parents.

"Teeth-clenching suspenseful at times and deliciously creepy at others, Fahy . . . delivers a classic horror story." Publ Wkly

Falkner, Brian

Brain Jack. Random House 2010 349p $17.99; lib bdg $20.99

Grades: 7 8 9 10 **Fic**

1. Science fiction 2. Computers -- Fiction 3. New York (N.Y.) -- Fiction

ISBN 978-0-375-84366-2; 0-375-84366-3; 978-0-375-93924-2 lib bdg; 0-375-93924-5 lib bdg

LC 2008-43386

In a near-future New York City, fourteen-year-old computer genius Sam Wilson manages to hack into the AT&T network and sets off a chain of events that have a profound effect on human activity throughout the world.

"This fast-paced, cyber thriller is intelligent, well-written, and very intuitive to the possibilities and challenges we may face in our ever changing digital society." Libr Media Connect

The **project**. Random House 2011 275p $17.99

Grades: 6 7 8 9 10 **Fic**

1. Adventure fiction 2. Time travel -- Fiction 3. National socialism -- Fiction 4. World War, 1939-1945 -- Fiction

ISBN 978-0-375-96945-4; 0-375-96945-4

LC 2010033449

After discovering a terrible secret hidden in the most boring book in the world, Iowa fifteen-year-olds Luke and Tommy find out that members of a secret Nazi organization intend to use this information to rewrite history.

"The wacky unbelievability of this story in no way detracts from its enjoyment. It reads like an action movie, with plenty of chases, explosions, and by-a-hair escapes." SLJ

Falls, Kat

Inhuman; Kat Falls. Scholastic Press 2013 384 p. $17.99

Grades: 7 8 9 10 **Fic**

1. Dystopian fiction 2. Apocalyptic fiction 3. Science fiction 4. Survival -- Fiction 5. Quarantine -- Fiction 6. Virus diseases -- Fiction 7. Father-daughter relationship--Fiction

ISBN 054537099X; 9780545370998

LC 2013026360

In this dystopian novel by Kat Falls, "the United States east of the Mississippi has been abandoned. Now called the Feral Zone, a reference to the virus that turned millions of people into bloodthirsty savages, the entire area is off-limits. . . . [Protagonist] Lane gets the shock of her life when she learns that someone close to her has crossed into the Feral Zone." (Publisher's note)

"Years ago, the U.S. was bisected by a pandemic (spread by biting) that causes humans to mutate into feral human-animal hybrids. When pampered teenager Lane is blackmailed into the Feral Zone, she joins the search for a cure and discovers the gray area between human and feral. While Lane and her love triangle are bland, the zombie-apocalypse-meets-wereanimals-gone-wild setup captures the imagination." (Horn Book)

Fama, Elizabeth

Overboard; Elizabeth Fama. Cricket Books 2002 158p. maps (Cloth: alk. paper) $15.95

Grades: 7 8 9 10 **Fic**

1. Muslims -- Fiction 2. Indonesia -- Fiction 3. Shipwrecks -- Fiction 4. Survival after airplane accidents, shipwrecks, etc. -- Fiction 5. Survival -- Fiction 6. Sumatra (Indonesia) -- Fiction

ISBN 0812626524; 9780553494365

LC 20020592

In this "novel based on a 1996 ferry accident off the coast of Sumatra, Emily, a 14-year-old American living in Indonesia with her doctor parents, boards an overcrowded, tilting ferry (without her parents' knowledge) after her uncle invites her to visit him on a nearby island. As the ship lists to 'an unnatural angle,' the captain distributes life vests. Emily hands hers to a younger boy who is trying to hang on to the railing. . . . The girl then becomes trapped in the life-vest locker, which immediately fills with water. . . . [The plot continues with a] chronicle of Emily's nightlong struggle to survive. . . . During the course of the evening, she [encounters] . . . a Muslim child who explains some of the tenets of his faith as they bob along in the water." (Publishers Weekly)

Fantaskey, Beth

Buzz kill; Beth Fantaskey. Houghton Mifflin Harcourt. 2014 362p $17.99

Grades: 8 9 10 11 12 **Fic**

1. Coaches (Athletics) -- Fiction; 2. Dating (Social customs) --Fiction; 3. High schools -- Fiction; 4. Murder -- Fiction; 5. Mystery and detective stories

ISBN: 0547393105; 9780547393100

LC 2013011423

"When the head football coach is killed, seventeen-year-old Millie, a school reporter obsessed with Nancy Drew, sets out to learn the truth and clear her assistant-coach father of any suspicion. She gets some unexpected help from dreamy quarterback Chase, who's hiding some secrets. This entertaining sleuth story is a good choice for teens now graduated from books featuring Millie's literary hero." Horn Book

Jessica's guide to dating on the dark side. Harcourt 2009 354p $17

Grades: 8 9 10 11 12 **Fic**

1. Vampires -- Fiction

ISBN 978-0-15-206384-9; 0-15-206384-6

LC 2007-49002

Seventeen-year-old Jessica, adopted and raised in Pennsylvania, learns that she is descended from a royal line of Romanian vampires and that she is betrothed to a vampire prince, who poses as a foreign exchange student while courting her.

"Fantaskey makes this premise work by playing up its absurdities without laughing at them. . . . The romance sizzles, the plot develops ingeniously and suspensefully, and the satire sings." Publ Wkly

Farinango, Maria Virginia

★ The **Queen** of Water. Delacorte Press 2011 352p $16.99; lib bdg $19.99

Grades: 8 9 10 11 12 **Fic**

1. Ecuador -- Fiction 2. Social classes -- Fiction

ISBN 978-0-385-73897-2; 0-385-73897-8; 978-0-385-90761-3 lib bdg; 0-385-90761-3 lib bdg

LC 2010-10512

"The complexities of class and ethnicity within Ecuadorian society are explained seamlessly within the context of the first-person narrative, and a glossary and pronunciation guide further help to plunge readers into the novel's world. By turns heartbreaking, infuriating and ultimately inspiring." Kirkus

Farish, Terry

★ The **good** braider; by Terry Farish. Marshall Cavendish 2012 221 p. (hardcover) $17.99

Grades: 9 10 11 12 **Fic**

1. Refugees -- Fiction 2. Sudanese Americans -- Fiction 3. Mother-daughter relationship -- Fiction 4. Immigrants -- Fiction 5. Portland (Me.) -- Fiction 6. Mothers and daughters -- Fiction 7. Sudan -- History -- Civil War, 1983-2005 -- Fiction

ISBN 0761462678; 9780761462675; 9780761462682

LC 2011033659

In this novel by Terry Farish, written "in . . . free verse," protagonist Viola tells "the story of her family's journey from war-torn Sudan, to Cairo, and finally to Portland, Maine. Here, in the sometimes too close embrace of the local Southern Sudanese Community, she dreams of South Sudan while she tries to navigate the strange world of America . . . a world that puts her into sharp conflict with her traditional mother." (Publisher's note)

Farizan, Sara

★ **If** you could be mine; a novel. Sara Farizan. Algonquin 2013 256 p. (hardcover) $16.95

Grades: 8 9 10 11 12 **Fic**

1. Sex reassignment surgery -- Fiction 2. Iran -- Social conditions -- Fiction 3. Iran -- Fiction 4. Love -- Fiction 5. Lesbians -- Fiction 6. Friendship -- Fiction 7. Best friends -- Fiction

ISBN 1616202513

LC 2013008931

This novel, set in Iran, 17-year-old Sahar, who has wanted to marry her best friend Nasrin since they were six years old, dreams of living openly with her lover. Nasrin prefers to accept an arranged marriage, while intending to continue their illicit affair. Exposed to a world of sexual diversity by her gay cousin and made desperate by Nasrin's impending marriage, Sahar explores the one legal option for the two of them to be together: her own sex reassignment surgery." (Publishers Weekly)

"Rich with details of life in contemporary Iran, this is a GLBTQ story that we haven't seen before in YA fiction." SLJ

Tell me again how a crush should feel; Sara Farizan. Algonquin Young Readers. 2014 304p $16.95

Grades: 9 10 11 12 **Fic**

1. Friendship -- Fiction; 2. High schools -- Fiction; 3. Iranian Americans -- Fiction; 4. Lesbians -- Fiction

ISBN: 161620284X; 9781616202842

LC 2014021580

The protagonist is "sixteen-year-old Iranian American Leila Azadi. . . . Afraid to tell her best friends and her conservative family that she is gay, Leila finds herself in a secret relationship with Saskia, a gorgeous, sophisticated new girl with a decidedly wicked side. As Saskia reveals herself to be a master manipulator, Leila turns to an unexpected ally, Lisa, an old friend who recently lost her brother in acar accident." (Horn Book Magazine)

"Farizan fashions an empowering romance featuring a lovable, awkward protagonist who just needs a little nudge of confidence to totally claim her multifaceted identity." Booklist

Farmer, Nancy

★ The **Ear,** the Eye, and the Arm; a novel. Puffin Books 1995 311p pa $6.99

Grades: 6 7 8 9 10 **Fic**

1. Science fiction 2. Zimbabwe -- Fiction

ISBN 978-0-14-131109-8; 0-14-131109-6

LC 95019982

First published 1994 by Orchard Books

A Newbery Medal honor book, 1995

In 2194 in Zimbabwe, General Matsika's three children are kidnapped and put to work in a plastic mine while three mutant detectives use their special powers to search for them

"Throughout the story, it's the thrilling adventure that will grab readers, who will also like the comic, tender characterizations." Booklist

A **girl** named Disaster. Orchard Bks. 1996 309p $19.95; pa $7.99

Grades: 6 7 8 9 **Fic**

1. Adventure fiction 2. Supernatural -- Fiction

ISBN 0-531-09539-8; 0-14-038635-1 pa

LC 96-15141

A Newbery Medal honor book, 1997

While journeying from Mozambique to Zimbabwe to escape an arranged marriage, eleven-year-old Nhamo struggles to escape drowning and starvation and in so doing comes close to the luminous world of the African spirits

"This story is humorous and heartwrenching, complex and multilayered." SLJ

★ The **house** of the scorpion. Atheneum Bks. for Young Readers 2002 380p $17.95; pa $7.99

Grades: 7 8 9 10 **Fic**

1. Science fiction 2. Cloning -- Fiction

ISBN 0-689-85222-3; 0-689-85223-1 pa

LC 2001-56594

A Newbery Medal honor book, 2003

In a future where humans despise clones, Matt enjoys special status as the young clone of El Patrón, the 140-year-old leader of a corrupt drug empire nestled between Mexico and the United States.

"This is a powerful, ultimately hopeful, story that builds on today's sociopolitical, ethical, and scientific issues and prognosticates a compelling picture of what the future could bring." Booklist

★ The **lord** of Opium; Nancy Farmer. Atheneum Books for Young Readers 2013 432 p. (hardcover) $17.99
Grades: 7 8 9 10 **Fic**
1. Fantasy fiction 2. Drug traffic -- Fiction 3. Science fiction 4. Cloning -- Fiction 5. Environmental degradation -- Fiction
ISBN 1442482540; 9781442482548
LC 2012030418
Sequel to: House of the scorpion (2002)
Here, "Matt was a clone of El Patrón, drug lord of Opium, but with El Patrón dead, Matt is now considered by international law to be fully human and El Patrón's rightful heir. But it's a corrupt land . . . ruled over by drug lords and worked by armies of Illegals turned into 'eejits,' or zombies. Matt wants to bring reform." (Kirkus Reviews)

Farrey, Brian

With or without you. Simon Pulse 2011 348p pa $8.99; ebook $7.99
Grades: 9 10 11 12 **Fic**
1. Wisconsin -- Fiction 2. Friendship -- Fiction 3. Hate crimes -- Fiction 4. Homosexuality -- Fiction
ISBN 978-1-4424-0699-5 pa; 978-1-4424-0700-8 ebook
LC 2010-38722
When eighteen-year-old best friends Evan and Davis of Madison, Wisconsin, join a community center group called "chasers" to gain acceptance and knowledge of gay history, there may be fatal consequences.
"Farrey paces his story beautifully, covering many contemporary issues for teens about coming out, friendship, relationships, and following a dangerous crowd simply for a sense of belonging." SLJ

Fehlbaum, Beth

Big fat disaster; Beth Fehlbaum. Merit Press, an imprint of F+W Media, Inc. 2014 288 p. (pb) $17.99
Grades: 7 8 9 10 **Fic**
1. Moving -- Fiction 2. Family life -- Fiction 3. Eating disorders -- Fiction 4. Overweight teenagers -- Fiction 5. Texas -- Fiction 6. Schools -- Fiction 7. High schools -- Fiction 8. Family problems -- Fiction 9. Compulsive eating -- Fiction 10. Moving, Household -- Fiction 11. Overweight persons -- Fiction 12. Family life -- Texas -- Fiction
ISBN 1440570485; 9781440570483
LC 2013044512
"Colby's life as the heavy daughter of a disapproving former Miss Texas beauty queen is difficult enough, but it gets worse very quickly once she discovers a photo of her politician father kissing another woman...Colby's experiences, while extreme, ring true, and the fast pace, lively and profane dialogue, and timely topic make it a quick and enjoyable read." (Kirkus)

Hope in Patience. WestSide Books 2010 312p $16.95
Grades: 10 11 12 **Fic**
1. School stories 2. Texas -- Fiction 3. Family life -- Fiction 4. Child sexual abuse -- Fiction 5. Post-traumatic stress disorder -- Fiction
ISBN 978-1-934813-41-6
LC 2010-31118
After years of sexual abuse by her stepfather, fifteen-year-old Ashley Asher starts a better life with her father and stepmother in Patience, Texas, but despite psychotherapy and new friends, she still suffers from Post Traumatic Stress Disorder.
"Teens who are attracted by . . . [Ashley's] honesty and her compelling story will come away with a deeper understanding of trauma and healing. This book will open hearts and might well save lives." SLJ

Fehler, Gene

Beanball; by Gene Fehler. Clarion Books 2008 119p $16
Grades: 7 8 9 10 **Fic**
1. School stories 2. Novels in verse 3. Baseball -- Fiction
ISBN 0-618-84348-5; 978-0-618-84348-0
LC 2007013058
Relates, from diverse points of view, events surrounding the critical injury of popular and talented high school athlete, Luke "Wizard" Wallace, when he is hit in the face by a fastball.
This is a "moving baseball novel in free verse. . . . This swift read will appeal to both reluctant readers and baseball players." KLIATT

Feinstein, John

Last shot; a Final Four mystery. Knopf 2005 251p $16.95; lib bdg $18.99
Grades: 6 7 8 9 **Fic**
1. Mystery fiction 2. Basketball -- Fiction 3. Journalists -- Fiction
ISBN 0-375-83168-1; 0-375-93168-6 lib bdg
LC 2004-26535
After winning a basketball reporting contest, eighth graders Stevie and Susan Carol are sent to cover the Final Four tournament, where they discover that a talented player is being blackmailed into throwing the final game.
"The action on the court is vividly described. . . . Mystery fans will find enough suspense in this fast-paced narrative to keep them hooked." SLJ
Other titles in this series are:
Vanishing act (2006)
Cover-up (2007)
Change-up (2009)
Rivalry (2010)

Foul trouble; by John Feinstein. Alfred A. Knopf 2013 400 p. (trade) $16.99
Grades: 8 9 10 11 12 **Fic**
1. College basketball -- Fiction 2. High school students -- Fiction 3. Basketball -- Fiction 4. African Americans -- Fiction
ISBN 0375869646; 9780375869648; 9780375871696; 9780375982460
LC 2012042982
In this basketball novel by John Feinstein, "Danny Wilcox is Terrell's best friend and teammate, and a top prospect himself, but these days it seems like everyone wants to get

close to Terrell: the sneaker guys, the money managers, the college boosters. They show up offering fast cars, hot girls, and cold, hard cash. They say they just want to help, but their kind of help could get Terrell disqualified." (Publisher's note)

"Danny works to guide his friend and teammate, Terrell Jamerson, through the trials and temptations of the college recruiting process, as agents, boosters, and other 'dudes' look to hitch a ride with the top recruit. Engaging characters (including real-life cameos), intense basketball action, and sports-writer Feinstein's behind-the-scenes background provide an authentic view of a system that can both promote and exploit young athletes." (Horn Book)

Feldman, Ruth Tenzer

Blue thread; Ruth Tenzer Feldman. Ooligan Press 2012 302 p. $12.95

Grades: 7 8 9 10 **Fic**

1. Historical fiction 2. Jewish women -- Fiction 3. Women's rights -- Fiction

ISBN 1932010416; 9781932010411

LC 2011024382

This young adult novel focuses on Miriam, a young Jewish girl in 1912 Portland, Oregon. "While her mother plans their trip to New York City to find her a husband, Miriam gets caught up in the fight for women's suffrage. At first she's nervous about going against her parents' wishes, but curiosity gets the better of her. . . . However, after a mysterious girl named Serakh whisks Miriam back to biblical times, her desire to be a larger part of the movement becomes stronger." (School Library Journal)

Felin, M. Sindy

Touching snow. Atheneum Books for Young Readers 2007 234p $16.99

Grades: 9 10 11 12 **Fic**

1. Child abuse -- Fiction 2. Stepfathers -- Fiction 3. New York (N.Y.) -- Fiction 4. Haitian Americans -- Fiction

ISBN 978-1-4169-1795-3; 1-4169-1795-0

LC 2006-14794

After her stepfather is arrested for child abuse, thirteen-year-old Karina's home life improves but while the severity of her older sister's injuries and the urging of her younger sister, their uncle, and a friend tempt her to testify against him, her mother and other well-meaning adults persuade her to claim responsibility.

"Although the resolution is brutal, this story is a compelling read from an important and much-needed new voice. Readers will cheer for the young narrator." SLJ

Fergus, Maureen

Recipe for disaster. Kids Can Press 2009 252p $18.95; pa $8.95

Grades: 7 8 9 **Fic**

1. Baking -- Fiction 2. Friendship -- Fiction

ISBN 978-1-55453-319-0; 1-55453-319-8; 978-1-55453-320-6 pa; 1-55453-320-1 pa

Francie was born to bake and dreams of one day starring in her own baking show. Her life is almost perfect until the new girl at school shows up.

"Francie is a delight. Her own special brand of humor touches every aspect of the tale. . . . This breezy, appealing read covers personal growth, the sacrifices of friendship, and the mistakes made along the way." SLJ

Ferguson, Alane

The **Christopher** killer; a forensic mystery. Viking/Sleuth 2006 274p $15.99

Grades: 9 10 11 12 **Fic**

1. Mystery fiction 2. Homicide -- Fiction 3. Forensic sciences -- Fiction 4. Father-daughter relationship -- Fiction

ISBN 0-670-06008-9

LC 2005-15806

On the payroll as an assistant to her coroner father, seventeen-year-old Cameryn Mahoney uses her knowledge of forensic medicine to catch the killer of a friend while putting herself in terrible danger.

"This is worlds away from the Nancy Drew college series in terms of gore, but CSI fans won't blink twice." Booklist

Other titles featuring Cameryn Mahoney are:
The angel of death (2006)
The circle of blood (2007)
The dying breath (2009)

The **circle** of blood; a forensic mystery. Viking 2007 238p $15.99

Grades: 9 10 11 12 **Fic**

1. Mystery fiction 2. Forensic sciences -- Fiction 3. Mother-daughter relationship -- Fiction

ISBN 978-0-670-06056-6

LC 2007-10420

Sequel to Angel of death (2006)

As she uses her knowledge of forensic medicine to investigate the death of a young runaway, seventeen-year-old Cameryn Mahoney, an assistant to her coroner father, worries that her secretive mother may be involved.

"This book is the best yet in the series, and the ending lets the reader know that there are more to come." Voice Youth Advocates

Followed by The dying breath (2009)

The **dying** breath; a forensic mystery. Viking 2009 234p $16.99

Grades: 9 10 11 12 **Fic**

1. Mystery fiction 2. Forensic sciences -- Fiction

ISBN 978-0-670-06314-7

LC 2009-2170

Sequel to The circle of blood (2007)

When her ex-boyfriend starts stalking her, seventeen-year-old Cameryn must use her knowledge of forensic sciences to protect herself.

"This is page-turning suspense from the opening scene, with enough gory details to attract fans of CSI and other forensic shows. Moreover, strong characterization and relationships, particularly the one between Camryn and the gruff medical examiner who serves as her mentor, make this more than a satisfying genre read." Kirkus

Ferraiolo, Jack D.

★ **Sidekicks**. Amulet 2011 309p $16.95

Grades: 6 7 8 9 **Fic**

1. Superheroes -- Fiction

ISBN 978-0-8109-9803-2; 0-8109-9803-3

"By all outward appearances, Bright Boy is an average middle-school student, but at night, he becomes the sidekick to superhero Rogue Warrior. . . . Ferraiolo is delightfully unafraid to inject irreverence into the superhero formula, adding plenty of humor to the high-adventure high jinks." Booklist

Ferris, Jean

Of sound mind. Farrar, Straus & Giroux 2001 215p hardcover o.p. pa $6.95

Grades: 7 8 9 10 **Fic**

1. Deaf 2. Friendship 3. Deaf -- Fiction 4. Family problems 5. Friendship -- Fiction 6. American Sign Language 7. People with disabilities

ISBN 0-374-35580-0; 0-374-45584-8 pa

LC 00-68123

Tired of interpreting for his deaf family and resentful of their reliance on him, high school senior Theo finds support and understanding from Ivy, a new student who also has a deaf parent. "Grades seven to ten." (Bull Cent Child Books)

"Both a thought-provoking study of just when being deaf matters and when it does not, and an unusually rich coming-of-age story that explores universal issues of family responsibility, emotional maturation, love, and loss." Booklist

Fforde, Jasper

★ The **last** Dragonslayer; Jasper Fforde. Hodder & Stoughton 2010 281 p. (The Chronicles of Kazam) $16.99; (hbk.) $16.99

Grades: 7 8 9 10 **Fic**

1. Magic -- Fiction 2. Dragons -- Fiction 3. Employment agencies -- Fiction

ISBN 978-0547738475; 1444707175; 1444707191; 9781444707175; 9781444707199

LC 2010551874

In this book by Jasper Fforde, part of the Chronicles of Kazam series, "magic is fading. . . . Fifteen-year-old foundling Jennifer Strange runs Kazam, an employment agency for magicians -- but it's hard to stay in business when magic is drying up. And then the visions start, predicting the death of the world's last dragon at the hands of an unnamed Dragonslayer. If the visions are true, everything will change for Kazam -- and for Jennifer." (Publisher's note)

The **song** of the Quarkbeast; Jasper Fforde. Houghton Mifflin Harcourt 2013 304 p. (The chronicles of Kazam) $16.99

Grades: 7 8 9 10 **Fic**

1. Magic 2. Fantasy fiction

ISBN 054773848X; 9780547738482

LC 2012047318

This is the second book in Jasper Fforde's Chronicles of Kazam series. Here, now "that magical power is on the rise again, the despotic King Snodd IV hopes to cash in, specifically by putting the wizards who work at Kazam Mystical Arts Management under his control by proposing they merge with iMagic, the rival house led by the Amazing Blix, a questionable character with a new royal appointment: Court Mystician." (Publishers Weekly)

Fichera, Liz

Hooked; Liz Fichera. Harlequin Books 2013 368 p. $9.99

Grades: 9 10 11 12 **Fic**

1. Love stories 2. Golf -- Fiction 3. School sports -- Fiction

ISBN 0373210728; 9780373210725

In this young adult romance story, by Liz Fichera, part of the "Harlequin Teen" series, Fred Oday finds herself as the first girl on her school's golf team. She is worried about being assigned to the boys' team and what it will do to her popularity, but she also can't help noticing the attractive Ryan Berenger who she's been assigned to work with by the coach.

Fiedler, Lisa

Romeo's ex; Rosaline's story. Henry Holt 2006 246p $16.95

Grades: 8 9 10 11 12 **Fic**

1. Poets 2. Authors 3. Dramatists 4. Love stories

ISBN 978-0-8050-7500-7; 0-8050-7500-3

LC 2005-35692

In a story based on the Shakespeare play, sixteen-year-old Roseline, who is studying to be a healer, becomes romantically entangled with the Montague family even as her beloved young cousin, Juliet Capulet, defies the family feud to secretly marry Romeo.

"This novel manages to be both witty and multilayered, leaving readers with plenty to ponder." Publ Wkly

Fienberg, Anna

Number 8. Walker 2007 288p $16.95

Grades: 7 8 9 10 **Fic**

1. Singers -- Fiction 2. Family life -- Fiction 3. Mathematics -- Fiction 4. Organized crime -- Fiction

ISBN 978-0-8027-9660-8; 0-8027-9660-5

LC 2007-14706

While hiding out from the mob in the suburbs with his mother, a singer, Jackson uses his fascination with math and numbers to make friends, but strange phone calls and even greater threats endanger not only Jackson and his mother, but his new girlfriend, as well.

"The fact that each character has an idiosyncratic passion that somehow helps them understand the others adds dimension to an already effective suspense plot." Bull Cent Child Books

Fink, Mark

The **summer** I got a life. WestSide 2009 196p $15.95

Grades: 7 8 9 **Fic**

1. Love stories 2. Wisconsin -- Fiction 3. People with disabilities

ISBN 978-1-934813-12-6; 1-934813-12-5

"Andy is pumped that his freshman year is over and his vacation is about to begin. Then his dad's promotion changes everything. Instead of Hawaii, Andy is spending two weeks on a farm in Wisconsin with his somewhat odd, but well-meaning, aunt and uncle. Once there, though, he finds that things aren't so bad particularly when he spots 'the most incredible-looking girl he has ever seen.' . . . Andy discovers that an accident at age four has left Laura confined to a wheelchair. . . . This is an engaging novel filled with life lessons, a little romance, humor, sports, and fraternal love." SLJ

Finn, Mary

★ **Belladonna**. Candlewick Press 2011 371p $16.99

Grades: 7 8 9 10 **Fic**

1. Artists 2. Painters 3. Horses -- Fiction

ISBN 978-0-7636-5106-0; 0-7636-5106-0

LC 2010038707

This novel is set in "rural England in 1757, [where] Thomas Rose is on the verge-of becoming a man. Clever, but unable to learn reading and writing . . . Tom meets the enigmatic Hélène, a circus performer who goes by the name of Ling . . .Enchanted with Ling's stories of her life in the circus as much as with the girl herself, Tom commits to helping her find her beloved horse, Belladonna . . . Their search leads them to George Stubbs, known in the village as a horse butcher . . . the teens discover that Stubbs is a painter who is completing an anatomical study of horses that involves dissection of the animals. Stubbs takes Tom on as an apprentice and secures Ling a position in the household of the wealthy family that purchased Belladonna, not knowing that the girl's ultimate goal is to escape with her horse." (School Libr J)

"A touch of intrigue and interesting details about horses, early necropsy, and everyday life add a rich frame to this historical coming-of-age story, unique in both its setting and subject." Booklist

Finneyfrock, Karen

The **sweet** revenge of Celia Door; by Karen Finneyfrock. Viking 2013 272 p. (hardcover) $16.99

Grades: 7 8 9 10 **Fic**

1. School stories 2. Revenge -- Fiction 3. Teenagers -- Fiction 4. Gays -- Fiction 5. Poetry -- Fiction 6. Schools -- Fiction 7. High schools -- Fiction 8. Hershey (Pa.) -- Fiction 9. Family life -- Pennsylvania -- Hershey -- Fiction

ISBN 0670012750; 9780670012756

LC 2011047221

In this teen novel, by Karen Finneyfrock, "Celia Door enters her freshman year . . . with giant boots, dark eyeliner, and a thirst for revenge against Sandy Firestone. . . . But then Celia meets Drake, the cool new kid from New York City who entrusts her with his deepest, darkest secret. When Celia's quest for justice threatens her relationship with Drake, she's forced to decide which is sweeter: revenge or friendship." (Publisher's note)

Fischer, Jackie

An **egg** on three sticks; [by] Jackie Moyer Fischer. Thomas Dunne Books 2004 309p pa $12.95

Grades: 9 10 11 12 **Fic**

1. Mental illness -- Fiction 2. San Francisco (Calif.) -- Fiction 3. Mother-daughter relationship -- Fiction

ISBN 0-312-31775-1

LC 2003-9126

In the San Francisco Bay Area in the early 1970s, twelve-year-old Abby watches her mother fall apart and must take on the burden of holding her family together

"With acutely observed detail, Fischer describes a young adult's pull between the universal struggles of adolescence and the surreal anguish of losing a parent to disease." Booklist

Fisher, Catherine

Darkwater; by Catherine Fisher. Penguin Group USA 2012 229p (hardcover) $16.99

Grades: 6 7 8 9 10 11 12 **Fic**

1. Sin 2. Teenagers -- Fiction 3. Private schools -- Fiction 4. Soul -- Fiction 5. Twins -- Fiction 6. England -- Fiction 7. Schools -- Fiction 8. Brothers -- Fiction 9. Supernatural -- Fiction 10. Great Britain -- History -- Edward VII, 1901-1910 -- Fiction

ISBN 9780803738188

LC 2011048063

In author Catherine Fisher's book, "Sarah Trevelyan would give anything to regain the power and wealth her family has lost, so she makes a bargain with Azrael, Lord of Darkwater Hall. He gives her one hundred years and the means to accomplish her objective--in exchange for her soul. Fast-forward a hundred years to Tom, a fifteen-year-old boy who dreams of attending Darkwater Hall School but doesn't believe he has the talent. Until he meets a professor named Azrael, who offers him a bargain. Will Sarah be able to stop Tom from making the same mistake she did a century ago?" (Publisher's note)

Incarceron. Dial Books 2010 442p $17.99

Grades: 7 8 9 10 **Fic**

1. Fantasy fiction 2. Prisoners -- Fiction

ISBN 978-0-8037-3396-1; 0-8037-3396-8

LC 2008-46254

First published 2007 in the United Kingdom

To free herself from an upcoming arranged marriage, Claudia, the daughter of the Warden of Incarceron, a futuristic prison with a mind of its own, decides to help a young prisoner escape.

"Complex and inventive, with numerous and rewarding mysteries, this tale is certain to please." Publ Wkly

Followed by Sapphique (2011)

The **Margrave**. Dial Books for Young Readers 2011 464p (Relic master) $16.99

Grades: 6 7 8 9 **Fic**

1. Fantasy fiction 2. Apprentices -- Fiction

ISBN 978-0-8037-3676-4; 0-8037-3676-2

LC 2010043237

Their quest to find a secret relic with great power leads Master Galen and his sixteen-year-old apprentice Raffi into the Pit of Maar and the deep evil world at the heart of the Watch.

"The conclusion to Fisher's science-fantasy quartet satisfies." Kirkus

The **dark** city. Dial Books for Young Readers 2011 376p (Relic master) $16.99

Grades: 6 7 8 9 **Fic**

1. Fantasy fiction 2. Apprentices -- Fiction
ISBN 978-0-8037-3673-3; 0-8037-3673-8
LC 2010028801

"Relic Master Galen injured both his body and his mind when he dismantled an ancient technological artifact. While his physical injuries have healed, the loss of his psychic gifts has left him reluctantly dependent on his talented young apprentice, Raffi. Together they travel the dangerous road to the ruined Antaran city of Tasceron, where Galen hopes to reclaim his abilities from a shadowy figure known only as the Crow." Booklist

The **hidden** Coronet. Dial Books for Young Readers 2011 421p (Relic master) $16.99
Grades: 6 7 8 9 **Fic**

1. Fantasy fiction 2. Apprentices -- Fiction
ISBN 978-0-8037-3675-7; 0-8037-3675-4
LC 2010039315

Sixteen-year-old Raffi and Master Galen continue to evade the Watch as they seek the Coronet, a potent ancient relic that could be their only hope for defeating the power that is destroying Anara.

"The climactic integration of visionary mysticism and gee-whiz gadgetry, rendered bittersweet by all-too human failures, leads directly to a cliffhanger ending." Kirkus

The **lost** heiress. Dial Books for Young Readers 2011 375p (Relic master) $16.99
Grades: 6 7 8 9 **Fic**

1. Fantasy fiction 2. Apprentices -- Fiction
ISBN 978-0-8037-3674-0; 0-8037-3674-6
LC 2010038156

Even though the city of Tasceron and its emperor have fallen, when Master Galen and his sixteen-year-old apprentice Raffi hear a rumor that the heiress to the throne still lives, they must try to find her and keep her safe.

"Separate plot threads intertwine in a satisfying climax, posing puzzles to keep readers ensnared while providing pleasing narrative momentum to the overall series." Kirkus

The **obsidian** mirror; by Catherine Fisher. Dial Books 2013 384 p. (hardcover) $17.99
Grades: 7 8 9 10 11 12 **Fic**

1. Fantasy fiction 2. Science fiction 3. Fathers -- Fiction 4. Time travel -- Fiction 5. Missing persons -- Fiction
ISBN 0803739699; 9780803739697
LC 2012019459

This book is the first in a trilogy from Catherine Fisher. The "mirror of the title, a dangerous gateway to other time periods, is being pursued by not one but three equally unpleasant and obsessive mad scientists. One of them, Oberon Venn, is the master of spooky Wintercombe Abbey. . . . Jake Wilde, Venn's teenage godson and his equal in arrogance, has been expelled from boarding school and shipped off to Wintercombe, where the boy plans to accuse Venn of having murdered Jake's father." (Publishers Weekly)

The **oracle** betrayed; book one of The Oracle Prophecies. by Catherine Fisher. 1st American ed; Greenwillow Books 2004 341p (Oracle prophecies) $16.99; lib bdg $17.89; pa $6.99
Grades: 7 8 9 10 **Fic**

1. Fantasy fiction
ISBN 0-06-057157-8; 0-06-057158-6 lib bdg; 0-06-057159-4 pa
LC 2003-48498

After she is chosen to be "Bearer-of-the-god," Mirany questions the established order and sets out, along with a musician and a scribe, to find the legitimate heir of the religious leader known as the Archon.

"This [is] a well-developed world with its own culture, some sharply realized settings, and several strong, distinctive characters." Booklist

Other titles in this series :

Day of the scarab: book three of The Oracle Prophecies (2006)

The Sphere of Secrets: book two of The Oracle Prophecies (2005)

Sapphique. Dial Books 2011 460p $17.99
Grades: 7 8 9 10 **Fic**

1. Fantasy fiction 2. Computers -- Fiction 3. Prisoners -- Fiction 4. Identity (Psychology) -- Fiction
ISBN 978-0-8037-3397-8; 0-8037-3397-6
LC 2009-31479

Sequel to: Incarceron (2010)

After his escape from the sentient prison, Incarceron, Finn finds that the Realm is not at all what he expected, and he does not know whether he is to be its king, how to free his imprisoned friends, or how to stop Incarceron's quest to be free of its own nature.

"Fisher's superb world-building marks this title, effectively drawing the reader in to a place so rife with secrets even its inhabitants don't entirely understand the depth of its illusions." Bull Cent Child Books

Fishman, Seth

The **well's** end; Seth Fishman. G.P. Putnam's Sons. 2014 347pp $17.99
Grades: 9 10 11 12 **Fic**

1. Boarding schools--Fiction 2. Father-daughter relationship--Fiction 3.Colorado--Fiction 4. Viruses--Fiction 5. Science fiction
ISBN: 0399159908; 9780399159909
LC 2013022716

Booklist (February 2014)

"When a bizarre disease that accelerates aging locks down her boarding school's campus, sixteen-year-old Mia and her friends stage a daring escape. If they can reach her father's secretive, subterranean office at mysterious Fenton Electronics, they will find a cure--and, hopefully, an explanation. This suspenseful sci-fi adventure ends with a cliffhanger that will leave readers eager for another installment." Horn Book

FitzGerald, Helen

Deviant; Helen FitzGerald. Soho Teen 2013 248 p. (hardcover) $17.99
Grades: 10 11 12 **Fic**

1. Mystery fiction 2. Orphans -- Fiction 3. Science

fiction 4. Behavior -- Fiction 5. Families -- Fiction
ISBN 1616951397; 9781616951399
LC 2012033455

In this book, "Abigail Thorn was given up by her mother as a newborn," so at 16, she's "surprised to learn that her birth mother has just died, leaving her a letter, a large sum of money, and a one-way plane ticket to Los Angeles to live with a family Abigail never knew existed. . . . Abigail gradually begins to let down her guard around her new older sister . . . , but she still senses that something is not right within her privileged new family." (Publishers Weekly)

"This thriller has great character development and will keep readers hooked until the cliff-hanger ending... There's quite a bit of crude language in this one, but overall it's a great action-filled mystery." SLJ

Fitzpatrick, Huntley

My life next door; by Huntley Fitzpatrick. Dial Books 2012 394 p.

Grades: 9 10 11 12 **Fic**

1. Love stories 2. Teenagers -- Fiction 3. Family life -- Fiction 4. Love -- Fiction 5. Conduct of life -- Fiction 6. Politics, Practical -- Fiction
ISBN 0803736991; 9780803736993
LC 2011027166

This novel by Huntley Fitzpatrick is "about family, friendship, first romance, and how to be true to one person you love without betraying another . . . The Garretts are everything the Reeds are not. Loud, numerous, messy, affectionate. And every day from her balcony perch, seventeen-year-old Samantha Reed wishes she was one of them . . . until one summer evening, Jase Garrett climbs her terrace and changes everything. As the two fall fiercely in love, Jase's family makes Samantha one of their own. Then in an instant, the bottom drops out of her world and she is suddenly faced with an impossible decision." (Publisher's note)

What I thought was true; by Huntley Fitzpatrick. Dial. 2014 409p $17.99

Grades: 9 10 11 12 Fic

1. Dating (Social customs)--Fiction 2. Islands--Fiction 3. Social classes--Fiction 4. Connecticut--Fiction 5. Love stories
ISBN: 0803739095; 9780803739093
LC 2013027029

A "love story [that] shows the clash between classes in a New England beach community. . . Gwen, whose mother is a house cleaner, has . . . [a poor] reputation among the members of the boys' swim team, including rich Cass. . . . After a humiliating run-in with him at a party, it's hard for Gwen to believe that he wants more from her than a quick fling, but over the course of the summer, he gradually wins her trust and her heart." (Publishers Weekly)

"A teenage girl struggles with class divisions, sex and the tricky art of communication. Gwen . . . is an islander, while Cass Somers is a rich boy . . . The two have had some romantic moments, but miscommunication, misinterpretation and fear keep them from moving forward. . . . Whatstarts out as snappy chick-lit writing quickly becomes deeper and more complex . . . A late revelation will surprise readers as much as it does Gwen; natural dialogue and authentic characters abound. Much deeper than the pretty cover lets on." Kirkus

Flack, Sophie

★ **Bunheads.** Poppy 2011 294p $17.99

Grades: 8 9 10 11 12 **Fic**

1. Ballet -- Fiction 2. New York (N.Y.) -- Fiction 3. Dating (Social customs) -- Fiction
ISBN 978-0-316-12653-3; 0-316-12653-5
LC 2011009715

Hannah Ward, nineteen, revels in the competition, intense rehearsals, and dazzling performances that come with being a member of Manhattan Ballet Company's corps de ballet, but after meeting handsome musician Jacob she begins to realize there could be more to her life.

"Readers, both dancers and 'pedestrians' (the corps' term for nondancers), will find Hannah's struggle a gripping read." Publ Wkly

Flake, Sharon G.

Bang! Jump at the Sun/Hyperion Books for Children 2005 298p hardcover o.p. pa $7.99

Grades: 8 9 10 11 12 **Fic**

1. Violence -- Fiction 2. Family life -- Fiction 3. African Americans -- Fiction
ISBN 0-7868-1844-1; 0-7868-4955-X pa
LC 2005-47434

A teenage boy must face the harsh realities of inner city life, a disintegrating family, and destructive temptations as he struggles to find his identity as a young man.

"This disturbing, thought-provoking novel will leave readers with plenty of food for thought and should fuel lively discussions." SLJ

Pinned; Sharon G. Flake. Scholastic Press 2012 228 p. $17.99

Grades: 9 10 11 12 **Fic**

1. Friendship -- Fiction 2. Best friends -- Fiction 3. High schools -- Fiction 4. African Americans -- Fiction 5. Learning disabilities -- Fiction 6. People with disabilities -- Fiction
ISBN 0545057183; 9780545057189; 9780545057332
LC 2012009239

This novel by Sharon G. Flake is "about a teen boy and girl, each tackling disabilities. Autumn is outgoing and has lots of friends. Adonis is shy and not so eager to connect with people. But even with their differences, the two have one thing in common--they're each dealing with a handicap. For Autumn, who has a learning disability, reading is a painful struggle that makes it hard to focus in class. . . . Adonis is confined to a wheelchair. But he's a strong reader who loves books." (Publisher's note)

Fleischman, Paul

Seek. Simon Pulse 2003 167p pa $7.99

Grades: 7 8 9 10 **Fic**

1. Radio -- Fiction 2. Fathers -- Fiction
ISBN 0-689-85402-1
First published 2001 by Front St./Cricket Bks.

Rob becomes obsessed with searching the airwaves for his long-gone father, a radio announcer.

"Fleischman has orchestrated a symphony that is both joyful and poignant with this book designed for reader's theatre." Voice Youth Advocates

Fletcher, Christine

★ **Ten** cents a dance. Bloomsbury U.S.A. Children's Books 2008 356p $16.95
Grades: 9 10 11 12 **Fic**

1. Dancers -- Fiction 2. Poverty -- Fiction 3. Chicago (Ill.) -- Fiction 4. Conduct of life -- Fiction 5. World War, 1939-1945 -- Fiction

ISBN 978-1-59990-164-0; 1-59990-164-1

LC 2007-50737

In 1940s Chicago, fifteen-year-old Ruby hopes to escape poverty by becoming a taxi dancer in a nightclub, but the work has unforeseen dangers and hiding the truth from her family and friends becomes increasingly difficult.

"The descriptions of nightlife are lively and engaging, and they bring to light race, class, and gender issues in 1940s Chicago, which are fodder for discussion. Leisure readers will enjoy this novel, but it will also be useful in the classroom as a historical snapshot." Voice Youth Advocates

Fletcher, Ralph

The **one** o'clock chop; [by] Ralph Fletcher. 1st ed.; Henry Holt 2007 183p $16.95
Grades: 7 8 9 10 **Fic**

1. Cousins -- Fiction 2. Boats and boating -- Fiction

ISBN 978-0-8050-8143-5; 0-8050-8143-7

LC 2006035470

In New York, fourteen-year-old Matt spends the summer of 1973 digging clams to earn money for his own boat and falling for Jazzy, a beautiful and talented girl from Hawaii who happens to be his first cousin.

"Plenty of universal teen fascinations and concerns exist for those readers willing to enter Matt's world and give themselves over to this smoothly paced and competently written novel." SLJ

Fletcher, Susan

Alphabet of dreams. Atheneum Books for Young Readers 2006 294p map $16.95
Grades: 6 7 8 9 10 **Fic**

1. Iran -- Fiction 2. Dreams -- Fiction 3. Zoroastrianism -- Fiction

ISBN 0-689-85042-5

Fourteen-year-old Mitra, of royal Persian lineage, and her five-year-old brother Babak, whose dreams foretell the future, flee for their lives in the company of the magus Melchoir and two other Zoroastrian priests, traveling through Persia as they follow star signs leading to a newlyborn king in Bethlehem. Includes historical notes

"The characters are vivid and whole, the plot compelling, and the setting vast." Voice Youth Advocates

Ancient, strange, and lovely. Atheneum Books for Young Readers 2010 315p il (The dragon chronicles) $16.99
Grades: 6 7 8 9 **Fic**

1. Fantasy fiction 2. Dragons -- Fiction 3. Poaching -- Fiction

ISBN 978-1-4169-5786-7; 1-4169-5786-3

LC 2009053797

Fourteen-year-old Bryn must try to find a way to save a baby dragon from a dangerous modern world that seems to have no place for something so ancient.

"This book offers a wondrous mix of dystopic science fiction and magical fantasy. . . . Fletcher has done an outstanding job of creating a believable place and space for this story to unfold. The plot flows smoothly and quickly with a lot of action." SLJ

Dragon's milk. Atheneum Pubs. 1989 242p hardcover o.p. pa $5.99
Grades: 7 8 9 10 **Fic**

1. Fantasy fiction 2. Dragons -- Fiction

ISBN 0-689-31579-1; 0-689-71623-0 pa

LC 88-35059

Kaeldra, an outsider adopted by an Elythian family as a baby, possesses the power to understand dragons and uses this power to try to save her younger sister who needs dragon's milk to recover from an illness

"High-fantasy fans will delight in the clash of swords, the flash of magic, the many escape-and-rescue scenes." Booklist

Other titles in this series are:
Flight of the Dragon Kyn (1993)
Sign of the dove (1996)

Flinn, Alex

Beastly. HarperTeen 2007 304p $16.99; lib bdg $17.89; pa $8.99
Grades: 6 7 8 9 10 **Fic**

1. Fantasy fiction

ISBN 978-0-06-087416-2; 0-06-087416-3; 978-0-06-087417-9 lib bdg; 0-06-087417-1 lib bdg; 978-0-06-196328-5 pa; 0-06-196328-3 pa

LC 2006-36241

A modern retelling of "Beauty and the Beast" from the point of view of the Beast, a vain Manhattan private school student who is turned into a monster and must find true love before he can return to his human form.

This "is creative enough to make it an engaging read. . . . [This is an] engrossing tale that will have appeal for fans of fantasy and realistic fiction." Voice Youth Advocates

Breaking point; [by] Alex Flinn. HarperTempest 2002 241p hardcover o.p. pa $6.99
Grades: 9 10 11 12 **Fic**

1. School stories 2. Friendship -- Fiction

ISBN 0-06-623847-1; 0-06-623848-X; 9780064473712 pa

LC 2001-39504

"Gate-Brickell Christian is a toney private school attended by the rich and privileged—and a few despised offspring of the staff, like Paul Richmond. . . . Charlie, the magnetic class ringleader, becomes the center of Paul's world. . . . Paul's loyalty to Charlie takes him from vandalism (battering mailboxes) to cheating . . . to, finally, leaving a Charlie-made bomb in a classroom." Bull Cent Child Books

★ **Breathing** underwater. HarperCollins Pubs. 2001 263p hardcover o.p. pa $8.99
Grades: 9 10 11 12 **Fic**

1. Domestic violence -- Fiction

ISBN 0-06-029198-2; 0-06-447257-4 pa

LC 00-44933

Sent to counseling for hitting his girlfriend, Caitlin, and ordered to keep a journal, sixteen-year-old Nick recounts his relationship with Caitlin, examines his controlling behavior and anger, and describes living with his abusive father.

"This book attempts to understand the root of domestic violence. Flinn has created sympathetic characters who are struggling with their insecurities. While it is difficult at first to be sympathetic towards Nick, it becomes easier as he examines his life and relationships. This is a good book to use in discussion with teens who have anger issues." Book Rep

Followed by Diva (2006)

Cloaked. HarperTeen 2011 341p $16.99

Grades: 6 7 8 9 **Fic**

1. Fairy tales 2. Magic -- Fiction 3. Shoes -- Fiction 4. Animals -- Fiction 5. Princesses -- Fiction 6. Missing persons -- Fiction

ISBN 978-0-06-087422-3; 0-06-087422-8

LC 2009-53387

Seventeen-year-old Johnny is approached at his family's struggling shoe repair shop in a Miami, Florida, hotel by Alorian Princess Victoriana, who asks him to find her brother who was turned into a frog.

"A diverting, whimsical romp through fairy-tale tropes." Bull Cent Child Books

A **kiss** in time. HarperTeen 2009 384p $16.99; pa $8.99

Grades: 7 8 9 10 11 12 **Fic**

1. Witches -- Fiction 2. Princesses -- Fiction

ISBN 978-0-06-087419-3; 0-06-087419-8; 978-0-06-087421-6 pa; 0-06-087421-X pa

LC 2008-22582

Sixteen-year-old Princess Talia persuades seventeen-year-old Jack, the modern-day American who kissed her awake after a 300-year sleep, to take her to his Miami home, where she hopes to win his love before the witch who cursed her can spirit her away.

This is a "clever and humorous retelling of 'Sleeping Beauty.' . . . Alternating between the teenagers' distinctive points of view, Flinn skillfully delineates how their upbringings set them apart while drawing parallels between their family conflicts. Fans of happily-ever-after endings will delight in the upbeat resolution." Publ Wkly

Flores-Scott, Patrick

Jumped in; Patrick Flores-Scott. Christy Ottaviano Books, Henry Holt and Company 2013 304 p. (hardback) $16.99

Grades: 8 9 10 **Fic**

1. Gangs 2. Friendship 3. Slam poetry 4. Poetry -- Fiction 5. Schools -- Fiction 6. High schools -- Fiction 7. Mexican Americans -- Fiction 8. Des Moines (Wash.) -- Fiction 9. Interpersonal relations -- Fiction 10. Family life -- Washington (State) -- Fiction

ISBN 0805095144; 9780805095142

LC 2013018844

In this book, "grunge-rock devotee Sam has been trying to avoid the attention of teachers and other students ever since his mom left town two years earlier. Then the equally quiet Luis Cárdenas arrives in Sam's English class. . . . Sam doesn't see Luis' true colors until Ms. Cassidy announces that the class will have a poetry slam. Luis not only throws himself into creating a poem, he inspires Sam to do the same." (Kirkus Reviews)

Fogelin, Adrian

The **big** nothing; 1st ed; Peachtree 2004 235p $14.95

Grades: 7 8 9 10 **Fic**

1. Pianists -- Fiction 2. Family life -- Fiction

ISBN 1-56145-326-9

LC 2004-6327

Thirteen-year-old Justin Riggs struggles to cope with major family problems, including a brother who might be heading for the Persian Gulf, but finds an escape in piano lessons and the dream of a romance with a popular girl.

"Serious and humorous by turns, this seemingly simple story is actually quite complex but not weighty and will be enthusiastically embraced." SLJ

The **real** question. Peachtree 2006 234p $15.95

Grades: 7 8 9 10 **Fic**

1. Father-son relationship -- Fiction

ISBN 1-56145-383-8

LC 2006013996

Fisher Brown, a sixteen-year-old over-achiever, is on the verge of academic burnout when he impulsively decides to stop cramming for the SATs for one weekend and accompany his ne'erdowell neighbor to an out-of-town job repairing a roof.

"Fisher's first-person narration is dead-on. . . . This amazing title . . . should be required reading for every teen . . . who feels the weight of a parent's expectations but cannot quite figure out what to do about it." Voice Youth Advocates

Foley, Jessie Ann

★ **Carnival** at Bray: a novel; Jessie Ann Foley. Elephant Rock Books. 2014 235p $12.95

Grades: 9 10 11 12 **Fic**

1. Bildungsromans 2. Ireland--Fiction 3. Rock music--Fiction 4. Teenage girls--Fiction 5. Americans--Ireland--Fiction

ISBN: 0989515591; 9780989515597

LC 2014937608

Printz Honor Book (2015)

Kirkus Best Teen Books (2014)

"This promising debut, set in the heyday of grunge, tells the story of Maggie Lynch, a displaced Chicagoan and grunge music fan, living in a quiet town (Bray) on the Irish Sea. Maggie was uprooted from her friends, her music scene, and her beloved Uncle Kevin when her romantically fickle mother married her latest boyfriend, resulting in a move to his hometown. During her time of difficult adjustment to Ireland, Maggie falls in love with Eion the very moment a devastating loss hits her family, leading to rebellion and a journey to Rome to see Nirvana and fulfill Uncle Kevin's wish for her...Foley has also populated Bray with a host of quirky, loving, and memorable background characters, which enriches the story. Recommended for teens who enjoy travelogue romance stories or novels about rock music." SLJ

Fombelle, Timothee De

Vango: between sky and earth. By Timothee de Fombelle. Candlewick Press. 2014 432p $17.99

Grades: 9 10 11 12 **Fic**

1. False accusation — Fiction; 2. Clergy — Fiction; 3. Friendship— Fiction; 4. Historical fiction; 5. Adventure fiction

ISBN: 9780763671969; 0763671967

LC 2013955696

YALSA Best Fiction for Young Adults: Top Ten (2015)

"Minutes from joining the priest hood in 1934, Vango, who was found washed ashore on a tiny Ital ian is land as a toddler, must suddenly avoid both arrest and asimultaneous assassination attempt. Establishing his innocence while on the run across Europe requires untangling his mysterious past." (Kirkus Reviews)

"de Fombelle has written a brilliant, wonderfully exciting story of flight and pursuit, filled with colorful characters and head-scratching mystery. As the novel proceeds, the suspense is ratcheted up to breathtaking levels as the boy remains only one step ahead of his relentless pursuers." Booklist

Fontes, Justine

Benito runs. Darby Creek 2011 104p (Surviving Southside) lib bdg $27.93; pa $7.99

Grades: 7 8 9 10 **Fic**

1. Fathers -- Fiction 2. Hispanic Americans -- Fiction 3. Post-traumatic stress disorder -- Fiction

ISBN 978-0-7613-6151-0 lib bdg; 0-7613-6151-0; 978-0-7613-6165-7 pa; 0-7613-6165-0 pa

LC 2010023820

"Running away is the only option.Benito's father, Xavier, had been in Iraq for more than a year. When he returns, Benito's family life is not the same. Xavier suffers from PTSD--post-traumatic stress disorder--and yells constantly. He causes such a scene at a school function that Benny is embarrassed to go to back to Southside High. Benny can't handle seeing his dad so crazy, so he decides to run away." Publisher's note

This "well-written [story reinforces] the importance of family, friends, values, and thoughtful decision-making. . . . [An] excellent [purchase, this book] will attract and engage reluctant readers." SLJ

Ford, John C.

★ The **morgue** and me. Viking 2009 313p $17.99

Grades: 8 9 10 11 12 **Fic**

1. Mystery fiction 2. Homicide -- Fiction 3. Michigan -- Fiction 4. Journalists -- Fiction 5. Criminal investigation -- Fiction

ISBN 978-0-670-01096-7; 0-670-01096-0

LC 2009-1956

Eighteen-year-old Christopher, who plans to be a spy, learns of a murder cover-up through his summer job as a morgue assistant and teams up with Tina, a gorgeous newspaper reporter, to investigate, despite great danger.

"Ford spins a tale that's complex but not confusing, never whitewashing some of the harsher crimes people commit. The result is a story that holds its own as a mainstream mystery as well as a teen novel." Publ Wkly

Ford, Michael

The **poisoned** house. Albert Whitman 2011 319p $16.99

Grades: 6 7 8 9 10 **Fic**

1. Ghost stories 2. Supernatural -- Fiction 3. London (England) -- Fiction 4. Household employees -- Fiction 5. Great Britain -- History -- 19th century -- Fiction

ISBN 978-0-8075-6589-6; 0-8075-6589-X

LC 2010048250

As the widowed master of an elegant house in Victorian-era London slips slowly into madness and his tyrannical housekeeper takes on more power, a ghostly presence distracts a teenaged maidservant with clues to a deadly secret.

"This ghost story is light fare, chilling, and suspenseful." SLJ

Ford, Michael Thomas

Suicide notes; a novel. HarperTeen 2008 295p $16.99; pa $8.99

Grades: 9 10 11 12 Adult **Fic**

1. Suicide -- Fiction 2. Homosexuality -- Fiction 3. Psychiatric hospitals -- Fiction

ISBN 978-0-06-073755-9; 0-06-073755-7; 978-0-06-073757-3 pa; 0-06-073757-3 pa

LC 2008-19199

Brimming with sarcasm, fifteen-year-old Jeff describes his stay in a psychiatric ward after attempting to commit suicide.

Ford's "characterizations run deep, and without too much contrivance the teens' interactions slowly dislodge clues about what triggered Jeff's suicide attempt." Publ Wkly

Z. HarperTeen 2010 276p $16.99; lib bdg $17.89

Grades: 7 8 9 10 **Fic**

1. Science fiction 2. Games -- Fiction 3. Zombies -- Fiction

ISBN 978-0-06-073758-0; 0-06-073758-1; 978-0-06-073759-7 lib bdg; 0-06-073759-X lib bdg

LC 2009-44005

In the year 2032, after a virus that turned people into zombies has been eradicated, Josh is invited to join an underground gaming society, where the gamers hunt zombies and the action is more dangerous than it seems.

"This book is a thriller, and the clever plot and characters will have readers hoping for more." SLJ

Forman, Gayle

I was here; Gayle Forman. Viking. 2015 288p $18.99

Grades: 9 10 11 12 **Fic**

1. Friendship — Fiction; 2. Grief — Fiction; 3. Mystery and detective stories; 4. Suicide — Fiction; 5. Washington (State) —Fiction; 6. Secrets — Fiction; 7. Female friendship — Fiction

ISBN: 0451471474; 9780451471475

LC 2014011445

"Cody struggles to figure out why Meg took her own life and puzzles over a suspicious line in her friend's suicide email. The distraught but determined teen begins to encrypt files on Meg's laptop, which lead her to a suicide support group and posts from . . . a Pied Piper-type character who encourages suicide. As she goes further down the rabbit hole, Cody comes to the realization that she needs to forgive Meg, and, more importantly, herself." (School Library Journal)

"An engrossing and provocative look at the devastating finality of suicide, survivor's guilt, the complicated nature of responsibility and even the role of the Internet in life-and-death decisions." Kirkus

★ **If** I stay; a novel. Dutton Children's Books 2009 201p $16.99
Grades: 7 8 9 10 **Fic**

1. Coma -- Fiction 2. Death -- Fiction 3. Oregon -- Fiction 4. Medical care -- Fiction
ISBN 978-0-525-42103-0; 0-525-42103-3
LC 2008-23938

While in a coma following an automobile accident that killed her parents and younger brother, seventeen-year-old Mia, a gifted cellist, weights whether to live with her grief or join her family in death.

"Intensely moving, the novel will force readers to take stock of their lives and the people and things that make them worth living." Publ Wkly

Followed by: Where she went (2011)

Just one day; Gayle Forman. Dutton Books 2013 320 p. (hardcover: alk. paper) $17.99
Grades: 9 10 11 12 **Fic**

1. Love stories 2. Voyages and travels -- Fiction 3. Love -- Fiction 4. Europe -- Fiction 5. Actors and actresses -- Fiction 6. Self-actualization (Psychology) -- Fiction
ISBN 0525425918; 9780525425915
LC 2012030798

In this story, recent high school graduate Allyson meets Dutch actor Willem and "the two take an impulsive trip to Paris, but Willem disappears and Allyson is left stranded. Back in the U.S., Allyson is unable to wipe Willem from her mind, and her carefully planned future takes unexpected turns. . . . In college, Allyson breaks away from her mother's expectations, realizes her passion for theater and language, and tries to gather clues about Willem's whereabouts." (Publishers Weekly)

Where she went. Dutton Books 2011 264p $16.99
Grades: 7 8 9 10 **Fic**

1. Musicians -- Fiction 2. Rock music -- Fiction 3. Violoncellos -- Fiction 4. New York (N.Y.) -- Fiction
ISBN 978-0-525-42294-5; 0-525-42294-3
LC 2010-13474

In this sequel to If I stay, Adam, now a rising rock star, and Mia, a successful cellist, reunite in New York and reconnect after the horrific events that tore them apart when Mia almost died in a car accident three years earlier.

"Both characters spring to life, and their pain-filled back story and current realities provide depth and will hold readers fast." Kirkus

Forster, Miriam

★ **City** of a Thousand Dolls; Miriam Forster. HarperTeen 2013 368 p. (hardcover) $17.99
Grades: 9 10 11 12 **Fic**

1. Fantasy fiction 2. Mystery fiction 3. Fantasy 4. Orphans -- Fiction
ISBN 0062121308; 9780062121301
LC 2012004289

In this book, "Nisha has lived in the City of a Thousand Dolls for 10 years, ever since her parents abandoned her there. Unlike the other girls there, she was never placed in one of the city's Houses to be trained. Nisha's only status comes from her position as the assistant to the Matron, a placement that allows her access to any house on the grounds. When someone begins killing girls on the eve of the Royal Prince's arrival to claim his bride, terror and chaos ensue." (School Library Journal)

Foxlee, Karen

The **anatomy** of wings. Alfred A. Knopf 2009 361p $16.99; lib bdg $19.99
Grades: 8 9 10 11 12 **Fic**

1. Sisters -- Fiction 2. Suicide -- Fiction 3. Australia -- Fiction 4. Bereavement -- Fiction 5. Family life -- Fiction
ISBN 978-0-375-85643-3; 0-375-85643-9; 978-0-375-95643-0 lib bdg; 0-375-95643-3 lib bdg
LC 2008-19373

First published 2007 in Australia

After the suicide of her troubled teenage sister, eleven-year-old Jenny struggles to understand what actually happened.

Jenny's "observations are . . . poetic and washed with magic realism. . . . With heart-stopping accuracy and sly symbolism, Foxlee captures the small ways that humans reveal themselves, the mysterious intensity of female adolescence, and the surreal quiet of a grieving house, which slowly and with astonishing resilience fills again with sound and music." Booklist

The **midnight** dress; Karen Foxlee. Alfred A. Knopf 2013 288 p. $16.99
Grades: 9 10 11 12 **Fic**

1. Magic -- Fiction 2. Female friendship -- Fiction 3. Clothing and dress -- Fiction 4. Sewing -- Fiction 5. Schools -- Fiction 6. Australia -- Fiction 7. Alcoholism -- Fiction 8. Friendship -- Fiction 9. Mystery and detective stories 10. Single-parent families -- Fiction 11. Eccentrics and eccentricities -- Fiction
ISBN 0375856455; 9780375856457; 9780375956454; 9780449818213
LC 2012029108

In this book by Karen Foxlee, "Rose doesn't expect to fall in love with the . . . town of Leonora. Nor does she expect to become fast friends with . . . Pearl Kelly, organizer of the high school float at the annual Harvest Festival parade. Pearl convinces Rose to visit Edie Baker, once a renowned dressmaker, now a rumored witch. Together Rose and Edie hand-stitch [a dress] for Rose to wear at the Harvest Festival--a dress that will have long-lasting consequences." (Publisher's note)

"After arriving in Australian beach town Leonora, self-contained, morose Rose is befriended by outgoing Pearl. Pearl tells Rose about the annual harvest festival and urges her to start thinking about a gown. Enter the enigmatic Edie Baker, an old dressmaker. There are many story lines within Foxlee's complex novel; they coalesce into a dream-like, eerie whole told in mesmerizing, sensuous prose." (Horn Book)

Frank, E. R.

★ **America**; a novel. Atheneum Pubs. 2002 242p $18

Grades: 9 10 11 12 **Fic**

1. Foster home care -- Fiction 2. Racially mixed people -- Fiction

ISBN 0-689-84729-7

LC 2001-22984

Teenage America, a not-black, not-white, not-anything boy who has spent many years in institutions for disturbed, antisocial behavior, tries to piece his life together

The author "exposes with compassion, clarity, and deeply unsetting detail the profound shame and horror of abuse as well as the erratic nature of a medical system that tries to reclaim the victims. . . . A piercing, unforgettable novel." Booklist

Life is funny; a novel. Puffin Books 2002 263p pa $7.99

Grades: 7 8 9 10 **Fic**

1. Family life -- Fiction 2. Brooklyn (New York, N.Y.) -- Fiction

ISBN 0-14-230083-7

LC 2001-48436

First published 2000 by DK Ink

The lives of a number of young people of different races, economic backgrounds, and family situations living in Brooklyn, New York, become intertwined over a seven year period.

"The voices ring true, and the talk is painful, vulgar, rough, sexy, funny, fearful, furious, gentle." Booklist

Wrecked. Atheneum Books for Young Readers 2005 247p $15.95

Grades: 8 9 10 11 12 **Fic**

1. Bereavement -- Fiction 2. Traffic accidents -- Fiction

ISBN 0-689-87383-2

LC 2004-18448

After a car accident seriously injures her best friend and kills her brother's girlfriend, sixteen-year-old Anna tries to cope with her guilt and grief, while learning some truths about her family and herself.

"This story is compulsively readable both because Anna is likable and imperfect and because Frank's writing is so fluid." SLJ

Frank, Hillary

Better than running at night. Houghton Mifflin 2002 263p $17; pa $10

Grades: 9 10 11 12 **Fic**

1. School stories

ISBN 0-618-10439-9; 0-618-25073-5 pa

LC 2002-218

"Ellie's a freshman at art college, and her new life is bringing her all the changes she could have desired. She's in an intense and strange introductory class, which is causing her to rethink her artistic priorities; more significantly, she's in her first serious and sexual relationship." Bull Cent Child Books

"With honesty, wit, and a wild first-person narrative, this first novel breaks boundaries in YA fiction." Booklist

The **view** from the top. Dutton 2010 232p il $16.99

Grades: 9 10 11 12 **Fic**

1. Maine -- Fiction 2. Friendship -- Fiction 3. Family life -- Fiction 4. Dating (Social customs) -- Fiction

ISBN 978-0-525-42241-9; 0-525-42241-2

LC 2009-26143

Anabelle and her fellow high school graduates navigate their way through a disastrous summer of love and friendship in the small coastal town of Normal, Maine.

"This quirky love story about falling for yourself first will appeal to teens' hearts and heads." Booklist

Franklin, Emily

The **half** life of planets; a novel. [by] Emily Franklin and Brendan Halpin. Disney Hyperion Books 2010 247p $16.99

Grades: 7 8 9 10 **Fic**

1. Astronomy -- Fiction 2. Rock music -- Fiction 3. Bereavement -- Fiction 4. Family life -- Fiction 5. Asperger's syndrome -- Fiction

ISBN 978-1-4231-2111-4; 1-4231-2111-2

LC 2010-4606

An unlikely romance develops between a science-minded girl who is determined to reclaim her reputation and a boy with Asperger's Syndrome.

"The discursive story favors dialogue and introspection over action and can border on melodrama, but the characters' candid perspectives ring true and the romance should have readers longing for connections as deeply felt." Publ Wkly

The **other** half of me. Delacorte Press 2007 247p $15.99; pa $6.50

Grades: 8 9 10 11 12 **Fic**

1. Artists -- Fiction 2. Sisters -- Fiction 3. Identity (Psychology) -- Fiction

ISBN 978-0-385-73445-5; 0-385-73445-X; 978-0-385-73446-2 pa; 0385-73446-8 pa

LC 2006-36825

Feeling out of place in her athletic family, artistic sixteen-year-old Jenny Fitzgerald, whose biological father was a sperm donor, finds her half sister through the Sibling Donor Registry and contacts her, hoping that this will finally make her feel complete.

"Franklin offers readers an engaging protagonist whose humor and unusual situation highlight the lonely and displaced feelings common to many teens." SLJ

Frazier, Angie

The **Eternal** Sea. Scholastic Press 2011 362p $17.99

Grades: 8 9 10 11 12 **Fic**

1. Adventure fiction 2. Egypt -- Fiction 3. Supernatural -- Fiction

ISBN 978-0-545-11475-2; 0-545-11475-6

Sequel to: Everlasting (2010)

Realizing that the magic of Umandu, the stone that grants immortality, is not done, seventeen-year-old Camille accompanies Oscar, Ira, and Randall to Egypt, where all their lives are in grave danger.

"Readers who enjoy sea romances won't go wrong." SLJ

Everlasting. Scholastic Press 2010 329p $17.99
Grades: 8 9 10 11 12 **Fic**

1. Adventure fiction 2. Australia -- Fiction 3. Shipwrecks -- Fiction 4. Supernatural -- Fiction 5. Seafaring life -- Fiction 6. Father-daughter relationship -- Fiction

ISBN 978-0-545-11473-8; 0-545-11473-X

LC 2009-20519

In 1855, seventeen-year-old Camille sets out from San Francisco, California, on her last sea voyage before entering a loveless marriage, but when her father's ship is destroyed, she and a friend embark on a cross-Australian quest to find her long-lost mother who holds a map to a magical stone.

"Although this novel takes place in the nineteenth century, many of the themes are relevant for today's teens. The author does a nice job of developing strong and funny characters while keeping the plot moving at a readable pace." Voice Youth Advocates

Followed by: The eternal sea (2011)

Fredericks, Mariah

Crunch time. Atheneum Bks. for Young Readers 2006 317p $15.95
Grades: 9 10 11 12 **Fic**

1. School stories 2. Friendship -- Fiction

ISBN 0-689-86938-X

LC 2004-20008

Four students, who have formed a study group to prepare for the SAT exam, sustain each other through the emotional highs and lows of their junior year in high school. "Grades seven to ten." (Bull Cent Child Books)

"Fredericks writes about high school academics and social rules with sharp insight and spot-on humor." Booklist

The **girl** in the park; Mariah Fredericks. Schwartz & Wade Books 2012 217 p. $16.99
Grades: 10 11 12 **Fic**

1. Mystery fiction 2. Crime -- Fiction 3. Girls -- Fiction 4. New York (N.Y.) -- Fiction 5. Murder -- Fiction 6. Schools -- Fiction 7. High schools -- Fiction 8. Mystery and detective stories

ISBN 0375868437; 9780375868436; 9780375899072; 9780375968433

LC 2011012309

This young adult mystery novel by Mariah Frederick follows teenage social life in New York City. "When Wendy Geller's body is found in Central Park after the night of a rager, . . . Shy Rain, once Wendy's best friend, knows there was more to Wendy than just 'party girl.' As she struggles to separate the friend she knew from the tangle of gossip and headlines, Rain becomes determined to discover the truth about the murder." (Publisher's note)

Head games. Atheneum Books for Young Readers 2004 260p $15.95
Grades: 7 8 9 10 **Fic**

1. School stories 2. Dating (Social customs) -- Fiction

ISBN 0-689-85532-X

LC 2003-17012

Two teenagers connect online in a roleplaying game which leads them into their own face-to-face, half-acknowledged courtship.

"This novel realistically portrays young adults trying to find themselves, fit in, and resist the labels put on them." SLJ

Freitas, Donna

★ The **possibilities** of sainthood. Farrar, Straus & Giroux 2008 272p $16.95
Grades: 7 8 9 10 11 12 **Fic**

1. School stories 2. Saints -- Fiction 3. Catholics -- Fiction 4. Family life -- Fiction 5. Rhode Island -- Fiction 6. Italian Americans -- Fiction

ISBN 978-0-374-36087-0; 0-374-36087-1

LC 2007-33298

While regularly petitioning the Vatican to make her the first living saint, fifteen-year-old Antonia Labella prays to assorted patron saints for everything from help with preparing the family's fig trees for a Rhode Island winter to getting her first kiss from the right boy.

"With a satisfying ending, this novel about the realistic struggles of a chaste teen is a great addition to all collections." SLJ

The **Survival** Kit. Farrar Straus Giroux 2011 351p $16.99
Grades: 7 8 9 10 **Fic**

1. Death -- Fiction 2. Bereavement -- Fiction

ISBN 978-0-374-39917-7; 0-374-39917-4

LC 2010041294

After her mother dies, sixteen-year-old Rose works through her grief by finding meaning in a survival kit that her mother left behind.

"The premise of the survival kit, a real-life tradition from Freitas's own mother, begs to be discussed and glued-and-scissored with friends, students, teachers, and librarians. A copy of The Survival Kit would be a worthy addition for a teen coping with her own loss or struggling to help friends or family cope with theirs." Voice Youth Advocates

This gorgeous game. Farrar, Straus and Giroux 2010 208p $16.99
Grades: 9 10 11 12 **Fic**

1. Priests -- Fiction 2. Authorship -- Fiction 3. Sexual harassment -- Fiction 4. Colleges and universities -- Fiction 5. Teacher-student relationship -- Fiction

ISBN 978-0-374-31472-9; 0-374-31472-1

LC 2009-18309

Seventeen-year-old Olivia Peters, who dreams of becoming a writer, is thrilled to be selected to take a college fiction seminar taught by her idol, Father Mark, but when the priest's enthusiasm for her writing develops into something more, Olivia shifts from wonder to confusion to despair.

"Young women who have found themselves the object of obsession will relate to the protagonist's ordeal and be inspired by her decision to speak out no matter the consequences." Publ Wkly

Freymann-Weyr, Garret

★ **After** the moment. Houghton Mifflin Harcourt 2009 328p $16
Grades: 8 9 10 11 12 **Fic**

1. Stepfamilies -- Fiction 2. Dating (Social customs) -- Fiction
ISBN 978-0-618-60572-9; 0-618-60572-X
LC 2008-36109

When seventeen-year-old Leigh changes high schools his senior year to help his stepsister, he finds himself falling in love with her emotional disturbed friend, although he is still attached to a girl back home.

"This is an expertly crafted story about a complicated first love." Publ Wkly

My heartbeat. Houghton Mifflin 2002 154p $15
Grades: 7 8 9 10 **Fic**

1. Siblings -- Fiction 2. Homosexuality -- Fiction
ISBN 0-618-14181-2
LC 2001-47059

Michael L. Printz Award honor book, 2003

As she tries to understand the closeness between her older brother and his best friend, fourteen-year-old Ellen finds her relationship with each of them changing

"This beautiful novel tells a frank, upbeat story of teen bisexual love in all its uncertainty, pain, and joy. . . . The fast, clipped dialogue will sweep teens into the story, as will Ellen's immediate first-person, present-tense narrative." Booklist

Stay with me. Houghton Mifflin 2006 308p $16
Grades: 9 10 11 12 **Fic**

1. Sisters -- Fiction 2. Suicide -- Fiction 3. New York (N.Y.) -- Fiction
ISBN 0-618-60571-1; 978-0-618-60571-2
LC 2005-10754

When her sister kills herself, sixteen-year-old Leila goes looking for a reason and, instead, discovers great love, her family's true history, and what her own place in it is.

"This novel pushes the markers of YA fiction onward and upward." Booklist

Friedman, Aimee

The **year** my sister got lucky. Scholastic 2008 370p $16.99
Grades: 7 8 9 10 **Fic**

1. Moving -- Fiction 2. Sisters -- Fiction 3. Country life -- Fiction 4. New York (State) -- Fiction 5. City and town life -- Fiction
ISBN 978-0-439-92227-2; 0-439-92227-5
LC 2007-16416

When fourteen-year-old Katie and her older sister, Michaela, move from New York City to upstate New York, Katie is horrified by the country lifestyle but is even more shocked when her sister adapts effortlessly, enjoying their new life, unlike Katie.

"Friedman gets the push and pull of the sister bond just right in this delightful, funny, insightful journey." Booklist

Friedman, Robin

Nothing. Flux 2008 232p pa $9.95
Grades: 7 8 9 10 **Fic**

1. Novels in verse 2. Jews -- Fiction 3. Bulimia -- Fiction 4. Family life -- Fiction
ISBN 978-0-7387-1304-5; 0-7387-1304-X
LC 2008-08184

Despite his outward image of popular, attractive high-achiever bound for the Ivy League college of his father's dreams, high school senior Parker sees himself as a fat, unattractive failure and finds relief for his overwhelming anxieties in ever-increasing bouts of binging and purging.

"The novel does a good job of letting readers inside the head of someone who is suffering from an eating disorder. Compelling reading." SLJ

Friend, Natasha

★ **Bounce**; [by] Natasha Friend. Scholastic Press 2007 188p $16.99
Grades: 6 7 8 9 **Fic**

1. Moving -- Fiction 2. Remarriage -- Fiction 3. Stepfamilies -- Fiction
ISBN 978-0-439-85350-7; 0-439-85350-8
LC 2006038126

Thirteen-year-old Evyn's world is turned upside-down when her father, widowed since she was a toddler, suddenly decides to remarry a woman with six children, move with Ev and her brother from Maine to Boston, and enroll her in private school.

The author "presents, through hip conversations and humor, believable characters and a feel-good story with a satisfying amount of pathos." SLJ

For keeps. Viking 2010 267p $16.99
Grades: 8 9 10 11 12 **Fic**

1. School stories 2. Massachusetts -- Fiction 3. Father-daughter relationship -- Fiction 4. Mother-daughter relationship -- Fiction
ISBN 978-0-670-01190-2; 0-670-01190-8
LC 2009-22472

Just as sixteen-year-old Josie and her mother finally begin trusting men enough to start dating seriously, the father Josie never knew comes back to town and shakes up what was already becoming a difficult mother-daughter relationship.

"The book discusses sex and abortion, and includes adult language and underage drinking. Many readers will be able to relate to this protagonist, whose strength and maturity set a positive example. Friend skillfully portrays the challenges of adolescence while telling an engaging story with unique and genuine characters." SLJ

Lush. Scholastic Press 2006 178p $16.99
Grades: 7 8 9 10 **Fic**

1. Fathers -- Fiction 2. Alcoholism -- Fiction
ISBN 0-439-85346-X
LC 2005-031333

Unable to cope with her father's alcoholism, thirteen-year-old Sam corresponds with an older student, sharing her family problems and asking for advice.

"Friend adeptly takes a teen problem and turns it into a believable, sensitive, character-driven story, with realistic dialogue." Booklist

My life in black and white; by Natasha Friend. Penguin Group USA 2012 294 p. (hardcover) $17.99; (paperback) $8.99
Grades: 8 9 10 11 **Fic**

1. Sisters 2. Self-perception 3. Self-consciousness 4. Boxing -- Fiction 5. Friendship -- Fiction 6. Peer pressure -- Fiction 7. Self-acceptance -- Fiction 8. Beauty, Personal -- Fiction 9. Dating (Social customs) -- Fiction

ISBN 067001303X; 9780670013036; 9780670784943
LC 2011021436

Author Natasha Friend tells the story of Lexi and her best friend Taylor. "After finding her boyfriend . . . and Taylor making out at a party, . . . an argument quickly escalates, leading to an accident that changes Lexi's life forever. . . . It isn't until her sister, Ruthie, and [friend] Theo . . . are honest with her that Lexi starts peeling away the plastic life she once had and discovers the real one underneath." (Kirkus Reviews)

Perfect. Milkweed Editions 2004 172p $16.95; pa $6.95
Grades: 6 7 8 9 **Fic**

1. Bulimia -- Fiction 2. Bereavement -- Fiction

ISBN 1-57131-652-3; 1-57131-651-5 pa
LC 2004-6371

Following the death of her father, thirteen-year-old Isabelle uses bulimia as a way to avoid her mother's and ten-year-old sister's grief, as well as her own.

"Isabelle's grief and anger are movingly and honestly portrayed, and her eventual empathy for her mother is believable and touching." Booklist

Friesen, Gayle

The **Isabel** factor. KCP Fiction 2005 252p $16.95; pa $6.95
Grades: 7 8 9 10 **Fic**

1. Camps -- Fiction 2. Friendship -- Fiction

ISBN 1-55337-737-0; 1-55337-738-9 pa

"Anna and Zoe are inseparable—at least until Zoe breaks her arm and Anna finds herself on her way to summer camp without her best friend. . . . By the time Zoe arrives at camp (with her arm still in a sling), Anna is already embroiled in keeping peace between the individualistic Isabel and everyone else in Cabin 7. . . . Girls addicted to friendship stories will welcome this particularly well-crafted novel." Booklist

Friesner, Esther M.

Spirit's princess; Esther Friesner. 1st ed. Random House Childrens Books 2012 449 p. (trade) $17.99; (paperback) $10.99; (ebook) $53.97; (lib bdg.) $20.99
Grades: 7 8 9 10 **Fic**

1. Family -- Fiction 2. Father-daughter relationship -- Fiction 3. Children with physical disabilities -- Fiction 4. Magic -- Fiction 5. Shamans -- Fiction 6. Spirits -- Fiction 7. Sex role -- Fiction 8. Japan -- History -- To 645 -- Fiction

ISBN 0375869077; 9780375869075; 9780375873140; 9780375873157; 9780375899904; 9780375969072
LC 2011010468

In the book by Esther Friesner, "Himiko's chieftain father adores her, as do her older brother and her father's wives. Despite their love and affection, none of them takes Himiko seriously when she insists she is a shaman. Himiko herself isn't sure she can achieve her goal; with one leg lame since she was a child, she can't do a shaman's dances. Though the current shaman insists Himiko will be her heir, it can't happen until Himiko is ready to stand up to her father." (Kirkus Reviews)

Friesner, Esther M.

Nobody's princess; [by] Esther Friesner. Random House 2007 305p hardcover o.p. pa $7.99
Grades: 6 7 8 9 10 **Fic**

1. Adventure fiction 2. Sex role -- Fiction 3. Classical mythology -- Fiction 4. Helen of Troy (Legendary character) -- Fiction

ISBN 978-0-375-87528-1; 0-375-87528-X; 978-0-375-87529-8 pa; 0-375-87529-8 pa
LC 2006-06515

Determined to fend for herself in a world where only men have real freedom, headstrong Helen, who will be called queen of Sparta and Helen of Troy one day, learns to fight, hunt, and ride horses while disguised as a boy, and goes on an adventure throughout the Mediterranean world.

This "is a fascinating portrait. . . . Along the way, Friesner skillfully exposes larger issues of women's rights, human bondage, and individual destiny. It's a rollicking good story." Booklist

Followed by: Nobody's prize (2008)

Nobody's prize. Random House 2008 320p $16.99; lib bdg $19.99
Grades: 6 7 8 9 **Fic**

1. Adventure fiction 2. Sex role -- Fiction 3. Jason (Greek mythology) -- Fiction 4. Helen of Troy (Legendary character) -- Fiction

ISBN 978-0-375-87531-1; 0-375-87531-X; 978-0-375-97531-8 lib bdg; 0-375-97531-4 lib bdg
LC 2007-08395

Still longing for adventure, Princess Helen of Sparta maintains her disguise as a boy to join her unsuspecting brothers as part of the crew of the Argo, the ship commanded by Prince Jason in his quest for the Golden Fleece.

"Friesner is an accomplished writer who is able to interweave a contemporary feel for these ancient characters with pieces of history and mythology. She can also be funny. . . . It is possible for readers to begin with this book. . . . But it is surely best enjoyed as part of a series, and libraries with the first book will want to make sure fans get their second helping." Voice Youth Advocates

Sphinx's princess. Random House 2009 370p il map $17.99; lib bdg $20.99
Grades: 8 9 10 11 12 **Fic**

1. Queens 2. Queens -- Fiction 3. Egypt -- History -- Fiction

ISBN 978-0-375-85654-9; 0-375-85654-4; 978-0-375-95654-6 lib bdg; 0-375-95654-9 lib bdg
LC 2009-13719

Although she is a dutiful daughter, Nefertiti's dancing abilities, remarkable beauty, and intelligence garner attention near and far, so much so that her family is summoned to the Egyptian royal court, where Nefertiti becomes a pawn in the power play of her scheming aunt, Queen Tiye.

"Dramatic plot twists, a powerful female subject, and engrossing details of life in ancient Egypt make for lively historical fiction." Booklist

Followed by: Sphinx's queen (2010)

Sphinx's queen. Random House 2010 352p $17.99; lib bdg $29.99

Grades: 8 9 10 11 12 **Fic**

1. Queens 2. Queens -- Fiction 3. Egypt -- History -- Fiction

ISBN 978-0-375-85657-0; 0-375-85657-9; 978-0-375-95657-7 lib bdg; 0-375-95657-3 lib bdg

LC 2010-13769

Sequel to: Sphinx's princess (2009)

Chased after by the prince and his soldiers for a crime she did not commit, Nefertiti finds temporary refuge in the wild hills along the Nile's west bank before returning to the royal court to plead her case to the Pharaoh.

This is written "in fine prose that expresses the questioning of religion that most young people experience as they approach maturity. . . . This deeply moral book tells a good story; or, rather, this good story reveals deeply moral truths." SLJ

Spirit's princess; Esther Friesner. 1st ed. Random House Childrens Books 2012 449 p. (trade) $17.99; (paperback) $10.99; (ebook) $53.97; (lib bdg.) $20.99

Grades: 7 8 9 10 **Fic**

1. Family -- Fiction 2. Father-daughter relationship -- Fiction 3. Physically handicapped children -- Fiction 4. Magic -- Fiction 5. Shamans -- Fiction 6. Spirits -- Fiction 7. Sex role -- Fiction

ISBN 0375869077; 9780375869075; 9780375873140; 9780375873157; 9780375899904; 9780375969072

LC 2011010468

In the book by Esther Friesner, "Himiko's chieftain father adores her, as do her older brother and her father's wives. Despite their love and affection, none of them takes Himiko seriously when she insists she is a shaman. Himiko herself isn't sure she can achieve her goal; with one leg lame since she was a child, she can't do a shaman's dances. Though the current shaman insists Himiko will be her heir, it can't happen until Himiko is ready to stand up to her father." (Kirkus Reviews)

Threads and flames. Viking 2010 390p $17.99

Grades: 6 7 8 9 10 **Fic**

1. Jews -- Fiction 2. Fires -- Fiction 3. Immigrants -- Fiction 4. New York (N.Y.) -- Fiction 5. Polish Americans -- Fiction 6. Triangle Shirtwaist Company, Inc. -- Fiction

ISBN 978-0-670-01245-9; 0-670-01245-9

After recovering from typhus, thirteen-year-old Raisa leaves her Polish shtetl for America to join her older sister, and goes to work at the Triangle Shirtwaist factory.

"Friesner's sparkling prose makes the immigrant experience in New York's Lower East Side come alive. . . . Readers will turn the pages with rapt attention to follow the characters' intrepid, risk-all adventures in building new lives." Booklist

Frost, Gregory

Lord Tophet; a Shadowbridge novel. by Gregory Frost. Del Rey/Ballantine Books 2008 222 p. (paperback) $14

Grades: 9 10 11 12 **Fic**

1. Occult fiction 2. Fantasy fiction 3. Magic -- Fiction 4. Puppeteers -- Fiction 5. Women storytellers -- Fiction

ISBN 0345497597; 9780345497598

LC 2008006642

This book is part of the Shadowbridge series by Gregory Frost. Here, "daughter of the legendary shadow-puppeteer Bardsham, Leodora has inherited her father's skills . . . and his enemies. Together with her manager—Soter, keeper of her father's darkest secrets, and a gifted young musician named Diverus, Leodora has traveled from span to span, her masked performances given under the stage name Jax, winning fame and fortune." (Publisher's note)

Shadowbridge; [by] Gregory Frost. Ballantine Books 2008 255p pa $14

Grades: 9 10 11 12 **Fic**

1. Fantasy fiction 2. Orphans -- Fiction

ISBN 978-0-345-49758-1 pa; 0-345-49758-9 pa

LC 2007033139

"Orphaned 16-year-old Leodora, a talented puppeteer and storyteller, is forced to hide her identity and gender as she travels the spans and tunnels of the ocean-crossing Shadowbridge in Frost's exciting first of a diptych. . . . Frost (Fitcher's Brides) draws richly detailed human characters and embellishes his multilayered stories with intriguing creatures—benevolent sea dragons, trickster foxes, death-eating snakes and capricious gods—that make this fantasy a sparkling gem of mythic invention and wonder." SLJ

Frost, Helen

★ The **braid**. Farrar, Straus and Giroux 2006 95p $16

Grades: 7 8 9 10 **Fic**

1. Novels in verse 2. Canada -- Fiction 3. Sisters -- Fiction 4. Scotland -- Fiction 5. Immigrants -- Fiction

ISBN 0-374-30962-0

LC 2005-40148

Two Scottish sisters, living on the western island of Barra in the 1850s, relate, in alternate voices and linked narrative poems, their experiences after their family is forcible evicted and separated with one sister accompanying their parents and younger siblings to Cape Breton, Canada, and the other staying behind with other family on the small island of Mingulay.

"The book will inspire both students and teachers to go back and study how the taut poetic lines manage to contain the powerful feelings." Booklist

★ **Crossing** stones. Farrar, Straus and Giroux 2009 184p $16.99

Grades: 6 7 8 9 10 **Fic**

1. War stories 2. Novels in verse 3. Soldiers -- Fiction 4. Family life -- Fiction 5. Women -- Suffrage -- Fiction

6. World War, 1914-1918 -- Fiction
ISBN 0-374-31653-8; 978-0-374-31653-2
LC 2008-20755

In their own voices, four young people, Muriel, Frank, Emma, and Ollie, tell of their experiences during the first World War, as the boys enlist and are sent overseas, Emma finishes school, and Muriel fights for peace and women's suffrage.

"Beautifully written in formally structured verse. . . . This [is a] beautifully written, gently told story." Voice Youth Advocates

Hidden. Farrar Straus Giroux 2011 147p $16.99
Grades: 6 7 8 9 10 **Fic**

1. Novels in verse 2. Camps -- Fiction 3. Friendship -- Fiction
ISBN 0-374-38221-2; 978-0-374-38221-6
LC 2010-24854

When Wren Abbott and Darra Monson are eight years old, Darra's father steals a minivan. He doesn't know that Wren is hiding in the back. Years later, in a chance encounter at camp, the girls face each other for the first time.

"This novel in verse stands out through its deliberate use of form to illuminate emotions and cleverly hide secrets in the text." Booklist

Keesha's house. Frances Foster Bks./Farrar, Straus & Giroux 2003 116p hardcover o.p. pa $8
Grades: 7 8 9 10 **Fic**

1. Home -- Fiction
ISBN 0-374-34064-1; 0-374-40012-1 pa
LC 2002-22698

Michael L. Printz Award honor book, 2004

Seven teens facing such problems as pregnancy, closeted homosexuality, and abuse each describe in poetic forms what caused them to leave home and where they found home again

"Spare, eloquent, and elegantly concise. . . . Public, private, or correctional educators and librarians should put this must-read on their shelves." Voice Youth Advocates

Frost, Mark

Alliance; Mark Frost. Random House Inc 2014 352 p. (The Paladin Prophecy) (hardback) $17.99
Grades: 7 8 9 10 **Fic**

1. Supernatural -- Fiction 2. Secret societies -- Fiction 3. Superheroes -- Fiction 4. Good and evil -- Fiction
ISBN 0375870466; 9780375870460
LC 2013041891

"This second entry in the Paladin Prophecy trilogy brings readers up to date and includes a list in the first chapter to show the strengths possessed by the main characters. Basically, this is another book involving the adventures of a group of young people against the forces of evil, set against a school backdrop...There are discoveries, including caves and a hidden lab, very real threats, and of course, more villains in book two, which ends on a cliff-hanger—with the final confrontation for the fate of the world still to come in the third book." (VOYA)

Fukuda, Andrew

The **Prey**; Andrew Fukuda. St Martins Press 2013 336 p. $18.99
Grades: 7 8 9 10 11 12 **Fic**

1. Horror fiction 2. Occult fiction 3. Survival skills -- Fiction
ISBN 1250005116; 9781250005113
LC 2013002667

This teen horror thriller, by Andrew Fukuda, is book 2 of the "Hunt" series. "With death only a heartbeat away, Gene and the remaining humans must find a way . . . to escape the hungry predators chasing them through the night. . . . Their escape takes them to a refuge of humans living high in the mountains. Gene and his friends think they're finally safe, but not everything here is as it seems." (Publisher's note)

Funke, Cornelia, 1958-

Fearless; Cornelia Funke. Little, Brown Books for Young Readers 2013 432 p. (hardcover) $19.99
Grades: 6 7 8 9 **Fic**

1. Fantasy fiction 2. Brothers -- Fiction 3. Blessing and cursing -- Fiction 4. Fantasy 5. Magic -- Fiction 6. Adventure and adventurers -- Fiction
ISBN 0316056103; 9780316056106
LC 2012028742

This fantasy novel, by Cornelia Funke, translated by Oliver Latsch, is part of the "Mirrorworld" series. "Jacob Reckless has . . . tried everything to shake the Fairy curse that traded his life for his brother's. . . . But . . . they hear of one last possibility . . .: a crossbow that can kill thousands, or heal one, when shot through the heart. But a Goyl treasure hunter is also searching for the prized crossbow." (Publisher's note)

"Adroitly building on layers of European fairy tale, Funke's original, rapid-fire narrative fearlessly transports Jacob and a bevy of ominous, multifaceted fantastical characters through a dark, decaying landscape in which death waits and honor is rare. Provocative, harrowing, engrossing." Kirkus

★ **Reckless**; written and illustrated by Cornelia Funke; translated by Oliver Latsch. Little, Brown 2010 394p il $19.99
Grades: 6 7 8 9 **Fic**

1. Fantasy fiction 2. Adventure fiction 3. Magic -- Fiction 4. Brothers -- Fiction
ISBN 978-0-316-05609-0; 0-316-05609-X; 031605609X; 9780316056090
LC 2010006877

Jacob and Will Reckless have looked out for each other ever since their father disappeared, but when Jacob discovers a magical mirror that transports him to a warring world populated by witches, giants, and ogres, he keeps it to himself until Will follows him one day, with dire consequences.

"The fluid, fast-paced narrative exposes Jacob's complex character, his complicated sibling relationship and a densely textured world brimming with vile villains and fairy-tale detritus." Kirkus

Fusco, Kimberly Newton

Tending to Grace. Knopf 2004 167p $14.95
Grades: 7 8 9 10 **Fic**

1. Aunts -- Fiction 2. Mothers -- Fiction 3. Speech

disorders -- Fiction
ISBN 0-375-82862-1

LC 2003-60406

When Cornelia's mother runs off with a boyfriend, leaving her with an eccentric aunt, Cornelia must finally confront the truth about herself and her mother.

"This quiet, beautiful first novel makes the search for home a searing drama." Booklist

Gagnon, Michelle

Don't let go; Michelle Gagnon. Harper. 2014 335p $17.99

Grades: 7 8 9 10 11 12 **Fic**

1. Dystopian fiction 2. Computer hackers--Fiction 3. Conspiracies--Fiction 4. Experiments--Fiction 5. Foster home care--Fiction 6. Abandoned children--Fiction
ISBN: 0062102966; 9780062102966

LC 2014001880

"This novel by Michelle Gagnon is the "finale to the Don't Turn Around trilogy," in which "Noa Torson is out of options. On the run with Peter and the two remaining teens of Persephone's Army, and with quickly failing health, she is up against immeasurable odds. The group is outnumbered, outsmarted, and outrun. But they will not give up. They know they must return to where this all began." (Publisher's note)

"Noa and three friends are on the run. They are toting heavy backpacks loaded with hard drives that contain the encrypted information they need to bring to the authorities to prove what experiments Pike has been doing on live people...A look into a future marred by what powerful people will do to fulfill their needs and wants is a little scary. It is heartening to see that young people who discover the truth can band together and battle what seems like overwhelming odds to triumph in the end." VOYA

Don't Look Now; Michelle Gagnon. Harpercollins Childrens Books 2013 336 p. $17.99

Grades: 7 8 9 10 11 12 **Fic**

1. Computer hackers -- Fiction 2. Abandoned children -- Fiction 3. Experiments -- Fiction 4. Foster home care -- Fiction 5. Dystopian fiction
ISBN 0062102931; 9780062102935

LC 2013021823

In this book, by Michelle Gagnon, "Noa Torsen is on the run. Having outsmarted the sinister Project Persephone, Noa and her friend Zeke now move stealthily across the country . . . Back in Boston, Peter anxiously follows Noa's movements from his computer, using his hacker skills to feed her the information she needs to stay alive. . . . It will take everything Noa and Peter have to bring down the Project before it gets them first." (Publisher's note)

"Still suffering strange side effects from her stint as a human lab rat at Pike & Dolan, Noa (Don't Turn Around) leads a group of homeless teens bent on sabotaging the corporation. In Boston, her "hacktivist" friend Peter and his ex-girlfriend, Amanda, uncover new evidence that places them all in danger. This tense, suspenseful tech-thriller will engage readers from beginning to end." (Horn Book)

Don't turn around; by Michelle Gagnon. Harper 2012 320 p. (trade bdg.) $17.99

Grades: 7 8 9 10 11 12 **Fic**

1. Dystopian fiction 2. Teenagers -- Fiction 3. Conspiracies -- Fiction 4. Computer hackers -- Fiction 5. Experiments -- Fiction 6. Foster home care -- Fiction 7. Abandoned children -- Fiction
ISBN 0062102907; 9780062102904

LC 2012009691

This book tells the story of "[t]eenage hackers Noa and Peter." Orphan Noa escapes a hospital after waking up from an operation she has no memory of. After having his computer seized when he investigated his father's files, "Peter enlists his hacktivist group /ALLIANCE/ (of which Noa is a member) to" investigate and counterattack. "The attack only serves to dig the teens in deeper when they uncover a frightening conspiracy of human experimentation and corporate malfeasance." (Kirkus Reviews)

Strangelets; by Michelle Gagnon. Soho Teen 2013 1 p. (alk. paper) $17.99

Grades: 8 9 10 11 12 **Fic**

1. Horror fiction 2. Mystery fiction 3. Science fiction 4. Escapes -- Fiction 5. Survival -- Fiction 6. Near-death experiences -- Fiction
ISBN 1616951370; 9781616951375

LC 2012038333

This book by Michelle Gagnon shows the "horror endured by six teens trapped in a hospital-like bunker. They come from every point on the globe: cancer-stricken Sophie from California, petty thief Declan from Ireland, military trainee Anat from Israel, hiker Nico from Switzerland, shy Yosh from Japan, and studious Zain from India." They must figure out why they are there. (Publishers Weekly)

Gaiman, Neil

Interworld; [by] Neil Gaiman [and] Michael Reaves. Eos 2007 239p $16.99; lib bdg $17.89

Grades: 6 7 8 9 10 **Fic**

1. Science fiction 2. Space and time -- Fiction
ISBN 978-0-06-123896-3; 978-0-06-123897-0 lib bdg

LC 2007-08617

At nearly fifteen years of age, Joey Harker learns that he is able to travel between dimensions. Soon, he joins a team of different versions of himself, each from another dimension, to fight the evil forces striving to conquer all the worlds.

This offers "vivid, well-imagined settings and characters. . . . [A] rousing sf/fantasy hybrid." Booklist

Galante, Cecilia

The **patron** saint of butterflies. Bloomsbury 2008 292p $16.95

Grades: 6 7 8 9 10 **Fic**

1. Cults -- Fiction 2. Christian life -- Fiction
ISBN 978-1-59990-249-4; 1-59990-249-4

LC 2007-51368

When her grandmother takes fourteen-year-old Agnes, her younger brother, and best friend Honey and escapes Mount Blessing, a Connecticut religious commune, Agnes clings to the faith she loves while Honey looks toward a future free of control, cruelty, and preferential treatment.

"If both girls occasionally seem wise beyond their years, readers will nevertheless cheer them on as they ponder the limits of faith and duty." SLJ

The **sweetness** of salt. Bloomsbury 2010 311p $16.99
Grades: 9 10 11 12 **Fic**

1. Sisters -- Fiction 2. Vermont -- Fiction 3. Family life -- Fiction 4. Self-perception -- Fiction
ISBN 978-1-59990-512-9; 1-59990-512-4
LC 2010-03477

After graduating from high school, class valedictorian Julia travels to Poultney, Vermont, to visit her older sister, and while she is there she learns about long-held family secrets that have shaped her into the person she has grown up to be.

"What makes this novel great is its simplicity. It is poignant without becoming overbearing; it is quiet yet speaks volumes. It contains a realness that is almost uncomfortable to face at times. . . . This is an excellent novel, one that deserves to be read." Voice Youth Advocates

The **summer** of May. Aladdin 2011 252p $16.99
Grades: 5 6 7 8 **Fic**

1. Anger -- Fiction 2. Summer -- Fiction 3. Teachers -- Fiction 4. Loss (Psychology) -- Fiction 5. Mother-daughter relationship -- Fiction
ISBN 1-4169-8023-7; 978-1-4169-8023-0
LC 2010-15879

An angry thirteen-year-old girl and her hated English teacher spend a summer school class together, learning surprising things about each other.

"May's voice is sometimes humorous, at times heartbreaking, and always authentic. . . . A taut and believable novel." SLJ

Gallagher, Liz

The **opposite** of invisible. Wendy Lamb Books 2008 153p $15.99; lib bdg $18.99
Grades: 8 9 10 11 12 **Fic**

1. Art -- Fiction 2. Friendship -- Fiction 3. Seattle (Wash.) -- Fiction 4. Dating (Social customs) -- Fiction
ISBN 978-0-375-84152-1; 0-375-84152-0; 978-0-375-94329-4 lib bdg; 0-375-94329-3 lib bdg
LC 2007-11334

Artistic Seattle high school sophomore Alice decides to emerge from her cocoon and date a football player, which causes a rift between her and her best friend, a boy who wants to be more than just friends.

"With its striking setting and diverse cast of well-developed characters, Gallagher's debut—like Alice—shines." Voice Youth Advocates

Gant, Gene

The **Thunder** in His Head. Lightning Source Inc 2012 200 p. (paperback) $14.99
Grades: 9 10 11 12 **Fic**

1. Divorce -- Fiction 2. Gay teenagers -- Fiction
ISBN 1613725728; 9781613725726

In this book, "Kyle Manning is a tall, strong, openly gay sixteen-year-old who makes decent grades and plays on his school's basketball team. He's a good kid who cares deeply about his family and friends. But his life has become a mess" due to his parents' divorce. "As Kyle struggles with his fear and frustration, he grows angrier and more erratic. Then he meets Dwight Varley, a buff, attractive athlete from another school." Will having Dwight make things better or worse? (Publisher's note)

García, Cristina, 1958-

Dreams of significant girls. Simon & Schuster Books for Young Readers 2011 238p $16.99
Grades: 9 10 11 12 **Fic**

1. School stories 2. Summer -- Fiction 3. Friendship -- Fiction 4. Switzerland -- Fiction
ISBN 978-1-4169-7920-3; 1-4169-7920-4
LC 2010002585

In the 1970s, a teenaged Iranian princess, a German-Canadian girl, and a Cuban-Jewish girl from New York City become friends when they spend three summers at a Swiss boarding school.

"The girls' personal awakenings feel organic, and the narrative handles mature themes well, including abortion, family connections to Nazis, and sexual awakenings. García's boarding school setting feels vibrantly alive, an international home away from home that readers should find as magical as do the protagonists." Publ Wkly

Garcia, Kami

Beautiful creatures; by Kami Garcia & Margie Stohl. Little, Brown and Co. 2010 563p $17.99
Grades: 7 8 9 10 **Fic**

1. Love stories 2. School stories 3. Supernatural -- Fiction 4. South Carolina -- Fiction 5. Extrasensory perception -- Fiction 6. United States -- History -- 1861-1865, Civil War -- Fiction
ISBN 0-316-04267-6; 978-0-316-04267-3
LC 2008-51306

ALA YALSA Morris Award Finalist, 2010

This novel is set in a small South Carolina town. Ethan is powerfully drawn to Lena, a new classmate with whom he shares a psychic connection and whose family hides a secret that my be revealed on her sixteenth birthday. "Grades eight to ten." (Bull Cent Child Books)

"The intensity of Ethan and Lena's need to be together is palpable, the detailed descriptions create a vivid, authentic world, and the allure of this story is the power of love. The satisfying conclusion is sure to lead directly into a sequel." SLJ

Followed by Beautiful darkness (2010)

Beautiful darkness; by Kami Garcia & Margaret Stohl. Little, Brown 2010 503p $17.99; pa $9.99
Grades: 8 9 10 11 12 **Fic**

1. Love stories 2. Supernatural -- Fiction 3. South Carolina -- Fiction 4. Extrasensory perception -- Fiction
ISBN 978-0-316-07705-7; 0-316-07705-7; 978-0-316-07704-0 pa; 0-316-07704-6 pa
LC 2010-7015

Sequel to: Beautiful creatures (2010)

In a small southern town with a secret world hidden in plain sight, sixteen-year-old Lena, who possesses supernatural powers and faces a life-altering decision, draws away from her true love, Ethan, a mortal with frightening visions.

"The southern gothic atmosphere, several new characters, and the surprising fate of one old favorite will keep readers going until the next book, which promises new surprises as '18 moons' approaches." Booklist

Garden, Nancy

Endgame. Harcourt 2006 287p $17

Grades: 8 9 10 11 12 **Fic**

1. School stories 2. Bullies -- Fiction 3. Violence -- Fiction 4. Family life -- Fiction

ISBN 0-15-205416-2; 978-0-15-205416-8

LC 2005-19486

Fifteen-year-old Gray Wilton, bullied at school and ridiculed by an unfeeling father for preferring drums to hunting, goes on a shooting rampage at his high school.

"This is a hard-hitting and eloquent look at the impact of bullying, and the resulting destruction of lives touched by the violence." SLJ

Gardner, Sally

★ **Maggot** moon; Sally Gardner. Candlewick Press 2013 288 p. (reinforced) $16.99

Grades: 7 8 9 10 11 12 **Fic**

1. Dystopian fiction 2. Alternative histories

ISBN 0763665533; 9780763665531

LC 2012947247

Costa Children's Book Award Winner 2012

In this dystopian novel, "Standish Treadwell, 15, has lost parents, neighbors, best friend: All disappeared from Zone Seven, a post-war occupied territory, into the hellish clutches of the Motherland. Now a new horror approaches. . . . Standish and [his friend] Hector spin fantasies about the far-off tantalizing consumer culture they glimpsed on television (now banned), but they lack a vision of the future beyond vague dreams of rescue." (Kirkus Reviews)

★ The **red** necklace; a story of the French Revolution. Dial Books 2008 378p $16.99

Grades: 8 9 10 11 12 **Fic**

1. Adventure fiction 2. Gypsies -- Fiction 3. Orphans -- Fiction 4. Social classes -- Fiction 5. France -- History -- 1789-1799, Revolution -- Fiction

ISBN 978-0-8037-3100-4; 0-8037-3100-0

LC 2007-39813

In the late eighteenth-century, Sido, the twelve-year-old daughter of a self-indulgent marquis, and Yann, a fourteen-year-old Gypsy orphan raised to perform in a magic show, face a common enemy at the start of the French Revolution.

"Scores are waiting to be settled on every page; this is a heart-stopper." Booklist

Followed by: The silver blade (2009)

The **Silver** Blade. Dial Books 2009 362p $16.99

Grades: 8 9 10 11 12 **Fic**

1. Adventure fiction 2. Magic -- Fiction 3. France -- History -- 1789-1799, Revolution -- Fiction

ISBN 978-0-8037-3377-0; 0-8037-3377-1

LC 2009-9282

Sequel to: The red necklace (2008)

As the Revolution descends into the ferocious Reign of Terror, Yann, now an extraordinary practioner of magic, uses his skills to confound his enemies and help spirit refugees out of France, but the question of his true identity and the kidnapping of his true love, Sido, expose him to dangers that threaten to destroy him.

"A luscious melodrama, rich in sensuous detail from horrific to sublime, with an iridescent overlay of magic." Kirkus

Garner, Em

Contaminated; by Em Garner. Egmont USA 2013 336 p. (hardcover) $17.99; (ebook) $17.99

Grades: 7 8 9 10 **Fic**

1. Horror fiction 2. Dystopian fiction 3. Horror stories 4. Science fiction 5. Mothers -- Fiction

ISBN 1606843540; 9781606843543; 9781606843550

LC 2012024472

This book is set two years after "a diet drink with genetically modified ingredients transformed countless Americans into mindlessly violent animals" Now, "the Contaminated are controlled by electronic collars, and the unclaimed are housed in kennels like that in which Velvet Ellis, 17, finds her mother." Velvet and her sister's "shaky hold on normal life is finally upended when Velvet brings their mother home, facing anger and fear from neighbors and eviction from their landlord." (Kirkus Reviews)

Garsee, Jeannine

Before, after, and somebody in between. Bloomsbury 2007 342p $16.95

Grades: 8 9 10 11 12 **Fic**

1. School stories 2. Poor -- Fiction 3. Alcoholism -- Fiction 4. Family life -- Fiction 5. Cleveland (Ohio) -- Fiction

ISBN 978-1-59990-022-3; 1-59990-022-X

LC 2006-27975

After dealing with an alcoholic mother and her abusive boyfriend, a school bully, and life on the wrong side of the tracks in Cleveland, Ohio, high school sophomore Martha Kowalski expects to be happy when she moves in with a rich family across town, but finds that the "rich life" has problems of its own.

"Readers who live in better conditions can experience the underside of life from her dead-on observations. Martha is just a hairsbreadth away from being sucked under like so many around her. Readers will be pulling for her to beat the odds." SLJ

Say the word. Bloomsbury Children's Books 2009 360p $16.99

Grades: 9 10 11 12 **Fic**

1. Ohio -- Fiction 2. Lesbians -- Fiction 3. Bereavement -- Fiction 4. Family life -- Fiction

ISBN 978-1-59990-333-0; 1-59990-333-4

LC 2008-16476

After the death of her estranged mother, who left Ohio years ago to live with her lesbian partner in New York City, seventeen-year-old Shawna Gallagher's life is transformed by revelations about her family, her best friend, and herself.

"This sensitive and heart-wrenching story slowly unfolds into a gripping read featuring realistically flawed characters who undergo genuine growth." Booklist

Garvey, Amy

Cold kiss. HarperTeen 2011 292p $17.99; ebook $9.99

Grades: 9 10 11 12 **Fic**

1. School stories 2. Dead -- Fiction 3. Future life -- Fiction 4. Parapsychology -- Fiction

ISBN 978-0-06-199622-1; 978-0-06-210335-2 ebook

LC 2010040421

When her boyfriend is killed in a car accident, high school student Wren Darby uses her hidden powers to bring him back from the dead, never imagining the consequences that will result from her decision.

"Garvey sidesteps zombie tropes by keeping the focus on Wren's emotional state and the consequences of her actions, painting a delicate portrait of first love, loss, and a 'girl who thought love came with ownership papers.'" Publ Wkly

Glass Heart; Amy Garvey. 1st ed. HarperTeen 2012 310 p. (hardcover) $17.99

Grades: 9 10 11 12 **Fic**

1. Horror fiction 2. Magic -- Fiction 3. Psychics -- Fiction 4. Horror stories 5. Psychic ability -- Fiction

ISBN 0061996246; 9780061996245

LC 2011052410

In this book by Amy Garvey, protagonist Wren has discovered "new magical abilities that include the power to resurrect the dead. . . . Desperate to learn more . . . Wren presses her mother for help. Unfortunately, secrecy, shame and pain keep her from teaching Wren. . . . Looking to her new friends, who have abilities of their own, Wren begins leading a secret life full of spells and excitement. But while Fiona seems mostly fun and frivolous, Bay is dark and dangerous." (Kirkus Reviews)

Gee, Maurice

★ **Salt.** Orca Book Publishers 2009 252p map (The Salt trilogy) $18; pa $12.95

Grades: 6 7 8 9 10 **Fic**

1. Fantasy fiction 2. Extrasensory perception -- Fiction

ISBN 978-1-55469-209-5; 1-55469-209-1; 978-1-55469-369-6 pa; 1-55469-369-1 pa

"Hari lives in Blood Burrow, a hellacious, rat-infested slum. . . . Pearl is a pampered daughter of Company, her only purpose in life to be married off to cement one of her father's political alliances. When both young people, who share rare psychic gifts, revolt against their fates, they find themselves on a desperate journey across a hostile landscape, with the forces of Company at their heels. . . . A compelling tale of anger and moral development that also powerfully explores the evils of colonialism and racism." Publ Wkly

Other titles in this series are:

Gool (2010)

The Limping Man (2011)

Gelbwasser, Margie

Inconvenient. Flux 2010 305p pa $9.95

Grades: 7 8 9 10 **Fic**

1. School stories 2. Alcoholism -- Fiction 3. Immigrants -- Fiction 4. Popularity -- Fiction 5. Russian Americans -- Fiction 6. Jews -- United States -- Fiction

ISBN 978-0-7387-2148-4; 0-7387-2148-4

LC 2010025578

While fifteen-year-old Russian-Jewish immigrant Alyssa tries desperately to cope with her mother's increasingly out-of-control alcoholism by covering for her and pretending things are normal, her best friend Lana attempts to fit in with the popular crowd at their high school.

"This will be a hit with girls who like realistic fiction that focuses on the complexity of human relationships." Voice Youth Advocates

Gensler, Sonia

The **revenant.** Alfred A. Knopf 2011 336p $16.99; lib bdg $19.99

Grades: 7 8 9 10 **Fic**

1. Ghost stories 2. School stories 3. Oklahoma -- Fiction 4. Teachers -- Fiction 5. Cherokee Indians -- Fiction 6. Cherokee National Female Seminary -- Fiction

ISBN 978-0-375-86701-9; 0-375-86701-5; 978-0-375-96701-6 lib bdg; 0-375-96701-X lib bdg

LC 2010-28701

When seventeen-year-old Willemina Hammond fakes credentials to get a teaching position at a school for Cherokee girls in nineteenth-century Oklahoma, she is haunted by the ghost of a drowned student.

"Gensler makes a solid debut with an eerie and suspenseful work of historical fiction in which everyone is a murder suspect. . . . The layers of detail address the complex social structure of the period, and Gensler's characters and dialogue are believably crafted." Publ Wkly

George, Jessica Day

★ **Princess** of glass. Bloomsbury Children's Books 2010 266p $16.99

Grades: 6 7 8 9 10 **Fic**

1. Fairy tales 2. Princesses -- Fiction

ISBN 978-1-59990-478-8; 1-59990-478-0

In the midst of maneuverings to create political alliances through marriage, sixteen-year-old Poppy, one of the infamous twelve dancing princesses, becomes the target of a vengeful witch while Prince Christian tries to save her.

"In a clever reworking of the Cinderella story, George once again proves adept at spinning her own magical tale." Booklist

★ **Princess** of the midnight ball. Bloomsbury Children's Books 2009 280p $16.99

Grades: 6 7 8 9 10 **Fic**

1. Fairy tales

ISBN 978-1-59990-322-4; 1-59990-322-9

LC 2008-30310

A retelling of the tale of twelve princesses who wear out their shoes dancing every night, and of Galen, a former soldier now working in the king's gardens, who follows them in hopes of breaking the curse.

"Fans of fairy-tale retellings . . . will enjoy this story for its magic, humor, and touch of romance." SLJ

Sun and moon, ice and snow. Bloomsbury 2008 336p $16.95
Grades: 7 8 9 10 11 12 **Fic**

1. Fairy tales 2. Fantasy fiction
ISBN 1-59990-109-9; 978-1-59990-109-1
LC 2007030848

A girl travels east of the sun and west of the moon to free her beloved prince from a magic spell.

"George has adapted Norse myths and fairy tales to create this eerily beautiful, often terrifying world. . . . Mystery, adventure, and the supernatural, and a touch of love are woven together to create a vivid, well-crafted, poetic fantasy." Booklist

George, Madeleine

The **difference** between you and me; Madeleine George. Viking 2012 256 p.
Grades: 9 10 11 12 **Fic**

1. Schools -- Fiction 2. Lesbians -- Fiction 3. High schools -- Fiction 4. Protest movements -- Fiction
ISBN 9780670011285
LC 2011012192

This young adult novel uses a trio of alternating narrators to tell the story of "self-proclaimed misfit and outspoken manifesto-author Jesse [who] deals daily with the hazards of being out and proud in high school. She's also carrying on a secret affair with image-conscious Emily, the girlfriend of a popular boy at school. Meeting weekly in the bathroom of the local public library, the two experience an inexplicable chemistry, even though Emily will barely acknowledge Jesse at any other time. Switching perspective among Emily, Jesse and a third girl, Esther, this . . . tale . . . explor[es] . . . attraction and shame. Jesse hides her relationship from her warmly quirky and accepting parents not because it is with a girl, but because she knows they will disapprove of its secrecy." (Kirkus)

★ **Looks**. Viking 2008 240p $16.99; pa $7.99
Grades: 8 9 10 11 12 **Fic**

1. School stories 2. Obesity -- Fiction 3. Friendship -- Fiction 4. Anorexia nervosa -- Fiction
ISBN 978-0-670-06167-9; 0-670-06167-0; 978-0-14-241419-4 pa; 0-14-241419-0 pa
LC 2007-38218

"Meghan and Aimee are on opposite ends of the outcast spectrum. Meghan is extremely overweight. . . . Aimee, on the other hand, is classic anorexic. Both girls have been hurt by one of the popular girls at school. They join forces to bring Cara down in a stunning bit of public humiliation. . . . The story will make readers think about the various issues touched upon, and it is difficult to put down." SLJ

Geras, Adele

Ithaka. Harcourt 2006 360p $17; pa $6.95
Grades: 7 8 9 10 **Fic**

1. Trojan War -- Fiction 2. Classical mythology -- Fiction 3. Odysseus (Greek mythology) -- Fiction
ISBN 0-15-205603-3; 0-15-206104-5 pa
LC 2005-7569

Companion volume to: Troy

The island of Ithaka is overrun with uncouth suitors demanding that Penelope choose a new husband, as she patiently awaits the return of Odysseus from the Trojan War.

This book "can introduce young people to the power of story in Homer's epics as well as being a beautifully written story in its own right." Voice Youth Advocates

★ **Troy**. Harcourt 2001 340p hardcover o.p. pa $6.95
Grades: 7 8 9 10 **Fic**

1. Trojan War -- Fiction
ISBN 0-15-216492-8; 0-15-204570-8 pa
LC 00-57262

"Mythology buffs will savor the author's ability to embellish stories of old without diminishing their original flavor, while the uninitiated will find this a captivating introduction to a pivotal event in classic Greek literature." Publ Wkly

Gier, Kerstin

Emerald green; Kerstin Gier; translated by Anthea Bell. Henry Holt and Co 2013 464 p. (hardback) $17.99
Grades: 7 8 9 10 **Fic**

1. Love stories 2. Time travel -- Fiction 3. Secret societies -- Fiction 4. Love -- Fiction 5. England -- Fiction 6. London (England) -- Fiction 7. Great Britain -- History -- Fiction 8. Family life -- England -- London -- Fiction
ISBN 0805092676; 9780805092677
LC 2013017885

Sequel to: Sapphire blue

In the conclusion to author Kerstin Gier's Ruby Red trilogy, Gwen has "recently learned that she is the Ruby, the final member of the time-traveling Circle of Twelve, and since then nothing has been going right. She suspects the founder of the Circle, Count Saint-German, is up to something nefarious, but nobody will believe her. And she's just learned that her charming time-traveling partner, Gideon, has probably been using her all along." (Publisher's note)

"The conclusion to the Ruby Red series has as many twists as the two previous books in the trilogy. Gwen has endured danger and flirted with romance throughout the two weeks (!) since she learned she's the final member of the time-traveling Circle of Twelve. Now, the questions aren't resolved until the final few pages as she tries to counteract the plans of the dastardly Count Saint-Germain. The best-selling series has been blessed with a clever heroine, a hysterical gargoyle, and a guy as good looking as he is enigmatic. With loooong lives ahead of them, perhaps this not the end after all. " (Booklist)

★ **Ruby** red. Henry Holt 2011 330p $16.99
Grades: 7 8 9 10 **Fic**

1. Family life -- Fiction 2. Time travel -- Fiction 3. London (England) -- Fiction 4. Secret societies -- Fiction
ISBN 978-0-8050-9252-3; 0-8050-9252-8
LC 2010-49223

"Sixteen-year-old Londoner Gwyneth Shepherd comes from a family of time travelers. The gene was supposed to have skipped Gwen, but sneaks up on her unexpectedly in the middle of class one day and hurls her way back to the 18th century, where she meets an insufferable-turns-lovable time-traveling boy named Gideon." TeenVogue.com

"Adventure, humor, and mystery all have satisfying roles here." Booklist

Sapphire blue; Kerstin Gier; translated from the German by Anthea Bell. Henry Holt 2012 362 p. (hc) $16.99

Grades: 7 8 9 10 **Fic**

1. Fantasy fiction 2. Time travel -- Fiction 3. Secret societies -- Fiction 4. England -- Fiction 5. London (England) -- Fiction 6. Great Britain -- History -- Fiction 7. Family life -- England -- London -- Fiction

ISBN 0805092668; 9780805092660

LC 2011034011

Sequel to: Ruby red

In this young adult fantasy novel, by Kerstin Gier, "16-year-old Gwen continues her time-traveling adventures as the newest member of the Circle of Twelve. . . . Her life's now controlled by . . . a secret society monitoring time travel. . . . All 12 time travelers must be introduced into the chronograph so the Circle can be closed, and the Guardians have assigned Gwen and irresistible Gideon de Villiers the task of locating four missing time travelers." (Kirkus Reviews)

Giles, Gail

Dark song. Little, Brown 2010 292p $16.99

Grades: 8 9 10 11 12 **Fic**

1. Criminals -- Fiction 2. Family life -- Fiction

ISBN 978-0-316-06886-4; 0-316-06886-1

LC 2010-06888

After her father loses his job and she finds out that her parents have lied to her, fifteen-year-old Ames feels betrayed enough to become involved with a criminal who will stop at nothing to get what he wants.

"Suspense lovers will savor this fast-paced psychological thriller." Voice Youth Advocates

Girls like us; Gail Giles. Candlewick Press 2014 224 p. $16.99

Grades: 9 10 11 12 **Fic**

1. Roommates -- Fiction 2. Friendship -- Fiction 3. People with disabilities -- Fiction

ISBN 0763662674; 9780763662677

LC 2013944011

" In compelling, engaging, and raw voices, 18-year-olds Biddy and Quincy, newly independent, intellectually disabled high-school graduates, narrate their growing friendship and uneasy transition into a life of jobs, real world apartments, and facing cruel prejudice... Giles (Dark Song, 2010) offers a sensitive and affecting story of two young women learning to thrive in spite of their hard circumstances." (Booklist)

Playing in traffic. Simon Pulse 2006 176p pa $7.99

Grades: 10 11 12 **Fic**

1. School stories 2. Homicide -- Fiction

ISBN 978-1-4169-0926-2; 1-4169-09265

LC 2006274249

First published 2004 by Roaring Brook Press

Shy and unremarkable, seventeen-year-old Matt Lathrop is surprised and flattered to find himself singled out for the sexual attentions of the alluring Skye Colbly, until he discovers the evil purpose behind her actions.

"The book is fast paced and written in short chapters that will keep a reluctant reader going. The language is realistic for this MTV generation and sex plays a big part in the story. Although the book is suggested for ages 12 years and up, I recommend that you consider it for grades 10 through 12." Libr Media Connect

Right behind you. Little, Brown 2007 292p hardcover o.p. pa $7.99

Grades: 8 9 10 11 12 **Fic**

1. Homicide -- Fiction 2. Family life -- Fiction 3. Psychotherapy -- Fiction

ISBN 978-0-316-16636-2; 0-316-16636-7; 978-0-316-16637-9 pa; 0-316-16637-5 pa

LC 2007-12336

After spending over four years in a mental institution for murdering a friend in Alaska, fourteen-year-old Kip begins a completely new life in Indiana with his father and stepmother under a different name, but not only has trouble fitting in, he finds there are still problems to deal with from his childhood.

"The story-behind-the-headlines flavor gives this a voyeuristic appeal, while the capable writing and sympathetic yet troubled protagonist will suck readers right into the action." Bull Cent Child Books

Shattering Glass. Simon Pulse 2003 215p pa $7.99

Grades: 7 8 9 10 **Fic**

1. School stories 2. Violence -- Fiction

ISBN 978-0-689-85800-0; 0-689-85800-0

First published 2002 by Roaring Brook Press

When Rob, the charismatic leader of the senior class, turns the school nerd into Prince Charming, his actions lead to unexpected violence.

"Tricky, surprising, and disquieting, this tension-filled story is a psychological thriller as well as a book about finding oneself and taking responsibility." Booklist

★ **What** happened to Cass McBride? a novel. Little, Brown and Company 2006 211p $16.99; pa $7.99

Grades: 11 12 **Fic**

1. Suicide -- Fiction 2. Kidnapping -- Fiction 3. Family life -- Fiction

ISBN 978-0-316-16638-6; 0-316-16638-3; 978-0-316-16639-3 pa; 0-316-16639-1 pa

LC 2005-37298

After his younger brother commits suicide, Kyle Kirby decides to exact revenge on the person he holds responsible.

"Often brutal, this outstanding psychological thriller is recommended for older teens." Voice Youth Advocates

Giles, Lamar

Fake ID; L.R. Giles. Amistad 2014 320 p. (hardback) $17.99

Grades: 8 9 10 11 12 **Fic**

1. Homicide -- Fiction 2. Witnesses -- Fiction 3.

Conspiracies -- Fiction 4. African Americans -- Fiction 5. Mystery and detective stories 6. Witness protection programs -- Fiction
ISBN 0062121847; 9780062121844
LC 2013032149

"Nick Pearson's real name is Tony Bordeaux. A high schooler in Witness Protection, this is the fourth new identity and home for Nick in the last few years. It's all because his father keeps falling into his old criminal habits...Teen readers will especially relate to the likable everyman and African American main character. His burgeoning relationship with Reya, despite being grounded in tragedy, is one of the more charming aspects of the plot. A twist reveal at the novel's climax will shock many and will leave fans of mystery and suspense books extremely satisfied." (School Library Journal)

Gill, David Macinnis

Black hole sun. Greenwillow Books 2010 340p $16.99

Grades: 8 9 10 11 12 **Fic**

1. Science fiction 2. Miners -- Fiction 3. Mars (Planet) -- Fiction
ISBN 978-0-06-167304-7; 0-06-167304-8
LC 2009-23050

"Durango is the 16-year-old chief of a team of mercenaries who eke out a living on Mars by earning meager commissions for their dangerous work. Their current job, and the main thrust of this high-energy, action-filled, science-fiction romp, is to protect South Pole miners from the Dræu, a cannibalistic group who are after the miners' treasure. . . . Throughout the novel, the dialogue crackles with expertly delivered sarcastic wit and venom. . . . Readers will have a hard time turning the pages fast enough as the body count rises to the climactic, satisfying ending." Booklist

Invisible sun; by David Macinnis Gill. 1st ed. Greenwillow Books 2012 370 p. (Black Hole Sun Trilogy) (paperback) $9.99; (trade bdg.) $16.99

Grades: 8 9 10 11 **Fic**

1. Science fiction 2. Mars (Planet) -- Fiction 3. Adventure fiction
ISBN 9780062073334; 006207332X; 9780062073327
LC 2011002841

Sequel to Black Hole Sun.

This science fiction adventure story, by David Macinnis Gill, is the sequel to "Black Hole Sun," continuing to describe how "Martian freedom fighters Durango and Vienne infiltrate an evil government compound in search of missing data they hope will render the planet safe from future harm. This . . . novel is packed with . . . death-defying escapes, ambushes and . . . shootouts." (Kirkus)

Shadow on the sun; David Macinnis Gill. 1st ed. Greenwillow Books, an imprint of HarperCollins Publishers 2013 432 p. (Black Hole Sun Trilogy) (hardcover) $17.99

Grades: 8 9 10 11 **Fic**

1. Science fiction 2. Mars (Planet) -- Fiction
ISBN 0062073354; 9780062073358
LC 2013008361

This young adult science fiction novel, by David Macinnis Gill, is the sequel to "Invisible Sun." "Ex-Regulators Durango and Vienne are at it again in a race against time on a dangerous Martian landscape. Shocked to have learned that his father heads up the enemy forces who captured him at the end of the previous book, wisecracking teen soldier Durango fights to escape the clutches of his evil dad and to reunite with his ex-assassin sidekick and love interest, Vienne." (Kirkus Reviews)

"This sequel doesn't stand alone, and Gill inserts just enough left turns and red herrings to keep seasoned series readers guessing. . . . A refreshingly nondystopic sci-fi adventure." Kirkus

Soul enchilada. Greenwillow Books 2009 368p $16.99; lib bdg $17.89

Grades: 7 8 9 10 **Fic**

1. Devil -- Fiction 2. Grandfathers -- Fiction 3. Racially mixed people -- Fiction
ISBN 978-0-06-167301-6; 0-06-167301-3; 978-0-06-167302-3 lib bdg; 0-06-167302-1 lib bdg
LC 2008-19486

When, after a demon appears to repossess her car, she discovers that both the car and her soul were given as collateral in a deal made with the Devil by her irrascible grandfather, eighteen-year-old Bug Smoot, given two-days' grace, tries to find ways to outsmart the Devil as she frantically searches for her conveniently absent relative.

"Bug is a refreshingly gutsy female protagonist with an attitude that will win over readers searching for something different." Booklist

Gilman, Charles

Professor Gargoyle; Charlie Ward. Quirk Books 2012 175 p. (hardcover) $13.99

Grades: 7 8 9 10 **Fic**

1. Horror fiction 2. School stories 3. Monsters 4. Teachers 5. Middle schools
ISBN 1594745919; 9781594745911
LC 2011946052

In this novel by Charles Gilman "Strange things are happening at Lovecraft Middle School. Rats are leaping from lockers. Students are disappearing. The school library is a labyrinth of secret corridors. And the science teacher is acting very peculiar -- in fact, he just might be a monster-in-disguise. Twelve-year-old Robert Arthur knew that seventh grade was going to be weird, but this is ridiculous!"(Publisher's note)

Gilman, David

The **devil's** breath. Delacorte Press 2008 391p (Danger zone) $15.99; lib bdg $18.99

Grades: 7 8 9 10 11 12 **Fic**

1. Adventure fiction 2. Namibia -- Fiction 3. Environmental protection -- Fiction
ISBN 978-0-385-73560-5; 978-0-385-90546-6 lib bdg
LC 2007-46744

When fifteen-year-old Max Gordon's environmentalist-adventurer father goes missing while working in Namibia and Max becomes the target of a would-be assassin at his school in England, he decides he must follow his father to Africa and find him before they both are killed.

"The action is relentless. . . . Gilman has a flair for making the preposterous seem possible." Booklist

Other titles in this series are:
Ice claw (2010)
Blood sun (2011)

Gilmore, Kate

The **exchange** student. Houghton Mifflin 1999 216p $15; pa $6.95

Grades: 7 8 9 10 **Fic**

1. Science fiction 2. Endangered species -- Fiction 3. Wildlife conservation -- Fiction 4. Extraterrestrial beings -- Fiction

ISBN 0-395-57511-7; 0-618-68948-6 pa

LC 97-47162

When her mother arranges to host one of the young people coming to Earth from Chela, Daria is both pleased and intrigued by the keen interest shown by the Chelan in her work breeding endangered species

"Gilmore makes a farfetched premise seem more reasonable with everyday details of life in the twenty-first century, sympathetic characters, and logical consequences. . . . A story that will appeal to readers on many levels." Booklist

Gleason, Colleen

The **clockwork** scarab; Colleen Gleason. Chronicle Books 2013 356 p. (Stoker & Holmes) (alk. paper) $17.99

Grades: 7 8 9 10 **Fic**

1. Mystery fiction 2. Historical fiction 3. Scarabs -- Fiction 4. Time travel -- Fiction 5. Scarabs 6. Secret societies -- Fiction 7. Detective and mystery stories 8. Mystery and detective stories 9. Time travel 10. Secret societies 11. Great Britain -- History -- 1837-1901 -- Fiction 12. London (England) -- History -- 19th century -- Fiction 13. London (England) -- History -- 19th century

ISBN 1452110700; 9781452110707

LC 2012036578

This is the first book in Colleen Gleason's Stoker and Holmes series. The "narrative switches between two young women living in 1889 London: observant and cerebral Alvermina Holmes (she goes by Mina . . .), the niece of Sherlock Holmes; and Evaline Stoker, the headstrong (and physically strong) younger sister to Bram, and member of a proud line of vampire hunters." They "investigate the connection between the disappearance of a young woman and several recent murders." (Publishers Weekly)

Goeglein, T. M.

Cold fury; T.M. Goeglein. G.P. Putnam's Sons 2012 312 p. (hardcover) $17.99

Grades: 8 9 10 11 12 **Fic**

1. Mafia -- Fiction 2. Chicago (Ill.) -- Fiction 3. Missing persons -- Fiction 4. Violence -- Fiction 5. Secret societies -- Fiction 6. Mystery and detective stories

ISBN 0399257209; 9780399257209

LC 2011025824

This book by T. M. Goeglein follows "Sara Jane Rispoli . . . a normal sixteen-year-old coping with school and a budding romance--until her parents and brother are kidnapped and she discovers her family is deeply embedded in the Chicago Outfit (aka the mob). Now on the run from a masked assassin, rogue cops and her turncoat uncle, Sara Jane is chased and attacked at every turn, fighting back with cold fury as she searches for her family." (Publisher's note)

Goelman, Ari

The **path** of names; by Ari Goelman. Arthur A. Levine Books 2013 352 p. (hard cover: alk. paper) $16.99

Grades: 7 8 9 10 **Fic**

1. Ghost stories 2. Mystery fiction 3. Camps -- Fiction 4. Magic -- Fiction 5. Cabala -- Fiction 6. Labyrinths -- Fiction 7. Magic tricks -- Fiction 8. Camps 9. Magic 10. Cabala 11. Labyrinths 12. Brothers and sisters -- Fiction 13. Jews -- United States -- Fiction 14. Magic tricks 15. Brothers and sisters 16. Jews -- United States

ISBN 0545474302; 9780545474306; 9780545474313; 9780545540148

LC 2012030554

This book features Dahlia whom "her parents have sent . . . to Camp Arava. . . . When Dahlia first sees two young girls disappear through the cabin wall, she's convinced it's a great magic trick, but soon she realizes that they're actually ghosts. . . . These strange phenomena begin to converge around a mysterious garden maze on the campgrounds, a maze that is rumored to be connected to the disappearance of children and that is ferociously guarded by the skulking camp caretaker." (Bulletin of the Center for Children's Books)

"Thirteen-year-old magic nerd Dahlia loathes her Jewish summer camp until she starts dreaming about a Jewish teen in 1940s New York City who seems to be connected to a pair of ghosts haunting the camp. Readers with an interest in Jewish mysticism will enjoy the book's paranormal elements and tweens will appreciate the realistic relationships among the campers." (Horn Book)

Going, K. L.

★ **Fat** kid rules the world. Putnam 2003 187p $17.99; pa $6.99

Grades: 7 8 9 10 **Fic**

1. Obesity -- Fiction 2. Musicians -- Fiction 3. Friendship -- Fiction

ISBN 0-399-23990-1; 0-14-240208-7 pa

LC 2002-67956

Michael L. Printz Award honor book, 2004

Seventeen-year-old Troy, depressed, suicidal, and weighing nearly 300 pounds, gets a new perspective on life when a homeless teenager who is a genius on guitar wants Troy to be the drummer in his rock band

"Going has put together an amazing assortment of characters. . . . This is an impressive debut that offers hope for all kids." Booklist

★ **King** of the screwups. Houghton Mifflin Harcourt 2009 310p $17

Grades: 9 10 11 12 **Fic**

1. Uncles -- Fiction 2. Homosexuality -- Fiction 3. Father-son relationship -- Fiction

ISBN 978-0-15-206258-3; 0-15-206258-0

LC 2008-25113

After getting in trouble yet again, popular high school senior Liam, who never seems to live up to his wealthy father's expectations, is sent to live in a trailer park with his gay "glam-rocker" uncle.

"Readers—screwups or not—will empathize as Liam, utterly likable despite his faults, learns to be himself." Publ Wkly

Saint Iggy. Harcourt 2006 260p $17

Grades: 9 10 11 12 **Fic**

1. Poor -- Fiction 2. Drug abuse -- Fiction 3. Family life -- Fiction

ISBN 0-15-205795-1; 978-0-15-205795-4

LC 2005-34857

Iggy Corso, who lives in city public housing, is caught physically and spiritually between good and bad when he is kicked out of high school, goes searching for his missing mother, and causes his friend to get involved with the same dangerous drug dealer who deals to his parents.

"Teens will connect with Iggy's powerful sense that although he notices everything, he is not truly seen and accepted himself." Booklist

Goldblatt, Stacey

Stray; a novel. Delacorte Press 2007 276p $15.99; lib bdg $18.99

Grades: 7 8 9 10 11 12 **Fic**

1. Dogs -- Fiction 2. Dating (Social customs) -- Fiction 3. Mother-daughter relationship -- Fiction

ISBN 978-0-385-73443-1; 0-385-73443-3; 978-0-385-90448-3 lib bdg; 0-385-90448-7 lib bdg

LC 2006-31828

Natalie's mother, a veterinarian with a dogs-only practice, has the sixteen-year-old on such a short leash that, when the teenaged son of her old school friend comes to stay with them for the summer, Natalie is tempted to break her mother's rules and follow her own instincts for a change.

"This fresh treatment of a familiar teen feeling will attract readers who love dogs as well as a good first-love story." Booklist

Golden, Christopher

The **sea** wolves; by Christopher Golden & Tim Lebbon; with illustrations by Greg Ruth. Harper 2012 384 p. $16.99

Grades: 7 8 9 10 **Fic**

1. Sea stories 2. Adventure fiction 3. Monsters 4. Supernatural 5. Pirates -- Fiction 6. Supernatural -- Fiction 7. Adventure and adventurers -- Fiction

ISBN 0061863203; 9780061863202; 9780061863219

LC 2011010031

This young adult fantasy adventure novel by Christopher Golden and Tim Lebbon follows "Jack London . . . a writer who lived his own real-life adventures. But . . . even he couldn't set down [all his adventures] in writing. Terrifying, mysterious, bizarre, and magical. . . . Clinging to life after he is captured in an attack by savage pirates, Jack is unprepared for what he faces at the hands of the crew and their charismatic, murderous captain, Ghost. For these mariners are not mortal men but hungry beasts chasing gold and death across the North Pacific. Jack's only hope lies with Sabine—a sad, sultry captive of Ghost's insatiable hunger. But on these waters, nothing is as it seems, and Sabine may be hiding dangerous secrets of her own." (Publisher's note)

The **wild**; by Christopher Golden & Tim Lebbon; with illustrations by Greg Ruth. Harper 2011 348p il (The secret journeys of Jack London) $15.99; lib bdg $16.89

Grades: 7 8 9 10 **Fic**

1. Authors 2. Novelists 3. Adventure fiction 4. Wolves -- Fiction 5. Short story writers 6. Supernatural -- Fiction 7. Wilderness survival -- Fiction 8. Gold mines and mining -- Fiction 9. Yukon River valley (Yukon and Alaska) -- Fiction

ISBN 978-0-06-186317-2; 0-06-186317-3; 978-0-06-186318-9 lib bdg; 0-06-186318-1 lib bdg

LC 2010-07475

Seventeen-year-old Jack London makes the arduous journey to the Yukon's gold fields in 1893, becoming increasingly uneasy about supernatural forces in the wilderness that seem to have taken a special interest in him.

"Golden and Lebbon write with a gritty assurance that brings the fantasy elements . . . down to earth. . . . Occasional sketches add a bit of cinematic drama." Booklist

Golding, Julia

Secret of the sirens; [by] Julia Golding. 1st Marshall Cavendish ed.; Marshall Cavendish 2007 357p (The companions quartet) $16.99

Grades: 7 8 9 10 **Fic**

1. Supernatural -- Fiction 2. Mythical animals -- Fiction 3. Environmental protection -- Fiction

ISBN 978-0-7614-5371-0; 0-7614-5371-7

LC 2006052799

First published 2006 in the United Kingdom

Upon moving to her aunt's seaside home in the British Isles, Connie becomes part of a secret society that shelters mythical creatures, and must use her ability to communicate with these beings to protect them from evil and the incursions of humans.

This "packs a serious environmental message, yet never feels heavyhanded. . . . The contemporary setting and its modern villains . . . make for an entertaining read." Publ Wkly

Other titles in this series are:

The gorgon's gaze (2007)

Mines of the minotaur (2008)

The chimera's curse (2008)

Goldman, Steven

★ **Two** parties, one tux, and a very short film about the Grapes of Wrath. Bloomsbury Children's Books 2008 307p $16.99

Grades: 7 8 9 10 **Fic**

1. School stories 2. Friendship -- Fiction 3. Homosexuality -- Fiction 4. Dating (Social customs) -- Fiction

ISBN 978-1-59990-271-5; 1-59990-271-0

LC 2008-11587

Mitch, a shy and awkward high school junior, negotiates the difficult social situations he encounters, both with girls and with his best friend David, after David reveals to him that he is gay.

"With fitting touches of rough language and situations and on-target characters, this witty and skillfully developed story creates a compelling picture of high school life." Voice Youth Advocates

Golds, Cassandra

The **museum** of Mary Child. Kane Miller 2009 329p $16.99

Grades: 6 7 8 9 10 **Fic**

1. Dolls -- Fiction 2. Museums -- Fiction

ISBN 978-1-935279-13-6; 1-935279-13-0

LC 2009-922719

"Lonely Heloise wants only to be loved, but lives as if jailed in the house of her stern and sometimes cruel godmother. One day Heloise uncovers a beautiful doll, Maria, hidden under the floorboards of her room, and it is love at first sight. Heloise hides Maria from her godmother, whose personal Ten Commandments include forbidding play, 'pretty clothes' and the possession of a doll. . . . Once Maria is discovered, Heloise finds out the horrible truth about the museum that adjoins her godmother's cottage and is thrust down a strange and magical path that reveals how sheltered she has been. . . . Golds's novel is pure fun, filled with mystery and nearly impossible to put down." Publ Wkly

Gonzalez, Julie

Imaginary enemy. Delacorte Press 2008 241p $15.99; lib bdg $18.99

Grades: 6 7 8 9 10 **Fic**

1. Imaginary playmates -- Fiction

ISBN 978-0-385-73552-0; 0-385-73552-9; 978-0-385-90530-5 lib bdg; 0-385-90530-0 lib bdg

LC 2007-45752

Although her impetuous behavior, smart-mouthed comments, and slacker ways have landed her in trouble over the years, sixteen-year-old Jane has always put the blame on her "imaginary enemy," until a new development forces her to decide whether or not to assume responsibility for her actions.

"Gonzalez has written a witty, realistic novel . . . peppered with funny, authentic dialogue." Booklist

Goobie, Beth

Before wings; a novel. Orca Bk. Pubs. 2001 203p hardcover o.p. pa $8.95

Grades: 7 8 9 10 **Fic**

1. Camps -- Fiction 2. Death -- Fiction

ISBN 1-55143-161-0; 1-55143-163-7 pa

LC 00-105582

"Fifteen-year-old Adrien barely survived a brain aneurysm two years earlier, and is haunted by the fact that she could die from another one at any time. In fact, issues of life and death completely fill her world at Camp Lakeshore, owned and operated by her Aunt Erin, a woman with a haunted past of her own. Adrien bonds with Paul, a teen who is convinced that he has dreamt of his own death and that it will happen on his next birthday. She also seems to be experiencing events in the lives of five girls, a group of campers who died long ago in a tragic accident." SLJ

"Full of magic realism and beautifully written, this is a story of good triumphing over evil, life triumphing over death, the power of love, friendship, and the hope for an afterlife." Booklist

Goodman, Alison

★ **Eon**: Dragoneye reborn. Viking 2009 531p $19.99

Grades: 7 8 9 10 **Fic**

1. Fantasy fiction 2. Magic -- Fiction 3. Dragons -- Fiction 4. Sex role -- Fiction 5. Apprentices -- Fiction

ISBN 978-0-670-06227-0; 0-670-06227-8

LC 2008-33223

Sixteen-year-old Eon hopes to become an apprentice to one of the twelve energy dragons of good fortune and learn to be its main interpreter, but to do so will require much, including keeping secret that she is a girl.

"Entangled politics and fierce battle scenes provide a pulse-quickening pace, while the intriguing characters add interest and depth." Booklist

Followed by: Eona: The last Dragoneye (2011)

Eona: the last Dragoneye. Viking 2011 637p il $19.99

Grades: 7 8 9 10 **Fic**

1. Fantasy fiction 2. Magic -- Fiction 3. Dragons -- Fiction 4. Apprentices -- Fiction

ISBN 978-0-670-06311-6; 0-670-06311-8

LC 2011-02997

Sequel to: Eon: Dragoneye reborn (2009)

Eon has been revealed as Eona, the first female Dragoneye in hundreds of years. Along with fellow rebels Ryko and Lady Dela, she is on the run from High Lord Sethon's army. The renegades are on a quest for the black folio, stolen by the drug-riddled Dillon; they must also find Kygo, the young Pearl Emperor, who needs Eona's power and the black folio if he is to wrest back his throne from the self-styled "Emperor" Sethon.

"One of those rare and welcome fantasies that complicate black-and-white morality." Kirkus

Singing the Dogstar blues. Viking 2003 261p $16.99

Grades: 7 8 9 10 **Fic**

1. Time travel 2. Science fiction

ISBN 0-670-03610-2

LC 2002-12161

First published 1998 in Australia

In a future Australia, the saucy eighteen-year-old daughter of a famous newscaster and a sperm donor teams up with a hermaphrodite from the planet Choria in a time travel adventure that may significantly change both of their lives

"This wildly entertaining novel successfully mixes adventure, humor, mystery, and sf into a fast-paced, thrilling story that will apeal to a wide audience." Booklist

Goodman, Shawn

Kindness for weakness; Shawn Goodman. 1st ed. Delacorte Press 2013 272 p. (ebook) $50.97; (library) $19.99; (hardcover) $16.99

Grades: 9 10 11 12 **Fic**

1. Gangs -- Fiction 2. Juvenile delinquency -- Fiction 3. Brothers -- Fiction 4. Self-esteem -- Fiction 5. Drug

dealers -- Fiction
ISBN 0375991026; 9780307982070; 9780375991028; 9780385743242
LC 2012015772

In this book, Shawn Goodman "introduces 15-year-old James, who is caught running drugs for his older brother and sentenced to a year in juvie. Despite a rough initiation to the program, James—inspired by books recommended to him by his English teacher—does his best to stay out of trouble; however, his emotional and physical strength are tested time and again by corrupt, belligerent guards and boys who pressure him into joining a gang." (Publishers Weekly)

Something like hope. Delacorte Press 2011 193p $16.99; lib bdg $19.99
Grades: 9 10 11 12 **Fic**
1. African Americans -- Fiction 2. Juvenile delinquency -- Fiction
ISBN 978-0-385-73939-9; 978-0-385-90786-6 lib bdg
LC 2009-53657

"Smart, angry, and desperate, Shavonne, 17, is in juvenile detention again, and in her present-tense, first-person narrative, she describes the heartbreaking brutality that she suffered before she was locked up, as well as the harsh treatment, and sometimes the kindness, she encounters in juvie." (Booklist)

The author "delivers a gritty, frank tale that doesn't shrink from the harshness of the setting but that also provides a much-needed redemption for both Shavonne and readers." Kirkus

Gordimer, Nadine

★ The **house** gun. Penguin Books 1999 294p pa $15
Grades: 9 10 11 12 **Fic**
1. Homicide -- Fiction 2. South Africa -- Fiction
ISBN 0-14-027820-6
First published 1998 by Farrar, Straus & Giroux

"A house gun, like a house cat: a fact of ordinary daily life. How else can you defend yourself against intruders and thieves in post-apartheid South Africa? The respected executive director of an insurance company, Harald, and his doctor wife, Claudia, are faced with something that could never happen to them: Their son, Duncan, has murdered a man." Publisher's note

"Gordimer is above all a writer of ideas, and she engages her audience in the discourse of morality and ethical conduct without deteriorating into the tedious language of a civics lesson." Women's Rev Books

My son's story. Penguin Books 1991 277p pa $9.95
Grades: 9 10 11 12 **Fic**
1. South Africa -- Fiction
ISBN 0-14-015975-4
LC 91-17273
First published 1990 by Farrar, Straus & Giroux

"When Will skips school to slip off to a movie theater near Johannesburg, he is shocked to see his father. An ordinary mishap, but his father is no ordinary man. He is a "colored" and revered anti-apartheid hero, and his female companion is a white activist fiercely dedicated to the cause. As Will struggles with confusion and bitterness," Publisher's note

This is a "thoughtful, poised, quietly poignant novel that not only recognizes the value and cost of political commitment, but also takes account of recent developments in South Africa and Eastern Europe in a way that Gordimer's previous work did not." Christ Sci Monit

Gorman, Carol

Games. HarperCollinsPublishers 2007 279p $16.99; lib bdg $17.89
Grades: 6 7 8 9 **Fic**
1. School stories 2. Games -- Fiction
ISBN 978-0-06-057027-9; 0-06-057027-X; 978-0-06-057028-6 lib bdg; 0-06-057028-8 lib bdg
LC 2006-31759

When fourteen-year-old rivals Boot Quinn and Mick Sullivan fight once too often, the new principal devises the punishment of having to play games together at his office, where they learn which battles are worth fighting.

"This novel is a great book for middle school students, well scripted, realistic, and entertaining. The characters are true and understandable." Voice Youth Advocates

Gormley, Beatrice

Poisoned honey; a story of Mary Magdalene. Alfred A. Knopf 2010 306p $16.99; lib bdg $19.99
Grades: 9 10 11 12 **Fic**
1. Saints 2. Apostles 3. Jews -- Fiction 4. Saints -- Fiction 5. Jerusalem -- Fiction 6. Demoniac possession -- Fiction 7. Bible -- History of Biblical events -- Fiction
ISBN 978-0-375-85207-7; 0-375-85207-7; 978-0-375-95207-4 lib bdg; 0-375-95207-1 lib bdg
LC 2009-5095

Relates events from the life of a girl who would grow up to be a close follower of Jesus Christ, interspersed with stories of the Apostle Matthew. Includes author's note distinguishing what Scripture says of Mary Magdalene from later traditions.

"Fast paced and vivid, the novel will appeal most strongly to Christians, but other readers will find the portrait of a person, and a time, memorably real." SLJ

Goto, Hiromi

★ **Half** World; illustrations by Jillian Tamaki. Viking 2010 221p il $16.99
Grades: 7 8 9 10 **Fic**
1. Fantasy fiction 2. Mother-daughter relationship -- Fiction
ISBN 978-0-670-01220-6; 0-670-01220-3

"Raised in impoverished circumstances by her single mother, overweight 14-year-old Melanie is the target of ridicule at school and leads a lonely, introverted life. Then an evil being named Mr. Glueskin kidnaps her mother, forcing Melanie to travel to Half World, a colorless land that has been sundered from the realms of flesh and spirit, its deceased inhabitants cursed to relive the most traumatic moments of their lives. . . . Goto writes the hellish Half World as miserably surreal yet horrifyingly believable. . . . It's a fast-moving and provocative journey with cosmically high stakes, and one that should readily appeal to fans of dark, nightmarish fantasy." Publ Wkly

Gould, Sasha

Cross my heart; Sasha Gould. Delacorte Press 2011 263 p. (hc) $17.99

Grades: 9 10 11 12 **Fic**

1. Historical fiction 2. Young adult literature 3. Secret societies 4. Love -- Fiction 5. Sex role -- Fiction 6. Secret societies -- Fiction 7. Mystery and detective stories 8. Italy -- History -- 16th century -- Fiction 9. Venice (Italy) -- History -- 16th century -- Fiction

ISBN 0385741502; 9780375985409; 9780375990076; 9780385741507

LC 2011012357

This novel, by Sasha Goul, takes place in "Venice, 1585. When 16-year-old Laura della Scala['s] . . . older sister, Beatrice, . . . drown[s], she is given no time to grieve. Instead, Laura's father removes her from the convent where he forcibly sent her years earlier and orders her to marry Beatrice's fiance. . . . Panicked, Laura betrays a powerful man to earn her way into the Segreta, a shadowy society of women who deal in only one currency--secrets." (Publisher's note)

Grace, Amanda

In too deep; Amanda Grace. Flux 2012 228 p. $9.95

Grades: 7 8 9 10 11 12 **Fic**

1. Rape -- Fiction 2. Honesty -- Fiction 3. False accusation -- Fiction 4. High school students -- Fiction 5. Teenagers -- Conduct of life -- Fiction 6. Rumor -- Fiction 7. Schools -- Fiction 8. High schools -- Fiction 9. Conduct of life -- Fiction

ISBN 0738726001; 9780738726007

LC 2011028806

In this young adult novel, a "girl gets caught in a lie she didn't tell but doesn't have the courage to correct. . . . Samantha wants to spark some romantic interest from her best friend and secret heartthrob Nick, so she makes a play for popularity-magnet Carter. He rebuffs her, but someone sees her leaving his bedroom in tears and jumps to the false conclusion that Carter assaulted her. Sam doesn't hear about the resulting rumors until she returns to school. Soon she feels too overwhelmed by social pressure to deny them. Sam finds many opportunities to confess the truth, but she can't bring herself to exonerate Carter. . . . Complicating matters, Sam knows that because of the deception, she's likely to lose Nick, who finally has declared his love for her." (Kirkus)

Graff, Lisa

★ **Lost** in the sun; Lisa Graff. Philomel Books. 2015 289p$16.99

Grades: 4 5 6 7 8 9 **Fic**

1. Brothers — Fiction 2. Friendship — Fiction 3. Guilt —Fiction 4. Remarriage — Fiction 5. Tricks — Fiction

ISBN: 0399164065; 9780399164064

LC 2014027868

"Trent Zimmerman is consumed by rage. The universe has been manifestly unfair to him and he doesn't know how to handle it. Seven months ago, he struck a hockey puck at a bad angle, sending it like a missile into the chest of a boy with a previously undiagnosed heart ailment. That boy died and Trent feels responsible...Weighty matters deftly handled with humor and grace will give this book wide appeal." SLJ

Grant, Christopher

Teenie. Alfred A. Knopf 2010 264p $16.99; lib bdg $19.99; ebook $10.99

Grades: 9 10 11 12 **Fic**

1. School stories 2. Family life -- Fiction 3. African Americans -- Fiction 4. Dating (Social customs) -- Fiction 5. Brooklyn (New York, N.Y.) -- Fiction

ISBN 978-0-375-86191-8; 978-0-375-96191-5 lib bdg; 978-0-375-89779-5 ebook

LC 2010-35377

High school freshman Martine, longing to escape Brooklyn and her strict parents, is trying to get into a study-abroad program but when her long-time crush begins to pay attention to her and her best friend starts an online relationship, Teenie's mind is on anything but her grades.

"Realistic descriptions of teenage life and appealing characters make for an enjoyable reading experience." SLJ

Grant, K. M.

Blood red horse. Walker & Co. 2005 277p $16.95; pa $8.99

Grades: 6 7 8 9 **Fic**

1. Horses -- Fiction 2. Crusades -- Fiction 3. Middle Ages -- Fiction

ISBN 0-8027-8960-9; 0-8027-7734-8 pa

LC 2005-42280

First published 2004 in the United Kingdom

A special horse named Hosanna changes the lives of two English brothers and those around them as they fight with King Richard I against Saladin's armies during the Third Crusades.

This "story . . . transcends boundaries of gender and genre, with something to offer fans of equestrian fare, historical fiction, and battlefield drama alike." Booklist

Other titles in this series are:

Green jasper (2006)

Blaze of silver (2007)

Blue flame; book one of the Perfect Fire trilogy. Walker & Co. 2008 246p (Perfect fire trilogy) $16.99

Grades: 7 8 9 10 **Fic**

1. Middle Ages -- Fiction 2. Knights and knighthood -- Fiction 3. France -- History -- 0-1328 -- Fiction

ISBN 978-0-8027-9694-3; 0-8027-9694-X

LC 2007-51384

In 1242 in the restive Languedoc region of France, Parsifal, having been charged as a child to guard an important religious relic, has lived in hiding for much of his life until he befriends a young couple on opposite sides of the escalating conflict between the Catholics and the Cathars.

"Characters are as complex as the moral issues they face, and Grant's nuanced, thought-provoking look at the religious conflicts they face will resonate today." Booklist

Other books in this series are Paradise red (2010)

White heat (2009)

★ **How** the hangman lost his heart. Walker & Co. 2007 244p $16.95

Grades: 7 8 9 10 **Fic**

1. Adventure fiction

ISBN 978-0-8027-9672-1; 0-8027-9672-9

LC 2006-53182

When her Uncle Frank is executed for treason against England's King George in 1746, and his severed head is mounted on a pike for public viewing, daring Alice tries to reclaim the head for a proper burial, finding an unlikely ally in the softhearted executioner, while incurring the wrath of the royal guard.

"The story is filled with action and interesting characters. . . . This is a rousing read." SLJ

Paradise red; by K.M. Grant. Walker & Co. 2010 279 p. (hardcover) $17.99

Grades: 7 8 9 10 **Fic**

1. Love stories 2. Fantasy fiction 3. Albigenses -- Fiction 4. Middle Ages -- Fiction 5. Knights and knighthood -- Fiction 6. France -- History -- Louis IX, 1226-1270 -- Fiction 7. Languedoc (France) -- History -- 13th century -- Fiction 8. Montségur (France) -- History -- 13th century -- Fiction

ISBN 0802796966; 9780802796967

LC 2009054214

This is the final book in K.M. Grant's Perfect Fire trilogy. The novel "concludes the story of Raimon's quest to save the mystical blue flame which is at the heart of his love for the land he grew up in. This runs alongside the complicated story of his relationship with Yolanda who has made a political marriage to one of the enemy." (School Librarian)

White heat. Walker & Co. 2009 260p (Perfect fire trilogy) $16.99

Grades: 7 8 9 10 **Fic**

1. Inquisition -- Fiction 2. Middle Ages -- Fiction 3. Knights and knighthood -- Fiction 4. France -- History -- 0-1328 -- Fiction

ISBN 978-0-8027-9695-0; 0-8027-9695-8

LC 2008-46984

Sequel to: Blue heat (2008)

As the conflict in Languedoc, also called Occitan, intensifies, Raimon, having escaped the pyre, suppresses his longing to find his beloved Yolanda and, together with Parsifal, carries the Blue Flame to the mountains where it serves to rally loyal Occitanians to organize against the formidable French forces set to invade their beloved country.

"With thorough scholarship and an immersion into medieval sights, sounds, and points of view, Grant invites readers on a thrilling trip back in time." Horn Book

Grant, Michael, 1954-

★ **Gone.** HarperTeen 2008 576p $17.99; lib bdg $18.89; pa $9.99

Grades: 7 8 9 10 **Fic**

1. Supernatural -- Fiction 2. Good and evil -- Fiction

ISBN 978-0-06-144876-8; 978-0-06-144877-5 lib bdg; 978-0-06-144878-2 pa

LC 2007-36734

In a small town on the coast of California, everyone over the age of fourteen suddenly disappears, setting up a battle between the remaining town residents and the students from a local private school, as well as those who have "The Power" and are able to perform supernatural feats and those who do not.

"A tour de force that will leave readers dazed, disturbed, and utterly breathless." Booklist

Other titles in this series are:

Hunger (2009)

Lies (2010)

Plague (2011)

Fear (2012)

Grant, Vicki

Quid pro quo. Orca 2005 160p $16.95; pa $7.95

Grades: 7 8 9 10 **Fic**

1. Mystery fiction 2. Lawyers -- Fiction 3. Missing persons -- Fiction 4. Mother-son relationship -- Fiction

ISBN 1-55143-394-X; 1-55143-370-2 pa

"Cyril Floyd MacIntyre, 13, is perplexed over the disappearance of his mother, a 28-year-old law-school graduate. . . . Cyril becomes involved in a web of intrigue and deceit searching for her. His discovery of resurfacing shady characters who played a role in Andy's disappearance makes for a suspense-filled, well-plotted legal thriller." SLJ

Res judicata. Orca Book Publishers 2008 172p pa $9.95

Grades: 7 8 9 10 **Fic**

1. Mystery fiction 2. Lawyers -- Fiction 3. Criminals -- Fiction 4. Mother-son relationship -- Fiction

ISBN 978-1-55143940-2; 1-55143940-9

Cyril MacIntyre is on the case again, working for his eccentric mother and giving new meaning to the term "legal aid" in this sequel to Quid Pro Quo.

"The novel features laugh-out-loud bits between mother and son and plenty of hilarious insights from Cyril about life and the law. Students who enjoy quick-witted writing and good mysteries will enjoy how well Vicki Grant cracks the case." Libr Media Connect

Gratton, Tessa

The **blood** keeper; Tessa Gratton. Random House Books for Young Readers 2012 432 p. (hardback) $17.99

Grades: 9 10 11 12 **Fic**

1. Love stories 2. Magic -- Fiction 3. Supernatural -- Fiction

ISBN 0375867341; 9780375867347; 9780375897696; 9780375967344

LC 2011049532

This book follows "Mab Prowd, [for whom] the practice of blood magic is as natural as breathing. . . . Growing up on an isolated farm in Kansas with other practitioners may have kept her from making friends her own age, but it has also given her a sense of purpose -- she's connected to the land and protective of the magic. . . . But one morning . . . she encounters Will, a local boy who is trying to exorcise some mundane personal demons." (Publisher's note)

"A perfect book for those who loved Wuthering Heights and are looking for an essentially American gothic." Kirkus

Gratz, Alan

★ **Samurai** shortstop. Dial Books 2006 280p hardcover o.p. pa $7.99

Grades: 7 8 9 10 **Fic**

1. School stories 2. Baseball -- Fiction 3. Tokyo (Japan) -- Fiction 4. Father-son relationship -- Fiction

ISBN 0-8037-3075-6; 978-0-8037-3075-5; 0-14-241099-3 pa; 978-0-14-24099-8 pa

LC 2005-22081

While obtaining a Western education at a prestigious Japanese boarding school in 1890, sixteen-year-old Toyo also receives traditional samurai training which has profound effects on both his baseball game and his relationship with his father. This book features some scenes of graphic violence.

"This is an intense read about a fascinating time and place in world history." Publ Wkly

Something rotten; a Horatio Wilkes mystery. Dial Books 2007 207p $16.99; pa $6.99

Grades: 8 9 10 11 12 **Fic**

1. Poets 2. Authors 3. Dramatists 4. Mystery fiction 5. Homicide -- Fiction 6. Tennessee -- Fiction

ISBN 978-0-8037-3216-2; 0-8037-3216-3; 978-0-14-241297-8 pa; 0-14-241297-X pa

LC 2006-38484

In a contemporary story based on Shakespeare's play, Hamlet, Horatio Wilkes seeks to solve the murder of his friend Hamilton Prince's father in Denmark, Tennessee.

"Readers will find this enjoyable as a pleasure read and surprisingly painless as a curricular entry." Bull Cent Child Books

Followed by: Something wicked (2008)

Gray, Claudia

Evernight. HarperTeen 2008 327p (Evernight) $16.99; lib bdg $17.89; pa $8.99

Grades: 8 9 10 11 12 **Fic**

1. Horror fiction 2. School stories 3. Vampires -- Fiction

ISBN 978-0-06-128439-7; 0-06-128439-4; 978-0-06-128443-4 lib bdg; 0-06-128443-2 lib bdg; 978-0-06-128444-1 pa; 0-06-128444-0 pa

LC 2007-36733

Bianca has been "uprooted from her small hometown and enrolled at Evernight Academy, an eerie Gothic boarding school where the students are somehow too perfect. . . . Bianca knows she doesn't fit in. Then she meets Lucas. . . . Lucas ignores the rules, stands up to the snobs, and warns Bianca to be careful—even when it comes to caring about him. . . . But the connection between Bianca and Lucas can't be denied. Bianca will risk anything to be with Lucas, but dark secrets are fated to tear them apart." (Publisher's note) "Grades eight to ten." (Bull Cent Child Books)

"Gray's writing hooks readers from the first page and reels them in with surprising plot twists and turns. . . . A must-have for fans of vampire stories." SLJ

Spellcaster; Claudia Gray. HarperTeen 2013 400 p. (hardback) $17.99

Grades: 8 9 10 11 12 **Fic**

1. Occult fiction 2. Witches -- Fiction 3. Love stories 4. Horror stories 5. Magic -- Fiction 6. Schools -- Fiction 7. High schools -- Fiction 8. Rhode Island -- Fiction 9. Blessing and cursing -- Fiction 10. Family life -- Rhode Island -- Fiction

ISBN 0061961205; 9780061961205

LC 2012025331

This young adult paranormal romance story, by Claudia Gray, follows a teenage girl with magical powers. "Descended from witches, Nadia can sense that a spell has been cast over the tiny Rhode Island town--a sickness infecting everyone and everything in it. The magic at work is darker and more powerful than anything she's come across and has sunk its claws most deeply into Mateo . . . her rescuer, her friend, and the guy she yearns to get closer to even as he pushes her away." (Publisher's note)

Steadfast; a Spellcaster novel. Claudia Gray. HarperTeen 2014 352 p. (hardcover bdg.) $17.99

Grades: 8 9 10 11 12 **Fic**

1. Imaginary places 2. Magic -- Fiction 3. Horror stories 4. Schools -- Fiction 5. Witches -- Fiction 6. High schools -- Fiction 7. Rhode Island -- Fiction 8. Blessing and cursing -- Fiction 9. Family life -- Rhode Island -- Fiction

ISBN 0061961221; 9780061961229

LC 2013015445

Sequel to: Spellcaster

"The first barrier between our world and the evil entity known as The One Beneath has been breached and redemption is impossible—unless untrained teen witch Nadia, along with her steadfast Mateo and friend Verlaine, can resist a seemingly invincible sorceress' power and a demon's meddling, all while remaining true to their friendship and ideals...Gray uses unique and lyrical free-verse spells, spoken by both Nadia and the dark sorceress Elizabeth, as inroads to sets of memories—a clever tactic that helps readers understand motivation while providing backstories that make it easy to bond with Nadia and her friends. The ending will provide terrific fodder for book discussions, so make sure you have enough copies to go around." (Booklist)

Gray, Keith

★ **Ostrich** boys. Random House 2010 297p $17.99; lib bdg $20.99

Grades: 8 9 10 11 12 **Fic**

1. Death -- Fiction 2. Scotland -- Fiction 3. Friendship -- Fiction 4. Great Britain -- Fiction

ISBN 978-0-375-85843-7; 0-375-85843-1; 978-0-375-95843-4 lib bdg; 0-375-95843-6 lib bdg

LC 2008-21729

After their best friend Ross dies, English teenagers Blake, Kenny, and Sim plan a proper memorial by taking his ashes to Ross, Scotland, an adventure-filled journey that tests their loyalty to each other and forces them to question what friendship means.

"Gray's writing is cheeky, crisp, and realistic. He has created funny, bright characters whom readers cannot help but root for." SLJ

Green, John

★ An **abundance** of Katherines. Dutton Books 2006 227p $16.99

Grades: 9 10 11 12 **Fic**

1. Mathematics -- Fiction

ISBN 0-525-47688-1; 978-0-525-47688-7

LC 2006-4191

Michael L. Printz Award honor book, 2007

Having been recently dumped for the nineteenth time by a girl named Katherine, recent high school graduate and former child prodigy Colin sets off on a road trip with his best friend to try to find some new direction in life while also trying to create a mathematical formula to explain his relationships.

This "is an enjoyable, thoughtful novel that will attract readers interested in romance, math, or just good storytelling." Voice Youth Advocates

★ The **fault** in our stars; John Green. Dutton Books 2012 318p.

Grades: 9 10 11 12 **Fic**

1. Love stories 2. Cancer -- Patients -- Fiction 3. Terminally ill children -- Fiction 4. Love -- Fiction 5. Cancer -- Fiction

ISBN 9780525478812

LC 2011045783

Odyssey Award Winner (2013)

This book tells the story of "Hazel Lancaster and Augustus Waters [who] are very different: She's a sensitive poetry aficionado; he's a hunky ex-basketball player. But their paths (and stars) cross in a cancer support group for teens. . . . Hazel yearns to travel to Amsterdam to meet her favorite author, and Augustus leaps to help even as their respective cancers threaten to derail her dream." (Washington Post)

★ **Looking** for Alaska. Dutton Books 2005 221p $15.99; pa $7.99

Grades: 9 10 11 12 **Fic**

1. School stories 2. Death -- Fiction 3. Birmingham (Ala.) -- Fiction

ISBN 0-525-47506-0; 0-14-240251-6 pa

LC 2004-10827

Michael L. Printz Award, 2006

Sixteen-year-old Miles' first year at Culver Creek Preparatory School in Alabama includes good friends and great pranks, but is defined by the search for answers about life and death after a fatal car crash

"The language and sexual situations are aptly and realistically drawn, but sophisticated in nature. Miles's narration is alive with sweet, self-deprecating humor, and his obvious struggle to tell the story truthfully adds to his believability." SLJ

Paper towns. Dutton Books 2008 305p $17.99

Grades: 9 10 11 12 **Fic**

1. Mystery fiction 2. Florida -- Fiction 3. Missing persons -- Fiction

ISBN 978-0-525-47818-8; 0-525-47818-3

LC 2007-52659

One month before graduating from his Central Florida high school, Quentin "Q" Jacobsen basks in the predictable boringness of his life until the beautiful and exciting Margo Roth Spiegelman, Q's neighbor and classmate, takes him on a midnight adventure and then mysteriously disappears.

"The writing is . . . stellar, with deliciously intelligent dialogue and plenty of mind-twisting insights. . . . Language and sex issues might make this book more appropriate for older teens, but it is still a powerfully great read." Voice Youth Advocates

★ **Will** Grayson, Will Grayson; [by] John Green & David Levithan. Dutton 2010 310p $17.99

Grades: 9 10 11 12 **Fic**

1. Obesity -- Fiction 2. Theater -- Fiction 3. Homosexuality -- Fiction 4. Chicago (Ill.) -- Fiction 5. Dating (Social customs) -- Fiction

ISBN 978-0-525-42158-0; 0-525-42158-0

LC 2008-48979

When two teens, one gay and one straight, meet accidentally and discover that they share the same name, their lives become intertwined as one begins dating the other's best friend, who produces a play revealing his relationship with them both.

"Each character comes lovingly to life, especially Tiny Cooper, whose linebacker-sized, heart-on-his-sleeve personality could win over the grouchiest of grouches. . . . Their story, along with the rest of the cast's, will have readers simultaneously laughing, crying and singing at the top of their lungs." Kirkus

Green, Sally

Half bad; Sally Green. Viking, published by the Penguin Group 2014 416 p. (hardback) $18.99

Grades: 9 10 11 12 **Fic**

1. Witches -- Fiction 2. England -- Fiction 3. Prisoners -- Fiction 4. Toleration -- Fiction 5. Good and evil -- Fiction 6. Fathers and sons -- Fiction 7. Family life -- England -- Fiction

ISBN 0670016780; 9780670016785

LC 2013041190

In this book, by Sally Green, "witches live alongside humans: White witches, who are good; Black witches, who are evil; and sixteen-year-old Nathan, who is both. Nathan's father is the world's most powerful and cruel Black witch, and his mother is dead. He is hunted from all sides. Trapped in a cage, beaten and handcuffed, Nathan must escape before his seventeenth birthday, at which point he will receive three gifts from his father and come into his own as a witch--or else he will die." (Publisher's note)

"In a world divided by two factions at war, Nathan is caught in the middle, for he is neither a White Witch nor a Black Witch, but a Half Code-half White and half Black... Told at times in first- and second-person, the story allows unique insights into Nathan's perspectives, including the fast-paced escapes and heart-wrenching torment. An interesting spin on the paranormal that runs adjacent to some important social issues, Half Bad leaves readers questioning if the division between good and evil is ever as simple as black and white." (VOYA)

Greenberg, Joanne

I never promised you a rose garden; a novel. Henry Holt 2009 291p pa $15

Grades: 7 8 9 10 11 12 Adult **Fic**
1. Mentally ill -- Fiction 2. Psychotherapy -- Fiction
ISBN 978-0-8050-8926-4; 0-8050-8926-8
LC 2010-275768

First published 1964

Chronicles the three-year battle of a mentally ill, but perceptive, teenage girl against a world of her own creation, emphasizing her relationship with the doctor who gave her the ammunition of self-understanding with which to destroy that world of fantasy.

"The hospital world and Deborah's fantasy world are strikingly portrayed, as is the girl's violent struggle between sickness and health, a struggle given added poignancy by youth, wit, and courage." Libr J

Griffin, Adele

★ **All** you never wanted; Adele Griffin. Alfred A. Knopf 2012 225 p. (hard cover) $16.99
Grades: 9 10 11 12 **Fic**
1. Popularity -- Fiction 2. Self-destructive behavior 3. Sibling rivalry -- Fiction 4. Personal appearance -- Fiction 5. Wealth -- Fiction 6. Sisters -- Fiction
ISBN 9780307974662; 9780375870811; 9780375870828; 9780375970825
LC 2012020504

Author Adele Griffith tells a story of a sibling rivalry. "Alex has it all--brains, beauty, popularity, and a dangerously hot boyfriend. Her little sister Thea wants it all, and she's stepped up her game to get it. Even if it means spinning the truth to win the attention she deserves. Even if it means uncovering a shocking secret her older sister never wanted to share. Even if it means crying wolf. (Publisher's note)

The **Julian** game. G.P. Putnam's Sons 2010 200p $16.99
Grades: 8 9 10 11 12 **Fic**
1. School stories 2. Bullies -- Fiction
ISBN 978-0-399-25460-4; 0-399-25460-9
LC 2010-2281

In an effort to improve her social status, a new scholarship student at an exclusive girls' school uses a fake online profile to help a popular girl get back at her ex-boyfriend, but the consequences are difficult to handle.

This is a "perceptive novel. . . . Canny use of details makes Griffin's characters fully realized and believable. . . . Strong pacing and a sympathetic protagonist ought to keep readers hooked." Publ Wkly

Tighter. Alfred A. Knopf 2011 216p $16.99; lib bdg $19.99; ebook $10.99
Grades: 9 10 11 12 **Fic**
1. Ghost stories 2. Death -- Fiction 3. Nannies -- Fiction 4. Rhode Island -- Fiction 5. Mental illness -- Fiction 6. Social classes -- Fiction
ISBN 978-0-375-86645-6; 978-0-375-96645-3 lib bdg; 978-0-375-89643-9 ebook
LC 2010-25301

Based on Henry James's "The Turn of the Screw," tells the story of Jamie Atkinson's summer spent as a nanny in a small Rhode Island beach town, where she begins to fear that the estate may be haunted, especially after she learns of two deaths that occurred there the previous summer.

"Griffin interweaves subtle commentary about social class, drug abuse and mental illness into this marvelous homage while winding the suspense knob all the way to 11. Whether or not the ghosts are real, Jamie's alienation and addiction are, and readers will feel her growing claustrophobia at each turn of the page." Kirkus

Where I want to be. G.P. Putnam's Sons 2005 150p pa $6.99
Grades: 7 8 9 10 **Fic**
1. Death -- Fiction 2. Sisters -- Fiction 3. Rhode Island -- Fiction 4. Mental illness -- Fiction
ISBN 0-399-23783-6; 0-14-240948-0 pa
LC 2004-1887

Two teenaged sisters, separated by death but still connected, work through their feelings of loss over the closeness they shared as children that was later destroyed by one's mental illness, and finally make peace with each other

"Thoughtful, unique, and ultimately life-affirming, this is a fascinating take on the literary device of a main character speaking after death." SLJ

Griffin, Claire J.

Nowhere to run; Claire J. Griffin. 1st ed. Namelos llc 2013 118 p. (hardcover) $18.95
Grades: 7 8 9 10 **Fic**
1. School stories 2. Juvenile delinquency -- Fiction
ISBN 1608981444; 9781608981441; 9781608981458
LC 2012951212

In this novel, by Claire J. Griffin, "Calvin has Deej--and a coach who thinks Calvin can win the championship in the 100-meter dash, a little brother who looks up to him, a boss who trusts him with the keys to the car shop, and Momma, who made him promise to stay in school. And then there's Junior, the girlfriend of Calvin's dreams. . . . But when Calvin and Deej get suspended from school on a trumped-up charge, things start to fall apart." (Publisher's note)

Griffin, N.

★ The **whole** stupid way we are; N. Griffin. Atheneum Books for Young Readers 2013 368 p. (hardcover) $16.99
Grades: 9 10 11 12 **Fic**
1. Friendship -- Fiction 2. Dysfunctional families -- Fiction 3. Maine -- Fiction 4. Best friends -- Fiction 5. Family problems -- Fiction
ISBN 1442431555; 9781442431553; 9781442431584
LC 2012002595

In this young adult novel, by N. Griffin, "the friendship between optimistic Dinah Beach and depressed, nihilistic Skint Gilbert is tested. . . . Skint thinks constantly about human cruelty; Dinah wants playful distractions. Skint lives with a father suffering from dementia and a mother who is bitter, angry and occasionally violent; Dinah takes care not to bring up Skint's family . . . ," until one day when she decides to help. (Kirkus Reviews)

Griffin, Paul

Ten Mile River. Dial Books 2008 188p $16.99
Grades: 8 9 10 11 12 **Fic**
1. Homeless persons -- Fiction 2. Runaway teenagers

-- Fiction 3. Juvenile delinquency -- Fiction
ISBN 978-0-8037-3284-1; 0-8037-3284-8
LC 2007-047870

Having escaped from juvenile detention centers and foster care, two teenaged boys live on their own in an abandoned shack in a New York City park, making their way by stealing, occasionally working, and trying to keep from being arrested.

"The language is tough but convincing, the setting authentic, the characters memorable and their struggles played out with a complexity that respects the audience's intelligence." Publ Wkly

Burning blue; by Paul Griffin. Dial Books 2012 288 p. (hardcover) $17.99
Grades: 9 10 11 12 **Fic**

1. Love stories 2. Accidents -- Fiction 3. Popularity -- Fiction 4. Beauty, Personal -- Fiction 5. Computer hackers -- Fiction 6. Disfigured persons -- Fiction 7. Mystery and detective stories
ISBN 0803738153; 9780803738157
LC 2012003578

Author Paul Griffin's protagonist "Nicole Castro, the most beautiful girl in her wealthy New Jersey high school, is splashed with acid on the left side of her perfect face, [and] the whole world takes notice. But quiet loner Jay Nazarro does more than that--he decides to find out who did it. Jay understands how it feels to be treated like an outsider, and he also has a secret: He's a brilliant hacker. But the deeper he digs, the more danger he's in--and the more he falls for Nicole. Too bad everyone is turning into a suspect, including Nicole herself." (paulgriffinstories.net)

★ The **Orange** Houses. Dial Books 2009 147p $16.99
Grades: 9 10 11 12 **Fic**

1. Veterans -- Fiction 2. People with disabilities -- Fiction 3. Illegal aliens -- Fiction 4. Mental illness -- Fiction 5. Bronx (New York, N.Y.) -- Fiction 6. Africans -- United States -- Fiction
ISBN 978-0-8037-3346-6; 0-8037-3346-1
LC 2008-46259

"Tamika, a fifteen-year-old hearing-impaired girl, Jimmi, an eighteen-year-old veteran who stopped taking his antipsychotic medication, and sixteen-year-old Fatima, an illegal immigrant from Africa, meet and connect in their Bronx, New York, neighborhood." (Publisher's note) "Grades eight to twelve." (Bull Cent Child Books)

"Griffin's . . . prose is gorgeous and resonant, and he packs the slim novel with defeats, triumphs, rare moments of beauty and a cast of credible, skillfully drawn characters. A moving story of friendship and hope under harsh conditions." Publ Wkly

★ **Stay** with me. Dial Books for Young Readers 2011 288p il $16.99
Grades: 10 11 12 **Fic**

1. Dogs -- Fiction 2. Family life -- Fiction 3. Restaurants -- Fiction
ISBN 978-0-8037-3448-7
LC 2011001287

Fifteen-year-olds Mack, a high school dropout but a genius with dogs, and Céce, who hopes to use her intelligence to avoid a life like her mother's, meet and fall in love at the restaurant where they both work, but when Mack lands in prison he pushes Céce away and only a one-eared pit-bull can keep them together.

"A stellar story, with genuine dialogue and drama, this is a book that will appeal greatly to teens, especially dog lovers." SLJ

Grimes, Nikki

★ **Bronx** masquerade. Dial Bks. 2002 167p $16.99; pa $5.99
Grades: 7 8 9 10 **Fic**

1. School stories 2. African Americans -- Fiction 3. Bronx (New York, N.Y.) -- Fiction
ISBN 0-8037-2569-8; 0-14-250189-1 pa
LC 00-31701

While studying the Harlem Renaissance, students at a Bronx high school read aloud poems they've written, revealing their innermost thoughts and fears to their formerly clueless classmates

"Funny and painful, awkward and abstract, the poems talk about race, abuse, parental love, neglect, death, and body image. . . . Readers will enjoy the lively, smart voices that talk bravely about real issues and secret fears. A fantastic choice for readers' theater." Booklist

Dark sons. Jump at the Sun 2005 216p $15.99
Grades: 6 7 8 9 10 **Fic**

1. Novels in verse 2. Stepfamilies -- Fiction 3. Father-son relationship -- Fiction
ISBN 0-7868-1888-3
LC 2004-54208

Alternating poems compare and contrast the conflicted feelings of Ishmael, son of the Biblical patriarch Abraham, and Sam, a teenager in New York City, as they try to come to terms with being abandoned by their fathers and with the love they feel for their younger stepbrothers.

"The simple words eloquently reveal what it's like to miss someone. . . . but even more moving is the struggle to forgive and the affection each boy feels for the baby that displaces him. The elemental connections and the hope . . . will speak to a wide audience." Booklist

A **girl** named Mister. Zondervan 2010 223p $15.99
Grades: 8 9 10 11 **Fic**

1. Saints 2. Novels in verse 3. Pregnancy -- Fiction 4. Christian life -- Fiction 5. African Americans -- Fiction
ISBN 978-0-310-72078-2; 0-310-72078-8
LC 2010-10830

A pregnant teenager finds support and forgiveness from God through a book of poetry presented from the Virgin Mary's perspective.

"Writing in lovely prose with lyrical, forthright language that avoids over-moralizing while driving home the big issues of teen pregnancy, award-winning Nikki Grimes just may help a few young women make different choices. At the same time, she effectively makes the case for parents and schools to continue to educate, educate, educate." Voice Youth Advocates

★ **Jazmin's** notebook. Dial Bks. 1998 102p $15.99
Grades: 6 7 8 9 **Fic**

1. Authorship -- Fiction 2. African Americans -- Fiction
ISBN 0-8037-2224-9

LC 97-5850

A Coretta Scott King honor book for text, 1999

Jazmin, an Afro-American fourteen-year-old who lives with her older sister in a small Harlem apartment in the 1960s, finds strength in writing poetry and keeping a record of the events in her sometimes difficult life

"An articulate, admirable heroine, Jazmin leaps over life's hurdles with agility and integrity." Publ Wkly

Grossman, Nancy

A **world** away; Nancy Grossman. Hyperion 2012 394 p. $16.99
Grades: 7 8 9 10 **Fic**

1. Bildungsromans 2. Amish -- Fiction 3. Adolescence -- Fiction 4. Aunts -- Fiction 5. Self-realization -- Fiction
ISBN 1423151534; 9781423151531

LC 2011032890

This book is the story of 16-year-old Eliza, who "feels trapped by the conservative traditions of her Amish community. During her 'rumspringa,' a time when Amish teenagers are allowed to 'step out of the plain world,' she" works as "a nanny . . . . Eliza is thrilled with her new contemporary wardrobe and the modern conveniences available to her, but she didn't anticipate falling in love with a neighbor . . . or discovering secrets that will significantly change her view of her family." (Publishers Weekly)

Grove, S. E.

★ The **glass** sentence; S. E. Grove. Viking 2014 il maps $17.99
Grades: 6 7 8 9 10 **Fic**

1. Fantasies; 2. Kidnapping — Fiction; 3. Maps — Fiction; 4. Historical fiction
ISBN: 0670785024; 9780670785025

LC 2013025832

Blue Ribbon Awards (2014)

First volume in the author's Mapmakers trilogy. "In the Great Disruption of 1799, time itself broke apart and fragmented, stranding countries and continents in different time periods, some of them thousands of years apart. Thirteen-year-old Sophia lives with her Uncle Shadrack in New Occident Boston, discovering the magic and science of maps. When her uncle is kidnapped by those seeking a powerful artifact, Sophia must journey through a dangerous, shattered landscape to seek out help and answers." SLJ

"In a world fractured into disparate eras during the Great Disruption, Sophia Tims is entrusted with the Tracing Glass (containing a memory thought to be the cause of the Disruption) when her uncle, the cartographer Shadrack Elli, is kidnapped. An intricate fantasy with a Gilded-Age feel, this solidly constructed quest features maps of all kinds and unusual steampunk-flavored elements." Horn Book

Guibord, Maurissa

★ **Warped.** Delacorte Press 2011 339p $16.99; lib bdg $19.99
Grades: 7 8 9 10 **Fic**

1. Magic -- Fiction 2. Tapestry -- Fiction 3. Time travel -- Fiction 4. Great Britain -- History -- 1485-1603, Tudors -- Fiction
ISBN 0-385-73891-9; 0-385-90758-3 lib bdg; 978-0-385-73891-0; 978-0-385-90758-3 lib bdg

LC 2009-53654

When seventeen-year-old Tessa Brody comes into possession of an ancient unicorn tapestry, she is thrust into sixteenth-century England, where her life is intertwined with that of a handsome nobleman. "Grades seven to ten." (Bull Cent Child Books)

"This has it all—fantasy, romance, witchcraft, life-threatening situations, detective work, chase scenes, and a smattering of violence. Imaginative and compelling, it's impossible to put down." SLJ

Gurtler, Janet

I'm not her. Sourcebooks Fire 2011 288p pa $9.99
Grades: 7 8 9 10 **Fic**

1. Cancer -- Fiction 2. Sisters -- Fiction 3. Identity (Psychology) -- Fiction
ISBN 978-1-4022-5636-3; 1-4022-5636-1

Brainy Tess Smith is the younger sibling of the beautiful, popular, volleyball-scholarship-bound Kristina. When Kristina is diagnosed with bone cancer, it drastically changes both sisters' lives.

"This quick and heartbreaking read realistically shows how one person's illness affects an entire community." SLJ

Haas, Abigail

Dangerous girls; by Abigail Haas. Simon Pulse 2013 400 p. (hardback) $16.99
Grades: 10 11 12 **Fic**

1. Homicide -- Fiction 2. Female friendship -- Fiction 3. Teenagers -- Conduct of life -- Fiction 4. Aruba -- Fiction 5. Murder -- Fiction 6. Friendship -- Fiction 7. Best friends -- Fiction 8. Trials (Murder) -- Fiction 9. Mystery and detective stories
ISBN 1442486597; 9781442486591

LC 2013008216

In this book, "an American teen languishes in an Aruba jail, charged with the brutal murder of her best friend. When Anna Chevalier's on-the-rise father moves her . . . to tony Hillcrest Prep, she quickly makes friends with the charismatic Elise. . . .They and their posse of rich and beautiful teens party hard and often; the centerpiece of their senior year is their unsupervised trip to Aruba--where Elise's stabbing death brings their perpetual celebration to a grinding halt." (Kirkus Reviews)

"Anna's wild spring break ends abruptly when her best friend Elise is found murdered. Anna is the primary suspect--she narrates from an Aruban jail, awaiting her trial. Anna's flashbacks reveal additional suspects on the island, but also rivalries, romances, and betrayals among Anna, Elise, and their friends. Anna's riveting unreliable narration will keep readers guessing until the final page." (Horn Book)

Haddix, Margaret Peterson

Full ride; Margaret Peterson Haddix. Simon & Schuster Books for Young Readers 2013 352 p. (hardcover) $16.99

Grades: 6 7 8 9 10 11 12 **Fic**

1. Scholarships -- Fiction 2. Family secrets 3. Ohio -- Fiction 4. Schools -- Fiction 5. Secrets -- Fiction 6. Criminals -- Fiction 7. High schools -- Fiction 8. Mothers and daughters -- Fiction

ISBN 1442442786; 9781442442788; 9781442442795; 9781442442801

LC 2012038146

"Her father in prison for embezzlement, fourteen-year-old Becca and her mother flee to an Ohio suburb to hide from the media and start new lives. Years later, a chain of events reveals layers of secrets behind Becca's father's crimes, his victims, and her mother's motivations. Haddix deftly emphasizes relatable issues: moving, losing faith in a parent, and falling out of economic comfort." (Horn Book)

Just Ella. Simon & Schuster Bks. for Young Readers 1999 185p hardcover o.p. pa $5.99

Grades: 7 8 9 10 **Fic**

1. Sex role -- Fiction 2. Princesses -- Fiction

ISBN 0-689-82186-7; 0-689-83128-5 pa

LC 98-8384

In this continuation of the Cinderella story, fifteen-year-old Ella finds that accepting Prince Charming's proposal ensnares her in a suffocating tangle of palace rules and royal etiquette, so she plots to escape

"In lively prose, with well-developed characters, creative plot twists, wit, and drama, Haddix transforms the Cinderella tale into an insightful coming-of-age story." Booklist

Leaving Fishers. Simon & Schuster Bks. for Young Readers 1997 211p hardcover o.p. pa $5.99

Grades: 7 8 9 10 **Fic**

1. Cults -- Fiction

ISBN 0-689-81125-X; 0-689-86793-X pa

LC 96-47857

After joining her new friends in the religious group called Fishers of Men, Dorry finds herself immersed in a cult from which she must struggle to extricate herself

"The novel does a credible job of showing the effect of a cult on a vulnerable person, without disavowing strong religious beliefs." Child Book Rev Serv

Uprising. Simon & Schuster Books for Young Readers 2007 346p $16.99; pa $7.99

Grades: 6 7 8 9 10 **Fic**

1. Fires -- Fiction 2. Strikes -- Fiction 3. Triangle Shirtwaist Company, Inc. -- Fiction

ISBN 978-1-4169-1171-5; 1-4169-1171-5; 978-1-4169-1172-2 pa; 1-4169-1172-3 pa

LC 2006-34870

In 1927, at the urging of twenty-one-year-old Harriet, Mrs. Livingston reluctantly recalls her experiences at the Triangle Shirtwaist factory, including miserable working conditions that led to a strike, then the fire that took the lives of her two best friends, when Harriet, the boss's daughter, was only five years old. Includes historical notes.

"This deftly crafted historical novel unfolds dramatically with an absorbing story and well-drawn characters who readily evoke empathy and compassion." SLJ

Hahn, Mary Downing, 1937-

Mister Death's blue-eyed girls; Mary Downing Hahn. Clarion Books 2012 330 p. $16.99

Grades: 8 9 10 11 12 **Fic**

1. Mystery fiction 2. Historical fiction 3. Homicide -- Fiction 4. Grief -- Fiction 5. Murder -- Fiction 6. Coming of age -- Fiction 7. Baltimore (Md.) -- History -- 20th century -- Fiction

ISBN 0547760620; 9780547760629

LC 2011025950

In this work of historical fiction, "[t]he high-school year is almost over, there's a party in the park and Mister Death will soon be there, rifle in hand. . . . Two girls, Cheryl and Bobbi Jo, never make it to school the next day, their bloody bodies found in the park where they were shot. [Mary Downing] Hahn's . . . story traces the effects of a crime on everyone involved, including Buddy Novak, accused of a crime he didn't commit." (Kirkus Reviews)

Hahn, Rebecca

A **creature** of moonlight; Rebecca Hahn. Houghton Mifflin Harcourt 2014 224 p. $17.99

Grades: 7 8 9 10 11 12 **Fic**

1. Fantasy fiction 2. Dragons -- Fiction 3. Princesses -- Fiction 4. Fantasy 5. Magic -- Fiction 6. Flowers -- Fiction 7. Identity -- Fiction 8. Forests and forestry -- Fiction

ISBN 054410935X; 9780544109353

LC 2013020188

In this novel, by Rebecca Hahn, "as the only heir to the throne, Marni should have been surrounded by wealth and privilege, not living in exile--but now the time has come when she must choose between claiming her birthright as princess of a realm whose king wants her dead, and life with the father she has never known: a wild dragon who is sending his magical woods to capture her." (Publisher's note)

"Marni lives in a shack at the edge of the woods with her Gramps, where she tends flowers, as she's done for most of her life. Yet change is afoot... This book's greatest strength lies in the vivid woodland scenes and the rich detail that describes the mystical pieces of Marni's tale." (School Library Journal)

Haines, Kathryn Miller

★ The **girl** is murder. Roaring Brook Press 2011 352p $16.99

Grades: 7 8 9 10 **Fic**

1. Mystery fiction 2. Social classes -- Fiction 3. Missing persons -- Fiction 4. New York (N.Y.) -- Fiction 5. Father-daughter relationship -- Fiction

ISBN 978-1-59643-609-1; 1-59643-609-3

LC 2010-32935

In 1942 New York City, fifteen-year-old Iris grieves for her mother who committed suicide, and secretly helps her father with his detective business since he, having lost a leg at Pearl Harbor, struggles to make ends meet. "Grades six to ten." (Bull Cent Child Books)

This is "a smart offering that gives both mysteries and historical fiction a good name. . . . The mystery is solid, but what makes this such a standout is the cast. . . . The characters, young and old, leap off the pages." Booklist

The **girl** is trouble; Kathryn Miller Haines. Roaring Brook Press 2012 336p. $17.99
Grades: 6 7 8 **Fic**
1. Mystery fiction 2. Historical fiction 3. Women detectives -- Fiction
ISBN 9781596436107
LC 2011031806

This book is set in "the Fall of 1942 and Iris's world is rapidly changing. Her Pop is back from the war with a missing leg, limiting his ability to do the physically grueling part of his detective work. Iris is dying to help, especially when she discovers that one of Pop's cases involves a boy at her school. Now, instead of sitting at home watching Deanna Durbin movies, Iris is sneaking out of the house, double crossing her friends, and dancing at the Savoy till all hours of the night. There's certainly never a dull moment in the private eye business." (Publisher's note)

Halam, Ann

★ **Dr.** Franklin's island. Wendy Lamb Bks. 2002 245p hardcover o.p. pa $6.50
Grades: 9 10 11 12 **Fic**
1. Science fiction 2. Genetic engineering -- Fiction 3. Survival after airplane accidents, shipwrecks, etc. -- Fiction
ISBN 0-385-73008-X; 0-440-23781-5 pa
LC 2001-50691

First published 2001 in the United Kingdom

When their plane crashes over the Pacific Ocean, three science students are left stranded on a tropical island and then imprisoned by a doctor who is performing horrifying experiments on humans involving the transfer of animal genes

"This exciting and well-developed book . . . will appeal to fans of horror and adventure. . . . However, the book is not for the squeamish. The description of the dead bodies found in the aftermath of the plane explosion and the physical changes the girls experience during their experiments is gruesomely detailed." SLJ

Snakehead. Wendy Lamb Books 2008 289p il map $16.99; lib bdg $19.99
Grades: 6 7 8 9 10 **Fic**
1. Gods and goddesses -- Fiction 2. Classical mythology -- Fiction 3. Medusa (Greek mythology) -- Fiction 4. Perseus (Greek mythology) -- Fiction
ISBN 978-0-375-84108-8; 978-0-375-94108-5 lib bdg
LC 2007-28318

Compelled by his father Zeus to accept the evil king Polydectes's challenge to bring the head of the monstrous Medusa to the Aegean island of Serifos, Perseus, although questioning the gods' interference in human lives, sets out, accompanied by his beloved Andromeda, a princess with her own harsh destiny to fulfill.

"Mythology buffs will appreciate the plethora of classical figures, while periodic references to contemporary culture (e.g., a band of rich, rowdy teens are dubbed the Yacht Club kids) and occasional slang drive the story home for the target audience without sacrificing its heroic dimensions." Publ Wkly

Hale, Marian

The **goodbye** season. Henry Holt and Co. 2009 271p $16.99
Grades: 7 8 9 10 **Fic**
1. Texas -- Fiction 2. Bereavement -- Fiction 3. Family life -- Fiction 4. Household employees -- Fiction 5. Mother-daughter relationship -- Fiction
ISBN 978-0-8050-8855-7; 0-8050-8855-5
LC 2008-50275

In Canton, Texas, seventeen-year-old Mercy's dreams of a different life than her mother's are postponed by harsh circumstances, including the influenza epidemic of 1918-19, which forces her into doing domestic work for a loving, if troubled, family.

This is a "compelling, tautly written novel." SLJ

Hale, Shannon

★ **Book** of a thousand days; illustrations by James Noel Smith. Bloomsbury Children's Books 2007 305p il $17.95
Grades: 7 8 9 10 **Fic**
1. Love stories 2. Fantasy fiction
ISBN 978-1-59990-051-3; 1-59990-051-3
LC 2006-36999

Fifteen-year-old Dashti, sworn to obey her sixteen-year-old mistress, the Lady Saren, shares Saren's years of punishment locked in a tower, then brings her safely to the lands of her true love, where both must hide who they are as they work as kitchen maids.

This is a "captivating fantasy filled with romance, magic, and strong female characters." Booklist

The **Goose** girl. Bloomsbury Children's Books 2003 383p $17.95; pa $8.99
Grades: 6 7 8 9 **Fic**
1. Fairy tales 2. Princesses -- Fiction
ISBN 1-58234-843-X; 1-58234-990-8 pa
LC 2002-28336

On her way to marry a prince she's never met, Princess Anidori is betrayed by her guards and her lady-in-waiting and must become a goose girl to survive until she can reveal her true identity and reclaim the crown that is rightfully hers

"A fine adventure tale full of danger, suspense, surprising twists, and a satisfying conclusion." Booklist

Other titles in this series are:
Enna burning (2004)
River secrets (2006)
Forest born (2009)

Hall, Teri

Away. Dial Books 2011 234 p. $16.99
Grades: 5 6 7 8 **Fic**
1. Science fiction 2. Resistance to government -- Fiction
ISBN 9780803735026; 0803735022
LC 2011001163

After helping heal Malgam, Rachel learns that her father is still living in the devastated territory of Away, captured by members of another clan who are planning to use him to make a deal with the government on the other side of the Line, and she joins the rescue party that must risk much to save him.

"This worthy sequel . . . continues to build a dystopian world rich with suspense and moral choices." Kirkus

The **Line**. Dial Books 2010 219p $16.99
Grades: 5 6 7 8 **Fic**

1. Science fiction

ISBN 978-0-8037-3466-1; 0-8037-3466-2
LC 2009-12301

Rachel thinks that she and her mother are safe working for Ms. Moore at her estate close to The Line, an invisible border of the Unified States, but when Rachel has an opportunity to Cross into the forbidden zone, she is both frightened and intrigued

This "sets readers up for a series about another world that might have come from situations too close to our own." Libr Media Connect

Halpern, Julie

Get well soon. Feiwel & Friends 2007 193p $16.95; pa $8.99
Grades: 7 8 9 10 **Fic**

1. Mental illness -- Fiction 2. Psychiatric hospitals -- Fiction

ISBN 0-312-36795-3; 978-0-312-36795-4; 0-312-58148-3 pa; 978-0-312-58148-0 pa
LC 2006-32358

When her parents confine her to a mental hospital, Anna, an overweight teenage girl who suffers from panic attacks, describes her experiences in a series of letters to a friend.

"Halpern creates a narrative that reflects the changes in Anna with each passing day that includes self-reflection and a good dose of humor." Voice Youth Advocates

Have a nice day; Julie Halpern. Feiwel and Friends 2012 325 p. $16.99
Grades: 7 8 9 10 11 12 **Fic**

1. Mental illness -- Fiction 2. Self-perception 3. Parent-child relationship

ISBN 0312606605; 9780312606602

In author Julie Halpern's book, "Anna Bloom has just come home from a three-week stay in a mental hospital. She feels...okay. It's time to get back to some sort of normal life, whatever that means. She has to go back to school, where teachers and friends are dying to know what happened to her, but are too afraid to ask. And Anna is dying to know what's going on back at the hospital with her crush, Justin, but is too afraid to ask. Meanwhile, Anna's parents are"t getting along, and she wonders if she's the cause of her family's troubles." (Publisher's note)

Into the wild nerd yonder. Feiwel and Friends 2009 247p $16.99
Grades: 9 10 11 12 **Fic**

1. School stories 2. Siblings -- Fiction 3. Friendship -- Fiction 4. Popularity -- Fiction 5. Dungeons & dragons (Game) -- Fiction

ISBN 978-0-312-38252-0; 0-312-38252-9
LC 2008-34751

When high school sophomore Jessie's long-term best friend transforms herself into a punk and goes after Jessie's would-be boyfriend, Jessie decides to visit "the wild nerd yonder" and seek true friends among classmates who play Dungeons and Dragons.

"Descriptions of high school cliques . . . are hilarious and believable. . . . This novel is particularly strong in showing how teen friendships evolve and sometimes die away, and how adolescents redefine themselves." SLJ

Halpin, Brendan

A **really** awesome mess; Trish Cook and Brendan Halpin. Egmont USA 2013 288 p. (hardcover) $17.99
Grades: 9 10 11 12 **Fic**

1. Private schools -- Fiction 2. Chinese Americans -- Fiction 3. Emotionally disturbed children -- Fiction 4. Schools -- Fiction 5. Psychotherapy -- Fiction 6. Boarding schools -- Fiction 7. Emotional problems -- Fiction

ISBN 160684363X; 9781606843635
LC 2012045978

In this book, "a group of teens at a live-in institution for troubled young people bond, pull off a caper and overcome their issues. . . . Emmy, adopted from China by white parents, feels out of place and unwanted in her family. She is sent to Heartland Academy after retaliating against a tormentor at school. . . . Justin, who resents his father's absence, comes to Heartland following a suicide attempt and after being caught receiving oral sex from a girl he met earlier that day." (Kirkus Reviews)

"Having found themselves at Heartland Academy, a reform school for troubled youth, Justin, Emmy, and a band of misfit teens attempt to sneak out for one really awesome night of fun and adventure. With Eleanor & Park-esque protagonists and a cast reminiscent of Girl, Interrupted, this is a satisfying story about trauma and laughter, and the power of friendship." (Horn Book)

★ **Shutout**. Farrar, Straus and Giroux 2010 183p $16.99
Grades: 6 7 8 9 **Fic**

1. Soccer -- Fiction 2. Friendship -- Fiction

ISBN 978-0-374-36899-9; 0-374-36899-6
LC 2009-32972

Fourteen-year-old Amanda and her best friend Lena start high school looking forward to playing on the varsity soccer team, but when Lena makes varsity and Amanda only makes junior varsity, their long friendship rapidly changes.

"The dialogue is spot-on, and the characters are fully fleshed out. . . . While there is plenty of soccer action for fans of the sport, the book will also appeal to teens looking for a solid friendship story." SLJ

Hamilton, K. R. (Kersten R.)

In the forests of the night; Kersten Hamilton. Clarion Books 2011 295 p. $16.99
Grades: 7 8 9 10 **Fic**

1. Fantasy fiction 2. Goblins -- Fiction 3. Zoos -- Fiction 4. Magic -- Fiction 5. Finn MacCool -- Fiction 6. Irish Americans -- Fiction 7. Imaginary creatures

-- Fiction 8. People with mental disabilities -- Fiction
ISBN 0547435606; 9780547435602
LC 2011009846

This book is the second in Kersten Hamilton's Goblin Wars series. Here, "Teagan and her friends must cope with the aftermath of escaping from the Dark Man's forces as well as new dangers. As she picks up the pieces of her life, Teagan begins a tentative relationship with goblin hunter Finn and struggles with her newly revealed goblin heritage." (School Library Journal)

"In her second book, high schooler Teagan (who found out in Tyger, Tyger that she's half-goblin) is back safely from Mag Mell. While she, her little brother Aiden, and love interest Finn Mac Cumhaill (Finn MacCool from Irish folklore) regroup at home in Chicago, wicked forces track them. Well-incorporated folklore elements blend nicely with everyday concerns (e.g., Teagan's post-high-school plans; best friend/boyfriend rivalry)." (Horn Book)

Tyger tyger; by Kersten Hamilton. Clarion Books 2010 308p (Goblin wars) $17
Grades: 7 8 9 10 **Fic**

1. Fantasy fiction 2. Magic -- Fiction 3. Goblins -- Fiction 4. Irish Americans -- Fiction 5. Children with mental disabilities -- Fiction
ISBN 978-0-547-33008-2; 0-547-33008-1
LC 2010-01337

Soon after the mysterious and alluring Finn arrives at her family's home, sixteen-year-old Teagan Wylltson and her disabled brother are drawn into the battle Finn's family has fought since the thirteenth century, when Finn MacCumhaill angered the goblin king. "Grades eight to ten." (Bull Cent Child Books)

"Laced with humor, packed with surprises and driven by suspense, the plot grabs readers from the start using the stylistic tactics of the best fantasy writing. Major characters are beautifully drawn, and many of the secondary characters are equally distinct." Kirkus

Followed by: In the forests of the night (2011) and When the Stars Threw Down Their Spears (2013)

When the stars threw down their spears; by Kersten Hamilton. Clarion Books 2013 400 p. (hardback) $16.99
Grades: 7 8 9 10 **Fic**

1. Love stories 2. Magic -- Fiction 3. Goblins -- Fiction 4. Zoos -- Fiction 5. Finn MacCool -- Fiction 6. Chicago (Ill.) -- Fiction 7. Irish Americans -- Fiction 8. Imaginary creatures -- Fiction 9. People with mental disabilities -- Fiction
ISBN 0547739648; 9780547739649
LC 2012029195

In this novel by Kersten Hamilton "magical creatures are tumbling through mysterious portals from Mag Mell, the world-between-worlds, into the streets of Chicago. Meanwhile, the romance between seventeen-year-old Teagan, who is part goblin, and the alluring bad boy Finn Mac Cumhaill is heating up . . . which is awkward, to say the least, considering he is bound by a family curse to fight goblins his entire life." (Publisher's note)

"In this third book, Teagan and her friends deal with the evil creatures seeping out of Mag Mell and into the streets of Chicago. Teagan and Finn work together to fight the darkness while their love continues to grow, even though it's now forbidden. Fans of fast-paced adventures and Irish folklore will find the two components nicely intertwined." (Horn Book)

Hamilton, Kiki

The **faerie** ring. Tor Teen 2011 343p $17.99
Grades: 7 8 9 10 **Fic**

1. Fantasy fiction 2. Fairies -- Fiction 3. Orphans -- Fiction 4. Thieves -- Fiction 5. London (England) -- Fiction 6. Great Britain -- History -- 19th century -- Fiction
ISBN 978-0-7653-2722-2; 0-7653-2722-8
LC 2011021577

"In 1871 London, a ragged girl pickpocket steals a ring that enforces a truce between the British Crown and the Faery world, setting off a struggle between the realms. . . . The story keeps suspense high with one crisis after another, until it escalates into a final exciting showdown." Kirkus

Hamley, Dennis

Without warning; Ellen's story 1914-1918. [by] Dennis Hamley. 1st U.S. ed.; Candlewick Press 2007 326p $17.99
Grades: 6 7 8 9 **Fic**

1. World War, 1914-1918 -- Fiction
ISBN 978-0-7636-3338-7; 0-7636-3338-0
LC 2007025248

First published 2006 in the United Kingdom with title: Ellen's people

During World War I, an English teenager leaves the safety of home and begins a journey of self-discovery that takes her close to the front lines to pursue her calling as a nurse.

"This intense narrative dramatically offers insight into the effects of World War I on the English home front. . . . This is a highly readable selection with many well-drawn characters." SLJ

Han, Jenny

The **summer** I turned pretty. Simon & Schuster Books for Young Readers 2009 276p $16.99
Grades: 7 8 9 10 **Fic**

1. Summer -- Fiction 2. Beaches -- Fiction 3. Vacations -- Fiction 4. Friendship -- Fiction
ISBN 978-1-4169-6823-8; 1-4169-6823-7
LC 2008-27070

Belly spends the summer she turns sixteen at the beach just like every other summer of her life, but this time things are very different.

"Romantic and heartbreakingly real. . . . The novel perfectly blends romance, family drama, and a coming-of-age tale, one that is substantially deeper than most." SLJ

Other titles in this series are:
It's not summer without you (2010)
We'll always have summer (2011)

Hand, Elizabeth

Illyria; a novel. Viking 2010 135p $15.99
Grades: 10 11 12 **Fic**

1. Poets 2. Authors 3. Dramatists 4. Acting -- Fiction 5. Incest -- Fiction 6. Cousins -- Fiction 7. Theater

-- Fiction
ISBN 978-0-670-01212-1; 0-670-01212-2
First published 2007 in the United Kingdom

Teenage cousins Madeleine and Rogan, who share twin souls and a sexual relationship, are cast in a school production of Twelfth Night that forces them to confront their respective strengths and future prospects.

"The edgy subject matter, explicit but not gratuitous, relegates this novel to mature readers, but it's beautifully written, rich in theatrical detail and intensely realized characters." Publ Wkly

Radiant days; a novel. by Elizabeth Hand. Viking 2012 287 p.
Grades: 9 10 11 12 **Fic**
1. Graffiti -- Fiction 2. Time travel -- Fiction 3. Women artists -- Fiction 4. Creation (Literary, artistic, etc.) -- Fiction 5. Europe -- Fiction 6. Washington (D.C.) -- Fiction 7. Women art students -- Fiction
ISBN 9780670011353
LC 2011020578

Sequel to: Illyria

This book tells the story of "a 20th-century teen artist and 19th-century French poet Arthur Rimbaud," who discover a shared connection with art through time travel. Author Elizabeth Hand "alternates between Merle's first-person, past-tense story and a third-person account of Rimbaud during the Franco-Prussian War of 1871-72, laced with excerpts from his poems and letters." (Kirkus Reviews)

Includes bibliographical references

Hannan, Peter

My big mouth; 10 songs I wrote that almost got me killed. Scholastic Press 2011 235p il $16.99
Grades: 6 7 8 9 **Fic**
1. School stories 2. Bullies -- Fiction 3. Rock music -- Fiction 4. Bands (Music) -- Fiction
ISBN 978-0-545-16210-4; 0-545-16210-6
LC 2010034426

"Hannan's abundant cartoons set the tone for the misadventures of Davis Delaware, the new kid in ninth grade. Davis's attempts to blend in quickly land him on the wrong side of school bully Gerald 'the Butcher' when he forms a band with Gerald's cute girlfriend, Molly, and her dweeby friend, Edwin. . . . Hannan's edgy, exaggerated style suits the humor-driven narrative well. Give this to readers who enjoy light, entertaining realistic fiction." SLJ

Handler, Daniel, 1970-

★ **Why** we broke up; art by Maira Kalman. Little, Brown 2012 354p il $19.99
Grades: 8 9 10 11 12 **Fic**
1. Man-woman relationship -- Fiction 2. Breaking up (Interpersonal relations) 3. Letters -- Fiction 4. Dating (Social customs) -- Fiction
ISBN 978-0-316-12725-7
LC 2011009714

Printz Honor Book (2012)

Sixteen-year-old Min Green writes a letter to Ed Slaterton in which she breaks up with him, documenting their relationship and how items in the accompanying box, from bottle caps to a cookbook, foretell the end.

Hardy, Janice

The **shifter**. Balzer + Bray 2009 370p (The Healing Wars) $16.99; pa $7.99
Grades: 7 8 9 10 **Fic**
1. War stories 2. Fantasy fiction 3. Orphans -- Fiction 4. Sisters -- Fiction
ISBN 978-0-06-174704-5; 0-06-174704-1; 978-0-06-174708-3 pa; 0-06-174708-4 pa
LC 2008-47673

Nya is an orphan struggling for survival in a city crippled by war. She is also a Taker—with her touch, she can heal injuries, pulling pain from another person into her own body. But unlike her sister, Tali, and the other Takers who become Healers' League apprentices, Nya's skill is flawed: She can't push that pain into pynvium, the enchanted metal used to store it. All she can do is shift it into another person

"The ethical dilemmas raised . . . provide thoughtful discussion material and also make the story accessible to more than just fantasy readers." Booklist

Other titles in this series are:
Blue fire (2010)
Darkfall (2011)

Harland, Richard

Liberator; Richard Harland. 1st ed. Simon & Schuster Book for Young Readers 2012 487 p. maps (paperback) $9.99; (hardcover) $17.99
Grades: 6 7 8 9 10 **Fic**
1. Steampunk fiction 2. Revolutions -- Fiction 3. Social conflict -- Fiction 4. Fantasy 5. Social classes -- Fiction
ISBN 9781442423343; 1442423331; 9781442423336; 9781442423350
LC 2010050911

Second title in the author's steampunk series. "After the Filthies revolted, Col Porpentine and his family were among the few swanks to stay aboard the juggernaut now called the 'Liberator.' But the new regime has troubles galore: A saboteur stalks the halls, an anti-Swank zealot joins the Revolutionary Council and people are disappearing. It's hard for Col to maintain a blossoming romance with revolutionary Filthy Riff in this atmosphere." (Kirkus Reviews)

Worldshaker. Simon & Schuster Books for Young Readers 2010 388p $16.99
Grades: 6 7 8 9 10 **Fic**
1. Fantasy fiction 2. Social classes -- Fiction
ISBN 978-1-4169-9552-4; 1-4169-9552-8
LC 2009-16924

Sixteen-year-old Col Porpentine is being groomed as the next Commander of Worldshaker, a juggernaut where elite families live on the upper decks while the Filthies toil below, but when he meets Riff, a Filthy girl on the run, he discovers how ignorant he is of his home and its residents.

"Harland's steampunk alternate history is filled with oppression, class struggle, and war, showing their devastation on a personal level through Col's privileged eyes. . . . The writing is sharp and the story fast-paced, demonstrating that, despite his elite status, Col may be just as trapped as any Filthy." Publ Wkly

Harmel, Kristin

When you wish; [by] Kristin Harmel. 1st ed.; Delacorte Press 2008 273p $15.99; lib bdg $18.99
Grades: 7 8 9 10 **Fic**

1. Fame -- Fiction 2. Singers -- Fiction 3. Father-daughter relationship -- Fiction 4. Mother-daughter relationship -- Fiction
ISBN 978-0-385-73475-2; 0-385-73475-1; 978-0-385-90474-2 lib bdg; 0-385-90474-6 lib bdg
LC 2007020472

When sixteen-year-old pop singing sensation Star Beck learns that her father, who left when she was three, has been writing to her for six years, she disguises herself, leaves her controlling mother and adoring fans behind, and goes to find him—and, perhaps, a normal life—in St. Petersburg, Florida.

"Harmel has created a character and a story that will have wide appeal. There is enough complexity to hold the interest of a more demanding reader, even while remaining basically an entertaining reading experience." KLIATT

Harmon, Michael B.

Brutal; [by] Michael Harmon. Alfred A. Knopf 2009 229p $16.99; lib bdg $19.99
Grades: 9 10 11 12 **Fic**

1. Moving -- Fiction 2. Bullies -- Fiction 3. California -- Fiction 4. Father-daughter relationship -- Fiction
ISBN 978-0-375-84099-9; 0-375-84099-0; 978-0-375-94099-6 lib bdg; 0-375-94099-5 lib bdg
LC 2008-4718

Forced to leave Los Angeles for life in a quiet California wine town with a father she has never known, rebellious sixteen-year-old Poe Holly rails against a high school system that allows elite students special privileges and tolerates bullying of those who are different.

"Harmon's dialogue is crystal clear and authentic, his youth characters intelligent, and his adult characters finely drawn." Booklist

★ The **last** exit to normal. Alfred A. Knopf 2008 275p $15.99; lib bdg $18.99
Grades: 9 10 11 12 **Fic**

1. Montana -- Fiction 2. Child abuse -- Fiction 3. Homosexuality -- Fiction 4. Father-son relationship -- Fiction
ISBN 978-0-375-84098-2; 0-375-84098-2; 978-0-375-94098-9 lib bdg; 0-375-94098-7 lib bdg
LC 2007-10107

Yanked out of his city life and plunked down into a small Montana town with his father and his father's boyfriend, seventeen-year-old Ben, angry and resentful about the changed circumstances of his life, begins to notice that something is not quite right with the little boy next door and determines to do something about it.

The author "unwinds a complex, emotionally charged story of a boy trying to fix not only those who are broken around him, but himself as well." Libr Media Connect

Under the bridge; by Michael Harmon. 1st ed. Alfred A. Knopf 2012 259 p. (paperback) $8.99; (hardcover) $16.99; (ebook) $50.97; (library) $19.99
Grades: 9 10 11 12 **Fic**

1. Urban fiction 2. Brothers -- Fiction 3. Skateboarding -- Fiction 4. Drug dealers -- Fiction 5. Spokane (Wash.) -- Fiction
ISBN 0375866469; 9780375859304; 9780375866463; 9780375896422; 9780375966460
LC 2011036368

In this teenage novel, by Michael Harmon, "Tate's younger brother Indy is probably the best skateboarder in Spokane. . . . But when Indy clashes with his father one too many times and drops out of school, it's up to Tate to win his brother back from the seedier elements of Spokane." (Publisher's note)

Harness, Cheryl

Just for you to know. HarperCollins 2006 308p $16.99; lib bdg $17.89
Grades: 5 6 7 8 **Fic**

1. Death -- Fiction 2. Family life -- Fiction
ISBN 0-06-078313-3; 0-06-078314-1 lib bdg
LC 2006-281855

In Independence, Missouri, in 1963, twelve-year-old Carmen already has her hands full dealing with a dreamy mother, a sometimes reckless father, and five noisy little brothers, but must find a way to hold onto her own dreams when tragedy strikes.

"Carmen's pain and loneliness are brought to life through her narrative. The writing flows nicely." SLJ

Harper, Suzanne

The **Juliet** club. Greenwillow Books 2008 402p $17.99; lib bdg $18.89
Grades: 8 9 10 11 12 **Fic**

1. Poets 2. Authors 3. Dramatists 4. Italy -- Fiction 5. Letters -- Fiction
ISBN 978-0-06-136691-8; 0-06-136691-9; 978-0-06-136692-5 lib bdg; 0-06-136692-7 lib bdg
LC 2007-41315

When high school junior Kate wins an essay contest that sends her to Verona, Italy, to study Shakespeare's 'Romeo and Juliet' over the summer, she meets both American and Italian students and learns not just about Shakespeare, but also about star-crossed lovers—and herself.

"An amalgam of familiar Shakespearean plot elements, character names, and devices make up this delightful, light, and romantic read. . . . The chapter titles are each given act and scene designations to keep the structure of a play. Following the formula of a Shakespearean comedy, the novel ends with a grand ball where misunderstandings are resolved and couples are revealed in a magical evening." Voice Youth Advocates

The **secret** life of Sparrow Delaney. Greenwillow Books 2007 364p $16.99; lib bdg $17.89
Grades: 7 8 9 10 **Fic**

1. Family life -- Fiction 2. Spiritualism -- Fiction
ISBN 978-0-06-113158-5; 0-06-113158-X; 978-0-06-113159-2 lib bdg; 0-06-113159-8 lib bdg
LC 2006-41339

In Lily Dale, New York, a community dedicated to the religion of Spiritualism, tenth-grader Sparrow Delaney, the youngest daughter in an eccentric family of psychics, agonizes over whether or not to reveal her special abilities in order to help a friend.

"For all of the imagination the author displays in inventing a spirit world, she shows equal skill in probing the nuances of tender emotions, too." Publ Wkly

Harrington, Hannah

Speechless; Hannah Harrington. Harlequin Teen 2012 268 p. (paperback) $9.99

Grades: 9 10 11 12 **Fic**

1. Gossip -- Fiction 2. Bullies -- Fiction 3. Hate crimes -- Fiction 4. Schools -- Fiction 5. Secrets -- Fiction 6. Bullying -- Fiction 7. High schools -- Fiction 8. Interpersonal relations -- Fiction

ISBN 0373210523; 9780373210527

LC 2012471034

"Chelsea Knot falls from the top of her high school's social ladder to hated loser in one night when she informs the police of an attack on a gay student by a couple of popular basketball players. It's partially her fault she instigated the attack by gossiping about the teen and spreading his secret to the student body. Trapped between guilt and broken pride, Chelsea takes a vow of silence to keep herself from causing any more harm." (Booklist)

Harris, Carrie

Bad taste in boys. Delacorte Press 2011 201p $17.99

Grades: 6 7 8 9 10 **Fic**

1. Horror fiction 2. School stories 3. Zombies -- Fiction 4. Football -- Fiction 5. Steroids -- Fiction

ISBN 978-0-385-73968-9; 0-385-73968-0

LC 2010040027

Future physician Kate Grable is horrified when her high school's football coach gives team members steroids, but the drugs turn players into zombies and Kate must find an antidote before the flesh-eating monsters get to her or her friends.

"Teens will admire how Kate uses her brains to win the hearts of her male classmates. The plot moves along quickly, making readers feel as if they were watching an actual zombie movie. The short chapters are filled with light humor along with a silly, gory edge that will make readers laugh, rather than cringe." SLJ

Harris, Joanne

Runemarks. Alfred A. Knopf 2008 526p map $18.99; lib bdg $21.99

Grades: 7 8 9 10 11 12 **Fic**

1. Fantasy fiction 2. Magic -- Fiction 3. Norse mythology -- Fiction

ISBN 978-0-375-84444-7; 978-0-375-94444-4 lib bdg; 0-375-84444-9; 0-375-94444-3 lib bdg

LC 2007-28928

Maddy Smith, who bears the mysterious mark of a rune on her hand, learns that she is destined to join the gods of Norse mythology and play a role in the fate of the world.

"Harris demonstrates a knack for moving seamlessly between the serious and comic. . . . She creates a glorious and complex world replete with rune-based magic spells, bickering gods, exciting adventures, and difficult moral issues." Publ Wkly

Harrison, Cora

I was Jane Austen's best friend; illustrated by Susan Hellard. Delacorte Press 2010 342p il $17.99; lib bdg $20.99

Grades: 7 8 9 10 **Fic**

1. Authors 2. Novelists 3. Cousins -- Fiction 4. Diaries -- Fiction 5. Friendship -- Fiction 6. Great Britain -- History -- 1714-1837 -- Fiction

ISBN 0-385-73940-0; 0-385-90787-7 lib bdg; 978-0-385-73940-5; 978-0-385-90787-3 lib bdg

LC 2010-15309

In a series of journal entries, Jenny Cooper describes her stay with cousin Jane Austen in the 1790s. "Grades five to eight." (Bull Cent Child Books)

"This is a lovely, simple coming-of-age story with a strong historical setting. . . . The situations and locations are unmistakable and will be pleasingly familiar to readers of Austen's works." Voice of Youth Advocates

Harstad, Johan

★ **172** hours on the moon; Johan Harstad; translation by Tara F. Chace. Little, Brown and Company 2012 351 p. $17.99

Grades: 9 10 11 12 **Fic**

1. Horror fiction 2. Science fiction 3. Young adult literature 4. Moon -- Fiction 5. Astronauts -- Fiction 6. Space flight to the moon -- Fiction 7. United States. National Aeronautics and Space Administration -- Fiction

ISBN 0316182885; 9780316182881

LC 2011025414

This novel by Johan Harstad tells of "three teenagers [who] join an expedition to the Moon in 2019 and find horror there. . . . [They are] Mia, a Norwegian punk rocker, Midori, a Japanese girl rebelling against her restrictive culture, and Antoine, a French boy devastated by a broken romance. . . . The group intends to shelter for a week in a previously secret lab that NASA had established on the Moon in the 1970s. As soon as the group arrives, however, things start to go horribly wrong." (Kirkus Reviews)

Hartinger, Brent

Geography Club. HarperTempest 2003 226p hardcover o.p. pa $8.99

Grades: 9 10 11 12 **Fic**

1. School stories 2. Clubs -- Fiction 3. Homosexuality -- Fiction

ISBN 0-06-001221-8; 0-06-001223-4 pa

LC 2001-51736

A group of gay and lesbian teenagers finds mutual support when they form the "Geography Club" at their high school.

"Hartinger grasps the melodrama and teen angst of high school well. . . . Frank language and the intimation of sexual activity might put off some readers." Voice Youth Advocates

Other titles in this series are:

The Order of the Poison Oak (2005)

Split screen (2007)

Project Sweet Life. HarperTeen 2009 282p $16.99
Grades: 6 7 8 9 **Fic**
1. Friendship -- Fiction 2. Summer employment -- Fiction
ISBN 978-0-06-082411-2; 0-06-082411-5
LC 2008-19644

When their fathers insist that they get summer jobs, three fifteen-year-old friends in Tacoma, Washington, dedicate their summer vacation to fooling their parents into thinking that they are working, which proves to be even harder than having real jobs would have been.

This "will keep readers laughing and engaged." SLJ

Hartman, Rachel

★ **Seraphina**; a novel. by Rachel Hartman. Random House 2012 465 p. (hardcover) $17.99
Grades: 7 8 9 10 11 12 **Fic**
1. Fantasy fiction 2. Dragons -- Fiction 3. Kings and rulers -- Fiction 4. Fantasy 5. Music -- Fiction 6. Secrets -- Fiction 7. Identity -- Fiction 8. Courts and courtiers -- Fiction 9. Self-actualization (Psychology) -- Fiction
ISBN 9780375866562; 9780375896583; 9780375966569; 0375866566
LC 2011003015

William C. Morris Award (2013)
Boston Globe-Horn Book Honor: Fiction (2013).

In this book, "[a]fter 40 years of peace between human and dragon kingdoms, their much-maligned treaty is on the verge of collapse. Tensions are already high with an influx of dragons, reluctantly shifted to human forms, arriving for their ruler Ardmagar Comonot's anniversary. But when Prince Rufus is found murdered in the fashion of dragons--that is, his head has been bitten off--things reach a fever pitch." (Booklist)

Hartnett, Sonya

★ The **ghost's** child. Candlewick Press 2008 176p $16.99
Grades: 8 9 10 11 12 **Fic**
1. Ghost stories 2. Voyages and travels -- Fiction
ISBN 978-0-7636-3964-8; 0-7636-3964-8
LC 2008-30817

When a mysterious child appears in her living room one day, the elderly Maddy tells him the story of her love for the wild and free-spirited Feather, who tried but failed to live a conventional life with her, and her search for him on a fantastical voyage across the seas.

"Those who enjoy fables or magical realism will be spellbound by this redemptive story of a search for love, love lost and love (of a sort) found again. . . . [Written in] exquisite prose." Publ Wkly

★ **Surrender**. Candlewick Press 2006 248p $16.99; pa $7.99
Grades: 9 10 11 12 **Fic**
1. Dogs -- Fiction 2. Brothers -- Fiction 3. Family life -- Fiction
ISBN 0-7636-2768-2; 07636-3423-9 pa
LC 2005-54259

Michael L. Printz Award honor book, 2007

As he is dying, a twenty-year-old man known as Gabriel recounts his troubled childhood and his strange relationship with a dangerous counterpart named Finnigan.

"From the gripping cover showing a raging inferno to the blood-chilling revelation of the final chapter, this page-turner is a blistering yet dense psychological thriller." Voice Youth Advocates

Thursday's child. Candlewick Press 2002 261p hardcover o.p. pa $7.99
Grades: 7 8 9 10 **Fic**
1. Poverty -- Fiction 2. Australia -- Fiction 3. Farm life -- Fiction 4. Family life -- Fiction
ISBN 0-7636-1620-6; 0-7636-2203-6 pa
LC 2001-25223

Harper Flute recounts her Australian farm family's poverty during the Depression, her father's cowardice, and her younger brother Tin's obsession for digging tunnels and living underground

"This coming-of-age story with allegorical overtones will burrow into young people's deepest hopes and fears, shining light in the darkest inner rooms." Booklist

Hartnett, Sonya, 1968-

Butterfly. Candlewick Press 2010 232p $16.99
Grades: 7 8 9 10 11 12 **Fic**
1. Australia -- Fiction 2. Family life -- Fiction
ISBN 0-7636-4760-8; 978-0-7636-4760-5
LC 2009046549

In 1980s Australia, nearly fourteen-year-old Ariella "Plum" Coyle fears the disapproval of her friends, feels inferior to her older brothers, and hates her awkward, adolescent body but when her glamorous neighbor befriends her, Plum starts to become what she wants to be—until she discovers her neighbor's ulterior motive.

"The deliberate pacing, insight into teen angst, and masterful word choice make this a captivating read to savor." SLJ

What the birds see. Candlewick Press 2003 196p $15.99
Grades: 7 8 9 10 **Fic**
1. Missing children -- Fiction
ISBN 0-7636-2092-0
LC 2002-73717

While the residents of his town concern themselves with the disappearance of three children, a lonely, rejected nine-year-old boy worries that he may inherit his mother's insanity

"Tightly composed and ripe with symbolism, this complex book will offer opportunities for rich discussion." SLJ

Harvey, Alyxandra

Haunting Violet. Walker Books for Young Readers 2011 352p $17.99
Grades: 6 7 8 9 **Fic**
1. Ghost stories 2. Mystery fiction 3. Spiritualism -- Fiction 4. Social classes -- Fiction
ISBN 978-0-8027-9839-8; 0-8027-9839-X
LC 2010-31077

Sixteen-year-old Violet Willoughby has been part of her mother's Spiritualist scam since she was nine, but during an 1872 house party in Hampshire, England, she is horrified to learn that she can actually see ghosts, one of whom wants Violet to solve her murder.

"A well-paced, clever and scary supernatural-suspense story." Kirkus

Hearts at stake. Walker & Co. 2010 248p (The Drake chronicles) $16.99; pa $9.99

Grades: 8 9 10 11 12 **Fic**

1. Siblings -- Fiction 2. Vampires -- Fiction 3. Friendship -- Fiction

ISBN 978-0-8027-9840-4; 0-8027-9840-3; 978-0-8027-2074-0 pa; 0-8027-2074-9 pa

LC 2009-23156

As her momentous sixteenth birthday approaches, Solange Drake, the only born female vampire in 900 years, is protected by her large family of brothers and her human best friend Lucy from increasingly persistent attempts on her life by the powerful vampire queen and her followers.

"Witty, sly, and never disappointing." Booklist

Other titles in this series are:

Blood feud (2010)

Out for blood (2011)

Harvey, Sarah N.

Death benefits. Orca Book Publishers 2010 212p pa $12.95

Grades: 6 7 8 9 **Fic**

1. Old age -- Fiction 2. Grandfathers -- Fiction

ISBN 978-1-55469-226-2 pa; 1-55469-226-1 pa

Royce is pressed into service as a caregiver for his ninety-five-year-old grandfather and gradually comes to appreciate the cantankerous old man.

"Harvey's writing is energetic, and Royce's snarky narration is sure to keep readers' attention." Publ Wkly

Plastic. Orca Book Publishers 2010 120p (Orca soundings) pa $9.95

Grades: 7 8 9 10 **Fic**

1. Friendship -- Fiction 2. Plastic surgery -- Fiction

ISBN 978-1-55469-252-1; 1-55469-252-0

Trying to save his best friend from the horrors of plastic surgery, Jack ends up on the front line of a protest of unscrupulous surgeons.

"This novel is characteristically fast paced and of high interest. Information about both the pros and the cons of plastic surgery is included without detracting from the plot. Plastic does a good job of exploring an important societal issue while telling a timely tale." SLJ

Hassan, Michael

★ **Crash** and Burn; by Michael Hassan. 1st ed. Balzer + Bray 2013 544 p. (hardcover) $14.99

Grades: 9 10 11 12 **Fic**

1. School stories 2. School shootings -- Fiction 3. Schools -- Fiction 4. Violence -- Fiction 5. High schools -- Fiction 6. Emotional problems -- Fiction 7. Interpersonal relations -- Fiction

ISBN 0062112929; 9780062112903

LC 2012004280

In this book, "Steven 'Crash' Crashinsky becomes a hero when he saves more than a thousand people at his high school by confronting his armed and dangerous classmate, David 'Burn' Burnett, during a chilling hostage situation. Crash signs a book deal to write about events leading up to the crisis, his understanding of Burn, and the final secret Burn shared with him that horrible day." (School Library Journal)

Hattemer, Kate

The **vigilante** poets of Selwyn Academy. Alfred A. Knopf 2014 323p $16.99

Grades: 8 9 10 11 12 **Fic**

1. Arts -- Fiction 2. Creative ability -- Fiction; 3. Friendship -- Fiction 4. Reality television programs -- Fiction 5. Minnesota -- Fiction 6. Poetry --Fiction 7. School stories

ISBN: 0385753780

LC 2013014325

"Witty, sarcastic Ethan and his three friends decide to take down the reality TV show, 'For Art's Sake,' that is being filmed at their high school, the esteemed Selwyn Arts Academy, where each student is more talented than the next. While studying Ezra Pound in English class, the friends are inspired to write a vigilante long poem and distribute it to the student body, detailing the evils of 'For Art's Sake.'" (Publisher's note)

"In this place of immense talent, Ethan is immensely relatable as the voice of the average (that is, socially awkward) teen. Hattemer writes with a refreshing narrative style, crafting both believable characters and a cohesive, well-plotted story. Romance, while in the air, takes a sideline to friendship, which proves to be the book's heart and soul. Relying on the passion and ideals that drive adolescence, this has a vibrancy and authenticity that will resonate with anyone who has fought for their beliefs or who has loved a hamster." Booklist

Hautman, Pete

All-in. Simon & Schuster Books for Young Readers 2007 181p hardcover o.p. pa $5.99

Grades: 7 8 9 10 **Fic**

1. Poker -- Fiction 2. Gambling -- Fiction 3. Las Vegas (Nev.) -- Fiction

ISBN 978-1-4169-1325-2; 1-4169-1325-4; 978-1-4169-1326-9 pa; 1-4169-1326-9 pa

LC 2006-23871

Sequel to No limit (2005)

Having won thousands of dollars playing high-stakes poker in Las Vegas, seventeen-year-old Denn Doyle hits a losing streak after falling in love with a young casino card dealer named Cattie Hart.

"Skillfully using the multiple-voice approach, Hautman brings to life the intricacies of poker, crafting a thrilling story of loss, good versus evil, and redemption." Voice Youth Advocates

★ The **big** crunch. Scholastic Press 2011 280p $17.99

Grades: 8 9 10 11 12 **Fic**

1. School stories 2. Dating (Social customs) -- Fiction

ISBN 978-0-545-24075-8; 0-545-24075-1

LC 2010-40011

"Wes Andrews has just ended a suffocating relationship with Izzy. June is new to the school—her sixth in the last four years. Like Wes, she's not looking to get entangled. . . . But in the high-school world of 'users, posers, geeks, skanks, preps, gangstas, macho-morons, punks, burnouts, and so forth,' the two relatively normal, nice kids do find each other . . . eventually. Hautman uses a third-person point of view to weave a humorous and bittersweet tale of romance and the convoluted, uncertain paths that bring two people together. A poignant and quiet tale in which the only special effect is love—refreshing." Kirkus

Blank confession. Simon & Schuster Books for Young Readers 2010 170p $16.99
Grades: 7 8 9 10 **Fic**

1. School stories 2. Bullies -- Fiction 3. Drug traffic -- Fiction
ISBN 978-1-4169-1327-6; 1-4169-1327-0
LC 2009-50169

A new and enigmatic student named Shayne appears at high school one day, befriends the smallest boy in the school, and takes on a notorious drug dealer before turning himself in to the police for killing someone.

"Masterfully written with simple prose, solid dialogue and memorable characters, the tale will grip readers from the start and keep the reading in one big gulp, in the hope of seeing behind Shayne's mask. A sure hit with teen readers." Kirkus

★ The **Cydonian** pyramid; Pete Hautman. Candlewick Press 2013 368 p. (Klaatu Diskos) $16.99
Grades: 7 8 9 10 11 12 **Fic**

1. Science fiction 2. Time travel -- Fiction
ISBN 0763654043; 9780763654047
LC 2012942673

This novel, by Pete Hautman, is part of the "Klaatu Diskos" series. "More than half a millennium in the future, in the shadow of the looming Cydonian Pyramid, a pampered girl named Lah Lia has been raised for one purpose: to be sacrificed. . . . But just as she is about to be killed, a strange boy appears from the diskos, providing a cover of chaos that allows her to escape and launching her on a time-spinning journey in which her fate is irreversibly linked to his." (Publisher's note)

★ **Godless**. Simon & Schuster Books for Young Readers 2004 208p $15.95; pa $8.99
Grades: 7 8 9 10 **Fic**

1. Religion -- Fiction
ISBN 0-689-86278-4; 1-4169-0816-1 pa
LC 2003-10468

When sixteen-year-old Jason Bock and his friends create their own religion to worship the town's water tower, what started out as a joke begins to take on a power of its own

"The witty text and provocative subject will make this a supremely enjoyable discussion-starter as well as pleasurable read." Bull Cent Child Books

Hole in the sky. Simon & Schuster Bks. for Young Readers 2001 179p $16; pa $11.95
Grades: 7 8 9 10 **Fic**

1. Science fiction
ISBN 0-689-83118-8; 1-4169-6822-9 pa
LC 00-58324

In a future world ravaged by a mutant virus, sixteen-year-old Ceej and three other teenagers seek to save the Grand Canyon from being flooded, while trying to avoid capture by a band of renegade Survivors

"Readers will appreciate the novel's intense action and fascinating premise." Horn Book Guide

How to steal a car. Scholastic Press 2009 170p $16.99
Grades: 7 8 9 10 **Fic**

1. Theft -- Fiction 2. Family life -- Fiction
ISBN 978-0-545-11318-2; 0-545-11318-0
LC 2008-54146

Fifteen-year-old, suburban high school student Kelleigh, who has her learner's permit, recounts how she began stealing cars one summer, for reasons that seem unclear even to her.

"A sharply observed, subversive coming-of-age tale." Kirkus

★ **Invisible**. Simon & Schuster Books for Young Readers 2005 149p $15.95; pa $7.99
Grades: 7 8 9 10 **Fic**

1. Friendship -- Fiction 2. Mental illness -- Fiction
ISBN 0-689-86800-6; 0-689-86903-7 pa
LC 2004-2484

Doug and Andy are unlikely best friends—one a loner obsessed by his model trains, the other a popular student involved in football and theater—who grew up together and share a bond that nothing can sever

"With its excellent plot development and unforgettable, heartbreaking protagonist, this is a compelling novel of mental illness." SLJ

The **Klaatu** terminus; Pete Hautman. Candlewick Press. 2014 358p (Klaatu Diskos) $16.99
Grades: 7 8 9 10 11 12 **Fic**

1. Apocalyptic fiction; 2. Science fiction; 3. Dystopian fiction
ISBN: 0763654051; 9780763654054
LC 2013944132

In this final volume of the Klaatu Diskos trilogy Tucker and Lia " join together in the end stage of their journey through the millennia and the final confrontation with the murderous Lah Sept; Tucker uncovers his own role in Lah Sept history. Pulling together elaborate strands of thefirst two books, this conclusion rewards readers with a surprising yet cogent and satisfying chronicle across time." Horn Book

★ The **obsidian** blade; Pete Hautman. Candlewick Press 2012 308 p. (Klaatu Diskos)
Grades: 7 8 9 10 11 12 **Fic**

1. Science fiction 2. Uncles -- Fiction 3. Time travel -- Fiction 4. Missing persons -- Fiction 5. Supernatural 6. Religion -- Fiction 7. Supernatural -- Fiction 8. Space and time -- Fiction
ISBN 9780763654030
LC 2011018617

In this book, which is the first in a series, "[o]ne day Tucker sees his father disappear through a strange disk in the air and then come back an hour later changed, . . . but offering no explanation. . . . Tucker . . . realizes that . . . the disks . . . appear to be portals to other times and places. The disks are unpredictable, though, and their passages seem to lead to sites where violent, traumatic events are occurring." (Bulletin of the Center for Children's Books)

Snatched; [by] Pete Hautman and Mary Logue. Putnam 2006 200p (Bloodwater mysteries) $15.99
Grades: 7 8 9 10 **Fic**

1. Mystery fiction 2. Kidnapping -- Fiction
ISBN 0-399-24377-1
LC 2005-28558

Too curious for her own good, Roni, crime reporter for her high school newspaper, teams up with Brian, freshman science geek, to investigate the beating and kidnapping of a classmate.

"Give this solid marks for plotting and characterization, as well as for suspense." Booklist

Other titles in this series are:
Skullduggery (2007)
Doppelganger (2008)

★ **Sweetblood.** Simon & Schuster Bks. for Young Readers 2003 180p $16.95; pa $6.99
Grades: 7 8 9 10 **Fic**

1. Diabetes -- Fiction
ISBN 0-689-85048-4; 0-689-87324-7 pa
LC 2002-11179

"Lucy Szabo has been an insulin-dependent diabetic since she was 6, and now, at age 16, she has developed an interesting theory that links vampirism with diabetic ketoacidosis." SLJ

"Hautman does an outstanding job of making Lucy's theory and her struggle to accept herself credible. . . . Lucy's clever, self-deprecating voice is endlessly original." Booklist

What boys really want? Pete Hautman. Scholastic Press 2012 297 p. (hbk.) $17.99
Grades: 8 9 10 11 **Fic**

1. Friendship 2. High school students -- Fiction 3. Dating (Social customs) 4. Jealousy 5. Plagiarism 6. High school students 7. Interpersonal relations
ISBN 0545113156; 9780545113151
LC 2011278706

In this book, "Lita has never told Adam that she is behind the snarky and irreverent teen advice blog 'Miz Fitz,' or that she has basically sabotaged all of his romantic relationships. . . . Adam hasn't confided the fact that he's getting most of his information for his . . . book on what boys want from girls . . . from the internet, specifically Miz Fitz's blog. As Adam barrels forward with his project, Lita . . . [is] jealous: writing is her territory, not his." (Bulletin of the Center for Children's Books)

"The book moves along at a snappy pace...This is fresh, realistic YA fiction at its best." SLJ

Hawkins, Rachel

Demonglass; a Hex Hall novel. Hyperion 2011 359p $16.99
Grades: 7 8 9 10 **Fic**

1. Ghost stories 2. Magic -- Fiction 3. Witches -- Fiction 4. Supernatural -- Fiction 5. Great Britain -- Fiction 6. Father-daughter relationship -- Fiction
ISBN 978-1-4231-2131-2; 1-4231-2131-7
LC 2010-10511

Sequel to: Hex Hall (2010)

After learning that she is capable of dangerous magic, Sophie Mercer goes to England with her father, friend Jenna, and Cal hoping to have her powers removed, but soon she learns that she is being hunted by the Eye—and haunted by Elodie.

"Narrator Sophie's delivery is . . . delightfully bold, and the many action scenes lend a cinematic feel." Booklist

Hex Hall. Disney/Hyperion Books 2010 323p $16.99
Grades: 7 8 9 10 **Fic**

1. School stories 2. Witches -- Fiction 3. Supernatural -- Fiction
ISBN 1423121309; 9781423121305

When Sophie attracts too much human attention for a prom-night spell gone horribly wrong, she is exiled to Hex Hall, an isolated reform school for witches, faeries, and shapeshifters. "Grades seven to ten." (Bull Cent Child Books)

"Sixteen-year-old Sophie Mercer, whose absentee father is a warlock, discovered both her heritage and her powers at age 13. While at her school prom, Sophie happens upon a miserable girl sobbing in the bathroom and tries to perform a love spell to help her out. It misfires, and Sophie finds herself at Hecate (aka Hex) Hall, a boarding school for delinquent Prodigium (witches, warlocks, faeries, shape-shifters, and the occasional vampire). What makes this fast-paced romp work is Hawkins' wry humor and sharp eye for teen dynamics." Booklist

Followed by: Demonglass (2011)

School spirits; Rachel Hawkins. Hyperion 2013 304 p. (hardcover) $17.99
Grades: 7 8 9 10 **Fic**

1. Occult fiction 2. School stories 3. Monsters -- Fiction 4. Magic -- Fiction 5. Schools -- Fiction 6. High schools -- Fiction 7. Supernatural -- Fiction
ISBN 1423148495; 9781423148494
LC 2012046402

This young adult paranormal novel, by Rachel Hawkins, is part of the "Hex Hall" series. "Izzy and her mom move to a new town, but . . . discover it's not as normal as it appears. A series of hauntings has been plaguing the local high school, and Izzy is determined to . . . investigate. But assuming the guise of an average teenager is easier said than done. For a tough girl who's always been on her own, it's strange to suddenly make friends and maybe even have a crush." (Publisher's note)

Haydu, Corey Ann

★ **OCD** love story; Corey Ann Haydu. Simon Pulse 2013 352 p. (alk. paper) $17.99
Grades: 9 10 11 12 **Fic**

1. Love stories 2. Obsessive-compulsive disorder -- Fiction 3. Psychotherapy -- Fiction 4. Interpersonal relations -- Fiction
ISBN 1442457325; 9781442457324
LC 2012021545

In this book, when "Bea kisses a strange boy during a blackout at a school dance, it's clear she's a little eccentric, but it isn't until her therapist slips several pamphlets about OCD into Bea's hands that" her problem becomes clear. "Bea's need to perform certain rituals, even at the risk of alienating those she loves, becomes all-consuming. The one bright spot in Bea's life is a budding romance with Beck, the boy from the school dance, who resurfaces in Bea's group-therapy sessions." (Kirkus Reviews)

"Bea and Beck both have debilitating obsessive-compulsive disorder. As they begin dating, they must navigate their feelings for each other and the complications of their individual compulsions. Thanks to some leaps of faith and a lot of therapy, the teens get a happy ending. Haydu explores a sweet, unconventional romance in this compulsively readable novel." (Horn Book)

Hayes, Rosemary

Payback. Frances Lincoln 2009 207p pa $8.95
Grades: 7 8 9 10 **Fic**

1. Muslims -- Fiction

ISBN 978-1-84507-935-2 pa; 1-84507-935-3 pa

Halima, a teenaged Muslim girl living in London, discovers her father owes a favor to a distant relative in Pakistan and must repay the debt by forcing Halima into marriage

"In this tale of clashing cultures set against a backdrop of strong family ties and traditional Muslim faith, Hayes writes clearly and concisely, switching the narrative voice among the characters and letting the dynamics of the story simmer and build realistically." SLJ

Headley, Justina Chen

★ **North** of beautiful. Little, Brown 2009 373p $16.99
Grades: 7 8 9 10 11 12 **Fic**

1. Aesthetics -- Fiction

ISBN 978-0-316-02505-8; 0-316-02505-4

LC 2008-09260

Headley's "finely crafted novel traces a teen's uncharted quest to find beauty. Two things block Terra's happiness: a port-wine stain on her face and her verbally abusive father. . . . A car accident brings her together with Jacob, an Asian-born adoptee with unconventional ideas. . . . The author confidently addresses very large, slippery questions about the meaning of art, travel, love and of course, beauty." Publ Wkly

Healey, Karen

Guardian of the dead. Little, Brown 2010 345p $17.99
Grades: 9 10 11 12 **Fic**

1. School stories 2. Magic -- Fiction 3. Maoris -- Fiction 4. Fairies -- Fiction 5. New Zealand -- Fiction

ISBN 978-0-316-04430-1

LC 2009-17949

Eighteen-year-old New Zealand boarding school student Ellie Spencer must use her rusty tae kwon do skills and new-found magic to try to stop a fairy-like race of creatures from Maori myth and legend that is plotting to kill millions of humans in order to regain their lost immortality.

"Fast-paced adventure and an unfamiliar, frightening enemy set a new scene for teen urban fantasy." Kirkus

The **shattering.** Little, Brown 2011 311p $17.99
Grades: 7 8 9 10 **Fic**

1. Mystery fiction 2. Suicide -- Fiction 3. Homicide -- Fiction 4. New Zealand -- Fiction 5. Supernatural -- Fiction

ISBN 978-0-316-12572-7; 0-316-12572-5

LC 2010047996

When a rash of suicides disturbs Summerton, an oddly perfect tourist town on the west coast of New Zealand, the younger siblings of the dead boys become suspicious and begin an investigation that reveals dark secrets and puts them in grave danger.

"Juggling multiple viewpoints, Healey skillfully keeps her characters on an emotional roller-coaster even as they deal with physical threats. The climax delivers a gut punch that only underscores the sensitivity of the subject matter (without lessening the thrill at all)." Publ Wkly

When we wake. Little, Brown Books for Young Readers 2013 304 p. (hardcover) $17.99
Grades: 7 8 9 10 11 12 **Fic**

1. Science fiction 2. Dystopian fiction 3. Australia -- Fiction

ISBN 031620076X; 9780316200769

LC 2012028739

"Sixteen-year-old Tegan is just like every other girl living in 2027--But on what should have been the best day of Tegan's life, she dies--and wakes up a hundred years in the future, locked in a government facility with no idea what happened. . . . But the future isn't all she hoped it would be, and when . . . secrets come to light, Tegan must make a choice: Does she keep her head down and survive, or fight for a better future?" (Publisher's note)

While we run. Little Brown & Co. 2014 336p $18.00
Grades: 7 8 9 10 11 12 **Fic**

1. Cryonics -- Fiction; 2. Science fiction; 3. Australia--Fiction

ISBN: 031623382X; 9780316233828

LC 2013022281

This is a sequel to When we wake. In the previous installment " Tegan and Abdi revealed the government's plan to populate a new planet with cryogenically frozen slaves. Abdi begins narrating six months after their capture by the government. Like its predecessor, Run succeeds simply as a sci-fi thriller, but it's elevated by its social commentary, emphasizing the importance of fighting for justice in a world that has little of it." Horn Book

Hearn, Julie

Hazel; a novel. Atheneum Books for Young Readers 2009 389p $17.99
Grades: 8 9 10 11 **Fic**

1. Slavery -- Fiction 2. Social classes -- Fiction 3. Racially mixed people -- Fiction

ISBN 978-1-4169-2504-0; 1-4169-2504-X

LC 2008-53961

Thirteen-year-old Hazel leaves her comfortable, if somewhat unconventional, London home in 1913 after her father has a breakdown, and goes to live in the Caribbean on her grandparents' sugar plantation where she discovers some shocking family secrets.

"Hearn's characters vividly reveal class distinctions and racial prejudices prevalent in 1913." Voice Youth Advocates

★ **Ivy**; a novel. Atheneum Books for Young Readers 2008 355p $17.99; pa $9.99
Grades: 8 9 10 11 12 **Fic**

1. Artists -- Fiction 2. Criminals -- Fiction 3. Drug abuse -- Fiction 4. London (England) -- Fiction 5. Great Britain -- History -- 19th century -- Fiction
ISBN 978-1-4169-2506-4; 1-4169-2506-6; 978-1-4169-2507-1 pa; 1-4169-2507-4 pa
LC 2007-045463

In mid-nineteenth-century London, young, mistreated, and destitute Ivy, whose main asset is her beautiful red hair, comes to the attention of an aspiring painter of the pre-Raphaelite school of artists who, with the connivance of Ivy's unsavory family, is determined to make her his model and muse.

"Quirky characters, darkly humorous situations, and quick action make this enjoyable historical fiction." SLJ

The **minister's** daughter. Atheneum Books for Young Readers 2005 263p hardcover o.p. pa $7.99
Grades: 7 8 9 10 **Fic**

1. Witchcraft -- Fiction 2. Supernatural -- Fiction 3. Salem (Mass.) -- Fiction 4. Great Britain -- History -- 1642-1660, Civil War and Commonwealth -- Fiction
ISBN 0-689-87690-4; 0-689-87691-2 pa
LC 2004-18324

In 1645 in England, the daughters of the town minister successfully accuse a local healer and her granddaughter of witchcraft to conceal an out-of-wedlock pregnancy, but years later during the 1692 Salem trials their lie has unexpected repercussions.

"With its thought-provoking perceptions about human nature, magic and persecution, this tale will surely cast a spell over readers." Publ Wkly

Heath, Jack

The **Lab**. Scholastic Press 2008 311p $17.99
Grades: 7 8 9 10 **Fic**

1. Science fiction 2. Adventure fiction 3. Spies -- Fiction 4. Genetic engineering -- Fiction
ISBN 978-0-545-06860-4; 0-545-06860-6

"A gritty dystopic world exists under the iron rule of the mega-corporation Chao-Sonic, with only a few vigilante groups around to act as resistance. Six of Hearts is easily the best agent on one such group, the Deck, and he is fiercely dedicated to justice, using his extensive genetic modifications to his advantage. . . . The compelling and memorable protagonist stands out even against the intricately described and disturbing city whose vividness makes the place's questionable fate a suspenseful issue in its own right." Bull Cent Child Books

Followed by: Remote control (2010)

Money run; by Jack Heath. 1st American ed. Scholastic Press 2013 245 p. (hardcover) $17.99
Grades: 8 9 10 **Fic**

1. Crime -- Fiction 2. Adventure fiction 3. Stealing -- Fiction 4. Assassins -- Fiction 5. Theft 6. Thieves 7. Assassins 8. Robbers and outlaws -- Fiction
ISBN 0545512662; 9780545512664
LC 2013004005

In this book, "Ashley and Benjamin are two teen partners in crime--real crime, as in major heists--who rely on their youth to avoid suspicion. . . . Their prey today happens to be a billionaire businessman who has sponsored an essay contest with a prize of $10,000 (Ash has won with an essay ghostwritten by Benjamin), but that's peanuts compared to the $2 million they hope to loot." (Kirkus Reviews)

Remote control. Scholastic Press 2010 326p $17.99
Grades: 7 8 9 10 **Fic**

1. Science fiction 2. Adventure fiction 3. Spies -- Fiction 4. Genetic engineering -- Fiction
ISBN 978-0-545-07591-6; 0-545-07591-2
Sequel to: The Lab (2008)
First published 2007 in Australia

Agent Six of Hearts, 16-year-old superhuman, is on a mission. His brother Kyntak has been kidnapped. A strange and sinister new figure is rising in power. Six is suspected of being a double agent. The Deck has been put into lockdown by the Queen of Spades. A mysterious girl has appeared who acts as Six's guardian angel. Who can he trust?

"The technothriller begun in The Lab (2008) takes several intriguing twists . . . on its way to a satisfying, if temporary, resolution." Booklist

Hegamin, Tonya

M +O 4evr; [by] Tonya Cherie Hegamin. Houghton Mifflin Co. 2008 165p $16
Grades: 8 9 10 11 **Fic**

1. Death -- Fiction 2. Slavery -- Fiction 3. Lesbians -- Fiction 4. Friendship -- Fiction 5. Family life -- Fiction
ISBN 978-0-618-49570-2; 0-618-49570-3
LC 2007-34293

In parallel stories, Hannah, a slave, finds love while fleeing a Maryland plantation in 1842, and in the present, Opal watches her life-long best friend, Marianne, pull away and eventually lose her life in the same Pennsylvania ravine where Hannah died.

"Hegamin's first novel is richly imaginative as it deals with difficult subjects. . . . [The] parallel stories of love and loss blend seamlessly in this small book that packs a big wallop." SLJ

Hegedus, Bethany

Between us Baxters. WestSide Books 2009 306p $17.95
Grades: 7 8 9 10 **Fic**

1. Friendship -- Fiction 2. Race relations -- Fiction
ISBN 978-1-934813-02-7; 1-934813-02-8

"In 1959, in Holcolm County, GA, there is a palpable tension. Times are slowly changing, causing resentment among some folks and optimism among others. The volatile mix sets the tone for this story of family, friendship, and racial discrimination. . . .When suspicious fires, vandalism, and threats to successful black business owners cause fear and distrust among the townspeople, the strength of Polly and Timbre Ann's bond is tested. . . . The connection between the two girls and their families is beautifully described and believable, and the richness of the characters is apparent. The pacing of the story is deliberate and suspenseful with twists and turns that add to the bittersweet conclusion." SLJ

Hemphill, Helen

Long gone daddy. Front Street 2006 176p $16.95

Grades: 8 9 10 11 12 **Fic**

1. Grandfathers -- Fiction 2. Christian life -- Fiction 3. Las Vegas (Nev.) -- Fiction 4. Father-son relationship -- Fiction

ISBN 1-932425-38-1

LC 2005-25105

Young Harlan Q. Stank gets a taste of life in the fast lane when he accompanies his preacher father on a road trip to Las Vegas to bury his grandfather and to fulfill the terms of the old man's will.

"Many teens will see their own questions about faith, worship, and independence in Harlan's heart-twisting feelings." Booklist

Hemphill, Stephanie

Hideous love; the story of the girl who wrote Frankenstein. Stephanie Hemphill. Balzer + Bray, an imprint of HarperCollinsPublishers 2013 320 p. (hardcover bdg.) $17.99

Grades: 9 10 11 12 **Fic**

1. Novels in verse 2. Historical fiction 3. Love -- Fiction 4. Authorship -- Fiction

ISBN 0061853313; 9780061853319

LC 2013000237

This book is a "fictionalized verse biography of" author Mary Shelley. Stephanie Hemphill "explores the particular challenges facing a gifted female artist who allies herself with a renowned male poet. Central to the plot is the parentage of Mary Wollstonecraft Godwin Shelley, daughter of Mary Wollstonecraft, the pioneering feminist philosopher who died days after Mary was born, and William Godwin, a radical political philosopher who espoused free love for all but his daughters." (Kirkus Reviews)

Sisters of glass; Stephanie Hemphill. Alfred A. Knopf 2012 150 p. $16.99

Grades: 7 8 9 10 **Fic**

1. Love stories 2. Novels in verse 3. Historical fiction 4. Families -- Fiction 5. Family life -- Fiction 6. Venice (Italy) -- Fiction 7. Venice (Italy) 8. Glass blowing and working -- Fiction

ISBN 0375861092; 0375961097; 9780375861093; 9780375961090

LC 2011277551

This book presents "[a] . . . tale of destiny, fidelity, and true love" set in "fourteenth-century Murano, Italy (of glassmaking renown) and . . . told through verse. . . . Maria is disdainful of her training to be a society woman and yearns instead to spend her time with her art or in the family's furnaces with Luca, an employee whose skill with glass is the marvel that leads Maria, who once aspired to be a glassblower, to fall in love with him." (Booklist)

★ **Wicked** girls; a novel of the Salem witch trials. Balzer + Bray 2010 408p il $17.99; lib bdg $17.89

Grades: 7 8 9 10 11 12 **Fic**

1. Novels in verse 2. Trials -- Fiction 3. Witchcraft -- Fiction 4. Salem (Mass.) -- Fiction

ISBN 0-06-185328-3; 0-06-185329-1 lib bdg; 978-0-06-185328-9; 978-0-06-185329-6 lib bdg

LC 2010-9593

This is "a fictionalized account of the Salem witch trials told from the perspectives of three of the real young women living in Salem in 1692. Ann Putnam Jr. plays the queen bee. When her father suggests that a spate of illnesses within the village is the result of witchcraft, Ann . . . puts in motion a chain of events that will change the lives of the people around her forever. Mercy Lewis, the beautiful servant in Ann's house, inspires adulation in some and envy in others. With a troubled past, she seizes her only chance at safety. Margaret Walcott, Ann's cousin, is desperately in love and consumed with fiery jealousy. She is torn between staying loyal to her friends and pursuing the life she dreams of with her betrothed." (Publisher's note) "Middle school, high school." (Horn Book)

"Hemphill's raw, intimate poetry probes behind the abstract facts and creates characters that pulse with complex emotion." Booklist

Includes bibliographical references

Henderson, Jan-Andrew

Bunker 10. Harcourt 2007 253p $17

Grades: 7 8 9 10 **Fic**

1. Virtual reality -- Fiction 2. Genetic engineering -- Fiction

ISBN 978-0-15-206240-8; 0-15-206240-8

LC 2006-38694

Something is going terribly wrong at the top secret Pinewood Military Installation as the teenage geniuses who study and work there are about to discover a horrible truth.

"Henderson ably balances intriguing plot twists and hauntingly well-developed characters with gripping pace and dramatic showdowns." Bull Cent Child Books

Henderson, Jason

★ **Vampire** rising. HarperTeen 2010 249p (Alex Van Helsing) $16.99

Grades: 6 7 8 9 10 **Fic**

1. Horror fiction 2. School stories 3. Vampires -- Fiction 4. Supernatural -- Fiction

ISBN 978-0-06-195099-5; 0-06-195099-8

LC 2009-39663

At a boarding school in Switzerland, fourteen-year-old Alex Van Helsing learns that vampires are real, that he has a natural ability to sense them, and that an agency called the Polidorium has been helping his family fight them since 1821.

"Henderson references Mary Shelley's Frankenstein to weave a great story line full of action, suspense, and adventure. The satisfying story captivates readers with a modern-day spin of James Bond meets Dracula." SLJ

Another title about Alex Van Helsing is:
Voice of the undead (2011)
The Triumph of Death (2012)

The **Triumph** of Death; Jason Henderson. HarperTeen 2012 310 p.
Grades: 8 9 10 11 12 **Fic**
1. Vampires 2. Occult fiction 3. Adventure fiction 4. Horror stories 5. Witches -- Fiction 6. Vampires -- Fiction 7. Supernatural -- Fiction
ISBN 9780061951039
LC 2012004297

This young adult paranormal adventure, by Jason Henderson, is book three of the "Alex Van Helsing" series. "There is a famous painting in Madrid that holds the key to an apocalypse only Alex Van Helsing can stop . . . [and] a newly risen vampire queen threatens the fate of the world. . . . Teaming up with a motorcycle-riding witch, Alex jets between Switzerland, the UK, and Spain in a frantic race to prevent the queen from . . . [plunging] the world into darkness." (Publisher's note)

Henry, April

Torched. G.P. Putnam's Sons 2009 224p $16.99
Grades: 8 9 10 11 **Fic**
1. Terrorism -- Fiction 2. Environmental movement -- Fiction
ISBN 978-0-399-24645-6; 0-399-24645-2
LC 2008-01145

In order to save her parents from going to jail for possession of marijuana, sixteen-year-old Ellie must help the FBI uncover the intentions of a radical environmental group by going undercover.

"The mix of politics and thrilling action will grab teens. . . . This suspenseful story will spark discussion about what it means to fight for right 'by any means necessary.'" Booklist

Hepler, Heather

The **cupcake** queen. Dutton 2009 242p $16.99; pa $7.99
Grades: 6 7 8 9 **Fic**
1. Baking -- Fiction 2. Moving -- Fiction 3. Family life -- Fiction
ISBN 978-0-525-42157-3; 0-525-42157-2; 978-0-14-241668-6 pa; 0-14-241668-1 pa
LC 2008-48971

While longing to return to life in New York City, thirteen-year-old Penny helps her mother and grandmother run a cupcake bakery in Hog's Hollow, tries to avoid the beastly popular girls, to be a good friend to quirky Tally, and to catch the eye of enigmatic Marcus.

"An endearing and poignant story about standing up to adversity and finding peace in what it is, rather than holding out for what it could be." Publ Wkly

Herbach, Geoff

Nothing special; Geoff Herbach. Sourcebooks Inc. 2012 290 p. (paperback) $9.99; (ebook) $9.99
Grades: 6 7 8 9 10 **Fic**
1. Friendship -- Fiction 2. Dysfunctional families -- Fiction 3. Teenagers -- Conduct of life -- Fiction
ISBN 1402265077; 9781402265075; 9781402265099

In this book, author Geoff Herbach tells the story of Felton, a football and track star who deals with his girlfriend Aleah abroad in Germany and "the possibility that his younger brother Andrew could be falling apart. Andrew has convinced their mother to let him go to band camp, but Felton discovers that Andrew, usually the sane member of the family, has in fact run away to Florida. An impromptu road trip with erstwhile best friend Gus turns up surprising reasons for Andrew's escape." (Kirkus Reviews)

Stupid fast. Sourcebooks 2011 311p pa $9.99
Grades: 6 7 8 9 10 **Fic**
1. Boys -- Fiction 2. Football -- Fiction
ISBN 978-1-4022-5630-1; 1-4022-5630-2

"Herbach is at his peak limning the confusion and frustration of a young man who no longer recognizes his own body, and Felton's self-deprecating take on his newly awarded A-list status is funny and compelling." Bull Cent Child Books

Herlong, Madaline

The **great** wide sea; [by] M. H. Herlong. Viking Children's Books 2008 283p $16.99; pa $6.99
Grades: 7 8 9 10 **Fic**
1. Sailing -- Fiction 2. Brothers -- Fiction 3. Bereavement -- Fiction 4. Father-son relationship -- Fiction 5. Survival after airplane accidents, shipwrecks, etc. -- Fiction
ISBN 978-0-670-06330-7; 0-670-06330-4; 978-0-14-241670-9 pa; 0-14-241670-3 pa
LC 2008-08384

Still mourning the death of their mother, three brothers go with their father on an extended sailing trip off the Florida Keys and have an adventure at sea

"Herlong makes the most of the three boys' characters, each exceptionally well developed here, to make this as much a novel of brotherhood as a sea story." Bull Cent Child Books

Hernandez, David

No more us for you. HarperTeen 2009 281p $16.99
Grades: 9 10 11 12 **Fic**
1. School stories 2. Death -- Fiction 3. California -- Fiction 4. Friendship -- Fiction 5. Bereavement -- Fiction
ISBN 978-0-06-117333-2; 0-06-117333-9
LC 2008-19203

Teenagers Isabel and Carlos find themselves growing closer after a car crash forces them to confront difficult issues. "Grades eight to twelve." (Bull Cent Child Books)

"Hernandez builds Isabel and Carlos into characters that readers come to root for and love." Voice Youth Advocates

★ **Suckerpunch.** HarperTeen 2008 217p $17.89
Grades: 9 10 11 12 **Fic**
1. Brothers -- Fiction 2. Drug abuse -- Fiction 3. Child abuse -- Fiction 4. Hispanic Americans -- Fiction 5. Father-son relationship -- Fiction
ISBN 978-0-06-117330-1; 0-06-117331-2

Accompanied by two friends, teenage brothers Marcus and Enrique head on a road trip to confront the abusive father who walked out on them a year earlier.

"The author's imagery, sometimes subtle, sometimes searing, invariably hits its mark." Publ Wkly

Herrick, Steven

By the river. Front Street 2006 238p $16.95
Grades: 8 9 10 11 12 **Fic**

1. Death -- Fiction 2. Brothers -- Fiction 3. Australia -- Fiction 4. Single parent family -- Fiction
ISBN 1-932425-72-1
LC 2005-23967

First published 2004 in the United Kingdom

A fourteen-year-old describes, through prose poems, his life in a small Australian town in 1962, where, since their mother's death, he and his brother have been mainly on their own to learn about life, death, and love.

"The poems are simple but potent in their simplicity, blending together in a compelling, evocative story of a gentle, intelligent boy growing up and learning to deal with a sometimes-ugly little world that he . . . will eventually escape." Voice Youth Advocates

Cold skin. Front Street 2009 279p $17.95
Grades: 8 9 10 11 12 **Fic**

1. Mystery fiction 2. Novels in verse 3. Homicide -- Fiction 4. Australia -- Fiction 5. Country life -- Fiction
ISBN 978-1-59078-572-0; 1-59078-572-X
LC 2008-18620

In a rural Australian coal mining town shortly after World War II, teenaged Eddie makes a startling discovery when he investigates the murder of a local high school girl.

"The strongest plot element is the mystery, which is well developed and has a surprising yet satisfying outcome. Some sexual scenarios make this most appropriate for older teens. Overall, a multilayered and affecting read." SLJ

The **wolf.** Front Street 2007 214p $17.95
Grades: 8 9 10 11 12 **Fic**

1. Novels in verse 2. Australia -- Fiction 3. Domestic violence -- Fiction 4. Father-daughter relationship -- Fiction
ISBN 978-1-932425-75-8; 1-932425-75-6
LC 2006-12072

Sixteen-year-old Lucy, living in the shadow of her violent father, experiences a night of tenderness, danger and revelation as she and Jake, her fifteen-year-old neighbor, search for a legendary wolf in the Australian outback.

"Herrick's verse style perfectly suits this emotionally taut survival story. . . . Readers will find this novel compelling, its fast-moving narrative rewarding." SLJ

Hesse, Karen

Safekeeping; Karen Hesse. Feiwel and Friends 2012 294 p. ill., map $17.99
Grades: 7 8 9 10 11 12 **Fic**

1. Alternative histories 2. Revolutions -- Fiction 3. Voyages and travels -- Fiction
ISBN 1250011345; 9781250011343
LC 2012288414

In this book, a "group of rebels called the American People's Party has taken control" in the U.S. "Radley, an American teenager returning home from doing volunteer work in Haiti, finds her parents gone and her Vermont home abandoned. Not knowing whom to trust or where she'll be safe, she sets out on foot to Canada, befriending a reticent girl along the way. The two form a tentative friendship and manage to cross into Canada." (Publishers Weekly)

Hesser, Terry Spencer

Kissing doorknobs. Delacorte Press 1998 149p hardcover o.p. pa $6.50
Grades: 7 8 9 10 **Fic**

1. Friendship -- Fiction 2. Family life -- Fiction 3. Mental illness -- Fiction 4. Obsessive-compulsive disorder -- Fiction
ISBN 0-385-32329-8; 0-440-41314-1 pa
LC 97-26937

Fourteen-year-old Tara describes how her increasingly strange compulsions begin to take over her life and affect her relationships with her family and friends

"An honest, fresh, and multilayered story to which readers will instantly relate. . . . The prose is forthright, economical, and peppered with wry humor." SLJ

Hiaasen, Carl

Skink -- no surrender; Carl Hiaasen; Alfred A. Knopf. 2014 281p $18.99
Grades: 9 10 11 12 Fic

1. Missing children -- Fiction 2. Wilderness areas -- Fiction 4. Florida -- Fiction 5. Mystery fiction
ISBN: 0375870512; 9780375870514; 9780375970511
LC 2014006036

"Richard and his cousin Malley are best friends. But while Richard is pretty levelheaded, Malley tends to get into trouble. So Richard is only mildly surprised to discover that she's run off with a guy she met on the Internet in order to avoid being sent to boarding school in New Hampshire. Richard wants to go find her, and luckily he runs into what may be the perfect person to help him do just that: a ragged, one-eyed ex-governor of Florida named Skink. With Skink at the helm, the two set off across Florida in search of Richard's cousin." Booklist

"A high stakes, action-packed comedy with a lot of heart." VOYA

Higgins, F. E.

The **Eyeball** Collector. Feiwel & Friends 2009 251p $14.99
Grades: 7 8 9 10 **Fic**

1. Horror fiction 2. Mystery fiction
ISBN 978-0-312-56681-4; 0-312-56681-6

"In what the author dubs a 'polyquel' that partially bridges her Black Book of Secrets (2007) and its prequel Bone Magician (2008), Higgins sends a suddenly penniless young orphan from the filthy streets of Urbs Umida's South Side to an extravagantly rococo estate house in search of vengeance for his family's ruin. . . . Readers with a taste for lurid prose, macabre twists, riddles, exotic poisons, high-society caricatures, murderous schemes and scenes of stomach-churning degeneracy will find some or all of these in every chapter, and though the author trots in multiple characters and references from previous episodes, this one stands sturdily on its own." Kirkus

Higgins, Jack

★ **Sure** fire; [by] Jack Higgins with Justin Richards. G.P. Putnam's Sons 2007 237p $16.99
Grades: 6 7 8 9 **Fic**

1. Adventure fiction 2. Spies -- Fiction 3. Twins -- Fiction 4. Fathers -- Fiction
ISBN 978-0-399-24784-2; 0-399-24784-X
LC 2007008144

First published 2006 in the United Kingdom

Resentful of having to go and live with their estranged father after the death of their mother, fifteen-year-old twins, Rich and Jade, soon find they have more complicated problems when their father is kidnapped and their attempts to rescue him involve them in a dangerous international plot to control the world's oil.

This is a "standout YA spy novel. . . . Each chapter ends with a cliff-hanger, maintaining the high level of suspense." Publ Wkly

Other titles in this series are:
Death run (2008)
Sharp shot (2009)
First strike (2010)

Higgins, M. G.

Bi-Normal; M. G. Higgins. Saddleback Pub 2013 191 p. (paperback) $9.95
Grades: 7 8 9 10 11 12 **Fic**

1. School stories 2. Gay teenagers -- Fiction
ISBN 1622500040; 9781622500048

In this book, "a teen football player with a girlfriend discovers he has feelings for another boy. When Brett first notices his attraction to Zach, a boy who sits next to him in art class, he wants to push it away Brett and his friends are the kind of guys who ogle girls' bodies and pick on boys they perceive as gay. As his feelings intensify, however, Brett is torn between acting on his attraction and acting out of his denial." (Kirkus Reviews)

Higson, Charles

The **dead**; [by] Charlie Higson. Hyperion 2011 485p map $16.99
Grades: 8 9 10 **Fic**

1. Horror fiction 2. Zombies -- Fiction
ISBN 978-1-4231-3412-1; 1-4231-3412-5

As a disease turns everyone over sixteen into brainless, decomposing, flesh-eating creatures, a group of teenagers head to London. Ed, Jack, Bam and the other students at Rowhurst School learn more about the Disaster, and meet an adult who seems to be immune to the disease.

"With the book's immense cast and substantial body count, it doesn't pay to get too attached to any one character, while the intense descriptions of violence and sickness will get under readers' skin." Publ Wkly

★ The **enemy**. Hyperion/DBG 2010 440p $16.99; pa $8.99
Grades: 9 10 11 12 **Fic**

1. Horror fiction 2. Zombies -- Fiction 3. London (England) -- Fiction
ISBN 978-1-4231-3175-5; 1-4231-3175-4; 978-1-4231-3312-4 pa; 1-4231-3312-9 pa

First published 2009 in the United Kingdom

"Nearly two years ago, the world changed; everyone over 16 became horrifically ill and began to crave fresh meat. As supplies are exhausted and the vicious grown-ups grow braver, Arrum and Maxie, along with their band of refugees, must embark on a perilous journey across London to reach the safest spot in the city: Buckingham Palace. . . . Intrigue, betrayal and the basic heroic-teens-against-marauding-adults conflict give this work a high place on any beach-reading list." Kirkus

Followed by: The dead (2011)

Hijuelos, Oscar

Dark Dude. Atheneum Books for Young Readers 2008 439p $16.99; pa $9.99
Grades: 7 8 9 10 **Fic**

1. Wisconsin -- Fiction 2. Cuban Americans -- Fiction
ISBN 978-1-4169-4804-9; 1-4169-4804-X; 978-1-4169-4945-9 pa; 1-4169-4945-3 pa
LC 2008-00959

In the 1960s, Rico Fuentes, a pale-skinned Cuban American teenager, abandons drug-infested New York City for the picket fence and apple pie world of Wisconsin, only to discover that he still feels like an outsider and that violent and judgmental people can be found even in the wholesome Midwest.

"Hijuelos weaves a compelling and insightful tale of one outsider's coming-of-age. . . . The resolution is quick and tidy, but the imagery is rich and the content sure to engage teen readers." Voice Youth Advocates

Hill, C. J.

Erasing time; C. J. Hill. Katherine Tegen Books 2012 361 p. $17.99
Grades: 8 9 10 11 **Fic**

1. Secrecy -- Fiction 2. Resistance to government 3. Future life 4. Science fiction 5. Twins -- Fiction 6. Sisters -- Fiction 7. Time travel -- Fiction 8. Government, Resistance to -- Fiction
ISBN 0062123920; 9780062123923
LC 2011044624

Slayers; friends and traitors. by C. J. Hill. Feiwel & Friends 2013 390 p. $16.99
Grades: 7 8 9 10 11 12 **Fic**

1. Dragons -- Fiction 2. Teenagers -- Fiction
ISBN 1250024617; 9781250024619

In this book, by C. J. Hill, "Tori's got a problem. She thought she'd have one more summer to train as a dragon Slayer, but time has run out. When Tori hears the horrifying sound of dragon eggs hatching, she knows the Slayers are in trouble. In less than a year, the dragons will be fully grown and completely lethal. The Slayers are well-prepared, but their group is still not complete, and Tori is determined to track down Ryker--the mysterious missing Slayer." (Publisher's note)

"When Tori breaks the rules that keep the dragon slayers safe, all the slayers are endangered unless they can figure out which one of them is a traitor. A steamy love triangle takes center stage over the dragon-fighting in this installment; though many characters from the first book only show up fleetingly, fans of Slayers will find plenty to entertain them." (Horn Book)

Hill, Will

Department 19. Razorbill 2011 540p
Grades: 10 11 12 **Fic**

1. Horror fiction 2. Homicide -- Fiction 3. Vampires -- Fiction 4. Supernatural -- Fiction 5. Great Britain -- Fiction

ISBN 1595144064; 9781595144065

LC 2010-54252

After watching his father's murder, sixteen-year-old Jamie Carpenter joins Department 19, a secret government agency, where he learns of the existence of vampires and the history that ties him to the team destined to stop them. "Grades eight to ten." (Bull Cent Child Books)

"This is a nonstop thrill ride right up to the cliffhanger ending. This cinematic adrenaline rush has the makings of a surefire hit." Publ Wkly

The **rising**; Will Hill. Razorbill 2012 576 p.
Grades: 10 11 12 **Fic**

1. Vampires 2. Supernatural 3. Dracula, Count (Fictional character) 4. Adventure fiction

ISBN 1595144072; 9781595144072

In this novel, by Will Hill, "Sixteen-year-old Jamie Carpenter's life was violently upended when he was brought into Department 19, a classified government agency of vampire hunters. . . . But being the new recruit at the Department isn't all weapons training and covert missions. Jamie's own mother has been turned into a vampire--and now Jamie will stop at nothing to wreak revenge on her captors." (Publisher's note)

Hills, Lia

★ The **beginner's** guide to living. Farrar, Straus and Giroux 2010 221p il $17.99
Grades: 9 10 11 12 **Fic**

1. School stories 2. Bereavement -- Fiction

ISBN 978-0-374-30659-5; 0-374-30659-1

LC 2009-19248

Struggling to cope with his mother's sudden death and growing feelings of isolation from his father and brother, seventeen-year-old Will turns to philosophy for answers to life's biggest questions, while finding some solace in a new love.

"Almost nothing escapes Will's notice (though his perceptiveness alone doesn't produce answers), and the mosaic of imagery and musings in his poetic, staccato narration offers thought-provoking ideas about grief and the universal drive to find a purpose. Although this novel begins with a death, it is a celebration of life, companionship, and love." Publ Wkly

Hinton, S. E.

★ The **outsiders**. Viking 1967 188p $17.99; pa $9.99
Grades: 7 8 9 10 **Fic**

1. Social classes -- Fiction 2. Juvenile delinquency -- Fiction

ISBN 0-670-53257-6; 0-14-038572-X pa

ALA YALSA Margaret A. Edwards Award (1988)

"This remarkable novel by a seventeen-year-old girl gives a moving, credible view of the outsiders from the inside—their loyalty to each other, their sensitivity under tough crusts, their understanding of self and society." Horn Book

Hinwood, Christine

The **returning**. Dial Books 2011 302p map $17.99
Grades: 6 7 8 9 10 **Fic**

1. War stories 2. Villages -- Fiction

ISBN 978-0-8037-3528-6; 0-8037-3528-6

LC 2010-08398

First published 2009 in Australia with title: Bloodflower

When the twelve-year war between the Uplanders and Downlanders is over and Cam returns home to his village, questions dog him, from how he lost an arm to why he was the only one of his fellow soldiers to survive, such that he must leave until his own suspicions are resolved.

"Themes of rebuilding and redemption are powerful, but it is in the small, acutely observed details of debut author Hinwood's world that her story truly shines." Publ Wkly

Hirsch, Jeff

The **eleventh** plague. Scholastic Press 2011 278p $17.99
Grades: 7 8 9 10 **Fic**

1. Science fiction

ISBN 978-0-545-29014-2; 0-545-29014-7

LC 2010048966

Twenty years after the start of the war that caused the Collapse, fifteen-year-old Stephen, his father, and grandfather travel post-Collapse America scavenging, but when his grandfather dies and his father decides to risk everything to save the lives of two strangers, Stephen's life is turned upside down.

This "novel is an impressive story with strong characters. . . . Hirsch delivers a tight, well-crafted story." Publ Wkly

Hoban, Julia

Willow. Dial Books 2009 329p $16.99
Grades: 9 10 11 12 **Fic**

1. Guilt -- Fiction 2. Orphans -- Fiction 3. Bereavement -- Fiction 4. Self-mutilation -- Fiction

ISBN 978-0-8037-3356-5; 0-8037-3356-9

LC 2008-33064

Sixteen-year-old Willow, who was driving the car that killed both of her parents, copes with the pain and guilt by cutting herself, until she meets a smart and sensitive boy who is determined to help her stop.

"Hoban's appropriately complex portrayal of cutting makes this a good choice on a crucial subject." Kirkus

Hoban, Russell, 1925-2011

Soonchild; Russell Hoban; illustrated by Alexis Deacon. Candlewick 2012 144 p. (hardback) $15.99
Grades: 9 10 11 12 **Fic**

1. Occult fiction 2. Shamans -- Fiction 3. Arctic

regions -- Fiction 4. Inuit -- Fiction 5. Eskimos -- Fiction 6. Pregnancy -- Fiction 7. Supernatural -- Fiction 8. Father and child -- Fiction
ISBN 9780763659202
LC 2011048373

In this book, set "[s]omewhere in the Arctic Circle, Sixteen-Face John, a shaman, learns that his first child, a soonchild, cannot hear the World Songs from her mother's womb. The World Songs are what inspire all newborns to come out into the world, and John must find them for her. But how? The answer takes him through many lifetimes and many shape-shifts, as well as encounters with beasts, demons and a mysterious benevolent owl spirit, Ukpika." (Publisher's note)

Hobbs, Valerie

Sonny's war. Farrar, Straus & Giroux 2002 215p hardcover o.p. pa $7.95
Grades: 7 8 9 10 **Fic**
1. Vietnam War, 1961-1975 -- Fiction
ISBN 0-374-37136-9; 0-374-46970-9 pa
LC 2002-23891

In the late 1960s, fourteen-year-old Cory's life is greatly changed by the sudden death of her father and her brother's tour of duty in Vietnam

"Hobbs writes like a dream . . . but the Cory she conjures up for us is as real as real, completely believable in all her teenage vulnerability and sharp-eyed observation." Horn Book Guide

Hobbs, Will

Beardance. Atheneum Pubs. 1993 197p il pa $5.99
Grades: 7 8 9 10 **Fic**
1. Bears -- Fiction 2. Ute Indians -- Fiction
ISBN 0-689-31867-7; 0-689-87072-8 pa
LC 92-44874

Sequel to Bearstone

While accompanying an elderly rancher on a trip into the San Juan Mountains, Cloyd, a Ute Indian boy, tries to help two orphaned grizzly cubs survive the winter and, at the same time, completes his spirit mission.

"The story offers plenty of action and memorable characters, and the descriptions of Ute rituals and legends, the setting, and Cloyd's first experiences with spirit dreams are particularly well done." Horn Book Guide

Bearstone. Atheneum Pubs. 1989 154p hardcover o.p. pa $4.99
Grades: 7 8 9 10 **Fic**
1. Ute Indians -- Fiction
ISBN 0-689-87071-X pa
LC 89-6641

"The growth and maturity that Cloyd acquires as the summer progresses is juxtaposed poetically against the majestic Colorado landscape. Hobbs has creatively blended myth and reality as Cloyd forges a new identity for himself." Voice Youth Advocates

Followed by Beardance (1993)

Crossing the wire. HarperCollins 2006 216p $15.99; lib bdg $16.89; pa $5.99
Grades: 5 6 7 8 **Fic**
1. Mexicans -- Fiction 2. Illegal aliens -- Fiction
ISBN 978-0-06-074138-9; 0-06-074138-4; 978-0-06-074139-6 lib bdg; 0-06-074139-2 lib bdg; 978-0-06-074140-2 pa; 0-06-074140-6 pa
LC 2005-19697

Fifteen-year-old Victor Flores journeys north in a desperate attempt to cross the Arizona border and find work in the United States to support his family in central Mexico.

This is "an exciting story in a vital contemporary setting." Voice Youth Advocates

Downriver. Atheneum Pubs. 1991 204p hardcover o.p. pa $6.99
Grades: 7 8 9 10 **Fic**
1. White-water canoeing -- Fiction
ISBN 0-689-31690-9; 0-440-22673-2 pa
LC 90-1044

Fifteen-year-old Jessie and the other rebellious teenage members of a wilderness survival school team abandon their adult leader, hijack his boats, and try to run the dangerous white water at the bottom of the Grand Canyon

"The book is exquisitely plotted, with nail-biting suspense and excitement." SLJ

Leaving Protection. HarperCollins 2004 178p il map $15.99; pa $5.99
Grades: 7 8 9 10 **Fic**
1. Alaska -- Fiction 2. Fishing -- Fiction 3. Buried treasure -- Fiction
ISBN 0-688-17475-2; 0-380-73312-9 pa
LC 2003-15545

Sixteen-year-old Robbie Daniels, happy to get a job aboard a troller fishing for king salmon off southeastern Alaska, finds himself in danger when he discovers that his mysterious captain is searching for long-buried Russian plaques that lay claim to Alaska and the Northwest

This "nautical thriller brims with detail about the fishing life and weaves in historical facts as well. . . . Robbie's doubts build to a climactic finale involving a dramatic and fateful storm at sea, grippingly rendered. Fans of maritime tales will relish the atmosphere and the bursts of action." Publ Wkly

★ The **maze.** Morrow Junior Bks. 1998 198p $15.99; pa $5.99
Grades: 7 8 9 10 **Fic**
1. Condors -- Fiction 2. Runaway teenagers -- Fiction
ISBN 0-688-15092-6; 0-380-72913-X pa
LC 98-10791

Rick, a fourteen-year-old foster child, escapes from a juvenile detention facility near Las Vegas and travels to Canyonlands National Park in Utah where he meets a bird biologist working on a project to reintroduce condors to the wild

"Hobbs spins an engrossing yarn, blending adventure with a strong theme, advocating the need for developing personal values." Horn Book Guide

Take me to the river. HarperCollins 2011 184p $15.99; lib bdg $16.89

Grades: 5 6 7 8 **Fic**

1. Cousins -- Fiction 2. Canoes and canoeing -- Fiction

ISBN 978-0-06-074144-0; 0-06-074144-9; 978-0-06-074145-7 lib bdg; 0-06-074145-7 lib bdg

LC 2010003147

When North Carolina fourteen-year-old Dylan Sands joins his fifteen-year-old cousin Rio in running the Rio Grande River, they face a tropical storm and a fugitive kidnapper.

"The story unfolds in a disarming manner. The pace is quick, and the challenges are relentless, but the writing is so grounded in physical details and emotional realism that every turn of events seems convincing within the context of the story." Booklist

Wild Man Island. HarperCollins Pubs. 2002 184p $15.99; lib bdg $16.89; pa $5.99

Grades: 6 7 8 9 **Fic**

1. Wilderness survival -- Fiction

ISBN 0-688-17473-6; 0-06-029810-3 lib bdg; 0-380-73310-2 pa

LC 2001-39818

After fourteen-year-old Andy slips away from his kayaking group to visit the wilderness site of his archaeologist father's death, a storm strands him on Admiralty Island, Alaska, where he manages to survive, encounters unexpected animal and human inhabitants, and looks for traces of the earliest prehistoric immigrants to America

"A well-paced adventure, this novel combines survival saga, mystery, and archaeological expedition." Voice Youth Advocates

Hocking, Amanda

Wake; Amanda Hocking. St. Martin's Griffin 2012 309 p. (hardback) $17.99

Grades: 7 8 9 10 **Fic**

1. Occult fiction 2. Fantasy fiction 3. Sirens (Mythology) -- Fiction 4. Love -- Fiction 5. Sisters -- Fiction 6. Supernatural -- Fiction 7. Seaside resorts -- Fiction

ISBN 1250008123; 9781250008121; 9781429956581

LC 2012014630

This is the first in Amanda Hocking's Watersong series. Here, "Gemma Fisher is happy—she's a star on the swim team, her family is loving and supportive, and the crush-worthy boy next door returns her interest. The only downside: three gorgeous but creepy new girls who have her in their sights." These girls ultimately turn out to be Sirens who trick Gemma into drinking potion that turns her into a Siren as well. (Publishers Weekly)

Followed by Lullaby (2012) and Tidal (2013)

Hodge, Rosamund

Cruel Beauty; Rosamund Hodge. Balzer + Bray, an imprint of HarperCollinsPublishers 2014 352 p. (hardcover) $17.99

Grades: 8 9 10 11 12 **Fic**

1. Love stories 2. Imaginary places 3. Magic -- Fiction 4. Fantasy

ISBN 0062224735; 9780062224736

LC 2013015418

In this book, by Rosamund Hodge, "betrothed to the evil ruler of her kingdom, Nyx has always known her fate was to marry him, kill him, and free her people from his tyranny. On her seventeenth birthday, when she moves into his castle high on the kingdom's mountaintop, nothing is as she expected. Nyx knows she must save her homeland at all costs, yet she can't resist the pull of her sworn enemy--who's gotten in her way by stealing her heart." (Publisher's note)

"Hodge's story infuses elements of Greek mythology and classic fairy tales. The plot moves quickly, and the characters are well formed; their transgressions make them interesting and authentic. The complex relationship between Nyx and Ignifex is especially engaging. An entertaining read for teens who enjoy romantic fantasy." (School Library Journal)

Hodkin, Michelle

The **evolution** of Mara Dyer; Michelle Hodkin. Simon & Schuster Books for Young Readers 2012 527 p. (hardcover) $17.99

Grades: 7 8 9 10 11 12 **Fic**

1. Stalkers -- Fiction 2. Supernatural -- Fiction 3. Post-traumatic stress disorder -- Fiction 4. Love -- Fiction 5. Florida -- Fiction

ISBN 1442421797; 9781442421790; 9781442421813

LC 2012019195

Sequel to: The unbecoming of Mara Dyer

In this novel by Michelle Hodkin, part of the Mara Dyer Trilogy, "Mara continues her relationship with wealthy Noah. . . . Meanwhile, Mara insists that her supposedly dead former boyfriend, Jude, continues to stalk her. She is being treated as an outpatient for PTSD after causing (as she originally believed) the deaths of Jude and her friends. . . . Noah uses his wits and wealth to try to protect her and to investigate the possibility that Jude indeed survived." (Kirkus)

The **unbecoming** of Mara Dyer. Simon & Schuster 2011 456p $16.99

Grades: 7 8 9 10 11 12 **Fic**

1. School stories 2. Family life -- Fiction 3. Supernatural -- Fiction 4. Post-traumatic stress disorder -- Fiction

ISBN 978-1-4424-2176-9; 1-4424-2176-2

LC 2010050862

Seventeen-year-old Mara cannot remember the accident that took the lives of three of her friends but, after moving from Rhode Island to Florida, finding love with Noah, and more deaths, she realizes uncovering something buried in her memory might save her family and her future.

"The characters are real and wonderful, and the supernatural story is riveting." SLJ

Hoffman, Alice

The **foretelling**. Little, Brown 2005 167p hardcover o.p. pa $7.99

Grades: 7 8 9 10 **Fic**

1. Amazons -- Fiction 2. Sex role -- Fiction

ISBN 0-316-01018-9; 0-316-15409-1 pa

LC 2004-25102

Growing up the daughter of an Amazon queen who shuns her, Rain rebels against the ways of her tribe through her sisterlike relationship with Io and her feelings for a boy from a tribe of wanderers.

The "first-person narration is accessible while evoking a sense of otherworldliness. . . . The story unfolds at a measured pace with little dialogue, but the language makes it compulsively readable." SLJ

Green angel. Scholastic Press 2003 116p pa $5.99
Grades: 7 8 9 10 **Fic**

1. Gardening -- Fiction

ISBN 0-439-44384-9; 0-545-20411-9 pa

LC 2002-6980

Haunted by grief and by her past after losing her family in a fire, fifteen-year-old Green retreats into her ruined garden as she struggles to survive emotionally and physically on her own

"A powerfully written and thought-provoking selection." SLJ

Green witch. Scholastic Press 2010 135p $17.99
Grades: 7 8 9 10 11 12 **Fic**

1. Orphans -- Fiction 2. Gardening -- Fiction 3. Bereavement -- Fiction 4. Storytelling -- Fiction 5. Supernatural -- Fiction 6. Missing persons -- Fiction

ISBN 978-0-545-14195-6; 0-545-14195-8

LC 2009-17606

A year after her world was nearly destroyed, sixteen-year-old Green has become the one villagers turn to for aid, especially to record their stories, but Green will need the help of other women who, like herself, are believed to be witches if she is to find her best friend and her one true love.

"Haunting, philosophical, and filled with poetic imagery . . . this book will leave an indelible mark." Publ Wkly

★ **Incantation.** Little, Brown 2006 166p hardcover o.p. pa $8.99
Grades: 8 9 10 11 12 **Fic**

1. Spain -- Fiction 2. Prejudices -- Fiction 3. Inquisition -- Fiction 4. Jews -- Persecutions -- Fiction

ISBN 978-0-316-01019-1; 0-316-01019-7; 978-0-316-15428-4 pa; 0-316-15428-8 pa

LC 2005-37301

During the Spanish Inquisition, sixteen-year-old Estrella, brought up a Catholic, discovers her family's true Jewish identity, and when their secret is betrayed by Estrella's best friend, the consequences are tragic. Includes some scenes of graphic violence.

"Hoffman's lyrical prose and astute characterization blend to create a riveting, horrific tale that unites despair with elements of hope." SLJ

Hoffman, Mary

★ The **falconer's** knot; a story of friars, flirtation and foul play. Bloomsbury Children's Books 2007 297p $16.95
Grades: 7 8 9 10 **Fic**

1. Love stories 2. Renaissance -- Fiction 3. Religious life -- Fiction

ISBN 978-1-59990-056-8; 1-59990-056-4

LC 2006-16365

Silvano and Chiara, teens sent to live in a friary and a nunnery in Renaissance Italy, are drawn to one another and dream of a future together, but when murders are committed in the friary, they must discover who is behind the crimes before they can realize their love.

"Hoffman creates utterly engaging characters and vivid settings, and she skillfully turns up the suspense, wrapping her varied plot threads into a satisfying whole." Booklist

Hoffman, Nina Kiriki

A **stir** of bones. Viking 2003 211p $15.99
Grades: 7 8 9 10 **Fic**

1. Ghost stories 2. Wife abuse -- Fiction

ISBN 0-670-03551-3

LC 2003-5029

Fourteen-year-old Susan Blackstrom "begins the painful process of breaking away from her abusive father, with help from allies both human and supernatural. A chance encounter with three classmates leads Susan to an abandoned house that . . . harbors an uncommonly substantial ghost named Nathan. . . . Richly endowed with complex relationships, a strange and subtle brand of magic, evocative language, and suspenseful storytelling, this will draw readers into a world less safe and simple than it seems at first glance." Booklist

Hokenson, Terry

The **winter** road; 1st ed.; Front Street 2006 175p $16.95
Grades: 7 8 9 10 **Fic**

1. Survival after airplane accidents, shipwrecks, etc. -- Fiction

ISBN 1-932425-45-4

LC 2005027030

Seventeen-year-old Willa, still grieving over the death of her older brother and the neglect of her father, decides to fly a small plane to fetch her mother from Northern Ontario, but when the plane crashes she is all alone in the snowy wilderness.

"The mortal challenges Willa faces make for a gripping narrative, one sharpened by visceral details." Booklist

Holder, Nancy

Crusade; by Nancy Holder and Debbie Viguie. Simon Pulse 2010 470p $16.99
Grades: 7 8 9 10 11 **Fic**

1. Horror fiction 2. Sisters -- Fiction 3. Vampires -- Fiction 4. Supernatural -- Fiction

ISBN 978-1-4169-9802-0; 1-4169-9802-0

LC 2010-9094

An international team of six teenaged vampire hunters, trained in Salamanca, Spain, goes to New Orleans seeking to rescue team-member Jenn's younger sister as the vampires escalate their efforts to take over the Earth.

"The cinematic writing and apocalyptic scenario should find a ready audience." Publ Wkly

Followed by: Damned (2011)

Damned; by Nancy Holder and Debbie Viguie. Simon Pulse 2011 $16.99; pa $9.99
Grades: 7 8 9 10 **Fic**

1. Horror fiction 2. Vampires -- Fiction 3. Supernatural

-- Fiction
ISBN 978-1-4169-9804-4; 1-4169-9804-7; 978-1-4169-9805-1 pa; 1-4169-9805-5 pa
LC 2011005474

As the newly appointed Hunter, teenager Jenn leads the fighting teams who defend against the Cursed Ones--the vampires who are taking over Earth--but an even more sinister force now threatens the teams of hunters, with the fate of humanity at stake.

Holland, L. Tam

The **counterfeit** family tree of Vee Crawford-Wong; by L. Tam Holland. 1st ed. Simon & Schuster BFYR 2013 368 p. (hardcover) $17.99
Grades: 9 10 11 12 **Fic**

1. School stories 2. Truthfulness and falsehood -- Fiction 3. China -- Fiction 4. Schools -- Fiction 5. Families -- Fiction 6. High schools -- Fiction 7. Chinese Americans -- Fiction
ISBN 144241264X; 9781442412644; 9781442412651; 9781442412668
LC 2012014542

In this book, Vee has to write an essay on family history, but all he "knows about his Texas grandparents is that their annual Christmas card always makes his mother cry; his father, meanwhile, left China for college and never looked back. Already in trouble for lackluster academics, Vee can't get his parents to talk about their pasts, so he completes the essay by inventing a backstory for his father's family in a fishing village along the Yangtze. After he gets away with that, he's on a roll." (Publishers Weekly)

Holub, Josef

An **innocent** soldier; translated by Michael Hofmann. Arthur A. Levine Books 2005 231p $16.99
Grades: 8 9 10 11 12 **Fic**

1. War stories 2. Russia -- Fiction 3. France -- History -- 1799-1815 -- Fiction
ISBN 0-439-62771-0

A sixteen-year-old farmhand is tricked into fighting in the Napoleonic Wars by the farmer for whom he works, who secretly substitutes him for the farmer's own son.

"This is a well-wrought psychological tale. . . . [It] has a lot to offer to those seeking to build a deep historical fiction collection." SLJ

Hooper, Mary

Fallen Grace. Bloomsbury 2011 309p $16.99
Grades: 7 8 9 10 **Fic**

1. Orphans -- Fiction 2. Poverty -- Fiction 3. Sisters -- Fiction 4. London (England) -- Fiction 5. People with mental disabilities -- Fiction 6. Swindlers and swindling -- Fiction 7. Funeral rites and ceremonies -- Fiction 8. Great Britain -- History -- 19th century -- Fiction
ISBN 978-1-59990-564-8; 1-59990-564-7
LC 2010-25498

In Victorian London, impoverished fifteen-year-old orphan Grace takes care of her older but mentally unfit sister Lily, and after enduring many harsh and painful experiences, the two become the victims of a fraud perpetrated by the wealthy owners of several funeral businesses.

Hooper "packs her brisk Dickensian fable with colorful characters and suspenseful, satisfying plot twists. The sobering realities of child poverty and exploitation are vividly conveyed, along with fascinating details of the Victorian funeral trade." Kirkus

Includes bibliographical references

Velvet; by Mary Hooper. 1st U.S. ed. Bloomsbury 2012 323 p. (hardcover) $16.99
Grades: 9 10 11 **Fic**

1. Historical fiction 2. Orphans -- Fiction 3. Spiritualists -- Fiction 4. London (England) -- History -- 19th century -- Fiction 5. Great Britain -- History -- Victoria, 1837-1901 -- Fiction
ISBN 159990912X; 9781599909127
LC 2012005205

In this novel, by Mary Hooper, "Velvet is a laundress in a Victorian steam laundry. . . . The laundry is scalding, back-breaking work and Velvet is desperate to create a better life. Then she is noticed by Madame Savoya, a famed medium, who asks Velvet to come work for her. At first she is dazzled by the young yet beautifully dressed and bejeweled Madame. But Velvet soon realizes that Madame Savoya is not all that she says she is, and Velvet's very life may be in danger." (Publisher's note)

Includes bibliographical references

Hopkins, Ellen

★ **Burned**. Margaret K. McElderry Books 2006 532p $16.95
Grades: 9 10 11 12 **Fic**

1. Novels in verse 2. Mormons -- Fiction 3. Sex role -- Fiction 4. Child abuse -- Fiction 5. Family life -- Fiction
ISBN 1-4169-0354-2; 978-1-4169-0354-3
LC 2005-32461

Seventeen-year-old Pattyn, the eldest daughter in a large Mormon family, is sent to her aunt's Nevada ranch for the summer, where she temporarily escapes her alcoholic, abusive father and finds love and acceptance, only to lose everything when she returns home.

"The free verses, many in the form of concrete poems, create a compressed and intense reading experience with no extraneous dialogue or description. . . . This book will appeal to teens favoring realistic fiction and dramatic interpersonal stories." Voice Youth Advocates

Identical. Margaret K. McElderry Books 2008 565p $17.99
Grades: 10 11 12 **Fic**

1. Novels in verse 2. Twins -- Fiction 3. Sisters -- Fiction 4. Child sexual abuse -- Fiction
ISBN 978-1-4169-5005-9; 1-4169-5005-2
LC 2007-32463

Sixteen-year-old identical twin daughters of a district court judge and a candidate for the United States House of Representatives, Kaeleigh and Raeanne Gardella desperately struggle with secrets that have already torn them and their family apart.

This book "tells the twins' story in intimate and often-graphic detail. Hopkins packs in multiple issues including eating disorders, drug abuse, date rape, alcoholism, sexual abuse, and self-mutilation as she examines a family that 'puts the dys in dysfunction.' . . . Gritty and compelling, this is not a comfortable read, but its keen insights make it hard to put down." SLJ

Rumble; Ellen Hopkins. Margaret K. McElderry Books. 2014 546p $19.99
Grades: 8 9 10 11 12 **Fic**

1. Family problems -- Fiction 2. Grief -- Fiction 3. High schools -- Fiction; 4. Novels in verse 5. Suicide -- Fiction
ISBN: 1442482842; 9781442482845
LC 2013037681

In this verse novel, "Matthew Turner doesn't have faith in anything. Not in family--his is a shambles after his younger brother was bullied into suicide. Not in so-called friends who turn their backs when things get tough. Not in some all-powerful creator who lets too much bad stuff happen. . . . No matter what his girlfriend Hayden says about faith and forgiveness, there's no way Matt's letting go of blame." (Publisher's note)

"Matt is a wonderfully faceted character that readers will alternately sympathize with and dislike. His actions are directly related to his emotional turmoil, and teens will understand his pain and admire his intellect, even while shaking their heads over his actions.." SLJ

Smoke; Ellen Hopkins. 1st ed. Margaret K. McElderry Books 2013 560 p. (hardcover) $19.99
Grades: 9 10 11 12 **Fic**

1. Rape -- Fiction 2. Homicide -- Fiction 3. Novels in verse 4. Grief -- Fiction 5. Mormons -- Fiction 6. Sisters -- Fiction 7. Runaways -- Fiction 8. Emotional problems -- Fiction
ISBN 9781416983286; 1416983287
LC 2012038452

Sequel to: Burned

In this sequel to Ellen Hopkins' "Burned," sisters Pattyn and Jackie "wrestle with guilt and fear after one kills the father who battered them." Pattyn stays with a family of farm workers while hiding from police. "Meanwhile, 15-year-old Jackie is stuck at home, narrating her own half of the story. Through free-verse poems . . . , the shooting's details emerge. A schoolmate raped Jackie; blaming Jackie, Dad broke her ribs and loosened her teeth; Pattyn's gun stopped Dad forever." (Kirkus Reviews)

Tricks. Margaret K. McElderry Books 2009 627p $18.99
Grades: 10 11 12 **Fic**

1. Novels in verse 2. Family life -- Fiction 3. Prostitution -- Fiction
ISBN 978-1-4169-5007-3
LC 2009-20297

Five troubled teenagers fall into prostitution as they search for freedom, safety, community, family, and love.

"Hopkins's pithy free verse reveals shards of emotion and quick glimpses of physical detail. It doesn't matter that the first-person voices blur, because the stories are distinct and unmistakable. Graphic sex, rape, drugs, bitter loneliness, despair—and eventually, blessedly, glimmers of hope." Kirkus

Hopkinson, Nalo

The **Chaos**; Nalo Hopkinson. Margaret K. McElderry Books 2012 241p. (hardcover) $16.99
Grades: 7 8 9 10 11 12 **Fic**

1. Science fiction 2. Toronto (Ont.) -- Fiction 3. Siblings 4. Racially mixed people -- Fiction 5. Supernatural 6. Canada -- Fiction 7. Identity -- Fiction 8. Supernatural -- Fiction 9. Brothers and sisters -- Fiction 10. Family life -- Canada -- Fiction 11. Interpersonal relations -- Fiction
ISBN 1416954880; 9781416954880; 9781442409552
LC 2011018154

In this young adult science fiction novel, "Scotch's womanly build and mixed heritage (white Jamaican dad, black American mom) made her the target of small-town school bullies. Since moving to Toronto, she's found friends and status. . . . When a giant bubble appears at an open-mic event, Scotch dares her brother, Rich, to touch it. He disappears, a volcano rises from Lake Ontario and chaos ripples across city and world, transforming reality in ways bizarre." (Kirkus Reviews)

Hornby, Nick, 1957-

★ **Slam.** G.P. Putnam's Sons 2007 309p $19.99; (audiobook) $29.95
Grades: 8 9 10 11 12 **Fic**

1. Skateboarders 2. Skateboarding -- Fiction 3. Teenage fathers -- Fiction
ISBN 9780399250484; 0399250484; 9780143142836
LC 2007-14146

In this book by Nick Hornby, "for 16-year-old Sam, life is about to get extremely complicated. He and his girlfriend--make that ex-girlfriend--Alicia have gotten themselves into a bit of trouble." When she gets pregnant, "Sam is suddenly forced to grow up and struggle with the familiar fears and inclinations that haunt us all." (Publisher's note)

The author "pens a first novel for teens that is a sweet and funny story about mistakes and choices. . . . Recommend this delightful and poignant novel to older teens who will laugh and weep with Sam." Voice Youth Advocates

Horner, Emily

A **love** story starring my dead best friend. Dial Books 2010 259p $16.99
Grades: 9 10 11 12 **Fic**

1. Love stories 2. School stories 3. Death -- Fiction 4. Bullies -- Fiction 5. Lesbians -- Fiction
ISBN 978-0-8037-3420-3; 0-8037-3420-4
LC 2009-23820

As she tries to sort out her feelings of love, seventeen-year-old Cass, a spunky math genius with an introverted streak, finds a way to memorialize her dead best friend.

"With its John Green-esque set pieces, mad road trips, fortuitous stranger encounters, thoroughly teased-out friendship drama, and optimistic romanticism—not to mention a fresh treatment of a lesbian heroine—this entertaining . . . [book] has something for everyone." Horn Book

Horowitz, Anthony

Raven's gate; book one of the Gatekeepers. [by] Anthony Horowitz. 1st ed; Scholastic Press 2005 254p (Gatekeepers) $17.95; pa $7.99

Grades: 6 7 8 9 **Fic**

1. Witchcraft -- Fiction 2. Supernatural -- Fiction
ISBN 0-439-67995-8; 0-439-68009-7 pa
LC 2004-21512

Sent to live in a foster home in a remote Yorkshire village, Matt, a troubled fourteen-year-old English boy, uncovers an evil plot involving witchcraft and the site of an ancient stone circle.

"The creepy activities and the overall atmosphere of fear are well defined, and once the action starts, it doesn't let up. . . . This powerful struggle between good and evil is a real page-turner." SLJ

Other titles in the Gatekeepers series are:
Evil star (2006)
Nightrise (2007)
Necropolis (2009)

★ **Stormbreaker.** Philomel Books 2001 192p (An Alex Rider adventure) $17.99; pa $7.99
Grades: 5 6 7 8 **Fic**

1. Adventure fiction 2. Spies -- Fiction 3. Orphans -- Fiction 4. Terrorism -- Fiction
ISBN 0-399-23620-1; 0-14-240611-2 pa
LC 00-63683

First published 2000 in the United Kingdom

After the death of the uncle who had been his guardian, fourteen-year-old Alex Rider is coerced to continue his uncle's dangerous work for Britain's intelligence agency, MI6

"Horowitz thoughtfully balances Alex's super-spy finesse with typical teen insecurities to create a likable hero living a fantasy come true. An entertaining, nicely layered novel." Booklist

Other titles about Alex Rider are:
Point blank (2002)
Skeleton key (2003)
Eagle strike (2004)
Scorpia (2005)
Alex Rider, the gadgets (2006)
Ark angel (2006)
Snakehead (2007)
Crocodile tears (2009)
Scorpia rising (2011)

Horvath, Polly

The **Corps** of the Bare-Boned Plane. Farrar, Straus and Giroux 2007 261p $17
Grades: 7 8 9 10 11 12 **Fic**

1. Death -- Fiction 2. Uncles -- Fiction 3. Cousins -- Fiction 4. Islands -- Fiction 5. Airplanes -- Fiction 6. Bereavement -- Fiction
ISBN 978-0-374-31553-5; 0-374-31553-1
LC 2006-41281

When their parents are killed in a train accident, cousins Meline and Jocelyn, who have little in common, are sent to live with their wealthy, eccentric, and isolated Uncle Marten on his island off the coast of British Columbia, where they are soon joined by other oddly disconnected and troubled people.

"The savagely dark humor allows Horvath to place her characters in increasingly bizarre psychic positions, building to an almost painful crescendo in a remarkable examination of the extremes of emotional distress." Horn Book

Houck, Colleen

Tiger's curse. Sterling 2011 402p $17.95
Grades: 8 9 10 11 12 **Fic**

1. India -- Fiction 2. Circus -- Fiction 3. Tigers -- Fiction 4. Orphans -- Fiction 5. Immortality -- Fiction
ISBN 978-1-4027-8403-3
LC 2010-33191

Seventeen-year-old Oregon teenager Kelsey forms a bond with a circus tiger who is actually one of two brothers, Indian princes Ren and Kishan, who were cursed to live as tigers for eternity, and she travels with him to India where the tiger's curse may be broken once and for all.

The author "tells a good story filled with chaste romance that will keep readers turning pages to the inconclusive ending." Booklist

Other titles in this series are:
Tiger's quest (2011)
Tiger's voyage (2011)

Houston, Julian

New boy. Houghton Mifflin Co. 2005 282p $16
Grades: 8 9 10 11 12 **Fic**

1. School stories 2. Prejudices -- Fiction 3. African Americans -- Fiction
ISBN 0-618-43253-1
LC 2004-27207

"As the first black student in an elite Connecticut boarding school in the late 1950s, Rob Garrett, 16, knows he is making history. . . . When his friends in the South plan a sit-in against segregation, he knows he must be part of it. . . . The honest first-person narrative makes stirring drama. . . . This brings up much for discussion about then and now." Booklist

Howard, A. G.

Unhinged: a novel; by A. G. Howard. Amulet Books. 2014 400p $17.95
Grades: 9 10 11 12 **Fic**

1. Characters in literature -- Fiction 2. Mental illness --Fiction 3. Mother-daughter relationship-- Fiction 4. Supernatural -- Fiction
ISBN: 1419709712; 9781419709715
LC 2013026395

In this sequel to Splintered (2013) Alyssa Gardner, a descendant of Alice Liddell, Lewis Carroll's inspiration for Alice and Wonderland, " has been down the rabbit hole. . . . Now all she has to do is graduate high school. That would be easier without her mother, freshly released from an asylum, acting overly protective and suspicious. It would be much simpler if the mysterious Morpheus didn't show up for school one day to tempt her with another dangerous quest in the dark, challenging Wonderland." (Publisher's note)

"Alyssa left Wonderland (in Splintered) a year ago, but now her dreams foreshadow new trouble there. When Wonderland's inhabitants enter the human realm, Alyssa's two worlds collide. Though a romantic triangle and Alyssa's identity struggle bog down this second installment, fans will be intrigued by the cliffhanger ending, which hints at future trips to Wonderland--and to "the looking-glass world, Any-Elsewhere." Horn Book

Sequel to: Splintered

Howard, J. J.

That time I joined the circus; J.J. Howard. Point 2013 272 p. (hardcover) $17.99

Grades: 7 8 9 10 **Fic**

1. Circus -- Fiction 2. Absent mothers -- Fiction 3. Florida -- Fiction 4. Friendship -- Fiction 5. Best friends -- Fiction 6. New York (N.Y.) -- Fiction 7. Mothers and daughters -- Fiction 8. Single-parent families -- Fiction

ISBN 0545433819; 9780545433815

LC 2012016715

In this novel, 17-year-old Lexi lives with her father Gavin, a musician in New York City. Her "long-absent mother . . . has apparently joined the circus. When Gavin dies unexpectedly, leaving his daughter penniless, her only option is to track down her mother in Florida. Failing to find her, Lexi gratefully accepts work with the Circus Europa." (Publishers Weekly)

Howard, Jonathan L.

Katya's World; Jonathan L. Howard. A Strange Chemistry pbk. orig. Osprey Pub Co 2012 332 p. (paperback) $9.99

Grades: 9 10 11 12 **Fic**

1. Science fiction 2. Dystopian fiction

ISBN 1908844132; 9781908844132

LC 2012464526

In this book, Katya Kuriakova lives on the watery planet Russalka, which was founded by Russian colonists from Earth, and which was violently attacked a decade before. She "is excited about apprenticing on her uncle Lukyan's submarine, but much goes wrong on her debut voyage, including the sub getting commandeered by a military officer and his pirate prisoner, surprise attacks, and a conspiracy that could threaten all of Russalka." (Publishers Weekly)

Howe, Katherine

Conversion; by Katherine Howe. G. P. Putnam's Sons. 2014 432p $18.88

Grades: 7 8 9 10 11 12 Fic

1. Epidemics -- Fiction 2. Friendship -- Fiction 3. High schools -- Fiction 4. Massachusetts -- Fiction 5. Salem (Mass.) -- Fiction 6. Witchcraft -- Fiction

ISBN: 0399167773; 9780399167775

LC 2014000397

When girls start experiencing strange tics and other mysterious symptoms at Colleen's high school, her small town of Danvers, Massachusetts, falls victim to rumors that lead to full-blown panic, and only Colleen connects their fate to the ill-fated Salem Village, where another group of girls suffered from a similarly bizarre epidemic three centuries ago.

"A simmering blend of relatable high-school drama with a persistent pinprick of unearthliness in the background." Booklist

Howell, Simmone

Everything beautiful. Bloomsbury Children's Books 2008 292p $16.99

Grades: 9 10 11 **Fic**

1. Camps -- Fiction 2. Religious life -- Fiction 3. People with physical disbilities -- Fiction

ISBN 978-1-59990-042-1; 1-59990-42-4

LC 2008-17211

When sixteen-year-old Riley unwillingly attends a religious summer camp, she forms a deep bond with another camper who happens to be wheelchair bound.

"What could be a clichéd situation–the bond between two outcasts–is instead touching and believable. . . . This novel will appeal to sensitive teens who will root for Riley and the other camp underdogs." SLJ

Howells, Amanda

The **summer** of skinny dipping; a novel. Sourcebooks Fire 2010 295p pa $8.99

Grades: 9 10 11 12 **Fic**

1. Love stories 2. Death -- Fiction 3. Ocean -- Fiction 4. Cousins -- Fiction 5. Swimming -- Fiction

ISBN 978-1-4022-3862-8

LC 2009-49926

While spending the summer in the Hamptons, sixteen-year-old Mia is disappointed that her cousin Corinne has grown so distant, but when she meets the irresistible and adventurous boy next door, everything changes for the better.

"With a lyrical yet straightforward voice and a layered plot, this novel will live on for more than a summer." SLJ

Howland, Leila

Nantucket blue; Leila Howland. 1st ed. Hyperion 2013 304 p. (reinforced) $16.99

Grades: 8 9 10 11 12 **Fic**

1. Summer -- Fiction 2. Female friendship -- Fiction 3. Interpersonal relations -- Fiction 4. Grief -- Fiction 5. Divorce -- Fiction 6. Friendship -- Fiction 7. Best friends -- Fiction 8. Dating (Social customs) -- Fiction 9. Nantucket Island (Mass.) -- Fiction

ISBN 1423160517; 9781423160519

LC 2012035121

"Lacrosse-champ Cricket Thompson has always been welcomed by her best friend Jules's affluent family. But when Nina, Jules's mother, dies suddenly, big changes ensue. Expecting her usual warm reception, Cricket shows up at Jules's family home on Nantucket to find herself shunned. There's some emotional heaviness to the story, but it's also a breezy, beach-ready tale of self-awakening and first love." (Horn Book)

Hrdlitschka, Shelley

Allegra; by Shelley Hrdlitschka. Orca Book Publishers 2013 280 p. (paperback) $12.95; (ebook) $12.99; (ebook) $12.99

Grades: 7 8 9 10 **Fic**

1. School stories 2. Teacher-student relationship -- Fiction 3. Performing arts high schools 4. Teacher-student relationships

ISBN 1459801970; 9781459801974; 9781459801981 pdf; 9781459801998

LC 2012952952

In this book, Allegra, daughter of two musicians, is thrilled to be at Deer Lake School for the Fine and Performing Arts. She "has her sights set on becoming a professional dancer. However, her excitement is dimmed by the school's requirement that she take a music-theory class. Despite her initial reluctance, Allegra soon begins to enjoy the class due to the charisma of its young and attractive teacher,"

Mr. Rocchelli. Is their relationship too close? (School Library Journal)

Sister wife. Orca 2008 269p pa $12.95
Grades: 8 9 10 11 12 **Fic**
1. Polygamy -- Fiction
ISBN 978-1-55143-927-3; 1-55143-927-1
In a remote polygamist community, Celeste struggles to accept her destiny while longing to be free to live her life her way.
"This compelling story combines with authentic characters to pique the interest of a wide array of teens and get them talking about faith and free will." Voice Youth Advocates

Hubbard, Amanda
But I love him; [by] Amanda Grace. Flux 2011 253p pa $9.95
Grades: 7 8 9 10 **Fic**
1. School stories 2. Abused women -- Fiction 3. Washington (State) -- Fiction 4. Dating (Social customs) -- Fiction
ISBN 978-0-7387-2594-9; 0-7387-2594-3
LC 2010-50131
Traces, through the course of a year, Ann's transformation from a happy A-student, track star, and popular senior to a solitary, abused woman whose love for the emotionally-scarred Connor has taken away everything—even herself.
"A great shared read for parents and teens." Voice Youth Advocates

Ripple; [by] Mandy Hubbard. Razorbill 2011 260p $16.99
Grades: 8 9 10 11 12 **Fic**
1. Love stories 2. Fantasy fiction 3. Sirens (Mythology)
ISBN 978-1-59514-423-2; 1-59514-423-4
"Lexi, 18, is responsible for the death of Steven, her friend Siena's brother and the only boy she ever loved. That was two years ago, right before discovering that she is a siren, cursed to swim each night and sing out haunting melodies that will lure men to their deaths in the water. She has been protecting herself and those around her by keeping everyone at a distance and swimming in an isolated lake where no one will hear her song. But as the new school year begins, Lexi finds herself pursued by two boys whom she can't ignore. . . . In this new twist on a supernatural romance, Hubbard expands the genre by including both a siren and a nix in among the high school drama. . . . Fans of girl dramas, mysteries, and fantasy romance will devour the story." SLJ

Hubbard, Jennifer R.
Try not to breathe; Jennifer R. Hubbard. Viking 2012 233 p. (hardcover) $16.99
Grades: 10 11 12 **Fic**
1. Friendship -- Fiction 2. Teenagers -- Suicide -- Fiction 3. Mentally ill -- Institutional care -- Fiction 4. Suicide -- Fiction 5. Interpersonal relations -- Fiction
ISBN 0670013900; 9780670013906
LC 2011012203
In this book, a "half-hearted suicide attempt lands Ryan at a facility for adolescents with emotional problems. He makes friends and recovers, but now that he's home again, he's not quite sure how to re-enter his life, especially when he meets a girl named Nicki, who keeps pressuring him to share his secrets. . . . He gradually realizes that he has the inner resources to cope with rejection and uncertainty." (Bulletin of the Center for Children's Books)

★ **And** we stay; Jenny Hubbard. Delacorte Press 2014 240 p. (hc) $16.99
Grades: 9 10 11 12 **Fic**
1. High school students -- Fiction 2. Teenagers -- Suicide -- Fiction 3. Poetry -- Fiction 4. Schools -- Fiction 5. Suicide -- Fiction 6. High schools -- Fiction 7. Amherst (Mass.) -- Fiction 8. Boarding schools -- Fiction 9. Interpersonal relations -- Fiction
ISBN 0385740573; 9780375989551; 9780385740579
LC 2013002236
In this book, by Jenny Hubbard "high school senior Paul Wagoner walks into his school library with a stolen gun, . . . threatens his girlfriend Emily Beam, then takes his own life. In the wake of the tragedy, an angry and guilt-ridden Emily is shipped off to boarding school in Amherst, Massachusetts, where she encounters a ghostly presence who shares her name. The spirit of Emily Dickinson and two quirky girls offer helping hands, but it is up to Emily to heal her own damaged self." (Publisher's note)
"Budding poets may particularly appreciate Emily's story, but there is certainly something for anyone looking for a good read with a strong, believable female lead who is working her hardest to overcome tragedy." SLJ

★ **Paper** covers rock. Delacorte Press 2011 183p audiobook $46.75; audiobook $46.75; audiobook $42.00; $16.99; lib bdg $19.99; ebook $10.99
Grades: 9 10 11 12 **Fic**
1. School stories 2. Death -- Fiction 3. North Carolina -- Fiction 4. Conduct of life -- Fiction
ISBN 9781464021572; 9781464021565; 9781464021657; 978-0-385-74055-5; 978-0-375-98954-4 lib bdg; 978-0-375-89942-3 ebook
LC 2010-23462
In this book, set at a "boys' boarding school, 16-year-old Alex is devastated when he fails to save a drowning friend. When questioned, Alex and his friend Glenn, who was also at the river, begin weaving their web of lies. . . . Caught in the web with Alex and Glenn is their English teacher, Miss Dovecott, fresh out of Princeton, who suspects there's more to what happened at the river when she perceives guilt in Alex's writing for class." (Booklist)
This is "a powerful story of how the truth can easily be manipulated, how actions can be misinterpreted, and how fragile adolescent friendships and alliances can be." Voice Youth Advocates

Hubbard, Kirsten
Like Mandarin. Delacorte Press 2011 308p $17.99; lib bdg $20.99
Grades: 8 9 10 11 12 **Fic**
1. School stories 2. Wyoming -- Fiction 3. Friendship -- Fiction 4. Family life -- Fiction
ISBN 978-0-385-73935-1; 0-385-73935-4; 978-0-385-90784-2 lib bdg; 0-385-90784-2 lib bdg
LC 2009-53653

When shy, awkward fourteen-year-old Grace Carpenter is paired with the beautiful and wild Mandarin on a school project, an unlikely, explosive friendship begins, but all too soon, Grace discovers that Mandarin is a very troubled, even dangerous, girl.

"With a flair for metaphors and character description, Hubbard's writing exposes the deep emotions and conflicts that have rippled through most of Grace and Mandarin's lives. These small-town girls could be found anywhere." Voice Youth Advocates

Wanderlove; Kirsten Hubbard. Delacorte Press 2012 338 p. (hc) $17.99
Grades: 10 11 12 **Fic**

1. Travel -- Fiction 2. Children -- Travel 3. Central America -- Fiction 4. Love -- Fiction 5. Artists -- Fiction
ISBN 0385739370; 9780375897511; 9780385739375; 9780385907859

LC 2011007435

In this book, "Bria decides to do the most un-Bria-like thing she can think of: she signs up alone for a tour to Central America. When she finds out her traveling companions are a group of middle-aged tourists rather than the young, carefree backpackers on the brochure, she's thoroughly disappointed. . . . She breaks from her tour group and joins a girl named Starling and her brother Rowan to pursue what she considers a more authentic traveling experience." (Bulletin of the Center for Children's Books)

"With an extraordinary setting, delicately rendered and well informed by Hubbard's years as a guide to Central American travel on About.com, this becomes a wonderful story of kindred souls in a land of beauty, illuminated by Hubbard's own drawings." Booklist

Hudson, Tara

Hereafter. HarperTeen 2011 407p $17.99
Grades: 8 9 10 11 12 **Fic**

1. Ghost stories 2. Oklahoma -- Fiction 3. Family life -- Fiction 4. Future life -- Fiction 5. Good and evil -- Fiction 6. Near-death experiences -- Fiction
ISBN 978-0-06-202677-4; 0-06-202677-1

LC 2010045622

Amelia, long a ghost, forms a strong bond with eighteen-year-old Joshua, who nearly drowned where she did and who awakens in her long-forgotten senses and memories even as Eli, a spirit, tries to draw her away.

"A must for collections given the genre's popularity." Booklist

Hughes, Dean

Search and destroy. Atheneum Books for Young Readers 2006 216p $16.95
Grades: 7 8 9 10 **Fic**

1. Vietnam War, 1961-1975 -- Fiction
ISBN 0-689-87023-X

LC 2005-11255

Recent high school graduate Rick Ward, undecided about his future and eager to escape his unhappy home life, joins the army and experiences the horrors of the war in Vietnam.

"This is a compelling, insightful story about the emotional, physical, and psychological scars that wars leave upon soldiers." Booklist

Humphreys, Chris

The **hunt** of the unicorn. Alfred A. Knopf 2011 345p $16.99; lib bdg $19.99; e-book $16.99
Grades: 6 7 8 9 **Fic**

1. Fantasy fiction 2. Unicorns -- Fiction
ISBN 978-0-375-85872-7; 0-375-85872-7; 978-0-375-95872-4 lib bdg; 0-375-95872-4; 978-0-375-89624-8 e-book

LC 2010-30852

Despite strange dreams and her ailing father's firm belief in the family lore of a long-ago ancestor's connection to the mythical unicorn, fifteen-year-old New Yorker Elayne remains skeptical until, during a school visit to the unicorn tapestries in the Cloisters, she finds herself entering a tumultuous world where she must fulfill the legacy of her ancestors by taming the unicorn and bringing a tyrant to justice.

"This is wish fulfillment at its finest, with Elayne playing the everyday gal turned spunky heroine. . . . With references to our world's overpopulation and pollution, there is a heady dose of environmentalism here, but it is nicely tempered with a fair amount of humor and adventure." Bull Cent Child Books

Huntley, Amy

The **everafter**. Balzer + Bray 2009 144p $16.99; lib bdg $17.89; pa $8.99
Grades: 7 8 9 10 **Fic**

1. Dead -- Fiction 2. Death -- Fiction 3. Friendship -- Fiction 4. Lost and found possessions -- Fiction
ISBN 978-0-06-177679-3; 0-06-177679-3; 978-0-06-177680-9 lib bdg; 0-06-177680-7 lib bdg; 978-0-06-177681-6 pa; 0-06-177681-5 pa

LC 2008-46149

ALA YALSA Morris Award Finalist, 2010

Madison Stanton doesn't know where she is or how she got there. But she does know this—she is dead. And alone in a vast, dark space. The only company Maddy has in this place are luminescent objects that turn out to be all the things she lost while she was alive. And soon she discovers that, with these artifacts, she can re-experience—and even—change moments from her life.

"This fresh take on a teen's journey of self-exploration is a compelling and highly enjoyable tale. Huntley expertly combines a coming-of-age story with a supernatural mystery that keeps readers engrossed until the climactic ending. This touching story will appeal to those looking for a ghost story, romance, or family drama." SLJ

Hurley, Tonya

★ **Ghostgirl**. Little, Brown 2008 328p $17.99
Grades: 7 8 9 10 **Fic**

1. Ghost stories 2. School stories 3. Death -- Fiction 4. Popularity -- Fiction
ISBN 978-0-316-11357-1; 0-316-11357-3

LC 2007-31541

After dying, high school senior Charlotte Usher is as invisible to nearly everyone as she always felt, but despite what she learns in a sort of alternative high school for dead teens, she clings to life while seeking a way to go to the Fall Ball with the boy of her dreams.

"Hurley combines afterlife antics, gothic gore, and high school hell to produce an original, hilarious satire. . . . Tim Burton and Edgar Allan Poe devotees will die for this fantastic, phantasmal read." SLJ

Other titles in this series are:
Ghostgirl: Homecoming (2009)
Ghostgirl: Lovesick (2010)

Hurwin, Davida

Freaks and revelations; a novel. by Davida Wills Hurwin. Little, Brown and Co. 2009 234p $16.99
Grades: 10 11 12 **Fic**

1. California -- Fiction 2. Drug abuse -- Fiction 3. Prejudices -- Fiction 4. Homosexuality -- Fiction
ISBN 978-0-316-04996-2; 0-316-04996-4
LC 2008-47384

Tells, in two voices, of events leading up to a 1980 incident in which fourteen-year-old Jason, a gay youth surviving on the streets as a prostitute, and seventeen-year-old Doug, a hate-filled punk rocker, have a fateful meeting in a Los Angeles alley.

"Sympathetic to both characters without shying away from brutality—physical or emotional—the finely crafted story leads to a powerful climax of hope and redemption that will stay with readers." Publ Wkly

Huser, Glen

Stitches. Groundwood Books 2003 198p hardcover o.p. pa $6.95
Grades: 7 8 9 10 **Fic**

1. Canada -- Fiction 2. Bullies -- Fiction 3. Sex role -- Fiction 4. Puppets and puppet plays -- Fiction
ISBN 0-88899-553-9; 0-88899-578-4 pa
LC 2003-363167

This story of two outsiders who become friends is set in rural Alberta. The protagonists "are Chantelle, who has a limp and a scarred face, and Travis, a boy completely unselfconscious about his love for puppets and sewing. Both kids have ragtaggle families. . . . Chantelle and Travis joined forces back in fifth grade, when she rescued him from the boys who called him 'girlie'; junior high brings new challenges as the teasing gets uglier and, eventually, violent."

"Teachers will use this book in their classrooms, but it will appeal to leisure readers as well." Voice Youth Advocates

Hyde, Catherine Ryan

Becoming Chloe. Random House 2006 215p $15.95; pa $8.99
Grades: 9 10 11 12 **Fic**

1. Homeless persons -- Fiction 2. Voyages and travels -- Fiction
ISBN 0-375-83258-0; 0-375-83260-2 pa
LC 2005-18949

"This thought-provoking story of the power of hope . . . blends the realities of street life with the wonder of cross-country exploration." Voice Youth Advocates

Jumpstart the world. Alfred A. Knopf 2010 186p $16.99; lib bdg $19.99
Grades: 9 10 11 12 **Fic**

1. School stories 2. Moving -- Fiction 3. Transgender people-- Fiction 4. Apartment houses -- Fiction 5. Mother-daughter relationship -- Fiction
ISBN 978-0-375-86665-4; 978-0-375-96665-1 lib bdg; 978-0-375-89677-4 ebook
LC 2010-02511

Sixteen-year-old Elle falls in love with Frank, the neighbor who helps her adjust to being on her own in a big city, but learning that he is transgendered turns her world upside-down.

"For a book loaded with issues—there is even treatment of mental illness—this is a plain good read. These characters are funny, complex, and engaging. . . . There are many teens today who need this book." Voice Youth Advocates

The **year** of my miraculous reappearance. Alfred A. Knopf 2007 228p $15.99; lib bdg $18.99
Grades: 7 8 9 10 **Fic**

1. Siblings -- Fiction 2. Alcoholism -- Fiction 3. Down syndrome -- Fiction
ISBN 978-0-375-83257-4; 978-0-375-93257-1 lib bdg; 0-375-83257-2; 0-375-93257-7 lib bdg
LC 2006-29194

Thirteen-year-old Cynnie has had to deal with her mother's alcoholism and stream of boyfriends all her life, but when her grandparents take custody of her brother, Bill, who has Down Syndrome, Cynnie becomes self-destructive and winds up in court-mandated Alcoholics Anonymous meetings.

"Cynnie's love for and devotion to Bill are wholly believable, as are her attempts to snare a stable adult presence in her life. Secondary characters are multidimensional and well drawn." Booklist

Ibbitson, John

The **Landing**; a novel. KCP Fiction 2008 160p $17.95; pa $7.95
Grades: 7 8 9 10 **Fic**

1. Canada -- Fiction 2. Uncles -- Fiction 3. Violinists -- Fiction
ISBN 978-1-55453-234-6; 1-55453-234-5; 978-1-55453-238-4 pa; 1-55453-238-8 pa

Ben thinks he will always be stuck at Cook's Landing, barely making ends meet like his uncle. But when he meets a wealthy widow from New York City, he sees himself there too. When she hires him to play his violin, he realizes his gift could unlock the possibilities of the world. Then, during a stormy night on Lake Muskoka, everything changes.

"With lovely prose, Ibbitson brings to life the rugged beauty and the devastating poverty of the Lake Muskoka region. His characters are as strong and remote as their surroundings." Voice Youth Advocates

Ingold, Jeanette

The **Big** Burn. Harcourt 2002 295p $17; pa $6.95
Grades: 7 8 9 10 **Fic**

1. Forest fires -- Fiction
ISBN 0-15-216470-7; 0-15-204924-X pa
LC 2001-5667

Three teenagers battle the flames of the Big Burn of 1910, one of the century's biggest wildfires

"A solid adventure story with a well-realized setting." Booklist

Includes bibliographical references (p. {293}-295)

Hitch. Harcourt, Inc 2005 272p $17; pa $6.95
Grades: 7 8 9 10 **Fic**

1. Montana -- Fiction 2. Great Depression, 1929-1939 -- Fiction

ISBN 0-15-204747-6; 0-15-20561-9 pa

LC 2004-19447

To help his family during the Depression and avoid becoming a drunk like his father, Moss Trawnley joins the Civilian Conservation Corps, helps build a new camp near Monroe, Montana, and leads the other men in making the camp a success.

This is "a credible, involving story. . . . Both [the author's] writing style and her 1930s setting feels totally true to the time." Booklist

Mountain solo. Harcourt 2003 309p $17; pa $6.95
Grades: 7 8 9 10 **Fic**

1. Violinists -- Fiction 2. Family life -- Fiction

ISBN 0-15-202670-3; 0-15-205358-1 pa

LC 2003-42326

Back at her childhood home in Missoula, Montana, after a disastrous concert in Germany, a teenage violin prodigy contemplates giving up life with her mother in New York City and her music as she, her father, stepmother, and stepsister hike to a pioneer homesite where another violinist once faced difficult decisions of his own

"Mountain Solo is a good read for anyone fascinated by the power of music and its effects on individuals' lives." SLJ

Includes bibliographical references (p. {307}-309)

Jacobs, John Hornor

The **Shibboleth** by John Hornor Jacobs. Carolrhoda Lab. 2014 393p $17.95
Grades: 9 10 11 12 **Fic**

1. Ability — Fiction; 2. Bullies — Fiction; 3. Memory — Fiction; 4. Psychiatric hospitals — Fiction; 5. Supernatural — Fiction

ISBN: 0761390081; 9780761390084

LC 2013009535

Second title in the author's Twelve-fingered boy trilogy

"Branded a 'candy' dealer for doling out drugs, Shreve is incarcerated in a juvenile detention center at first, but after he frightens a nurse there, he's sent to a mental hospital, where he's drugged for schizophrenia. What his keepers don't know is that he's not schizophrenic at all. Instead, he's a shibboleth, a being that can read minds and possess the bodies of others." (Kirkus Reviews)

"Polydactyl hero Shreve, now sixteen, escapes from Tulaville Psychiatric Hospital to seek Hiram Quincrux--the monster behind an insomnia epidemic causing mayhem in the U.S.--and pit his own "extranatural" powers, his shibboleth, against Quincrux's. The sheer weirdness of it all will captivate readers and involve them in a memorable second installment that nicely sets up what's sure to be a dramatic conclusion." Horn Book

★ The **twelve-**fingered boy; John Hornor Jacobs. Carolrhoda Lab. 2013 264 p. $17.95
Grades: 9 10 11 12 **Fic**

1. Fantasy fiction 2. Teenagers -- Fiction 3. Ability -- Fiction 4. Bullies -- Fiction 5. Supernatural -- Fiction 6. Juvenile detention homes -- Fiction

ISBN 0761390073; 9780761390077

LC 2012015292

This is the first in a trilogy from John Hornor Jacobs about superhuman teens. "Fifteen-year-old Shreve Cannon is passing the time in Pulaski Juvenile Detention Center, . . . when he's assigned a new roommate: Jack Graves, a small, quiet 13-year old with 12 fingers and uncontrollable telekinetic abilities. When a stranger named Mr. Quincrux shows up, sporting nasty mental powers and an uncomfortable interest in Jack, the boys . . . break out of juvie and go on the run." (Publishers Weekly)

Jacobson, Jennifer, 1958-

The **complete** history of why I hate her; [by] Jennifer Richard Jacobson. Atheneum Books for Young Readers 2010 181p $16.99
Grades: 7 8 9 10 **Fic**

1. Maine -- Fiction 2. Cancer -- Fiction 3. Resorts -- Fiction 4. Sisters -- Fiction 5. Personality disorders -- Fiction

ISBN 978-0-689-87800-8; 0-689-87800-1

LC 2008-42959

Wanting a break from being known only for her sister's cancer, seventeen-year-old Nola leaves Boston for a waitressing job at a summer resort in Maine, but soon feels as if her new best friend is taking over her life.

"A compelling story of self-discovery with plenty of insights into the motivations that drive relationships." Booklist

Jaden, Denise

Losing Faith. Simon Pulse 2010 381p pa $9.99
Grades: 7 8 9 10 11 12 **Fic**

1. School stories 2. Cults -- Fiction 3. Death -- Fiction 4. Sisters -- Fiction 5. Bereavement -- Fiction 6. Christian life -- Fiction

ISBN 978-1-4169-9609-5; 1-4169-9609-5

LC 2010-7296

Brie tries to cope with her grief over her older sister Faith's sudden death by trying to learn more about the religious "home group" Faith secretly joined and never talked about with Brie or her parents.

"With pitch-perfect portrayals of high school social life and a nuanced view into a variety of Christian experiences of faith, this first novel gives readers much to think about." SLJ

Never enough; Denise Jaden. 1st Simon Pulse paperback ed. Simon Pulse 2012 372 p. (paperback) $9.99
Grades: 9 10 11 12 **Fic**

1. Personal appearance 2. High school students 3. Parent-child relationship 4. Sisters -- Fiction 5. Popularity -- Fiction 6. Photography -- Fiction 7. Family problems -- Fiction 8. Eating disorders --

Fiction 9. Self-realization -- Fiction
ISBN 1442429070; 9781442429079
LC 2011033407

Author Denise Jaden tells the story "from the perspective of high school junior Loann, who lives in the shadow of her more beautiful and gifted older sister, Claire. Loann's feelings of inadequacy and resentment are overtaken by fear when she discovers that her sister is going to extreme measures to remain thin . . . Loann's horror intensifies when she realizes her parents are incapable of handling Claire's eating disorder and finding a solution. While struggling to understand her sister, Loann is drawn to a boy at school with serious problems of his own." (Publishers Weekly)

Jaffe, Michele

Bad kitty. HarperCollins Publishers 2006 268p il hardcover o.p. pa $8.99
Grades: 9 10 11 12 **Fic**

1. Mystery fiction 2. Las Vegas (Nev.) -- Fiction
ISBN 0-06-078108-4; 978-0-06-078108-8; 0-06-078110-6 pa; 978-0-06-078110-1 pa
LC 2005-5733

While vacationing with her family in Las Vegas, seventeen-year-old Jasmine stumbles upon a murder mystery that she attempts to solve with the help of her friends, recently arrived from California.

"Readers will likely find themselves quickly clawing their way through this fun novel." Publ Wkly

Followed by: Kitty kitty (2008)

Rosebush. Razorbill 2010 326p $16.99
Grades: 8 9 10 11 12 **Fic**

1. Mystery fiction 2. Traffic accidents -- Fiction
ISBN 978-1-59514-353-2; 1-59514-353-X

Instead of celebrating Memorial Day weekend on the Jersey Shore, Jane is in the hospital surrounded by teddy bears, trying to piece together what happened last night. One minute she was at a party, wearing fairy wings and cuddling with her boyfriend. The next, she was lying near-dead in a rosebush after a hit-and-run.

"Compulsively readable, the novel bristles with red herrings, leading readers down one tempting plot branch after another, each one blooming with plausibility. The characters are skillfully cultivated through flashbacks, and the insecure, people-pleasing Jane grows believably as she takes on the mystery." Booklist

James, Rebecca

Beautiful malice; a novel. Bantam Books 2010 260p $25
Grades: 9 10 11 12 **Fic**

1. Australia -- Fiction 2. Friendship -- Fiction 3. Bereavement -- Fiction
ISBN 978-0-553-80805-6
LC 2010-6255

To escape the media attention generated by her sister's murder, a grieving seventeen-year-old Australian girl moves away and meets a vibrant new friend who harbors a dangerous secret.

This "novel will grab your attention on the first page, and you won't want to turn away even after the last page has been turned." Voice Youth Advocates

Jansen, Hanna

★ **Over** a thousand hills I walk with you; translated from the German by Elizabeth D. Crawford. Carolrhoda Books 2006 342p $16.95
Grades: 7 8 9 10 **Fic**

1. Rwanda -- Fiction
ISBN 1-57505-927-4; 978-1-57505-927-3
LC 2005-21123

Original German edition, 2002

"Eight-year-old Jeanne was the only one of her family to survive the 1994 Rwanda genocide. Then a German family adopted her, and her adoptive mother now tells Jeanne's story in a compelling fictionalized biography that stays true to the traumatized child's bewildered viewpoint." Booklist

Jaramillo, Ann

La linea. Roaring Brook Press 2006 131p $16.95; pa $7.99
Grades: 5 6 7 8 **Fic**

1. Mexicans -- Fiction 2. Siblings -- Fiction 3. Immigrants -- Fiction
ISBN 1-59643-154-7; 0-312-37354-6 pa
LC 2005-20133

When fifteen-year-old Miguel's time finally comes to leave his poor Mexican village, cross the border illegally, and join his parents in California, his younger sister's determination to join him soon imperils them both.

"A gripping contemporary survival adventure, this spare first novel is also a heart-wrenching family story of courage, betrayal, and love." Booklist

Jarzab, Anna

All unquiet things. Delacorte Press 2010 339p $17.99
Grades: 8 9 10 11 12 **Fic**

1. School stories 2. Mystery fiction 3. Homicide -- Fiction 4. California -- Fiction 5. Social classes -- Fiction
ISBN 978-0-385-73835-4; 0-385-73835-8; 978-0-385-90723-1 lib bdg; 0-385-90723-0 lib bdg
LC 2009-11557

After the death of his ex-girlfriend Carly, northern California high school student Neily joins forces with Carly's cousin Audrey to try to solve her murder.

The **opposite** of hallelujah; Anna Jarzab. Delacorte Press 2012 452 p. (hc) $16.99
Grades: 7 8 9 10 **Fic**

1. Ex-nuns -- Fiction 2. Secrets -- Fiction 3. Sisters -- Fiction 4. Nuns -- Fiction 5. Guilt -- Fiction 6. Guilt 7. Ex-nuns 8. Sisters 9. Children's secrets
ISBN 0385738366; 9780375894084; 9780385738361; 9780385907248
LC 2012010882

In this book by Anna Jarzab "Caro's parents drop the bombshell news that [her sister] Hannah is returning to live with them. . . . Unable to understand Hannah, Caro resorts to telling lies about her mysterious reappearance. . . . And as she unearths a clue from Hannah's past--one that could save Hannah from the dark secret that possesses her--Caro begins to see her sister in a whole new light." (Publisher's note)

Jayne, Hannah

Truly, madly, deadly; by Hannah Jayne. Sourcebooks Fire 2013 272 p. (paperback) $9.99
Grades: 9 10 11 12 **Fic**

1. School stories 2. Stalkers -- Fiction 3. Murder -- Fiction 4. Dating violence -- Fiction
ISBN 1402281218; 9781402281211
LC 2012046383

In this book, "high school junior Sawyer Dodd is still reeling from her boyfriend's death in a drunk driving accident when she receives a note from an 'admirer' that simply reads, 'You're welcome.' Meanwhile, Sawyer's former friend Maggie is making her life at school miserable, and her parents want her to attend therapy. When a second person is killed, Sawyer realizes that her admirer/stalker is closer than she suspected and knows everything about her life." (Publishers Weekly)

Jenkins, A. M.

Beating heart; a ghost story. HarperCollins Publishers 2006 244p $15.99; pa $8.99
Grades: 9 10 11 12 **Fic**

1. Ghost stories 2. Moving -- Fiction 3. Divorce -- Fiction
ISBN 0-06-054607-7; 0-06-054609-3 pa
LC 2005-05071

Following his parents' divorce, seventeen-year-old Evan moves with his mother and sister into an old house where the spirit of a teenager who died there awakens and mistakes him for her long-departed lover.

"Both accessible and substantive, this book will be an easy sell to teens." Booklist

Night road. HarperTeen 2008 362p $16.99; lib bdg $17.89; pa $8.99
Grades: 8 9 10 11 12 **Fic**

1. Horror fiction 2. Vampires -- Fiction 3. Automobile travel -- Fiction
ISBN 978-0-06-054604-5; 0-06-054604-2; 978-0-06-054605-2 lib bdg; 0-06-054605-0 lib bdg; 978-0-06-054606-9 pa; 0-06-054606-9 pa
LC 2007-31703

Battling his own memories and fears, Cole, an extraordinarily conscientious vampire, and Sandor, a more impulsive acquaintance, spend a few months on the road, trying to train a young man who recently joined their ranks.

"The real strength of the novel lies in the noirish atmosphere, accessible prose, and crisp, sharp dialogue." Horn Book

Repossessed. HarperTeen 2007 218p $15.99
Grades: 7 8 9 10 **Fic**

1. School stories 2. Devil -- Fiction 3. Demoniac possession -- Fiction
ISBN 978-0-06-083568-2; 0-06-083568-0
LC 2007-09142

Michael L. Printz Award honor book, 2008

A fallen angel, tired of being unappreciated while doing his pointless, demeaning job, leaves Hell, enters the body of a seventeen-year-old boy, and tries to experience the full range of human feelings before being caught and punished, while the boy's family and friends puzzle over his changed behavior.

"Funny and clever. . . . It's a quick, quirky and entertaining read, with some meaty ideas in it, too." Kliatt

Jennings, Richard W.

Ghost town. Houghton Mifflin 2009 167p $16
Grades: 7 8 9 10 **Fic**

1. Ghost towns -- Fiction 2. Imaginary playmates -- Fiction 3. Business enterprises -- Fiction
ISBN 978-0-547-19471-4; 0-547-19471-4
LC 2008036781

Thirteen-year-old Spencer Honesty and his imaginary friend, an Indian called Chief Leopard Frog, improbably achieve fame and riches in the abandoned town of Paisley, Kansas, when Spencer begins taking photographs with his deceased father's ancient camera and Chief Leopard Frog has his poems published by a shady businessman in the Cayman Islands.

"Jennings has a dry wit, and the protagonist's matter-of-fact observations make the most outlandish scenes seem possible. This is a coming-of-age story/tall tale that's full of charm." SLJ

Jeschonek, Robert T.

My favorite band does not exist. Clarion Books 2011 327p $16.99
Grades: 8 9 10 11 12 **Fic**

1. Fantasy fiction
ISBN 978-0-547-37027-9; 0-547-37027-X

Sixteen-year-old Idea Deity, who believes that he is a character in a novel who will die in the sixty-fourth chapter, has created a fictional underground rock band on the internet which, it turns out, may actually exist, and whose members are wondering who is broadcasting all their personal information.

"Jeschonek has created a quirky, time and space-bending adventure that might just gather a cult following of its own. . . . Libraries looking for a strong addition to their science-fiction collections will want to invest in this sophisticated novel." SLJ

Jimenez, Francisco

★ **Breaking** through. Houghton Mifflin 2001 195p il $15; pa $6.95
Grades: 7 8 9 10 11 12 **Fic**

1. Migrant labor -- Fiction 2. Mexican Americans -- Fiction
ISBN 0-618-01173-0; 0-618-34248-6 pa
LC 2001-16941

Having come from Mexico to California ten years ago, fourteen-year-old Francisco is still working in the fields but fighting to improve his life and complete his education

"For all its recounting of deprivation, this is a hopeful book, told with rectitude and dignity." Horn Book

★ The **circuit** : stories from the life of a migrant child. Houghton Mifflin 1999 $16
Grades: 7 8 9 10 11 12 **Fic**

1. Family life -- Fiction 2. Migrant labor -- Fiction 3. Mexican Americans -- Fiction
ISBN 0-395-7902-1; 978-0-395-97902-0

First published 1997 by University of New Mexico Press

The story "begins in Mexico when the author is very young and his parents inform him that they are going on a very long trip to 'El Norte.' What follows is a series of stories of the family's unending migration from one farm to another as they search for the next harvesting job. Each story is told from the point of view of the author as a young child. The simple and direct narrative stays true to this perspective. . . . Lifting the story up from the mundane, Jiménez deftly portrays the strong bonds of love that hold this family together." Publ Wkly

★ **Reaching** out. Houghton Mifflin 2008 196p $16; pa $6.99

Grades: 7 8 9 10 11 12 **Fic**

1. California -- Fiction 2. Mexican Americans -- Fiction 3. Father-son relationship -- Fiction

ISBN 978-0-618-03851-0; 0-618-03851-5; 978-0-547-25030-4 pa; 0-547-25030-4 pa

Sequel to: Breaking through (2001)

A Pura Belpre Author Award honor book, 2009

"Papa's raging depression intensifies young Jiménez's personal guilt and conflict in the 1960s. . . . He is the first in his Mexican American migrant family to attend college in California. . . . Like his other fictionalized autobiographies, The Circuit (1997) and Breaking Through (2001), this sequel tells Jiménez's personal story in self-contained chapters that join together in a stirring narrative. . . . The spare episodes will draw readers with the quiet daily detail of work, anger, sorrow, and hope." Booklist

Jinks, Catherine

Babylonne; [by] Catherine Jinks. Candlewick Press 2008 384p map $18.99

Grades: 7 8 9 10 11 12 **Fic**

1. War stories 2. Orphans -- Fiction 3. Middle Ages -- Fiction

ISBN 978-0-7636-3650-0; 0-7636-3650-9

LC 2007-21958

In the violent and predatory world of thirteenth-century Languedoc, Pagan's sixteen-year-old daughter disguises herself as a boy and runs away with a priest who claims to be a friend of her dead father and mother, not knowing whether or not she can trust him, or anyone.

"Complete with snappy dialogue, humorous asides, and colorful descriptions . . . this novel stands on its own as a very fine historical fiction book about a period in history that is not commonly written about for teens." Voice Youth Advocates

★ **Evil** genius. Harcourt 2007 486p $17

Grades: 7 8 9 10 **Fic**

1. School stories 2. Crime -- Fiction 3. Genius -- Fiction 4. Australia -- Fiction 5. Good and evil -- Fiction

ISBN 978-0-15-205988-0; 0-15-205988-1

LC 2006-14476

First published 2005 in Australia

Child prodigy Cadel Piggot, an antisocial computer hacker, discovers his true identity when he enrolls as a first-year student at an advanced crime academy.

"Cadel's turnabout is convincingly hampered by his difficulty recognizing appropriate outlets for rage, and Jinks' whiplash-inducing suspense writing will gratify fans of Anthony Horowitz's high-tech spy scenarios." Booklist

Other titles about Cadel Piggot are:

Genius squad (2008)

Genius wars (2010)

Genius squad. Harcourt 2008 436p $17

Grades: 7 8 9 10 **Fic**

1. Crime -- Fiction 2. Genius -- Fiction 3. Australia -- Fiction 4. Good and evil -- Fiction

ISBN 978-0-15-205985-9; 0-15-205985-7

After the Axis Institute is blown up, fifteen-year-old Cadell Piggot is unhappily stuck in foster care with constant police surveillance to protect him from the evil Prosper English until he gets an offer to join a mysterious group called Genius Squad.

"Readers who loved Evil Genius will find this sequel as gripping, devilish and wonderfully dark as its predecessor." Publ Wkly

The **genius** wars. Harcourt 2010 378p $17

Grades: 7 8 9 10 **Fic**

1. Science fiction 2. Crime -- Fiction 3. Genius -- Fiction 4. Australia -- Fiction 5. Good and evil -- Fiction

ISBN 978-0-15-206619-2; 0-15-206619-5

LC 2009-49979

Fifteen-year-old genius Cadel Piggot Greenaus sets aside his new, crime-free life when his best friend Sonja is attacked, and he crosses oceans and continents trying to track down his nemesis Prosper English, breaking whatever rules he must.

"The climax is taut, absorbing and tantalizingly ambiguous." Kirkus

Living hell. Harcourt 2010 256p $17

Grades: 7 8 9 10 **Fic**

1. Science fiction

ISBN 978-0-15-206193-7; 0-15-206193-2

LC 2009-18938

Chronicles the transformation of a spaceship into a living organism, as seventeen-year-old Cheney leads the hundreds of inhabitants in a fight for survival while machines turn on them, treating all humans as parasites.

"Jinks' well-thought-out environs and rational characters help ground this otherwise out-of-control interstellar thriller." Booklist

The **abused** werewolf rescue group. Harcourt 2011 409p $16.99

Grades: 8 9 10 11 12 **Fic**

1. Mystery fiction 2. Werewolves -- Fiction

ISBN 978-0-15-206615-4; 0-15-206615-2

When Tobias wakes up in a hospital with no memory of the night before, a mysterious man tells him he has a dangerous condition, and he finds himself involved with a group of werewolves convinced he needs their help.

Jinks "weaves an action-packed story that has a tempo all its own. The constant plot twists and turns thrust the characters into bizarre situations that are at times as humorous as they are scary." SLJ

The **reformed** vampire support group. Houghton Mifflin Harcourt 2009 362p $17; pa $8.99
Grades: 8 9 10 11 12 **Fic**
1. Mystery fiction 2. Vampires -- Fiction
ISBN 978-0-15-206609-3; 0-15-206609-8; 978-0-547-41166-8 pa; 0-547-41166-9 pa
LC 2008-25115

Fifteen-year-old vampire Nina has been stuck for fifty-one years in a boring support group for vampires, and nothing exciting has ever happened to them—until one of them is murdered and the others must try to solve the crime.

"Those tired of torrid bloodsucker stories or looking for a comic riff on the trend will feel refreshed by the vomitous, guinea-pig-drinking accidental heroics of Nina and her pals." Kirkus

Followed by: The abused werewolf rescue group (2011)

Jocelyn, Marthe

Folly. Wendy Lamb Books 2010 249p $15.99; lib bdg $18.99
Grades: 8 9 10 11 12 **Fic**
1. London (England) -- Fiction 2. Abandoned children -- Fiction 3. Household employees -- Fiction 4. Foundling Hospital (London, England) -- Fiction 5. Great Britain -- History -- 19th century -- Fiction
ISBN 978-0-385-73846-0; 0-385-73846-3; 978-0-385-90731-6 lib bdg; 0-385-90731-1 lib bdg
LC 2009-23116

In a parallel narrative set in late nineteenth-century England, teenaged country girl Mary Finn relates the unhappy conclusion to her experiences as a young servant in an aristocratic London household while, years later, young James Nelligan describes how he comes to leave his beloved foster family to live and be educated at London's famous Foundling Hospital.

"Mary's spry narration (James's chapters unfold in third-person) combined with the tale's texture and fervent emotion will seduce readers." Horn Book Guide

Would you. Wendy Lamb Books 2008 165p $15.99; lib bdg $18.99; pa $6.50
Grades: 8 9 10 11 12 **Fic**
1. Coma -- Fiction 2. Sisters -- Fiction 3. Family life -- Fiction 4. Medical care -- Fiction 5. Traffic accidents -- Fiction
ISBN 978-0-375-83703-6; 0-375-83703-5; 978-0-375-93703-3 lib bdg; 0-375-93703-X lib bdg; 978-0-375-83704-3 pa; 0-375-83704-3 pa
LC 2007-18913

When her beloved sister, Claire, steps in front of a car and winds up in a coma, Nat's anticipated summer of working, hanging around with friends, and seeing Claire off to college is transformed into a nightmare of doctors, hospitals, and well-meaning neighbors.

"Jocelyn captures a teen's thoughts and reactions in a time of incredible anguish without making her overly dramatic. Readers will fly through the pages of this book, crying, laughing, and crying some more." SLJ

John, Antony

Five flavors of dumb. Dial Books 2010 337p $16.99
Grades: 7 8 9 10 **Fic**
1. Deaf -- Fiction 2. Rock musicians -- Fiction 3. Seattle (Wash.) -- Fiction
ISBN 978-0-8037-3433-3; 0-8037-3433-6
LC 2009-44449

Eighteen-year-old Piper is profoundly hearing impaired and resents her parent's decision raid her college fund to get cochlear implants for her baby sister. She becomes the manager for her classmates' popular rock band, called Dumb, giving her the chance to prove her capabilities to her parents and others, if only she can get the band members to get along.

"Readers interested in any of the narrative strands . . . will find a solid, satisfyingly complex story here." Bull Cent Child Books

Johnson, Alaya Dawn

★ The **summer** prince; Alaya Dawn Johnson. Arthur A. Levine Books 2013 304 p. (jacketed hardcover: alk. paper) $17.99
Grades: 9 10 11 12 **Fic**
1. Science fiction 2. Artists -- Fiction 3. Resistance to government -- Fiction 4. Love -- Fiction 5. Brazil -- Fiction 6. Government, Resistance to -- Fiction 7. Kings, queens, rulers, etc. -- Fiction
ISBN 0545417791; 9780545417792; 9780545417808; 9780545520775
LC 2012022236

Rainbow List (2014)
Lambda Literary Awards Finalist (2014)

This speculative fiction novel, by Alaya Dawn Johnson, takes place in "a futuristic Brazil. . . . In the midst of this vibrant metropolis, June Costa creates art that's sure to make her legendary. But her dreams of fame become something more when she meets Enki, the bold new Summer King. . . . Together, June and Enki will stage explosive, dramatic projects that Palmares Tres will never forget. They will add fuel to a growing rebellion against the government's strict limits on new tech." (Publisher's note)

Johnson, Angela

★ **Heaven.** Simon & Schuster Bks. for Young Readers 1998 138p $16.95; pa $7.99
Grades: 6 7 8 9 **Fic**
1. Parent and child 2. Adoption -- Fiction 3. African Americans -- Fiction
ISBN 0-689-82229-4; 1-4424-0342-X pa
LC 98-3291

Coretta Scott King Award for text, 1999

Fourteen-year-old Marley's seemingly perfect life in the small town of Heaven is disrupted when she discovers that her father and mother are not her real parents

"In spare, often poetic prose . . . Johnson relates Marley's insightful quest into what makes a family." SLJ

Sweet, hereafter; Angela Johnson. 1st ed. Simon and Schuster Books for Young Readers 2010 118 p. (paperback) $7.99; (hardcover) $16.99

Grades: 7 8 9 10 Fic

1. Iraq War, 2003- -- Fiction 2. African Americans -- Fiction

ISBN 0689873859; 9780689873867; 9780689873850; 0689873867

LC 2009027618

"Grades seven to ten." (Bull Cent Child Books)

"Johnson concludes the trilogy that began with Heaven (1998) and The First Part Last (2003). . . . Johnson's stripped-down, poetic prose is filled with shattering emotional truths about war's incalculable devastation, love's mysteries, and the bewildering, necessary search for happiness." Booklist

"With heartfelt empathy, we share in Shoogy's personal loss and her need for a new direction. Characters from the two other titles reappear, and we get a glimpse of how their lives are moving forward. This book belongs in all junior and senior high school collections, especially those who already own the first two titles. . . . Johnson now has one more well-woven character development novel to her name." Libr Media Connect

★ **Toning** the sweep. Orchard Bks. 1993 103p hardcover o.p. pa $5.99

Grades: 6 7 8 9 Fic

1. Death -- Fiction 2. Family life -- Fiction 3. Grandmothers -- Fiction 4. African Americans -- Fiction

ISBN 0-531-05476-4; 0-531-08626-7 lib bdg; 978-0-590-48142-7 pa; 0-590-48142-8 pa

LC 92-34062

Coretta Scott King Award for text

On a visit to her grandmother Ola, who is dying of cancer in her house in the desert, fourteen-year-old Emmie hears many stories about the past and her family history and comes to a better understanding of relatives both dead and living

"Full of subtle nuance, the novel is overlaid with meaning about the connections of family and the power of friendship." SLJ

★ The **first** part last. Simon & Schuster Bks. for Young Readers 2003 131p $15.95

Grades: 7 8 9 10 Fic

1. Infants -- Fiction 2. Teenage fathers -- Fiction 3. African Americans -- Fiction

ISBN 0-689-84922-2

LC 2002-36512

Michael L. Printz Award, 2004

Bobby's carefree teenage life changes forever when he becomes a father and must care for his adored baby daughter.

"Brief, poetic, and absolutely riveting." SLJ

Johnson, Angela, 1961-

★ A **certain** October; Angela Johnson. Simon & Schuster Books For Young Readers 2012 176 p. (hardback) $16.99

Grades: 7 8 9 10 11 12 Fic

1. Bildungsromans 2. Death -- Fiction 3. Guilt -- Fiction 4. Teenagers -- Fiction 5. Autism -- Fiction 6. Friendship -- Fiction 7. High schools -- Fiction

ISBN 9781442417267; 9780689865053; 9780689870651

LC 2012001595

In this book, "when a terrible accident occurs, Scotty feels responsible for the loss of someone she hardly knew, and the world goes wrong. She cannot tell what is a dream and what is real. Her friends are having a hard time getting through to her and her family is preoccupied with their own trauma. But the prospect of a boy, a dance, and the possibility that everything can fall back into place soon help Scotty realize that she is capable of adding her own flavor to life." (Publisher's note)

Johnson, Christine

Claire de Lune. Simon Pulse 2010 336p $16.99

Grades: 7 8 9 10 Fic

1. Werewolves -- Fiction 2. Mother-daughter relationship -- Fiction

ISBN 978-1-4169-9182-3; 1-4169-9182-4

LC 2009-36269

On her sixteenth birthday Claire discovers strange things happening and when her mother reveals their family secret which explains the changes, Claire feels her world, as she has known it to be, slowly slipping away.

"Strong characters and major plot twists coupled with a new twist on werewolf mythology make this a fun and entertaining read that will satisfy fans of the genre." SLJ

Followed by Nocturne (2011)

Nocturne; a Claire de Lune novel. Simon Pulse 2011 355p $16.99

Grades: 7 8 9 10 Fic

1. School stories 2. Werewolves -- Fiction 3. Supernatural -- Fiction 4. Identity (Psychology) -- Fiction 5. Mother-daughter relationship -- Fiction

ISBN 978-1-4424-0776-3

LC 2010032068

Sequel to Claire de Lune (2010)

After the tragic events of the summer, Claire wants to worry about nothing but finding the perfect dress for the Autumn Ball, but her worst nightmares come true when someone learns that she is a werewolf, placing everyone she knows at risk.

Johnson, Harriet McBryde

★ **Accidents** of nature. Holt 2006 229p $16.95

Grades: 9 10 11 12 Fic

1. Camps -- Fiction 2. People with disabilities -- Fiction 3. Cerebral palsy -- Fiction

ISBN 0-8050-7634-4; 978-0-8050-7634-9

LC 2005-24598

Having always prided herself on blending in with "normal" people despite her cerebral palsy, seventeen-year-old Jean begins to question her role in the world while attending a summer camp for children with disabilities.

"This book is smart and honest, funny and eye-opening. A must-read." SLJ

Johnson, J. J.

★ The **theory** of everything; by Jen Wichman. Peachtree Publishers 2012 334 p. ill. (hardcover) $16.95

Grades: 7 8 9 10 Fic

1. Bereavement -- Fiction 2. Interpersonal relations -- Fiction 3. Grief -- Fiction 4. Friendship -- Fiction

5. Best friends -- Fiction 6. New York (State) -- Fiction 7. Loss (Psychology) -- Fiction 8. Family life -- New York (State) -- Fiction
ISBN 1561456233; 9781561456239
LC 2011020973

In this novel, by J. J. Johnson, "ever since Sarah Jones's best friend Jamie died in a freak accident, life has felt sort of . . . random. Sarah has always followed the rules. . . . Now what? . . . In a last ditch effort to pull it together, Sarah ends up working for Roy, a local eccentric who owns a Christmas tree farm, and who might also be trying to understand the rules, patterns, and connections in life." (Publisher's note)

Johnson, Lindsay Lee

Worlds apart. Front Street 2005 166p il $16.95
Grades: 7 8 9 10 **Fic**

1. Moving -- Fiction 2. Psychiatric hospitals -- Fiction
ISBN 1-932425-28-4
LC 2005-12052

A thirteen-year-old daughter of a surgeon finds herself wrenched away from a comfortable lifestyle to a home on the grounds of a mental hospital, where her father has accepted a five year contract.

"This story brings bias and prejudice to the forefront in a discussable and readable narrative." SLJ

Johnson, LouAnne

Muchacho. Alfred A. Knopf 2009 197p $15.99; lib bdg $18.99
Grades: 8 9 10 **Fic**

1. Bildungsromans 2. Teenagers -- Fiction 3. Mexican Americans -- Fiction 4. School stories 5. New Mexico -- Fiction
ISBN 978-0-375-86117-8; 0-375-86117-3; 978-0-375-96117-5 lib bdg; 0-375-96117-8 lib bdg
LC 2009-1768

Living in a neighborhood of drug dealers and gangs in New Mexico, high school junior Eddie Corazon, a juvenile delinquent-in-training, falls in love with a girl who inspires him to rethink his life and his choices.

"Eddie's first-person narration and street language will hold teenagers' interest. Set in New Mexico, one of the states with the highest dropout rates among Hispanics, this novel unveils the social pressures and struggles of teens living in inner cities." Kirkus

Johnson, Maureen

★ **13** little blue envelopes. HarperCollins Publishers 2005 317p $15.99; pa $8.99
Grades: 8 9 10 11 12 **Fic**

1. Aunts -- Fiction 2. Europe -- Fiction 3. Voyages and travels -- Fiction
ISBN 0-06-054141-5; 0-06-054143-1 pa
LC 2005-02658

When seventeen-year-old Ginny receives a packet of mysterious envelopes from her favorite aunt, she leaves New Jersey to criss-cross Europe on a sort of scavenger hunt that transforms her life.

"Equal parts poignant, funny and inspiring, this tale is sure to spark wanderlust." Publ Wkly

Followed by: The last little blue envelope (2011)

★ The **madness** underneath; Maureen Johnson. G. P. Putnam's Sons 2013 304 p. (Shades of London) (hardback) $17.99
Grades: 6 7 8 9 10 **Fic**

1. Ghost stories 2. Occult fiction 3. Mystery fiction 4. Ghosts -- Fiction 5. Murder -- Fiction 6. England -- Fiction 7. Schools -- Fiction 8. Boarding schools -- Fiction 9. London (England) -- Fiction
ISBN 039925661X; 9780399256615
LC 2012026755

This paranormal mystery novel, by Maureen Johnson, is book two of "The Shades of London Trilogy." "After her near-fatal run-in with the Jack the Ripper copycat, Rory Devereaux . . . [has] become a human terminus, with the power to eliminate ghosts on contact. . . . The Ripper may be gone, but now there is a string of new inexplicable deaths threatening London. Rory has evidence that the deaths are no coincidence. Something much more sinister is going on." (Publisher's note)

The **name** of the star. G. P. Putnam's Sons 2011 384p $16.99
Grades: 6 7 8 9 10 **Fic**

1. Ghost stories 2. School stories 3. Homicide -- Fiction 4. Witnesses -- Fiction 5. London (England) -- Fiction
ISBN 978-0-399-25660-8; 0-399-25660-1; 9780399256608; 0399256601
LC 2011009003

"Johnson's trademark sense of humor serves to counterbalance some grisly murders in this page-turner, which opens her Shades of London series. . . . As one mutilated body after another turns up, Johnson . . . amplifies the story's mysteries with smart use of and subtle commentary on modern media shenanigans and London's infamously extensive surveillance network. . . . Readers looking for nonstop fun, action, and a little gore have come to the right place." Publ Wkly

Scarlett fever. Point/Scholastic 2010 336p $16.99
Grades: 7 8 9 10 **Fic**

1. School stories 2. Actors -- Fiction 3. Family life -- Fiction 4. New York (N.Y.) -- Fiction 5. Hotels and motels -- Fiction 6. Dating (Social customs) -- Fiction
ISBN 978-0-439-89928-4; 0-439-89928-1
Sequel to: Suite Scarlett (2008)

Fifteen-year-old Scarlett, who is beginning to get over her breakup with Eric, stays busy as assistant to her theatrical-agent friend who is not only promoting Scarlett's brother Spencer, but also a new client whose bad-boy brother has transferred to Scarlett's school.

"While the novel may be enjoyed for the light if slightly madcap romance that it is, it is notable for its attention to social class and to the Martins' struggles with money." SLJ

Suite Scarlett. Scholastic Point 2008 353p $16.99
Grades: 6 7 8 9 10 **Fic**

1. Authorship -- Fiction 2. Family life -- Fiction 3. New York (N.Y.) -- Fiction 4. Hotels and motels --

Fiction
ISBN 978-0-439-89927-7; 0-439-89927-3
LC 2007-041903

Fifteen-year-old Scarlett Marvin is stuck in New York City for the summer working at her quirky family's historic hotel, but her brother's attractive new friend and a seasonal guest who offers her an intriguing and challenging writing project improve her outlook.

"Utterly winning, madcap Manhattan farce, crafted with a winking, urbane narrative and tight, wry dialogue." Booklist

Another title about Scarlett is:
Scarlett fever (2010)

Johnson, Peter

★ **What** happened. Front Street 2007 133p $16.95
Grades: 8 9 10 11 12 **Fic**

1. Traffic accidents -- Fiction 2. Father-son relationship -- Fiction
ISBN 978-1-932425-67-3; 1-932425-67-5
LC 2006-12028

When Duane is involved in a hit-and-run accident during a snowstorm, passengers Kyle and his younger brother must face Duane's powerful father, a man whose hatred of their own absent father may lead him to harm the boys.

"The voice that Johnson has given this boy . . . is breathtakingly good, each word conspiring with every other word to create an irresistibly seductive tone that is a haunting combination of sadness and fragile hope." Booklist

Johnson, Varian

Saving Maddie. Delacorte Press 2010 231p $16.99; lib bdg $19.99
Grades: 9 10 11 12 **Fic**

1. Clergy -- Fiction 2. Religion -- Fiction 3. Family life -- Fiction 4. South Carolina -- Fiction
ISBN 978-0-385-73804-0; 0-385-73804-8; 978-0-385-90708-8 lib bdg; 0-385-90708-7 lib bdg
LC 2010-277721

"Joshua and Maddie, both preacher's kids, were best friends when they were younger, until Maddie's father moved the family to Norfolk. Now Maddie's back in town. Her father, having refused to pay her tuition at Brown, has sent her to an aunt's house to straighten up after years of too much boys and booze. Joshua, PK that he is, is sure he can save Maddie, but angry and hostile, she has resolved to stay the way she is." (Booklist)

Johnston, E. K.

Prairie fire; E. K. Johnston. Carolrhoda Books. 2015 304p $18.99
Grades: 7 8 9 10 Fic

1. Adventure fiction 2. Bards and bardism -- Fiction 3. Dragons -- Fiction 4. Fame -- Fiction 5. Family life -- Canada -- Fiction 6. High schools -- Fiction 7. Friendship -- Fiction
ISBN: 146773909X; 9781467739092; 9781467761819; 9781467776790; 9781467776806; 9781467776813
LC 2014008995

"Every dragon slayer owes the Oil Watch a period of service, and young Owen was no exception. What made him different was that he did not enlist alone. His two closest friends stood with him shoulder to shoulder. . . . But the arc of history is long and hardened by dragon fire. Try as they might, Owen and his friends could not twist it to their will." (Publisher's note)

"There is a little something for everyone in this sequel to the acclaimed The Story of Owen. Fantasy fans will love returning to an alternate world in which the armed forces slay dragons...A fantasy YA novel that steers clear of love triangles, teen angst, and a tidy ending is hard to come by; Prairie Fire and its prequel are must-haves." SLJ

The **story** of Owen: dragon slayer of Trondheim; E. K. Johnston. Carolrhoda Lab. 2014 305p $17.95
Grades: 7 8 9 10 11 12 **Fic**

1. Adventure fiction 2. Bards and bardism -- Fiction 3. Dragons -- Fiction 4. Fame -- Fiction 5. Family life -- Canada -- Fiction 6. High schools -- Fiction 7. Canada -- Fiction
ISBN: 9781467710664; 1467710660
LC 2013020492

In this book, author E. K. Johnston, "envisions an Earth nearly identical to our own, with one key difference: dragons. . . . After 16-year-old Siobhan McQuaid agrees to become the bard for dragon-slayer-in-training Owen Thorskard, who has moved with his famous dragon-slaying family to her small Ontario town, she winds up at the center of a grassroots effort to understand an odd spike in dragon numbers." Publishers Weekly

"Humor, pathos and wry social commentary unite in a cleverly drawn, marvelously diverse world. Refreshingly, the focus is on the pair as friends and partners, not on potential romance." Kirkus

Jolin, Paula

In the name of God. Roaring Brook Press 2007 208p $16.95
Grades: 8 9 10 11 12 **Fic**

1. Syria -- Fiction 2. Muslims -- Fiction 3. Family life -- Fiction 4. Islamic fundamentalism -- Fiction
ISBN 978-1-59643-211-6; 1-59643-211-X
LC 2006-23834

Determined to follow the laws set down in the Qur'an, seventeen-year-old Nadia becomes involved in a violent revolutionary movement aimed at supporting Muslim rule in Syria and opposing the Western politics and materialism that increasingly affect her family.

"The well-written prose and short chapters give stories in the news a face and a character. Readers of this book will not be able to read or watch the news in the same way." Voice Youth Advocates

Jones, Allan Frewin

Destiny's path; [by] Frewin Jones. HarperTeen 2009 329p $16.99
Grades: 8 9 10 11 12 **Fic**

1. War stories 2. Magic -- Fiction 3. Wales -- Fiction 4. Princesses -- Fiction 5. Fate and fatalism -- Fiction
ISBN 978-0-06-087146-8; 0-06-087146-6
LC 2009-14587

Sequel to: Warrior princess (2009)

When fifteen-year-old Princess Branwen tries to turn away from her destiny as the one who will save Wales from the Saxons, the Shining Ones send an owl in the form of a young girl called Blodwedd to guide her and Rhodri on the right path.

"Branwen's compelling story leaves readers waiting for the sequel." Booklist

Followed by: The emerald flame (2010)

Jones, Patrick

Chasing tail lights. Walker & Co. 2007 294p hardcover o.p. pa $7.99

Grades: 9 10 11 12 **Fic**

1. Incest -- Fiction 2. Michigan -- Fiction 3. Family life -- Fiction 4. Child sexual abuse -- Fiction

ISBN 978-0-8027-9628-8; 0-8027-9628-1; 978-0-8027-9762-9 pa; 0-8027-9762-8 pa

LC 2006-27657

Seventeen-year-old Christy wants only to finish high school and escape her Flint, Michigan, home, where she cooks, cleans, cares for her niece, and tries to fend off her half-brother, a drug dealer who has been abusing her since she was eleven.

The author "tackles a lot of relevant issues here. . . . His look at teen rebellion and the misunderstandings it can engender is full of hard-to-face truths, and his ultimate faith in teens' ability to survive tough circumstances may inspire readers." Bull Cent Child Books

The **tear** collector. Walker & Company 2009 263p $16.99

Grades: 7 8 9 10 **Fic**

1. School stories 2. Michigan -- Fiction 3. Family life -- Fiction 4. Supernatural -- Fiction

ISBN 978-0-8027-8710-1; 0-8027-8710-X

LC 2008-55868

As one of an ancient line of creatures who gain energy from human tears, seventeen-year-old Cassandra offers sympathy to anyone at her school or the hospital where she works, but she yearns to be fully human for the boy she loves, even if it means letting her family down.

"Cassandra is a complex character who readers will identify with as she struggles to understand who she really is, where her loyalties lie, and how to take control of her own destiny. Those looking for a new spin on the vampire story should find this one satisfying." SLJ

Jones, Traci L.

Finding my place. Farrar Straus Giroux 2010 181p $16.99

Grades: 6 7 8 9 **Fic**

1. School stories 2. Moving -- Fiction 3. Friendship -- Fiction 4. Prejudices -- Fiction 5. Race relations -- Fiction 6. African Americans -- Fiction

ISBN 978-0-374-33573-1; 0-374-33573-7

LC 2008-54433

After moving to an affluent suburb of Denver in 1975, ninth-grader Tiphanie feels lonely at her nearly all-white high school until she befriends another "outsider" and discovers that prejudice exists in many forms.

"Tiphanie is refreshingly witty and open-minded. . . . Jones handles the intricacies of race relations splendidly and excels in the frankness of her prose. . . . This immediate, engaging novel will appeal to readers of all backgrounds." Booklist

Standing against the wind; 1st ed.; Farrar, Straus and Giroux 2006 184p $16

Grades: 6 7 8 9 **Fic**

1. School stories 2. African Americans -- Fiction 3. City and town life -- Fiction

ISBN 978-0-374-37174-6; 0-374-37174-1

LC 2005-51226

As she tries to escape her poor Chicago neighborhood by winning a scholarship to a prestigious boarding school, shy and studious eighth-grader Patrice discovers that she has more options in life than she previously realized.

"Handled without obscenity, the lively street talk will draw readers to the gripping story of a contemporary kid who works to make her dreams come true." Booklist

Joseph, Lynn

Flowers in the sky; by Lynn Joseph. HarperTeen 2013 240 p. (hardcover) $17.99

Grades: 8 9 10 11 12 **Fic**

1. Bildungsromans 2. New York (N.Y.) -- Fiction 3. Brothers and sisters -- Fiction 4. Love -- Fiction 5. Immigrants -- Fiction 6. Coming of age -- Fiction 7. Dominican Republic -- Fiction 8. Dominican Americans -- Fiction

ISBN 0060297948; 9780060297947

LC 2012038122

In this novel, by Lynn Joseph, "fifteen-year-old Nina Perez . . . must leave her . . . lush island home in Samana, Dominican Republic, when she's sent . . . to live with her brother, Darrio, in New York, to seek out a better life. . . . But then she meets . . . [a] tall, green-eyed boy . . . , who just might help her learn to see beauty in spite of tragedy." (Publisher's note)

Joyce, Graham, 1954-

The **exchange**. Viking 2008 241p $16.99

Grades: 7 8 9 10 **Fic**

1. Tattooing -- Fiction 2. Supernatural -- Fiction 3. Single parent family -- Fiction 4. Dating (Social customs) -- Fiction

ISBN 978-0-670-06207-2; 0-670-06207-3

LC 2007-32160

Cursed by the elderly recluse whose home she and a friend were creeping through late one night, fourteen-year-old Caz soon finds her life disintegrating and realizes she must find a way of lifting the curse—or at least understanding its power.

"Joyce has crafted a bizarre, magically realistic tale. . . . It's a wild ride with subtly moralistic undertones and a surprisingly happy ending that will stay with readers." Booklist

Juby, Susan

Another kind of cowboy. HarperTeen 2007 344p $16.99

Grades: 8 9 10 11 12 **Fic**

1. Horses -- Fiction 2. Friendship -- Fiction 3. Horsemanship -- Fiction 4. Homosexuality -- Fiction

5. British Columbia -- Fiction
ISBN 0-06-076517-8; 978-0-06-076517-0
LC 2006-36336

In Vancouver, British Columbia, two teenage dressage riders, one a spoiled rich girl and the other a closeted gay sixteen-year-old boy, come to terms with their identities and learn to accept themselves.

"Wry humor infuses this quiet story with a gentle warmth, and the secondary characters are well developed." Booklist

Getting the girl; a guide to private investigation, surveillance, and cookery. [by] S. Juby. HarperTeen 2008 341p $16.99; lib bdg $17.89; pa $8.99
Grades: 6 7 8 9 10 **Fic**

1. School stories 2. Mystery fiction 3. Popularity -- Fiction
ISBN 978-0-06-076525-5; 0-06-076525-9; 978-0-06-076527-9 lib bdg; 0-06-076527-5 lib bdg; 978-0-06-076528-6 pa; 0-06-076528-3 pa
LC 2008-00788

Ninth-grader Sherman Mack investigates the "Defilers," a secret group at his British Columbia high school that marks certain female students as pariahs, at first because he is trying to protect the girl he has a crush on, but later as a matter of principle.

Juby "applies her signature brand of humor to a detective novel. . . . [This offers a] strong and memorable female cast. . . . Here's hoping that Juby delivers on the promise of sequels." Horn Book

Kade, Stacey

The **ghost** and the goth. Hyperion 2010 281p $16.99
Grades: 8 9 10 11 12 **Fic**

1. Ghost stories 2. School stories
ISBN 1-4231-2197-X; 978-1-4231-2197-8
LC 2010-8135

After being hit by a bus and killed, a high school homecoming queen gets stuck in the land of the living, with only a loser classmate—who happens to be able to see and hear ghosts—to help her.

'The tale is absorbing, and Kade successfully portrays a typical present-day high school. This novel will appeal to fans of romances and ghost stories alike." SLJ

Followed by: Queen of the dead (2011)

The **rules**; Stacey Kade. Hyperion 2013 416 p. $17.99
Grades: 7 8 9 10 11 12 **Fic**

1. Science fiction 2. Schools -- Fiction 3. Identity -- Fiction 4. High schools -- Fiction 5. Genetic engineering -- Fiction 6. Fathers and daughters -- Fiction 7. Extraterrestrial beings -- Fiction 8. Interpersonal relations -- Fiction
ISBN 9781423153283
LC 2012033732

In this book, rescued "from a genetics lab by her adoptive father, Ariane Tucker has spent the last ten years hiding" that she's "a human-extraterrestrial hybrid, created by GenTex Labs as part of Project Paper Doll. She must follow 'the rules' set out by her father to avoid being detected by her classmates or GTX. Blend in, do not get noticed, trust no one, and never forget that they are searching for her." But Ariane breaks the rules when she catches the eye of Zane Bradshaw. (Voice of Youth Advocates)

The **ghost** and the goth. Hyperion 2010 281p $16.99
Grades: 8 9 10 11 12 **Fic**

1. Ghost stories 2. School stories
ISBN 1-4231-2197-X; 978-1-4231-2197-8
LC 2010-8135

After being hit by a bus and killed, a high school homecoming queen gets stuck in the land of the living, with only a loser classmate—who happens to be able to see and hear ghosts—to help her.

"The tale is absorbing, and Kade successfully portrays a typical present-day high school. This novel will appeal to fans of romances and ghost stories alike." SLJ

Queen of the dead. Hyperion 2011 266p $16.99
Grades: 8 9 10 11 12 **Fic**

1. Ghost stories 2. Family life -- Fiction 3. Secret societies -- Fiction
ISBN 978-1-4231-3467-1; 1-4231-3467-2
LC 2010029226

Will gets involved with The Order, a group consisting of ghost-talkers like himself, as he continues to help spirits into the light, while Alona, his vain, self-centered, and cranky spirit guide begins to learn the value of helping others.

"This sequel to The Ghost and the Goth (2010) has exchanged some of the lighter humor for a more complex story line. Characters are more fully developed, and the momentum is stronger." Booklist

Kagawa, Julie

The **Eternity** Cure; Julie Kagawa. Harlequin Books 2013 448 p. (hardcover) $16.99
Grades: 7 8 9 10 11 12 **Fic**

1. Science fiction 2. Vampires -- Fiction 3. Epidemics -- Fiction
ISBN 0373210698; 9780373210695

This vampire novel, by Julie Kagawa, is part of the "Blood of Eden" series. "Allie will follow the call of blood to save her creator, Kanin, from the psychotic vampire Sarren. But when the trail leads to Allie's birthplace in New Covington, what Allie finds there will change the world forever. . . . There's a new plague on the rise, a strain of the Red Lung virus that wiped out most of humanity generations ago--and this strain is deadly to humans and vampires alike." (Publisher's note)

★ The **immortal** rules; a legend begins. Julie Kagawa. Harlequin Teen 2012 504 p. (Blood of Eden) (hardcover) $18.99
Grades: 7 8 9 10 11 12 **Fic**

1. Love stories 2. Diseases -- Fiction 3. Vampires -- Fiction
ISBN 0373210515; 9780373210510
LC 2011279454

In this book, "[r]abids, vicious hybrid creatures born of the plague, prowl the land beyond the walled vampire cities. . . . When Allie is savagely attacked by a rabid, . . . a mysterious vampire offers her the choice of a human death or 'life' as a vampire. . . . Allie's determination to remain more human than monster is put to the test, particularly when she joins a band of humans on a desperate journey to safety on the island of Eden. Particularly when she falls in love." (Kirkus)

"Kagawa wraps excellent writing and skillful plotting around a well-developed concept and engaging characters, resulting in a fresh and imaginative thrill-ride that deserves a wide audience." Pub Wkly

Kamata, Suzanne

Gadget Girl; the art of being invisible. Suzanne Kamata. GemmaMedia 2013 256 p. (pbk.) $14.95

Grades: 9 10 11 12 **Fic**

1. Cerebral palsy -- Fiction 2. Mother-daughter relationship -- Fiction 3. France -- Fiction 4. Artists -- Fiction 5. Coming of age -- Fiction 6. Paris (France) -- Fiction 7. Cartoons and comics -- Fiction 8. Mothers and daughters -- Fiction 9. Single-parent families -- Fiction 10. People with disabilities -- Fiction

ISBN 1936846381; 9781936846382

LC 2012051566

Asian/Pacific American Awards for Literature: Young Adult Literature Honor (2014)

In this book by Suzanne Kamata, "Aiko, who has cerebral palsy . . . is the 14-year-old secretive creator of a manga comic starring Lisa Cook as Gadget Girl. Aiko also serves as the reluctant muse to her midwestern American mother, an award-winning sculptor who has been invited to Paris, even as she longs for a connection to her birth father in Japan." (Booklist)

"For Aiko Cassidy, it's hard enough sitting at the "invisible" table and dealing with trespassing geeks. It's harder when her cerebral palsy makes guys notice her in all the wrong ways...Awkwardly and believably, this sensitive novel reveals an artistic teen adapting to family, disability and friendships in all their flawed beauty." (Kirkus)

Kantor, Melissa

Girlfriend material. Disney/Hyperion Books 2009 251p $15.99

Grades: 7 8 9 10 **Fic**

1. Summer -- Fiction

ISBN 978-1-4231-0849-8; 1-4231-0849-3

Kate has never had a boyfriend. But while crashing at her mother's wealthy friends' home at Cape Cod for the summer, Kate meets Adam. But when her breezy summer romance with Adam becomes more complicated, Kate asks herself if she is girlfriend material.

"The changes in Kate are both gradual and realistic. . . . Her emotional journey and acute self-consciousness are likely to strike a chord." Publ Wkly

The **breakup** bible; a novel. Hyperion Books for Children 2007 272p $15.99

Grades: 8 9 10 11 12 **Fic**

1. Dating (Social customs) -- Fiction

ISBN 978-0-7868-0962-2

Jennifer thinks she and Max are the perfect couple, until he decides he just wants to be friends.

"Written with wit and featuring a few fine plot twists, this will have teen girls nodding sympathetically." Booklist

Karim, Sheba

Skunk girl. Farrar, Straus & Giroux 2009 231p $16.95

Grades: 8 9 10 11 12 **Fic**

1. School stories 2. Muslims -- Fiction 3. Family life -- Fiction 4. New York (State) -- Fiction 5. Pakistani Americans -- Fiction 6. Dating (Social customs) -- Fiction

ISBN 978-0-374-37011-4; 0-374-37011-7

LC 2008-7482

Nina Khan is not just the only Asian or Muslim student in her small-town high school in upstate New York, she is also faces the legacy of her "Supernerd" older sister, body hair, and the pain of having a crush when her parents forbid her to date.

This novel is "rife with smart, self-deprecating humor." Kirkus

Karp, Jesse

Those that wake. Harcourt 2011 329p

Grades: 9 10 11 12 **Fic**

1. Science fiction 2. New York (N.Y.) -- Fiction 3. Identity (Psychology) -- Fiction

ISBN 978-0-547-55311-5

"Things have been bleak in New York City ever since 'Big Black,' the explosion that destroyed Con Edison and the two-week aftermath of darkness, rioting, looting, and murder. Residents interact with their cell phones more than with one another. For four New Yorkers, though, things are much worse than bleak. One day Laura wakes to find that no one remembers her existence. Mal's brother is missing, and his only lead is that Tommy was running errands for someone in an empty office tower that doesn't seem to conform to the laws of physics. . . . With plenty of action, challenging ideas, and bizarre antagonists, this one should appeal to a broad section of teens." SLJ

Kaslik, Ibolya

Skinny; [by] Ibi Kaslik. Walker & Company 2006 244p $16.95

Grades: 11 12 **Fic**

1. Sisters -- Fiction 2. Anorexia nervosa -- Fiction 3. Father-daughter relationship -- Fiction

ISBN 978-0-8027-9608-0; 0-8027-9608-7

LC 2006-42140

First published 2004 in Canada

After the death of their father, two sisters struggle with various issues, including their family history, personal relationships, and an extreme eating disorder

"It's refreshing that Gigi's anorexia and briefly described lesbian romance are treated as only parts of a larger story, and the girls' grief following their father's death and the pressures they face growing up with immigrant parents add depth to the novel. . . . This is an ambitious, often moving offering, and older readers will likely connect with the raw emotions and intelligent insights into a family's secrets, pain, and enduring love." Booklist

Katcher, Brian

★ **Almost** perfect. Delacorte Press 2009 360p $17.99

Grades: 9 10 11 12 Fic

1. School stories 2. Missouri -- Fiction 3. Transgender people -- Fiction 4. Single parent family -- Fiction 5. Dating (Social customs) -- Fiction

ISBN 978-0-385-73664-0; 0-385-73664-9

LC 2008-37659

Stonewall Children's and Young Adult Literature Award, 2011

With his mother working long hours and in pain from a romantic break-up, eighteen-year-old Logan feels alone and unloved until a zany new student arrives at his small-town Missouri high school, keeping a big secret.

"The author tackles issues of homophobia, hate crimes and stereotyping with humor and grace in an accessible tone that will resonate with teens who may not have encountered the issue of transgender identity before." Kirkus

Playing with matches. Delacorte Press 2008 294p $15.99; lib bdg $18.99

Grades: 8 9 10 11 12 Fic

1. School stories 2. Missouri -- Fiction 3. Burns and scalds -- Fiction 4. Dating (Social customs) -- Fiction

ISBN 978-0-385-73544-5; 0-385-73544-8; 978-0-385-90525-1 lib bdg; 0-385-90525-4 lib bdg

LC 2007-27654

While trying to find a girl who will date him, Missouri high school junior Leon Sanders befriends a lonely, disfigured female classmate.

"This is a strong debut novel with a cast of quirky, multidimensional characters struggling with issues of acceptance, sexuality, identity, and self-worth." SLJ

Kate, Lauren

The **betrayal** of Natalie Hargrove. Penguin Young Readers Group 2009 235p pa $9.99

Grades: 9 10 11 12 Fic

1. School stories 2. Contests -- Fiction 3. Social classes -- Fiction 4. South Carolina -- Fiction

ISBN 978-1-59514-265-8; 1-59514-265-7

LC 2009-18481

South Carolina high school senior Nat has worked hard to put her trailer-park past behind her, and when she and her boyfriend are crowned Palmetto Prince and Princess everything would be perfect, except that a prank they played a few nights before went horribly awry.

"Lots of adjectives can be applied to this debut effort—mean, smutty, decadent—and all of them should be taken as compliments." Booklist

Kaye, Marilyn

Demon chick. Henry Holt 2009 215p $16.99

Grades: 7 8 9 10 Fic

1. Hell -- Fiction 2. Politics -- Fiction 3. Mother-daughter relationship -- Fiction

ISBN 0-8050-8880-6; 978-0-8050-8880-9

LC 2008-50280

Sixteen-year-old Jessica discovers that her mother, a charismatic presidential candidate, sold Jessica's soul to the devil in exchange for political power.

"There's a little political commentary, a little Machiavellianism, a little about responsibility and guilt and loyalty, but the weighty issues are handled with a light touch, thanks to Jessica, whose wry observations and dialogue keep the narrative snappy. . . . This is one hell worth visiting." Horn Book

Kearney, Meg

The **girl** in the mirror; a novel in poems and journal entries. Meg Kearney. Persea Books 2012 168 p. (trade pbk.: alk. paper) $15

Grades: 9 10 11 12 Fic

1. Novels in verse 2. Grief -- Fiction 3. Adoptees -- Fiction 4. Identity (Psychology) -- Fiction 5. Adoption -- Fiction

ISBN 0892553855; 9780892553853

LC 2011045052

Sequel to: The secret of me

This book, the sequel to "The Secret of Me," is "told in verse and journal entries." The protagonist's "father passed away on the same day that a letter with non-identifying information about her birth mother arrived from the adoption agency. . . . She . . . joins her older coworkers in late-night partying and drinking. . . . When her change in lifestyle results in losing close friends and a near rape, Lizzie realizes that she no longer recognizes the girl she sees in the mirror." (Kirkus Reviews)

"Kearney tenderly explores Lizzie's anger, sadness, and ambivalence about her identity as she grapples with whether to risk being hurt by the mother she never knew or to approach the future without first claiming her past." Pub Wkly

Includes bibliographical references

Kehoe, Stasia Ward

The **sound** of letting go; by Stasia Ward Kehoe. Viking 2014 388p $17.99

Grades: 7 8 9 10 11 12 Fic

1. Autism — Fiction 2. Family problems — Fiction 3. High schools — Fiction 4. Jazz — Fiction 5. Novels in verse

ISBN: 0670015539; 9780670015535

LC 2013013098

A novel in verse. "For sixteen years, Daisy has been good. A good daughter, helping out with her autistic younger brother uncomplainingly. A good friend, even when her best friend makes her feel like a third wheel. When her parents announce they're sending her brother to an institution--without consulting her--Daisy's furious, and decides the best way to be a good sister is to start being bad. She quits jazz band and orchestra, slacks in school, and falls for bad-boy Dave." (Publisher's note)

"This painfully honest portrait of a family in crisis raises questions about love, responsibility, and self-sacrifice as it moves gracefully to a difficult but realistic resolution." Pub Wkly

Kelly, Tara

Harmonic feedback. Henry Holt and Company 2010 280p $16.99

Grades: 9 10 11 12 Fic

1. Drug abuse -- Fiction 2. Rock music -- Fiction 3. Washington (State) -- Fiction 4. Asperger's syndrome -- Fiction

ISBN 978-0-8050-9010-9; 0-8050-9010-X

LC 2009-24150

When Drea and her mother move in with her grandmother in Bellingham, Washington, the sixteen-year-old finds finds that she can have real friends, in spite of her Asperger's, and that even when you love someone it doesn't make life perfect.

"The novel's strength lies in Drea's dynamic personality: a combination of surprising immaturity, childish wonder, and profound insight. Her search for stability and need to escape being labeled is poignant and convincing." Publ Wkly

Kenneally, Miranda

Racing Savannah; Miranda Kenneally. Sourcebooks Fire 2013 304 p. (tp: alk. paper) $9.99

Grades: 8 9 10 11 12 **Fic**

1. Horsemanship -- Fiction 2. Love 3. Horses 4. Love -- Fiction 5. Horses -- Fiction 6. Tennessee -- Fiction
ISBN 1402284764; 9781402284762
LC 2013023322

In this book, by Miranda Kenneally, "Savannah has always been much more comfortable around horses than boys. Especially boys like Jack Goodwin. . . . She knows the rules: no mixing between the staff and the Goodwin family. But Jack has no such boundaries. With her dream of becoming a jockey, Savannah isn't exactly one to follow the rules either." (Publisher's note)

"Kenneally (Stealing Parker, 2012) again looks at sports through a female lens, this time tackling male-dominated horse racing, in this fourth Hundred Oaks novel. Savannah, her widowed horse-trainer father, and her father's pregnant girlfriend move to Tennessee's Cedar Hill, a farm that trains horses for races including the Kentucky Derby...The author's knack for weaving forbidden romance, breezy dialogue, and details of this lesser-known sports venue places it in the winner's circle for reluctant readers and chick-lit fans." (Booklist)

Stealing Parker; Miranda Kenneally. Paw Prints 2012 242 p. (paperback) $8.99; (prebind) $17.99

Grades: 9 10 11 12 **Fic**

1. School stories 2. Children of gay parents -- Fiction
ISBN 1402271875; 1451768125; 9781402271878; 9781451768121

In this book, "when Parker's mother comes out, Parker's family falls apart: . . . Parker herself gives up her beloved softball and takes up kissing guys in order to prove that she's nothing like her mother. At the behest of her best friend, Drew, she becomes the manager of the boys' baseball team, where she quickly become attracted to and confused by the good-looking new coach." (Bulletin of the Center for Children's Books)

Kephart, Beth

Dangerous neighbors; a novel. Egmont USA 2010 176p $16.99; lib bdg $19.99

Grades: 7 8 9 10 **Fic**

1. Death -- Fiction 2. Guilt -- Fiction 3. Twins -- Fiction 4. Sisters -- Fiction 5. Bereavement -- Fiction 6. Philadelphia (Pa.) -- Fiction 7. Centennial Exhibition (1876: Philadelphia, Pa.) -- Fiction
ISBN 978-1-60684-080-1; 1-60684-080-0; 978-1-60684-106-8 lib bdg; 1-60684-106-8 lib bdg
LC 2010-11249

Set against the backdrop of the 1876 Centennial Exhibition in Philadelphia, Katherine cannot forgive herself when her beloved twin sister dies, and she feels that her only course of action is to follow suit.

"Exceptionally graceful prose . . . and flashbacks are so realistically drawn and deftly integrated that readers will be as startled as Katherine to find themselves yanked out of morose memories and surrounded by noisy fairgoers." Bull Cent Child Books

Dr. Radway's Sarsaparilla Resolvent; by Beth Kephart; illustrated by William Sulit. Temple Univ Pr 2013 198 p. ill. (paperback) $15.95

Grades: 6 7 8 9 **Fic**

1. Grief -- Fiction 2. Police brutality -- Fiction
ISBN 0984042962; 9780984042968

This book by Beth Kephart follows 14-year-old protagonist William Quinn. "With his father in the Cherry Hill prison and his genially wayward older brother, Francis, recently beaten to death by a brutal policeman, his mother has ground herself into unbearable, paralyzing grief, and the boy has to find a way to save them both. . . . Gradually, William finds a way to make right some terrible wrongs." (Kirkus Reviews)

Going over; Beth Kephart; Chronicle Books. 2014 262p $17.99

Grades: 8 9 10 11 12 **Fic**

1. Berlin Wall (1961-1989) 2. Family life--Germany--Fiction 3. Berlin (Germany)--Fiction 4. Love stories
ISBN: 1452124574; 9781452124575
LC 2012046894

"Ada lives among the rebels, punkers, and immigrants of Kreuzberg in West Berlin. Stefan lives in East Berlin, in a faceless apartment bunker of Friedrichshain. Bound by love and separated by circumstance, their only chance for a life together lies in a high-risk escape. But will Stefan find the courage to leap? Or will forces beyond his control stand in his way?" Publisher's note

"In a present-tense narration alternating between Ada's first-person and Stefan's second-person, the young lovers on opposite sides of the Berlin Wall in 1983 plan for Stefan's escape to the West. Kephart works romantic chemistry into a danger-packed plot with moving results in this captivating glimpse into an underrepresented era that will appeal to older readers with a taste for literary historical fiction." Horn Book

★ The **heart** is not a size. HarperTeen 2010 244p $16.99

Grades: 7 8 9 10 **Fic**

1. Poverty -- Fiction 2. Friendship -- Fiction 3. Volunteer work -- Fiction
ISBN 978-0-06-147048-6; 0-06-147048-1
LC 2008-55721

Fifteen-year-old Georgia learns a great deal about herself and her troubled best friend Riley when they become part of a group of suburban Pennsylvania teenagers that go to Anapra, a squatters village in the border town of Juarez, Mexico, to undertake a community construction project.

"Kephart's prose is typically poetic. She pens a faster-paced novel that explores teens' inner selves. . . . The writing is vivid, enabling readers to visualize Anapra's desolation and hope." Voice Youth Advocates

House of Dance. HarperTeen 2008 263p $16.99; lib bdg $17.89; pa $10.99
Grades: 7 8 9 10 **Fic**

1. Death -- Fiction 2. Cancer -- Fiction 3. Dancers -- Fiction 4. Grandfathers -- Fiction 5. Mother-daughter relationship -- Fiction

ISBN 978-0-06-142928-6; 0-06-142928-7; 978-0-06-142929-3 lib bdg; 0-06-142929-5 lib bdg; 978-0-06-142930-9 pa; 0-06-142930-9 pa

LC 2007-26011

During one of her daily visits across town to visit her dying grandfather, fifteen-year-old Rosie discovers a dance studio that helps her find a way to bring her family members together.

This is "distinguished more by its sharp, eloquent prose than by its plot. . . . Poetically expressed memories and moving dialogue both anchor and amplify the characters' emotions." Publ Wkly

Nothing but ghosts. HarperTeen 2009 278p $17.95
Grades: 8 9 10 11 12 **Fic**

1. Art -- Fiction 2. Mothers -- Fiction 3. Gardening -- Fiction 4. Bereavement -- Fiction 5. Loss (Psychology) -- Fiction

ISBN 978-0-06-166796-1; 0-06-166796-X

LC 2008-26024

After her mother's death, sixteen-year-old Katie copes with her grief by working in the garden of an old estate, where she becomes intrigued by the story of a reclusive millionaire, while her father, an art restorer, manages in his own way to come to terms with the death of his wife.

"Kephart's evocative writing and gentle resolution offer healing and hope as her characters come to terms with their losses." Publ Wkly

★ **Small** damages; Beth Kephart. Philomel Books 2012 304 p. $17.99
Grades: 10 11 12 **Fic**

1. Spain -- Fiction 2. Adoption -- Fiction 3. Teenage pregnancy -- Fiction 4. Cooking -- Fiction 5. Pregnancy -- Fiction 6. Ranch life -- Spain -- Fiction 7. Interpersonal relations -- Fiction

ISBN 0399257489; 9780399257483

LC 2011020947

As Beth Kephart's character is "provided by her mother with only the barest of details about a couple that wishes to adopt her baby, Kenzie finds herself an unofficial apprentice in the kitchen of the home of a successful bull breeder connected to the prospective adoptive parents. . . . Her initially strained relationship with terse Estela, the marvelous chef charged with her safekeeping, eventually melts into a mutual trust." (Kirkus Reviews)

Undercover. HarperTeen 2007 278p $16.99; lib bdg $17.89; pa $8.99
Grades: 8 9 10 11 12 **Fic**

1. School stories 2. Poetry -- Fiction 3. Family life -- Fiction

ISBN 978-0-06-123893-2; 0-06-123893-7; 978-0-06-123894-9 lib bdg; 0-06-123894-5 lib bdg; 978-0-06-123895-6 pa; 0-06-123895-3 pa

LC 2007-2981

High school sophomore Elisa is used to observing while going unnoticed except when classmates ask her to write love notes for them, but a teacher's recognition of her talent, a "client's" desire for her friendship, a love of ice skating, and her parent's marital problems draw her out of herself.

"Kephart tells a moving story. . . . Readers will fall easily into the compelling premise and Elisa's memorable, graceful voice." Booklist

You are my only; a novel. Egmont USA 2011 240p $16.99
Grades: 7 8 9 10 **Fic**

1. Kidnapping -- Fiction 2. Home schooling -- Fiction 3. Mother-daughter relationship -- Fiction

ISBN 978-1-60684-272-0; 1-60684-272-2

LC 2010052662

Tells, in their separate voices and at a space of fourteen years, of Emmy, whose baby has been stolen, and Sophie, a teenager who defies her nomadic, controlling mother by making friends with a neighbor boy and his elderly aunts.

This is "a psychologically taut novel. . . . Succinct, emotionally packed chapters capture similarities between mother and daughter, the depth of their despair, their common desire to be free, and their poetic vision of the world." Publ Wkly

Keplinger, Kody

A **midsummer's** nightmare; a novel. by Kody Keplinger. Poppy 2012 291 p. $17.99
Grades: 9 10 11 12 **Fic**

1. Young adult literature 2. Family life 3. Stepfamilies 4. Illinois -- Fiction 5. Remarriage -- Fiction 6. Conduct of life -- Fiction 7. Family problems -- Fiction 8. Fathers and daughters -- Fiction

ISBN 0316084220; 9780316084222

LC 2011026949

This young adult novel by Kody Keplinger tells how "Whitley Johnson's dream summer with her divorce dad has turned into a nightmare. She's just met his new fiancee and her kids. . . . Worse, she totally doesn't fit in with her dad's perfect new country-club family. So Whitley acts out. . . . It will take all [of her friends and step family] to help Whitley get through her anger and begin to put the pieces of her [life] together." (Publisher's note)

Kerbel, Deborah

Mackenzie, lost and found. Dundurn Press 2008 251p pa $12.99
Grades: 7 8 9 10 **Fic**

1. Jerusalem -- Fiction 2. Culture conflict -- Fiction

ISBN 978-1-55002-852-2; 1-55002-852-9

"Fifteen-year-old Mackenzie is uprooted from her native Canada and forced to move to Israel when her archaeologist father takes a visiting professorship at The Hebrew University of Jerusalem. . . . She soon begins to make friends and learn the language, while engaging in a forbidden romance with a Palestinian boy named Nasir. When Mack finds herself in the middle of a plot involving stolen antiquities after Nasir's father enlists his help in illegally digging up and selling artifacts, she must choose between protecting her first real boyfriend and obeying the law. . . . This solid coming-of-age story offers a unique setting and a likeable young heroine." Voice Youth Advocates

Kerr, M. E.

Gentlehands. Harper & Row 1978 183p hardcover o.p. pa $5.99

Grades: 7 8 9 10 **Fic**

1. Criminals -- Fiction 2. Grandfathers -- Fiction 3. Social classes -- Fiction

ISBN 978-0-06-447067-4 pa; 0-06-447067-9 pa

LC 77-11860

ALA YALSA Margaret A. Edwards Award (1993)

"Buddy Boyle falls for Skye and her affluent, breezy way of life. Finding his own parents not 'cultured' enough for this new relationship, Buddy turns to his grandfather, whose love of opera and other refinements make him more suitable to make Skye's acquaintance. A shocking surprise awaits Buddy when Mr. DeLucca, pursuer of an infamous Nazi, finally identifies his quarry." Shapiro. Fic for youth. 3rd edition

If I love you, am I trapped forever? Marshall Cavendish 2008 178p $16.99

Grades: 8 9 10 11 12 **Fic**

1. School stories 2. Newspapers -- Fiction 3. Dating (Social customs) -- Fiction 4. Father-son relationship -- Fiction

ISBN 978-0-7614-5545-5

LC 2007051768

A reissue of the title first published 1973 by Harper & Row

Alan, a popular senior high school student, faces painful changes after a new student, Duncan "Doomed" Stein, comes to town and starts an influential underground newspaper.

"Extremely humorous at times, the story is also occasionally touched with sadness and poignancy." Horn Book Guide

Kessler, Jackie

Loss; Jackie Morse Kessler. Graphia 2012 258 p. pa $8.99

Grades: 8 9 10 11 12 **Fic**

1. Fantasy fiction 2. Plague -- Fiction 3. Bullies -- Fiction 4. Apocalyptic fiction 5. Schools -- Fiction 6. Diseases -- Fiction 7. Self-esteem -- Fiction 8. Time travel -- Fiction 9. High schools -- Fiction 10. Four Horsemen of the Apocalypse -- Fiction

ISBN 0547712154; 9780547712154

LC 2011031490

This young adult novel is part of Jackie Morse Kessler's Riders of the Apocalypse

series in which "[f]ifteen-year-old Billy Ballard is the kid that everyone picks on. But things change drastically when Death tells Billy he must stand in as Pestilence, the White Rider of the Apocalypse. Now armed with a Bow that allows him to strike with disease from a distance, Billy lashes out at his tormentors . . . and accidentally causes an outbreak of meningitis. Horrified by his actions, Billy begs Death to take back the Bow. For that to happen, says Death, Billy must track down the real White Rider, and stop him from unleashing something awful on humanity . . . that could make the Black Plague look like a summer cold. Does one bullied teenager have the strength to stand his ground—and the courage to save the world?" (Publisher's note)

Kessler, Jackie Morse

Breath; Jackie Morse Kessler. Graphia 2013 336 p. (paperback) $8.99

Grades: 8 9 10 11 12 **Fic**

1. Death -- Fiction 2. Depression (Psychology) -- Fiction 3. Four Horsemen of the Apocalypse -- Fiction

ISBN 0547970439; 9780547970431

LC 2012023509

In this book by Jackie Morse Kessler, "the fourth and final title in the 'Riders of the Apocalypse' series, Death is suicidal. Because his soul mate did not follow him into the world of sadness and dying, the Grim Reaper has decided to end it all, a decision that will mean the end of humanity. Fortunately, he doesn't consider the fact that high-school senior Xander Atwood, although similarly depressed, might worm his way into Death's heart and provide insight that could change his mind." (Booklist)

"Kessler once again highlights a common teen affliction, this time depression, in her allegory of hopelessness turned to hope. . . . The series is a strong and unique attempt to encourage troubled teens to consider their options and accept the help they need, while exposing all readers to the pain their friends may be experiencing." Booklist

Khoury, Jessica

Origin; Jessica Khoury. Razorbill 2012 393 p. $17.99

Grades: 6 7 8 **Fic**

1. Science fiction 2. Immortality -- Fiction 3. Science -- Experiments -- Fiction 4. Rain forests -- Fiction 5. Indigenous peoples -- Fiction

ISBN 1595145958; 9781595145956

LC 2012014447

In this young adult novel by Jessica Khoury "Pia has grown up in a secret laboratory hidden deep in the Amazon rainforest. She was raised by a team of scientists who have created her to be the start of a new immortal race. But on the night of her seventeenth birthday . . . and sneaks outside the compound for the first time in her life . . . Pia meets Eio, a boy from a nearby village. Together, they embark on a race against time to discover the truth about Pia's origin." (Publisher's note)

Kiely, Brendan

★ The **gospel** of winter; Brendan Kiely. Simon & Schuster 2014 304 p. $17.99

Grades: 9 10 11 12 **Fic**

1. Priests -- Fiction 2. Child sexual abuse -- Fiction

ISBN 1442484896; 9781442484894

Kiely's gutsy debut addresses abuse in the Catholic Church. The year is 2001, the events of 9/11 are only two months old, and 16-year-old Aidan's family is falling apart. Aidan finds comfort in snorting lines of Adderall, swiping drinks from his father's wet bar, and forming a friendship with Father Greg of Most Precious Blood, the town's Catholic church. The scandal among the Boston archdiocese in early 2002 gets Aidan's town's attention, and when it does, Aidan's feelings of rage and denial and fear come to a head. This is challenging, thought-provoking material, presented in beautiful prose that explores the ways in which acts rendered in the name of love can both destroy and heal." (Booklist)

Kiem, Elizabeth

Dancer, daughter, traitor, spy; by Elizabeth Kiem. Soho Teen 2013 288 p. (alk. paper) $17.99

Grades: 9 10 11 12 **Fic**

1. Clairvoyance -- Fiction 2. Russian Americans -- Fiction 3. Soviet Union -- Foreign relations -- United States -- Fiction 4. Spies -- Fiction 5. Soviet Union -- Relations -- United States -- Fiction 6. United States -- Relations -- Soviet Union -- Fiction 7. Brooklyn (New York, N.Y.) -- History -- 20th century -- Fiction

ISBN 1616952636; 9781616952631

LC 2013006502

This book by Elizabeth Kiem is set in "the 'Russia by the Sea' neighborhood of Brighton Beach, Brooklyn. Marina and her father escape there following the State Psychiatric Directorate's institutionalization of her mother, Sveta, a celebrated Bolshoi dancer, who had a vision of a terrible past event the regime must keep hidden. . . . Marina and her father cannot shake the suspicion and danger Sveta's vision put them under." (Publishers Weekly)

"The disappearance of a star ballerina in Soviet Russia shatters the life of her daughter. Bright, 17-year-old Marya is the daughter of the Bolshoi's star ballerina and her scientist husband, and she's a dancer herself...The pacing is somewhat uneven, but there are enough twists to surprise and engage readers to the end. A compelling portrait of a young woman on the verge of adulthood, caught up in the domestic secrets of her parents and the enmity of two countries." (Kirkus)

Kinch, Michael

The **fires** of New SUN; a Blending time novel. Michael Kinch. Flux 2012 275 p. (Blending time) $9.95

Grades: 9 10 11 12 **Fic**

1. Africa -- Fiction 2. Dystopian fiction 3. Deserts -- Fiction 4. Science fiction 5. Survival -- Fiction 6. Violence -- Fiction 7. Friendship -- Fiction

ISBN 0738730769; 9780738730769

LC 2011035527

This dystopian thriller novel, by Michael Kinch, is set "in the harsh African desert. . . . Jaym and D'Shay . . . have helped dozens of Nswibe refugees cross the African desert. . . . They've finally reunited with their friend, Reya, and found safe haven at a New SUN outpost, a cavern fortress hidden in the Blue Mountains. But their troubles are just beginning. . . . As a massive [renegade] attack looms, the three friends are quickly drawn into a deadly battle." (Publisher's note)

The **rebels** of New SUN; a Blending time novel. Michael Kinch. Flux 2013 288 p. (Blending time) $9.99

Grades: 9 10 11 12 **Fic**

1. Africa -- Fiction 2. Dystopian fiction 3. Deserts -- Fiction 4. Science fiction 5. Survival -- Fiction 6. Violence -- Fiction 7. Friendship -- Fiction

ISBN 073873151X; 9780738731513

LC 2012028409

This dystopian thriller novel, by Michael Kinch, is book three of the "Blending Time" series. "Before the 'gades secure the savannah and wipe out the New SUN resistance, Reya, D'Shay, Jaym, and a handful of other rebels launch a daring mission to infiltrate . . . Chewena's capital city. . . . To free the country from GlobeTran's . . . control, they seek out allies and information that could help the resistance . . . return power to the people of Africa." (Publisher's note)

Kinch, Michael P.

The **blending** time; [by] Michael Kinch. Flux 2010 254p pa $9.95

Grades: 10 11 12 **Fic**

1. Science fiction 2. Africa -- Fiction 3. Violence -- Fiction

ISBN 978-0-7387-2067-8

LC 2010-24149

In the harsh world of 2069, ravaged by plagues and environmental disasters, friends Jaym, Reya, and D'Shay are chosen to help repopulate Africa as their mandatory Global Alliance work, but civil war and mercenaries opposed to the Blending Program separate them and threaten their very lives.

"Determinedly multiethnic, fast-paced, and with plentiful gore and violence, the book will draw reluctant readers who enjoy action and adventure." Booklist

Kincy, Karen

Other. Flux 2010 326p pa $9.95

Grades: 9 10 11 12 **Fic**

1. Homicide -- Fiction 2. Supernatural -- Fiction 3. Self-acceptance -- Fiction 4. Washington (State) -- Fiction

ISBN 978-0-7387-1919-1

LC 2010-5297

Gwen Williams is like any seventeen-year-old except that she is a shapeshifter living in Klikamuks, Washington, where not everyone tolerates "Others" like Gwen, but when someone begins killing Others she must try to embrace her true self and find the killer before she becomes the next victim.

"The emotional turmoil of the characters is evident and will appeal to readers who have felt misunderstood or as if they don't belong—teenagers." SLJ

Kindl, Patrice

Keeping the castle; a tale of romance, riches, and real estate. by Patrice Kindl. Viking Childrens Books 2012 261 p. $16.99; (hardcover) $16.99

Grades: 7 8 9 10 11 **Fic**

1. Love stories 2. Regency novels 3. Marriage -- Fiction 4. Castles -- Fiction 5. Courtship -- Fiction 6. Social classes -- Fiction 7. Great Britain -- History -- 1789-1820 -- Fiction 8. England -- Social life and customs -- 19th century -- Fiction

ISBN 0670014389; 9780670014385

LC 2011033185

In this book, "[s]eventeen-year-old Althea Crawley is . . . on a quest to marry rich so that she may secure the family's only inheritance, a dilapidated castle on the edge of the North Sea. . . . Marriage prospects in tiny Lesser Hoo are slim, to say the least, until dashing and wealthy Lord Boring arrives on the scene. Matters are further complicated by a revolving cast of potential suitors, including Lord Boring's cousin, Mr. Fredericks." (Booklist)

King, A. S.

★ **Ask** the passengers; a novel. by A.S. King. Little, Brown 2012 304 p. (hardcover) $17.99

Grades: 9 10 11 12 **Fic**

1. Moving -- Fiction 2. Identity -- Fiction 3. Love stories 4. Love -- Fiction 5. Gossip -- Fiction 6. Schools -- Fiction 7. Lesbians -- Fiction 8. Prejudices -- Fiction 9. High schools -- Fiction 10. Family problems -- Fiction

ISBN 0316194689; 9780316194686

LC 2011053207

This book by A.S. King follows teenage protagonist Astrid, "her closeted BFF, Kristina, and Dee, a star hockey player she met while working for a local catering company. Sparks fly between Astrid and Dee, causing Astrid to feel even more distanced and confused. . . . She's in love with Dee, but she's not sure if she's a lesbian. She's ignoring all of the labels and focusing on what she feels." (Kirkus Reviews)

★ **Everybody** sees the ants; by A.S. King. Little, Brown 2011 282p. $17.99; ebook $9.99

Grades: 9 10 11 12 **Fic**

1. Family -- Fiction 2. Domestic relations 3. Teenagers -- Fiction 4. Dreams -- Fiction 5. Arizona -- Fiction 6. Bullies -- Fiction 7. Family life -- Fiction 8. Grandfathers -- Fiction 9. Missing persons -- Fiction 10. Vietnam War, 1961-1975 -- Fiction

ISBN 978-0-316-12928-2; 978-0-316-19181-4 ebook; 9780316129275

LC 2010049434

Overburdened by his parents' bickering and a bully's attacks, fifteen-year-old Lucky Linderman begins dreaming of being with his grandfather, who went missing during the Vietnam War, but during a visit to Arizona, his aunt and uncle and their beautiful neighbor, Ginny, help him find a new perspective.

"Blending magic and realism, this is a subtly written, profoundly honest novel about a kid falling through the cracks and pulling himself back up." Booklist

★ **Glory** O'Brien's history of the future: a novel; by A.S. King; Little, Brown & Co. 2014 306p $18.00

Grades: 9 10 11 12 **Fic**

1. Best friends -- Fiction 2. Clairvoyance -- Fiction 3. Eccentrics and eccentricities -- Fiction 4. Father-daughter relationship -- Fiction 5. Friendship -- Fiction 6. Photography -- Fiction 7. Suicide -- Fiction

ISBN: 0316222720; 9780316222723

LC 2013041670

In this novel, the main character Gloria "begins to experience an astonishing new power to see a person's infinite past and future. From ancient ancestors to many generations forward, Glory is bombarded with visions--and what she sees ahead of her is terrifying. . . . Glory makes it her mission to record everything she sees, hoping her notes will somehow make a difference. . . . She may not see a future for herself, but she'll do anything to make sure this one doesn't come to pass." (Publisher's note)

"Imbuing Glory's narrative with a graceful, sometimes dissonant combination of anger, ambivalence, and hopefulness that resists tidy resolution, award-winning King presents another powerful, moving, and compellingly complex coming-of-age story." Booklist

★ **Please** ignore Vera Dietz. Alfred A. Knopf 2010 326p $16.99; lib bdg $19.99; ebook $16.99

Grades: 9 10 11 12 **Fic**

1. Death -- Fiction 2. Friendship -- Fiction

ISBN 978-0-375-86586-2; 978-0-375-96586-9 lib bdg; 978-0-375-89617-0 ebook

LC 2010-12730

A Michael L. Printz honor book, 2011

When her best friend, whom she secretly loves, betrays her and then dies under mysterious circumstances, high school senior Vera Dietz struggles with secrets that could help clear his name.

This "is a gut-wrenching tale about family, friendship, destiny, the meaning of words, and self-discovery." Voice Youth Advocates

★ **Reality** Boy; A.S. King. Little, Brown and Co. 2013 368 p. $18

Grades: 10 11 12 **Fic**

1. Special education -- Fiction 2. Reality television programs -- Fiction 3. Fame -- Fiction 4. Family problems -- Fiction 5. Emotional problems -- Fiction 6. Dating (Social customs) -- Fiction 7. Self-actualization (Psychology) -- Fiction

ISBN 0316222704; 9780316222709

LC 2012048432

Author A. S. King's book looks at "a boy saddled with the nickname the Crapper because of his infamous behavior at age five on a reality show, Network Nanny. Now almost 17, Gerald Faust is ostracized by his peers, barely keeping his violent urges at bay, and grateful for his spot in special ed because" it is a safe place for him. Although "the Network Nanny episodes about Gerald's family framed him as the problem child among his siblings, the truth was more disturbing, as King shows in flashbacks." (Publishers Weekly)

"When Gerald was five, TV's Network Nanny came to his house to help solve his behavior problems. Now nearly seventeen, Gerald bears the emotional scars of having his deeply dysfunctional childhood nationally televised. When Gerald meets Hannah, he discovers he's not the only one with a messed-up family. As always, King's societal critique is spot-on and scathing." (Horn Book)

Kirby, Jessi

Golden; Jessi Kirby. 1st ed. Simon & Schuster Books for Young Readers 2013 288 p. (hardcover) $16.99

Grades: 7 8 9 10 11 12 **Fic**

1. Love stories 2. Mystery fiction 3. Diaries -- Fiction 4. Love -- Fiction 5. Choice -- Fiction 6. Family

problems -- Fiction 7. Mothers and daughters -- Fiction
ISBN 1442452161; 9781442452169; 9781442452183; 9781442452251

LC 2012042216

In this novel, by Jessi Kirby, "seventeen-year-old Parker Frost has never taken the road less traveled. . . . Julianna Farnetti and Shane Cruz are remembered as the golden couple of Summit Lakes High . . . but Julianna's journal tells . . . . the secrets that were swept away with her the night that Shane's jeep plunged into an icy river. . . . Reading Julianna's journal gives Parker . . . reasons to question what really happened the night of the accident." (Publisher's note)

"Kirby's . . . third novel is inspirational and contemplative in its mood and tone. Multifaceted characters and dashes of mystery and romance come together in a successful mediation on the value of taking an active role in one's life." Pub Wkly

Moonglass. Simon & Schuster Books for Young Readers 2011 232p $16.99; ebook $9.99

Grades: 8 9 10 11 12 **Fic**

1. Guilt -- Fiction 2. Moving -- Fiction 3. Beaches -- Fiction 4. Suicide -- Fiction 5. California -- Fiction 6. Father-daughter relationship -- Fiction
ISBN 978-1-4424-1694-9; 1-4424-1694-7; 978-1-4424-1696-3 ebook; 1-4424-1696-3 ebook

LC 2010-37389

At age seven, Anna watched her mother walk into the surf and drown, but nine years later, when she moves with her father to the beach where her parents fell in love, she joins the cross-country team, makes new friends, and faces her guilt.

"Kirby creates a cast of sympathetic and credible characters, each imperfect but well intentioned. There's action as well as introspection here." Booklist

Kirkpatrick, Katherine

Between two worlds; by Katherine Kirkpatrick. Wendy Lamb Books. 2014 304p $16.99

Grades: 10 11 12 **Fic**

1. Eskimos -- Fiction 2. Inuit -- Fiction 3. Race relations -- Fiction 4. Peary, Robert E. (Robert Edwin), 1856-1920 -- Fiction 5. Arctic regions -- Exploration -- Fiction
ISBN: 0385740476; 9780375872211; 9780375989476; 9780385740470

LC 2013014735

"In 1900, sixteen-year-old Greenland Inuit girl Billy Bah sets out to rescue Lieutenant Peary, his ship stuck in the ice during a polar expedition. Though torn between cultures, having spent a year with Peary's family in America, Billy Bah ultimately feels she must risk her life to find him. A compelling tale with enthralling details of the stark, beautiful Greenland landscape." Horn Book Guide

Kittle, Katrina

Reasons to be happy. Sourcebooks Jabberwocky 2011 281p pa $7.99

Grades: 7 8 9 10 **Fic**

1. School stories 2. Bulimia -- Fiction 3. Popularity -- Fiction 4. Bereavement -- Fiction 5. Personal appearance -- Fiction
ISBN 978-1-4022-6020-9; 1-4022-6020-2

LC 2011020276

Eighth-grader Hannah Carlisle feels unattractive compared to her movie star parents and cliquish Beverly Hills classmates, and when her mother's cancer worsens and her father starts drinking heavily, Hannah's grief and anger turn into bulimia, which only her aunt, a documentary filmmaker, understands.

"Hannah's believability as a character as well as the realistic, painful depiction of bulimia make this a standout." Booklist

Kittredge, Caitlin

The **Iron** Thorn. Delacorte Press 2011 493p (Iron Codex) $17.99; lib bdg $20.99

Grades: 7 8 9 10 **Fic**

1. Fantasy fiction
ISBN 0-385-73829-3; 0-385-90720-6 lib bdg; 978-0-385-73829-3; 978-0-385-90720-0 lib bdg

LC 2010-00972

In an alternate 1950s, mechanically gifted fifteen-year-old Aoife Grayson, whose family has a history of going mad at sixteen, must leave the totalitarian city of Lovecraft and venture into the world of magic to solve the mystery of her brother's disappearance and the mysteries surrounding her father and the Land of Thorn.

"Steampunk fans will delight in this first title in the sure-to-be-popular Iron Codex series. . . . There's plenty of tame but satisfying romance, too, and plot twists galore. Aoife is a caustic-tongued, feisty, and independent young woman, with plenty of nerve and courage." Booklist

The **nightmare** garden; Caitlin Kittredge. Delacorte Press 2012 417 p. (The iron codex) (hardback) $17.99

Grades: 7 8 9 10 **Fic**

1. Fantasy fiction 2. Adventure fiction 3. Steampunk fiction 4. Metaphysics -- Fiction 5. Voyages and travels -- Fiction 6. Fantasy 7. Magic -- Fiction
ISBN 9780375985690; 9780385738316; 9780385907217

LC 2011038306

Sequel to: The Iron Thorn.

This book is the second novel in Caitlin Kittredge's 'Iron Codex' series. "Spoiled, inconsistent, often-thoughtless heroine Aoife Grayson nearly destroyed the world when she broke the Lovecraft Engine and sundered the gates between the worlds of human and Fae. But she's not going to let a little thing like that stop her, so she sets off on an exhausting, somewhat episodic adventure through the steampunk-horror '50s nightmare that is her world . . . . The ending promises even bigger adventures to come." (Kirkus)

Kizer, Amber

A **matter** of days; Amber Kizer. 1st ed. Delacorte Press 2013 288 p. (ebook) $50.97; (hardcover) $16.99; (library) $19.99

Grades: 7 8 9 10 **Fic**

1. Apocalyptic fiction 2. Voyages and travels 3. Science fiction 4. Survival -- Fiction 5. Epidemics -- Fiction 6. Virus diseases -- Fiction 7. Brothers and

sisters -- Fiction
ISBN 0385908040; 9780375898259; 9780385739733; 9780385908047
LC 2012012200

In this book, "Nadia and Rabbit's military doctor uncle, Bean, visited them and insisted on injecting them with a vaccine for a 'new bug.' Not long afterward, the disease XRD TB . . . starts ravaging the world, and 16-year-old Nadia and 11-year-old Rabbit are the only survivors in their entire town. With the assorted survival gear their uncle ordered for them, they attempt to make their way from their Seattle suburb to their grandfather in West Virginia." (Publishers Weekly)

"This post-apocalyptic tale is particularly frightening as it doesn't take place in some distant, imagined future. A solid, realistically imagined survival tale with a strong female protagonist." Kirkus

Meridian. Delacorte Press 2009 305p $16.99; lib bdg $19.99
Grades: 7 8 9 10 **Fic**
1. Death -- Fiction 2. Angels -- Fiction 3. Colorado -- Fiction 4. Supernatural -- Fiction 5. Good and evil -- Fiction
ISBN 978-0-385-73668-8; 0-385-73668-1; 978-0-385-90621-0 lib bdg; 0-385-90621-8 lib bdg
LC 2008-35666

On her sixteenth birthday, Meridian is whisked off to her great-aunt's home in Revelation, Colorado, where she learns that she is a Fenestra, the half-human, half-angel link between the living and the dead, and must learn to help human souls to the afterlife before the dark forces reach them.

"The author brings a fresh voice to the realm of teen paranormal romantic fiction. . . . The characters are compelling and the themes of good and evil, life and death will keep readers engaged." SLJ

Followed by: Wildcat fireflies (2011)

Wildcat fireflies. Delacorte Press 2011 508p $16.99
Grades: 7 8 9 10 **Fic**
1. Death -- Fiction 2. Angels -- Fiction 3. Supernatural -- Fiction 4. Good and evil -- Fiction
ISBN 978-0-385-73971-9; 0-385-73971-0
LC 2010-30405

Sequel to: Meridian (2010)

Teenaged Meridian Sozu, a half-human, half-angel link between the living and the dead known as a Fenestra, hits the road with Tens, her love and sworn protector, in hopes of finding another person with Meridian's ability to help souls transition safely into the afterlife.

"Some of the day-to-day events may be hard to believe, but this is a book about angels and demons after all; fans will forgive." Kirkus

Klass, David

Firestorm. Frances Foster Books 2006 289p (The Caretaker trilogy) $17
Grades: 8 9 10 11 12 **Fic**
1. Science fiction
ISBN 0-374-32307-0
LC 2005-52112

After learning that he has been sent from the future for a special purpose, eighteen-year-old Jack receives help from an unusual dog and a shape-shifting female fighter.

"The sobering events and tone are leavened with engaging humor, and the characters are multidimensional. The relentless pace, coupled with issues of ecology, time travel, self-identity, and sexual awakening, makes for a thrilling and memorable read." SLJ

Other books in the Caretaker Trilogy are:
Whirlwind (2008)
Timelock (2009)

★ **You** don't know me; a novel. Foster Bks. 2001 262p $17
Grades: 7 8 9 10 **Fic**
1. School stories 2. Child abuse -- Fiction
ISBN 0-374-38706-0
LC 00-22709

Fourteen-year-old John creates alternative realities in his mind as he tries to deal with his mother's abusive boyfriend, his crush on a beautiful, but shallow classmate and other problems at school

"Klass is effective with John's deliberately distanced voice, his constant dancing with and away from reality, . . . and his brittle and even dorky defenses, and the rising tension is suspenseful." Bull Cent Child Books

Klass, Sheila Solomon

Soldier's secret; the story of Deborah Sampson. Henry Holt 2009 215p $17.95
Grades: 6 7 8 9 10 **Fic**
1. Soldiers 2. Memoirists 3. Soldiers -- Fiction 4. United States -- History -- 1775-1783, Revolution -- Fiction
ISBN 978-0-8050-8200-5; 0-8050-8200-X
LC 2008-36783

During the Revolutionary War, a young woman named Deborah Sampson disguises herself as a man in order to serve in the Continental Army.

In this novel, Sampson "is strong, brave, and witty. . . . Klass doesn't shy away from the horrors of battle; she also is blunt regarding details young readers will wonder about, like how Sampson dealt with bathing, urination, and menstruation. . . . Sampson's romantic yearnings for a fellow soldier . . . is given just the right notes or restraint and realism." Booklist

Klause, Annette Curtis

★ **Blood** and chocolate. Delacorte Press 1997 264p hardcover o.p. pa $6.50
Grades: 7 8 9 10 **Fic**
1. Horror fiction 2. Werewolves -- Fiction
ISBN 0-385-32305-0; 0-440-22668-6 pa
LC 96-35247

Having fallen for a human boy, a beautiful teenage werewolf must battle both her packmates and the fear of the townspeople to decide where she belongs and with whom

"Klause's imagery is magnetic, and her language fierce, rich, and beautiful. . . . Passion and philosophy dovetail superbly in this powerful, unforgettable novel for mature teens." Booklist

★ **The silver** kiss. Delacorte Press 1990 198p hardcover o.p. pa $5.99
Grades: 8 9 10 11 12 **Fic**
1. Death -- Fiction 2. Vampires -- Fiction
ISBN 0-385-30160-X; 0-440-21346-0 pa
LC 89-48880

"One evening, when 17-year-old Zoë is sitting in the park contemplating her mother's imminent death due to cancer, her father's lack of support, and her best friend's move, she meets Simon. Simon is startlingly handsome and strangely compelling. As their friendship grows over time, Simon reveals to Zoë his true identity: he is a vampire, trying to kill his younger vampire brother." SLJ

"There's inherent romantic appeal in the vampire legend, and Klause weaves all the gory details into a poignant love story that becomes both sensuous and suspenseful." Booklist

Klein, Lisa M.

Cate of the Lost Colony; by Lisa Klein. Bloomsbury 2010 329p $16.99
Grades: 8 9 10 11 12 **Fic**
1. Poets 2. Queens 3. Authors 4. Explorers 5. Historians 6. Courtiers 7. Travel writers 8. Orphans -- Fiction 9. Lumbee Indians -- Fiction 10. Roanoke Island (N.C.) -- History -- Fiction
ISBN 978-1-59990-507-5; 1-59990-507-8
LC 2010-8299

When her dalliance with Sir Walter Ralegh is discovered by Queen Elizabeth in 1587, lady-in-waiting Catherine Archer is banished to the struggling colony of Roanoke, where she and the other English settlers must rely on a Croatoan Indian for their survival. Includes author's note on the mystery surrounding the Lost Colony.

"This robust, convincing portrait of the Elizabethan world with complex, rounded characters wraps an intriguingly plausible solution to the 'lost colony' mystery inside a compelling love story of subtle thematic depth." Kirkus

Includes bibliographical references

Lady Macbeth's daughter. Bloomsbury 2009 291p $16.99
Grades: 7 8 9 10 **Fic**
1. Poets 2. Authors 3. Dramatists 4. Kings 5. Homicide -- Fiction 6. Scotland -- Fiction 7. Witchcraft -- Fiction 8. Kings and rulers -- Fiction 9. People with physical disabilities -- Fiction
ISBN 978-1-59990-347-7; 1-59990-347-4
LC 2009-6717

In alternating chapters, ambitious Lady Macbeth tries to bear a son and win the throne of Scotland for her husband, and Albia, their daughter who was banished at birth and raised by three weird sisters, falls in love, learns of her parentage, and seeks to free Scotland from tyranny in this tale based on Shakespeare's Macbeth.

"The writing is crisp and clear and makes good use of Shakespeare's language and its times. The characters are well-developed and the story being told from the perspective of the mother and daughter makes for age-old conflict. This tale will keep readers asking the ultimate question of whether or not power is ultimately worth the price." Libr Media Connect

Ophelia. Bloomsbury Children's Books 2006 328p $16.95
Grades: 9 10 11 12 **Fic**
1. Poets 2. Authors 3. Dramatists 4. Princes -- Fiction 5. Homicide -- Fiction
ISBN 978-1-58234-801-8; 1-58234-801-4
LC 2005-32601

In a story based on Shakespeare's Hamlet, Ophelia tells of her life in the court at Elsinore, her love for Prince Hamlet, and her escape from the violence in Denmark.

"Teens need not be familiar with Shakespeare's original to enjoy this fresh take—with the added romance and a strong heroine at its center." Publ Wkly

Kluger, Steve

My most excellent year; a novel of love, Mary Poppins, & Fenway Park. Dial Books 2008 403p $16.99; pa $8.99
Grades: 8 9 10 11 12 **Fic**
1. Friendship -- Fiction 2. Boston (Mass.) -- Fiction
ISBN 978-0-8037-3227-8; 0-8037-3227-9; 978-0-14-241343-2 pa; 0-14-2413437 pa
LC 2007-26651

"Three bright and funny Brookline, MA, eleventh graders look back on their most excellent year—ninth grade—for a school report. Told in alternating chapters by each of them, this enchanting, life-affirming coming-of-age story unfolds through instant messages, emails, memos, diary entries, and letters. . . . This is a rich and humorous novel for older readers." SLJ

Knight, Karsten

Embers & echoes; Karsten Knight. Simon & Schuster Books for Young Readers 2012 480 p. (hardcover) $16.99
Grades: 9 10 11 12 **Fic**
1. Occult fiction 2. Sisters -- Fiction 3. Teenagers -- Fiction 4. Gods -- Fiction 5. Goddesses -- Fiction 6. Tricksters -- Fiction 7. Miami (Fla.) -- Fiction 8. Supernatural -- Fiction
ISBN 1442450304; 9781442450301
LC 2011046357

In this young adult fantasy novel, "high school sophomore and reincarnated volcano goddess Ashline heads off to Miami, following a vision of her missing younger sister. There, she teams up with an Aztec night god and a Roman dawn goddess to thwart a villainous millionaire and her sadistic henchgods, rescue her other sister from a netherworldly dimension, and keep the loves and lies of her past incarnations from leaking into this one." (Kirkus)

Knowles, Jo

Jumping off swings; [by] Jo Knowles. Candlewick Press 2009 230p $16.99
Grades: 10 11 12 **Fic**
1. Pregnancy -- Fiction
ISBN 0-7636-3949-4; 978-0-7636-3949-5
LC 2009-4587

When Josh 'leads Ellie to the back seat of his van after a party, Ellie gets pregnant and Josh reacts with shame and heartbreak, while their confidantes, Caleb and Corinne grapple with their own complex emotions." (Publisher's note) "Grades seven to ten." (Bull Cent Child Books)

"With so many protagonists in the mix, it is no small feat that each character is fully developed and multidimensional—there are no villains or heroes here, only kids groping their way through a desperate situation. . . . [This is] a moving tale with a realistically unresolved ending." Kirkus

★ **Living** with Jackie Chan; by Jo Knowles. Candlewick Press 2013 384 p. $16.99
Grades: 10 11 12 Fic
1. Teenage fathers 2. Guilt -- Fiction 3. Uncles -- Fiction
ISBN 0763662801; 9780763662806
LC 2012955157

"Overcome with guilt after getting Ellie pregnant (Jumping Off Swings), Josh moves in with his karate-obsessed, incessantly cheerful uncle. He starts senior year at a new school, attends his uncle's karate classes, and makes a new friend-who-might-be-more. Josh is a sensitive guy whose pain is palpable; readers will root for him as he--slowly--conquers the demons of his past." (Horn Book)

See you at Harry's; Jo Knowles. 1st ed. Candlewick Press 2012 310 p. $16.99
Grades: 6 7 8 9 10 11 Fic
1. Siblings -- Fiction 2. Bereavement -- Fiction 3. Restaurants -- Fiction 4. Gay teenagers -- Fiction 5. Family 6. Grief -- Fiction 7. Family life -- Fiction 8. Homosexuality -- Fiction 9. Family problems -- Fiction 10. Brothers and sisters -- Fiction
ISBN 9780763654078
LC 2011018619

In this children's novel, "seventh grader Fern . . . relates the . . . tragedies of her family. Her high-school-freshman older brother Holden has come to the place in his life where he's acknowledged that he's gay. . . . Fern offers him support and love. . . . And then there's 3-year-old Charlie, always messy, often annoying, but deeply loved. Fern's busy, distracted parents leave all of the kids wanting for more attention--until a tragic accident tears the family apart." (Kirkus Reviews)

Knox, Elizabeth

Dreamhunter; book one of the Dreamhunter duet. Farrar, Straus & Giroux 2006 365p (Dreamhunter duet) $19; pa $8.99
Grades: 7 8 9 10 Fic
1. Fantasy fiction 2. Dreams -- Fiction
ISBN 0-374-31853-0; 0-312-53571-6 pa
LC 2005-46366

First published 2005 in the United Kingdom

In a world where select people can enter "The Place" and find dreams of every kind to share with others for a fee, a fifteen-year-old girl is training to be a dreamhunter when her father disappears, leaving her to carry on his mysterious mission. "Grades nine to twelve." (Bull Cent Child Books)

This first of a two-book series is "a highly original exploration of the idea of a collective unconscious, mixed with imagery from the raising of Lazarus and with the brave, dark qualities of the psyche of an adolescent female." Horn Book Guide

Followed by Dreamquake (2007)

Dreamquake; book two of the Dreamhunter duet. Farrar, Straus & Giroux 2007 449p map (Dreamhunter duet) $19
Grades: 7 8 9 10 Fic
1. Fantasy fiction 2. Dreams -- Fiction
ISBN 978-0-374-31854-3; 0-374-31854-9
LC 2006-48109

Sequel to Dreamhunter

Michael L. Printz Award honor book, 2008

Aided by her family and her creation, Nown, Laura investigates the powerful Regulatory Body's involvement in mysterious disappearances and activities and learns, in the process, the true nature of the Place in which dreams are found.

The author's "haunting, invigorating storytelling will leave readers eager to return to its puzzles—and to reap its rewards." Booklist

Mortal fire; by Elizabeth Knox. 1st ed. Frances Foster Books 2013 448 p. (hardcover) $17.99
Grades: 7 8 9 10 11 Fic
1. Occult fiction 2. Fantasy fiction 3. Magic -- Fiction 4. Identity -- Fiction 5. Stepbrothers -- Fiction 6. Islands of the Pacific -- Fiction
ISBN 0374388296; 9780374388294
LC 2012040872

This novel, set in a fictional area of New Zealand, stars Canny, a "16-year-old Ma'eu, taciturn, antisocial, and exceptionally gifted in math." She has what she calls "Extra," an "ethereal script that Canny alone can see, attached to plants, buildings, or nothing at all." When she and friends "come upon a valley dense with the Extra, Canny realizes that there is more to her visions than her own oddness—there are people, the Zarenes, whose existence is interwoven with this magical language." (Publishers Weekly)

Knutsson, Catherine

Shadows cast by stars; Catherine Knutsson. 1st ed. Atheneum Books for Young Readers 2012 456 p. (hardcover) $17.99; (paperback) $9.99
Grades: 7 8 9 10 Fic
1. Blood 2. Science fiction 3. Plague -- Fiction 4. Twins -- Fiction 5. Spirits -- Fiction 6. Family life -- Fiction 7. Brothers and sisters -- Fiction 8. Indians of North America -- Fiction
ISBN 1442401915; 9781442401914; 9781442401938; 9781442401921
LC 2011038419

Author Catherine Knutsson tells the story of Native American Cassandra Mercredi. The "sixteen-year-old . . . [may] be immune to Plague, but that doesn't mean she's safe--government forces are searching for those of aboriginal heritage to harvest their blood. When a search threatens Cassandra and her family, they flee to the Island: a mysterious and idyllic territory protected by the Band, a group of guerilla warriors--and by an enigmatic energy barrier that keeps outsiders out and the spirit world in." (Publisher's note)

Koertge, Ronald

Lies, knives and girls in red dresses; Ron Koertge; illustrated by Andrea Dezso. Candlewick 2012 96 p. ill. (hardcover) $17.99

Grades: 9 10 11 **Fic**

1. Fairy tales 2. Orphans -- Fiction 3. Princesses -- Fiction 4. Novels in verse

ISBN 0763644064; 9780763644062

LC 2011047027

This illustrated poetry collection "retells 23 classic fairy tales in free verse, written from the perspectives of iconic characters like Little Red Riding Hood, as well as maligned or minor figures such as the Mole from Thumbelina and Cinderella's stepsisters. . . . Several stories trade happily ever after for disappointment and discontent, as with the danger-addicted queen in Rumpelstiltskin." (Publishers Weekly)

"The well-crafted poetry is firmly rooted in the experiences of regular teens and addresses subjects that range from breakups to baseball. . . . Appealing and accessible." Booklist

★ **Margaux** with an X; [by] Ron Koertge. Candlewick Press 2004 165p $15.99; pa $6.99

Grades: 7 8 9 10 **Fic**

1. Domestic violence -- Fiction

ISBN 0-7636-2401-2; 0-7636-2679-1 pa

LC 2003-65279

Margaux, known as a "tough chick" at her Los Angeles high school, makes a connection with Danny, who, like her, struggles with the emotional impact of family violence and abuse.

This book "excels in character development. It is an intriguing story that constantly provokes readers' curiosity. . . . [The author's] language at times is advanced, an accurate reflection of his characters' intellectual capacity." SLJ

Now playing; Stoner & Spaz II. [by] Ron Koertge. Candlewick Press 2011 208p $16.99

Grades: 8 9 10 11 12 **Fic**

1. School stories 2. Drug abuse -- Fiction 3. Cerebral palsy -- Fiction 4. Self-acceptance -- Fiction 5. Dating (Social customs) -- Fiction

ISBN 978-0-7636-5081-0; 0-7636-5081-1

LC 2010040151

Sequel to: Stoner & Spaz (2002)

High schooler Ben Bancroft, a budding filmmaker with cerebral palsy, struggles to understand his relationship with drug-addict Colleen while he explores a new friendship with A.J., who shares his obsession with movies and makes a good impression on Ben's grandmother.

"Koertge writes sharp dialogue and vivid scenes." Publ Wkly

★ **Shakespeare** makes the playoffs; [by] Ron Koertge. Candlewick Press 2010 170p lib bdg $15.99; pa $5.99

Grades: 6 7 8 9 **Fic**

1. Novels in verse 2. Poetry -- Fiction 3. Baseball -- Fiction

ISBN 978-0-7636-4435-2 lib bdg; 0-7636-4435-8 lib bdg; 978-0-7636-5852-6 pa

LC 2009-14519

Fourteen-year-old Kevin Boland, poet and first baseman, is torn between his cute girlfriend Mira and Amy, who is funny, plays Chopin on the piano, and is also a poet.

Stoner & Spaz; [by] Ron Koertge. Candlewick Press 2002 169p hardcover o.p. pa $6.99

Grades: 8 9 10 11 12 **Fic**

1. School stories 2. Cerebral palsy -- Fiction

ISBN 0-7636-1608-7; 0-7636-2150-1 pa

LC 2001-43050

A troubled youth with cerebral palsy struggles toward self-acceptance with the help of a drug-addicted young woman

"Funny, touching, and surprising, it is a hopeful yet realistic view of things as they are and as they could be." Booklist

Followed by: Now Playing: Stoner & Spaz II (2011)

★ **Strays;** [by] Ron Koertge. Candlewick Press 2007 167p $16.99

Grades: 7 8 9 10 11 12 **Fic**

1. Orphans -- Fiction 2. Foster home care -- Fiction

ISBN 978-0-7636-2705-8; 0-7636-2705-4

LC 2007-24096

After his parents are killed in a car accident, high school senior Sam wonders whether he will ever feel again or if he will remain numbed by grief.

"Though Koertge never soft pedals the horrors faced by some foster children, this thoughtful novel about the lost and abandoned is a hopeful one." Booklist

Koja, Kathe

Buddha boy. Speak 2004 117p pa $5.99

Grades: 7 8 9 10 **Fic**

1. School stories 2. Artists -- Fiction 3. Buddhism -- Fiction 4. Conduct of life -- Fiction

ISBN 0-14-240209-5

LC 2004041669

First published 2003 by Farrar, Straus & Giroux

Justin spends time with Jinsen, the unusual and artistic new student whom the school bullies torment and call Buddha Boy, and ends up making choices that impact Jinsen, himself, and the entire school.

"A compelling introduction to Buddhism and a credible portrait of how true friendship brings out the best in people." Publ Wkly

Headlong. Farrar, Straus and Giroux 2008 195p $16.95

Grades: 8 9 10 11 12 **Fic**

1. School stories 2. Orphans -- Fiction 3. Social classes -- Fiction

ISBN 978-0-374-32912-9; 0-374-32912-5

LC 2007-23612

High school sophomore Lily opens herself to new possibilities when, despite warnings, she becomes friends with 'ghetto girl' Hazel, a new student at the private Vaughn School which Lily, following in her elitist mother's footsteps, has attended since preschool.

"Class, identity and friendship are the intersecting subjects of this intelligent novel. . . . [The author] relays this story with her usual insight and, through her lightning-fast characterizations, an ability to project multiple perspectives simultaneously." Publ Wkly

Kissing the bee. Farrar, Straus and Giroux 2007 121p $16
Grades: 8 9 10 11 12 **Fic**

1. Love stories 2. School stories 3. Bees -- Fiction 4. Friendship -- Fiction
ISBN 978-0-374-39938-2; 0-374-39938-7
LC 2006-37378

While working on a bee project for her advanced biology class, quiet high school senior Dana reflects on her relationship with gorgeous best friend Avra and Avra's boyfriend Emil, whom Dana secretly loves.

The "understated, tightly focused language evokes vivid scenes and heady emotions." Publ Wkly

Konigsberg, Bill

★ **Openly** straight; Bill Konigsberg. Arthur A. Levine Books 2013 336 p. (hard cover: alk. paper) $17.99
Grades: 8 9 10 11 **Fic**

1. School stories 2. Gay teenagers -- Fiction 3. Schools -- Fiction 4. Identity -- Fiction 5. Homosexuality -- Fiction 6. Massachusetts -- Fiction 7. Preparatory schools -- Fiction 8. Gay teenagers 9. Homosexuality 10. Identity (Psychology) 11. Preparatory schools -- Massachusetts
ISBN 0545509890; 9780545509893; 9780545509909
LC 2012030552

Lambda Literary Awards Finalist (2014)

In this book, "Coloradan Rafe Goldberg has always been the token gay kid. He's been out since eighth grade. His parents and community are totally supportive. . . . On the outside, Rafe seems fine, but on the inside, he's looking for change, which comes with the opportunity to reinvent himself at the prestigious Natick Academy in Massachusetts. There for his junior year, Rafe cloaks his gayness in order to be just like one of the other guys." All is well until he falls for a straight friend. (Kirkus Reviews)

"Rafe is sick of being the poster child for all things gay at his uber-liberal Colorado high school, so when he gets into a Massachusetts boarding school for his junior year, he decides to reboot himself as "openly straight." Konigsberg slyly demonstrates how thoroughly assumptions of straightness are embedded in everyday interactions. For a thought-provoking take on the coming-out story, look no further." (Horn Book)

Konigsburg, E. L.

Silent to the bone. Atheneum Bks. for Young Readers 2000 261p hardcover o.p. pa $5.99
Grades: 7 8 9 10 **Fic**

1. Mystery fi ction 2. Siblings -- Fiction
ISBN 0-689-83601-5; 0-689-83602-3 pa
LC 00-20043

When he is wrongly accused of gravely injuring his baby half-sister, thirteen-year-old Branwell loses his power of speech and only his friend Connor is able to reach him and uncover the truth about what really happened

"A compelling mystery that is also a moving story of family, friendship, and seduction." Booklist

Kontis, Alethea

Enchanted; Alethea Kontis. Harcourt 2012 308 p.
Grades: 9 10 11 12 **Fic**

1. Fantasy fiction 2. Frogs -- Fiction 3. Magic -- Fiction 4. Fractured fairy tales 5. Princes 6. Fairy tales
ISBN 0547645708; 9780547645704
LC 2011027317

This young adult fantasy book presents the "fairy-tale mashup" story of the adventures of a girl named Sunday Woodcutter and her six siblings. Sunday becomes friends with the enchanted frog Grumble and unwittingly helps him transform back into Prince Rumbold. Author Alethea Kontis "has . . . woven just about every fairy character tale readers might half-remember into the fabric of her story: the beanstalk, the warrior maiden, Cinderella and Sleeping Beauty and some darker ones, too." (Kirkus)

Korman, Gordon

The **Juvie** three. Hyperion 2008 249p lib bdg $15.99
Grades: 7 8 9 10 **Fic**

1. Friendship -- Fiction 2. Juvenile delinquency -- Fiction
ISBN 978-1-4231-0158-1; 1-4231-0158-8
LC 2008-19087

Gecko, Arjay, and Terence, all in trouble with the law, must find a way to keep their halfway house open in order to stay out of juvenile detention.

"Korman keeps lots of balls in the air as he handles each boy's distinct voice and character—as well as the increasingly absurd situation—with humor and flashes of sadness." Booklist

Son of the mob. Hyperion Bks. for Children 2002 262p hardcover o.p. pa $7.99
Grades: 7 8 9 10 **Fic**

1. Mafia -- Fiction
ISBN 0-7868-0769-5; 0-7868-1593-0 pa
LC 2002-68672

Seventeen-year-old Vince's life is constantly complicated by the fact that he is the son of a powerful Mafia boss, a relationship that threatens to destroy his romance with the daughter of an FBI agent

"The fast-paced, tightly focused story addresses the problems of being an honest kid in a family of outlaws—and loving them anyway. Korman doesn't ignore the seamier side of mob life, but even when the subject matter gets violent . . . he keeps things light by relating his tale in the first-person voice of a humorously sarcastic yet law-abiding wise guy." Horn Book

Another title about Vince is:
Son of the mob: Hollywood hustle (2004)

Son of the mob: Hollywood hustle. Hyperion 2004 268p $15.99
Grades: 9 10 11 12 **Fic**

1. Mafia -- Fiction 2. California -- Fiction
ISBN 0-7868-0918-3
LC 2004-44181

Sequel to Son of the mob

Eighteen-year-old Vince Luca, son of mob boss Anthony Luca, goes away to college in southern California hoping to escape his past, but soon his brother and a series of "uncles" appear at his dorm, and before long he is caught up in criminal activity once again

"Teens will love this hilarious latest chapter of Vince's life. . . . {This} is a wonderful sauce filled with brilliant characterization, sneaky plot twists, and humor that will make teens fall off their chairs with laughter." Voice Youth Advocates

Kositsky, Lynne

The **thought** of high windows. Kids Can Press 2004 175p hardcover o.p. pa $6.95

Grades: 7 8 9 10 **Fic**

1. Jews -- Fiction 2. Holocaust, 1933-1945 -- Fiction

ISBN 1-55337-621-8; 1-55337-622-6 pa

"Esther describes her life as one of a group of Jewish children taken from Germany to France by the Red Cross during World War II. The novel begins when she is 15 and living in a French castle; her childhood in Berlin is described through flashbacks. . . . Based on true events, this is an immediate, painfully honest story." SLJ

Koss, Amy Goldman

Poison Ivy. Roaring Brook Press 2006 166p $16.96

Grades: 7 8 9 10 **Fic**

1. School stories 2. Bullies -- Fiction

ISBN 1-59643-118-0

LC 2005-17256

In a government class three popular girls undergo a mock trial for their ruthless bullying of a classmate.

"Realistic dialogue and fast-paced action will hold interest, and the final verdict is unsettling, but not unexpected." SLJ

Side effects; 1st ed.; Roaring Brook Press 2006 143p $16.95

Grades: 6 7 8 9 **Fic**

1. Cancer -- Fiction

ISBN 978-1-59643-167-6; 1-59643-167-9

LC 2005-31473

Everything changes for Isabelle, not quite fifteen, when she is diagnosed with lymphoma—but eventually she survives and even thrives.

"Koss refuses to glamorize Issy's illness or treatment. Instead, she settles for an honesty and frankness that will both challenge and enlighten readers." Booklist

Kostick, Conor

★ **Epic**. Viking 2007 364p $17.99

Grades: 7 8 9 10 **Fic**

1. Fantasy fiction 2. Video games -- Fiction

ISBN 0-670-06179-4; 978-0-670-06179-2

LC 2006-19958

On New Earth, a world based on a video role-playing game, fourteen-year-old Erik pursuades his friends to aid him in some unusual gambits in order to save his father from exile and safeguard the futures of each of their families.

"There is intrigue and mystery throughout this captivating page-turner. Veins of moral and ethical social situations and decisions provide some great opportunities for discussion. Well written and engaging." SLJ

Other titles in this series are:

Edda (2011)

Saga (2008)

Kraus, Daniel

Rotters. Delacorte Press 2011 448p $16.99; lib bdg $19.99; ebook $10.99

Grades: 9 10 11 12 **Fic**

1. School stories 2. Iowa -- Fiction 3. Moving -- Fiction 4. Bullies -- Fiction 5. Grave robbing -- Fiction 6. Father-son relationship -- Fiction

ISBN 978-0-385-73857-6; 978-0-385-90737-8 lib bdg; 978-0-375-89558-6 ebook

LC 2010005174

Sixteen-year-old Joey's life takes a very strange turn when his mother's tragic death forces him to move from Chicago to rural Iowa with the father he has never known, and who is the town pariah.

"Disturbing characters and grotesque details make for a tale of death that ultimately exhumes truths about life." Horn Books Guide

Scowler; Daniel Kraus. Delacorte Press 2013 304 p. (glb) $19.99

Grades: 9 10 11 12 **Fic**

1. Horror fiction 2. Meteorites -- Fiction 3. Adult child abuse victims -- Fiction 4. Horror stories 5. Iowa -- Fiction 6. Violence -- Fiction 7. Mentally ill -- Fiction 8. Farm life -- Iowa -- Fiction 9. Family life -- Iowa -- Fiction

ISBN 0375990941; 9780307980878; 9780375990946; 9780385743099

LC 2012005363

Odyssey Award (2014)

"This literary horror novel[, by Daniel Kraus,] gives readers insight into the mind of a controlling homicidal man and the son who must stop him. . . . Nineteen-year-old Ry Burke . . . wishes for anything to distract him from the grim memories of his father's physical and emotional abuse. Then a meteorite falls from the sky, bringing with it not only a fragment from another world but also the arrival of a ruthless man intent on destroying the entire family." (Publisher's note)

"A Midwestern gothic family saga that will hook readers--or scare them away." Kirkus

Krisher, Trudy

Fallout. Holiday House 2006 315p $17.95

Grades: 7 8 9 10 **Fic**

1. Friendship -- Fiction 2. Prejudices -- Fiction

ISBN 978-0-8234-2035-3; 0-8234-2035-3

LC 2006-41193

The move of an unconventional Hollywood family to a coastal North Carolina town in the early 1950s results not only in an unlikely friendship between high school age Genevieve and newcomer Brenda but also in a challenge to traditional ways of thinking.

"This is an excellent novel for teens searching for a good story with a well-paced and action-filled plot that challenges them to think about the importance of voicing their opinions." SLJ

Krokos, Dan

False memory; Dan Krokos. Disney Press 2012 327 p. $17.99

Grades: 6 7 8 9 **Fic**

1. Secrecy -- Fiction 2. Teenagers -- Fiction 3. Genetic transformation 4. Science fiction 5. Memory -- Fiction 6. Genetic engineering -- Fiction

ISBN 1423149769; 9781423149767

LC 2011053532

In author Dan Krokos' book, "Miranda North wakes up alone on a park bench with no memory. In her panic, she releases a mysterious energy that incites pure terror in everyone around her . . . Miranda discovers she was trained to be a weapon and is part of an elite force of genetically-altered teens who possess flawless combat skills and powers strong enough to destroy a city . . . Then Miranda uncovers a dark truth that sets her team on the run. Suddenly her past doesn't seem to matter when there may not be a future." (Publisher's note)

Krovatin, Christopher

Heavy metal and you. Scholastic 2005 186p $16.95; pa $7.99

Grades: 9 10 11 12 **Fic**

1. School stories 2. Rock music -- Fiction 3. New York (N.Y.) -- Fiction

ISBN 0-439-73648-X; 0-439-74399-0 pa

LC 2004-23645

High schooler Sam begins losing himself when he falls for a preppy girl who wants him to give up getting wasted with his best friends and even his passion for heavy metal music in order to become a better person.

"From the terrific cover and portrait of selfish love to the clever CD player icons indicating narrative switches . . . this is an authentic portrayal of an obsession with music. Teens don't have to like heavy metal to appreciate this novel, which is guaranteed to attract readers looking for a book to reach their death-metal souls." Booklist

Kuehn, Stephanie

★ **Charm** & strange; by Stephanie Kuehn. 1st ed. St. Martin's Griffin 2013 224 p. (hardcover) $17.99

Grades: 9 10 11 12 **Fic**

1. School stories 2. Mystery fiction 3. Sexual abuse -- Fiction 4. Mental illness -- Fiction 5. Psychological abuse -- Fiction

ISBN 1250021944; 9781250021946

LC 2013003247

William C. Morris Award (2014)

This book follows Andrew Winston Winters, known as Win. Present-day "Win is smart, competitive and untrusting, estranged from his former roommate, Lex, his one ally and defender. The reasons for Win's self-loathing and keyed-up anxiety won't be fully revealed until story's end. What exactly does he expect to happen during the full moon? Why has he fallen out with Lex? Win's privileged childhood, when he was known as Drew, is another mystery." (Kirkus Reviews)

"Kuehn . . . keeps us on constant edge regarding exactly what genre of book it is that we're reading." Booklist

Complicit; Stephanie Kuehn. St. Martin's Griffin 2014 256 p. (hardback) $19.99

Grades: 8 9 10 11 12 **Fic**

1. Orphans -- Fiction 2. Mental illness -- Fiction 3. Private schools -- Fiction 4. Brothers and sisters -- Fiction 5. Amnesia -- Fiction 6. Schools -- Fiction

ISBN 1250044596; 9781250044594

LC 2014008117

"Cate is out of juvie. For her little brother, 17-year-old Jamie, that's bad. It's been two years since Cate horribly injured a rival by setting a barn on fire. This was the last in a long series of tempestuous, violent acts Cate committed since she and Jamie were adopted following the murder of their mother...Her confidence is what's so invigorating: every page shows a firm, surprising choice, whether you like it or not. Cate, naturally, is the main event, the alternatingly irrational, gentle, explosive, and enigmatic center of this fast, black whirlpool of a novel." (Booklist)

Kwasney, Michelle D.

Blue plate special. Chronicle Books 2009 366p $16.99

Grades: 8 9 10 11 12 **Fic**

1. Forgiveness -- Fiction 2. Mother-daughter relationship -- Fiction

ISBN 978-0-8118-6780-1; 0-8118-6780-3

LC 2009-5322

In alternating chapters, the lives of three teenage girls from three different generations are woven together as each girl learns about forgiveness, empathy, and self-respect.

Kwasney's "protagonists are distinctive and empathetic, her narratives meticulously structured and realistic, exposing the unpredictability—and sometimes unfairness—that life can bring." Publ Wkly

L'Engle, Madeleine

A **wrinkle** in time. Farrar, Straus & Giroux 1962 211p $17; pa $7.99

Grades: 5 6 7 8 9 10 **Fic**

1. Fantasy fiction

ISBN 0-374-38613-7; 0-312-36754-6 pa

ALA YALSA Margaret A. Edwards Award (1998)

Awarded The Newbery Medal, 1963

"A brother and sister, together with a friend, go in search of their scientist father who was lost while engaged in secret work for the government on the tesseract problem. A tesseract is a wrinkle in time. The father is a prisoner on a forbidding planet, and after awesome and terrifying experiences, he is rescued, and the little group returns safely to Earth and home." Child Books Too Good to Miss

This book "makes unusual demands on the imagination and consequently gives great rewards." Horn Book

Other titles in this series are:

A swiftly tilting planet (1978)

A wind in the door (1973)

LaFaye, A.

Stella stands alone; [by] A. LaFaye. Simon & Schuster Books for Young Readers 2008 245p map $16.99

Grades: 7 8 9 10 **Fic**

1. Orphans -- Fiction 2. African Americans -- Fiction 3. Swindlers and swindling -- Fiction 4. Reconstruction (1865-1876) -- Fiction

ISBN 978-1-4169-1164-7; 1-4169-1164-2

LC 2007-38725

Fourteen-year-old Stella, orphaned just after the Civil War, fights to keep her family's plantation and fulfill her father's desire to turn land over to the people who have worked on it for generations, but first she must find her father's hidden deed and will.

"Readers will be drawn along by Stella's refusal to act helpless and sweet and her discovery of strength and kindness in unexpected places. The sadness and anger, and the wrenching legacy of slavery are present throughout." Booklist

Laban, Elizabeth

The **Tragedy** Paper; Elizabeth LaBan. Alfred A. Knopf 2013 320 p. $17.99

Grades: 7 8 9 10 11 12 **Fic**

1. Love stories 2. School stories 3. Albinos and albinism -- Fiction 4. Schools -- Fiction 5. High schools -- Fiction 6. Boarding schools -- Fiction 7. Dating (Social customs) -- Fiction 8. Interpersonal relations -- Fiction

ISBN 0375870407; 9780375870408; 9780375970405; 9780375989124

LC 2012011294

This novel by Elizabeth Laban "follows the story of Tim Macbeth, a seventeen-year-old albino and a recent transfer to the prestigious Irving School. . . . He finds himself falling for the quintessential 'It' girl, Vanessa Sheller. . . . Vanessa is into him, too, but she can kiss her social status goodbye if anyone ever finds out. Tim and Vanessa begin a clandestine romance, but looming over them is the Tragedy Paper, Irving's version of a senior year thesis." (Publisher's note)

LaCour, Nina

★ The **Disenchantments**; Nina LaCour. Dutton Children's Books 2012 308 p. (hardcover) $16.99

Grades: 9 10 11 12 **Fic**

1. Bildungsromans 2. Teenagers -- Fiction 3. Friendship -- Fiction 4. Bands (Music) -- Fiction 5. Pacific Northwest -- Fiction 6. Artists -- Fiction 7. Secrets -- Fiction 8. Best friends -- Fiction 9. Automobile travel -- Fiction 10. Northwest, Pacific -- Fiction

ISBN 9780525422198

LC 2011021953

In this book, "[a]fter Colby graduates from high school, his . . . plans to spend a year traveling through Europe go up in smoke. . . . He . . . commit[s] himself to playing chauffeur for [his friend] Bev's . . . band . . . on their first . . . summer tour. Chronicling the band's road trip, . . .this . . . coming-of-age story expresses how a teen in limbo learns . . . lessons about disappointment, love, and the pursuit of dreams." (Publishers Weekly)

Everything leads to you; Nina LaCour. Dutton Books 2014 320 p. (hardback) $17.99

Grades: 9 10 11 12 **Fic**

1. Love -- Fiction 2. Summer -- Fiction 3. Secrets -- Fiction 4. Motion picture industry -- Fiction 5. Families -- Fiction 6. Lesbians -- Fiction 7. Set designers -- Fiction

ISBN 0525425888; 9780525425885

LC 2014004799

"Eighteen-year-old production design intern Emi is getting over her first love and trying to establish her place in the Los Angeles film industry...When she and her best friend Charlotte find a letter hidden in the possessions of a recently deceased Hollywood film legend at an estate sale, they begin searching for its intended recipient. Eventually that leads to Ava, a beautiful teen to whom Emi is immediately attracted. ..This one is highly enjoyable and highly recommended." (School Library Journal)

Hold still; with illustrations by Mia Nolting. Dutton 2009 229p il

Grades: 9 10 11 12 **Fic**

1. Suicide -- Fiction 2. Friendship -- Fiction 3. Bereavement -- Fiction

ISBN 0-525-42155-6; 978-0-525-42155-9

LC 2010-275162

Ingrid didn't leave a note. Three months after her best friend's suicide, Caitlin finds what she left instead: a journal, hidden under Caitlin's bed.

"Interspersed with drawings and journal entries, the story of Caitlin's journey through her grief is both heart-wrenching and realistic. . . . LaCour strikes a new path through a familiar story, leading readers with her confident writing and savvy sense of prose." Kirkus

LaFevers, Robin

★ **Dark** triumph; by Robin LaFevers. Houghton Mifflin Harcourt 2013 400 p. $17.99

Grades: 9 10 11 12 **Fic**

1. Fantasy fiction 2. Death -- Fiction 3. Assassins -- Fiction 4. Gods -- Fiction 5. Love -- Fiction 6. Brittany (France) -- History -- 1341-1532 -- Fiction 7. France -- History -- Charles VIII, 1483-1498 -- Fiction

ISBN 0547628382; 9780547628387

LC 2012033555

In this novel, by Robin LaFevers, book 2 of the "His Fair Assassin Trilogy," "Sybella's duty as Death's assassin in 15th-century France forces her return home to the personal hell that she had finally escaped. . . . While Sybella is a weapon of justice wrought by the god of Death himself, He must give her a reason to live. When she discovers an unexpected ally imprisoned in the dungeons, will a daughter of Death find something other than vengeance to live for?" (Publisher's note)

"LaFevers weaves the 'crazed, tangled web' of Sybella's life...with force, suspense and subtle tenderness. The prose's beauty inspires immediate re-reads of many a sentence, but its forward momentum is irresistible. An intricate, masterful page-turner about politics, treachery, religion, love and healing." Kirkus

★ **Grave** mercy; by Robin LaFevers. Houghton Mifflin 2012 549 p.
Grades: 9 10 11 12 **Fic**

1. Love stories 2. Historical fiction 3. Executions and executioners 4. Gods -- Fiction 5. Death -- Fiction 6. Assassins -- Fiction 7. Courts and courtiers -- Fiction 8. Brittany (France) -- History -- 1341-1532 -- Fiction 9. France -- History -- Charles VIII, 1483-1498 -- Fiction
ISBN 9780547628349
LC 2011039893

This book is a "historical romance with a . . . recreation of 15th-century Brittany. At its center is 17-year-old Ismae, . . . [who,] fleeing her thuggish husband, is taken in by the convent of St. Mortain. . . . Ismae is trained as an assassin. . . [and] dispatched to the court of Anne of Brittany to keep track of Duval, the duchess's . . . older brother. Reluctantly, she falls in love with him, knowing . . . that she may someday be called upon to end his life." (Publishers Weekly)

★ **Mortal** heart; by Robin LaFevers . Houghton Mifflin Harcourt. 2014 464p $17.99
Grades: 9 10 11 12 **Fic**

1. Assassins -- Fiction 2. Convents -- Fiction 3. Death --Fiction 4. Gods -- Fiction; 5. Nuns -- Fiction 6. Brittany (France) -- History -- 1341-1532 -- Fiction 7. France --History -- Charles VIII, 1483-1498 -- Fiction
ISBN: 0547628404; 9780547628400
LC 2014001877

In this book, the conclusion of the His Fair Assassin trilogy, "Annith, overskilled and underused daughter of Mortain, god of Death, rebels against her abbess's decree that she remain immured in the convent as Mortain's seeress. Her rebellious escape to the world of politics, murder, and romance revolutionizes Annith's understanding of her nature and identity and brings about her sexual awakening." (Horn Book Magazine)

"The protagonists' sometimes-contradictory natures enrich their characters, and the intertwined relationships of realistic and Netherworld personages add depth to their personal stories. A plethora of strong females and their romantic relationships will have wide appeal for teens." SLJ

Laird, Elizabeth

The **betrayal** of Maggie Blair. Houghton Mifflin 2011 423p il $16.99
Grades: 7 8 9 10 **Fic**

1. Uncles -- Fiction 2. Witchcraft -- Fiction 3. Scotland -- History -- 17th century -- Fiction
ISBN 978-0-547-34126-2; 0-547-34126-1
LC 2010-25120

In seventeenth-century Scotland, sixteen-year-old Maggie Blair is sentenced to be hanged as a witch but escapes to the home of her uncle, placing him and his family in great danger as she risks her life to save them all from the King's men.

"Laird seamlessly weaves a fairly comprehensive history lesson into an engaging, lively story." Bull Cent Child Books

A **little** piece of ground; [by] Elizabeth Laird; with Sonia Nimr. Haymarket Books 2006 216p pa $9.95
Grades: 6 7 8 9 10 **Fic**

1. Israel-Arab conflicts -- Fiction
ISBN 978-1-931859-38-7; 1-931859-38-8
LC 2006008707

During the Israeli occupation of Ramallah in the West Bank of Palestine, twelve-year-old Karim and his friends create a secret place for themselves where they can momentarily forget the horrors of war.

"Throughout this powerful narrative, the authors remain true to Karim's character and reactions. He is a typical self-centered adolescent. . . . [This book] deserves serious attention and discussion." SLJ

Lake, Nick

Blood ninja II: the revenge of Lord Oda. Simon and Schuster Books for Young Readers 2010 377p $16.99
Grades: 7 8 9 10 11 **Fic**

1. Japan -- Fiction 2. Ninja -- Fiction 3. Vampires -- Fiction
ISBN 978-1-4169-8629-4; 1-4169-8629-4
LC 2010-10110

Sequel to: Blood ninja (2009)

In sixteenth-century Japan, Taro, a vampire like all ninja warriors, tries to protect his mother and defeat the power-hungry Lord Oda, who he believed was dead.

"Ghosts and Zen Buddhist philosophy add a surprising and sometimes effective depth to the story." Booklist

★ **Hostage** Three; by Nick Lake. Bloomsbury 2013 320 p. (hardback) $17.99
Grades: 9 10 11 12 **Fic**

1. Pirates -- Fiction 2. Hostages -- Fiction 3. Father-daughter relationship -- Fiction 4. Yachts -- Fiction 5. Survival -- Fiction 6. Fathers and daughters -- Fiction 7. Adventure and adventurers -- Fiction
ISBN 1619631237; 9781619631236
LC 2013002686

"The last way seventeen-year-old Amy wants to spend the summer after high school is sailing around the world with her father and new stepmother. When Somali pirates hijack the family's yacht, the sullen, entitled teen forms a surprising bond with one of their captors. Lake's sensitive character development and sophisticated storytelling (including alternate endings) helps elicit readers' sympathies for his complex characters." (Horn Book)

In darkness; Nick Lake. Bloomsbury 2012 341 p.
Grades: 8 9 10 11 12 **Fic**

1. Haiti -- Fiction 2. Earthquakes -- Fiction 3. Gangs -- Fiction 4. Survival -- Fiction 5. Violence -- Fiction 6. Haiti Earthquake, Haiti, 2010 -- Fiction 7. Haiti Earthquake, Haiti, 2010 8. Haiti -- History -- Revolution, 1791-1804 -- Fiction 9. Haiti -- History -- Revolution, 1791-1804
ISBN 9781599907437
LC 2011022350

Michael L. Printz Award (2013)

"This . . . novel, set in Haiti, alternates between the narration of a contemporary fifteen-year-old, trapped in the rubble following the 2010 earthquake, and the story of Toussaint L'Ouverture, the legendary eighteenth-century leader of Haiti's anti-colonial revolution. The two become aware of each other through dreams; Shorty experiences Toussaint's reality while Toussaint perceives the bewildering future setting in which Shorty lives. . . . [B]oth share graphic depictions of the cruelty and violence of the protagonists' lives. Shorty tells of his pre-earthquake life in quick allusions and references that eventually cohere into a complete story." (Bulletin of the Center for Children's Books)

Lam, Laura

Pantomime; Laura Lam. Strange Chemistry 2013 394 p. (pbk.) $9.99

Grades: 9 10 11 12 **Fic**

1. Fantasy fiction 2. Magic -- Fiction 3. Circus -- Fiction 4. Fantasy 5. Love stories 6. Love -- Fiction 7. Runaways -- Fiction 8. Circus 9. Runaways

ISBN 190884437X; 9781908844378; 9781908844385

LC 2012540335

"R.H. Ragona's Circus of Magic is the greatest circus of Ellada. Nestled among the glowing blue Penglass -- remnants of a mysterious civilisation long gone -- are wonders beyond the wildest imagination. . . . Iphigenia Laurus, or Gene, the daughter of a noble family, is uncomfortable in corsets and crinoline, and prefers climbing trees to debutante balls. Micah Grey, a runaway living on the streets, joins the circus as an aerialist's apprentice and soon becomes the circus's rising star." (Publisher's note)

"At around page 90 in Lam's impressive debut fantasy novel, there's a reveal so stunning that it makes it difficult to discuss without spoilers... Using a flashback structure to show both why noble-born Iphigenia Laurus runs away and joins the circus and how she changes her identity to become trapeze-artist Micah Grey, Pantomime does feature standard YA elements such as parental estrangement and problematic romance—yet marvelously transfigures them." (Booklist)

Lanagan, Margo

★ The **brides** of Rollrock Island; Margo Lanagan. Alfred A. Knopf 2012 305 p. (hardback) $17.99

Grades: 9 10 11 12 **Fic**

1. Selkies -- Fiction 2. Magic 3. Fantasy fiction 4. Magic -- Fiction 5. Islands -- Fiction 6. Witches -- Fiction

ISBN 0375869190; 9780375869198; 9780375969195; 9780375989308

LC 2011047466

This novel, by Margo Lenagan, takes place around "remote Rollrock Island, [where] men go to sea to make their livings--and to catch their wives. The witch Misskaella knows the way of drawing a girl from the heart of a seal . . . [a]nd for a price a man may buy himself a lovely sea-wife. . . . But from his first look into [her] . . . eyes, he will be just as transformed as she. He will be equally ensnared. And the witch will have her true payment." (Publisher's note)

★ **Tender** morsels. Alfred A. Knopf 2008 436p $16.99; lib bdg $19.99

Grades: 10 11 12 **Fic**

1. Fantasy fiction

ISBN 978-0-375-84811-7; 0-375-84811-8; 978-0-375-94811-4 lib bdg; 0-375-94811-2 lib bdg

LC 2008-04155

Michael L. Printz Award honor book, 2009

A young woman who has endured unspeakable cruelties is magically granted a safe haven apart from the real world and allowed to raise her two daughters in this alternate reality, until the barrier between her world and the real one begins to break down.

The author "touches on nightmarish adult themes, including multiple rape scenarios and borderline human-animal sexual interactions, which reserve this for the most mature readers. . . . Drawing alternate worlds that blur the line between wonder and horror, and characters who traverse the nature of human and beast, this challenging, unforgettable work explores the ramifications of denying the most essential and often savage aspects of life." Booklist

Lancaster, Mike A.

The **future** we left behind; Mike A. Lancaster. Egmont USA 2012 367 p. (hardback) $16.99

Grades: 7 8 9 10 **Fic**

1. Science fiction 2. Cults -- Fiction 3. England -- Fiction 4. Computer programs -- Fiction 5. Family life -- England -- Fiction 6. Technological innovations -- Fiction

ISBN 1606844105; 9781606844106; 9781606844113

LC 2012003794

Sequel to: Human.4

This sequel to "Human.4" is set in the future. Here, "Peter is the son of the man who saved the world by inventing robot bees. Destined by his wealthy genius father for a future in science, Peter rebels against both by enrolling in a literature class and befriending Alpha, a girl in a wacky religious cult. Alpha is a Strakerite, following the ancient tapes of Kyle Straker. Kyle and his girlfriend Lilly believed humans are regularly upgraded by aliens. Skeptical at first, Peter is soon convinced." (Kirkus)

★ **Human.4**. Egmont USA 2011 231p $16.99

Grades: 7 8 9 10 **Fic**

1. Science fiction 2. Computers -- Fiction 3. Family life -- Fiction

ISBN 978-1-6068-4099-3; 1-6068-4099-1

LC 2010030313

Twenty-first century fourteen-year-old Kyle was hypnotized when humanity was upgraded to 1.0 and he, incompatible with the new technology, exposes its terrifying impact in a tape-recording found by the superhumans of the future.

"Lancaster fashions a fast-paced, upsetting little thriller punctuated by ominous editorial notes that translate Kyle's details for the futuristic audience." Booklist

Lane, Andrew

Black ice; Andrew Lane. Farrar Straus Giroux 2013 288 p. (Sherlock Holmes. The legend begins) (hardcover) $17.99

Grades: 5 6 7 8 **Fic**

1. Mystery fiction 2. Holmes, Sherlock (Fictional character) -- Fiction 3. Murder -- Fiction 4. Mystery

and detective stories
ISBN 0374387699; 9780374387693
LC 2012004996

This novel, by Andrew Lane, is the third book of the "Sherlock Holmes: The Legend Begins" series. "When Sherlock and Amyus Crowe, his American tutor, visit Sherlock's brother, Mycroft, in London, all they are expecting is lunch and some polite conversation. What they find shocks both of them to the core: a locked room, a dead body, and Mycroft holding a knife. . . . Threatened with the gallows, Mycroft needs Sherlock to save him." (Publisher's note)

Rebel fire; Andrew Lane. Farrar Straus Giroux 2012 343 p. (Sherlock Holmes. The legend begins) $16.99
Grades: 5 6 7 8 **Fic**
1. Mystery fiction 2. Holmes, Sherlock (Fictional character) -- Fiction 3. Mystery and detective stories
ISBN 0374387680; 9780374387686
LC 2011000124

This novel, by Andrew Lane, is part of the "Sherlock Holmes: The Legend Begins" series. "Fourteen-year-old Sherlock Holmes knows that Amyus Crowe, his mysterious American tutor, has some dark secrets. But he didn't expect to find John Wilkes Booth, the notorious assassin, apparently alive and well in England--and Crowe somehow mixed up in it. . . . And so begins an adventure that will take Sherlock across the Atlantic, to the center of a deadly web." (Publisher's note)

Includes bibliographical references

Lane, Dakota

Gothic Lolita; a mystical thriller. words and photographs by Dakota Lane. Atheneum Books for Young Readers 2008 194p il $17.99
Grades: 8 9 10 11 12 **Fic**
1. Weblogs -- Fiction 2. Bereavement -- Fiction 3. Racially mixed people -- Fiction
ISBN 978-1-4169-1396-2; 1-4169-1396-3
LC 2008-15390

Lane "focuses on two half-Japanese, half-American girls who forge an unusual bond over their blogs, loneliness and fascination with the gothic Lolita subculture. Chelsea is in L.A. and Miya is in Japan. . . . Readers will find themselves quickly engrossed." Publ Wkly

Lange, Erin Jade

Butter; Erin Jade Lange. Bloomsbury 2012 296 p. (hardback) $16.99
Grades: 8 9 10 11 12 **Fic**
1. Eating habits 2. Suicide -- Fiction 3. Teenagers -- Fiction 4. Obesity -- Fiction 5. Eating disorders -- Fiction
ISBN 1599907801; 9781599907802
LC 2011045509

In author Erin Jade Lange's book, a "lonely obese boy everyone calls 'Butter' is about to make history. He is going to eat himself to death-live on the Internet-and everyone is invited to watch. When he first makes the announcement online to his classmates, Butter expects pity, insults, and possibly sheer indifference. What he gets are morbid cheerleaders rallying around his deadly plan. Yet as their dark encouragement grows, it begins to feel a lot like popularity . . . But what happens when Butter reaches his suicide deadline?" (Publisher's note)

Larbalestier, Justine

How to ditch your fairy. Bloomsbury 2008 307p $16.99
Grades: 6 7 8 9 10 **Fic**
1. Magic -- Fiction 2. Fairies -- Fiction
ISBN 978-1-59990-301-9; 1-59990-301-6
LC 2008-02408

In a world in which everyone has a personal fairy who tends to one aspect of daily life, fourteen-year-old Charlie decides she does not want hers—a parking fairy—and embarks on a series of misadventures designed to rid herself of the invisible sprite and replace it with a better one, like her friend Rochelle's shopping fairy.

"Charlie is totally likable, smart, and sarcastic, a perfectly self-involved, insecure teen. At its core, this is a typical coming-of-age story, but the addition of the fairies, the slightly alternative setting, and the made-up slang make it much more." SLJ

★ **Liar.** Bloomsbury Children's Books 2009 376p $16.99
Grades: 9 10 11 12 **Fic**
1. Honesty -- Fiction 2. Werewolves -- Fiction
ISBN 978-1-59990-305-7; 1-59990-305-9
LC 2009-12581

Compulsive liar Micah promises to tell the truth after revealing that her boyfriend has been murdered.

"Micah's narrative is convincing, and in the end readers will delve into the psyche of a troubled teen and decide for themselves the truths and lies. This one is sure to generate discussion." SLJ

Magic lessons. Razorbill 2006 275p $16.99; pa $7.99
Grades: 8 9 10 11 12 **Fic**
1. Magic -- Fiction 2. Australia -- Fiction 3. Space and time -- Fiction 4. New York (N.Y.) -- Fiction
ISBN 1-59514-054-9; 1-59514-124-3 pa
LC 2005-23870

Sequel to Magic or madness (2005)

When fifteen-year-old Reason is pulled through the magical door connecting New York City with the Sydney, Australia, home of her grandmother, she encounters an impossibly ancient man who seems to have some purpose in mind for her.

"Larbalestier creates complex relationships among her characters, and their realistic flaws, combined with the sense of danger throughout, make this a good choice for even reluctant readers." SLJ

Followed by Magic's child (2007)

Magic or madness. Razorbill 2005 288p $16.99; pa $7.99
Grades: 8 9 10 11 12 **Fic**
1. Magic -- Fiction 2. Australia -- Fiction 3. Grandmothers -- Fiction 4. Space and time -- Fiction 5.

New York (N.Y.) -- Fiction
ISBN 1-59514-022-0; 1-59514-124-3 pa
LC 2004-18263

From the Sydney, Australia home of a grandmother she believes is a witch, fifteen-year-old Reason Cansino is magically transported to New York City, where she discovers that friends and foes can be hard to distinguish

"Readers looking for layered, understated fantasy will follow the looping paths of Larbalestier's fine writing . . . with gratitude and awe." Booklist

Other titles about Reason Cansino are:
Magic lessons (2006)
Magic's child (2007)

Larson, Kirby

★ **Hattie** Big Sky. Delacorte Press 2006 289p hardcover o.p. pa $6.99
Grades: 6 7 8 9 10 **Fic**

1. Montana -- Fiction 2. Orphans -- Fiction 3. World War, 1914-1918 -- Fiction 4. Frontier and pioneer life -- Fiction
ISBN 0-385-73313-5; 0-385-73595-2 pa
LC 2005-35039

A Newbery Medal honor book, 2007

After inheriting her uncle's homesteading claim in Montana, sixteen-year-old-orphan Hattie Brooks travels from Iowa in 1917 to make a home for herself, befriends a German-American family and encounters some unexptected problems related to the war in Europe. "Grades six to nine." (Bull Cent Child Books)

This is "a richly textured novel full of memorable characters." Booklist

Hattie ever after; Kirby Larson. Delacorte Press 2013 240 p. (hc) $16.99
Grades: 6 7 8 9 10 **Fic**

1. Historical fiction 2. Orphans -- Fiction 3. Reporters and reporting -- Fiction 4. Self-reliance -- Fiction 5. San Francisco (Calif.) -- History -- 20th century -- Fiction
ISBN 0385737467; 9780307979681; 9780385737463; 9780385906685
LC 2012007068

Sequel to: Hattie Big Sky

In this novel, by Newbury Honor award-winning author Kirby Larson, "after leaving Uncle Chester's homestead claim, orphan Hattie Brooks throws a lasso around a new dream, even bigger than the Montana sky. She wants to be a reporter . . . , go to Grand Places, and do Grand Things, like Hattie's hero Nellie Bly. Another girl might be stymied by this, but . . . nothing can squash her desire to write for a big city newspaper." (Publisher's note)

Includes bibliographical references

Laskas, Gretchen Moran

The **miner's** daughter. Simon & Schuster Books for Young Readers 2007 250p $15.99
Grades: 8 9 10 11 12 **Fic**

1. Family life -- Fiction 2. Coal mines and mining -- Fiction 3. Great Depression, 1929-1939 -- Fiction
ISBN 978-1-4169-1262-0; 1-4169-1262-2
LC 2006-00684

Sixteen-year-old Willa, living in a Depression-era West Virginia mining town, works hard to help her family, experiences love and friendship, and finds an outlet for her writing when her family becomes part of the Arthurdale, West Virginia, community supported by Eleanor Roosevelt.

"Richly drawn characters and plot make this an excellent novel that explores the struggles endured by many in America in the 1930s." SLJ

Lasky, Kathryn

★ **Ashes.** Viking 2010 318p $16.99
Grades: 6 7 8 9 10 11 12 **Fic**

1. Germany -- Fiction 2. National socialism -- Fiction
ISBN 978-0-670-01157-5; 0-670-01157-6
LC 2009-33127

In 1932 Berlin, thirteen-year-old Gaby Schramm witnesses the beginning of Hitler's rise to power, as soldiers become ubiquitous, her beloved literature teacher starts wearing a jewelled swastika pin, and the family's dear friend, Albert Einstein, leaves the country while Gaby's parents secretly bury his books and papers in their small yard.

"Gaby's questioning but assertive nature helps form a compelling, readable portrait of pre-WWII Germany." Publ Wkly

Chasing Orion. Candlewick Press 2010 362p $17.99
Grades: 6 7 8 9 **Fic**

1. Friendship -- Fiction 2. Poliomyelitis -- Fiction
ISBN 978-0-7636-3982-2; 0-7636-3982-6
LC 2009007327

In 1952, when Georgie is eleven years old, her family moves to a new Indiana neighborhood where her teenaged neighbor has polio and is in an iron lung.

"A truly extraordinary page-turner that embraces life's big and small aspects with humor and a healthy respect for its profound contradictions." Kirkus

Hawksmaid; the untold story of Robin Hood and Maid Marian. Harper 2010 292p $16.99
Grades: 5 6 7 8 **Fic**

1. Falconry -- Fiction 2. Robin Hood (Legendary character) -- Fiction 3. Maid Marian (Legendary character) -- Fiction
ISBN 978-0-06-000071-4; 0-06-000071-6

In twelfth-century England, Matty grows up to be a master falconer, able to communicate with the devoted birds who later help her and Fynn, also known as Robin Hood, to foil Prince John's plot to steal the crown.

"Lasky nicely weaves details of 12th-century life into this suspenseful adventure whose fantasy ending may surprise but will certainly please readers." SLJ

Lone wolf. Scholastic Press 2010 219p il map (Wolves of the Beyond) $16.99
Grades: 5 6 7 8 **Fic**

1. Fantasy fiction 2. Wolves -- Fiction
ISBN 978-0-545-09310-1; 0-545-09310-4
LC 2009-17007

Abandoned by his pack, a baby wolf with a mysterious mark on his deformed paw survives and embarks on a journey that will change the world of the wolves of the Beyond.

"Lasky merges anthropomorphic fantasy with realistic details about wolves and bears to produce an almost plausible emotional narrative, complete with dialogue and personalities. . . . The author builds a captivating world of forest, snow and volcanoes populated by intelligent animals and weaves a compelling story sure to bring readers back for the second installment." Kirkus

Other titles in this series are:
Shadow wolf (2010)
Watch wolf (2011)
Frost worlf (2011)

Lavender, William

Aftershocks. Harcourt 2006 344p $17

Grades: 8 9 10 11 12 **Fic**

1. Sex role -- Fiction 2. Earthquakes -- Fiction 3. Chinese Americans -- Fiction 4. San Francisco (Calif.) -- Fiction 5. Father-daughter relationship -- Fiction

ISBN 0-15-205882-6

LC 2005-19695

In San Francisco from 1903 to 1908, teenager Jessie Wainwright determines to reach her goal of becoming a doctor while also trying to care for the illegitimate child of a liaison between her father and their Chinese maid.

This "is readable historical fiction about an engrossing event in U.S. history." Voice Youth Advocates

Lawlor, Laurie

Dead reckoning; a pirate voyage with Captain Drake. Simon & Schuster Books for Young Readers 2005 254p $15.95

Grades: 7 8 9 10 **Fic**

1. Orphans -- Fiction 2. Pirates -- Fiction 3. Seafaring life -- Fiction

ISBN 0-689-86577-5

LC 2004-21682

Emmet, a fifteen-year-old orphan, learns hard lessons about survival when he sails from England in 1577 as a servant aboard the Golden Hind—the ship of his cousin, the explorer and pirate Francis Drake—on its three-year circumnavigation of the world.

"The tone is dark and grim, and there are scenes that might horrify younger readers. . . . But the story is authentic and harrowing, and the historical details are well done. This book would be perfect for older teens who love historical fiction, or want more on pirates." SLJ

He will go fearless; [by] Laurie Lawlor. Simon & Schuster Books for Young Readers 2006 210p $15.95

Grades: 5 6 7 8 **Fic**

1. Father-son relationship -- Fiction 2. Overland journeys to the Pacific -- Fiction

ISBN 0-689-86579-1

LC 2005-06129

With the Civil War ended and Reconstruction begun, fifteen-year-old Billy resolves to make the dangerous and challenging journey West in search of real fortune – his true father.

"Danger, adventure, and survival combine to make this a richly detailed story." SLJ

The **two** loves of Will Shakespeare. Holiday House 2006 278p $16.95

Grades: 9 10 11 12 **Fic**

1. Poets 2. Authors 3. Dramatists 4. Great Britain -- History -- 1485-1603, Tudors -- Fiction

ISBN 0-8234-1901-0; 978-0-8234-1901-2

LC 2005-52537

After falling in love, eighteen-year-old Will Shakespeare, a bored apprentice in his father's glove business and often in trouble for various misdeeds, vows to live an upstanding life and pursue his passion for writing.

"Quoting lines from Shakespeare's sonnets and highlighting the dismal treatment of women in that brutally repressive society, the author creates both a vivid setting and a feckless protagonist, equally credible as an adolescent and as a product of his times." Booklist

Lawson, Mary

Crow Lake. Dial Press (NY) 2002 291p hardcover o.p. pa $14

Grades: 11 12 Adult **Fic**

1. Canada -- Fiction 2. Orphans -- Fiction 3. Poverty -- Fiction

ISBN 0-385-33611-X; 0-385-33763-9 pa

LC 2001-53779

"Four children living in northern Ontario struggle to stay together after their parents die in an auto accident. . . . Kate Morrison narrates the tale in flashback mode, starting with the fatal car accident that leaves seven-year-old Kate; her toddler sister, Bo; 19-year-old Luke; and 17-year-old Matt to fend for themselves. At first they are divided up among relatives, but the plan changes when Luke gives up his teaching college scholarship to get a job and try to keep them together." Publ Wkly

"Lawson achieves a breathless anticipatory quality in her surprisingly adept first novel, in which a child tells the story, but tells it very well indeed." Booklist

Le Guin, Ursula K.

The **farthest** shore. Pocket Books 2004 259p $15

Grades: 6 7 8 9 **Fic**

1. Fantasy fiction

ISBN 978-1-416-50964-6; 1-416-50964-X

First published 1972 by Atheneum Pubs.

This book continues "the story of Ged and introduces a new hero, Arren, the young prince who travels with the Archmage Ged on his last perilous mission. The writing has, as the concept has, a majestic intricacy; to appreciate it the reader must enjoy ornate language, the grave discussion of life and death and love, and courage, and the tongue-rolling exotic names of a legendary land." Bull Cent Child Books

Gifts. Harcourt 2004 274p $17; $17; pa $7.95

Grades: 7 8 9 10 **Fic**

1. Fantasy fiction

ISBN 9780152051235; 0-15-205123-6; 0-15-205124-4 pa

LC 2003-21449

"Brantors, or chiefs, of the various clans of the Uplands have powers passed down through generations, powers to call animals to the hunt, start fires, cast a wasting disease, or undo the very essence of a life or thing. The clans live isolated from the inhabitants of the Lowland cities in an uneasy truce, where each people's ambitions are kept at bay by fear of the other's vengeance. Two Upland teenagers, Gry and Orrec, have grown from childhood friendship into romance and also into a repudiation of their hereditary powers. . . . Rejecting traditions that bind them to roles unwanted and undesired, Gry and Orrec decide to leave their homes and seek a freer if less privileged life in the Lowlands. . . . Grades seven to twelve." (Bull Cent Child Books)

"Although intriguing as a coming-of-age allegory, Orrec's story is also rich in . . . earthy magic and intelligent plot twists." Booklist

The **lathe** of heaven; a novel. Scribner 2008 184p pa $15
Grades: 11 12 Adult **Fic**

1. Science fiction 2. Dreams -- Fiction
ISBN 978-1-4165-5696-1; 1-4165-5696-6
LC 2007047222

First published 1971 by Scribner

Science fiction classic about a character whose dreams alter reality.

"The author has done some profound research in psychology, cerebrophysiology and biochemistry. . . . In addition, her perceptions of such matters as geopolitics, race, socialized medicine and the patient/shrink relationship are razor-sharp and more than a little cutting." Natl Rev

★ The **left** hand of darkness. Ace Books 2000 304p pa $13.95
Grades: 9 10 11 12 **Fic**

1. Science fiction 2. Extrasensory perception -- Fiction
ISBN 0-441-00731-7

A reissue of the title first published 1969 by Walker & Company

ALA YALSA Margaret A. Edwards Award (2004)

"This is a tale of political intrigue and danger on the world of Gethen, the Winter planet. Genly Ai, high official of the Eukeman—the commonwealth of worlds—is on Gethen to convince the royalty to join the Federation. He soon becomes a pawn in Gethen's power struggles, set against the elaborate mores of the Gethenians, a unisex hermaphroditic people whose intricate sexual physiology plays a key role in the conflict. Allied with Estraven, fallen lord, Genly is forced to cross the savage and impassable Gobrin Ice." Shapiro. Fic for Youth. 3d edition

Powers. Harcourt 2007 502p map $17; pa $7.99
Grades: 7 8 9 10 **Fic**

1. Fantasy fiction
ISBN 978-0-15-205770-1; 0-15-205770-6; 978-0-15-206674-1 pa; 0-15-206674-8 pa
LC 2006-13549

Sequel to Voices (2006)

When young Gavir's sister is brutally killed, he escapes from slavery and sets out to explore the world and his own psychic abilities.

"Le Guin uses her own prodigious power as a writer to craft lyrical, precise sentences, evoking a palpable sense of place and believable characters." SLJ

Voices. Harcourt 2006 341p $17
Grades: 7 8 9 10 **Fic**

1. Fantasy fiction
ISBN 978-015-205678-0; 0-15-205678-5
LC 2005020753

Sequel to Gifts (2004)

Young Memer takes on a pivotal role in freeing her war-torn homeland from its oppressive captors.

"While her prose is simple and unadorned, Le Guin's superior narrative voice and storytelling power make even small moments ring with truth, and often with beauty." SLJ

Followed by Powers (2007)

★ A **wizard** of Earthsea; [by] Ursula K. Le Guin; illustrated by Ruth Robbins. Bantam trade pbk. ed.; Bantam Books 2004 182p il pa $15
Grades: 6 7 8 9 **Fic**

1. Fantasy fiction 2. Science fiction 3. Magic -- Fiction
ISBN 0-553-38304-3; 978-0-553-38304-1
LC 2004558962

A reissue of the title first published 1968 by Parnassus Press

ALA YALSA Margaret A. Edwards Award (2004)

A boy grows to manhood while attempting to subdue the evil he unleashed on the world as an apprentice to the Master Wizard.

A "powerful fantasy-allegory. Though set as prose, the rhythms of the langauge are truly and consistently poetical." Read Ladders for Hum Relat. 5th edition

Other titles in this series are:
The Tombs of Atuan (1971)
The farthest shore (1972)
Tehanu (1990)

Leavitt, Lindsey

Going vintage; by Lindsey Leavitt. 1st U.S. ed. Bloomsbury 2013 320 p. (hardcover) $16.99
Grades: 7 8 9 10 **Fic**

1. School stories 2. Sisters -- Fiction 3. Dating (Social customs) -- Fiction 4. Lists -- Fiction 5. Schools -- Fiction 6. California -- Fiction 7. High schools -- Fiction 8. Family life -- California -- Fiction
ISBN 1599907879; 9781599907871
LC 2012023269

In this book, "after discovering her boyfriend has a serious online relationship with another girl, Mallory very publicly dumps him on his social media site. She complicates the situation by deciding to try to fulfill a to-do list her grandmother crafted at the beginning of her junior year of high school in 1962, a time Mallory thinks must have been much simpler than today. . . . She's aided by her loyal younger sister, Ginnie, and the growing affection of her ex's cousin, charming Oliver." (Kirkus)

Sean Griswold's head. Bloomsbury 2011 276p $16.99
Grades: 7 8 9 10 **Fic**

1. School stories 2. Family life -- Fiction 3.

Pennsylvania -- Fiction 4. Multiple sclerosis -- Fiction
ISBN 978-1-59990-498-6; 1-59990-498-5
LC 2010-06949

After discovering that her father has multiple sclerosis, fifteen-year-old Payton begins counselling sessions at school, which lead her to become interested in a boy in her biology class, have a falling out with her best friend, develop an interest in bike riding, and eventually allow her to come to terms with life's uncertainties.

"Leavitt capably handles the issues of chronic illness with sensitivity, making this an insightful, humorous, and ultimately uplifting family drama." Bull Cent Child Books

Leavitt, Martine

My book of life by Angel; Martine Leavitt. Farrar, Straus and Giroux Books for Young Readers 2012 252 p. $17.99; (hardback) $17.99; (ebook) $12.95

Grades: 8 9 10 11 **Fic**

1. Novels in verse 2. Runaway teenagers -- Fiction 3. Juvenile prostitution -- Fiction 4. Runaways -- Fiction 5. Drug abuse -- Fiction 6. Prostitution -- Fiction 7. Vancouver (B.C.) -- Fiction
ISBN 0374351236; 9780374351236; 9781554983179
LC 2011044563

This "novel in verse tells the story of 16-year-old Angel, who has been working as a prostitute in Vancouver. . . . After Angel's friend Serena disappears, Angel decides to give up" the drugs her pimp Call feeds her "and try to return home. Angel's withdrawal is severe . . . but it's nothing compared to the pain she feels when Call brings home an 11-year-old girl, Melli, to follow in Angel's footsteps. Angel is determined to keep Melli safe, even while other women continue to disappear." (Publishers Weekly)

Lecesne, James

Absolute brightness. HarperTeen 2008 472p $17.99; lib bdg $18.89

Grades: 7 8 9 10 **Fic**

1. Cousins -- Fiction 2. New Jersey -- Fiction 3. Good and evil -- Fiction 4. Homosexuality -- Fiction
ISBN 978-0-06-125627-1; 0-06-125627-7; 978-0-06-125628-8 lib bdg; 0-06-125628-5 lib bdg
LC 2007-02988

ALA YALSA Morris Award Finalist, 2009

In the beach town of Neptune, New Jersey, Phoebe's life is changed irrevocably when her gay cousin moves into her house and soon goes missing.

"This thoughtful novel is beautifully written; its themes are haunting, and in spite of the central tragedy, it's often laugh-out-loud funny." Kliatt

Lee, Harper, 1926-

★ **To** kill a mockingbird; Harper Lee. 50th anniversary ed; Harper 2010 323p $25.00

Grades: 8 9 10 11 12 Adult **Fic**

1. Alabama -- Fiction 2. Race relations -- Fiction
ISBN 9780061743528

A reissue of the title first published 1960 by Lippincott

"Scout, as Jean Louise is called, is a precocious child. She relates her impressions of the time when her lawyer father, Atticus Finch, is defending a black man accused of raping a white woman in a small Alabama town during the 1930's. Atticus's courageous act brings the violence and injustice that exists in their world sharply into focus as it intrudes into the lighthearted life that Scout and her brother Jem have enjoyed until that time." Shapiro. Fic for Youth. 3d edition

Lee, Tanith

Piratica; being a daring tale of a singular girl's adventure upon the high seas. Presented most handsomely by the notorious Tanith Lee. Dutton Children's Books 2004 288p $17.99

Grades: 6 7 8 9 **Fic**

1. Adventure fiction 2. Pirates -- Fiction 3. Sex role -- Fiction
ISBN 0-525-47324-6

First published 2003 in the United Kingdom

A bump on the head restores Art's memories of her mother and the exciting life they led, so the sixteen-year-old leaves Angels Academy for Young Maidens, seeks out the pirates who were her family before her mother's death, and leads them back to adventure on the high seas.

"Piratica is a refreshing, tongue-in-cheek, tangled tale that will entice readers who crave adventure and fantasy." SLJ

Piratica II: return to Parrot Island; being the return of a most intrepid heroine to sea and secrets. Dutton Children's Books 2006 320p $17.99

Grades: 6 7 8 9 **Fic**

1. Adventure fiction 2. Pirates -- Fiction 3. Sex role -- Fiction
ISBN 0-525-47769-1

Art Blastside is bored with life ashore, so she jumps at the chance to return to sea.

"Lee's writing is complex, and she uses her skill to craft subtle pundit humor and lush description." Voice Youth Advocates

Lee, Ying S.

A **spy** in the house. Candlewick Press 2010 335p (The Agency) $16.99

Grades: 8 9 10 11 12 **Fic**

1. Mystery fiction 2. Orphans -- Fiction 3. Household employees -- Fiction 4. Swindlers and swindling -- Fiction 5. Great Britain -- History -- 19th century -- Fiction
ISBN 978-0-7636-4067-5; 0-7636-4067-0
LC 2009-32736

Rescued from the gallows in 1850s London, young orphan and thief Mary Quinn is offered a place at Miss Scrimshaw's Academy for Girls where she is trained to be part of an all-female investigative unit called The Agency and, at age seventeen, she infiltrates a rich merchant's home in hopes of tracing his missing cargo ships.

"Lee fills the story with classic elements of Victorian mystery and melodrama. Class differences, love gone awry, racial discrimination, London's growing pains in the 1850s, and the status of women in society are all addressed. Historical details are woven seamlessly into the plot, and descriptive writing allows readers to be part of each scene." SLJ

Other titles in this series are:

The body at the tower (2010)

The traitor in the tunnel (2012)

LeFlore, Lyah

The **world** is mine; [by] Lyah B. LeFlore; with illustrations by DL Warfield. Simon Pulse 2009 269p il (Come up) pa $8.99

Grades: 7 8 9 10 **Fic**

1. School stories 2. Maryland -- Fiction 3. Family life -- Fiction 4. Music industry -- Fiction 5. African Americans -- Fiction

ISBN 978-1-4169-7963-0; 1-4169-7963-8

LC 2009-6900

Maryland high school juniors and best friends Blue Reynolds and Collin Andrews seem to have it all, and when they decide to become party promoters, anything can happen—including being pitted against parents, jealous girlfriends, and even one another.

"Teens, especially the hip-hop obsessed, will relate to the characters' stratospheric aspirations, their struggles to balance their passions with parental demands, as well as the sharp dialogue and narration." Publ Wkly

Leitch, Will

Catch. Razorbill 2005 288p pa $7.99

Grades: 9 10 11 12 **Fic**

1. Illinois -- Fiction

ISBN 1-59514-069-7

LC 2005-08146

Teenager Tim Temples must decide if he wants to leave his comfortable life in a small town and go to college.

"This substantive title will entice both male and female YA readers with its thoughtful, authentic, and romantic young man's voice." Booklist

Lennon, Tom

When love comes to town; Tom Lennon. Albert Whitman 2013 304 p. (reinforced) $15.99

Grades: 8 9 10 11 12 **Fic**

1. Historical fiction 2. Gay teenagers -- Fiction 3. Gays -- Fiction 4. Ireland -- Fiction 5. Coming out (Sexual orientation) -- Fiction

ISBN 0807589160; 9780807589168

LC 2012020160

In this novel, by Tom Lennon, "the year is 1990, and in his hometown of Dublin, Ireland, Neil Byrne plays rugby, keeps up with the in-crowd at his school, and is just a regular guy. A guy who's gay. It's a secret he keeps from the wider world as he explores the city at night and struggles to figure out how to reveal his real self--and to whom." (Publisher's note)

Leonard, Julia Platt

Cold case. Aladdin 2011 281p $15.99

Grades: 6 7 8 9 **Fic**

1. Mystery fiction 2. Spies -- Fiction 3. Brothers -- Fiction 4. Homicide -- Fiction 5. Family life -- Fiction 6. Restaurants -- Fiction

ISBN 978-1-4424-2009-0; 1-4424-2009-X

LC 2010041854

When thirteen-year-old Oz Keillor finds a dead body in his family's Santa Fe, New Mexico, restaurant, he is determined to solve the mystery in which his older brother is implicated, but which also involves their long-dead father, who was accused of being a spy.

"The well-plotted double mystery is propped up by a few choice details about restaurant life, some sly red herrings, and a cast of nicely rounded characters." Booklist

Leroux, Gaston

The **phantom** of the opera; introduction by Anne Perry. Modern Library 2002 xxiii, 286p (The Modern Library Classics) pa $8.95

Grades: 9 10 11 12 **Fic**

1. Paris (France) -- Fiction

ISBN 0-375-76113-6

LC 2002-67075

First published 1911 by The Bobbs-Merrill Company

This love story/thriller relates the tale of the mysterious masked terror who inhabits the cellars of the Paris Opera House

Les Becquets, Diane

Love, Cajun style. Bloomsbury 2005 296p $16.95; pa $7.95

Grades: 9 10 11 12 **Fic**

1. Aunts -- Fiction 2. Louisiana -- Fiction 3. Friendship -- Fiction 4. Family life -- Fiction

ISBN 1-58234-674-7; 1-59990-030-0 pa

LC 2005-11948

Teenage Lucy learns about life and love with the help of her friends and saucy Tante Pearl over the course of one hot Louisiana summer before her senior year of high school.

"This is romantic, real, and lots of fun." Booklist

★ **Season** of ice. Bloomsbury U.S.A. Children's Books 2008 281p $16.95

Grades: 8 9 10 11 12 **Fic**

1. Lakes -- Fiction 2. Maine -- Fiction 3. Stepfamilies -- Fiction 4. Missing persons -- Fiction 5. Father-daughter relationship -- Fiction

ISBN 978-1-59990-063-6; 1-59990-063-7

LC 2007-30845

When seventeen-year-old Genesis Sommer's father disappears on Moosehead Lake near their small-town Maine home in mid-November, she must cope with the pressure of keeping her family together, even while rumors about the event plague her.

This is "a heartbreaking story from the very beginning, but Les Becquets turns it into something well beyond a mere tearjerker. . . . It's a tender story of a tough, smart, loving girl who finds that she can rise to the challenge of what she's lost because of what she's gained. Readers will understand her and admire her, and find her difficult indeed to forget." Bull Cent Child Books

Leslea, Newman

October mourning; a song for Matthew Shepard. Lesléa Newman. Candlewick 2012 xi, 111 p.p

Grades: 10 11 12 **Fic**

1. Poetry -- Collections 2. Gays -- Fiction 3. Novels in verse 4. Murder -- Fiction 5. Hate crimes -- Fiction 6. Laramie (Wyo.) -- Fiction

ISBN 0763658073; 9780763658076

LC 2011048358

Stonewall Honor Book (2013)

In this book "lesbian literary icon [Lesléa] Newman offers a 68-poem tribute to Matthew Shepard, . . . [who] was lured from a bar by two men who drove him to the outskirts of town, beat him mercilessly, tied him to a fence and left him to die. This cycle of poems, meant to be read sequentially as a whole, incorporates Newman's reflections on Shepard's killing and its aftermath, using a number of . . . literary devices to portray. . . that fateful night and the trial that followed." (Kirkus Reviews)

Includes bibliographical references.

Lessing, Doris May

The **sweetest** dream; [by] Doris Lessing. HarperCollins Pubs. 2002 478p hardcover o.p. pa $13.95

Grades: 11 12 Adult **Fic**

1. Feminism -- Fiction 2. London (England) -- Fiction

ISBN 0-06-621334-7; 0-06-093755-6 pa

LC 2002-279950

"While Frances Lennox, uncomplaining and unsentimental about her roles as a 1960s earth mother for a string of "screwed up" post-war children, serves up endless nurturing at the crowded kitchen table of a large North London house, her ex- husband pursues revolution on all-expenses-paid trips and conferences. Occasionally he drops by for free meals or to dump one of the children, or wives, of another failed marriage on Frances's doorstep." Amazon.com

"Lessing's understanding of relationships—both personal and political—has always been keen; now . . . it is unparalleled. This novel is warm and heartfelt, old-fashioned and ambitious in its historical sweep." New Statesman (1913)

Lester, Joan Steinau

Black, white, other. Zondervan 2011 222p $15.99

Grades: 7 8 9 10 **Fic**

1. Divorce -- Fiction 2. Slavery -- Fiction 3. California -- Fiction 4. Family life -- Fiction 5. Grandmothers -- Fiction 6. Race relations -- Fiction 7. Racially mixed people -- Fiction

ISBN 978-0-310-72763-7; 0-310-72763-4

LC 2011015208

Twenty miles from Oakland, California, where fires have led to racial tension, multi-racial fifteen-year-old Nina faces the bigotry of long-time friends, her parents' divorce, and her brother's misbehavior, while learning of her great-great grandmother Sarah's escape from slavery.

"Lester . . . conjures a credible plot and complications; divorce is a fact of life and racially mixed heritage is conspicuously becoming one. The simple contrapuntal narrative of Sarah Armstrong's escaping slavery distinguishes the book emotionally and psychologically, raising it above other issue-oriented YA novels. Lester writes with social sensitivity and an ear for teen language and concerns. This is engaging treatment of a challenging subject that comes with little precedent." Publ Wkly

Includes bibliographical references

Lester, Julius

★ **Day** of tears; a novel in dialogue. Hyperion 2005 177p hardcover o.p. pa $7.99

Grades: 7 8 9 10 **Fic**

1. Slavery -- Fiction 2. African Americans -- Fiction

ISBN 0-7868-0490-4; 1-42310-409-9 pa

Coretta Scott King Award for text

Emma has taken care of the Butler children since Sarah and Frances's mother, Fanny, left. Emma wants to raise the girls to have good hearts, as a rift over slavery has ripped the Butler household apart. Now, to pay off debts, Pierce Butler wants to cash in his slave "assets", possibly including Emma.

"The horror of the auction and its aftermath is unforgettable. . . . The racism is virulent (there's widespread use of the n-word). The personal voices make this a stirring text for group discussion." Booklist

★ **Guardian.** Amistad/HarperTeen 2008 129p $16.99; lib bdg $17.89

Grades: 7 8 9 10 **Fic**

1. Lynching -- Fiction 2. Race relations -- Fiction 3. Southern States -- Fiction 4. African Americans -- Fiction

ISBN 978-0-06-155890-0; 0-06-155890-7; 978-0-06-155891-7 lib bdg; 0-06-155891-5 lib bdg

LC 2008-14251

In a rural southern town in 1946, a white man and his son witness the lynching of an innocent black man. Includes historical note on lynching.

"The author's understated, haunting prose is as compelling as it is dark; . . . [the story] leaves a deep impression." Publ Wkly

Includes bibliographical references

Time's memory. Farrar, Straus & Giroux 2006 230p $17

Grades: 8 9 10 11 12 **Fic**

1. Slavery -- Fiction 2. African Americans -- Fiction

ISBN 0-374-37178-4; 978-0-374-37178-4

LC 2005-47716

Ekundayo, a Dogon spirit brought to America from Africa, inhabits the body of a young African American slave on a Virginia plantation, where he experiences loss, sorrow, and reconciliation in the months preceding the Civil War.

"More than a picture of slavery through the eyes of those enslaved or their captors, Lester's narrative evokes spiritual images of Mali's Dogon people." SLJ

Letting Ana go; Anonymous. Simon Pulse 2013 304 p. $17.99

Grades: 9 10 11 12 **Fic**

1. Anorexia nervosa -- Fiction 2. Diet -- Fiction 3. Diaries -- Fiction 4. Food habits -- Fiction 5. Family problems -- Fiction 6. Self-perception -- Fiction

ISBN 1442472235; 9781442472235

LC 2012037458

This book provides an "account of one girl's battle with anorexia. . . . The unnamed narrator begins her story as a healthy, well-adjusted teen from a privileged family. Her overweight mother struggles with food issues on a daily basis and receives little emotional support from her husband. . . . Witnessing the deterioration of her parents' marriage, the teen becomes overwhelmed by a flood of conflicting emotions and channels her need for order into restricting what she eats." (School Library Journal)

Levchuk, Lisa

★ **Everything** beautiful in the world. Farrar, Straus & Giroux 2008 203p $16.95

Grades: 9 10 11 12 **Fic**

1. School stories 2. Cancer -- Fiction 3. Teachers -- Fiction 4. New Jersey -- Fiction 5. Family life -- Fiction

ISBN 978-0-374-32238-0; 0-374-32238-4

LC 2007-16603

Toward the end of the disco era, seventeen-year-old Edna refuses to visit her mother, who is in a New York City hospital undergoing cancer treatment, and barely speaks to her father, who finally puts her in psychotherapy, while her crush on an art teacher turns into a full-blown affair.

"Edna's narrative is fascinating. She is funny and scathing. . . . Her voice is so engrossing that the book is difficult to put down." Voice Youth Advocates

Levine, Ellen, 1939-2012

In trouble. Carolrhoda Lab 2011 200p $17.95

Grades: 7 8 9 10 **Fic**

1. Rape -- Fiction 2. Abortion -- Fiction 3. Pregnancy -- Fiction 4. Family life -- Fiction 5. New York (State) -- Fiction

ISBN 978-0-7613-6558-7; 0-7613-6558-3; 9780761365587; 0761365583

LC 2010051448

In 1950s New York, sixteen-year-old Jamie's life is unsettled since her father returned from serving time in prison for refusing to name people as Communists, when her best friend turns to Jamie for help with an unplanned pregnancy.

"The author's notes and acknowledgments draw together the past and present, making the book a good choice for required reading in sociology or advanced American history classes. In Trouble should be available in every library serving young adults." SLJ

Levine, Gail Carson

Ella enchanted. HarperCollins Pubs. 1997 232p $16.99; lib bdg $17.89; pa $6.50

Grades: 5 6 7 8 **Fic**

1. Fairy tales 2. Fantasy fiction

ISBN 0-06-027510-3; 0-06-027511-1 lib bdg; 0-06-440705-5 pa

LC 96-30734

A Newbery Medal honor book, 1998

"Ella is blessed by a fairy at birth with the gift of obedience. But the blessing is a horror for Ella, who must literally do what everyone tells her, from sweeping the floor to giving up a beloved heirloom necklace. After her mother dies, and her covetous, caustic father leaves on a trading trip, Ella's world is turned upside down. She battles both ogres and wicked stepsisters, makes friends and loses them, and must deny her love for her prince, Charmont, to save his life and his realm. In making this ultimate sacrifice, she breaks the curse." (Booklist)

"As finely designed as a tapestry, Ella's story both neatly incorporates elements of the original tale and mightily expands them." Booklist

Ever. HarperCollinsPublishers 2008 256p $16.99; lib bdg $17.89; pa $6.99

Grades: 5 6 7 8 **Fic**

1. Winds -- Fiction 2. Immortality -- Fiction 3. Fate and fatalism -- Fiction 4. Gods and goddesses -- Fiction

ISBN 978-0-06-122962-6; 0-06-122962-8; 978-0-06-122963-3 lib bdg; 0-06-122963-6 lib bdg; 978-0-06-122964-0 pa; 0-06-122964-4 pa

LC 2007-32289

Fourteen-year-old Kezi and Olus, Akkan god of the winds, fall in love and together try to change her fate—to be sacrificed to a Hyte god because of a rash promise her father made—through a series of quests that might make her immortal.

"Levine conducts a riveting journey, offering passion and profound pondering along the way." Publ Wkly

Fairest. HarperCollins 2006 326p $16.99

Grades: 6 7 8 9 **Fic**

1. Fairy tales 2. Singing -- Fiction

ISBN 978-0-06-073408-4; 0-06-073408-6

LC 2006-00337

In a land where beauty and singing are valued above all else, Aza eventually comes to reconcile her unconventional appearance and her magical voice, and learns to accept herself for who she truly is.

"The plot is fast-paced, and Aza's growth and maturity are well crafted and believable." SLJ

Levine, Kristin

★ The **best** bad luck I ever had. Putnam 2009 266p $16.99

Grades: 5 6 7 8 **Fic**

1. Friendship -- Fiction 2. Prejudices -- Fiction 3. Family life -- Fiction 4. Country life -- Fiction 5. Race relations -- Fiction

ISBN 978-0-399-25090-3; 0-399-25090-5

LC 2008-11570

In Moundville, Alabama, in 1917, twelve-year-old Dit hopes the new postmaster will have a son his age, but instead he meets Emma, who is black, and their friendship challenges accepted ways of thinking and leads them to save the life of a condemned man.

"Tension builds just below the surface of this energetic, seamlessly narrated . . . novel. . . . Levine handles the setting with grace and nuance." Publ Wkly

★ The **lions** of Little Rock; Kristin Levine. G. P. Putnam's Sons 2012 298p.

Grades: 5 6 7 8 **Fic**

1. School stories 2. African Americans -- Fiction 3. School integration -- Fiction 4. Schools -- Fiction 5. Friendship -- Fiction 6. Bashfulness -- Fiction 7. Middle schools -- Fiction 8. Race relations -- Fiction 9. Family life -- Arkansas -- Fiction

ISBN 9780399256448

LC 2011031835

This book presents a "portrait of 1958 Little Rock, Ark., the tumultuous year when the governor refused integration by closing local high schools. The story is told through the . . . voice of painfully quiet 12-year-old Marlee Nisbett, who makes a rare friend in Liz, a new student at her middle school. Liz instills some much-needed confidence in Marlee, but when it's revealed that Liz is 'passing" as a white student, Liz must leave school abruptly, putting their friendship to the test. The girls meet in secret, and Marlee joins an antisegregationist organization, both actions inviting serious risk amid escalating racist threats." (Publishers Weekly)

Levithan, David

★ **Every** day; by David Levithan. Alfred A. Knopf 2012 336 p. (hard cover) $16.99

Grades: 9 10 11 12 **Fic**

1. Love stories 2. Occult fiction 3. Teenagers -- Fiction 4. Love -- Fiction 5. Interpersonal relations -- Fiction

ISBN 0307931889; 9780307931887; 9780307931894; 9780307975638; 9780375971112

LC 2012004173

This book follows A, "who takes over the body of a different person each day at midnight. Right around A's 6,000th day on the planet, A meets Rhiannon—girlfriend of current host body Justin—and falls in love. A is careful not to disrupt the lives of the bodies he/she inhabits (A doesn't identify as male or female), but that starts to change as A pursues Rhiannon." (Publishers Weekly)

"Levithan's self-conscious, analytical style marries perfectly with the plot...Readers will devour his trademark poetic wordplay and cadences that feel as fresh as they were when he wrote Boy Meets Boy (2003)." Kirkus

Every you, every me; photographs by Jonathan Farmer. Alfred A. Knopf 2011 248p il $16.99; lib bdg $19.99; ebook $10.99

Grades: 9 10 11 12 **Fic**

1. School stories 2. Friendship -- Fiction 3. Mental illness -- Fiction

ISBN 978-0-375-86098-0; 978-0-375-96098-7 lib bdg; 978-0-375-89621-7 ebook

LC 2010048723

Evan is haunted by the loss of his best friend, but when mysterious photographs start appearing, he begins to fall apart as he starts to wonder if she has returned, seeking vengeance.

"The book is written for high school students who enjoy suspense but also for those who face depression in everyday life. Mental illness and loss touch all of us and this book shows what can happen to survivors self destructive behaviors." Voice Youth Advocates

Love is the higher law. Alfred A. Knopf 2009 167p $15.99; lib bdg $18.99

Grades: 8 9 10 11 12 **Fic**

1. Homosexuality -- Fiction 2. New York (N.Y.) -- Fiction 3. September 11 terrorist attacks, 2001 -- Fiction

ISBN 978-0-375-83468-4; 0-375-83468-0; 978-0-375-93468-1 lib bdg; 0-375-93468-5 lib bdg

LC 2008-40886

Three New York City teens express their reactions to the bombing of the World Trade Center on September 11, 2001, and its impact on their lives and the world.

"The author's prose has never been deeper in thought or feeling. His writing here is especially pure—unsentimental, restrained, and full of love for his characters and setting. . . . Levithan captures the mood of post-9/11 New York exquisitely, slashed open to reveal a deep heart." SLJ

Marly's ghost; a remix of Charles Dickens' A Christmas Carol. with illustrations by Brian Selznick. Dial Books 2006 167p il hardcover o.p. pa $6.99

Grades: 7 8 9 10 **Fic**

1. Ghost stories 2. Valentine's Day -- Fiction

ISBN 0-8037-3063-2; 0-14-240912-X pa

LC 2005-16183

The spirit of Ben's girlfriend Marly returns with three other ghosts to haunt him with a painful journey though Valentine's Days past, present, and future.

"The magical realism is powerful throughout. . . . A solid story to mark the holiday." Booklist

★ **Two** boys kissing; by David Levithan. Alfred A. Knopf 2013 208 p. (hardcover library binding) $19.99

Grades: 8 9 10 11 12 **Fic**

1. School stories 2. Gay teenagers -- Fiction 3. Gays -- Fiction 4. Love -- Fiction 5. Homosexuality -- Fiction 6. Social change -- Fiction

ISBN 0307931900; 0375971122; 9780307931900; 9780307931917; 9780375971129

LC 2012047089

Stonewall Honor Book: Children and Young Adult (2014)

Lambda Literary Awards Winner - LGBT Children's/YA (2014)

In this book, students Craig and Henry are trying to set a world record for the longest kiss They "are no longer dating, throwing an element of uncertainty into an act that's romantic, political, and personal. Neil and Peter have been dating for a year and are beginning to wonder what's next. Avery, 'born a boy that the rest of the world saw as a girl,' and Ryan are caught up in the dizzying excitement of meeting someone new. And Cooper is rapidly losing himself into a digital oblivion." (Publishers Weekly)

"Craig and Harry attempt to break the world record for longest kiss, which, in turn, affects the lives of the people around them. Narrated by a ghostly chorus of past generations of gay men who died of AIDS, Levithan's latest novel weaves together an informed (sometimes melodramatic) perspective on the past with the present-day stories of seven boys constructing their own sexual identities." (Horn Book)

Levitin, Sonia

Strange relations. Alfred A. Knopf 2007 298p hardcover o.p. pa $6.50

Grades: 7 8 9 10 **Fic**

1. Jews -- Fiction 2. Hawaii -- Fiction 3. Cousins -- Fiction 4. Religion -- Fiction

ISBN 978-0-375-83751-7; 0-375-83751-5; 978-0-440-23963-5 pa; 0-440-23963-X pa

LC 2006-33275

Fifteen-year-old Marne is excited to be able to spend her summer vacation in Hawaii, not realizing the change in her lifestyle it would bring staying with her aunt, seven cousins, and uncle who is a Chasidic rabbi.

"It's rare to find such well-developed characters, empathetic and sensitive religious treatment, and carefully crafted plotlines in one novel." SLJ

Lewis, Stewart

The **secret** ingredient; Stewart Lewis. Delacorte Press 2013 256 p. (hc) $17.99

Grades: 7 8 9 10 **Fic**

1. Cooking -- Fiction 2. Mothers -- Fiction 3. Interpersonal relations -- Fiction 4. Self-realization -- Fiction 5. Los Angeles (Calif.) -- Fiction

ISBN 0385743319; 9780375991066; 9780385743310

LC 2012027203

This novel by Stewart Lewis is a "journey of family, food, romance, and self-discovery as Olivia, a teen chef living in L.A., finds a vintage cookbook and begins a search for her birthmother that will change her life forever. A new job leads Olivia to a gorgeous, mysterious boy named Theo. And as Olivia cooks the recipes from a vintage cookbook she stumbles upon, she begins to wonder if the mother she's never known might be the secret ingredient she's been lacking." (Publisher's note)

"Adopted by two dads, Olivia begins to sense a void in her life. Serendipitously, Olivia finds her supposedly "nameless" birth mother but quickly realizes that maybe the secret ingredient to a fulfilled life is appreciating what one already has. Lewis's mature protagonist adapts remarkably well to her nontraditional life in this story that limns themes of adolescence, adoption, illness, and financial instability." (Horn Book)

Lewis, Sylvia

Beautiful decay; Sylvia Lewis. Running Press Teens 2013 303 p. $9.95

Grades: 7 8 9 10 11 12 **Fic**

1. Supernatural -- Fiction 2. Alienation (Social psychology) -- Fiction

ISBN 0762446110; 9780762446117

LC 2012951788

This "paranormal horror novel" follows "17-year-old Ellie. . . . A touch of her bare skin can cause anyone or anything to decay. No one wants to be near her, even though she wears gloves to avoid contact with anyone. . . .Things at school improve when Nate, the new guy, seems more curious than grossed out by her. . . . Ellie finds the strength she didn't know she had to break away from her lonely, 'bleached and gloved' existence to help him." (School Library Journal)

"Ellie Miller lives a lonely life. Her parents are rarely home when she is, her mother spends her time bleaching the house, and her only friend, Mackenzie, lives two states away and communicates via computer. Isolated by classmates due to an "immunity disorder," she wears gloves and dares not touch anything or anyone...Fans of paranormal will flock to Lewis' fast-paced debut that offers a unique take on being different. Many questions are left unanswered, laying the groundwork for a sequel." (Booklist)

LeZotte, Ann Clare

T4; a novel in verse. written by Ann Clare LeZotte. Houghton Mifflin Co. 2008 108p $14

Grades: 6 7 8 9 10 **Fic**

1. Novels in verse 2. Deaf -- Fiction 3. Euthanasia -- Fiction 4. Germany -- History -- 1933-1945 -- Fiction

ISBN 978-0-547-04684-6; 0-547-04684-7

LC 2007-47737

When the Nazi party takes control of Germany, thirteen-year-old Paula, who is deaf, finds her world-as-she-knows-it turned upside down, as she is taken into hiding to protect her from the new law nicknamed T4.

"This novel will have a lasting effect on readers, giving insight into an often-forgotten aspect of the horrors of the Third Reich." SLJ

Libby, Alisa M.

The **king's** rose. Dutton Children's Books 2009 320p $17.99

Grades: 7 8 9 10 **Fic**

1. Queens 2. Kings 3. Queens -- Fiction 4. Kings and rulers -- Fiction 5. Great Britain -- History -- 1485-1603, Tudors -- Fiction

ISBN 978-0-525-47970-3; 0-525-47970-8

LC 2008-14338

Catharine Howard recounts the events in her life that led to her being groomed for marriage at the age of fifteen to King Henry VIII, her failure to produce an heir to the throne, and her quick execution.

"While numerous sexual encounters are part of the political reality, they are subtly handled. A real treat for lovers of historical fiction." SLJ

Liberty, Anita

The **center** of the universe; yep, that would be me. Simon Pulse 2008 291p il pa $9.99

Grades: 10 11 12 **Fic**

1. School stories 2. Girls -- Fiction

ISBN 978-1-4169-5789-8; 1-4169-5789-8

LC 2007-940383

An angst-ridden fictional memoir of Anita Liberty's last two years in high school is presented through diary entries, poems, sarcastic advice, scorecards of parental infractions, and definitions of SAT vocabulary words.

"Female readers should laugh aloud throughout this fast, entertaining read, and especially appreciate the interesting epilogue continuing the author's post-high school experiences before ending with her present fulfilling circumstances." Voice Youth Advocates

Lieberman, Leanne

Lauren Yanofsky hates the holocaust; Leanne Lieberman. Orca Book Publishers 2013 240 p. (paperback) $12.95; (ebook) $12.99

Grades: 7 8 9 10 **Fic**

1. Jews -- Fiction 2. Holocaust, 1939-1945 -- Fiction

ISBN 1459801091; 9781459801097; 9781459801103 pdf; 9781459801110

LC 2012952950

In this novel, by Leanne Lieberman, "Lauren Yanofsky doesn't want to be Jewish anymore. Her father, a noted Holocaust historian, keeps giving her Holocaust memoirs to read, and her mother doesn't understand why Lauren hates the idea of Jewish youth camps and family vacations to Holocaust memorials. But when Lauren sees some of her friends . . . playing Nazi war games, she is faced with a terrible choice: betray her friends or betray her heritage." (Publisher's note)

"Lieberman . . . smoothly weaves humor and knowledge about Judaism through Lauren's story. Lauren's narration is contemplative and from the heart, and readers should relate to her attempts to identify her beliefs and tackle life's big questions." Pub Wkly

Lindskold, Jane M.

Thirteen orphans; [by] Jane Lindskold. Tor 2008 367p il $24.95

Grades: 11 12 Adult **Fic**

1. Fantasy fiction

ISBN 978-0-7653-1700-1; 0-7653-1700-1

LC 2008-34085

In an alternate world inspired by ancient Chinese lore and magic, Brenda learns about her magical ancestry after an attack on her father and finds herself among a band of orphans who each represent an animal from the Chinese zodiac.

The author "has created a convincing tale of a young woman entering adulthood, assuming responsibility for herself and for others, and making sometimes-wrenching decisions." SLJ

Lipsyte, Robert

★ The **contender**. Harper & Row 1967 182p hardcover o.p. pa $5.99

Grades: 7 8 9 10 **Fic**

1. Boxing -- Fiction 2. African Americans -- Fiction 3. Harlem (New York, N.Y.) -- Fiction

ISBN 0-06-447039-3

ALA YALSA Margaret A. Edwards Award (2001)

"After a street fight in which he is the chief target, Alfred wanders into a gym in his neighborhood. He decides not only to improve his physical condition but also to become a boxer. Because of this interest Alfred's life is completely changed. He assumes a more positive outlook on his immediate future, even within the confines of a black ghetto." Shapiro. Fic for Youth. 3d edition

Followed by The brave (1991) and The chief (1993)

One fat summer. Harper & Row 1977 152p hardcover o.p. pa $5.99

Grades: 7 8 9 10 **Fic**

1. Obesity -- Fiction 2. Weight loss -- Fiction

ISBN 0-06-023895-X; 0-06-447073-3 pa

LC 76-49746

ALA YALSA Margaret A. Edwards Award (2001)

"This is far superior to most of the summer-of-change stories; any change that takes place is logical and the protagonist learns by action and reaction to be both self-reliant and compassionate." Bull Cent Child Books

Followed by Summer rules (1981) and The summerboy (1982)

Raiders night. HarperTempest 2006 232p hardcover o.p. pa $6.99

Grades: 9 10 11 12 **Fic**

1. Rape -- Fiction 2. Football -- Fiction 3. Drug abuse -- Fiction

ISBN 978-0-06-059946-1; 0-06-059946-4; 978-0-06-059948-5 pa; 0-06-059948-0 pa

LC 2005-17865

Matt Rydeck, co-captain of his high school football team, endures a traumatic season as he witnesses the rape of a rookie player by teammates and grapples with his own use of performance-enhancing drugs.

This is "is a riveting and chilling look inside contemporary high school football." Publ Wkly

Lisle, Holly

★ The **Ruby** Key. Orchard Books 2008 361p (Moon & sun) $16.99; pa $7.99

Grades: 5 6 7 8 **Fic**

1. Fantasy fiction 2. Siblings -- Fiction

ISBN 978-0-545-00012-3; 0-545-00012-2; 978-0-545-00013-0 pa; 0-545-00013-0 pa

LC 2007-30217

In a world where an uneasy peace binds Humans and Nightlings, fourteen-year-old Genna and her twelve-year-old brother Dan learn of their uncle's plot to gain immortality in exchange for human lives, and the two strike their own bargain with the Nightling lord, which sets them on a dangerous journey along the Moonroads in search of a key.

"Lisle's fertile imagination provides the nightworlds with monsters . . . but it is her clever plotting in this . . . fantasy, leading up to a thrilling finish . . . That will bewitch her audience." Horn Book

The **silver** door. Orchard Books 2009 366p (Moon & sun) $17.99

Grades: 5 6 7 8 **Fic**

1. War stories 2. Fantasy fiction

ISBN 978-0-545-00014-7; 0-545-00014-9

LC 2008-40153

When Genna is chosen as the Sunrider of prophecy, her destiny is to unite the magic of the sun and the moon for the good of both Nightlings and humans.

"This second book of the Moon & Sun series has jarring stop-start feel, but the complexities of the interlaced human and nightling societies continue to unfold in fascinating way, creating a multi-hued, fully realized world for readers to explore." Horn Book

Littke, Lael

Lake of secrets. Holt & Co. 2002 202p $16.95

Grades: 7 8 9 10 **Fic**

1. Mystery fiction 2. Reincarnation -- Fiction 3. Mystery and detective stories

ISBN 0-8050-6730-2

LC 2001-39933

Having arrived in her mother's home town to try to find her long-missing brother, who disappeared three years before she was born, fifteen-year-old Carlene finds herself haunted by memories from a past life

"The realistic characters and plot make the idea compelling, and the story will intrigue teens." Booklist

Little, Kimberley Griffiths

★ **Circle** of secrets. Scholastic Press 2011 326p $17.99

Grades: 5 6 7 8 **Fic**

1. Ghost stories 2. Guilt -- Fiction 3. Mother-daughter relationship -- Fiction

ISBN 978-0-545-16561-7; 0-545-16561-X

LC 2011000889

A year after her mother has deserted the family, eleven-year-old Shelby goes to stay with her, deep in the Louisiana bayou, where they both confront old hurts and regrets.

"The gently spooky ghost angle is handled nicely with some religious overtones. A very dramatic climax leads to a sweet, satisfying ending with some surprising twists and with reconciliation occurring for several characters." Kirkus

The **healing** spell. Scholastic Press 2010 354p $17.99

Grades: 5 6 7 8 **Fic**

1. Coma -- Fiction 2. Guilt -- Fiction

ISBN 978-0-545-16559-4; 0-545-16559-8

LC 2009-28016

Twelve-year-old Livie is living with a secret and it's crushing her. She knows she is responsible for her mother's coma, but she can't tell anyone. It's up to her to find a way to wake her momma up.

"Little explores the extremes of childhood guilt and its consequences in this harsh yet well-crafted story about fully drawn people. The bayou, with its rich culture, is an atmospheric character that overlays the story with mystery and dread." Booklist

Littman, Sarah

Life, after; [by] Sarah Darer Littman. Scholastic Press 2010 281p $17.99

Grades: 7 8 9 10 11 12 **Fic**

1. Terrorism -- Fiction 2. Immigrants -- Fiction

ISBN 978-0-545-15144-3; 0-545-15144-9

After a terrorist attack kills Dani's aunt and unborn cousin, life in Argentina—private school, a boyfriend, a loving family—crumbles quickly. In order to escape a country that is sinking under their feet, Dani and her family move to the United States.

The author "weaves sensitively articulated themes . . . and credible teen banter into an emotionally complex tale." Booklist

Lloyd, Alison

Year of the tiger. Holiday House 2010 194p $16.95

Grades: 5 6 7 8 **Fic**

1. Adventure fiction 2. Archery -- Fiction 3. Social classes -- Fiction

ISBN 978-0-8234-2277-7; 0-8234-2277-1

LC 2009033651

First published 2008 in Australia

In ancient China, Hu and Ren forge an unlikely alliance in an effort to become expert archers and, ultimately, to save their city from invading barbarians.

"Brimming with details of daily life in the Han Dynasty, this fast-paced story alternates in the third person between Hu and Ren." Kirkus

Lloyd, Saci

★ The **carbon** diaries 2015. Holiday House 2009 330p il map $17.95

Grades: 8 9 10 11 12 **Fic**

1. Science fiction 2. Family life -- Fiction 3. Great Britain -- Fiction 4. Conservation of natural resources -- Fiction

ISBN 978-0-8234-2190-9; 0-8234-2190-2

LC 2008-19712

First published 2008 in the United Kingdom

In 2015, when England becomes the first nation to introduce carbon dioxide rationing in a drastic bid to combat climate change, sixteen-year-old Laura documents the first year of rationing as her family spirals out of control.

"Deeply compulsive and urgently compulsory reading." Booklist

Includes bibliographical references

Followed by The carbon diaries 2017 (2010)

The **carbon** diaries 2017. Holiday House 2010 326p il map $17.95

Grades: 8 9 10 11 12 **Fic**

1. Science fiction 2. College students -- Fiction 3. London (England) -- Fiction 4. Conservation of natural resources -- Fiction

ISBN 978-0-8234-2260-9; 0-8234-2260-7

Sequel to: The carbon diaries 2015 (2009)

First published 2009 in the United Kingdom

Two years after England introduces carbon dioxide rationing to combat climatic change, eighteen-year-old Laura chronicles her first year at a London university as natural disasters and political upheaval disrupt her studies.

"The friction of living life in times of radical upheaval remains potent, sobering, and awfully exciting." Booklist

Lo, Malinda

Adaptation; Malinda Lo. Little, Brown Books for Young Readers 2012 400 p. (hardcover) $17.99

Grades: 9 10 11 12 **Fic**

1. Mystery fiction 2. Secrecy -- Fiction 3. Lesbians -- Fiction 4. Love -- Fiction 5. Science fiction 6. Conspiracies -- Fiction 7. Sexual orientation -- Fiction 8. Genetic engineering -- Fiction 9. Extraterrestrial beings -- Fiction

ISBN 0316197963; 9780316197960

LC 2012005489

Author Malinda Lo tells the story of "Reese and David, traveling home after a disastrous debate tournament, [who] are in a near-fatal car accident near a mysterious government facility. The tension is relentless until the teens make it safely back to San Francisco, at which point romantic entanglements (Reese falls for Amber, but maybe she likes David too) detract from the strange abilities Reese and David are developing and the conspiracies they begin to unravel (with lots of men in black after the)." (Kirkus)

Ash. Little, Brown and Co. 2009 264p $16.99; pa $8.99

Grades: 8 9 10 11 **Fic**

1. Fairy tales 2. Love stories 3. Fairies -- Fiction 4. Stepfamilies -- Fiction

ISBN 978-0-316-04009-9; 0-316-04009-6; 978-0-316-04010-5 pa; 0-316-04010-X pa

LC 2009-17471

ALA YALSA Morris Award Finalist, 2010

In this variation on the Cinderella story, Ash grows up believing in the fairy realm that the king and his philosophers have sought to suppress, until one day she must choose between a handsome fairy cursed to love her and the King's Huntress whom she loves.

"Part heart-pounding lesbian romance and part universal coming-of-age story, Lo's powerful tale is richly embroidered with folklore and glittering fairy magic that will draw fans of Sharon Shinn's earthy, herb-laced fantasies." Booklist

Followed by Huntress (2011)

Huntress. Little, Brown 2011 371p map $17.99
Grades: 9 10 11 12 **Fic**

1. Fairy tales 2. Love stories 3. Fairies -- Fiction 4. Lesbians -- Fiction 5. Voyages and travels -- Fiction

ISBN 978-0-316-04007-5; 0-316-04007-X

LC 2010-38827

"A 'Tam Lin'-inspired rendition of fairy society blends nicely with the author's Chinese and I Ching-inspired human society, creating a delicate, unusual setting; and although the expeditionary plot has an overly deliberate pace, the episodes are varied and emotional enough to retain interest. Most notably, the inclusion of gay characters in a young adult fantasy, and the natural unfolding of their relationship, comes as a refreshing change." Horn Book

Inheritance; by Malinda Lo. Little, Brown and Co. 2013 470 p. $18
Grades: 9 10 11 12 **Fic**

1. Love stories 2. Teenagers -- Fiction 3. Human-alien encounters -- Fiction 4. Love -- Fiction 5. Science fiction 6. Kidnapping -- Fiction 7. Conspiracies -- Fiction 8. Sexual orientation -- Fiction 9. Genetic engineering -- Fiction 10. Extraterrestrial beings -- Fiction

ISBN 0316198005; 9780316198004

LC 2012048433

Sequel to: Adaptation

In this book, by Malinda Lo, "after a car accident, mortally injured Reese and David are revived by an injection of alien DNA that has given the teens special abilities. They are kidnapped by brutal government forces. . . . Returned home, Reese and David are caught in a web of intrigue and lies. . . . The fate of the world seems to be at risk as the government, a secret faction of the government, and the aliens square off at the United Nations." (School Library Journal)

"Reese (Adaptation) juggles her discovery that the government has been working for decades with aliens called the Imria and her feelings for her Imrian ex and her new guy. When huge secrets are revealed, romantic alliances get back-burnered as Reese tries to understand what's next for Earth. Clever plot and strong world-building are this sequel's strengths." (Horn Book)

Lockhart, E.

The **boy** book; a study of habits and behaviors, plus techniques for taming them. Delacorte Press 2006 193p $15.95; lib bdg $17.99
Grades: 8 9 10 11 12 **Fic**

1. School stories 2. Friendship -- Fiction 3. Dating (Social customs) -- Fiction

ISBN 978-0-385-73208-6; 0-385-73208-2; 978-0-385-90239-7 lib bdg; 0-385-90239-5 lib bdg

LC 2006-4601

A high school junior continues her quest for relevant data on the male species, while enjoying her freedom as a newly licensed driver and examining her friendship with a clean-living vegetarian classmate.

"Lockhart achieves the perfect balance of self-deprecating humor and self-pity in Ruby, and thus imbues her with such realism that she seems almost to fly off the page." Voice Youth Advocates

The **boyfriend** list; (15 guys, 11 shrink appointments, 4 ceramic frogs, and me, Ruby Oliver) Delacorte Press 2005 240p hardcover o.p. pa $8.95
Grades: 9 10 11 12 **Fic**

1. School stories 2. Washington (State) -- Fiction 3. Dating (Social customs) -- Fiction

ISBN 0-385-73206-6; 0-385-73207-4 pa

LC 2004-6691

A Seattle fifteen-year-old explains some of the reasons for her recent panic attacks, including breaking up with her boyfriend, losing all her girlfriends, tensions between her performance-artist mother and her father, and more.

"Readers will find many of Ruby's experiences familiar, and they'll appreciate the story as a lively, often entertaining read." Booklist

Other titles about Ruby Oliver are:

The boy book (2006)

Real live boyfriends (2010)

The treasure map of boys (2009)

★ **Dramarama.** Hyperion 2007 311p $15.99
Grades: 7 8 9 10 11 12 **Fic**

1. School stories 2. Actors -- Fiction 3. Friendship -- Fiction

ISBN 0-7868-3815-9; 978-0-7868-3815-8

LC 2006-49599

Spending their summer at Wildewood Academy, an elite boarding school for the performing arts, tests the bond between best friends Sadye and Demi.

"Teens will identify strongly with both the heartbreak and the humor in this authentic portrayal of friendships maturing and decaying." SLJ

★ The **disreputable** history of Frankie Landau-Banks. Hyperion 2008 352p $16.99; pa $8.99
Grades: 7 8 9 10 11 12 **Fic**

1. School stories

ISBN 0-7868-3818-3; 0-7868-3819-1 pa; 978-0-7868-3818-9; 978-0-7868-3819-6 pa

Michael L. Printz Award honor book, 2009

"On her return to Alabaster Prep . . . [Frankie] attracts the attention of gorgeous Matthew . . . [who] is a member of the Loyal Order of the Basset Hounds, an all-male Alabaster secret society. . . . Frankie engineers her own guerilla membership by assuming a false online identity. . . . Lockhart creates a unique, indelible character. . . . Teens will be galvanized." Booklist

How to be bad; [by] E. Lockhart, Sarah Mlynowski [and] Lauren Myracle. HarperTeen 2008 325p $16.99; lib bdg $17.89

Grades: 9 10 11 12 **Fic**

1. Friendship -- Fiction 2. Automobile travel -- Fiction
ISBN 978-0-06-128422-9; 0-06-128422-X; 978-0-06-128423-6 lib bdg; 0-06-128423-8 lib bdg
LC 2007-52946

Told in alternating voices, Jesse, Vicks, and Mel, hoping to leave all their worries and woes behind, escape their small town by taking a road trip to Miami.

"Whip-smart dialogue and a fast-moving, picaresque plot that zooms from lump-in-the-throat moments to all-out giddiness will keep readers going, and it's a testimony to how real these girls seem that the final chapters are profoundly satisfying rather than tidy." Publ Wkly

Real live boyfriends; yes, boyfriends, plural, if my life weren't complicated I wouldn't be Ruby Oliver. Delacorte Press 2010 224p $16.99; lib bdg $19.99

Grades: 8 9 10 11 **Fic**

1. School stories 2. Seattle (Wash.) -- Fiction 3. Dating (Social customs) -- Fiction
ISBN 978-0-385-73428-8; 0-385-73428-X; 978-0-385-90438-4 lib bdg; 0-385-90438-X lib bdg
LC 2009-41988

Now a senior at her Seattle prep school, Ruby continues her angst-filled days coping with the dilemmas of boyfriends, college applications, her parents' squabbling, and realizing that her "deranged" persona may no longer apply.

The **treasure** map of boys; Noel, Jackson, Finn, Hutch, Gideon--and me, Ruby Oliver. Delacorte Press 2009 244p $15.99; lib bdg $18.99

Grades: 8 9 10 11 12 **Fic**

1. School stories 2. Friendship -- Fiction 3. Seattle (Wash.) -- Fiction 4. Dating (Social customs) -- Fiction
ISBN 978-0-385-73426-4; 0-385-73426-3; 978-0-385-90437-7 lib bdg; 0-385-90437-1 lib bdg
LC 2008-33062

A Seattle sixteen-year-old juggles therapy, running a school bake sale, coping with her performance artist mother, growing distant from an old friend, and conflicting feelings about her ex-boyfriend and potential new boyfriends.

"Replete with wordplay, footnotes and . . . lots of laugh-out-loud moments, this is a worthy follow-up." Kirkus

★ **We** were liars; E. Lockhart. Delacorte Press 2014 240 p. (hardback) $17.99

Grades: 7 8 9 10 11 12 **Fic**

1. Summer -- Fiction 2. Wealth -- Fiction 3. Love 4. Family life 5. Love -- Fiction 6. Amnesia -- Fiction 7. Families -- Fiction 8. Friendship -- Fiction
ISBN 038574126X; 9780375989940; 9780385741262
LC 2013042127

"Cadence Sinclair Easton comes from an old-money family, headed by a patriarch who owns a private island off of Cape Cod. Each summer, the extended family gathers at the various houses on the island, and Cadence, her cousins Johnny and Mirren, and friend Gat (the four "Liars"), have been inseparable since age eight....The story, while lightly touching on issues of class and race, more fully focuses on dysfunctional family drama, a heart-wrenching romance between Cadence and Gat, and, ultimately, the suspense of what happened during that fateful summer. The ending is a stunner that will haunt readers for a long time to come." (School Library Journal)

London, Alex

Guardian; Alex London. Philomel Books. 2014 340p $17.99

Grades: 7 8 9 **Fic**

1. Epidemics — Fiction 2. Gays — Fiction 3. Science fiction 4. Social classes — Fiction 5. Dystopian fiction
ISBN: 0399165762; 9780399165764
LC 2013025938

"It's a grave new world when the revolution a reluctant hero inspired could mean the death of everyone he tried to save, including himself. In this sequel to Proxy (2013), radical groups form in the wake of the Jubilee. The Reconciliation staunchly endorses tech-free purity, while Machinists demand a renaissance of the networks. Reluctant 16-year-old hero Syd is paraded as a political puppet, labeled a savior by supporters and marked a target by the opposition. His importance as a mascot for the Reconciliation necessitates a bodyguard, 17-year-old Liam. Liam is strong (he has a killer metal hand), silent (too shy for vocal eloquence) and will do anything to remain near Syd for reasons other than professional integrity. Amid political upheaval, an illness begins to spread, rendering victims' blue blood black and diminishing their mental faculties. Syd has been a hesitant political figure but knows he is the only hope for ending the illness." (Kirkus)

"Nonstop action and breakneck pace characterize this exceptional thriller. London provides his audience with an intricate plot, enriched by fine world-building and believable characters. The ample backstory will enable readers to enjoy Guardian without having read Proxy, although most will want to read these in sequence. This thought-provoking and breathtaking novel belongs in all collections serving young adults." VOYA

London, Jack

★ The **call** of the wild; pictures by Wendell Minor. Atheneum Books for Young Readers 1999 112p il $24; pa $4.95

Grades: 5 6 7 8 9 10 11 12 Adult **Fic**

1. Dogs -- Fiction
ISBN 0-689-81836-X; 1-4165-0019-7 pa
LC 97-45019

First published 1903 by Macmillan

"Buck, half-St. Bernard, half-Scottish sheepdog, is stolen from his comfortable home in California and pressed into service as a sledge dog in the Klondike. At first he is abused by both man and dog, but he learns to fight ruthlessly. He becomes lead dog on a sledge team, after bettering Spitz, the vicious old leader, in a brutal fight to the death. In John Thornton, he finally finds a master whom he can respect and love. When Thornton is killed by Indians, Buck breaks away to the wilds and becomes the leader of a wolf pack, returning each year to the site of Thornton's death." Reader's Ency. 4th edition

White Fang; Jack London. Scholastic 2001 252p. hardcover o.p. rpt $5.99

Grades: 7 8 9 10 11 12 Adult **Fic**

1. Dogs -- Fiction

ISBN 9780439236195 rpt

LC 98-19241

First published 1906

White Fang "is about a dog, a cross-breed, sold to Beauty Smith. This owner tortures the dog to increase his ferocity and value as a fighter. A new owner Weedom Scott, brings the dog to California, and, by kind treatment, domesticates him. White Fang later sacrifices his life to save Scott." Haydn. Thesaurus of Book Dig

Long, Ruth Frances

The **treachery** of beautiful things; by Ruth Frances Long. Dial Books 2012 363 p. (hardcover) $17.99

Grades: 7 8 9 10 11 12 **Fic**

1. Fantasy fiction 2. Fairies -- Fiction 3. Forests and forestry -- Fiction 4. Fantasy 5. Love -- Fiction 6. Kings, queens, rulers, etc. -- Fiction

ISBN 0803735804; 9780803735804

LC 2011027165

In this book by Ruth Long, "the trees swallowed her brother whole, and Jenny was there to see it. Now seventeen, she revisits the woods where Tom was taken. . . . She's lured into the trees, where she finds strange and dangerous creatures. . . . Among them is Jack, mercurial and magnetic, with secrets of his own. Determined to find her brother, with or without Jack's help, Jenny struggles to navigate a faerie world where stunning beauty masks some of the most treacherous evils." (Publisher's note)

Longshore, Katherine

Gilt; by Katherine Longshore. Viking 2012 406 p. $17.99; (hardcover) $17.99

Grades: 9 10 11 12 **Fic**

1. Historical fiction 2. Female friendship -- Fiction 3. Great Britain -- History -- 1485-1603, Tudors -- Fiction 4. Courts and courtiers -- Fiction 5. Kings, queens, rulers, etc. -- Fiction 6. Great Britain -- History -- Henry VIII, 1509-1547 -- Fiction

ISBN 0670013994; 9780670013999

LC 2011028214

This book is set in the court of English king Henry VIII. When "Kitty Tylney's best friend, Catherine Howard, worms her way into King Henry VIII's heart and brings Kitty to court, she's thrust into a world filled with fabulous gowns, sparkling jewels, and elegant parties. . . . But court is also full of secrets, lies, and sordid affairs, and as Kitty witnesses Cat's meteoric rise and fall as queen, she must figure out how to keep being a good friend." (Publisher's note)

Tarnish; by Katherine Longshore. Viking 2013 448 p. (hardcover) $17.99

Grades: 9 10 11 12 **Fic**

1. Historical fiction 2. Great Britain -- History -- 1485-1603, Tudors -- Fiction 3. Love -- Fiction 4. Sex role -- Fiction 5. Kings, queens, rulers, etc. -- Fiction 6. Great Britain -- History -- Henry VIII, 1509-1547 -- Fiction 7. Great Britain -- History -- Henry VIII, 1509-1547

ISBN 0670014001; 9780670014002

LC 2012032988

This book is the companion to Katherine Longshore's novel "Gilt" and looks at the relationship between Anne Boleyn and Thomas Wyatt. Wyatt bets Anne that he can turn court favor to her side if she does as he asks. If the plan succeeds, he will have her in his bed because she will want to be there. After some thought she concedes and their game of courtly love begins. He pursues her and she encourages it. Soon she realizes that Wyatt's plan is working"—and that they're in love. (School Library Journal)

Love, D. Anne

Defying the diva; [by] D. Anne Love. Margaret K. McElderry Books 2008 257p $16.99

Grades: 7 8 9 10 **Fic**

1. School stories 2. Bullies -- Fiction

ISBN 978-1-4169-3481-3; 1-4169-3481-2

LC 2007-10945

During Haley's freshman year of high school, a campaign of gossip and bullying causes her to be socially ostracized, but after spending the summer living with her aunt, working at a resort, making new friends, and dating a hunky lifeguard, she learns how to stand up for herself and begins to trust again.

"Concluding with a serious author's note on harassment, which includes information on getting help, this text skillfully captures the painful reality of teen bullying while also telling Haley's humorous and sincere story of growing up." Kirkus

Semiprecious. Margaret K. McElderry Books 2006 293p $16.95; pa $6.99

Grades: 5 6 7 8 **Fic**

1. Family life -- Fiction

ISBN 978-0-689-85638-9; 0-689-85638-5; 978-0-689-87389-8 pa; 0-689-87389-1 pa

LC 2005-14906

Uprooted and living with an aunt in 1960s Oklahoma, thirteen-year-old Garnet and her older sister Opal brave their mother's desertion and their father's recovery from an accident, learning that "the best home of all is the one you make inside yourself"

"An involving novel of hurt, healing, and adjustment." Booklist

Low, Dene

The **entomological** tales of Augustus T. Percival; Petronella saves nearly everyone. Houghton Mifflin 2009 196p $16.00

Grades: 7 8 9 10 **Fic**

1. Uncles -- Fiction 2. Insects -- Fiction 3. Missing persons -- Fiction

ISBN 0-547-15250-7; 978-0-547-15250-9

Petronella's fashionable friends are arriving at her country estate near London to celebrate her sixteenth birthday and her coming out party. During the festivities, important guests are disappearing, kidnapping notes are appearing, many of the clues are insects, and Uncle Augustus (who has developed a bug eating compulsion) is surreptitiously devouring evidence.

"Archetypical characters are skillfully drawn, time and place are clearly evoked, and excitement and intrigue abound amid the hilarity." SLJ

Lowitz, Leza

Jet Black and the ninja wind; Leza Lowitz, Shogo Oketani. Tuttle Publishing 2013 319 p. $17.99
Grades: 9 10 11 12 **Fic**

1. Ninja -- Fiction 2. Family secrets -- Fiction 3. Japan -- Fiction 4. Secrets -- Fiction 5. Buried treasure -- Fiction 6. Family life -- Japan -- Fiction 7. Adventure and adventurers -- Fiction
ISBN 480531284X; 9784805312841
LC 2013023578

Asian/Pacific American Awards for Literature: Young Adult Lit (2014)

In this book, by Leza Lowitz and Shogo Oketani, "Seventeen-year-old Jet Black is a ninja. There's only one problem—she doesn't know it. Others do, however, and they're scheming to capture her and uncover her secrets. When her mother dies, Jet knows only that she must go to Japan to protect a family treasure hidden in her ancestral land. . . . Stalked by bounty hunters and desperately in love with the man who's been sent to kill her, Jet must be strong enough to protect the treasure." (Publisher's note)

"At her mother's insistence, Rika Kuroi, nicknamed Jet Black, has spent her young life training in the art of combat and ninja techniques-with no idea why. Her mother dies before explaining, and when Jet travels to her family's village in Japan to lay her mother's ashes to rest, she is plunged into a complicated web of ancient mysteries and family secrets... Give this book to anime fans or anyone seeking an engaging and thought-provoking read." (School Library Journal)

Lowry, Lois, 1937-

Gathering blue. Houghton Mifflin 2000 215p $16; pa $8.95
Grades: 5 6 7 8 **Fic**

1. Artists 2. Orphans 3. Science fiction 4. People with physical disabilities
ISBN 0-618-05581-9; 0-385-73256-2 pa
LC 00-24359

Lame and suddenly orphaned, Kira is mysteriously removed from her squalid village to live in the palatial Council Edifice, where she is expected to use her gifts as a weaver to do the bidding of the all-powerful Guardians

"Lowry has once again created a fully realized world full of drama, suspense, and even humor." SLJ

The **giver**. Houghton Mifflin 1993 180p $17; pa $8.95
Grades: 6 7 8 9 10 **Fic**

1. Science fiction
ISBN 0-395-64566-2; 0-385-73255-4 pa
LC 92-15034

Awarded the Newbery Medal, 1994

Given his lifetime assignment at the Ceremony of Twelve, Jonas becomes the receiver of memories shared by only one other in his community and discovers the terrible truth about the society in which he lives.

"A riveting, chilling story that inspires a new appreciation for diversity, love, and even pain. Truly memorable." SLJ

★ **Son**; by Lois Lowry. Houghton Mifflin 2012 393 p. $17.99
Grades: 6 7 8 9 10 11 12 **Fic**

1. Science fiction 2. Dystopian fiction 3. Amnesia -- Fiction 4. Mothers -- Fiction 5. Secrecy -- Fiction 6. Identity -- Fiction 7. Mother-child relationship -- Fiction 8. Mother and child -- Fiction 9. Separation (Psychology) -- Fiction
ISBN 0547887205; 9780547887203
LC 2012014034

Author Lois Lowry tells the story of "14-year-old Claire, [who] has no contact with her baby Gabe until she surreptitiously bonds with him in the community Nurturing Center. . . . After living for years with Alys, a childless healer, Claire's memory returns. Intent on finding Gabe, she . . . encounters the sinister Trademaster and exchanges her youth for his help in finding her child, now living in the same village as middle-aged Jonas and his wife Kira. Elderly and failing, Claire reveals her identity to Gabe, who must use his unique talent to save the village." (Kirkus Reviews)

Lu, Marie

★ **Champion**; a Legend novel. Marie Lu. G.P. Putnam's Sons, an imprint of Penguin Group (USA) 2013 384 p. (hardback) $18.99
Grades: 8 9 10 11 12 **Fic**

1. Love -- Fiction 2. Dystopian fiction 3. Plague -- Fiction 4. Science fiction
ISBN 0399256776; 9780399256776
LC 2013028221

In this novel, by Marie Lu, "June and Day have sacrificed so much for the people of the Republic—and each other—and now their country is on the brink of a new existence. June is back in the good graces of the Republic, working within the government's elite circles as Princeps Elect while Day has been assigned a high level military position. But neither could have predicted the circumstances that will reunite them once again." (Publisher's note)

"Having been diagnosed with a terminal illness, Day (Legend; Prodigy) takes care of his brother, Eden, victim of the Republic's experiments in biological warfare. International diplomacy raises the stakes in this final volume of the trilogy, but readers will likely care more about whether Day and June (the Republic's prodigy) can repair their passionate romance. Lu's storytelling is compulsively readable." (Horn Book)

★ **Legend**. G. P. Putnam's Sons 2011 305p $17.99
Grades: 8 9 10 11 12 **Fic**

1. War stories 2. Science fiction 3. Plague -- Fiction 4. Siblings -- Fiction 5. Soldiers -- Fiction 6. Criminals -- Fiction 7. Resistance to government -- Fiction
ISBN 978-0-399-25675-2; 0-399-25675-X
LC 2011002003

"What was once the western United States is now home to the Republic, a nation perpetually at war with its neighbors. Born into an elite family in one of the Republic's wealthiest districts, fifteen-year-old June is a prodigy being groomed for success in the Republic's highest military circles. Born into the slums, fifteen-year-old Day is the country's most wanted criminal. But his motives may not be as malicious as they seem." Publisher's note

"The characters are likable, the plot moves at a good pace, and the adventure is solid." SLJ

★ **Prodigy**; a Legend novel. Marie Lu. G. P. Putnam's Sons 2012 384 p. (Legend) $17.99
Grades: 8 9 10 11 12 **Fic**

1. Science fiction 2. Dystopian fiction 3. Fugitives from justice -- Fiction 4. Resistance to government -- Fiction 5. War -- Fiction 6. Soldiers -- Fiction 7. Criminals -- Fiction 8. Assassination -- Fiction 9. Government, Resistance to -- Fiction
ISBN 0399256768; 9780399256769
LC 2012003773

This young adult science fiction adventure novel, by Marie Lu, is the sequel to her novel "Legend." "Injured and on the run, it has been seven days since June and Day barely escaped Los Angeles and the Republic with their lives. Day is believed dead. . . . June is now the Republic's most wanted traitor. Desperate for help, they turn to the Patriots--a vigilante rebel group sworn to bring down the Republic. But can they trust them?" (Publisher's note)

"This is a well-molded mixture of intrigue, romance, and action, where things can change with almost any turn of the page, and frequently do." Booklist

Lubar, David

Hidden talents. TOR Bks. 1999 213p il hardcover o.p. pa $5.99
Grades: 6 7 8 9 **Fic**

1. School stories 2. Extrasensory perception -- Fiction
ISBN 0-312-86646-1; 0-7653-4265-0 pa
LC 99-24560

When thirteen-year-old Martin arrives at an alternative school for misfits and problem students, he falls in with a group of boys with psychic powers and discovers something surprising about himself

The author "serves up great fun, along with an insight or two for those whose powers are only too human." Publ Wkly

Sleeping freshmen never lie. Dutton Books 2005 279p $16.99; pa $6.99
Grades: 7 8 9 10 **Fic**

1. School stories 2. Authorship -- Fiction
ISBN 0-525-47311-4; 0-14-240780-1 pa
LC 2004-23067

While navigating his first year of high school and awaiting the birth of his new baby brother, Scott loses old friends and gains some unlikely new ones as he hones his skills as a writer

"The plot is framed by Scott's journal of advice for the unborn baby. The novel's absurd, comical mood is evident in its entries. . . . The author brings the protagonist to three-dimensional life by combining these introspective musings with active, hilarious narration." SLJ

Lucier, Makiia

A **death**-struck year; Makiia Lucier. Houghton Mifflin Harcourt 2014 288 p. (hardback) $17.99
Grades: 9 10 11 12 **Fic**

1. Nurses -- Fiction 2. Epidemics -- Fiction 3. Influenza -- Fiction 4. Portland (Or.) -- Fiction 5. Influenza Epidemic, 1918-1919 -- Fiction 6. Portland (Or.) -- History -- 20th century -- Fiction 7. Influenza Epidemic, 1918-1919 -- Oregon -- Portland
ISBN 0544164504; 9780544164505
LC 2013037482

In this novel, by Makiia Lucier, "the Spanish influenza is devastating the East Coast–but Cleo Berry knows it is a world away from the safety of her home in Portland, Oregon. Then the flu moves into the Pacific Northwest. Schools, churches, and theaters are shut down. The entire city is thrust into survival mode–and into a panic. Seventeen-year-old Cleo is told to stay put in her quarantined boarding school, but when the Red Cross pleads for volunteers, she cannot ignore the call for help." (Publisher's note)

"A teen girl struggles to survive the Spanish influenza pandemic of 1918...Readers will be swept up in the story as Cleo builds friendships and manages to find hope amid disease and death. A notable debut." (Kirkus)

Includes bibliographical references

Luedeke, Lisa

Smashed; Lisa Luedeke. Margaret K. McElderry Books 2012 323 p.
Grades: 9 10 11 12 **Fic**

1. Alcoholism -- Fiction 2. Field hockey players -- Fiction 3. Teenagers -- Alcohol use -- Fiction 4. High schools -- Fiction 5. Emotional problems -- Fiction
ISBN 1442427795; 9781442427792; 9781442427952
LC 2011030515

In this novel by Lisa Luedeke "Katie Martin is a field hockey star on the fast track to a college scholarship. Her relationship with alcohol has always been a little questionable, but things get bleak really quickly when she takes up with bad boy Alec Osborne. . . . On a rain-soaked, alcohol-drenched night, one impulsive decision threatens Katie's dreams, leaving her indebted to Alec in the worst possible way." (Author's note)

Lundgren, Jodi

Leap; [edited by Alison Kooistra] Second Story Press 2011 217p $11.95
Grades: 6 7 8 9 10 **Fic**

1. Dance -- Fiction 2. Friendship -- Fiction 3. Family life -- Fiction
ISBN 978-1-897187-85-2; 1-897187-85-8

Having just turned 15 and gone through her parents' divorce, Natalie and her best friend Sasha are going to be practicing with their dance team all summer, but her friendship with Sasha goes on the rocks, and her relationship with her boyfriend Kevin who is Sasha's brother goes too far.

"This novel, with its luminous descriptions of dance and frank discussions of sexuality and relationships, will captivate teens looking for a story they can relate to." SLJ

Luper, Eric

Bug boy. Farrar, Straus and Giroux 2009 248p $16.99
Grades: 7 8 9 10 **Fic**

1. Gambling -- Fiction 2. Horse racing -- Fiction 3. New York (State) -- Fiction 4. Father-son relationship -- Fiction 5. Swindlers and swindling -- Fiction
ISBN 978-0-374-31000-4; 0-374-31000-9
LC 2008-26730

In 1934 Saratoga, New York, just as fifteen-year-old Jack Walsh finally realizes his dream of becoming a jockey, complications arise in the form of a female bookie, an unexpected visit from his father, and a man who wants him to "fix" a race.

"This well-written, engaging story effectively captures the desperate times of the Depression and the hard-edged world of horse racing." SLJ

Seth Baumgartner's love manifesto. Balzer + Bray 2010 293p $16.99
Grades: 8 9 10 11 12 **Fic**

1. Golf -- Fiction 2. Love -- Fiction 3. Dating (Social customs) -- Fiction 4. Father-son relationship -- Fiction
ISBN 978-0-06-182753-2; 0-06-182753-3
LC 2009-29706

After his girlfriend breaks up with him and he sees his father out with another woman, high school senior Seth Baumgartner, who has a summer job at the country club and is preparing for a father-son golf tournament, launches a podcast in which he explores the mysteries of love.

"Luper weaves together many themes—trust and secrets, lies and truth, love, lust and, of course, golf—in a way that even the most introspection-hating male reader will eat with a spoon." Kirkus

Lupica, Mike

The **batboy**. Philomel Books 2010 247p $17.99
Grades: 5 6 7 8 **Fic**

1. Baseball -- Fiction 2. Mother-son relationship -- Fiction
ISBN 978-0-399-25000-2; 0-399-25000-X
LC 2009015067

Even though his mother feels baseball ruined her marriage to his father, she allows fourteen-year-old Brian to become a bat boy for the Detroit Tigers, who have just drafted his favorite player back onto the team.

Lupica gives "his readers a behind-the-scenes look at major league sports. In this novel, he adds genuine insights into family dynamics and the emotional state of his hero." Booklist

The **big** field. Philomel Books 2008 243p $17.99
Grades: 5 6 7 8 **Fic**

1. Baseball -- Fiction 2. Father-son relationship -- Fiction
ISBN 978-0-399-24625-8; 0-399-24625-8
LC 2007-23647

When fourteen-year-old baseball player Hutch feels threatened by the arrival of a new teammate named Darryl, he tries to work through his insecurities about both Darryl and his remote and silent father, who was once a great ballplayer too.

"Writing in typically fluid prose and laying in a strong supporting lineup, Lupica strikes the right balance between personal issues and game action." Booklist

Hero. Philomel Books 2010 289p $17.99
Grades: 6 7 8 9 **Fic**

1. Adventure fiction 2. Death -- Fiction 3. Politics -- Fiction 4. Family life -- Fiction 5. Superheroes -- Fiction 6. Father-son relationship -- Fiction
ISBN 978-0-399-25283-9; 0-399-25283-5
LC 2010-01772

Fourteen-year-old Zach learns he has the same special abilities as his father, who was the President's globe-trotting troubleshooter until "the Bads" killed him, and now Zach must decide whether to use his powers in the same way at the risk of his own life.

"Lupica effectively unfolds this high-adventure story." Booklist

Miracle on 49th Street. Philomel Books 2006 246p $17.99; pa $7.99
Grades: 5 6 7 8 **Fic**

1. Basketball -- Fiction 2. Father-daughter relationship -- Fiction
ISBN 0-399-24488-3; 0-14-240942-1 pa
LC 2005-32648

After her mother's death, twelve-year-old Molly learns that her father is a basketball star for the Boston Celtics.

"Lupica creates intriguing, complex characters . . . and he paces his story well, with enough twists and cliff-hangers to keep the pages turning." SLJ

Ben be able to pull it together for his team and for himself?" (Publisher's note)

Summer ball; [by] Mike Lupica. Philomel Books 2007 244p $17.99
Grades: 6 7 8 9 **Fic**

1. Camps -- Fiction 2. Basketball -- Fiction
ISBN 978-0-399-24487-2
LC 2006021781

Thirteen-year-old Danny must prove himself all over again for a disapproving coach and against new rivals at a summer basketball camp.

"Lupica breathes life into both characters and story. Danny is . . . sympathetic and engaging. He is surrounded by a cast of supporting characters who add humor and whose interactions ring true." SLJ

Lurie, April

The **latent** powers of Dylan Fontaine. Delacorte Press 2008 208p $15.99; lib bdg $18.99
Grades: 8 9 10 11 12 **Fic**

1. Family life -- Fiction 2. New York (N.Y.) -- Fiction
ISBN 978-0-385-73125-6; 978-0-385-90153-6 lib bdg
LC 2007-32313

Fifteen-year-old Dylan's friend Angie is making a film about him while he is busy trying to keep his older brother from getting caught with drugs, to deal with his mother having left the family, and to figure out how to get Angie to think of him as more than just a friend.

"This is a story about guys, primarily . . . brothers; fathers and sons; lonely young men who are feeling somewhat lost. Any reader will care for each one of them. Lurie does a wonderful job of making them real." KLIATT

Lyga, Barry

★ The **astonishing** adventures of Fanboy & Goth Girl. Houghton Mifflin 2006 311p $16.95
Grades: 8 9 10 11 12 **Fic**

1. School stories 2. Friendship -- Fiction 3. Cartoons

and caricatures -- Fiction
ISBN 0-618-72392-7

LC 2005-33259

A fifteen-year-old "geek" who keeps a list of the high school jocks and others who torment him, and pours his energy into creating a great graphic novel, encounters Kyra, Goth Girl, who helps change his outlook on almost everything, including himself.

"This engaging first novel has good characterization with genuine voices. . . . The book is compulsively readable." Voice Youth Advocates

Followed by: Goth Girl rising (2009)

Boy toy. Houghton Mifflin 2007 410p $16.95
Grades: 10 11 12 **Fic**

1. School stories 2. Child sexual abuse -- Fiction
ISBN 978-0-618-72393-5; 0-618-72393-5

LC 2006-39840

After five years of fighting his way past flickers of memory about the teacher who molested him and the incident that brought the crime to light, eighteen-year-old Josh gets help in coping with his molestor's release from prison when he finally tells his best friends the whole truth.

The author "tackles this incredibly sensitive story with boldness and confidence. He does not shy away from graphic descriptions of Josh's past and even makes the audacious choice of showing young Josh enjoying the attention . . . [Josh] works hard at healing himself and moving into healthy adulthood, and by the end of this well-written, challenging novel, the reader has high hopes that he will make it." Voice Youth Advocates

Game; by Barry Lyga. Little, Brown and Co. 2013 528 p. (hardcover) $17.99
Grades: 10 11 12 **Fic**

1. Mystery fiction 2. Serial killers -- Fiction 3. Murder -- Fiction 4. Psychopaths -- Fiction 5. New York (N.Y.) -- Fiction
ISBN 0316125873; 9780316125871

LC 2012040157

Sequel to: I hunt killers

This is Barry Lyga's follow-up to "Hunt Killers." It "focuses on 17-year-old Jazz, the son of the world's most prolific serial killer, but expands his world by fleshing out previously minor characters. Jazz is called upon to help the NYPD hunt Hat-Dog, a brutal killer who might be connected to Jazz's now-escaped father, Billy Dent. Meanwhile, Jazz's girlfriend, Connie, starts receiving mysterious information about Jazz's past." (Publishers Weekly)

Goth girl rising. Houghton Mifflin Harcourt 2009 390p $17
Grades: 8 9 10 11 12 **Fic**

1. School stories 2. Psychotherapy -- Fiction
ISBN 978-0-547-07664-5; 0-547-07664-9

Sequel to: The astonishing adventures of Fanboy and Goth Girl (2006)

"After six months in a mental hospital, Kyra, the newly shaven-headed heroine of The Astonishing Adventures of Fan Boy and Goth Girl (2006), has only one plan: to exact embarrassing revenge on sweet, loyal Fan Boy for not contacting her while she was away. . . . Goth teens and fans of the first novel will be drawn into the darkness that is her life." Kirkus

Hero-type. Houghton Mifflin Co. 2008 295p $16
Grades: 7 8 9 10 **Fic**

1. School stories 2. Maryland -- Fiction 3. Patriotism -- Fiction 4. Heroes and heroines -- Fiction
ISBN 978-0-547-07663-8; 0-547-07663-0

LC 2008-7276

Feeling awkward and ugly is only one reason sixteen-year-old Kevin is uncomfortable with the publicity surrounding his act of accidental heroism, but when a reporter photographs him apparently being unpatriotic, he steps into the limelight to encourage people to think about what the symbols of freedom really mean.

"Leavened by much humor . . . this neatly plotted look at what real patriotism and heroism mean will get readers thinking." KLIATT

★ **I** hunt killers; by Barry Lyga. Little, Brown 2012 359 p.
Grades: 10 11 12 **Fic**

1. Mystery fiction 2. Serial killers -- Fiction 3. Father-son relationship -- Fiction 4. Teenagers -- Conduct of life -- Fiction 5. Murder -- Fiction 6. Psychopaths -- Fiction 7. Conduct of life -- Fiction 8. Fathers and sons -- Fiction
ISBN 9780316125840

LC 2011025418

This book tells the story of Jasper, a 17-year-old boy whose father "is the most notorious serial killer of the 21st century" and who has found that "having a normal life is a struggle. . . . Now living with his Gramma, Jasper finds himself investigating another serial killer with help from his best friend Howie." (Kirkus Reviews)

Followed by: Game (2013)

Lynch, Chris, 1962-

★ **Angry** young man. Simon & Schuster BFYR 2011 167p $16.99
Grades: 7 8 9 10 **Fic**

1. Brothers -- Fiction 2. Conduct of life -- Fiction 3. Single parent family -- Fiction 4. Mother-son relationship -- Fiction
ISBN 0-689-84790-4; 978-0-689-84790-5

LC 2009-52832

Eighteen-year-old Robert tries to help his half-brother Xan, a seventeen-year-old misfit, to make better choices as he becomes increasingly attracted to a variety of protesters, anarchists, and the like.

"For those who wonder about the roots of homegrown terror and extremism, . . . Lynch pushes the spotlight from the individual to society in a story that can be brutal and ugly, yet isn't devoid of hope." Publ Wkly

The **Big** Game of Everything. HarperTeen 2008 275p $16.99; lib bdg $17.89
Grades: 7 8 9 10 **Fic**

1. Golf -- Fiction 2. Family life -- Fiction 3. Grandfathers -- Fiction 4. Summer employment --

Fiction
ISBN 978-0-06-074034-4; 0-06-074034-5; 978-0-06-074035-1 lib bdg; 0-06-074035-3 lib bdg
LC 2007-49578

Jock and his eccentric family spend the summer working at Grampus's golf complex, where they end up learning the rules of "The Big Game of Everything."

"This Printz Honor-winning author offers up another touching and offbeat novel full of delightfully skewed humor." Voice Youth Advocates

Casualties of war; Chris Lynch. Scholastic Press 2013 192 p. (hc) $16.99
Grades: 8 9 10 11 12 **Fic**
1. War stories 2. Soldiers -- Fiction 3. Vietnam War, 1961-1975 -- Fiction 4. Airmen -- Fiction 5. Agent Orange -- Fiction 6. Agent Orange 7. United States. Air Force -- Fiction 8. Vietnam -- History -- 1945-1975 -- Fiction 9. Vietnam War, 1961-1975 10. United States. Air Force 11. Vietnam -- History -- 1945-1975
ISBN 0545270235; 9780545270236; 9780545270243
LC 2012014434

This book concludes "[Chris] Lynch's Vietnam War series . . . with the final narrative of four friends caught in the chaos of war. Morris, Ivan and Rudi have told their stories; it's Beck's turn. Beck, now in the Air Force, was always the smart one, the one bound for college. . . . And in Vietnam, Beck does feel as if he has 'just been handed the keys to the universe itself.' He is, literally, above it all, as he watches the war from on high in his C-123 aircraft." (Kirkus)

★ **Hothouse.** HarperTeen 2010 198p $16.99
Grades: 8 9 10 11 12 **Fic**
1. Death -- Fiction 2. Friendship -- Fiction 3. Bereavement -- Fiction 4. Fire fighters -- Fiction 5. Father-son relationship -- Fiction
ISBN 978-0-06-167379-5; 0-06-167379-X
LC 2010-3145

Teens D.J. and Russell, life-long friends and neighbors, had drifted apart but when their firefighter fathers are both killed, they try to help one another come to terms with the tragedy and its aftermath.

"Lynch fully commits to the first-person voice, giving into Russ' second-by-second conflicts and contradictions. The author also has a strong grasp of the garrulous slaps and punches that make up many male relationships. Russ' friendships are so real they hurt. The story hurts, too, but that's how it should be." Booklist

★ **Inexcusable.** Atheneum Books for Young Readers 2005 165p $16.95; pa $6.99
Grades: 8 9 10 11 12 **Fic**
1. School stories 2. Rape -- Fiction 3. Football -- Fiction
ISBN 0-689-84789-0; 1-416-93972-5 pa
LC 2004-30874

High school senior and football player Keir sets out to enjoy himself on graduation night, but when he attempts to comfort a friend whose date has left her stranded, things go terribly wrong

"This finely crafted and thought-provoking page-turner carefully conveys that it is simply inexcusable to whitewash wrongs, and that those responsible should (and hopefully will) pay the price." SLJ

Pieces; Chris Lynch. Simon & Schuster Books for Young Readers 2013 176 p. (hardcover) $16.99
Grades: 7 8 9 10 11 12 **Fic**
1. Bereavement 2. Donation of organs, tissues, etc. 3. Death -- Fiction 4. Grief -- Fiction 5. Brothers -- Fiction 6. Interpersonal relations -- Fiction 7. Donation of organs, tissues, etc. -- Fiction
ISBN 1416927034; 9781416927037; 9781442453111
LC 2011042049

In this book, "a year after his 20-year-old brother Duane died in a diving accident, 18-year-old Eric still can't seem to move forward. In an attempt to keep the 'nothingness that is filling the Duane space' from taking hold, he reaches out to three of the donors who received his brother's 'pieces.' After meeting shy, redheaded Phil, brassy Barry and sweet single mom Melinda, Eric finds himself constantly asking the questions, 'Who are these people? Who are they, to me? Who am I, to them?'" (Kirkus Reviews)

Lynch, Janet Nichols

My beautiful hippie; Janet Nichols Lynch. Holiday House 2013 186 p. (hardcover) $16.95
Grades: 10 11 12 **Fic**
1. Bildungsromans 2. Hippies -- Fiction 3. Historical fiction 4. Feminism -- Fiction 5. Pianists -- Fiction 6. Coming of age -- Fiction 7. Vietnam War, 1961-1975 -- Fiction 8. Family life -- California -- Fiction 9. San Francisco (Calif.) -- History -- 20th century -- Fiction
ISBN 0823426033; 9780823426034
LC 2012016563

In this novel, by Janet Nichols Lynch, "it's 1967 and Joanne's San Francisco neighborhood has become inundated with hippies . . . , which thrills her but appalls the rest of her family. In the midst of preparations for her sister's wedding, Joanne meets Martin . . . and begins to see him secretly. Over the course of the next year, Joanne discovers a world of drugs, anti-war demonstrations, and psychedelic dances that both fascinates and frightens her." (Publisher's note)

Lyne, Jennifer H.

Catch rider; by Jennifer H. Lyne. Clarion Books 2013 288 p. (hardcover) $16.99
Grades: 9 10 11 12 **Fic**
1. Poor -- Fiction 2. Horses -- Fiction 3. Uncles -- Fiction 4. Virginia -- Fiction 5. Horse shows -- Fiction 6. Horsemanship -- Fiction 7. Social classes -- Fiction 8. Single-parent families -- Fiction 9. Family life -- Virginia -- Fiction
ISBN 0547868715; 9780547868714
LC 2012022616

In this book, "Sidney Criser might still be 14, but that doesn't stop her from driving the junk car her uncle gave her an hour over mountains to clean stalls at a rich woman's barn. Sid grew up tough, and she can ride anything, but times are desperate: Since her father's death, her mother has taken up with a no-good abuser who threatens to move them to California. Her mother's lost her job, and . . . her uncle Wayne, who's long been Sidney's mainstay, is just about to drink himself to death." (Kirkus)

Lyon, Steve

The **gift** moves. Houghton Mifflin 2004 230p $15

Grades: 5 6 7 8 **Fic**

1. Science fiction

ISBN 0-618-39128-2

LC 2003-12293

In a futuristic United States devoid of wealth and material things, a teenage baker befriends a talented weaver's apprentice who holds a dark secret.

"Lyon mixes elements of magical realism with a coming-of-age story, incorporating issues that teens will relate to. . . . This is an unusual story that is sure to inspire much thought and contemplation." SLJ

Lyons, Mary E.

Letters from a slave boy; the story of Joseph Jacobs. Atheneum Books for Young Readers 2007 197p il map $15.99; pa $5.99

Grades: 6 7 8 9 **Fic**

1. Letters -- Fiction 2. Slavery -- Fiction 3. African Americans -- Fiction

ISBN 978-0-689-87867-1; 0-689-87867-2; 978-0-689-87868-8 pa; 0-689-87868-0 pa

LC 2006-01277

A fictionalized look at the life of Joseph Jacobs, son of a slave, told in the form of letters that he might have written during his life in pre-Civil War North Carolina, on a whaling expedition, in New York, New England, and finally in California during the Gold Rush.

"The 'letters' are short and the pace is quick. The dialect and spelling give authenticity without making the text difficult to read and understand. . . . This title stands on its own, but children who appreciated the forthright perspective of the first book will want to read this one as well." SLJ

★ **Letters** from a slave girl; the story of Harriet Jacobs. Scribner 1992 146p il hardcover o.p. pa $5.99; pa $5.99

Grades: 6 7 8 9 **Fic**

1. Slaves 2. Letters -- Fiction 3. African Americans -- Fiction

ISBN 0-684-19446-5; 1-4169-3637-8 pa; 9781416936374 pa

LC 91-45778

This is a fictionalized version of the life of Harriet Jacobs, told in the form of letters that she might have written during her slavery in North Carolina and as she prepared for escape to the North in 1842. Glossary. Bibliography.

This "is historical fiction at its best. . . . Mary Lyons has remained faithful to Jacobs's actual autobiography throughout her readable, compelling novel. . . . Her observations of the horrors of slavery are concise and lucid. The letters are written in dialect, based on Jacobs's own writing and on other slave narrations of the period." Horn Book

Maas, Sarah J.

Crown of midnight; by Sarah J. Maas. Bloomsbury 2013 432 p. (hardcover) $17.99

Grades: 9 10 11 12 **Fic**

1. Occult fiction 2. Assassins -- Fiction 3. Fantasy 4. Love -- Fiction 5. Courts and courtiers -- Fiction 6. Kings, queens, rulers, etc. -- Fiction

ISBN 1619630621; 9781619630628

LC 2013009063

Sequel to: Throne of glass

This is the second book in Sarah J. Maas's Throne of Glass series. "After being named the King's Champion in 'Throne of Glass' (2012), Celaena Sardothien serves as the king of Adarlan's personal assassin—at least, she pretends to. . . . If the king catches Celaena disobeying his orders, he will execute her closest friends. However, she can't stomach advancing his agenda, especially if it means murdering innocents in cold blood." (Kirkus Reviews)

Throne of glass; Sarah J. Maas. Bloomsbury 2012 406 p. (hardback) $17.99

Grades: 10 11 12 **Fic**

1. Fantasy fiction 2. Contests -- Fiction 3. Assassins -- Fiction 4. Fantasy 5. Princes -- Fiction 6. Prisoners -- Fiction 7. Courts and courtiers -- Fiction

ISBN 1599906953; 9781599906959

LC 2012011229

An assassin whose work "has landed her in a slave-labor prison no one has ever survived. A year into her sentence, the Crown Prince offers to sponsor Celaena in a competition with 23 other criminals and murderers that, should she win, will result in her freedom. The only catch? She'll become the king's personal assassin for four years, the same dark-hearted king who sentenced her to imprisonment." (Kirkus Reviews)

Maberry, Jonathan

Dust & decay. Simon & Schuster 2011 519p $17.99; ebook $9.99

Grades: 8 9 10 11 12 **Fic**

1. Horror fiction 2. Zombies -- Fiction 3. Brothers -- Fiction

ISBN 978-1-4424-0235-5; 978-1-4424-0237-9 ebook

LC 2010050305

Sequel to Rot & ruin (2010)

In post-apocalyptic America, fifteen-year-old Benny Imura and his friends set out into the great Rot & Ruin hoping to find a better future but are soon pitted against zombies, wild animals, insane murderers, and the horrors of Gameland.

"The language is easy to comprehend, the characters are relatable, and the action-filled plot keeps the story moving. The western elements, seldom seen in teen fiction, are a welcome addition." Voice Youth Advocates

★ **Rot** & ruin. Simon & Schuster Books for Young Readers 2010 458p $17.99

Grades: 9 10 11 12 **Fic**

1. Horror fiction 2. Zombies -- Fiction 3. Brothers -- Fiction

ISBN 978-1-4424-0232-4; 1-4424-0232-6

LC 2009-46041

In a post-apocalyptic world where fences and border patrols guard the few people left from the zombies that have overtaken civilization, fifteen-year-old Benny Imura is finally convinced that he must follow in his older brother's footsteps and become a bounty hunter.

"In turns mythic and down-to-earth, this intense novel combines adventure and philosophy to tell a truly memorable zombie story." Publ Wkly

Followed by: Dust & decay (2011)

MacColl, Michaela

Nobody's secret; by Michaela MacColl. Chronicle Books 2013 288 p. (reinforced) $16.99

Grades: 7 8 9 10 **Fic**

1. Mystery fiction 2. Historical fiction 3. Poets -- Fiction 4. Amherst (Mass.) -- History -- 19th century -- Fiction 5. Women poets, American -- 19th century

ISBN 1452108609; 9781452108605

LC 2012030364

In this book, when "15-year-old Emily Dickinson meets and flirts with a handsome stranger, she feels the first flicker of romance. Then the young man is found dead in her family's pond, and the budding poet is sure that he was a victim of foul play. Determined to see that justice is done, she and her younger sister, Vinnie, investigate and discover that he is James Wentworth, heir to a fortune from which his aunt and uncle have defrauded him. Suspecting murder, Emily sets out to solve the case." (School Library Journal)

Prisoners in the palace; how Victoria became queen with the help of her maid, a reporter, and a scoundrel; a novel of intrigue and romance. Chronicle Books 2010 367p $16.99

Grades: 7 8 9 10 **Fic**

1. Queens 2. Orphans -- Fiction 3. London (England) -- Fiction 4. Household employees -- Fiction 5. Great Britain -- History -- 19th century -- Fiction

ISBN 978-0-8118-7300-0; 0-8118-7300-5

LC 2010-8257

Recently orphaned and destitute, seventeen-year-old Liza Hastings earns a position as a lady's maid to sixteen-year-old Princess Victoria at Kensington Palace in 1836, the year before Victoria becomes Queen of England.

"This novel is full of historical detail, vivid settings, and richly drawn characters, and themes of friendship and romance give the story teen appeal." Booklist

Promise the night. Chronicle Books 2011 $16.99

Grades: 6 7 8 9 **Fic**

1. Women air pilots -- Fiction

ISBN 978-0-8118-7625-4; 0-8118-7625-X

LC 2011010938

This novel explores the early life of Beryl Markham, who grew up on a farm in Kenya, and became the first person to fly solo across the Atlantic from east to west.

"MacColl vividly portrays her headstrong protagonist . . . with fierce, exuberant spirit." Booklist

MacCullough, Carolyn

Always a witch. Clarion Books 2011 276p $16.99

Grades: 8 9 10 11 12 **Fic**

1. Witches -- Fiction 2. Time travel -- Fiction 3. Good and evil -- Fiction

ISBN 978-0-547-22485-5; 0-547-22485-0

LC 2011008148

Haunted by her grandmother's prophecy that she will soon be forced to make a terrible decision, witch Tamsin Greene risks everything to travel back in time to 1887 New York to confront the enemy that wants to destroy her family.

This is "an enjoyable magical adventure." Kirkus

Drawing the ocean. Roaring Brook Press 2006 170p $16.95

Grades: 7 8 9 10 **Fic**

1. Ghost stories 2. Death -- Fiction 3. Twins -- Fiction 4. Siblings -- Fiction

ISBN 978-1-59643-092-1; 1-59643-092-3

LC 2005-31471

A gifted artist, Sadie is determined to fit in at her new school, but her deceased twin brother Ollie keeps appearing to her.

"Characters of every age come to life with vivid descriptions and dialogue that make this spare mood piece work." SLJ

MacCready, Robin Merrow

Buried. Dutton Books 2006 198p $16.99; pa $6.99

Grades: 8 9 10 11 12 **Fic**

1. Children of alcoholics -- Fiction 2. Mother-daughter relationship -- Fiction 3. Obsessive-compulsive disorder -- Fiction

ISBN 978-0-525-47724-2; 0-525-47724-1; 978-0-14-241141-4 pa; 0-14-241141-8 pa

LC 2006-03870

When her alcoholic mother goes missing, seventeen-year-old Claudine begins to spin out of control, despite her attempts to impose order on every aspect of her life.

"Readers who came for the issues may find themselves reaching for the tissues as Claudine finally finds closure with her mother." Bull Cent Child Books

MacCullough, Carolyn

Once a witch. Clarion Books 2009 292p $16

Grades: 8 9 10 11 12 **Fic**

1. Sisters -- Fiction 2. Witches -- Fiction 3. Time travel -- Fiction 4. Good and evil -- Fiction 5. New York (N.Y.) -- Fiction

ISBN 978-0-547-22399-5; 0-547-22399-4

LC 2008-49234

Born into a family of witches, seventeen-year-old Tamsin is raised believing that she alone lacks a magical "Talent," but when her beautiful and powerful sister is taken by an age-old rival of the family in an attempt to change the balance of power, Tamsin discovers her true destiny.

"The book will appeal to teen readers who enjoy stories with romance, magic, or time travel, along with hardcore fantasy aficionados, and it is appropriate for all young adult collections." Voice Youth Advocates

Followed by: Always a witch (2011)

Stealing Henry. Roaring Brook Press 2005 196p $16.95

Grades: 9 10 11 12 **Fic**

1. Siblings -- Fiction 2. Child abuse -- Fiction 3. Runaway teenagers -- Fiction 4. Mother-daughter

relationship -- Fiction
ISBN 1-596-43045-1

LC 2004-17550

The experiences of high-schooler Savannah, following her decision to take her eight-year-old half brother from his abusive father and their oblivious mother, are interspersed with the earlier story of her mother, Alice, as she meets Savannah's father and unexpectedly becomes pregnant.

"Young adult readers will find this [book] fascinating and appealing." Libr Media Connect

MacDonald, Anne Louise

Seeing red. KCP Fiction 2009 220p $17.95; pa $8.95

Grades: 6 7 8 9 **Fic**

1. Dreams -- Fiction 2. Extrasensory perception -- Fiction

ISBN 978-1-55453-291-9; 1-55453-291-4; 978-1-55453-292-6 pa; 1-55453-292-2 pa

"From the time he was a young child, Frankie's dreams invoked meaningful colors and seemed like premonitions that he was powerless to change. . . . He develops an unexpected friendship with an unpopular classmate whom he is convinced is a mind reader and who also sees colors. The dilemmas faced by Frankie and some of the other characters are intriguing as they struggle with their fears, disappointments, and aspirations. The story has several touching moments and unexpected turns in a plot." SLJ

Macdonald, Maryann

Odette's secrets; by Maryann Macdonald. Bloomsbury 2013 240 p. (hardback) $16.99

Grades: 6 7 8 9 **Fic**

1. Novels in verse 2. Hidden children (Holocaust) 3. France -- History -- 1940-1945, German occupation -- Fiction 4. Identity -- Fiction 5. Jews -- France -- Fiction 6. Holocaust, Jewish (1939-1945) -- Fiction 7. World War, 1939-1945 -- France -- Fiction 8. France -- History -- German occupation, 1940-1945 -- Fiction

ISBN 159990750X; 9781599907505

LC 2012015549

This biographical story-in-verse, by Maryann Macdonald, takes place in Nazi-occupied France. "Odette is a young Jewish girl living in Paris during a dangerous time. . . . After Odette's father enlists in the French army and her mother joins the Resistance, Odette is sent to the countryside until it is safe to return. On the surface, she leads the life of a regular girl . . . but inside, she is burning with secrets about the life she left behind and her true identity." (Publisher's note)

MacHale, D. J.

★ The **pilgrims** of Rayne. Simon & Schuster Books for Young Readers 2007 547p (Pendragon) $16.99; pa $8.99

Grades: 7 8 9 10 **Fic**

1. Fantasy fiction 2. Adventure fiction

ISBN 978-1-4169-1416-7; 1-4169-1416-1; 978-1-4169-1417-4 pa; 1-4169-1417-X pa

LC 2006038131

With Saint Dane seemingly on the verge of toppling all of the territories, Pendragon and Courtney set out to rescue Mark and find themselves traveling—and battling—their way through different worlds as they try to save all of Halla.

This is "packed . . . with nonstop action, mind-boggling plot twists, and well-imagined locales." Voice Youth Advocates

Other titles in this series are:
The merchant of death (2002)
The lost city of Faar (2003)
The never war (2003)
The reality bug (2003)
Black water (2004)
The rivers of Zadaa (2005)
Quillan games (2006)
Raven rise (2008)
The soldiers of Halla (2009)

Raven rise; [by] D.J. MacHale. 1st ed.; Simon & Schuster Books for Young Readers 2008 544p (Pendragon) $17.99

Grades: 7 8 9 10 **Fic**

1. Fantasy fiction 2. Adventure fiction

ISBN 978-1-4169-1418-1; 1-4169-1418-8

LC 2007046886

While Pendragon is trapped on Ibara, Alder returns to Denduron and reluctantly goes into battle again, and other Travelers face obstacles of various sorts, Saint Dane gains the power he seeks on Second Earth and makes his push to destroy and rebuild Halla.

Storm; D. J. MacHale; Razorbill. 2014 481p $17.99

Grades: 5 6 7 8 **Fic**

1.Dystopian -- fiction 2. Adventure -- fiction

ISBN: 1595146679; 9781595146670

LC 2013047604

In this second title in the author's SYLO Chronicles, "Tucker and his friends Tori, Kent and Olivia escaped from Pemberwick Island and the air-and-sea battle that raged around it to land in Portland. . . . Taking refuge in a hospital, the teens find a few other survivors but not a lot of additional information. A looping radio transmission encourages survivors to go west, where a force is gathering to fight back. Division threatens, as the teens argue about what to do: join this resistance or find refuge. Tucker just wants some payback for the death of his best friend in the previous book. Tucker's search for the moral right leads to the concept of the 'lesser evil' in ways he could never have anticipated and keeps readers completely involved every step of the way." (Kirkus)

SYLO; by D.J. MacHale. Penguin Group USA 2013 416 p. (hardcover) $17.99

Grades: 5 6 7 8 9 **Fic**

1. Dystopian fiction 2. Adventure fiction

ISBN 1595146652; 9781595146656

This is the first book in a proposed trilogy from D.J. MacHale. Here, Tucker Pierce has a small but satisfying life on a small island. But when the island is quarantined by the U.S. Navy, things start to fall apart. . . . People start dying. The girl he wants to get to know a whole lot better, Tori, is captured along with Tucker and imprisoned behind barbed wire." They must escape to the mainland and try to figure out what this SYLO organization that is imprisoning them is. (Kirkus Reviews)

Maciel, Amanda

Tease. Amanda Maciel; Balzer + Bray. 2014 328p $17.99

Grades: 9 10 11 12 **Fic**

1. Bullying -- Fiction; 2. High schools -- Fiction; 3. Suicide

ISBN: 0062305301; 9780062305305

LC 2013043067

"Sara is climbing the high school social ladder when a new girl, Emma, steals her spotlight. Sara and her friends retaliate with pranks, rumors, and social media warfare, but all are shocked when Emma commits suicide. Sara is a fragile, conflicted narrator struggling to understand her role in Emma's death. A complex and thought-provoking examination of modern teen bullying." Horn Book

Mackall, Dandi Daley

★ **Eva** underground. Harcourt 2006 239p $17

Grades: 9 10 11 12 **Fic**

1. Poland -- Fiction 2. Communism -- Fiction 3. Father-daughter relationship -- Fiction

ISBN 0-15-205462-6; 978-0-15-205462-5

LC 2005-04195

In 1978, a high school senior is forced by her widowed father to move from their comfortable Chicago suburb to help with an underground education movement in communist Poland.

"Poland behind the Iron Curtain is rarely found in modern young adult literature, and Mackall has done a superb job in captivating high reader interest in this unique setting." Libr Media Connect

The **silence** of murder. Alfred A. Knopf 2011 327p $16.99; lib bdg $19.99

Grades: 7 8 9 10 **Fic**

1. Mystery fiction 2. Homicide -- Fiction 3. Siblings -- Fiction 4. People with mental disabilities -- Fiction

ISBN 978-0-375-86896-2; 978-0-375-96896-9 lib bdg

LC 2010035991

Sixteen-year-old Hope must defend her developmentally disabled brother (who has not spoken a word since he was seven) when he is accused of murdering a beloved high school baseball coach.

"The well-plotted mystery is intriguing, and Hope's determined efforts to solve it have an authentic feel." Booklist

Mackel, Kathy

★ **Boost.** Dial Books 2008 248p $16.99; pa $7.99

Grades: 6 7 8 9 **Fic**

1. Steroids -- Fiction 2. Basketball -- Fiction

ISBN 978-0-8037-3240-7; 0-8037-3240-6; 978-0-14-241539-9 pa; 0-14-241539-1 pa

LC 2007-49441

Thirteen-year-old Savvy's dreams of starting for her elite basketball team are in danger when she is accused of taking steroids

"Mackel has turned a tough subject in the world of teen competitive sports into a highly readable blend of intense action, interfamily relationships, and intrigue." SLJ

Mackey, Weezie Kerr

Throwing like a girl; [by] Weezie Kerr Mackey. Marshall Cavendish 2007 271p $16.99

Grades: 6 7 8 9 **Fic**

1. School stories 2. Softball -- Fiction 3. Family life -- Fiction

ISBN 978-0-7614-5342-0

LC 2006030233

After moving from Chicago to Dallas in the spring of her sophomore year, fifteen-year-old Ella finds that joining the softball team at her private school not only helps her make friends, it also provides unexpected opportunities to learn and grow.

"Readers will be delighted with how well the athletics and the girly stuff work in tandem." Booklist

Mackler, Carolyn

★ The **earth,** my butt, and other big, round things. Candlewick Press 2003 246p $15.99; pa $8.99

Grades: 7 8 9 10 **Fic**

1. School stories 2. Obesity -- Fiction 3. Family life -- Fiction 4. New York (N.Y.) -- Fiction

ISBN 0-7636-1958-2; 0-7636-2091-2 pa

LC 2002-73921

Michael L. Printz Award honor book, 2004

Feeling like she does not fit in with the other members of her family, who are all thin, brilliant, and good-looking, fifteen-year-old Virginia tries to deal with her self-image, her first physical relationship, and her disillusionment with some of the people closest to her

"The e-mails [Virginia] exchanges . . . and the lists she makes (e.g., 'The Fat Girl Code of Conduct') add both realism and insight to her character. The heroine's transformation into someone who finds her own style and speaks her own mind is believable—and worthy of applause." Publ Wkly

Guyaholic; a story of finding, flirting, forgetting . . . and the boy who changes everything. Candlewick Press 2007 176p $16.99; pa $7.99

Grades: 9 10 11 12 **Fic**

1. Dating (Social customs) -- Fiction

ISBN 978-0-7636-2537-5; 0-7636-2537-X; 978-0-7636-280107 pa; 0-7636-2801-8 pa

LC 2007-24098

Sequel to Vegan virgin Valentine (2004)

V is "still living with her grandparents and still sleeping around. Then a hockey puck hits her in the head, and she literally falls into the arms of Sam Almond. . . . V comes across as an engaging character whose struggles seem very real. The details of her road trip are written with humor and verve, and the sex, while prevelant, is not graphic. There's also a sweetness here that makes V and Sam worth rooting for." Booklist

Tangled. HarperTeen 2010 308p $16.99

Grades: 8 9 10 11 12 **Fic**

1. Vacations -- Fiction 2. Friendship -- Fiction 3. Caribbean region -- Fiction 4. New York (State) -- Fiction

ISBN 978-0-06-173104-4; 0-06-173104-8

LC 2009-7286

The lives of four very different teenagers become entangled in ways that none of them could have imagined after a short stay at a Caribbean resort

"The various viewpoints weave together to create a compelling and cohesive whole. Themes of understanding, respecting others, and the power of good communication are carefully and effectively woven throughout a story that begs for discussion." SLJ

Vegan virgin Valentine. Candlewick Press 2004 228p $16.99; pa $8.99

Grades: 9 10 11 12 **Fic**

1. School stories 2. Aunts -- Fiction

ISBN 0-7636-2155-2; 0-7636-2613-9 pa

LC 2004-45774

Mara's niece, who is only one-year-younger, moves in bringing conflict between the two teenagers because of their opposite personalities

"Racily narrated by likeable Mara, this fast-paced coming-of-age story is charged with sarcasm, angst, honesty, and hope. Many teen girls will recognize parts of themselves within its pages." Voice Youth Advocates

Followed by Guyaholic (2007)

MacLean, Jill

Nix Minus One; by Jill Maclean. Pajama Press 2013 296 p. (hardcover) $21.95

Grades: 7 8 9 10 **Fic**

1. School stories 2. Novels in verse

ISBN 192748524X; 9781927485248

This novel in verse focuses on 15-year-old Nix. "Formerly known as 'Fatty Humbolt,' he is struggling with his crush on Loren Cody, the girlfriend of the best player on the hockey team, and his love-hate relationship with his older sister, Roxy." Nix is shy while Roxy is the opposite. "Then Roxy falls for Bryan Sykes, a popular but notorious cad and politician's son, and Nix is forced to come out of his shell and find his voice." (School Library Journal)

★ The **nine** lives of Travis Keating. Fitzhenry & Whiteside 2008 217p pa $11.95

Grades: 5 6 7 8 **Fic**

1. Cats -- Fiction 2. Bullies -- Fiction

ISBN 978-1-55455-104-0; 1-55455-104-8

After his mother's death, Travis Keating and his father move to Ratchet, Newfoundland, to start a new life. Things are tough for Travis (Hud, the school bully, being the toughest) until, putting aside his own problems, he starts to care for a colony of feral cats.

"This is a solid piece of contemporary fiction with an interesting story. It should have broad appeal." SLJ

Madden, Kerry

Gentle's Holler. Viking 2005 237p $16.99; pa $6.99

Grades: 5 6 7 8 **Fic**

1. Poverty -- Fiction 2. Family life -- Fiction

ISBN 0-670-05998-6; 0-14-240751-8 pa

LC 2004-18424

In the early 1960s, twelve-year-old songwriter Livy Two Weems dreams of seeing the world beyond the Maggie Valley, North Carolina, holler where she lives in poverty with her parents and eight brothers and sisters, but understands that she must put family first.

"Livy's narration rings true and is wonderfully voiced, and Madden's message about the importance of forgiveness will be well received." SLJ

Other titles in this series are:

Louisiana's song (2007)

Jessie's mountain (2008)

Madigan, L. K.

★ **Flash** burnout; a novel. Houghton Mifflin 2009 332p $16

Grades: 9 10 11 12 **Fic**

1. School stories 2. Friendship -- Fiction 3. Photographers -- Fiction 4. Dating (Social customs) -- Fiction

ISBN 978-0-547-19489-9; 0-547-19489-7

LC 2010-278252

ALA YALSA The William C. Morris YA Debut Award (2010)

"When he snapped a picture of a street person for his photography homework, Blake never dreamed that the woman in the photo was his friend Marissa's long-lost meth addicted mom. Blake's participation in the ensuing drama opens up a world of trouble, both for him and for Marissa." Publisher's note

"This rich romance explores the complexities of friendship and love, and the all-too-human limitations of both. It's a sobering, compelling, and satisfying read for teens." Booklist

The **mermaid's** mirror. Houghton Mifflin Harcourt 2010 316p $16

Grades: 8 9 10 11 12 **Fic**

1. Magic -- Fiction 2. Surfing -- Fiction 3. California -- Fiction 4. Family life -- Fiction 5. Mermaids and mermen -- Fiction 6. Father-daughter relationship -- Fiction

ISBN 978-0-547-19491-2; 0-547-19491-9

LC 2010-6771

Lena, almost sixteen, has always felt drawn to the waters of San Francisco Bay despite the fears of her father, a former surfer, but after she glimpses a beautiful woman with a tail, nothing can keep Lena from seeking the mermaid in the dangerous waves at Magic Crescent Cove.

"The characters . . . are well rounded and integrated into the plot. . . . With highly imagistic descriptions and savvy dialogue, Madigan offers a rewarding and credible story that uses fantasy elements to bare truths about family ties." Booklist

Madison, Bennett

Lulu Dark and the summer of the Fox; a mystery. by Bennett Madison. Razorbill 2006 $10.99

Grades: 7 8 9 10 **Fic**

1. Mystery fiction

ISBN 1-59514-086-7

LC 2006004960

When a mysterious person called the Fox begins to threaten young starlets, Lulu Dark investigates, even though she suspects that her own mother—an aging actress—might be behind it all.

"Teens will enjoy this smart, funny chick-lit heroine who has real problems and a satirical outlook." SLJ

★ **September** Girls; Bennett Madison. Harpercollins Childrens Books 2013 352 p. (hardcover) $17.99

Grades: 9 10 11 12 **Fic**

1. Love stories 2. Summer -- Fiction 3. Mermaids and mermen -- Fiction

ISBN 0061255637; 9780061255632

In this young adult, magical realist novel, by Bennett Madison, "Sam is spending the summer in a beach town filled with beautiful blond girls. . . . Sam finds himself in an unexpected summer romance when he falls for one of the Girls, DeeDee. But as they get closer, she pulls away without explanation. Sam knows that if he is going to win her back, he'll have to learn the Girls' secret." (Publisher's note)

Magnin, Joyce

Carrying Mason; [by] Joyce Magnin. Zonderkidz 2011 153p $14.99

Grades: 5 6 7 8 **Fic**

1. Family life -- Fiction 2. Country life -- Fiction 3. People with mental disabilities -- Fiction

ISBN 978-0-310-72681-4; 0-310-72681-6

LC 2011014462

In rural Pennsylvania in 1958, when thirteen-year-old Luna's best friend Mason dies, she decides to move in with his mentally disabled mother and care for her as Mason did.

"Gently, deliberately paced, Luna's first-person tale provides a fresh look at mental disabilities and the additional burden of negative attitudes. While Ruby's disability is apparent, this effort also celebrates her capabilities. Although the primary focus is Luna, her quirky father, supportive mother and boy-crazy older sister are also sufficiently developed to provide additional depth. A quiet coming-of-age tale with heart offers a fresh look at mentally disabled adults." Kirkus

Magoon, Kekla

37 things I love (in no particular order) Kekla Magoon. Henry Holt 2012 218 p. (hc) $16.99

Grades: 9 10 11 12 **Fic**

1. Young adult literature 2. Girls 3. Grief 4. Family life 5. Coma -- Fiction 6. Grief -- Fiction 7. Schools -- Fiction 8. High schools -- Fiction 9. Interpersonal relations -- Fiction 10. Self-actualization (Psychology) -- Fiction

ISBN 0805094652; 9780805094657

LC 2011031998

This young adult novel by Kekla Magoon follows Ellis, who "only has four days of her sophomore year left. . . . Her father has been in a coma for years, . . . and her already-fragile relationship with her mother is strained over whether or not to remove him from life support. Her best friend fails even to notice that anything is wrong and Ellis feels like her world is falling apart. But when all seems bleak, Ellis finds comfort in the most unexpected places." (Publisher's note)

Camo girl. Aladdin 2010 218p $16.99

Grades: 5 6 7 8 **Fic**

1. Friendship -- Fiction 2. Prejudices -- Fiction 3. Racially mixed people -- Fiction

ISBN 978-1-4169-7804-6; 1-4169-7804-6

A novel about a biracial girl living in the suburbs of Las Vegas examines the friendships that grow out of, and despite, her race.

"Magoon . . . offers a sensitive and articulate portrayal of a pair of middle-school outsiders. . . . This poetic and nuanced story addresses the courage it takes to truly know and support someone, as well as the difficult choices that come with growing up." Publ Wkly

Fire in the streets; by Kekla Magoon. 1st Aladdin hardcover ed. Aladdin 2012 336 p. $15.99

Grades: 7 8 9 10 **Fic**

1. Historical fiction 2. Black nationalism -- Fiction 3. African Americans -- Civil rights -- Fiction 4. Racism -- Fiction 5. African Americans -- Fiction 6. Black Panther Party -- Fiction 7. Brothers and sisters -- Fiction 8. Civil rights movements -- Fiction 9. United States -- History -- 20th century -- Fiction 10. Chicago (Ill.) -- History -- 20th century -- Fiction

ISBN 1442422300; 9781442422308

LC 2011039129

Sequel to: The rock and the river

This historical novel by Kekla Magoon, is set "in the sweltering Chicago summer of 1968. [Maxie] is a Black Panther--or at least she wants to be one. . . . At fourteen, she's allowed to help out in the office, but she certainly can't help patrol the streets. Then Maxie realizes that there is a traitor in their midst, and if she can figure out who it is, it may be her ticket to becoming a real Panther. But when she learns the truth, the knowledge threatens to destroy her world." (Publisher's note)

★ **How** it went down; Kekla Magoon, Henry Holt & Co. 2014 336p $17.99

Grades: 9 10 11 12 Fic

1. African Americans -- Fiction 2. Death -- Fiction 3. Race relations -- Fiction 4. Witnesses -- Fiction 5. United States -- Race relations -- Fiction 6. Murder -- Fiction

ISBN: 0805098690; 9780805098693; 9781250068231

LC 2014027402

Coretta Scott King Author Award Honor Book (2015)

"When 16-year-old Tariq, a black teen, is shot and killed by a white man, every witness has a slightly different perception of the chain of events leading up to the murder. Family, friends, gang members, neighbors, and a well-meaning but self-serving minster make up the broad cast of characters...With a great hook and relatable characters, this will be popular for fans of realistic fiction. The unique storytelling style and thematic relevance will make it a potentially intriguing pick for classroom discussion." SLJ

The **rock** and the river. Aladdin 2009 290p $15.99

Grades: 7 8 9 10 **Fic**

1. Brothers -- Fiction 2. Chicago (Ill.) -- Fiction 3. African Americans -- Fiction 4. Black Panther Party -- Fiction

ISBN 978-1-4169-7582-3; 1-4169-7582-9

LC 2008-29170

ALA EMIERT Coretta Scott King John Steptoe New Talent Award (2010)

In 1968 Chicago, fourteen-year-old Sam Childs is caught in a conflict between his father's nonviolent approach to seeking civil rights for African Americans and his older brother, who has joined the Black Panther Party.

This "novel will make readers feel what it was like to be young, black, and militant 40 years ago, including the seething fury and desperation over the daily discrimination that drove the oppressed to fight back." Booklist

Maguire, Gregory

Egg & spoon; Gregory Maguire; Candlewick Press. 2014 475p $17.99

Grades: 7 8 9 10 11 12 **Fic**

1. Baba Yaga (Legendary Character) --Fiction 2. Mistaken identity --Fiction 3. Monks --Fiction 4. Princes --Fiction 5. Teenage girls --Fiction 6. Poor —Fiction 7. Girls —Fiction 8. Russia — Fiction

ISBN: 0763672203; 9780763672201

LC 2014931834

Boston Globe-Horn Book Honor: Fiction (2015)

"With one brother conscripted into the Tsar's army and another bound to serve a local landowner, Elena is left alone to care for her widowed and ailing mother in early 20th-century Russia. When an elegant train bearing a noble her age rolls through their barren village, Elena and her counterpart, Cat, accidentally swap places. . . . The author weaves a lyrical tale full of magic and promise, yet checkered with the desperation of poverty and the treacherous prospect of a world gone completely awry. Egg and Spoon is a beautiful reminder that fairy tales are at their best when they illuminate the precarious balance between lighthearted childhood and the darkness and danger of adulthood." SLJ

Mah, Adeline Yen

Chinese Cinderella and the Secret Dragon Society; [by] Adeline Yen Mah. 1st ed; HarperCollins 2005 242p $15.99; lib bdg $16.89

Grades: 5 6 7 8 **Fic**

1. Martial arts -- Fiction 2. World War, 1939-1945 -- Fiction

ISBN 0-06-056734-1; 0-06-056735-X lib bdg

LC 2004-8852

During the Japanese occupation of parts of China, twelve-year-old Ye Xian is thrown out of her father's and stepmother's home, joins a martial arts group, and tries to help her aunt and the Americans in their struggle against the Japanese invaders.

"Full of adventure and contrivance, this somewhat old-fashioned, plot-driven novel is clear about the values that are important to the author. . . . These young people are courageous, creative, and open-minded." SLJ

Mahoney, Karen

The **iron** witch. Flux 2011 299p $9.95

Grades: 6 7 8 9 10 **Fic**

1. Magic -- Fiction 2. Alchemy -- Fiction 3. Orphans -- Fiction 4. Kidnapping -- Fiction

ISBN 0-7387-2582-X; 978-0-7387-2582-6

LC 2010037692

Seventeen-year-old Donna Underwood is considered a freak, cursed by the magical heritage that destroyed her alchemist parents, but when vicious wood elves abduct her best friend Navin, Donna must betray all her parents fought for and join the battle between the humans and the fey.

"Adventurous, dark and dangerous. The Iron Witch will have teen readers clamoring for more." Libr Media Connect

Mahy, Margaret

The **Magician** of Hoad. Margaret K. McElderry Books 2009 411p $18.99

Grades: 7 8 9 10 **Fic**

1. Fantasy fiction 2. Magicians -- Fiction

ISBN 978-1-4169-7807-7; 1-4169-7807-0

LC 2008-23000

A young farm boy who possesses mysterious powers is chosen by the king to be the court's royal magician.

"Mahy majestically deploys the poetic language of fantasy to portray the changes and challenges of adolescence; here, and epic quest for identity is wrapped up in terror, romance, surprise, and suspense—always sustained by luminous imagery and intelligent, musical prose." Horn Book

Maizel, Rebecca

Infinite days; a vampire queen novel. St. Martin's Griffin 2010 325p (Vampire queen) pa $9.99

Grades: 7 8 9 10 **Fic**

1. School stories 2. Vampires -- Fiction 3. Supernatural -- Fiction

ISBN 978-0-312-64991-3; 0-312-64991-6

At a New England boarding school, Lenah Beaudonte tries to act like a normal sixteen-year-old although she was, before a hundred-year hibernation, a centuries-old vampire queen whose bloodthirsty, abandoned coven is seeking her.

"The story is filled with action, romance, longing, deception, and sacrifice. It will leave vampire fans thirsting for more." SLJ

Stolen nights; a Vampire queen novel. Rebecca Maizel. St. Martin's Griffin 2013 303 p. (paperback) $9.99

Grades: 7 8 9 10 **Fic**

1. Love -- Fiction 2. Vampires -- Fiction 3. Supernatural -- Fiction 4. Schools -- Fiction 5. Boarding schools -- Fiction

ISBN 0312649924; 9780312649920

LC 2012038339

This book, the second in author Rebecca Maizel's Vampire Queen series, follows Lenah Beaudonte . . . a vampire who has just become human again. . . . Lenah and her lover, Rhode, are now both human teens. . . . [T]hey are confronted . . . by the Aeris, a sort of supernatural communion of the elements, who . . .give them a choice: they can either go back to their original times . . . or stay in the present day with the caveat of not being able to be romantically linked to each other." (VOYA)

"At first, this novel seems to lack luster in its genre, but timeless themes of love and the search for identity, in addition to the cliff-hanger ending, leave readers pondering Lenah's choices and keenly anticipating the next installment." SLJ

Malaghan, Michael

Greek ransom. Andersen Press 2010 264p pa $9.99

Grades: 5 6 7 8 **Fic**

1. Adventure fiction 2. Siblings -- Fiction 3. Kidnapping -- Fiction

ISBN 978-184270-786-9; 1-84270-786-8

"Nick and Callie Latham are on the Greek island of Theta with their archaeologist parents for a working vacation. Then the children discover that Mum and Dad have lost the family's money in a reckless bid to locate the lost treasure of King Akanon. A shifty businessman kidnaps the couple in order to acquire it for himself. After Nick and Callie barely escape capture themselves, it's up to them to find a way to free their parents. . . . Readers will be on the edge of their seats throughout to see what happens next. . . . The relationship between Nick and Callie is spot-on, and kids will enjoy this high-spirited tale." SLJ

Malchow, Alex

The **Sword** of Darrow; [by] Alex and Hal Malchow. BenBella 2011 531p map $17.99

Grades: 5 6 7 8 **Fic**

1. Fantasy fiction 2. Magic -- Fiction 3. Fairies -- Fiction 4. Princesses -- Fiction

ISBN 978-1-9356-1846-1; 1-9356-1846-6

LC 2011012233

"For 10 years the people of Sonnencrest endured the cruel and tyrannical rule of the Goblins. Then Princess Babette, the only surviving member of the royal family, and Darrow, a crippled boy, become the unlikely forces in the fight against the oppressors. The authors paint convincing portraits of the characters. . . . Readers will be drawn to this fledgling rebellion and follow it to its spectacular success. Magic, monsters, and wizards add to the excitement." SLJ

Maldonado, Torrey

Secret Saturdays. G.P. Putnam's Sons 2010 195p $16.99

Grades: 6 7 8 9 **Fic**

1. School stories 2. African Americans -- Fiction 3. Single parent family -- Fiction 4. Racially mixed people -- Fiction

ISBN 978-0-399-25158-0; 0-399-25158-8

LC 2009-10361

Twelve-year-old boys living in a rough part of New York confront questions about what it means to be a friend, a father, and a man.

"Maldonado convincingly portrays roughneck playgrounds where boys are expected to be 'hard' and . . . Justin's narration resonates with the authenticity of a preteen doing his best in an urban landscape that has taught him all he knows. . . . The book remains a moving portrayal of the hope to be found through honest relationships." Publ Wkly

Malley, Gemma

The **Declaration**. Bloomsbury 2007 300p $16.95

Grades: 7 8 9 10 **Fic**

1. Science fiction 2. Immortality -- Fiction 3. Great Britain -- Fiction

ISBN 978-1-59990-119-0; 1-59990-119-6

LC 2006-102138

In 2140 England, where drugs enable people to live forever and children are illegal, teenaged Anna, an obedient "Surplus" training to become a house servant, discovers that her birth parents are trying to find her.

This is "gripping. . . . The indoctrinated teen's awakening to massive injustice makes compulsive reading." Booklist

Other titles in this series are:

The legacy (2011)

The resistance (2008)

Mancusi, Mari

Scorched; Mari Mancusi. Sourcebooks Fire 2013 352 p. (hc: alk. paper) $16.99

Grades: 9 10 11 12 **Fic**

1. Occult fiction 2. Fantasy fiction 3. Eggs -- Fiction 4. Dragons -- Fiction 5. Grandfathers -- Fiction 6. Supernatural -- Fiction 7. Adventure and adventurers -- Fiction

ISBN 1402284586; 9781402284588

LC 2013011799

In this book, Trinity's kooky grandfather impulsively buys a "supposed dragon egg. Before she can determine how to rescue both their home and the once-reputable West Texas museum they run from foreclosure, twin brothers . . . appear from the future. Both brothers are there to collect Trinity. Both want possession of the egg. Both want to save the world from an apocalyptic future via starkly different but equally menacing means. Whom can Trinity trust?" (Kirkus Reviews)

Mangum, Lisa

After hello; Lisa Mangum. Shadow Mountain 2012 272 p. (hardbound: alk. paper) $17.99

Grades: 7 8 9 10 **Fic**

1. Friendship -- Fiction 2. Photographers -- Fiction 3. Man-woman relationship -- Fiction 4. Trust -- Fiction 5. New York (N.Y.) -- Fiction 6. Dating (Social customs) -- Fiction 7. Interpersonal relations -- Fiction

ISBN 1609070100; 9781609070106

LC 2012017735

Author Lisa Mangum focuses on Sara, a girl whose "first trip to New York City . . . turns into 24 hours she will never forget. An amateur photographer, Sara walks around the city taking pictures; when a boy named Sam wanders into her lens, she is intrigued by him and follows him on his missions to find and trade things for people . . . As Sam and Sara travel from St. John the Divine Cathedral to Central Park and Times Square, they meet a string of artists and musicians and reluctantly discuss their turbulent pasts." (Barnes & Noble)

Manivong, Laura

Escaping the tiger. Harper 2010 216p il $15.99

Grades: 6 7 8 9 Fic

1. Refugees -- Fiction 2. Family life -- Fiction
ISBN 978-0-06-166177-8; 0-06-166177-5
LC 2009-24095

In 1982, twelve-year-old Vonlai, his parents, and sister, Dalah, escape from Laos to a Thai refugee camp, where they spend four long years struggling to survive in hopes on one day reaching America.

"This compelling novel offers significant historical background. This is certainly a book to prompt purposeful discussion to increase historical and multicultural awareness." SLJ

Mankell, Henning

★ A **bridge** to the stars. Delacorte Press 2007 164p $15.99; lib bdg $18.99; pa $8.99

Grades: 6 7 8 9 Fic

1. Father-son relationship -- Fiction
ISBN 978-0-385-73495-0; 0-385-73495-6; 978-0-385-90489-6 lib bdg; 0-385-90489-4 lib bdg; 978-0-440-24042-6 pa; 0-440-24042-5 pa
LC 2006-26901

In Sweden in 1956, eleven-year-old Joel and his father, a logger who was once a sailor, live alone with their secrets, including Joel's secret society that meets at night and his father's new romantic interest.

This is a "quiet but deeply satisfying coming-of-age story. . . . Those who welcome character-driven fiction will treasure this beautifully realized novel." Booklist

Other titles in this series are:
Shadows in the twilight (2008)
When the snow fell (2009)

Shadow of the leopard; [translated from the Swedish by Anna Paterson] Annick Press; Distributed in the U.S.A. by Firefly Books 2009 177p $19.95; pa $10.95

Grades: 10 11 12 Fic

1. Adultery -- Fiction 2. Amputees -- Fiction 3. Mozambique -- Fiction 4. Family life -- Fiction
ISBN 978-1-55451-200-3; 978-1-55451-199-0 pa
Sequel to Secrets of the fire (2003)
First published in Australia with title: The fury in the fire

Sofia, who lost her legs as a child, is now grown up with children in Mozambique, but when she discovers that Armando, the father of her children, is cheating on her, she leaves him, igniting his terrible rage.

"Readers will remember the indomitable Sofia—whose tale is based on real events—long after they close the book." Kirkus

Manning, Sarra

Guitar girl. Dutton Children's Books 2004 217p hardcover o.p. pa $6.99

Grades: 9 10 11 12 Fic

1. Musicians -- Fiction 2. Great Britain -- Fiction
ISBN 0-525-47234-7; 0-14-240318-0 pa
LC 2004-299584
First published 2003 in the United Kingdom

"Wryly funny, often sincere, and sometimes pressed into banshee-like behavior, Molly is endearing in her attempts to reach maturity, sort out what's important, and decide what needs to be left behind." SLJ

Mantchev, Lisa

Eyes like stars. Feiwel and Friends 2009 356p $16.99

Grades: 8 9 10 11 12 Fic

1. Magic -- Fiction 2. Actors -- Fiction 3. Orphans -- Fiction 4. Theater -- Fiction 5. Books and reading -- Fiction
ISBN 978-0-312-38096-0; 0-312-38096-8
LC 2008-15317

Thirteen-year-old Bertie strives to save Theater Illuminata, the only home she has ever known, but is hindered by the Players who magically live on there, especially Ariel, who is willing to destroy the Book at the center of the magic in order to escape into the outside world.

"The story contains enough mystery and mayhem to keep readers engaged, even as they analyze." Voice Youth Advocates

Other titles in this series include:
Perchance to dream (2010)
So silver bright (2011)

Manzano, Sonia

★ The **revolution** of Evelyn Serrano; Sonia Manzano. Scholastic 2012 205 p. $17.99

Grades: 6 7 8 9 10 Fic

1. Historical fiction 2. Puerto Ricans -- Fiction 3. Identity -- Fiction 4. Grandmothers -- Fiction 5. New York (N.Y.) -- History -- 20th century -- Fiction 6. East Harlem (New York, N.Y.) 7. Protest movements -- New York (State) -- New York
ISBN 0545325056; 9780545325059; 9780545325066
LC 2012009240
Pura Belpré Author Honor Book (2013)

This novel, by Sonia Manzano, is set "in New York's El Barrio in 1969. . . . The Young Lords, a Puerto Rican activist group, dump garbage in the street and set it on fire, igniting a powerful protest. When Abuela steps in to take charge, Evelyn is thrust into the action. . . . Evelyn learns important truths about her Latino heritage and the history makers who shaped a nation." (Publisher's note)

Includes bibliographical references

Marchetta, Melina

★ **Finnikin** of the rock. Candlewick Press 2010 399p map $18.99

Grades: 8 9 10 11 12 Fic

1. Fantasy fiction
ISBN 0-7636-4361-0; 978-0-7636-4361-4
LC 2009-28046

In this fantasy novel, "Finnikin was only a child during the five days of the unspeakable, when the royal family of Lumatere were brutally murdered, and an imposter seized the throne. . . . Finnikin, now on the cusp of manhood, is compelled to join forces with an arrogant and enigmatic young novice named Evanjalin, who claims that her dark dreams will lead the exiles to a surviving royal child and a way to pierce the cursed barrier and regain the land of Lumatere." (Publisher's note)

"The skillful world building includes just enough detail to create a vivid sense of place, and Marchetta maintains suspense with unexpected story arcs. It is the achingly real characters, though, and the relationships that emerge through the captivating dialogue that drive the story. Filled with questions about the impact of exile and the human need to belong, this standout fantasy quickly reveals that its real magic lies in its accomplished writing." Booklist

★ **Froi** of the exiles. Candlewick 2012 608 p.
Grades: 8 9 10 11 12 **Fic**

1. Exiles 2. War stories 3. Fantasy fiction
ISBN 9780763647599

In this fantasy book, "Froi, a former street thief who has started a new life in Lumatere, is sent to Charyn in disguise to assassinate its king, but his worldview is shaken by revelations about his own unknown past. Tensions between the two kingdoms ratchet up, and Froi's loyalties are tested as he becomes entrenched in the chaotic political situation in Charyn and is drawn to its unpredictable princess, Quintana, who has been horribly abused in an attempt to break Charyn's curse." (Publishers Weekly)

★ **Jellicoe** Road. HarperTeen 2008 419p $17.99; lib bdg $18.89
Grades: 9 10 11 12 **Fic**

1. School stories 2. Australia -- Fiction 3. Abandoned children -- Fiction 4. Identity (Psychology) -- Fiction
ISBN 978-0-06-143183-8; 0-06-143183-4; 978-0-06-143184-5 lib bdg; 0-06-143184-2 lib bdg

LC 2008-00760

First published 2006 in Australia with title: On the Jellicoe Road

Michael L. Printz Award, 2009

Abandoned by her drug-addicted mother at the age of eleven, high school student Taylor Markham struggles with her identity and family history at a boarding school in Australia.

"Readers may feel dizzied and disoriented, but as they puzzle out exactly how Hannah's narrative connects with Taylor's current reality, they will find themselves ensnared in the story's fascinating, intricate structure. A beautifully rendered mystery." Kirkus

The **piper's** son. Candlewick Press 2011 328p $17.99
Grades: 9 10 11 12 **Fic**

1. Australia -- Fiction 2. Musicians -- Fiction 3. Bereavement -- Fiction 4. Family life -- Fiction
ISBN 978-0-7636-4758-2; 0-7636-4758-6

LC 2010-39168

"Award-winning author Melina Marchetta reopens the story of the group of friends from her acclaimed novel Saving Francesca - but five years have passed, and now it's Thomas Mackee who needs saving. After his favorite uncle was blown to bits on his way to work in a foreign city, Tom watched his family implode. He quit school and turned his back on his music and everyone that mattered, including the girl he can't forget...An unflinching look at family, forgiveness, and the fierce inner workings of love and friendship, The Piper's Son redefines what it means to go home again." Publisher's Note

"A memorable portrait of first love, surviving grief, and the messy contradictions and fierce bonds that hold friends and family together." Booklist

★ **Quintana** of Charyn; Melina Marchetta. Candlewick Press 2013 528 p. (Lumatere chronicles) $18.99
Grades: 8 9 10 11 12 **Fic**

1. War stories 2. Fantasy fiction
ISBN 0763658359; 9780763658359

LC 2012955120

This is the conclusion of Melina Marchetta's trilogy which began with "Finnikin of the Rock." Here, "the kingdoms of Lumatere and Charyn attempt to bridge past atrocities through a new generation of leaders. Although tragedies arise, unity and healing are core themes, compared to the horrors of the previous books. As the title suggests, Quintana--the rightful ruler of Charyn, hidden following the uprising in the kingdom in Froi of the Exiles--is at the center of this final book." (Publishers Weekly)

Saving Francesca. Knopf 2004 243p hardcover o.p. pa $8.95
Grades: 9 10 11 12 **Fic**

1. School stories 2. Australia -- Fiction 3. Mental illness -- Fiction 4. Mother-daughter relationship -- Fiction
ISBN 0-375-82982-2; 0-375-82983-0 pa

LC 2004-3926

Sixteen-year-old Francesca could use her outspoken mother's help with the problems of being one of a handful of girls at a parochial school that has just turned co-ed, but her mother has suddenly become severely depressed

This book "has great characterizations, witty dialogue, a terrific relationship between Francesca and her younger brother, and a sweet romance. Teens will relate to this tender novel and will take to heart its solid messages and realistic treatment of a very real problem." SLJ

Followed by The piper's son (2011)

Marcus, Kimberly

Exposed. Random House 2011 260p $16.99; lib bdg $19.99
Grades: 8 9 10 **Fic**

1. School stories 2. Novels in verse 3. Rape -- Fiction 4. Guilt -- Fiction 5. Friendship -- Fiction 6. Photography -- Fiction
ISBN 0-375-86693-0; 0-375-96693-5 lib bdg; 978-0-375-86693-7; 978-0-375-89724-5 e-book; 978-0-375-96693-4 lib bdg

LC 2009-51545

High school senior Liz, a gifted photographer, can no longer see things clearly after her best friend accuses Liz's older brother of a terrible crime.

"The narrative largely zooms in on Liz's pain and her struggle to ground herself in her photography and gain admission to art school as events swirl around her. As a result of tethering the narrative to Liz's perspective, the ongoing discussion of Kate's rape and ensuing trial are not heavy-handed or gratuitous. In Liz, Marcus has created a sympathetic lead. A worthy addition to any collection." SLJ

Marillier, Juliet

Child of the prophecy. TOR Bks. 2002 528p il map (Sevenwaters trilogy) $26.95; pa $15.95

Grades: 11 12 Adult **Fic**
1. Fantasy fiction
ISBN 0-312-84881-1; 0-312-87036-1 pa
LC 2001-57480

Sequel to Son of the shadows (2001)

"As the daughter of Niamh of the Sevenwaters Clan, Fainne possesses a magic born of the land itself. Instructed by her grandmother, the sorceress Oonagh, Fainne believes she has a destiny to bring about a terrible change in the world. . . . The author captures the feel of myth in this Celtic-laced saga that belongs in most fantasy collections." Libr J

Cybele's secret. Alfred A. Knopf 2008 432p $17.99; lib bdg $20.99
Grades: 7 8 9 10 **Fic**
1. Magic -- Fiction 2. Turkey -- Fiction 3. Sisters -- Fiction 4. Supernatural -- Fiction
ISBN 978-0-375-83365-6; 0-375-83365-X; 978-0-375-93365-3 lib bdg; 0-375-93365-4 lib bdg
LC 2008-4758

Scholarly eighteen-year-old Paula and her merchant father journey from Transylvania to Istanbul to buy an ancient pagan artifact rumored to be charmed, but others, including a handsome Portuguese pirate and an envoy from the magical Wildwood, want to acquire the item, as well.

This is a "honeyed draught of a [novel]. . . . Marillier embroiders Ottoman Empire cultural details into every fold and drape of her story." Booklist

Daughter of the forest. TOR Bks. 2000 400p (Sevenwaters trilogy) hardcover o.p. pa $15.95
Grades: 11 12 Adult **Fic**
1. Fantasy fiction
ISBN 0-312-84879-X; 0-312-87530-4 pa
LC 00-25216

"As the only daughter and youngest child of Lord Colum of Sevenwaters, Sorcha grows up protected and pampered by her six older brothers. When a sorceress's evil magic ensorcels Colum's sons, transforming them into swans, only Sorcha's efforts can break the curse. . . . The author's keen understanding of Celtic paganism and early Irish Christianity adds texture to a rich and vibrant novel that belongs in most fantasy collections." Libr J

Other titles in the Sevenwaters trilogy are:
Child of the prophecy (2002)
Son of the shadows (2001)

Raven flight; a Shadowfell novel. Juliet Marillier. Alfred A. Knopf 2013 416 p.
Grades: 7 8 9 10 **Fic**
1. Occult fiction 2. Fantasy fiction 3. Fantasy 4. Magic -- Fiction 5. Orphans -- Fiction 6. Insurgency -- Fiction 7. Voyages and travels -- Fiction
ISBN 9780375869556; 9780375969553
LC 2012039483

This is the second volume of Juliet Marillier's Shadowfell series. Here, "Neryn's time among the rebels has left her stronger and healthier but no closer to grasping her power and becoming a true Caller. When a potential ally sets a time limit for rebelling against tyrannical King Keldec, Neryn can no longer hide and sets off to find the Hag of the Isles and the Lord of the North." (Kirkus Reviews)

Shadowfell; Juliet Marillier. Alfred A. Knopf 2012 410 p. map (trade) $16.99
Grades: 7 8 9 10 11 12 **Fic**
1. Fantasy fiction 2. Magic -- Fiction 3. Adventure fiction 4. Fantasy 5. Orphans -- Fiction 6. Insurgency -- Fiction 7. Voyages and travels -- Fiction
ISBN 0375869549; 9780375869549; 9780375969546; 9780375983665
LC 2011041050

Originally published: Sydney, N.S.W.: Pan Macmillan, 2012.

In this novel by Juliet Marillier "Fifteen-year-old Neryn is alone in the land of Alban, where the oppressive king has ordered anyone with magical strengths captured and brought before him. Eager to hide her own canny skill--a uniquely powerful ability to communicate with the fairy-like Good Folk--Neryn sets out for the legendary Shadowfell, a home and training ground for a secret rebel group determined to overthrow the evil King Keldec." (Publisher's note)

Son of the shadows. TOR Bks. 2001 462p (Sevenwaters trilogy) $25.95; pa $14.95
Grades: 11 12 Adult **Fic**
1. Fantasy fiction
ISBN 0-312-84880-3; 0-312-87529-0 pa
LC 2001-17387

Sequel to Daughter of the forest (2000)

"Sorcha has brought her British husband home and raised her children, including the gorgeous Niamh and her darker sister, Liadan, in peace. But evil stalks the land again when a tattooed outlaw appears to unsettle the alliances that keep Sevenwaters safe. And with whom but that Painted Man will our heroine—Liadan—fall passionately in love? Marillier's virtuosic pacing and vivid, filmic style make this an engaging continuation of one of last year's best fantasies." Booklist

Followed by Child of the prophecy (2002)

Wildwood dancing. Knopf 2007 416p $16.99; lib bdg $18.99
Grades: 7 8 9 10 **Fic**
1. Magic -- Fiction 2. Sisters -- Fiction 3. Supernatural -- Fiction
ISBN 0-375-83364-1; 0-375-93364-6 lib bdg
LC 2006-16075

Five sisters who live with their merchant father in Transylvania use a hidden portal in their home to cross over into a magical world, the Wildwood.

This is told "with a striking sense of place, magical elements, beautifully portrayed characters, strong heroines, and an emotional core that touches the heart." Voice Youth Advocates

Followed by: Cybele's secret (2008)

Marino, Peter

★ **Dough** Boy. Holiday House 2005 221p hardcover o.p. pa $6.95
Grades: 7 8 9 10 **Fic**
1. School stories 2. Bullies -- Fiction 3. Obesity --

Fiction 4. Family life -- Fiction
ISBN 0-8234-1873-1; 0-8234-2096-5 pa
LC 2004-40593

Overweight, fifteen-year-old Tristan, who lives happily with his divorced mother and her boyfriend Frank, suddenly finds that he must deal with intensified criticism about his weight and other aspects of his life when Frank's popular but troubled, nutrition-obsessed daughter moves in.

"Readers will easily feel the boy's anger and will applaud his resilience and resolve to remain true to himself." Publ Wkly

Mariz, Rae

The **Unidentified**. Balzer + Bray 2010 296p $16.99
Grades: 7 8 9 10 **Fic**
1. School stories 2. Science fiction
ISBN 978-0-06-180208-9; 0-06-180208-5
LC 2009-54254

In a futuristic alternative school set in a shopping mall where video game-playing students are observed and used by corporate sponsors for market research, Katey "Kid" Dade struggles to figure out where she fits in and whether she even wants to.

"An all-too-logical extrapolation of today's trends, this story of conformity, rebellion, and seeking one's identity is evocative of Scott Westerfeld and Cory Doctorow, injecting a dystopian setting with an optimistic, antiestablishment undercurrent." Publ Wkly

Markandaya, Kamala

Nectar in a sieve; with an introduction by Indira Ganesan and a new afterword by Thrity Umrigar. Signet Classics 2010 204p pa $7.95
Grades: 9 10 11 12 Adult **Fic**
1. India -- Fiction 2. Farm life -- Fiction
ISBN 978-0-451-53172-8

First published 1954 in the United Kingdom; first United States edition published 1955 by Day

"This realistic novel of peasant life in a southern Indian village portrays the struggle that Nathan and Rukmani must make to survive. Their first child is a daughter, Irawaddy, and there follow five other children, all sons, after an interval of seven years. Hardships are innumerable and insurmountable, whether they are disasters of nature such as drought, or such manmade catastrophes as the coming of a tannery to their village and a subsequent labor conflict. After many crises, Nathan and Rukmani come to the city to seek help from one of their sons, but he has disappeared. Nathan, finally destroyed by privation, dies, believing to the end that his life with Rukmani has been a happy one." Shapiro. Fic for Youth. 3d edition

Includes bibliographical references

Marr, Melissa

Wicked lovely. HarperTeen 2007 328p il $16.99; lib bdg $17.89
Grades: 8 9 10 11 12 **Fic**
1. Fantasy fiction 2. Fairies -- Fiction 3. Kings and rulers -- Fiction
ISBN 978-0-06-121465-3; 0-06-121465-5; 978-0-06-121466-0 lib bdg; 0-06-121466-3 lib bdg
LC 2007-09143

Seventeen-year-old Aislinn, who has the rare ability to see faeries, is drawn against her will into a centuries-old battle between the Summer King and the Winter Queen, and the survival of her life, her love, and summer all hang in the balance.

"This story explores the themes of love, commitment, and what it really means to give of oneself for the greater good to save everyone else. It is the unusual combination of past legends and modern-day life that gives a unique twist to this 'fairy' tale." SLJ

Other titles in this series are:
Darkest mercy (2011)
Fragile eternity (2009)
Ink exchange (2008)
Radiant shadows (2010)

Marriott, Zoe

The **swan** kingdom. Candlewick Press 2008 272p $16.99; pa $8.99
Grades: 6 7 8 9 10 11 12 **Fic**
1. Fantasy fiction 2. Magic -- Fiction
ISBN 978-0-7636-3481-0; 0-7636-3481-6; 978-0-7636-4293-8 pa; 0-7636-4293-2 pa
LC 2007-38291

When Alexa's mother is killed, her father marries a cunning and powerful woman and her brothers disappear, sending Alexa on a long, dangerous journey as she attempts to harness the mystical power she inherited from her mother and restore the kingdom to its proper balance.

"The mix of magic, royalty and romance will compel many teens." Publ Wkly

Marsden, Carolyn, 1950-

My Own Revolution; Carolyn Marsden. Candlewick Press 2012 174 p. $16.99
Grades: 7 8 9 10 11 12 **Fic**
1. Czechoslovakia -- Fiction 2. Communist countries -- Fiction 3. Resistance to government -- Fiction
ISBN 0763653950; 9780763653958
LC 2012942296

This novel takes place "in 1960s Czechoslovakia, [where] . . . fourteen-year-old Patrik rebels against the communist regime in small ways whenever he gets the chance. . . . But anti-Party sentiment is risky, and when party interference cuts a little too close to home, Patrik and his family find themselves faced with a decision . . . that will change everything." (Publisher's note)

Sahwira; an African friendship. [by] Carolyn Marsden and Philip Matzigkeit. Candlewick Press 2009 189p $15.99
Grades: 5 6 7 8 **Fic**
1. Clergy -- Fiction 2. Friendship -- Fiction 3. Race relations -- Fiction
ISBN 978-0-7636-3575-6; 0-7636-3575-8

The strong friendship between two boys, one black and one white, who live on a mission in Rhodesia, begins to unravel as protests against white colonial rule intensify in 1964.

"The book looks beyond race to examine questions about the meaning of being Christian, fear of Communism, family loyalty, and ethical choices. Marsden and Matzigkeit . . . deftly navigate the dynamic forces at play in the two boys' lives. . . . The story crosses genres to bring in elements of historical fiction, intrigue, and mystery." Bull Cent Child Books

Marsden, John, 1950-

Hamlet: a novel. Candlewick Press 2009 229p $16.99

Grades: 10 11 12 **Fic**

1. Poets 2. Authors 3. Dramatists 4. Denmark -- Fiction 5. Princes -- Fiction 6. Homicide -- Fiction

ISBN 978-0-7636-4451-2; 0-7636-4451-X

LC 2009-7331

This is a retelling of Shakespeare's play. Grieving for the recent death of his beloved father and appalled by his mother's quick remarriage to his uncle, Hamlet, heir to the Danish throne, struggles with conflicting emotions, particularly after his father's ghost appeals to him to avenge his death.

"The setting is contemporary, but feels timeless. Marsden stays true to Shakespeare's text, while modernizing the dialogue. He makes the prince a sympathetic teen who is struggling with his hormones, his grief, and the fact that his uncle is now his stepfather. . . . This is a wonderful treatment of the play: engaging, gripping, dark, and lovely." SLJ

Incurable. Scholastic 2008 245p (The Ellie chronicles) pa $7.99

Grades: 7 8 9 10 **Fic**

1. War stories 2. Australia -- Fiction

ISBN 978-0-439-78322-4 pa; 0-439-78322-4 pa

First published 2005 in Australia

Ellie has struggled to put the war behind her and lead a normal life. Although what's normal about your parents having been murdered; trying to run a farm and go to school; and bringing up a young boy who's hiding terrible secrets about his past?

The **other** side of dawn. Scholastic 2007 319p pa $8.99

Grades: 7 8 9 10 **Fic**

1. War stories 2. Australia -- Fiction

ISBN 978-0-439-85805-2

Sequel to The night is for hunting. Another title in the author's series which began with Tomorrow, when the war began

First published 1999 in Australia

Ellie and her friends, five Australian teenagers who survived the enemy invasion of their country, use guerrilla tactics to support a major counterattack by New Zealand troops.

"As were the previous titles, this final book is chockful of action sequences that are undeniably gripping if not always completely believable. The characters, on the other hand, feel quite real." Horn Book

Tomorrow, when the war began. Houghton Mifflin 1995 286p pa $9.99

Grades: 7 8 9 10 **Fic**

1. War stories 2. Australia -- Fiction

ISBN 9780439829106; 0395706734

LC 94-29299

First published 1993 in Australia

"Australian teenager Ellie and six of her friends return from a winter break camping trip to find their homes burned or deserted, their families imprisoned, and their country occupied by a foreign military force in league with a band of disaffected Australians. As their shock wears off, the seven decide they must stick together if they are to survive. After a life-threatening skirmish with the occupiers, the teens retreat to their isolated campsite in the bush country and make plans to fight a guerilla war against the invaders. . . . " (SLJ)

While I live. Scholastic 2007 299p (The Ellie chronicles) $16.99

Grades: 7 8 9 10 **Fic**

1. War stories 2. Australia -- Fiction

ISBN 978-0-439-78318-7; 0-439-78318-6

Officially the war is over, but Ellie can not seem to escape it and resume a normal life especially after her parents are murdered and she becomes the ward of an unscrupulous lawyer who wants to acquire her family's property.

"Fans of 16-year-old Ellie Linton . . . will be overjoyed that she's back in an exciting series of her own. The realistic and shocking war-related violence that characterized the earlier titles is just as prevalent here." SLJ

Other titles about Ellie Linton are:

Circle of flight (2009)

Incurable (2008)

Marsh, Katherine

★ **Jepp,** who defied the stars; Katherine Marsh. Hyperion 2012 385 p. (hardback) $16.99

Grades: 6 7 8 9 10 **Fic**

1. Bildungsromans 2. Dwarfs -- Fiction 3. Historical fiction 4. Renaissance -- Fiction 5. Voyages and travels -- Fiction 6. Courts and courtiers -- Fiction 7. Europe -- History -- 16th century -- Fiction

ISBN 1423135008; 9781423135005

LC 2011053065

This book tells the story of "a 15-year-old dwarf named Jepp. . . . The first of the book's three sections finds a battered and beaten Jepp being transported ignobly in a cage to an unknown destination; along the way, he recalls the events that led him there, from his humble upbringing in an inn to becoming a court dwarf in Brussels. . . . Jepp's fortunes continue to wax and wane in the later sections, as he arrives at the island castle of astronomer Tycho Brahe." (Publishers Weekly)

★ The **night** tourist; [by] Katherine Marsh. 1st ed.; Hyperion Books for Children 2007 232p $17.99

Grades: 6 7 8 9 **Fic**

1. Death -- Fiction 2. Classical mythology -- Fiction

ISBN 978-1-4231-0689-0; 1-4231-0689-X

LC 2007013311

After fourteen-year-old classics prodigy Jack Perdu has a near fatal accident he meets Euri, a young ghost who introduces him to New York's Underworld, where those who died in New York reside until they are ready to move on, and Jack vows to find his dead mother there.

"Mixing numerous references to mythology and classical literature with deft touches of humor and extensive historical details . . . this intelligent and self-assured debut will compel readers from its outset and leave them satisfied." Publ Wkly

Marshall, Catherine

Christy. Avon Books 2006 576p pa $6.99

Grades: 9 10 11 12 **Fic**

1. Teachers -- Fiction 2. Appalachian region -- Fiction

ISBN 0-380-00141-1

A reissue of the title first published 1967 by McGraw-Hill

"A spirited young woman leaves the security of her home to become a teacher in Cutter Gap, Kentucky. It is 1912 and the needs of the Appalachian people are great. Christy learns much from the poverty and superstition of the mountain folk. Marshall's Christian faith and ideals are intertwined in the plot, which includes a love story." Shapiro. Fic for Youth. 3d edition

Martin, Ann M., 1955-

Here today. Scholastic 2004 308p $16.95; pa $5.99

Grades: 5 6 7 8 **Fic**

1. Mothers -- Fiction 2. Family life -- Fiction

ISBN 0-439-57944-9; 0-439-57945-7 pa

LC 2004-41620

In 1963, Ellie's mother was crowned a grocery store beauty queen, her classmates treated her cruelly, and President Kennedy was killed. It was also when Ellie realized that in trying to keep her life together she had to let pieces of it go

"Martin paints a well-articulated picture of the times, but it is her memorable child and adult characters that shine here." SLJ

Martin, C. K. Kelly

★ **I** know it's over. Random House 2008 244p $16.99; lib bdg $19.99

Grades: 9 10 11 12 **Fic**

1. Love stories 2. School stories 3. Canada -- Fiction 4. Pregnancy -- Fiction

ISBN 978-0-375-84566-6; 978-0-375-94566-3 lib bdg

LC 2007-29180

Sixteen-year-old Nick, still trying to come to terms with his parents' divorce, experiences exhilaration and despair in his relationship with his girlfriend Sasha especially when, after instigating a trial separation, she announces that she is pregnant.

"This measured but heartbreaking rendering of an all-too-common situation would be a great choice for mixed-gender book groups." Bull Cent Child Books

The **lighter** side of life and death. Random House Children's Books 2010 231p $16.99; lib bdg $19.99

Grades: 9 10 11 12 **Fic**

1. School stories 2. Theater -- Fiction 3. Remarriage -- Fiction

ISBN 978-0-375-84588-8; 0-375-84588-7; 978-0-375-95588-4 lib bdg; 0-375-95588-7 lib bdg

LC 2009-15608

After the last, triumphant night of the school play, fifteen-year-old Mason loses his virginity to his good friend and secret crush, Kat Medina, which leads to enormous complications at school just as his home life is thrown into turmoil by his father's marriage to a woman with two children.

"This is not your ordinary teen romance. It's heavy on the sex but carefully nuanced. . . . The layers of emotion, so rarely evoked by young men in YA novels, give a depth and authenticity to Mason's personality that expose his naïveté and occasional bewilderment. The book's other characters are equally complex. . . . A more genuine representation of teen life would be hard to find." Booklist

Yesterday; C.K. Kelly Martin. Random House 2012 368 p. (hardcover library binding) $19.99

Grades: 9 10 11 12 **Fic**

1. Occult fiction 2. Mystery fiction 3. Interpersonal relations -- Fiction 4. Science fiction 5. Memory -- Fiction 6. Schools -- Fiction 7. Identity -- Fiction 8. High schools -- Fiction 9. Family life -- Canada -- Fiction 10. Canada -- History -- 20th century -- Fiction

ISBN 0375866507; 0375966501; 9780375866500; 9780375896446; 9780375966507

LC 2011023994

In this book, "[h]er father's recent death and the move from New Zealand to Toronto with her mother and sister in 1985 have left Freya Kallas seriously disoriented and plagued by headaches. Worse, her memories have puzzling gaps. . . . What do Freya's dreams of living another life mean? . . . Freya is sure the boy she spots on a school field trip has the answers she needs. Though she doesn't know his name and he doesn't recognize her, Freya, increasingly desperate, can't let him go." (Kirkus)

Martin, Rafe

Birdwing; [by] Rafe Martin. 1st ed; Arthur A. Levine Books 2005 359p $16.99

Grades: 6 7 8 9 **Fic**

1. Fairy tales 2. Young adult literature -- Works

ISBN 0-439-21167-0

LC 2004-11695

Prince Ardwin, known as Birdwing, the youngest of six brothers turned into swans by their stepmother, is unable to complete the transformation back into human form, so he undertakes a journey to discover whether his feathered arm will be a curse or a blessing to him.

"The many original characters and unusual adventure scenes ensure that readers will remember this well-paced fantasy." Booklist

Martin, T. Michael

The **end** games; T. Michael Martin. Balzer + Bray 2013 384 p. (hardcover) $17.99

Grades: 9 10 11 12 **Fic**

1. Science fiction 2. Zombies -- Fiction 3. Brothers -- Fiction 4. Survival -- Fiction 5. West Virginia --

Fiction
ISBN 0062201808; 9780062201805
LC 2012038108

This novel, by T. Michael Martin, "takes place in rural West Virginia after a zombie apocalypse. Seventeen-year-old Michael and his baby brother . . . have managed to stay alive by following the Instructions of a mysterious Games Master. They spend their nights fighting the Bellows, grotesque, flesh-eating creatures. But the brothers may not survive much longer. The Bellows are evolving. And the others in The Game don't always follow the rules." (Publisher's note)

Martinez, Jessica

Virtuosity. Simon Pulse 2011 294p $16.99
Grades: 8 9 10 11 12 **Fic**
1. Musicians -- Fiction 2. Drug abuse -- Fiction 3. Violinists -- Fiction 4. Chicago (Ill.) -- Fiction 5. Mother-daughter relationship -- Fiction
ISBN 978-1-4424-2052-6; 1-4424-2052-9
LC 2010042513

This is a "riveting novel. . . . The portrayal of Carmen's world . . . is unique and convincing. . . . Even readers without much interest in music will enjoy this exceptional novel." SLJ

Martinez, Victor

★ **Parrot** in the oven; a novel. Cotler Bks. 1996 216p $19.99; pa $5.99
Grades: 7 8 9 10 **Fic**
1. Family life -- Fiction 2. Mexican Americans -- Fiction
ISBN 0-06-026704-6; 0-06-447186-1 pa
LC 96-2119

Manny relates his coming of age experiences as a member of a poor Mexican American family in which the alcoholic father only adds to everyone's struggle

The author "maintains the authenticity of his setting and characterizations through a razor-sharp combination of tense dialogue, coursing narrative and startlingly elegant imagery." Publ Wkly

Martino, Alfred C.

Over the end line. Houghton Mifflin Harcourt 2009 304p $17
Grades: 10 11 12 **Fic**
1. Soccer -- Fiction 2. Friendship -- Fiction 3. Popularity -- Fiction
ISBN 978-0-15-206121-0; 0-15-206121-5
LC 2008-46464

After scoring the winning goal in the county soccer championship, New Jersey high school senior Jonny finally attains some of the popularity enjoyed by his best friend Kyle, until a devastating event changes everything.

"The author's portrayal of a graphic sex scene and use of explicit language add to the novel's tension. Martino sets out to touch upon issues such as 'the meaning of friendship, the power of the celebrated athlete, and the interactions between teen guys and girls.' He succeeds in dealing with these issues in a compelling manner." Voice Youth Advocates

Mary-Todd, Jonathan

Shot down; Jonathan Mary-Todd. Darby Creek 2012 92 p. (lib. bdg. : alk. paper) $27.93
Grades: 7 8 9 10 11 12 **Fic**
1. Adventure fiction 2. Apocalyptic fiction 3. Survival skills -- Fiction 4. Survival after airplane accidents, shipwrecks, etc. -- Fiction 5. Science fiction 6. Hunting -- Fiction 7. Kentucky -- Fiction 8. Survival -- Fiction
ISBN 0761383298; 9780761383291
LC 2012006864

This young adult novel, by Jonathan Mary-Todd, is a post-apocalyptic adventure story. "When a bullet knocks Malik and the Captain's hot-air balloon out of the sky, Malik goes into wilderness survival mode. . . . Whatever the crisis, he's always counted on the Gene Matterhorn Wilderness Survival Guidebook when things got crazy. Now he and the Captain are in the middle of miles of Kentucky wilderness, being chased by manhunters." (Publisher's note)

Mason, Bobbie Ann

★ **In** country; a novel. Harper Perennial 2005 245, 16p pa $14.99
Grades: 11 12 Adult **Fic**
1. Kentucky -- Fiction 2. Veterans -- Fiction 3. Vietnam War, 1961-1975 -- Fiction
ISBN 978-0-06-083517-0; 0-06-083517-6
LC 2006-273518
First published 1985

"Sam, 17, is obsessed with the Vietnam War and the effect it has had on her life—losing a father she never knew and now living with Uncle Emmett, who seems to be suffering from the effects of Agent Orange. In her own forthright way, she tries to sort out why and how Vietnam has altered the lives of the vets of Hopewell, Kentucky. . . . A harshly realistic, well-written look at the Vietnam War as well as the story of a young woman maturing." SLJ

Mason, Prue

Camel rider; [by] Prue Mason. 1st U.S. ed.; Charlesbridge 2007 204p $15.95
Grades: 6 7 8 9 **Fic**
1. War stories 2. Deserts -- Fiction 3. Wilderness survival -- Fiction
ISBN 978-1-58089-314-5; 1-58089-314-7
LC 2006034125

Two expatriates living in a Middle Eastern country, twelve-year-old Adam from Australia and Walid from Bangladesh, must rely on one another when war breaks out and they find themselves in the desert, both trying to reach the same city with no water, little food, and no common language.

"The suspense is sustained and the wildly improbable happy ending is very satisfying." SLJ

Mass, Wendy

Heaven looks a lot like the mall; a novel. Little, Brown 2007 251p $16.99
Grades: 8 9 10 11 12 **Fic**
1. School stories 2. Coma -- Fiction 3. Shopping centers and malls -- Fiction
ISBN 978-0-316-05851-3; 0-316-05851-3
LC 2007-12333

When high school junior Tessa Reynolds falls into a coma after getting hit in the head during gym class, she experiences heaven as the mall where her parents work, and she revisits key events from her life, causing her to reevaluate herself and how she wants to live.

"Tessa's journey and authentic voice is one that readers will appreciate. . . . Funny, thought-provoking, and at times heartbreaking, this story will entertain and inspire readers." SLJ

Jeremy Fink and the meaning of life. Little, Brown 2006 289p $15.99; pa $6.99

Grades: 5 6 7 8 **Fic**

1. Conduct of life -- Fiction 2. Father-son relationship -- Fiction

ISBN 978-0-316-05829-2; 0-316-05829-7; 978-0-316-05849-0 pa; 0-316-05849-1 pa

LC 2005037291

Just before his thirteenth birthday, Jeremy Fink receives a keyless locked box—set aside by his father before his death five years earlier—that purportedly contains the meaning of life.

"Mass fashions an adventure in which both journey and destination are worth the trip." Horn Book

A **mango** -shaped space; a novel. Little, Brown 2003 220p $16.95

Grades: 5 6 7 8 **Fic**

1. School stories 2. Synesthesia -- Fiction

ISBN 0-316-52388-7

LC 2002-72989

Afraid that she is crazy, thirteen-year-old Mia, who sees a special color with every letter, number, and sound, keeps this a secret until she becomes overwhelmed by school, changing relationships, and the loss of something important to her

"Mass skillfully conveys Mia's emotions, and readers will be intrigued with this fictional depiction of an actual, and fascinating, condition." Horn Book Guide

Massey, David

Torn; David Massey. Scholastic 2013 288 p. $17.99

Grades: 9 10 11 12 **Fic**

1. Missing children -- Fiction 2. Afghan War, 2001- -- Fiction 3. War -- Fiction 4. Soldiers -- Fiction 5. Afghanistan -- Fiction 6. Medical care -- Fiction 7. Afghan War, 2001

ISBN 0545496454; 9780545496452

LC 2012024405

In this novel by David Massey, set "in war-torn Afghanistan, a girl walks right into a hail of bullets: Elinor watches it with her own eyes. The young British army medic risks the line of fire to rescue her, only to realize the girl is gone. To find the missing, mysterious child, Elinor enlists the help of an American Navy SEAL. But in all the confusion, with coalition troops fighting every day to maintain a fragile peace, does Ben have something to hide?" (Publisher's note)

Massey, a former counter-terrorism consultant, brings an air of authenticity to this intense novel that explores the power of friendships formed in combat as well as war's effect on one young woman's idealism." (Horn Book)

Masson, Sophie

Snow, fire, sword; 1st American ed.; Eos 2006 359p $15.99; lib bdg $16.89

Grades: 6 7 8 9 **Fic**

1. Fantasy fiction 2. Magic -- Fiction

ISBN 978-0-06-079091-2; 0-06-079091-1; 978-0-06-079092-9 lib bdg; 0-06-079092-X lib bdg

LC 2005-18149

In the mythical, Indonesia-like country of Jayangan, a village girl and an apprentice swordmaker embark on a magical journey to defeat a hidden evil that threatens their land.

"The sense of a permeable membrane between spirit worlds and contemporary reality will fascinate many readers, as will the shifting images of water buffaloes and motorbikes, villages and cities, and sacred and secular ways." Booklist

The **madman** of Venice. Delacorte Press 2010 276p $17.99; lib bdg $20.99

Grades: 6 7 8 9 **Fic**

1. Missing persons -- Fiction

ISBN 978-0-385-73843-9; 0-385-73843-9; 978-0-385-90729-3 lib bdg; 0-385-90729-X lib bdg

LC 2009022369

First published 2009 in the United Kingdom

"An exotic setting and delicious intrigue combine to make intense historical fiction in this tale of missing persons, murder, and, of course, romance. English merchant Master Ashby heads to Venice in 1602 to investigate the murder of his agent Salerio and the strange disappearance of a young Jewish girl accused of witchcraft by the cruel, conniving wife of the Count of Montemaro. . . . Ashby and his alchemist friend Dr. Leone soon find themselves entangled in a morass that involves Venetian pirates, mistaken identities, and the poisoning of the Count." SLJ

Master, Irfan

★ A **beautiful** lie; by Irfan Master. Albert Whitman 2012 301 p. (hardcover) $16.99

Grades: 7 8 9 10 **Fic**

1. Deception -- Fiction 2. India -- History -- Fiction 3. Father-son relationship -- Fiction 4. Honesty -- Fiction 5. Terminally ill -- Fiction 6. Fathers and sons -- Fiction 7. India -- History -- Partition, 1947 -- Fiction 8. Pakistan -- History -- 20th century -- Fiction

ISBN 0807505978; 9780807505977

LC 2011051132

In this book by Irfan Master, set "in India in 1947, the country is coming apart -- and so is thirteen-year-old Bilal's life. He is determined to protect his dying father from the news of Partition, news that he knows will break his father's heart. With spirit and determination, and with the help of his good friends, Bilal builds an elaborate deception, even printing false pages of the local newspaper to hide the signs of national unrest." (Publisher's note)

Matas, Carol

After the war. Simon & Schuster Bks. for Young Readers 1996 116p map hardcover o.p. pa $4.99

Grades: 7 8 9 10 **Fic**

1. Jews -- Fiction 2. Holocaust, 1933-1945 -- Fiction
ISBN 0-689-80350-8; 0-689-80722-8
LC 95-43613

After being released from Buchenwald at the end of World War II, fifteen-year-old Ruth risks her life to lead a group of children across Europe to Palestine

"Rich in texture and simple in its honesty, this story resonates with feeling." Voice Youth Advocates

The **whirlwind**. Orca 2007 128p pa $8.95
Grades: 6 7 8 9 **Fic**

1. Jews -- Fiction 2. Immigrants -- Fiction 3. World War, 1939-1945 -- Fiction
ISBN 978-1-55143-703-3 pa; 1-55143-703-1 pa

"Benjamin Friedman, a 15-year-old Jewish boy, fears for his life in Nazi Germany. Fortunately, his family is able to escape Hitler, arriving in Seattle in the summer of 1941. Ben is relieved to be there but is upset and confused by his experiences. . . . This unique and thought-provoking story shows what prejudice and indifference to suffering and wrongdoing can lead to. It imparts an understanding of the Holocaust and World War II." SLJ

Matson, Morgan

Amy & Roger's epic detour. Simon and Schuster Books for Young Readers 2010 343p il $16.99
Grades: 9 10 11 12 **Fic**

1. Death -- Fiction 2. Guilt -- Fiction 3. Fathers -- Fiction 4. Bereavement -- Fiction 5. Automobile travel -- Fiction
ISBN 978-1-4169-9065-9; 1-4169-9065-8
LC 2009-49988

After the death of her father, Amy, a high school student, and Roger, a college freshman, set out on a carefully planned road trip from California to Connecticut. "Grades eight to twelve." (Bull Cent Child Books)

"This entertaining and thoughtful summertime road trip serves up slices of America with a big scoop of romance on the side." Kirkus

★ **Second** chance summer; Morgan Matson. Simon & Schuster Books For Young Readers 2012 468 p. (hardback) $16.99
Grades: 9 10 11 12 **Fic**

1. Cancer -- Fiction 2. Family -- Fiction 3. Vacations -- Fiction 4. Love -- Fiction 5. Terminally ill -- Fiction 6. Pocono Mountains (Pa.) -- Fiction 7. Interpersonal relations -- Fiction 8. Family life -- Pennsylvania -- Fiction
ISBN 1416990674; 9781416990673; 9781416990680; 9781439157527
LC 2011052241

In this young adult novel, Taylor and her parents and older brother and younger sister are headed to their lake house in the Poconos for the summer so her father, who is dying of cancer, can spend his last summer there. "Returning to their lake house after a five-year absence fills [Taylor] with dread: she'll have to face her estranged best friend as well as the boy she left without saying goodbye." (Publishers Weekly)

Since you've been gone; Morgan Matson; Simon & Schuster Books for Young Readers. 2014 464p $17.99
Grades: 7 8 9 10 **Fic**

1. Best friends -- Fiction 2. Dating (Social customs) -- Fiction 3. Family life -- Connecticut -- Fiction 4. Friendship -- Fiction 5. Self-reliance -- Fiction 6. Connecticut -- Fiction
ISBN: 1442435003; 9781442435001; 9781442435018
LC 2013041617

"Emily feels lost when her best friend, Sloane, disappears without explanation. But Sloane left Emily a daunting to-do list (with items like 'kiss a stranger'), and Emily bravely takes on each task, finding new friends, confidence, and a crush along the way. A perfectly awkward protagonist; well-rounded, quirky supporting characters; and spot-on dialogue make this novel of self-discovery stand out." Horn Book

Matthews, Andrew

The **way** of the warrior. Dutton Children's Books 2008 152p $15.99
Grades: 7 8 9 10 **Fic**

1. Samurai -- Fiction
ISBN 978-0-525-42063-7; 0-525-42063-0

"In 1565, when Jimmu is 10 years old, he witnesses his father commit seppuku, a ritual suicide, to avoid bringing dishonor to his family. . . . Jimmu spends the next seven years learning the art of the samurai . . . with the sole intention of avenging his father . . . . The . . . story is an honest and engaging portrayal of a young man's struggle to do the right thing. . . . The vivid depictions of a soldier's life in 16th-century Japan will captivate samurai enthusiasts, and the amount of action that Matthews packs into this relatively short novel will appeal to reluctant readers." SLJ

Matthews, L. S.

The **outcasts**. Delacorte Press 2007 259p $15.99; lib bdg $18.99
Grades: 7 8 9 10 **Fic**

1. School stories 2. Supernatural -- Fiction
ISBN 978-0-385-73367-0; 978-0-385-90382-0 lib bdg
LC 2006-50872

First published 2005 in the United Kingdom

A much-anticipated school trip to England's West Country turns into a life-changing adventure for five high school misfits when they fall into another dimension while exploring the house in which they are staying.

"A fun, wild, and thoughtfully layered adventure." Booklist

Mattison, Booker T.

Unsigned hype; a novel. Revell 2009 207p pa $9.99
Grades: 7 8 9 10 **Fic**

1. Rap music -- Fiction 2. Christian life -- Fiction 3. African Americans -- Fiction
ISBN 978-0-8007-3380-3; 0-8007-3380-0
LC 2008-54966

Fifteen-year-old Tory Tyson dreams of producing hip hop records, and as he rapidly begins to experience success doing just that, he finds that he must make choices between the way he has been raised by his single, God-fearing mother and the folks he meets in the music world.

This "novel has an authentic voice, taking readers into the world of New York City hip-hop through the wide eyes of a kid who's still refreshingly innocent." Publ Wkly

May, Kyla

Kiki; my stylish life. by Kyla May. Scholastic Inc. 2013 96 p.

Grades: 7 8 9 10 11 12 **Fic**

1. Diaries -- Fiction 2. Friendship -- Fiction 3. Fashion -- Fiction 4. Popularity -- Fiction 5. Best friends -- Fiction 6. Elementary schools -- Fiction 7. Friendship

ISBN 9780545445122; 9780545496131; 9780545496803; 0545496136

LC 2012034246

In this book by Kyla May, "Kiki, Coco, and Lulu are the BEST of friends. They even have their very own club! But Mika, the new girl, is shaking things up on Lotus Lane. This first book is written as Kiki's diary--with illustrations and doodles throughout. Kiki LOVES creating cool outfits, hanging out with friends, and collecting fun facts." (Publisher's note)

Mayall, Beth

Mermaid Park. Razorbill 2005 248p $16.99

Grades: 7 8 9 10 **Fic**

1. Swimming -- Fiction 2. Family life -- Fiction 3. Summer employment -- Fiction

ISBN 1-59514-029-8

Sixteen-year-old Amy escapes family difficulties by immersing herself in her job at a mermaid-themed water show.

"This is a good read that deals with real growing-up issues." SLJ

Mazer, Harry

★ **Snow** bound. Delacorte Press 1973 146p hardcover o.p. pa $5.99

Grades: 7 8 9 10 **Fic**

1. Runaway children -- Fiction 2. Wilderness survival -- Fiction

ISBN 0-440-96134-3

LC 72-7958

"Tony Laporte is angry when his parents will not allow him to keep a stray dog, so he takes off in his mother's old car. Driving without a license in the middle of a snowstorm that soon becomes a blizzard, Tony picks up a hitchhiker, Cindy Reichert. Trying to impress the slightly older girl with his driving skill, Tony wrecks the car, leaving the two stranded in a desolate area far from a main highway, with little likelihood of rescue for days." Shapiro. Fic for Youth. 3d edition

A **boy** at war; a novel of Pearl Harbor. Simon & Schuster Bks. for Young Readers 2001 104p il hardcover o.p. pa $4.99

Grades: 7 8 9 10 **Fic**

1. Pearl Harbor (Oahu, Hawaii), Attack on, 1941 -- Fiction

ISBN 0-689-84161-2; 0-689-84160-4 pa

LC 00-49687

While fishing with his friends off Honolulu on December 7, 1941, teenaged Adam is caught in the midst of the Japanese attack and through the chaos of the subsequent days tries to find his father, a naval officer who was serving on the U.S.S. Arizona when the bombs fell

"Mazer's graphic, sensory descriptions give the narrative immediacy, putting readers alongside Adam, watching with him as 'pieces of the ship and pieces of men rained down around him.' . . . This is a thought-provoking, sobering account of the human costs of war." Horn Book Guide

Other titles in this series are:

A boy no more (2004)

Heroes don't run (2005)

The **last** mission. Dell 1981 188p pa $5.99

Grades: 7 8 9 10 **Fic**

1. Jews -- Fiction 2. Prisoners of war -- Fiction 3. World War, 1939-1945 -- Fiction

ISBN 0-440-94797-9

First published 1979 by Delacorte Press

In 1944 a 15-year-old Jewish boy tells his family he will travel in the West but instead, enlists in the United States Air Corps and is subsequently taken prisoner by the Germans.

"Told in a rapid journalistic style, occasionally peppered with barrack-room vulgarities, the story is a vivid and moving account of a boy's experience during World War II as well as a skillful, convincing portrayal of his misgivings as a Jew on enemy soil and of his ability to size up—in mature human fashion—the misery around him." Horn Book

Mazer, Norma Fox

After the rain. Morrow 1987 291p hardcover o.p. pa $5.99

Grades: 6 7 8 9 **Fic**

1. Death -- Fiction 2. Grandfathers -- Fiction

ISBN 0-688-06867-7; 0-380-75025-2 pa

LC 86-33270

A Newbery Medal honor book, 1988

After discovering her grandfather is dying, fifteen-year-old Rachel gets to know him better than ever before and finds the experience bittersweet

"A powerful book, dealing with death and dying and the strength of family affection." Horn Book

Girlhearts. HarperCollins Pubs. 2001 210p hardcover o.p. lib bdg $16.89; pa $6.99

Grades: 6 7 8 9 **Fic**

1. Death -- Fiction 2. Orphans -- Fiction 3. Mothers and daughters

ISBN 0-688-13350-9; 0-688-06866-9 lib bdg; 0-380-72290-9 pa

LC 00-63202

Thirteen-year-old Sarabeth Silver's life is turned upside-down when her mother dies suddenly, leaving her orphaned, confused, and at the mercy of everyone who seems to know what is best for her

"Mazer's intimate portrait of grief is convincing and well drawn." Horn Book Guide

★ The **missing** girl. HarperTeen 2008 288p $16.99; lib bdg $17.89

Grades: 7 8 9 10 **Fic**

1. Sisters -- Fiction 2. Kidnapping -- Fiction 3. New York (State) -- Fiction 4. Child sexual abuse -- Fiction
ISBN 978-0-06-623776-3; 978-0-06-623777-0 lib bdg
LC 2007-09136

In Mallory, New York, as five sisters, aged eleven to seventeen, deal with assorted problems, conflicts, fears, and yearnings, a mysterious middle-aged man watches them, fascinated, deciding which one he likes the best.

"Fans of . . . classic tales of high-tension peril will appreciate the way this successfully plays on their deepest fears." Bull Cent Child Books

McBay, Bruce

Waiting for Sarah; {by} Bruce McBay & James Heneghan. Orca Book Publishers 2003 170p pa $7.95

Grades: 9 10 11 12 **Fic**

1. Canada -- Fiction 2. Orphans -- Fiction 3. People with physical disabilities -- Fiction
ISBN 1-55143-270-6
LC 2002-117768

After Mike loses his family and is severely injured in a car accident, he withdraws until he meets mysterious Sarah, a girl who is not who she seems

"This is a well-developed novel that shatters the teen perceptions of invincibility, as well as dealing with loss, handicaps, and positive ways to break through grief." Lib Media Connect

McBride, Lish

Hold me closer, necromancer. Henry Holt 2010 342p $16.99

Grades: 9 10 11 12 **Fic**

1. Dead -- Fiction 2. Magic -- Fiction 3. Werewolves -- Fiction 4. Supernatural -- Fiction 5. Seattle (Wash.) -- Fiction
ISBN 978-0-8050-9098-7; 0-8050-9098-3
LC 2009-50768

Sam LaCroix, a Seattle fast-food worker and college dropout, discovers that he is a necromancer, part of a world of harbingers, werewolves, satyrs, and one particular necromancer who sees Sam as a threat to his lucrative business of raising the dead.

"With fine writing, tight plotting, a unique and uniquely odd cast of teens, adults, and children, and a pace that smashes through any curtain of disbelief, this sardonic and outrageous story's only problem is that it must, like all good things, come to an end." Booklist

McBride, Regina

The **fire** opal. Delacorte Press 2010 293p $16.99; lib bdg $19.99

Grades: 7 8 9 10 **Fic**

1. Ireland -- Fiction 2. Family life -- Fiction 3. Supernatural -- Fiction 4. Celtic mythology -- Fiction
ISBN 978-0-385-73781-4; 0-385-73781-5; 978-0-385-90692-0 lib bdg; 0-385-90692-7 lib bdg
LC 2009-07573

While invading English soldiers do battle in sixteenth-century Ireland, Maeve grows up with a mystical connection to a queen who, centuries before, faced enemies of her own.

"Filled with fantastic creatures and hair-raising adventure, this mystical, imaginative tale should appeal to fantasy fans of all ages. A compelling, addictive read." Voice Youth Advocates

McCafferty, Megan

Bumped. Balzer + Bray 2011 323p $16.99

Grades: 9 10 11 12 **Fic**

1. Twins -- Fiction 2. Sisters -- Fiction 3. Viruses -- Fiction 4. Pregnancy -- Fiction 5. New Jersey -- Fiction
ISBN 978-0-06-196274-5; 0-06-196274-0
LC 2010-30704

In 2036 New Jersey, when teens are expected to become fanatically religious wives and mothers or high-priced Surrogettes for couples made infertile by a widespread virus, sixteen-year-old identical twins Melody and Harmony find in one another the courage to believe they have choices.

"The book's carefree sexuality and exploitation makes it uncomfortable, scandalous, and not easily forgotten—there's little doubt that's exactly what McCafferty is going for." Publ Wkly

Thumped; Megan McCafferty. Balzer + Bray 2012 290 p. (hardback) $17.99

Grades: 9 10 11 12 **Fic**

1. Science fiction 2. Dystopian fiction 3. Teenage mothers -- Fiction 4. Teenage pregnancy -- Fiction 5. Twins -- Fiction 6. Honesty -- Fiction 7. Pregnancy -- Fiction 9. Infertility -- Fiction
ISBN 0061962767; 9780061962769
LC 2011042149

This book is the sequel to Megan McCafferty's science fiction novel 'Bumped' about the pregnancies of teenage twin girls twins Melody and Harmony in a future dystopian United States. "After a virus destroyed the ability of anyone over the age of 18 to reproduce, teen pregnancy became big business. . . . [T]his book . . . makes the deliberate point that teenage pregnancy and sex without love can seriously damage both the teens and society." (Kirkus Reviews)

"The well-paced plot and the twins' alternating narratives will keep readers engaged... A worthwhile read for teens beginning to think about their personal reproductive choices." LJ

Sloppy Firsts Crown Publishers 2001 280p $13.99

Grades 9 10 11 12 **Fic**

1. High school students -- Fiction. 2. Teenage girls -- Fiction. 3. Bildungsromans. 4. New Jersey -- Fiction.
ISBN 0609807900

"When her best friend, Hope Weaver, moves away from Pineville, New Jersey, hyperobservant sixteen-year-old Jessica Darling is devastated. A fish out of water at school and a stranger at home, Jessica feels more lost than ever now that the only person with whom she could really communicate has gone. How is she supposed to deal with the boy- and shopping-crazy girls at school, her dad's obsession with her track meets, her mother salivating over big sister Bethany's lavish wedding, and her nonexistent love life?" (Publisher's Note)

"When her best friend, Hope, moves away after Jess's brother dies of a drug overdose, sixteen-year-old Jess copes with loss of the only friend who understands her. Diary entries and monthly letters to Hope reflect Jess's longing for love but refusal to settle for just anyone, and reveal her rivalry with her perfect, engaged sister...The author shines with painfully honest portrayals of a variety of relationships, from simple best-friend pacts to complex family interactions in a house where the death of the only son is never mentioned. Ultimately, the author exposes the harm teens do to themselves and to one another, and juxtaposes their resilience alongside their destruction." VOYA

Other titles about Jessica Darling are:
Second Helpings (2003)
Charmed Thirds (2006)
Fourth Comings (2007)
Perfect Fifths (2009)

McCaffrey, Anne

Dragon's kin; {by} Anne McCaffrey, Todd McCaffrey. Del Rey 2003 304p $24.95
Grades: 9 10 11 12 **Fic**

1. Fantasy fiction
ISBN 0-345-46198-3

"On the planet Pern, the colonists prepare for the return of the Red Star and the deadly fall of Thread, which consumes any organic matter it touches. When the mines that provide the planet with minerals for metalworking and coal for heat play out, a pair of young people discover a heretofore hidden power of the watchwhers, the lowly kin of dragonkind, and learn a new way to provide assistance for the people of Pern. . . . Personable characters and superb storytelling make this an excellent choice for sf collections and essential for Pern fans of all ages. Highly recommended." Libr J

Dragonflight; volume 1 of The Dragonriders of Pern. Ballantine Bks. 1978 337p il (Dragonriders of Pern) hardcover o.p. pa $12.95
Grades: 8 9 10 11 12 Adult **Fic**

1. Fantasy fiction 2. Science fiction 3. Dragons -- Fiction
ISBN 0-345-27749-X; 0-345-48426-6 pa
LC 78-16707

First published 1968 in paperback. Based on two award winning stories entitled: Weyr search and Dragonrider. Many titles co-written by Todd McCaffrey

ALA YALSA Margaret A. Edwards Award (1999)

The planet Pern, originally colonized from Earth but long out of contact with it, has been periodically threatened by the deadly silver Threads which fall from the wandering Red Star. To combat them a life form on the planet was developed into winged, fire-breathing dragons. Humans with a high degree of empathy and telepathic power are needed to train and preserve these creatures. As the story begins, Pern has fallen into decay, the threat of the Red Star has been forgotten, the Dragonriders and dragons are reduced in number and in disrepute, and the evil Lord Fax has begun conquering neighboring holds.

Fantasy titles set on Pern include:
All the Weyrs of Pern (1991)
The chronicles of Pern: first fall (1993)
Dragon Harper (2007)
Dragon's fire (2006)
Dragon's kin (2003)
Dragon's time (2011)
Dragondrums (1979)
Dragonquest (1971)
Dragonsdawn (1988)
Dragonseye (1997)
Dragonsinger (1977)
Dragonsong (1976)
The masterharper of Pern (1998)
Morets: Dragonlady of Pern (1983)
Nerilka's story (1986)
The Renegades of Pern (1989)
The skies of Pern (2001)
White dragon (1978)

McCaffrey, Todd J.

Dragongirl; [by] Todd McCaffrey. Del Rey-Ballantine Books 2010 482p map (Dragonriders of Pern) $26; ebook $26
Grades: 9 10 11 12 Adult **Fic**

1. Fantasy fiction 2. Dragons -- Fiction
ISBN 978-0-345-49116-9; 978-0-345-52191-0 ebook
LC 2010-14672

Sequel to Dragonheart (2008)

"Once again, the Red Star appears in the skies over Pern, triggering the fall of Thread, a corrosive and deadly spaceborn spore that comes in Passes that last approximately 50 years. This time, however, the dragons bred by the colonists of Pern to fight Thread are dying from a mysterious plague, and the population of Pern faces extinction. While gold-dragon rider Fiona concentrates on learning to heal sick and injured dragons and their riders, the harper Kindan and ex-dragon rider Lorana search for a cure." Libr J

McCahan, Erin

I now pronounce you someone else. Arthur A. Levine Books 2010 258p $16.99
Grades: 8 9 10 11 **Fic**

1. Michigan -- Fiction 2. Family life -- Fiction 3. Stepfathers -- Fiction 4. Dating (Social customs) -- Fiction 5. Mother-daughter relationship -- Fiction
ISBN 978-0-545-08818-3; 0-545-08818-6
LC 2009-35992

Eighteen-year-old Bronwen has long felt that she was switched with another child at birth, and so although she loves Jared, she must decide if she is ready to be married or should, instead, live on her own first.

"Told in lively first-person narrative, this intelligent romance teaches a hard but relevant lesson about living dreams and letting them go." Publ Wkly

McCall, Guadalupe Garcia

★ **Under** the mesquite. Lee & Low Books 2011 224p $17.95
Grades: 7 8 9 10 11 12 **Fic**

1. Texas -- Fiction 2. Cancer -- Fiction 3. Family life -- Fiction 4. Mexican Americans -- Fiction
ISBN 978-1-60060-429-4; 1-60060-429-3; 978-1-60060-875-9 ebook
LC 2010052567

Throughout her high school years, as her mother battles cancer, Lupita takes on more responsibility for her house and seven younger siblings, while finding refuge in acting and writing poetry. Includes glossary of Spanish terms.

"With poignant imagery and well-placed Spanish, the author effectively captures the complex lives of teenagers in many Latino and/or immigrant families." Kirkus

McCarry, Sarah

All our pretty songs; by Sarah McCarry. 1st ed. St. Martin's Griffin 2013 234 p. (paperback) $9.99; (hardcover) $18.99

Grades: 9 10 11 12 **Fic**

1. Music -- Fiction 2. Supernatural -- Fiction 3. Triangles (Interpersonal relations) -- Fiction 4. Love -- Fiction 5. Musicians -- Fiction 6. Friendship -- Fiction 7. Best friends -- Fiction

ISBN 1250040884; 9781250027085; 9781250040886

LC 2013003451

This novel by Sarah McCarry is about "two best friends who grew up like sisters: charismatic, mercurial, and beautiful Aurora, and the devoted, watchful narrator. Their unbreakable bond is challenged when a mysterious and gifted musician named Jack comes between them. They're not the only ones who have noticed Jack's gift; his music has awakened an ancient evil--and a world both above and below which may not be mythical at all." (Publisher's note)

"Art and music run rampant through an unnamed narrator's journey with her best friend, strikingly beautiful Aurora, as frightening and elusive strangers promise drugs, fame, and love. The writing is rich and lush, yet conveys immediacy and is comprehensible even when the events are not...The descent into the underworld is riveting as the heroine tries to fight for her loved ones' fates. Raw sex and foul language accompany the shadow world that promises fame and one's heart's desire, and only faith in the narrator makes the journey endurable. Brilliant in concept and execution." (School Library Journal)

McCarthy, Maureen

Rose by any other name. Roaring Brook Press 2008 336p $17.95

Grades: 9 10 11 12 **Fic**

1. Australia -- Fiction 2. Family life -- Fiction 3. Automobile travel -- Fiction

ISBN 978-1-59643-372-4; 1-59643-372-8

LC 2007-18406

First published 2006 in Australia

During a road trip with her mother from Melbourne to Fairy Point, Australia, to see her dying grandmother, nineteen-year-old Rose gains a new perspective on events of the previous year, when family problems, the end of a long-term friendship, and bad personal choices dramatically transformed her near-perfect life.

"This complex coming-of-age novel, which explores both universal self-destructive tendencies and resilience, will resonate with teen readers as well as many adults." Booklist

McCarthy, Susan Carol

True fires. Bantam Books 2004 306p hardcover o.p. pa $13

Grades: 9 10 11 12 **Fic**

1. Florida -- Fiction 2. Race relations -- Fiction 3. Segregation in education -- Fiction

ISBN 0-553-80170-8; 0-553-38104-0 pa

LC 2003-70885

"Recently widowed, Franklin Dare moves his family to Florida to start a new life in the lush citrus groves. But his young children catch the eye of a corrupt sheriff, K.A. DeLuth, who proclaims Daniel's hair too 'kinked' and Rebecca's nose too wide and bans them from Lake Esther Elementary (according to Florida law, any child deemed one-eighth black or more cannot attend an all-white school). Only unimpeachable evidence that Franklin has no black blood—in fact, he is part Croatan Indian—will result in the children's readmittance. . . . The ending may present more questions than answers, but it doesn't take away from McCarthy's flawless dialogue, warm characters and compassionate wit, all of which service a moving story about the powers of love and justice." Publ Wkly

McCaughrean, Geraldine

Cyrano. Harcourt 2006 114p $16

Grades: 7 8 9 10 **Fic**

1. Soldiers 2. Love stories 3. France -- History -- 1589-1789, Bourbons -- Fiction

ISBN 978-0-15-205805-0; 0-15-205805-2

LC 2006-05445

Ashamed of his ugliness, long-nosed Cyrano de Bergerac, a brilliant seventeenth-century poet and expert swordsman in the French army, helps a rival woo and win Roxane, the beautiful cousin Cyrano loves in silence.

"The story has something for everyone—action, adventure, and romance. The dynamically drawn characters jump off the page. Staying true to Edmond Rostand's original tale, McCaughrean introduces a new generation to the swashbuckling hero." SLJ

★ The **death** -defying Pepper Roux. Harper 2010 328p $16.99; lib bdg $17.89

Grades: 5 6 7 8 **Fic**

1. Adventure fiction 2. Fate and fatalism -- Fiction

ISBN 978-0-06-183665-7; 0-06-183665-6; 978-0-06-183666-4 lib bdg; 0-06-183666-4 lib bdg

LC 2009-39665

Having been raised believing he will die before he reaches the age of fourteen, Pepper Roux runs away on his fourteenth birthday in an attempt to elude his fate, assumes another identity, and continues to try to outrun death, no matter the consequences.

"McCaughrean's exuberant prose and whirling humor animate an unforgettable cast of characters." Booklist

★ The **glorious** adventures of the Sunshine Queen. Harper 2011 325p $16.99

Grades: 5 6 7 8 **Fic**

1. Adventure fiction 2. Theater -- Fiction

ISBN 978-0-06-200806-0; 0-06-200806-4

LC 2010021958

When a diphtheria outbreak forces twelve-year-old Cissy to leave her Oklahoma hometown in the 1890s, she and her two classmates embark on a wild adventure down the

Missouri River with a team of traveling actors who are living on a dilapidated paddle steamer.

"McCaughrean invests her characters with humanity and shows a farcical sense for dialogue, while her arch narrative voice, includes the theatrical and clever turns of phrase." Booklist

★ The **kite** rider; a novel. HarperCollins Pubs. 2002 272p maps hardcover o.p. pa $6.99

Grades: 5 6 7 8 **Fic**

1. Kites -- Fiction 2. China -- History -- Yüan dynasty, 1260-1368

ISBN 0-06-623874-9; 0-06-441091-9 pa

LC 2001-39522

In thirteenth-century China, after trying to save his widowed mother from a horrendous second marriage, twelve-year-old Haoyou has life-changing adventures when he takes to the sky as a circus kite rider and ends up meeting the great Mongol ruler Kublai Khan

"The story is a genuine page-turner. . . . McCaughrean fully immerses her memorable characters in the culture and lore of the ancient Chinese and Mongols, which make this not only a solid adventure story but also a window to a fascinating time and place." Booklist

Not the end of the world; a novel. HarperTempest 2005 244p $16.99; lib bdg $17.89

Grades: 7 8 9 10 **Fic**

1. Noah's ark -- Fiction

ISBN 0-06-076030-3; 0-06-076031-1 lib bdg

LC 2004-14786

Noah's daughter, daughters-in-law, sons, wife, and the animals describe what it was like to be aboard the ark while they watched everyone around them drown.

"This frightening retelling of the biblical Noah's Ark story is written beautifully and with brutal clarity." Voice Youth Advocates

The **white** darkness. HarperTempest 2007 384p hardcover o.p. pa $8.99

Grades: 8 9 10 11 12 **Fic**

1. Antarctica -- Fiction 2. Wilderness survival -- Fiction

ISBN 978-0-06-089035-3; 0-06-089035-5; 978-0-06-089037-7 pa; 0-06-089037-1 pa

LC 2006-02503

First published 2005 in the United Kingdom

Michael L. Printz Award, 2008

Taken to Antarctica by the man she thinks of as her uncle for what she believes to be a vacation, Symone—a troubled fourteen year old—discovers that he is dangerously obsessed with seeking Symme's Hole, an opening that supposedly leads into the center of a hollow Earth.

"McCaughrean's lyrical language actively engages the senses, plunging readers into a captivating landscape that challenges the boundaries of reality." Booklist

McClintock, Norah

Masked; written by Norah McClintock. Orca Book Publishers 2010 108p (Orca soundings) pa $9.95

Grades: 7 8 9 10 **Fic**

1. Mystery fiction

ISBN 978-1-55469-364-1; 1-55469-364-0

Rosie walks in on an armed robbery in her father's convienence store. Who is that masked man? And why is the loser from school there?

"Tight plotting, swift pacing, and tension that intensifies with each page mark this entry in the always-reliable Orca Soundings series for reluctant readers." Booklist

Taken. Orca Book Publishers 2009 166p pa $12.95

Grades: 7 8 9 10 **Fic**

1. Kidnapping -- Fiction 2. Wilderness survival -- Fiction

ISBN 978-1-55469-152-4; 1-55469-152-4

"After two girls from a nearby town go missing everyone goes on high alert, suspecting a serial killer, and while walking home, Stephanie is grabbed from behind and injected with a drug that knocks her out. She awakens hours later to find herself tied up in an abandoned cabin deep in a densely wooded area. . . . Her harrowing journey back to safety propels this plot-driven, fast-paced tale forward. . . . Told in the first person, this suspenseful survival story is sure to have strong appeal." Kirkus

McClymer, Kelly

Must love black. Simon Pulse 2008 167p pa $8.99

Grades: 6 7 8 9 **Fic**

1. Twins -- Fiction 2. Sisters -- Fiction 3. Babysitters -- Fiction

ISBN 978-1-4169-6994-5; 1-4169-4903-8

"Philippa does not consider herself a Goth but she loves the color black. When she answers a classified ad for a summer nanny position, it is the advertisement's one specification 'must love black' that attracts her to the job. . . . McClymer's novel combines understated gothic elements with traditional teen romance tropes and succeeds as a light and funny read." SLJ

McCormick, Patricia, 1956-

★ **Cut**. Front St. 2000 168p $16.95

Grades: 7 8 9 10 **Fic**

1. Self-mutilation -- Fiction 2. Psychiatric hospitals -- Fiction

ISBN 1-88691-061-8

LC 00-34840

While confined to a mental hospital, thirteen-year-old Callie slowly comes to understand some of the reasons behind her self-mutilation, and gradually starts to get better

"Realistic, sensitive, and heartfelt." Voice Youth Advocates

My brother's keeper. Hyperion Books for Children 2004 187p $15.99

Grades: 7 8 9 10 **Fic**

1. Baseball -- Fiction 2. Brothers -- Fiction 3. Drug abuse -- Fiction

ISBN 0-7868-5173-2

LC 2004-55233

Thirteen-year-old Toby, a prematurely gray-haired Pittsburgh Pirates fan and baseball card collector, tries to cope with his brother's drug use, his father's absence, and his mother dating Stanley the Food King.

"This is a clever and believable first-person narrative by a responsible, caring, and appealing kid who is doing his utmost to hold together people he loves." Booklist

Never fall down; a novel. Patricia McCormick. Balzer + Bray 2012 216 p.
Grades: 9 10 11 12 **Fic**

1. Genocide -- Fiction 2. Musicians -- Fiction 3. Human rights -- Fiction 4. Cambodian refugees -- Fiction 5. Cambodia -- History -- 1975- -- Fiction 6. Soldiers -- Fiction 7. Party of Democratic Kampuchea -- Fiction 8. Cambodia -- History -- 1975-1979 -- Fiction 9. Cambodia -- History -- 1975-1979
ISBN 0061730939; 9780061730931

LC 2011052211

In this book, "drawing on hundreds of hours of interviews with Arn Chorn-Pond, who was eleven in 1975 when the Khmer Rouge gained control of Cambodia, [author Patricia] McCormick creates a . . . portrait of genocide as seen through a boy's eyes. . . . He becomes a motivating force for fellow prisoners such as Mek, the music teacher enlisted to teach the boys how to play patriotic songs on traditional instruments. . . . Mek wants to die, too, but Arn won't let him." (Horn Book Magazine)

Includes bibliographical references and index

Purple Heart. Balzer + Bray 2009 198p $16.99; lib bdg $17.89; pa $8.99
Grades: 7 8 9 10 **Fic**

1. Memory -- Fiction 2. Soldiers -- Fiction 3. Hospitals -- Fiction 4. Iraq War, 2003- -- Fiction 5. Brain -- Wounds and injuries -- Fiction
ISBN 978-0-06-173090-0; 0-06-173090-4; 978-0-06-173091-7 lib bdg; 0-06-173091-2 lib bdg; 978-0-06-173092-4 pa; 0-06-173092-0 pa

LC 2009-1757

While recuperating in a Baghdad hospital from a traumatic brain injury sustained during the Iraq War, eighteen-year-old soldier Matt Duffy struggles to recall what happened to him and how it relates to his ten-year-old friend, Ali.

"Strong characters heighten the drama. . . . McCormick raises moral questions without judgment and will have readers examining not only this conflict but the nature of heroism and war." Publ Wkly

★ **Sold.** Hyperion 2006 263p $15.99
Grades: 9 10 11 12 **Fic**

1. Nepal -- Fiction 2. Slavery -- Fiction 3. Prostitution -- Fiction
ISBN 0-7868-5171-6; 978-0-7868-5171-3

LC 2006-49594

Thirteen-year-old Lakshmi leaves her poor mountain home in Nepal thinking that she is to work in the city as a maid only to find that she has been sold into the sex slave trade in India and that there is no hope of escape.

"In beautiful clear prose and free verse that remains true to the child's viewpoint, first-person, present-tense vignettes fill in Lakshmi's story. The brutality and cruelty are ever present ('I have been beaten here, / locked away, / violated a hundred times / and a hundred times more'), but not sensationalized. . . . An unforgettable account of sexual slavery as it exists now." Booklist

McDaniel, Lurlene

Breathless. Delacorte Press 2009 165p $13.99
Grades: 8 9 10 11 12 **Fic**

1. Cancer -- Fiction 2. Suicide -- Fiction 3. Siblings -- Fiction 4. Friendship -- Fiction
ISBN 978-0-385-90458-2; 0-385-90458-4

LC 2008-18427

A high school diving champion develops bone cancer in this story told from the points of view of the diver, his best friend, his sister, and his girlfriend.

"This is a heartstrings-tugging read that retains the central character's dignity and peace in the face of insurmountable odds. A sensitive book on a delicate topic." SLJ

Hit and run; [by] Lurlene McDaniel. 1st ed.; Delacorte Press 2007 180p $10.99
Grades: 8 9 10 11 12 **Fic**

1. School stories 2. Traffic accidents -- Fiction
ISBN 978-0-385-73161-4

LC 2006012738

Events surrounding the hit and run accident of a popular high school student are told from the viewpoints of those involved, including the victim.

This "demonstrates the power of love and making choices. McDaniel, known for her inspiring novels, has a simplistic style, but a weighty message—it's the way you respond to a given situation that defines who you are and who you will be." SLJ

McDevitt, Jack

Moonfall. HarperCollins Pubs. 1998 464p hardcover o.p. pa $7.99
Grades: 9 10 11 12 **Fic**

1. Science fiction 2. Comets -- Fiction 3. Space colonies -- Fiction
ISBN 0-06-105036-9; 0-06-105112-8 pa

LC 98-147774

"The discovery of an interstellar comet on a collision course with the moon spells catastrophic destruction not only for Moonbase—Earth's first lunar colony—but for the planet itself. . . . McDevitt chronicles the countdown from sighting to impact to aftermath in taut vignettes that display the best and worst of humanity's reaction to impending doom. Compulsively readable." Libr J

McDonald, Abby

The **anti-**prom. Candlewick Press 2011 280p $16.99
Grades: 8 9 10 11 **Fic**

1. School stories
ISBN 978-0-7636-4956-2; 0-7636-4956-2

LC 2010-39170

On prom night, Bliss, Jolene, and Meg, students from the same high school who barely know one another, band together to get revenge against Bliss's boyfriend and her best friend, whom she caught together in the limousine they rented.

"McDonald instills more intelligence than you'd expect from such a plot while not skimping on the simple pleasures, either." Booklist

Boys, bears, and a serious pair of hiking boots. Candlewick Press 2010 293p $16.99
Grades: 9 10 11 12 **Fic**

1. Canada -- Fiction 2. Social action -- Fiction 3. Self-perception -- Fiction 4. Wilderness areas -- Fiction 5. Environmental protection -- Fiction
ISBN 978-0-7636-4382-9; 0-7636-4382-3
LC 2009-26015

Seventeen-year-old Jenna, an ardent vegetarian and environmentalist, is thrilled to be spending the summer communing with nature in rural Canada, until she discovers that not all of the rugged residents there share her beliefs.

McDonald "composes a fun summer read, closely examining the conflict between sticking to one's beliefs and learning the art of compromise." Publ Wkly

McDonald, Ian

Be my enemy; by Ian McDonald. Pyr 2012 280 p. (hardcover) $16.95
Grades: 7 8 9 10 **Fic**

1. Science fiction 2. Kidnapping -- Fiction 3. Technology -- Fiction 4. Father-son relationship -- Fiction
ISBN 1616146788; 9781616146788
LC 2012018572

Sequel to: Planesrunner (2011)

This book by Ian McDonald is the second in the Everness Series. "Everett Singh has escaped with the Infundibulum from the clutches of Charlotte Villiers and the Order, but at a terrible price. His father is missing, banished to one of the billions of parallel universes of the Panoply of All Worlds, and Everett and the crew of the airship Everness have taken a wild Heisenberg jump to a random parallel plane." (Publisher's note)

Empress of the sun; by Ian McDonald. Pyr 2014 290 p. (Everness) (hardback) $17.99
Grades: 7 8 9 10 **Fic**

1. War stories 2. Airships -- Fiction 3. Human-alien encounters -- Fiction 4. Science fiction 5. Adventure and adventurers -- Fiction
ISBN 1616148659; 9781616148652
LC 2013036315

In this book by Ian McDonald, "the The airship Everness [enters an] . . . alternate Earth unlike any her crew has ever seen. Everett, Sen, and the crew find themselves above a plain that goes on forever in every direction without any horizon. There they find an Alderson Disc, an astronomical megastructure of incredibly strong material. Then they meet the Jiju, the dominant species on a plane where the dinosaurs didn't die out. War between their kingdoms is inevitable, total and terrible." (Publisher's note)

"The marvelous Everness series takes readers to a world with highly evolved dinosaurs in this third voyage through parallel universes...Fans might wish for more focus on the original Everett, but eventually, the three storylines weave themselves together nicely, setting up another sequel with hints of forthcoming romance. Endlessly fascinating and fun." (Kirkus)

★ **Planesrunner.** Pyr 2011 (Everness) 269p $16.95
Grades: 6 7 8 9 **Fic**

1. Science fiction
ISBN 978-1-61614-541-5; 1-61614-541-2
LC 2011032751

When fourteen-year-old Everett Singh's scientist father is kidnapped from the streets of London, he leaves a mysterious app on Everett's computer giving him access to the Infundibulum—a map of parallel earths—which is being sought by technologically advanced dark powers that Everett must somehow elude while he tries to rescue his father.

"McDonald writes with scientific and literary sophistication, as well as a wicked sense of humor. Add nonstop action, eccentric characters, and expert universe building, and this first volume of the Everness series is a winner." Publ Wkly

McDonald, Janet

Chill wind. Farrar, Straus & Giroux 2002 134p hardcover o.p. pa $6.95
Grades: 7 8 9 10 **Fic**

1. Public welfare -- Fiction 2. New York (N.Y.) -- Fiction 3. Teenage mothers -- Fiction 4. African Americans -- Fiction
ISBN 0-374-39958-1; 0-374-41183-2 pa
LC 2001-54785

Afraid that she will have nowhere to go when her welfare checks are stopped, nineteen-year-old high school dropout Aisha tries to figure out how she can support herself and her two young children in New York City

"McDonald writes with such honesty, wit, and insight that you want to quote from every page and read the story aloud to share the laughter and anguish, fury and tenderness." Booklist

Harlem Hustle. Frances Foster Books 2006 182p $16
Grades: 8 9 10 11 **Fic**

1. Rap music -- Fiction 2. African Americans -- Fiction 3. Harlem (New York, N.Y.) -- Fiction
ISBN 978-0-374-37184-5; 0-374-37184-9
LC 2005-52108

Eric "Hustle" Samson, a smart and streetwise seventeen-year-old dropout from Harlem, aspires to rap stardom, a dream he naively believes is about to come true.

"The author nails the hip-hop lingo and the street slang, and her characters strike just the right attitude. . . . Young adults will love this book." SLJ

Off-color. Farrar, Straus and Giroux 2007 163p $16
Grades: 7 8 9 10 11 12 **Fic**

1. Single parent family -- Fiction 2. Racially mixed people -- Fiction 3. Brooklyn (New York, N.Y.) -- Fiction 4. Mother-daughter relationship -- Fiction
ISBN 0-374-37196-2
LC 2006-47334

Fifteen-year-old Cameron living with her single mother in Brooklyn finds her search for identity further challenged when she discovers that she is the product of a biracial relationship.

"McDonald dramatizes the big issues from the inside, showing the hard times and the joy in fast-talking dialogue that is honest, insulting, angry, tender, and very funny." Booklist

McDonnell, Margot

Torn to pieces. Delacorte Press 2008 258p $15.99; lib bdg $18.99

Grades: 8 9 10 11 12 **Fic**

1. Friendship -- Fiction 2. Grandparents -- Fiction 3. Missing persons -- Fiction 4. Mother-daughter relationship -- Fiction

ISBN 978-0-385-73559-9; 0-385-73559-6; 978-0-385-90542-8 lib bdg; 0-385-90542-4 lib bdg

LC 2007-41536

When her mother disappears during a business trip, seventeen-year-old Anne discovers that her family harbors many dark secrets.

"This teen thriller . . . builds to a gripping conclusion with a final twist that will shock and satisfy teen readers." Booklist

McEntire, Myra

Hourglass. Egmont USA 2011 390p $17.99

Grades: 7 8 9 10 **Fic**

1. Science fiction 2. Orphans -- Fiction 3. Homicide -- Fiction 4. Siblings -- Fiction 5. Parapsychology -- Fiction 6. Space and time -- Fiction

ISBN 1-60684-144-0; 978-1-60684-144-0

LC 2010-43618

Seventeen-year-old Emerson uses her power to manipulate time to help Michael, a consultant hired by her brother, to prevent a murder that happened six months ago. "Grades seven to ten." (Bull Cent Child Books)

"Em is an entertainingly cheeky narrator and appealingly resilient heroine. . . . McEntire deftly juggles plot, characters and dialogue; her portrait of grief is particularly poignant." Kirkus

McGarry, Katie

★ **Dare** You to; by Katie McGarry. Harlequin Books 2013 480 p. (hardcover) $17.99

Grades: 9 10 11 12 **Fic**

1. Love stories 2. Dysfunctional families -- Fiction 3. Man-woman relationship -- Fiction

ISBN 0373210639; 9780373210633

This book is a "coming-of-age love story" which follows "tattooed, pierced 'skater girl' Beth and high school baseball star Ryan. . . . Raised on opposite sides of the tracks, both teens contend with selfish, manipulative parents who use their children to satisfy their own desires; both also have mentors and family members offering guidance and support. . . . Beth's compulsive efforts to rescue her drug-addicted mother . . . captures their greatest obstacle." (Publishers Weekly)

Pushing the limits. Harlequin Teen 2012 403 p.

Grades: 9 10 11 12 **Fic**

1. Love stories

ISBN 0373210493; 9780373210497

LC 2011287989

In this young adult novel by Katie McGarry "[n]o one knows what happened the night Echo Emerson went from popular girl with jock boyfriend to gossiped-about outsider with 'freaky' scars on her arms. . . . [W]hen Noah Hutchins, the smoking-hot, girl-using loner in the black leather jacket, explodes into her life with his tough attitude and surprising understanding, Echo's world shifts in ways she could never have imagined." (Author's note)

McGhee, Alison

All rivers flow to the sea. Candlewick Press 2005 168p $15.99

Grades: 8 9 10 11 12 **Fic**

1. Sisters -- Fiction 2. Bereavement -- Fiction 3. Traffic accidents -- Fiction 4. Adirondack Mountains (N.Y.) -- Fiction

ISBN 0-7636-2591-4

LC 2004-54609

After a car accident in the Adirondacks leaves her older sister Ivy brain-dead, seventeen-year-old Rose struggles with her grief and guilt as she slowly learns to let her sister go.

"This somber, philosophical look at loss and the reestablishment of identity is sensitive and perceptive, and includes passages of beautiful writing. Supporting characters are complex and lovingly rendered." Booklist

McGowan, Anthony

The **knife** that killed me. Delacorte Press 2010 216p $16.99

Grades: 10 11 12 **Fic**

1. School stories 2. Gangs -- Fiction 3. Bullies -- Fiction 4. Homicide -- Fiction 5. Friendship -- Fiction 6. Great Britain -- Fiction

ISBN 978-0-385-73822-4; 0-385-73822-6

LC 2009-11662

Paul Varderman, a secondary student in an English Catholic School, is a loner until, just as he is becoming friends with 'the freaks,' the school bully encourages Paul to join his gang and gives him a knife to carry as an incentive.

"Depicting brutality without a hint of glamour, this tale of alienation and reaction cuts deeply into school culture and the teenage mind." Kirkus

McGowan, Keith

The **witch's** guide to cooking with children; illustrated by Yoko Tanaka. Henry Holt and Co. 2009 180p il $15.99

Grades: 5 6 7 8 **Fic**

1. Witches -- Fiction 2. Siblings -- Fiction

ISBN 978-0-8050-8668-3; 0-8050-8668-4

LC 2008-50269

Eleven-year-old inventor Sol must recover his self-confidence if he and his eight-year-old sister, Connie, are to escape the clutches of Hansel and Gretel's witch, to whom they have been led by their new stepmother and the man they believe to be their father.

"McGowan's modern retelling of the Hansel and Gretel plot is nuanced, fascinating, and gratifyingly dark without being graphic or horrific. . . . Tanaka's frequent softly shaded monochromatic illustrations are atmospheric and haunting, and the human figures' oversized eyes and exaggerated noses echo the disturbing strangeness of the story. Hand this to kids who like their folktales on the scary side." Bull Cent Child Book

McGuigan, Mary Ann

Morning in a different place. Front Street 2009 195p $17.95

Grades: 7 8 9 10 **Fic**

1. Friendship -- Fiction 2. Race relations -- Fiction 3. African Americans -- Fiction 4. Bronx (New York, N.Y.) -- Fiction

ISBN 978-1-59078-551-5; 1-59078-551-7

LC 2007-17547

In 1963 in the Bronx, New York, eighth-graders Fiona and Yolanda help one another face hard decisions at home despite family and social opposition to their interracial friendship, but Fiona is on her own when popular classmates start paying attention to her and give her a glimpse of both a different way of life and a new kind of hatefulness.

This book is "never didactic. McGuigan's writing is spare and low-key, and her metaphors are acute." Booklist

McKay, Hilary

★ **Saffy's** angel. Margaret K. McElderry Bks. 2002 152p $16; pa $4.99

Grades: 5 6 7 8 **Fic**

1. Adoption -- Fiction 5. Family life -- Fiction

ISBN 0-689-84933-8; 0-689-84934-6 pa

LC 2001-44110

First published 2001 in the United Kingdom

After learning that she was adopted, thirteen-year-old Saffron's relationship with her eccentric, artistic family changes, until they help her go back to Italy where she was born to find a special momento of her past

"Like the Casson household itself, the plot is a chaotic whirl that careens off in several directions simultaneously. But McKay always skillfully draws each clearly defined character back into the story with witty, well-edited details; rapid dialogue; and fine pacing." Booklist

Other titles in this series are:
Indigo's star (2004)
Permanent Rose (2005)
Caddy ever after (2006)
Forever Rose (2008)

McKay, Sharon E.

Enemy territory; Sharon McKay. Annick Press 2012 184 p. $21.95

Grades: 6 7 8 9 10 11 12 **Fic**

1. Toleration -- Fiction 2. Friendship 3. Israel-Arab conflicts -- Fiction

ISBN 1554514312; 9781554514311

In author Sharon E. McKay's book, "Sam, an Israeli teen whose leg may have to be amputated, and Yusuf, a Palestinian teen who has lost his left eye, find themselves uneasy roommates in a Jerusalem hospital. One night, the boys decide to slip away while the nurses aren't looking and go on an adventure to the Old City. . . . They band together to find their way home and to defend themselves against unfriendly locals, arrest by the military police, and an encounter with a deadly desert snake." (Publisher's note)

Thunder over Kandahar; photographs by Rafal Gerszak. Annick Press 2010 260p il $21.95; pa $12.95

Grades: 7 8 9 10 11 12 **Fic**

1. Afghanistan -- Fiction 2. Afghan War, 2001- -- Fiction

ISBN 978-1-55451-267-6; 1-55451-267-0; 978-1-55451-266-9 pa; 1-55451-266-2 pa

"When her British and American-educated parents' return to Afghanistan is cut short by a terrible attack, 14-year-old Yasmine is sent to Kandahar for safety. Instead, the driver abandons her and her friend Tamanna along the way, and they must travel on their own through Taliban-controlled mountains. . . . In spite of unrelenting violence, along with grinding poverty, restrictive customs, and the horrors of war, what shines through this sad narrative is the love Afghans have for their country. . . . [The author] traveled to Afghanistan and provides numerous credits for this gripping tale." SLJ

McKenzie, Nancy

Grail prince; {by} Nancy Affleck McKenzie. Del Rey 2003 510p pa $14.95

Grades: 9 10 11 12 **Fic**

1. Great Britain -- History -- 0-1066 -- Fiction

ISBN 0-345-45648-3

LC 2002-94133

In this sequel to Queen of Camelot, "the story focuses on Sir Galahad, son of Lancelot and Guinevere's cousin, Elaine. Legend says that when the Holy Grail and the spear of King Macsen, along with the sword Excalibur, are in the hands of the king, Britain will be forever invincible. Galahad's quest to find these relics, undertaken at Arthur's command, is for him a journey into manhood as well as one of expiation." Libr J

"Brimming with romance, myth, and magic, this intriguing retelling of an ever-appealing fable will appease fans eager for new twists and turns in the lives and times of King Arthur and the knights of the Round Table." Booklist

Guinevere's gamble. Alfred A. Knopf 2009 361p (The Chrysalis Queen quartet) $16.99; lib bdg $19.99

Grades: 7 8 9 10 **Fic**

1. Kings 2. Merlin (Legendary character) -- Fiction 3. Guinevere (Legendary character) -- Fiction 4. Great Britain -- History -- 0-1066 -- Fiction 5. Morgan le Fay (Legendary character) -- Fiction

ISBN 978-0-375-84346-4; 0-375-84346-9; 978-0-375-94346-1 lib bdg; 0-375-94346-3 lib bdg

LC 2008-50617

Sequel to: Guinevere's gift (2008)

Thirteen-year-old Guinevere learns more about her destiny when she accompanies her aunt and uncle to an important council of Welsh kings and finds that she has a powerful enemy in the High King's sister Morgan.

"Readers who are familiar with Arthurian legends as well as those who are not will find this continuing story enjoyable." SLJ

Guinevere's gift. Alfred A. Knopf 2008 327p (The Chrysalis Queen quartet) $15.99; lib bdg $18.99

Grades: 7 8 9 10 **Fic**

1. Cousins -- Fiction 2. Guinevere (Legendary character) -- Fiction 3. Great Britain -- History -- 0-1066 -- Fiction

ISBN 978-0-375-84345-7; 0-375-84345-0; 978-0-375-94345-4 lib bdg; 0-375-94345-5 lib bdg

LC 2007-28782

When the orphaned Guinevere is twelve years old, living with Queen Alyse and King Pellinore of Gwynedd, she fearlessly helps rescue her cousin from kidnappers who are plotting to seize the palace and overthrow the king, even as the queen despairs of Guinevere's rebellious nature.

"Adventure seekers can be content with this tale of a heroine and her castle while dedicated legend fans will appreciate where it fits in the overall tapestry." Bull Cent Child Books

Another title in this series is:
Guinevere's gamble (2009)

McKernan, Victoria

Shackleton's stowaway. Knopf 2005 336p $15.95; lib bdg $17.99

Grades: 7 8 9 10 **Fic**

1. Explorers 2. Adventure fiction 3. Survival after airplane accidents, shipwrecks, etc. -- Fiction

ISBN 0-375-82691-2; 0-375-92691-7 lib bdg

LC 2004-10313

A fictionalized account of the adventures of eighteen-year-old Perce Blackborow, who stowed away for the 1914 Shackleton Antarctic expedition and, after their ship Endurance was crushed by ice, endured many hardships, including the loss of the toes of his left foot to frostbite, during the nearly two-year return journey across sea and ice

"This book provides historical information for history and geography classes who are interested in exploration, the Antarctic, and early history of great sea voyages." Libr Media Connect

The **devil's** paintbox. Alfred A. Knopf 2009 359p $16.99; lib bdg $19.99

Grades: 6 7 8 9 10 **Fic**

1. Orphans -- Fiction 2. Siblings -- Fiction 3. Frontier and pioneer life -- Fiction 4. Overland journeys to the Pacific -- Fiction

ISBN 978-0-375-83750-0; 0-375-83750-7; 978-0-375-93750-7 lib bdg; 0-375-93750-1 lib bdg

LC 2008-4749

In 1866, fifteen-year-old Aidan and his thirteen-year-old sister Maddy, penniless orphans, leave drought-stricken Kansas on a wagon train hoping for a better life in Seattle, but find there are still many hardships to be faced.

This is a "gripping novel. . . . Attention to detail and steady pacing keep readers fully engaged." Publ Wkly

McKinley, Robin

★ **Beauty**; a retelling of the story of Beauty & the beast. Harper & Row 1978 247p $15.99; pa $5.99

Grades: 7 8 9 10 **Fic**

1. Fairy tales

ISBN 0-06-024149-7; 0-06-440477-3 pa

LC 77-25636

"McKinley's version of this folktale is embellished with rich descriptions and settings and detailed characterizations. The author has not modernized the story but varied the traditional version to attract modern readers. The values of love, honor, and beauty are placed in a magical setting that will please the reader of fantasy." Shapiro. Fic for Youth. 3d edition

The **blue** sword. Greenwillow Bks. 1982 272p $17.99; pa $6.99

Grades: 7 8 9 10 **Fic**

1. Fantasy fiction

ISBN 0-688-00938-7; 0-441-06880-4 pa

LC 82-2895

A Newbery Medal honor book, 1983

Harry, bored with her sheltered life in the remote orange-growing colony of Daria, discovers magic in herself when she is kidnapped by a native king with mysterious powers.

"This is a zesty, romantic, heroic fantasy with an appealing stalwart heroine, a finely realixed mythical kingdom, and a grounding in reality." Booklist

The **hero** and the crown. Greenwillow Bks. 1985 246p lib bdg $16.99

Grades: 6 7 8 9 **Fic**

1. Fantasy fiction

ISBN 0-688-02593-5

LC 84-4074

Awarded the Newbery Medal, 1985

"A prequel rather than sequel to 'The Blue Sword' [1982], McKinley's second novel set in the . . . mythical kingdom of Damar centers on Aerin, daughter of a Damarian king and his second wife, a witchwoman from the feared, demon-ridden North. The narrative follows Aerin as she seeks her birthright, becoming first a dragon killer and eventually the savior of the kingdom." Booklist

The author "has in this suspenseful prequel . . . created an utterly engrossing fantasy, replete with a fairly mature romantic subplot as well as adventure." N Y Times Book Rev

Chalice. G.P. Putnam's Sons 2008 263p $18.99

Grades: 7 8 9 10 11 12 **Fic**

1. Fantasy fiction 2. Bees -- Fiction

ISBN 978-0-399-24676-0; 0-399-24676-2

LC 2008-704

A beekeeper by trade, Mirasol's life changes completely when she is named the new Chalice, the most important advisor to the new Master, a former priest of fire.

"The fantasy realm is evoked in thorough and telling detail. . . . A lavish and lasting treat." Publ Wkly

Dragonhaven. G.P. Putnam's Sons 2007 342p $17.99

Grades: 7 8 9 10 11 12 **Fic**

1. Fantasy fiction 2. Dragons -- Fiction
ISBN 978-0-399-24675-3; 0-399-24675-4
LC 2007-8197

When Jake Mendoza, who lives in the Smokehill National Park where his father runs the Makepeace Institute of Integrated Dragon Studies, goes on his first solo overnight in the park, he finds an infant dragon whose mother has been killed by a poacher.

Readers "will be engaged by McKinley's well-drawn characters and want to root for the Smokehill community's fight to save the ultimate endangered species." SLJ

Pegasus. G.P. Putnam's Sons 2010 404p $18.99
Grades: 8 9 10 11 12 **Fic**

1. Fantasy fiction 2. Magic -- Fiction 3. Princesses -- Fiction 4. Pegasus (Greek mythology) -- Fiction
ISBN 0-399-24677-0; 978-0-399-24677-7
LC 2010-2279

Because of a thousand-year-old alliance between humans and pegasi, Princess Sylvi is ceremonially bound to Ebon, her own pegasus, on her twelfth birthday, but the closeness of their bond becomes a threat to the status quo and possibly to the safety of their two nations.

"McKinley's storytelling is to be savored. She lavishes page after page upon rituals and ceremonies, basks in the awe of her intricately constructed world, and displays a masterful sense of pegasi physicality and mannerisms." Booklist

McKinney-Whitaker, Courtney

The **last** sister: a novel; Courtney McKinney-Whitaker. University of South Carolina Press. 2014 232p (Young Palmetto books) $39.95
Grades: 7 8 9 10 **Fic**

1. Cherokee Indians--Fiction 2. Frontier and pioneer life--South Carolina--Fiction 3. South Carolina--History--1775-1865--Fiction 4. Native Americans--Wars--Fiction 5. Historical fiction
ISBN: 1611174295; 9781611174298; 9781611174304
LC 2014011484

This historical novel is "set during the Anglo-Cherokee War (1758-61), . . . traces a young woman's journey through grief, vengeance, guilt, and love in the unpredictable world of the early American frontier. After a band of fellow settlers fakes a Cherokee raid to conceal their murder of her family, seventeen-year-old Catriona 'Catie' Blair embarks on a quest to report the crime and bring the murderers to justice." (Publisher's note)

"This historical novel is set in the Carolinas during the Cherokee Wars, concurrent with Thomas Jefferson and John Adams writing the Declaration of Independence and George Washington navigating the Delaware River. Seventeen-year-old Catie Blair is forced to conjure up maturity and responsibility when tragedy strikes her family...A unique historical fiction title with a compelling plot and unique backdrop, taking place during a little-known skirmish in a pivotal time of American history." SLJ

McKissack, Fredrick, 1939-2013

Shooting star. Atheneum Books for Young Readers 2009 273p $16.99
Grades: 8 9 10 11 12 **Fic**

1. School stories 2. Football -- Fiction 3. Steroids -- Fiction 4. African Americans -- Fiction
ISBN 978-1-4169-4745-5; 1-4169-4745-0
LC 2008-55525

Jomo Rogers, a naturally talented athlete, starts taking performance enhancing drugs in order to be an even better high school football player, but finds his life spinning out of control as his game improves.

"Profane and scatological language abounds, but it is not outside the realm of what one could hear any day in a school locker room. Top-notch sports fiction." SLJ

McLaren, Clemence

Inside the walls of Troy; a novel of the women who lived the Trojan War. Atheneum Bks. for Young Readers 1996 199p hardcover o.p. pa $5.99
Grades: 7 8 9 10 **Fic**

1. Helen of Troy (Legendary character) -- Fiction
ISBN 0-689-31820-0; 0-689-87397-2 pa
LC 93-8127

The events surrounding the famous battle between the Greeks and the Trojans are told from the points of view of two women, the beautiful Helen and the prophetic Cassandra

"These ancient stories are made as fresh and vivid as any modern tale by the electrifying characters and sensual details." Booklist

McLaughlin, Lauren

Scored. Random House 2011 226p $17.99; lib bdg $20.99
Grades: 6 7 8 9 10 **Fic**

1. Science fiction
ISBN 978-0-375-86820-7; 978-0-375-96820-4 lib bdg
LC 2010028113

In the not-so-distant future, teenaged Imani must struggle within a world where a monolithic corporation assigns young people a score that will determine the rest of their lives.

"The bold, aggressive narrative condemns both No Child Left Behind–style testing and current financial policies, cautioning about what could happen to social mobility in the face of stark inequity." Kirkus

McLoughlin, Jane

At Yellow Lake. Frances Lincoln Children's Books 2012 358 p. (paperback) $8.99
Grades: 7 8 9 10 **Fic**

1. Mystery fiction 2. Teenagers -- Fiction 3. Native Americans -- Fiction
ISBN 1847802877; 9781847802873

In this book by Jane McLoughlin, "Etta, Peter and Jonah all find themselves at a cabin by the shore of Yellow Lake. . . . Jonah has come to Yellow Lake to try to get in touch with his Ojibwe roots. Peter is there to bury a lock of his mother's hair -- her final request. Etta is on the run from her mother's creepy boyfriend. . . . But as the three take shelter in the cabin . . . they soon realise that they have inadvertently stumbled onto the scene of a horrifying crime." (Publisher's note)

McMann, Lisa

Wake. Simon Pulse 2008 210p $15.99; pa $8.99

Grades: 7 8 9 10 **Fic**

1. School stories 2. Dreams -- Fiction

ISBN 978-1-4169-5357-9; 1-4169-5357-4; 978-1-4169-7447-5 pa; 1-4169-7447-4 pa

LC 2007036267

Ever since she was eight years old, high school student Janie Hannagan has been uncontrollably drawn into other people's dreams, but it is not until she befriends an elderly nursing home patient and becomes involved with an enigmatic fellow-student that she discovers her true power.

"A fast pace, a great mix of teen angst and supernatural experiences, and an eerie, attention-grabbing cover will make this a hit." Booklist

Other titles in this series are:
Fade (2009)
Gone (2010)

McMullan, Margaret

Cashay. Houghton Mifflin Harcourt 2009 166p $15

Grades: 7 8 9 10 **Fic**

1. Anger -- Fiction 2. Mentoring -- Fiction 3. Bereavement -- Fiction 4. Racially mixed people -- Fiction

ISBN 978-0-547-07656-0; 0-547-07656-8

LC 2008-36111

When her world is turned upside down by her sister's death, a mentor is assigned to fourteen-year-old Cashay to help her through her anger and grief.

"Cashay's spirited voice and non-frothy prose will draw both confirmed and newer fans of inner-city drama." Kirkus

★ **Sources** of light. Houghton Mifflin 2010 233p $15

Grades: 6 7 8 9 **Fic**

1. Photography -- Fiction 2. Race relations -- Fiction 3. African Americans -- Civil rights -- Fiction

ISBN 978-0-547-07659-1; 0-547-07659-2

LC 2009-49708

"When 14-year-old Samantha Thomas moves to Jackson, Miss., in 1962, following her father's death in Vietnam, she learns about love and hate all in the same year. Her mother meets Perry Walker, a photographer who teaches Sam about taking photographs and seeing the world in new ways, but what she begins seeing and pondering is the racial situation in Jackson—lunch-counter sit-ins, voter-registration protests and the violent reprisals of many in the white community, including the father of the boy she begins to like. . . . This offers a superb portrait of a place and time and a memorable character trying to make sense of a world both ugly and beautiful." Kirkus

McNab, Andy

Traitor; [by] Andy McNab and Robert Rigby. G.P. Putnam's Sons 2005 265p $15.99

Grades: 7 8 9 10 **Fic**

1. Spies -- Fiction 2. Orphans -- Fiction 3. Grandfathers -- Fiction

ISBN 0-399-24464-6

LC 2005-6701

"Orphaned Londoner Danny Watts wants nothing to do with his estranged grandfather, a traitor who went MIA years ago, until the British military offers Danny a proposition: find his grandfather and he'll receive a scholarship. . . . With help from his best friend, Elena, he sets off to find his relative and the truth. . . . The well-crafted language includes a few coarse phrases. . . . With its brisk plot and unpredictable characters, this story of intrigue rises above many standard adventure stories." Booklist

Other titles in this series are:
Payback (2006)
Avenger (2007)
Meltdown (2008)

McNamee, Eoin

The **Navigator**. Wendy Lamb Books 2007 342p il (Navigator trilogy) $15.99; pa $6.99

Grades: 6 7 8 9 **Fic**

1. Fantasy fiction 2. Time -- Fiction

ISBN 978-0-375-83910-8; 0-375-83910-0; 978-0-385-73554-4 pa; 0-385-73554-5 pa

LC 2006-26691

Owen has always been different, and not only because his father committed suicide, but he is not prepared for the knowledge that he has a mission to help the Wakeful—the custodians of time—to stop the Harsh from reversing the flow of time.

McNamee "shows a deft hand in writing for children. Excellent world-building, a thrilling and propulsive plot, internal consistency and a multitude of child heroes guarantee a following for this exciting fantasy." Kirkus

Other titles in this series are:
City of Time (2008)
The Frost Child (2009)

McNamee, Graham

★ **Acceleration**. Wendy Lamb Bks. 2003 210p hardcover o.p. pa $6.99

Grades: 8 9 10 11 12 **Fic**

1. Mystery fiction 2. Canada -- Fiction 3. Homicide -- Fiction

ISBN 0-385-73119-1; 0-440-23836-6 pa

LC 2003-3708

Stuck working in the Lost and Found of the Toronto Transit Authority for the summer, seventeen-year-old Duncan finds the diary of a serial killer and sets out to stop him

"Never overexploits the sensational potential of the subject and builds suspense layer upon layer, while injecting some surprising comedy relief." Booklist

Beyond; a ghost story. by Graham McNamee. Wendy Lamb Books 2012 226 p. (trade) $15.99

Grades: 9 10 11 12 **Fic**

1. Supernatural -- Fiction 2. Shades and shadows -- Fiction 3. Near-death experiences -- Fiction 4. Ghosts -- Fiction

ISBN 0385737750; 9780375851650; 9780375897597; 9780385737753; 9780385906876

LC 2011043610

This book by Graham McNamee follows "Jane, [who is] no stranger to near-death experiences. Her shadow has forced her to drink drain cleaner and held her down on a train track as a speeding train approached. After a recent nail-gun 'accident' to the skull causes her to flat-line, Jane returns to the living with her shadow even more determined to kill her." (Kirkus Reviews)

McNaughton, Janet

An **earthly** knight. HarperCollins Publishers 2004 261p $15.99; lib bdg $16.89

Grades: 7 8 9 10 **Fic**

1. Fantasy fiction

ISBN 0-06-008992-X; 0-06-008993-8 lib bdg

LC 2003-9561

First published 2003 in Canada

In 1162 in Scotland, sixteen-year-old Jenny Avenel falls in love with the mysterious Tam Lin while being courted by the king's brother and must navigate the tides of tradition and the power of ancient magic to define her own destiny.

"The author does an excellent job of interweaving legend and history to create an exciting and engaging tale." SLJ

McNeal, Laura

Dark water. Alfred A. Knopf 2010 287p $16.99; lib bdg $19.99

Grades: 7 8 9 10 **Fic**

1. Fires -- Fiction 2. Divorce -- Fiction 3. California -- Fiction 4. Family life -- Fiction 5. Illegal aliens -- Fiction 6. Homeless persons -- Fiction

ISBN 978-0-375-84973-2; 0-375-84973-4; 978-0-375-94973-9 lib bdg; 0-375-94973-9 lib bdg

LC 2009-43249

Living in a cottage on her uncle's southern California avocado ranch since her parent's messy divorce, fifteen-year-old Pearl Dewitt meets and falls in love with an illegal migrant worker, and is trapped with him when wildfires approach his makeshift forest home.

"Notable for well-drawn characters, an engaging plot and, especially, hauntingly beautiful language, this is an outstanding book." Kirkus

The **decoding** of Lana Morris; [by] Laura & Tom McNeal. Alfred A. Knopf 2007 289p $15.99

Grades: 7 8 9 10 11 12 **Fic**

1. Drawing -- Fiction 2. Nebraska -- Fiction 3. People with disabilities -- Fiction 4. Supernatural -- Fiction 5. Foster home care -- Fiction

ISBN 0-375-83106-1; 978-0-375-83106-5

LC 2006-23950

For sixteen-year-old Lana life is often difficult, with a flirtatious foster father, an ice queen foster mother, a houseful of special needs children to care for, and bullies harrassing her, until the day she ventures into an antique shop and buys a drawing set that may change her life.

This is "a colorful character drama with genuine spice and impact." Bull Cent Child Books

★ **Zipped**; [by] Laura and Tom McNeal. Knopf 2003 283p hardcover o.p. pa $7.99

Grades: 9 10 11 12 **Fic**

1. Stepfamilies -- Fiction

ISBN 0-375-81491-4; 0-375-83098-7 pa

LC 2002-2781

At the end of their sophomore year in high school, the lives of four teenagers are woven together as they start a tough new job, face family problems, deal with changing friendships, and find love

"There's a realism here that takes the narrative beyond the problem novel and into one of relationships, their difficult demands in the face of human complexity and frailty, and their nonetheless often satisfying rewards. The book never loses sight of the kids at the heart of this, however, which keeps this accessible to the teens it's about." Bull Cent Child Books

McNeal, Tom

★ **Far** far away; by Tom McNeal. 1st ed. Alfred A. Knopf Books for Young Readers 2013 371 p. (hardcover) $17.99; (ebook) $53.97; (library) $20.99

Grades: 7 8 9 10 **Fic**

1. Occult fiction 2. Fantasy fiction 3. Ghosts -- Fiction 4. Friendship -- Fiction 5. Supernatural -- Fiction 6. Missing persons -- Fiction

ISBN 0375849726; 9780375849725; 9780375896989; 9780375949722

LC 2012020603

Parents' Choice: Gold Medal Fiction (2013)

This book "is narrated by the ghost of Jacob Grimm . . . , unhappily caught in the Zwischenraum (a plane of existence between life and death). For now, he is the nearly constant companion of Jeremy Johnson," who hears voices. This ability "has made him an object of derision for many in his little town, though—thrillingly—not to the electrifyingly vibrant Ginger Boultinghouse, who is more than happy to lure Jeremy into more trouble than he's ever encountered." (School Library Journal)

McNicoll, Sylvia

Last chance for Paris. Fitzhenry & Whiteside 2008 204p pa $11.95

Grades: 6 7 8 9 **Fic**

1. Twins -- Fiction 2. Wolves -- Fiction 3. Siblings -- Fiction

ISBN 978-1-5545-5061-6 pa; 1-5545-5061-0 pa

Fourteen-year-old Zanna goes to the Alberta ice fields with her father and twin brother, Martin, where they find a wolf pup which they name Paris. When Martin is lost, Paris helps find him.

"Written with elements of wry humor and romance, this Canadian novel features a narrator whose disarmingly candid opinions make her an appealing guide for readers who usually veer away from backwoods or survival stories." Booklist

McNish, Cliff

Angel. Carolrhoda Books 2008 312p $16.95

Grades: 7 8 9 10 **Fic**

1. School stories 2. Angels -- Fiction 3. Bullies -- Fiction 4. Popularity -- Fiction 5. Mental illness --

Fiction
ISBN 978-0-8225-8900-6; 0-8225-8900-1
LC 2007-9664

An unlikely friendship develops between fourteen-year-olds Stephanie, an angel-obsessed social outcast, and Freya, a popular student whose visions of angels sent her to a mental institution and who is now seeing a dark angel at every turn.

"The author beautifuly melds a tale of the fantastic and the mundane." Voice Youth Advocates

McPhee, Peter

New blood. James Lorimer 2008 167p pa $8.95
Grades: 6 7 8 9 10 **Fic**

1. School stories 2. Canada -- Fiction 3. Bullies -- Fiction
ISBN 978-1-55028-996-1; 1-55028-996-9

When his family moves from the tough streets of Glasgow to Winnipeg, Canada, Callum finds that his high school days of dealing with bullies are far from over.

"The Scottish culture, which becomes a colorful character, adds to the fullness of the story. The writing, rich in dialogue, does not waste words and keeps the reader involved and cheering for this gutsy hero who fights his fear to stand against abuse aimed at himself and others." Voice Youth Advocates

McQuein, Josin L.

Arclight; Josin L. McQuein. 1st ed. Greenwillow Books, an imprint of HarperCollins Publishers 2013 416 p. (hardcover) $17.99
Grades: 8 9 10 11 12 **Fic**

1. Orphans 2. Fantasy fiction 3. Science fiction 4. Amnesia -- Fiction 5. Identity -- Fiction
ISBN 0062130145; 9780062130143
LC 2013002929

In this book, "Marina was pulled from the Dark at the cost of nine lives, and she is paying the price. Ostracized and abused by those whose parents died for her sake, Marina is all but alone in the Arclight, a safe zone where it is never dark. The Fade live in the Dark—chameleons, they steal humans from the light to an unknown fate. Marina dreams of their voices and frets that she has no memory of her life before her rescue." She seeks answers about her past. (Publishers Weekly)

McQuerry, Maureen Doyle

The **Peculiars**; a novel. Maureen Doyle McQuerry. Amulet Books 2012 359 p. (hardback) $16.95
Grades: 7 8 9 10 11 12 **Fic**

1. Fantasy fiction 2. Voyages and travels -- Fiction 3. Father-daughter relationship -- Fiction 4. Goblins -- Fiction 5. Identity -- Fiction 6. Abnormalities, Human -- Fiction 7. Adventure and adventurers -- Fiction
ISBN 1419701789; 9781419701788
LC 2012000844

This is the story of Lena Mattacascar, who at age 18 "travel[s] to Scree, an uncharted wilderness of 'indigenous folks' and deported convicts," sitting on the train with young librarian "Jimson Quiggley," with "marshal Thomas Saltre" watching them. "Lena cannot stop thinking about her mysterious father" or the possibility that she's part Peculiar (goblin). "Scree is the place where Lena's questions might be answered, but arriving there just multiplies them." (Publishers Weekly)

McVoy, Terra Elan

After the kiss. Simon Pulse 2010 382p $16.99
Grades: 9 10 11 12 **Fic**

1. School stories 2. Novels in verse 3. Moving -- Fiction 4. Atlanta (Ga.) -- Fiction
ISBN 978-1-4424-0211-9
LC 2009-44220

In alternating chapters, two high school senior girls in Atlanta reveal their thoughts and frustrations as they go through their final semester of high school.

This is "a poignant tale of two girls on the brink of adulthood faced with real decisions about their future, who they want to be, and what role boys will play in their decisions." SLJ

Pure. Simon Pulse 2009 330p $16.99
Grades: 8 9 10 11 12 **Fic**

1. Friendship -- Fiction 2. Christian life -- Fiction 3. Dating (Social customs) -- Fiction
ISBN 978-1-4169-7872-5; 1-4169-7872-0
LC 2008-33404

Fifteen-year-old Tabitha and her four best friends all wear purity rings to symbolize their pledge to remain virgins until they marry, but when one admits that she has broken the pledge each girl must reexamine her faith, friendships, and what it means to be pure.

"Tabitha's blooming romance with Jake and her positive relationship with her supportive, if somewhat quirky, parents add pleasant undercurrents to a book that girls of a spiritual bent will enjoy." SLJ

McWilliams, Kelly

Doormat; a novel. Delacorte Press 2004 131p $15.95; lib bdg $17.99
Grades: 6 7 8 9 **Fic**

1. Theater -- Fiction 2. Pregnancy -- Fiction 3. Friendship -- Fiction
ISBN 0-385-73168-X; 0-385-90204-2 lib bdg
LC 2003-19675

Fourteen-year-old Jaime has always been a doormat, but her diary reveals how getting the lead in a school play, finding her first boyfriend, discovering her dream, and helping her best friend cope with being pregnant transform her life.

"McWilliams' first-person, present-tense vignettes are taut, funny, and touching, the dialogue is authentic, and both the teen and adult characters ring true." Booklist

Mead, Alice

Dawn and dusk. Farrar, Straus and Giroux 2007 151p $16
Grades: 6 7 8 9 **Fic**

1. Refugees -- Fiction 2. Iran-Iraq War, 1980-1988 -- Fiction
ISBN 0-374-31708-9; 978-0-374-31708-9
LC 2006-40850

As thirteen-year-old Azad tries desperately to cling to the life he has known, the political situation in Iran during the war with Iraq finally forces his family to flee their home and seek safety elsewhere.

"Azad is an appealing protagonist, and it is his simple and direct story that will draw readers through the complexities of a multinational ethnic longing for self-determination that remains at the heart of an international tinderbox." SLJ

★ **Swimming** to America; Alice Mead. 1st ed; Farrar, Straus and Giroux 2005 153p $16

Grades: 6 7 8 9 **Fic**

1. Immigrants -- Fiction

ISBN 0-374-38047-3

LC 2004-53249

Eighth grader Linda Berati struggles to understand who she is within the context of her mother's secrecy about the family background, her discomfort with her old girlfriends, her involvement with the family problems of her Cuban-American friend Ramon, and an opportunity to attend a school for "free spirits" like herself.

Written with "sensitivity and optimism. . . . [This is] an informative, empathetic, contemporary portrait of the immigrant experience." SLJ

Mebus, Scott

Gods of Manhattan. Dutton Children's Books 2008 372p (Gods of Manhattan) $17.99

Grades: 6 7 8 9 **Fic**

1. Fantasy fiction 2. Adventure fiction 3. Space and time -- Fiction 4. Gods and goddesses -- Fiction

ISBN 978-0-525-47955-0; 0-525-47955-4

LC 2007-18113

"Rory, 13, and his sister Bridget, 9, live in present-day New York City unaware of the spirits from Manhattan's or 'Mannahatta's' past that coexist alongside them. Rory has a gift for seeing this other world but has repressed this ability until the day he notices a cockroach riding a rat, an ancient Indian warrior, a papier-mâché boy, and other oddities. . . . The use of real historical figures and events lends authenticity to this compulsively readable and fast-paced fantasy." SLJ

Other titles in this series are:

Spirits in the park (2009)

The sorcerer's secret (2010)

Mecum, Ryan

Zombie haiku; Ryan Mecum. HOW Books 2008 139 p. ill. (some col.) (pbk.) $9.99

Grades: 9 10 11 12 **Fic**

1. Haiku 2. Zombies -- Fiction 3. Poetry -- Collections 4. Humorous poetry -- Collections 5. Haiku -- Humor 6. Zombies -- Humor 7. Zombies -- Poetry

ISBN 1600610706; 9781600610707

LC 2008008678

This book is a collection of haikus written from the perspective of an author who "managed to chronicle his change from artist to [zombie] . . . after being attacked by an undead mob." (booklistforworms.blogspot.com) In this book, "you'll find . . . three-line poems (all in the classic 5-7-5 syllable structure), and follow the undead poet on a journey through deserted streets and barricaded doors. Experience every . . . moment of the eventual downfall of the human race from the point of view of a zombie, and gain insight to help you survive." (firestormcafe.com)

Medina, Meg

★ **Milagros**; girl from Away. Henry Holt and Co. 2008 279p $17.89

Grades: 6 7 8 9 **Fic**

1. Magic -- Fiction 2. Islands -- Fiction 3. Rays (Fishes) -- Fiction 4. Mother-daughter relationship -- Fiction

ISBN 978-0-8050-8230-2; 0-8050-8230-1

LC 2007-46939

Twelve-year-old Milagros barely survives an invasion of her tiny, Caribbean island home, escapes with the help of mysterious sea creatures, reunites briefly with her pirate-father, and learns about a mother's love when cast ashore on another island.

"Medina's use of magical realism keeps readers tantalizingly off-balance as she navigates among settings. . . . [This] haunting tale . . . will remain with readers." Horn Book

★ **Yaqui** Delgado wants to kick your ass; Meg Medina. Candlewick Press 2013 272 p. (reinforced) $16.99

Grades: 9 10 11 12 **Fic**

1. School stories 2. Bullies -- Fiction

ISBN 0763658596; 9780763658595

LC 2012943645

Pura Belpre Author Award (2014)

In this novel, by Meg Medina, "a Latina teen is targeted by a bully at her new school--and must discover resources she never knew she had. One morning before school, some girl tells Piddy Sanchez that Yaqui Delgado hates her and wants to . . . [beat her up.] . . . As the harassment escalates, avoiding Yaqui and her gang starts to take over Piddy's life. Is there any way for Piddy to survive without closing herself off or running away?" (Publisher's note)

Meehan, Kierin

★ **Hannah's** winter. Kane/Miller Book Publishers 2009 212p $15.95

Grades: 5 6 7 8 **Fic**

1. Adventure fiction

ISBN 978-1-933605-98-2; 1-933605-98-7

First published 2001 in Australia

Hannah would much rather be back in Australia, starting high school with her friends. But Japan turns out to be nothing like she'd imagined. When Hannah and her new friend Miki find an ancient message in the stationery shop, they are drawn into involving a mysterious riddle.

"Meehan utilizes beautifully crafted similes and metaphors as she creates a loving and detailed portrayal of Japan and its people. . . . The tale remains so grounded in reality that it never defies belief. A fine fantasy." Kirkus

Meehl, Brian

Suck it up. Delacorte Press 2008 323p $15.99; pa $8.99

Grades: 8 9 10 11 **Fic**

1. Vampires -- Fiction

ISBN 978-0-385-73300-7; 0-385-73300-3; 978-0-440-42091-0 pa; 0-440-42091-1 pa

LC 2007-27995

After graduating from the International Vampire League, a scrawny, teenaged vampire named Morning is given the chance to fulfill his childhood dream of becoming a superhero when he embarks on a League mission to become the first vampire to reveal his identity to humans and to demonstrate how peacefully-evolved, blood-substitute-drinking vampires can use their powers to help humanity.

This "an original and light variation on the current trend in brooding teen vampire protagonists. . . . Puns abound in this lengthy, complicated romp. . . . Teens will find it delightful." Booklist

You don't know about me. Delacorte Press 2011 406p $17.99; ebook $10.99; lib bdg $20.99
Grades: 9 10 11 12 **Fic**

1. Homosexuality -- Fiction 2. Christian life -- Fiction 3. Automobile travel -- Fiction 4. Father-son relationship -- Fiction 5. Mother-son relationship -- Fiction
ISBN 978-0-385-73909-2; 978-0-375-89715-3 ebook; 978-0-385-90771-2 lib bdg
LC 2010-17101

Billy has spent his almost-sixteen years with four cardinal points—Mother, Christ, Bible, and Home-school—but when he sets off on a wild road trip to find the father he thought was dead, he learns much about himself and life.

"The humor, action, and edgy social commentary make this a book a mature reader, with knowledge and interest of the works of Mark Twain, might enjoy." Voice Youth Advocates

Meldrum, Christina

★ **Madapple.** Alfred A. Knopf 2008 410p il $16.99; lib bdg $19.99
Grades: 9 10 11 12 **Fic**

1. Trials -- Fiction 2. Miracles -- Fiction 3. Mother-daughter relationship -- Fiction
ISBN 978-0-375-85176-6; 978-0-375-95176-3 lib bdg
LC 2007-49653

ALA YALSA Morris Award finalist, 2009

A girl who has been brought up in near isolation is thrown into a twisted web of family secrets and religious fundamentalism when her mother dies and she goes to live with relatives she never knew she had.

"A markedly intelligent offering mixing lush descriptions of plants, history, science and religion, this should surely spark interest among a wide array of readers." Kirkus

Include bibliographical references

Melling, O. R.

The **book** of dreams. Amulet Books 2009 698p map (Chronicles of Faerie) $19.95
Grades: 7 8 9 10 **Fic**

1. Magic -- Fiction 2. Canada -- Fiction 3. Fairies -- Fiction 4. Native Americans -- Fiction 5. Voyages and travels -- Fiction
ISBN 978-0-8109-8346-5; 0-8109-8346-X
LC 2008-24689

Sequel to The Light-Bearer's daughter (2007)

Now thirteen and depressed, Dana has been living with her father and his new wife in Canada for two years, and when she finds that her gateway to the land of Faerie has been mysteriously shattered, she must travel the length and breadth of Canada to find the secret that will re-open the Faerie world.

"The author's exploration of folk traditions across cultures makes the book unique." Voice Youth Advocates

The **Hunter's** Moon. Amulet Books 2005 284p (Chronicles of Faerie) $16.95; pa $7.95
Grades: 7 8 9 10 **Fic**

1. Magic -- Fiction 2. Ireland -- Fiction
ISBN 0-8109-5857-0; 0-8109-9214-0 pa
LC 2004-22216

First published 1992 in Ireland

Two teenage cousins, one Irish, the other from the United States, set out to find a magic doorway to the Faraway Country, where humans must bow to the little people.

"This novel is a compelling blend of Irish mythology and geography. Characters that breathe and connect with readers, and a picturesque landscape that shifts between the present and the past, bring readers into the experience." SLJ

Other available titles in this series are:
The book of dreams (2009)
The Light-Bearer's daughter (2007)
The Summer King (2006)

The **Light-**Bearer's daughter. Amulet Books 2007 348p map (Chronicles of Faerie) hardcover o.p. pa $7.95
Grades: 7 8 9 10 11 **Fic**

1. Magic -- Fiction 2. Ireland -- Fiction
ISBN 978-0-8109-0781-2; 0-8109-0781-X; 978-0-8109-7123-3 pa; 0-8109-7123-2 pa
LC 2006-33517

Sequel to The Summer King (2006)

In exchange for the granting of her heart's desire, twelve-year-old Dana agrees to make an arduous journey to Lugnaquillia through the land of Faerie in order to warn King Lugh, second in command to the High King, that an evil destroyer has entered the Mountain Kingdom.

"The richly integrated, vivid fantasy scenes balance the strident calls for environmental protection and world peace, and the characters' private passages through 'layers of storied memory' will bring the issues home for readers." Booklist

Followed by The book of dreams (2009)

The **Summer** King. Amulet Books 2006 359p map (Chronicles of Faerie) $16.95
Grades: 7 8 9 10 **Fic**

1. Magic -- Fiction 2. Ireland -- Fiction
ISBN 0-8109-5969-0
LC 2005-15083

Seventeen-year-old Laurel returns to her grandparents' home in Ireland, where she encounters the roly-poly man, a cluricaun who sets Laurel on a quest to free her twin sister, thought to be dead, to live with her lover in the legendary world of Faerie.

"Fans of Melling's first title in the Chronicles of Faerie, The Hunter's Moon (2005), will recognize similarly thrilling action, fascinating Irish mythology, and magnificently detailed magic." Booklist

Meloy, Maile

★ The **apothecary**. G. P. Putnam's Sons 2011 353p $16.99

Grades: 6 7 8 9 **Fic**

1. Adventure fiction 2. Alchemy -- Fiction 3. Cold war -- Fiction

ISBN 978-0-399-25627-1; 0-399-25627-X

LC 2010045003

This novel follows a fourteen-year-old American girl whose life unexpectedly changes when she moves to London in 1952 and gets swept up in a race to save the world from nuclear war

"With evocative, confident prose and equally atmospheric spot art from Schoenherr, adult author Meloy's first book for young readers is an auspicious one." Publ Wkly

The **apprentices**; by Maile Meloy; illustrated by Ian Schoenherr. G.P. Putnam's Sons, an imprint of Penguin Group (USA) Inc. 2013 432 p. (hardcover) $16.99

Grades: 6 7 8 9 **Fic**

1. Magic -- Fiction 2. Alchemy -- Fiction 3. Voyages and travels -- Fiction 4. Adventure and adventurers -- Fiction 5. Southeast Asia -- History -- 1945- -- Fiction

ISBN 9780399162459

LC 2012048715

In this book by Maile Meloy is the sequel to "The Apothecary". "Janie, now 16, is alone at an elite American boarding school, unaware of the whereabouts of her first boyfriend, Benjamin, and his apothecary father. After she is wrongly expelled, she realizes she is the victim of a nefarious scheme, which again poses a threat to world peace. The . . . plot spans the globe as the heroes find their way back to each other." (Publishers Weekly)

Meminger, Neesha

Shine, coconut moon. Margaret K. McElderry Books 2009 256p $16.99; pa $8.99

Grades: 7 8 9 10 **Fic**

1. School stories 2. Prejudices -- Fiction 3. East Indian Americans -- Fiction 4. September 11 terrorist attacks, 2001 -- Fiction

ISBN 978-1-4169-5495-8; 1-4169-5495-3; 978-1-4424-0305-5 pa; 1-4424-0305-5 pa

LC 2008-9836

In the days and weeks following the terrorist attacks on September 11, 2001, Samar, who is of Punjabi heritage but has been raised with no knowledge of her past by her single mother, wants to learn about her family's history and to get in touch with the grandparents her mother shuns.

"Meminger's debut book is a beautiful and sensitive portrait of a young woman's journey from self-absorbed navet to selfless, unified awareness." SLJ

Mesrobian, Carrie

Sex and violence; by Carrie Mesrobian. Carolrhoda Lab 2013 304 p. (reinforced) $17.95

Grades: 10 11 12 **Fic**

1. School stories 2. Violence -- Fiction 3. Sex -- Fiction 4. Psychotherapy -- Fiction 5. Emotional problems -- Fiction 6. Interpersonal relations -- Fiction

ISBN 1467705977; 9781467705974

LC 2012047181

William C. Morris Honor Book (2014)

In this book, a teen boy "is brutally beaten in a communal shower by two classmates after he hooks up with one of their former girlfriends, setting the stage for a difficult recovery. After the assault that leaves Evan in the hospital, his father whisks him off to his own boyhood home in Minnesota, where he's uneasily sucked into a tightknit group spending their last summer at home getting high and hanging out before going off to college." (Kirkus Reviews)

"The absence of sentimentality and melodrama in favor of frank dialogue and bruising honesty is a gasp of fresh air." Booklist

Metzger, Lois

A **trick** of the light; by Lois Metzger. 1st ed. Balzer + Bray 2013 208 p. (hardcover) $17.99

Grades: 9 10 11 12 **Fic**

1. Family life -- Fiction 2. Anorexia nervosa -- Fiction 3. Schools -- Fiction 4. High schools -- Fiction 5. Family problems -- Fiction 6. Eating disorders -- Fiction

ISBN 006213308X; 9780062133083

LC 2012019039

In this book by Lois Metzger, "[t]he story of 15-year-old Mike Welles's descent into anorexia is narrated by the disease itself, the insidious voice inside his head preying on his every vulnerability. The voice waits patiently for an opening, which comes in the form of Mike's parents' marital crisis and his insecurity around a new crush, pushing Mike to exercise, coaching him to subsist on next to nothing, and encouraging a friendship with Amber, who is also anorexic." (Publishers Weekly)

"This is a somewhat familiar story told in a new way. . . . A chilling, straightforward novel written with depth and understanding." SLJ

Meyer, Carolyn

Beware, Princess Elizabeth. Harcourt 2001 214p (Young royals) hardcover o.p. pa $5.95

Grades: 7 8 9 10 **Fic**

1. Queens 2. Sisters 3. Princesses

ISBN 0-15-202659-2; 0-15-204556-2 pa

LC 00-11700

After the death of her father, King Henry VIII, in 1547, thirteen-year-old Elizabeth must endure the political intrigues and dangers of the reigns of her half-brother Edward and her half-sister Mary before finally becoming Queen of England eleven years later

"The story moves along swiftly with hints of romance, life-and-death plots, and snippets of everyday life." Book Rep

Cleopatra confesses. Simon & Schuster Books for Young Readers 2011 289p $16.99

Grades: 6 7 8 9 **Fic**

1. Queens -- Fiction 2. Princesses -- Fiction

ISBN 978-1-4169-8727-7; 1-4169-8727-4

LC 2010025989

Princess Cleopatra, the third (and favorite) daughter of King Ptolemy XII, comes of age in ancient Egypt, accumulating power and discovering love.

Meyer's "lush, detail-rich prose ably evokes Cleopatra's life as a young princess, beginning at age 10 and continuing on until she turns 22. . . . Narrating with the poise and confidence of a born leader, this Cleopatra should win readers over." Publ Wkly

Includes bibliographical references

Duchessina; a novel of Catherine de' Medici. Harcourt 2007 261p (Young royals) $17

Grades: 7 8 9 10 **Fic**

1. Queens 2. Regents 3. Italy -- Fiction 4. Queens -- Fiction 5. Orphans -- Fiction

ISBN 978-0-15-205588-2; 0-15-205588-6

LC 2006028876

While her tyrannical family is out of favor in Italy, young Catherine de Medici is raised in convents, then in 1533, when she is fourteen, her uncle, Pope Clement VII, arranges for her marriage to prince Henri of France, who is destined to become king.

"With meticulous historical detail, sensitive characterizations, and Catherine's strong narration, Meyer's memorable story of a fascinating young woman who relies on her intelligence, rather than her beauty, will hit home with many teens." Booklist

The **true** adventures of Charley Darwin. Harcourt 2009 321p il $17

Grades: 7 8 9 10 **Fic**

1. Natural history -- Fiction 2. Voyages around the world -- Fiction 3. Beagle Expedition (1831-1836) -- Fiction

ISBN 978-0-15-206194-4; 0-15-206194-0

LC 2008-17451

In nineteenth-century England, young Charles Darwin rejects the more traditional careers of physician and clergyman, choosing instead to embark on a dangerous five-year journey by ship to explore the natural world.

"Meyer's writing has a light touch that capitalizes on the humorous, romantic, and exciting events in the man's life while introducing his scientific pursuits and the beliefs of his time. . . . This novel paints a readable and detailed portrait of the young Charles Darwin." SLJ

Includes bibliographical references

Meyer, L. A.

Bloody Jack; being an account of the curious adventures of Mary Jacky Faber, ship's boy. Harcourt 2002 278p hardcover o.p. pa $6.95

Grades: 7 8 9 10 **Fic**

1. Adventure fiction 2. Orphans -- Fiction 3. Pirates -- Fiction 4. Sex role -- Fiction 5. Seafaring life -- Fiction

ISBN 0-15-216731-5; 0-15-205085-X pa

LC 2002-759

Reduced to begging and thievery in the streets of 18th-century London, a thirteen-year-old orphan disguises herself as a boy and connives her way onto a British warship set for high sea adventure in search of pirates

"From shooting a pirate in battle to foiling a shipmate's sexual attack to surviving when stranded alone on a Caribbean island, the action in Jacky's tale will entertain readers with a taste for adventure." Booklist

Other titles in this series are:

Curse of the blue tattoo (2004)

In the belly of The Bloodhound (2006)

The mark of the golden dragon (2011)

Mississippi Jack (2007)

My bonny light horseman (2008)

Rapture of the deep (2009)

Under the Jolly Roger (2005)

The wake of the Lorelei Lee (2010)

Viva Jacquelina! being an account of the further adventures of Jacky Faber, over the hills and far away. written by L.A. Meyer. Harcourt 2012 p. cm. $16.99

Grades: 7 8 9 10 **Fic**

1. Spies 2. Spain -- History -- Fiction 3. Adventure fiction 4. Historical fiction 5. Spies -- Fiction 6. Sex role -- Fiction 7. Seafaring life -- Fiction 8 Europe -- History -- 1789-1815 -- Fiction 9. Great Britain -- History -- George III, 1760-1820 -- Fiction

ISBN 9780547763507

LC 2011041931

This young adult adventure novel, by L. A. Meyer, continues the "Bloody Jack Adventures" series. "Once again under the thumb of British Intelligence, Jacky is sent to Spain to spy for the Crown during the early days of the nineteenth-century Peninsular War. She finds herself in the company of guerilla freedom fighters, poses for the famous artist Goya, runs with the bulls, is kidnapped by the Spanish Inquisition, and travels with a caravan of gypsies." (Publisher's note)

Meyer, Marissa, 1984-

★ **Cinder**; Marissa Meyer. Feiwel & Friends 2012 320 p. $17.99

Grades: 7 8 9 10 11 12 **Fic**

1. Fairy tales 2. Science fiction 3. Robots -- Fiction

ISBN 9780312641894

LC 2011036123

In this book, "as plague ravages the overcrowded Earth, observed by a ruthless lunar people, Cinder, a gifted mechanic and cyborg, becomes involved with handsome Prince Kai and must uncover secrets about her past in order to protect the world in this futuristic take on the Cinderella story." (Publisher's note)

Followed by: Scarlet (2013)

★ **Cress**; Marissa Meyer. Feiwel & Friends 2014 560 p. $18.99

Grades: 7 8 9 10 11 12 **Fic**

1. Fugitives from justice -- Fiction 2. Human-alien encounters -- Fiction

ISBN 0312642970; 9780312642976

In this book by Marissa Meyer, third in her Lunar Chronicles series, "Cinder and Captain Thorne are fugitives on the run, now with Scarlet and Wolf in tow. Together, they're plotting to overthrow Queen Levana and prevent her army from invading Earth. Their best hope lies with Cress, a girl trapped on a satellite since childhood. When a daring rescue of Cress goes awry, the group is splintered. Meanwhile, Queen Levana will let nothing prevent her marriage to Emperor Kai." (Publisher's note)

"Cress fills in more historical details about Earth and Luna's relationship—most of which will be of no surprise to the reader—and Cinder's rebirth as a cyborg. Fans of Scarlet and Wolf may be disappointed that their relationship takes a backseat to the newly introduced pairing. As always, Meyer excels at interweaving new characters that extend beyond the archetypes of their fairy tale into the main story. Readers will eagerly await the final installment of this highly appealing and well-constructed series." (School Library Journal)

★ **Scarlet**; Marissa Meyer. Feiwel and Friends 2013 464 p. $17.99
Grades: 7 8 9 10 11 12 **Fic**
1. Science fiction 2. Fractured fairy tales 3. Cyborgs -- Fiction 4. Missing persons -- Fiction 5. Extraterrestrial beings -- Fiction
ISBN 0312642962; 9780312642969
LC 2012034060

This novel, by Marissa Meyer, is the second book of the "Lunar Chronicles" series. "Cinder, the cyborg mechanic, . . . [is] trying to break out of prison. . . . [Meanwhile,] Scarlet Benoit's grandmother is missing. . . . When Scarlet encounters Wolf, a street fighter who may have information . . . , she is loath to trust this stranger. . . . As Scarlet and Wolf unravel one mystery, they encounter another when they meet Cinder." (Publisher's note)

Meyer, Stephenie
★ **Twilight**. Little, Brown and Co. 2005 498p $17.99; pa $8.99
Grades: 8 9 10 11 12 **Fic**
1. School stories 2. Vampires -- Fiction 3. Washington (State) -- Fiction
ISBN 0-316-16017-2; 0-316-01584-9 pa
LC 2004-24730

When seventeen-year-old Bella leaves Phoenix to live with her father in Forks, Washington, she meets an exquisitely handsome boy at school for whom she feels an overwhelming attraction and who she comes to realize is not wholly human.

"Realistic, subtle, succinct, and easy to follow, . . . [this book] will have readers dying to sink their teeth into it." SLJ

Other titles in this series are:
Breaking dawn (2008)
Eclipse (2007)
New moon (2006)

Meyer, Susan
Black radishes; [by] Susan Lynn Meyer. Delacorte Press 2010 228p map $16.99; lib bdg $19.99
Grades: 5 6 7 8 **Fic**
1. Jews -- France -- Fiction 2. Holocaust, 1933-1945 -- Fiction
ISBN 978-0-385-73881-1; 0-385-73881-1; 978-0-385-90748-4 lib bdg; 0-385-90748-6 lib bdg
LC 2009-47613

"Set in France during World War II, this historical novel follows eleven-year-old Gustave as his family escapes Paris for safer quarters in the small, provincial town of Saint-Georges. . . . Not long after Gustave's family arrives in Saint-Georges, the Nazis invade and occupy Paris and establish a demarcation line between occupied northern France and unoccupied Vichy France in the south. . . . The episodic narrative offers abundant detail, and the wartime dangers, especially Gustave's father's illicit travel between occupied and unoccupied zones, adds considerable suspense. Gustave's growth over the course of the novel is both realistic and relatable, making this an appealing topical entry for the upper elementary/middle school set." Bull Cent Child Books

Meyerhoff, Jenny
Queen of secrets. Farrar, Straus and Giroux 2010 230p $16.99
Grades: 8 9 10 11 12 **Fic**
1. School stories 2. Cousins -- Fiction 3. Orphans -- Fiction 4. Grandparents -- Fiction 5. Jews -- United States -- Fiction
ISBN 978-0-374-32628-9; 0-374-32628-2
LC 2008-55561

Fifteen-year-old Essie Green, an orphan who has been raised by her secular Jewish grandparents in Michigan, experiences conflicting loyalties and confusing emotions when her aunt, uncle, and cousin move back from New York, and her very religious cousin tries to fit in with the other football players at Essie's high school, one of whom is Essie's popular new boyfriend.

"Compelling characters, dramatic tension, and thoughtful exploration of how teenagers create their own identity amid familial and cultural influences should give this story wide appeal." Publ Wkly

Michael, Jan
★ **City** boy. Clarion Books 2009 186p $16
Grades: 5 6 7 8 **Fic**
1. Orphans -- Fiction 2. Country life -- Fiction
ISBN 978-0-547-22310-0; 0-547-22310-2
LC 2008-37418

First published in the United Kingdom with title: Leaving home

In the southern African country of Malawi, after the AIDS-related deaths of both of his parents, a boy leaves his affluent life in the city to live in a rural village, sharing a one-roomed hut with his aunt, his cousins, and other orphans.

"This is a powerful portrait of poverty and hardship, evenly balanced with shades of hope. Michael's simple prose subtly layers detail, building full-bodied descriptions of landscapes and characters, leaving no room for shortcuts. . . . A stoic tale of surviving life's uncertainties." Kirkus

Michaelis, Antonia
The **dragons** of darkness; translated from the German by Anthea Bell. Amulet Books 2010 548p il $18.95
Grades: 8 9 10 11 12 **Fic**
1. Fantasy fiction 2. Magic -- Fiction 3. Nepal -- Fiction 4. Dragons -- Fiction
ISBN 978-0-8109-4074-1; 0-8109-4074-4
LC 2009-3051

Two boys from very different backgrounds are thrown together by magic, mayhem, and a common foe as they battle deadly dragons in the wilderness of Nepal.

"Ably translated from German, crammed with magic realism, colors, fairytales, dreams, and contemporary conflicts, this novel is not the average dragons-in-an-alien-world fantasy. Here people make love, are kind to strangers, struggle to survive, and sometimes are casually murdered. . . . Serious fantasy fans will be fascinated by this original and well-told tale." Voice Youth Advocates

Tiger moon; translated from the German by Anthea Bell. Amulet Books 2008 453p pa $9.95; $19.95

Grades: 8 9 10 11 12 **Fic**

1. India -- Fiction 2. Tigers -- Fiction 3. Thieves -- Fiction 4. Princesses -- Fiction 5. Storytelling -- Fiction

ISBN 0-8109-4499-5 pa; 0-8109-9481-X; 978-0-8109-4499-2 pa; 978-0-8109-9481-2

LC 2007-22823

Sold to be the eighth wife of a rich and cruel merchant, Safia, also called Raka, tries to escape her fate by telling stories of Farhad the thief, his companion Nitish the white tiger, and their travels across India to retrieve a famous jewel that will save a kidnapped princess from becoming the bride of a demon king. "Grades eight to ten." (Bull Cent Child Books)

"The plot is fast paced and exciting, and the story gives an excellent overview of the conflicts of India at the time of British occupation, and of Hindu religious beliefs." SLJ

Michaels, Rune

★ **Genesis** Alpha; [by] Rune Michaels. 1st ed.; Atheneum Books for Young Readers 2007 193p $15.99

Grades: 7 8 9 10 **Fic**

1. Brothers -- Fiction 2. Homicide -- Fiction 3. Video games -- Fiction 4. Genetic engineering -- Fiction

ISBN 978-1-4169-1886-8; 1-4169-1886-8

LC 2007001446

When thirteen-year-old Josh's beloved older brother, Max, is arrested for murder, the victim's sister leads Josh to evidence of Max's guilt—and her own—hidden in their favorite online role-playing game. Josh, who was conceived to save Max's life years earlier, must consider whether he shares that guilt.

"Skillfully interweaving science fiction and cyberspace into a murder mystery, Michaels gives readers a story that is not only difficult to put down but also poses questions that will linger long after the last page is turned." Voice Youth Advocates

Nobel genes. Simon & Schuster 2010 181p $16.99

Grades: 6 7 8 9 10 **Fic**

1. Mentally ill -- Fiction 2. Mother-son relationship -- Fiction 3. Manic-depressive illness -- Fiction

ISBN 978-1-4169-1259-0; 1-4169-1259-2

LC 2009-36665

A boy whose manic-depressive mother has always told him that his father won a Nobel Prize, spends his time taking care of her and searching for clues to the identity of the Nobel Prizewinning sperm donor, eventually finding a truth he must learn to accept.

This is a "skillful, deeply disconcerting tale. . . . Michaels . . . makes effective use of first-person narration to give readers a highly believable protagonist and a riveting, from-the-trenches look at what it is like to live with a parent who suffers from a serious mental illness." Publ Wkly

The **reminder**. Atheneum Books for Young Readers 2008 182p $16.99; pa $8.99

Grades: 6 7 8 9 10 **Fic**

1. Robots -- Fiction 2. Mothers -- Fiction 3. Bereavement -- Fiction

ISBN 978-1-4169-4131-6; 1-4169-4131-2; 978-1-4424-0253-9 pa; 1-4424-0253-9 pa

LC 2008-15391

A teenaged girl who hears her dead mother's voice makes a startling discovery after breaking into her father's industrial robotics lab and finding his latest secret project: a lifelike replica of her mother's head that looks, talks, moves, and even smiles just like her mother.

"An intriguing story about loss and survival, with elements of science fiction." Booklist

Mieville, China

★ **Railsea**; China Mieville. Del Rey/Ballantine Books 2012 424 p. ill. (hbk. : alk. paper) $18.00

Grades: 7 8 9 10 **Fic**

1. Adventure fiction 2. Steampunk fiction 3. Railroads -- Fiction 4. Imaginary places -- Fiction

ISBN 0345524527; 9780345524522; 9780345524546

LC 2012009516

This book presents "a steampunk spin on 'Moby-Dick' . . . . Instead of chasing whales on the sea, the crew of the diesel train Medes hunt moldywarpes—enormous, man-eating, molelike creatures who are only one of the countless menacing species who burrow in the perilous earth beneath a tangled ocean of train tracks. And it is one moldywarpe in particular, the great Mocker-Jack, that Captain Naphi is after—it's trendy for any captain worth her iron to have such a defining obsession, and she is fully aware that they hunt metaphor in beast form. Aboard for the grand adventure is your hero, young Sham (don't call him Ishmael)." (Booklist)

★ **Un** Lun Dun. Ballantine Books 2007 432p il hardcover o.p. pa $9

Grades: 5 6 7 8 9 **Fic**

1. Fantasy fiction 2. Young adult literature -- Works

ISBN 978-0-345-49516-7; 0-345-49516-0; 978-0-345-45844-5 pa; 0-345-45844-3 pa

LC 2007-296921

When 12-year-old Zanna and her friend Deeba find a secret entrance leading out of London and into the strange city of Un Lun Dun, it appears that an ancient prophesy is coming true at last

"Miéville's fantastical city is vivid and splendidly crafted. . . . The story is exceptional and the action moves along at a quick pace." SLJ

Mikaelsen, Ben

Ghost of Spirit Bear; [by] Ben Mikaelsen. 1st ed.; HarperCollins Publishers 2008 154p $16.99; lib bdg $17.89

Grades: 6 7 8 9 **Fic**

1. School stories 2. Bullies -- Fiction

ISBN 978-0-06-009007-4; 0-06-009007-3; 978-0-06-009008-1 lib bdg; 0-06-009008-1 lib bdg

LC 2007036732

After a year in exile on an Alaskan island as punishment for severely beating a fellow student, Cole Matthews returns to school in Minneapolis having made peace with himself and his victim--but he finds that surviving the violence and hatred of high school is even harder than surviving in the wilderness.

This is "gripping and fast moving. . . [this novel] will appeal to boys especially and to reluctant readers." KLIATT

Touching Spirit Bear. HarperCollins Pubs. 2001 241p $15.99; lib bdg $16.89; pa $5.99

Grades: 6 7 8 9 **Fic**

1. Bears -- Fiction 2. Wilderness survival -- Fiction 3. Indians of North America -- Alaska 4. Juvenile delinquents -- Rehabilitation

ISBN 0-380-97744-3; 0-06-029149-4 lib bdg; 0-380-80560-X pa

LC 00-40702

After his anger erupts into violence, Cole, in order to avoid going to prison, agrees to participate in a sentencing alternative based on the native American Circle Justice, and he is sent to a remote Alaskan Island where an encounter with a huge Spirit Bear changes his life

"Mikaelsen's portrayal of this angry, manipulative, damaged teen is dead on. . . . Gross details about Cole eating raw worms, a mouse, and worse will appeal to fans of the outdoor adventure/survival genre." SLJ

Miklowitz, Gloria D.

The **enemy** has a face. Eerdmans Bks. for Young Readers 2003 139p $16; pa $8

Grades: 7 8 9 10 **Fic**

1. Missing persons 2. Palestinian Arabs 3. Arab-Israeli conflict 4. Jews -- United States 5. Missing persons -- Fiction

ISBN 0-8028-5243-2; 0-8028-5261-0 pa

LC 2002-9233

Netta and her family have relocated temporarily from Israel to Los Angeles, and when her seventeen-year-old brother mysteriously disappears, she becomes convinced that he has been abducted by Palestinian terrorists

"Almost unbearably suspenseful, the plot will keep readers turning pages as fast as they can. Nicely interspersed with the events is a thoughtful examination of some of the reasons behind the age-old strife between Palestinians and Israelis. Readers come away with a greater understanding of the conflict, and Netta is given the opportunity to modify her attitude about her former enemies." SLJ

Milford, Kate

The **Boneshaker**; [illustrations by Andrea Offermann] Clarion Books 2010 372p il $17

Grades: 5 6 7 8 9 **Fic**

1. Bicycles -- Fiction 2. Missouri -- Fiction 3. Demonology -- Fiction 4. Supernatural -- Fiction

ISBN 978-0-547-24187-6; 0-547-24187-9

LC 2009-45350

When Jake Limberleg brings his traveling medicine show to a small Missouri town in 1913, thirteen-year-old Natalie senses that something is wrong and, after investigating, learns that her love of automata and other machines make her the only one who can set things right.

"Natalie is a well-drawn protagonist with sturdy supporting characters around her. The tension built into the solidly constructed plot is complemented by themes that explore the literal and metaphorical role of crossroads and that thin line between good and evil." Kirkus

The **Broken** Lands; by Kate Milford; with illustrations by Andrea Offermann. Clarion Books 2012 455 p. ill. (hardback) $16.99

Grades: 5 6 7 8 9 10 **Fic**

1. Bridges -- Fiction 2. Supernatural -- Fiction 3. New York (N.Y.) -- Fiction 4. New York (N.Y.) -- History -- 1865-1898 -- Fiction 5. Coney Island (New York, N.Y.) -- History -- 19th century -- Fiction

ISBN 0547739664; 9780547739663

LC 2011049466

This book, a prequel to "Kate Milford's 'The Boneshaker,' [is] set in . . . nineteenth-century Coney Island and New York City. Few crossroads compare to the one being formed by the Brooklyn Bridge and the East River, and as the bridge's construction progresses, forces of unimaginable evil seek to bend that power to their advantage. . . . Can the teenagers Sam, a card sharp, and Jin, a fireworks expert, stop them before it's too late?" (Publisher's note)

Miller, Ashley Edward

Colin Fischer; Ashley Edward Miller & Zack Stentz. Razorbill 2012 228 p. (hardcover) $17.99

Grades: 9 10 11 **Fic**

1. Mystery fiction 2. Bullies -- Fiction 3. Schools -- Fiction 4. High schools -- Fiction 5. Mystery and detective stories 6. Asperger's syndrome -- Fiction

ISBN 1595145788; 9781595145789

LC 2012014274

This book focuses on Colin Fischer, "whose Asperger's means he has difficulty reading social cues despite his high intelligence. When a melee breaks out in the [school] cafeteria one day, culminating in a gun's going off, Colin is convinced that as the nearest person to the gun he's likely to be suspected of being the shooter. He therefore decides to bring his inquisitive nature and love of logic to the problem and solve the mystery himself." (Bulletin of the Center for Children's Books)

Miller, Kirsten

All you desire; can you trust your heart? Razorbill 2011 423p $17.99

Grades: 6 7 8 9 10 **Fic**

1. Love stories 2. Reincarnation -- Fiction 3. Fate and fatalism -- Fiction

ISBN 978-1-59514-323-5; 1-59514-323-8

Haven Moore and Iain Morrow have been living a blissful life in Rome, an ocean way from the Ouroboros Society and its diabolical leader. But paradise is not to last. The mysterious disappearance of Haven's best friend, Beau, sends the pair running back to New York, where they encounter the Horae, an underground group of women who have spent centuries scheming to destroy Adam Rosier.

"A multi-layered mystery with (mostly) rounded characters." Kirkus

The **eternal** ones. Razorbill 2010 411p $17.99
Grades: 6 7 8 9 10 **Fic**

1. Love stories 2. Faith -- Fiction 3. Tennessee -- Fiction 4. Reincarnation -- Fiction 5. New York (N.Y.) -- Fiction 6. Fate and fatalism -- Fiction

ISBN 978-1-59514-308-2; 1-59514-308-4

LC 2010-22775

Seventeen-year-old Haven Moore leaves East Tennessee to attend the Fashion Institute of Technology in New York City, where she meets playboy Iain Morrow, whose fate may be tied to hers through a series of past lives.

"Miller's writing elevates the supernatural romance well beyond typical fare, and Haven's mix of naïveté and determination makes her a solid, credible heroine." Publ Wkly

Followed by: All you desire (2011)

How to lead a life of crime; Kirsten Miller. Razorbill 2013 358 p. (hardcover) $18.99
Grades: 9 10 11 12 **Fic**

1. School stories 2. Criminals -- Fiction 3. Ghosts -- Fiction 4. Schools -- Fiction 5. Survival -- Fiction

ISBN 1595145184; 9781595145185

LC 2012031576

In this young adult novel, by Kirsten Miller, "the Mandel Academy . . . has been training young criminals for over a century. Only the most ruthless . . . graduate. The rest disappear. Flick . . . has risen to the top of his class. But then Mandel recruits a fierce new competitor who also happens to be Flick's old flame. They've been told only one of them will make it out of the Mandel Academy. Will they find a way to save each other--or will the school destroy them both?" (Publisher's note)

Miller, Sarah

The **lost** crown. Atheneum Books for Young Readers 2011 412p $17.99
Grades: 8 9 10 11 12 **Fic**

1. Emperors 2. Sisters -- Fiction 3. Kings and rulers -- Fiction 4. World War, 1914-1918 -- Fiction 5. Russia -- History -- 1905, Revolution -- Fiction

ISBN 978-1-4169-8340-8; 1-4169-8340-6

LC 2010037001

In alternating chapters, Grand Duchesses Olga, Tatiana, Maria, and Anastasia tell how their privileged lives as the daughters of the tsar in early twentieth-century Russia are transformed by world war and revolution.

"Each Grand Duchess comes across as a unique personality. . . . Like the best historical novels, this allows modern-day teens to see themselves in very different people." Booklist

Miss Spitfire; reaching Helen Keller. Atheneum Books for Young Readers 2007 208p $16.99
Grades: 7 8 9 10 11 **Fic**

1. Deaf 2. Authors 3. Memoirists 4. Humanitarians 5. Deaf -- Fiction 6. Blind -- Fiction 7. Teachers -- Fiction 8. Teachers of the deaf 9. Inspirational writers 10. Teachers of the blind 11. Social welfare leaders

ISBN 978-1-4169-2542-2; 1-4169-2542-2

LC 2006014738

At age twenty-one, partially-blind, lonely but spirited Annie Sullivan travels from Massachusetts to Alabama to try and teach six-year-old Helen Keller, deaf and blind since age two, self-discipline and communication skills. Includes historical notes and timeline.

"This excellent novel is compelling reading even for those familiar with the Keller/Sullivan experience." SLJ

Includes bibliographical references

Miller, Walter M.

★ A **canticle** for Leibowitz; a novel. by Walter M. Miller, Jr. Lippincott 1960 320p hardcover o.p. pa $13.95
Grades: 9 10 11 12 Adult **Fic**

1. Science fiction

ISBN 0-06-089299-4

"Here is science fiction of the highest literary excellence and thematic intelligence. A monastery founded by the scientist Leibowitz is discovered decades after an atomic war. In the first part of the book a young novice in the monastery is the protagonist; in the second part we see scholars in a new period of enlightenment; and in the final section we observe man's proclivity for repeating mistakes and the apparent inevitability of history's repeating itself." Shapiro. Fic for Youth. 3d edition

Miller-Lachmann, Lyn

Gringolandia; a novel. Curbstone Press 2009 279p $16.95
Grades: 9 10 11 12 **Fic**

1. Chile -- Fiction 2. Wisconsin -- Fiction 3. Political activists -- Fiction 4. Father-son relationship -- Fiction 5. Post-traumatic stress disorder -- Fiction

ISBN 978-1-931896-49-8; 1-931896-49-6

LC 2008-36990

In 1986, when seventeen-year-old Daniel's father arrives in Madison, Wisconsin, after five years of torture as a political prisoner in Chile, Daniel and his eighteen-year-old "gringa" girlfriend, Courtney, use different methods to help this bitter, self-destructive stranger who yearns to return home and continue his work.

"This poignant, often surprising and essential novel illuminates too-often ignored political aspects of many South Americans' migration to the United States." Kirkus

Mills, Sam

The **viper** within; [by] Sam Mills. 1st American ed.; Alfred A. Knopf 2008 296p $16.99; lib bdg $19.99
Grades: 7 8 9 10 **Fic**

1. Cults -- Fiction 2. Divorce -- Fiction 3. Religion -- Fiction 4. Kidnapping -- Fiction

ISBN 978-0-375-84465-2; 0-375-84465-1; 978-0-375-94465-9 lib bdg; 0-375-94465-6 lib bdg

LC 2007031952

Bitter and angry after his parents' divorce, Jon joins a cult, The Religion of Hebetheus, at his high school and soon becomes embroiled in a plot to kidnap a fellow student and suspected terrorist, but their plans go terribly wrong.

"Thought provoking, tension packed, and suspenseful, Mill's novel forces readers to grapple with multiple perspectives on terrorism, cults, religion, victimization, fidelity, embedded misogyny and conscience." Voice Youth Advocates

Mills, Tricia

Heartbreak river. Razorbill 2009 248p pa $8.99

Grades: 7 8 9 10 **Fic**

1. Death -- Fiction 2. Guilt -- Fiction 3. Rivers -- Fiction 4. Colorado -- Fiction 5. Rafting (Sports) -- Fiction

ISBN 978-1-59514-256-6

LC 2008-21062

When her father dies while whitewater rafting, sixteen-year-old Alex feels responsible, but when tragedy strikes again she must face her deepest fears in order to reclaim her love of the Colorado river where she grew up—and of the boy she grew up with.

"Mills builds suspense in both the romance and the moving drama of family secrets and loss. The fast talk and Alex's first-person narrative are right on, especially in the quarrels. Best of all is the setting, which is powerfully described in scenes of Alex struggling to overcome her phobia and return to the wild rushing river she loves." Booklist

Min, Katherine

Secondhand world; a novel. Knopf 2006 269p hardcover o.p. pa $13.95

Grades: 11 12 Adult **Fic**

1. Family life -- Fiction 2. Korean Americans -- Fiction 3. Parent-child relationship -- Fiction

ISBN 978-0-307-26344-5; 978-0-307-27499-1 pa

LC 2006-41038

The book "opens by introducing readers to 18-year-old Isadora Myung Hee Sohn, known as Isa to her mother and friends and Myung Hee to her father. Isa tells the absorbing story of a young woman's struggle to overcome the obstacles of growing up Korean American in Albany, NY, during the 1970s. True to that stereotypically liberated period, Isa gets involved with sex, drugs, and rock'n'roll. . . . Touching and bittersweet, this novel is filled with universal themes presented through Isa's eyes and should resonate with teen readers of both today and yesterday." Libr J

Minato, Kanae

Confessions: a novel. Kanae Minato; translated by Stephen Snyder. Mulholland Books/Little, Brown & Co. 2014 234p $15.00

Grades: 11 12 Adult **Fic**

1. Accidents -- Fiction 2. Revenge -- Fiction 3. Teacher-student relationship -- Fiction 4. Schools -- Fiction 5. Mystery fiction 6. Teachers -- Fiction

ISBN: 0316200921; 9780316200929

LC 2014937563

Alex Award (2015)

"Yuko Moriguchi leads a relatively simple life, teaching middle school and raising her four-year-old daughter, Manami, on her own. But when Manami is murdered in a sick act of hatred, Yuko decides the legal system is unreliable and plans her own revenge...This award-winning debut novel is a creepy and mesmerizing psychological thriller that challenges the conventions of right vs. wrong, good vs. evil, and law vs. justice. There are no happy endings here, but Minato has pieced together an intriguing puzzle that will keep readers glued to their seats." LJ

Minchin, Adele

★ The **beat** goes on. Simon & Schuster Books for Young Readers 2004 212p hardcover o.p. pa $11.95

Grades: 9 10 11 12 **Fic**

1. Cousins -- Fiction 2. Great Britain -- Fiction 3. AIDS (Disease) -- Fiction

ISBN 0-689-86611-9; 1-4169-6755-9 pa

First published 2001 in the United Kingdom

"Fifteen-year-old Leyla must keep her cousin's secret: Emma is HIV positive, and only her mother and Leyla know. The secret becomes a burden, especially when Leyla must lie to her parents in order to work with Emma's support group on their special project—to teach other HIV-positive teens how to play the drums. In spite of its heavy Briticisms and a didactic tone, this is one of the better YA books about HIV. The facts of transmission and symptoms are clearly presented, as are Emma's struggles to lead a normal, healthy life. . . . Minchin educates young readers while telling a gripping story that will keep personal tragedy aficionados turning the pages to the hopeful yet realistic conclusion." Booklist

Miranda, Megan

Hysteria; by Megan Miranda. Walker 2013 336 p. (hardback) $17.99

Grades: 9 10 11 12 **Fic**

1. School stories 2. Memory -- Fiction 3. Homicide -- Fiction 4. Boarding schools -- Fiction

ISBN 0802723101; 9780802723109

LC 2012015780

In this novel, by Megan Miranda, "Mallory killed her boyfriend, Brian. She can't remember the details . . . but everyone knows it was self-defense, so she isn't charged. . . . In desperate need of a fresh start, Mallory is sent to . . . a fancy prep school where no one knows her. . . . Then, one of her new classmates turns up dead. As suspicion falls on Mallory, she must find a way to remember the details of both deadly nights so she can prove her innocence." (Publisher's note)

Mitchard, Jacquelyn

★ **All** we know of heaven; a novel. HarperTeen 2008 312p $16.99; lib bdg $17.89

Grades: 7 8 9 10 11 12 **Fic**

1. Death -- Fiction 2. Bereavement -- Fiction 3. Traffic accidents -- Fiction

ISBN 978-0-06-134578-4; 0-06-134578-4; 978-0-06-134579-1 lib bdg; 0-06-134579-2 lib bdg

When Maureen and Bridget, two sixteen-year-old best friends who look like sisters, are in a terrible car accident and one of them dies, they are at first incorrectly identified at the hospital, and then, as Maureen achieves a remarkable recovery, she must deal with the repercussions of the accident, the mixup, and some choices she made while she was getting better.

"Riveting, compassionate and psychologically nuanced. . . . Utterly gripping." Publ Wkly

The **midnight** twins. Razorbill 2008 235p $16.99; pa $8.99
Grades: 6 7 8 9 **Fic**
1. Twins -- Fiction 2. Telepathy -- Fiction 3. Clairvoyance -- Fiction
ISBN 978-1-59514-160-6; 1-59514-160-X; 978-1-59514-226-9 pa; 1-59514-226-6 pa
LC 2007-31139

Identical twins Meredith and Mallory Brynn have always shared one another's thoughts, even as they dream, but their connection diminishes as they approach their thirteenth birthday, and one begins to see the future, the other the past, leading them to discover that a high school student they know is doing horrible things that place the twins, and others, in grave danger.

"The plot moves quickly, propelled by the mysteries of the sisters' relationship. . . . The girls' supernatural knowledge is a delicious bonus." Publ Wkly

Other titles about Meredith and Mallory are:
Look both ways (2009)
Watch for me by moonlight (2010)

Mitchell, David

★ **Black** swan green; a novel. Random House 2006 294p hardcover o.p.
Grades: 11 12 Adult **Fic**
1. Boys 2. Adolescence 3. Family life 4. Sexual instinct 5. England -- Fiction 6. Authorship -- Fiction 7. Family life -- Fiction 8. Teenage boys -- Fiction 9. Great Britain -- Fiction 10. England -- Worcestershire 11. Speech disorders -- Fiction
ISBN 0-8129-7401-8 pa; 1-4000-6379-5; 978-0-8129-7401-0 pa; 978-1-4000-6379-6
LC 2005052914

This is a novel by the author of Cloud Atlas (2004). "Black Swan Green tracks a single year in what is, for thirteen-year-old Jason Taylor, the sleepiest village in muddiest Worcestershire in a dying Cold War England, 1982." (Publisher's note)

"The author does not pull any punches when it comes to the casual cruelty that adolescent boys can inflict on one another, but it is this very brutality that underscores the sweetness of which they are also capable. With its British slang and complex twists and turns, this title is not a selection for reluctant readers, but teens who enjoy multifaceted coming-of-age stories will be richly rewarded." SLJ

Mitchell, Saundra

The **vespertine**. Harcourt 2011 296p $16.99
Grades: 8 9 10 11 12 **Fic**
1. Clairvoyance -- Fiction 2. Baltimore (Md.) -- Fiction
ISBN 978-0-547-48247-7; 0-547-48247-7

It's the summer of 1889, and Amelia van den Broek is new to Baltimore and eager to take in all the pleasures the city has to offer. But her gaiety is interrupted by disturbing, dreamlike visions she has only at sunset—visions that offer glimpses of the future. Soon, friends and strangers alike call on Amelia to hear her prophecies. However, a forbidden romance with Nathaniel, an artist, threatens the new life Amelia is building in Baltimore.

"Nathaniel's forbidden charms will most certainly have readers swooning. . . . There's . . . considerable fun to be had here, and Amelia's supernatural power is believably portrayed." Bull Cent Child Books

Mitchell, Todd

The **secret** to lying. Candlewick Press 2010 328p $17.99
Grades: 9 10 11 12 **Fic**
1. School stories
ISBN 978-0-7636-4084-2
LC 2009032484

Fifteen-year-old James lies about himself to be considered "cool" when he gets into an exclusive boarding school. "Grades nine to twelve." (Bull Cent Child Books)

"Mitchell paints a vivid picture of teenage social and mental health issues, neither overdramatizing nor understating their impact, and the result is a great read." Publ Wkly

Mlawski, Shana

Hammer of witches; by Shana Mlawski. Tu Books 2013 400 p. (reinforced) $18.95
Grades: 6 7 8 9 **Fic**
1. Fantasy fiction 2. Storytelling -- Fiction 3. America -- Exploration -- Fiction 4. Magic -- Fiction 5. Wizards -- Fiction 6. Explorers -- Fiction 7. America -- Discovery and exploration -- Spanish -- Fiction
ISBN 1600609872; 9781600609879
LC 2012048627

In this novel, by Shana Mlawski, "Baltasar Infante . . . encounters a monster straight out of stories one night . . . Captured by . . . a mysterious witch-hunting arm of the Spanish Inquisition, . . . the Inquisitor demands he reveal the whereabouts of Amir al-Katib, a legendary Moorish sorcerer who can bring myths and the creatures within them to life. Now Baltasar must escape, find al-Katib, and defeat a dreadful power that may destroy the world." (Publisher's note)

"Newcomer Mlawski delivers a fast-paced coming-of-age adventure, respectfully evoking the complexities and cultural landscape of the period. She draws from a variety of sources, including Jewish and Biblical myth, offering an accessible, attention-grabbing story that seamlessly inserts its magical elements into historical fact." Pub Wkly

Mlynowski, Sarah

Don't even think about it; Sarah Mlynowski. Delacorte Press. 2014 336p $17.99
Grades: 7 8 9 10 **Fic**
1. Extrasensory perception — Fiction 2. High schools — Fiction 3. New York (N.Y.) — Fiction 5. Telepathy — Fiction
ISBN: 0385737386; 9780385737388; 9780385906623
LC 2012050777

"When a group of Manhattan 10th graders inadvertently receives telepathic abilities from tainted flu shots, things rapidly get chaotic (and noisy). Finding out too much information dramatically upends family relationships, friendships, and romances. . . . Filled with heartbreak, hilarity, and some brutal truths, Mlynowski's novel will leave readers thinking about the gaps between our private and public selves and the lies we tell others and ourselves." Pub Wkly

Gimme a call. Delacorte Press 2010 301p $17.99; lib bdg $20.99

Grades: 7 8 9 10 **Fic**

1. School stories 2. Time travel -- Fiction

ISBN 978-0-385-73588-9; 0-385-73588-X; 978-0-385-90574-9 lib bdg; 0-385-90574-2 lib bdg

LC 2009-20020

"When Devi's high-school sweetheart breaks up with her right before their senior prom, she is devastated. Not only is she dateless but she is also friendless and relegated to a mediocre college because she has concentrated on her boyfriend instead of academics. . . . In a fresh twist on time travel, she contacts her freshman self via cell phone and proceeds to change their future. Of course, one small change leads to others, and both girls begin to wonder about the wisdom of this collaboration. Mlynowski has given herself a complicated, challenging story, and she is particularly effective in conveying the differences in maturity and perspective between a freshman and a senior." Booklist

Ten things we did (and probably shouldn't have) HarperTeen 2011 357p $16.99; ebook $9.99

Grades: 7 8 9 10 **Fic**

1. Friendship -- Fiction 2. Connecticut -- Fiction

ISBN 978-0-06-170124-5; 0-06-170124-6; 978-0-06-208461-3 ebook; 0-06-208461-5 ebook

LC 2010-45556

Sixteen-year-old April, a high school junior, and her friend Vi, a senior, get a crash course in reality as the list of things they should not do becomes a list of things they did while living parent-free in Westport, Connecticut, for the semester.

"With wit, energy, and an uncanny understanding of teenage logic, Mlynowski . . . weighs the pros and cons of independence in this modern cautionary tale. . . . Mlynowski avoids sermonizing, offering 10 madcap and remarkably tense escapades that will have readers laughing, cringing, and guessing how April will get out of the next pickle." Publ Wkly

Mochizuki, Ken

Beacon Hill boys. Scholastic Press 2002 201p $16.95; pa $5.99

Grades: 7 8 9 10 **Fic**

1. Japanese Americans -- Fiction

ISBN 0-439-26749-8; 0-439-24906-6 pa

LC 2002-2343

In 1972 in Seattle, a teenager in a Japanese American family struggles for his own identity, along with a group of three friends who share his anger and confusion

"The author nicely balances universal experiences of male adolescence . . . with scenes that bring readers right into the complicated era, and his important, thought-provoking story asks tough questions about racial and cultural identity, prejudice, and family." Booklist

Molloy, Michael

Peter Raven under fire. Scholastic 2005 502p il maps $17.95

Grades: 6 7 8 9 **Fic**

1. Sea stories 2. Adventure fiction

ISBN 0-439-72454-6

"In 1800, continuous war has depleted France's treasury, but Napoleon still wants to expand his empire. To this end, he needs money to defeat the superior British Navy and to exploit Louisiana for the greatest gain. In England, midshipman Peter Raven, 13, is assigned to HMS Torren. When powerful, sadistic pirates murder everyone on the ship except Peter and jack-of-all-trades Matthew Book, the protagonist finds himself apprenticed to a British spy. . . . Fast paced with multiple plot twists. . . . Molloy's writing is intelligent and engaging." SLJ

Moloney, James

Black taxi. HarperCollins Publishers 2005 264p hardcover o.p. lib bdg $16.89

Grades: 9 10 11 12 **Fic**

1. Mystery fiction 2. Crime -- Fiction 3. Automobiles -- Fiction 4. Great Britain -- Fiction

ISBN 0-06-055937-3; 0-06-055938-1 lib bdg

LC 2003-27848

When Rosie agrees to take care of her grandfather's Mercedes while he is in jail, she gets more than she bargained for, including being thrust into the middle of a jewel heist mystery and being attracted to a dangerous boy.

"Love and larceny are center stage in this British import, which is best suited to older readers even though it has no explicit language or dicey situations. Only the main characters are developed, but the story is entertaining enough to appeal to fans of lightweight mystery who also relish a hint of romance." Booklist

The **Book** of Lies. HarperCollinsPublishers 2007 360p $16.99; lib bdg $17.89

Grades: 5 6 7 8 **Fic**

1. Fantasy fiction 2. Magic -- Fiction 3. Orphans -- Fiction

ISBN 978-0-06-057842-8; 0-06-057842-4; 978-0-06-057843-5 lib bdg; 0-06-057843-2 lib bdg

LC 2006-29874

On the night he was brought to an orphanage, Marcel's memories were taken by a sorceror and replaced with new ones by his Book of Lies, but Bea, a girl with the ability to make herself invisible, was watching and is determined to help him discover his true identity.

"Readers who enjoy the mixture of mystery, riddles, action, and camaraderie will be pleased that the open-ended conclusion leads to a planned sequel." Booklist

Monaghan, Annabel

A **girl** named Digit; by Annabel Monaghan. Houghton Mifflin Harcourt 2012 187 p. $16.99; $16.99

Grades: 7 8 9 **Fic**

1. School stories 2. Terrorism -- Fiction 3. Cryptography -- Fiction 4. Kidnapping -- Fiction 5. Interpersonal relations -- Fiction 6. Adventure and adventurers -- Fiction

ISBN 054766852X; 9780547668529; 9780544022485

LC 2011012239

In this book, "saddled with the nickname Digit, Farrah resolved to fit in once she reached high school by hiding her math skills. Then Farrah stumbles upon an eco-terrorist organization after their suicide bomb attack on JFK Airport, and the terrorists want her dead. . . . Farrah's FBI protector, the cute, young rookie agent John Bennett, . . . works with

Farrah to uncover a blackmail scheme involving the attack's bomber." (Kirkus Reviews)

Monninger, Joseph

★ **Finding** somewhere. Delacorte Press 2011 $17.99; lib bdg $20.99; e-book $17.99

Grades: 7 8 9 10 **Fic**

1. Horses -- Fiction 2. Friendship -- Fiction 3. Automobile travel -- Fiction

ISBN 978-0-385-73942-9; 978-0-385-90789-7 lib bdg; 978-0-375-86214-4 e-book

LC 2010053551

Sixteen-year-old Hattie and eighteen-year-old Delores set off on a road trip that takes unexpected turns as they discover the healing power of friendship and confront what each of them is fleeing from.

"Monniger's writing is delicious, evocative and, especially during horse-focused scenes, moving. Horse story, road trip, coming-of-age tale: It's any and all of these, but mostly a tender and authentic voyage into the mind of a wise, funny and wholly likable protagonist." Kirkus

★ **Hippie** chick. Front Street 2008 156p $16.95

Grades: 8 9 10 11 12 **Fic**

1. Manatees -- Fiction 2. Shipwrecks -- Fiction 3. Survival after airplane accidents, shipwrecks, etc. -- Fiction

ISBN 978-1-59078-598-0; 1-59078-598-3

LC 2007-51976

After her sailboat capsizes, fifteen-year-old Lolly Emmerson is rescued by manatees and taken to a mangrove key in the Everglades, where she forms a bond with her aquatic companions while struggling to survive.

"It's an affecting account, beautifully told." SLJ

Wish. Delacorte Press 2010 193p $17.99; lib bdg $20.99

Grades: 6 7 8 9 10 **Fic**

1. Sharks -- Fiction 2. Wishes -- Fiction 3. Siblings -- Fiction 4. Cystic fibrosis -- Fiction

ISBN 978-0-385-73941-2; 0-385-73941-9; 978-0-385-90788-0 lib bdg; 0-385-90788-5 lib bdg

LC 2010-09958

Bee's brother, Tommy, knows everything there is to know about sharks. He also knows that his life will be cut short by cystic fibrosis. And so does Bee. That's why she wants to make his wish-foundation-sponsored trip to swim with a great white shark an unforgettable memory. Only when Bee takes Tommy to meet a famous shark attack survivor and hard-core surfer does Tommy have the chance to live one day to the fullest.

"Fans of Monninger's other works will recognize the fluid, thoughtful writing and vivid characters, and this could be an eye-opener for shark aficionados looking to take their interest beyond the glitz of shark week." Bull Cent Child Books

Mont, Eve Marie

A **breath** of Eyre. Kensington/Kteen 2012 342 p.

Grades: 9 10 11 12 **Fic**

1. Love stories 2. Fantasy fiction 3. Supernatural -- Fiction 4. Eyre, Jane (Fictional character) 5. Books and reading

ISBN 9780758269485

In this book, "Emma Townsend has always believed in stories. . . . Perhaps it's because she feels like an outsider at her . . . school, or because her stepmother doesn't come close to filling the void left by her mother's death. And her only romantic prospect . . . is . . . a long-time friend who just adds to Emma's confusion. But escape soon arrives in a . . . copy of 'Jane Eyre.'. . . Reading of Jane's isolation sparks a deep sense of kinship. Then . . . a lightning storm catapults Emma right into Jane's body and her nineteenth-century world. . . . Emma has a sense of belonging she's never known"and an attraction to the brooding Mr. Rochester. Now, moving between her two realities and uncovering secrets in both, Emma must decide . . . [where] her destiny lies." (Publisher's note)

Moore, Carley

The **stalker** chronicles; Carley Moore. Farrar Straus Giroux 2012 230 p. (hardcover) $16.99

Grades: 8 9 10 11 12 **Fic**

1. School stories 2. Divorce -- Fiction 3. Interpersonal relations -- Fiction 4. Best friends -- Fiction 5. New York (State) -- Fiction 6. Family life -- New York (State) -- Fiction

ISBN 9780374371807; 9781429961752

LC 2011013093

This book features "Cammie, a high-school sophomore, whose history has involved such intense interest in guys . . . that she's now known around school as a stalker. When cute new guy Toby turns up in her small town, Cammie's determined that she'll change her ways, . . . and finally get the relationship she's been longing for. . . . The dissolution of Cammie's parents' marriage . . . brings her dysfunctional patterns into sharp relief." (Bulletin of the Center for Children's Books)

Moore, Derrick

Always upbeat / All that; Stephanie Perry Moore; All that / Stephanie Perry Moore & Derrick Moore. Saddleback 2012 314 p. $14.95

Grades: 7 8 9 10 11 12 **Fic**

1. Football players 2. Cheerleading -- Fiction 3. High school students -- Fiction

ISBN 1616518847; 9781616518844

This book by Stephanie Perry Moore and Derrick Moore "deliver[s] a pair of intersecting but distinct stories from the points of view of a cheerleader and a quarterback at a predominantly African-American Atlanta high school. Spoiled, confident Charli Black and driven athlete Blake Strong have been together for two years. Now, at the start of their junior year, they are growing apart. Blake wants to 'take [their] relationship to the next level,' but Charli wants to wait." (Kirkus Reviews)

Moore, Kelly

★ **Amber** House; by Kelly Moore, Tucker Reed, and Larkin Reed. Arthur A. Levine Books 2012 349 p. (hardback) $17.99

Grades: 9 10 11 12 **Fic**

1. Death -- Fiction 2. Friendship -- Fiction 3.

Grandmothers -- Fiction 4. Family secrets -- Fiction 5. Haunted houses -- Fiction 6. Visions -- Fiction 7. Maryland -- Fiction 8. Psychic ability -- Fiction 9. Mystery and detective stories 10. Brothers and sisters -- Fiction

ISBN 0545434165; 9780545434164; 9780545434171; 9780545469739

LC 2012014729

In this first title of the authors' proposed trilogy, protagonist "Sarah Parsons has never seen Amber House, the grand Maryland estate that's been in her family for three centuries. She's never walked its hedge maze nor found its secret chambers; she's never glimpsed the shades that haunt it, nor hunted for lost diamonds in its walls. But all of that is about to change. After her grandmother passes away, Sarah and her friend Jackson decide to search for the diamonds, and the house comes alive." (Publisher's note)

Neverwas; by Kelly Moore, Tucker Reed, and Larkin Reed. Arthur A. Levine Books 2014 320 p. (Amber House trilogy) (hardback) $17.99

Grades: 9 10 11 12 **Fic**

1. Historical fiction 2. Alternative histories 3. Love -- Fiction 4. Visions -- Fiction 5. Maryland -- Fiction 6. Dwellings -- Fiction 7. Supernatural -- Fiction 8. Psychic ability -- Fiction 9. Family life -- Maryland -- Fiction

ISBN 0545434181; 9780545434188; 9780545434195

LC 2013020546

This second title in the authors' Amber House trilogy "presents a stark departure from the preceding volume; gone are the creepy ghost children and specters in mirrors, now replaced by Sarah's confident knowledge that these ghosts are there to guide her. The authors' vision of this alternate, broken United States slowly comes into focus, rather as a ghost might materialize in the background. Sure, ghosts are scary, but a world where the Holocaust lasted for 75 years and may continue? That's inconceivably frightening. A wild ride that leaves its readers breathless for the final installment." (Kirkus)

Moore, Perry

Hero. Hyperion 2007 428p $16.99

Grades: 7 8 9 10 11 12 **Fic**

1. Science fiction 2. Superheroes -- Fiction 3. Homosexuality -- Fiction 5. Father-son relationship -- Fiction

ISBN 978-1-4231-0195-6; 1-4231-0195-2

Thom Creed, the gay son of a disowned superhero, finds that he, too, has special powers and is asked to join the very League that rejected his father, and it is there that Thom finds other misfits whom he can finally trust.

"The combination of mystery, fantasy, thriller, and romance create a delightful and compelling read." Voice Youth Advocates

Moore, Peter

Red moon rising. Hyperion 2011 328p $16.99

Grades: 7 8 9 10 **Fic**

1. Vampires -- Fiction 2. Werewolves -- Fiction

ISBN 978-1-4231-1665-3; 1-4231-1665-8

LC 2009-40375

In a world where vampires dominate and werewolves are despised, a teenaged half-vampire discovers his recessive werewolf genes are developing with the approaching full moon.

"The details are imaginative and believable, as are the social interactions at school and in Danny's home." Booklist

V is for villain; Peter Moore. Hyperion. 2014 336p $17.99

Grades: 7 8 9 10 Fic

1. Ability -- Fiction 2. Brothers -- Fiction 3. Good and evil -- Fiction 4. Superheroes -- Fiction 5. Adventure fiction

ISBN: 1423157494; 9781423157496

LC 2013026304

"When Brad makes friends who are more into political action than weight lifting, he's happy to join a new crew-especially since it means spending more time with Layla, a girl who may or may not have a totally illegal, totally secret super-power. And with her help, Brad begins to hone a dangerous new power of his own." (Publisher's note)

"Some of the characterizations in this quasi-dystopian novel can be a little heavy-handed, but with plenty of plot twists, dastardly conspiracies, and a snarky narrator, the latest from Moore . . . has lots of sparkle." Booklist

Moran, Katy

Bloodline. Candlewick Press 2009 297p il map $16.99

Grades: 7 8 9 10 **Fic**

1. War stories 2. Adventure fiction 3. Middle Ages -- Fiction 4. Great Britain -- History -- 0-1066 -- Fiction

ISBN 978-07636-4083-5; 0-7636-4083-2

LC 2008-21413

While traveling through early seventh-century Britain trying to stop an impending war, Essa, who bears the blood of native British tribes and of the invading Anglish, makes discoveries that divide his loyalties.

"Essa is a complex, sympathetic protagonist: prickly and quick of temper, but also clever, determined and of unflinching integrity. If his struggle is authentically gory and ultimately tragic, it is not without glimpses of love and hope." Kirkus

Followed by: Bloodline rising (2011)

Bloodline rising. Candlewick Press 2011 328p map $16.99

Grades: 7 8 9 10 **Fic**

1. Slaves -- Fiction 2. Criminals -- Fiction 3. Middle Ages -- Fiction 4. Great Britain -- History -- 0-1066 -- Fiction

ISBN 978-0-7636-4508-3; 0-7636-4508-7

LC 2010-46692

Sequel to: Bloodline (2009)

Cai, a thief in seventh-century Constantinople, finds himself held captive on a trading ship bound for Britain—the home his father, a ruthless barbarian assassin, fled long ago—where he discovers that his Anglish captors know more about the secrets of his family than he does.

"At its heart, this is the story of a boy's turbulent relationship with his father, torn between resentment and admiration, rivalry and respect, which renders the tale both as intimate as heartbreak and universal as hope. Grim, lyrical and unforgettable." Kirkus

Moranville, Sharelle Byars

A **higher** geometry. Henry Holt 2006 212p $16.95

Grades: 8 9 10 11 **Fic**

1. School stories 2. Sex role -- Fiction 3. Mathematics -- Fiction

ISBN 978-0-8050-7470-3; 0-8050-7470-8

LC 2005-21699

While grieving the death of her grandmother in 1959, teenager Anna is torn between her aspirations to study math in college and her family's expectations that she will marry and become a homemaker after high school.

"Readers will easily connect with the romance that's both thrilling and nurturing and with Anna's steady resolve to follow her passion for numbers and challenge a world of expectations." Booklist

Morden, Simon

The **lost** art. David Fickling Books 2008 521p $16.99; lib bdg $19.99

Grades: 8 9 10 11 12 **Fic**

1. Science fiction 2. Religion and science -- Fiction

ISBN 978-0-385-75147-6; 0-385-75147-8; 978-0-385-75148-3 lib bdg; 0-385-75148-6 lib bdg

LC 2007-35591

A millennium after a devastating war changed the direction of Earth's rotation, when the Church keeps science and technology suppressed, magician-like Benzamir and Va, a killer-for-hire turned monk, seek Solomon, who is surreptitiously spreading technology for nefarious purposes.

"This original and engaging science fiction adventure features adult protagonists, though they deal with classic coming-of-age questions about their place in the world." Horn Book Guide

Morel, Alex

Survive; Alex Morel. Razorbill 2012 259 p. $17.99

Grades: 9 10 11 12 **Fic**

1. Suicide -- Fiction 2. Wilderness survival -- Fiction 3. Survival after airplane accidents, shipwrecks, etc. -- Fiction 4. Arctic regions -- Fiction 5. Wilderness areas -- Fiction 6. Aircraft accidents -- Fiction

ISBN 1595145109; 9781595145109

LC 2012012138

In this book by Alex Morel, "Jane is on a plane on her way home to Montclair, New Jersey, from a mental hospital. She is about to kill herself. Just before she can swallow a lethal dose of pills, the plane hits turbulence and everything goes black. Jane wakes up amidst piles of wreckage and charred bodies on a snowy mountaintop. There is only one other survivor: a boy named Paul, who inspires Jane to want to fight for her life for the first time." (Publisher's note)

Morgan, Nicola

The **highwayman's** footsteps. Candlewick Press 2007 354p $16.99

Grades: 6 7 8 9 **Fic**

1. Adventure fiction

ISBN 978-0-7636-3472-8; 0-7636-3472-7

LC 2007-25997

In eighteenth-century England, William runs away from his father, only to be captured by an armed highwayman who turns out to be a girl. Together, they seek vengeance against William's cruel father and the soldiers who killed the girl's parents.

"Alfred Noyes' romantic epic . . . provides the jumping off point for this beautifully written historical novel. . . . Excellent for both recreational reading and curriculum support in the humanities." Booklist

Morgan, Page

The **beautiful** and the cursed; by Page Morgan. 1st ed. Delacorte Press 2013 352 p. (library) $21.99; (hardcover) $18.99

Grades: 7 8 9 10 11 12 **Fic**

1. Love stories 2. Gargoyles -- Fiction 3. Brothers and sisters -- Fiction 4. Sisters -- Fiction 5. Supernatural -- Fiction 6. Paris (France) -- History -- 1870-1940 -- Fiction 7. France -- History -- Third Republic, 1870-1940 -- Fiction

ISBN 0385743114; 9780375990953; 9780385743112

LC 2012022378

In this book by Page Morgan, "Ingrid, her sister Gabby, and their mom arrive at the abandoned abbey that they plan to turn into an art gallery. Grayson, Ingrid's twin brother, had procured the place and was supposed to meet them there. Grayson, however, does not show up and the girls are surprised to learn that he has actually been missing for several days. . . . [Ingrid] and Gabby . . .discover a world of living gargoyles that can transform into humans." (Children's Literature)

Morgenroth, Kate

Echo. Simon & Schuster 2007 144p $15.99

Grades: 7 8 9 10 **Fic**

1. Death -- Fiction 2. Post-traumatic stress disorder -- Fiction

ISBN 1-4169-1438-2; 978-1-4169-1438-9

LC 2005-32984

After Justin witnesses his brother's accidental shooting death, he must live with the repercussions, as the same horrific day seems to happen over and over.

Moriarty, Jaclyn

★ A **corner** of white; Jaclyn Moriarty. Arthur A. Levine Books 2013 384 p. (Colors of Madeleine trilogy) (hardcover) $17.99

Grades: 7 8 9 10 11 12 **Fic**

1. Fantasy fiction 2. Epistolary fiction 3. Color -- Fiction 4. Magic -- Fiction 5. England -- Fiction 6. Princesses -- Fiction 7. Missing persons -- Fiction 8. Cambridge (England) -- Fiction 9. Interpersonal relations -- Fiction

ISBN 0545397367; 9780545397360

LC 2012016582

Boston Globe-Horn Book Honor: Fiction (2013).

This opening volume of a fantasy series from Jaclyn Moriarty focuses on 14-year-old Madeleine, who "lives in Cambridge, England, with her zany mother in uncertain circumstances, having run away from their fabulously privileged international existence. Meanwhile, Elliot lives in Bonfire, The Farms, Cello, a parallel reality. . . . Through a crack between their worlds, they begin exchanging letters." (Kirkus Reviews)

"Australian writer Moriarty's marvelously original fantasy is quirky and clever... [she] captures the proud iconoclasm of many homeschoolers and does not shy away from tenderness and poignancy." BookList

★ The **cracks** in the kingdom; Jaclyn Moriarty. Arthur A. Levine Books, an imprint of Scholastic Inc. 2014 480 p. (The colors of Madeleine) (hardcover : alk. paper) $18.99

Grades: 7 8 9 10 11 12 **Fic**

1. Princesses 2. Fantasy fiction 3. Missing persons 4. Color -- Fiction 5. Magic -- Fiction 6. England -- Fiction 7. Missing persons -- Fiction 8. Cambridge (England) -- Fiction 9. Interpersonal relations -- Fiction

ISBN 0545397383; 9780545397384; 9780545397391

LC 2013022827

"In this lively follow-up to A Corner of White (Scholastic, 2013), Moriarty chronicles the ever-intertwining lives of Cambridge resident Madeline Tully and her secret correspondent Elliot Baranski, a quick-witted farm boy from the Kingdom of Cello...The RYA's work around Cello expands an already complex and intricately drawn world. Readers will be clamoring for the next title after the thrilling yet satisfying conclusion." (School Library Journal)

The **ghosts** of Ashbury High. Arthur A. Levine Books 2010 480p $18.99

Grades: 8 9 10 11 12 **Fic**

1. School stories 2. Australia -- Fiction

ISBN 978-0-545-06972-4; 0-545-06972-6

LC 2009-32651

Student essays, scholarship committee members' notes, and other writings reveal interactions between a group of modern-day students at an exclusive New South Wales high school and their strange connection to a young Irishman transported to Australia in the early 1800s.

"The off-the-rails zaniness . . . is . . . satisfying, and in between all the irreverence, Moriarty slips in plenty of sharp-eyed, poignant observations." SLJ

Feeling sorry for Celia St. Martin's Press 2001 276p $9.27

Grades 7 8 9 10 11 12 **Fic**

1. Teenage girls -- Fiction. 2. Epistolary fiction. 3. Bildungsromans. 4. Australia -- Fiction.

"Life is pretty complicated for Elizabeth Clarry. Her best friend Celia keeps disappearing, her absent father suddenly reappears, and her communication with her mother consists entirely of wacky notes left on the fridge...But Elizabeth is on the verge of some major changes. She may lose her best friend, find a wonderful new friend, kiss the sexiest guy alive, and run in a marathon.

So much can happen in the time it takes to write a letter..." (Publisher's Note)

"Life isn't going well for high school student Elizabeth Clarry. Her absentee father just moved back to Australia from Canada for a year, and now he wants to spend "quality time" with her. She's getting anonymous love notes from a boy who refuses to tell her his name. Worst of all, her best friend has run away and joined the circus... Eventually, Elizabeth learns to stop obsessing over the flighty, thoughtless Celia and comes to appreciate her own gifts. Her intelligence and wry sense of humor come through strongly in her letters to her mother and her friends. Elizabeth's ditzy mother and new pen pal are especially vivid characters." SLJ

The **year** of secret assignments. Arthur A. Levine Books 2004 340p $16.95; pa $7.99

Grades: 8 9 10 11 12 **Fic**

1. School stories 2. Australia -- Fiction 3. Friendship -- Fiction

ISBN 0-439-49881-3; 0-439-49882-1 pa

LC 2003-14278

Three female students from Ashbury High write to three male students from rival Brookfield High as part of a pen pal program, leading to romance, humiliation, revenge plots, and war between the schools

"There are a few coarse moments—a reference to a blow job and some caustic outbursts. . . . This is an unusual novel with an exhilarating pace, irrepressible characters, and a screwball humor that will easily attract teens." Booklist

Other titles set at Ashbury High are:

The ghosts of Ashbury High (2010)

The murder of Bindy Mackenzie (2006)

Moriarty, Laura

The **center** of everything. Hyperion 2003 291p $22.95; pa $14

Grades: 9 10 11 12 **Fic**

1. Kansas -- Fiction 2. Single parent family -- Fiction 3. Mother-daughter relationship -- Fiction

ISBN 1-401-30031-6; 0-7868-8845-8 pa

LC 2002-32898

"Any map clearly shows that Kansas is the center of everything. Ten-year-old Evelyn Bucknow notices it on every map that she sees and truly believes that is where she belongs—in the center. Unfortunately, Evelyn is forced to parent her mother, a flighty, unrealistically romantic woman who is having an affair with her married boss. . . . Fortunately, Evelyn takes the events of her life and her mother's life and learns her lessons, with a few glitches along the way. Young people will find Evelyn appealing and real despite the book's setting in the age of Ronald Reagan and big hair, and they will respond positively to her determination." Voice Youth Advocates

Morpurgo, Michael

An **elephant** in the garden. Feiwel and Friends 2011 199p $16.99

Grades: 6 7 8 9 **Fic**

1. Zoos -- Fiction 2. Elephants -- Fiction 3. World War, 1939-1945 -- Fiction

ISBN 978-0-312-59369-8; 0-312-59369-4

Lizzie and Karl's mother is a zoo keeper; the family has become attached to an orphaned elephant named Marlene, who will be destroyed as a precautionary measure so she and the other animals don't run wild should the zoo be hit by bombs. The family persuades the zoo director to let Marlene stay in their garden instead. When the city is bombed, the family flees with thousands of others, but how can they walk the same route when they have an elephant in tow, and keep themselves safe?

"This well-paced, heartwarming narrative by a master storyteller will appeal to readers on several levels—as a tale of adventure and suspense, as a commentary on human trauma and animal welfare during war, as a perspective on the hardships facing the German people in the final months of World War II, and as a tribute to the rich memories and experiences of an older generation." SLJ

Half a man; Michael Morpurgo, illustrated by Gemma O'Callaghan. Candlewick Press. 2015 64p $16.99

Grades: 7 8 9 10 **Fic**

1. Grandparent and child -- Fiction; 2. Veterans -- Fiction; 3. World War, 1939-1945 -- Fiction; 4. Grandfathers -- Fiction

ISBN: 0763677477; 9780763677473

LC 2014939339

In this book, "author Michael Morpurgo evokes the post-war Britain of his childhood. . . . From a young age, Michael was both fascinated by and afraid of his grandfather. Grandpa's ship was torpedoed during the Second World War, leaving him with terrible burns. . . . As he grows older, Michael stays with his grandfather during the summer holidays and learns the story behind Grandpa's injuries, finally getting to know the real man behind the solemn figure from his childhood." (Publisher's note)

"Morpurgo has penned an extraordinary little book of pain and triumph. It is a fictionalized tale but is based on the heroic work of Dr. McIndoe, a pioneering plastic surgeon who treated severely burned soldiers during World War II... This title will resonate with a variety of readers . . . and is an outstanding choice for reluctant readers. With our returning wounded warriors of today, this is a timely and superb addition to all collections and not to be missed." SLJ

★ **Private** Peaceful. Scholastic Press 2004 202p $16.95; pa $5.99

Grades: 7 8 9 10 **Fic**

1. Great Britain -- Fiction 2. World War, 1914-1918 -- Fiction

ISBN 0-439-63648-5; 0-439-63653-1 pa

LC 2003-65347

First published 2003 in the United Kingdom

When Thomas Peaceful's older brother is forced to join the British Army, Thomas decides to sign up as well, although he is only fourteen years old, to prove himself to his country, his family, his childhood love, Molly, and himself

"In this World War I story, the terse and beautiful narrative of a young English soldier is as compelling about the world left behind as about the horrific daily details of trench warfare. . . . Suspense builds right to the end, which is shocking, honest, and unforgettable." Booklist

Morris, Gerald

★ The **squire's** tale. Houghton Mifflin 1998 212p (The squire's tales) $15; pa $5.50

Grades: 6 7 8 9 **Fic**

1. Magic -- Fiction 2. Knights and knighthood -- Fiction 3. Gawain (Legendary character) -- Fiction 4. Gawain (Legendary character) -- Fiction

ISBN 0-395-86959-5; 0-440-22823-9 pa

LC 97-12447

In medieval England, fourteen-year-old Terence finds his tranquil existence suddenly changed when he becomes the squire of the young Gawain of Orkney and accompanies him on a long quest, proving Gawain's worth as a knight and revealing an important secret about his own true identity

"Well-drawn characters, excellent, snappy dialogue, detailed descriptions of medieval life, and a dry wit put a new spin on this engaging tale of the characters and events of King Arthur's time." Booklist

Other titles in this series are:

The squire, his knight, & his lady (1999)

The savage damsel and the dwarf (2000)

Parsifal's page (2001)

The ballad of Sir Dinadan (2003)

The princess, the crone, and the dung-cart knight (2004)

The lionness & her knight (2005)

The quest of the Fair Unknown (2006)

The squire's quest (2009)

The legend of the king (2010)

Morris, Paula

Ruined; a novel. Point 2009 309p $16.99

Grades: 6 7 8 9 10 **Fic**

1. Ghost stories 2. New Orleans (La.) -- Fiction

ISBN 978-0-545-04215-4; 0-545-04215-1

Set in New Orleans, this is "the story of 15-year-old Rebecca Brown, a proud New Yorker sent to live with a family friend while her father travels overseas. Ostracized as an outsider, Rebecca struggles to fit in and cope with her new surroundings. When she befriends Lisette, a ghost who has haunted the cemetery ever since her mysterious death 155 years earlier, Rebecca is drawn into an eerie story of betrayal, loss, old curses and family secrets. . . . This moody tale thoroughly embraces the rich history, occult lore and complex issues of race, ethnicity, class and culture that have defined New Orleans for centuries." Publ Wkly

Morrison, Toni, 1931-

Sula. Knopf 1974 174p hardcover o.p. pa $14

Grades: 11 12 Adult **Fic**

1. Ohio -- Fiction 2. Poverty -- Fiction 3. Friendship -- Fiction 4. African Americans -- Fiction

ISBN 0-394-48044-9; 1-4000-3343-8 pa

This "is the story of two black women friends and of their community of Medallion, Ohio. The community has been stunted and turned inward by the racism of the larger society. The rage and disordered lives of the townspeople are seen as a reaction to their stifled hopes. The novel follows the lives of Sula and Nel from childhood to maturity to death." Merriam-Webster's Ency of Lit

Morton-Shaw, Christine

The **riddles** of Epsilon. Katherine Tegen Books 2005 375p $16.99; lib bdg $17.89

Grades: 7 8 9 10 **Fic**

1. Supernatural -- Fiction

ISBN 0-06-072819-1; 0-06-072820-5 lib bdg

LC 2004-14641

After moving with her parents to a remote English island, fourteen-year-old Jess attempts to dispel an ancient curse by solving a series of riddles, aided by Epsilon, a supernatural being.

Moses, Shelia P.

Joseph. Margaret K. McElderry Books 2008 174p $16.99; pa $8.99
Grades: 7 8 9 10 **Fic**

1. Drug abuse -- Fiction 2. African Americans -- Fiction 3. Mother-son relationship -- Fiction
ISBN 978-1-4169-1752-6; 1-4169-1752-7; 978-4169-9442-8 pa; 1-4169-9442-4 pa

Fourteen-year-old Joseph tries to avoid trouble and keep in touch with his father, who is serving in Iraq, as he and his alcoholic, drug-addicted mother move from one homeless shelter to another.

"Moses creates a compelling character in Joseph. His struggle to survive his current situation intact is fascinating to read. . . . Negative influences such as drug dealers and users are described in a clear, cold light. Education and hard work are praised for their positive influences. Middle school and junior high teens will enjoy this story." Voice Youth Advocates

The **legend** of Buddy Bush. Margaret K. McElderry Books 2004 216p $15.95
Grades: 6 7 8 9 **Fic**

1. Race relations 2. African Americans -- Fiction 3. Family life -- North Carolina
ISBN 0-689-85839-6
LC 2003-8024

In 1947, twelve-year-old Pattie Mae is sustained by her dreams of escaping Rich Square, North Carolina, and moving to Harlem when her Uncle Buddy is arrested for attempted rape of a white woman and her grandfather is diagnosed with a terminal brain tumor.

"Patti Mae's first-person voice, steeped in the inflections of the South, rings true, and her observations richly evoke a time, place, and a resilient African American community." Booklist

Another title about Buddy Bush is:
The return of Buddy Bush (2005)

Moskowitz, Hannah

Break. Simon Pulse 2009 262p pa $8.99
Grades: 9 10 11 12 **Fic**

1. Allergy -- Fiction 2. Brothers -- Fiction 3. Fractures -- Fiction 4. Family life -- Fiction 5. Mental illness -- Fiction
ISBN 978-1-4169-8275-3; 1-4169-8275-2
LC 2008-42816

To relieve the pressures of caring for a brother with life-threatening food allergies, another who is a fussy baby, and parents who are at odds with one other, seventeen-year-old Jonah sets out to break every bone in his body in hopes of becoming stronger.

"Some readers will find Moskowitz's sickening premise a stretch. But for those with a taste for the macabre and an aversion to the sentimental, it's hard not to be taken in by the book's strong central relationships and Moskowitz's unapologetic, single-minded dedication to her unsavory task." Booklist

★ **Teeth**; Hannah Moskowitz. Simon Pulse 2013 242 p. $17.99
Grades: 9 10 11 12 **Fic**

1. Fantasy fiction 2. Mermaids and mermen -- Fiction 3. Mermen -- Fiction 4. Islands -- Fiction 5. Brothers -- Fiction 6. Loneliness -- Fiction 7. Supernatural -- Fiction 8. Cystic fibrosis -- Fiction
ISBN 1442465328; 9781442449466; 9781442465329
LC 2012019114

This novel, by Hannah Moskowitz, offers a "gritty, romantic modern fairy tale. . . . Rudy's . . . family moves to a remote island in a last attempt to save his sick younger brother. . . . Then he meets Diana, who makes him wonder what he even knows about love, and Teeth, who makes him question what he knows about anything. . . . He soon learns that Teeth has terrible secrets . . . that will force Rudy to choose between his own happiness and his brother's life." (Publisher's note)

Mosley, Walter

47. Little, Brown 2005 232p $16.99
Grades: 7 8 9 10 **Fic**

1. Magic -- Fiction 2. Slavery -- Fiction 3. African Americans -- Fiction
ISBN 0-316-11035-3
LC 2004-12500

Number 47, a fourteen-year-old slave boy growing up under the watchful eye of a brutal master in 1832, meets the mysterious Tall John, who introduces him to a magical science and also teaches him the meaning of freedom.

"Time travel, shape-shifting, and intergalactic conflict add unusual, provocative elements to this story. And yet, well-drawn characters; lively dialogue filled with gritty, regional dialect; vivid descriptions; and poignant reflections ground it in harsh reality." SLJ

Fortunate son. Little, Brown and Co. 2006 313p hardcover o.p. pa $13.99
Grades: 11 12 Adult **Fic**

1. Brothers -- Fiction 2. Race relations -- Fiction
ISBN 978-0-316-11471-4; 0-316-11471-5; 978-0-316-06628-0 pa; 0-316-06628-1 pa
LC 2005-24477

"Tommy was born out of wedlock with a hole in his heart; he's also lame and black. Eric, on the other hand, glows with health; he is so beautiful that people want to touch him—and he's white. For a few years, the boys live together after Tommy's mother and Eric's widowed doctor father fall in love after meeting in the hospital ward. Then Tommy's mother dies, and Tommy is wrested from the only family he's known. Eric grows up leading a life that appears blessed, but with Tommy gone, he's lost all that is important to him. Tommy, meanwhile, ends up on the street but feels lucky simply to be alive. . . . The writing is crisp and the plotting impeccable." Libr J

Moss, Jenny

Shadow. Scholastic Press 2010 377p $17.99

Grades: 7 8 9 10 **Fic**

1. Fairy tales 2. Kings and rulers -- Fiction

ISBN 978-0-545-03641-2; 0-545-03641-0

LC 2009-14209

When Shadow, whose job all her life has been to stay close to the young queen and prevent her prophecied death at the age of sixteen, fails in her task and the castle is thrown into chaos, she escapes along with a young knight, embarking upon a journey that eventually reveals her true identity.

"With its dashing knights, pretentious queen, and put-upon protagonist, the story starts out like any other garden-variety fairytale, but it soon takes a turn for the darkly subversive world of pagan religions and political scheming. . . . A nuanced coming of age story with a fairy-tale setting, this is sure to please." Bull Cent Child Books

Moulton, Courtney Allison

Angelfire; 1st ed. Katherine Tegen Books 2011 453 p. (trade bdg.) $17.99

Grades: 7 8 9 10 **Fic**

1. Horror fiction 2. Horror stories 3. Souls -- Fiction 4. Youths' writings 5. Angels -- Fiction 6. Monsters -- Fiction 7. Reincarnation -- Fiction

ISBN 9780062002327; 9780062002341

LC 2010012821

A seventeen-year-old girl discovers that she has the reincarnated soul of an ancient warrior destined to battle the reapers --creatures who devour humans and send their souls to Hell. --Grades nine to twelve. -- (Bull Cent Child Books)

"The author has introduced a dark and compelling world of action and intrigue, albeit with enough 'normal' drama and humor sprinkled throughout to lighten it. . . . Older junior and senior high school readers will find themselves engrossed in the story until its powerful conclusion—then anxiously awaiting the second installment." Voice Youth Advocates

Mourlevat, Jean-Claude

★ **Winter's** end; translated by Anthea Bell. Candlewick Press 2009 415p lib bdg $21.99

Grades: 8 9 10 11 12 **Fic**

1. Fantasy fiction 2. Adventure fiction 3. Orphans -- Fiction 4. Despotism -- Fiction 5. Resistance to government -- Fiction

ISBN 978-0-7636-4450-5; 0-7636-4450-1

LC 2009-8456

Fleeing across icy mountains from a pack of terrifying dog-men sent to hunt them down, four teenagers escape from their prison-like boarding schools to take up the fight against the tyrannical government that murdered their parents fifteen years earlier.

"Teeming with heroic acts, heartbreaking instances of sacrifice and intriguing characters . . . the book will keep readers absorbed and set imaginations spinning." Publ Wkly

Mowll, Joshua

Operation Red Jericho; [illustrated by Benjamin Mowll, Julek Heller, Niroot Puttapipat] Candlewick Press 2005 271p il map (The Guild of Specialists) hardcover o.p. pa $8.99

Grades: 9 10 11 12 **Fic**

1. Adventure fiction 2. Uncles -- Fiction 3. Siblings -- Fiction

ISBN 0-7636-2634-1; 0-7636-3475-1 pa

LC 2005-45382

The posthumous papers of Rebecca MacKenzie document her adventures, along with her brother Doug, in 1920s China as the teenaged siblings are sent to live aboard their uncle's ship where they become involved in the dangerous activities of a mysterious secret society called the Honourable Guild of Specialists.

"Some readers may pore over the details in this novel; others will simply appreciate the comic adventure." SLJ

Operation Storm City. Candlewick Press 2009 273p il (The Guild of Specialists) $16.99

Grades: 7 8 9 10 **Fic**

1. Adventure fiction 2. China -- Fiction 3. Siblings -- Fiction

ISBN 978-0-7636-4224-2; 0-7636-4224-X

LC 2008-19703

Siblings Becca and Doug discover important clues to their missing parents' expedition route and the location of Ur-Can, the fabled Storm City, and they embark on a perilous journey to the Takla Makan desert, racing against their Guild enemies by steam train, riverboat, and airship across the Himalayas, trying to save not only their parents, but the entire planet.

"For readers who love adventure stories and can handle a greater level of complexity, this whirlwind of travel, fighting, and impending disaster is a great trip." Voice Youth Advocates

Operation typhoon shore. Candlewick Press 2006 272p il map (The Guild of Specialists) $15.99

Grades: 7 8 9 10 **Fic**

1. Adventure fiction 2. China -- Fiction 3. Ships -- Fiction 4. Uncles -- Fiction 5. Siblings -- Fiction

ISBN 978-0-7636-3122-2; 0-7636-3122-1

LC 2006-47481

Sequel to Operation Red Jericho (2005)

In the spring of 1920, teenaged siblings Rebecca and Doug MacKenzie continue their adventures on their uncle's ship, sailing through a typhoon into the Celebes Sea in pursuit of a missing "gyrolabe" which may be connected to the disappearance of their parents.

"This book rolls along with plenty of action and fun. Readers will be captivated by the story line, but also will be intrigued by all of the sketches, photographs, newspaper clippings, and foldout information on technology." SLJ

Mulder, Michelle

Out of the box. Orca Book Publishers 2011 150p pa $9.95

Grades: 6 7 8 9 **Fic**

1. Aunts -- Fiction 2. Family life -- Fiction 3. Mother-daughter relationship -- Fiction

ISBN 978-1-55469-328-3 pa; 1-55469-328-4 pa

Ellie's passion for tango music leads to an interest in Argentine history and a desire to separate herself from her parents' problems.

"Ellie's narration authentically conveys her gradual growth, the insecurities that surround her developing friendships, her role in a dysfunctional family, and the pleasure she takes in music. Adults and their relationships are portrayed credibly. . . . A bit of Argentine history rounds out the believable plot." SLJ

Muller, Rachel Dunstan

Squeeze; written by Rachel Dunstan Muller. Orca Book Publishers 2010 166p (Orca sports) pa $9.95

Grades: 6 7 8 9 **Fic**

1. Caves -- Fiction 2. Brothers -- Fiction 3. Accidents -- Fiction

ISBN 978-1-55469-324-5; 1-55469-324-1

On a caving trip with his older brother, Byron discovers a new cave but has to make some life-or-death decisions when his brother is seriously injured.

"A fast-paced, compulsively readable book. . . . Information about caving is woven seamlessly into the narrative, and descriptions of the beauty of underground rock formations are often quite lyrical." SLJ

Mulligan, Andy

Trash. David Fickling Books 2010 232p $16.99; lib bdg $19.99

Grades: 6 7 8 9 **Fic**

1. Mystery fiction 2. Poverty -- Fiction 3. Political corruption -- Fiction 4. Refuse and refuse disposal -- Fiction

ISBN 978-0-385-75214-5; 0-385-75214-8; 978-0-385-75215-2 lib bdg; 0-385-75215-6 lib bdg

LC 2010-15940

Fourteen-year-olds Raphael and Gardo team up with a younger boy, Rat, to figure out the mysteries surrounding a bag Raphael finds during their daily life of sorting through trash in a third-world country's dump.

"While on the surface the book reads like a fast-paced adventure title, it also makes a larger statement about the horrors of poverty and injustice in the world. . . . Trash is a compelling read." SLJ

Mullin, Mike

Ashfall. Tanglewood 2011 466p $16.99

Grades: 9 10 11 12 **Fic**

1. Science fiction 2. Volcanoes -- Fiction 3. Wilderness survival -- Fiction

ISBN 978-1-933718-55-2

LC 2011007133

"Mullin puts his characters through hell, depicting numerous deaths in detail. . . . There's also cannibalism and a rape before the novel comes to a believable ending. . . . The book is well written and its protagonists are well-drawn, particularly the nontraditional and mechanically inclined Darla. Although more appropriate for older teens due to its violence, this is a riveting tale of survival." Publ Wkly

Sunrise; Mike Mullin. Tanglewood Publishing. 2014 546p $17.99

Grades: 9 10 11 12 **Fic**

1. Science fiction 2. Volcanoes -- Fiction 3. Wilderness survival -- Fiction

ISBN: 1939100011; 9781939100016

LC 2013050876

In this final book of the Ashfall Trilogy, "the Yellowstone supervolcano nearly wiped out the human race. Now, almost a year after the eruption, the survivors seem determined to finish the job. Communities wage war on each other, gangs of cannibals roam the countryside, and what little government survived the eruption has collapsed completely. The ham radio has gone silent. Sickness, cold, and starvation are the survivors' constant companions." (Publisher's note)

"The writing, even in transitory moments of peace, never lets readers forget that potential catastrophe lurks around every corner. A story about how hope is earned, as heart-pounding as it is heart-wrenching." Kirkus

Murdoch, Emily

★ **If** you find me; Emily Murdoch. St. Martin's Griffin 2013 256 p. (hardback) $17.99

Grades: 9 10 11 12 **Fic**

1. Abandoned children -- Fiction 2. Children of drug addicts -- Fiction 3. Sisters -- Fiction 4. Foundlings -- Fiction 5. Family secrets -- Fiction 6. Abused children -- Fiction

ISBN 1250021529; 9781250021526

LC 2013002656

This is the story of "14-year-old Carey and her younger sister, Nessa, [who] were kidnapped, hidden in the backwoods of Tennessee, and raised apart from society by their meth-addicted mother. After having abandoned the girls for months, she contacts the girls' father, who rescues them from the trailer where they've been living on their own, whisking them away to his gorgeous home, his understanding new wife, and her less understanding daughter." (Publishers Weekly)

Murdock, Catherine Gilbert

★ **Dairy** Queen; a novel. Houghton Mifflin 2006 275p $16

Grades: 7 8 9 10 **Fic**

1. Football -- Fiction 2. Farm life -- Fiction

ISBN 0-618-68307-0

LC 2005-19077

After spending her summer running the family farm and training the quarterback for her school's rival football team, sixteen-year-old D.J. decides to go out for the sport herself, not anticipating the reactions of those around her.

"D. J.'s voice is funny, frank, and intelligent, and her story is not easily pigeonholed." Voice Youth Advocates

Front and center. Houghton Mifflin 2009 256p (The dairy queen trilogy) $16

Grades: 7 8 9 10 **Fic**

1. Farm life -- Fiction 2. Basketball -- Fiction

ISBN 978-0-618-95982-2; 0-618-95982-3

LC 2009-24167

Sequel to: The off season (2007)

"In the third and final book . . . about farm girl, linebacker, and basketball star D.J. Schwenk, the self-aggrandizing heroine must decide her future: is she up to playing basketball for the Big Ten schools that are starting to recruit her, or should she choose a smaller college, where the game is less brutal but also less challenging? . . . D.J.'s voice is intimate and compelling, her story both universal and unique, familiar and eye-opening." Horn Book

The **off** season. Houghton Mifflin 2007 277p $16
Grades: 7 8 9 10 **Fic**
1. Football -- Fiction 2. Farm life -- Fiction
ISBN 978-0-618-68695-7; 0-618-68695-9
LC 2006029278

Sequel to: Dairy Queen (2006)

High school junior D.J. staggers under the weight of caring for her badly injured brother, her responsibilities on the dairy farm, a changing relationship with her friend Brian, and her own athletic aspirations.

This "depicts a believably maturing D.J., a young woman whose character shines through even as she struggles to find her voice. Readers will root for her at every tragicomic turn." SLJ

Followed by: Front and center (2009)

Princess Ben; being a wholly truthful account of her various discoveries and misadventures, recounted to the best of her recollection, in four parts. written by Catherine Gilbert Murdock. Houghton Mifflin 2008 344p $16; pa $8.99
Grades: 7 8 9 10 **Fic**
1. Fairy tales 2. Magic -- Fiction 3. Princesses -- Fiction 4. Courts and courtiers -- Fiction
ISBN 978-0-618-95971-6; 0-618-95971-8; 978-0-547-22325-4 pa; 0-547-22325-0 pa
LC 2007-34300

A girl is transformed, through instruction in life at court, determination, and magic, from sullen, pudgy, graceless Ben into Crown Princess Benevolence, a fit ruler of the kindgom of Montagne as it faces war with neighboring Drachensbett.

"Murdock's prose sweeps the reader up and never falters, blending a formal syntax and vocabulary with an intimate tone that bonds the reader with Ben." Horn Book

Wisdom's kiss; a thrilling and romantic adventure, incorporating magic, villany and a cat. written by Catherine Gilbert Murdock. Houghton Mifflin 2011 284p $16.99
Grades: 7 8 9 10 **Fic**
1. Fairy tales 2. Cats -- Fiction 3. Orphans -- Fiction 4. Soldiers -- Fiction 5. Princesses -- Fiction 6. Supernatural -- Fiction 7. Household employees -- Fiction
ISBN 978-0-547-56687-0; 0-547-56687-5
LC 2011003708

Princess Wisdom, who yearns for a life of adventure beyond the kingdom of Montagne, Tips, a soldier keeping his true life secret from his family, Fortitude, an orphaned maid who longs for Tips, and Magic the cat form an uneasy alliance as they try to save the kingdom from certain destruction. Told through diaries, memoirs, encyclopedia entries, letters, biographies, and a stage play.

"Packed with double entendres, humorous dialogue and situations, and a black cat that will capture the reader's imagination, this is a joyful, timeless fantasy that teens will savor." Booklist

Murphy, Jim

Desperate journey. Scholastic Press 2006 278p il map $16.99
Grades: 5 6 7 8 **Fic**
1. Family life -- Fiction
ISBN 0-439-07806-7
LC 2006-02526

In the mid-1800s, with both her father and her uncle in jail on an assault charge, Maggie, her brother, and her ailing mother rush their barge along the Erie Canal to deliver their heavy cargo or lose everything.

This is a "gripping novel." Booklist

Murphy, Rita

Looking for Lucy Buick. Delacorte Press 2005 165p $15.95; lib bdg $17.99
Grades: 7 8 9 10 **Fic**
1. Family life -- Fiction 2. Abandoned children -- Fiction
ISBN 0-385-72939-1; 0-385-90176-3 lib bdg
LC 2004-20128

Following the death of her favorite adoptive aunt, Lucy goes searching for her biological family who abandoned her in an old Buick eighteen years before.

"What wins the day are the people in Lucy's life, living and dead . . . who pop off the pages, and Murphy's voice . . . which tells the story with a steadfastness and sweetness." Booklist

Murray, Martine

How to make a bird. Arthur A. Levine Books 2010 233p $17.99
Grades: 7 8 9 10 **Fic**
1. Australia -- Fiction 2. Bereavement -- Fiction 3. Family life -- Fiction 4. Runaway teenagers -- Fiction
ISBN 978-0-439-66951-1; 0-439-66951-0
LC 2009-27453

When seventeen-year-old, small-town Australian girl Manon Clarkeson leaves home in the middle of the night, wearing her mother's long, inappropriate red silk dress and riding her bike, she is heading for Melbourne, not exactly sure what she is looking for but not wanting to stay at home alone with her father anymore.

"Although Mannie's defining attributes—acute self-consciousness and claustrophobic intensity—are hallmarks of many YA heroines, Murray's powerful lyrical voice and close observation breathe new life into them. . . . The novel offers an especially vivid sense of place—the harsh but open rural landscape and densely populated yet lonely, urban Melbourne." Kirkus

Murray, Yxta Maya

The **good** girl's guide to getting kidnapped. Razorbill 2010 251p $16.99; pa $9.99
Grades: 9 10 11 12 **Fic**
1. Gangs -- Fiction 2. California -- Fiction 3. Kidnapping -- Fiction 4. Foster home care -- Fiction 5. Mexican Americans -- Fiction
ISBN 978-1-59514-272-6; 1-59514-272-X; 978-1-59514-341-9 pa; 1-59514-341-6 pa
LC 2009-21091

Fifteen-year-old Michelle Pena, born into a powerful Mexican American gang family, tries to reconcile her gangster legacy with the girl she has become—a nationally ranked runner and academic superstar.

This book "is action-packed, as it raises relevant questions of identity and loyalty. This fast-paced story, heavy with street dialogue and slang, should have ample teen appeal." Publ Wkly

Mussi, Sarah

★ The **door** of no return. Margaret K. McElderry Books 2008 394p $17.99; pa $8.99

Grades: 8 9 10 11 12 **Fic**

1. Adventure fiction 2. Ghana -- Fiction 3. Blacks -- Fiction 4. Homicide -- Fiction 5. Great Britain -- Fiction 6. Buried treasure -- Fiction

ISBN 978-1-4169-1550-8; 1-4169-1550-8; 978-1-4169-6825-2 pa; 1-4169-6825-3 pa

LC 2007-18670

Sixteen-year-old Zac never believed his grandfather's tales about their enslaved ancestors being descended from an African king, but when his grandfather is murdered and the villains come after Zac, he sets out for Ghana to find King Baktu's long-lost treasure before the murderers do.

"This exciting narrative takes place in England and Africa; in jungles, dark caves, and on the sea. . . . Overall, this is a complex, masterful story for confident readers." SLJ

Myers, Anna

Assassin; [by] Anna Myers. Walker & Company 2005 212p $16.95

Grades: 7 8 9 10 **Fic**

1. Actors 2. Lawyers 3. Presidents 4. Murderers 5. State legislators 6. Members of Congress

ISBN 0-8027-8989-7

LC 2005042275

In alternating passages, a young White House seamstress named Bella and the actor John Wilkes Booth describe the events that lead to the latter's assassination of Abraham Lincoln.

"The novel offers a good opportunity for discussion about the assassin, his motivations, and, in this case, how he drew an unsuspecting girl into his scheme." SLJ

Spy! [by] Anna Myers. Walker & Co. 2008 211p $16.99

Grades: 5 6 7 8 9 **Fic**

1. Revolutionaries 2. Spies -- Fiction 3. Orphans -- Fiction 4. Teachers -- Fiction

ISBN 978-0-8027-9742-1; 0-8027-9742-3

LC 2008-254

In 1774, twelve-year-old Jonah becomes a pupil of Nathan Hale, who inspires him to question his beliefs about the impending revolution, and two years later, Jonah makes a decision that leads to Nathan's execution.

"Set against clearly delineated historical events, the story employs personal thoughts and feelings to show the conflicts facing the colonists. This well-written novel is a good supplement to American history studies." SLJ

Tulsa burning. Walker & Co. 2002 152p $16.95; pa $6.95

Grades: 7 8 9 10 **Fic**

1. Riots -- Fiction 2. Race relations -- Fiction

ISBN 0-8027-8829-7; 0-8027-7696-5 pa

LC 2002-23457

In 1921, fifteen-year-old Noble Chase hates the sheriff of Wekiwa, Oklahoma, and is more than willing to cross him to help his best friend, a black man, who is injured during race riots in nearby Tulsa

"In this emotional page-turner, Myers expertly captures an era of poisonous racism while conveying the strong, true voice of a courageous young man." Booklist

The **grave** robber's secret. Walker & Co. 2011 196p $16.99

Grades: 7 8 9 10 **Fic**

1. Homicide -- Fiction 2. Grave robbing -- Fiction

ISBN 978-0-8027-2183-9; 0-8027-2183-4

LC 2010018097

In Philadelphia in the 1800s, twelve-year-old Robbie is forced to help his father rob graves, then when he suspects his dad of murder, Robbie makes a life-changing decision.

"The story is well written and the characterization is excellent. Readers will connect to Robby on several levels and will feel for Martha Burke." Libr Media Connect

Myers, Edward

★ **Storyteller**; by Edward Myers. Clarion Books 2008 283p $16

Grades: 6 7 8 9 **Fic**

1. Fairy tales 2. Storytelling -- Fiction 3. Kings and rulers -- Fiction

ISBN 978-0-618-69541-6; 0-618-69541-9

LC 2007031031

Jack, a seventeen-year-old storyteller, goes to the royal city seeking his fortune and soon attracts the attention of the grief-stricken king, his beautiful eldest daughter, and his cruel young son, and he attempts to help them—and the entire kingdom—through his stories.

"This old-fashioned story has the timeless appeal of adventure, humor, and light romance, all woven together by an able teller of tales." Booklist

Myers, Walter Dean, 1937-

All the right stuff; by Walter Dean Myers. HarperTeen 2012 213 p.

Grades: 8 9 10 11 12 **Fic**

1. Bildungsromans 2. Mentoring -- Fiction 3. Soup kitchens -- Fiction 4. Social contract -- Fiction 5. African Americans -- Harlem (New York, N.Y.) -- Fiction 6. Coming of age -- Fiction 7. Conduct of life -- Fiction 8. African Americans -- Fiction 9. Harlem (New York, N.Y.) -- Fiction

ISBN 9780061960871; 9780061960888

LC 2011024251

This novel tells the story of Paul DuPree, a 16-year-old boy who "has taken on two jobs: work in a soup kitchen and the required mentoring of a young basketball player. At the soup kitchen, he meets Elijah Jones, the project's driving force and resident philosopher," who helps Paul understand "how one person's decisions and actions might affect the entire community" as he mentors teenage mother Keisha and comes to terms with the death of his father." (Kirkus)

Amiri & Odette; a love story. a poem by Walter Dean Myers; paintings by Javaka Steptoe. Scholastic Press 2009 un il $17.99
Grades: 7 8 9 10 **Fic**
1. Fairy tales 2. Love stories 3. Novels in verse 4. African Americans -- Fiction 5. Young adult literature -- Works
ISBN 978-0-590-68041-7; 0-590-68041-2
LC 2008-11563

Presents a modern, urban retelling in verse of the ballet in which brave Amiri falls in love with beautiful Odette and fights evil Big Red for her on the streets of the Swan Lake Projects.

"Myers's verse is almost overwrought—as it should be to suit the story, and the intensity of teenage love. The melodrama combines with an energy and beat that—heightened by dynamic text design—makes this ideal for performance. Steptoe's collage-on-cinderblock illustrations have a roughness, darkness, and density that suit the tone." SLJ

Carmen; an urban adaptation of the opera. Egmont USA 2011 various pagings $16.99
Grades: 8 9 10 11 12 **Fic**
1. Love -- Fiction 2. Hispanic Americans -- Fiction 3. Young adult literature -- Works
ISBN 978-1-60684-115-0; 1-60684-115-7; 978-1-60684-199-0 e-book
LC 2011002491

A policeman's obsessive love for a tempestuous wig factory worker ends in tragedy in this updated version of Bizet's Carmen, set in Spanish Harlem, and told in screenplay format.

"Myers seamlessly pulls off the drama's transportation to a contemporary urban setting and, true to form, renders it accessible to today's teens. . . . An excellent choice for reluctant readers, urban or otherwise." SLJ

★ The **Cruisers**; Walter Dean Myers. Scholastic Press 2010 126 p. $15.99
Grades: 6 7 8 9 **Fic**
1. Schools -- Fiction 2. Newspapers -- Fiction 3. Middle schools -- Fiction 4. Race relations -- Fiction 5. African Americans -- Fiction 6. Freedom of speech -- Fiction
ISBN 978-0-439-91626-4; 0-439-91626-7; 9780439916264
LC 2009052426

Friends Zander, Kambui, LaShonda, and Bobbi, caught in the middle of a mock Civil War at DaVinci Academy, learn the true cost of freedom of speech when they use their alternative newspaper, The Cruiser, to try to make peace.

"A finely crafted look at smart, urban underachievers. . . . [The book offers] fleet pacing, a spot-on voice, good characters, great dialogue, smart ideas, and an unusual story that can maneuver whip-quick from light to heavy and right back again." Booklist

Another title in this series is:
The Cruisers: checkmate (2011)

★ **Darius** & Twig; Walter Dean Myers. 1st ed. Harper, an imprint of HarperCollinsPublishers 2013 208 p. (hardcover) $17.99
Grades: 8 9 10 11 12 **Fic**
1. Friendship -- Fiction 2. Harlem (New York, N.Y.) -- Fiction 3. Running -- Fiction 4. Authorship -- Fiction 5. Best friends -- Fiction 6. New York (N.Y.) -- Fiction 7. African Americans -- Fiction 8. Dominican Americans -- Fiction
ISBN 0061728233; 9780061728235; 9780061728242
LC 2012050678

Coretta Scott King Honor Book: Author (2014)

In this book by Walter Dean Myers, "Harlem teenager Darius, a writer, wants to get out of his neighborhood and make it to college, but his grades aren't good enough. He's hoping that if he can get a story published, he might nab a college scholarship. His best friend Twig is a track star, and sees athletics as his escape. Both are skeptical of the hype they are fed about how hard work pays off, and they face obstacles ranging from school bullies . . . to indifferent educators." (Publishers Weekly)

"This encouraging text may inspire teens who feel trapped by their surroundings...Told in Darius's voice, the prose is poetic but concise. This would be a worthwhile addition to any middle or high school media center or public library shelf and would make a valuable book for discussion in a middle school classroom." VOYA

Dope sick. HarperTeen/Amistad 2009 186p $16.99; lib bdg $17.89
Grades: 8 9 10 11 12 **Fic**
1. Drug abuse -- Fiction 2. Supernatural -- Fiction 3. African Americans -- Fiction 4. Harlem (New York, N.Y.) -- Fiction
ISBN 978-0-06-121477-6; 0-06-121477-9; 978-0-06-121478-3 lib bdg; 0-06-121478-7 lib bdg
LC 2008-10568

Seeing no way out of his difficult life in Harlem, seventeen-year-old Jeremy "Lil J" Dance flees into a house after a drug deal goes awry and meets a weird man who shows different turning points in Lil J's life when he could have made better choices.

"Myers uses street-style lingo to cover Lil J's sorry history of drug use, jail time, irresponsible fatherhood and his own childhood grief. A didn't-see-that-coming ending wraps up the story on a note of well-earned hope and will leave readers with plenty to think about." Publ Wkly

★ **Fallen** angels; Walter Dean Myers. Scholastic Paperbacks 2008 336 p. hardcover o.p. (pbk.) $7.99
Grades: 8 9 10 11 12 Adult **Fic**
1. Vietnam War, 1961-1975 -- Fiction 2. African American soldiers -- Fiction
ISBN 9780545055765; 0545055768
First published 1988
ALA YALSA Margaret A. Edwards Award (1994)

"Black, seventeen, perceptive and sensitive, Richie (the narrator) has enlisted and been sent to Vietnam; in telling the story of his year of active service, Richie is candid about the horror of killing and the fear of being killed, the fear and bravery and confusion and tragedy of the war." Bull Cent Child Books

"Except for occasional outbursts, the narration is remarkably direct and understated; and the dialogue, with morbid humor sometimes adding comic relief, is steeped in natural vulgarity, without which verisimilitude would be unthinkable. In fact, the foul talk, which serves as the story's linguistic setting, is not nearly as obscene as the events." Horn Book

Game. HarperTeen 2008 218p $16.99; lib bdg $17.89

Grades: 8 9 10 11 12 **Fic**

1. School stories 2. Basketball -- Fiction 3. Czech Americans -- Fiction 4. African Americans -- Fiction 5. Harlem (New York, N.Y.) -- Fiction

ISBN 978-0-06-058294-4; 978-0-06-058295-1 lib bdg

LC 2007-18370

If Harlem high school senior Drew Lawson is going to realize his dream of playing college, then professional, basketball, he will have to improve at being coached and being a team player, especially after a new—white—student threatens to take the scouts' attention away from him.

"Basketball fans will love the long passages of detailed court action. . . . The authentic thoughts of a strong, likable, African American teen whose anxieties, sharp insights, and belief in his own abilities will captivate readers of all backgrounds." Booklist

Harlem summer. Scholastic Press 2007 176p il $16.99

Grades: 6 7 8 9 **Fic**

1. African Americans -- Fiction 2. Harlem Renaissance -- Fiction

ISBN 978-0-439-36843-8; 0-439-36843-X

LC 2006-46812

In 1920s Harlem, sixteen-year-old Mark Purvis, an aspiring jazz saxophonist, gets a summer job as an errand boy for the publishers of the groundbreaking African American magazine, "The Crisis," but soon finds himself on the enemy list of mobster Dutch Shultz.

"Readers will be delighted to accompany the teen on his action-packed adventures." Booklist

★ **Hoops**; a novel. Delacorte Press 1981 183p hardcover o.p. pa $5.99

Grades: 7 8 9 10 **Fic**

1. Basketball -- Fiction 2. African Americans -- Fiction

ISBN 0-440-93884-8 pa

LC 81-65497

ALA YALSA Margaret A. Edwards Award (1994)

"This story offers the reader some fast, descriptive basketball action, a love story between Lonnie and girlfriend Mary-Ann, peer friendship problems, and gangster intrigues. Most importantly, however, it portrays the growth of a trusting and deeply caring father-son relationship between [the coach] Cal and [fatherless] Lonnie." Voice Youth Advocates

Invasion! Walter Dean Myers. Scholastic Press 2013 224 p. $17.99

Grades: 7 8 9 10 **Fic**

1. Friendship 2. African American soldiers 3. Normandy (France), Attack on, 1944 4. War -- Fiction 5. Soldiers -- Fiction 6. African American soldiers -- Fiction

ISBN 0545384281; 9780545384285; 9780545384292; 9780545576598

LC 2013005595

In this book by Walter Dean Myers, "old friends Josiah 'Woody' Wedgewood and Marcus Perry see each other in England prior to the invasion of Normandy. Woody is with the 29th Infantry, and Marcus, who's black, is with the Transportation Corps, the segregation of their Virginia hometown following them right into wartime. Their friendship frames the story, as the two occasionally encounter each other in the horrific days ahead." (Kirkus Reviews)

"Myers eloquently conveys how exhausting war is physically and emotionally. . . . [T]his novel can be hard to read, but it is also hard to put down." SLJ

Kick; [by] Walter Dean Myers and Ross Workman. HarperTeen 2011 197p $16.99; lib bdg $17.89

Grades: 7 8 9 10 **Fic**

1. Police -- Fiction 2. Soccer -- Fiction 3. Mentoring -- Fiction 4. New Jersey -- Fiction 5. Family life -- Fiction 6. Criminal investigation -- Fiction

ISBN 978-0-06-200489-5; 0-06-200489-1; 978-0-06-200490-1 lib bdg; 0-06-200490-5 lib bdg

LC 2010-18441

Told in their separate voices, thirteen-year-old soccer star Kevin and police sergeant Brown, who knew his father, try to keep Kevin out of juvenile hall after he is arrested on very serious charges.

"Workman is a genuine talent, writing short, declarative sentences that move that narrative forward with assurance and a page-turning tempo. Myers, of course, is a master. . . . The respective voices and characters play off each other as successfully as a high-stakes soccer match." Booklist

Lockdown. Amistad 2010 247p $16.99; lib bdg $17.89

Grades: 8 9 10 11 12 **Fic**

1. Old age -- Fiction 2. Friendship -- Fiction 3. African Americans -- Fiction 4. Juvenile delinquency -- Fiction

ISBN 978-0-06-121480-6; 0-06-121480-9; 978-0-06-121481-3 lib bdg; 0-06-121481-7 lib bdg

LC 2009-7287

Coretta Scott King Author Award honor book, 2011

Teenage Reese, serving time at a juvenile detention facility, gets a lesson in making it through hard times from an unlikely friend with a harrowing past.

"Reese's first-person narration rings with authenticity. . . . Myers' storytelling skills ensure that the messages he offers are never heavy-handed." Booklist

★ **Monster**; illustrations by Christopher Myers. HarperCollins Pubs. 1999 281p il $14.95; lib bdg $14.89; pa $8.99

Grades: 7 8 9 10 **Fic**

1. Trials -- Fiction 2. African Americans -- Fiction

ISBN 0-06-028077-8; 0-06-028078-6 lib bdg; 0-06-440731-4 pa

LC 98-40958

Michael L. Printz Award, 2000

While on trial as an accomplice to a murder, sixteen-year-old Steve Harmon records his experiences in prison and in the courtroom in the form of a film script as he tries to come to terms with the course his life has taken.

"Balancing courtroom drama and a sordid jailhouse setting with flashbacks to the crime, Myers adeptly allows each character to speak for him or herself, leaving readers to judge for themselves the truthfulness of the defendants, witnesses, lawyers, and, most compellingly, Steve himself." Horn Book Guide

Oh, Snap! by Walter Dean Myers. Scholastic 2013 128 p. (hardcover) $17.99

Grades: 6 7 8 9 **Fic**

1. Theft 2. Journalists

ISBN 0439916291; 9780439916295

This is the fourth book in Walter Dean Myers's Cruisers series. Here, the "four budding urban journalists are psyched that their underground publication, 'The Cruiser,' was named the third-best school newspaper in the city, an honor that doesn't sit well with the official school newspaper, which ups its game. This pushes narrator Zander to hastily get involved with the case of Phat Tony, a wannabe rapper classmate who may be involved in a robbery." (Booklist)

★ **Riot**. Egmont 2009 164p $16.99; lib bdg $19.99; pa $8.99

Grades: 7 8 9 10 11 12 **Fic**

1. Riots -- Fiction 2. Race relations -- Fiction 3. Irish Americans -- Fiction 4. African Americans -- Fiction 5. Racially mixed people -- Fiction

ISBN 978-1-60684-000-9; 1-60684-000-2; 978-1-60684-042-9 lib bdg; 1-60684-042-8 lib bdg; 978-1-60684-209-6 pa; 1-60684-209-9 pa

LC 2009-14638

In 1863, fifteen-year-old Claire, the daughter of an Irish mother and a black father, faces ugly truths and great danger when Irish immigrants, enraged by the Civil War and a federal draft, lash out against blacks and wealthy "swells" of New York City.

"In this fast, dramatic novel told in screenplay format, Myers takes on a controversial historical conflict that is seldom written about. . . . There are no easy resolutions, idealized characters, or stereotypes, and the conflicts are unforgettable." Booklist

Scorpions. Harper & Row 1988 216p $16.99; lib bdg $16.89; pa $5.99

Grades: 6 7 8 9 **Fic**

1. African Americans -- Fiction 2. Juvenile delinquency -- Fiction

ISBN 0-06-024364-3; 0-06-024365-1 lib bdg; 0-06-447066-0 pa

LC 85-45815

A Newbery Medal honor book, 1989

Set in Harlem, this "story presents a brutally honest picture of the tragic influence of gang membership and pressures on a young black adolescent. Jamal Hicks, age twelve, reluctantly follows the orders of his older brother, now serving time in prison for robbery, and takes his place as leader of the Scorpions. When Jamal's leadership is challenged, disaster follows and Jamal learns some tragic lessons about friendship and owning a gun." Child Book Rev Serv

★ **Slam!** Scholastic Press 1996 266p hardcover o.p. pa $5.99

Grades: 7 8 9 10 **Fic**

1. School stories 2. Basketball -- Fiction 3. African Americans -- Fiction

ISBN 0-590-48667-5; 0-590-48668-3 pa

LC 95-46647

Coretta Scott King Award for text

Seventeen-year-old "Slam" Harris is counting on his noteworthy basketball talents to get him out of the inner city and give him a chance to succeed in life, but his coach sees things differently

Myers "descriptions of Slam on the court . . . use crisp details, not flowery language, to achieve their muscular poetry, and Myers is equally vivid in relating the torment Slam feels as he stares at a page of indecipherable algebra formulas. . . . [This is an] admirably realistic coming-of-age novel." Booklist

A **star** is born; Walter Dean Myers. Scholastic 2012 176 p. (Cruisers) (ebook) $17.99; (hardcover) $17.99

Grades: 6 7 8 9 **Fic**

1. School stories 2. Autism -- Fiction 3. Siblings -- Fiction 4. Gifted children -- Fiction 5. Theater -- Fiction 6. Middle schools -- Fiction 7. African Americans -- Fiction 8. Brothers and sisters -- Fiction 9. Harlem (New York, N.Y.) -- Fiction

ISBN 9780545512688; 9780439916288

LC 2011030333

This book is the third in the Cruisers series. "For 14-year-old LaShonda Powell, real life is a lot tougher than solving for x and y in algebra class. She's been offered a full scholarship to the Virginia Woolf Society Program for Young Ladies, thanks to her costume designs for the recent class play, and if she completes the program, she'll qualify for future college scholarships. The problem is that LaShonda lives in a group home with her autistic brother, Chris, and the two are inseparable." (Kirkus)

Street love. Amistad/Harper Tempest 2006 134p $15.99; lib bdg $16.89

Grades: 8 9 10 11 12 **Fic**

1. Novels in verse 2. Love -- Fiction 3. African Americans -- Fiction

ISBN 978-0-06-028079-6; 0-06-028079-4; 978-0-06-028080-2 lib bdg; 0-06-028080-8 lib bdg

LC 2006-02457

This story told in free verse is set against a background of street gangs and poverty in Harlem in which seventeen-year-old African American Damien takes a bold step to ensure that he and his new love will not be separated.

"The realistic drama on the street and at home tells a gripping story." Booklist

★ **Sunrise** over Fallujah. Scholastic Press 2008 290p $17.99

Grades: 8 9 10 11 12 **Fic**

1. Iraq War, 2003- -- Fiction 2. African Americans --

Fiction
ISBN 978-0-439-91624-0; 0-439-91624-0
LC 2007-25444

"Instead of heading to college as his father wishes, Robin leaves Harlem and joins the army to stand up for his country after 9/11. While stationed in Iraq with a war looming that he hopes will be averted, he begins writing letters home to his parents and to his Uncle Richie. . . . Myers brilliantly freeze-frames the opening months of the current Iraq War by realistically capturing its pivotal moments in 2003 and creating a vivid setting. Memorable characters share instances of wry levity that balance the story without deflecting its serious tone." SLJ

Myracle, Lauren, 1969-

★ **Bliss.** Amulet Books 2008 444p $16.95
Grades: 9 10 11 12 **Fic**
1. Horror fiction 2. School stories 3. Occultism -- Fiction 4. Atlanta (Ga.) -- Fiction
ISBN 978-0-8109-7071-7; 0-8109-7071-6
LC 2007-50036

Having grown up in a California commune, Bliss sees her aloof grandmother's Atlanta world as a foreign country, but she is determined to be nice as a freshman at an elite high school, which makes her the perfect target for Sandy, a girl obsessed with the occult.

"Catering to teens with a taste for horror, this carefully plotted occult thriller set in 1969-1970 combines genre staples with creepy period particulars." Publ Wkly

The **infinite** moment of us; by Lauren Myracle. Amulet Books 2013 336 p. (hardback) $17.95
Grades: 9 10 11 12 **Fic**
1. Love stories 2. Foster children -- Fiction 3. Love -- Fiction 4. Atlanta (Ga.) -- Fiction 5. Family life -- Georgia -- Fiction 6. Dating (Social customs) -- Fiction 7. Assertiveness (Psychology) -- Fiction
ISBN 1419707930; 9781419707933
LC 2013017135

This book is a love story between two high school graduates. "Poised and accomplished, Wren has always done what her parents have expected of her, while Charlie is a foster child, self-conscious about his often unpleasant upbringing, but fiercely protective of his current family." The story is an "account of two young people whose insecurities and personal histories weigh on the romance they work to build with each other." (Publishers Weekly)

Peace, love, and baby ducks. Dutton Children's Books 2009 292p $16.99; pa $8.99
Grades: 8 9 10 11 12 **Fic**
1. Sisters -- Fiction 2. Atlanta (Ga.) -- Fiction
ISBN 978-0-525-47743-3; 0-525-47743-8; 978-0-14-241527-6 pa; 0-14-241527-8 pa
LC 2008-34221

Fifteen-year-old Carly's summer volunteer experience makes her feel more real than her life of privilege in Atlanta ever did, but her younger sister starts high school pretending to be what she is not, and both find their relationships suffering.

"Myracle empathetically explores issues of socioeconomic class, sibling rivalry, and parental influence in a story that is deeper and more nuanced than the title and cutesy cover." Booklist

Shine. Amulet Books 2011 359p $16.95
Grades: 10 11 12 **Fic**
1. Friendship -- Fiction 2. Hate crimes -- Fiction 3. Homosexuality -- Fiction 4. North Carolina -- Fiction
ISBN 0-8109-8417-2; 978-0-8109-8417-2
LC 2010-45017

When her best friend falls victim to a vicious hate crime, sixteen-year-old Cat sets out to discover the culprits in her small North Carolina town.

"Readers will find themselves thinking about Cat's complicated rural community long after the mystery has been solved." Publ Wkly

ttyl Harry N Abrams 2014 182p $8.95
Grades 7 8 9 10 11 12 **Fic**
1. Friendship -- Fiction 2. Interpersonal relations -- Fiction 3. High Schools -- Fiction

"It's time for a new generation of readers to discover the phenomenally bestselling and beloved series, told entirely in messages and texts. With a fresh look and updated cultural references, the notorious list-topping series is ready for the iPhone generation. First published in 2004 (holy moly!), ttyl and its sequels follow the ups and downs of high school for the winsome threesome, three very different but very close friends: wild Maddie (mad maddie), bubbly Angela (SnowAngel), and reserved Zoe (zoegirl)..." (Publisher's Note)

"Told entirely in instant messages, this modern epistolary tale prompts both tears and LOL (laughing out loud). Best buds SnowAngel (Angela), zoegirl (Zoe), and mad maddie (Maddie) IM with one another constantly when not in school. Tenth grade is tough, with obnoxious trendy classmates, unfair parents, and sex. Friends can help each other get through the year, but only if they manage to stay together...But best friends are always there for each other, and a series of emergencies pushes them further apart and then brings them back together, closer than ever." Kirkus

Other titles in the series are:
ttfn (2014)
l8r, g8r (2014)
yolo (2014).

Na, An

★ A **step** from heaven. Front St. 2000 156p $15.95
Grades: 7 8 9 10 **Fic**
1. Family life -- Fiction 2. Korean Americans -- Fiction
ISBN 1-88691-058-8
LC 00-41083

Michael L. Printz Award, 2002

A young Korean girl and her family find it difficult to learn English and adjust to life in America

"This isn't a quick read, especially at the beginning when the child is trying to decipher American words and customs, but the coming-of-age drama will grab teens and make them think of their own conflicts between home and outside. As in the best writing, the particulars make the story universal." Booklist

★ **Wait** for me. Putnam 2006 169p hardcover o.p. pa $7.99
Grades: 8 9 10 11 12 **Fic**
1. Deaf -- Fiction 2. Sisters -- Fiction 3. Korean Americans -- Fiction 4. Mother-daughter relationship -- Fiction
ISBN 0-399-24275-9; 0-14-240918-9 pa
LC 2005-30931

As her senior year in high school approaches, Mina yearns to find her own path in life but working at the family business, taking care of her little sister, and dealing with her mother's impossible expectations are as stifling as the southern California heat, until she falls in love with a man who offers a way out.

"This is a well-crafted tale, sensitively told. . . . The mother-daughter conflict will resonate with teens of any culture who have wrestled parents for the right to choose their own paths." Bull Cent Child Books

Nader, Elisa

Escape from Eden; Elisa Nader. Adams Media Corp 2013 272 p. $17.95
Grades: 9 10 11 12 **Fic**
1. Cults -- Fiction 2. Escapes -- Fiction 3. Christian fundamentalism -- Fiction
ISBN 1440563926; 9781440563928

"At 16, Mia is disenchanted with Edenton, the religious cult compound in the South American jungle where she has lived for six years. She learns to hide her disloyal thoughts from the Reverend and his potential spies, but it is difficult to avoid Edenton's subtle influence on her mind. Only when Mia is called to the community's "Prayer Circle"—actually a forced prostitution scheme perpetrated by the so-called spiritual leader—does she grasp the truth about their commune...The brutal, horrific climactic scene is far less credible as those building up to it. Still, many readers will find Mia's first-person narrative a riveting read, from the slow burn of her growing sexual awareness to the many fast-paced action scenes." (Booklist)

Nadin, Joanna

Wonderland. Candlewick Press 2011 208p $16.99
Grades: 9 10 11 12 **Fic**
1. Friendship -- Fiction 2. Bereavement -- Fiction 3. Great Britain -- Fiction 4. Conduct of life -- Fiction 5. Father-daughter relationship -- Fiction
ISBN 978-0-7636-4846-6; 0-7636-4846-9
LC 2010-38715

Sixteen-year-old Jude hopes to finally become who she wants to be, away from tiny Churchtown and the father who cannot get over her mother's death, by joining a prestigious drama program in London until Stella, her wild childhood friend, returns and causes Jude to wonder if she really wants to be the center of attention, after all.

"This is more of a psychological thriller than a book about bad girls. Once they reach this surprising disclosure, teens will think about the book differently and maybe even read it again." SLJ

Nadol, Jen

The **mark**. Bloomsbury 2010 228p $16.99
Grades: 9 10 11 12 **Fic**
1. Death -- Fiction 2. Kansas -- Fiction 3. Orphans -- Fiction 4. Clairvoyance -- Fiction 5. Fate and fatalism -- Fiction
ISBN 978-1-59990-431-3; 1-59990-431-4
LC 2009-16974

While in Kansas living with an aunt she never knew existed and taking a course in philosophy, sixteen-year-old Cass struggles to learn what, if anything, she should do with her ability to see people marked to die within a day's time.

"Nadol's story is more than a modern take on the Cassandra story of Greek myth, and the author uses her protagonist's moral torment (and a philosophy course she takes) to touch on schools of philosophical thought, from Aristotle to Plato. As in life, there are no tidy endings, but the engrossing narration and realistic characters create a deep, lingering story." Publ Wkly

Followed by The vision (2011)

The **vision**. Bloomsbury Children's Books 2011 232p $16.99
Grades: 9 10 11 12 **Fic**
1. Death -- Fiction 2. Orphans -- Fiction 3. Illinois -- Fiction 4. Clairvoyance -- Fiction 5. Fate and fatalism -- Fiction 6. Undertakers and undertaking -- Fiction
ISBN 978-1-59990-597-6
LC 2011004927

Sequel to The mark (2010)

Seventeen-year-old Cassie, now working in a funeral home on the outskirts of Chicago, continues to try to learn about death and her ability to identify people who will soon die, but her efforts to get help from others like herself only prove that she is on her own.

"For those willing to ponder difficult questions and appreciate the opportunity to come to their own conclusions, Cassie's visions will resonate long after the last page is turned." Kirkus

Naidoo, Beverley

★ **Burn** my heart. HarperCollins 2009 209p $15.99; lib bdg $16.89
Grades: 7 8 9 10 11 12 **Fic**
1. Kenya -- Fiction 2. Friendship -- Fiction 3. Race relations -- Fiction
ISBN 978-0-06-143297-2; 0-06-143297-0; 978-0-06-143298-9 lib bdg; 0-06-143298-9 lib bdg
LC 2008-928322

First published 2007 in the United Kingdom

This "is an interesting story of which few people will be aware but might wish to know more. This solid novel would be a good multicultural addition to a teen collection." Voice Youth Advocates

and sisters

Namioka, Lensey

Mismatch; a novel. Delacorte Press 2006 217p $15.95; lib bdg $17.99
Grades: 7 8 9 10 **Fic**
1. Prejudices -- Fiction 2. Chinese Americans -- Fiction 3. Japanese Americans -- Fiction 4. Dating (Social customs) -- Fiction
ISBN 0-385-73183-3; 0-385-90220-4 lib bdg

Their families clash when Andy, a Japanese-American teenaged boy, starts dating Sue, a Chinese-American teenaged girl.

"A story that is current, relevant, and upbeat." SLJ

★ An **ocean** apart, a world away. Delacorte Press 2002 197p hardcover o.p. pa $5.50

Grades: 5 6 7 8 **Fic**

1. Chinese -- United States -- Fiction

ISBN 0-385-73002-0; 0-440-22973-1 pa

LC 2002-73550

Despite the odds facing her decision to become a doctor in 1920's Nanking, China, teenaged Yanyan leaves her family to study at Cornell University where, along with hard work, she finds prejudice and loneliness as well as friendship and a new sense of accomplishment

"Without heavy messages, Namioka explores what it means to be independent." Booklist

Nance, Andrew

Daemon Hall; [by] Andrew Nance; with illustrations by Coleman Polhemus. Henry Holt 2007 259p $16.95

Grades: 7 8 9 10 **Fic**

1. Horror fiction 2. Authorship -- Fiction

ISBN 978-0-8050-8171-8; 0-8050-8171-2

LC 2006-31044

Famous horror story writer R. U. Tremblin comes to the town of Maplewood to hold a short story writing contest, offering the five finalists the chance to spend what turns out to be a terrifying—and deadly—night with him in a haunted house.

"Readers looking for creepy chills and thrills will find plenty of satisfaction in this fast-paced book." Booklist

Return to Daemon Hall: evil roots; with illustrations by Coleman Polhemus. Henry Holt 2011 240p il $16.99

Grades: 7 8 9 10 **Fic**

1. Horror fiction 2. Authors -- Fiction 3. Contests -- Fiction 4. Authorship -- Fiction 5. Storytelling -- Fiction

ISBN 978-0-8050-8748-2; 0-8050-8748-6

LC 2010048609

Sequel to: Daemon Hall (2007)

Wade and Demarius go to author Ian Tremblin's home as judges of the second writing contest but soon are mysteriously transported to Daemon Hall, where they and the three finalists must tell—and act out—the stories each has written.

"Polhemus' stark artwork builds the mood, with heavy lines and crosshatching complementing the campfire nature of the tales." Kirkus

Nanji, Shenaaz

Child of dandelions. Front Street 2008 214p $17.95

Grades: 7 8 9 10 11 12 **Fic**

1. Generals 2. Presidents 3. Uganda -- Fiction 4. Family life -- Fiction 5. East Indians -- Fiction

ISBN 978-1-93242-593-2; 1-93242-593-4

LC 2007-31576

In Uganda in 1972, fifteen-year-old Sabine and her family, wealthy citizens of Indian descent, try to preserve their normal life during the ninety days allowed by President Idi Amin for all foreign Indians to leave the country, while soldiers and others terrorize them and people disappear.

"This is an absorbing story rich with historical detail and human dynamics." Bull Cent Child Books

Napoli, Donna Jo

Alligator bayou. Wendy Lamb Books 2009 280p $16.99; lib bdg $19.99

Grades: 6 7 8 9 10 **Fic**

1. Uncles -- Fiction 2. Prejudices -- Fiction 3. Country life -- Fiction 4. Italian Americans -- Fiction

ISBN 978-0-385-74654-0; 0-385-74654-7; 978-0-385-90891-7 lib bdg; 0-385-90891-1 lib bdg

LC 2008-14504

Fourteen-year-old Calogero Scalise and his Sicilian uncles and cousin live in small-town Louisiana in 1898, when Jim Crow laws rule and anti-immigration sentiment is strong, so despite his attempts to be polite and to follow American customs, disaster dogs his family at every turn.

"Napoli's skillful pacing and fascinating detail combine in a gripping story that sheds cold, new light on Southern history and on the nature of racial prejudice." Booklist

Beast. Atheneum Bks. for Young Readers 2000 260p hardcover o.p. pa $8

Grades: 7 8 9 10 **Fic**

1. Fairy tales 2. Iran -- Fiction

ISBN 0-689-83589-2; 0-689-87005-1 pa

LC 99-89923

"The reader is immersed in the imagery and spirituality of ancient Persia. . . . Although Napoli uses Farsi (Persian) and Arabic words in the text (there is a glossary), this only adds to the texture and richness of her remarkable piece of writing." Book Rep

★ **Bound**. Atheneum Books for Young Readers 2004 186p hardcover o.p. pa $5.99

Grades: 8 9 10 11 12 **Fic**

1. China -- Fiction 2. Sex role -- Fiction

ISBN 0-689-86175-3; 0-689-86178-8 pa

LC 2004-365

In a novel based on Chinese Cinderella tales, fourteen-year-old stepchild Xing-Xing endures a life of neglect and servitude, as her stepmother cruelly mutilates her own child's feet so that she alone might marry well

The author "fleshes out and enriches the story with well-rounded characters and with accurate information about a specific time and place in Chinese history; the result is a dramatic and masterful retelling." SLJ

The **great** god Pan. Wendy Lamb Bks. 2003 149p $15.95; lib bdg $17.99

Grades: 7 8 9 10 **Fic**

1. Pan (Greek deity) -- Fiction 2. Classical mythology -- Fiction

ISBN 0-385-32777-3; 0-385-90120-8 lib bdg

LC 2002-13139

A retelling of the Greek myths about Pan, both goat and god, whose reed flute frolicking leads him to a meeting with

Iphigenia, a human raised as the daughter of King Agamemnon and Queen Clytemnestra

"Filling in gaps that appear in other myths about Pan and Iphigenia, Napoli creates a novel filled with breathtaking language about nature, music, and desire. Teen readers will swoon." Booklist

Hush; an Irish princess' tale. Atheneum Books for Young Readers 2007 308p $16.99

Grades: 8 9 10 11 12 **Fic**

1. Ireland -- Fiction 2. Slavery -- Fiction 3. Princesses -- Fiction 4. Middle Ages -- Fiction

ISBN 978-0-689-86176-5; 0-689-86176-1

LC 2007-2676

Fifteen-year-old Melkorka, an Irish princess, is kidnapped by Russian slave traders and not only learns how to survive but to challenge some of the brutality of her captors, who are fascinated by her apparent muteness and the possibility that she is enchanted.

This is a "powerful survival story. . . . Napoli does not shy from detailing practices that will make readers wince . . . and the Russian crew repeatedly gang-rapes an older captive. . . . The tension over Mel's hopes for escape paces this story like a thriller." Publ Wkly

The **magic** circle. Dutton Children's Bks. 1993 118p hardcover o.p. pa $4.99

Grades: 9 10 11 12 **Fic**

1. Fairy tales 2. Witchcraft -- Fiction

ISBN 0-525-45127-7; 0-14-037439-6 pa

LC 92-27008

After learning sorcery to become a healer, a good-hearted woman is turned into a witch by evil spirits and she fights their power until her encounter with Hansel and Gretel years later

"The strength of Napoli's writing and the clarity of her vision make this story fresh and absorbing. A brilliantly conceived and beautifully executed novel that is sure to be appreciated by thoughtful readers." SLJ

The **smile**. Dutton Children's Books 2008 260p $17.99

Grades: 7 8 9 10 **Fic**

1. Artists -- Fiction 2. Renaissance -- Fiction

ISBN 978-0-525-47999-4; 0-525-47999-6

LC 2007-48522

In Renaissance Italy, Elisabetta longs for romance, and when Leonardo da Vinci introduces her to Guiliano de Medici, whose family rules Florence but is about to be deposed, she has no inkling of the romance—and sorrow—that will ensue.

"Napoli skillfully draws readers into the vibrant settings . . . with tangible, sensory details that enliven the novel's intriguing references to history and art. Elisabetta's strength and individuality . . . will captivate readers." Booklist

Storm; Donna Jo Napoli. Simon & Schuster. 2014 350p $17.99

Grades: 8 9 10 11 12 **Fic**

1. Animals — Fiction; 2. Floods — Fiction; 3. Noah's ark — Fiction; 4. Survival after airplane accidents, shipwrecks, etc. — Fiction

ISBN: 1481403028; 9781481403023

LC 2013026808

National Jewish Book Award: Children's and Young Adult (2014)

"A Paula Wiseman book."

This young adult novel, by Donna Jo Napoli, is a re-imagining of the Noah flood myth. "After days of downpour, her family lost, Sebah . . . is tempted just to die in the flames rather than succumb to a slow, watery death. Instead, she and her companion, a boy named Aban, build a raft. What they find on the stormy seas is beyond imagining: a gigantic ark. But Sebah does not know what she'll find on board, and Aban is too weak to leave their raft." (Publisher's note)

"Exhausted and grief-stricken, Sebah finds herself in a cage with a pair of bonobos, with whom she soon bonds. The characters that Napoli creates to flesh out her retelling of the classic story add both veracity and depth.." Horn Book

The **wager**. Henry Holt 2010 262p il $16.99

Grades: 8 9 10 11 12 **Fic**

1. Fairy tales 2. Devil -- Fiction

ISBN 978-0-8050-8781-9; 0-8050-8781-8

LC 2009-23436

Having lost everything in a tidal wave in 1169 Sicily, nineteen-year-old Don Giovanni makes a simple-sounding wager with a stranger he recognizes as the devil but, while desperate enough to surrender his pride and good looks for three years, he is not willing to give up his soul.

"Evocative of Hermann Hesse's Siddhartha, this marvelous story is well told, and the rich, sophisticated language will grip skilled readers." SLJ

Naslund, Sena Jeter

Four spirits; a novel. Morrow 2003 524p hardcover o.p. pa $14.95

Grades: 9 10 11 12 **Fic**

1. Race relations -- Fiction 2. Birmingham (Ala.) -- Fiction

ISBN 0-06-621238-3; 0-06-093669-X pa

LC 2003-51170

"The book's last act, involving the murder of four protesters at a sit-in, is violent and shocking and leads to one of the few sermons in contemporary literature that I can recall as vital and moving. . . . Naslund brings a measure of dignity and moral complexity to her portrayal of a city that came to be known as 'Bombingham.'" N Y Times Book Rev

Nayeri, Daniel

Another Faust; [by] Daniel & Dina Nayeri. Candlewick Press 2009 387p $16.99

Grades: 9 10 11 12 **Fic**

1. School stories 2. Devil -- Fiction 3. Supernatural -- Fiction 4. New York (N.Y.) -- Fiction

ISBN 978-0-7636-3707-1; 0-7636-3707-6

LC 2008-940873

Years after vanishing, five teens reappear with a strange governess, and when they enter New York City's most prestigious high school, they soar to suspicious heights with the help of their benefactor's extraordinary "gifts."

"The writing is clever and stylish . . . It's an absorbing, imaginative read, with a tense climax." Publ Wkly

Followed by Another Pan (2010)

Another Pan; [by] Daniel & Dina Nayeri. Candlewick Press 2010 393p $16.99
Grades: 9 10 11 12 **Fic**

1. Fantasy fiction 2. Peter Pan (Fictional character)
ISBN 978-0-7636-3712-5

LC 2010-6606

Companion volume to Another Faust (2009)

While attending an elite prep school where their father is a professor, Wendy and John Darling discover a book which opens the door to other worlds, to Egyptian myths long thought impossible, and to the home of an age-old darkness.

"Teens who like their fantasy layered and with multifaceted characters will enjoy this thought-provoking read." SLJ

Naylor, Phyllis Reynolds

Alice in April. Atheneum Pubs. 1993 164p hardcover o.p. pa $5.99
Grades: 5 6 7 8 **Fic**

1. School stories 2. Family life -- Fiction
ISBN 0-689-31805-7; 978-1-442-42757-0 pa; 1-442-42757-4 pa

LC 92-17016

While trying to survive seventh grade, Alice discovers that turning thirteen will make her the Woman of the House at home, so she starts a campaign to get more appreciated for taking care of her father and older brother

"Deftly written dialogue and an empathetic tone neatly balance substantial themes with plain good fun." Publ Wkly

Alice in rapture, sort of. Atheneum Pubs. 1989 166p hardcover o.p. pa $5.99
Grades: 5 6 7 8 **Fic**

1. Family life -- Fiction
ISBN 0-689-31466-3; 1-442-42362-5 pa

LC 88-8174

The summer before she enters the seventh grade becomes the summer of Alice's first boyfriend, and she discovers that love is about the most mixed-up thing that can possibly happen to you, especially since she has no mother to go to for advice

"A book that is wise, perceptive, and hilarious." SLJ

Faith, hope, and Ivy June. Delacorte Press 2009 280p $16.99; lib bdg $19.99
Grades: 5 6 7 8 **Fic**

1. School stories 2. Young adult literature -- Works
ISBN 978-0-385-73615-2; 0-385-73615-0; 978-0-385-90588-6 lib bdg; 0-385-90588-2 lib bdg

LC 2008-19625

During a student exchange program, seventh-graders Ivy June and Catherine share their lives, homes, and communities, and find that although their lifestyles are total opposites they have a lot in common.

"This finely crafted novel . . . depicts a deep friendship growing slowly through understanding. As both girls wait out tragedies at the book's end, they cling to hope—and each other—in a thoroughly real and unaffected way. Naylor depicts Appalachia with sympathetic realism." Kirkus

Intensely Alice. Atheneum Books for Young Readers 2009 269p $16.99; pa $6.99
Grades: 7 8 9 10 **Fic**

1. Summer -- Fiction 2. Maryland -- Fiction
ISBN 978-1-4169-7551-9; 1-4169-7551-9; 978-1-4169-7554-0 pa; 1-4169-7554-3 pa

LC 2008-49047

During the summer between her junior and senior years of high school, Maryland teenager Alice McKinley volunteers at a local soup kitchen, tries to do "something wild" without getting arrested, and wonders if her trip to Chicago to visit boyfriend Patrick will result in a sleepover.

"As candid, funny, and touching as the rest of the series." Booklist

Incredibly Alice. Atheneum Books for Young Readers 2011 278p $16.99
Grades: 7 8 9 10 **Fic**

1. School stories 2. Theater -- Fiction 3. Family life -- Fiction 4. Young adult literature -- Works 5. Dating (Social customs) -- Fiction
ISBN 978-1-4169-7553-3; 1-4169-7553-5

LC 2010036982

Maryland teenager Alice McKinley spends her last semester of high school performing in the school play, working on the student paper, worrying about being away from her boyfriend, who will be studying in Spain, and anticipating her future in college.

"Realistic and satisfying, Alice and friends' bittersweet senior year's ending and their preparations for adulthood's exciting and intimidating world will resonate with any high school female." Voice Youth Advocates

★ **Reluctantly** Alice. Atheneum Pubs. 1991 182p $16; pa $4.99
Grades: 7 8 9 10 **Fic**

1. School stories 2. Family life -- Fiction 3. Young adult literature -- Works 4. Children's literature -- Works -- Grades two through six
ISBN 0-689-31681-X; 0-689-81688-X pa

LC 90-37956

Alice experiences the joys and embarrassments of seventh grade while advising her father and older brother on their love lives

"Naylor combines laugh-out-loud scenes with moments of sudden gentleness. . . . The characters are complex, the dialogue is droll, the junior high world authentic." Booklist

Other titles about Alice are:
Achingly Alice (1998)
Alice alone (2001)
Alice in-between (1994)
Alice in lace (1996)
Alice in the know (2006)
Alice on her way (2005)
Alice on the outside (1999)
Alice the brave (1995)
All but Alice (1992)
Almost Alice (2008)
Intensely Alice (2009)
Dangerously Alice (2007)
The grooming of Alice (2000)
Including Alice (2004)

Outrageously Alice (1997)
Patiently Alice (2003)
Simply Alice (2002)

Neely, Cynthia

Unearthly; [by] Cynthia Hand. HarperTeen 2011 435p $17.99
Grades: 7 8 9 10 **Fic**

1. School stories 2. Angels -- Fiction 3. Moving -- Fiction 4. Wyoming -- Fiction 5. Supernatural -- Fiction
ISBN 978-0-06-199616-0; 0-06-199616-5
LC 2010-17849

Sixteen-year-old Clara Gardner's purpose as an angel-blood begins to manifest itself, forcing her family to pull up stakes and move to Jackson, Wyoming, where she learns that danger and heartbreak come with her powers.

"Hand avoids overt discussion of religion while telling an engaging and romantic tale with a solid backstory. Her characters deal realistically with the uncertainty of being on the cusp of maturity without wrapping themselves in angst." Publ Wkly

Neff, Henry H.

The **hound** of Rowan. Random House 2007 414p il (The tapestry) $17.99; lib bdg $20.99; pa $6.99
Grades: 6 7 8 9 **Fic**

1. School stories 2. Magic -- Fiction
ISBN 978-0-375-83894-1; 0-375-83894-5; 978-0-375-93894-8 lib bdg; 0-375-93894-4 lib bdg; 978-0-375-83895-8 pa; 0-375-83895-3 pa
LC 2006-20970

After glimpsing a hint of his destiny in a mysterious tapestry, twelve-year-old Max McDaniels becomes a student at Rowan Academy, where he trains in "mystics and combat" in preparation for war with an ancient enemy that has been kidnapping children like him.

"Max's intelligence and goodhearted nature give the story a solid emotional core even as the surprising twists and turns keep the pages turning." Voice Youth Advocates

Other titles in this series are:
The second siege (2008)
The fiend and the forge (2011)

Nelson, Blake

Destroy all cars. Scholastic Press 2009 218p $17.99
Grades: 7 8 9 10 **Fic**

1. School stories 2. Ecology -- Fiction 3. Social action -- Fiction
ISBN 978-0-545-10474-6; 0-545-10474-2
LC 2008-34850

Through assignments for English class, seventeen-year-old James Hoff rants against consumerism and his classmates' apathy, puzzles over his feelings for his ex-girlfriend, and expresses disdain for his emotionally-distant parents.

Nelson "offers an elegant and bittersweet story of a teenager who is finding his voice and trying to make meaning in a world he often finds hopeless." Publ Wkly

Recovery Road. Scholastic Press 2011 310p $17.99
Grades: 9 10 11 12 **Fic**

1. Alcoholism -- Fiction 2. Drug abuse -- Fiction 3. Drug addicts -- Rehabilitation -- Fiction
ISBN 978-0-545-10729-7; 0-545-10729-6
LC 2010-31288

"Madeline is sent away to Spring Meadows to help with a drinking and rage problem she has. It's a pretty intense place, but there is the weekly movie night in town--where Madeline meets Stewart, who's at another rehab place nearby. They fall for each other during a really crazy time in their lives. Madeline gets out and tries to get back on her feet, waiting for Stewart to join her. When he does, though, it's not the ideal recovery world Madeline dreamed of." (Publisher's note)

The author "gives a hard, honest appraisal of addiction, its often-fatal consequences, and the high probability of relapse. This is an important story that pulls no punches." Publ Wkly

Rock star, superstar; by Blake Nelson. Viking 2004 229p hardcover o.p. pa $6.99
Grades: 9 10 11 12 **Fic**

1. Musicians -- Fiction 2. Rock music -- Fiction
ISBN 0-670-05933-1; 0-14-240574-4 pa
LC 2003-27556

When Pete, a talented bass player, moves from playing in the school jazz band to playing in a popular rock group, he finds the experience exhilarating even as his new fame jeopardizes his relationship with girlfriend Margaret.

"A brilliant, tender, funny, and utterly believable novel about music and relationships. . . . Pete is one of the best male protagonists in recent YA fiction and the other characters are equally strong." SLJ

They came from below. Tor 2007 299p $17.95
Grades: 7 8 9 10 **Fic**

1. Beaches -- Fiction 2. Supernatural -- Fiction 3. Marine pollution -- Fiction
ISBN 978-0-7653-1423-9; 0-7653-1423-1
LC 2007-09542

While vacationing on Cape Cod, best friends Emily, age sixteen, and Reese, seventeen, meet Steve and Dave, who seem too good to be true, and whose presence turns out to be related to a dire threat of global pollution.

"Offering wittiness, suspense and ideologies borrowed from Eastern religions, Nelson reaches a new level of depth and creativity with this intriguing depiction of one very weird summer." Publ Wkly

Nelson, James

On the volcano. G.P. Putnam's Sons 2011 275p $16.99
Grades: 7 8 9 10 **Fic**

1. Violence -- Fiction 2. Volcanoes -- Fiction 3. Wilderness areas -- Fiction 4. Frontier and pioneer life -- Fiction
ISBN 978-0-399-25282-2; 0-399-25282-7
LC 2008-53557

In the 1870s, sixteen-year-old Katie has grown up in a remote cabin on the edge of a volcano with her father and their friend Lorraine, the only people she has ever seen, but, after eagerly anticipating it for so long, her first trip into a town ultimately brings tragedy into their lives.

"Nelson has created a moving tale of frontier life. Katie shows tremendous fighting spirit as she deal with the trials in her life. . . . [This] is perfect for historical fiction fans." Voice Youth Advocates

Nelson, Jandy

★ **I'll** give you the sun. Jandy Nelson. Dial Books for Young Readers. 2014 384p $17.99

Grades: 9 10 11 12 **Fic**

1. Artists — Fiction; 2. Death — Fiction; 3. Gays — Fiction; 4. Grief — Fiction; 5. Twins — Fiction; 6. California — Fiction; 7. Love stories

ISBN: 0803734964; 9780803734968

LC 2014001596

Michael L. Printz Award (2015)

Stonewall Honor Book: Children's & Young Adult Literature (2015)

In this novel by Jandy Nelson, "Jude and her twin brother, Noah, are incredibly close. At thirteen, isolated Noah draws constantly and is falling in love with the charismatic boy next door, while daredevil Jude cliff-dives and wears red-red lipstick and does the talking for both of them. But three years later, Jude and Noah are barely speaking. Something has happened to wreck the twins in different and dramatic ways." Publisher's note

"Nelson's prose is replete with moments of stunning emotional clarity, and her characters are as irresistible to the reader as they are to each other," Bulletin Center Child Books

★ The **sky** is everywhere. Dial Books 2010 275p il $17.99

Grades: 9 10 11 12 **Fic**

1. Sisters -- Fiction 2. Musicians -- Fiction 3. Bereavement -- Fiction

ISBN 978-0-8037-3495-1; 0-8037-3495-6

LC 2009-22809

In the months after her sister dies, seventeen-year-old Lennie falls into a love triangle and discovers the strength to follow her dream of becoming a musician.

"This is a heartfelt and appealing tale. Girls who gobble up romantic and/or weep-over fiction will undoubtedly flock to this realistic, sometimes funny, and heartbreaking story." SLJ

"Nelson's prose is replete with moments of stunning emotional clarity, and her characters are as irresistible to the reader as they are to each other," Bulletin Center Child Books

Nelson, R. A.

Breathe my name. Razorbill 2007 314p hardcover o.p. pa $8.99

Grades: 8 9 10 11 12 **Fic**

1. School stories 2. Homicide -- Fiction 3. Mentally ill -- Fiction 4. Mother-daughter relationship -- Fiction

ISBN 978-1-59514-094-4; 978-1-59514-186-6 pa

LC 2007-3272

Since her adoption, seventeen-year-old Frances has lived a quiet suburban life, but soon after she begins falling for the new boy at school, she receives a summons from her birth mother, who has just been released after serving eleven years for smothering Frances's younger sisters.

"With major twists and turns in the last 50 pages, this book will keep readers riveted until the very end." SLJ

Days of Little Texas. Alfred A. Knopf 2009 388p $16.99; lib bdg $19.99

Grades: 8 9 10 11 12 **Fic**

1. Ghost stories 2. Slavery -- Fiction 3. Supernatural -- Fiction 4. Good and evil -- Fiction 5. Christian life -- Fiction 6. Evangelistic work -- Fiction

ISBN 978-0-375-85593-1; 0-375-85593-9; 978-0-375-95593-8 lib bdg; 0-375-95593-3 lib bdg

LC 2008-33855

Sixteen-year-old Ronald Earl King, who has been a charismatic evangelist since he was ten years old, is about to preach at a huge revival meeting on the grounds of an old plantation, where, with confusing help from the ghost of a girl he could not heal, he becomes engaged in an epic battle between good and evil.

"Chapters are brief, the pace is rapid, and the tension is high as Ronald wrestles with demons both temporal and spiritual to find his place in the world. An affecting and sharply written story." SLJ

Nelson, Vaunda Micheaux

No crystal stair; a documentary novel of the life and work of Lewis Michaux, Harlem bookseller. by Vaunda Micheaux Nelson; art work by R. Gregory Christie. Carolrhoda Lab 2012 188p. ill.

Grades: 6 7 8 9 10 11 12 **Fic**

1. Harlem (New York, N.Y.) 2. African American authors 3. Booksellers and bookselling 4. African Americans -- Books and reading 5. Bookstores -- New York (State) -- New York

ISBN 9780761361695

LC 2011021251

Coretta Scott King Author Honor Book (2013)

This "biographical novel presents the life and work of a man whose Harlem bookstore became an intellectual, literary haven for African Americans from 1939 until 1975. [The book proceeds t]hrough alternating voices of actual family members, acquaintances, journalists, and the subject himself, [Lewis] Michaux. . . . Influenced by the nationalism of Marcus Garvey and the intellect of Frederick Douglass, he believed that black people needed to educate themselves . . . [and h]e opened the National Memorial African Bookstore. . . . He accumulated works by black writers and talked to customers and passersby about cultural awareness and self-improvement. His bookstore attracted Harlem residents; civil-rights activists, including Malcolm X and Muhammad Ali; and political attention." (School Libr J)

Ness, Patrick, 1971-

The **Ask** and the Answer; a novel. Candlewick Press 2009 519p (Chaos walking) $18.99

Grades: 8 9 10 11 12 **Fic**

1. Science fiction 2. Telepathy -- Fiction 3. Space colonies -- Fiction 4. Social problems -- Fiction

ISBN 978-0-7636-4490-1; 0-7636-4490-0

LC 2009-7329

Sequel to: The knife of never letting go (2008)

Alternate chapters follow teenagers Todd and Viola, who become separated as the Mayor's oppressive new regime takes power in New Prentisstown, a space colony where residents can hear each other's thoughts.

"Provocative questions about gender bias, racism, the meaning of war and the price of peace are thoughtfully threaded throughout a breathless, often violent plot peopled with heartbreakingly real characters." Kirkus

Followed by: Monsters of men (2010)

★ The **knife** of never letting go. Candlewick Press 2008 479p (Chaos walking) $18.99

Grades: 8 9 10 11 12 **Fic**

1. Boys -- Fiction 2. Science fiction 3. Dystopian fiction 4. Psychics -- Fiction 5. Telepathy -- Fiction 6. Space colonies -- Fiction

ISBN 978-0-7636-3931-0; 0-7636-3931-1

LC 2007-52334

Pursued by power-hungry Prentiss and mad minister Aaron, young Todd and Viola set out across New World searching for answers about his colony's true past and seeking a way to warn the ship bringing hopeful settlers from Old World.

"This troubling, unforgettable opener to the Chaos Walking trilogy is a penetrating look at the ways in which we reveal ourselves to one another, and what it takes to be a man in a society gone horribly wrong." Booklist

Monsters of men. Candlewick Press 2010 603p (Chaos walking) $18.99; pa $9.99

Grades: 8 9 10 11 12 **Fic**

1. War stories 2. Science fiction 3. Telepathy -- Fiction 4. Space colonies -- Fiction 5. Social problems -- Fiction

ISBN 978-0-7636-4751-3; 0-7636-4751-9; 978-0-7636-5665-2 pa; 0-7636-5665-8 pa

Sequel to: The Ask and the Answer (2009)

As a world-ending war surges to life around them, Todd and Viola face monstrous decisions, questioning all they have ever known as they try to step back from the darkness and find the best way to achieve peace.

"The Chaos Walking trilogy comes to a powerful conclusion in this grueling but triumphant tale." Publ Wkly

★ A **monster** calls; a novel. Candlewick Press 2011 204p il $15.99

Grades: 6 7 8 9 10 **Fic**

1. School stories 2. Cancer -- Fiction 3. Monsters -- Fiction 4. Great Britain -- Fiction 5. Loss (Psychology) -- Fiction 6. Mother-son relationship -- Fiction

ISBN 978-0-7636-5559-4; 0-7636-5559-7

LC 2010040741

"Conor O'Malley is struggling with his mother's illness and terrorized by nightmares which seem to come to life. The monster who visits him tells Conor three allegorical stories, each time instructing Conor that he will have to tell his own truth in the fourth and final story. Conor's daily life and "truth" are even more haunting than the monster." (Library Media Connection)

This is a "profoundly moving, expertly crafted tale of unaccountable loss. . . . A singular masterpiece, exceptionally well-served by Kay's atmospheric and ominous illustrations." Publ Wkly

More than this; Patrick Ness. Candlewick Press 2013 480 p. $19.99

Grades: 9 10 11 12 **Fic**

1. Death -- Fiction 2. Dystopian fiction

ISBN 0763662585; 9780763662585

LC 2013943065

In this book, "teenage Seth is experiencing his own death in painful detail. In the next chapter, he wakes up physically weak, covered in bandages and strange wounds, and wonders if he is in Hell or the future or somewhere else entirely. . . . He is plagued by intense flashbacks of his life before he died. . . . Upon discovering two other young people . . . Seth begins to learn the Matrix-like truth about what has happened to the rest of humanity." (School Library Journal)

Neumeier, Rachel

The **City** in the Lake. Alfred A. Knopf 2008 304p $15.99; lib bdg $18.99

Grades: 8 9 10 11 12 **Fic**

1. Fantasy fiction 2. Magic -- Fiction

ISBN 978-0-375-84704-2; 0-375-84704-9; 978-0-375-94704-9 lib bdg; 0-375-94704-3 lib bdg

LC 2008-08941

Seventeen-year-old Timou, who is learning to be a mage, must save her mysterious, magical homeland, The Kingdom, from a powerful force that is trying to control it.

"Neumeier structures her story around archetypal fantasy elements. . . . It's the poetic, shimmering language and fascinating unfolding of worlds that elevates this engrossing story beyond its formula." Booklist

Newbery, Linda

At the firefly gate. David Fickling Books 2007 152p hardcover o.p. pa $6.50

Grades: 5 6 7 8 **Fic**

1. Supernatural -- Fiction 2. World War, 1939-1945 -- Fiction

ISBN 978-0-385-75113-1; 978-0-440-42188-7 pa

LC 2006-01796

After moving with his parents from London to Suffolk near a former World War II airfield , Henry sees the shadowy image of a man by the orchard gate and feels an unusual affinity with an eldery woman who lives next door

"This is a well-written book, with an old-fashioned tone, that emphasizes character and feelings over plot. It's for thoughtful readers who appreciate a book that lingers in their minds." SLJ

Flightsend. David Fickling Books 2010 241p $15.99; lib bdg $18.99

Grades: 7 8 9 10 **Fic**

1. Moving -- Fiction 2. Bereavement -- Fiction

ISBN 978-0-385-75203-9; 0-385-75203-2; 978-0-385-75205-3 lib bdg; 0-385-75205-9 lib bdg

First published 1999 in the United Kingdom

Just when her life seems to be falling apart, an English teen named Charlie gains a fresh perspective when she and her mother relocate to a rural village.

"The characters are wonderfully developed. The leisurely plot unfolds quietly, meandering through Charlie's life and endearing her to readers." SLJ

Newton, Robert

Runner. Alfred A. Knopf 2007 209p $15.99; lib bdg $18.99

Grades: 6 7 8 9 **Fic**

1. Poverty -- Fiction 2. Running -- Fiction 3. Criminals -- Fiction

ISBN 978-0-375-83744-9; 978-0-375-93744-6 lib bdg; 0-375-83744-2; 0-375-93744-7 lib bdg

LC 2006-29275

In Richmond, Australia, in 1919, fifteen-year-old Charlie Feehan becomes an errand boy for a notorious mobster, hoping that his ability to run will help him, his widowed mother, and his baby brother to escape poverty.

"Rich dialogue in Australian dialect creates a colorful picture of the historical urban setting, suspenseful plot, and warm characterizations." SLJ

Nichols, Janet

Messed up; [by] Janet Nichols Lynch. Holiday House 2009 250p $17.95

Grades: 7 8 9 10 **Fic**

1. School stories 2. California -- Fiction 3. Family life -- Fiction 4. Abandoned children -- Fiction 5. Hispanic Americans -- Fiction

ISBN 978-0-8234-2185-5; 0-8234-2185-6

LC 2008-22577

Fifteen-year-old RD is repeating the eighth grade, planning to have an easy year, but after his grandmother walks out her boyfriend is no longer able to care for him, which leaves RD to fend for himself while avoiding being caught.

"A memorable story of grit and survival, and helping hands along the way." Kirkus

Nicholson, William

Seeker. Harcourt 2006 413p (Noble warriors) $17; pa $7.95

Grades: 7 8 9 10 **Fic**

1. Fantasy fiction

ISBN 978-0-15-205768-8; 0-15-205768-4; 978-0-15-205866-1 pa; 0-15-205866-4 pa

LC 2005-17171

"Seeker, Morning Star, and Wildman are three teens who hope to join the Nomana, a society of noble warriors and worshippers of the All and Only (the god who makes all things). . . . Conjuring up a plan to prove their worth, this motley trio plays a key role in foiling the murderous plans of the royalty in a nearby town." Bull Cent Child Books

"The classic coming-of-age tale is combined with a rich setting of cold villains, strange powers, and disturbing warriors." Voice Youth Advocates

Other titles in this series are:

Jango (2007)

Noman (2008)

Nielsen, Susin

The **reluctant** journal of Henry K. Larsen; Susin Nielsen. Tundra Books of Northern New York 2012 243 p. (hardcover) $17.95

Grades: 7 8 9 10 11 12 **Fic**

1. Bullies 2. Grief 3. Diaries

ISBN 1770493727; 9781770493728

LC 2011938782

In this novel, by Susin Nielsen, "thirteen-year-old Henry's happy life abruptly ends when his older brother kills the boy who bullied him in school and then takes his own life. Henry refers to this tragedy as 'IT.' He moves to a new city . . . for a fresh start. To help him cope with IT, Henry's therapist recommends he keep a journal. Henry hates the suggestion but soon finds himself recording his thoughts and feelings constantly, even updating it multiple times per day." (Kirkus Reviews)

Nilsson, Per

★ **You** & you & you; translated by Tara Chace. Front Street 2005 301p $16.95

Grades: 9 10 11 12 **Fic**

1. Sweden -- Fiction 2. Friendship -- Fiction

ISBN 1-932425-19-5

LC 2004-30660

Original Swedish edition, 1998

Young Anon, who marches to the beat of a different drummer in galoshes to protect himself from radiation, touches the lives of all around him, resulting in disillusionment, loss, love, and more than a few surprises.

"Swedish magical realism comes alive in this mature, sometimes graphically sexual and violent, ultimately breathtaking and inspiring tale. . . . Many of the older YA readers to whom this book is directed will likely come away with a feeling of being somehow transformed or at least being given much to ponder." SLJ

Nix, Garth, 1963-

Clariel: the lost Abhorsen. Garth Nix. HarperCollins. 2014 400p $18.99

Grades: 7 8 9 10 **Fic**

1. Magic — Fiction; 2. Fantasy fiction

ISBN: 006156155X; 9780061561559

LC 2013047958

In this title, part of the author's Old Kingdom fantasy series, "Clariel is the daughter of one of the most notable families in the Old Kingdom, with blood relations to the Abhorsen and, most important, to the King. She dreams of living a simple life but discovers this is hard to achieve when a dangerous Free Magic creature is loose in the city, her parents want to marry her off to a killer, and there is a plot brewing against the old and withdrawn King Orrikan." (Publisher's note)

"Nix's intricate world building reveals more Old Kingdom history and its ever-shifting alliance between the political and magical. Themes of freedom and destiny underpin Clariel's harrowing, bittersweet story, and readers will delight in the telling." Booklist

A **confusion** of princes; by Garth Nix. HarperTeen 2012 337 p.

Grades: 8 9 10 11 12 **Fic**

1. Science fiction 2. Princes 3. Adventure fiction 4. Inheritance and succession -- Fiction 5. Princes --

Fiction 6. Adventure and adventurers -- Fiction
ISBN 9780060096946; 9780060096953
LC 2011042308

This book tells the story of "a vast empire of 10 million biologically and mechanically augmented princes," where prince "Khemri discovers that--assassination attempts and imperial interference aside--royal life isn't what he'd been led to believe. While on a secret mission, he meets Raine, a young woman who changes his perspective and Khemri begins trying to fulfill his true potential. Aurealis Award-winning author [Garth] Nix develops an empire . . . with an emphasis on house loyalty and political machinations." (Booklist)

Mister Monday; Keys to the kingdom, book one. Scholastic 2003 361p (Keys to the kingdom) $15.99; pa $5.99
Grades: 6 7 8 9 **Fic**
1. Fantasy fiction 2. Young adult literature -- Works
ISBN 0-439-70370-0; 0-439-55123-4 pa
LC 2004-540574

Arthur Penhaligon is supposed to die at a young age, but is saved by a key that is shaped like the minute hand of a clock. The key causes bizarre creatures to come from another realm, bringing with them a plague. A man named Mister Monday will stop at nothing to get the key back. Arthur goes to a mysterious house that only he can see, so that he can learn the truth about himself and the key

"The first in a seven part series for middle graders is every bit as exciting and suspenseful as the author's previous young adult novels." SLJ

Other titles in the Keys to the Kingdom series are:
Grim Tuesday (2004)
Drowned Wednesday (2005)
Sir Thursday (2006)
Lady Friday (2007)
Superior Saturday (2008)
Lord Sunday (2010)

★ **Sabriel.** HarperCollins Pubs. 1996 292p hardcover o.p. pa $7.99
Grades: 7 8 9 10 **Fic**
1. Fantasy fiction
ISBN 0-06-027322-4; 0-06-447183-7 pa
LC 96-1295

First published 1995 in Australia

Sabriel, daughter of the necromancer Abhorsen, must journey into the mysterious and magical Old Kingdom to rescue her father from the Land of the Dead.

"The final battle is gripping, and the bloody cost of combat is forcefully presented. The story is remarkable for the level of originality of the fantastic elements . . . and for the subtle presentation, which leaves readers to explore for themselves the complex structure and significance of the magic elements." Horn Book

Other titles in this series are:
Abhorsen (2003)
Across the wall (2005)
Clariel (2014)
Lirael, daughter of the Clayr (2001)

Shade's children. HarperCollins Pubs. 1997 310p $18.99; pa $6.99
Grades: 7 8 9 10 **Fic**
1. Science fiction
ISBN 0-06-027324-0; 0-06-447196-9 pa
LC 97-3841

In a savage postnuclear world, four young fugitives attempt to overthrow the bloodthirsty rule of the Overlords with the help of Shade, their mysterious mentor

"Grim, unusual, and fascinating." Horn Book

Nixon, Joan Lowery

Nightmare. Delacorte Press 2003 166p hardcover o.p. lib bdg $17.99; pa $5.99
Grades: 6 7 8 9 **Fic**
1. Mystery fiction 2. Camps -- Fiction 3. Homicide -- Fiction
ISBN 0-385-73026-8; 0-385-90151-8 lib bdg; 0-4402-3773-4 pa
LC 2003-43434

Emily is sent to a camp for underachievers where she discovers a murderer on the staff who might provide an explanation for her recurring nightmares

"Elements of suspense and mystery are cleverly integrated with the teen's problems resulting from what she witnessed as a child. Readers will once again fall under Nixon's spell as they enjoy this page-turner." SLJ

The **haunting.** Delacorte Press 1998 184p hardcover o.p. pa $5.50
Grades: 7 8 9 10 **Fic**
1. Ghost stories 2. Ghosts -- Fiction 3. Haunted houses -- Fiction
ISBN 0-385-32247-X; 0-440-22008-4 pa
LC 97-32658

When her mother inherits an old plantation house in the Louisiana countryside, fifteen-year-old Lia seeks to rid it of the evil spirit that haunts it

"This title has it all - a hint of romance, some really scary scenes, and a plucky heroine who successfully routs both outer and inner demons." Horn Book Guide

Noel, Alyson

Radiance. Square Fish 2010 183p pa $7.99
Grades: 5 6 7 8 **Fic**
1. Ghost stories 2. Dead -- Fiction 3. Future life -- Fiction
ISBN 978-0-312-62917-5; 0-312-62917-6
LC 2010015840

After crossing the bridge into the afterlife, a place called Here where the time is always Now, Riley's existence continues in much the same way as when she was alive until she is given the job of Soul Catcher and, together with her teacher Bodhi, returns to earth for her first assignment, a ghost called the Radiant Boy who has been haunting an English castle for centuries and resisted all previous attempts to get him across the bridge.

"Narrating in a contemporary voice with an honest and comfortable cadence, Riley is imperfect, but always likable. . . . In the midst of this wildly fanciful setting, Noël is able to capture with nail-on-the-head accuracy common worries and concerns of today's tweens." SLJ

Other titles in this series are:
Dreamland (2011)
Shimmer (2011)

Nolan, Han

Crazy. Harcourt 2010 348p $17
Grades: 7 8 9 10 **Fic**

1. School stories 2. Friendship -- Fiction 3. Bereavement -- Fiction 4. Mental illness -- Fiction 5. Father-son relationship -- Fiction
ISBN 978-0-15-205109-9; 0-15-205109-0
LC 2009-49969

Fifteen-year-old loner Jason struggles to hide father's declining mental condition after his mother's death, but when his father disappears he must confide in the other members of a therapy group he has been forced to join at school.

"Nolan leavens this haunting but hopeful story with spot-on humor and a well-developed cast of characters." Booklist

North, Pearl

The **boy** from Ilysies. Tor 2010 316p $17.99
Grades: 7 8 9 10 **Fic**

1. Fantasy fiction 2. Books and reading -- Fiction
ISBN 978-0-7653-2097-1; 0-7653-2097-5
LC 2010-36676

Sequel to Libyrinth (2009)

Cast out of the Libyrinth after being tricked into committing a crime, young Po may return only if he completes a dangerous mission to retrieve a legendary artifact that could either be the answer to all of the Libyrinth's problems, or could destroy the world.

"North has created that rare thing: a second book in a series that is stronger than the first." SLJ

Libyrinth. Tor Teen 2009 332p $17.95
Grades: 7 8 9 10 **Fic**

1. Fantasy fiction 2. Books and reading -- Fiction
ISBN 978-0-7653-2096-4; 0-7653-2096-7
LC 2009-1514

In a distant future where Libyrarians preserve and protect the ancient books that are housed in the fortress-like Libyrinth, Haly is imprisoned by Eradicants, who believe that the written word is evil, and she must try to mend the rift between the two groups before their war for knowledge destroys them all.

"Among this novel's pleasures are the many anonymous quotations scattered throughout, snatches of prose that Haly hears as she goes about her chores . . . all of which are carefully identified at the end. The complex moral issues posed by this thoughtful and exciting tale are just as fascinating." Publ Wkly

Followed by: The boy from Ilysies (2010)

North, Phoebe

Starglass; by Phoebe North. 1st ed. Simon & Schuster Books for Young Readers 2013 448 p. (hardcover) $17.99
Grades: 7 8 9 10 **Fic**

1. Jews -- Fiction 2. Underground movements -- Fiction 3. Interplanetary voyages -- Fiction 4. Science fiction 5. Insurgency -- Fiction 6. Fathers and daughters -- Fiction
ISBN 1442459530; 9781442459533; 9781442459557
LC 2012021171

In this book by Phoebe North, "[o]n a generation ship that left Earth 500 years ago, a teenager grapples with disillusionment and emotional isolation as her society nears the planet it intends to land on. Terra lives with her harsh, alcoholic father and awaits her adult job assignment . . . from the strict ruling Council." She "discovers a secret rebellion aboard the Asherah." (Kirkus Reviews)

Northrop, Michael

Gentlemen. Scholastic Press 2009 234p $16.99
Grades: 8 9 10 **Fic**

1. School stories 2. Crime -- Fiction 3. Guilt -- Fiction 4. Teachers -- Fiction 5. Missing persons -- Fiction
ISBN 978-0-545-09749-9; 0-545-09749-5
LC 2008-38971

When three teenaged boys suspect that their English teacher is responsible for their friend's disappearance, they must navigate a maze of assorted clues, fraying friendships, violence, and Dostoevsky's "Crime and Punishment" before learning the truth.

"The brutal narration, friendships put through the wringer and the sense of dread that permeates the novel will keep readers hooked through the violent climax and its aftermath." Publ Wkly

Trapped. Scholastic Press 2011 225p $17.99
Grades: 7 8 9 10 **Fic**

1. School stories 2. Blizzards -- Fiction
ISBN 978-0-545-21012-6; 0-545-21012-7
LC 2010-36595

Seven high school students are stranded at their New England high school during a week-long blizzard that shuts down the power and heat, freezes the pipes, and leaves them wondering if they will survive.

"Northrop is cooly brilliant in his setup, amassing the tension along with the snow, shrewdly observing the shifting social dynamics within the group." Bull Cent Child Books

Norville, Rod

Moonshine express; with a history of moonshine today and yesterday. Four Seasons Pub. 2003 xxix, 195p pa $13.95
Grades: 6 7 8 9 **Fic**

1. Moonshining -- Fiction
ISBN 1-89129-99-2

"Thirteen-year-old Rob McKinley's world is falling apart. His mother has died and his father is drinking heavily. Rob's barely coping with the support of his friend, Katie. They live on the edge of a north Florida swamp sprinkled with half-breed Seminole moon shiners. Rob and Katie are stunned when they stumble across respectable community citizens behind a local moonshine distribution ring." Publisher's note

"This is an edge-of-the-seat thriller." SLJ

Nowlin, Laura

If he had been with me; Laura Nowlin. Sourcebooks Fire 2013 336 p. (tp : alk. paper) $9.99

Grades: 9 10 11 12 **Fic**

1. Love stories 2. Friendship -- Fiction 3. Love -- Fiction

ISBN 1402277822; 9781402277825

LC 2012041338

In this book by Laura Nowlin, "in eighth grade, Autumn and Finny stop being friends due to an unexpected kiss. They drift apart and find new friends, but their friendship keeps asserting itself at parties, shared holiday gatherings and random encounters. In the summer after graduation, Autumn and Finny reconnect and are finally ready to be more than friends. But on August 8, everything changes, and Autumn has to rely on all her strength to move on." (Kirkus Reviews)

Nussbaum, Susan

★ **Good** kings bad kings; a novel. by Susan Nussbaum. Algonquin Books of Chapel Hill 2013 336 p. $23.95

Grades: 10 11 12 Adult **Fic**

1. Youth with disabilities -- Fiction 2. People with disabilities -- Institutional care -- Fiction 3. Institutional care -- Employees -- Fiction 4. Children with disabilities -- Institutional care -- Fiction

ISBN 1616202637; 9781616202637

LC 2013001350

PEN/Bellwether Prize for Socially Engaged Fiction (2012)

A "look at life inside an institution for disabled juveniles. Located next to the old Chicago stockyards, the Illinois Learning and Life Skills Center is hardly as nurturing as its name suggests. Formerly state-run, ILLC is now operated by a private company whose main interest is in maximizing profits; while Whitney-Palm cuts costs and corners, ILLC's doctors get kickbacks for ordering millions of dollars in unnecessary tests for their patients. One of the "houseparents" is sexually abusing a terrified incest survivor; one of the guards is a brutal bully who eventually breaks a boy's jaw. Even the well-meaning employees are so exhausted and overstretched due to staff cuts that one wheelchair-bound kid dies of third-degree burns from a scalding shower when left unsupervised. Nussbaum unfolds her story in a polyphonic narrative whose colorful individual voices somewhat mitigate the parade of grim particulars." Kirkus

Nuzum, K. A.

A **small** white scar; [by] K.A. Nuzum. 1st ed.; Joanna Cotler Books 2006 180p $15.99; lib bdg $16.89

Grades: 6 7 8 9 **Fic**

1. Twins -- Fiction 2. Brothers -- Fiction 3. Cowhands -- Fiction 4. People with mental disabilities-- Fiction

ISBN 978-0-06-075639-0; 0-06-075639-X; 978-0-06-075640-6 lib bdg; 0-06-075640-3 lib bdg

LC 2005017721

While trying to live his dream of crossing the plains to La Junta to become the radio champoin, Will Bennon must face troubling past issues when his twin brother, Denny, comes along for the adventure and acts as a constant reminder of Will's past. (Publisher's Note)

"The images of the stark 1940s Colorado countryside suffering from drought, and the wild animals that populate it, are clearly drawn with poetic turns of phrase. Characters, plot, and theme all combine to make a compelling story." SLJ

Nye, Naomi Shihab

Going going. Greenwillow Books 2005 232p il $15.99; lib bdg $16.89

Grades: 7 8 9 10 **Fic**

1. Small business -- Fiction 2. Political activists -- Fiction

ISBN 0-688-16185-5; 0-06-029366-7 lib bdg

LC 2004-10146

In San Antonio, Texas, sixteen-year-old Florrie leads her friends and a new boyfriend in a campaign which supports small businesses and protests the effects of chain stores.

The "novel's strong message belongs honestly to Florrie, whose vivid individualism will engage readers. Nye evokes history through small details, inviting readers to view their own cities and towns with a new perspective." Horn Book Guide

★ **Habibi.** Simon & Schuster Bks. for Young Readers 1997 259p $16; pa $5.99

Grades: 7 8 9 10 **Fic**

1. Jewish-Arab relations -- Fiction

ISBN 0-689-80149-1; 0-689-82523-4 pa

LC 97-10943

When fourteen-year-old Liyanne Abboud, her younger brother, and her parents move from St. Louis to a new home between Jerusalem and the Palestinian village where her father was born, they face many changes and must deal with the tensions between Jews and Palestinians

"Poetically imaged and leavened with humor, the story renders layered and complex history understandable through character and incident." SLJ

Nyembezi, C. L. Sibusiso

The **rich** man of Pietermaritzburg; [by Sibusiso Nyembezi; translated by Sandile Ngidi] Aflame Books 2008 200p pa $15.95

Grades: 10 11 12 Adult **Fic**

1. South Africa -- Fiction 2. Swindlers and swindling -- Fiction

ISBN 978-0-9552339-9-9; 0-9552339-9-2

Original Zulu edition, 1961

"A stranger from the city comes to a rural South African village claiming he is a benefactor on a mission to save the people in this traditional, pastoral place from a life of poverty and ignorance. In an attempt to elevate his status in the tribe's eyes, the black Ndebenkulu brags that in the city 'whites call me an esquire.' This pompous stranger soon manages to divide and disrupt the entire clan. . . . Classism, racism, and encroaching capitalism are keenly represented in this touching, endearing, and sadly prescient tale." SLJ

O'Brien, Annemarie

Lara's gift; by Annemarie O'Brien. Alfred A. Knopf 2013 176 p. (hardcover) $16.99; (ebook) $50.97; (library binding) 19.99

Grades: 5 6 7 8 9 **Fic**

1. Historical fiction 2. Dogs -- Fiction 3. Borzoi -- Fiction 4. Visions -- Fiction 5. Sex role -- Fiction 6. Family life -- Russia -- Fiction 7. Fathers and daughters

-- Fiction 8. Russia -- History -- 1904-1914 -- Fiction
ISBN 0307931749; 9780307931740; 9780307975485; 9780375971051
LC 2012034070

In this book, on "a remote estate in 1910s Russia, Lara must prove herself capable of following in her father's footsteps as the head of a prestigious borzoi breeding kennel. There are so many things between her and the realization of her dream. That she is female is the biggest obstacle, but she must also hide the fact that she has visions of future occurrences that involve the dogs and the dangerous wolves that populate the estate." (Kirkus Reviews)

O Guilin, Peadar

The **inferior**. David Fickling Books 2008 439p $16.99

Grades: 8 9 10 11 12 **Fic**

1. Science fiction 2. Hunting -- Fiction 3. Cannibalism -- Fiction
ISBN 978-0-385-75145-2; 0-385-75145-1
LC 2007-34496

In a brutal world where hunting and cannibalism are necessary for survival, something is going terribly wrong as even the globes on the roof of the world are fighting, but one young man, influenced by a beautiful and mysterious stranger, begins to envision new possibilities.

This is an "epic story of survival, betrayal, and community. . . . This well-paced fantasy/science fiction blend perfectly introduces community conflict at a base level. . . . Easy to follow and intriguing at every turn, TheInferior will hold readers from page to page, chapter to chapter, to the very end." SLJ

O'Brien, Caragh M.

Birthmarked. Roaring Brook Press 2010 362p map $16.99

Grades: 6 7 8 9 10 **Fic**

1. Science fiction 2. Midwives -- Fiction 3. Genetic engineering -- Fiction
ISBN 978-1-59643-569-8; 1-59643-569-0
LC 2010-281716

In a future world baked dry by the sun and divided into those who live inside the wall and those who live outside it, sixteen-year-old midwife Gaia Stone is forced into a difficult choice when her parents are arrested and taken into the city.

"Readers who enjoy adventures with a strong heroine standing up to authority against the odds will enjoy this compelling tale." SLJ

O'Brien, Johnny

Day of the assassins; a Jack Christie novel. [illustrated by Nick Hardcastle] Templar Books 2009 211p il $15.99

Grades: 5 6 7 8 **Fic**

1. Princes 2. Science fiction 3. Adventure fiction 4. Time travel -- Fiction 5. World War, 1914-1918 -- Fiction
ISBN 978-0-7636-4595-3; 0-7636-4595-8
LC 2009023630

Fifteen-year-old Jack is sent to 1914 Europe as a pawn in the battle between his long-lost father, who has built a time machine, and a secret network of scientists who want to prevent him from trying to use it to change history for the better.

"From an explosive escape out of captivity to a much-anticipated scene that decides the fate of World War I, the end of the book has plenty of action. Historical information and photographs about the events and people central to the period enhance this title even more." SLJ

Another title about Jack is:
Day of deliverance (2010)

O'Brien, Robert C.

★ **Z** for Zachariah. Atheneum Pubs. 1975 246p hardcover o.p. pa $7.99

Grades: 7 8 9 10 **Fic**

1. Science fiction
ISBN 0-689-30442-0; 1-416-93921-0 pa

Seemingly the only person left alive after a nuclear war, a sixteen-year-old girl is relieved to see a man arrive into her valley until she realizes that he is a tyrant and she must somehow escape.

"The journal form is used by O'Brien very effectively, with no lack of drama and contrast, and the pace and suspense of the story are adroitly maintained until the dramatic and surprising ending." Bull Cent Child Books

O'Connell, Mary

★ The **sharp** time; Mary O'Connell. 1st ed. Delacorte Press 2011 229 p.

Grades: 9 10 11 12 **Fic**

1. Dropouts 2. Orphans -- Fiction 3. Bereavement -- Fiction 4. Grief -- Fiction 5. Revenge -- Fiction 6. High schools -- Fiction 7. Vintage clothing -- Fiction 8. Interpersonal relations -- Fiction 9. Teacher-student relationships -- Fiction
ISBN 9780375899294; 9780375989483; 9780385740487
LC 2010044170

In this book, "[a]fter algebra teacher Mrs. Bennett inappropriately chides ADD-suffering Sandinista Jones . . . for not paying attention in class, the 18-year-old, whose single mother has recently died, gives up on school and life. . . . To fill her days, the teen quickly finds a job at the Pale Circus, a vintage clothing store, a companion in heartache with co-worker and 'druggie Robin Hood' Bradley and in possession of a handgun. . . . It takes a village, or at least a street full of eclectic shop workers in her rundown Kansas City neighborhood, to raise Sandinista out of despair. From her newfound community, comprised of the HIV-positive Pale Circus owner, Erika of Erika's Erotic Confections, a sympathetic pawn-shop owner and friendly Trappist monks, she finds faith, the will to go on in and unexpected beauty in an often cruel world." (Kirkus)

O'Connell, Tyne

True love, the sphinx, and other unsolvable riddles; a comedy in four voices. [by] Tyne O'Connell. 1st U.S. ed.; Bloomsbury 2007 225p $16.95

Grades: 7 8 9 10 **Fic**

1. Love stories 2. School stories 3. Friendship -- Fiction
ISBN 978-1-59990-050-6; 1-59990-050-5
LC 2007002596

While on a class trip in Egypt, two teenaged best friends from an American private boys' school and two teenaged best friends from a British private girls' school meet each other, and must endure many misunderstandings on their path to true love.

"This flirty, fun romcom, told from four distinctive points of view, reads like an old-time comedy of errors. O'Connell describes Egypt with such vitality and richness that it shines as a separate character." SLJ

O'Connor, Sheila

★ **Sparrow** Road. G. P. Putnam's Sons 2011 247p $16.99

Grades: 5 6 7 8 **Fic**

1. Artists -- Fiction

ISBN 978-0-399-25458-1; 0-399-25458-7

LC 2010-28290

Twelve-year-old Raine spends the summer at a mysterious artists colony and discovers a secret about her past.

This is a "beautifully written novel. . . . Readers finding themselves in this quiet world will find plenty of space to imagine and dream for themselves." Kirkus

O'Dell, Scott

★ **Island** of the Blue Dolphins; illustrated by Ted Lewin. 50th anniversary ed.; Houghton Mifflin Books for Children 2010 177p il $22

Grades: 5 6 7 8 **Fic**

1. Native Americans -- Fiction 2. Wilderness survival -- Fiction

ISBN 978-0-547-42483-5; 0-547-42483-3

A reissue of the newly illustrated edition published 1990; first published 1960

Awarded the Newbery Medal, 1961

Left alone on a beautiful but isolated island off the coast of California, a young Indian girl spends eighteen years, not only merely surviving through her enormous courage and self-reliance, but also finding a measure of happiness in her solitary life.

The edition illustrated by Ted Lewin "features twelve full-page, full-color watercolors in purple and blue hues that are appropriate to the island setting. This handsome gift-edition version includes a new introduction by Lois Lowry to commemorate the book's fiftieth anniversary." Horn Book Guide

Sing down the moon. Houghton Mifflin 1970 137p hardcover o.p. pa $6.99

Grades: 5 6 7 8 **Fic**

1. Navajo Indians -- Fiction

ISBN 0-395-10919-1; 978-0-547-40632-9 pa; 0-547-40632-0 pa

A Newbery Medal honor book, 1971

A young Navajo girl recounts the events of 1864 when her tribe was forced to march to Fort Sumner as prisoners of the white soldiers

"There is a poetic sonority of style, a sense of identification, and a note of indomitable courage and stoicism that is touching and impressive." Saturday Rev

Streams to the river, river to the sea; a novel of Sacagawea. Houghton Mifflin 1986 191p hardcover o.p. pa $6.99

Grades: 5 6 7 8 **Fic**

1. Interpreters 2. Guides (Persons) 3. Native Americans -- Fiction

ISBN 0-395-40430-4; 0-618-96642-0 pa

LC 86-936

A young Indian woman, accompanied by her infant and cruel husband, experiences joy and heartbreak when she joins the Lewis and Clark Expedition seeking a way to the Pacific.

"An informative and involving choice for American history students and pioneer-adventure readers." Bull Cent Child Books

Thunder rolling in the mountains; [by] Scott O'Dell and Elizabeth Hall. Houghton Mifflin 1992 128p map $17

Grades: 5 6 7 8 **Fic**

1. Nez Perce Indians -- Fiction

ISBN 0-395-59966-0

LC 91-15961

This account of the defeat of the Nez Perce Indians in 1877 by the United States Army is narrated by Chief Joseph's daughter.

"This is a sad, dark-hued story told in Mr. O'Dell's lean, affecting prose." Child Book Rev Serv

★ **Zia**. Houghton Mifflin 1976 179p hardcover o.p. pa $6.95

Grades: 5 6 7 8 **Fic**

1. Native Americans -- Fiction 2. Christian missions -- Fiction

ISBN 0-395-24393-9; 978-0-547-40633-6 pa; 0-547-40633-9 pa

LC 75-44156

A young Indian girl, Zia, caught between the traditional world of her mother and the present world of the Mission, is helped by her aunt Karana whose story was told in the Island of the Blue Dolphins.

"Zia is an excellent story in its own right, written in a clear, quiet, and reflective style which is in harmony with the plot and characterization." SLJ

O'Hearn, Kate

Kira. Kane Miller 2009 309p (Shadow of the dragon) $16.99

Grades: 6 7 8 9 **Fic**

1. Fantasy fiction 2. Dragons -- Fiction 3. Prisoners -- Fiction

ISBN 978-1-935279-05-1; 1-935279-05-X

"Kira is twelve, and strong willed. The daughter of a retired dragon knight, she yearns for adventure and dreams of following in her father's footsteps astride her own magnificent mount. But this can never happen. According to the 'stupid laws' of the kingdom, she must be married by thirteen." Publisher's note

"With plenty of exciting action sequences, this debut fantasy will appeal to girls clamoring for a hearty heroine, and the cliff-hanger ending will have readers checking the release date for the next book." Booklist

Another title in this series is:
Elspeth (2010)

O'Neal, Eilis

★ The **false** princess. Egmont USA 2010 319p $16.99

Grades: 6 7 8 9 **Fic**

1. Magic -- Fiction 2. Princesses -- Fiction 3. Witchcraft -- Fiction 4. Conspiracies -- Fiction

ISBN 978-1-60684-079-5; 1-60684-079-7

LC 2009040903

For sixteen years, Nalia has been raised as the princess of Thorvaldor, but one day she learns that her real name is Sinda and that she is part of a complicated plot that would change the future of her country forever.

This is a "compelling fantasy, which is filled with magic, political drama, and romance." Publ Wkly

O'Rourke, Erica

Tangled; Erica O'Rourke. KTeen/Kensington 2012 ix, 326 p.p (trade pbk.) $9.95

Grades: 7 8 9 10 **Fic**

1. Occult fiction 2. Magic -- Fiction 3. Interpersonal relations -- Fiction 4. Secrets -- Fiction 5. Friendship -- Fiction 6. Magic 7. Secrecy 8. Friendship

ISBN 0758267053; 9780758267054

LC 2011277358

Sequel to: Torn.

This is the second in the "Torn" trilogy. To help her dead friend's sister, Mo must "summon Luc for help. But help for Constance comes with a price—the Quartoren, leaders of the Arcs, want Mo to repair the ley lines from which they draw their power." Several others require her attention as well, pulling Mo in several directions and exacerbating her struggle of living in both the human and magical worlds. (Kirkus)

Torn. Kensington 2011 310p pa $9.95

Grades: 7 8 9 10 **Fic**

1. Magic -- Fiction 2. Homicide -- Fiction 3. Friendship -- Fiction

ISBN 978-0-7582-6703-0; 0-7582-6703-7

Mo Fitzgerald knows about secrets. But when she witnesses her best friend's murder, she discovers Verity was hiding things she never could have guessed. To find the answers she needs and the vengeance she craves, Mo will have to enter a world of raw magic and shifting alliances. And she'll have to choose between two very different, equally dangerous guys.

"O'Rourke's heroine is refreshing: determined, spunky, and unpredictable. . . . Torn should . . . satisfy readers with an insatiable thirst for well-written, fast-paced fantasy and leave them eager for the next installment in the series." SLJ

Oaks, J. Adams

Why I fight; a novel. Atheneum Books for Young Readers 2009 228p $16.99; pa $8.99

Grades: 8 9 10 11 12 **Fic**

1. Uncles -- Fiction 2. Violence -- Fiction 3. Criminals -- Fiction

ISBN 978-1-4169-1177-7; 1-4169-1177-4; 978-1-4424-0254-6 pa; 1-4424-0254-7 pa

LC 2007-46433

After his house burns down, twelve-year-old Wyatt Reaves takes off with his uncle, and the two of them drive from town to town for six years, earning money mostly by fighting, until Wyatt finally confronts his parents one last time.

"Oaks' first novel is a breathtaking debut with an unforgettable protagonist. . . . The voice Oaks has created for Wyatt to tell his painful and poignant story is a wonderful combination of the unlettered and the eloquent." Booklist

Oates, Joyce Carol, 1938-

★ **Big** Mouth & Ugly Girl. HarperCollins Pubs. 2002 265p hardcover o.p. pa $7.99

Grades: 7 8 9 10 **Fic**

1. School stories 2. Friendship -- Fiction

ISBN 0-06-623756-4; 0-06-447347-3 pa

LC 2001-24601

When sixteen-year-old Matt is falsely accused of threatening to blow up his high school and his friends turn against him, an unlikely classmate comes to his aid.

"Readers will be propelled through these pages by an intense curiosity to learn how events will play out. Oates has written a fast-moving, timely, compelling story." SLJ

★ **Freaky** green eyes. Harper Tempest 2003 341p hardcover o.p. pa $6.99

Grades: 7 8 9 10 **Fic**

1. Domestic violence -- Fiction

ISBN 0-06-623757-2 lib bdg; 0-06-447348-1 pa

LC 2002-32868

Fifteen-year-old Frankie relates the events of the year leading up to her mother's mysterious disappearance and her own struggle to discover and accept the truth about her parents' relationship.

"Oates pulls readers into a fast-paced, first-person thriller. . . . An absorbing page-turner." Booklist

Two or three things I forgot to tell you; Joyce Carol Oates. HarperTeen 2012 277 p. (trade bdg.) $17.99

Grades: 9 10 11 12 **Fic**

1. School stories 2. Secrecy -- Fiction 3. Teenagers -- Suicide -- Fiction 4. Secrets -- Fiction 5. Friendship -- Fiction 6. Self-esteem -- Fiction 7. Preparatory schools -- Fiction 8. Cutting (Self-mutilation) -- Fiction

ISBN 0062110470; 9780062110473

LC 2012009699

This novel, by Joyce Carol Oates, tells a "story of three teenage girls in crisis. . . . In part one, Merissa . . . secretly embraces cutting. Part two flashes back to 15 months earlier, when . . . Tink, a former child star, transfers into their junior class and changes everything. Part three picks back up in the winter of their senior year and focuses on Nadia, who falls prey to sexts and cyberbullying." (Kirkus)

Obreht, Tea

★ The **tiger's** wife; a novel. 1st ed. Random House 2011 337 p. (hbk. : acid-free paper) $25

Grades: 11 12 Adult **Fic**

1. Storytelling 2. Balkan Peninsula 3. Legends -- Europe 4. Orphans -- Fiction 5. Grandfathers -- Fiction 6. Women physicians -- Fiction 7. Orphans 8.

Grandfathers 9. Women physicians 10. Orphanages -- Fiction 11. Balkan Peninsula -- Fiction 12. Grandparent and child -- Fiction
ISBN 0385343833; 9780385343831
LC 2010-09612
Orange Broadband Prize for Fiction (2011)

"The evolving story of the tiger's wife . . . forms one of three strands that sustain the novel, the other two being Natalia's efforts to care for orphans and a wayward family who, to lift a curse, are searching for the bones of a long-dead relative; and several of her grandfather's stories about Gavran Gailé, the deathless man, whose appearances coincide with catastrophe and who may hold the key to all the stories that ensnare Natalia." Publ Wkly

"Moments of breathtaking magic, wildness, and beauty are paired with chilling episodes in which superstition overrides reason; fear and hatred smother compassion; and inexplicable horror rules. Every word, every scene, every thought is blazingly alive in this many-faceted, spellbinding, and rending novel of death, succor, and remembrance. " Booklist

Ockler, Sarah

The **Book** of Broken Hearts; by Sarah Ockler. 1st Simon Pulse hardcover ed. Simon Pulse 2013 368 p. (hardcover) $16.99
Grades: 9 10 11 12 **Fic**
1. Love stories 2. Family life -- Fiction 3. Argentine Americans -- Fiction
ISBN 1442430389; 9781442430389
LC 2012033041

In this romance novel, by Sarah Ockler, "Jude has learned a lot from her older sisters, but the most important thing is this: The Vargas brothers are notorious heartbreakers. . . . Now Jude is the only sister still living at home, and she's spending the summer helping her ailing father restore his vintage motorcycle--which means hiring a mechanic to help out. Is it Jude's fault he happens to be cute? And surprisingly sweet? And a Vargas?" (Publisher's note)

Fixing Delilah. Little, Brown 2010 308p $16.99
Grades: 8 9 10 11 12 **Fic**
1. Vermont -- Fiction 2. Bereavement -- Fiction 3. Single parent family -- Fiction 4. Depression (Psychology) -- Fiction
ISBN 978-0-316-05209-2; 0-316-05209-4
LC 2010-08631

Delilah Hannaford "used to be a good student, but she can't seem to keep it together anymore. Her 'boyfriend' isn't much of a boyfriend. And her mother refuses to discuss the fight that divided their family eight years ago. Falling apart, it seems, is a Hannaford tradition. Over a summer of new friendships, unexpected romance, and moments that test the complex bonds between mothers and daughters, Delilah must face her family's painful past." (Publisher's note)

Delilah "tells her own story in a lyrical and authentic voice; the thoughtful reader will get lost in her anguish, her triumphs, and her eventual resolution." Voice Youth Advocates

Twenty boy summer. Little, Brown and Co. 2009 290p $16.99
Grades: 8 9 10 11 12 **Fic**
1. Vacations -- Fiction 2. California -- Fiction 3. Friendship -- Fiction 4. Bereavement -- Fiction
ISBN 978-0-316-05159-0; 0-316-05159-4
LC 2008-14196

While on vacation in California, sixteen-year-old best friends Anna and Frankie conspire to find a boy for Anna's first kiss, but Anna harbors a painful secret that threatens their lighthearted plan and their friendship.

"Often funny, this is a thoughtful, multilayered story about friendship, loss, and moving on." SLJ

Okorafor, Nnedi

Akata witch. Viking 2011 349p $16.99
Grades: 6 7 8 9 **Fic**
1. Fantasy fiction 2. Witchcraft -- Fiction 3. Albinos and albinism -- Fiction
ISBN 978-0-670-01196-4; 0-670-01196-7

"Although 12-year-old Sunny is Nigerian, she was born in America, and her Nigerian classmates see her as an outsider. Worse, she's an albino, an obvious target for bullies and suspected of being a ghost or a witch. Things change, however, when she has a vision of impending nuclear war. Then her classmate Orlu and his friend Chichi turn out to be Leopard People—witches—and insist that she is, too. . . . This tale is filled with marvels and is sure to appeal to teens whose interest in fantasy goes beyond dwarves and fairies." Publ Wkly

The **shadow** speaker; [by] Nnedi Okorafor-Mbachu. Jump at the Sun/Hyperion Books for Children 2007 336p hardcover o.p. pa $8.99
Grades: 7 8 9 10 **Fic**
1. Fantasy fiction 2. Science fiction 3. West Africa -- Fiction 4. Sahara Desert -- Fiction
ISBN 978-1-4231-0033-1; 1-4231-0033-6; 978-1-4231-0036-2 pa; 1-4231-0036-0 pa
LC 2007-13313

In West Africa in 2070, after fifteen-year-old "shadow speaker" Ejii witnesses her father's beheading, she embarks on a dangerous journey across the Sahara to find Jaa, her father's killer, and upon finding her, she also discovers a greater purpose to her life and to the mystical powers she possesses.

"Okorafor-Mbachu does an excellent job of combining both science fiction and fantasy elements into this novel. . . . The action moves along at a quick pace and will keep most readers on their toes and wanting more at the end of the novel." Voice Youth Advocates

Oliver, Jana

Soul thief; [by] Jana Oliver. St. Martin's Griffin 2011 339p (A demon trappers novel) pa $9.99
Grades: 7 8 9 10 **Fic**
1. Orphans -- Fiction 2. Demonology -- Fiction 3. Apprentices -- Fiction 4. Supernatural -- Fiction 5. Atlanta (Ga.) -- Fiction
ISBN 978-0-312-61479-9
LC 2011019930

Sequel to The demon trapper's daughter (2011)

In 2018 Atlanta, Georgia, seventeen-year-old apprentice Demon Trapper Riley Blackthorne must deal with unwanted fame, an unofficial bodyguard, an overprotective friend, the Vatican's own Demon Trappers, and an extremely powerful Grade Five demon who is stalking her.

Oliver, Jana G.

The **demon** trapper's daughter; a demon trapper novel. [by] Jana Oliver. St. Martin's Griffin 2011 355p pa $9.99

Grades: 7 8 9 10 **Fic**

1. Demonology -- Fiction 2. Apprentices -- Fiction 3. Supernatural -- Fiction 4. Atlanta (Ga.) -- Fiction 5. Father-daughter relationship -- Fiction

ISBN 978-0-312-61478-2; 0-312-61478-0

LC 2010-38860

In 2018 Atlanta, Georgia, after a demon threatens seventeen-year-old Riley Blackthorne's life and murders her father, a legendary demon trapper to whom she was apprenticed, her father's partner, Beck, steps in to care for her, knowing she hates him.

"With a strong female heroine, a fascinating setting, and a complex, thrill-soaked story, this series is off to a strong start." Publ Wkly

Followed by Soul thief (2011)

Oliver, Lauren

Before I fall. The Bowen Press 2010 470p $17.99

Grades: 9 10 11 12 **Fic**

1. School stories 2. Dead -- Fiction 3. Popularity -- Fiction 4. Self-perception -- Fiction

ISBN 006172680X; 9780061726804; 978-0-06-172680-4; 0-06-172680-X

LC 2009-7288

After she dies in a car crash, teenage Samantha relives the day of her death over and over again until, on the seventh day, she finally discovers a way to save herself.

"This is a compelling book with a powerful message that will strike a chord with many teens." Booklist

★ **Delirium**. HarperCollins 2011 441p $17.99

Grades: 8 9 10 11 **Fic**

1. Science fiction 2. Love -- Fiction 3. Maine -- Fiction 4. Resistance to government -- Fiction

ISBN 978-0-06-172682-8; 0-06-172682-6

LC 2010-17839

Lena looks forward to receiving the government-mandated cure that prevents the delirium of love and leads to a safe, predictable, and happy life, until ninety-five days before her eighteenth birthday and her treatment, she falls in love.

This book is a "deft blend of realism and fantasy. . . . The story bogs down as it revels in romance—Alex is standard-issue perfection—but the book never loses its A Clockwork Orange–style bite regarding safety versus choice." Booklist

Pandemonium; Lauren Oliver. 1st ed.; HarperCollinsPublishers 2012 375p $17.99

Grades: 8 9 10 11 **Fic**

1. Science fiction 2. Love -- Fiction 3. Resistance to government -- Fiction

ISBN 978-0-06-197806-7

LC 2011024241

Sequel to Delirium (2011)

After falling in love, Lena and Alex flee their oppressive society where love is outlawed and everyone must receive "the cure"—an operation that makes them immune to the delirium of love—but Lena alone manages to find her way to a community of resistance fighters, and although she is bereft without the boy she loves, her struggles seem to be leading her toward a new love.

Panic; Lauren Oliver. Harper, an imprint of HarperCollinsPublishers 2014 416 p. (hardcover bdg.) $17.99

Grades: 9 10 11 12 **Fic**

1. Young adult literature 2. City and town life -- Fiction 3. Games -- Fiction 4. Risk-taking (Psychology) -- Fiction

ISBN 0062014552; 9780062014559

LC 2013008472

Written by Lauren Oliver, this young adult novel describes how "Heather never thought she would compete in Panic, a legendary game played by graduating seniors, where the stakes are high and the payoff is even higher. . . . Dodge has never been afraid of Panic. . . . For Heather and Dodge, the game will bring new alliances, unexpected revelations, and the possibility of first love for each of them." (Publisher's note)

"There's not much to do in tiny Carp, New York, so a group of teenagers take it upon themselves to create their own excitement through Panic, a risky game with potentially deadly sets of challenges... The bleak setting, tenacious characters, and anxiety-filled atmosphere will draw readers right into this unique story. Oliver's powerful return to a contemporary realistic setting will find wide a readership with this fast-paced and captivating book." (School Library Journal)

Requiem; Lauren Oliver. Harper 2013 432 p. (hardcover) $18.99

Grades: 8 9 10 11 12 **Fic**

1. Science fiction 2. Resistance to government -- Fiction 3. Love -- Fiction 4. Maine -- Fiction 5. Marriage -- Fiction 6. Friendship -- Fiction 7. Best friends -- Fiction 8. Government, Resistance to -- Fiction

ISBN 0062014536; 9780062014535

LC 2012030236

Sequel to: Pandemonium

This young adult novel, by Lauren Oliver, is the conclusion to the "Delirium" trilogy. "The nascent rebellion . . . has ignited into an all-out revolution . . . , and Lena is at the center of the fight. After rescuing Julian from a death sentence, Lena and her friends fled to the Wilds. But the Wilds are no longer a safe haven. . . . As Lena navigates the increasingly dangerous terrain of the Wilds, her best friend, Hana, lives a safe, loveless life in Portland." (Publisher's note)

Olsen, Gregg

Envy. Splinter 2011 285p (Empty Coffin) $17.95

Grades: 9 10 11 12 **Fic**

1. Twins -- Fiction 2. Sisters -- Fiction 3. Suicide -- Fiction 4. Parapsychology -- Fiction 5. Washington

(State) -- Fiction
ISBN 978-1-4027-8957-1
LC 2011017797

Fifteen-year-old twins Hayley and Taylor Ryan of Port Gamble, WA, known as "Empty Coffin" because of a local legend, investigate a former friend's Christmas suicide and, along the way, discover a secret from their own past.

This is "is a stark, emotionless narrative, a cynical rumination on the nature of evil and man's darkness." Publ Wkly

Olsen, Sylvia

The **girl** with a baby. Sono Nis Press 2004 203p pa $8.95

Grades: 7 8 9 10 **Fic**

1. Teenage mothers -- Fiction 2. Native Americans -- Fiction
ISBN 1-55039-142-9

This "novel tells of teenage mother Jane, 14, who wants to stay in school and raise her baby, Destiny, to be respectful of tradition and smart in the new ways. Jane's family left the reservation because of resentment against Dad, who is white; now in a white area, they face prejudice for being Indian. . . . Jane's home . . . is drawn without romanticism, and . . . Jane's first-person narrative never denies how hard life is, and how thrilling." Booklist

★ **White** girl. Sono Nis Press 2004 235p pa $8.95

Grades: 7 8 9 10 **Fic**

1. Prejudices -- Fiction 2. Native Americans -- Fiction
ISBN 1-5503-9147-X

"Until she was fourteen, Josie was pretty ordinary. Then her Mom meets Martin, 'a real ponytail Indian,' and before long, Josie finds herself living on a reserve outside town, with a new stepfather, a new stepbrother, and a new name 'Blondie.'" Publisher's note

"The talk is contemporary and relaxed, and the characters will hold readers as much as the novel's extraordinary sense of place." Booklist

Omololu, Cynthia Jaynes

Dirty little secrets; [by] C.J. Omololu. Walker & Co. 2010 212p $16.99

Grades: 8 9 10 11 12 **Fic**

1. School stories 2. Death -- Fiction 3. Compulsive behavior -- Fiction 4. Mother-daughter relationship -- Fiction
ISBN 978-0-8027-8660-9; 0-8027-8660-X
LC 2009-22461

When her unstable mother dies unexpectedly, sixteen-year-old Lucy must take control and find a way to keep the long-held secret of her mother's compulsive hoarding from being revealed to friends, neighbors, and especially the media.

"As a valuable new addition to heartbreaking but honest books about teens immersed in emotionally distressed families, . . . this potent and creatively woven page-turner brings a traumatic situation front and center." SLJ

Oppel, Kenneth

Airborn. Eos 2004 355p $16.99; lib bdg $17.89

Grades: 7 8 9 10 **Fic**

1. Fantasy fiction 2. Airships -- Fiction 3. Imaginary creatures
ISBN 0-06-053180-0; 0-06-053181-9 lib bdg
LC 2003-15642

Michael L. Printz Award honor book, 2005

Matt, a young cabin boy aboard an airship, and Kate, a wealthy young girl traveling with her chaperone, team up to search for the existence of mysterious winged creatures reportedly living hundreds of feet above the Earth's surface.

"This rousing adventure has something for everyone: appealing and enterprising characters, nasty villains, and a little romance." SLJ

Other titles in this series are:
Skybreaker (2005)
Starclimber (2009)

Half brother. Scholastic Press 2010 375p $17.99

Grades: 7 8 9 10 **Fic**

1. Canada -- Fiction 2. Research -- Fiction 3. Chimpanzees -- Fiction 4. Family life -- Fiction
ISBN 978-0-545-22925-8; 0-545-22925-1
LC 2010-2696

In 1973, when a renowned Canadian behavioral psychologist pursues his latest research project—an experiment to determine whether chimpanzees can acquire advanced language skills—he brings home a baby chimp named Zan and asks his thirteen-year-old son to treat Zan like a little brother.

"Oppel has taken a fascinating subject and molded it into a topnotch read. Deftly integrating family dynamics, animal-rights issues, and the painful lessons of growing up, Half Brother draws readers in from the beginning and doesn't let go." SLJ

Skybreaker. Eos 2005 369p il hardcover o.p. lib bdg $17.89; pa $6.99

Grades: 7 8 9 10 **Fic**

1. Fantasy fiction 2. Airships -- Fiction
ISBN 0-06-053227-0; 0-06-053228-9 lib bdg; 0-06-053229-7 pa
LC 2005-08386

Matt Cruse, a student at the Airship Academy, and Kate de Vries, a young heiress, team up with a gypsy and a daring captain, to find a long-lost airship, rumored to carry a treasure beyond imagination.

This "starts with a bang and doesn't let up until the satisfying ending. . . . This worthy companion to Airborn maintains its roller-coaster thrills in true swashbuckling style." SLJ

Starclimber. Eos 2009 390p $17.99; lib bdg $18.89

Grades: 7 8 9 10 **Fic**

1. Fantasy fiction 2. Airships -- Fiction 3. Outer space -- Exploration -- Fiction
ISBN 978-0-06-085057-9; 0-06-085057-4; 978-0-06-085058-6 lib bdg; 0-06-085058-2 lib bdg
LC 2008019747

As members of the first crew of astralnauts, Matt Cruse and Kate De Vries journey into outer space on the Starclimber and face a series of catastrophes that threaten the survival of all on board.

This "is a thrilling roller-coaster ride of a book, full of humor and derring-do and guaranteed to keep readers up long past midnight." SLJ

Such wicked intent; Kenneth Oppel. Simon & Schuster Books For Young Readers 2012 320 p. (hardback) $16.99; (paperback) $9.99

Grades: 7 8 9 10 **Fic**

1. Love stories 2. Death -- Fiction 3. Friendship -- Fiction 4. Horror stories 5. Dead -- Fiction 6. Twins -- Fiction 7. Alchemy -- Fiction 8. Brothers -- Fiction 9. Supernatural -- Fiction 10. Geneva (Republic) -- History -- 18th century -- Fiction

ISBN 1442403187; 9781442403185; 9781442403208; 9781442403192

LC 2011042843

This book by Kenneth Oppel is part of the "Apprenticeship of Victor Frankenstein" series. "[T]hree weeks after [his twin] Konrad's death, Victor plucks a mysterious box from the still-warm ashes of the books of the Dark Library. Demonstrating tremendous hubris, Victor aims to return Konrad to the living world and still win Elizabeth, Konrad's grief-stricken love and the boys' childhood friend." (Kirkus Reviews)

This dark endeavor; the apprenticeship of Victor Frankenstein. Simon & Schuster Books for Young Readers 2011 298p $17.99

Grades: 7 8 9 10 **Fic**

1. Horror fiction 2. Twins -- Fiction 3. Alchemy -- Fiction 4. Brothers -- Fiction

ISBN 1-4424-0315-2; 1-4424-0317-9 ebook; 978-1-4424-0315-4; 978-1-4424-0317-8 ebook

LC 2011016974

When his twin brother falls ill in the family's chateau in the independent republic of Geneva in the eighteenth century, sixteen-year-old Victor Frankenstein embarks on a dangerous and uncertain quest to create the forbidden Elixir of Life described in an ancient text in the family's secret Biblioteka Obscura.

"Written in a readable approximation of early 19th-century style, Oppel's . . . tale is melodramatic, exciting, disquieting, and intentionally over the top." Publ Wkly

Orenstein, Denise Gosliner

Unseen companion. Katherine Tegen Bks. 2003 357p lib bdg $16.89; pa $7.99

Grades: 7 8 9 10 **Fic**

1. Inuit -- Fiction

ISBN 0-06-052057-4 lib bdg; 0-06-052058-2 pa

LC 2002-152944

In rural Alaska in 1969, the lives of several teenagers come together while trying to find out what happened to a sixteen-year-old boy who is missing

"In distinctive voices, the four narrators tell their own involving stories. . . . A sensitive observer and a compelling storyteller, Orenstein offers a novel that is both touching and harsh." Booklist

Oron, Judie

Cry of the giraffe; based on a true story. Annick Press 2010 193p map $21.95; pa $12.95

Grades: 8 9 10 11 12 **Fic**

1. Jews -- Ethiopia -- Fiction 2. Jews -- Persecutions -- Fiction

ISBN 978-1-55451-272-0; 978-1-55451-271-3 pa

Labeled outcasts by their Ethiopian neighbors because of their Jewish faith, 13-year-old Wuditu and her family make the arduous trek on foot to Sudan in the hope of being transported to Yerusalem and its promise of a better life. Based on real events.

"Oron's novel shows with brutal, unflinching detail the horrors of refugee life and child slavery and the shocking vulnerability of young females in the developing world, and she offers a sobering introduction to a community and historical episodes rarely covered in books for youth." Booklist

Ortiz Cofer, Judith

Call me Maria; a novel. Orchard Books 2004 127p $16.95

Grades: 7 8 9 10 **Fic**

1. Identity 2. Puerto Ricans -- Fiction

ISBN 0-439-38577-6

LC 2004-2674

Fifteen-year-old Maria leaves her mother and their Puerto Rican home to live in the barrio of New York with her father, feeling torn between the two cultures in which she has been raised.

"Through a mixture of poems, letters, and prose, María gradually reveals herself as a true student of language and life. . . . Understated but with a brilliant combination of all the right words to convey events, Cofer aptly relates the complexities of María's two homes, her parents' lives, and the difficulty of her choice between them." SLJ

If I could fly. Farrar Straus & Giroux 2011 195p $16.99

Grades: 8 9 10 11 12 **Fic**

1. Pigeons -- Fiction 2. Singers -- Fiction 3. Family life -- Fiction 4. Puerto Ricans -- Fiction

ISBN 978-0-374-33517-5; 0-374-33517-6

LC 2010022309

When fifteen-year-old Doris's mother, a professional singer, returns to Puerto Rico and her father finds a girlfriend, Doris cares for a neighbor's pigeons and relies on friends as she begins to find her own voice and wings.

"A familiar story of mother/daughter relationships delivered lyrically, simply and inspirationally." Kirkus

Osa, Nancy

Cuba 15. Delacorte Press 2003 277p hardcover o.p. pa $7.95

Grades: 7 8 9 10 **Fic**

1. Cuban Americans -- Fiction

ISBN 0-385-73021-7; 0-385-73233-3 pa

LC 2002-13389

Violet Paz, who is half Cuban American, half Polish American, reluctantly prepares for her upcoming "quince," a Spanish nickname for the celebration of an Hispanic girl's fifteenth birthday

"Violet's hilarious, cool first-person narrative veers between slapstick and tenderness, denial and truth." Booklist

Osterlund, Anne

Academy 7. Speak 2009 259p pa $8.99

Grades: 8 9 10 11 12 **Fic**

1. School stories 2. Science fiction 3. Fathers -- Fiction
ISBN 978-0-14-241437-8; 0-14-241437-9

LC 2008-41323

Aerin Renning and Dane Madousin struggle as incoming students at the most exclusive academy in the Universe, both hiding secrets that are too painful to reveal, not realizing that those very secrets link them together.

This story, "with details of spacecraft, flight, and other worlds, will appeal to readers who crave adventure." Booklist

Aurelia. Speak 2008 246p pa $8.99

Grades: 8 9 10 11 **Fic**

1. Mystery fiction 2. Princesses -- Fiction
ISBN 978-0-14-240579-6; 0-14-240579-5

LC 2007-36074

The king sends for Robert, whose father was a trusted spy, when someone tries to assassinate Aurelia, the stubborn and feisty crown princess of Tyralt.

"Osterlund's characters are both believable, relatable, and enviable, which makes this book enjoyable to read. Even though the book might seem to fit the mold of a quintessential princess fairy tale, Aurelia's spitfire attitude and her resulting actions lend the story a unique twist." Voice Youth Advocates

Followed by: Exile (2011)

Exile. Speak 2011 295p pa $8.99

Grades: 8 9 10 11 **Fic**

1. Princesses -- Fiction 2. Voyages and travels -- Fiction
ISBN 978-0-14-241739-3; 0-14-241739-4

LC 2010009645

Sequel to Aurelia (2008)

In exile, Princess Aurelia is free of responsibilities, able to travel the country and meet the people of Tyralt, but when her journey erupts in a fiery conflagration that puts the fate of the kingdom in peril, she and her companion Robert must determine whether they have the strength and the will to complete their mission.

Ostlere, Cathy

★ **Karma**; a novel in verse. Razorbill 2011 517p map $18.99

Grades: 7 8 9 10 11 12 **Fic**

1. Novels in verse 2. India -- Fiction 3. Violence -- Fiction 4. Culture conflict -- Fiction
ISBN 978-1-59514-338-9; 1-59514-338-6

"The novel's pace and tension will compel readers to read at a gallop, but then stop again and again to turn a finely crafted phrase, whether to appreciate the richness of the language and imagery or to reconsider the layers beneath a thought. This is a book in which readers will consider the roots and realities of destiny and chance. Karma is a spectacular, sophisticated tale that will stick with readers long after they're done considering its last lines." SLJ

Ostow, Micol

Emily Goldberg learns to salsa. Razorbill 2006 200p $16.99

Grades: 7 8 9 10 **Fic**

1. Jews -- Fiction 2. Family life -- Fiction 3. Puerto Ricans -- Fiction 4. Racially mixed people -- Fiction
ISBN 1-59514-081-6

LC 2006-14651

Forced to stay with her mother in Puerto Rico for weeks after her grandmother's funeral, half-Jewish Emily, who has just graduated from a Westchester, New York high school, does not find it easy to connect with her Puerto Rican heritage and relatives she had never met.

This is "a moving story that has a solid plotline and plenty of family secrets." Booklist

★ **So** punk rock (and other ways to disappoint your mother) a novel. with art by David Ostow. Flux 2009 246p il pa $9.95

Grades: 8 9 10 11 12 **Fic**

1. School stories 2. New Jersey -- Fiction 3. Rock music -- Fiction 4. Bands (Music) -- Fiction 5. Jews -- United States -- Fiction
ISBN 978-0-7387-1471-4; 0-7387-1471-2

LC 2009-8216

Four suburban New Jersey students from the Leo R. Gittleman Jewish Day School form a rock band that becomes inexplicably popular, creating exhiliration, friction, confrontation, and soul-searching among its members.

The "comic-strip-style illustrations are true show-stoppers. . . . A rollicking, witty, and ultra-contemporary book that drums on the funny bone and reverberates through the heart." Booklist

Owen, James A.

Here, there be dragons; written and illustrated by James A. Owen. Simon & Schuster Books for Young Readers 2006 326p il (The Chronicles of the Imaginarium Geographica) $17.95

Grades: 8 9 10 11 12 **Fic**

1. Poets 2. Fantasy fiction
ISBN 978-1-4169-1227-9; 1-4169-1227-4

LC 2005-30486

Three young men are entrusted with the Imaginarium Geographica, an atlas of fantastical places to which they travel in hopes of defeating the Winter King whose bid for power is related to the First World War raging in the Real World.

"From the arresting prologue, the reader is gripped by a finely crafted fantasy tale and compelled to continue. . . . This superb saga has interesting characters and plenty of action." Voice Youth Advocates

Other titles in this series are:
The search for the Red Dragon (2007)
The indigo king (2008)
The shadow dragons (2009)
The dragon's apprentice (2010)

Otsuka, Julie

★ **When** the emperor was divine; a novel. Knopf 2002 141p hardcover o.p. pa $10.95

Grades: 11 12 Adult **Fic**

1. California -- Fiction 2. Japanese Americans -- Evacuation and relocation, 1942-1945 -- Fiction

ISBN 0-375-41429-0; 0-385-72181-1 pa

LC 2002-20814

This novel traces the "fortunes of a Japanese-American family from the spring of 1942—when President Roosevelt's evacuation order came through—to the spring of 1946. In four brief chapters, we follow a mother, daughter and son from their comfortable home in Berkeley through their five months in a temporary 'assembly center' (a converted stable at a racetrack south of San Francisco) to an internment camp in Topaz, Utah, where they spend three years." N Y Times Book Rev

Otsuka "demonstrates a breathtaking restraint and delicacy throughout this supple and devastating first novel." Booklist

Padian, Maria

Jersey tomatoes are the best. Alfred A. Knopf 2011 344p $16.99; lib bdg $19.99

Grades: 7 8 9 10 **Fic**

1. Camps -- Fiction 2. Ballet -- Fiction 3. Tennis -- Fiction 4. Friendship -- Fiction 5. Anorexia nervosa -- Fiction

ISBN 978-0-375-86579-4; 0-375-86579-9; 978-0-375-96579-1 lib bdg; 0-375-96579-3 lib bdg

LC 2010-11827

When fifteen-year-old best friends Henry and Eve leave New Jersey, one for tennis camp in Florida and one for ballet camp in New York, each faces challenges that put her long-cherished dreams of the future to the test.

"Padian's writing and plotting are clean and clear, and her handling of the duo's dilemmas never stoops to melodrama. An excellent read for sports lovers who desire some meaty beefsteak in their stories." Booklist

Paley, Sasha

Huge. Simon & Schuster Books for Young Readers 2007 259p $15.99

Grades: 7 8 9 **Fic**

1. Camps -- Fiction 2. Obesity -- Fiction 3. Friendship -- Fiction

ISBN 978-1-4169-3517-9; 1-4169-3517-7

LC 2007-03510

When Wilhelmina and April find themselves roommates at a fat camp, both with very different goals, they find they have very little in common until they are both humiliated by the same person.

"The characters are sharply drawn, and the often-amusing story does a good job of showing how everyday concerns are often overshadowed by the issue of weight." Booklist

Palma, Felix J.

The **map** of the sky; a novel. by Felix J. Palma. 1st Atria Books hardcover ed. Atria Books 2012 594 p. (hardcover : alk. paper) $26.00; (paperback) $16.00; (ebook) $24.99

Grades: 6 7 8 9 10 11 12 Adult **Fic**

1. Time travel -- Fiction 2. Extraterrestrial beings -- Fiction 3. Wells, H. G. (Herbert George), 1866-1946 -- Fiction 4. Fiances -- Fiction 5. Writers -- Fiction 6. Socialites -- New York (State) -- New York -- Fiction

ISBN 1451660316; 9781451660319; 9781451660326; 9781921942907

LC 2012028794

Sequel to: The map of time

In this book by Felix J. Palma, "H. G. Wells . . . meet[s] . . . Garrett Serviss, the man who dared write a sequel to his 'War of the Worlds.'. . . An alcohol-infused sense of camaraderie and adventure inspire the two men to set off to view a hidden secret -- a Martian kept in a locked room in the Natural History Museum. As alien forces converge on London, a group of citizens struggle to preserve the once-proud city against destruction." (Library Journal)

The **map** of time; Félix J. Palma ; translated by Nick Caistor. Atria Books 2011 611p. $26.00

Grades: 6 7 8 9 10 11 12 Adult **Fic**

1. Science fiction 2. Historical fiction 3. Time travel -- Fiction

ISBN 9781439167397; 1439167397; 143916746X; 9781439167465

LC 2010047304

Originally published in Spain in 2008.

Col. ill. on lining papers.

This book, the first in a trilogy is a "thriller that explores the ramifications of time travel in three intersecting narratives. In the opening chapter, set in 1896 England, aristocratic Andrew Harrington plans to take his own life, despondent over the death years earlier of his lover, the last victim of Jack the Ripper. Meanwhile, 21-year-old Claire Haggerty plots to escape her restrictive role as a woman in Victorian society by journeying to the year 2000. A new commercial concern, Murray's Time Travel, offers such a trip for a hefty fee. Finally, Scotland Yarder Colin Garrett believes that the fatal wound on a murder victim could only have been caused by a weapon from the future. Linking all three stories is H.G. Wells, the author of The Time Machine." (Publisher"s Wkly)

Palmer, Robin

The **Corner** of Bitter and Sweet; by Robin Palmer. Penguin Group USA 2013 400 p. $9.99

Grades: 7 8 9 10 11 12 **Fic**

1. Children of alcoholics -- Fiction 2. Television personalities -- Fiction 3. Mother-daughter relationship -- Fiction

ISBN 0142412503; 9780142412503

In this book by Robin Palmer, "a teenage girl and her showbiz mom are forced to re-evaluate their relationship after rehab. . . . To learn how to cope, Annabelle joins Alateen. But when Janie scores a role in a new movie with hot young superstar Billy Barrett, Annabelle frets that if anything goes wrong, it could put her mom right back on the bottle. Fortunately she's distracted by her own crush on small-town boy Matt and the lure of a college photography fellowship." (Kirkus Reviews)

Geek charming. Speak 2009 338p pa $7.99

Grades: 7 8 9 10 **Fic**

1. School stories 2. Popularity -- Fiction

ISBN 0-14-241122-1; 978-0-14-241122-3

LC 2008-25918

Rich, spoiled, and popular high school senior Dylan is coerced into doing a documentary film with Josh, one of the school's geeks, who leads her to realize that the world does not revolve around her.

This is "a lighthearted contemporary novel filled with snappy dialogue. . . . Rather than following the predictable route of having opposites fall in love, Palmer . . . offers a slightly more original and plausible alternative." Publ Wkly

Paolini, Christopher

★ **Eragon.** Knopf 2003 509p (Inheritance) $18.95; lib bdg $20.99; pa $6.99

Grades: 7 8 9 10 **Fic**

1. Fantasy fiction 2. Dragons -- Fiction

ISBN 0-375-82668-8; 0-375-92668-2 lib bdg; 0-440-23848-X pa

LC 2003-47481

First published 2002 in different form by Paolini International

In Aagaesia, a fifteen-year-old boy of unknown lineage called Eragon finds a mysterious stone that weaves his life into an intricate tapestry of destiny, magic, and power, peopled with dragons, elves, and monsters

"This unusual, powerful tale . . . is the first book in the planned Inheritance trilogy. . . . The telling remains constantly fresh and fluid, and [the author] has done a fine job of creating an appealing and convincing relationship between the youth and the dragon." Booklist

Other titles in this series are:

Brisningr (2008)

Eldest (2005)

Papademetriou, Lisa

Drop. Alfred A. Knopf 2008 169p $15.99; lib bdg $18.99

Grades: 8 9 10 11 12 **Fic**

1. Gambling -- Fiction

ISBN 978-0-375-84244-3; 0-375-84244-6; 978-0-375-94244-0 lib bdg; 0-375-94244-0 lib bdg

LC 2008-02568

Sixteen-year-old math prodigy Jerrica discovers she has the ability to predict outcomes in blackjack and roulette, and joins forces with Sanjay and Kat to develop her theories while helping them get the money they desperately need.

"The characters are well drawn and the excitement of the gambling scenes is well executed. Additionally, some surprising details about the teens turn the story upside down, unraveling everything that readers thought they knew about them. A page-turner." SLJ

M or F? a novel. [by] Lisa Papademetriou and Chris Tebbetts. Razorbill 2005 296p $16.99

Grades: 8 9 10 11 12 **Fic**

1. Friendship -- Fiction 2. Homosexuality -- Fiction

ISBN 1-59514-034-4

LC 2005008149

Gay teen Marcus helps his friend Frannie chat up her crush online, but then becomes convinced that the crush is falling for him instead.

"This is a creative, funny romance, written with style and sophistication." Booklist

Paquette, Ammi-Joan

Nowhere girl. Walker & Co. 2011 246p $16.99

Grades: 6 7 8 9 **Fic**

1. Fathers -- Fiction 2. Voyages and travels -- Fiction

ISBN 978-0-8027-2297-3; 0-8027-2297-0

LC 2010049591

Fair-skinned and blond-haired, thirteen-year-old Luchi was born in a Thai prison where her American mother was being held and she has never had any other home, but when her mother dies Luchi sets out into the world to search for the family and home she has always dreamed of.

"The classic quest story gets expanded here with contemporary details in spare lyrical prose that intensify the perilous, archetypal journey. . . . The realistic specifics . . . make the story of betrayal and kindness immediate and universal." Booklist

Park, Linda Sue, 1960-

Click; [by] Linda Sue Park [et al.] Arthur A. Levine Books 2007 217p $16.99

Grades: 7 8 9 10 **Fic**

1. Adventure fiction 2. Photojournalism -- Fiction

ISBN 0-439-41138-6; 978-0-439-41138-7

LC 2006-100069

"Ten distinguished authors each write a chapter of this intriguing novel of mystery and family, which examines the lives touched by a photojournalist George Keane, aka Gee. . . . The authors' distinctive styles remain evident; although readers expecting a more straightforward or linear story may find the leaps through time and place challenging, the thematic currents help the chapters gel into a cohesive whole." Publ Wkly

A **long** walk to water; based on a true story. Clarion Books 2010 121p map $16

Grades: 6 7 8 9 10 **Fic**

1. Refugees 2. Relief workers 3. Water -- Fiction 4. Africans -- Fiction 5. Refugees -- Fiction 6. Sudan -- History -- Civil War, 1983-2005 -- Fiction

ISBN 0-547-25127-0; 978-0-547-25127-1

LC 2009-48857

When the Sudanese civil war reaches his village in 1985, eleven-year-old Salva becomes separated from his family and must walk with other Dinka tribe members through southern Sudan, Ethiopia, and Kenya in search of safe haven. Based on the life of Salva Dut, who, after emigrating to America in 1996, began a project to dig water wells in Sudan.

This is a "spare, immediate account. . . . Young readers will be stunned by the triumphant climax of the former refugee who makes a difference." Booklist

Parker, Amy Christine

★ **Gated;** by Amy Christine Parker. 1st ed. Random House Inc 2013 339 p. (hardcover) $17.99; (library) $20.99

Grades: 9 10 11 12 **Fic**

1. Love stories 2. Cults -- Fiction 3. Utopias -- Fiction 4. Survival -- Fiction 5. Religious leaders -- Fiction

ISBN 0449815978; 9780449815977; 9780449815984

LC 2012048123

In this book, 17-year-old "Lyla is part of the Community, a group of families led by the charismatic Pioneer, who has secluded them from the outside world in anticipation of the imminent apocalypse. With Pioneer's prophesied deadline fast approaching, Lyla struggles with her faith and resolve. A chance encounter with Cody, a boy from the outside, further tempts her away from the way of the Community, but when events escalate," she may have to make a difficult choice. (Publishers Weekly)

"Part of a select few who will survive the end of the world, Lyla and her family live in the Community, led by prophet Pioneer, and she can barely remember her old life. Then an outsider raises questions she shouldn't be asking, and Pioneer does not appreciate questions. Slowly mounting action builds suspense in this coming-of-age story and examination of cult mentality." (Horn Book)

Parker, Robert B.

The **boxer** and the spy. Philomel Books 2008 210p $17.99

Grades: 7 8 9 10 11 **Fic**

1. Mystery fiction 2. Boxing -- Fiction

ISBN 978-0-399-24775-0; 0-399-24775-0

LC 2007-23689

Fifteen-year-old Terry, an aspiring boxer, uncovers the mystery behind the unexpected death of a classmate.

"The lessons about human nature and life are effective and compelling without ever approaching a preachy level." Voice Youth Advocates

Chasing the bear; a young Spenser novel. Philomel Books 2009 169p $14.99

Grades: 7 8 9 10 **Fic**

1. Bullies -- Fiction 2. Friendship -- Fiction 3. Kidnapping -- Fiction 4. Child abuse -- Fiction

ISBN 978-0-399-24776-7; 0-399-24776-9

LC 2008-52725

Spenser reflects back to when he was fourteen-years-old and how he helped his best friend Jeannie when she was abducted by her abusive father.

"A clean, sharp jab of a read." Booklist

The **Edenville** Owls. Philomel Books 2007 194p $17.99

Grades: 6 7 8 9 **Fic**

1. Mystery fiction 2. Teachers -- Fiction 3. Basketball -- Fiction 4. Friendship -- Fiction

ISBN 978-0-399-24656-2; 0-399-24656-8

LC 2006-34533

Fourteen-year-old Bobby, living in a small Massachusetts town just after World War II, finds himself facing many new challenges as he tries to pull together his coachless basketball team, cope with new feelings for his old friend Joanie, and discover the identity of the mysterious stranger who seems to be threatening his teacher.

"The poignant, well-articulated coming-of-age moments deepen the heart-pounding suspense." Booklist

Parkinson, Curtis

Domenic's war; a story of the Battle of Monte Cassino. Tundra Books 2006 191p pa $9.95

Grades: 6 7 8 9 **Fic**

1. World War, 1939-1945 -- Fiction

ISBN 0-88776-751-6

"Based on actual experiences, this World War II novel tells the stories of Italians living near Monte Cassino, caught between the German army and the Allied forces. Young Domenic Luppino and his family live north of the fighting, but fear the advancing troops. Fifteen-year-old Antonio lost his entire family when fighting moved into the town, and now he's on his own. Both boys face hardships and risk their lives for friends and family. Their stories of strength, resourcefulness, and survival are deftly placed within the context of the Monte Cassino campaign and will give readers a poignant look at the ways in which the war affected average citizens." SLJ

Parkinson, Siobhán

Long story short. Roaring Brook Press 2011 160p $16.99

Grades: 6 7 8 9 10 **Fic**

1. Ireland -- Fiction 2. Siblings -- Fiction 3. Runaway children -- Fiction

ISBN 978-1-59643-647-3; 1-59643-647-6

LC 2010-29023

Fourteen-year-old Jono and his eight-year-old sister Julie run away when, soon after their grandmother's death, their alcoholic mother hits Julie, but when the police find them in Galway, Jono learns he is in big trouble.

"A deeply affecting story about what can go wrong when adults fail children and the choices available to them are all bad." Publ Wkly

Patneaude, David

Thin wood walls. Houghton Mifflin 2004 231p $16

Grades: 7 8 9 10 **Fic**

1. World War, 1939-1945 -- Fiction 2. Japanese Americans -- Evacuation and relocation, 1942-1945 -- Fiction

ISBN 0-618-34290-7

LC 2004-1014

When the Japanese bomb Pearl Harbor, Joe Hamada and his family face growing prejudice, eventually being torn away from their home and sent to a relocation camp in California, even as his older brother joins the United States Army to fight in the war.

"Basing his story on extensive research and interviews, the author does a fine job of bringing the daily experience up close through the story of an American kid torn from home." Booklist

Paton Walsh, Jill

★ A **parcel** of patterns. Farrar, Straus & Giroux 1983 136p hardcover o.p. pa $5.95

Grades: 7 8 9 10 **Fic**

1. Plague -- Fiction 2. Great Britain -- Fiction

ISBN 0-374-35750-1; 0-374-45743-3 pa

LC 83-48143

Mall Percival tells how the plague came to her Derbyshire village of Eyam in the year 1665, how the villagers determined to isolate themselves to prevent further spread of the disease, and how three-fourths of them died before the end of the following year.

"Historical in broad outline, the narrative blends superb characterizations, skillful plotting, and convincing speech for a hauntingly memorable story that offers a richly textured picture of the period." Child Book Rev Serv

Paton, Alan

Cry, the beloved country. Scribner Classics 2003 316p $28; pa $15

Grades: 7 8 9 10 11 12 Adult **Fic**

1. Zulus (African people) 2. Race relations -- Fiction 3. Anglican and Episcopal clergy

ISBN 0-7432-6195-X; 0-7432-6217-4 pa

First published 1948

"Reverend Kumalo, a black South African preacher, is called to Johannesburg to rescue his sister. There he learns that his son Absalom has been accused of murdering a young white attorney whose interests and sympathies had been with the natives. Despite this, the attorney's father comes to the aid of the minister to help the natives in their struggle to survive a drought." Shapiro. Fic for Youth. 3d edition

Patrick, Cat

Forgotten; a novel. Little, Brown 2011 288p $17.99

Grades: 7 8 9 10 11 **Fic**

1. School stories 2. Memory -- Fiction 3. Family life -- Fiction 4. Dating (Social customs) -- Fiction

ISBN 978-0-316-09461-0; 0-316-09461-7

LC 2010-43032

Sixteen-year-old London Lane forgets everything each night and must use notes to struggle through the day, even to recall her wonderful boyfriend, but she "remembers" future events and as her "flashforwards" become more disturbing she realizes she must learn more about the past lest it destroy her future.

"Patrick raises philosophical issues of real interest. . . . Thoughtful readers will enjoy the mind games, romance readers will enjoy the relationship dynamics, and all readers will find themselves inexorably pulled into a logical yet surprising and compelling finish." Booklist

The **Originals**; Cat Patrick. 1st ed. Little, Brown and Co. 2013 304 p. (hardcover) $18

Grades: 8 9 10 11 12 **Fic**

1. Sisters -- Fiction 2. Human cloning -- Fiction 3. Dating (Social customs) -- Fiction 4. Cloning -- Fiction 5. Individuality -- Fiction 6. Single-parent families -- Fiction

ISBN 0316219436; 9780316219433

LC 2012029853

In this novel, by Cat Patrick, "17-year-olds Lizzie, Ella, and Betsey Best grew up as identical triplets . . . until they discovered a shocking family secret. They're actually closer than sisters, they're clones . . . , hiding from a government agency that would expose them. . . . Then Lizzie meets Sean Kelly. . . . As their relationship develops, Lizzie realizes that she's not a carbon copy of her sisters; she's an individual with unique dreams and desires." (Publisher's note)

Revived; by Cat Patrick. 1st ed. Little, Brown & Co. 2012 336 p. (hardcover) $17.99; (paperback) $8.99

Grades: 7 8 9 10 11 12 **Fic**

1. Drugs -- Testing 2. Secrecy -- Fiction 3. Science -- Experiments -- Fiction 4. Death -- Fiction 5. Drugs -- Fiction 6. High schools -- Fiction 7. Moving, Household -- Fiction

ISBN 0316094625; 9780316094627; 9780316094634

LC 2011026950

This book, by Cat Patrick, follows Daisy, who since the age of five has been "part of a top-secret clinical trial for a drug called Revive that can bring the deceased back to life. . . . Daisy uncovers some secrets within the program: a mysterious extra case file, a new test batch of Revive, some unexplained car crashes, and the erratic behavior of the mysterious man at the top, nicknamed God." (Bulletin of the Center for Children's Books)

Patrick, Denise Lewis

A **matter** of souls. Denise Lewis Patrick. Carolrhoda Lab. 2014 186p $16.95

Grades: 7 8 9 10 11 12 **Fic**

1. African Americans — Southern States — Fiction; 2. Race relations — Fiction; 3. Southern States — History — Fiction; 4. American short stories; 5. African Americans — History; 6. Southern States — Fiction

ISBN: 0761392807; 9780761392804

LC 2013017597

Through a series of vignettes the author "considers the souls of black men and women across centuries and continents. In each, she takes the measure of their dignity, describes their dreams, and catalogs their fears. Brutality, beauty, laughter, rage, and love all take their turns in each story, but the final impression is of indomitable, luminous, and connected souls." (Publisher's note)

"Eight short stories with long memory cut to the quick-all the more as they could be true. Patrick's tales from the distant and not-so-distant past shed fresh light on interracial and intraracial conflicts that shape and often distort the realities of African-Americans. . . . The plots and characters change from one story to the next, but each one artfully tells a poignant truth without flinching. Shocking, informative and powerful, this volume offers spectacular literary snapshots of black history and culture." Kirkus

Patron, Susan

Behind the masks; the diary of Angeline Reddy. Susan Patron. Scholastic 2012 293 p. ill., map (paper-over-board) $12.99

Grades: 5 6 7 8 9 **Fic**

1. Mystery fiction 2. Diaries -- Fiction 3. Thieves -- Fiction 4. Gold mines and mining -- Fiction 5. Frontier and pioneer life -- California -- Fiction 6. Lawyers -- Fiction 7. Mystery and detective stories 8. Robbers and outlaws -- Fiction 9. California -- History -- 19th century -- Fiction

ISBN 9780545304375

LC 2011023826

"[T]his Dear America series title [is] set in Bodie, California, in 1880. Fourteen-year-old diarist and would-be dramatist Angeline Reddy does not believe her father, criminal lawyer Patrick Reddy, has been murdered. Convinced his disappearance is purposeful, Angie investigates his 'demise' and tries to bring him back to their rough-and-tumble mining community. Assisted by friends, a dashing young Wells Fargo clerk, and the members of a local theater troupe, . . . Angie offers a revealing look at frontier life "especially preoccupations with thespian entertainments, racial and social prejudices, and vigilante justice."(Booklist)

Patt, Beverly

★ **Best** friends forever; a World War II scrapbook. with illustrations by Shula Klinger. Marshall Cavendish 2010 92p il $17.99

Grades: 5 6 7 8 **Fic**

1. Friendship -- Fiction 2. World War, 1939-1945 -- Fiction 3. Japanese Americans -- Evacuation and relocation, 1942-1945 -- Fiction

ISBN 978-0-7614-5577-6; 0-7614-5577-9

LC 2008-20875

Fourteen-year-old Louise keeps a scrapbook detailing the events in her life after her best friend, Dottie, a Japanese-American girl, and her family are sent to a relocation camp during World War II.

"If the drama of the girls separation isn't enough, a romantic subplot and the antics of Dottie's goofy dog (living with Louise in her absence) will surely keep young readers interested. This heartwarming tale of steadfast friendship makes a wonderful access point for learning more about World War II and Japanese internment." SLJ

Includes bibliographical references

Patterson, James

Homeroom diaries. by James Patterson & Lisa Papademetriou ; illustrated by Keino. Little, Brown and Co. 2014 246p $18.00

Grades: 7 8 9 10 **Fic**

1. Diaries — Fiction 2. Foster home care — Fiction 3. Friendship — Fiction 4. High schools — Fiction 5. Teenage girls —Fiction

ISBN: 0316207624; 9780316207621

LC 2013016061

"Margaret 'Cuckoo' Clarke recently had a brief stay in a mental institution following an emotional breakdown, but she's turning over a new leaf with her 'Operation Happiness.' She's determined to beat down the bad vibes of the Haters, the Terror Teachers, and all of the trials and tribulations of high school by writing and drawing in her diary." (Publisher's note)

"Cuckoo is a well-developed and accessible protagonist. She is introspective and she copes with life's difficulties by spending a lot of time in her head and writing alternative endings to movies in her journal. Despite the fact that serious issues (a negligent mother, an attempted sexual assault, and an incident of cyberbullying) are at play, the lighthearted tone adds levity to the work." SLJ

Maximum Ride: the angel experiment. Little, Brown 2005 422p (Maximum Ride) $16.99

Grades: 7 8 9 10 **Fic**

1. Science fiction 2. Genetic engineering -- Fiction

ISBN 0-316-15556-X

LC 2004-18623

After the mutant Erasers abduct the youngest member of their group, the "bird kids," who are the result of genetic experimentation, take off in pursuit and find themselves struggling to understand their own origins and purpose.

"Smart-mouthed sympathetic characters and copious butt-kicking make this fast read pure escapist pleasure." Horn Book Guide

Other titles in this series are:

School's out - forever (2006)

Saving the world and other extreme sports (2007)

Final warning (2008)

Max (2009)

Fang (2010)

Angel (2011)

Patterson, Valerie O.

The **other** side of blue. Clarion Books 2009 223p $16

Grades: 7 8 9 10 **Fic**

1. Artists -- Fiction 2. Curacao -- Fiction 3. Bereavement -- Fiction 4. Mother-daughter relationship -- Fiction

ISBN 978-0-547-24436-5; 0-547-24436-3

LC 2008-49233

The summer after her father drowned off the island of Curacao, Cyan and her mother, a painter, return to the house they stay at every summer, along with the daughter of her mother's fiance, but Cyan blames her mother and spends her time trying to find out what really happened to her father

"In her memorable first-person voice, filled with the minute observations of a young artist, Cyan sketches out with believable detail the beautiful setting, the unspoken family tension, and her fragile recovery of hope after loss." Booklist

Pattou, Edith

East. Harcourt 2003 498p hardcover o.p. pa $8.95

Grades: 7 8 9 10 **Fic**

1. Fairy tales 2. Bears -- Fiction

ISBN 0-15-204563-5; 0-15-205221-6 pa

LC 2003-2338

A young woman journeys to a distant castle on the back of a great white bear who is the victim of a cruel enchantment

"Readers with a taste for fantasy and folklore will embrace Pattou's . . . lushly rendered retelling of 'East of the Sun and West of the Moon'." Publ Wkly

Pauley, Kimberly

Cat Girl's day off; Kimberly Pauley. Tu Books 2012 334 p. (hardcover : alk. paper) $17.95

Grades: 6 7 8 9 10 **Fic**

1. Cats -- Fiction 2. Mystery fiction 3. Adventure fiction 4. High school students -- Fiction 5. Parapsychology -- Juvenile literature 6. Schools -- Fiction 7. High schools -- Fiction 8. Chicago (Ill.) -- Fiction 9. Mystery and detective stories 10. Human-animal communication -- Fiction 11. Family life -- Illinois -- Chicago -- Fiction 12. Motion pictures -- Production and direction -- Fiction

ISBN 1600608833; 9781600608834; 9781600608841

LC 2011042997

In this young adult novel, "High school sophomore Natalie 'Nat' Ng has a 'Talent' she's not proud of: the ability to talk to cats. Her younger sister is a 'supergenius' with chameleonlike abilities; her older sister is proficient in truth divination and levitation, and has X-ray vision; and her parents work for the Bureau of Extrasensory Regulation and Management. When a film crew comes to Nat's Chicago high school to shoot a takeoff of 'Ferris Bueller's Day Off' things get fishy: the female star isn't acting like herself, and Nat learns from a cat that celebrity blogger Easton West may not be who she claims to be. Along with her friends Oscar and Melly, Nat gets dragged into a whirlwind adventure to find out what happened to the real Easton." (Publishers Weekly)

Paulsen, Gary

Crush; the theory, practice, and destructive properties of love. Gary Paulsen. Wendy Lamb Books 2012 136 p.

Grades: 5 6 7 8 **Fic**

1. Love -- Fiction 2. Humorous fiction 3. Crushes -- Fiction 4. High school students -- Fiction 5. Dating (Social customs) -- Fiction 6. Humorous stories 7. Interpersonal relations -- Fiction

ISBN 0385742304; 9780307974532; 9780375990540; 9780385742306; 9780385742313

LC 2011028915

In this book, "Tina, aka the most beautiful girl he's ever seen, has stolen Kevin's heart, although she's blissfully oblivious to the effect she has on him. . . . Rather than reveal his ardor outright, Kevin decides it's safer to first make a scientific study of just how love works by setting up romantic opportunities for his victims (otherwise known as study subjects). He starts by trying to create a candlelit dinner for his parents, although he accidentally causes a fire." (Kirkus Reviews)

The **island**. Orchard Bks. 1988 202p hardcover o.p. pa $5.99

Grades: 8 9 10 11 12 **Fic**

1. Islands -- Fiction

ISBN 0-531-05749-6; 0-439-78662-2 pa

LC 87-24761

Fifteen-year-old Wil discovers himself and the wonders of nature when he leaves home to live on an island in northern Wisconsin.

"With humor and psychological genius, Paulsen develops strong adolescent characters who lend new power to youth's plea to be allowed to apply individual skills in their risk-taking." Voice Youth Advocates

Nightjohn. Delacorte Press 1993 92p $15.95; pa $5.99

Grades: 7 8 9 10 **Fic**

1. Reading -- Fiction 2. Slavery -- Fiction 3. African Americans -- Fiction

ISBN 0-385-30838-8; 0-440-21936-1 pa

LC 92-1222

Twelve-year-old Sarny's brutal life as a slave becomes even more dangerous when a newly arrived slave offers to teach her how to read

"Paulsen is at his best here: the writing is stark and bare-boned, without stylistic pretensions of any kind. The narrator's voice is strong and true, the violence real but stylized with an almost mythic tone. . . . The simplicity of the text will make the book ideal for older reluctant readers who can handle violence but can't or won't handle fancy writing in long books. Best of all, the metaphor of reading as an act of freedom speaks for itself through striking action unembroidered by didactic messages." Bull Cent Child Books

The **Schernoff** discoveries. Delacorte Press 1997 103p pa $4.99

Grades: 5 6 7 8 **Fic**

1. School stories 2. Friendship -- Fiction

ISBN 0440414636

LC 96045390

This "novel, narrated by a 14-year-old, self-confessed geek, focuses on the narrator's friend, Harold. Equally geeky and brainy as well, Harold takes the lead in {a} . . . series of adventures ranging from the unusual but pragmatic (enrolling in home economics to meet girls) to the sneaky and possibly suicidal (taking revenge on the football players who broke his slide rule by giving them a cake flavored with 43 boxes of chocolate laxatives)." (Booklist)

"The tone is breezy, funny, and sometimes touching (but not too mushy) and bound to keep the most reluctant reader chuckling." Bull Cent Child Books

Soldier's heart; a novel of the Civil War. Delacorte Press 1998 106p $15.95; pa $5.99

Grades: 7 8 9 10 **Fic**

1. Post-traumatic stress disorder -- Fiction 2. United States -- History -- Civil War, 1861-1865

ISBN 0-385-32498-7; 0-440-22838-7 pa

LC 98-10038

"This compelling and realistic depiction of war is based on a true story. . . . Paulsen's writing is crisp and fast-paced, and this soldier's story will haunt readers long after they finish reading the novel." Book Rep

★ **Woods** runner. Wendy Lamb Books 2010 164p $15.99; lib bdg $18.99

Grades: 6 7 8 9 **Fic**

1. Spies -- Fiction 2. Soldiers -- Fiction 3. Kidnapping -- Fiction 4. Native Americans -- Fiction 5. Frontier and pioneer life -- Fiction

ISBN 978-0-385-73884-2; 0-385-73884-6; 978-0-385-90751-4 lib bdg; 0-385-90751-6 lib bdg

LC 2009-27397

From his 1776 Pennsylvania homestead, thirteen-year-old Samuel, who is a highly-skilled woodsman, sets out toward New York City to rescue his parents from the band of British soldiers and Indians who kidnapped them after slaughtering most of their community. Includes historical notes.

"Paulsen fortifies this illuminating and gripping story with interspersed historical sections that offer details about frontier life and the war (such as technology, alliances, and other period information), helping place Sam's struggles in context." Publ Wkly

Pausewang, Gudrun

Dark hours; translated by John Brownjohn. Annick Press 2006 208p $21.95

Grades: 6 7 8 9 **Fic**

1. Refugees -- Fiction 2. World War, 1939-1945 -- Fiction

ISBN 1-55451-042-2

A story "what it was like for German children at the end of the war, when the Russians and the Allies were bombing their country. Gisel, 15, flees her village home. Separated from her mother and grandmother in the crowds of refugees, she must care for herself and her younger siblings after all are trapped under the rubble of a bombed building. The story centers on the adventure of brave kids surviving on their own." Booklist

"Well written with suspense and powerful sentiments, this story will spark discussion." SLJ

Traitor; translated from the German by Rachel Ward. Carolrhoda Books 2006 220p hardcover o.p. pa $9.95

Grades: 7 8 9 10 **Fic**

1. Germany -- Fiction 2. Prisoners of war -- Fiction 3. World War, 1939-1945 -- Fiction

ISBN 0-8225-6195-6; 0-7613-6571-0 pa

LC 2005-33379

During the closing months of World War II, a fifteen-year-old German girl must decide whether or not to help an escaped Russian prisoner of war, despite the serious consequences if she does so.

"Pausewang presents an exciting and thought-provoking novel." SLJ

Peacock, Shane

Eye of the crow. Tundra Books 2007 264p (The boy Sherlock Holmes) $24.99; pa $9.95

Grades: 6 7 8 9 10 **Fic**

1. Mystery fiction 2. Great Britain -- History -- 19th century -- Fiction

ISBN 978-0-88776-850-7; 0-88776-850-4; 978-0-88776-919-1 pa; 0-88776-919-5 pa

"A young woman is brutally murdered in a dark back street of Whitechapel; a young Arab is discovered with the bloody murder weapon; and a thirteen-year-old Sherlock Holmes, who was seen speaking with the alleged killer as he was hauled into jail, is suspected to be his accomplice. . . . Although imaginative reconstruction of Holmes childhood has been the subject of literary and cinematic endeavors, Peacock's take ranks among the most successful." Bull Cent Child Books

Other titles in this series are:
Death in the air (2008)
The dragon turn (2011)
The secret fiend (2010)
Vanishing girl (2009)

Pearce, Jackson

As you wish. HarperTeen 2009 298p $16.99

Grades: 6 7 8 9 **Fic**

1. School stories 2. Wishes -- Fiction 3. Artists -- Fiction 4. Popularity -- Fiction 5. Homosexuality -- Fiction

ISBN 006166152X; 0061661538; 0061661546; 9780061661525; 9780061661532; 9780061661549

LC 2008-44033

When a genie arrives to grant sixteen-year-old Viola's wish to feel she belongs, as she did before her best friend/boyfriend announced that he is gay, her delay in making wishes gives her and the mysterious Jinn time to fall in love.

"Written in alternating chapters between Jinn and Viola, the story unfolds to rapidly change from the regular 'genie in the bottle' saga to a poignant tale of love and sacrifices made in the name of love. . . . The result is a fabulous fantasy from a first time author." Voice Youth Advocates

Sisters red. Little, Brown 2010 328p $16.99

Grades: 9 10 11 12 **Fic**

1. Sisters -- Fiction 2. Werewolves -- Fiction 3. Supernatural -- Fiction

ISBN 978-0-316-06868-0

LC 2009-44734

After a Fenris, or werewolf, killed their grandmother and almost killed them, sisters Scarlett and Rosie March devote themselves to hunting and killing the beasts that prey on teenaged girls, learning how to lure them with red cloaks and occasionally using the help of their old friend, Silas, the woodsman's son.

"Told by the sisters in alternating chapters, this well-written, high-action adventure grabs readers and never lets go." SLJ

Pearce, Jacqueline

Manga touch; [by] Jacqueline Pearce. Orca Books 2007 105p pa $8.95

Grades: 6 7 8 **Fic**

1. Travel -- Fiction

ISBN 978-1-55143-746-0 pa; 1-55143-746-5 pa

Dana takes a school trip to Japan to learn about Japanese culture and artwork. She surprisingly discovers she has a lot to learn about people as well as manga art.

"Readers will enjoy the skillful way Pearce weaves in facts regarding Japanese culture while still keeping things interesting." Voice Youth Advocates

Pearson, Joanna

The **rites** & wrongs of Janice Wills. Arthur A. Levine Books 2011 218p $16.99

Grades: 8 9 10 11 12 **Fic**

1. School stories 2. Anthropology -- Fiction 3. North Carolina -- Fiction

ISBN 978-0-545-19773-1; 0-545-19773-2

LC 2010029348

Aspiring anthropologist Janice Wills reports on the sociocultural ordeals of being an almost-seventeen-year-old in Melva, North Carolina, including "Beautiful Rich Girls," parties, and the Miss Livermush pageant.

"This anthropological observation-style novel is unique and provides a great social commentary on the life of teenagers. It is a cute story that includes mentions of bisexuality, some strong language, and the hint that the Hot Theater Guy might push Janice too far, but it remains a fun look at life in small town Southern society." Voice Youth Advocates

Pearson, Mary E.

★ The **adoration** of Jenna Fox; [by] Mary E. Pearson. Henry Holt and Co. 2008 272p $16.95; pa $8.99

Grades: 7 8 9 10 11 12 Fic

1. Science fiction 2. Bioethics -- Fiction

ISBN 978-0-8050-7668-4; 0-8050-7668-9; 978-0-312-59441-1 pa; 0-312-59441-0 pa

LC 2007-27314

In the not-too-distant future, when biotechnological advances have made synthetic bodies and brains possible but illegal, a seventeen-year-old girl, recovering from a serious accident and suffering from memory lapses, learns a startling secret about her existence.

"The science . . . and the science fiction are fascinating, but what will hold readers most are the moral issues of betrayal, loyalty, sacrifice, and survival." Booklist

Followed by The Fox inheritance (2011)

Fox forever; Mary E. Pearson. Henry Holt and Company 2013 304 p. (hardcover) $17.99

Grades: 7 8 9 10 11 12 Fic

1. Science fiction 2. Dystopian fiction 3. Bioethics -- Fiction 4. Biotechnology -- Fiction 5. Medical ethics -- Fiction 6. Government, resistance to -- Fiction

ISBN 0805094342; 9780805094343

LC 2012027677

This young adult novel, by Mary E. Pearson, is the conclusion to the "Jenna Fox Chronicles." "After . . . 260 years as a disembodied mind in a little black box, [Lock Jenkins] has a . . . body. But . . . he'll have to return the Favor he accepted from the . . . Network. Locke must infiltrate the home of a government official by gaining the trust of his daughter, seventeen-year-old Raine, and he soon finds himself pulled deep into the world of the resistance--and into Raine's life." (Publisher's note)

The **Fox** Inheritance; [by] Mary E. Pearson. Henry Holt 2011 384p $16.99

Grades: 7 8 9 10 11 12 Fic

1. Science fiction 2. Bioethics -- Fiction

ISBN 0805088296; 9780805088298

LC 2011004800

Sequel to: The adoration of Jenna Fox (2008)

Two-hundred-sixty years after a terrible accident destroyed their bodies, sixteen-year-old Locke and seventeen-year-old Kara have been brought back to life in newly bioengineered bodies, with many questions about the world they find themselves in and more than two centuries of horrible memories of being trapped in a digital netherworld wondering what would become of them.

"Pearson delivers another spellbinding thriller. . . . A dazzling blend of science fiction, mystery, and teen friendship drama." Publ Wkly

★ The **miles** between; [by] Mary E. Pearson. Henry Holt 2009 266p $16.99

Grades: 9 10 11 12 Fic

1. School stories 2. Friendship -- Fiction

ISBN 978-0-8050-8828-1; 0-8050-8828-8

LC 2008-50277

Seventeen-year-old Destiny keeps a painful childhood secret all to herself until she and three classmates from her exclusive boarding school take off on an unauthorized road trip in search of "one fair day."

"Pearson skillfully separates truth from illusion and offers an uplifting book, in which grace and redemption are never left to chance." Booklist

A **room** on Lorelei Street; [by] Mary E. Pearson. Henry Holt 2005 266p $16.95

Grades: 9 10 11 12 Fic

1. Texas -- Fiction 2. Alcoholism -- Fiction 3. Family life -- Fiction

ISBN 0-8050-7667-0

LC 2004-54015

To escape a miserable existence taking care of her alcoholic mother, seventeen-year-old Zoe rents a room from an eccentric woman, but her earnings as a waitress after school are minimal and she must go to extremes to cover expenses.

"Readers drawn to rescue dramas may particularly appreciate this story of a girl who's trying against odds to rescue herself." Bull Cent Child Books

Peck, Dale

Sprout. Bloomsbury 2009 277p $16.99

Grades: 9 10 11 12 Fic

1. Kansas -- Fiction 2. Friendship -- Fiction 3. Homosexuality -- Fiction 4. Father-son relationship -- Fiction

ISBN 978-1-59990-160-2; 1-59990-160-9

LC 2008-40922

ALA GLBTRT Stonewall Book Award Honor Book (2010)

Moving from Long Island to Kansas after his mother dies, a teenaged boy nicknamed Sprout is surprised to find new friends, a fascinating landscape, and romantic love.

"Sharply witty and bittersweet, this story . . . is a stellar step ahead for young adult literature's traditional examination of the life of the heroic antihero. Finely honed characters and an engaging voice make it an easy book for teen readers who like emotional challenges as well as word tricks to love." Voice Youth Advocates

Peck, Richard

The **river** between us. Dial Bks. 2003 164p $16.99; pa $6.99

Grades: 7 8 9 10 Fic

1. Race relations -- Fiction 2. Racially mixed people -- Fiction

ISBN 0-8037-2735-6; 0-14-240310-5 pa

LC 2002-34815

During the early days of the Civil War, the Pruitt family takes in two mysterious young ladies who have fled New Orleans to come north to Illinois

"The harsh realities of war are brutally related in a complex, always surprising plot that resonates on mutiple levels." Horn Book Guide

Peck, Robert Newton

★ A **day** no pigs would die. Knopf 1973 150p $25; pa $5.50

Grades: 6 7 8 9 Fic

1. Pigs -- Fiction 2. Shakers -- Fiction 3. Family life -- Fiction 4. Autobiographical stories 5. Father-son relationship -- Fiction

ISBN 0-394-48235-2; 0-679-85306-5 pa

"Rob lives a rigorous life on a Shaker farm in Vermont in the 1920s. Since farm life is earthy, this book is filled with Yankee humor and explicit descriptions of animals mating. A painful incident that involves the slaughter of Rob's beloved pet pig is instrumental in urging him toward adulthood. The death of his father completes the process of his accepting responsibility." Shapiro. Fic for Youth. 3d edition

Peet, Mal

★ **Life**; an exploded diagram. Candlewick Press 2011 385p il $17.99

Grades: 9 10 11 12 **Fic**

1. War stories 2. Family life -- Fiction 3. Great Britain -- Fiction 4. Social classes -- Fiction

ISBN 978-0-7636-5227-2; 978-0-7636-5631-7 ebook

LC 2010042742

In 1960s Norfolk, England, seventeen-year-old Clem Ackroyd lives with his mother and grandmother in a tiny cottage, but his life is transformed when he falls in love with the daughter of a wealthy farmer in this tale that flashes back through the stories of three generations.

"This [book] is mesmerizing through the sheer force and liveliness of its prose, as well as its unpredictable, inexorable plot. . . . Peet's subtle, literary play with narrative voice, style, and chronology make this a satisfyingly sophisticated teen novel. Outstanding." Horn Book

★ **Tamar**. Candlewick Press 2007 424p $17.99

Grades: 8 9 10 11 12 **Fic**

1. Netherlands -- Fiction 2. Grandfathers -- Fiction 3. World War, 1939-1945 -- Fiction

ISBN 978-0-7636-3488-9; 0-7636-3488-3

LC 2006-51837

In 1995, 15-year-old Tamar inherits a box containing a series of coded messages from his late grandfather. The messages show Tamar the life that his grandfather lived during World War II the life of an Allied undercover operative in Nazi-occupied Holland.

"Peet's plot is tightly constructed, and striking, descriptive language, full of metaphor, grounds the story." Booklist

Pennington, Kate

Brief candle; [by] Kate Pennington. Hodder Children's 2004 262p pa $12.95

Grades: 6 7 8 9 **Fic**

1. Poets 2. Authors 3. Novelists

ISBN 0-12-92965-2

"Along with losing herself in romantic poetry, 14-year-old Emily Bronte loves to wander the wild landscape around her father's parsonage. . . . Her two passions thrillingly collide when she encounters a distraught young man, whose courtship of a girl outside his station has left him jobless and desperate. . . . Pennington's homage offers the most to teens familiar with Bronte's Wuthering Heights. . . . But even readers without much previous knowledge about the book's underpinnings . . . will enjoy the universally accessible view of an ill-fated love and the dreamy restless teen who acts on its behalf." SLJ

Perera, Anna

★ **Guantanamo** boy. Albert Whitman 2011 339p $17.99

Grades: 7 8 9 10 11 12 **Fic**

1. Cousins -- Fiction 2. Muslims -- Fiction 3. Torture -- Fiction 4. Prisoners -- Fiction 5. Prejudices -- Fiction 6. Guantanamo Bay Naval Base (Cuba) -- Detention Camp -- Fiction

ISBN 978-0-8075-3077-1; 0-8075-3077-8

LC 2010048016

Six months after the events of September 11, 2001, Khalid, a Muslim fifteen-year-old boy from England is kidnapped during a family trip to Pakistan and imprisoned in Guantanamo Bay, Cuba, where he is held for two years suffering interrogations, water-boarding, isolation, and more for reasons unknown to him.

"Readers will feel every ounce of Khalid's terror, frustration, and helplessness in this disturbing look at a sad, ongoing chapter in contemporary history." Publ Wkly

Perez, Ashley Hope

The **knife** and the butterfly; Ashley Hope Pérez. Carolrhoda Lab 2012 209 p.

Grades: 9 10 11 12 **Fic**

1. Gangs -- Fiction 2. Juvenile delinquency -- Fiction 3. Salvadoran Americans -- Fiction 4. Juvenile detention homes -- Fiction

ISBN 0761361561; 9780761361565

LC 2011021236

"Fifteen-year-old Salvadoran Martín 'Azael' Arevalo awakens in a cell remembering bits and pieces of a fight in a Houston park between his gang, Mara Salvatrucha or MS-13, and Crazy Crew. Yet he cannot recall how the fight ended or why he is behind bars again. . . . Azael finds himself assigned to the secret observation of a white 17-year-old girl named Alexis 'Lexi' Allen, although he fails to see any connection the two might have had on the outside. While Azael hates Lexi at the beginning, he finds himself beginning to empathize with the struggles she has faced over her life." (Kirkus)

What can(t) wait. Carolrhoda 2011 234p $17.95

Grades: 7 8 9 10 **Fic**

1. Family life -- Fiction 2. Mexican Americans -- Fiction

ISBN 978-0-7613-6155-8; 0-7613-6155-3

LC 2010-28175

"Pérez fills a hole in YA lit by giving Marisa an authentic voice that smoothly blends Spanish phrases into dialogue and captures the pressures of both Latina life and being caught between two cultures." Kirkus

Perez, Marlene

Dead is a battlefield; Marlene Perez. Graphia 2012 227 p.

Grades: 7 8 9 10 **Fic**

1. Zombies -- Fiction 2. Perfumes -- Fiction 3. Supernatural -- Fiction 4. Female friendship -- Fiction 5. High school students -- Fiction 6. High schools -- Fiction 7. Interpersonal relations -- Fiction

ISBN 0547607342; 9780547607344

LC 2011031489

In this young adult novel, a "high-school freshman learns that she's one of a group of women who fight evil beasties in her supernatural town of Nightshade, Calif. In this sixth installment of the "Dead Is . . ." series, Jessica discovers to her dismay that she's a "virago," a woman warrior destined to fight paranormal baddies. Jessica worries, too, about her very best friend in the whole world, Eva, who's been acting strangely since she discovered a new perfume. . . . Jessica also finds herself attracted to Dominic . . . while she's juggling dates with Connor. . . . Meanwhile, Eva joins the groupies hanging around creepy Edgar and becomes ever more hostile toward Jessica, even trying to bite her. It seems that Edgar's perfume turns girls into zombies. Now Jessica has to find a cure and drive Edgar out of town." (Kirkus)

Dead is a killer tune; Marlene Perez. Graphia 2012 204 p. (paperback) $7.99

Grades: 8 9 10 11 12 **Fic**

1. Accidents -- Fiction 2. Bands (Music) -- Fiction 3. Mystery fiction 4. Music -- Fiction 5. High schools -- Fiction 6. Supernatural -- Fiction 7. Interpersonal relations -- Fiction

ISBN 0547608349; 9780547608341

LC 2012014798

Author Marlene Perez tells the story of a Battle of the Bands competition. "Jessica's romance with Dominic hasn't exactly progressed smoothly . . . Dominic's band, Side Effects May Vary, finds competition in an out-of-town act followed by a large entourage of obsessed fans--Hamlin, fronted by Brett Piper. When the most competitive bands start losing members to recklessness and bizarre accidents, Jessica must not only get to the bottom of the mystery, but also step into the spotlight as a musician herself." (Kirkus)

Dead is just a dream; by Marlene Perez. Houghton Mifflin Harcourt 2013 164 p. (Dead is) (hardback) $16.99

Grades: 8 9 10 **Fic**

1. Fantasy fiction 2. Clowns -- Fiction 3. Homicide -- Fiction 4. Murder -- Fiction 5. Schools -- Fiction 6. Nightmares -- Fiction 7. High schools -- Fiction 8. Supernatural -- Fiction 9. Psychic ability -- Fiction 10. Interpersonal relations -- Fiction

ISBN 0544102622; 9780544102620

LC 2013003883

"Jessica and her virago friends are back in this latest Dead Is series entry. This time they're in the midst of four murders, all seemingly connected to creepy paintings being installed in the homes of Nightshade's most influential citizens. Just when the girls think they've solved the mystery, a bloody clown begins to stalk Jessica, confounding their original suspicions...Girl drama, sweet romance, and murder—what more could young teens want in a breezy read?" Booklist

Dead is the new black. Harcourt 2008 190p pa $7.95

Grades: 7 8 9 10 **Fic**

1. School stories 2. Cheerleading -- Fiction 3. Supernatural -- Fiction 4. Extrasensory perception -- Fiction

ISBN 978-0-15-206408-2; 0-15-206408-7

LC 2007027677

While dealing with her first boyfriend and suddenly being pressed into service as a substitute cheerleader, seventeen-year-old Daisy Giordano, daughter and sister of psychics but herself a 'normal', attempts to help her mother discover who is behind a series of bizarre attacks on teenage girls in their little town of Nightshade, California.

"This is the witty and humorous first installment in a series; it provides romance, mystery, friendship, adventure, and the supernatural all rolled up in a fast-paced, plot-twisting story." SLJ

Other titles in this series are:
Dead is a state of mind (2009)
Dead is so last year (2009)
Dead is just a rumor (2010)
Dead is not an option (2011)

Perkins, Lynne Rae

★ **As** easy as falling off the face of the earth. Greenwillow Books 2010 352p il $16.99

Grades: 8 9 10 11 12 **Fic**

1. Adventure fiction 2. Chance -- Fiction 3. Accidents -- Fiction

ISBN 978-0-06-187090-3; 0-06-187090-0

LC 2009-42524

A teenaged boy encounters one comedic calamity after another when his train strands him in the middle of nowhere, and everything comes down to luck.

"The real pleasure is Perkins' relentlessly entertaining writing. . . . Wallowing in the wry humor, small but potent truths, and cheerful implausibility is an absolute delight." Booklist

★ **Criss** cross. Greenwillow Books 2005 337p $16.99; lib bdg $17.89; pa $6.99

Grades: 6 7 8 9 **Fic**

1. Nineteen sixties -- Fiction

ISBN 0-06-009272-6; 0-06-009273-4 lib bdg; 0-06-009274-2 pa

LC 2004-54023

Awarded the Newbery Medal, 2006

Teenagers in a small town in the 1960s experience new thoughts and feelings, question their identities, connect, and disconnect as they search for the meaning of life and love.

"Debbie . . . and Hector . . . narrate most of the novel. Both are 14 years old. Hector is a fabulous character with a wry humor and an appealing sense of self-awareness. . . . The descriptive, measured writing includes poems, prose, haiku, and question-and-answer formats. There is a great deal of humor in this gentle story." SLJ

Perkins, Mitali

Secret keeper. Delacorte Press 2009 225p $16.99; lib bdg $19.99

Grades: 7 8 9 10 **Fic**

1. India -- Fiction 2. Sisters -- Fiction 3. Family life -- Fiction

ISBN 978-0-385-73340-3; 0-385-73340-2; 978-0-385-90356-1 lib bdg; 0-385-90356-1 lib bdg

LC 2008-21475

In 1974 when her father leaves New Delhi, India, to seek a job in New York, Ashi, a tomboy at the advanced age of sixteen, feels thwarted in the home of her extended family in Calcutta where she, her mother, and sister must stay, and when her father dies before he can send for them, they must remain with their relatives and observe the old-fashioned traditions that Ashi hates.

"The plot is full of surprising secrets rooted in the characters' conflicts and deep connections with each other. The two sisters and their mutual sacrifices are both heartbreaking and hopeful." Booklist

Perkins, Stephanie

Anna and the French kiss. Dutton 2010 372p $16.99

Grades: 7 8 9 10 **Fic**

1. School stories 2. France -- Fiction 3. Foreign study -- Fiction 4. Paris (France) -- Fiction

ISBN 978-0-525-42327-0; 0-525-42327-3

LC 2009-53290

"Perkin's debut surpasses the usual chick-lit fare with smart dialogue, fresh characters and plenty of tingly interactions, all set amid pastries, parks and walks along the Seine in arguably the most romantic city in the world." Kirkus

Lola and the boy next door. Dutton Books 2011 338p $16.99

Grades: 9 10 11 12 **Fic**

1. Costume -- Fiction 2. San Francisco (Calif.) -- Fiction 3. Dating (Social customs) -- Fiction 4. Father-daughter relationship -- Fiction

ISBN 978-0-525-42328-7

LC 2011015533

"Perkins's novel goes a bit deeper than standard chick-lit fare, and Lola is a sympathetic protagonist even when readers disagree with her decisions. . . . Step back—it's going to fly off the shelves." SLJ

Perl, Erica S.

Vintage Veronica. Alfred A. Knopf 2010 279p $16.99; lib bdg $19.99

Grades: 9 10 11 12 **Fic**

1. Work -- Fiction 2. Obesity -- Fiction 3. Friendship -- Fiction 4. Summer employment -- Fiction 5. Clothing and dress -- Fiction

ISBN 978-0-375-85923-6; 0-375-85923-3; 978-0-375-95923-3 lib bdg; 0-375-95923-8 lib bdg

LC 2009-5280

After getting a job at a vintage clothing shop and quickly bonding with two older girls, fifteen-year-old Veronica finds herself making bad decisions in order to keep their friendship.

"Provides a realistic snapshot of teen dating, dotted with descriptions of some adorable-sounding outfits and filled with well-rounded characters from a variety of subcultures. The protagonist is a self-described 'fat girl' who is not obsessed with losing weight—a much-needed character in young adult fiction. An enjoyable read filled with quirky characters." SLJ

Pesci, David

★ **Amistad**; the thunder of freedom. Marlowe & Co. 1997 292p hardcover o.p. pa $12.95

Grades: 11 12 Adult **Fic**

1. Presidents 2. Senators 3. Trials -- Fiction 4. Slavery -- Fiction 5. Members of Congress 6. Secretaries of state 7. Amistad (Schooner) -- Fiction

ISBN 1-56924-748-X; 1-56924-703-X pa

LC 96-54050

"In August 1839, Singbe-Pleh, a Mende tribesman, led his fellow African captives aboard the Spanish ship Amistad in successful revolt. The Africans took over the ship but could not sail it back to Africa. They were captured and put on trial in Connecticut. . . . The case was politically charged, with pro-slavery President Van Buren's administration wanting to give the Africans to Spain, abolitionists rallying for their freedom, and former President John Quincy Adams eventually defending them before the Supreme Court. Pesci deftly blends the facts of this fascinating historical episode with story." SLJ

Peterfreund, Diana

Across a star-swept sea; Diana Peterfreund. Balzer + Bray, an imprint of HarperCollinsPublishers 2013 464 p. (hardcover bdg.) $17.99

Grades: 9 10 11 12 **Fic**

1. Spy stories 2. Science fiction 3. Spies -- Fiction 4. Social classes -- Fiction 5. Government, Resistance to -- Fiction

ISBN 0062006169; 9780062006165

LC 2013003082

This book, a retelling of "The Scarlet Pimpernel," is a follow-up to Diana Peterfreund's "For Darkness Shows the Stars." Here, on "a Pacific island in a high-tech future, 16-year-old Persis Blake seems the epitome of a lady: beautiful, charming, stylish . . . shallow and stupid. The Wild Poppy, her alter ego, is clever, courageous and noble, crossing the sea to rescue aristos imprisoned by the tyrannical revolution." (Kirkus Reviews)

For darkness shows the stars; by Diana Peterfreund. Balzer + Bray 2012 407 p. (hardback) $17.99

Grades: 9 10 11 12 **Fic**

1. Science fiction 2. Farmers -- Fiction 3. Apocalyptic fiction 4. Man-woman relationship -- Fiction 5. Love -- Fiction 6. Social classes -- Fiction 7. Family problems -- Fiction

ISBN 0062006142; 9780062006141

LC 2011042126

Elliot North fights to save her family's land and her own heart in this post-apocalyptic reimaging of Jane Austen's 'Persuasion.'

"The story stands on its own, a richly envisioned portrait of a society in flux, a steely yet vulnerable heroine, and a young man who does some growing up." Publ Wkly

Peters, Julie Anne, 1952-

By the time you read this, I'll be dead. Disney/Hyperion Books 2010 200p $16.99

Grades: 8 9 10 11 12 **Fic**

1. Bullies -- Fiction 2. Obesity -- Fiction 3. Suicide -- Fiction 4. Depression (Psychology) -- Fiction

ISBN 1-4231-1618-6; 978-1-4231-1618-9

LC 2009-8315

High school student Daelyn Rice, who has been bullied throughout her school career and has more than once attempted suicide, again makes plans to kill herself, in spite of the persistent attempts of an unusual boy to draw her out.

"Powerfully portrayed in the first person, the protagonist's account offers compelling insight into just how spiritually and emotionally devastating bullying can be." Voice Youth Advocates

Between Mom and Jo. Little, Brown 2006 232p $16.99

Grades: 7 8 9 10 **Fic**

1. Lesbians -- Fiction 2. Prejudices -- Fiction 3. Family life -- Fiction 4. Mother-son relationship -- Fiction

ISBN 0-316-73906-5

LC 2005-22012

Fourteen-year-old Nick has a three-legged dog named Lucky 2, some pet fish, and two mothers, whose relationship complicates his entire life as they face prejudice, work problems, alcoholism, cancer, and finally separation.

"A powerful, moving examination of the relationships we forge within the family we are given." Horn Book Guide

Define normal; a novel. Little, Brown 2000 196p $14.95; pa $5.95

Grades: 7 8 9 10 **Fic**

1. Friendship 2. School stories 3. Peer counseling 4. Family problems 5. Parent and child

ISBN 0-316-70631-0; 0-316-73489-6 pa

LC 99-42774

When she agrees to meet with Jasmine as a peer counselor at their middle school, Antonia never dreams that this girl with the black lipstick and pierced eyebrow will end up helping her deal with the serious problems she faces at home and become a good friend

"Readers who are looking for believable characters and a good story about friendship, being different, and growing wiser will appreciate Define 'Normal'" Voice Youth Advocates

It's our prom (so deal with it) a novel. by Julie Anne Peters. 1st ed. Little, Brown 2012 342 p. (paperback) $8.99; (hardcover) $17.99

Grades: 9 10 11 12 **Fic**

1. Lesbians -- Fiction 2. Bisexuals -- Fiction 3. High school students -- Fiction 4. Interpersonal relations -- Fiction 5. Proms -- Fiction 6. Popularity -- Fiction 7. Bisexuality -- Fiction 8. High schools -- Fiction 9. Family problems -- Fiction

ISBN 9780316131445; 031613158X; 9780316131582

LC 2011031756

This novel, by Julie Anne Peters, describes what happens when "Azure's principal gives her the chance to turn the school's traditional (and boring) senior prom into an event that will appeal to everyone. . . . Soon Azure manages to convince her best friends . . . to join . . . as well. . . . [T]he three friends are . . . determined to succeed—if Luke's and Azure's secret crushes on Radhika don't push the committee members, and their friendships, to the breaking point first." (Publisher's note)

★ **Luna**; a novel. Little, Brown 2003 248p hardcover o.p. pa $7.99

Grades: 9 10 11 12 **Fic**

1. Siblings -- Fiction 2. Transgender youth -- Fiction

ISBN 0-316-73369-5; 0-316-01127-4 pa

LC 2003-58913

Regan's brother Liam can't stand the person he is during the day... His true self, Luna, only reveals herself at night. In the secrecy of his basement bedroom Liam transforms himself into the beautiful girl he longs to be, with help from his sister's clothes and make up...But are Liam's family and friends ready to welcome Luna into their lives. Compelling and provoacative, this is an unforgettable novel about a transgender teen's struggle for self-identity and acceptance. (Publisher's Note)

"The author gradually reveals the issues facing a transgender teen, educating readers without feeling too instructional (Luna and Regan discuss lingo, hormones and even sex change operations). Flashbacks throughout help round out the story, explaining Liam/Luna's longtime struggle with a dual existence, and funny, sarcastic-but-strong Regan narrates with an authentic voice that will draw readers into this new territory." Publ Wkly

Rage; a love story. Alfred A. Knopf 2009 293p $16.99; lib bdg $19.99

Grades: 9 10 11 12 **Fic**

1. Sisters -- Fiction 2. Lesbians -- Fiction 3. Child abuse -- Fiction 4. Abused women -- Fiction 5. Homosexuality -- Fiction

ISBN 978-0-375-85209-1; 0-375-85209-3; 978-0-375-95209-8 lib bdg; 0-375-95209-8 lib bdg

LC 2008-33500

At the end of high school, Johanna finally begins dating the girl she has loved from afar, but Reeve is as much trouble as she claims to be as she and her twin brother damage Johanna's self-esteem, friendships, and already precarious relationship with her sister.

"The appeal of Johanna and Reeve's romance is its edgy, tragic drama, and Johanna's take on things offers keen insight into why kind, sane people allow themselves to be hit and then make excuses for their abusers. . . . The issues raised here are important and thought-provoking while never overpowering the appeal of the story itself." Bull Cent Child Books

She loves you, she loves you not-- Little, Brown 2011 278p $17.99

Grades: 9 10 11 12 **Fic**

1. Mothers -- Fiction 2. Colorado -- Fiction 3. Lesbians -- Fiction 4. Family life -- Fiction

ISBN 978-0-316-07874-0; 0-316-07874-3

LC 2010-22853

The author "skillfully depicts the self-obsessed, tumultuous life of a heartbroken teenager, adding just enough action to draw along a plot that might otherwise be tepid. While the book alludes to the girls' sexual relations, the descriptions are not graphic and should not deter high school libraries from adding this title to their LGBTQ collection." Libr Media Connect

Peterson, Lois J.

Beyond repair; [by] Lois Peterson. Orca Book Publishers 2011 121p (Orca currents) pa $9.95

Grades: 6 7 8 9 **Fic**

1. Bereavement -- Fiction

ISBN 978-1-55469-816-5; 1-55469-816-2

Cam, still grieving over the death of his father, is worried that he is being stalked.

"Compact, dialogue driven writing keeps the atmosphere tense as Cam races toward a confrontation with his father's killer. . . . A resonant, quick read from a reliable reluctant reader series." Booklist

Silver rain; [by] Lois Peterson. Orca Book Publishers 2010 181p pa $9.95

Grades: 6 7 8 9 **Fic**

1. Missing persons -- Fiction 2. Great Depression, 1929-1939 -- Fiction

ISBN 978-1-55469-280-4; 1-55469-280-6

Elsie's father has disappeared and, as the Depression wears on, the family becomes desperate for money.

"Terse, grim, and funny, the plainspoken narrative from Elsie's viewpoint beautifully conveys a child's sense of the times." Booklist

Peterson, Will

Triskellion; [by] Will Peterson. Candlewick Press 2008 365p $16.99

Grades: 6 7 8 9 **Fic**

1. Twins -- Fiction 2. Siblings -- Fiction 3. Supernatural -- Fiction

ISBN 978-0-7636-3971-6; 0-7636-3971-0

After their parents' divorce, Rachel and Adam are sent to live with their grandmother in the English village of Triskellion, where they find danger and paranormal activity as they discover hidden secrets that some will kill to keep buried.

"The plot moves along at a brisk pace, and there's plenty of adventure, dark and creepy atmosphere, and a touch of the paranormal." SLJ

Triskellion 2: The burning. Candlewick Press 2009 461p $16.99

Grades: 6 7 8 9 **Fic**

1. Twins -- Fiction 2. Siblings -- Fiction 3. Archeology -- Fiction 4. Supernatural -- Fiction

ISBN 978-0-7636-4223-5; 0-7636-4223-1

LC 2009006657

Fourteen-year-old twins Adam and Rachel, pursued by both their former 'Hope Project' benefactors and followers of a zombie-like figure, flee London for Paris, Seville, and finally Morocco, where they unearth an ancient secret more startling than the first.

This is an "action-packed sequel. . . . [It is] imaginative and centered on two likable teens." SLJ

Petrucha, Stefan

The **Rule** of Won. Walker & Co. 2008 227p $16.99

Grades: 8 9 10 11 12 **Fic**

1. School stories 2. Clubs -- Fiction 3. Supernatural -- Fiction 4. Books and reading -- Fiction

ISBN 978-0-8027-9651-6; 0-8027-9651-6

LC 2008-00255

Caleb Dunne, the quintessential slacker, is pressured by his girlfriend to join a high school club based on The Rule of Won, which promises to fulfill members' every "crave," but when nonbelievers start being ostracized and even hurt, Caleb must act.

"The book is fast paced and gripping enough to draw in reluctant readers. . . . Raising questions about issues such as personal responsibility, freedom of speech and the press, and standing up for unpopular beliefs, this novel would be a terrific choice for book-group and class discussions." SLJ

Split. Walker Books for Young Readers 2010 257p $16.99

Grades: 7 8 9 10 **Fic**

1. Computers -- Fiction 2. Space and time -- Fiction

ISBN 978-0-8027-9372-0; 0-8027-9372-X

LC 2009-8889

After his mother dies, Wade Jackson cannot decide whether to become a musician or a scholar, so he does both—splitting his consciousness into two distinct worlds.

"The shifting action keeps the fast-paced dual plots moving, and teens will be entertained by the two Wades' embodiment of the tension between being success oriented and following your whims." Booklist

★ **Teen,** Inc. [by] Stefan Petrucha. Walker 2007 244p $16.95

Grades: 8 9 10 11 12 **Fic**

1. Orphans -- Fiction 2. Pollution -- Fiction 3. Business ethics -- Fiction

ISBN 978-0-8027-9650-9; 0-8027-9650-8

LC 2007-2368

Fourteen-year-old Jaiden has been raised by NECorp. since his parents were killed when he was a baby, so when he discovers that the corporation has been lying about producing illegal levels of mercury emissions, he and his two friends decide to try to do something about it.

"Witty and provocative without being preachy, this novel has both daring characters and a heady plot." Booklist

Pfeffer, Susan Beth

Blood wounds. Harcourt 2011 248p $16.99

Grades: 7 8 9 10 **Fic**

1. Homicide -- Fiction 2. Family life -- Fiction 3. Stepfamilies -- Fiction 4. Self-mutilation -- Fiction

ISBN 978-0-547-49638-2

LC 2011009602

Willa seems to have a perfect life as a member of a loving blended family until the estranged father she barely remembers murders his wife and children, then heads toward Willa and her mother.

"This intense psychological drama, showing the brightest and darkest sides of humanity, offers remarkable acts of courage and disturbing images of domestic violence. Willa's frankly portrayed grief, confusion, and uncertainties will have a strong impact on readers." Publ Wkly

Life as we knew it. Harcourt 2006 337p $17

Grades: 7 8 9 10 **Fic**

1. Science fiction 2. Family life -- Fiction 3. Natural disasters -- Fiction

ISBN 0-15-205826-5; 978-0-15-205826-5

LC 2005-36321

Through journal entries sixteen-year-old Miranda describes her family's struggle to survive after a meteor hits the moon, causing worldwide tsunamis, earthquakes, and volcanic eruptions.

"Each page is filled with events both wearying and terrifying and infused with honest emotions. Pfeffer brings cataclysmic tragedy very close." Booklist

Other titles in this series are:
The dead & gone (2008)
This world we live in (2010)
The shade of the moon (2013)

Philbin, Joanna

The **daughters**. Little, Brown 2010 275p il $16.99

Grades: 6 7 8 9 **Fic**

1. School stories 2. Fame -- Fiction 3. Wealth -- Fiction 4. Friendship -- Fiction

ISBN 978-0-316-04900-9; 0-316-04900-X

In New York City, three fourteen-year-old best friends who are all daughters of celebrities watch out for each other as they try to strike a balance between ordinary high school events, such as finding a date for the homecoming dance, and family functions like walking the red carpet with their famous parents.

This is a "fun, quick read. . . . Readers will be intrigued by the well-drawn characters and their growth over the course of several months." SLJ

Other titles in this series are:
The daughters break the rules (2010)
The daughters take the stage (2011)

Philbrick, W. R.

★ The **last** book in the universe; by Rodman Philbrick. Blue Sky Press (NY) 2001 223p hardcover o.p. pa $5.99

Grades: 9 10 11 12 **Fic**

1. Science fiction 2. Epilepsy -- Fiction

ISBN 0-439-08758-9; 0-439-08759-7 pa

LC 99-59878

Expanded from a short story in Tomorrowland edited by Michael Cart, published 1999 by Scholastic Press

After an earthquake has destroyed much of the planet, an epileptic teenager nicknamed Spaz begins the heroic fight to bring human intelligence back to the Earth of a distant future

"Enthralling, thought-provoking, and unsettling." Voice Youth Advocates

Phillips, Suzanne

★ **Burn**; a novel. Little, Brown and Co. 2008 279p $16.99

Grades: 9 10 11 12 **Fic**

1. School stories 2. Bullies -- Fiction 3. Post-traumatic stress disorder -- Fiction

ISBN 978-0-316-00165-6; 0-316-00165-1

LC 2007-43520

Bullied constantly during his freshman year in high school, Cameron's anger and isolation grows, leading to deadly consequences.

"This is an intense story with brutal descriptions of the abuse Cameron suffers. . . . There is understanding to be gained for everyone who reads this timely title." SLJ

Pierce, Tamora

Alanna: the first adventure. Atheneum 2014 249p (Song of the Lioness) $19.99

Grades: 7 8 9 10 **Fic**

1. Fantasy fiction 2. Knights and knighthood -- Fiction 3. Gender role -- Fiction

ISBN 9781481439589; 1481439588

First published 1983

"Neither Alanna nor her twin brother Thom were happy with their father's decision to send Alanna to a convent and Thom to court. The two decide to switch places and Alanna posing as 'Alan' becomes a page at court while Tom goes to the convent to learn sorcery. Alanna finds life as a page hard, particularly as she is lighter and smaller than the other pages, but she struggles hard to overcome these disadvantages. She makes many friends at court, including . . . Prince Jonathan whose life she saves using her magical gift of healing." (Voice of Youth Advocates)

Other titles in this series are:
In the hand of the goddess (1984);
The woman who rides like a man (1986);
Lioness rampant (1988)

Bloodhound. Random House 2009 551p il (Beka Cooper) $18.99; lib bdg $21.99; pa $10.99

Grades: 7 8 9 10 **Fic**

1. Fantasy fiction 2. Police -- Fiction 3. Counterfeits and counterfeiting -- Fiction

ISBN 978-0-375-81469-3; 0-375-81469-8; 978-0-375-91469-0 lib bdg; 0-375-91469-2 lib bdg; 978-0-375-83817-0 pa; 0-375-83817-1 pa

LC 2008025838

Sequel to Terrier (2006)

Having been promoted from "Puppy" to "Dog," Beka, now a full-fledged member of the Provost's Guard, and her former partner head to a neighboring port city to investigate a case of counterfeit coins.

"Quirky, endearing characters save the story." Booklist

Followed by Mastiff (2011)

★ **First** test. Random House 1999 216p (Protector of the small) hardcover o.p. pa $5.99

Grades: 6 7 8 9 **Fic**

1. Fantasy fiction 2. Sex role -- Fiction 3. Knights and knighthood -- Fiction

ISBN 0-679-88914-0; 0-679-98914-5 lib bdg; 0-679-88917-5 pa

LC 98-30903

First title in the Protector of the small series. Ten-year-old Keladry of Mindalen, daughter of nobles, serves as a page but must prove herself to the males around her if she is ever to fulfill her dream of becoming a knight

"Pierce spins a whopping good yarn, her plot balanced on a solid base of action and characterization." Bull Cent Child Books

Other titles in this series are:
Page (2001)
Squire (2002)
Lady knight (2002)

Mastiff. Random House 2011 593p (Beka Cooper) $18.99; lib bdg $21.99; e-book $10.99

Grades: 7 8 9 10 **Fic**

1. Fantasy fiction 2. Police -- Fiction 3. Kidnapping -- Fiction 4. Kings and rulers -- Fiction

ISBN 978-0-375-81470-9; 978-0-375-91470-6 lib bdg; 978-0-375-89328-5 e-book

LC 2011024152

Sequel to Bloodhound (2009)

Beka, having just lost her fiance in a slaver's raid, is able to distract herself by going with her team on an important hunt at the queen's request, unaware that the throne of Tortall depends on their success.

"This novel provides both crackerjack storytelling and an endearingly complex protagonist." Kirkus

★ **Melting** stones. Scholastic Press 2008 312p $17.99

Grades: 8 9 10 11 12 **Fic**

1. Fantasy fiction 2. Magic -- Fiction

ISBN 978-0-545-05264-1; 0-545-05264-5

LC 2007045036

Residents of the island of Starns send for help from Winding Circle temple, and when prickly green mage Rosethorn and young stone mage trainee Evvy respond, Evvy finds that the problem is with a long-dormant volcano and tries to use her talents to avert the looming destruction.

This "is a riveting story that has many inventive and exciting plot twists and turns. . . . The story features excellent character development." SLJ

★ **Sandry's** book. Scholastic Press 1997 252p (Circle of magic) hardcover o.p. pa $6.99

Grades: 6 7 8 9 **Fic**

1. Fantasy fiction 2. Magic -- Fiction

ISBN 0-590-55356-9; 0-590-55408-5 pa

LC 95-39540

Four young misfits find themselves living in a strictly disciplined temple community where they become friends while also learning to do crafts and to use their powers, especially magic

"Pierce has created an excellent new world where magic is a science and utterly believable and populated it with a cast of well-developed characters." Booklist

Other available titles in this series are:
Tris's book (1998)
Daja's book (1998)
Briar's book (1999)

Terrier. Random House 2006 581p il map (Beka Cooper) hardcover o.p. pa $9.99

Grades: 7 8 9 10 **Fic**

1. Fantasy fiction 2. Magic -- Fiction 3. Police -- Fiction

ISBN 978-0-375-81468-6; 0-375-81468-X; 978-0-375-83816-3 pa; 0-375-83816-3 pa

LC 2006-14834

When sixteen-year-old Beka becomes "Puppy" to a pair of "Dogs," as the Provost's Guards are called, she uses her police training, natural abilities and a touch of magic to help them solve the case of a murdered baby in Tortall's Lower City.

"Pierce deftly handles the novel's journal structure, and her clear homage to the police-procedural genre applies a welcome twist to the girl-legend-in-the-making story line." Booklist

Other titles featuring Beka Cooper are:
Bloodhound (2009)
Mastiff (2011)

★ **Trickster's** choice. Random House 2003 422p $17.95; pa $8.95

Grades: 7 8 9 10 **Fic**

1. Fantasy fiction

ISBN 0-375-81466-3; 0-375-82879-6 pa

LC 2003-5202

Alianne must call forth her mother Alanna's courage and her father's wit in order to survive on the Copper Isles in a royal court rife with political intrigue and murderous conspiracy

"This series opener is packed with Pierce's alluring mix of fantasy, adventure, romance, and humor, making the book an essential purchase for school and public libraries." Voice Youth Advocates

Another title in this series is:
Trickster's queen (2004)

Wild magic. Atheneum 2015 (The immortals) $19.99

Grades: 7 8 9 10 **Fic**

1. Fantasy fiction 2. Magic -- Fiction 3. Human-animal communication -- Fiction

ISBN 9781481440233; 1481440233

First published 1992

"Thirteen-year-old Daine has always had a special connection with animals, but only when she's forced to leave home does she realize it's more than a knack--it's magic. With this wild magic, not only can Daine speak to animals, but she can also make them obey her. Daine takes a job handling horses for the Queen's Riders, where she meets the master mage Numair and becomes his student. Under Numair's guidance, Daine explores the scope of her magic." (Publisher's note)

Other titles in this series are:
Wolf-speaker (1994)
Emperor mage (1995)
The realms of the gods (1996)

The **will** of the empress. Scholastic Press 2005 550p $17.99; pa $8.99

Grades: 8 9 10 11 12 **Fic**

1. Fantasy fiction

ISBN 0-439-44171-4; 0-439-44172-2 pa

LC 2005-02874

On visit to Namorn to visit her vast landholdings and her devious cousin, Empress Berenene, eighteen-year-old Sandry must rely on her childhood friends and fellow mages, Daja, Tris, and Briar, despite the distance that has grown between them

"This novel begins two years after the Circle of Magic and The Circle Opens series. . . . Readers will enjoy being reacquainted with these older but still very well-developed characters." SLJ

Pierson, D. C.

Crap kingdom; by DC Pierson. Viking 2013 368 p. (hardcover) $17.99

Grades: 7 8 9 10 11 12 **Fic**

1. Fantasy fiction 2. Humorous fiction 3. Heroes -- Fiction

ISBN 067001432X; 9780670014323

LC 2012015578

In this comic novel, by D. C. Pierson, "with [a] . . . mysterious yet oddly ordinary-looking prophecy, Tom's fate is sealed: he's . . . whisked away to a magical kingdom to be its Chosen One. There's just one problem: The kingdom is mostly made of garbage from Earth. . . . When Tom turns down the job of Chosen One, he thinks he's making a smart decision. But when Tom discovers he's been replaced by his best friend Kyle, . . . Tom wants Crap Kingdom back--at any cost." (Publisher's note)

Pignat, Caroline

Greener grass; the famine years. Red Deer Press 2009 276p pa $12.95

Grades: 7 8 9 10 **Fic**

1. Famines -- Fiction 2. Ireland -- Fiction

ISBN 978-0-88995-402-1; 0-88995-402-X

"In 1847, 15-year-old Kit is jailed for digging up potatoes on confiscated land to feed her starving family, and during the three weeks that she is incarcerated, she reflects on the past year in Ireland: the blight, the famine, evictions, and deaths. . . . True to Kat's voice, the plain, rhythmic language . . . is lyrical but never ornate. The tension in the story and in the well-developed characters is always rooted in daily detail." Booklist

Followed by: Wild geese (2010)

Wild geese. Red Deer Press 2010 335p pa $12.95

Grades: 7 8 9 10 **Fic**

1. Irish -- Fiction 2. Canada -- Fiction 3. Immigrants -- Fiction 4. Seafaring life -- Fiction

ISBN 978-0-88995-432-8 pa; 0-88995-432-1 pa

Sequel to: Greener grass (2009)

"Kit, pursued as a criminal, has safely made it on board an immigrant 'coffin' ship bound for Canada, disguised as a boy and accompanied by Mick, her best friend. Along the way, with historically gritty authenticity, she encounters a lethal fever, near-starvation conditions and terrifying storms. . . . When she finally reaches Canada, there is more disease and separation." Kirkus

Pike, Aprilynne

Earthbound. Penguin Group USA 2013 352 p. $17.99

Grades: 7 8 9 10 **Fic**

1. Occult fiction 2. Science fiction

ISBN 1595146504; 9781595146502

This is the first book in a series from Aprilynne Pike. Here, plane crash survivor Tavia "is in rehab and finishing her senior year online. She has time to look at the world with attentive eyes, and what she sees is often unnerving: glowing triangles on the historic houses of Portsmouth, N.H., or pedestrians who flicker. She tries to attribute these visions to the brain injury she sustained in the crash, but she can't dismiss the stalker with a blond ponytail so easily." (Publishers Weekly)

"The characters are well developed and the narrative is easy to follow... Pike does take a while to get to the heart of the matter, but overall the story is compelling. Readers of supernatural romances will be clamoring." SLJ

Wings. HarperTeen 2009 294p $16.99; lib bdg $17.89; pa $8.99

Grades: 7 8 9 10 **Fic**

1. Fantasy fiction 2. Plants -- Fiction 3. Trolls -- Fiction 4. Fairies -- Fiction

ISBN 978-0-06-166803-6; 0-06-166803-6; 978-0-06-166804-3 lib bdg; 0-06-166804-4 lib bdg; 978-0-06-166805-0 pa; 0-06-166805-2 pa

LC 2008-24653

When a plant blooms out of fifteen-year-old Laurel's back, it leads her to discover the fact that she is a faerie and that she has a crucial role to play in keeping the world safe from the encroaching enemy trolls.

"Replete with budding romance, teen heroics, a good smattering of evil individuals, and an ending that serves up a ready sequel, this novel nonetheless provides an unusual approach to middle level fantasy through its startlingly creative premise that faeries are of the plant world and not the animal world. . . . Both male and female fantasy readers will enjoy this fast-paced action fantasy." Voice Youth Advocates

Other titles in this series are:

Illusions (2011)

Spells (2010)

Pitcher, Annabel

★ **Ketchup** clouds; a novel. by Annabel Pitcher. Little, Brown and Company 2013 272 p. $18

Grades: 8 9 10 11 12 **Fic**

1. Grief -- Fiction 2. Guilt -- Fiction 3. Secrets -- Fiction 4. England -- Fiction 5. Epistolary fiction 6. Letters -- Fiction 7. Bath (England) -- Fiction 8. Grief 9. Guilt 10. Family life -- England -- Fiction 11. Bath (England) 12. Children's secrets 13. Families -- England

ISBN 031624676X; 9780316246767

LC 2012044116

In this book, by Annabel Pitcher, "Zoe has an unconventional pen pal-Mr. Stuart Harris, a Texas Death Row inmate and convicted murderer. But then again, Zoe has an unconventional story to tell. A story about how she fell for two boys, betrayed one of them, and killed the other." (Publisher's note)

"Guilt-ridden British teen Zoe feels responsible for the fates of two brothers--Max, the hot guy with whom she's been making out; and Aaron, with whom she's in love. Zoe's original turns of phrase and sprightly narrative style give her story quick, light momentum and moments of lyricism. Sharp, articulate perceptions and a measure of suspense make this an engaging read." (Horn Book)

My sister lives on the mantelpiece; a novel. Annabel Pitcher. 1st US ed. Little, Brown & Co. 2012 214 p. (hardcover) $17.99

Grades: 6 7 8 9 10 **Fic**

1. Grief -- Fiction 2. England -- Fiction 3. Family

problems -- Fiction
ISBN 0316176907; 9780316176903
LC 2011027350

In this book, Annabel Pitcher tells a story about "grief, prejudice, religion, bullying, and familial instability. . . . Jamie and his family are still dealing with his sister Rose's death in a terrorist bombing five years earlier. . . . The family falls apart--their mother runs off with another man, and their alcoholic father moves from London to the Lake District with the children, where he lavishes attention on Rose's urn. . . . Jamie's pivotal friendship with a Muslim girl, Sunya, is a standout." (Publishers Weekly)

Pixley, Marcella

Without Tess. Farrar Straus Giroux 2011 280p $16.99

Grades: 7 8 9 10 **Fic**

1. Death -- Fiction 2. Guilt -- Fiction 3. Sisters -- Fiction 4. Mental illness -- Fiction 5. Jews -- United States -- Fiction
ISBN 978-0-374-36174-7; 0-374-36174-6
LC 2011001469

Fifteen-year-old Lizzie Cohen recalls what it was like growing up with her imaginative but disturbed older sister Tess, and how she is striving to reclaim her own life since Tess died.

The author "plumbs the emotional depths of a tough subject with sensitivity and insight into the complexities of human nature and sibling bonds." Kirkus

Platt, Chris

Astra. Peachtree 2010 144p $15.95

Grades: 5 6 7 8 **Fic**

1. Horses -- Fiction 2. Father-daughter relationship -- Fiction
ISBN 978-1-56145-541-6; 1-56145-541-5
LC 2010001654

Forbidden to ride after her mother's death in a riding accident, thirteen-year-old Lily nurses her mother's beloved horse, Astra, back to health, hoping that someday Astra will win the Tevis Cup endurance race

"Filled with information about endurance racing as well as a cast of interesting supporting characters, including the dishy new boy in town, this novel is a quick and enjoyable read." SLJ

Plum, Amy

Die for me. HarperTeen 2011 344p $17.99

Grades: 8 9 10 11 **Fic**

1. Love stories 2. Dead -- Fiction 3. Sisters -- Fiction 4. Bereavement -- Fiction 5. Supernatural -- Fiction
ISBN 978-0-06-200401-7; 0-06-200401-8
LC 2010-30785

After their parents are killed in a car accident, sixteen-year-old Kate Mercier and her older sister Georgia, each grieving in her own way, move to Paris to live with their grandparents and Kate finds herself powerfully drawn to the handsome but elusive Vincent who seems to harbor a mysterious and dangerous secret.

"Plum deftly navigates the real world and the fantastical. Her characters are authentic, and their romances are believable. Plum introduces a world and a story that are sure to intrigue teen readers and will easily attract fans of the Twilight series." Booklist

Plum-Ucci, Carol

Fire will fall. Harcourt 2010 485p $18

Grades: 8 9 10 11 **Fic**

1. Spies -- Fiction 2. Diseases -- Fiction 3. Terrorism -- Fiction 4. New Jersey -- Fiction 5. Supernatural -- Fiction
ISBN 978-0-15-216562-8; 0-15-216562-2
LC 2009-23854

Sequel to: Stream of Babel (2008)

Moved to a mansion in the South Jersey Pine Barrens, four teenagers, trying to recover from being poisoned by terrorists, struggle with health issues, personal demons, and supernatural events, as operatives try to track down the terror cell.

"The compelling characters, dramatic situations, and page-turning pace of this thriller will keep readers enthralled right up to the climax." SLJ

Streams of Babel. Harcourt 2008 424p $17

Grades: 8 9 10 11 **Fic**

1. Spies -- Fiction 2. Computers -- Fiction 3. Terrorism -- Fiction 4. New Jersey -- Fiction
ISBN 978-0-15-216556-7; 0-15-216556-8
LC 2007-26503

Six teens face a bioterrorist attack on American soil as four are infected with a mysterious disease affecting their small New Jersey neighborhood and two others, both brilliant computer hackers, assist the United States Intelligence Coalition in tracking the perpetrators.

The "story's threads are brought together in ways designed to keep readers on the edge of their seats. . . . Fans of suspense will discover a thrilling ride." Voice Youth Advocates

Followed by: Fire will fall (2010)

Poblocki, Dan

The **nightmarys**. Random House 2010 325p $16.99; lib bdg $19.99

Grades: 6 7 8 9 **Fic**

1. Mystery fiction 2. Supernatural -- Fiction
ISBN 978-0-375-84256-6; 0-375-84256-X; 978-0-375-94256-3 lib bdg; 0-375-94256-4 lib bdg
LC 2009-50690

Seventh-grader Timothy July and his new friend Abigail try to break a curse that is causing them and others to be tormented by their greatest fears brought to life.

Poblocki "offers plenty of grisly, cinematically creepy imagery for readers who like a good scare, and the tightly wound narrative and ongoing tension between Timothy and Abigail will keep readers holding their breath until even after what they think is the climax." Publ Wkly

Polak, Monique

The **middle** of everywhere. Orca Book Publishers 2009 200p pa $12.95

Grades: 7 8 9 10 **Fic**

1. Inuit -- Fiction 2. Arctic regions -- Fiction 3. Québec (Province) -- Fiction 4. Wilderness survival -- Fiction
ISBN 978-1-55469-090-9; 1-55469-090-0

Noah spends a school term in George River, in Quebec's Far North, trying to understand the Inuit culture, which he finds both threatening and puzzling.

"Although the survival-adventure details will engage reluctant readers, the story has elements of romance when Noah strives to impress an Inuit classmate." SLJ

What world is left. Orca Book Pub. 2008 215p pa $12.95

Grades: 7 8 9 10 11 12 **Fic**

1. Jews -- Netherlands -- Fiction 2. Holocaust, 1933-1945 -- Fiction 3. World War, 1939-1945 -- Netherlands -- Fiction 4. Netherlands -- History -- 1940-1945, German occupation -- Fiction

ISBN 978-1-5514-3847-4; 1-5514-3847-X

"Growing up in a secular Jewish home in Holland, Anneke cares little about Judaism, so she has no faith to lose when, in 1943, her family is deported to Theresienstadt, the Nazi concentration camp. . . . Based on the experiences of the author's mother . . . this novel is narrated in Anneke's first-person, present-tense voice. The details are unforgettable. . . . An important addition to the Holocaust curriculum." Booklist

Pollock, Tom

★ The **city's** son; Tom Pollock. Flux 2012 460p $16.99

Grades: 6 7 8 **Fic**

1. London (England) -- Fiction 2. Magic -- Fiction 3. Supernatural -- Fiction 4. Family problems -- Fiction

ISBN 9780738734309

LC 2012010589

This novel, by Tom Pollock, follows "teenage graffiti artist Beth Bradley . . . [and] Filius, the ragged crown prince of London's underworld. . . . Reach, the malign god of demolition, is on a rampage . . . to lay claim to the skyscraper throne. Caught up in helping Filius raise an alleyway army to battle Reach, Beth soon forgets her old life. But when the enemy claims her best friend, Beth must choose between the acceptance she finds in the streets and the life she left behind." (Publisher's note)

Pon, Cindy

Fury of the phoenix. Greenwillow Books 2011 362p $17.99

Grades: 9 10 11 12 **Fic**

1. China -- Fiction 2. Supernatural -- Fiction 3. Voyages and travels -- Fiction 4. Father-son relationship -- Fiction

ISBN 978-0-06-173025-2

LC 2010-11700

Sequel to Silver phoenix (2009)

When Ai Ling leaves her home and family to accompany Chen Yong on his quest to find his father, haunted by the ancient evil she thought she had banished to the underworld, she must use her growing supernatural powers to save Chen Yong from the curses that follow her.

★ **Silver** phoenix; beyond the kingdom of Xia. Greenwillow Books 2009 338p $17.99; lib bdg $18.89; pa $8.99

Grades: 9 10 11 12 **Fic**

1. China -- Fiction 2. Supernatural -- Fiction 3. Voyages and travels -- Fiction 4. Father-daughter relationship -- Fiction

ISBN 978-0-06-173021-4; 0-06-173021-1; 978-0-06-178033-2 lib bdg; 0-06-178033-2 lib bdg; 978-0-06-173024-5 pa; 0-06-173024-6 pa

LC 2008-29149

With her father long overdue from his journey and a lecherous merchant blackmailing her into marriage, seventeen-year-old Ai Ling becomes aware of a strange power within her as she goes in search of her parent.

"Pon's writing, both fluid and exhilarating, shines whether she's describing a dinner delicacy or what it feels like to stab an evil spirit in the gut. There's a bit of sex here, including a near rape, but it's all integral to a saga that spins and slashes as its heroine tries to find her way home." Booklist

Followed by Fury of the phoenix (2011)

Porter, Sarah

Lost voices. Houghton Mifflin Harcourt 2011 291p $16.99

Grades: 7 8 9 10 **Fic**

1. Singing -- Fiction 2. Supernatural -- Fiction 3. Mermaids and mermen -- Fiction

ISBN 978-0-547-48250-7; 0-547-48250-7

LC 2011008438

Assaulted and left on the cliffs outside of her grim Alaskan fishing village by her abusive, alcoholic uncle, fourteen-year-old Luce expects to die when she tumbles into the icy waters below, but when she instead transforms into a mermaid she is faced with struggles and choices she could never have imagined.

"Porter's writing is expressive and graceful. . . . A captivatingly different story." Booklist

Porter, Tracey

Lark. HarperTeen 2011 183p $15.99

Grades: 8 9 10 11 12 **Fic**

1. Homicide -- Fiction 2. Virginia -- Fiction 3. Bereavement -- Fiction 4. Supernatural -- Fiction

ISBN 978-0-06-112287-3; 0-06-112287-4

LC 2010021959

"When sixteen-year-old Lark is raped and murdered, her two friends Nyetta and Eve must deal with the aftermath. Nyetta is being haunted by Lark, who wants someone to acknowledge her pain before she becomes trapped in the tree where she died. Eve, who has been estranged from Lark ever since she left the swimming team after an assistant coach fondled her, must process her long-repressed feelings as she falls in love with Ian, a boy Lark also admired. Unable to face her fears, Nyetta falls further into her own emotional darkness until she connects with Eve, and together the girls are able to free Lark's soul." (VOYA)

"The concise narrative holds deep and honest emotions as the characters go through the stages of dealing with Lark's untimely and gruesome death. An excellent addition to YA collections." SLJ

Portman, Frank

Andromeda Klein. Delacorte Press 2009 424p $17.99; lib bdg $20.99

Grades: 8 9 10 11 12 **Fic**

1. Deaf -- Fiction 2. Tarot -- Fiction 3. Libraries -- Fiction 4. Occultism -- Fiction 5. People with disabilities -- Fiction 6. Books and reading -- Fiction

ISBN 978-0-385-73525-4; 0-385-73525-1; 978-0-385-90512-1 lib bdg; 0-385-90512-2 lib bdg

LC 2009-15879

High school sophomore Andromeda, an outcast because she studies the occult and has a hearing impairment and other disabilities, overcomes grief over terrible losses by enlisting others' help in her plan to save library books—and finds a kindred spirit along the way.

"Andromeda is a compelling character, whose reclaiming of misheard words and misspelled text messages gives her unique and likable flavor. . . . For readers who are occult fans, this quirky text will be a self-satisfied joy." Kirkus

★ **King** Dork. Delacorte Press 2006 344p il hardcover o.p. pa $8.99

Grades: 10 11 12 **Fic**

1. School stories 2. Fathers -- Fiction 3. Short story writers

ISBN 0-385-73291-0; 978-0-385-73291-8; 0-385-73450-6 pa; 978-0-385-73450-9 pa

LC 2005-12556

High school loser Tom Henderson discovers that "The Catcher in the Rye" may hold the clues to the many mysteries in his life.

"Mature situations, casual sexual experiences, and allusions to Salinger suggest an older teen audience, who will also best appreciate the appended bandography and the very funny glossary." Booklist

Potter, Ryan

Exit strategy. Flux 2010 303p pa $9.95

Grades: 8 9 10 11 12 **Fic**

1. Summer -- Fiction 2. Michigan -- Fiction 3. Steroids -- Fiction 4. Friendship -- Fiction

ISBN 978-0-7387-1573-5; 0-7387-1573-5

LC 2009-27697

Seventeen-year-old Zach, his best friend (and state wrestling champion) Tank, and Tank's twin sister Sarah, an Ivy League-bound scholar, are desperate to leave their depressing hometown of Blaine, Michigan, after next year's graduation, but plans go awry when Zach uncovers a steroid scandal and falls in love with Sarah.

"Packed with suspense and drama, with some romance and a fight, this book is bound to be popular among the male crowd. Just make sure you get it into the right hands; mature themes exist, including extramarital affairs, underage drinking, and anger management." Libr Media Connect

Powell, Laura

Burn mark; by Laura Powell. Bloomsbury Children's Books 2012 403p. (hardback) $17.99

Grades: 7 8 9 10 11 12 **Fic**

1. Occult fiction 2. Witches -- Fiction 3. Supernatural -- Fiction 4. England -- Fiction 5. London (England) -- Fiction

ISBN 1599908433; 9781599908434

LC 2011034464

This young adult fantasy, by Laura Powell, is set "in a modern world where witches are hunted down and burned at the stake. . . . Glory is from a family of witches, and is desperate to develop her 'Fae' powers. . . . Lucas is the son of the Chief Prosecutor for the Inquisition with a privileged life very different from the witches he is being trained to prosecute. And then one day, both Glory and Lucas develop the Fae . . . [and] their lives are inextricably bound together." (Publisher's note)

The **game** of triumphs. Alfred A. Knopf 2011 269p $16.99; lib bdg $19.99; ebook $10.99

Grades: 7 8 9 10 **Fic**

1. Games -- Fiction 2. Tarot -- Fiction 3. Supernatural -- Fiction 4. Space and time -- Fiction 5. London (England) -- Fiction

ISBN 978-0-375-86587-9; 0-375-86587-X; 978-0-375-96587-6 lib bdg; 0-375-96587-4 lib bdg; 978-0-375-89774-0 ebook

LC 2010021813

Fifteen-year-old Cat and three other London teens are drawn into a dangerous game in which Tarot cards open doorways into a different dimension and while there is everything to win, losing can be fatal.

"Original and engrossing." Kirkus

The **Master** of Misrule; Laura Powell. Alfred A. Knopf 2012 363 p. (trade hardcover) $16.99

Grades: 7 8 9 10 11 12 **Fic**

1. Games -- Fiction 2. Tarot -- Fiction 3. Supernatural -- Fiction 4. England -- Fiction 5. Role playing -- Fiction 6. Space and time -- Fiction 7. London (England) -- Fiction

ISBN 0375865888; 9780375865664; 9780375865886; 9780375897849; 9780375965883

LC 2011021135

Sequel to: The Game of Triumphs

In this book, "despite holding the Triumphs that promise answers to their various back stories (including the murder of Cat's parents, Blaine's abusive stepfather and Flora's comatose sister, all related to the Game of Triumphs), resolution eludes Cat and her friends. They must fight the Fool, now the Master of Misrule, whom they released in the first volume, not only for their own success, but to save the world." (Kirkus Reviews)

"This fast-paced novel mixes fantasy and reality in an intricately described setting... Packed with mystery, action, and even a hint of romance, The Master of Misrule will appeal to fans of role-playing games or anyone seeking an adventurous read." VOYA

Powell, Randy

Swiss mist. Farrar, Straus & Giroux 2008 210p $16.95

Grades: 6 7 8 9 10 **Fic**

1. Divorce -- Fiction

ISBN 978-0-374-37356-6; 0-374-37356-6

LC 2007-27680

Follows Milo from fifth grade, when his mother and philosopher father get divorced, through tenth grade, when his mother has married a wealthy businessman and Milo is still a bit of a loner, looking for the meaning of life.

"This book is rewardingly remarkable for the characters and bits of truth that Milo never stops pursuing, even as he learns that truth is not what matters most." SLJ

★ **Three** clams and an oyster. Farrar, Straus & Giroux 2002 216p hardcover o.p. pa $6.95
Grades: 7 8 9 10 **Fic**

1. Football -- Fiction 2. Friendship -- Fiction
ISBN 0-374-37526-7; 0-374-40007-5 pa
LC 2001-54833

During their humorous search to find a fourth player for their flag football team, three high school juniors are forced to examine their long friendship, their individual flaws, and their inability to try new experiences

"Sometimes philosophical, sometimes comical, but always touching, Randy Powell writes an unusually moving story of adolescent male friends." Book Rep

Powell, William Campbell

Expiration day; William Campbell Powell. Tor Teen 2014 336 p. (hardback) $17.99
Grades: 8 9 10 11 12 **Fic**

1. Bildungsromans 2. Science fiction 3. Robots -- Fiction 4. Diaries -- Fiction 5. England -- Fiction 6. Coming of age -- Fiction
ISBN 0765338289; 9780765338280
LC 2013025453

In this book, by William Campbell Powell, "it is the year 2049, and humanity is on the brink of extinction. . . . Tania Deeley has always been told that she's a rarity: a human child in a world where most children are sophisticated androids manufactured by Oxted Corporation. . . . Though she has always been aware of the existence of teknoids, it is not until her first day at The Lady Maud High School for Girls that Tania realizes that her best friend, Siân, may be one." (Publisher's note)

"The author pays homage to the genre's giants while combining realistic characters (both human and android) and detailed worldbuilding with an unpredictably optimistic conclusion." (Kirkus)

Power, Susan

★ The **grass** dancer. Putnam 1994 300p hardcover o.p. pa $7.99
Grades: 11 12 Adult **Fic**

1. Dakota Indians -- Fiction
ISBN 0-399-13911-7; 0-425-14962-5 pa
LC 93-47199

"Set on a North Dakota reservation, 'The Grass Dancer' tells the story of Harley Wind Soldier, a young Sioux trying to understand his place among people whose intertwined lives and shared heritage move backward in time in the narrative from the 1980's to the middle of the last century." N Y Times Book Rev

This "is a passionate portrayal of universal human emotions and a vivid account of Native American history and culture." SLJ

Powers, J. L.

This thing called the future; a novel. Cinco Puntos 2011 213p $16.95
Grades: 8 9 10 11 12 **Fic**

1. Sick -- Fiction 2. South Africa -- Fiction 3. Mother-daughter relationship -- Fiction
ISBN 978-1-933693-95-8; 1-933693-95-9

Powers "composes a compelling, often harrowing portrait of a struggling country, where old beliefs and rituals still have power, but can't erase the problems of the present. Readers will be fully invested in Khosi's efforts to secure a better future." Publ Wkly

Pratchett, Terry

★ The **amazing** Maurice and his educated rodents. HarperCollins Pubs. 2001 241p hardcover o.p. pa $6.99
Grades: 7 8 9 10 **Fic**

1. Fantasy fiction 2. Cats -- Fiction 3. Rats -- Fiction
ISBN 0-06-001233-1; 0-06-001235-8 pa
LC 2001-42411

A talking cat, intelligent rats, and a strange boy cooperate in a Pied Piper scam until they try to con the wrong town and are confronted by a deadly evil rat king

"In this laugh-out-loud fantasy, his first 'Discworld' novel for younger readers, Pratchett rethinks a classic story and comes up with a winner." SLJ

★ **Dodger**; by Terry Pratchett. HarperCollins 2012 360 p. (hardback) $17.99
Grades: 7 8 9 10 **Fic**

1. Lifesaving 2. Love stories 3. Historical fiction 4. Humorous fiction 5. Conduct of life -- Fiction 6. Adventure and adventurers -- Fiction 7. Todd, Sweeney (Legendary character) -- Fiction 8. London (England) -- History -- 19th century -- Fiction 9. Great Britain -- History -- Victoria, 1837-1901 -- Fiction
ISBN 0062009494; 9780062009494; 9780062009500
LC 2012022155

Michael L. Printz Honor Book (2013)

Author Terry Pratchett presents a story of historical fiction. "Dodger is a guttersnipe and a tosher . . . [and] a petty criminal but also (generally) one of the good guys. One night he rescues a beautiful young woman and finds himself hobnobbing quite literally with the likes of Charlie Dickens . . . and Ben Disraeli . . . And when he attempts to smarten himself up to impress the damsel in distress, he unexpectedly comes face to face with . . . Sweeney Todd." (Kirkus)

I shall wear midnight. Harper 2010 355p $16.99
Grades: 7 8 9 10 **Fic**

1. Ghost stories 2. Fantasy fiction 3. Fairies -- Fiction 4. Witches -- Fiction
ISBN 978-0-06-143304-7; 0-06-143304-7
LC 2010-24442

Sequel to: Wintersmith (2006)

Fifteen-year-old Tiffany Aching, the witch of the Chalk, seeks her place amid a troublesome populace and tries to control the ill-behaved, six-inch-high Wee Free Men who follow her as she faces an ancient evil that agitates against witches.

"The final adventure in Pratchett's Tiffany Aching series brings this subset of Discworld novels to a moving and highly satisfactory conclusion." Publ Wkly

★ **Only** you can save mankind. HarperCollins 2005 207p hardcover o.p. lib bdg $16.89; pa $6.99
Grades: 5 6 7 8 **Fic**

1. War stories 2. Computer games -- Fiction
ISBN 0-06-054185-7; 0-06-054186-5 lib bdg; 0-06-054187-3 pa

First published 1992 in the United Kingdom

Twelve-year-old Johnny endures tensions between his parents, watches television coverage of the Gulf War, and plays a computer game called Only You Can Save Mankind, in which he is increasingly drawn into the reality of the alien ScreeWee

This is "a wild ride, full of Pratchett's trademark humor; digs at primitive, low-resolution games . . . ; and some not-so-subtle philosophy about war and peace." Booklist

Other titles in this trilogy are:
Johnny and the dead (2006)
Johnny and the bomb (2006)

★ **Nation**. HarperCollins 2008 367p $16.99; lib bdg $17.89; pa $8.99
Grades: 7 8 9 10 11 12 **Fic**

1. Islands -- Fiction 2. Tsunamis -- Fiction 3. Survival after airplane accidents, shipwrecks, etc. -- Fiction
ISBN 978-0-06-143301-6; 0-06-143301-2; 978-0-06-143302-3 lib bdg; 0-06-143302-0 lib bdg; 978-0-06-143303-0 pa; 0-06-143303-9 pa

LC 2008-20211

Boston Globe-Horn Book Award: Fiction (2009)

After a devastating tsunami destroys all that they have ever known, Mau, an island boy, and Daphne, an aristocratic English girl, together with a small band of refugees, set about rebuilding their community and all the things that are important in their lives.

"Quirky wit and broad vision make this a fascinating survival story on many levels." Booklist

★ The **Wee** Free Men. HarperCollins Pubs. 2003 263p hardcover o.p. pa $9.99
Grades: 7 8 9 10 **Fic**

1. Fantasy fiction 2. Witches -- Fiction
ISBN 0-06-001236-6; 0-06-201217-7 pa

LC 2002-15396

A young witch-to-be named Tiffany teams up with the Wee Free Men, a clan of six-inch-high blue men, to rescue her baby brother and ward off a sinister invasion from Fairyland

"Pratchett invites readers into his well-established realm of Discworld where action, magic, and characters are firmly rooted in literary reality. Humor ripples throughout, making tense, dangerous moments stand out in stark contrast." Bull Cent Child Books

Other titles about Tiffany are:
A hat full of sky (2004)
I shall wear midnight (2010)
Wintersmith (2006)

Preller, James

★ **Bystander**. Feiwel and Friends 2009 226p $16.99
Grades: 5 6 7 8 **Fic**

1. School stories 2. Moving -- Fiction 3. Bullies -- Fiction 4. Divorce -- Fiction 5. Family life -- Fiction
ISBN 0312379064; 9780312379063

LC 2008-28554

Thirteen-year-old Eric discovers there are consequences to not standing by and watching as the bully at his new school hurts people, but although school officials are aware of the problem, Eric may be the one with a solution.

"Although there are no pat answers, the message (that a bystander is hardly better than an instigator) is clear, and Preller's well-shaped characters, strong writing, and realistic treatment of middle-school life deliver it cleanly." Booklist

Preus, Margi

★ **Heart** of a samurai; based on the true story of Nakahama Manjiro. Abrams/Amulet 2010 301p il $15.95
Grades: 7 8 9 10 11 12 **Fic**

1. Interpreters 2. Japanese -- United States -- Fiction 3. Survival after airplane accidents, shipwrecks, etc. -- Fiction
ISBN 978-0-8109-8981-8; 0-8109-8981-6

LC 2009-51634

A Newbery Medal honor book, 2011

In 1841, rescued by an American whaler after a terrible shipwreck leaves him and his four companions castaways on a remote island, fourteen-year-old Manjiro, who dreams of becoming a samurai, learns new laws and customs as he becomes the first Japanese person to set foot in the United States.

The author "mixes fact with fiction in a tale that is at once adventurous, heartwarming, sprawling, and nerve-racking in its depictions of early anti-Asian sentiment. She succeeds in making readers feel every bit as 'other' as Manjiro, while showing America at its best and worst through his eyes." Publ Wkly

Includes bibliographical references

Shadow on the mountain; a novel inspired by the true adventures of a wartime spy. by Margi Preus. Amulet Books 2012 286 p. (alk. paper) $16.95
Grades: 6 7 8 9 **Fic**

1. Adventure fiction 2. Historical fiction 3. World War, 1939-1945 4. Spies -- Fiction 5. Norway -- History -- German occupation, 1940-1945 -- Fiction 6. World War, 1939-1945 -- Underground movements -- Norway -- Fiction
ISBN 1419704249; 9781419704246

LC 2012015623

This juvenile historical fiction novel, by Margi Preus, "recounts the adventures of a 14-year-old Norwegian boy named Espen during World War II. After Nazi Germany invades and occupies Norway, Espen and his friends are swept up in the Norwegian resistance movement. Espen gets his start by delivering illegal newspapers, then graduates to the role of courier and finally becomes a spy, dodging the Gestapo along the way." (Publisher's note)

Includes bibliographical references.

Price, Charlie

★ **Dead** connection. Roaring Brook Press 2006 225p $16.95

Grades: 8 9 10 11 12 **Fic**

1. Ghost stories 2. Homicide -- Fiction
ISBN 1-59643-114-8; 978-1-59643-114-0
LC 2005-17138

A loner who communes with the dead in the town cemetery hears the voice of a murdered cheerleader and tries to convince the adults that he knows what happened to her

"Readers will like the edginess and be intrigued by the extrasensory elements as well as the darker turns the mystery takes. This is something different." Booklist

★ **Desert** Angel. Farrar Straus Giroux 2011 176p $15.99

Grades: 8 9 10 11 12 **Fic**

1. Violence -- Fiction 2. California -- Fiction 3. Illegal aliens -- Fiction 4. Mexican Americans -- Fiction
ISBN 978-0-374-31775-1; 0-374-31775-5
LC 2010044122

"Price's pacing is tight, aided by direct, clipped prose that underscores Scotty's brutality and Angel's fragile emotional state. Both the best and worst of humanity shine through in this gripping novel." Publ Wkly

The **interrogation** of Gabriel James. Farrar Straus Giroux 2010 170p $16.99

Grades: 9 10 11 12 **Fic**

1. Montana -- Fiction 2. Homicide -- Fiction 3. Criminal investigation -- Fiction
ISBN 978-0-374-33545-8; 0-374-33545-1
LC 2009-37309

As an eyewitness to two murders, a Montana teenager relates the shocking story behind the crimes in a police interrogation interspersed with flashbacks.

"The author writes intriguing and believable characters and keeps a stream of realism moving through the story even when neither readers nor Gabriel are really sure what's going on. Patience from readers won't be required, though, as plenty of action keeps the narrative moving while the plot details unfold. The result is not only suspense but a memorable and believable characterization. Top notch." Kirkus

Price, Lissa

Enders; by Lissa Price. Delacorte Press 2014 288 p. (hc : alk. paper) $17.99

Grades: 7 8 9 10 **Fic**

1. Brainwashing 2. Teenagers -- Fiction 3. Science -- Experiments -- Fiction 4. Science fiction
ISBN 0385742495; 9780375990618; 9780385742498
LC 2013011679

Sequel to: Starters

In this book by Lissa Price, the conclusion to her Starters series, "someone is after Starters like Callie and Michael--teens with chips in their brains. They want to experiment on anyone left over from Prime Destinations--Starters who can be controlled and manipulated. With the body bank destroyed, Callie no longer has to rent herself out to creepy Enders. But Enders can still get inside her mind and make her do things she doesn't want to do." (Publisher's note)

"Some glossed-over twists stretch believability, though the threat (and villain's secret plan), smaller-scale than in Starters, is personal in a creepy way. Metals can be controlled remotely, and Callie's modified chip keeps her awake and aware, leading to a delightfully disturbing climax. It's not as intense as Starters, but it offers some answers and a solid conclusion that will repay readers." (Kirkus)

Starters; Lissa Price. Delacorte Press 2012 336 p. (paperback) $9.99; (ebook) $53.97; (glb) $20.99; (hardcover) $17.99

Grades: 7 8 9 10 **Fic**

1. Science fiction 2. Orphans -- Fiction 3. Intergenerational relations -- Fiction 4. Brothers and sisters -- Fiction
ISBN 9780385742481; 0385742371; 9780307975232; 9780375990601; 9780385742375
LC 2011040820

In this book, "[w]hen a deadly virus wipes out the entire population of the U.S. save the elderly and the young, . . . the result is a dysfunctional society polarized between young 'Starters' and the increasingly long-lived 'Enders.' Children who are unclaimed by surviving relatives are institutionalized, and many -- like Callie and her little brother, Tyler -- learn to fend for themselves in virtual hiding from the law to escape that fate." (Bulletin of the Center for Children's Books)

Price, Nora

Zoe letting go; Nora Price. Razorbill 2012 279 p. $17.99

Grades: 8 9 10 11 12 **Fic**

1. Rehabilitation -- Fiction 2. Eating disorders -- Fiction 3. Diaries -- Fiction 4. Letters -- Fiction 5. Friendship -- Fiction 6. Anorexia nervosa -- Fiction 7. Emotional problems -- Fiction
ISBN 1595144668; 9781595144669
LC 2012012257

This book tells the story of 16-year-old Zoe, who "finds herself in a small rehabilitation center for girls with eating disorders," which she feels "must be some kind of mistake" because "she feels in control of her cautious dietary habits. Through letters to her mysteriously silent best friend, Elise, as well as a personal journal," it becomes clear that Zoe is in denial and "that she is, in fact, a girl with a disorder that is spiraling out of control." (School Library Journal)

Priestly, Chris

Mister Creecher. Bloomsbury 2011 390p $16.99

Grades: 6 7 8 9 **Fic**

1. Horror fiction 2. Frankenstein's monster (Fictional character)
ISBN 978-1-59990-703-1; 1-59990-703-8

Billy is a street urchin, a pickpocket, and a petty thief. Mister Creecher is a giant of a man whose appearance terrifies everyone he meets. A bond develops between these two misfits as they embark on a bloody journey that will take them from London northward on the trail of their target . . . Doctor Victor Frankenstein.

"Priestly's love of Shelley is evident. Here, he restores Shelley's original creature—not a lurching, moaning monster but an eloquent, profoundly flawed being—imbuing him with the deep desire to be loved and accepted." Booklist

Prinz, Yvonne

The **Vinyl** Princess. HarperTeen 2010 313p $16.99

Grades: 8 9 10 11 12 **Fic**

1. Music -- Fiction 2. Zines -- Fiction 3. Weblogs -- Fiction 4. California -- Fiction 5. Sound recordings -- Fiction

ISBN 978-0-06-171583-9; 0-06-171583-2

LC 2009-14270

Allie, a sixteen-year-old who is obsessed with LPs, works at the used record store on Telegraph Ave. and deals with crushes—her own and her mother's—her increasingly popular blog and zine, and generally grows up over the course of one summer in her hometown of Berkeley, California.

Prinz "writes with a genuine passion for music that readers who live to listen will recognize, and in this heartfelt, often-hilarious story, she shows the profound ways that music can shape lives." Booklist

Proimos, James

12 things to do before you crash and burn. Roaring Brook Press 2011 121p $14.99

Grades: 7 8 9 10 **Fic**

1. Uncles -- Fiction 2. Bereavement -- Fiction 3. Father-son relationship -- Fiction

ISBN 978-1-59643-595-7; 1-59643-595-X

LC 2010043935

Sixteen-year-old James 'Hercules' Martino completes twelve tasks while spending two weeks in Baltimore with his Uncle Anthony, and gains insights into himself, his uncle, and his recently deceased father, a self-help author and daytime talk show host who was beloved by the public but a terrible father.

"Proimos fully inhabits the mind and voice of his hero, whose almost mythic journey offers moments hilarious, heartbreaking, and triumphant." Publ Wkly

Prose, Francine

After. HarperCollins Pubs. 2003 330p $15.99; lib bdg $16.89

Grades: 7 8 9 10 **Fic**

1. School stories 2. Conspiracies -- Fiction 3. School violence -- Fiction

ISBN 0-06-008081-7; 0-06-008082-5 lib bdg

LC 2002-14386

In the aftermath of a nearby school shooting, a grief and crisis counselor takes over Central High School and enacts increasingly harsh measures to control students, while those who do not comply disappear

"This drama raises all-too-relevant questions about the fine line between safety as a means of protection versus encroachment on individual rights and free will. Sure to spur heated discussions." Publ Wkly

Touch. HarperTeen 2009 262p $16.99; lib bdg $17.89

Grades: 7 8 9 10 **Fic**

1. School stories 2. Friendship -- Fiction 3. Family life -- Fiction 4. Stepmothers -- Fiction

ISBN 978-0-06-137517-0; 0-06-137517-9; 978-0-06-137518-7 lib bdg; 0-06-137518-7 lib bdg

LC 2008-20208

Ninth-grader Maisie's concepts of friendship, loyalty, self-acceptance, and truth are tested to their limit after a schoolbus incident with the three boys who have been her best friends since early childhood.

"Readers will be fascinated by this convincing tale and the questions that it raises, from its gripping first chapter to its poignant and surprising conclusion." Voice Youth Advocates

The **turning**; by Francine Prose. HarperTeen 2012 256 p. (hardcover) $17.99

Grades: 7 8 9 10 **Fic**

1. Ghost stories 2. Horror fiction 3. Babysitters -- Fiction 4. Ghosts -- Fiction

ISBN 0061999660; 9780061999666

LC 2012019090

This book by Francine Prose is an "epistolary retelling of Henry James's 'The Turn of the Screw' [which] traces a contemporary babysitter's supernatural encounters. The protagonist, Jack, is hoping to earn some money for college when he agrees to care for orphan siblings on Crackstone's Landing, a remote island without phones, Internet, or TV. . . . Jack is spooked by two ethereal figures, perhaps the ghosts of the children's former governess and her beau." (Publishers Weekly)

Provoost, Anne

In the shadow of the ark; translated by John Nieuwenhuizen. Arthur A. Levine Books 2004 368p $17.95

Grades: 9 10 11 12 **Fic**

1. Noah's ark -- Fiction

ISBN 0-439-44234-6

LC 2003-9622

Original Dutch edition, 2001

This is a "story of the biblical Flood, recounted by Re Jana, whose family leaves the marshes to find the ark. The passion Re Jana finds with Ham, son of the Builder, leads to a place on the ark, but this 'safe haven,' with the stink and sounds of the animals, starvation, and repeated (if not lustful) rapes by Ham's brothers, tests her in every way, even as she carries new life into the New World. Exquisitely detailed and intelligently written, this is a YA novel only in the broadest sense; no one would blink if it appeared on an adult list." Booklist

Pullman, Philip, 1946-

★ The **golden** compass; his dark materials book I. [appendix illustrations by Ian Beck] Deluxe 10th anniversary ed.; Alfred A. Knopf 2006 399p il $22.95

Grades: 7 8 9 10 11 12 **Fic**

1. Fantasy fiction

ISBN 978-0-375-83830-9; 0-375-83830-9

LC 2005-32556

First published 1995 in the United Kingdom with title: Northern lights

This first title in a fantasy trilogy "introduces the characters and sets up the basic conflict, namely, a race to unlock the mystery of a newly discovered type of charged particles simply called 'dust' that may be a bridge to an alternate universe. The action follows 11-year-old protagonist Lyra Belacqua from her home at Oxford University to the frozen wastes of the North on a quest to save dozens of kidnapped children from the evil 'Gobblers,' who are using them as part of a sinister experiment involving dust." Libr J [review of 1996 edition]

Other titles in the His dark materials series are:
The amber spyglass (2000)
The subtle knife (1997)

Once upon a time in the North; illustrated by John Lawrence. Knopf 2008 95p il $12.99
Grades: 7 8 9 10 11 12 **Fic**

1. Fantasy fiction
ISBN 978-0-375-84510-9; 0-375-84510-0
LC 2007-43993

Prequel to: The golden compass

In a time before Lyra Silvertongue was born, the tough American balloonist Lee Scoresby and the great armoured bear Iorek Byrnison meet when Lee and his hare daemon Hester crash-land their trading balloon onto a port in the far Arctic North and find themselves right in the middle of a political powder keg.

"The precise narrative prose is spiced up with Lee's flights of 'oratorical flamboyancy,' and the sardonic banter between Lee and his daemon Hester is as amusing as ever. [Illustrated with] engraved spot illustrations and 'reproduced' documents." Horn Book

Purcell, Kim

Trafficked; by Kim Purcell. Viking 2012 384 p.
Grades: 9 10 11 12 **Fic**

1. Slavery -- Fiction 2. Young adult literature 3. Immigrants -- United States -- Fiction 4. Juvenile prostitution 5. Human trafficking -- Fiction 6. Los Angeles (Calif.) -- Fiction 7. Moldovans -- United States -- Fiction
ISBN 0670012807; 9780670012800
LC 2011011530

In this young adult novel by Kim Purcell, "[w]hen Hannah's parents are killed in an explosion in a café in the breakaway republic of Transnistria, she and her grandmother are hard pressed to make ends meet in their Moldovan home. . . . Hannah decides to take an offer to go to America as a nanny for a Russian family. . . . What she finds in America is a harsh reality check; yes, she is a nanny to a reasonably wealthy family, but the family confiscates her return ticket, she is forbidden to leave the house or even speak English, and no money is forthcoming. She is also under threat from a family friend to . . . [who] imports Russian girls as prostitutes. . . . Hannah is constantly worried about what will happen to her." (Bulletin of the Center for Children's Books)

Qamar, Amjed

★ **Beneath** my mother's feet. Atheneum Books for Young Readers 2008 198p $16.99
Grades: 7 8 9 10 **Fic**

1. Poverty -- Fiction 2. Pakistan -- Fiction 3. Sex role -- Fiction 4. Household employees -- Fiction
ISBN 978-1-4169-4728-8; 1-4169-4728-0
LC 2007-19001

When her father is injured, fourteen-year-old Nazia is pulled away from school, her friends, and her preparations for an arranged marriage, to help her mother clean houses in a wealthy part of Karachi, Pakistan, where she finally rebels against the destiny that is planned for her.

This novel "provides a fascinating glimpse into a world remarkably distant from that of most American teens, and would be an excellent suggestion for readers who want to know about how other young people live." SLJ

Quick, Barbara

A **golden** web. HarperTeen 2010 266p $16.99
Grades: 7 8 9 10 **Fic**

1. Biologists 2. Italy -- Fiction 3. Anatomy -- Fiction 4. Sex role -- Fiction 5. Middle Ages -- Fiction
ISBN 978-0-06-144887-4; 0-06-144887-7
LC 2009-14265

In fourteenth-century Bologna, Alessandra Giliani, a brilliant young girl, defies convention and risks death in order to attend medical school at the university so that she can study anatomy.

"Alessandra's intellectual curiosity is wonderfully depicted, her philosophical musings are entertaining, and her commitment to the pursuit of biological knowledge enlivens the plot. Quick's prose is fluid and authentic, bright and engaging." Publ Wkly

Quick, Matthew

Boy21; by Matthew Quick. Little, Brown and Co. 2012 250 p.
Grades: 8 9 10 11 12 **Fic**

1. Basketball -- Fiction 2. Friendship -- Fiction 3. Race relations -- Fiction 4. Boys -- Psychology -- Fiction 5. High school students -- Fiction 6. Violence -- Fiction 7. High schools -- Fiction 8. Pennsylvania -- Fiction 9. African Americans -- Fiction
ISBN 0316127973; 9780316127974
LC 2010047995

In this book, high school basketball player "Finley . . . take[s] under his wing Russell Washington, the . . . son of a family friend. Boy21, as Russell now calls himself, was a phenom . . . until his parents were killed and he withdrew into an outer-space obsession and refused to play ball. . . . Just as Boy21 begins to get his life back together, Finley's goes into a tailspin when [his girlfriend] Erin is run down by an enemy of her brother." (Bulletin of the Center for Children's Books)

Forgive me, Leonard Peacock; by Matthew Quick. Little, Brown and Co. 2013 288 p. $18
Grades: 9 10 11 12 **Fic**

1. School stories 2. Suicide -- Fiction 3. School shootings -- Fiction
ISBN 0316221333; 9780316221337
LC 2012031410

This book by Matthew Quick follows "Leonard Peacock . . . a teenager who feels let down by adults and out of step with his sheeplike classmates. Foreseeing only more unhappiness and disappointment in life (and harboring a secret that's destroying him), Leonard packs up his grandfather's WWII handgun and heads to school, intending to kill his former best friend and then himself. First, though, he will visit the important people in his life." (Publishers Weekly)

"Eighteen-year-old Leonard Peacock is packing a handgun and planning to kill his former best friend, then himself. Over the course of one intense day (with flashbacks), Leonard's existential crisis is delineated through an engaging first-person narrative supplemented with letters from the future that urge Leonard to believe in a "life beyond the bermorons" at school. Complicated characters and ideas mark this memorable story." (Horn Book)

Sorta like a rockstar; a novel. Little, Brown 2010 355p $16.99; pa $8.99
Grades: 7 8 9 10 11 **Fic**

1. School stories 2. Homeless persons -- Fiction 3. Depression (Psychology) -- Fiction
ISBN 978-0-316-04352-6; 0-316-04352-4; 978-0-316-04353-3 pa; 0-316-04353-2 pa
LC 2008-46746

Although seventeen-year-old Amber Appleton is homeless, living in a school bus with her unfit mother, she is a relentless optimist who visits the elderly at a nursing home, teaches English to Korean Catholic women with the use of rhythm and blues music, and befriends a solitary Vietnam veteran and his dog, but eventually she experiences one burden more than she can bear and slips into a deep depression.

"This book is the answer to all those angst-ridden and painfully grim novels in the shortcut lingo of short attention-span theater. Hugely enjoyable." SLJ

Quintero, Isabel

★ **Gabi,** a girl in pieces. Isabel Quintero. Cinco Puntos Press. 2014 208p $17.95
Grades: 9 10 11 12 **Fic**

1. Family problems — Fiction; 2. Gays — Fiction; 3. High schools — Fiction; 4. Mexican Americans — Fiction; 5. Pregnancy — Fiction; 6. Diaries--Fiction
ISBN: 1935955942; 9781935955948; 9781935955955
LC 2014007658

William C. Morris Award (2015)

"Sixteen-year-old Gabi Hernandez has a lot to deal with during her senior year. Her best friend Cindy is pregnant; her other best friend Sebastian just got kicked out of his house for coming out to his strict parents; her meth addict dad is trying to quit, again; and her super religious Tía Bertha is constantly putting a damper on Gabi's love life. In lyrical diary entries peppered with the burgeoning poet's writing, Spanglish, and phone conversations, Quintero gives voice to a complex, not always likable but totally believable teen who struggles to figure out her own place in the world. Believing she's not Mexican enough for her family and not white enough for Berkeley, Gabi still meets every challenge head-on with vulgar humor and raw honesty." Booklist

Quintero, Sofia

★ **Efrain's** secret. Alfred A. Knopf 2010 265p $16.99; lib bdg $19.99
Grades: 8 9 10 11 12 **Fic**

1. School stories 2. Violence -- Fiction 3. Drug traffic -- Fiction 4. Hispanic Americans -- Fiction 5. Bronx (New York, N.Y.) -- Fiction
ISBN 978-0-375-84706-6; 0-375-84706-5; 978-0-375-94706-3 lib bdg; 0-375-94706-X lib bdg
LC 2009-8493

Ambitious high school senior and honor student Efrain Rodriguez makes some questionable choices in pursuit of his dream to escape the South Bronx and attend an Ivy League college.

"Quintero imbues her characters with unexpected grace and charm. . . . Mostly, though, it is Quintero's effortless grasp of teen slang that gives her first-person story its heart." Booklist

Rabin, Staton

Black powder. Margaret K. McElderry Books 2005 245p $16.95
Grades: 6 7 8 9 **Fic**

1. Science fiction 2. African Americans -- Fiction
ISBN 0-689-86876-4

After his best friend is shot and killed, fourteen-year-old Langston borrows his science teacher's time machine and travels from Los Angeles in 2010 to Oxford, England, in 1278 to try to prevent Roger Bacon from publishing his formula for gunpowder.

This is "a touching story of two great scientific minds discovering the humanity behind the ideas. Langston is particularly well-developed as an intelligent, mostly responsible African-American finding his way." SLJ

Raedeke, Christy

The **daykeeper's** grimoire. Flux 2010 352p (Prophecy of days) pa $9.95
Grades: 7 8 9 10 **Fic**

1. Mayas -- Fiction 2. Scotland -- Fiction 3. Prophecies -- Fiction 4. Conspiracies -- Fiction 5. Secret societies -- Fiction
ISBN 978-0-7387-1576-6; 0-7387-1576-X
LC 2009-30668

Caity Mac Fireland of San Francisco accompanies her parents to an isle off the coast of Scotland where she finds a Mayan relic and, guided by a motley crew of advisors, uncovers an incredible secret that an elite group of power-brokers will stop at nothing to control.

"A delightful heroine, she's funny, frank, and mostly true to the way a real teen would act if she found herself in such an odd circumstance. Readers will want to follow Caity's adventure." Booklist

Followed by: The serpent's coil (2011)

The **serpent's** coil. Flux 2011 298p (Prophecy of days) $9.95
Grades: 7 8 9 10 **Fic**

1. Travel -- Fiction 2. Prophecies -- Fiction 3. Conspiracies -- Fiction 4. Native Americans -- Fiction
ISBN 978-0-7387-1577-3; 0-7387-1577-8
LC 2011004573

While attending a boarding school that allows her to travel around the globe, Caity continues her mission to fulfill a Mayan prophecy and mobilize the world's young people to stop the devastating global reign of the Fraternitas.

"Conspiracies abound in the second book of the Prophecy of Days series, which, if possible, moves at an even greater pace than the first. Raedeke weaves together an impressive array of mysticism, ancient knowledge, and conspiracy theories while keeping the main plot, if not all the details, easy to follow." Voice Youth Advocates

Raf, Mindy

The **symptoms** of my insanity; Mindy Raf. Dial 2013 384 p. (hardcover) $17.99

Grades: 8 9 10 11 12 **Fic**

1. School stories 2. Puberty -- Fiction 3. Teenage girls -- Fiction 4. Mothers -- Fiction 5. High schools -- Fiction 6. Hypochondria -- Fiction

ISBN 0803732414; 9780803732414

LC 2012024708

"Izzy is running out of time to complete her art portfolio, her ever-expanding chest is the brunt of ogling and inappropriate jokes, and her mother's rare stomach cancer has probably returned. Naturally, the high school sophomore assumes that her body's idiosyncrasies must be a sign of a developing disease. There's still some hope for Izzy when popular basketball player Blake shows an interest in her. His affection is a ruse for a hazing prank, however, and when a cellphone photo of Izzy's bare breast goes viral, she becomes known as 'Boobgirl' around school." Kirkus

"While the plot is predictable . . . Izzy's self-deprecating humor and wry observations bring fresh air to tired tropes. Raf's background in comedy serves her well and gives her protagonist an authenticity that will make readers feel invested in her story. A fairly standard contribution to the genre, but a solid one." SLJ

Rainfield, Cheryl

★ **Scars**; Cheryl Rainfield. WestSide Books 2010 248p. $16.95

Grades: 9 10 11 12 **Fic**

1. Memory -- Fiction 2. Lesbians -- Fiction 3. Self-mutilation -- Fiction 4. Child sexual abuse -- Fiction 5. Artists -- Fiction 6. Emotional problems -- Fiction 7. Cutting (Self-mutilation) -- Fiction

ISBN 9781934813324

LC 2009052076

This novel tells the story of "Kendra, fifteen, [who] hasn't felt safe since she began to recall devastating memories of childhood sexual abuse—especially because she still can't remember the most important detail—her abuser's identity. Frightened, Kendra believes someone is always watching and following her, leaving menacing messages only she understands. . . . To relieve the pressure, Kendra cuts; aside from her brilliantly expressive artwork, it's her only way of coping. Since her own mother is too self-absorbed to hear her cries for help, Kendra finds support in others instead: from her therapist and her art teacher, from Sandy, the close family friend who encourages her artwork, and from Meghan, the classmate who's becoming a friend and maybe more." (Publisher's note)

"The excellent resource section covers widely respected books, Web sites, organizations, and help lines for youth seeking information on extreme abuse, cutting, same-sex attraction, and dissociation. This book will be a particular comfort and source of insight for teens facing any of these challenges, but whatever their life experience, they will be on the edge of their seats, rooting for Kendra to unravel the mystery that shadows her life. This is one heck of a good book!" SLJ

Stained; by Cheryl Rainfield. Harcourt, Houghton Mifflin Harcourt 2013 304 p. $16.99

Grades: 9 10 11 12 **Fic**

1. Kidnapping -- Fiction 2. Survival skills -- Fiction 3. Birthmarks -- Fiction 4. Body image -- Fiction 5. Psychopaths -- Fiction 6. Sexual abuse -- Fiction 7. Beauty, Personal -- Fiction

ISBN 0547942087; 9780547942087

LC 2012047540

In this book by Cheryl Rainfield, "Sarah Meadows longs for 'normal.' Born with a port wine stain covering half her face, all her life she's been plagued by stares, giggles, bullying, and disgust. But when she's abducted on the way home from school, Sarah is forced to uncover the courage she never knew she had, become a hero rather than a victim, and learn to look beyond her face to find the beauty and strength she has inside. It's that—or succumb to a killer." (Publisher's note)

Rallison, Janette

How to take the ex out of ex-boyfriend. G. P. Putnam's Sons 2007 265p hardcover o.p. pa $7.99

Grades: 7 8 9 10 **Fic**

1. School stories 2. Politics -- Fiction 3. Dating (Social customs) -- Fiction

ISBN 978-0-399-24617-3; 0-399-24617-7; 978-0-14-241269-5 pa; 0-14-241269-4 pa

LC 2006-26543

Giovanna rashly breaks up with her boyfriend when he refuses to help her twin brother with his campaign for Student Council president, but fixing her mistake may be more difficult for her than she realizes.

This "is more serious in its treatment of issues and meatier than others like it, making it engaging yet an easy fun read that will appeal to many teen girls." Voice Youth Advocates

Just one wish. G. P. Putnam's Sons 2009 264p $16.99; pa $7.99

Grades: 7 8 9 10 **Fic**

1. Actors -- Fiction 2. Cancer -- Fiction 3. Siblings -- Fiction

ISBN 978-0-399-24618-0; 0-399-24618-5; 978-0-14-241599-3 pa; 0-14-241599-5 pa

LC 2008-9297

Seventeen-year-old Annika tries to cheer up her little brother Jeremy before his surgery to remove a cancerous tumor by bringing home his favorite television actor, Steve Raleigh, the star of "Teen Robin Hood"

"Annika's wacky encounters . . . and anxiety for her brother make the story both comical and poignant." Horn Book Guide

Randall, Thomas

Dreams of the dead. Bloomsbury Children's Books 2009 276p (The waking) pa $8.99

Grades: 8 9 10 11 12 **Fic**

1. School stories 2. Death -- Fiction 3. Japan -- Fiction

4. Supernatural -- Fiction
ISBN 978-1-59990-250-0; 1-59990-250-8
LC 2008-30844

After her mother dies, sixteen-year-old Kara and her father move to Japan, where he teaches and she attends school, but she is haunted by a series of frightening nightmares and deaths that might be revenge—or something worse

"The story has suspense, mystery, and horror. It will be a great hit with fans of manga, anime, or Japanese culture." SLJ

Followed by: Spirits of the Noh (2011)

Spirits of the Noh. Bloomsbury U.S.A. Children's Books 2010 264p (The waking) $8.99
Grades: 8 9 10 11 12 **Fic**

1. Horror fiction 2. School stories 3. Japan -- Fiction
4. Monsters -- Fiction 5. Supernatural -- Fiction
ISBN 978-1-59990-251-7; 1-59990-251-6
LC 2009018251

Sequel to: Dreams of the dead (2009)

Just as Kara and her friends at the Monju-no-Chie school in Japan are beginning to get over the horrifying deaths of two students, another monster emerges to terrorize the school.

"Using all the usual horror elements, Randall constructs a fine teen chiller complete with mean-girl drama, a dash of romance and the angst of teens who believe that adults do not understand them." Kirkus

Rapp, Adam

The **children** and the wolves; Adam Rapp. Candlewick Press 2011 152 p. $16.99
Grades: 8 9 10 **Fic**

1. Kidnapping -- Fiction 2. Psychological fiction 3. Juvenile delinquency -- Fiction 4. Drug abuse -- Fiction
5. Single parent family -- Fiction
ISBN 0763653373; 9780763653378
LC 2011013676

This book by Printz Honor-winning author Adam Rapp presents a story "about three disaffected teens and a kidnapped child. Three teenagers—a sharp, well-to-do girl named Bounce and two struggling boys named Wiggins and Orange—are holding a four-year old girl hostage in Orange's basement. The little girl answers to 'the Frog'and seems content to play a video game about wolves all day long, a game that parallels the reality around her. As the stakes grow higher and the guilt and tension mount, Wiggins cracks and finally brings Frog to a trusted adult." (Publisher's note)

★ **Punkzilla.** Candlewick Press 2009 244p $16.99
Grades: 10 11 12 **Fic**

1. Brothers -- Fiction 2. Drug abuse -- Fiction 3. Runaway teenagers -- Fiction
ISBN 978-0-7636-3031-7; 0-7636-3031-4
LC 2008-935655

ALA YALSA Printz Award Honor Book (2010)

"Punkzilla" is on a mission to see his older brother "P", before "P" dies of cancer. Still buzzing from his last hit of meth, he embarks on a days-long trip from Portland, Ore. to Memphis, Tenn., writing letters to his family and friends. Along the way, he sees a sketchier side of America and worries if he will make it to see his brother in time.

"Jamie, who has ADD, details every step (being taken advantage of sexually, getting jumped, befriending a female-to-male transsexual, losing his virginity) in expletive-filled, stream-of-consciousness narration with insights into seedy roadside America . . . and his own situation. . . . The teenager's singular voice and observations make for an immersive reading experience." Publ Wkly

★ **Under** the wolf, under the dog. Candlewick Press 2004 310p $16.99
Grades: 9 10 11 12 **Fic**

1. Suicide -- Fiction 2. Illinois -- Fiction 3. Family life -- Fiction
ISBN 0-7636-1818-7
LC 2004-50255

"Steve currently resides in a facility for troubled youth, but most are here for drug abuse or suicidal tendencies, and he doesn't really fit in either category. What's led him here, as he describes in his journal, is a series of life depredations that have sent him reeling into irrationality: his mother's long, horrible, and unsuccessful bout with cancer, his father's concomitant catatonic depression, his brother's drug-induced haze and subsequent suicide, and his own unintentional self-woundings along the way, from a lacerated leg to an injury that eventually results in blindness in one eye." Bull Cent Child Books

Raskin, Joyce

My misadventures as a teenage rock star; written by Joyce Raskin; illustrations by Carol Chu. Graphia 2011 107p il pa $8.99
Grades: 7 8 9 10 **Fic**

1. Popularity -- Fiction 2. Rock music -- Fiction 3. Family life -- Fiction 4. Bands (Music) -- Fiction
ISBN 978-0-547-39311-7 pa; 0-547-39311-3 pa
LC 2010-27456

Fourteen-year-old Alex, a short, pasty, shy, greasy-haired girl with acne, gains self-confidence when her brother convinces her to play bass in a rock band, but she finds that being 'cool' has its drawbacks.

"The unintimidating length and layout, direct prose, and swift-moving plot make thsi a particularly fine choice for reluctant readers." Bull Cent Child Books

Ravel, Edeet

The **saver.** Groundwood Books/House of Anansi Press 2008 214p $17.95; pa $8.95
Grades: 7 8 9 10 11 **Fic**

1. Death -- Fiction 2. Uncles -- Fiction 3. Orphans -- Fiction
ISBN 978-0-88899-882-8; 0-88899-882-1; 978-0-88899-883-5 pa; 0-88899-883-X pa

When 17-year-old Fern's mother dies of a heart attack, she has to make her own way in the world. She takes over her mother's housecleaning jobs, takes a job as a janitor, and adds two other part-time jobs. Then her Uncle Jack, whom she's never met, shows up to help her.

"Written as a series of letters to an imaginary friend on another planet, this is a compelling story of determination and the will to survive." SLJ

Razzell, Mary

★ **Snow** apples. Groundwood Books 2006 209p hardcover o.p. pa $6.95

Grades: 10 11 12 **Fic**

1. Pregnancy -- Fiction 2. British Columbia -- Fiction 3. Mother-daughter relationship -- Fiction

ISBN 0-88899-741-8; 978-0-88899-741-8; 0-88899-728-0 pa; 978-0-88899-728-9 pa

First published 1984 in Canada

"In isolated, rural British Columbia, as World War II is ending, Sheila Brary turns 16 and yearns for a life different from the sad existence of her mother. Struggling to raise four sons and a daughter mostly on her own, the woman has turned hard and cold, always angry at her bright and emotional daughter who reminds her too much of her unfaithful, undependable husband. . . . The teen wins one struggle with her mother and manages to finish high school, while she loses another with her own awakening sexuality and finds herself desperate and pregnant. When she runs off to Vancouver, her distant father helps her to abort the pregnancy and then abandons her one last time. Sheila survives a terrifying miscarriage on her own, returns to her family long enough to see what her mother has sacrificed, and starts a new life with promise and support. This is a quiet, introspective novel that takes a while to build its power, and it has some stunningly dramatic scenes." SLJ

Reed, Amy

Crazy; Amy Reed. Simon Pulse 2012 367 p. (hardcover) $16.99; (hardcover) $16.99

Grades: 10 11 12 **Fic**

1. Love stories 2. Mental illness -- Fiction 3. Interpersonal relations -- Fiction 4. Email -- Fiction 5. Emotional problems -- Fiction 6. Washington (State) -- Fiction

ISBN 1442413476; 9781442413474; 9781442413498

LC 2011032804

This book tells the story of "a romance marred by mental illness. Connor knows that Izzy will never fall in love with him the way he's fallen for her. But somehow he's been let into her crazy, exhilarating world and become her closest confidante. But the closer they get, the more Connor realizes that Izzy's highs are too high and her lows are too low. And the frenetic energy that makes her shine is starting to push her into a much darker place. As Izzy's behavior gets increasingly erratic and self-destructive, Connor gets increasingly desperate to stop her from plummeting. He knows he can't save her from her pain...but what if no one else can?" (Publisher's note)

Over you; by Amy Reed. 1st Simon Pulse hardcover ed. Simon Pulse 2013 299 p. (hardcover) $16.99

Grades: 9 10 11 12 **Fic**

1. Communal living -- Fiction 2. Female friendship -- Fiction 3. Nebraska -- Fiction 4. Friendship -- Fiction 5. Family problems -- Fiction 6. Farm life -- Nebraska -- Fiction 7. Mothers and daughters -- Fiction

ISBN 1442456965; 9781442456969

LC 2012023492

In this book, 17-year-old friends Max and Sadie spend a summer on a communal farm. "Max welcomes the hippie residents (which include Sadie's absentee mother), yurts, and grueling farm work, but Sadie--volatile, self-absorbed, and always the center of attention--quickly grows bored and irate. After Sadie is quarantined with mono, Max has even more freedom to explore her own thoughts, interests, and desires--including a love/hate crush on a surly older boy that surprises even Max." (Publishers Weekly)

Reed, Jaime

Living violet; the Cambion chronicles. Jaime Reed. Dafina KTeen Books 2012 311 p. (paperback) $9.95

Grades: 9 10 11 12 **Fic**

1. Love stories 2. Supernatural -- Fiction 3. High school students -- Fiction 4. Paranormal fiction 5. Teenagers

ISBN 0758269242; 9780758269249

LC 2011275889

This book is a "supernatural boy-meets-girl romance. Samara doesn't understand" women's attraction to "her co-worker, Caleb . . . . When Caleb kills a would-be date-rapist in front of Samara to protect her friend, he's forced to reveal his nature to her. He's a Cambion, meaning he shares his body with an extra soul, that of a seductive incubus that draws the women to him to fulfill its life-sucking nutritional needs." (Kirkus Reviews)

Reedy, Trent

Words in the dust. Arthur A. Levine Books 2011 266p $17.99

Grades: 5 6 7 8 **Fic**

1. Literacy -- Fiction 2. Sex role -- Fiction 3. Birth defects -- Fiction

ISBN 0-545-26125-2; 978-0-545-26125-8

LC 2010-26160

Zulaikha, a thirteen-year-old girl in Afghanistan, faces a series of frightening but exhilarating changes in her life as she defies her father and secretly meets with an old woman who teaches her to read, her older sister gets married, and American troops offer her surgery to fix her disfiguring cleft lip.

"The evolution of key relationships presents a nuanced look at family dynamics and Afghan culture. Though unsentimental and fraught with tragedy, Reedy's narrative offers hope and will go a long way toward helping readers understand the people behind the headlines." Publ Wkly

Rees, Celia

The **fool's** girl. Bloomsbury 2010 297p $16.99

Grades: 8 9 10 11 12 **Fic**

1. Poets 2. Authors 3. Dramatists 4. Adventure fiction 5. London (England) -- Fiction 6. Great Britain -- History -- 1485-1603, Tudors -- Fiction

ISBN 978-1-59990-486-3; 1-59990-486-1

LC 2009-51894

Violetta and Feste have come to London to rescue a holy relic taken from a church in Illyria by the evil Malvolio, and once there, they tell the story of their adventures to playwright William Shakespeare, who turns it into a play.

"Expertly livening the proceedings with intrigues, japes, kisses, mildly bawdy comments, . . . colorful characters, plot twists, quick violence, and an occasional breath of the supernatural, Rees dishes up a quick-paced tale that builds to a suspenseful climax." Booklist

Pirates! the true and remarkable adventures of Minerva Sharpe and Nancy Kington, female pirates. Bloomsbury 2003 379p $16.95; pa $8.95

Grades: 9 10 11 12 **Fic**

1. Sea stories 2. Adventure fiction 3. Jamaica -- Fiction 4. Pirates -- Fiction

ISBN 1-582-34816-2; 1-582-34665-8 pa

LC 2003-51861

In 1722, after arriving with her brother at the family's Jamaican plantation where she is to be married off, sixteen-year-old Nancy Kington escapes with her slave friend, Minerva Sharpe, and together they become pirates traveling the world in search of treasure.

"There's action aplenty . . . with storms and sea battles and a devilish suitor hot on the heels of an innocent (except for the odd murder here and there) heroine. Add popcorn and a supersized soda, and you've got a rousing Saturday matinee." Bull Cent Child Books

Sovay. Bloomsbury 2008 404p $16.99

Grades: 7 8 9 10 11 12 **Fic**

1. Thieves -- Fiction 2. Sex role -- Fiction 3. Social classes -- Fiction 4. Great Britain -- History -- 1714-1837 -- Fiction 5. France -- History -- 1789-1799, Revolution -- Fiction

ISBN 978-1-59990-203-6; 1-59990-203-6

LC 2008-4779

In 1794 England, the rich and beautiful Sovay, disguised as a highwayman, acquires papers that could lead to her father's arrest for treason, and soon her newly-awakened political consciousness leads her and a compatriot to France during the Revolution.

"Taking as her inspiration a traditional English ballad, also titled Sovay, . . . Rees produces an appealingly fast-paced and suspenseful historical novel with plenty of plot twists, dastardly villains, and a brave, resourceful young heroine." Voice Youth Advocates

Rees, Douglas C.

Vampire High. Delacorte Press 2003 226p $15.95; lib bdg $17.99

Grades: 7 8 9 10 **Fic**

1. School stories 2. Vampires -- Fiction

ISBN 0-385-73117-5; 0-385-90143-7 lib bdg

LC 2003-41992

When his family moves from California to New Sodom, Massachusetts and Cody enters Vlad Dracul Magnet School, many things seem strange, from the dark-haired, pale-skinned, supernaturally strong students to Charon, the wolf who guides him around campus on the first day

"There's barely a false note in this rollicking tale of horror, humor, and light romance that will appeal to both girls and boys." Booklist

Vampire High: sophomore year. Delacorte 2010 247p $16.99; lib bdg $17.89

Grades: 7 8 9 10 **Fic**

1. School stories 2. Vampires -- Fiction

ISBN 978-0-385-73725-8; 0-385-73725-4; 978-0-385-90657-9 lib bdg; 0-385-90657-9 lib bdg

When Cody's Goth cousin Turk moves into his house, enrolls at Vlad Dracul, and decides to turn an abandoned nineteenth-century mill into an art center, the vampire (Jenti) students are not pleased, and Cody's hopes for a great sophomore year are blighted.

"Rees's fast-paced and action-packed story line tackles important teen issues like identity, belonging, friendship, and acceptance in a way that is not overbearing or preachy. With lots of humor and strong, engaging characters, this novel has an appeal factor that is sure to make its mark (or bite) on readers of this genre." SLJ

Reese, James

The **strange** case of Doctor Jekyll and Mademoiselle Odile; James Reese. Roaring Brook Press 2012 357 p.

Grades: 9 10 11 12 **Fic**

1. Occult fiction 2. Fantasy fiction 3. Historical fiction 4. Witchcraft -- Fiction 5. Orphans -- Fiction 6. Shapeshifting -- Fiction 7. Characters in literature -- Fiction 8. Paris (France) -- History -- Siege, 1870-1871 -- Fiction 9. France -- History -- Occupation and evacuation, 1871-1873 -- Fiction

ISBN 1596436840; 9781596436848

LC 2010053366

In this novel, by James Reese, "desperate to find a cure for her brother Grel's mysterious progressive disease . . . Odile has gone to test some magicked salts on the monkeys, with horrific results. . . . She also runs into a young doctor named Jekyll. . . . Little does she know that Jekyll has been spying on her, so that when she does heal Grel, and in the process transforms him into a powerful, hulking, amoral male, Jekyll is watching." (Bulletin of the Center for Children's Books)

Reeve, Philip, 1966-

★ **Fever** Crumb. Scholastic Press 2010 325p $17.99

Grades: 6 7 8 9 10 **Fic**

1. Science fiction 2. Orphans -- Fiction 3. Sex role -- Fiction 4. London (England) -- Fiction

ISBN 978-0-545-20719-5; 0-545-20719-3

LC 2009-15457

Prequel to: The Hungry City Chronicles series

Foundling Fever Crumb has been raised as an engineer although females in the future London, England, are not believed capable of rational thought, but at age fourteen she leaves her sheltered world and begins to learn startling truths about her past while facing danger in the present.

"Reeve's captivating flights of imagination play as vital a role in the story as his endearing heroine, hiss-worthy villains, and nifty array of supporting characters." Booklist

Followed by A web of air (2011)

★ **Here** lies Arthur. Scholastic Press 2008 339p $16.99

Grades: 7 8 9 10 **Fic**

1. Kings 2. Magic -- Fiction 3. Great Britain -- History

-- 0-1066 -- Fiction
ISBN 978-0-545-09334-7; 0-545-09334-1
LC 2008-05787

When her village is attacked and burned, Gwyna seeks protection from the bard Myrddin, who uses Gwyna in his plan to transform young Arthur into the heroic King Arthur.

"Powerfully inventive. . . . Events rush headlong toward the inevitable ending, but Gwyna's observations illuminate them in a new way." Booklist

Scrivener's moon; the third book in the Fever Crumb series. Philip Reeve. Scholastic Press 2012 341 p. (Fever Crumb series) (hardcover) $17.99
Grades: 6 7 8 9 10 **Fic**

1. Steampunk fiction 2. Technology -- Fiction 3. Science fiction 4. England -- Fiction 5. Identity -- Fiction 6. England 7. London (England) -- Fiction 8. Dystopias 9. Mutation (Biology) -- Fiction 10. Technology 11. London (England) 12. Mutation (Biology) 13. Identity (Psychology)
ISBN 0545222184; 9780545222181
LC 2012008124

This young adult steampunk adventure novel, by Philip Reeve, is the conclusion to the "Fever Crumb" trilogy. "The Scriven people are brilliant, mad--and dead. All except one, whose monstrous creation is nearly complete--a giant city on wheels. New London terrifies the rest of the world, and an army of mammoth-riders gathers to fight it. Meanwhile, young Fever Crumb begins a hunt for Ancient technology in the icy strongholds of the north." (Publisher's note)

A **Web** of Air. Scholastic Press 2011 293p $17.99
Grades: 6 7 8 9 10 **Fic**

1. Science fiction 2. Flight -- Fiction 3. Orphans -- Fiction
ISBN 0-545-22216-8; 978-0-545-22216-7
LC 2010043341

Sequel to: Fever Crumb (2010)

Two years ago, Fever Crumb escaped the wartorn city of London in a traveling theater. Now, she arrives in the extraordinary city of Mayda, where buildings ascend the cliffs on funicular rails, and a mysterious recluse is building a machine that can fly.

"It's clear that Reeve . . . is building toward an epic, and his remarkable storytelling gifts, coupled with a trenchant understanding of human nature, make these projected volumes worth the wait." Horn Book

Reeves, Dia

Slice of cherry. Simon Pulse 2011 505p $16.99
Grades: 10 11 12 **Fic**

1. Texas -- Fiction 2. Sisters -- Fiction 3. Homicide -- Fiction 4. Supernatural -- Fiction 5. African Americans -- Fiction
ISBN 978-1-4169-8620-1; 1-4169-8620-0
LC 2010-21805

Portero, Texas, teens Kit and Fancy Cordelle share their infamous father's fascination with killing, and despite their tendency to shun others they bring two boys with similar tendencies to a world of endless possibilities they have discovered behind a mysterious door.

"The warm, fuzzy moral—that it's fine to be a serial killer as long as you're doing it to help others—will delight and entertain readers mature enough to appreciate that fictional morals needn't always coincide with real-life didacticism. This gleeful page-turner is a winner." Kirkus

Reger, Rob

Emily the Strange: the lost days; [by] Rob Reger and Jessica Gruner; illustrated by Rob Reger and Buzz Parker. Harper 2009 266p il $16.99; lib bdg $17.89
Grades: 7 8 9 10 **Fic**

1. Adventure fiction 2. Amnesia -- Fiction 3. Runaway teenagers -- Fiction
ISBN 978-0-06-145229-1; 0-06-145229-7; 978-0-06-145230-7 lib bdg; 0-06-145230-0 lib bdg
LC 2008027225

Emily the Strange has lost her memory and finds herself in the town of Blackrock with nothing more than her diary, her slingshot, and the clothes on her back

"The action moves along with no lulls, and none of the entries or illustrations are superfluous. This is a highly enjoyable read." SLJ

Other titles about Emily the Strange are:
Emily the Strange: stranger and stranger (2010)
Emily the Strange: dark times (2010)

Reichs, Kathleen J.

Seizure; [by] Kathy Reichs. Razorbill 2011 491p $17.99
Grades: 6 7 8 9 10 **Fic**

1. Adventure fiction 2. Supernatural -- Fiction
ISBN 9781595143945; 1595143947

"Tory Brennan, 14, and her friends are still trying to determine exactly what happened to them following the events of the series opener (Virals, 2010). The teens have been exposed to an experimental virus that altered their DNA, giving them characteristics comparable to wolves, enhancing their natural senses and creating a human pack. . . . Due to the economy, funding has been pulled on [Kit's father's] research project, necessitating a change of job and a move away from South Carolina and her pack mates. . . . Dodging bullets, slipping out after curfew, following obscure clues into underground tunnels, not to mention Cotillion duties and snarky classmates, are just part of the adventure. . . . Reichs taps into the angst of teens, fear of separation and the uncertainty of today's economy and wraps it all in an entertaining yarn of history, pirates and modern technology." Kirkus

Virals; [by] Kathy Reichs. Penguin/Razorbill 2010 454p map $17.99
Grades: 6 7 8 9 10 **Fic**

1. Mystery fiction 2. Viruses -- Fiction 3. Missing persons -- Fiction
ISBN 978-1-59514-342-6; 1-59514-342-4
LC 2010-42384

Tory Brennan is the leader of a band of teenage "sciphiles" who live on an island off the coast of South Carolina and when the group rescues a dog caged for medical testing, they are exposed to an experimental strain of canine parvovirus that changes their lives forever.

"From the opening sentence to the last word, readers will be absorbed in Tory Brennan's world. . . . Reichs has found a pitch-perfect voice for Tory that will ring true with today's teens, capturing and entirely new audience." Kirkus

Followed by: Seizure (2011)

Reid, Kimberly

My own worst frenemy; a Langdon Prep novel. Dafina KTeen Books 2011 276p (Langdon Prep novel) pa $9.95

Grades: 7 8 9 10 **Fic**

1. School stories 2. Mystery fiction 3. Theft -- Fiction

ISBN 978-0-7582-6740-5

Chanti Evans moves from the streets of Detroit to the exclusive Langdon prepatory school, where her upbringing immediately makes her a suspect in the string of thefts occurring on campus, and she must find the culprit and clear her name.

"This clever mystery with a biting look at class and privilege is a breath of fresh air." Kirkus

Reinhardt, Dana

A **brief** chapter in my impossible life. Wendy Lamb Books 2006 228p hardcover o.p. pa $8.99

Grades: 9 10 11 12 **Fic**

1. Jews -- Fiction 2. Adoption -- Fiction 3. Family life -- Fiction 4. Massachusetts -- Fiction

ISBN 0-385-74698-9; 0-375-84691-3 pa

LC 2005-3972

Sixteen-year-old atheist Simone Turner-Bloom's life changes in unexpected ways when her parents convince her to make contact with her biological mother, an agnostic from a Jewish family who is losing her battle with cancer.

"Besides offering insight into the customs of Hasidic Jews, this intimate story celebrates family love and promotes tolerance of diverse beliefs. Readers will quickly become absorbed in Simone's quest to understand her heritage and herself." Publ Wkly

Harmless. Wendy Lamb Books 2007 229p hardcover o.p. pa $8.99

Grades: 7 8 9 10 **Fic**

1. Truthfulness and falsehood -- Fiction

ISBN 0-385-74699-7; 978-0-385-74699-1; 0-553-49497-X pa; 978-0-553-49497-6 pa

When Anna, Emma, and Mariah concoct a story about why they are late getting home one Friday night, their lie has unimaginable consequences for the girls, their families, and the community.

"Reinhardt's thought-provoking story avoids preachiness in part because of the girls' strong, complex characterizations." Booklist

★ **How** to build a house; a novel. Wendy Lamb Books 2008 227p $15.99; lib bdg $18.99

Grades: 8 9 10 11 12 **Fic**

1. Divorce -- Fiction 2. Building -- Fiction 3. Tennessee -- Fiction 4. Stepfamilies -- Fiction 5. Volunteer work -- Fiction

ISBN 978-0-375-84453-9; 0-375-84453-8; 978-0-375-94454-3 lib bdg; 0-375-94454-0 lib bdg

LC 2007-33403

Seventeen-year-old Harper Evans hopes to escape the effects of her father's divorce on her family and friendships by volunteering her summer to build a house in a small Tennessee town devastated by a tornado.

"This meticulously crafted book illustrates how both homes and relationships can be resurrected through hard work, hope and teamwork." Publ Wkly

★ The **things** a brother knows. Wendy Lamb Books 2010 245p $16.99; lib bdg $19.99

Grades: 7 8 9 10 11 12 **Fic**

1. Brothers -- Fiction 2. Soldiers -- Fiction 3. Family life -- Fiction 4. Boston (Mass.) -- Fiction 5. Jews -- United States -- Fiction

ISBN 978-0-375-84455-3; 0-375-84455-4; 978-0-375-94455-9 lib bdg; 0-375-94455-9 lib bdg

Although they have never gotten along well, seventeen-year-old Levi follows his older brother Boaz, an ex-Marine, on a walking trip from Boston to Washington, D.C. in hopes of learning why Boaz is completely withdrawn.

"Reinhardt's poignant story of a soldier coping with survivor's guilt and trauma, and his Israeli American family's struggle to understand and help, is timely and honest." Booklist

We are the Goldens. by Dana Reinhardt. Wendy Lamb Books.. 2014 197p $16.99

Grades: 9 10 11 12 **Fic**

1. Divorce — Fiction 2. High schools — Fiction 3. Sexual abuse — Fiction 4. Sisters — Fiction 5. Teacher-student relationship — Fiction

ISBN: 0385742576; 9780375990656; 9780385742573; 9780385742580

LC 2013023351

"Reinhardt plunges into the dilemmas of sibling affection and loyalty. High schooler Nell's equilibrium shatters when she realizes her sister Layla is having an affair with a teacher. Nell's narrative (directly addressed to Layla as "you") explains how she arrived at the difficult decision to tell their parents. Nell's voice is engaging, clever, and colloquial, making this a speedy, engrossing read." Horn Book

Renn, Diana

Tokyo heist; by Diana Renn. Viking 2012 373 p. (hardcover) $17.99

Grades: 7 8 9 10 11 12 **Fic**

1. Mystery fiction 2. Art thefts -- Fiction 3. Tokyo (Japan) -- Fiction 4. Seattle (Wash.) -- Fiction 5. Mystery and detective stories 6. Fathers and daughters -- Fiction

ISBN 0670013323; 9780670013326

LC 2011043364

In this book "when sixteen-year-old Violet agrees to spend the summer with her father, an up-and-coming artist in Seattle, she has no idea what she's walking into. Her father's newest clients, the Yamada family, are the victims of a high-profile art robbery: van Gogh sketches have been stolen from their home, and, until they can produce the corresponding painting, everyone's lives are in danger." (Publisher's note)

"The plot has lots of twists and turns, leaving readers on edge, and a hint of romance... Teens will learn about Japanese culture, and fans of manga and art students will rejoice that they can relate to the protagonist and story." LJ

Rennison, Louise

★ **Angus,** thongs and full-frontal snogging; confessions of Georgia Nicolson. HarperCollins Pubs. 2000 247p hardcover o.p. pa $6.95

Grades: 7 8 9 10 **Fic**

1. Great Britain -- Fiction

ISBN 0-06-028814-0; 0-06-447227-2 pa

LC 99-40591

First published 1999 in the United Kingdom

Michael L. Printz Award honor book, 2001

Presents the humorous journal of a year in the life of Georgia, a fourteen-year-old British girl who tries to reduce the size of her nose, stop her mad cat from terrorizing the neighborhood animals, and win the love of handsome hunk Robbie.

"Georgia is a wonderful character whose misadventures are not only hysterically funny but universally recognizable." Booklist

Other titles about Georgia are:

Are these my basoomas I see before me? (2009)

Away laughing on a fast camel (2004)

Dancing in my nuddy-pants (2003)

Knocked out by my nunga-nungas (2002)

Love is a many trousered thing (2007)

On the bright side, I'm now the girlfriend of a sex god (2001)

Startled by his furry shorts (2006)

Stop in the name of pants (2008)

Then he ate my boy entrancers (2005)

Are these my basoomas I see before me? final confessions of Georgia Nicolson. HarperTeen 2009 310p $16.99; lib bdg $17.89

Grades: 7 8 9 10 **Fic**

1. Diaries -- Fiction 2. Theater -- Fiction 3. Great Britain -- Fiction 4. Dating (Social customs) -- Fiction

ISBN 978-0-06-145935-1; 0-06-145935-6; 978-0-06-145936-8 lib bdg; 0-06-145936-4 lib bdg

LC 2009-25449

British teenager Georgia Nicolson's humorous diary entries reveal the results as she finally chooses between potential boyfriends, but then becomes involved in a play with the one not chosen, further complicating her love life.

Stop in the name of pants! HarperTeen 2008 310p $16.99; lib bdg $17.89

Grades: 7 8 9 10 **Fic**

1. Diaries -- Fiction 2. Great Britain -- Fiction 3. Dating (Social customs) -- Fiction

ISBN 978-0-06-145932-0; 0-06-145932-1; 978-0-06-145933-7 lib bdg; 0-06-145933-X lib bdg

LC 2008-14686

In a series of humorous diary entries, British teenager Georgia Nicolson tries to decide between two potential boyfriends—Masimo from Pizzagogoland (Italy) or local boy Dave the Laugh.

The **taming** of the tights; Louise Rennison. HarperTeen 2013 306 p. (trade bdg.) $17.99

Grades: 7 8 9 10 11 12 **Fic**

1. Love stories 2. School stories 3. Actresses -- Fiction 4. Teenagers -- Fiction 5. Humorous stories 6. England -- Fiction 7. High schools -- Fiction 8. Performing arts -- Fiction 9. Yorkshire (England) -- Fiction 10. Dating (Social customs) -- Fiction

ISBN 0062226207; 9780062226204

LC 2013021359

Sequel to: A midsummer tights dream

"Tallulah (A Midsummer Tights Dream) and the Tree Sisters are back for another term at performing arts college where they comically reinterpret another Shakespeare play. But drama follows Tallulah offstage as she debates who is better boyfriend material: Cain or Charlie. Though the book is light on plot, readers will welcome the return of Tallulah's humorous musings and this distinctly British, quirky cast of characters." (Horn Book)

Withering tights. HarperTeen 2011 274p (Misadventures of Tallulah Casey) $16.99

Grades: 7 8 9 10 **Fic**

1. Camps -- Fiction 2. Acting -- Fiction

ISBN 0-06-179931-9; 978-0-06-179931-0

LC 2010045552

Self-conscious about her knobby knees but confident in her acting ability, fourteen-year-old Tallulah spends the summer at a Yorkshire performing arts camp that, she is surprised to learn, is for girls only.

"Tallulah is a vivacious and hilarious character who will speak to every girl." SLJ

Resau, Laura

The **indigo** notebook. Delacorte Press 2009 324p $16.99; lib bdg $19.99; pa $9.99

Grades: 7 8 9 10 11 12 **Fic**

1. Ecuador -- Fiction 2. Fathers -- Fiction 3. Single parent family -- Fiction 4. Mother-daughter relationship -- Fiction

ISBN 978-0-385-73652-7; 0-385-73652-5; 978-0-385-90614-2 lib bdg; 0-385-90614-5 lib bdg; 978-0-375-84524-6 pa; 0-375-84524-0 pa

LC 2008-40519

Fifteen-year-old Zeeta comes to terms with her flighty mother and their itinerant life when, soon after moving to Ecuador, she helps an American teenager find his birth father in a nearby village

"Observant, aware, and occasionally wry, Zeeta's first-person narration will attract readers and hold them." Booklist

Followed by: The ruby notebook (2010)

The **jade** notebook; Laura Resau. Delacorte Press 2012 365 p. (hc) $16.99

Grades: 9 10 11 12 **Fic**

1. Mexico -- Fiction 2. Fathers -- Fiction 3. Missing persons -- Fiction 4. Mother-daughter relationship -- Fiction 5. Secrets -- Fiction 6. Mazunte (Mexico) -- Fiction 7. Single-parent families -- Fiction

ISBN 0385740530; 9780375899416; 9780375989537; 9780385740531

LC 2011034861

Sequel to: The ruby notebook

This book is the "third in a series of novels focusing on Zeeta and her wanderlust-stricken mother. . . . Zeeta's decision to find her mom a job in Mazunte was no accident. Newly armed with a slew of hints about her father's background . . . she is madly hoping that it might be his hometown. . . . With her boyfriend, Wendell, by her side, she begins to fit together the pieces of the puzzle. Yet each answer uncovered seems to create more questions about her father's complex past." (Kirkus Reviews)

"The lush descriptions, intermittent action sequences, and sprinkling of fantasy all come together to form an engaging reading experience that will delight teens looking for a more mature story." SLJ

Red glass. Delacorte Press 2007 275p $15.99; lib bdg $18.99

Grades: 7 8 9 10 **Fic**

1. Mexico -- Fiction 2. Orphans -- Fiction 3. Guatemala -- Fiction 4. Family life -- Fiction 5. Automobile travel -- Fiction

ISBN 978-0-385-73466-0; 0-385-73466-2; 978-0-385-90464-3 lib bdg; 0-385-90464-9 lib bdg

LC 2007-02408

Sixteen-year-old Sophie has been frail and delicate since her premature birth, but discovers her true strength during a journey through Mexico, where the six-year-old orphan her family hopes to adopt was born, and to Guatemala, where her would-be boyfriend hopes to find his mother and plans to remain.

"The vivid characters, the fine imagery, and the satisfying story arc make this a rewarding novel." Booklist

The **ruby** notebook. Delacorte Press 2010 373p $16.99; lib bdg $19.99

Grades: 7 8 9 10 **Fic**

1. France -- Fiction 2. Single parent family -- Fiction 3. Mother-daughter relationship -- Fiction

ISBN 978-0-385-73653-4; 0-385-73653-3; 978-0-385-90615-9 lib bdg; 0-385-90615-3 lib bdg

LC 2009-51965

Sequel to: The indigo notebook (2009)

When sixteen-year-old Zeeta and her itinerant mother move to Aix-en-Provence, France, Zeeta is haunted by a mysterious admirer who keeps leaving mementoes for her, and when her Ecuadorian boyfriend comes to visit, their relationship seems to have changed.

"Weaving bits of magic, city lore and bittersweet romance into each of the many plot lines, Resau has again crafted a complex and satisfying novel. . . . Characters are rich and vibrant." Kirkus

★ **What** the moon saw; a novel. Delacorte Press 2006 258p $15.95; pa $5.99

Grades: 5 6 7 8 **Fic**

1. Country life -- Fiction 2. Grandparents -- Fiction

ISBN 0-385-73343-7; 0-440-23957-5 pa

LC 2006-04571

Fourteen-year-old Clara Luna spends the summer with her grandparents in the tiny, remote village of Yucuyoo, Mexico, learning about her grandmother's life as a healer, her father's decision to leave home for the United States, and her own place in the world.

This is an "exquisitely crafted narrative. . . . The characters are well developed. . . . Resau does an exceptional job of portraying the agricultural society sympathetically and realistically." SLJ

Restrepo, Bettina

Illegal. Katherine Tegen Books 2011 251p $16.99

Grades: 7 8 9 10 **Fic**

1. Texas -- Fiction 2. Mexicans -- Fiction 3. Illegal aliens -- Fiction

ISBN 978-0-06-195342-2; 0-06-195342-3

LC 2010-19451

Nora, a fifteen-year-old Mexican girl, faces the challenges of being an illegal immigrant in Texas when she and her mother cross the border in search of Nora's father.

"Restrepo's novel offers an unsparing immigrant story that is both gritty and redemptive. . . . This is urban realism meets quest tale, told with great emotional immediacy, and it will appeal to many teen readers." Bull Cent Child Books

Revis, Beth

Across the universe. Razorbill 2011 398p $17.99

Grades: 7 8 9 10 **Fic**

1. Science fiction 2. Dictators -- Fiction 3. Space vehicles -- Fiction

ISBN 978-1-59514-397-6; 1-59514-397-1

LC 2010-51834

Amy, a cryogenically frozen passenger aboard the vast spaceship Godspeed, is nearly killed when her cyro chamber is unplugged fifty years before Godspeed's scheduled landing. All she knows is that she must race to unlock Godspeed's hidden secrets before whoever woke her tries to kill again—and she doesn't know who she can trust on a ship ruled by a tyrant.

"Revis's tale hits all of the standard dystopian notes, while presenting a believable romance and a series of tantalizing mysteries that will hold readers' attention." Publ Wkly

A **million** suns. Razorbill 2012 400 p.

Grades: 9 10 11 12 **Fic**

1. Science fiction 2. Homicide -- Fiction 3. Space flight -- Fiction 4. Interplanetary voyages -- Fiction

ISBN 9781101552247; 9781595143983; 9781595145376

This book follows a girl named Amy, who has been cryogenically frozen and placed "aboard the spaceship Godspeed" along with over two-thousand others. She and "16-year-old leader Elder . . . deal with two puzzles: who is killing members of the ship, and where are the hidden clues left behind by the murderer Orion leading?" (Booklist) "Since Elder demanded that the tranquilizing drug Phydus be removed from the water supply, people have awakened to their real emotions, and many are violent, angry, or depressed. Elder is faced with the very real possibility of rebellion, which he doesn't have time for because he's desperately trying to figure out what has gone wrong with the ship's engines. Also, food supplies are running low and the ship is beginning to break down." (School Libr J)

Shades of Earth; An Across the Universe Novel. Beth Revis. Penguin Group USA 2013 400 p. $18.99

Grades: 9 10 11 12 **Fic**

1. Science fiction 2. Space colonies -- Fiction 3. Life on other planets -- Fiction

ISBN 1595143998; 9781595143990

This young adult science fiction adventure story, by Beth Revis, is the conclusion to the "Across the Universe" trilogy. "Amy and Elder have finally left the oppressive walls of the spaceship Godspeed behind. They're ready to start life afresh . . . on Centauri-Earth, the planet that Amy has traveled 25 trillion miles across the universe to experience. But this new Earth isn't the paradise Amy had been hoping for. . . . And if they're going to stay, they'll have to fight." (Publisher's note)

Rex, Adam

Fat vampire; a never coming of age story. Balzer + Bray 2010 324p $16.99

Grades: 9 10 11 12 **Fic**

1. School stories 2. Obesity -- Fiction 3. Vampires -- Fiction 4. Television programs -- Fiction

ISBN 978-0-06-192090-5

LC 2010-9616

After being bitten by a vampire, not only is fifteen-year-old Doug doomed eternally to be fat, but now he must also save himself from the desperate host of a public-access-cable vampire-hunting television show that is on the verge of cancellation.

"Rex successfully sustains the wonderfully dry humor and calculated silliness and then surprises the reader with a thoughtful, poignant, ambiguous ending that is bound to inspire discussion." Booklist

Reynolds, Jason

When I was the greatest; Jason Reynolds. Atheneum Books for Young Readers 2014 240 p. (hardcover) $17.99

Grades: 9 10 11 12 **Fic**

1. Street life 2. Teenagers -- Fiction 3. Neighborhoods -- Fiction 4. Brothers and sisters -- Fiction 5. Brooklyn (New York, N.Y.) -- Fiction 6. Family life -- New York (State) -- Brooklyn -- Fiction

ISBN 1442459476; 9781442459472

LC 2012045734

In this book by Jason Reynolds "Ali lives . . . in the Bed-Stuy neighborhood of Brooklyn and spends all of his free time with best friends Noodles and Needles. Needles was born with Tourette's syndrome . . . [and the] teens hang out on the stoop and streets, living life and getting in just a touch of mischief. When their friend Tasha gets them into a party-and not just any party, an exclusive, adults-only party-trouble escalates." (School Library Journal)

"Sixteen-year-old Ali is a walking contradiction. He's a lauded boxer-in-training who's afraid of stepping into the ring; a straight-laced, head-down kind of kid on a bad block in Bed-Stuy, a neighborhood rife with drugs and violence... With fresh, fast-paced dialogue, Reynolds' debut novel chronicles Ali's friendship with next-door brothers Needles and Noodles, flawed but unforgettable characters all their own, as the three prepare for the party of a lifetime—and pay the consequences for thrusting themselves into a more sordid encounter than any of them could have envisioned. When I Was the Greatest is urban fiction with heart, a meditation on the meaning of family, the power of friendship, and the value of loyalty." (Booklist)

Reynolds, Marilyn

Shut up! Morning Glory Press 2009 245p (True-to-life series from Hamilton High) $15.95; pa $9.95

Grades: 8 9 10 11 12 **Fic**

1. Brothers -- Fiction 2. Child sexual abuse -- Fiction

ISBN 978-1-932538-93-9; 1-932538-93-3; 978-1-932538-88-5 pa; 1-932538-88-7 pa

LC 2008-933535

Seventeen-year-old Mario promises he'll take care of his nine-year-old brother, Eddie, while their mother serves in the National Guard in Iraq and soon realizes that Eddie desperately needs help.

This book "presents a marginalized issue—sexual abuse of boys—in a frank, thoughtful, and sensitive manner." Voice Youth Advocates

Rhuday-Perkovich, Olugbemisola

8th grade superzero. Arthur A. Levine Books 2010 324p $16.99

Grades: 6 7 8 9 **Fic**

1. School stories 2. Politics -- Fiction 3. Volunteer work -- Fiction 4. Homeless persons -- Fiction 5. African Americans -- Fiction

ISBN 978-0-545-09676-8; 0-545-09676-6

LC 2009-19850

After halfheartedly joining his church youth group's project at a homeless shelter near his Brooklyn middle school, eighth-grade "loser" Reggie McKnight is inspired to run for school office on a platform of making a real difference in the community.

The author "manages to bring both passion and compassion to a story that has its moments of humor and genuine emotion, and will be highly useful for classroom discussion." Booklist

Rice-Gonzalez, Charles

Chulito; Charles Rice-González. 1st Magnus Books ed. Magnus Books 2011 317 p. (paperback) $14.95

Grades: 10 11 12 **Fic**

1. School stories 2. Gay teenagers -- Fiction 3. Gay youth -- Fiction 4. Bronx (New York, N.Y.) -- Fiction 5. Coming out (Sexual orientation) -- Fiction 6. Latin Americans -- New York (State) -- New York -- Fiction

ISBN 1936833034; 9781936833030

LC 2011279750

In this book, "Chulito is a 15-year-old Puerto Rican high school dropout, who is right at home among the hip-hop-loving, macho, 'anything to survive' neighbors in a tough section of the Bronx. Growing up, he is close to Carlos, who—like Chulito—lived with a single mother in the same building. But the boys grow apart when Carlos finishes high school and goes to Long Island to attend college—primarily because he is perceived as being gay." Chulito falls in love with Carlos. (Echo Magazine)

Rich, Naomi

Alis. Viking Children's Books 2009 274p $17.99
Grades: 7 8 9 10 **Fic**

1. Marriage -- Fiction 2. Religion -- Fiction 3. Runaway teenagers -- Fiction
ISBN 978-0-670-01125-4; 0-670-01125-8
LC 2008-23234

Raised within the strict religious confines of the Community of the Book, Alis flees from an arranged marriage to the much older Minister of her town and her life takes a series of unexpected twists before she returns to accept her fate.

"Rich's sympathetic portrayal of Alis and her desperate struggle to exercise free will in a theocracy will have audiences firmly gripped." Publ Wkly

Rich, Simon

Elliot Allagash; a novel. Random House 2010 227p $23
Grades: 11 12 Adult **Fic**

1. School stories 2. Money -- Fiction 3. Wealth -- Fiction 4. Friendship -- Fiction
ISBN 978-1-4000-6835-7
LC 2009-43885

"The book follows the trial by fire of the narrator, Seymour, an obese but grudgingly docile eighth-grader at a posh Manhattan private school. He's the sort of kid who puts up with the school's arcane policy of putting any student involved in a scrap in detention—which means Seymour is in detention every week just for getting beaten up. His life changes dramatically when another character, an arrogant little bastard who stands to inherit an unimaginable fortune, takes an interest in Seymour's future. . . . Before long Seymour is stealing test answers; accepting a devilish bargain to sneak into Harvard; and corrupting the simplistic social systems of school to rise to the top of its hierarchy, no matter what it costs. . . . Rich is always funny, and he nails the bogus solemnity of high-school social politics. A high-school romp that John Hughes should be so lucky to direct." Kirkus

Richards, Jame

Three rivers rising; a novel of the Johnstown flood. Alfred A. Knopf 2010 293p $16.99; lib bdg $19.99
Grades: 6 7 8 9 10 **Fic**

1. Novels in verse 2. Floods -- Fiction 3. Pennsylvania -- Fiction 4. Social classes -- Fiction
ISBN 978-0-375-85885-7; 0-375-85885-7; 978-0-375-95885-4 lib bdg; 0-375-95885-1 lib bdg
LC 2009-4251

Sixteen-year-old Celestia is a wealthy member of the South Fork Fishing and Hunting Club, where she meets and falls in love with Peter, a hired hand who lives in the valley below, and by the time of the torrential rains that lead to the disastrous Johnstown flood of 1889, she has been disowned by her family and is staying with him in Johnstown. Includes an author's note and historical timeline.

This is a "striking novel in verse. . . . Richards builds strong characters with few words and artfully interweaves the lives of these independent thinkers." Publ Wkly

Includes bibliographical references

Richards, Natalie D.

Six months later; by Natalie D. Richards. Sourcebooks Fire 2013 336 p. (tp : alk. paper) $9.99
Grades: 9 10 11 12 **Fic**

1. School stories 2. Memory -- Fiction 3. Secrets -- Fiction 4. High schools -- Fiction
ISBN 1402285515; 9781402285516
LC 2013012470

In this book, by Natalie Richards, "Chloe, an average student with a bit of a rebellious streak, wakes up in study hall one day not remembering the past six months. But suddenly she's popular, dating her longtime crush, being recruited by Ivy League colleges because of top SAT scores, and her best friend is no longer speaking to her. As Chloe tries to unravel her memories, she begins to uncover secrets more dangerous than she ever thought possible." (Publisher's note)

Richter, Conrad

The **light** in the forest. Everyman's Library 2005 176p $14.95; pa $6.50
Grades: 7 8 9 10 **Fic**

1. Delaware Indians -- Fiction 2. Frontier and pioneer life -- Fiction
ISBN 1-4000-4426-X; 1-4000-7788-5 pa
First published 1953 by Knopf

"A boy stolen in early childhood and brought up by the Delawares is at fifteen suddenly returned to the family he has forgotten. He resents his loss of independence, hates the brutality of the white man's civilization, and longs only for a return to the Indians whom he remembers as peace-loving and kind. His return to the Delawares does not, however, bring him peace; rather, he must make a bitter choice between helping his indian brothers kill agroup of unsuspecting white men or helping the white men escape. This is both vivid re-creation of outdoor life and a provocative study in conflicting loyalties." Horn Book

Riggs, Ransom

Miss Peregrine's home for peculiar children. Quirk Books 2011 352p il $17.99
Grades: 6 7 8 9 **Fic**

1. Ghost stories
ISBN 978-1-59474-476-1; 1-59474-476-9

"When Jacob's grandfather, Abe, a WWII veteran, is savagely murdered, Jacob has a nervous breakdown, in part because he believes that his grandfather was killed by a monster that only they could see. On his psychiatrist's advice, Jacob and his father travel from their home in Florida to Cairnholm Island off the coast of Wales, which, during the war, housed Miss Peregrine's Home for Peculiar Children. . . . Nearly 50 unsettling vintage photographs appear throughout, forming the framework of this dark but empowering tale, as Riggs creates supernatural backstories and identities for those pictured in them. . . . It's an enjoyable, eccentric read, distinguished by well-developed characters, a believable Welsh setting, and some very creepy monsters." Publ Wkly

Rinaldi, Ann

Come Juneteenth. Harcourt 2007 246p (Great episodes) $17; pa $6.99

Grades: 6 7 8 9 **Fic**

1. Slavery -- Fiction 2. Juneteenth -- Fiction 3. Family life -- Fiction 4. African Americans -- Fiction

ISBN 978-0-15-05947-7; 0-15-205947-4; 978-0-15-206392-4 pa; 0-15-206392-7 pa

LC 2006-21458

Fourteen-year-old Luli and her family face tragedy after failing to tell their slaves that President Lincoln's Emancipation Proclamation made them free.

"Luli's authentic voice demonstrates Rinaldi's ability to evoke the human side of history." SLJ

Girl in blue. Scholastic Press 2001 310p hardcover o.p. pa $5.99

Grades: 6 7 8 9 **Fic**

1. Spies 2. Gender role 3. Sex role 4. Spies -- Fiction 5. Sex role -- Fiction 6. United States -- History -- Civil War, 1861-1865

ISBN 0-439-07336-7; 0-439-67646-0 pa

LC 00-41945

To escape an abusive father and an arranged marriage, fourteen-year-old Sarah, dressed as a boy, leaves her Michigan home to enlist in the Union Army, and becomes a soldier on the battlefields of Virginia as well as a Union spy working in the house of Confederate sympathizer Rose O'Neal Greenhow in Washington, D.C.

"This first-person novel will engage readers through its sympathetic main character and exciting action." Booklist

★ The **fifth** of March; a story of the Boston Massacre. Harcourt Brace & Co. 1993 335p (Great episodes) pa $6.95

Grades: 7 8 9 10 **Fic**

1. Political leaders 2. Boston Massacre, 1770 -- Fiction

ISBN 0-15-205078-7 pa

LC 93-17821

Fourteen-year-old Rachel Marsh, an indentured servant in the Boston household of John and Abigail Adams, is caught up in the colonists' unrest that eventually escalates into the massacre of March 5, 1770.

"The story moves along briskly, and details of life in 18th-century Boston are woven into the narrative." SLJ

The **redheaded** princess. HarperCollinsPublishers 2008 214p $15.99; lib bdg $16.89

Grades: 6 7 8 9 **Fic**

1. Queens

ISBN 978-0-06-073374-2; 0-06-073374-8; 978-0-06-073375-9 lib bdg; 0-06-073375-6 lib bdg

LC 2007-18577

In 1542, nine-year-old Lady Elizabeth lives on an estate near London, striving to get back into the good graces of her father, King Henry VIII, and as the years pass she faces his death and those of other close relatives until she finds herself next in line to ascend the throne of England in 1558.

"The rich scene-setting and believable, appealing heroine will satisfy Rinaldi's many fans." Booklist

An **unlikely** friendship; a novel of Mary Todd Lincoln and Elizabeth Keckley. Harcourt 2007 241p $17

Grades: 6 7 8 9 **Fic**

1. Memoirists 2. Dressmakers 3. Slavery -- Fiction 4. Friendship -- Fiction 5. Spouses of presidents

ISBN 0-15-205597-5

LC 2005-30210

Relates the lives of Mary Todd Lincoln, raised in a wealthy Virginia family, and Lizzy Keckley, a dressmaker born a slave, as they grow up separately then become best friends when Mary's childhood dream of living in the White House comes true.

This "story is fascinating and filled with remarkable gems of historical memorabilia to create a very satisfying read." Voice Youth Advocates

Riordan, James

The **sniper**. Frances Lincoln Children's Books 2009 229p il pa $8.95

Grades: 9 10 11 12 **Fic**

1. War stories 2. Stalingrad, Battle of, 1942-1943 -- Fiction

ISBN 978-1-84507-885-0

This is the story of a teenage sniper recruited in 1942 to seek out and shoot German officers. At first Tania finds it impossible to kill, but after a shocking discovery goes on to kill as many as 84 Germans.

"There is a deep poignancy and a moral tone here, along with exciting action, heroism and anguish. . . . This fine volume will appeal to many readers." Kirkus

Ritter, John H.

Choosing up sides. Philomel Bks. 1998 166p $17.99; pa $5.99

Grades: 6 7 8 9 **Fic**

1. Baseball -- Fiction 2. Self-acceptance -- Fiction 3. Fathers and sons -- Fiction 4. Father-son relationship -- Fiction 5. Left- and right-handedness -- Fiction

ISBN 0-399-23185-4; 0-689-11840-5 pa

LC 97-39779

In 1921 thirteen-year-old Luke finds himself torn between accepting his left-handedness or conforming to the belief of his preacher-father that such a condition is evil and must be overcome

"This is an entertaining and thought-provoking coming-of-age story." Book Rep

Ruiz Zafon, Carlos

Marina; Carlos Ruiz Zafon ; translated by Lucia Graves. Little, Brown & Co. 2014 326p $19.00

Grades: 8 9 10 11 12 **Fic**

1. Love — Fiction; 2. Mystery fiction 3. Supernatural — Fiction

ISBN: 0316044717; 9780316044714

LC 2013016666

Original Spanish edition, 1999

"Set in Barcelona, Spain from late 1979 to May 1980, this gothic novel centers around 15-year-old boarding school student Oscar Drai. Instead of studying during his free time, the teen explores the city, and one day ends up in an area that seems deserted. Drawn in by music coming from an old dilapidated house, Oscar is given a scare by the owner, an eccentric and haunted German artist...With elements of romance, mystery, and horror, none of them overwhelming the other, this complex volume that hints at Mary Shelley's Frankenstein manages to weave together three separate stories for a cohesive and eerie result." SLJ

Robert, Na'ima B.

Boy vs. girl. Frances Lincoln Children's Books 2011 260p $15.95

Grades: 6 7 8 9 10 **Fic**

1. Twins -- Fiction 2. Muslims -- Fiction 3. Ramadan -- Fiction 4. Siblings -- Fiction 5. Great Britain -- Fiction 6. Pakistanis -- Great Britain -- Fiction

ISBN 978-1-84780-150-0; 1-84780-150-1

"Twins Farhana and Faraz determine to fast during Ramadan now that they are 16. . . . As first-generation Brits, they must respond to the demands of their Pakistani family, their secular schools, and their friends. . . . The characters are realistic. . . . A well-balanced chord is struck here between storytelling and exploring the complex and sometimes conflicting pulls of tradition, family, friends, and lifestyle." Booklist

From Somalia with love; [by] Na'ima B. Robert. Frances Lincoln Children's Books 2008 159p $15.95; pa $7.95

Grades: 7 8 9 10 **Fic**

1. Muslims -- Fiction 2. Father-daughter relationship -- Fiction

ISBN 978-1-84507-831-7; 1-84507-831-4; 978-1-84507-832-4 pa; 1-84507-832-2 pa

"Safia has grown up believing her father died in the fighting in Somalia. When she finds out that he is alive and on his way to London to join the family, she is apprehensive about the difference his presence will make in her life. . . . This is a unique title that will be popular in regions that have large Somali populations or where Randa Abdel-Fattah's books are popular." SLJ

Includes glossary

Roberts, Jeyn

Dark inside. Simon & Schuster Books for Young Readers 2011 327p $17.99

Grades: 7 8 9 10 **Fic**

1. Science fiction 2. Monsters -- Fiction 3. Good and evil -- Fiction

ISBN 978-1-4424-2351-0; 1-4424-2351-X

LC 2011008642

After tremendous earthquakes destroy the Earth's major cities, an ancient evil emerges, turning ordinary people into hunters, killers, and insane monsters but a small group of teens comes together in a fight for survival and safety.

"Well-balanced, realistic suspense." Kirkus

Rage within; Jeyn Roberts. Simon & Schuster Books for Young Readers 2012 357 p. (hardcover) $17.99

Grades: 7 8 9 10 **Fic**

1. Science fiction 2. Apocalyptic fiction 3. Monsters -- Fiction 4. Survival -- Fiction 5. Good and evil -- Fiction

ISBN 1442423544; 9781442423541; 9781442423565

LC 2011047396

Sequel to: Dark inside

In author Jeyn Roberts' "apocalyptic sequel to 'Dark Inside' . . . Aries, Clementine, Michael, and Mason have survived the first wave of the apocalypse that wiped out most of the world's population and turned many of the rest into murderous Baggers. Now they're hiding out in an abandoned house . . . trying to figure out their next move. As the Baggers begin to create a new world order, these four teens will have to trust and rely on each other in order to survive." (Publisher's note)

Robinson, A. M.

Vampire crush. HarperTeen 2011 404p pa $8.99

Grades: 7 8 9 10 **Fic**

1. Vampires -- Fiction

ISBN 978-0-06-198971-1 pa; 0-06-198971-1 pa

LC 2010-09397

Sixteen-year-old journalist Sophie McGee's junior year is filled with unexpected drama—and romance—when she discovers that her new classmates are hiding a dark secret, while the "boy next door" from her childhood re-enters her life.

"Sophie is smart, funny, and determined, and her narration adds humor and wit to the story. The quirky supporting cast is pretty much what you'd expect in a teen vampire tale. An original and entertaining entry to the genre that won't disappoint." Booklist

Robinson, Kim Stanley

Forty signs of rain. Bantam Books 2004 358p hardcover o.p. pa $7.99

Grades: 9 10 11 12 **Fic**

1. Science fiction 2. Washington (D.C.) -- Fiction

ISBN 0-553-80311-5; 0-553-58580-0 pa

LC 2003-63683

A "novel set in the very near future. Anna Quibler is a technocrat at the National Science Foundation while her husband, Charlie, takes care of their toddler and telecommutes as a legislative consultant to a senator. . . . When a Buddhist delegation, whose country is being flooded because of climate change, opens an embassy near the NSF, the Quiblers befriend them and teach them to work the system of politics and grants. The Buddhists, in turn, affect the scientists in delightful and unexpectedly significant ways." SLJ

The author's "portrayal of how actual scientists would deal with this disaster-in-the-making is utterly convincing. Robinson clearly cares deeply about our planet's future, and he makes the reader care as well." Publ Wkly

Other titles in this series are:

Fifty degrees below (2005)

Sixty days and counting (2007)

Rocco, John

Swim that rock. John Rocco & Jay Primiano. Candlewick Press 2014 293p $16.99

Grades: 7 8 9 10 **Fic**

1. Fishing — Fiction; 2. Rhode Island — Fiction; 3. Family life — Fiction; 4. Bildungsromans

ISBN: 0763669059; 9780763669058

LC 2013952797

In this book, by John Rocco and Jay Primiano, "a young working-class teen fights to save his family's diner after his father is lost in a fishing-boat accident. . . . In Narragansett Bay, scrabbling out a living as a quahogger isn't easy, but with the help of some local clammers, Jake is determined to work hard and earn enough money to ensure his family's security and save the diner in time." (Publisher's note)

"With a lushly detailed sense of place and character, the story examines a boy coming to terms with his situation." Horn Book

Rodman, Sean

Infiltration. Orca Book Publishers 2011 130p (Orca soundings) lib bdg $16.95; pa $9.95

Grades: 7 8 9 10 **Fic**

1. City and town life -- Fiction

ISBN 978-1-55469-986-5 lib bdg; 1-55469-986-X lib bdg; 978-1-55469-985-8 pa; 1-55469-985-1 pa

Bex breaks into locked and abandoned buildings just because he can, but when a new friend's behavior becomes more and more risky, he has to do the right thing.

This "is a fast-paced action-adventure story. . . . The page-turning suspense it generates and the fascinating hook of urban-exploration should grab any reader." Booklist

Roecker, Laura

The **Liar** Society; by Lisa and Laura Roecker. Sourcebooks Fire 2011 361p pa $9.99

Grades: 7 8 9 10 **Fic**

1. School stories 2. Mystery fiction 3. Secret societies -- Fiction

ISBN 978-1-4022-5633-2; 1-4022-5633-7

When Kate receives a mysterious e-mail from her dead friend Grace, she must prove that Grace's death was not an accident, but finds that her elite private school holds secrets so big people are willing to kill to protect them.

This is a "smartly paced and plotted first novel, full of twists, clues, and sleuthing. Add this to your go-to list of mysteries." Booklist

The **lies** that bind; Lisa and Laura Roecker. Sourcebooks Fire 2012 314 p. (The Liar Society) (tp : alk. paper) $9.99

Grades: 7 8 9 10 **Fic**

1. School stories 2. Missing persons -- Fiction 3. Secret societies -- Fiction 4. High schools -- Fiction

ISBN 1402270240; 9781402270246

LC 2012035855

This young adult school mystery, by Lisa and Laura Roecker, is part of "The Liar Society" series. "Kate has heard of messages from beyond the grave, but she never expected to find one in a fortune cookie. Especially from her best friend, Grace--who's supposed to be dead. At the elite Pemberly Brown Academy, . . . a popular girl has gone missing, and Kate owes it to Grace's memory to find out what happened. But in a school ruled by secret societies, who can she trust?" (Publisher's note)

Rorby, Ginny

Lost in the river of grass. Carolrhoda Lab 2011 255p $17.95

Grades: 7 8 9 10 **Fic**

1. Wilderness survival -- Fiction

ISBN 978-0-7613-5685-1; 0-7613-5685-1

LC 2009-53999

"In this authentic survival adventure, Sarah, a 13-year-old scholarship student, leaves her preppy classmates on a weekend trip to the Everglades and takes off with Andy, 15 . . . who offers her a brief guided tour in his airboat. After the boat sinks, they walk for three days through the swamp . . . until, finally, helicopters rescue them. What comes through best here is not only the teens' courage and mutual support but also the realism of their fights and weaknesses." Booklist

The **outside** of a horse; a novel. Dial Books for Young Readers 2010 343p $16.99

Grades: 7 8 9 10 **Fic**

1. Horses -- Fiction 2. Amputees -- Fiction 3. Veterans -- Fiction 4. Father-daughter relationship -- Fiction

ISBN 978-0-8037-3478-4; 0-8037-3478-6

LC 2009-25101

When her father returns from the Iraq War as an amputee with post-traumatic stress disorder, Hannah escapes by volunteering to work with rescued horses, never thinking that the abused horses could also help her father recover.

Hannah "comes across as a believable teen. As a backdrop to the story, Rorby has interwoven a good deal of disturbing information about animal cruelty. Horse lovers and most others will saddle up right away with this poignant tale." Booklist

Rosen, Renee

★ **Every** crooked pot. St. Martin's Griffin 2007 227p pa $8.95

Grades: 7 8 9 10 **Fic**

1. Birth defects -- Fiction 2. Father-daughter relationship -- Fiction

ISBN 978-0-312-36543-1; 0-312-36543-8

LC 2007-10457

"Rosen looks back at the life of Nina Goldman, whose growing up is tied to two pillars: a port-wine stain around her eye and her inimitable father, Artie. The birthmark, she hates; her father, she loves. Both shape her in ways that merit Rosen's minute investigation. . . . There's real power in the writing." Booklist

Rosenfield, Kat

Amelia Anne is dead and gone; Kat Rosenfield. Dutton Books 2012 304 p. (hardcover) $17.99

Grades: 9 10 11 12 **Fic**

1. Mystery fiction 2. Homicide -- Fiction 3. Young women -- Fiction 4. Murder -- Fiction 5. Community life -- Fiction 6. Summer resorts -- Fiction 7. Dating violence -- Fiction 8. Mystery and detective stories 9. Dating (Social customs) -- Fiction

ISBN 9780525423898

LC 2011029958

In this book, "[t]he lives of two girls on the cusp of something bigger intertwine on a dusty road in a small, dead-end New England town. Amelia has just finished college and is on her way to a summer beach rental with her boyfriend before going to acting school. Becca, just graduated from high school, is looking forward to college. . . .

Just hours before Amelia is beaten and left for dead, Becca's boyfriend breaks up with her--right after they have sex in the bed of his pickup." (Kirkus Reivews)

Roskos, Evan

★ **Dr.** Bird's advice for sad poets; Evan Roskos. Houghton Mifflin Harcourt 2013 320 p. $16.99

Grades: 9 10 11 12 **Fic**

1. Poetry -- Fiction 2. Siblings -- Fiction 3. Depression (Psychology) -- Fiction 4. Family problems -- Fiction 5. Depression, Mental -- Fiction

ISBN 054792853X; 9780547928531

LC 2012033315

William C. Morris Honor Book (2014)

This novel "portrays the struggle of 16-year-old James Whitman to overcome anxiety and depression. James blames himself for his older sister's expulsion from their home and estrangement from their bullying parents. [Evan] Roskos . . . sketches James as a boy who is far more comfortable inside his own head than in connecting with others (case in point, he hugs trees to make himself feel better and seeks advice from Dr. Bird, an imaginary pigeon therapist)." (Publishers Weekly)

"Author Roskos's strength lies in his refusal to tidy up the mess in James's life and in his relentless honesty about surviving with depression and anxiety." Horn Book

Rosoff, Meg

How I Live Now Wendy Lamb Books 2004 194p $16.95

Grades: 7 8 9 10 Fic

1. Cousins -- Fiction 2. War stories 3. Great Britain -- Fiction

ISBN 0385746776

To get away from her pregnant stepmother in New York City, fifteen-year-old Daisy goes to England to stay with her aunt and cousins, with whom she instantly bonds, but soon war breaks out and rips apart the family while devastating the land.

"Teens may feel that they have experienced a war themselves as they vicariously witness Daisy's worst nightmares. Like the heroine, readers will emerge from the rubble much shaken, a little wiser and with perhaps a greater sense of humanity." Publ Wkly

★ **Picture** me gone; by Meg Rosoff. G.P. Putnam's Sons 2013 256 p. $17.99

Grades: 7 8 9 **Fic**

1. Missing persons -- Fiction 2. Parent-child relationship -- Fiction 3. Coming of age -- Fiction 4. Mystery and detective stories 5. Fathers and daughters -- Fiction

ISBN 0399257659; 9780399257650

LC 2012048974

"Sensitive Londoner Mila, twelve, travels with her father, Gil, to upstate New York to search for Gil's boyhood friend, who has inexplicably disappeared. The subject of this road-trip novel--how much guilt and tragedy can a person bear before he gives up on life?--is adult, but the writing is up to Rosoff's usual standards of originality, depth, wit, and insight." (Horn Book)

★ **There** is no dog; Meg Rosoff. G. P. Putnam's Sons 2011 243p. $17.99

Grades: 7 8 9 **Fic**

1. Love stories 2. God -- Fiction 3. Man-woman relationship -- Fiction

ISBN 9780399257643

LC 2011020651

This book "looks at the world's natural disasters, injustices, and chaos and presents a[n] . . . explanation: God is a horny teenage boy. According to this . . . account, God, aka 'Bob,' was given Earth by his mother, who won the planet in a poker game. Bob showed flashes of brilliance during Creation, but he feels little responsibility for the planet. When he falls head-over-heels in lust with a beautiful zoo employee, Lucy, Bob's passion and growing anger toward those who would keep them apart is manifested through wildly fluctuating weather and rampant flooding." (Publishers Weekly)

Ross, Elizabeth

Belle epoque; Elizabeth Ross. Delacorte Press 2013 336 p. (ebook) $53.97; (library) $20.99; (hardcover) $17.99

Grades: 7 8 9 10 11 12 **Fic**

1. Love stories 2. Historical fiction 3. Female friendship -- Fiction 4. Runaways -- Fiction 5. Social classes -- Fiction 6. Conduct of life -- Fiction 7. Beauty, Personal -- Fiction 8. Interpersonal relations -- Fiction 9. Paris (France) -- History -- 1870-1940 -- Fiction 10. France -- History -- Third Republic, 1870-1940 -- Fiction

ISBN 0375990054; 9780375985270; 9780375990052; 9780385741460

LC 2012034694

William C. Morris Honor Book (2014)

In this book, "sixteen-year-old runaway Maude Pichon is ugly—so much so that she lands a job as a 'repoussoir,' an unattractive girl paid to be seen with a lovelier girl to make her appear even more beautiful by comparison . . . . Maude is humiliated by the idea, but her poverty leaves her few options." Then "chance sends a dashing composer Maude's way, and a countess hires her to befriend her independent-minded daughter, Isabelle." (Publishers Weekly)

"Ross models her plot on an 1866 story by Zola, "Les Repoussoirs," expanding its focus to highlight Maude's plight and using that to illuminate the chasm that existed between the wealthy and the poor... A refreshingly relevant and inspiring historical venture." Kirkus

Ross, Jeff

The **drop**. Orca Book Publishers 2011 157p (Orca sports) pa $9.95

Grades: 6 7 8 9 **Fic**

1. Snowboarding -- Fiction

ISBN 978-1-55469-392-4; 1-55469-392-6

When Alex and three other snowboarders find themselves in trouble in the remote mountains of British Columbia, Alex must confront his fears and lead them to safety.

"Readers need not be regular snowboarders to appreciate the extended descriptions of the sport: they will feel the exhilaration of every turn and jump. The writing is crisp, and the plot moves along quickly." SLJ

Rossetti, Rinsai

The **girl** with borrowed wings; by Rinsai Rossetti. Dial Books 2012 300 p. (hardcover) $17.99
Grades: 7 8 9 10 11 12 **Fic**

1. Cats -- Fiction 2. Voyages and travels -- Fiction 3. Father-daughter relationship -- Fiction 4. Love -- Fiction 5. Flying -- Fiction 6. Deserts -- Fiction 7. Shapeshifting -- Fiction
ISBN 0803735669; 9780803735668
LC 2011027164

This is Rinsai Rossetti's debut, a coming-of-age novel. Of "Thai descent, 17-year-old Frenenqer Paje has grown up" with "her coldly overbearing father . . . . [S]he disobeys her father by rescuing a mistreated cat" who "is actually a shapeshifting 'Free person' named Sangris . . . . By night, he flies Frenenqer around the world to places both real and magical, slowly chipping away at the defenses she has built up to withstand her father's callous cruelty." (Publishers Weekly)

Rossi, Veronica

Under the never sky; Veronica Rossi. HarperCollins 2012 376 p. (hardback) $17.99
Grades: 6 7 8 9 10 11 12 **Fic**

1. Science fiction 2. Apocalyptic fiction 3. Cannibalism -- Fiction 4. Man-woman relationship -- Fiction
ISBN 9780062072030
LC 2011044631

This book tells the story of "Aria [who] knows her chances of surviving in the outer wasteland--known as The Death Shop--are slim. . . . Then Aria meets an Outsider named Perry. He's wild--a savage--and her only hope of staying alive. A hunter for his tribe in a merciless landscape, Perry views Aria as sheltered and fragile--everything he would expect from a Dweller. . . . Opposites in nearly every way, Aria and Perry must accept each other to survive." (Publisher's note)

Roth, Veronica

Allegiant; Veronica Roth; [edited by] Molly O'Neill. Katherine Tegen Books 2013 544 p. (hardcover bdg.) $19.99
Grades: 9 10 11 12 **Fic**

1. Love stories 2. Dystopian fiction 3. Science fiction 4. Loyalty -- Fiction 5. Social classes -- Fiction 6. Courage 7. Loyalty 8. Families 9. Social classes 10. Identity (Philosophical concept)
ISBN 006202406X; 9780062024060
LC 2013941315

Sequel to: Insurgent

Author Veronica Roth presents the conclusion to her dystopian Divergent trilogy. "Tris and Tobias conarrate their adventures and attempt to understand their surroundings. As their true love relationship plays out, they venture beyond war-torn Chicago, only to uncover a new network of conspiracies and key revelations about eugenics, authority, and social duty." (Bookmarks)

"Roth shakes up her storytelling (and will do the same to some readers) in this highly anticipated, largely satisfying wrap-up to the Divergent trilogy...for those who have faithfully followed these five factions, and especially the Dauntless duo who stole hearts two books ago, this final installment will capture and hold attention until the divisive final battle has been waged." (Publishers Weekly)

★ **Divergent**. Katherine Tegen Books 2011 487p $17.99; ebook $9.99
Grades: 9 10 11 12 **Fic**

1. Science fiction 2. Courage -- Fiction 3. Family life -- Fiction 4. Social classes -- Fiction 5. Identity (Psychology) -- Fiction
ISBN 978-0-06-202402-2; 0-06-202402-7; 978-0-06-207701-1 ebook; 0-06-207701-5 ebook
LC 2010-40579

"Roth's nonstop action, excellent voice, and simple yet accessible writing style will draw in many new readers to the genre. The themes are particularly poignant for young adults trying to identify their place in the world—having the choice to follow in your parents' footsteps or do something new. . . . This is a fast-paced and fun read." Voice Youth Advocates

Insurgent; Veronica Roth. Katherine Tegen Books 2012 525 p.
Grades: 9 10 11 12 **Fic**

1. Science fiction 2. Courage -- Fiction 3. Apocalyptic fiction 4. Personality -- Fiction 5. Social classes -- Fiction 6. Families -- Fiction 7. Identity -- Fiction
ISBN 0062024043; 9780062024046
LC 2011053287

Sequel to: Divergent

In this "sequel to . . . 'Divergent' . . . a bleak post-apocalyptic Chicago ruled by 'factions' exemplifying different personality traits collapses into all-out civil war. With both the Dauntless and Abnegation factions shattered by the Erudite attack, Tris and her companions seek refuge with Amity and Candor, and even among the factionless. But the Erudite search for 'Divergents' continues relentlessly." (Kirkus Reviews)

Rothenberg, Jess

The **catastrophic** history of you & me; Jess Rothenberg. Dial Books 2012 375 p. (hardcover : alk. paper) $17.99
Grades: 9 10 11 12 **Fic**

1. Grief -- Fiction 2. Future life -- Fiction 3. Love stories 4. Love -- Fiction 5. Death -- Fiction
ISBN 0803737203; 9780803737204
LC 2011021631

This book, by Jess Rothenberg, begins "when her boyfriend Jacob tells her that he no longer loves her, [and] Brie's heart spontaneously tears in two and she dies. . . . [She] finds herself in the heavenly version of her favorite pizza joint, where she meets Patrick, resident Lost Soul and guide to all things post-mortem. He informs her that she will have to work her way through the five stages of grief with a series of visits to her old life." (Bulletin of the Center for Children's Books)

Rottman, S. L.

Out of the blue; written by S.L. Rottman. Peachtree Publishers 2009 297p $16.95
Grades: 6 7 8 9 **Fic**

1. Moving -- Fiction 2. Child abuse -- Fiction 3.

Military bases -- Fiction
ISBN 978-1-56145-499-0; 1-56145-499-0
LC 2008052839

After moving to Minot, North Dakota, with his mother, the new female base commander, Air Force dependent Stu Ballentyne gradually becomes aware that something terrible is going on in his neighbor's house.

"The story offers both a realistic interpretation of teenage life on an Air Force base and the teen's feeling of powerlessness upon witnessing child abuse—both physical and verbal—in action." SLJ

Rowell, Rainbow

★ **Eleanor** & Park; Rainbow Rowell. St. Martin's Griffin 2013 320 p. (hardcover) $18.99
Grades: 9 10 11 12 Adult **Fic**

1. Love stories 2. School stories 3. Bullies -- Fiction 4. Love -- Fiction 5. Schools -- Fiction 6. High schools -- Fiction 7. Dating (Social customs) -- Fiction
ISBN 1250012570; 9781250012579; 9781250031211
LC 2012042136

Printz Honor Book (2014)
Boston Globe-Horn Book Award: Fiction (2013).
Odyssey Honor Recording (2014)

This book tells the story of the friendship between half-Korean sophomore Park Sheridan and the new girl Eleanor. "Tall, with bright red hair and a dress code all her own, [Eleanor is] an instant target. Too nice not to let her sit next to him, Park is alternately resentful and guilty for not being kinder to her. When he realizes she's reading his comics over his shoulder, a silent friendship is born" that will become something more. (Publishers Weekly)

"Through Eleanor and Park's alternating voices, readers glimpse the swoon-inducing, often hilarious aspects of first love... Funny, hopeful, foulmouthed, sexy and tear-jerking, this winning romance will captivate teen and adult readers alike." Kirkus

★ **Fangirl**; by Rainbow Rowell. St. Martin's Griffin 2013 448 p. (hardcover) $18.99
Grades: 9 10 11 12 **Fic**

1. Fan fiction 2. School stories 3. Characters and characteristics in literature
ISBN 1250030951; 9781250030955
LC 2013013842

"Change-resistant college freshman Cather holes up in her dorm room, writing fantasy fanfiction. But as the year progresses, she is pushed outside her comfort zone by her snarky roommate, Reagan; by Levi, Reagan's ex-boyfriend (and eventually Cath's first love interest); and by her manic but well-meaning father. Rowell transitions seamlessly between Cath's strong interior voice and clever dialogue in this sophisticated coming-of-age novel." (Horn Book)

Rowen, Michelle

Reign check. Walker 2010 292p (Demon princess) $16.99; pa $9.99
Grades: 7 8 9 10 **Fic**

1. School stories 2. Fairies -- Fiction 3. Demonology -- Fiction 4. Friendship -- Fiction
ISBN 978-0-8027-2093-1; 0-8027-2093-5; 978-0-8027-9549-6 pa; 0-8027-9549-8 pa
LC 2009028796

Sixteen-year-old Nikki is again summoned to the Underworld to appear before the Demon Council, the king of the faerie realm enrolls at her small-town Canada high school to experience human life, and her mother begins dating one of her teachers.

"Another chilling, sometimes violent, romantic fantasy that moves from the mundane world to the Shadowlands to the dungeons of the Underground before Nikki can finish her Christmas shopping." Booklist

Reign or shine. Walker & Co. 2009 284p (Demon princess) $16.99; pa $9.99
Grades: 7 8 9 10 **Fic**

1. School stories 2. Moving -- Fiction 3. Demonology -- Fiction 4. Remarriage -- Fiction
ISBN 978-0-8027-8492-6; 0-8027-8492-5; 978-0-8027-9534-2 pa; 0-8027-9534-X pa
LC 2009000205

In small-town Canada after her mother's fourth marriage, sixteen-year-old Nikki learns that her long-lost father is king of the demons, a fact that threatens to destroy her newfound popularity and sense of belonging.

Rowen "skillfully balances a lighthearted teen voice with emotional maturity. . . . Nikki's engaging voice and several intriguing secondary characters make this a winner." Publ Wkly

Rowling, J. K., 1965-

★ **Harry** Potter and the Sorcerer's Stone; illustrations by Mary Grandpré. Arthur A. Levine Bks. 1998 309p il $22.99; pa $8.99
Grades: 4 5 6 7 8 9 10 **Fic**

1. Fantasy fiction 2. Witches -- Fiction
ISBN 0-590-35340-3; 0-590-35342-X pa
LC 97-39059

First published 1997 in the United Kingdom with title: Harry Potter and the Philosopher's Stone

Rescued from the outrageous neglect of his aunt and uncle, a young boy with a great destiny proves his worth while attending Hogwarts School for Witchcraft and Wizardry.

This "is a brilliantly imagined and beautifully written fantasy." Booklist

Other titles in this series are:
Harry Potter and the Chamber of Secrets (1999)
Harry Potter and the Deathly Hallows (2007)
Harry Potter and the Goblet of Fire (2000)
Harry Potter and the Half-Blood Prince (2005)
Harry Potter and the Order of the Phoenix (2003)
Harry Potter and the prisoner of Azkaban (1999).

Roy, Jennifer Rozines

★ **Mindblind**; [by] Jennifer Roy. Marshall Cavendish 2010 248p il $15.99
Grades: 7 8 9 10 11 **Fic**

1. Genius -- Fiction 2. Bands (Music) -- Fiction 3.

Asperger's syndrome -- Fiction
ISBN 978-0-7614-5716-9; 0-7614-5716-X
LC 2010-6966

Fourteen-year-old Nathaniel Clark, who has Asperger's Syndrome, tries to prove that he is a genius by writing songs for his rock band, so that he can become a member of the prestigious Aldus Institute, the premier organization for the profoundly gifted.

"Mature readers will empathize with Nathaniel as his friends, Jessa and Cooper, do. This book is for teens who appreciate a story about self-discovery, dreams, and friendship." Voice Youth Advocates

Rubens, Michael

Sons of the 613; Mike Rubens. Clarion Books 2012 305 p. (hardcover) $16.99

Grades: 7 8 9 10 **Fic**

1. Brothers -- Fiction 2. Bar mitzvah -- Fiction 3. Masculinity -- Fiction 4. Minnesota -- Fiction 5. Coming of age -- Fiction 6. Junior high schools -- Fiction 7. Jews -- United States -- Fiction 8. Family life -- Minnesota -- Fiction
ISBN 0547612168; 9780547612164
LC 2011044352

In this book by Michael Rubens, "Isaac's parents have abandoned him for a trip to Italy in the final days before his bar mitzvah. And even worse, his hotheaded older brother, Josh, has been left in charge. . . . When Josh declares that there is more to becoming a man than memorization, the mad 'quest' begins for Isaac. . . . But when Isaac begins to fall for Josh's girlfriend, Leslie, the challenges escalate from bad to worse." (Publisher's note)

Ruby, Laura

★ **Bad** apple. HarperTeen 2009 247p $16.99; pa $8.99

Grades: 8 9 10 11 12 **Fic**

1. School stories 2. Bullies -- Fiction 3. Divorce -- Fiction 4. Teacher-student relationship -- Fiction
ISBN 978-0-06-124330-1; 0-06-124330-2; 978-0-06-124333-2 pa; 0-06-124333-7 pa
LC 2009-1409

Tola Riley, a high school junior, struggles to tell the truth when she and her art teacher are accused of having an affair.

"Tola and her family are fascinating, quirky-yet-believable, and wholly likable. Ruby works in traditional fairy-tale elements . . . with wry humor." Booklist

Ruby, Lois

Shanghai shadows. Holiday House 2006 284p $16.95

Grades: 7 8 9 10 **Fic**

1. Jews -- Fiction 2. World War, 1939-1945 -- Fiction 3. Young adult literature -- Works
ISBN 0-8234-1960-6; 978-0-8234-1960-9
LC 2005-50342

From 1939 to 1945, a Jewish family struggles to survive in occupied China; young Ilse by remaining optimistic, her older brother by joining a resistance movement, her mother by maintaining connections to the past, and her father by playing the violin that had been his livelihood.

The author's "careful research, courageous characters, low-key descriptions of fear and misery, and understated examples of love, friendship, and courage will further readers' understanding and personalize the often-horrifying epoch." Booklist

Includes bibliographical references

The **secret** of Laurel Oaks. Tom Doherty Associates 2008 282p $16.95

Grades: 6 7 8 9 **Fic**

1. Ghost stories 2. Slavery -- Fiction
ISBN 978-0-7653-1366-9; 0-7653-1366-9
LC 2008-28395

While staying with her family in Louisiana's Laurel Oaks Plantation, purported to be one of the most haunted places in America, thirteen-year-old Lila is contacted by the ghost of a slave girl unjustly convicted of murder. Story inspired by the author's visit to the Myrtles Plantation in Louisiana.

"Ruby succeeds in writing a captivating story about a time long gone, portraying the horror of slavery effectively." Libr Media Connect

Ruditis, Paul

The **four** Dorothys. Simon Pulse 2007 236p (Drama!) pa $8.99

Grades: 7 8 9 10 **Fic**

1. School stories 2. Theater -- Fiction 3. Musicals -- Fiction
ISBN 978-1-4169-3391-5
LC 2006-928449

The students at the Orion Academy put on a musical based on the Wizard of Oz. Due to their egotism, four of them have the part of Dorothy, but as opening night approaches, the Dorothys drop out of the show one-by-one. Bryan Stark must find out why in order to keep the musical from being cancelled.

"Swift pacing and tightly layered subplots keep pages turning through this refreshing take on some familiar high school dramas." SLJ

Rudnick, Paul, 1957-

Gorgeous; by Paul Rudnick. 1st ed. Scholastic 2013 336 p. (hardcover) $18.99

Grades: 9 10 11 12 **Fic**

1. Fame -- Fiction 2. Magic -- Fiction 3. Princes -- Fiction 4. Identity -- Fiction 5. Beauty, Personal -- Fiction
ISBN 0545464269; 9780545464260
LC 2012046062

In this satirical modern fairy tale, Becky, a teenage girl from a trailer park, "receives three dresses from reclusive super-designer Tom Kelly, who knew Becky's late mother. The ensembles transform Becky into nothing less than the most beautiful woman in the world . . . with a couple catches." Suddenly she's "on the cover of 'Vogue,' dating a Hollywood hunk, and possibly in line to be the next queen of England." (Publishers Weekly)

Rue, Ginger

Brand new Emily; a novel. Tricycle Press 2009 240p $14.99

Grades: 7 8 9 10 **Fic**

1. School stories 2. Poets -- Fiction 3. Publicity -- Fiction 4. Popularity -- Fiction

ISBN 978-1-58246-269-1; 1-58246-269-0

LC 2008011357

Tired of being picked on by a trio of popular girls, fourteen-year-old poet Emily hires a major public relations firm to change her image and soon finds herself "re-branded" as Em, one of the most important teens not only in her middle school, but in celebrity magazines, as well.

"It's a smart premise, and besides having something pertinent to say about kindness, hubris and the perils of popularity, Rue also imparts insight into how celebrities are designed and marketed. . . . The material is so enjoyable that readers might not even notice that they've learned something." Kirkus

Ruiz Zafon, Carlos

The **Prince** of Mist; translated by Lucia Graves. Little, Brown 2010 320p $17.99

Grades: 6 7 8 9 10 **Fic**

1. Dead -- Fiction 2. Magic -- Fiction 3. Siblings -- Fiction 4. Shipwrecks -- Fiction 5. Supernatural -- Fiction 6. Europe -- History -- 1918-1945 -- Fiction

ISBN 978-0-316-04477-6; 0-316-04477-6

LC 2009-51256

In 1943, in a seaside town where their family has gone to be safe from war, thirteen-year-old Max Carver and sister, fifteen-year-old Alicia, with new friend Roland, face off against an evil magician who is striving to complete a bargain made before he died.

"Zafon is a master storyteller. From the first page, the reader is drawn into the mystery and suspense that the young people encounter when they move into the Fleischmann house. . . . This book can be read and enjoyed by every level of reader." Voice Youth Advocates

Rumley, Crickett

Never sit down in a hoopskirt and other things I learned in Southern belle hell. Egmont USA 2011 296p pa $8.99

Grades: 8 9 10 11 12 **Fic**

1. Etiquette -- Fiction 2. Grandmothers -- Fiction 3. Beauty contests -- Fiction 4. Father-daughter relationship -- Fiction

ISBN 978-1-60684-131-0; 1-60684-131-9

LC 2010043617

After being ousted from yet another elite boarding school, seventeen-year-old Jane returns to her Alabama hometown, where her grandmother persuades her to enter the Magnolia Maid pageant.

"Rumley works in nice points about shaking up the status quo while still keeping things light and bright." Booklist

Runholt, Susan

The **mystery** of the third Lucretia. Viking Childrens Books 2008 288p $16.99; pa $6.99

Grades: 5 6 7 8 **Fic**

1. Mystery fiction 2. Art -- Fiction 3. Friendship -- Fiction

ISBN 978-0-670-06252-2; 0-670-06252-9; 978-0-14-241338-8 pa; 0-14-241338-0 pa

LC 2007-24009

While traveling in London, Paris, and Amsterdam, fourteen-year-old best friends Kari and Lucas solve an international art forgery mystery.

"There are enough artistic details for fans of art mysteries and enough spying and fleeing for fans of detective adventure." Bull Cent Child Books

Other titles about Kari and Lucas are:

Rescuing Seneca Crane (2009)

The adventure at Simba Hill (2011)

Runyon, Brent

Surface tension; a novel in four summers. Alfred A. Knopf 2009 197p $16.99; lib bdg $19.99

Grades: 8 9 10 11 **Fic**

1. Vacations -- Fiction 2. Family life -- Fiction 3. New York (State) -- Fiction

ISBN 978-0-375-84446-1; 0-375-84446-5; 978-0-375-94446-8 lib bdg; 0-375-94446-X lib bdg

LC 2008-9193

During the summer vacations of his thirteenth through his sixteenth year at the family's lake cottage, Luke realizes that although some things stay the same over the years that many more change.

"With sensitivity and candor, Runyon reveals how life changes us all and how these unavoidable changes can be full of both turmoil and wonder." Kirkus

Rupp, Rebecca

After Eli; Rebecca Rupp. 1st ed. Candlewick 2012 245 p. (hardcover) $15.99; (ebook) $15.99

Grades: 7 8 9 10 **Fic**

1. Bildungsromans 2. Family -- Fiction 3. Brothers -- Fiction 4. Bereavement -- Fiction 5. Death -- Fiction 6. Books and reading -- Fiction 7. Interpersonal relations -- Fiction

ISBN 0763658103; 9780763658106; 9780763661946

LC 2011048344

In this book, "Daniel, a wry and thoughtful narrator, looks back on the summer when he was 14, three years after his older brother, Eli, died in Iraq at age 22." Daniel's "memories of larger-than-life Eli and his lingering anger about his death" are interwoven with "Daniel's day-to-day challenges, including his dysfunctional family . . . ; his frustrations with his . . . friends; his attraction to Isabelle, a . . . newcomer to town; and his nascent friendship with school outcast Walter." (Publishers Weekly)

Rush, Jennifer

Altered; by Jennifer Rush. 1st ed. Little, Brown and Co. 2013 336 p. (hardcover) $17.99

Grades: 7 8 9 10 11 12 **Fic**

1. Science fiction 2. Runaway teenagers -- Fiction 3. Memory -- Fiction 4. Identity -- Fiction 5. Runaways -- Fiction 6. Genetic engineering -- Fiction 7. Fathers and daughters -- Fiction

ISBN 0316197084; 9780316197083

LC 2012007545

This is the debut novel in a series from Jennifer Rush. Here, "homeschooled 18-year-old Anna Mason has a life ruled by secrecy. Her widower father works for a clandestine organization called the Branch, and four gorgeous genetically altered teenage boys live in the basement laboratory of their New York State farmhouse. . . . When the Branch tries to collect 'the units,' chaos erupts, and Sam, Anna, and the others take off on the run." (Publishers Weekly)

"[T]his debut's strengths--pacing and plot twists, especially--outweigh the deficits. Riveting." Kirkus

Russell, Randy

Dead rules. HarperTeen 2011 376p $16.99

Grades: 7 8 9 10 **Fic**

1. School stories 2. Dead -- Fiction 3. Future life -- Fiction 4. Supernatural -- Fiction

ISBN 978-0-06-19867-03; 0-06-19867-04

LC 2010032452

When high school junior Jana Webster dies suddenly, she finds herself in Dead School, where she faces choices that will determine when she, a Riser, will move on, but she strives to become a Slider instead, for the chance to be with the love of her life—even if it means killing him.

"Sarcastic quips and double entendres drive the story's humor, but it's the sensitivity of the supporting characters . . . that allows Jana (and readers) to see laughter within tragedy." Kirkus

Russon, Penni

Breathe. Greenwillow Books 2007 356p $16.99; lib bdg $17.89

Grades: 8 9 10 11 12 **Fic**

1. Magic -- Fiction 2. Greece -- Fiction 3. Australia -- Fiction

ISBN 978-0-06-079393-7; 0-06-079393-7; 978-0-06-079394-4 lib bdg; 0-06-079394-5 lib bdg

LC 2006000944

Sequel to Undine

First published 2005 in Australia

Although Undine is excited about leaving Tasmania for a trip to see her father in Greece, she is also conflicted about using the magic that wells up inside her and confused about her personal relationships, including the one with her best friend Trout.

"Russon's bracing, poetic voice and earthy, likable characters ground the story's esoteric symbolism, and many readers will find their own fear and love reflected in the beautiful, open-ended metaphors." Booklist

Rutkoski, Marie

The **shadow** society; Marie Rutkoski. Farrar, Straus and Giroux 2012 408 p. $17.99

Grades: 7 8 9 10 11 12 **Fic**

1. Science fiction 2. Alternative histories 3. Supernatural -- Fiction 4. Identity -- Fiction 5. Illinois -- Fiction 6. High schools -- Fiction 7. Foster home care -- Fiction

ISBN 0374349053; 9780374349059

LC 2011033158

In this novel by Marie Rutkoski "Darcy Jones doesn't remember anything before the day she was abandoned as a child outside a Chicago firehouse. . . . But she couldn't have guessed that she comes from an alternate world where the Great Chicago Fire didn't happen and deadly creatures called Shades terrorize the human population. Memories begin to haunt Darcy when a new boy arrives at her high school, and he makes her feel both desire and desired in a way she hadn't thought possible." (Publisher's note)

Ryan, Amy Kathleen

Flame; a Sky Chasers novel. Amy Kathleen Ryan. St. Martin's Griffin 2014 336 p. (Sky Chasers) (hardback) $18.99

Grades: 8 9 10 11 12 **Fic**

1. War stories 2. Airships -- Fiction 3. Science fiction

ISBN 0312621361; 9780312621360

LC 2013039416

"When this meaty, harrowing conclusion to the Sky Chasers series opens, the inhabitants of the vessel Empyrean are fleeing their destroyed spacecraft to join their former enemies on board the New Horizon. Action begins immediately, and the story shifts mainly among the points of view of Waverly, Kieran and Seth...The pace is at times methodical, and much of the suspense comes from characters' and readers' uncertainty as to whom to trust. Stakes are high, however, and readers witness graphic (though generally not gory) violence and bodily harm as the three teens work to both overthrow and defend Pastor Anne Mather, the New Horizon's leader. It all comes to a head in a climax that is tense and viscerally frightening. Detailed and gripping, with a thorough and satisfying resolution." (Kirkus)

Glow. St. Martin's Griffin 2011 307p (Sky chasers) $17.99

Grades: 8 9 10 11 12 **Fic**

1. Science fiction

ISBN 978-0-312-59056-7; 0-312-59056-3

LC 2011020385

Part of the first generation to be conceived in deep space, fifteen-year-old Waverly is expected to marry young and have children to populate a new planet, but a violent betrayal by the dogmatic leader of their sister ship could have devastating consequences.

"The themes of survival, morality, religion, and power are well developed, and the characters are equally complex. The author has also created a unique and vivid outer-space setting that is exciting and easy to imagine." SLJ

Spark; a Sky chasers novel. Amy Kathleen Ryan. 1st ed. St. Martin's Press 2012 309 p. (hardcover) $17.99; (paperback) $9.99

Grades: 8 9 10 11 12 **Fic**

1. Mystery fiction 2. Friendship -- Fiction 3. Parent-child relationship -- Fiction 4. Science fiction

ISBN 0312621353; 9780312621353; 9781250014160; 9781250031952

LC 2012004631

Author Amy Kathleen Ryan's character "Waverly Marshall has endured and committed terrible acts aboard the 'New Horizon.' . . . [Kieran] delivers sermons designed to promote both unity and loyalty. . . . Meanwhile, Seth . . . escapes the brig under mysterious circumstances and discovers a major threat to the ship. As Waverly, Kieran, [and] Seth . . . work . . . to keep the peace, secure the ship and rescue their parents from the 'New Horizon,' . . . political and moral questions arise." (Kirkus Reviews)

Zen & Xander undone. Houghton Mifflin Harcourt 2010 212p $16
Grades: 8 9 10 11 12 **Fic**
1. Death -- Fiction 2. Sisters -- Fiction 3. Bereavement -- Fiction 4. Family life -- Fiction
ISBN 978-0-547-06248-8; 0-547-06248-6

Two teenaged sisters try to come to terms with the death of their mother in very different ways.

"Literate, believable, funny, and sometimes profound, this book has broad appeal." Voice Youth Advocates

Ryan, Carrie

★ The **Forest** of Hands and Teeth. Delacorte Press 2009 310p
Grades: 9 10 11 12 **Fic**
1. Horror fiction 2. Orphans -- Fiction 3. Zombies -- Fiction
ISBN 978-0-385-73681-7; 978-0-385-90631-9 lib bdg
LC 2008-06494

Through twists and turns of fate, orphaned Mary seeks knowledge of life, love, and especially what lies beyond her walled village and the surrounding forest, where dwell the Unconsecrated, aggressive flesh-eating people who were once dead.

"Mary's observant, careful narration pulls readers into a bleak but gripping story of survival and the endless capacity of humanity to persevere. . . . Fresh and riveting." Publ Wkly

Other titles in this series are:
The dark and hollow places (2011)
The dead-tossed waves (2010)

Ryan, Patrick

Gemini bites. Scholastic Press 2011 231p $17.99
Grades: 8 9 10 11 12 **Fic**
1. Twins -- Fiction 2. Vampires -- Fiction 3. Homosexuality -- Fiction 4. Dating (Social customs) -- Fiction
ISBN 978-0-545-22128-3; 0-545-22128-5

"Judy and Kyle Renneker are sixteen-year-old fraternal twins in a rambling family of nine. They have a prickly history with each other and are, at least from Judy's perspective, constantly in fierce competition. Kyle has recently come out of the closet to his family and feels he might never know what it's like to date a guy. Judy, who has a history of pretending to be something she isn't in order to get what she wants, is pretending to be born-again in order to land a boyfriend who heads his own bible study." Publisher's note

"Writing with humor and empathy in equal measure, Ryan . . . presents a touching gay romance as well as a pair of well-rounded and entertaining narrators who come to respect each other." Publ Wkly

In Mike we trust; [by] P. E. Ryan. HarperTeen 2009 321p $16.99
Grades: 8 9 10 11 12 **Fic**
1. Uncles -- Fiction 2. Homosexuality -- Fiction 3. Swindlers and swindling -- Fiction
ISBN 978-0-06-085813-1; 0-06-085813-3
LC 2008-11722

As fifteen-year-old Garth is wrestling with the promise he made his mother to wait a while before coming out, his somewhat secretive uncle shows up unexpectedly for an extended visit.

"The author's use of language, at times brilliantly translucent, provides insightful dialogue. This contemporary coming-of-age story set in Richmond, VA, subtly and clearly provides a fresh perspective on teenage sexual identity by imbedding it into the context of the bigger issue of truth." SLJ

Ryan, Sara

Empress of the world. Viking 2001 213p $15.99
Grades: 9 10 11 12 **Fic**
1. Lesbians 2. Bisexuality 3. Schools 4. Homosexuality
ISBN 0-670-89688-8
LC 00-52758

Lambda Literary Awards Children's and Teen Finalist (2002)

"At a summer institute for gifted high-school students, Nicola finds herself attracted to another girl. Nic's uncertainty about whether she's either lesbian or bisexual is believably conveyed, and the dialogue is convincingly realistic. Despite a flimsily constructed conflict, YA readers are sure to embrace the believable passions in this summer romance." (Horn Book)

Ryan, Tom

Way to go; Tom Ryan. Orca Book Publishers 2012 214 p. (paperback) $12.95; (ebook) $12.99
Grades: 9 10 11 12 **Fic**
1. Cooks -- Fiction 2. Gay teenagers -- Fiction
ISBN 145980077X; 9781459800779; 9781459800786 pdf; 9781459800793 epub
LC 2011943726

In this book, "as summer vacation begins on the island of Cape Breton in Nova Scotia, 17-year-old Danny feels lost, with no career aspirations and the burden of hiding that he's gay. . . . When Danny starts working at a new restaurant as a dishwasher, he discovers a passion for cooking, becomes sous chef at the restaurant, and bonds with Lisa, a hip and sophisticated waitress from New York City with troubles of her own." (Publishers Weekly)

Sachar, Louis

The **cardturner**; a novel about a king, a queen, and a joker. Delacorte Press 2010 336p $17.99; lib bdg $20.99
Grades: 8 9 10 11 12 **Fic**
1. Uncles -- Fiction 2. Family life -- Fiction 3. Bridge (Game) -- Fiction
ISBN 978-0-385-73662-6; 0-385-73662-2; 978-0-385-90619-7 lib bdg; 0-385-90619-6 lib bdg
LC 2009-27585

"Alton gets roped into serving as a card turner for his great-uncle, Lester Trapp, a bridge whizz who recently lost his eyesight. . . . To Alton's surprise, he becomes enamored of the game and begins to bond with his crusty uncle. . . . With dry, understated humor, Alton makes the intricacies of bridge accessible, while his relationships with and observations about family members and friends . . . form a portrait of a reflective teenager whose life is infinitely enriched by connections he never expected to make." Publ Wkly

Saenz, Benjamin Alire

He forgot to say good-bye. Simon & Schuster 2008 321p $16.99

Grades: 8 9 10 11 **Fic**

1. Drug abuse -- Fiction 2. Mexican Americans -- Fiction

ISBN 978-1-4169-4963-3; 1-4169-4963-1

LC 2007-21959

Two teenaged boys with very different lives find that they share a common bond—fathers they have never met who left when they were small boys—and in spite of their differences, they become close when they each need someone who understands.

"The affirming and hopeful ending is well-earned for the characters and a great payoff for the reader. . . . Characters are well-developed and complex. . . . Overall it is a strong novel with broad teenage appeal." Voice Youth Advocates

★ **Sammy** and Juliana in Hollywood; by Benjamin Alire Saenz. Cinco Puntos Press 2004 294p hardcover o.p. pa $11.95

Grades: 9 10 11 12 **Fic**

1. Violence -- Fiction 2. New Mexico -- Fiction 3. Mexican Americans -- Fiction

ISBN 0-938317-81-4; 1-933693-99-1 pa

LC 2004-2414

As a Chicano boy living in the unglamorous town of Hollywood, New Mexico, and a member of the graduating class of 1969, Sammy Santos faces the challenges of "gringo" racism, unpopular dress codes, the Vietnam War, barrio violence, and poverty

★ **Aristotle** and Dante discover the secrets of the universe; Benjamin Alire Sáenz. Simon & Schuster Books for Young Readers 2012 359 p. (hardcover) $16.99

Grades: 9 10 11 12 **Fic**

1. Bildungsromans 2. Friendship -- Fiction 3. Gay teenagers -- Fiction 4. Mexican Americans -- Fiction 5. Families -- Fiction 6. Coming of age -- Fiction 7. Homosexuality -- Fiction 8. Mexican-Americans -- Fiction

ISBN 1442408928; 9781442408920

LC 2010033649

Michael L. Printz Honor Book (2013)

This book follows "fifteen-year-old Ari [who] is restless and bored when a boy named Dante offers to teach him to swim. . . . When Dante is almost hit by a car, Ari risks his life to save him and then pulls back emotionally from Dante's effusive gratitude, but it isn't until Dante moves away for the school year and begins experimenting with his sexuality . . . that Ari really has to confront the secrets of his own universe." (Bulletin of the Center for Children's Books)

★ **Last** night I sang to the monster; a novel. Cinco Puntos Press 2009 239p $16.95

Grades: 9 10 11 12 **Fic**

1. Alcoholism -- Fiction 2. Family life -- Fiction 3. Psychotherapy -- Fiction

ISBN 978-1-933693-58-3; 1-933693-58-4

LC 2009-15833

Eighteen-year-old Zach does not remember how he came to be in a treatment center for alcoholics. Through therapy and and the help of friends such as Rafael, his amnesia fades and he begins to heal. "Grades nine to twelve." (Bull Cent Child Books)

"Saenz' poetic narrative will captivate readers from the first sentence to the last paragraph of this beautifully written novel, which explores the painful journey of an adolescent through the labyrinth of addiction and alcoholism. It is also a celebration of life and a song of hope in celebration of family and friendship, one that will resonate loud and long with teens." Kirkus

Saldana, Rene

A **good** long way; by Rene Saldana, Jr. Piñata Books 2010 103p pa $10.95

Grades: 8 9 10 11 **Fic**

1. School stories 2. Texas -- Fiction 3. Brothers -- Fiction 4. Mexican Americans -- Fiction 5. Runaway teenagers -- Fiction

ISBN 978-1-55885-607-3; 1-55885-607-2

LC 2010-32989

Three Mexican American teenagers in a small-town in Texas struggle with difficulties at home and at school as they try to attain the elusive status of adulthood.

"This fast-paced novel will make readers think about their own lives and responsibilities." SLJ

Salerni, Dianne K.

We hear the dead. Sourcebooks Fire 2010 422p pa $9.99

Grades: 7 8 9 10 **Fic**

1. Mediums 2. Sisters -- Fiction 3. Spiritualism -- Fiction 4. New York (State) -- Fiction

ISBN 978-1-4022-3092-9; 1-4022-3092-3

The author "paints vivid scenes of life in upstate New York during a time when exposed ankles were shocking and the Underground Railroad offered a dangerous route to freedom for both conductors and slaves. Historical fiction at its best." SLJ

Sales, Leila

Mostly good girls. Simon Pulse 2010 347p $16.99

Grades: 9 10 11 12 **Fic**

1. School stories 2. Ability -- Fiction 3. Authorship -- Fiction 4. Friendship -- Fiction 5. Massachusetts -- Fiction

ISBN 978-1-4424-0679-7

LC 2010-7190

Sixteen-year-olds Violet and Katie, best friends since seventh grade despite differences in their family backgrounds and abilities, are pulled apart during their junior year at Massachusetts' exclusive Westfield School.

"This exploration of growing up, personal change and angst is well-written." Voice of Youth Advocates

Past perfect. Simon Pulse 2011 306p $16.99
Grades: 7 8 9 10 **Fic**

1. New England -- Fiction 2. Summer employment -- Fiction 3. Dating (Social customs) -- Fiction
ISBN 978-1-4424-0682-7; 1-4424-0682-8
LC 2011025811

Sixteen-year-old Chelsea knows what to expect when she returns for a summer of historical reenactment at Colonial Essex Village until she learns that her ex-boyfriend is working there, too, and then meets the very attractive Dan who works at a rival historical village

"Chelsea is an appealing narrator with a sharp sense of humor, and readers will tear through this novel to find out whether she reunites with Ezra or gets together with Dan from the rival museum. . . . This is a satisfying and fun read." SLJ

This song will save your life; Leila Sales. Farrar Straus & Giroux 2013 288 p. (hard) $17.99
Grades: 8 9 10 11 12 **Fic**

1. Bullies -- Fiction 2. Disc jockeys -- Fiction 3. Suicide -- Fiction 4. Popularity -- Fiction 5. High schools -- Fiction 6. Interpersonal relations -- Fiction
ISBN 0374351384; 9780374351380
LC 2012050408

In this book, "Elise has endured a lifetime of social isolation and bullying at school. Walking alone one night soon after a halfhearted suicide attempt, the 16-year-old inadvertently ends up at an underground nightclub. There, an aspiring musician befriends her, and she catches the eye of Char, a cute DJ who agrees to teach her to mix music. But as talented, driven Elise spends more nights sneaking out to learn how to DJ (and kiss Char), her double life spins out of control." (Publishers Weekly)

Salisbury, Graham

★ **Eyes** of the emperor. Wendy Lamb Books 2005 228p hardcover o.p. pa $6.99
Grades: 7 8 9 10 **Fic**

1. Japanese Americans -- Fiction 2. World War, 1939-1945 -- Fiction
ISBN 0-385-72971-5; 0-440-22956-1 pa
LC 2004-15142

Following orders from the United States Army, several young Japanese American men train K-9 units to hunt Asians during World War II.

"Based on the experiences of 26 Hawaiian-Americans of Japanese ancestry, this novel tells an uncomfortable story. Yet it tells of belief in honor, respect, and love of country." Libr Media Connect

★ **House** of the red fish. Wendy Lamb Books 2006 291p $16.95; lib bdg $17.99
Grades: 6 7 8 9 **Fic**

1. Japanese Americans -- Fiction 2. World War, 1939-1945 -- Fiction
ISBN 0-385-73121-3; 0-385-90145-3 lib bdg
LC 2006-07544

Over a year after Japan's attack on Pearl Harbor and the arrest of Tomi's father and grandfather, Tomi and his friends, battling anti-Japanese-American sentiment in Hawaii, try to find a way to salvage his father's sunken fishing boat.

"Many readers, even those who don't enjoy historical fiction, will like the portrayal of the work and the male camaraderie." Booklist

Lord of the deep. Delacorte Press 2001 182p hardcover o.p. pa $7.99
Grades: 5 6 7 8 **Fic**

1. Fishing 2. Stepfathers 3. Fishing -- Fiction 4. Stepfathers -- Fiction
ISBN 0-385-72918-9; 0-440-22911-1 pa
LC 00-60280

Working for Bill, his stepfather, on a charter fishing boat in Hawaii teaches thirteen-year-old Mikey about fishing, and about taking risks, making sacrifices, and facing some of life's difficult choices

"With its vivid Hawaiian setting, this fine novel is a natural for book-discussion groups that enjoy pondering moral ambiguity. Its action-packed scenes will also lure in reluctant readers." SLJ

★ **Under** the blood-red sun. Delacorte Press 1994 246p hardcover o.p. pa $5.99
Grades: 5 6 7 8 9 10 **Fic**

1. Hawaii -- Fiction 2. Japanese Americans -- Fiction 3. World War, 1939-1945 -- Fiction 4. Pearl Harbor (Oahu, Hawaii), Attack on, 1941 -- Fiction
ISBN 0-385-32099-X; 0-440-41139-4 pa
LC 94-444

Tomikazu Nakaji's biggest concerns are baseball, homework, and a local bully, until life with his Japanese family in Hawaii changes drastically after the bombing of Pearl Harbor in December 1941

"Character development of major figures is good, the setting is warmly realized, and the pace of the story moves gently though inexorably forward." SLJ

Followed by: House of the red fish (2006)

Salmon, Dena K.

Discordia; the eleventh dimension. Disney/Hyperion Books 2009 223p $16.99
Grades: 6 7 8 9 10 **Fic**

1. Fantasy fiction 2. Science fiction
ISBN 978-1-4231-1109-2; 1-4231-1109-5
LC 2010-280666

"Lance is your everyday New York City teen, juggling school and parents as best he can, but really living for the mystical online world of Discordia, where he comes alive as his alter ego, a level 17 zombie sorcerer. But the line between reality and online gaming blurs and then fades altogether when he and his friend MrsKeller are recruited to join the Awaken Myths Guild by TheGreatOne, a level 60 player. Suddenly, a snow day in the Big Apple becomes a journey though an unknown but oddly familiar landscape, where little—if anything—makes sense anymore. . . . This is Alice in Wonderland turned upside down and made into a whiz-bang, nonstop read for the modern gamer." Kirkus

Salter, Sydney

Swoon at your own risk. Graphia 2010 356p pa $8.99
Grades: 9 10 11 12 **Fic**

1. Grandmothers -- Fiction 2. Summer employment

-- Fiction 3. Dating (Social customs) -- Fiction
ISBN 978-0-15-206649-9; 0-15-206649-7

After a junior hear of dating disasters, Polly—the granddaughter of a famous advice columnist—swears off boys. But when her grandmother moves in for the summer, Polly mistakenly believes she'll be getting great advice when in reality, she discovers that her grandmother is a mancrazed sexagenarian.

"This book is a light read with an emotional awakening and enough romance to keep fans of the genre interested." SLJ

Samms, Olivia

Sketchy; Olivia Samms. Amazon Childrens Pub 2013 256 p. (hardcover) $16.99

Grades: 9 10 11 12 **Fic**

1. Occult fiction 2. Mystery fiction
ISBN 147781650X; 9781477816509

This novel, by Olivia Samms, is book one in "The Bea Catcher Chronicles." "Bea is starting over at Packard High School, in a city shaken from two assaults on young women. The latest victim, Willa Pressman-the one who surviveddoesn't remember a thing. But Bea has a disturbing new 'skill': she can see-and then draw-images from other people's minds. And when she looks at Willa, Bea is shocked by what she sketches." (Publisher's note)

Sanchez, Alex

Bait. Simon & Schuster Books for Young Readers 2009 239p $16.99

Grades: 7 8 9 10 **Fic**

1. Stepfathers -- Fiction 2. Mexican Americans -- Fiction 3. Child sexual abuse -- Fiction
ISBN 978-1-4169-3772-2; 1-4169-3772-2
LC 2008-38815

Diego keeps getting into trouble because of his explosive temper until he finally finds a probation officer who helps him get to the root of his anger so that he can stop running from his past.

"This groundbreaking novel brings to life an appealing young man who is neither totally a victim nor a victimizer, one who struggles to handle conflicts that derail many young lives. . . . High interest and accessible, this coming-of-age story belongs in every collection." SLJ

Getting it. Simon & Schuster 2006 210p $16.95; pa $8.99

Grades: 9 10 11 12 **Fic**

1. School stories 2. Friendship -- Fiction 3. Homosexuality -- Fiction 4. Mexican Americans -- Fiction
ISBN 978-1-4169-0896-8; 1-4169-0896-X; 978-1-4169-0898-2 pa; 1-4169-0898-6 pa
LC 2005-29905

Hoping to impress a sexy female classmate, fifteen-yearold Carlos secretly hires gay student Sal to give him an image makeover, in exchange for Carlos's help in forming a Gay-Straight Alliance at their Texas high school.

"This title's sexual frankness may make it a controversial choice, particularly for school libraries in more conservative communities, but its themes, appeal, and readability make it a nearly essential purchase." Voice Youth Advocates

Rainbow boys. Simon & Schuster 2001 233p hardcover o.p. pa $8.99

Grades: 10 11 12 **Fic**

1. School stories 2. Homosexuality -- Fiction
ISBN 0-689-84100-0; 0-689-85770-5 pa
LC 2001-20952

Three high school seniors, a jock with a girlfriend and an alcoholic father, a closeted gay, and a flamboyant gay rights advocate, struggle with family issues, gay bashers, first sex, and conflicting feelings about each other.

"Some of the language and sexual situations may be too mature for some readers, but overall there's enough conflict, humor and tenderness to make this story believable—and touching." Publ Wkly

Other titles featuring Nelson, Kyle, and Jason are:
Rainbow High (2004)
Rainbow road (2005)

Rainbow High. Simon & Schuster Books for Young Readers 2004 247p $16.95; pa $8.99

Grades: 10 11 12 **Fic**

1. School stories 2. Homosexuality -- Fiction
ISBN 0-689-85477-3; 0-689-85478-1 pa
LC 2003-8252

Sequel to Rainbow boys (2001)

Follows three gay high school seniors as they struggle with issues of coming out, safe sex, homophobia, being in love, and college choices.

Followed by Rainbow road (2005)

Rainbow road. Simon & Schuster 2005 243p $16.95; pa $8.99

Grades: 10 11 12 **Fic**

1. Homosexuality -- Fiction 2. Automobile travel -- Fiction
ISBN 0-689-86565-1; 1-4169-1191-X pa
LC 2004-25980

Sequel to Rainbow high (2003)

While driving across the United States during the summer after high school graduation, three young gay men encounter various bisexual and homosexual people and make some decisions about their own relationships and lives.

"Some mature romance scenes, occasional frank language, and an inclusion of transgender/transsexual/bisexual story lines translate into a tender book that will likely be appreciated and embraced by young adult readers." SLJ

So hard to say; Alex Sanchez. 1st ed; Simon & Schuster Books for Young Readers 2004 230p $14.95

Grades: 6 7 8 9 **Fic**

1. Homosexuality -- Fiction 2. Mexican Americans -- Fiction
ISBN 0-689-86564-3
LC 2003-21128

Thirteen-year-old Xio, a Mexican American girl, and Frederick, who has just moved to California from Wisconsin, quickly become close friends, but when Xio starts thinking of Frederick as her boyfriend, he must confront his feelings of confusion and face the fear that he might be gay.

"Adventurous, multifaceted, funny, and unpredictably insightful, Sanchez's novel . . . gels well-rounded characterizations with the universal excitement of first love." SLJ

Sandell, Lisa Ann

A **map** of the known world. Scholastic Press 2009 273p $16.99

Grades: 7 8 9 10 **Fic**

1. School stories 2. Art -- Fiction 3. Bereavement -- Fiction 4. Family life -- Fiction

ISBN 978-0-545-06970-0; 0-545-06970-X

LC 2008-50745

Devastated, along with her parents, by the death of her older brother and apprehensive about being a freshman in the same high school he attended, fourteen-year-old Cora finds unexpected solace in art.

Sandell's "fluid phrasing and choice of metaphors give her prose a quiet poetic ambience." Publ Wkly

★ **Song** of the sparrow. Scholastic Press 2007 394p $16.99; pa $8.99

Grades: 8 9 10 11 12 **Fic**

1. War stories 2. Knights and knighthood -- Fiction 3. Great Britain -- History -- 0-1066 -- Fiction

ISBN 978-0-439-91848-0; 0-439-91848-0; 978-0-439-91849-7 pa; 0-439-91849-9 pa

LC 2007-00016

In fifth-century Britain, nine years after the destruction of their home on the island of Shalott brings her to live with her father and brothers in the military encampments of Arthur's army, seventeen-year-old Elaine describes her changing perceptions of war and the people around her as she becomes increasingly involved in the bitter struggle against the invading Saxons.

The author "invents a unique and eloquently wrought addition to Arthurian lore in 44 verses. . . . The poetic narrative . . . evokes a remarkable range (and natural progression) of emotions." Publ Wkly

Sanders, Scott Loring

Gray baby; a novel. Houghton Mifflin Harcourt 2009 321p $17

Grades: 7 8 9 10 **Fic**

1. Homicide -- Fiction 2. Virginia -- Fiction 3. Alcoholism -- Fiction 4. Country life -- Fiction 5. Single parent family -- Fiction 6. Racially mixed people -- Fiction

ISBN 978-0-547-07661-4; 0-547-07661-4

LC 2008-36810

Clifton has grown up in rural Virginia with the memory of his African American father being beaten to death by policemen, causing his white mother to slip into alcoholism and depression, but after befriending an old man who listens to his problems, Clifton finally feels less alone in the world.

"Unflinching and raw, the story, set in the late 1980s, explores the destructiveness of racism." Horn Book Guide

The **Hanging** Woods; a novel. Houghton Mifflin 2008 326p $16

Grades: 10 11 12 **Fic**

1. Alabama -- Fiction 2. Homicide -- Fiction 3. Friendship -- Fiction 4. Country life -- Fiction

ISBN 978-0-618-88125-3

LC 2007-25773

In rural Alabama during the summer of 1975, three teenaged boys build a treehouse, try to keep a headless turkey alive, and become involved in a murder mystery.

This is a "compelling, but disturbing story, which features mature subject matter and language." Kirkus

Sanders, Shelly

Rachel's secret. Second Story Press 2012 248 p. $12.95

Grades: 6 7 8 9 10 **Fic**

1. Historical fiction 2. Antisemitism -- Fiction 3. Judaism -- Relations -- Christianity -- Fiction

ISBN 1926920376; 9781926920375

This book follows "14-year-old Rachel . . . living under Russian rule in Kishinev in 1903, [she] was one of the last people to see her Christian friend Mikhail alive when she witnessed his murder at the hands of disgruntled relatives who stood to lose out on an inheritance. His death is blamed on Jews, however, and a vicious pogrom is unleashed on the city. Rachel's anguish about knowing what happened stems from a justified fear of not being believed if she comes forward, thus evoking more turmoil. She also harbors guilt that her somewhat risky friendship with a non-Jewish boy somehow triggered the calamity. . . . [W]hile Rachel does act courageously and courtroom justice is meted out, virulent anti-Semitism still rules the day." (Booklist)

Sanderson, Brandon

The **Rithmatist**; Brandon Sanderson. Tor Teen 2013 384 p. ill. (hardcover) $17.99

Grades: 7 8 9 10 **Fic**

1. Fantasy fiction 2. Magic -- Fiction 3. Fantasy

ISBN 0765320320; 9780765320322

LC 2012043417

In this young adult fantasy novel, by Brandon Sanderson, "Joel wants to be a Rithmatist. Chosen by the Master in a mysterious inception ceremony, Rithmatists have the power to infuse life into two-dimensional figures known as Chalklings. Rithmatists are humanity's only defense against the Wild Chalklings--merciless creatures that leave mangled corpses in their wake. Having nearly overrun the territory of Nebrask, the Wild Chalklings now threaten all of the American Isles." (Publisher's note)

Sandler, Karen

Tankborn. Tu Books 2011 373p map $17.95

Grades: 7 8 9 10 **Fic**

1. Science fiction 2. Genetic engineering -- Fiction

ISBN 978-1-60060-662-5; 1-60060-662-8

LC 2011014589

Kayla and Mishalla, two genetically engineered non-human slaves (GENs), fall in love with higher-status boys, discover deep secrets about the creation of GENs, and in the process find out what it means to be human.

"Sandler has created a fascinating dystopian world. . . . The author's speculative vision of the darker side of future possibilities in genetic engineering and mind control is both chilling and thought-provoking." SLJ

Sax, Aline

★ The **war** within these walls; by Aline Sax; illustrated by Caryl Strzelecki; translated from the Dutch by Laura Watkinson. Eerdmans Books for Young Readers 2013 176 p. $17

Grades: 9 10 11 12 **Fic**

1. Jewish ghettos 2. World War, 1939-1945 -- Fiction 3. Jews -- Poland -- Fiction 4. Jews -- Poland 5. Holocaust, Jewish (1939-1945) -- Poland -- Fiction 6. Poland -- History -- Occupation, 1939-1945 -- Fiction 7. Holocaust, Jewish (1939-1945) -- Poland 8. Warsaw (Poland) -- History -- Warsaw Ghetto Uprising, 1943 -- Fiction

ISBN 0802854281; 9780802854285

LC 2013005663

Mildred L. Batchelder Honor Book (2014)

National Jewish Book Award: Winner, Children's and Young Adult (2013)

"The narrator lives with his parents and sister in what becomes the Warsaw Ghetto. He finds a secret escape from the ghetto and begins smuggling food, eventually joining with Mordechai Anielewicz's organized Resistance. The prose is spare; the book's format, with text on black or white pages and plentiful ink and wash illustrations, is dramatic and will grab young readers." (Horn Book)

Scaletta, Kurtis

Mamba Point. Alfred A. Knopf 2010 268p il $16.99; lib bdg $19.99

Grades: 5 6 7 8 **Fic**

1. Fear -- Fiction 2. Snakes -- Fiction

ISBN 978-0-375-86180-2; 0-375-86180-7; 978-0-375-96180-9 lib bdg; 0-375-96180-1 lib bdg

LC 2009-22084

After moving with his family to Liberia, twelve-year-old Linus discovers that he has a mystical connection with the black mamba, one of the deadliest snakes in Africa, which he is told will give him some of the snake's characteristics. Includes facts about the author's experiences as a thirteen-year-old American living in Liberia in 1982

Scaletta "has created an appealing, well-written protagonist whose everyday and extraordinary experiences . . . change his life in unexpected, positive ways. . . . The engaging first-person narrative and array of diversely drawn characters further enliven the novel." Booklist

Scarrow, Alex

Day of the predator. Walker Books for Young Readers 2011 404p (TimeRiders) $16.99

Grades: 7 8 9 10 **Fic**

1. Science fiction 2. Time travel -- Fiction

ISBN 978-0-8027-2296-6; 0-8027-2296-2

LC 2010040987

Sequel to: TimeRiders (2010)

With teens Maddy, Liam, and Sal on their first solo assignment for a secret agency, Liam is sent back in time to prevent the murder of the father of time travel by a terrorist group, but due to a nuclear accident, he ends up in the late cretaceous period where the biggest threat is not from the legendary tyrannosaur.

"Readers will be intrigued, puzzled—and ready for the next one." Kirkus

TimeRiders. Walker & Co. 2010 405p $16.99

Grades: 7 8 9 10 **Fic**

1. Science fiction 2. Time travel -- Fiction 3. Environmental protection -- Fiction 4. September 11 terrorist attacks, 2001 -- Fiction

ISBN 978-0-8027-2172-3; 0-8027-2172-9

LC 2009-53166

Rescued from imminent death, teens Maddy, Liam, and Sal join forces in 2001 Manhattan to correct changes in history made by other time travelers, using a "time bubble" surrounding the attack on the Twin Towers to hide their journeys.

"The characters are expertly developed, each displaying vulnerabilities and quirks that make them memorable as individuals. . . . This is a brilliantly paced, fascinating look at the ways in which one seemingly small change can ripple out to—literally—the end of the world." Bull Cent Child Books

Another title in this series is:

Day of the predator (2011)

Scheibe, Lindsey

Riptide; one summer, endless possibilities. Lindsey Scheibe. 1st ed. Flux 2013 277 p. (paperback) $9.99

Grades: 7 8 9 10 11 12 **Fic**

1. Surfing -- Fiction 2. Teenage girls -- Fiction 3. Friendship -- Fiction 4. Child abuse -- Fiction 5. Best friends -- Fiction 6. San Diego (Calif.) -- Fiction 7. Dating (Social customs) -- Fiction

ISBN 0738735949; 9780738735948

LC 2012048951

In this novel, by Lindsey Scheibe, "signing up for her first surf competition, Grace has just one summer to train and impress the university scouts who will be judging the comp. But summer is about more than just big waves. As romances ignite and her feelings for Ford threaten to reach the point of no return, Grace must face the biggest challenges of her life." (Publisher's note)

Scheidt, Erica Lorraine

★ **Uses** for boys; Erica Lorraine Scheidt. St. Martin's Press 2013 240 p. $9.99

Grades: 9 10 11 12 **Fic**

1. Love stories 2. Dating (Social customs) -- Fiction 3. Teenagers -- Conduct of life -- Fiction

ISBN 1250007119; 9781250007117

In this novel by Erica Lorraine Scheidt "Anna learns that if you give boys what they want, you can get what you need. But the price is high--the other kids make fun of her; the girls call her a slut. . . . Then comes Sam. When Anna actually meets a boy who is more than just useful, whose family eats dinner together, laughs, and tells stories, the truth about love becomes clear. And she finally learns how it feels to have something to lose--and something to offer." (Publisher's note)

Schindler, Holly

★ A **blue** so dark. Flux 2010 277p pa $9.95

Grades: 8 9 10 11 12 **Fic**

1. School stories 2. Artists -- Fiction 3. Schizophrenia -- Fiction 4. Mental illness -- Fiction 5. Mother-daughter relationship -- Fiction

ISBN 978-0-7387-1926-9

LC 2009-31360

As Missouri fifteen-year-old Aura struggles alone to cope with the increasingly severe symptoms of her mother's schizophrenia, she wishes only for a normal life, but fears that her artistic ability and genes will one day result in her own insanity.

"A haunting, realistic view of the melding of art, creativity, and mental illness and their collective impact on a young person's life." Booklist

Playing hurt. Flux 2011 303p pa $9.95

Grades: 7 8 9 10 **Fic**

1. Love stories 2. Resorts -- Fiction 3. Minnesota -- Fiction 4. Loss (Psychology) -- Fiction

ISBN 978-0-7387-2287-0; 0-7387-2287-1

LC 2010-44173

Chelsea Keyes, a high school basketball star whose promising career has been cut short by a terrible accident on the court, and Clint Morgan, a nineteen-year-old ex-hockey player who gave up his sport following a game-related tragedy, meet at a Minnesota lake resort and find themselves drawn together by the losses they have suffered.

"Both heartbreaking and thrilling, the emotional journey that Clint and Chelsea embark on together is more than a heady romance; the characters are realistically drawn, and the book does not shy away from the reality of the characters' experiences: anger and grief mixed with desire and yearning. The book speaks to personal struggles and triumphs and the ability of the human spirit to heal." Voice Youth Advocates

Schmatz, Pat

★ **Bluefish**. Candlewick Press 2011 226p $15.99

Grades: 5 6 7 8 **Fic**

1. School stories 2. Literacy -- Fiction 3. Teachers -- Fiction

ISBN 978-0-7636-5334-7; 0-7636-5334-9

LC 2010044815

Everything changes for thirteen-year-old Travis, a new student who is trying to hide a learning disability, when he meets a remarkable teacher and Velveeta, a sassy classmate with her own secrets.

"A cast of richly developed characters peoples this work of contemporary fiction, told in the third person from Travis' point of view, with first-person vignettes from Velveeta's perspective peppered throughout. . . . A story rife with unusual honesty and hope." Kirkus

Schmidt, Gary D.

★ **Lizzie** Bright and the Buckminster boy. Clarion Books 2004 219p $15; pa $6.99

Grades: 7 8 9 10 **Fic**

1. Race relations -- Fiction

ISBN 0-618-43929-3; 0-553-49495-3 pa

LC 2003-20967

A Newbery Medal honor book, 2005

In 1911, Turner Buckminster hates his new home of Phippsburg, Maine, but things improve when he meets Lizzie Bright Griffin, a girl from a poor, nearby island community founded by former slaves that the town fathers—and Turner's—want to change into a tourist spot

"Although the story is hauntingly sad, there is much humor, too. Schmidt's writing is infused with feeling and rich in imagery. With fully developed, memorable characters and a fascinating, little-known piece of history, this novel will leave a powerful impression on readers." SLJ

★ **Trouble**. Clarion Books 2008 297p $16

Grades: 6 7 8 9 10 **Fic**

1. Death -- Fiction 2. Prejudices -- Fiction 3. Family life -- Fiction 4. Traffic accidents -- Fiction 5. Cambodian Americans -- Fiction

ISBN 978-0-618-92766-1; 0-618-92766-2

LC 2007-40104

Fourteen-year-old Henry, wishing to honor his brother Franklin's dying wish, sets out to hike Maine's Mount Katahdin with his best friend and dog, but fate adds another companion—the Cambodian refugee accused of fatally injuring Franklin—and reveals troubles that predate the accident.

"Schmidt creates a rich and credible world peopled with fully developed characters who have a lot of complex reckoning to do. . . . [The author's prose] is flawless, and Henry's odyssey of growth and understanding is pitch-perfect and deeply satisfying." Bull Cent Child Books

★ The **Wednesday** wars. Clarion Books 2007 264p pa $6.99; $16

Grades: 5 6 7 8 **Fic**

1. Poets 2. School stories

ISBN 054723760X; 0618724834; 9780547237602; 9780618724833

LC 2006-23660

A Newbery Medal honor book, 2008

During the 1967 school year, on Wednesday afternoons when all his classmates go to either Catechism or Hebrew school, seventh-grader Holling Hoodhound stays in Mrs. Baker's classroom where they read the plays of William Shakespeare and Holling learns something of value about the world he lives in.

"The serious issues are leavened with ample humor, and the supporting cast . . . is fully dimensional. Best of all is the hero." Publ Wkly

Schneider, Robyn

★ The **beginning** of everything; by Robyn Schneider. 1st ed. Katherine Tegen Books 2013 336 p. (hardcover) $17.99

Grades: 9 10 11 12 **Fic**

1. School stories 2. Popularity -- Fiction 3. California -- Fiction 4. High schools -- Fiction 5. Debates and debating -- Fiction 6. Interpersonal relations -- Fiction 7. People with disabilities -- Fiction 8. Family life --

California -- Fiction
ISBN 0062217135; 9780062217134
LC 2012030976

In this book, after "finding his vapid girlfriend going down on another guy, Ezra Faulkner is seriously injured in a hit-and-run accident, leaving him out of the loop with the jock-and-cheerleader set. When senior year begins, he gravitates toward his old friend Toby, no stranger to tragedy himself. Toby and his debate team welcome Ezra to their lunch table when they find out that the prom king is as smart and funny as they are." (Kirkus Reviews)

Schraff, Anne E.

A **boy** called Twister; [by] Anne Schraff. Saddleback Educational 2010 180p (Urban underground) pa $8.95

Grades: 6 7 8 9 10 **Fic**

1. Moving -- Fiction 2. Fathers -- Fiction 3. Prisoners -- Fiction 4. Track athletics -- Fiction
ISBN 978-1-61651-002-2 pa; 1-61651-002-1 pa

"After his beloved mother dies, Kevin, 16, moves from Texas to his grandparents' home in California. He quickly settles in and makes new friends, begins a romance, stars on the track team, and confronts the school bully, Marco. Throughout it all, though, he keeps the secret that his dad was sent to prison for second-degree murder and died in a prison riot when Kevin was 6. . . . This small, fast-paced paperback will grab even reluctant readers with the suspenseful story, cool dialogue, and sports action, which never distracts from Kevin's personal struggle." Booklist

Schreck, Karen

While he was away; Karen Schreck. Sourcebooks Fire 2012 249 p. $8.99

Grades: 7 8 9 10 **Fic**

1. Love stories 2. Loneliness -- Fiction 3. Iraq War, 2003-2011 -- Fiction
ISBN 140226402X; 9781402264023

This book follows a couple, Penna and David, as David "leaves for a stint in Iraq. . . . Penna is anxious and devastated, but eventually she finds ways to cope. . . . In Iraq, David struggles with the mind-numbing work of patrols and the terror that interrupts it, and he focuses on an orphanage for Iraqi refugee children as a way to be useful. . . . Paralleling Penna's story is her discovery of a grandmother who lost her first husband in World War II." (Kirkus Reviews)

"With realistic characters and interesting dialogue, While He Was Away is both insightful and tragic." VOYA

Schrefer, Eliot

The **deadly** sister. Scholastic Press 2010 310p $17.99

Grades: 8 9 10 11 12 **Fic**

1. Mystery fiction 2. Sisters -- Fiction 3. Homicide -- Fiction
ISBN 978-0-545-16574-7; 0-545-16574-1
LC 2010-281733

Abby Goodwin has always covered for her sister, Maya, but now Maya has been accused of murder, and Abby's not sure she'll be able to cover for her sister anymore. Abby helps Maya escape. But when Abby begins investigating the death, she find that you can't trust anyone, not even the people you think you know.

"Well-drawn characters, realistic dialogue, and suspenseful twists and turns add to the appeal. Teens crave mystery, and this book will suit them just fine." SLJ

★ **Endangered**; Eliot Schrefer. Scholastic Press 2012 264 p. (reinforced) $17.99

Grades: 7 8 9 10 11 12 **Fic**

1. Animal sanctuaries -- Fiction 2. Wildlife conservation -- Fiction 3. Congo (Democratic Republic) -- Fiction 4. Apes -- Fiction 5. Bonobo -- Fiction 6. Divorce -- Fiction 7. Wildlife rescue -- Fiction 8. Racially mixed people -- Fiction 9. Blacks -- Congo (Democratic Republic) -- Fiction
ISBN 0545165768; 9780545165761
LC 2012030877

This book by Eliot Schrefer was a 2012 National Book Award Finalist for Young People's Literature. "When one girl has to follow her mother to her sanctuary for bonobos, she's not thrilled to be there. It's her mother's passion, and she'd rather have nothing to do with it. But when revolution breaks out and their sanctuary is attacked, she must rescue the bonobos and hide in the jungle. Together, they will fight to keep safe, to eat, and to survive." (Publisher's note)

★ **Threatened**; Eliot Schrefer. Scholastic Press 2014 288 p. (jacketed hardcover) $17.99

Grades: 7 8 9 10 11 12 **Fic**

1. Orphans 2. Chimpanzees 3. Animal rescue 4. Gabon -- Fiction 5. Adventure stories 6. Chimpanzees -- Fiction 7. Animal rescue -- Fiction 8. Gabon 9. Orphans -- Gabon -- Fiction 10. Wildlife rescue 11. Orphans -- Gabon
ISBN 0545551439; 9780545551434
LC 2013018599

In this juvenile story, by Eliot Schrefer, "Luc and Prof head into the rough, dangerous jungle in order to study the elusive chimpanzees. There, Luc finally finds a new family--and must act when that family comes under attack. . . . [It] is the story of a boy fleeing his present, a man fleeing his past, and a trio of chimpanzees who are struggling not to flee at all." (Publisher's note)

"After the death of his mother and sister, Luc is left in the hands of a moneylender, Monsieur Tatagani. One of many orphans forced to do Tatagani's bidding, Luc has found a way to be useful and earn a few coins wiping glasses in a bar in Gabon...There are times when Luc's voice as an uneducated orphan adolescent seems vivid and real, at other times less so. Still, the valor and soul of Luc is captivating. Fascinating and sure to lead to discussion." (School Library Journal)

Schreiber, Ellen

Vampire kisses. Katherine Tegen Books 2003 197p $15.99; lib bdg $16.89

Grades: 7 8 9 10 **Fic**

1. Vampires -- Fiction
ISBN 0-06-009334-X; 0-06-009335-8 lib bdg
LC 2002-155506

Sixteen-year-old Raven, an outcast who always wears black and hopes to become a vampire some day, falls in love with the mysterious new boy in town, eager to find out if he can make her dreams come true

"Schreiber uses a careful balance of humor, irony, pathos, and romance." Booklist

Other titles in this series are:
Vampire kisses 2: Kissing coffins (2005)
Vampire kisses 3: Vampireville (2006)
Vampire kisses 4: Dance with a vampire (2007)
Vampire kisses 5: The Coffin Club (2008)
Vampire kisses 6: Royal Blood (2009)
Vampire kisses 7: Love bites (2010)
Vampire kisses 8: Cryptic cravings (2011)

Schreiber, Joe

Au revoir, crazy European chick. Houghton Mifflin 2011 190p $16.99
Grades: 9 10 11 12 **Fic**
1. Adventure fiction 2. New York (N.Y.) -- Fiction
ISBN 978-0-547-57738-8
LC 2011009845

Perry's parents insist that he take Gobi, their quiet, Lithuanian exchange student, to senior prom but after an incident at the dance he learns that Gobi is actually a trained assassin who needs him as a henchman, behind the wheel of his father's precious Jaguar, on a mission in Manhattan.

"Perfect for action adventure junkies who will enjoy the car chases, thugs, graphic killing scenes, explosions, and a random bear fight, Schreiber's debut novel also contains enough humor, sexual tension, distinctive language, and character development to make this more than just a quick thrill read." Horn Book

★ **Perry's** killer playlist; by Joe Schreiber. Houghton Mifflin 2012 209 p. $16.99
Grades: 9 10 11 12 **Fic**
1. Adventure fiction 2. Europe -- Fiction 3. Assassins -- Fiction 4. Adventure and adventurers -- Fiction
ISBN 0547601174; 9780547601175
LC 2011041392

Sequel to: Au revoir, crazy European chick

This novel, by Joe Schreiber, is the sequel to the young adult adventure "Au Revoir, Crazy European Chick." "The last time [Perry] saw Gobi, five people were assassinated one crazy night in New York City. Well . . . Gobi shows up, and once again Perry is roped into a wild, nonstop thrill ride with a body count. Double crossings, kidnappings, CIA agents, arms dealers, boat chases in Venetian canals, and a shootout in the middle of a Santa Claus convention ensue." (Publisher's note)

Schroeder, Lisa

Chasing Brooklyn. Simon Pulse 2010 412p $15.99
Grades: 7 8 9 10 **Fic**
1. Novels in verse 2. Dreams -- Fiction 3. Bereavement -- Fiction
ISBN 978-1-4169-9168-7; 1-4169-9168-9
LC 2009-19442

As teenagers Brooklyn and Nico work to help each other recover from the deaths of Brooklyn's boyfriend—Nico's brother Lucca—and their friend Gabe, the two begin to rediscover their passion for life, and a newly blossoming passion for one another.

"Chasing Brooklyn is told in a verse format that enables the author to cut right to the emotional quick. The short sentences and minimal dialogue keep the focus on the pain and fear of the two main characters. . . . While the wrenching impact will leave readers raw, the ultimately hopeful ending is comforting. A quick read, but one with substance." SLJ

Far from you. Simon Pulse 2009 355p $15.99
Grades: 7 8 9 10 **Fic**
1. Novels in verse 2. Snow -- Fiction 3. Stepfamilies -- Fiction
ISBN 978-1-4169-7506-9; 1-4169-7506-3
LC 2008-25268

A novel-in-verse about sixteen-year-old Ali's reluctant road trip with her stepmother and new baby sister, and the terror that ensues after they end up lost in the snow-covered woods.

"Schroeder weaves Alice in Wonderland . . . references throughout the book to echo the topsy-turvy nature of her protagonist's life. It is this roller coaster of emotions to which many teen readers will relate. A quick, yet satisfying, novel in verse." SLJ

Schröder, Monika

My brother's shadow. Farrar Straus Giroux 2011 217p $16.99
Grades: 6 7 8 9 10 **Fic**
1. Germany -- Fiction 2. Journalism -- Fiction 3. Family life -- Fiction 4. Political activists -- Fiction 5. World War, 1914-1918 -- Fiction
ISBN 978-0-374-35122-9; 0-374-35122-8
LC 2010033107

In 1918 Berlin, Germany, sixteen-year-old Moritz struggles to do what is right on his newspaper job, in his relationship with his mother and sister who are outspoken socialists, and with his brother, who returns from the war physically and emotionally scarred.

"In this nuanced and realistic work of historical fiction, Schröder . . . immerses readers in her setting with meticulous details and dynamic characters that contribute to a palpable sense of tension." Publ Wkly

Schumacher, Julie

★ **Black** box; a novel. Delacorte Press 2008 168p $15.99; lib bdg $18.99
Grades: 8 9 10 11 12 **Fic**
1. School stories 2. Sisters -- Fiction 3. Family life -- Fiction 4. Depression (Psychology) -- Fiction
ISBN 978-0-385-73542-1; 0-385-73542-1; 978-0-385-90523-7 lib bdg; 0-385-90523-8 lib bdg
LC 2007-45774

When her sixteen-year-old sister is hospitalized for depression and her parents want to keep it a secret, fourteen-year-old Elena tries to cope with her own anxiety and feelings of guilt that she is determined to conceal from outsiders.

"The writing is spare, direct, and honest. Written in the first person, this is a readable, ultimately uplifting book about a difficult subject." SLJ

Schwab, Victoria

Near Witch. Hyperion Books 2011 282p $16.99

Grades: 7 8 9 10 **Fic**

1. Witches -- Fiction 2. Villages -- Fiction 3. Supernatural -- Fiction

ISBN 978-1-4231-3787-0; 1-4231-3787-6

LC 2010036289

Sixteen-year-old Lexi, who lives on an enchanted moor at the edge of the village of Near, must solve the mystery when, the day after a mysterious boy appears in town, children start disappearing.

"Part fairy tale, part legend with a little romance, this well-written mystery will capture the attention of teens." SLJ

Schwartz, Ellen

Cellular; written by Ellen Schwartz. Orca Book Publishers 2010 115p (Orca soundings) pa $9.95

Grades: 7 8 9 10 **Fic**

1. Leukemia -- Fiction 2. Friendship -- Fiction

ISBN 978-1-55469-296-5; 1-55469-296-2

When Brendan is diagnosed with leukemia, his life is turned upside down. With smothering family, and distant friends, all seems hopeless until he meets Lark, terminally ill, and yet full of life.

"In this emotional entry in the Orca Soundings series, Lark's sweetness and wisdom spin out on a trajectory that readers just know will not end happily for her, even though Brendan realizes she has touched his life mightily." Booklist

Schwartz, Virginia Frances

Send one angel down. Holiday House 2000 163p $15.95 **Fic**

1. Cousins -- Fiction 2. Slavery -- Fiction 3. Racially-mixed people 4. African Americans -- Fiction 5. Racially mixed people -- Fiction

ISBN 0-8234-1484-1

LC 99-52818

Abram, a young slave tries to hide the horrors of slavery from his younger cousin Eliza, a light-skinned slave who is the daughter of the plantation owner

"Schwartz's well-developed characters are full of humanity and personality, and the story vividly acknowledges the sustaining power of music . . . in the lives of the slaves. This is a profoundly moving tale that is ultimately hopeful but never glosses over the horrific treatment of slaves." Booklist

Scieszka, Jon, 1954-

Who done it? an investigation of murder most foul. conducted by Jon Scieszka and you, the reader. Soho Teen, an imprint of Soho Press, Inc. 2013 373 p. (hardcover) $17.99

Grades: 9 10 11 12 **Fic**

1. Mystery fiction 2. Humorous fiction 3. Authors -- Fiction 4. Humorous stories 5. Authorship -- Fiction

ISBN 1616951524; 9781616951528

LC 2012033468

In this juvenile mystery, by Jon Scieszka, "the most cantankerous book editor alive . . . is Herman Mildew. The anthology opens with an invitation to a party, care of this . . . monster, where more than 80 of the most . . . recognizable names in . . . fiction learn that they are suspects in his murder. All must provide alibis in brief first-person entries. The problem is that all of them are liars, all of them are fabulists, and all have something to hide." (Publisher's note)

Scott, Elizabeth

Between here and forever. Simon Pulse 2011 250p $16.99; ebook $9.99

Grades: 9 10 11 12 **Fic**

1. Coma -- Fiction 2. Sisters -- Fiction

ISBN 978-1-4169-9484-8; 978-1-4169-9486-2 ebook

LC 2010051366

When her older, "perfect" sister Tess has a car accident that puts her in a coma, seventeen-year-old Abby, who has always felt unseen in Tess's shadow, plans to bring her back with the help of Eli, a gorgeous boy she has met at the hospital, but her plans go awry when she learns some secrets about both Tess and Eli, enabling her to make some decisions about her own life.

"Abby's emotional growth from her experiences, conversations and introspection emerges ever so slowly but will satisfy many teen readers. Leisurely but gratifying." Kirkus

Grace. Dutton Books 2010 200p $16.99

Grades: 8 9 10 11 12 **Fic**

1. Fantasy fiction 2. Despotism -- Fiction 3. Insurgency -- Fiction

ISBN 978-0-525-42206-8; 0-525-42206-4

LC 2009-53285

Sixteen-year-old Grace travels on a decrepit train toward a border that may not exist, recalling events that brought her to choose life over being a suicide bomber, and dreaming of freedom from the extremist religion-based government of Keran Berj

"Moody and compelling, without the easy moralizing so common in dystopian settings." Kirkus

★ **Living** dead girl. Simon Pulse 2008 170p $16.99; pa $8.99

Grades: 9 10 11 12 **Fic**

1. Kidnapping -- Fiction 2. Child sexual abuse -- Fiction

ISBN 978-1-4169-6059-1; 1-4169-6059-7; 978-1-4169-6060-7 pa; 1-4169-6060-0 pa

LC 2007-943736

A novel about a 15-year-old girl who has spent the last five years being abused by a kidnapper named Ray and is kept powerless by Ray's promise to harm her family if she makes one false move.

"Scott's prose is spare and damning, relying on suggestive details and their impact on Alice to convey the unimaginable violence she repeatedly experiences. Disturbing but fascinating, the book exerts an inescapable grip on readers—like Alice, they have virtually no choice but to continue until the conclusion sets them free." Publ Wkly

Love you hate you miss you. HarperTeen 2009 276p $16.99; lib bdg $17.89; pa $8.99

Grades: 9 10 11 12 **Fic**

1. School stories 2. Death -- Fiction 3. Guilt -- Fiction

4. Alcoholism -- Fiction 5. Friendship -- Fiction
ISBN 978-0-06-112283-5; 0-06-112283-1; 978-0-06-112284-2 lib bdg; 0-06-112284-X lib bdg; 978-0-06-112285-9 pa; 0-06-112285-8 pa

LC 2008-31420

After coming out of alcohol rehabilitation, sixteen-year-old Amy sorts out conflicting emotions about her best friend Julia's death in a car accident for which she feels responsible.

"The pain, confusion, insights, and hope Amy expresses will speak to teen readers. The issue of binge drinking is handled clearly and bluntly, and without preaching: readers understand why Amy drinks and why she stops." Voice Youth Advocates

Miracle; Elizabeth Scott. Simon Pulse 2012 217 p. (hbk.) $16.99
Grades: 9 10 11 12 **Fic**

1. Aircraft accidents -- Fiction 2. Interpersonal relations -- Fiction 3. Post-traumatic stress disorder -- Fiction 4. Survival -- Fiction 5. Family life -- Fiction
ISBN 1442417064; 9781442417069

LC 2011008655

This book's main character, Megan, is the sole survivor of a plane crash, and is hailed as a miracle. "However, when Megan returns to her small, rural hometown, she feels overwhelmed by both the onslaught of well-wishers and the slowly returning memories of the crash and its victims. Megan is most challenged by her parents, who are unable to see beyond her miraculous escape and fail to recognize that she is suffering from post-traumatic stress disorder (PTSD) and seriously needs help." (Kirkus Reviews)

Perfect you. Simon Pulse 2008 304p pa $9.99
Grades: 7 8 9 10 **Fic**

1. School stories 2. Friendship -- Fiction 3. Family life -- Fiction
ISBN 978-1-4169-5355-5 pa; 1-4169-5355-8 pa

LC 2007-929324

"Kate's father quit his job and is now living his dream by selling infomercial vitamins at a mall kiosk. The teen's college-graduate brother is living on the couch, her mother is working two jobs, and her friend Anna isn't talking to her now that Anna has lost weight and become popular. Making Kate's life completely miserable, her overbearing grandmother has moved in, and Will, the boy Kate tries to pretend she doesn't like because of their contentious history, is constantly making approaches. . . . Scott does a good job portraying a teen who is simultaneously self-centered and sympathetic. . . . Supporting characters are well fleshed out, and the ending, while encouraging, isn't all sunshine and roses, making it believable as well as hopeful." SLJ

Stealing Heaven. HarperTeen 2008 307p $16.99; lib bdg $17.89; pa $8.99
Grades: 7 8 9 10 **Fic**

1. Thieves -- Fiction 2. Mother-daughter relationship -- Fiction
ISBN 978-0-06-112280-4; 0-06-112280-7; 978-0-06-112281-1 lib bdg; 0-06-112281-5 lib bdg; 978-0-06-112282-8 pa; 0-06-112282-3 pa

Eighteen-year-old Dani grows weary of her life as a thief when she and her mother move to a town where Dani feels like she can put down roots.

"Witty dialogue gives a new perspective full of hope to YAs who feel trapped between family and friends." KLIATT

Scott, Kieran, 1974-

Geek magnet; a novel in five acts. G.P. Putnam's Sons 2008 308p $16.99
Grades: 7 8 9 10 **Fic**

1. School stories 2. Theater -- Fiction 3. Dating (Social customs) -- Fiction
ISBN 978-0-399-24760-6; 0-399-24760-2

LC 2007-28707

Seventeen-year-old KJ Miller is determined to lose the label of "geek magnet" and get the guy of her dreams, all while stage managing the high school musical, with the help of the most popular girl in school.

"An enjoyable, touching read about self-discovery with a hopeful ending that avoids too-neat resolutions." Booklist

She's so dead to us. Simon & Schuster 2010 278p $16.99
Grades: 8 9 10 11 12 **Fic**

1. School stories 2. Friendship -- Fiction 3. New Jersey -- Fiction 4. Social classes -- Fiction
ISBN 978-1-4169-9951-5; 1-4169-9951-5

LC 2009-46739

Told in two voices, high school juniors Allie, who now lives on the poor side of town, and Jake, the "Crestie" whose family bought her house, develop feelings for one another that are complicated by her former friends, his current ones, who refuse to forgive her for her father's bad investment that cost them all.

"In this successful blend of class struggle, betrayal, and forbidden romance, Scott creates an unpredictable and timely story." Horn Book Guide

Followed by He's so not worth it (2011)

This is so not happening; Kieran Scott. Simon & Schuster. 2012 315 p. (hardcover) $16.99
Grades: 7 8 9 10 **Fic**

1. Love stories 2. Teenage parents -- Fiction 3. Dating (Social customs) -- Fiction 4. Babies -- Fiction 5. New Jersey -- Fiction 6. High schools -- Fiction 7. Social classes -- Fiction 8. Teenage fathers -- Fiction 9. Teenage mothers -- Fiction 10. Family life -- New Jersey -- Fiction
ISBN 1416999558; 9781416999553

LC 2011041612

In this book, the third in a series, "constantly thwarted lovers Ally and Jake finally establish a firm boyfriend-girlfriend relationship during their senior year in high school. . . . Ally learns that her former best friend Chloe is pregnant and saying that Jake is the father. Because the brief encounter between the two occurred outside of their formal relationship, Ally decides to forgive Jake and stick with him, even as he becomes ever more obsessed with the baby." (Kirkus Reviews)

Scott, Michael

★ The **alchemyst.** Delacorte Press 2007 375p (The secrets of the immortal Nicholas Flammel) $16.99; lib bdg $19.99

Grades: 7 8 9 10 **Fic**

1. Magic -- Fiction 2. Twins -- Fiction 3. Alchemy -- Fiction 4. Writers on science 5. Siblings -- Fiction

ISBN 978-0-385-73357-1; 0-385-73357-7; 978-0-385-90372-1 lib bdg; 0-385-90372-3 lib bdg

LC 2006-24417

While working at pleasant but mundane summer jobs in San Francisco, fifteen-year-old twins, Sophie and Josh, suddenly find themselves caught up in the deadly, centuries-old struggle between rival alchemists, Nicholas Flamel and John Dee, over the possession of an ancient and powerful book holding the secret formulas for alchemy and everlasting life.

"Scott uses a gigantic canvas for this riveting fantasy. . . . A fabulous read." SLJ

Other titles in this series are:
The magician (2008)
The sorceress (2009)
The necromancer (2010)
The warlock (2011)

The **enchantress**; Michael Scott. Delacorte Press 2012 517 p. $18.99

Grades: 7 8 9 10 **Fic**

1. Atlantis -- Fiction 2. Monsters -- Fiction 3. Time travel -- Fiction 4. Flamel, Nicolas, d. 1418 -- Fiction 5. Magic -- Fiction 6. Twins -- Fiction 7. Alchemists -- Fiction 8. Supernatural -- Fiction 9. Brothers and sisters -- Fiction

ISBN 0385735359; 9780385735353

LC 2012006497

In this book, the final installment of the "Secrets of the Immortal Nicholas Flamel" series, "Nicholas Flamel and his beloved wife, Perenelle, are making a final stand to save San Francisco from an attack of monsters large and small, launched from Alcatraz Island by Quetzalcoatl. Twins Josh (Gold) and Sophie (Silver) are being staged to take power from Aten and become rulers of an overthrown Danu Talis 10,000 years earlier." (Booklist)

"[Scott] fully fleshes out his main characters in their final roles, realistically and sometimes surprisingly melding their lives, their deaths, and their futures. This is a powerful and tidy conclusion to [the] series." Booklist

Scott, Mindi

Freefall. Simon Pulse 2010 315p pa $7.99

Grades: 8 9 10 11 12 **Fic**

1. Alcoholism -- Fiction 2. Bereavement -- Fiction 3. Rock musicians -- Fiction

ISBN 978-1-4424-0278-2; 1-4424-0278-4

LC 2010-12663

Seth, a bass guitar player in a teen rock band, deals with alcoholism, his best friend's death, and first love.

"Seth's character arc is fully realized, without the burden of too much introspection or weighty insight to bog down the pace of the narrative. . . . This is a solid exploration of what you can and can't do to help your friends, built on top of an engaging story of boy meets girl." Bull Cent Child Books

Live through this; Mindi Scott. Simon Pulse 2012 289 p. (hc) $16.99

Grades: 9 10 11 12 **Fic**

1. Stepfamilies -- Fiction 2. Family secrets -- Fiction 3. Child sexual abuse -- Fiction 4. Incest -- Fiction 5. Secrets -- Fiction 6. Sexual abuse -- Fiction 7. Family life -- Washington (State) -- Fiction

ISBN 1442440597; 9781442440593; 9781442440609; 9781442440616

LC 2012006006

In this young adult novel, by Mindi Scott, "Coley Sterling's . . . stepdad is a successful attorney who gives Coley and her siblings everything, and her mother . . . escaped ten years ago from the abuse of Coley's real father. But Coley is keeping a lot of secrets. She won't admit . . . that her almost-perfect life is her own carefully crafted façade. Now, Coley and Reece are getting closer, and a decade's worth of Coley's lies are on the verge of unraveling." (Publisher's note)

Includes bibliographical references

Scrimger, Richard

Me & death; an afterlife adventure. Tundra Books 2010 187p pa $12.95

Grades: 7 8 9 10 **Fic**

1. Death -- Fiction 2. Future life -- Fiction

ISBN 978-0-88776-796-8 pa; 0-88776-796-6 pa

"Jim isn't an easy guy to like. . . . While he is chasing another kid, he falls in front of an oncoming car. So begins his epic journey into the afterlife, in which he is shown scenes from his past by three different ghosts, all of whom have a key to his future in the real world. . . . Scrimger creates unpredictable, sad, and authentic scenes that enliven the story. . . . Scrimger's novel is a difficult, compelling read that taps into teens' fascination with death, as well as the line between good and bad behavior." Booklist

Seamon, Hollis

★ **Somebody** up there hates you; a novel. by Hollis Seamon. 1st ed. Algonquin 2013 256 p. (hardcover) $16.95

Grades: 9 10 11 12 **Fic**

1. Cancer -- Fiction 2. Parties -- Fiction 3. Terminally ill children -- Fiction 4. Terminally ill -- Fiction 5. Hospices (Terminal care) -- Fiction

ISBN 1616202602; 9781616202606

LC 2013008476

This book follows Richie, a 17-year-old with terminal cancer. "Richie's uncle takes him out for a night of partying; girls start paying attention to him (and not just Sylvie, the 15-year-old across the hall); there are pranks and fistfights; and Richie gets a chance to be a normal teenager—or as normal as possible, given that he's surrounded by nurses, never knows how he'll feel next, and the annoying harpist in the lobby just keeps playing." (Publishers Weekly)

Sedgwick, Marcus

My swordhand is singing. Wendy Lamb Books 2007 205p hardcover o.p. pa $6.99

Grades: 7 8 9 10 **Fic**

1. Horror fiction 2. Gypsies -- Fiction 3. Vampires

-- Fiction 4. Supernatural -- Fiction
ISBN 978-0-375-84689-2; 978-0-375-84690-8 pa
LC 2007-07051

In the dangerous dark of winter in an Eastern European village during the early seventeenth century, Peter learns from a gypsy girl that the Shadow Queen is behind the recent murders and reanimations, and his father's secret past may hold the key to stopping her.

"Sedgwick writes a compellingly fresh vampire story, combining elements from ancient myths and legends to create a believable and frightening tale." Voice Youth Advocates

★ **Revolver**. Roaring Brook Press 2010 204p $16.99
Grades: 7 8 9 10 **Fic**

1. Death -- Fiction 2. Siblings -- Fiction 3. Arctic regions -- Fiction 4. Alaska -- Gold discoveries -- Fiction
ISBN 978-1-59643-592-6; 1-59643-592-5
First published 2009 in the United Kingdom
A Michael L. Printz honor book, 2011

In an isolated cabin, fourteen-year-old Sig is alone with a corpse: his father, who has fallen through the ice and frozen to death only hours earlier. Then comes a stranger claiming that Sig's father owes him a share of a horde of stolen gold. Sig's only protection is a loaded Colt revolver hidden in the cabin's storeroom.

"Tight plotting and a wealth of moral concerns—good versus evil; faith, love, and hope; the presence of God; survival in a bleak landscape; trusting the lessons parents teach—make this a memorable tale." Horn Book

★ **She** is not invisible; Marcus Sedgwick. Roaring Brook Press 2014 224 p. (hardback) $16.99
Grades: 7 8 9 10 11 12 **Fic**

1. Mystery fiction 2. Blind 3. Missing persons 4. Brothers and sisters 5. Blind -- Fiction 6. Fathers -- Fiction 7. Missing persons -- Fiction 8. Mystery and detective stories 9. Brothers and sisters -- Fiction 10. People with disabilities -- Fiction
ISBN 1596438010; 9781596438019
LC 2013029561

"Laureth is sixteen, smart, self-doubting, and blind. She is also desperate to find her missing famous writer father -- desperate enough to boost her mother's credit card to buy two plane tickets from London to New York City, forge travel documents, and "abduct" her beloved seven-year-old brother in order to disguise her blindness... Laureth herself is worth the journey. The tricks she uses to negotiate in a sighted world.. her determination to fight the tendency of sighted people to treat blind people as stupid or deaf or, most insidiously, invisible -- all are presented matter-of-factly and sympathetically. Readers will applaud Laureth's believable evolution into a more confident -- and definitely more visible -- young woman." (Horn Book)

★ **White** crow. Roaring Brook Press 2011 234p $15.99
Grades: 8 9 10 11 12 **Fic**

1. Horror fiction 2. Villages -- Fiction 3. Friendship -- Fiction 4. Good and evil -- Fiction 5. Great Britain -- Fiction
ISBN 978-1-59643-594-0; 1-59643-594-1
LC 2010034053

Sixteen-year-old Rebecca moves with her father from London to a small, seaside village, where she befriends another motherless girl and they spend the summer together exploring the village's sinister history.

"Showing his customary skill with a gothic setting and morally troubled characters, Sedgwick keeps readers guessing to the very end." Publ Wkly

Seigel, Andrea

The **kid** table. Bloomsbury Children's Books 2010 306p $16.99
Grades: 10 11 12 **Fic**

1. Cousins -- Fiction 2. Family life -- Fiction
ISBN 978-1-59990-480-1
LC 2010-4540

Explores the quirky dynamics in an extended family full of close-knit cousins who both help and hinder each other as they celebrate holidays and momentous occasions together.

"Laugh-out-loud humor punctuates . . . [Ingrid's] clear-eyed musings about family and relationships, narrated in a perceptive, analytical, with-it voice. . . . Teen girls in particular will enjoy this unusual coming-of-age novel." Voice Youth Advocates

Like the red panda. Harcourt 2004 280p pa $13
Grades: 9 10 11 12 **Fic**

1. School stories 2. Orphans -- Fiction 3. Suicide -- Fiction 4. California -- Fiction
ISBN 0-15-603024-1
LC 2003-17164

"Seigel's novel is a keen portrait of young American angst and all its ironic posturing. The result veers between an earnest critique of the Columbine era and Heathers-like parody, which leaves its conclusion half tragedy, half punch line." Publ Wkly

Selfors, Suzanne

Coffeehouse angel. Walker & Co. 2009 276p $16.99
Grades: 7 8 9 10 **Fic**

1. School stories 2. Angels -- Fiction 3. Wishes -- Fiction 4. Grandmothers -- Fiction
ISBN 978-0-8027-9812-1; 0-8027-9812-8
LC 2008-33333

Sixteen-year-old Katrina's kindness to a man she finds sleeping behind her grandmother's coffeehouse leads to a strange reward as Malcolm, who is actually a teenage guardian angel, insists on rewarding her by granting her deepest wish.

"This light read is right for teens struggling with self-confidence issues. . . . Although the protagonist deals with loneliness, illness, aging, and competition in this coming-of-age novel, it is a humorous read." Voice Youth Advocates

Mad love. Walker Books for Young Readers 2011 323p $16.99
Grades: 7 8 9 10 **Fic**

1. Love stories 2. Authorship -- Fiction 3. Eros (Greek deity) -- Fiction 4. Manic-depressive illness -- Fiction

5. Mother-daughter relationship -- Fiction
ISBN 978-0-8027-8450-6; 0-8027-8450-X
LC 2010-23261

When her famous romance-novelist mother is secretly hospitalized in an expensive mental facility, sixteen-year-old Alice tries to fulfill her mother's contract with her publisher by writing a love story—with the help of Cupid.

"There's a bit of mythology, a bit of romance, a bit of the paranormal, and some real-life problems, but Selfors juggles them all assuredly. Serious ideas are handled carefully, while real humor is spread throughout the whole book. This book has real charm with great depth." Voice Youth Advocates

★ **Saving** Juliet. Walker & Co. 2008 242p $16.95
Grades: 7 8 9 10 11 12 **Fic**
1. Actors -- Fiction 2. Theater -- Fiction 3. Space and time -- Fiction
ISBN 978-0-8027-9740-7; 0-8027-9740-7
LC 2007-18528

Seventeen-year-old Mimi Wallingford's stage fright and fight with her mother on the closing night of Romeo and Juliet are nothing compared to the troubles she faces when she and her leading man are transported to Shakespeare's Verona, where she decides to give the real Juliet a happy ending.

This is "hilarious and often very clever. . . . Readers will have fun with the characters. . . . Mimi . . . is an honest savvy narrator." Publ Wkly

The **sweetest** spell; Suzanne Selfors. Walker & Co. 2012 404 p. (hardback) $16.99
Grades: 7 8 9 10 11 12 **Fic**
1. Love stories 2. Fantasy fiction 3. People with physical disabilities -- Fiction 4. Fantasy 5. Magic -- Fiction 6. Chocolate -- Fiction 7. Prejudices -- Fiction 8. People with disabilities -- Fiction
ISBN 0802723764; 9780802723765
LC 2011034591

This book follows "Emmeline . . . an outcast among her people, the Kell. When the king enslaves the men and her village is destroyed in a flood, Emmeline is taken in by Owen Oak and his family. She discovers that she can churn butter into chocolate -- a food that's been lost for years in the land of Anglund. Romance blossoms, but the two are separated when the girl is kidnapped for her magical abilities." (School Library Journal)

"Selfors's story line initially comes across as chaotic, but the pacing is strong, and the elements of her tale fall into place in a logical and entirely satisfying manner. An exhilarating, romantic, and frequently funny story of self-discovery." Pub Wkly

Selzer, Adam

How to get suspended and influence people; a novel. Delacorte Press 2007 183p $15.99; lib bdg $18.99
Grades: 6 7 8 9 **Fic**
1. School stories 2. Censorship -- Fiction 3. Motion pictures -- Fiction
ISBN 978-0-385-73369-4; 978-0-385-90384-4 lib bdg
LC 2006-20438

Gifted eighth-grader Leon Harris becomes an instant celebrity when the film he makes for a class project sends him to in-school suspension.

"This funny, fast-paced novel is filled with characters who epitomize the middle school experience, and it presents a lesson or two about free speech as well." SLJ

Another title about Leon is:
Pirates of the retail wasteland (2008)

I kissed a zombie, and I liked it. Delacorte Press 2010 177p lib bdg $12.99; pa $7.99
Grades: 7 8 9 10 **Fic**
1. Zombies -- Fiction 2. Vampires -- Fiction 3. Dating (Social customs) -- Fiction
ISBN 978-0-385-90497-1 lib bdg; 0-385-90497-5 lib bdg; 978-0-385-73503-2 pa; 0-385-73503-0 pa
LC 2009-24052

Living in the post-human era when the undead are part of everyday life, high schooler Alley breaks her no-dating rule when Doug catches her eye, but classmate Will demands to turn her into a vampire and her zombie boyfriend may be unable to stop him.

"With snappy dialogue and a light, funny touch, Selzer creates a readable examination of love, self-sacrifice, and where to draw the line before you lose yourself." Publ Wkly

Sepetys, Ruta

★ **Between** shades of gray; Ruta Sepetys. Philomel Books 2011 344p map $17.99
Grades: 8 9 10 11 12 **Fic**
1. Lithuania -- Fiction 2. Soviet Union -- Fiction
ISBN 978-0-399-25412-3; 0-399-25412-9
LC 2009-50092

In this novel by Ruta Sepetys, "Fifteen-year-old Lina is a Lithuanian girl living an ordinary life--until Soviet officers invade her home and tear her family apart. Separated from her father and forced onto a crowded train, Lina, her mother, and her young brother make their way to a Siberian work camp, where they are forced to fight for their lives." (Publisher's note)

"A harrowing page-turner, made all the more so for its basis in historical fact, the novel illuminates the persecution suffered by Stalin's victims (20 million were killed), while presenting memorable characters who retain their will to survive even after more than a decade in exile." Publ Wkly

★ **Out** of the Easy; Ruta Sepetys. Philomel Books 2013 352 p. $17.99
Grades: 9 10 11 12 **Fic**
1. Mystery fiction 2. Historical fiction 3. Prostitution -- Fiction 4. New Orleans (La.) -- Fiction 5. Murder -- Fiction 6. Prostitition -- Fiction 7. Conduct of life -- Fiction 8. Mothers and daughters -- Fiction 9. New Orleans (La.) -- History -- 20th century -- Fiction
ISBN 039925692X; 9780399256929
LC 2012016062

This book, by Ruta Sepetys, is set in "1950 [in] . . . the French Quarter of New Orleans. . . . Known among locals as the daughter of a brothel prostitute, Josie Moraine wants more out of life than the Big Easy has to offer. She devises a plan get out, but a mysterious death in the Quarter leaves Josie tangled in an investigation that will challenge her allegiance to her mother, her conscience, and Willie Woodley, the brusque madam on Conti Street." (Publisher's note)

Service, Pamela F.

Tomorrow's magic; [by] Pamela F. Service. 1st ed.; Random House 2007 437p $15.99; lib bdg $18.99; pa $7.99

Grades: 7 8 9 10 **Fic**

1. Fantasy fiction 2. Science fiction 3. Kings 4. Magic -- Fiction 5. Merlin (Legendary character) -- Fiction 6. Morgan le Fay (Legendary character) -- Fiction

ISBN 978-0-375-84087-6; 0-375-84087-7; 978-0-375-94087-3 lib bdg; 0-375-94087-1 lib bdg; 978-0-375-84087-6 pa; 0-375-84088-5 pa

LC 2006016131

First published in two volumes by Atheneum: Winter of magic's return (1985), Tomorrow's magic (1987)

Two novels in which a young, resurrected Merlin and two friends attempt to bring King Arthur back to Britain, then struggle against the evil plots of Morgan Le Fey to build a new and better civilization in the wake of a nuclear holocaust.

"Service has done a terrific job melding futuristic science fiction with ancient Arthurian legend." Horn Book Guide

Yesterday's magic; [by] Pamela F. Service. Random House 2008 216p $16.99

Grades: 7 8 9 10 **Fic**

1. Fantasy fiction 2. Science fiction 3. Kings 4. Magic -- Fiction 5. Merlin (Legendary character) -- Fiction 6. Morgan le Fay (Legendary character) -- Fiction

ISBN 978-0-375-85577-1; 0-375-85577-7

"When Heather McKenna is kidnapped by the sorceress Morgan LeFay, it is up to Heather's friend Welly and the wizard Merlin . . . to rescue her. Set 500 years in the future, following a nuclear devastation, the technological world has ground to a halt, but magic is beginning to take hold again." Publisher's note

The **Shadowhunter's** codex; being a record of the ways and laws of the Nephilim, the chosen of the Angel Raziel. as compiled by Cassandra Clare & Joshua Lewis. Margaret K. McElderry Books 2013 274 p. (hardcover : alk. paper) $19.99

Grades: 9 10 11 12 **Fic**

1. Fantasy fiction 2. Magic -- Fiction 3. Demonology -- Fiction 4. Supernatural -- Fiction

ISBN 1442416920; 9781442416925; 9781442496828

LC 2013008628

"Intended as the ultimate resource for the young Shadowhunter in Clare's enormously successful Mortal Instruments and Infernal Devices series, this serves as a behind-the-scenes guide to heroine Clary's world, as it is supposed to be her personal copy of the Codex. Including chapters and sections titled Bestiaire Part I: Demonologie; Angelic Magic; and The Rise of Nephilim in the World, it also sports scribblings and notes taken by Clary and her two friends, Simon and Jace, who occasionally snatched away her Codex to add their own thoughts...An excellent addendum to the complex world Clare has built and meant for the serious fan." (Booklist)

Shahan, Sherry

Death mountain; [by] Sherry Shahan. 1st ed.; Peachtree 2005 202p $15.95

Grades: 5 6 7 8 **Fic**

1. Wilderness survival -- Fiction

ISBN 1-56145-353-6

LC 2005010820

"A day trip to a mountain lake turns to disaster when lightning strikes a pack mule, a mud slide kills a horse, and hikers scatter, seeking shelter. Erin, 14, leaves her new friend Levi with the injured hikers to search for his sister, Mae, who has run off-trail in the confusion. . . . A great addition to the adventure-survival genre." SLJ

Shan, Darren

Lord Loss; [by] Darren Shan. 1st U.S. ed.; Little, Brown 2005 233p (Demonata) hardcover o.p. pa $8.99

Grades: 7 8 9 10 **Fic**

1. Horror fiction 2. Young adult literature -- Works

ISBN 0-316-11499-5; 0-316-01233-5 pa

LC 2005-0145

Presumably the only witness to the horrific and bloody murder of his entire family, a teenage boy must outwit not only the mental health professionals determined to cure his delusion, but also the demonic forces only he can see.

"The plot rolls along at high speed, but Shan is still quite adept when it comes to capturing Grubbs' roller-coaster emotions." Booklist

Other titles in this series are:

Demon thief (2006)

Slawter (2006)

Bec (2007)

Blood beast (2007)

Demon apocalypse (2008)

Death's shadow (2008)

Wolf island (2009)

Dark calling (2009)

The **thin** executioner. Little, Brown 2010 483p map $17.99

Grades: 10 11 12 **Fic**

1. Slavery -- Fiction 2. Conduct of life -- Fiction 3. Capital punishment -- Fiction 4. Voyages and travels -- Fiction

ISBN 978-0-316-07865-8; 0-316-07865-4

LC 2009-45606

In a nation of warriors where weakness is shunned and all crimes, no matter how minor, are punishable by beheading, young Jebel Rum, along with a slave who is fated to be sacrificed, sets forth on a quest to petition the Fire God for invincibility, but when the long and arduous journey is over, Jebel has learned much about fairness and the value of life.

"Readers will hate the villains, feel sorry for the innocent, and root for Tel Hesani and Jebel to complete their mission. This is a must-read for thrill seekers with a strong stomach looking for an action-packed adventure with a host of fantastical creatures." Voice Youth Advocates

Shanahan, Lisa

★ The **sweet,** terrible, glorious year I truly, completely lost it. Delacorte Press 2007 297p $15.99; lib bdg $18.99

Grades: 7 8 9 10 **Fic**

1. School stories 2. Theater -- Fiction 3. Family life -- Fiction

ISBN 978-0-385-73516-2; 0-385-73516-2; 978-0-385-90505-3 lib bdg; 0-385-90505-X lib bdg

LC 2006-101158

Fourteen-year-old Gemma Stone struggles to understand her shifting emotions as her older sister plans her wedding, she overcomes her nerves and tries out for the school play, and she gets to know one of the most notorious boys in her class.

"Shanahan's quirky characters are a riot, but the depth of Gemma's growth and heartbreak is profound." SLJ

Sharenow, Rob

★ **My** mother the cheerleader; a novel. Laura Geringer Books 2007 288p hardcover o.p. pa $8.99

Grades: 7 8 9 10 **Fic**

1. Race relations -- Fiction 2. New Orleans (La.) -- Fiction 3. School integration -- Fiction 4. Mother-daughter relationship -- Fiction

ISBN 978-0-06-114896-5; 0-06-114896-2; 978-0-06-114898-9 pa; 0-06-114898-9 pa

LC 2006-21716

Thirteen-year-old Louise uncovers secrets about her family and her neighborhood during the violent protests over school desegregation in 1960 New Orleans.

"Through inquisitive Louise's perspective, readers get a wrenching look at the era's turmoil and pervasive racism." Publ Wkly

Sharenow, Rob

The **Berlin** Boxing Club. HarperTeen 2011 404p il $17.99

Grades: 7 8 9 10 **Fic**

1. Boxers (Persons) 2. Boxing -- Fiction 3. Family life -- Fiction 4. Jews -- Germany -- Fiction 5. Berlin (Germany) -- Fiction 6. National socialism -- Fiction 7. Holocaust, 1933-1945 -- Fiction 8. Germany -- History -- 1933-1945 -- Fiction

ISBN 978-0-06-157968-4; 0-06-157968-8

LC 2010024446

In 1936 Berlin, fourteen-year-old Karl Stern, considered Jewish despite a non-religious upbringing, learns to box from the legendary Max Schmeling while struggling with the realities of the Holocaust.

"Readers will be drawn by the sports detail and by the close-up narrative of the daily oppression." Booklist

Shaw, Liane

Fostergirls. Second Story Press 2011 256p pa $11.95

Grades: 6 7 8 9 **Fic**

1. Foster home care -- Fiction

ISBN 978-1-897187-90-6; 1-897187-90-4

"Her name is Sadie, but she might as well be called Fostergirl. Grouphomegirl. That's how everyone thinks of her. Sadie doesn't care. . . . Her goal is to go unnoticed, to disappear. Nothing good comes from being noticed, especially if you're a fostergirl. Another new high school, another new group home. This one is lucky number 13, but who's counting? Except, this time there's a girl at her school named Rhiannon who won't let Sadie be invisible. In fact, she insists on being her friend. This friendship, and the dawning feeling that she finally belongs, might be able to restore Sadie's belief in others, and—ultimately—herself." (Publisher's note)

"Shaw's biggest challenge is making caustic, self-deprecating, and distrustful Sadie likable. Fortunately, she succeeds. Sadie, though tough as nails, narrates her story with an amusing edginess that works. Shaw keeps things PG-rated . . . while highlighting the reality of life as a foster child. . . . Readers seeking an honest account of how a girl without parents survives, this story delivers." Publ Wkly

Shaw, Susan

One of the survivors. Margaret K. McElderry Books 2009 199p $15.99

Grades: 6 7 8 9 **Fic**

1. School stories 2. Anger -- Fiction 3. Death -- Fiction 4. Fires -- Fiction 5. Guilt -- Fiction 6. Bereavement -- Fiction

ISBN 978-1-4169-6129-1; 1-4169-6129-1

LC 2008035965

When his classmates die in a school fire, fourteen-year-old Joey is haunted by their deaths and struggles to survive amidst suspicion and anger from the town.

"Shaw tackles a gut-wrenching situation in honest, solution-oriented terms that should appeal to reluctant readers. The novel is short, the plot and suspense build slowly, and the decisions required by the teens make for thought-provoking discussions." SLJ

Safe. Dutton Books 2007 168p $16.99

Grades: 7 8 9 10 **Fic**

1. Rape -- Fiction 2. Mothers -- Fiction

ISBN 978-0-525-47829-4; 0-525-47829-9

LC 2006-36428

When thirteen-year-old Tracy, whose mother died when she was three years old, is raped and beaten on the last day of school, all her feelings of security disappear and she does not know how to cope with the fear and dread that engulf her.

This is an "extraordinarily tender novel. . . . Intimate, first-person narrative honestly expresses Tracy's full range of emotions." Publ Wkly

Tunnel vision. Margaret K. McElderry Books 2011 272p $16.99

Grades: 7 8 9 10 **Fic**

1. Crime -- Fiction 2. Homicide -- Fiction 3. Witnesses -- Fiction 4. Organized crime -- Fiction

ISBN 978-1-4424-0839-5; 1-4424-0839-1

LC 2010036306

After witnessing her mother's murder, sixteen-year-old high school student Liza Wellington and her father go into the witness protection program.

"The author creates a completely believable character in Liza, who often reverts to childlike emotions only to learn the hard way that cold reality takes precedence over even dearly held wishes. Kudos for the unexpected double ending, both illusory and realistic, giving readers a choice." Kirkus

Shea, John

A **kid** from Southie; [by] John Red Shea and Michael Harmon. WestSide Books 2011 239p $16.95

Grades: 9 10 11 12 **Fic**

1. Boxing -- Fiction 2. Boston (Mass.) -- Fiction 3. Conduct of life -- Fiction 4. Organized crime -- Fiction 5. Mother-son relationship -- Fiction

ISBN 978-1-934813-53-9

LC 2010054022

Desperate to help his unemployed mother, seventeen-year-old Aiden O'Connor reluctantly begins working for the Irish mob in tough South Boston, despite his coach's efforts to convince him he could be a professional boxer.

"With lots of action, short chapters, and realistic but raw language, this one's a winner. The great cover will attract reluctant readers and the content will keep them turning the pages." SLJ

Shecter, Vicky Alvear

Cleopatra's moon. Arthur A. Levine Books 2011 353p $18.99

Grades: 8 9 10 11 12 **Fic**

1. Queens 2. Generals 3. Statesmen 4. Orators 5. Egypt -- Fiction 6. Princesses -- Fiction 7. Rome -- History -- Fiction

ISBN 978-0-545-22130-6; 0-545-22130-7

LC 2010028818

Cleopatra Selene, the only surviving daughter of Cleopatra and Marc Antony, recalls her life of pomp and splendor in Egypt and, after her parents' deaths, capitivity and treachery in Rome.

"This novel has romance, drama, heartbreak, and adventure, all rooted in an accurate and descriptive historical setting. Shecter writes about the world of ancient Egypt and Rome with wonderful detail. . . . Her characters are skillfully fictionalized." SLJ

Sheinmel, Alyssa B.

The **lucky** kind. Alfred A. Knopf 2011 201p $16.99; lib bdg $19.99

Grades: 8 9 10 11 12 **Fic**

1. Adoption -- Fiction 2. Friendship -- Fiction 3. Family life -- Fiction

ISBN 978-0-375-86785-9; 0-375-86785-6; 978-0-375-96785-6 lib bdg; 0-375-96785-0 lib bdg; 978-0-375-89866-2 e-book

LC 2010-27967

Having always felt secure within his small family, Manhattan high school junior Nick is unsettled to discover the existence of an older brother that his father put up for adoption many years ago.

"Nick's narration, ruminative yet straightforward, gives him a credible voice as he lurches unwillingly toward adulthood, and the book deftly conveys that he's really a good guy even if the situation is causing him to sink below his usual standards. The well-crafted family story offers an excellent stage for depicting the challenge facing every young adult—how to accept human responsibilty and frailty as we go through life." Bull Cent Child Books

Sheinmel, Courtney

Positively. Simon & Schuster Books for Young Readers 2009 216p $15.99

Grades: 6 7 8 9 10 **Fic**

1. Camps -- Fiction 2. Death -- Fiction 3. Friendship -- Fiction 4. Bereavement -- Fiction 5. Stepfamilies -- Fiction 6. AIDS (Disease) -- Fiction

ISBN 978-1-4169-7169-6; 1-4169-7169-6

LC 2008-35447

Thirteen-year-old Emmy, grieving over her mother who died of AIDS, resentful of having to live with her father and pregnant stepmother, and despairing about her future, finds hope at a summer camp for HIV-positive girls like herself. Includes facts about Elizabeth Glaser, one of the founders of the Pediatric AIDS Foundation.

"This valuable story discusses uncertainty, very human fears, and most important, hope. . . . It is a terrific introduction to a complex and important topic." Voice Youth Advocates

Sheldon, Dyan

Confessions of a Hollywood star. Candlewick Press 2006 202p $15.99

Grades: 7 8 9 10 **Fic**

1. Actors -- Fiction 2. Motion pictures -- Fiction

ISBN 0-7636-3075-6

Upon learning at the end of her senior year of high school that a Hollywood film is being made in her hometown, Lola stops at nothing to get a part and upstage her nemesis, Carla Santini.

"Lola's voice is once again an uproariously funny delight." Booklist

My perfect life. Candlewick Press 2002 201p $16.99; pa $5.99

Grades: 7 8 9 10 **Fic**

1. School stories 2. Interpersonal relations 3. Elections -- Fiction

ISBN 0-7636-1839-X; 0-7636-2436-5 pa

LC 2001-58118

Ella has no interest in running for class president at her suburban high school, but her off-beat friend Lola tricks her into challenging the rich and overbearing Carla Santini in a less-than-friendly race

"The story is entertaining and well written. The characters reflect the personalities and cliques of kids in any high school." SLJ

The **crazy** things girls do for love. Candlewick Press 2011 $15.99

Grades: 7 8 9 10 **Fic**

1. School stories 2. Environmental protection -- Fiction

ISBN 978-0-7636-5018-6; 0-7636-5018-8

LC 2010048434

When fashionista Sicilee, arty Maya, and antisocial Waneeda risk their reputations by joining Clifton Springs High School's Environmental Club to be near gorgeous new student Cody Lightfoot, each finds a new way of looking at the world.

"The details are laugh-out-loud funny. . . . With plenty of wry romance, the story builds to a save-the-trees climax that also brings a change in Cody." Booklist

Shepard, Jim

★ **Project** X; a novel. Alfred A. Knopf 2004 163p hardcover o.p. pa $12
Grades: 9 10 11 12 **Fic**

1. School stories 2. School violence -- Fiction
ISBN 1-4000-4071-X; 1-4000-3348-9 pa
LC 2003-47575

"Flake and Edwin are often bullied; at other times, they have the horrible feeling of being completely invisible to their classmates. Flake is even more alienated than Edwin and hatches a revenge plan involving guns that they call 'project x.' Disaster looms. . . . The vivid dialogue is sprinkled with profanity and is movingly expressive. This heartbreaking and wrenching novel will leave teens with plenty of questions and, hopefully, some answers." SLJ

Shepard, Sara

The **lying** game. HarperTeen 2010 307p $16.99
Grades: 9 10 11 12 **Fic**

1. Mystery fiction 2. Dead -- Fiction 3. Twins -- Fiction 4. Sisters -- Fiction 5. Homicide -- Fiction
ISBN 978-0-06-186970-9; 0-06-186970-8
LC 2010-40332

Seventeen-year-old Emma Paxton steps into the life of her long-lost twin Sutton to solve her murder, while Sutton looks on from her afterlife.

"Shepard keeps the action rolling and the clues confusing as she spends this installment uncovering the twins' characters but not solving the murder yet. Naturally, boys and fashion also figure into the story, fleshing out a distinctive scenario that should appeal to many teen girls." Kirkus

Shepherd, Megan

Her Dark Curiosity. Harpercollins Childrens Books 2014 432 p. $17.99
Grades: 9 10 11 12 **Fic**

1. Murder -- Fiction 2. Father-daughter relationship -- Fiction
ISBN 0062128051; 9780062128058

This sequel to The madman's daughter "continues with Juliet's return to London after her escape from her father's island. Life is somewhat easier for Juliet now that she is back—a former colleague of her father's has taken her under his wing so that she does not want for anything, she has a job developing grafted rose bushes, and her friend Lucy has welcomed her with open arms. But not all is well...While the novel can be read independently of the first title, as enough of the backstory is given to make what is happening clear, readers will have a more satisfying experience if familiar with the previous installment. The psychological questions that Prince/Jekyll raises as to evil, desire, and nature vs. nurture add a depth of richness not often seen in young adult literature." (School Library Journal)

The **madman's** daughter; Megan Shepherd. Balzer + Bray 2013 432 p. (trade bdg.) $17.99
Grades: 9 10 11 12 **Fic**

1. Mental illness -- Fiction 2. Science -- Experiments -- Fiction 3. Father-daughter relationship -- Fiction 4. Science fiction 5. Fathers and daughters -- Fiction 6. Characters in literature -- Fiction
ISBN 0062128027; 9780062128027
LC 2012004281

This book by Megan Shepherd follows the events of "H.G. Wells' 'The Island of Doctor Moreau,' as seen through the eyes of the doctor's daughter. . . . When she learns that her father inhabits an island far, far away, where he performs horrific experiments on animals via vivisection, Juliet makes her way there along with Montgomery, her father's assistant, and Edward Prince, a castaway they meet along the way." (Kirkus Reviews)

Sherlock, Patti

Letters from Wolfie. Viking 2004 232p $16.99; pa $6.99
Grades: 5 6 7 8 **Fic**

1. Dogs -- Fiction 2. Vietnam War, 1961-1975 -- Fiction
ISBN 0-670-03694-3; 0-14-240358-X pa
LC 2003-24316

Certain that he is doing the right thing by donating his dog, Wolfie, to the Army's scout program in Vietnam, thirteen-year-old Mark begins to have second thoughts when the Army refuses to say when and if Wolfie will ever return.

"In this topnotch novel, Sherlock weaves together numerous threads of emotion, information, and plot so seamlessly that readers will be surprised by how much they've learned by the time they finish this deceptively simple story." SLJ

Sherman, Delia

★ The **freedom** maze. Big Mouth House 2011 267p $16.95
Grades: 7 8 9 10 **Fic**

1. Slavery -- Fiction 2. Time travel -- Fiction 3. Race relations -- Fiction 4. Plantation life -- Fiction
ISBN 978-1-931520-30-0; 1-931520-30-5

"It's 1960, but on the decayed Fairchild sugar plantation in rural Louisiana, vestiges of a grimmer past remain-the old cottage, overgrown garden maze, relations between white and black races. Stuck for the summer in the family ancestral home under the thumb of her cranky, imperious grandmother, Sophie, 13, makes a reckless wish that lands her in 1860, enslaved-by her own ancestors. . . . Plantation life for whites and blacks unfolds in compelling, often excruciating detail. . . . Multilayered, compassionate and thought-provoking." Kirkus

Sherrard, Valerie

The **glory** wind. Fitzhenry & Whiteside 2011 222p pa $12.95
Grades: 5 6 7 8 **Fic**

1. Prejudices -- Fiction 2. Country life -- Fiction
ISBN 978-1-55455-170-5; 1-55455-170-6

Eleven-year-old Luke must come to terms with the moral prejudices of his small town in rural 1950s Ontario when he befriends Gracie, the daughter of a young widow who moves in next door.

"Luke's first person narration is fresh and emotionally true. . . . The haunting depiction of small-mindedness will leave readers wondering, as Luke comes to, about Gracie's true nature: heavenly child—or angel?" Kirkus

Sheth, Kashmira

Keeping corner. Hyperion 2007 281p hardcover o.p. pa $5.99

Grades: 7 8 9 10 11 12 **Fic**

1. Authors 2. Journalists 3. Essayists 4. Pacifists 5. Memoirists 6. India -- Fiction 7. Political leaders 8. Widows -- Fiction 9. Writers on politics 10. Women's rights -- Fiction

ISBN 978-0-7868-3859-2; 0-7868-3859-0; 978-0-7868-3860-8 pa; 0-7868-3860-4 pa

LC 2007-15314

In India in the 1940s, twelve-year-old Leela's happy, spoiled childhood ends when her husband since age nine, whom she barely knows, dies, leaving her a widow whose only hope of happiness could come from Mahatma Ghandi's social and political reforms.

Sheth "sets up a thrilling premise in which politics become achingly personal." Booklist

Shimko, Bonnie

★ The **private** thoughts of Amelia E. Rye. Farrar, Straus Giroux 2010 234p $16.99

Grades: 5 6 7 8 **Fic**

1. Friendship -- Fiction 2. Mother-daughter relationship -- Fiction

ISBN 978-0-374-36131-0; 0-374-36131-2

LC 2008048092

Growing up in a small town in upstate New York during the 1960s, 13-year-old Amelia E. Ryel, unwanted by her mother, searches for love and acceptance.

"The book is peopled with believable, multilayered characters. . . . Shimko's . . . story is original, and Amelia's distinctive voice and likable nature will have readers rooting for her in times of trouble and cheering her ultimate good fortune." Publ Wkly

Shinn, Sharon

Gateway. Viking 2009 280p $17.99

Grades: 6 7 8 9 10 **Fic**

1. Space and time -- Fiction 2. Chinese Americans -- Fiction

ISBN 978-0-670-01178-0; 0-670-01178-9

LC 2009-14002

While passing through the Arch in St. Louis, Missouri, a Chinese American teenager is transported to a parallel world where she is given a dangerous assignment.

The author's "fantasy finds the right balance between adventure and romance, while illuminating how seductive evil can be and that sometimes the best weapon one can possess is a skeptical mind." Publ Wkly

Shirvington, Jessica

Emblaze; Jessica Shirvington. Sourcebooks Fire 2013 464 p. (hardcover) $16.99

Grades: 10 11 12 **Fic**

1. Occult fiction 2. Fantasy fiction 3. Angels -- Fiction 4. Supernatural -- Fiction 5. Good and evil -- Fiction

ISBN 1402268467; 9781402268465

LC 2012037497

This book is the third installment of Jessica Shrivington's Embrace series. Here, "Violet and her Grigori brethren prepare for a battle of apocalyptic proportions. . . . Finding the time to focus and gain control over [her angel powers] is no easy feat with a father who has decided to finally show up and parent, the temptation of a partner who is also a forbidden soul mate, and an ex who plans to use her to help him open up the gates of hell." (Kirkus)

Embrace. Sourcebooks, Inc. 2012 397p

Grades: 10 11 12 **Fic**

1. Fantasy fiction 2. Angels -- Fiction 3. Teenagers -- Fiction

ISBN 9781402271250; 9781402268403

This book follows "seventeen-year-old Violet Eden, [whose] mother died in childbirth, leaving her to be raised by her detached, workaholic father. If it weren't for her best friend Steph and her trainer (and secret love) Lincoln, Violet would be very much alone. But on her 17th birthday, everything changes. Though finally being kissed by Lincoln is a dream come true, Violet learns that their romantic involvement is forbidden because he and Violet are both Grigori--half angel and half human. They're destined to be eternal partners in the battle against exiled angels on Earth, and romance would make things far too complicated. Furious with Lincoln for keeping this secret, Violet pushes him away, making room for the dark and seductive Phoenix to take hold of her heart." (Kirkus)

Shoemaker, Tim

Code of silence; Tim Shoemaker. Zondervan 2012 331 p. (hardcover) $14.99

Grades: 7 8 9 10 **Fic**

1. Youth -- Fiction 2. Secrecy -- Fiction 3. Deception -- Fiction 4. Witnesses -- Fiction 5. Christian life -- Fiction 6. Conduct of life -- Fiction 7. Robbers and outlaws -- Fiction

ISBN 9780310726531

LC 2011048880

In this crime novel for young adults by Tim Shoemaker, "thirteen-year-olds Cooper, Gordy, and Hiro are snacking at their favorite burger joint, Frank 'n Stein's, when they witness a brutal robbery. Two men, masked as a clown and Elvis, savagely beat the owner and steal his considerable stash of cash. The kids manage to escape, and with the security camera hard drive to boot, but Clown gets a good look at Cooper and swears he'll find him. Afraid to go to the police (the robbers were wearing cop pants), Cooper convinces his friends to enact a code of silence. As the maybe-crooked police and other possible suspects get closer to identifying the witnesses, the kids' lies to their parents, their teachers, and one another set off increasingly desperate maneuvers and dangerous infighting" (Booklist)

Showalter, Gena

Intertwined. Harlequin Teen 2009 440p $15.99

Grades: 7 8 9 10 **Fic**

1. Vampires -- Fiction 2. Werewolves -- Fiction 3. Supernatural -- Fiction

ISBN 978-0-373-21002-2; 0-373-21002-7

"Most sixteen-year-olds have friends. Aden Stone has four human souls living inside him: one can time travel, one can raise the dead, one can tell the future, and one can possess another human, and then he meets a girl who quiets the voices." Publisher's note

"This fast-paced, action-driven plot has many unexpected twists and turns. Well written, with a unique story line and strong characters." SLJ

Other titles in this series are:
Unraveled (2010)
Twisted (2011)

Shreve, Susan

The **lovely** shoes; [by] Susan Shreve. Arthur A. Levine Books 2011 252p $16.99

Grades: 6 7 8 9 **Fic**

1. Shoemakers 2. School stories 3. Birth defects -- Fiction 4. Mother-daughter relationship -- Fiction

ISBN 978-0-439-68049-3; 0-439-68049-2

LC 2010027937

In 1950s Ohio, ninth-grader Franny feels isolated and self-conscious at high school because of her deformed leg and feet, but her irrepressibly high-spirited mother is determined to find shoes for Franny to wear at the school dances.

"Celebrating the rewards of determination and a positive attitude, this atmospheric novel credibly depicts Franny's internal growth and changing attitude. The contrast between smalltown Ohio and splendorous Florence provides an intriguing framework for the book's classic themes." Publ Wkly

Shukert, Rachel, 1980-

Love me; Rachel Shukert. Delacorte Press. 2014 325p $17.99

Grades: 9 10 11 12 Fic

1. Actors and actresses — Fiction 2. Fame — Fiction 3. Hollywood (Los Angeles, Calif.) — History — 20th century — Fiction 4. Actresses — Fiction

ISBN: 0385741103; 9780375989858; 9780385741101

LC 2012047071

"Actresses Margo, Gabby, and Amanda return for another soap about making it big--and staying big--in late-1930s Tinseltown. Much of the focus is on each girl's heartache at the hands of the domineering men in their lives, both lovers and movie-studio bigwigs. This sequel to Starstruck is rife with far-fetched coincidences and melodrama, but it's all deliciously entertaining." Horn Book

Starstruck; by Rachel Shukert. Delacorte Press 2013 352 p. (ebook) $53.97; (library) $20.99; (hardcover) $17.99; (paperback) $9.99

Grades: 9 10 11 12 **Fic**

1. Fame -- Fiction 2. Actresses -- Fiction 3. Actors and actresses -- Fiction 4. Hollywood (Los Angeles, Calif.) -- History -- 20th century -- Fiction

ISBN 0375989846; 9780375984259; 9780375989841; 9780385741088; 9780385741095

LC 2012015771

This novel, by Rachel Shukert, follows a girl trying to become a star. When "Margaret . . . [is] discovered by a powerful agent, she can barely believe her luck. She's more than ready to escape her snobby private school and conservative Pasadena family for a chance to light up the silver screen. . . . Set in Old Hollywood, [the story] follows the lives of three teen girls as they live, love, and claw their way to the top in a world where being a star is all that matters." (Publisher's note)

Shulman, Mark

Scrawl. Roaring Brook Press 2010 234p $16.99

Grades: 6 7 8 9 10 **Fic**

1. School stories 2. Bullies -- Fiction 3. Diaries -- Fiction 4. Poverty -- Fiction 5. Self-perception -- Fiction

ISBN 978-1-59643-417-2; 1-59643-417-1

LC 2010-10521

When eighth-grade school bully Tod and his friends get caught committing a crime on school property, his penalty—staying after school and writing in a journal under the eye of the school guidance counsellor—reveals aspects of himself that he prefers to keep hidden.

"Blackmail, cliques, and a sense of hopelessness from both students and teachers sets up an unexpected ending that will leave readers with a new appreciation for how difficult high school can be. With the potential to occupy the rarified air of titles like S.E. Hinton's The Outsiders and Chris Crutcher's Staying Fat for Sarah Byrnes . . ., Scrawl paints the stereotypical school bully in a different, poignant light." Voice Youth Advocates

Shulman, Polly

Enthusiasm. G. P. Putnam's Sons 2006 198p hardcover o.p. pa $7.99

Grades: 7 8 9 10 **Fic**

1. School stories

ISBN 0-399-24389-5; 0-14-240935-9 pa

LC 2005-13490

Julie and Ashleigh, high school sophomores and Jane Austen fans, seem to fall for the same Mr. Darcy-like boy and struggle to hide their true feelings from one another while rehearsing for a school musical.

"While familiarity with Austen's world through her books or, more likely, the movie renditions will deepen readers' appreciation for Shulman's impressive . . . novel, it is by no means a prerequisite to enjoying this involving and often amusing narrative of friendship, courtship, and (of course) true love." Booklist

Shusterman, Neal, 1962-

★ **Antsy** does time. Dutton Children's Books 2008 247p $16.99

Grades: 5 6 7 8 **Fic**

1. School stories 2. Death -- Fiction

ISBN 978-0-525-47825-6; 0-525-47825-6

LC 2008-00459

Fourteen-year-old Anthony "Antsy" Bonano learns about life, death, and a lot more when he tries to help a friend with a terminal illness feel hopeful about the future.

"Featuring a terrific supporting cast led by Antsy's wise, acerbic mother, an expert blend of comedy and near tragedy, and the wry observations of a narrator . . . this will keep tween readers hooked from start to finish." Booklist

Bruiser. HarperTeen 2010 328p $16.99; lib bdg $17.89

Grades: 8 9 10 11 12 **Fic**

1. Twins -- Fiction 2. Siblings -- Fiction 3. Child abuse

-- Fiction 4. Supernatural -- Fiction
ISBN 978-0-06-113408-1; 0-06-113408-2; 978-0-06-113409-8 lib bdg; 0-06-113409-0 lib bdg
LC 2009-30930

Inexplicable events start to occur when sixteen-year-old twins Tennyson and Bronte befriend a troubled and misunderstood outcast, aptly nicknamed Bruiser, and his little brother, Cody.

"Narrated in turns by Tennyson, Bronte, Bruiser, and Bruiser's little brother, Cody, the story is a fascinating study in the art of self-deception and the way our best intentions for others are often based in the selfish desires of our deepest selves. . . . This eloquent and thoughtful story will most certainly leave its mark." Bull Cent Child Books

Downsiders. Simon & Schuster Bks. for Young Readers 1999 246p hardcover o.p. pa $8.99
Grades: 9 10 11 12 **Fic**

1. Subways -- Fiction 2. New York (N.Y.) -- Fiction
ISBN 0-689-80375-3; 1-4169-9747-4 pa
LC 98-38555

When fourteen-year-old Lindsay meets Talon and discovers the Downsiders world which had evolved from the subway built in New York in 1867 by Alfred Ely Beach, she and her new friend experience the clash of their two cultures.

"Shusterman has invented an alternate world in the Downside that is both original and humorous." Voice Youth Advocates

★ **Everlost**. Simon & Schuster Books for Young Readers 2006 313p (The Skinjacker trilogy) $16.95; pa $8.99
Grades: 8 9 10 11 12 **Fic**

1. Death -- Fiction 2. Future life -- Fiction 3. Traffic accidents -- Fiction
ISBN 978-0-689-87237-2; 0-689-87237-2; 978-1-4169-9749-8 pa; 1-4169-9749-0 pa
LC 2005-32244

When Nick and Allie are killed in a car crash, they end up in Everlost, or limbo for lost souls, where although Nick is satisfied, Allie will stop at nothing—even skinjacking—to break free.

"Shusterman has reimagined what happens after death and questions power and the meaning of charity. While all this is going on, he has also managed to write a rip-roaring adventure complete with monsters, blimps, and high-diving horses." SLJ

Other titles in this series are:
Everfound (2011)
Everwild (2009)

Full tilt; a novel. Simon & Schuster Bks. for Young Readers 2003 201p $16.95; pa $8.99
Grades: 7 8 9 10 **Fic**

1. Horror fiction 2. Brothers -- Fiction 3. Amusement parks -- Fiction
ISBN 0-689-80374-5; 1-4169-9748-2 pa
LC 2002-13867

When sixteen-year-old Blake goes to a mysterious, by-invitation-only carnival he somehow knows that it could save his comatose brother, but soon learns that much more is at stake if he fails to meet the challenge presented there by the beautiful Cassandra.

"Shusterman has created a surreal, scary fantasy, packed with suspenseful psychological drama." Booklist

UnSouled; Neal Shusterman. Simon & Schuster Books for Young Readers 2013 416 p. (Unwind trilogy) (hardback) $17.99
Grades: 6 7 8 9 10 11 12 **Fic**

1. Science fiction 2. Traffic accidents 3. Travel -- Fiction 4. Identity -- Fiction 5. Survival -- Fiction 6. Revolutionaries -- Fiction 7. Fugitives from justice -- Fiction
ISBN 1442423692; 9781442423695
LC 2013022703

In this book, the third in author Neal Shusterman's UnWholly series, "Lev and Connor are on the road again. Their destination is back to Ohio where Sonia, an antiques dealer with an important past, will help them end Unwinding once and for all. After a bizarre car accident . . . they wind up on a Native American reservation. Here, readers learn a lot more about Lev's past, and Connor meets up with Cam, the one and only Rewind." (School Library Journal)

"In the third of his projected four-volume Unwind 'dystology' Shusterman brings most of his central cast of teenage fugitives together and introduces an important new character, who is exempt from being unwound (legally disassembled for body parts) because she has a mild spectrum disorder. Frequent references to events in previous episodes slow the pace somewhat but the present-tense tale remains suspenseful, the overall premise is as hauntingly plausible as ever, and an electrifying revelation at the end points the way to a possible resolution." (Booklist)

The **Schwa** was here; [by] Neal Shusterman. 1st ed; Dutton Children's Books 2004 228p $15.99
Grades: 5 6 7 8 **Fic**

1. Friendship -- Fiction
ISBN 0-525-47182-0
LC 2004-45072

A Brooklyn eighth-grader nicknamed Antsy befriends the Schwa, an "invisible-ish" boy who is tired of blending into his surroundings and going unnoticed by nearly everyone.

"Antsy is one funny narrator. . . . Shusterman has created yet another very readable and refreshingly different story." Voice Youth Advocates

UnWholly; Neal Shusterman. Simon & Schuster Books For Young Readers 2012 402 p. (hardback) $17.99
Grades: 6 7 8 9 10 11 12 **Fic**

1. Science fiction 2. Identity -- Fiction 3. Survival skills -- Fiction 4. Survival -- Fiction 5. Revolutionaries -- Fiction 6. Fugitives from justice -- Fiction
ISBN 1442423668; 9781442423664; 9781442423688
LC 2012002729

Sequel to: Unwind

This sequel to Neal Shusterman's book "Unwind" follows "Cam . . . a product of unwinding; made entirely out of the parts of other unwinds, he is a teen who does not technically exist. A futuristic Frankenstein, Cam struggles with a search for identity and meaning. . . . And when the actions of a sadistic bounty hunter cause Cam's fate to become inextricably bound with the fates of Connor, Risa, and Lev, he'll have to question humanity itself." (Publisher's note)

Unwind. Simon & Schuster Books for Young Readers 2007 335p $17.99

Grades: 6 7 8 9 10 11 12 **Fic**

1. Science fiction

ISBN 1-4169-1204-5; 1-4169-1205-3 pa; 978-1-4169-1204-0; 978-1-4169-1205-7 pa

LC 2006032689

In a future world where those between the ages of thirteen and eighteen can have their lives "unwound" and their body parts harvested for use by others, three teens go to extreme lengths to uphold their beliefs—and, perhaps, save their own lives. "Grades eight to ten." (Bull Cent Child Books)

"Poignant, compelling, and ultimately terrifying." Voice Youth Advocates

Siegelson, Kim L.

Honey Bea; [by] Kim L. Siegelson. 1st ed; Jump at the Sun/Hyperion Books for Children 2006 276p $15.99

Grades: 7 8 9 10 **Fic**

1. Magic -- Fiction 2. Slavery -- Fiction 3. Plantation life -- Fiction

ISBN 0-7868-0853-5

LC 2003-61888

On a Louisiana sugar plantation, a young slave girl struggles with the magical powers that have been passed down from her grandmother and mother to her, unsure of the responsibilities and consequences that accompany this power.

"Siegelson crafts a mesmerizing tale heavy with the scent of honey and flowers and rooted in Louisiana soil." Booklist

Silbert, Leslie

★ The **intelligencer**. Atria Bks. 2004 335p hardcover o.p. pa $14

Grades: 9 10 11 12 **Fic**

1. Authors 2. Dramatists 3. Mystery fiction 4. Great Britain -- History -- 1485-1603, Tudors -- Fiction

ISBN 0-7434-3292-4; 0-7434-3293-2 pa

LC 2004-298225

This mystery "alternates between the present and the England of Elizabeth I and Christopher Marlowe. In addition to being a skilled and popular playwright, Marlowe was a spy, or intelligencer, for both Cecil and Essex, rivals for the favor of the Queen. Kate Morgan, a present-day Renaissance scholar working as a PI for a former agent still working clandestinely for the government, takes on a case involving a bound collection of coded reports of intelligencers gathered by an employee of Cecil, Essex, and others. The trail of the manuscript and its codes intersects with modern investigations involving murders, a crooked but charming art dealer, a charming but devious entrepreneur, a captured spy, Iranian prisons, Kate's father, a U.S. senator, and the current CIA director. There are a lot of strands, but the pace is quick and the action fascinating." SLJ

Silver, Eve

Rush; Eve Silver. Katherine Tegen Books 2013 368 p. (The game) (hardcover) $17.99

Grades: 9 10 11 12 **Fic**

1. Science fiction 2. Violence -- Fiction 3. Extraterrestrial beings -- Fiction 4. Combat -- Fiction 5. Interpersonal relations -- Fiction

ISBN 0062192132; 9780062192134

LC 2012025496

This young adult novel, by Eve Silver, is the first entry in "The Game" series. "Seventeen-year-old Miki Jones . . . wakes up . . . in a place called the lobby--pulled from her life, pulled through time and space into some kind of game in which she and a team of other teens are sent on missions to eliminate the Drau, terrifying and beautiful alien creatures." (Publisher's note)

Silvey, Craig

★ **Jasper** Jones; a novel. Alfred A. Knopf 2011 312p $16.99

Grades: 6 7 8 9 10 **Fic**

1. Mystery fiction 2. Homicide -- Fiction 3. Australia -- Fiction 4. Family life -- Fiction

ISBN 0-375-86666-3; 0-375-96666-8 lib bdg; 978-0-375-86666-1; 978-0-375-96666-8 lib bdg

LC 2010-9364

In small-town Australia, teens Jasper and Charlie form an unlikely friendship when one asks the other to help him cover up a murder until they can prove who is responsible.

"Silvey infuses his prose with a musician's sensibility—Charlie's pounding heart is echoed in the terse staccato sentences of the opening scenes, alternating with legato phrases laden with meaning. The author's keen ear for dialogue is evident in the humorous verbal sparring between Charlie and Jeffrey, typical of smart 13-year-old boys. . . . A richly rewarding exploration of truth and lies by a masterful storyteller." Kirkus

Simmons, Kristen

Article 5; Kristen Simmons. Tor Teen 2012 364 p.

Grades: 9 10 11 **Fic**

1. Science fiction 2. Dystopian fiction 3. Young adult literature 4. Mother-daughter relationship -- Fiction 5. Soldiers -- Fiction 6. Government, Resistance to -- Fiction

ISBN 0765329581; 9780765329585

LC 2011035411

This young adult dystopian novel, by Kristen Simmons, is set where "The Bill of Rights has been revoked, and replaced with the Moral Statutes. There are no more police--instead, there are soldiers. . . . Ember Miller . . . has perfected the art of keeping a low profile. . . . That is, until her mother is arrested for noncompliance with Article 5 of the Moral Statutes. And one of the arresting officers is none other than Chase Jennings . . . the only boy Ember has ever loved." (Publisher's note)

Three. Kristen Simmons. Tor. 2014 382p $17.99

Grades: 9 10 11 12 **Fic**

1. Fugitives from justice — Fiction; 2. Science fiction; 3. Dystopian fiction; 4. Resistance to government — Fiction

ISBN: 0765329603; 9780765329608; 9781429948036

LC 2013026344

Conclusion of the author's dystopian trilogy which began with Article 5 (2012) and Breaking point (2013). "When the book opens, Ember is sleeping in what remains of a destroyed resistance safe house along with the boy she loves, Chase, and a handful of others. As they continue to travel underground, they encounter the legendary resistance group, Three. This is a war story: Ember and her friends continually flee, camp out, strategize and fight, often at a moment's notice. Where earlier volumes' action sequences felt repetitive, these are suspenseful and immediate. Whom to trust and how far are rarely clear. Some interesting moral questions about pragmatism and violence arise, and no easy answers are given. Ember and Chase's relationship, including a gentle and warmly presented sex scene, gives the story both hope and warmth." Kirkus

A Tom Doherty Associates Book.

Simmons, Michael

The **rise** of Lubchenko. Razorbill 2006 217p $16.99

Grades: 8 9 10 11 12 **Fic**

1. France -- Fiction 2. Smallpox -- Fiction 3. Criminals -- Fiction 4. Terrorism -- Fiction 5. Father-son relationship -- Fiction

ISBN 1-59514-061-1; 978-1-59514-061-6

LC 2006-10038

Sequel to Finding Lubchenko (2005)

Suspecting that his father's business partner is selling smallpox virus to terrorists and murdering anyone who gets in his way, sixteen-year-old Evan Macalister once again travels to France with his friends, Ruben and Erika, to search for the mysterious Lubchenko, the elusive spymaster whose help they need to avert a major disaster.

Simner, Janni Lee

Bones of Faerie. Random House 2009 247p $16.99; lib bdg $19.99

Grades: 7 8 9 10 **Fic**

1. Fantasy fiction 2. Magic -- Fiction 3. Fairies -- Fiction

ISBN 978-0-375-84563-5; 978-0-375-94563-2 lib bdg

LC 2008-2022

Fifteen-year-old Liza travels through war-ravaged territory, accompanied by two companions, in a struggle to bridge the faerie and human worlds and to bring back her mother while learning of her own powers and that magic can be controlled.

This is a "compelling developed, highly vulnerable trio whose resolute defiance against the status quo will resonate with readers long after specific details of the story may be forgotten." Bull Cent Child Books

Followed by: Faerie winter (2011)

Faerie after; Janni Lee Simner. Random House Inc. 2013 272 p. (ebook) $50.97; (hardcover) $16.99; (library) $19.99

Grades: 7 8 9 10 **Fic**

1. Occult fiction 2. Fantasy fiction 3. Fairies -- Fiction 4. Magic -- Fiction 5. Coming of age -- Fiction

ISBN 0375870695; 9780307974556; 9780375870699; 9780375970696

LC 2012006430

Sequel to: Faerie winter

This is the third book in Janni Lee's Bones of Faerie trilogy. "Relative peace has descended upon Liza's town, where she practices her summoner magic and waits for her half-faerie baby sister to be born. But the forest is showing new dangers, though subtle ones," particularly a strange dust. "Liza's quest to find out what's wrong reveals fresh disasters." (Kirkus)

Faerie winter. Random House Children's Books 2011 270p $16.99; lib bdg $19.99

Grades: 7 8 9 10 **Fic**

1. Magic -- Fiction 2. Fairies -- Fiction 3. Mother-daughter relationship -- Fiction

ISBN 978-0-375-86671-5; 0-375-86671-X; 978-0-375-96671-2 lib bdg; 0-375-96671-4 lib bdg

LC 2010014250

Unable to get answers from her mother, sixteen-year-old Liza learns from Karin that while her own actions may have doomed the fairy and human worlds, she may be able to save them with more training, if the Faerie Queen can first be stopped.

"Simner tells a more streamlined story this time around and keeps up the dark atmospherics of her high-appeal blend of unsettling speculative-fiction scenarios." Booklist

Thief eyes. Random House 2010 272p $16.99

Grades: 7 8 9 10 **Fic**

1. Fantasy fiction 2. Magic -- Fiction 3. Iceland -- Fiction 4. Missing persons -- Fiction

ISBN 978-0-375-86670-8; 0-375-86670-1

LC 2009-18166

Haley's mother disappeared while on a trip to Iceland, and a year later, when her father takes her there to find out what happened, Haley finds herself deeply involved in an ancient saga that began with her Nordic ancestors.

"Simner skillfully weaves Haley and Ari's modern emotional struggles into the ancient saga and enlivens the story with an intriguing cast of characters from the original tale." Booklist

Simon, Charnan

Plan B. Darby Creek 2011 104p (Surviving Southside) lib bdg $27.93; pa $7.95

Grades: 7 8 9 10 **Fic**

1. School stories 2. Pregnancy -- Fiction

ISBN 978-0-7613-6149-7 lib bdg; 0-7613-6149-9 lib bdg; 978-0-7613-6163-3 pa; 0-7613-6163-4 pa

LC 2010023819

Lucy has her life planned out: she'll graduate and then join her boyfriend, Luke, at college in Austin. She'll become a Spanish teacher and of course they'll get married. But then Lucy gets pregnant. Together, she and Luke will have to make the most difficult decision of their lives.

This "well-written [story reinforces] the importance of family, friends, values, and thoughtful decision-making. . . . [An] excellent [purchase, this book] will attract and engage reluctant readers." SLJ

Simone, Ni-Ni

Upgrade U; Ni-Ni Simone. Dafina Books 2011 viii, 276 p.p $9.95

Grades: 10 11 12 **Fic**

1. Love stories 2. Friendship -- Fiction 3. College students -- Fiction 4. College basketball -- Fiction 5. African Americans -- Fiction 6. Basketball players -- Fiction 7. Dating (Social customs) -- Fiction 8. Interpersonal relations -- Fiction

ISBN 0758241917; 9780758241917

LC 2011282065

In this novel, "Seven McKnight, introduced in 'Shortie Like Mine' (2008), moves from Newark, N.J., to New Orleans, La., to join her best friend Shae and boyfriend Josiah at Stiles University. . . . Problem is, Josiah hasn't returned any of Seven's many texts or phone calls, and Seven is afraid. . . . As Seven and Josiah cycle through fighting and making up, Seven finds support in her band of new and old friends: insightful Shae; bold, flirtatious and social-networking-obsessed Khya and boa-clad next-door neighbor Courtney, who inserts himself into practically every conversation and outing. When Seven meets Zaire, a seemingly forthright, sophisticated New Orleans native, a love triangle develops--or is that a love quadrangle?" (Kirkus)

Singer, Nicky

Gem X. Holiday House 2008 311p $16.95

Grades: 7 8 9 10 **Fic**

1. Science fiction 2. Cloning -- Fiction 3. Genetic engineering -- Fiction 4. Political corruption -- Fiction

ISBN 978-0-8234-2108-4; 0-8234-2108-2

LC 2007-14975

Sixteen-year-old Maxo Strang, the most perfect human ever made, suddenly discovers a 'crack' in his face, which leads him to expose his community's dark underworld of secret scientific research and the city's corrupt supreme leader.

"This intelligent, fast-paced novel will appeal to those teens who . . . want speculative fiction with bite and satire." SLJ

Singleton, Linda Joy

Dead girl dancing; Linda Joy Singleton. Flux 2009 259 p. pa $9.95

Grades: 8 9 10 11 12 **Fic**

1. Fantasy fiction 2. Stalkers -- Fiction 3. Supernatural -- Fiction 4. Identity -- Fiction 5. Friendship -- Fiction 6. Future life -- Fiction 7. Self-esteem -- Fiction 8. Best friends -- Fiction 9. Emotional problems -- Fiction

ISBN 9780738714066

LC 2008044037

This paranormal young adult book, the second book in Linda Joy Singleton's "Dead Girl" series after "Dead Girl Watching," continues the story of Amber, who is a "Temp Lifer," or someone who has the ability to "step[. . .] into someone's life--and their body." In this installment, Amber is stuck in the body of "[her] boyfriend's older sister, who is getting ready to go wild on spring break--while being pursued by a psycho stalker and a Dark Lifer." (Publisher's note)

Dead girl in love; Linda Joy Singleton. Flux 2009 283 p. $9.95

Grades: 8 9 10 11 12 **Fic**

1. Fantasy fiction 2. Supernatural -- Fiction 3. Female friendship -- Fiction 4. Identity -- Fiction 5. Friendship -- Fiction 6. Future life -- Fiction 7. Best friends -- Fiction 8. Grandmothers -- Fiction 9. Mothers and daughters -- Fiction

ISBN 0738714070; 9780738714073

LC 2009009049

This paranormal young adult book, the third book in Linda Joy Singleton's "Dead Girl" series after "Dead Girl Dancing," continues the story of Amber, whose "dead grandmother keeps finding people who have big problems and then [Amber has] the freaky experience of stepping into their life—and their body!—to provide help. This time, [she's] in the body of [her] BFF, Alyce. Since Alyce and [Amber] know everything about each other," Amber thinks she "won't have to do a lot of detective work" with this case. However, she's alarmed to discover that a question she does have to answer is why Alyce's body is in a coffin. (Publisher's note)

Dead girl walking; [by] Linda Joy Singleton. Flux 2008 308p (Dead girl) $9.95

Grades: 8 9 10 11 12 **Fic**

1. School stories 2. Death -- Fiction 3. Future life -- Fiction

ISBN 978-0-7387-1405-9; 0-7387-1405-4

LC 2008012991

When Amber, a smart, middle-class, high school student, is hit by a truck, she meets her deceased grandmother in a dreamlike place, then takes a wrong turn and awakens in the body of a wealthy, beautiful, popular classmate with serious problems.

"This page-turner has wit, love, courage, adventure, and remarkable insight." SLJ

Sitomer, Alan Lawrence

The **secret** story of Sonia Rodriguez. Jump at the Sun/Hyperion Books For Children 2008 312p lib bdg $17.99

Grades: 7 8 9 10 **Fic**

1. Family life -- Fiction 2. Mexican Americans -- Fiction

ISBN 978-1-4231-1072-9; 1-4231-1072-2

LC 2007-45265

Tenth-grader Sonia reveals secrets about her life and her Hispanic family as she studies hard to become the first Rodriguez to finish high school.

"Sonia's immediate voice will hold teens with its mix of anger, sorrow, tenderness, and humor." Booklist

Skelton, Matthew

★ **Endymion** Spring. Delacorte Press 2006 392p il $17.95; lib bdg $19.99; pa $9.99

Grades: 5 6 7 8 **Fic**

1. Inventors 2. Printers 3. Magic -- Fiction 4. Books and reading -- Fiction

ISBN 0-385-73380-1; 0-385-90397-9 lib bdg; 0-385-73456-5 pa

LC 2006-46259

Having reluctantly accompanied his academic mother and pesky younger sister to Oxford, twelve-year-old Blake Winters is at loose ends until he stumbles across an ancient and magical book, secretly brought to England in 1453 by Gutenberg's mute apprentice to save it from evil forces, and which now draws Blake into a dangerous and life-threatening quest

"This book is certain to reach an audience looking for a page-turner, and it just might motivate readers to explore the . . . facts behind the fiction." SLJ

Skilton, Sarah

Bruised; by Sarah Skilton. Amulet Books 2013 288 p. $16.95

Grades: 9 10 11 12 **Fic**

1. Bildungsromans 2. Martial arts -- Fiction 3. Tae kwon do -- Fiction 4. Self-perception -- Fiction

ISBN 1419703870; 9781419703874

LC 2012042801

This book follows sixteen-year-old Imogen, a martial artist who "can break boards with her feet and toss a man twice her size, but when her skills are tested during a diner holdup, she cowers rather than acts, and a man dies. Having lost her confidence and her pride, Imogen is ready to give up martial arts until Ricky—another witness of the holdup—asks her to teach him how to throw a punch. While working with Ricky, Imogen makes discoveries about her passions and fears." (Publishers Weekly)

Skovron, Jon

Misfit. Amulet Books 2011 362p $16.95

Grades: 7 8 9 10 **Fic**

1. School stories 2. Demonology -- Fiction 3. Supernatural -- Fiction 4. Seattle (Wash.) -- Fiction 5. Single parent family -- Fiction

ISBN 978-1-4197-0021-7; 1-4197-0021-9

LC 2010048691

Seattle sixteen-year-old Jael must negotiate normal life in Catholic school while learning to control the abilities she inherited from her mother, a demon, and protect those she loves from Belial, the Duke of Hell.

This book features "a believable magical world that incorporates dry humor, mythological and biblical references, voodoo practices, exorcism, and romance. Although the supernatural element drives the plot, it is Jael's feeling of isolation and her search for family—even if her demonic maternal uncle smells like rotting fish—that motivates her courageous actions. She is an unlikely but wholly delightful heroine" Booklist

Skrypuch, Marsha Forchuk

Daughter of war. Fitzhenry & Whiteside 2008 210p pa $14.95

Grades: 9 10 11 12 **Fic**

1. Turkey -- Fiction 2. Armenian massacres, 1915-1923 -- Fiction

ISBN 978-1-55455-044-9; 1-55455-044-0

"In this powerful story of the Armenian genocide, Kevork witnesses the brutal suffering of his people as he travels, disguised as an Arab, through Turkey and Syria in search of his love, Marta. Upon their reunion, Kevork learns that Marta has escaped from a forced Turkish marriage and borne a child." SLJ

Skurzynski, Gloria

The **Virtual** War. Simon & Schuster Bks. for Young Readers 1997 152p hardcover o.p. pa $10.95

Grades: 6 7 8 9 **Fic**

1. Science fiction 2. Virtual reality -- Fiction

ISBN 0-689-81374-0; 1-4169-7577-2 pa

LC 96-35346

In a future world where global contamination has necessitated limited human contact, three young people with unique genetically engineered abilities are teamed up to wage a war in virtual reality

"Skurzynski's anti-war message is clear yet never didactic; her characters are complex and fully realized, the pacing brisk, and the story compelling." Bull Cent Child Books

Other titles in this series are:

The choice (2006)

The clones (2002)

The revolt (2005)

Skuse, C. J.

Rockoholic; C.J. Skuse. Scholastic 2012 358 p. (reinforced) $18.99

Grades: 9 10 11 12 **Fic**

1. Teenagers -- Fiction 2. Kidnapping -- Fiction 3. Rock musicians -- Fiction 4. Fame -- Fiction 5. Wales -- Fiction 6. Musicians -- Fiction 7. Friendship -- Fiction 8. Rock music -- Fiction 9. Best friends -- Fiction

ISBN 0545429609; 9780545429603

LC 2011046582

In this young adult novel, by C. J. Skuse, "Jody's addicted to Jackson Gatlin, frontman of The Regulators, and . . . she's front and center at his sold-out concert. But when she gets mashed in the moshpit . . . and bodysurfs backstage, she ends up with more than a mild concussion to deal with. By the next morning, the strung-out rock star is coming down in her garage. Jody . . . kind of kidnapped him. By accident. And now he doesn't want to leave." (Publisher's note)

Slade, Arthur G.

The **dark** deeps. Wendy Lamb Books 2010 310p (The hunchback assignments) $16.99; lib bdg $19.99

Grades: 7 8 9 10 **Fic**

1. Science fiction 2. Spies -- Fiction 3. Shipwrecks -- Fiction 4. Supernatural -- Fiction 5. London (England) -- Fiction 6. People with physical disabilities 7. Great Britain -- History -- 19th century -- Fiction

ISBN 978-0-385-73785-2; 0-385-73785-8; 978-0-385-90695-1 lib bdg; 0-385-90695-1 lib bdg

LC 2009052117

Sequel to: The hunchback assignments (2009)

Fourteen-year-old Modo, a shape-changing hunchback, and Octavia take on another mission as secret agents for the Permanent Association in Victorian London, investigating the cause behind the sinking of several ships in the same place.

"The pacing and plotting are as tight and engaging as in the opener. Slade does an excellent job of catching new readers up to speed without pedantic reportage that would bore those who have already read the first volume." Booklist

Empire of ruins; by Arthur Slade. Wendy Lamb Books 2011 293p (The hunchback assignments) $15.99; lib bdg $18.99

Grades: 7 8 9 10 **Fic**

1. Science fiction 2. Spies -- Fiction 3. Australia -- Fiction 4. Great Britain -- Fiction 5. People with physical disabilities

ISBN 978-0-385-73786-9; 0-385-73786-6; 978-0-385-90696-8 lib bdg; 0-385-90696-X lib bdg

LC 2010053419

While on an assignment in Queensland, Australia, to discover the truth behind a powerful weapon known as the God Face, Modo, a teenaged, shape-changing hunchback living in Victorian London, battles the evil machinations of the Clockwork Guild and makes an astounding discovery—one that hinges on Modo's true appearance.

"Another fun outing, sure to please series fans." Kirkus

The **hunchback** assignments; [by] Arthur Slade. Wendy Lamb Books 2009 278p $15.99; lib bdg $18.99

Grades: 7 8 9 10 **Fic**

1. Science fiction 2. Spies -- Fiction 3. Supernatural -- Fiction 4. London (England) -- Fiction 5. People with physical disabilities 6. Great Britain -- History -- 19th century -- Fiction

ISBN 978-0-385-73784-5; 0-385-73784-X; 978-0-385-90694-4 lib bdg; 0-385-90694-3 lib bdg

LC 2008-54378

In Victorian London, fourteen-year-old Modo, a shape-changing hunchback, becomes a secret agent for the Permanent Association, which strives to protect the world from the evil machinations of the Clockwork Guild.

"A solid story line and well-crafted writing make for a pleasing and evocative adventure." Booklist

Other titles in the series are:

The dark deeps (2010)

Empire of ruins (2011)

Jolted; Newton Starker's rules for survival. [by] Arthur Slade. Wendy Lamb Books 2009 227p $15.99; lib bdg $18.99

Grades: 5 6 7 8 **Fic**

1. School stories 2. Lightning -- Fiction

ISBN 978-0-385-74700-4; 0-385-74700-4; 978-0-385-90944-0 lib bdg; 0-385-90944-6 lib bdg

LC 2008-8632

First published 2008 in Canada

Many of Newton Starker's ancestors, including his mother, have been killed by lightning strikes, so when he enrolls at the eccentric Jerry Potts Academy of Higher Learning and Survival in Moose Jaw, Saskatchewan, he tries to be a model student so that he can avoid the same fate.

"The premise will snag readers immediately [and] . . . Slade's portrayal of Newton's sweep of emotions as he deals with his perceived fate–fear, fury, dogged determination–is especially convincing." Publ Wkly

Slater, Adam

The **Shadowing** : Hunted. Egmont 2011 208p $16.99

Grades: 7 8 9 10 **Fic**

1. Ghost stories 2. Horror fiction 3. Supernatural -- Fiction

ISBN 978-1-6068-426-1; 1-60684-261-7

"Callum Scott sees ghosts. . . . It's because he is a 'chime child,' born on a full moon between midnight Friday and dawn Saturday. . . . When a huge, particularly evil-looking black dog and a pale boy dripping blood start following him, he is unnerved. . . . The barrier between the human world and the demon realm is disintegrating like it does every hundred years, and only the chime children can keep humanity safe. Slater shows a knack for building tension and terror and readers . . . will gulp this series opener and ask for more." Booklist

Slayton, Fran Cannon

When the whistle blows. Philomel Books 2009 162p $16.99

Grades: 7 8 9 10 **Fic**

1. Railroads -- Fiction 2. Family life -- Fiction 3. Country life -- Fiction 4. West Virginia -- Fiction

ISBN 978-0-399-25189-4; 0-399-25189-8

LC 2008-38435

Jimmy Cannon tells about his life in the 1940s as the son of a West Virginia railroad man, loving the trains and expecting one day to work on the railroad like his father and brothers.

"Telling details and gentle humor help set the scene and reveal a great deal about these characters and their lives. . . . A polished paean to a bygone time and place." SLJ

Sleator, William

★ **Interstellar** pig. Dutton 1984 197p hardcover o.p. pa $6.99

Grades: 5 6 7 8 **Fic**

1. Science fiction

ISBN 0-14-037595-3 pa

LC 84-4132

Barney's boring seaside vacation suddenly becomes more interesting when the cottage next door is occupied by three exotic neighbors who are addicted to a game they call "Interstellar Pig."

The author "draws the reader in with intimations of danger and horror, but the climactic battle is more slapstick than horrific, and the victor's prize could scarcely be more ironic. Problematic as straight science fiction but great fun as a spoof on human-alien contact." Booklist

Another title about Barney is:

Parasite Pig (2002)

Singularity. Dutton 1985 170p hardcover o.p. pa $5.99

Grades: 7 8 9 10 **Fic**

1. Science fiction 2. Twins -- Fiction

ISBN 0-525-44161-1; 0-14-037598-8 pa

LC 84-26075

Sixteen-year-old twins Harry and Barry stumble across a gateway to another universe, where a distortion in time and space causes a dramatic change in their competitive relationship

"The book has a title with a fine double entendre and is an unusual, suspenseful yarn told by a master storyteller." Horn Book

★ The **duplicate**. Dutton 1988 154p hardcover o.p. pa $5.99

Grades: 7 8 9 10 **Fic**
1. Science fiction
ISBN 0-14-130431-6
LC 87-30562

Sixteen-year-old David, finding a strange machine that creates replicas of living organisms, duplicates himself and suffers the horrible consequences when the duplicate turns against him

"There are some points in the story when the roles of the clones (referred to as Duplicates A and B) become congested to the detriment of the book's pace, but fantasy fans will doubtless find the concept fresh enough and eerie enough to compensate for this, and Sleator is, as always, economical in casting and structuring his story." Bull Cent Child Books

Sloan, Brian

★ A **tale** of two summers. Simon & Schuster Books for Young Readers 2006 241p $15.95
Grades: 9 10 11 12 **Fic**
1. Theater -- Fiction 2. Friendship -- Fiction 3. Homosexuality -- Fiction
ISBN 978-0-689-87439-0; 0-689-87439-1
LC 2005-20697

Even though Hal is gay and Chuck is straight, the two fifteen-year-olds are best friends and set up a blog where Hal records his budding romance with a young Frenchman and Chuck falls for a summer theater camp diva.

"This book is for readers mature enough to handle some very direct, realistic, and often-humorous entries about heterosexuality, homosexuality, masturbation, and alcohol and marijuana use. This title would be ideal for discussion within Gay/Straight Alliance groups." Voice Youth Advocates

Sloan, Holly Goldberg

★ **I'll** be there. Little, Brown 2011 392p $17.99
Grades: 7 8 9 10 **Fic**
1. Brothers -- Fiction 2. Family life -- Fiction 3. Mental illness -- Fiction 4. Young adult literature -- Works 5. Father-son relationship -- Fiction
ISBN 978-0-316-12279-5; 0-316-12279-3
LC 2010-42994

Raised by an unstable father who keeps constantly on the move, Sam Border has long been the voice of his younger brother, Riddle, but everything changes when Sam meets Emily Bell and, welcomed by her family, the brothers are faced with normalcy for the first time.

"This riveting story will keep readers interested and guessing until the end." SLJ

Smelcer, John E.

The **Great** Death; [by] John Smelcer. Henry Holt and Co. 2009 166p $15.99
Grades: 6 7 8 9 **Fic**
1. Death -- Fiction 2. Orphans -- Fiction 3. Sisters -- Fiction 4. Epidemics -- Fiction 5. Native Americans -- Fiction 6. Voyages and travels -- Fiction
ISBN 978-0-8050-8100-8; 0-8050-8100-3
LC 2008-51113

As their Alaskan village's only survivors of sickness brought by white men one winter early in the twentieth century, sisters Millie, aged thirteen, and Maura, ten, make their way south in hopes of finding someone alive.

"An engaging tale of survival." Kirkus

★ The **trap**; [by] John Smelcer. Henry Holt and Co. 2006 170p $15.95
Grades: 6 7 8 9 **Fic**
1. Alaska -- Fiction 2. Grandfathers -- Fiction 3. Native Americans -- Fiction 4. Survival after airplane accidents, shipwrecks, etc. -- Fiction
ISBN 978-0-8050-7939-5; 0-8050-7939-4
LC 2005035740

In alternating chapters, seventeen-year-old Johnny Least-Weasel worries about his missing grandfather, and the grandfather, Albert Least-Weasel, struggles to survive, caught in his own steel trap in the Alaskan winter.

"In this story, Smelcer . . . seems to straddle the line flawlessly between an ancient legend and contemporary fiction. . . . His characters act with quiet dignity. . . . The suspense is played on an everyday level, which is why it works." Voice Youth Advocates

Smibert, Angie

Memento Nora. Marshall Cavendish 2011 184p $16.99
Grades: 8 9 10 11 12 **Fic**
1. Science fiction 2. Memory -- Fiction 3. Terrorism -- Fiction 4. Cartoons and caricatures -- Fiction 5. Resistance to government -- Fiction
ISBN 0-7614-5829-8; 978-0-7614-5829-6
LC 2010011816

In a near future in which terrorism is commonplace but memories of horrors witnessed can be obliterated by a pill, teens Nora, Winter, and Micah, create an underground comic to share with their classmates the experiences they want to remember.

This offers "a multi-threaded plot that manages to be both complex and comfortably easy to follow. . . . The fast pace encourages readers to fall headfirst into a gripping suspense-adventure ride." Bull Cent Child Books

Smith, Alexander Gordon

Lockdown. Farrar, Straus and Giroux 2009 273p (Escape from Furnace) $14.99
Grades: 7 8 9 10 **Fic**
1. Science fiction 2. Escapes -- Fiction 3. Prisoners -- Fiction
ISBN 978-0-374-32491-9; 0-374-32491-3
LC 2008-43439

When fourteen-year-old Alex is framed for murder, he becomes an inmate in the Furnace Penitentiary, where brutal inmates and sadistic guards reign, boys who disappear in the middle of the night sometimes return weirdly altered, and escape might just be possible.

"Once a plot is hatched, readers will be turning pages without pause, and the cliffhanger ending will have them anticipating the next installment. Most appealing is Smith's flowing writing style, filled with kid-speak, colorful adjectives, and amusing analogies." SLJ

Other titles in this series are:
Death sentence (2011)
Solitary (2010)

Smith, Andrew, 1959-

★ **Ghost** medicine. Feiwel & Friends 2008 357p $17.95
Grades: 8 9 10 11 12 **Fic**

1. Death -- Fiction 2. Friendship -- Fiction 3. Ranch life -- Fiction 4. West (U.S.) -- Fiction
ISBN 978-0-312-37557-7; 0-312-37557-3

Still mourning the recent death of his mother, seventeen-year-old Troy Stotts relates the events of the previous year when he and his two closest friends try to retaliate against the sheriff's son, who has been bullying them for years.

This novel "defies expectations via its sublime imagery and its elliptical narrative structure." Publ Wkly

Grasshopper jungle; by Andrew Smith. Dutton Juvenile 2014 432 p. (hardback) $18.99
Grades: 9 10 11 12 **Fic**

1. Praying mantis 2. Apocalyptic fiction 3. Iowa -- Fiction 4. Science fiction 5. Humorous fiction 6. Insects -- Fiction 7. Survival -- Fiction 8. Friendship -- Fiction 9. Gender identity -- Fiction 10. Family life -- Iowa -- Fiction
ISBN 0525426035; 9780525426035
LC 2013030265

Boston Globe-Horn Book Award: Fiction (2014)

Author Andrew Smith presents a "novel of the apocalypse [featuring] a (dead) mad scientist, a fabulous underground bunker, voracious giant praying mantises and gobs of messy violence. Narrated by hapless Polish-Iowan sophomore Austin Szerba, [it describes] the dead-end town of Ealing, Iowa; his girlfriend, Shann Collins, . . . and most importantly, his gay best friend, Robby Brees, to whom he finds himself as attracted as he is to Shann." (Kirkus)

"Award-winning author Smith has cleverly used a B movie science fiction plot to explore the intricacies of teenage sexuality, love, and friendship. Austin's desires might garner buzz and controversy among adults but not among the teenage boys who can identify with his internal struggles. This novel is proof that when an author creates solely for himself-as Smith notes in the acknowledgments section-the result is an original, honest, and extraordinary work that speaks directly to teens as it pushes the boundaries of young adult literature." (School Library Journal)

The **Marbury** lens. Feiwel and Friends 2010 358p $17.99
Grades: 10 11 12 **Fic**

1. Horror fiction 2. Kidnapping -- Fiction 3. London (England) -- Fiction
ISBN 978-0-312-61342-6; 0-312-61342-3
LC 2010-13007

After being kidnapped and barely escaping, sixteen-year-old Jack goes to London with his best friend Connor, where someone gives him a pair of glasses that send him to an alternate universe where war is raging, he is responsible for the survival of two younger boys, and Connor is trying to kill them all.

"This bloody and genuinely upsetting book packs an enormous emotional punch. Smith's characters are very well developed and the ruined alternate universe they travel through is both surreal and believable." Publ Wkly

★ **Passenger**; Andrew Smith. Feiwel and Friends 2012 465 p. $17.99
Grades: 9 10 11 12 **Fic**

1. Horror fiction 2. Occult fiction 3. Fantasy fiction 4. Survival -- Fiction 5. Kidnapping -- Fiction 6. London (England) -- Fiction 7. Kidnapping 8. London (England)
ISBN 125000487X; 9781250004871
LC 2012288522

This horror fantasy novel, by Andrew Smith, is the sequel to "The Marbury Lens." "Best friends Jack and Conner can't stay away from Marbury. It's partly because of their obsession with this alternate world and the unresolved war that still wages there. . . . The boys try to destroy the lens that transports them to Marbury. But that dark world is not so easily reckoned with." (Publisher's note)

★ 100 **sideways** miles. Andrew Smith. Simon & Schuster Books for Young Readers. 2014 288p
Grades: 9 10 11 12 **Fic**

1. Authors — Fiction 2. Best friends — Fiction 3. Dating (Social customs) — Fiction 4. Epilepsy — Fiction 5. Father-son relationship — Fiction 6. Friendship — Fiction 7. California — Fiction 8. Boys — Fiction
ISBN: 1442444959; 9781442444959
LC 2013030326

National Book Award Longlist (2014)

"Finn Easton has lived his life in the shadow of a book. As a child, Finn was severely injured and his mother killed in a freak accident: a dead horse landed on them when it fell off a truck that was traveling over a bridge. After the accident, his father took many of Finn's unique characteristics (his name, heterochromatic eyes, propensity to measure time in miles traveled by the Earth in orbit, struggle with epilepsy, and a particular scar along his back) and made them into a character in a Robert Heinlein-esque novel, The Lazarus Door...This will appeal to teens who like novels with a bit of an absurdist edge, such as Libba Bray's Going Bovine..." (School Library Journal)

Stick. Feiwel and Friends 2011 292p $17.99; ebook $9.99
Grades: 9 10 11 12 **Fic**

1. Brothers -- Fiction 2. Child abuse -- Fiction 3. Birth defects -- Fiction 4. Homosexuality -- Fiction 5. Runaway teenagers -- Fiction
ISBN 978-0-312-61341-9; 978-1-4299-9537-5 ebook
LC 2011023541

"Thirteen-year-old Stick was born with only one ear and secretly sadistic parents; for the slightest infraction, Stick s father will beat him and his older brother Bosten. After Dad finds out Bosten is gay, both boys, separately, run away." (Horn Book)

"Dark, painful, but ultimately hopeful, this is not a book for everyone, but in the right reader's hands, it will be treasured." Voice Youth Advocates

★ **Winger**; Andrew Smith. 1st ed. Simon & Schuster Books for Young Readers 2013 448 p. (hardcover) $16.99
Grades: 9 10 11 12 **Fic**

1. School stories 2. Rugby football -- Fiction 3. High

schools -- Fiction 4. Boarding schools -- Fiction 5. Interpersonal relations -- Fiction
ISBN 1442444924; 9781442444928; 9781442444942
LC 2011052750

In this novel, by Andrew Smith, "Ryan Dean West is a fourteen-year-old junior at a boarding school for rich kids. He's living in . . . the dorm for troublemakers, and rooming with the biggest bully on the rugby team. And he's madly in love with his best friend Annie, who thinks of him as a little boy. With the help of his . . . humor, rugby buddies, and his penchant for doodling comics, Ryan Dean manages to survive life's complications and even find some happiness along the way." (Publisher's note)

"Smith deftly builds characters--readers will suddenly realize they've effortlessly fallen in love with them--and he laces meaning and poignantly real dialogue into uproariously funny scatological and hormonally charged humor, somehow creating a balance between the two that seems to intensify both extremes. Bawdily comic but ultimately devastating, this is unforgettable." Kirkus

Smith, Cynthia Leitich

Blessed. Candlewick Press 2011 462p $17.99
Grades: 9 10 11 12 **Fic**

1. Texas -- Fiction 2. Orphans -- Fiction 3. Vampires -- Fiction 4. Werewolves -- Fiction 5. Restaurants -- Fiction 6. Supernatural -- Fiction
ISBN 978-0-7636-4326-3
LC 2010-38697

Even as teenaged Quincie Morris adjusts to her appetites as a neophyte vampire, she must clear her true love, the hybrid-werewolf Kieren, of murder charges; thwart the apocalyptic ambitions of Bradley Sanguini, the vampire-chef who "blessed" her; and keep her dead parents' restaurant up and running before she loses her own soul.

"A satisfying blend of excitement and intrigue, Blessed provides a fun and entertaining read. Appealing to high schoolers with a flair for fantasy, this book provides a twist on life as an 'eternal.'" Voice Youth Advocates

Eternal. Candlewick Press 2009 307p $17.99
Grades: 8 9 10 11 **Fic**

1. Angels -- Fiction 2. Vampires -- Fiction
ISBN 978-0-7636-3573-2
LC 2008-27658

When Miranda's guardian angel Zachary recklessly saves her from falling into an open grave and dying, the result is that she turns into a vampire and he is left to try to reinstate his reputation by finally doing the right thing.

"Readers should be hooked by this fully formed world, up through the action-packed finale." Publ Wkly

Feral curse. Cynthia Leitich Smith. Candlewick Press. 2014 272p $17.99
Grades: 9 10 11 12 **Fic**

1. Adopted children — Fiction 2. Shapeshifting — Fiction 3. Curses — Fiction 4. Fantasy fiction
ISBN: 076365910X; 9780763659103
LC 2013946609

Second title in the author's Feral fantasy series. This "installment begins in the small town of Pine Ridge, Texas. Kayla is a teenage werecat adopted at birth and raised by loving human parents. Isolated from the shifter world, she has hidden her inner cat from those she cares about. Driven by her love for Benjamin and an attempt to be open and honest, she reveals her true nature. The result is disastrous, ending in betrayal, regret, and rejection. Determined to "save" Kayla, Ben unleashes a mystical curse that ensnares shifters and ties them to enchanted carousel animals while causing his untimely death." SLJ

"Debut character Kayla--level-headed, religious, but also quietly proud of her shifter nature--holds her own. Witty banter keeps the tone light even as the stakes ramp up." Horn Book

Feral nights; Cynthia Leitich Smith. Candlewick Press 2013 304 p. $17.99
Grades: 9 10 11 12 **Fic**

1. Shapeshifting --Fiction 2. Fantasy fiction
ISBN 0763659096; 9780763659097
LC 2012942377

This young adult paranormal fantasy story, by Cynthia Leitich Smith, is the first entry in the series "Feral." "When sexy, free-spirited werecat Yoshi tracks his sister, Ruby, to Austin, he discovers that she is not only MIA, but also the key suspect in a murder investigation. Meanwhile, werepossum Clyde and human Aimee have set out to do a little detective work of their own, sworn to avenge the brutal killing of werearmadillo pal Travis." (Publisher's note)

Rain is not my Indian name. HarperCollins Pubs. 2001 135p $15.99; lib bdg $16.89
Grades: 6 7 8 9 **Fic**

1. Death -- Fiction 2. Photography -- Fiction 3. Native Americans -- Fiction
ISBN 0-688-17397-7; 0-06-029504-X lib bdg
LC 00-59705

Tired of staying in seclusion since the death of her best friend, a fourteen-year-old Native American girl takes on a photographic assignment with her local newspaper to cover events at the Native American summer youth camp

"The engaging first-person narrative convincingly portrays Rain's grieving process and addresses the varying degrees of prejudice she encounters." Horn Book Guide

Tantalize. Candlewick Press 2007 310p $16.99; pa $8.99
Grades: 9 10 11 12 **Fic**

1. Texas -- Fiction 2. Vampires -- Fiction 3. Werewolves -- Fiction 4. Restaurants -- Fiction 5. Supernatural -- Fiction
ISBN 0-7636-2791-7; 978-0-7636-2791-1; 0-7636-4059-X pa; 978-0-7636-4059-0 pa
LC 2005-58124

When multiple murders in Austin, Texas, threaten the grand reopening of her family's vampire-themed restaurant, seventeen-year-old, orphaned Quincie worries that her best friend-turned-love interest, Kieren, a werewolf-in-training, may be the prime suspect.

"Horror fans will be hooked by Kieren's quiet, hirsute hunkiness, and Texans by the premise that nearly everybody in their capitol is a shapeshifter." Publ Wkly

Followed by Blessed (2011)

Smith, Emily Wing

Back when you were easier to love. Dutton Books 2011 296p $16.99

Grades: 8 9 10 11 12 **Fic**

1. Love stories 2. Mormons -- Fiction 3. Automobile travel -- Fiction

ISBN 978-0-525-42199-3; 0-525-42199-8

LC 2010-13469

When her boyfriend Zan leaves high school in Utah a year early to attend Pitzer College, a broken-hearted Joy and Zan's best friend Noah take off on a road trip to California seeking "closure."

Smith "effectively reconstructs Zan and Joy's relationship. . . . Joy's voice is sturdy, and her articulations about loss and belief are thoughtful and often moving. Self-acceptance and both the comforts and restrictions of the Mormon religion and identity are central themes in this sweet story." Publ Wkly

★ The **way** he lived; [by] Emily Wing Smith. 1st ed.; Flux 2008 232p pa $9.95

Grades: 8 9 10 11 12 **Fic**

1. Death -- Fiction 2. Mormons -- Fiction

ISBN 978-0-7387-1404-2 pa

LC 2008024416

"Besides living in the same Mormon community in Utah, Tabbatha, Adlen, Miles, Claire, Norah and Lissa have something else in common: each had a special connection to Joel Espen, who died of dehydration after giving away his water during a badly planned Boy Scout expedition. In vignettes showing the six teens differing points of view, first-time author Smith probes into the psychologies of the survivors to demonstrate Joel's effect on their lives and their attempts to make sense of his death. . . . The author preserves each narrator's complexity. . . It's a testiment to Smith's skills that although her central character speaks only through other people's recollections, his identity emerges distinctly by the end of the novel." Publ Wkly

Smith, Hilary T.

Wild awake; Hilary T. Smith. 1st ed. Katherine Tegen Books, an imprint of HarperCollinsPublishers 2013 375 p. (hardcover) $17.99

Grades: 9 10 11 12 **Fic**

1. Bereavement -- Fiction 2. Dating (Social customs) -- Fiction 3. Secrets -- Fiction 4. Sisters -- Fiction 5. Mental illness -- Fiction

ISBN 0062184687; 9780062184689

LC 2012045524

In this young adult novel, by Hilary T. Smith, "Kiri Byrd . . . intends to devote herself to her music and win the Battle of the Bands with her bandmate and best friend, Lukas. Perhaps then . . . he will finally realize she's the girl of his dreams. But a phone call from a stranger shatters Kiri's plans. He says he has her sister Suki's stuff--her sister Suki, who died five years ago. This call throws Kiri into a spiral of chaos that opens old wounds and new mysteries." (Publisher's note)

Smith, Jennifer E.

The **comeback** season. Simon & Schuster Books for Young Readers 2008 246p $15.99

Grades: 6 7 8 9 10 **Fic**

1. Baseball -- Fiction 2. Bereavement -- Fiction 3. Family life -- Fiction 4. Chicago (Ill.) -- Fiction 5. Father-daughter relationship -- Fiction

ISBN 978-1-4169-3847-7; 1-4169-3847-8

LC 2007-17067

High school freshman Ryan Walsh, a Chicago Cubs fan, meets Nick when they both skip school on opening day, and their blossoming relationship becomes difficult for Ryan when she discovers that Nick is seriously ill and she again feels the pain of losing her father five years earlier.

"Smith deftly twines strands of grief, romance, baseball, family, and friendships lost and regained into this tale. . . . The present-tense narrative has an immediacy that will engage readers and the supporting cast is unusually vivid." Booklist

The **geography** of you and me. Jennifer E. Smith. Little, Brown & Co. 2014 352p $18.00

Grades: 7 8 9 10 11 12 **Fic**

1. Electric power failures — Fiction; 2. Love — Fiction; 3. Social classes — Fiction; 4. Voyages and travels — Fiction; 5. New York (N.Y.) — Fiction

ISBN: 0316254770; 9780316254779

LC 2013022845

"Owen and Lucy meet during a citywide blackout in New York and spend a memorable (chaste) night together. Soon afterward, Lucy's parents take her to Europe, and Owen and his dad move to San Francisco, but even on opposite sides of the world, they think about each other. Smith's fans will recognize the alternating narration; reflective, deliberate writing style; and serendipitous coincidences." Horn Book

The **statistical** probability of love at first sight; Jennifer E. Smith. 1st ed. Little, Brown 2012 236 p.

Grades: 9 10 11 12 **Fic**

1. Love stories 2. Weddings -- Fiction 3. Air travel -- Fiction 4. Love -- Fiction 5. England -- Fiction 6. Remarriage -- Fiction 7. London (England) -- Fiction 8. Fate and fatalism -- Fiction 9. Funeral rites and ceremonies -- Fiction

ISBN 9780316122382

LC 2010048704

In this book, "[a]lthough her mother has made peace with the situation, Hadley is still angry and hurt that her father left them for an Englishwoman. Rebooked on the next flight after missing her plane to London, where she's to be a bridesmaid in their wedding, Hadley is seated next to the English boy who helped her in the terminal. He comes to her rescue again after she confesses she suffers from claustrophobia. A good-looking Yale student, Oliver is smart, funny and thoughtful, though evasive about the purpose of his trip. Their mutual attraction is heightened by the limbo of air travel, but on arrival, they're separated. With just minutes to get to the wedding, Hadley . . . makes her way to the church and the father she's avoided seeing for a year." (Kirkus)

This is what happy looks like; Jennifer E. Smith. 1st ed. Poppy 2013 416 p. (hardcover) $17.99

Grades: 9 10 11 **Fic**

1. Love stories 2. Online dating -- Fiction 3. Teenage girls -- Fiction 4. Love -- Fiction 5. Maine -- Fiction

6. Actors and actresses -- Fiction
ISBN 0316212822; 9780316212823

LC 2012028755

In this novel, by Jennifer E. Smith, "when teenage movie star Graham Larkin accidentally sends small town girl Ellie O'Neill an email about his pet pig, the two seventeen-year-olds strike up a witty and unforgettable correspondence, discussing everything . . . except for their names or backgrounds. Then Graham finds out that Ellie's Maine hometown is the perfect location for his latest film, and he decides to take their relationship from online to in-person." (Publisher's note)

Smith, Lindsay

Sekret; Lindsay Smith. Roaring Brook Press. 2014 345p $17.99

Grades: 8 9 10 11 12 **Fic**

1. KGB — Fiction 2. Psychic ability — Fiction 3. Spies — Fiction 4. Soviet Union — History — 1953-1985 — Fiction;
ISBN: 1596438924; 9781596438927

LC 2013027913

"Yulia's father always taught her to hide her thoughts and control her emotions to survive the harsh realities of Soviet Russia. But when she's captured by the KGB and forced to work as a psychic spy with a mission to undermine the U.S. space program, she's thrust into a world of suspicion, deceit, and horrifying power." (Publisher's note)

"We the Living meets Genius Squad, this novel follows the misfortunes of Yulia, one of a group of psychic teens pressed into the service of the 1960s KGB. The concept is ambitious and the heroine fiery, but there is a surfeit of plot elements (including a hokey love triangle) and the writing is frequently turgid." Horn Book

Smith, Patricia Clark

Weetamoo, heart of the Pocassets. Scholastic 2003 203p il (Royal diaries) $10.95

Grades: 6 7 8 9 **Fic**

1. Pocasset Indians 2. Native Americans -- Fiction
ISBN 0-439-12910-9

LC 00-49243

The 1653-1654 diary of a fourteen-year-old Pocasset Indian girl, destined to become a leader of her tribe, describes how her life changes with the seasons, after a ritual fast she undertakes, and with her tribe's interaction with the English "Coat-men" of the nearby Plymouth Colony

This is "a lively yet ultimately tragic tale that vividly evokes the time period." Booklist

Smith, Roland

Elephant run. Hyperion Books for Children 2007 318p $15.99

Grades: 6 7 8 9 10 11 12 **Fic**

1. Elephants -- Fiction 2. Prisoners of war -- Fiction 3. World War, 1939-1945 -- Fiction
ISBN 978-1-4231-0402-5; 1-4231-0402-1

LC 2007-13310

Nick endures servitude, beatings, and more after his British father's plantation in Burma is invaded by the Japanese in 1941.

"The Burmese setting and the role of elephants in the lumbering industry are exceptionally well integrated into this wartime adventure tale." Bull Cent Child Books

★ **Peak.** Harcourt 2007 246p $17

Grades: 7 8 9 10 **Fic**

1. Mountaineering -- Fiction 2. Fathers and sons -- Fiction 3. Father-son relationship -- Fiction
ISBN 978-0-15-202417-8

LC 2006024325

After fourteen-year-old Peak Marcello is arrested for scaling a New York City skyscraper, he is sent to live with his long-lost father, who wants him to be the youngest person to reach the Everest summit.

"This is a thrilling, multifaceted adventure story. Smith includes plenty of mountaineering facts told in vivid detail. . . . But he also explores other issues, such as the selfishness that nearly always accompanies the intensely single-minded." Booklist

Tentacles. Scholastic Press 2009 318p $16.99

Grades: 5 6 7 8 **Fic**

1. Mystery fiction 2. Adventure fiction 3. Squids -- Fiction
ISBN 978-0-545-16688-1; 0-545-16688-8

LC 2009011125

After the mysterious disappearance of their parents, Marty and Grace go to live with their scientist uncle and accompany him on, what soon becomes, an increasingly dangerous expedition to New Zealand to track a giant squid.

Smith, Sarah

The **other** side of dark. Atheneum Books for Young Readers 2010 312p $16.99

Grades: 6 7 8 9 10 **Fic**

1. Ghost stories 2. Orphans -- Fiction 3. Supernatural -- Fiction 4. Boston (Mass.) -- Fiction 5. Race relations -- Fiction 6. African Americans -- Fiction
ISBN 978-1-4424-0280-5; 1-4424-0280-6

LC 2010-14690

Since losing both of her parents, fifteen-year-old Katie can see and talk to ghosts, which makes her a loner until fellow student Law sees her drawing of a historic house and together they seek a treasure rumored to be hidden there by illegal slave-traders.

The author "weaves complicated racial issues into a romantic, mysterious novel." Booklist

Smith, Sherri L.

★ **Flygirl.** G.P. Putnam's Sons 2009 275p $16.99

Grades: 7 8 9 10 **Fic**

1. Air pilots -- Fiction 2. Women air pilots -- Fiction 3. African Americans -- Fiction 4. World War, 1939-1945 -- Fiction
ISBN 978-0-399-24709-5; 0-399-24709-2

LC 2008-25407

During World War II, a light-skinned African American girl "passes" for white in order to join the Women Airforce Service Pilots.

"The details about navigation are exciting, but tougher than any flight maneuver are Ida Mae's loneliness, shame, and fear that she will be thrown out of the the military, feelings that culminate in an unforgettable climax." Booklist

Orleans; Sherri L. Smith. G.P. Putnam's Sons 2013 324 p. (hardcover) $17.99
Grades: 9 10 11 12 **Fic**
1. Science fiction 2. Viruses -- Fiction 3. New Orleans (La.) -- Fiction 4. Virus diseases -- Fiction
ISBN 0399252940; 9780399252945
LC 2012009634

This novel, by Sherri L. Smith, describes a dystopian New Orleans. "After a . . . severe outbreak of Delta Fever, the Gulf Coast has been quarantined. Years later, residents of the Outer States are under the assumption that life in the Delta is all but extinct . . . but in reality, a new primitive society has been born. Fen de la Guerre . . . , left with her tribe leader's newborn, . . . is determined to get the baby to a better life over the wall." (Publisher's note)

Smith-Ready, Jeri
Shade. Simon Pulse 2010 309p $17.99
Grades: 9 10 11 12 **Fic**
1. Ghost stories 2. Trials -- Fiction 3. Musicians -- Fiction 4. Supernatural -- Fiction 5. Baltimore (Md.) -- Fiction
ISBN 978-1-4169-9406-0
LC 2009-39487

Sixteen-year-old Aura of Baltimore, Maryland, reluctantly works at her aunt's law firm helping ghosts with wrongful death cases file suits in hopes of moving on, but it becomes personal when her boyfriend, a promising musician, dies and persistently haunts her.

Although "Smith-Ready's occasionally racy . . . [book] resolves almost none of the issues surrounding the Shift, leaving the door open for future books, it is a fully satisfying read on its own, with well-developed, believable characters. . . . Perhaps even more impressive is the understatement of the paranormal premise—Smith-Ready changes the world completely by simply changing our ability to see." Publ Wkly

Followed by Shift (2011)

Shift. Simon Pulse 2011 367p $17.99
Grades: 9 10 11 12 **Fic**
1. Ghost stories 2. Musicians -- Fiction 3. Supernatural -- Fiction 4. Baltimore (Md.) -- Fiction
ISBN 978-1-4169-9408-4
LC 2010036784

Sequel to Shade (2011)

Logan returns as a ghost, complicating sixteen-year-old Aura's budding relationship with Zachary, especially when they discover that Logan might be able to become solid again.

"Smith-Ready's strengths are well-developed core characters, dialogue, and the clever narrative tone. Mature language and content make this better suited for older teens." SLJ

This **side** of salvation. Jeri Smith-Ready. Simon Pulse. 2014 384p $17.99
Grades: 9 10 11 12 **Fic**
1. Cults — Fiction; 2. End of the world — Fiction; 3. Grief — Fiction; 4. Missing persons — Fiction; 5. Schools — Fiction; 6. Family life — Fiction
ISBN: 1442439483; 9781442439481
LC 2013019948

"Following the death of his soldier brother, David's grief-stricken parents have turned to religion--specifically a fundamentalist cult--for solace. His recovering-alcoholic father speaks only in Bible verses; his mother is fixated on the upcoming Rapture, or Rush. When his parents disappear, David must untangle the mystery. Chapter flashbacks to "Before the Rush" alternate with "Now" in this nuanced study of relationships, religion, and faith." Horn Book

Sniegoski, Tom
Sleeper code; by Tom Sniegoski. Razorbill 2006 278p (Sleeper conspiracy) pa $6.99
Grades: 8 9 10 11 12 **Fic**
1. Conspiracies -- Fiction 2. Sleep disorders -- Fiction 3. Multiple personality -- Fiction
ISBN 1-59514-052-2
LC 2006009102

Just when he has met a beautiful girl and his outlook is improving, sixteen-year-old narcoleptic Tom Lovett begins to suspect that his dreams and hallucinations of killing people may be something more real and terrifying.

"Readers looking for fast-paced action and espionage will enjoy this first book in the two-part Sleeper Conspiracy." SLJ

Snow, Carol
Snap. HarperTeen 2009 221p $16.99
Grades: 7 8 9 10 **Fic**
1. Beaches -- Fiction 2. Cameras -- Fiction 3. Friendship -- Fiction 4. Family life -- Fiction 5. Photography -- Fiction 6. Supernatural -- Fiction
ISBN 978-0-06-145211-6; 0-06-145211-4
LC 2009-14581

When fifteen-year-old Madison's parents, who are having problems, bring her to a seedy beachside town, she relies on some quirky new friends for help figuring out how her camera is taking pictures of people who are not there, and who later suffer tragedies.

"Snow's novel is a page-turning blend of romance, mystery, and the supernatural. . . . Characters are well developed." SLJ

Switch. HarperTeen 2008 215p $16.99; pa $8.99
Grades: 8 9 10 11 12 **Fic**
1. Supernatural -- Fiction
ISBN 978-0-06-145208-6; 0-06-145208-4; 978-0-06-145210-9 pa; 0-06-145210-6 pa
LC 2008020220

Living in a small beach community with her mother, fifteen-year-old Claire, an accomplished swimmer, discovers that, like her long-dead but, still very much present, grandmother, she has the ability to inhabit other people's bodies while asleep.

"Claire's quick-paced narration comes laced with bolts of sarcasm; the realistic problems blend successfully into a suspenseful, mystical story." Kirkus

Somper, Justin

Demons of the ocean. Little, Brown 2006 330p (Vampirates) $15.99

Grades: 6 7 8 9 **Fic**

1. Adventure fiction 2. Twins -- Fiction 3. Pirates -- Fiction 4. Vampires -- Fiction

ISBN 0-316-01373-0

When twins Connor and Grace's ship is wrecked in a storm and Connor is rescued by pirates, he believes that Grace has been taken aboard the mythical Vampirate's ship, and he is determined to find her.

"This winning fantasy features both pirates and vampires with adventure, bloodcurling action, and sinister characters." Voice Youth Advocates

Other titles in this series are:

Tide of terror (2007)

Blood Captain (2008)

Black heart (2009)

Empire of night (2010)

Sones, Sonya

One of those hideous books where the mother dies. Simon & Schuster Books for Young Readers 2004 268p $15.95; pa $6.99

Grades: 7 8 9 10 **Fic**

1. Actors -- Fiction 2. Bereavement -- Fiction 3. Father-daughter relationship -- Fiction

ISBN 0-689-85820-5; 1-416-90788-2 pa

LC 2003-9355

Fifteen-year-old Ruby Milliken leaves her best friend, her boyfriend, her aunt, and her mother's grave in Boston and reluctantly flies to Los Angeles to live with her father, a famous movie star who divorced her mother before Ruby was born

"Ruby's affable personality is evident in her humorous quips and clever wordplays. Her depth of character is revealed through her honest admissions, poignant revelations, and sensitive insights. . . . Ruby's story is gripping, enjoyable, and memorable." SLJ

Stop pretending; what happened when my big sister went crazy. HarperCollins Pubs. 1999 149p lib bdg $14.89; pa $6.99

Grades: 6 7 8 9 **Fic**

1. Sisters -- Fiction 2. Mental illness -- Fiction

ISBN 0-06-028386-6 lib bdg; 0-06-446218-8 pa

LC 99-11473

"Based on the journals Sones wrote at the age of 13 when her 19-year-old sister was hospitalized due to manic depression, the simply crafted but deeply felt poems reflect her thoughts, fears, hopes, and dreams during that troubling time." SLJ

What my girlfriend doesn't know. Simon & Schuster Books for Young Readers 2007 291p $16.99

Grades: 7 8 9 10 **Fic**

1. School stories 2. Artists -- Fiction 3. Boston (Mass.) -- Fiction 4. Dating (Social customs) -- Fiction

ISBN 978-0-689-87602-8; 0-689-87602-5

LC 2006-14682

Sequel to What my mother doesn't know (2001)

Fourteen-year-old Robin Murphy is so unpopular at high school that his name is slang for "loser," and so when he begins dating the beautiful and popular Sophie her reputation plummets, but he finds acceptance as a student in a drawing class at Harvard.

"Robin's believable voice is distinctive, and Sones uses her spare words (and a few drawings) to expert effect." Booklist

What my mother doesn't know. Simon & Schuster Bks. for Young Readers 2001 259p hardcover o.p. pa $7.99

Grades: 7 8 9 10 **Fic**

1. Novels in verse 2. Dating (Social customs) -- Fiction

ISBN 0-689-84114-0; 0-689-85553-2 pa

LC 00-52634

Sophie describes her relationships with a series of boys as she searches for Mr. Right

This is "a fast, funny, touching book. . . . The very short, sometimes rhythmic lines make each page fly. Sophie's voice is colloquial and intimate." Booklist

Followed by What my girlfriend doesn't know (2007)

Sonnenblick, Jordan

★ **After** ever after. Scholastic Press 2010 260p $16.99

Grades: 5 6 7 8 **Fic**

1. School stories 2. Cancer -- Fiction 3. Friendship -- Fiction 4. Family life -- Fiction

ISBN 978-0-439-83706-4; 0-439-83706-5

Jeffery's cancer is in remission but the chemotherapy and radiation treatments have left him with concentration problems, and he worries about school work, his friends, his family, and a girl who likes him

"Sonnenblick imbues Jeffrey with a smooth, likable, and unaffected voice. . . . As hilarious as it is tragic, and as honest as it is hopeful . . . [this book is] irresistable reading." Booklist

Drums, girls, & dangerous pie. Scholastic Press 2005 273p $16.99

Grades: 5 6 7 8 **Fic**

1. Brothers -- Fiction 2. Leukemia -- Fiction

ISBN 0-439-75519-0

LC 2004-62563

First published 2004 by Turning Tide Press

When his younger brother is diagnosed with leukemia, thirteen-year-old Steven tries to deal with his complicated emotions, his school life, and his desire to support his family.

"A story that could have morphed into melodrama is saved by reality, rawness, and the wit Sonnenblick infuses into Steven's first-person voice." Booklist

Notes from the midnight driver. Scholastic Press 2006 265p $16.99

Grades: 8 9 10 11 12 **Fic**

1. Old age -- Fiction 2. Musicians -- Fiction 3. Friendship -- Fiction

ISBN 0-439-75779-7

LC 2005-27972

After being assigned to perform community service at a nursing home, sixteen-year-old Alex befriends a cantankerous old man who has some lessons to impart about jazz guitar playing, love, and forgiveness.

The author "deftly infiltrates the teenage mind to produce a first-person narrative riddled with enough hapless confusion, mulish equivocation, and beleaguered deadpan humor to have readers nodding with recognition, sighing with sympathy, and gasping with laughter—often on the same page." Horn Book

★ **Zen** and the art of faking it. Scholastic Press 2007 264p $16.99; pa $7.99

Grades: 5 6 7 8 **Fic**

1. School stories 2. Zen Buddhism -- Fiction 3. Asian Americans -- Fiction

ISBN 978-0-439-83707-1; 0-439-83707-3; 978-0-439-83709-5 pa; 0-439-83709-X pa

LC 2006-28841

When thirteen-year-old San Lee moves to a new town and school for the umpteenth time, he is looking for a way to stand out when his knowledge of Zen Buddhism, gained in his previous school, provides the answer—and the need to quickly become a convincing Zen master.

The author gives readers "plenty to laugh at. . . . Mixed with more serious scenes, . . . lighter moments take a basic message about the importance of honesty and forgiveness and treat it with panache." Publ Wkly

Sorrells, Walter

★ **First** shot. Dutton Children's Books 2007 279p hardcover o.p. pa $7.99

Grades: 7 8 9 10 11 12 **Fic**

1. Mystery fiction 2. Homicide -- Fiction 3. Father-son relationship -- Fiction

ISBN 978-0-525-47801-0; 0-525-47801-9; 978-0-14-241421-7 pa; 0-14-241421-2 pa

As David enters his senior year of high school, a family secret emerges that could solve the mystery of why his mother was murdered two years ago.

"David's first person narration pulls readers into the young man's torment. . . . This is a fast-paced, intriguing read." Booklist

Whiteout. Dutton Children's Books 2009 312p (Hunted) $15.99

Grades: 7 8 9 10 **Fic**

1. Mystery fiction 2. Homicide -- Fiction 3. Blizzards -- Fiction 4. Minnesota -- Fiction 5. Mother-daughter relationship -- Fiction

ISBN 978-0-525-42141-2; 0-525-42141-6

Sixteen-year-old Chass makes her way through a Minnesota blizzard, seeking not only the murderer of a beloved music teacher, but also something belonging to the killer who has been chasing her mother and herself around the country.

"There is . . . plenty of suspense to propel even a reluctant reader, and a number of false turns to keep the reader guessing." Voice Youth Advocates

Soto, Gary

Accidental love; [by] Gary Soto. Harcourt 2006 179p $16

Grades: 6 7 8 9 **Fic**

1. Love stories 2. School stories 3. Hispanic Americans -- Fiction

ISBN 0-15-205497-9

LC 2004-29900

After unexpectedly falling in love with a "nerdy" boy, fourteen-year-old Marisa works to change her life by transferring to another school, altering some of her behavior, and losing weight.

This is a "warmhearted, humorous novel." SLJ

★ **Buried** onions. Harcourt Brace & Co. 1997 149p hardcover o.p. pa $6.95

Grades: 8 9 10 11 12 **Fic**

1. Violence -- Fiction 2. Mexican Americans -- Fiction

ISBN 0-15-201333-4; 0-15-206265-3 pa

LC 96-53112

When nineteen-year-old Eddie drops out of college, he struggles to find a place for himself as a Mexican American living in a violence-infested neighborhood of Fresno, California.

"Soto has created a beautiful, touching, and truthful story. . . . The lyrical language and Spanish phrases add to the immediacy of setting and to the sensitivity the author brings to his character's life." Voice Youth Advocates

★ **Taking** sides. Harcourt Brace Jovanovich 1991 138p hardcover o.p. pa $5.95

Grades: 5 6 7 8 **Fic**

1. Basketball -- Fiction 2. Hispanic Americans -- Fiction

ISBN 0-15-284076-1; 0-15-204694-1 pa

LC 91-11082

Fourteen-year-old Lincoln Mendoza, an aspiring basketball player, must come to terms with his divided loyalties when he moves from the Hispanic inner city to a white suburban neighborhood

This is a "light but appealing story. . . . Because of its subject matter and its clear, straightforward prose, it will be especially good for reluctant readers." SLJ

Includes glossary

Sparrow, Rebecca

The **year** Nick McGowan came to stay; [by] Rebecca Sparrow. 1st American ed.; Alfred A. Knopf 2008 198p $15.99; lib bdg $18.99

Grades: 8 9 10 11 **Fic**

1. School stories

ISBN 978-0-375-84570-3; 0-375-84570-4; 978-0-375-94570-0 lib bdg; 0-375-84570-9 lib bdg

LC 2007020758

First published 2006 in Australia

In her final year of high school in 1989, Australian teenager Rachel has her world turned upside down when the most popular (and disturbed) boy in school comes to live with her family for a semester.

"This book is full of laugh-out-loud moments. . . . Sparrow is adept at accurately portraying her teenage characters and placing them in realistic scenarios that most readers will find pertinent." SLJ

Speare, Elizabeth George

★ The **witch** of Blackbird Pond. Houghton Mifflin 1958 249p $17
Grades: 6 7 8 9 **Fic**

1. Puritans -- Fiction 2. Witchcraft -- Fiction
ISBN 0-395-07114-3
LC 58-11063

Awarded the Newbery Medal, 1959

"Headstrong and undisciplined, Barbados-bred Kit Tyler is an embarrassment to her Puritan relatives, and her sincere attempts to aid a reputed witch soon bring her to trial as a suspect." Child Books Too Good to Miss

Spillebeen, Geert

Age 14; translated by Terese Edelstein. Houghton Mifflin 2009 216p $16
Grades: 8 9 10 11 12 **Fic**

1. Soldiers -- Fiction 2. World War, 1914-1918 -- Fiction
ISBN 978-0-547-05342-4; 0-547-05342-8
LC 2010-277732

"Based on a true story, this spare, powerful novel . . . focuses on Patrick, a poor Irish kid who is just 13 when war breaks out. He dreams of escaping his dreary future and abusive dad and finding adventure and glory in the army. . . . The recruiters knowingly accept him into the service when he claims that he is a 17-year-old named John. . . . Spillebeen brings to the story to a realistic, grim conclusion." Booklist

Kipling's choice; written by Geert Spillebeen; translated by Terese Edelstein. Houghton Mifflin Co 2005 147p $16; pa $7.99
Grades: 7 8 9 10 **Fic**

1. Army officers 2. France -- Fiction 3. Children of prominent persons 4. World War, 1914-1918 -- Fiction
ISBN 0-618-43124-1; 0-618-80035-2 pa
LC 2004-20856

In 1915, mortally wounded in Loos, France, eighteen-year-old John Kipling, son of writer Rudyard Kipling, remembers his boyhood and the events leading to what is to be his first and last World War I battle.

"This well-written novel combines facts with speculation about John Kipling's short life and gruesome death. A riveting account of World War I." SLJ

Spinelli, Jerry

★ **Crash**. Knopf 1996 162p hardcover o.p. pa $6.99; lib bdg $17.99
Grades: 5 6 7 8 **Fic**

1. Football -- Fiction 2. Friendship -- Fiction 3. Grandfathers -- Fiction
ISBN 0440238579; 0679879579; 0679979573
LC 95030942

"Crash is a star football player. He torments Penn, a classmate who is everything Crash is not—friendly, small, and a pacifist. When his beloved grandfather comes to live with his family and suffers a debilitating stroke, Crash begins to see value in many of the things he has scorned." Horn Book Guide

Smiles to go. Joanna Cotler Books 2008 248p $16.99; lib bdg $17.89; pa $6.99
Grades: 6 7 8 9 10 **Fic**

1. School stories 2. Siblings -- Fiction 3. Friendship -- Fiction 4. Family life -- Fiction
ISBN 978-0-06-028133-5; 0-06-028133-2; 978-0-06-028134-2 lib bdg; 0-06-028134-0 lib bdg; 978-0-06-447197-8 pa; 0-06-447197-7 pa
LC 2007-29563

Will Tuppence's life has always been ruled by science and common sense but in ninth grade, shaken up by the discovery that protons decay, he begins to see the entire world differently and gains new perspective on his relationships with his little sister and two closest friends.

"What makes a Spinelli novel isn't plotting so much as character, dialogue, voice and humor. The Spinelli touch remains true in this funny and thoroughly enjoyable read." Publ Wkly

★ **Stargirl**. Knopf 2000 186p $15.95; lib bdg $17.99; pa $8.95
Grades: 7 8 9 10 **Fic**

1. School stories
ISBN 0-679-88637-0; 0-679-98637-5 lib bdg; 0-375-82233-X pa
LC 99-87944

In this story about the perils of popularity, the courage of nonconformity, and the thrill of first love, an eccentric student named Stargirl changes Mica High School forever

"As always respectful of his audience, Spinelli poses searching questions about loyalty to one's friends and oneself and leaves readers to form their own answers." Publ Wkly

Another title about Stargirl is:
Love, Stargirl (2007)

There's a girl in my hammerlock. Simon & Schuster Bks. for Young Readers 1991 199p hardcover o.p. pa $5.99
Grades: 5 6 7 8 **Fic**

1. School stories 2. Sex role -- Fiction 3. Wrestling -- Fiction
ISBN 1-4169-3937-7 pa
LC 91-8765

Thirteen-year-old Maisie joins her school's formerly all-male wrestling team and tries to last through the season, despite opposition from other students, her best friend, and her own teammates

The author "tackles a meaty subject—traditional gender roles—with his usual humor and finesse. The result, written in a breezy, first-person style, is a rattling good sports story that is clever, witty and tightly written." Publ Wkly

Spinner, Stephanie

Damosel; in which the Lady of the Lake renders a frank and often startling account of her wondrous life and times. Alfred A. Knopf 2008 198p $16.99; lib bdg $19.99
Grades: 7 8 9 10 **Fic**

1. Kings 2. Magic -- Fiction 3. Dwarfs -- Fiction 4. Fools and jesters -- Fiction 5. Great Britain -- History

-- 0-1066 -- Fiction
ISBN 978-0-375-83634-3; 0-375-83634-9; 978-0-375-93634-0 lib bdg; 0-375-93634-3 lib bdg
LC 2007-43519

Damosel, a rule-bound Lady of the Lake, and Twixt, a seventeen-year-old dwarf, relate their experiences as they strive to help King Arthur face Morgause, Morgan, and Mordred, one through her magic and the other through his humble loyalty.

"The magic is exciting and palpable. . . . Spinner's elegant language, strong characterizations, energetic dialogue, and lively plot combine in a memorable, accessible novel." Booklist

Quicksilver. Knopf 2005 229p hardcover o.p. pa $5.99
Grades: 7 8 9 10 **Fic**
1. Classical mythology -- Fiction
ISBN 0-375-82638-6; 0-440-23845-5 pa
LC 2004-10311

Hermes, Prince of Thieves and son of Zeus, relates why the seasons change, the history of the Trojan War, his friendship with Pegasus, and many more adventures.

"Spinner seamlessly weaves necessary background information about the cast of celestial characters into a narrative filled with thrilling action and violence that is drawn straight from the original stories. Teens will connect with Hermes' immediate, often very funny voice." Booklist

Quiver. Knopf 2002 177p $15.95; lib bdg $17.99; pa $5.99
Grades: 7 8 9 10 **Fic**
1. Atalanta (Greek mythology) -- Fiction
ISBN 0-375-81489-2; 0-375-91489-7 lib bdg; 0-440-23819-6 pa
LC 2002-5451

When her father commands that she produce an heir, the huntress Atalanta gives her suitors a seemingly impossible task in order to uphold her pledge of chastity, as the gods of ancient Greece look on

"Spinner gives this Greek myth a fresh face and makes Atalanta a strong heroine." SLJ

Spooner, Michael

Last Child. Henry Holt 2005 230p $16.95
Grades: 7 8 9 10 **Fic**
1. Smallpox -- Fiction 2. Mandan Indians -- Fiction
ISBN 0-8050-7739-1
LC 2005-9957

Caught between the worlds of the her Scottish father and her Mandan mother in what is now North Dakota, Rosalie fights to survive both the 1837 smallpox epidemic and the actions of a vengeful trader.

"Action-packed prose; sharp, witty dialogue; and strong characterization make this novel an entertaining read." Voice Youth Advocates

Spradlin, Michael P.

Keeper of the Grail. G.P. Putnam's Sons 2008 248p (The youngest Templar) $17.99
Grades: 6 7 8 9 **Fic**
1. Grail -- Fiction 2. Crusades -- Fiction 3. Middle Ages -- Fiction
ISBN 978-0-399-24763-7; 0-399-24763-7
LC 2007-36143

In 1191, fifteen-year-old Tristan, a youth of unknown origin raised in an English abbey, becomes a Templar Knight's squire during the Third Crusade and soon finds himself on a mission to bring the Holy Grail to safety.

"The deadly action, uncompromising in many of its descriptions, may take center stage, but Spradlin smartly doesn't neglect story. . . . The stirring story ends with a true cliff-hanger, priming fans for the next installment." Booklist

Other titles in this series are:
Trail of fate (2009)
Orphan of destiny (2010)

Springer, Nancy

★ **I** am Mordred; a tale from Camelot. Philomel Bks. 1998 184p hardcover o.p. pa $6.99
Grades: 7 8 9 10 **Fic**
1. Kings 2. Mordred (Legendary character) -- Fiction 3. Great Britain -- History -- 0-1066 -- Fiction
ISBN 0-399-23143-9; 0-698-11841-3 pa
LC 97-39740

"Mordred, the bad seed, the son of King Arthur and his sister, spends his youth learning who he is and then trying to deal with the prophecy made by Merlin that he will kill his father." SLJ

"Springer humanizes Arthurian archvillain Mordred in a thoroughly captivating and poignant tale." Booklist

I am Morgan le Fay; a tale from Camelot. Philomel Bks. 2001 227p hardcover o.p. pa $5.99
Grades: 7 8 9 10 **Fic**
1. Kings 2. Great Britain -- History -- 0-1066 -- Fiction 3. Morgan le Fay (Legendary character) -- Fiction
ISBN 0-399-23451-9; 0-698-11974-6 pa
LC 99-52847

In a war-torn England where her half-brother Arthur will eventually become king, the young Morgan le Fay comes to realize that she has magic powers and links to the faerie world

"Introspective, yet threaded with intrigue and adventure, this compelling study of the legendary villainess explores the ways that love, hate, jealousy, and the desire for power shape one young woman's fate and affect the destiny of others." Horn Book

★ The **case** of the missing marquess; an Enola Holmes mystery. Philomel Books 2006 216p pa $6.99; $10.99
Grades: 5 6 7 8 **Fic**
1. Mystery fiction 2. Missing persons -- Fiction
ISBN 0-14-240933-2 pa; 0-399-24304-6

Enola Holmes, much younger sister of detective Sherlock Holmes, must travel to London in disguise to unravel the disappearance of her missing mother. "Grades four to eight." (Bull Cent Child Books)

"Enola's loneliness, intelligence, sense of humor, and sheer pluck make her an extremely appealing heroine." SLJ

Other titles about Enola Holmes are:
The case of the left-handed lady (2007)
The case of the bizarre bouquets (2008)

The case of the peculiar pink fan (2008)
The case of the cryptic crinoline (2009)
The case of the gypsy good-bye (2010)

St. Crow, Lili

Strange angels. Razorbill 2009 293p pa $9.99
Grades: 8 9 10 11 12 **Fic**

1. Orphans -- Fiction 2. Vampires -- Fiction 3. Werewolves -- Fiction 4. Supernatural -- Fiction 5. Extrasensory perception -- Fiction
ISBN 978-1-59514-251-1; 1-59514-251-7
LC 2008-39720

Sixteen-year-old Dru's psychic abilities helped her father battle zombies and other creatures of the "Real World," but now she must rely on herself, a "werwulf"-bitten friend, and a half-human vampire hunter to learn who murdered her parents, and why.

"The book grabs readers by the throat, sets hearts beating loudly and never lets go." Kirkus

Other titles in this series are:
Betrayals (2009)
Defiance (2011)
Jealousy (2010)

St. James, James

Freak show. Dutton Children's Books 2007 297p $18.99
Grades: 8 9 10 11 12 **Fic**

1. School stories 2. Florida -- Fiction 3. Prejudices -- Fiction 4. Homosexuality -- Fiction 5. Female impersonators -- Fiction
ISBN 978-0-525-47799-0; 0-525-47799-3
LC 2006-29716

Having faced teasing that turned into a brutal attack, Christianity expressed as persecution, and the loss of his only real friend when he could no longer keep his crush under wraps, seventeen-year-old Billy Bloom, a drag queen, decides the only to become fabulous again is to run for Homecoming Queen at his elite, private school near Fort Lauderdale, Florida.

"Though the subject matter and language will likely prove controversial, it's nearly impossible to remain untouched after walking a mile in the stilettos of someone so unfailingly true to himself and so blisteringly funny." Publ Wkly

Stahler, David

Doppelganger; [by] David Stahler, Jr. HarperCollins Publishers 2006 258p hardcover o.p. pa $8.99
Grades: 8 9 10 11 12 **Fic**

1. Horror fiction 2. Child abuse -- Fiction 3. Family life -- Fiction 4. Supernatural -- Fiction
ISBN 978-0-06-087232-8; 0-06-087232-2; 978-0-06-087234-2 pa; 0-06-087234-9 pa
LC 2005-28484

When a sixteen-year-old member of a race of shape-shifting killers called doppelgangers assumes the life of a troubled teen, he becomes unexpectedly embroiled in human life—and it is nothing like what he has seen on television.

"This brooding story of literally stepping into someone else's shoes combines romance, horror, and angst to create a distinctive story of redemption. The abusive relationships in Chris's family are portrayed with realism and sensitivity." Voice Youth Advocates

Spinning out; by David Stahler Jr. Chronicle Books 2012 285p $16.99
Grades: 7 8 9 10 **Fic**

1. School stories 2. Theater -- Fiction 3. Friendship -- Fiction 4. Schizophrenia -- Fiction 5. Television scriptwriters 6. Mental illness -- Fiction
ISBN 978-0-8118-7780-0; 0-8118-7780-9
LC 2010039392

Frenchy and Stewart, two Northern Vermont high school seniors, try out for the school musical, 'Man of La Mancha,' but when Stewart is cast as Don Quixote he soon becomes obsessed with his role and Frenchy must try to overcome his own demons to help his friend stay grounded in reality.

"Stahler creates a solid narrator in Frenchy, ably balancing his grief, confusion over Stewart's deteriorating mental state, and elation at his dawning relationship with stage manager Kaela. The resulting denouement is chaotic and heart-wrenching." Publ Wkly

Standiford, Natalie

★ The **boy** on the bridge; Natalie Standiford. Scholastic Press 2013 256 p. (hardcover) $17.99
Grades: 9 10 11 12 **Fic**

1. Love stories 2. School stories 3. Dissenters -- Fiction 4. Foreign study -- Fiction 5. Soviet Union -- History -- 1953-1985 -- Fiction 6. American students -- Soviet Union 7. Saint Petersburg (Russia) -- History -- 20th century -- Fiction
ISBN 0545334810; 9780545334815
LC 2012033037

"In 1982, college student Laura travels to Russia to study but becomes involved in a romance with a young Russian man. Laura struggles to decide if he really loves her, or if he's using her to escape the oppressive Communist regime--as she and her fellow American students have been warned. The story's premise and unusual setting helps offset the occasionally flat writing." (Horn Book)

★ **Confessions** of the Sullivan sisters. Scholastic Press 2010 313p
Grades: 9 10 11 12 **Fic**

1. Sisters -- Fiction 2. Family life -- Fiction 3. Grandmothers -- Fiction 4. Baltimore (Md.) -- Fiction 5. Conduct of life -- Fiction 6. Inheritance and succession -- Fiction
ISBN 9780545107105
LC 2010014512

Upon learning on Christmas Day that their rich and imperious grandmother may soon die and disown the family unless the one who offended her deeply will confess, each of the three Sullivan sisters sets down her offenses on paper. "High school." (Horn Book)

"A step above most books about rich girls, their boys, and their toys in both style and substance." Booklist

★ **How** to say goodbye in Robot. Scholastic 2009 276p $17.99; pa $8.99

Grades: 9 10 11 12 **Fic**

1. Death -- Fiction 2. Friendship -- Fiction 3. Family life -- Fiction 4. Baltimore (Md.) -- Fiction

ISBN 978-0-545-10708-2; 0-545-10708-3; 978-0-545-10709-9 pa; 0-545-10709-1 pa

LC 2009-5256

After moving to Baltimore and enrolling in a private school, high school senior Beatrice befriends a quiet loner with a troubled family history.

"This is an honest and complex depiction of a meaningful platonic friendship and doesn't gloss over troubling issues. The minor characters, particularly the talk-show regulars, are quirky and depicted with sly humor. . . . An outstanding choice for a book discussion group." SLJ

Stanley, George Edward

Night fires; a novel. Aladdin 2009 183p $15.99

Grades: 7 8 9 10 **Fic**

1. Moving -- Fiction 2. Bereavement -- Fiction 3. Race relations -- Fiction

ISBN 978-1-4169-7559-5; 1-4169-7559-4

LC 2008051607

In 1922, thirteen-year-old Woodrow Harper and his recently-widowed mother move to his father's childhood home in Lawton, Oklahoma, where he is torn between the "right people" of the Ku Klux Klan and those who encourage him to follow the path of his "nigra-loving" father.

"A thought-provoking novel. . . . Stanley's highly charged, emotional story tells of a very dark period in this country's history." SLJ

Staples, Suzanne Fisher

Dangerous skies. Farrar, Straus & Giroux 1996 231p hardcover o.p. pa $7.95

Grades: 7 8 9 10 **Fic**

1. Friendship -- Fiction 2. Prejudices -- Fiction 3. African Americans -- Fiction

ISBN 0-374-31694-5; 0-374-41670-2 pa

LC 95-45529

"At twelve, white boy Buck and black girl Tunes Smith are best friends. . . . The adolescents' idyllic world of fishing and observing nature is shattered when their much older friend Jorge Rodrigues is murdered, and Tunes is accused of the crime. . . . Staples's beautifully written and chilling tale of contemporary racism should keep young adult readers turning pages until they reach the heart-breaking end." Voice Youth Advocates

★ **Shabanu**; daughter of the wind. Knopf 1989 240p hardcover o.p. pa $6.50

Grades: 8 9 10 11 12 **Fic**

1. Pakistan -- Fiction 2. Sex role -- Fiction

ISBN 0-394-84815-2; 0-440-23856-0 pa

LC 89-2714

A Newbery Medal honor book, 1990

When eleven-year-old Shabanu, the daughter of a nomad in the Cholistan Desert of present-day Pakistan, is pledged in marriage to an older man whose money will bring prestige to the family, she must either accept the decision, as is the custom, or risk the consequences of defying her father's wishes

"Interspersing native words throughout adds realism, but may trip up readers, who must be patient enough to find meaning through context. This use of language is, however, an important element in helping Staples paint an evocative picture of life in the desert that includes references to the hard facts of reality." Booklist

Other titles in this series are:
Haveli (1993)
The house of djinn (2008)

★ **Under** the Persimmon tree. Farrar, Straus & Giroux 2005 275p $17

Grades: 78 9 10 **Fic**

1. Afghanistan – Fiction 2. Pakistan -- Fiction

ISBN 0-374-38025-2

During the 2001 Afghan War, the lives of Najmal, a young refugee from Kunduz, Afghanistan, and Nusrat, an American-Muslim teacher who is awaiting her huband's return from Mazar-i-Sharif, intersect at a school in Peshawar, Pakistan.

"Staples weaves a lot of history and politics into her story. . . . But . . . it's the personal story . . . that compels as it takes readers beyond the modern stereotypes of Muslims as fundamentalist fanatics. There are no sweet reunions, but there's hope in heartbreaking scenes of kindness and courage." Booklist

Staunton, Ted

Acting up. Red Deer Press 2010 263p pa $12.95

Grades: 9 10 11 12 **Fic**

1. School stories 2. Canada -- Fiction 3. Family life -- Fiction 4. Conduct of life -- Fiction

ISBN 0-88995-441-0; 978-0-88995-441-0

Sequel to Sounding off (2004)

"Sam Foster, a normal teenager and drummer in the band ADHD, has maturity as his latest goal. Achieving this goal will put him well on the way to a parent-free weekend over spring break and getting his learner's permit. But as with most teenagers, circumstances have a way of preventing even the most enthusiastic teen from success. . . . Staunton has written a fast-paced coming-of-age novel that flows well. Teens will easily identify with the main characters and the hilarious antics that take place as he achieves maturity. There is mention of the effects of drinking alcohol and references to drug taking, but it is within the context of the story." Voice Youth Advocates

Stead, Rebecca

First light. Wendy Lamb Books 2007 328p $15.99; lib bdg $18.99; pa $6.99

Grades: 5 6 7 8 **Fic**

1. Supernatural -- Fiction 2. Greenhouse effect -- Fiction

ISBN 978-0-375-84017-3; 0-375-84017-6; 987-0-375-094017-0 lib bdg; 0-375-94017-0 lib bdg; 978-0-440-42222-8 pa; 0-440-42222-1 pa

LC 2006-39733

This "novel is an exciting, engaging mix of science fiction, mystery, and adventure. . . . Peter and Thea are fully developed main characters." SLJ

"The father of 12-year-old Peter is a glaciologist, his mother, a genetic scientist. Peter is thrilled when his father decides to take the family on his latest excursion to Greenland to study the effects of global warming. Fourteen-year-old Thea lives in a secret society called Gracehope under the Greenland ice. After finding a map that leads her to the surface, she becomes obsessed with seeing the sun and bringing her people back above ground. Peter and Thea accidentally meet on the surface and discover, through a secret kept by Peter's mother, that their destinies are unexpectedly joined." Booklist

Steele, Allen

Apollo's outcasts; by Allen Steele. Pyr 2012 311 p. (hardcover) $16.99

Grades: 7 8 9 10 **Fic**

1. Science fiction 2. People with disabilities 3. United States -- Fiction 4. Space colonies -- Fiction 5. Coups d'état -- Fiction 6. Regression (Civilization) -- Fiction 7. Children with disabilities -- Fiction

ISBN 1616146869; 9781616146863

LC 2012023582

This book from Hugo Award-winning author Allen Steele sends "a handful of kids to the Moon in the wake of a political coup in America. Jamey Barlowe, 16, was born on the Moon but raised on Earth; as a result of a low-gravity infancy, Jamey uses a multifunctional 'mobil' chair to get around. . . . Anxious to do something productive upon arriving in Apollo (and able to walk for the first time), Jamey joins the elite Lunar Search and Rescue, just in time to end up on the front lines." (Publishers Weekly)

Stein, Tammar

High dive. Alfred A. Knopf 2008 201p $15.99; lib bdg $18.99

Grades: 7 8 9 10 **Fic**

1. Europe -- Fiction 2. Vacations -- Fiction 3. Friendship -- Fiction 4. Loss (Psychology) -- Fiction 5. Single parent family -- Fiction

ISBN 978-0-375-83024-2; 0-375-83024-3; 978-0-375-93024-9 lib bdg; 0-375-93024-8 lib bdg

LC 2007049657

With her mother stationed in Iraq as an Army nurse, Vanderbilt University student Arden Vogel, whose father was killed in a traffic accident a few years earlier, impulsively ends up on a tour of Europe with a group of college girls she meets on her way to attend to some family business in Sardinia.

"Ideal for the thoughtful armchair traveler, this story is engaging enough for readers on the long flight to the enduring wonders of Europe and emerging adulthood." SLJ

Light years; a novel. Knopf 2005 263p hardcover o.p. pa $6.99

Grades: 7 8 9 10 **Fic**

1. Bereavement -- Fiction 2. Israel-Arab conflicts -- Fiction

ISBN 0-375-83023-5; 0-440-23902-8 pa

LC 2004-7776

Maya Laor leaves her home in Israel to study astronomy at the University of Virginia after the tragic death of her boyfriend in a suicide bombing.

"This well-paced first novel, a moving study of grief and recovery, is also a love story that should appeal particularly to students interested in other ways of seeing the world." SLJ

Includes bibliographical references

Kindred. Alfred A. Knopf 2011 266p $16.99; lib bdg $19.99

Grades: 7 8 9 10 **Fic**

1. Twins -- Fiction 2. Angels -- Fiction 3. Siblings -- Fiction 4. Supernatural -- Fiction 5. Good and evil -- Fiction

ISBN 978-0-375-85871-0; 0-375-85871-7; 978-0-375-95871-7 lib bdg; 0-375-95871-1 lib bdg

LC 2010-07071

Spiritual warfare breaks out when the Archangel Raphael and the Devil deliver assignments to eighteen-year-old fraternal twins Miriam and Moses.

"Skillfully intertwining family, medical, and supernatural dramas with a sweet romantic subplot, Stein . . . unleashes cosmic battles to play out among the inhabitants of smalltown Hamilton, Tenn., a setting replete with Civil War history. . . . Miriam's initial interpretation of her illness as divine punishment gives way to more complex theological reflections in this riveting tale, an angel book that stands out from the chorus." Publ Wkly

Steinmetz, Karen

The **mourning** wars. Roaring Brook Press 2010 232p $17.99

Grades: 7 8 9 10 **Fic**

1. Mohawk Indians -- Fiction 2. United States -- History -- 1702-1713, Queen Anne's War -- Fiction

ISBN 978-1-59643-290-1; 1-59643-290-X

LC 2010-11735

In 1704, Mohawk Indians attack the frontier village of Deerfield, Massachusetts, kidnapping over 100 residents, including seven-year-old Eunice Williams. Based on a true story.

"Eunice's largely imagined life makes a fascinating story with a setting that is vividly and dramatically evoked. The book will be especially useful in the classroom." Booklist

Includes bibliographical references

Sternberg, Libby

The **case** against my brother. Bancroft Press 2007 201p $19.95

Grades: 6 7 8 9 **Fic**

1. Brothers -- Fiction 2. Prejudices -- Fiction 3. Polish Americans -- Fiction

ISBN 978-1-890862-51-0; 1-890862-51-7

"In 1922, when their widowed mother dies, Carl Matiuski and his older brother, Adam, move to Portland, OR, to live with an uncle. . . . When [Adam] is accused of a crime he didn't commit, Carl steps in . . . to try to clear his brother's name. . . . Readers are easily swept up in the adventure as the eye-opening mystery unfolds." SLJ

Stevenson, Robin

★ A **thousand** shades of blue; [by] Robin Stevenson. Orca Book Publishers 2008 231p

Grades: 7 8 9 10 **Fic**

1. Bahamas -- Fiction 2. Sailing -- Fiction 3. Family

life -- Fiction
ISBN 1551439212; 9781551439211

A yearlong sailing trip to the Bahamas reveals deep wounds in Rachel's family and brings out the worst in Rachel.

"The author does a fantastic job of making each character relatable to teens and creates some major drama between Rachel's mother and one of the locals that keeps the reader interested. . . . The book flows very smoothly, making it an easy read for teens." Voice Youth Advocates

Stevenson, Robin H.

Dead in the water; [by] Robin Stevenson. Orca Book Publishers 2008 169p (Orca sports) pa $9.95
Grades: 6 7 8 9 **Fic**

1. Adventure fiction 2. Sailing -- Fiction 3. Endangered species -- Fiction
ISBN 978-1-5514-3962-4 pa; 1-5514-3962-X pa

"Simon ('Spacey') joins three other teenagers for a weeklong sailing course in British Columbia, Canada. . . . His weird shipmate, Olivia, insists that the men on a nearby cabin cruiser are smuggling abalone, a threatened shellfish species, and she persuades Simon to help her investigate. . . . Stevenson . . . delivers plenty of realistic, gripping detail about handling a boat in screaming winds and crashing waves, as well as a solid story about a crucial environmental issue." Booklist

Escape velocity. Orca Book Publishers 2011 232p pa $12.95
Grades: 6 7 8 9 **Fic**

1. Mother-daughter relationship -- Fiction
ISBN 978-1-55469-866-0; 1-55469-866-9

Forced to live with the mother who abandoned her at birth, Lou goes looking for truth in her mother's fiction.

"Lou is a fully rounded, attractive character. Zoe's emotional insensitivity toward her, while painful, becomes understandable as her believable back story emerges. Other characters are also nicely, authentically fleshed out, adding depth and a strong sense of reality. A quiet, moving exploration of what it means to be a mother—or a daughter—even when the relationship is unconventional." Kirkus

Out of order; written by Robin Stevenson. Orca Book Publishers 2007 221p pa $8.95
Grades: 8 9 10 11 12 **Fic**

1. School stories 2. Friendship -- Fiction
ISBN 978-1-55143-693-7; 1-55143-693-0

When Sophie moves to Victoria, she hopes to leave the bullying she experienced in Ontario behind, but when she makes two new friends who are polar opposites, she finds that friendships can both help and harm her sense of self.

"The visceral, emotional reactions of the characters ring true. . . . Despite weighty themes, this story is about friendship and self-worth." Voice Youth Advocates

Stevenson, Sarah Jamila

The **Latte** Rebellion. Flux 2011 328p pa $9.95
Grades: 8 9 10 11 12 **Fic**

1. School stories 2. Clubs -- Fiction 3. California -- Fiction 4. Family life -- Fiction 5. Racially mixed people -- Fiction
ISBN 978-0-7387-2278-8; 0-7387-2278-2
LC 2010-35002

When high school senior Asha Jamison is called a "towel head" at a pool party, she and her best friend Carey start a club to raise awareness of mixed-race students that soon sweeps the country, but the hubbub puts her Ivy League dreams, friendship, and beliefs to the test.

"The novel speaks directly to teenagers who are beginning to find their place in their world and figuring out how to make the world a better place for others. . . . This coming-of-age story is craftily written, fast paced and delivers a message of doing the right thing under difficult circumstances." Voice Youth Advocates

Stewart, Alex

Dragonwood; Alex Stewart. Evans 2010 56 p. pa $7.99
Grades: 7 8 9 10 **Fic**

1. Fantasy fiction 2. Mystery fiction 3. Elves -- Fiction 4. Criminals -- Fiction
ISBN 0237541351; 145174465X; 9780237541354; 9781451744651
LC 2011287528

This book is part of "the Shades series . . . from Britain" and "presents a fantasy story that dispenses with the massive casting and large chunks of world building" found in other fantasy stories. The story "follows a Halfling bounty hunter, Pip, who has been paid by an elven prince to track down and return the head of an orcish outlaw, who is rumored to have slain the prince's sister. He soon enough finds reason to doubt his employer's word, but Pip is sworn to carry out his mission one way or another." Author Alex Stewart offers "a conflicted-private-eye story in a fantasy setting." (Booklist)

Stiefvater, Maggie

Ballad; a gathering of faerie. Flux 2009 353p pa $9.95
Grades: 8 9 10 11 12 **Fic**

1. School stories 2. Magic -- Fiction 3. Fairies -- Fiction 4. Musicians -- Fiction 5. Supernatural -- Fiction
ISBN 978-0-7387-1484-4 pa; 0-7387-1484-4 pa
LC 2009-19393

Sequel to: Lament: the faerie queen's deception (2008)

When music prodigy James Morgan and his best friend, Deirdre, join a private conservatory for musicians, his talent attracts Nuala, a faerie muse who fosters and feeds on creative energies, but soon he finds himself battling the Queen of the Fey for the very lives of Deirdre and Nuala.

"The themes of music, faerie, and romance combined with a smart male voice wil satisfy realistic fantasy readers as well as existing and new readers of the series." Libr Media Connect

★ **Blue** Lily, Lily Blue; Maggie Stiefvater. Scholastic Press; 2014 400p $18.99
Grades: 9 10 11 12 **Fic**

1. Magic--Fiction 2.Occultism--Fiction 3. Dreams--Fiction 4. Family secrets--Fiction
ISBN: 9780545424967; 0545424968
LC 2014947741

Kirkus Best Books: Teen (2014)

In this third title in the author's Raven Cycle, "Blue Sargent has found things. For the first time in her life, she has friends she can trust, a group to which she can belong. The Raven Boys have taken her in as one of their own. Their problems have become hers, and her problems have become theirs. The trick with found things, though, is how easily they can be lost. Friends can betray. Mothers can disappear. Visions can mislead. Certainties can unravel." (Publisher's note)

"This atmospheric fantasy is far more character driven than the former book, with increased and especially satisfying interactions among players. . . . The book's luminous and lively prose takes unanticipated paths, some new and surprising, with others connecting to previous events, demonstrating meticulous plot design." VOYA

★ The **dream** thieves; Maggie Stiefvater. Scholastic 2013 416 p. (Raven cycle) (jacketed hardcover) $18.99

Grades: 8 9 10 11 12 **Fic**

1. Occult fiction 2. Fantasy fiction 3. Magic -- Fiction 4. Dreams -- Fiction 5. Paranormal fiction 6. Secrets -- Fiction

ISBN 0545424941; 9780545424943

LC 2013018731

This is the second book in Maggie Stiefvater's Raven Cycle series. Here, after "the transformative events at Cabeswater . . . , the context in which Gansey, Blue, Adam, Ronan, and Noah operate is further altered by the arrival of the Gray Man, a self-described hit man. . . . The Gray Man brings with him the machinations of larger, previously unknown forces as he takes orders from a voice on the phone to hunt the Greywaren, the identity of which is revealed early on." (Publishers Weekly)

"In this darker second book (The Raven Boys), Gansey, Blue, and the search for Glendower take a backseat to the exploration of Ronan's and Adam's tortured personalities. Stiefvater's descriptive prose reveals a complicated plot, multiple viewpoints, and detailed backstories. Many mysteries remain, but the cliffhanger ending makes it clear that Glendower will resurface as the main focus of book three." (Horn Book)

Forever. Scholastic Press 2011 390p $17.99

Grades: 9 10 11 12 **Fic**

1. Love stories 2. Werewolves -- Fiction 3. Supernatural -- Fiction

ISBN 978-0-545-25908-8

LC 2011023889

Sequel to Linger (2010)

A human girl and her werewolf boyfriend must fight for their love as death comes closing in.

"Stiefvater's emotional prose is rich without being melodramatic, and she clearly shares her fans' love of these characters." Booklist

Linger. Scholastic 2010 362p $17.99

Grades: 8 9 10 11 12 **Fic**

1. Werewolves -- Fiction 2. Supernatural -- Fiction

ISBN 978-0-545-12328-0; 0-545-12328-3

LC 2009-39500

Sequel to Shiver (2009)

As Grace hides the vast depth of her love for Sam from her parents and Sam struggles to release his werewolf past and claim a human future, a new wolf named Cole wins Isabel's heart but his own past threatens to destroy the whole pack.

"This riveting narrative, impossible to put down, is not only an excellent addition to the current fangs and fur craze but is also a beautifully written romance that, along with Shiver, will have teens clamoring for the third and final entry." Voice Youth Advocates

Followed by Forever (2011)

★ The **raven** boys; Maggie Stiefvater. Scholastic Press 2012 409 p. (hardcover) $18.99

Grades: 8 9 10 11 12 **Fic**

1. Magic -- Fiction 2. Supernatural -- Fiction 3. Paranormal fiction 4. Occultism -- Fiction 5. Clairvoyance -- Fiction

ISBN 0545424925; 9780545424929

LC 2012030880

This book is the first in Maggie Stiefvater's series the "Raven Cycle". It follows "16-year-old Blue Sargent, daughter of a small-town psychic, [who] has lived her whole life under a prophecy: If she kisses her true love, he will die. . . . She sees a vision of a dying Raven boy named Gansey. The Raven Boys--students at Aglionby, a nearby prep school, so-called because of the ravens on their school crest--soon encounter Blue in person." (Kirkus Reviews)

★ The **Scorpio** Races. Scholastic Press 2011 409p $17.99

Grades: 8 9 10 11 12 **Fic**

1. Love stories 2. Fantasy fiction 3. Horses -- Fiction 4. Racing -- Fiction 5. Orphans -- Fiction

ISBN 978-0-545-22490-1; 0-545-22490-X

LC 2011015775

"Stiefvater's narration is as much about atmospherics as it is about event, and the water horses are the environment in which Sean and Puck move, allies and rivals to the end. It's not a feel-good story—dread, loss, and hard choices are the islanders' lot. As a study of courage and loyalty tested, however, it is an utterly compelling read." Publ Wkly

★ **Shiver**. Scholastic 2009 392p $17.99; pa $8.99

Grades: 9 10 11 12 **Fic**

1. Werewolves -- Fiction 2. Supernatural -- Fiction

ISBN 978-0-545-12326-6; 0-545-12326-7; 978-0-545-12327-3 pa; 0-545-12327-5 pa

LC 2009-5257

In all the years she has watched the wolves in the woods behind her house, Grace has been particularly drawn to an unusual yellow-eyed wolf who, in his turn, has been watching her with increasing intensity.

"Stiefvater skillfully increases the tension throughout; her take on werewolves is interesting and original while her characters are refreshingly willing to use their brains to deal with the challenges they face." Publ Wkly

Other titles featuring the wolves of Mercy Falls are:

Forever (2011)

Linger (2010)

Stoffels, Karlijn

★ **Heartsinger**; translated by Laura Watkinson. Arthur A. Levine Books 2009 134p $16.99

Grades: 8 9 10 11 **Fic**

1. Fantasy fiction 2. Love -- Fiction 3. Voyages and travels -- Fiction

ISBN 978-0-545-06929-8; 0-545-06929-7; 978-0-545-06968-7 pa; 0-545-06968-8 pa

LC 2008-17785

In this meditation on various kinds of love, Mee travels across the country to the court of the Princess Esperanza, singing the life stories of some of the people he meets.

"Written with clarity and grace. . . . This unusual novel offers readers limpid writing, strong storytelling, and the unblinking recognition of love in many forms." Booklist

Stone, Mary Hanlon

Invisible girl. Philomel Books 2010 279p $16.99

Grades: 7 8 9 10 **Fic**

1. California -- Fiction 2. Popularity -- Fiction 3. Child abuse -- Fiction

ISBN 978-0-399-25249-5; 0-399-25249-5

LC 2009-27255

Thirteen-year-old Stephanie, whisked from Boston to Encino, California, to stay with family friends after her abusive, alcoholic mother abandons her, tries desperately to fit in with her "cousin's" popular group even as she sees how much easier it would be to remain invisible.

"This edgy fish-out-of-water story features a strong and sympathetic protagonist." Horn Book Guide

Stone, Tamara Ireland

Time between us; Tamara Ireland Stone. Hyperion 2012 384 p. (hardcover) $17.99

Grades: 7 8 9 10 **Fic**

1. Love stories 2. Time travel -- Fiction 3. Love -- Fiction 4. Illinois -- Fiction 5. High schools -- Fiction 6. Space and time -- Fiction 7. Family life -- Illinois -- Fiction

ISBN 142315956X; 9781423159568

LC 2011053368

This book by Tamara Ireland Stone follows "Anna and Bennett," a couple who "were never supposed to meet: she lives in 1995 Chicago and he lives in 2012 San Francisco. But Bennett's unique ability to travel through time and space brings him into Anna's life, and with him, a new world of adventure and possibility. As their relationship deepens, they face the reality that time might knock Bennett back where he belongs." (Publisher's note)

Stone, Tanya Lee

★ A **bad** boy can be good for a girl. Wendy Lamb Books 2006 228p hardcover o.p. pa $7.99

Grades: 9 10 11 12 **Fic**

1. School stories

ISBN 0-385-74702-0; 978-0-385-74702-8; 0-553-49509-7 pa; 978-0-553-49509-6 pa

LC 2006-272453

Josie, Nicolette, and Aviva all get mixed up with a senior boy who can talk them into doing almost anything he wants. In a blur of high school hormones and personal doubt, each girl struggles with how much to give up and what ultimately to keep for herself.

"The language is realistic and frank, and, while not graphic, it is filled with descriptions of the teens and their sexuality. This is not a book that will sit quietly on any shelf; it will be passed from girl to girl to girl." SLJ

Stork, Francisco X.

★ The **last** summer of the death warriors. Arthur A. Levine Books 2010 344p $17.99

Grades: 8 9 10 11 12 **Fic**

1. Death -- Fiction 2. Orphans -- Fiction 3. New Mexico -- Fiction 4. Mexican Americans -- Fiction

ISBN 978-0-545-15133-7; 0-545-15133-3

LC 2009-19853

"Seventeen-year-old Pancho Sanchez is sent to a Catholic orphanage after his father and sister die in the span of a few months. Though the cause of his sister's death is technically 'undetermined,' Pancho plans to kill the man he believes responsible. . . . When D.Q., a fellow resident dying from brain cancer, asks Pancho to accompany him to Albuquerque for experimental treatments, Pancho agrees—he'll get paid and it's where his sister's killer lives." Publ Wkly

"This novel, in the way of the best literary fiction, is an invitation to careful reading that rewards serious analysis and discussion. Thoughtful readers will be delighted by both the challenge and Stork's respect for their abilities." Booklist

★ **Marcelo** in the real world. Arthur A. Levine Books 2009 312p $17.99

Grades: 8 9 10 11 12 **Fic**

1. Autism -- Fiction 2. Asperger's syndrome -- Fiction

ISBN 0-545-05474-5; 978-0-545-05474-4

LC 2008-14729

ALA Schneider Family Book Award Honor Book (2010)

This book features "Marcelo Sandoval [who] is a 17-year-old looking forward to his senior year in high school. Living with something akin to Asperger's syndrome, Marcelo has spent his life learning step by step how to do things that many people learn intuitively. . . . Marcelo's father makes a deal with him: if he will spend the summer working at his father's law firm and successfully follow the rules of the real world, he can choose where he will spend his senior year." (Christian Century)

"Stork introduces ethical dilemmas, the possibility of love, and other 'real world' conflicts, all the while preserving the integrity of his characterizations and intensifying the novel's psychological and emotional stakes." Publ Wkly

Strasser, Todd

Boot camp. Simon & Schuster Books for Young Readers 2007 238p hardcover o.p. pa $6.99

Grades: 8 9 10 11 12 **Fic**

1. Torture -- Fiction 2. Juvenile delinquency -- Fiction

ISBN 978-1-4169-0848-7; 1-4169-0848-X; 978-1-4169-5942-7 pa; 1-4169-5942-4 pa

LC 2006-13634

After ignoring several warnings to stop dating his former teacher, Garrett is sent to Lake Harmony, a boot camp that uses brutal methods to train students to obey their parents.

"The ending is both realistic and disturbing. . . . Writing in the teen's mature and perceptive voice, Strasser creates characters who will provoke strong reactions from readers. . . . [This is a] fast-paced and revealing story." SLJ

Can't get there from here. Simon & Schuster Books for Young Readers 2004 198p $15.95
Grades: 7 8 9 10 **Fic**
1. Homeless persons -- Fiction 2. Runaway teenagers -- Fiction
ISBN 0-689-84169-8
LC 2003-170

Tired of being hungry, cold, and dirty from living on the streets of New York City with a tribe of other homeless teenagers who are dying, one by one, a girl named Maybe ponders her future and longs for someone to care about her

"While the events described in this cautionary tale are shocking, the language is not, making these all-too-real problems accessible to a wide readership." SLJ

Famous. Simon & Schuster Books for Young Readers 2011 257p $15.99
Grades: 7 8 9 10 **Fic**
1. Fame -- Fiction 2. Actors -- Fiction 3. Celebrities -- Fiction 4. Hollywood (Calif.) -- Fiction
ISBN 978-1-4169-7511-3; 1-4169-7511-X
LC 2009-48163

Sixteen-year-old Jamie Gordon had a taste of praise and recognition at age fourteen when her unflattering photograph of an actress was published, but as she pursues her dream of being a celebrity photographer, she becomes immersed in the dark side of fame.

"The book makes some astute observations about America's reality-television culture and its obsession with fame. . . . This well-crafted novel clearly belongs in all public, junior high, and high school libraries." Voice Youth Advocates

★ **Give** a boy a gun. Simon & Schuster Bks. for Young Readers 2000 146p hardcover o.p. pa $5.99
Grades: 9 10 11 12 **Fic**
1. School stories 2. Violence -- Fiction
ISBN 0-689-81112-8; 0-689-84893-5 pa

"Statistics, quotes, and facts related to actual incidents of school violence appear in dark print at the bottom of the pages. An appendix includes a chronology of school shootings in the United States, the author's own treatise on gun control, and places to get more information." SLJ

If I grow up. Simon & Schuster Books for Young Readers 2009 222p $16.99
Grades: 7 8 9 10 **Fic**
1. Gangs -- Fiction 2. Poverty -- Fiction 3. Violence -- Fiction 4. African Americans -- Fiction
ISBN 978-1-4169-2523-1; 1-4169-2523-6
LC 2008-00655

Growing up in the inner-city projects, DeShawn is reluctantly forced into the gang world by circumstances beyond his control.

"Strasser's writing puts the reader in the midst of the projects and offers totally real characters." Voice Youth Advocates

Includes bibliographical references

No place; Todd Strasser. Simon & Schuster Books for Young Readers 2014 272 p. (hardcover) $17.99
Grades: 7 8 9 10 **Fic**
1. Homelessness 2. Homeless persons -- Fiction 3. Poverty -- Fiction
ISBN 144245721X; 9781442457218
LC 2012043701

In this novel, by Todd Strasser, "It seems like Dan has it all. . . . Then his family loses their home. Forced to move into the town's Tent City, Dan feels his world shifting. . . . As Dan struggles to adjust to his new life, he gets involved with the people who are fighting for better conditions and services for the residents of Tent City. But someone wants Tent City gone, and will stop at nothing until it's destroyed." (Publisher's note)

"High school senior Dan Halprin is the star pitcher on the baseball team, has been offered a scholarship to Rice University, and is dating wealthy Talia. When his parents lose their jobs as a stockbroker and youth athletics coach, and then their home, the family is forced to move into Dignityville, a tent community in the center of town. Humiliated and angry, Dan struggles to maintain his self-confidence, relationships, and aspirations...Coping with their personal financial catastrophe, wanting to stay in their familiar town, finding work, accepting charity, and maintaining self-respect are issues that weigh heavily on Dan and his parents. Readers will be drawn into this contemporary story." (School Library Journal)

Wish you were dead. Egmont USA 2009 236p
Grades: 8 9 10 11 12 **Fic**
1. School stories 2. Weblogs -- Fiction 3. Kidnapping -- Fiction 4. Missing persons -- Fiction 5. New York (State) -- Fiction
ISBN 160684007X; 1606840495; 9781606840078; 9781606840498
LC 2009-14641

Madison, a senior at a suburban New York high school, tries to uncover who is responsible for the disappearance of her friends, popular students mentioned in the posts of an anonymous blogger, while she, herself, is being stalked online and in-person.

"The themes of bullying, tolerance, and friendship are issues to which readers can relate, as well as the inclusion of the IMing, blogging, texting, and social networking. This thriller will be popular and passed from one reader to another." Voice Youth Advocates

Stratton, Allan

★ **Borderline**. HarperTeen 2010 298p $16.99; lib bdg $17.89
Grades: 6 7 8 9 10 **Fic**
1. Muslims -- Fiction 2. Terrorism -- Fiction 3. Friendship -- Fiction 4. Prejudices -- Fiction 5. Father-son relationship -- Fiction
ISBN 978-0-06-145111-9; 0-06-145111-8; 978-0-06-145112-6 lib bdg; 0-06-145112-6 lib bdg
LC 2009-5241

Despite the strained relationship between them, teenaged Sami Sabiri risks his life to uncover the truth when his father is implicated in a terrorist plot.

This is "a powerful story and excellent resource for teaching tolerance, with a message that extends well beyond the timely subject matter." Publ Wkly

★ **Chanda's** secrets. Annick Press 2004 193p $19.95; pa $8.95
Grades: 7 8 9 10 **Fic**
1. Africa -- Fiction 2. AIDS (Disease) -- Fiction
ISBN 1-55037-835-X; 1-55037-834-1 pa
Michael L. Printz Award honor book, 2005
"The details of sub-Saharan African life are convincing and smoothly woven into this moving story of poverty and courage, but the real insight for readers will be the appalling treatment of the AIDS victims. Strong language and frank description are appropriate to the subject matter." SLJ
Another title about Chanda is:
Chanda's war (2007)

Chanda's wars; with an afterword by Roméo Dallaire. HarperCollinsPublishers 2008 384p $17.99; lib bdg $18.89; pa $8.99
Grades: 8 9 10 11 12 **Fic**
1. War stories 2. Africa -- Fiction 3. Orphans -- Fiction 4. Kidnapping -- Fiction
ISBN 978-0-06-087262-5; 0-06-087262-4; 978-0-06-087264-9 lib bdg; 0-06-087264-0 lib bdg; 978-0-06-087265-6 pa; 0-06-087265-9 pa
LC 2007-10829
Sequel to: Chanda's secrets (2004)
Chanda Kabelo, a teenaged African girl, must save her younger siblings after they are kidnapped and forced to serve as child soldiers in General Mandiki's rebel army.
"The characters are drawn without sentimentality, and the story is a moving portrayal of betrayal and love. The army's brutality and the traumas of the child soldiers are graphic and disturbing." Booklist

Strauss, Victoria

Passion blue; by Victoria Strauss. Marshall Cavendish Children 2012 346 p. (hardcover) $17.99
Grades: 7 8 9 10 11 12 **Fic**
1. Historical fiction 2. Convents -- Fiction 3. Women artists -- Fiction 4. Self-realization -- Fiction 5. Nuns -- Fiction 6. Magic -- Fiction 7. Artists -- Fiction 8. Talismans -- Fiction 9. Italy -- History -- 15th century -- Fiction
ISBN 0761462309; 9780761462309; 9780761462316
LC 2011040133
In this book by Victoria Strauss, when "Giulia is forced into a convent . . . she is surprised to learn of the beauty within, and that nuns and novices have vocations. . . . Her world expands as she learns the tools, materials, and techniques of great Renaissance painters. By chance, she meets a young male artisan repairing a convent masterpiece. They begin a clandestine romance. Her two desires -- painting and a husband -- war within as she contemplates her future." (School Library Journal)

Strohmeyer, Sarah

How Zoe made her dreams (mostly) come true; Sarah Strohmeyer. Balzer + Bray 2013 320 p. (pbk. bdg.) $9.99
Grades: 7 8 9 10 **Fic**
1. Amusement parks -- Fiction 2. Summer employment -- Fiction 3. Internship programs -- Fiction 4. Cousins -- Fiction 5. New Jersey -- Fiction
ISBN 0062187457; 9780062187451
LC 2012038163
In this book, "Zoe Kiefer, 17, and her cousin, Jess, are interns at Fairyland Kingdom, an over-the-top theme park in New Jersey. These internships are coveted. . . . Jess gets cast as a Little Red Riding Hood and Zoe is tasked with being the demanding Queen's personal assistant (aka slave). Zoe worries that these subpar positions won't put them in the running for the Dream and Do grant, a $25,000 prize that both girls desperately need." (School Library Journal)

Smart girls get what they want; by Sarah Strohmeyer. 1st ed. Harpercollins Childrens Books 2012 348 p. (tr. bdg.) $17.99; (paperback) $9.99
Grades: 7 8 9 10 11 12 **Fic**
1. Female friendship -- Fiction 2. Grading and marking (Education) 3. High school students -- Fiction 4. Friendship -- Fiction 5. Best friends -- Fiction 6. High schools -- Fiction 7. Interpersonal relations -- Fiction
ISBN 0061953407; 9780061953408; 9780061953415
LC 2011026094
Author Sarah Strohmeyer tells the story of Gigi, Neerja, and Bea, three friends who "stumble upon . . . [Neerja's sister] Parad's signature-less yearbook, making them think that maybe studying isn't everything. . . . When Gigi is accused of cheating on the AP Chemistry midterm along with Mike, a Man Clan wannabe who calls her 'Einstein,' the girls launch into action. Gigi finds herself running for student rep against Will, the new guy from California. . . . Neerja tries out for the lead in Romeo and Juliet and Bea convinces Gigi to join the ski team with her." (Kirkus Reviews)

Stroud, Jonathan

The **Amulet** of Samarkand. Hyperion Bks. for Children 2003 462p (Bartimaeus trilogy) $17.95; pa $7.99
Grades: 7 8 9 10 **Fic**
1. Fantasy fiction
ISBN 0-7868-1859-X; 0-7868-5255-0 pa
LC 2003-49904
Nathaniel, a magician's apprentice, summons up the djinni Bartimaeus and instructs him to steal the Amulet of Samarkand from the powerful magician Simon Lovelace.
"There is plenty of action, mystery, and humor to keep readers turning the pages. This title, the first in a trilogy, is a must for fantasy fans." SLJ
Other titles in this series are:
The golem's eye (2004)
Ptolemy's gate (2006)

★ **Heroes** of the valley. Hyperion Books for Children 2009 483p $17.99
Grades: 7 8 9 10 **Fic**
1. Adventure fiction 2. Middle Ages -- Fiction
ISBN 978-1-4231-0966-2; 1-4231-0966-X
"Twelve Houses control sections of a valley. Halli Sveinsson—at 15, the youngest child of the rulers of the House of Svein—goes against tradition when he sets out

to avenge the death of his murdered uncle, and his actions result in warfare among Houses for the first time in generations. . . . Smart, funny dialogue and prose, revealing passages about the exploits of the hero Svein, bouts of action and a touch of romance briskly move the story along." Publ Wkly

The **ring** of Solomon; a Bartimaeus novel. Disney/Hyperion Books 2010 398p $17.99
Grades: 7 8 9 10 **Fic**
1. Fantasy fiction 2. Kings 3. Magic -- Fiction 4. Jerusalem -- Fiction 5. Witchcraft -- Fiction
ISBN 978-1-4231-2372-9; 1-4231-2372-7
LC 2010015468

Wise-cracking djinni Bartimaeus finds himself at the court of King Solomon with an unpleasant master, a sinister servant, and King Solomon's magic ring.

"In this exciting prequel set in ancient Israel, Stroud presents an early adventure of his sharp-tongued djinn, Bartimaeus. . . . This is a superior fantasy that should have fans racing back to those books." Publ Wkly

Strykowski, Marcia

Call Me Amy; Marcia Strykowski. Midpoint Trade Books Inc 2013 180 p. (hardcover) $24.95
Grades: 6 7 8 **Fic**
1. Adolescence 2. Animal rescue
ISBN 1935462768; 9781935462767

In this novel, set in Maine in 1973, eighth-grader Amy Henderson is dealing with acne, her faraway best friend, and overall nervousness. "But the sudden appearance of an injured harbor seal brings her closer to two unlikely allies as they care for the seal, dubbed 'Pup,' in secret: loudmouthed Craig, whose carefree personality is a cover for underlying insecurities and family problems, and elderly Miss Cogshell, who proves to be worldly and kind." (Publishers Weekly)

"Well-drawn, sympathetic characters and the developing spark between Amy and Craig combine to create a pleasant, satisfying read." Kirkus

Stuber, Barbara

★ **Crossing** the tracks. Margarert K. McElderry Books 2010 258p $16.99
Grades: 6 7 8 9 **Fic**
1. Household employees -- Fiction 2. Father-daughter relationship -- Fiction
ISBN 978-1-4169-9703-0; 1-4169-9703-2
LC 2009-42672

In Missouri in 1926, fifteen-year-old Iris Baldwin discovers what family truly means when her father hires her out for the summer as a companion to a country doctor's invalid mother.

"Thought-provoking and tenderhearted, Iris's story is one of a mature young woman who faces life with courage and common sense. . . . This thoughtful novel offers strong character development and an engaging protagonist." SLJ

Sturtevant, Katherine

The **brothers** story; Katherine Sturtevant. 1st ed. Farrar, Straus & Giroux 2009 271 p. (reinforced) $16.99
Grades: 6 7 8 **Fic**
1. Twins -- Fiction 2. Brothers -- Fiction 3. Apprentices -- Fiction 4. People with mental disabilities -- Fiction
ISBN 0374309922; 9780374309923
LC 2008035513

"Kit's wrestling with situations of moral complexity leads him to question some of the era's culturally accepted religious mores, providing a subtle but enlightening exploration of class and gender roles. . . . An era comes alive in this tale of a young man's awakening to his life's call." Publ Wkly

"Readers will quickly empathize with Kit; his conflicted feelings toward his brother, a mixture of great tenderness and shame, are sensitively drawn. He experiences the beginnings of his sexual awakening in scenes that are occasionally ribald but never gratuitous. Sturtevant invokes the cacophony of noises, smells, and sights of London, along with the sorrows and kindnesses found in daily life." SLJ

A **true** and faithful narrative. Farrar, Straus & Giroux 2006 247p $17
Grades: 6 7 8 9 **Fic**
1. London (England)--Fiction
ISBN 0-374-37809-6
LC 2005046922

In London in the 1680s, Meg—now sixteen years old—tries to decide whether to marry either of the two men who court her, taking into account both love and her writing ambitions.

The author "offers readers a story depicted with great clarity and many vivid details of everyday life. Written in the first-person, the narrative reveals Meg as a strong-willed yet vulnerable young woman who emerges as a well-rounded, convincing individual." Booklist

Sullivan, Laura L.

Guardian of the Green Hill; [illustrations by David Wyatt] Henry Holt and Company 2011 293p il $16.99
Grades: 5 6 7 8 **Fic**
1. Fantasy fiction 2. Fairies -- Fiction 3. Siblings -- Fiction 4. Supernatural -- Fiction
ISBN 978-0-8050-8985-1; 0-8050-8985-3
LC 2010029231

After the Midsummer War ends, Meg Morgan faces a madman in the battle for control of the last bastion of fairies in England, aided by her siblings Rowan, Silly, and James, and American neighbors Dickie Rhys, and Finn Fachan.

"Sullivan's writing has a timelessness that contrasts nicely with Meg's distinctly modern ideas and weaves a compelling story that will pull readers along." SLJ

Under the green hill. Henry Holt and Company 2010 308p $16.99
Grades: 5 6 7 8 **Fic**
1. Fantasy fiction 2. Fairies -- Fiction 3. Siblings -- Fiction 4. Supernatural -- Fiction
ISBN 978-0-8050-8984-4; 0-8050-8984-5
LC 2009-50772

While staying with distant relatives in England, Americans Rowan, Meg, Silly, and James Morgan, with their neighbors Dickie Rhys and Finn Fachan, learn that one of them must fight to the death in the Midsummer War required by the local fairies

"Sullivan draws heavily on her knowledge of Middle English folklore and creates a story rich with memorable characters and evocative language." SLJ

Sullivan, Tara

Golden boy; Tara Sullivan. G.P. Putnam's Sons, an imprint of Penguin Group (USA) Inc. 2013 368 p. (hardcover) $16.99

Grades: 7 8 9 10 11 12 **Fic**

1. Voyages and travels -- Fiction 2. Albinos and albinism -- Fiction 3. Survival -- Fiction 4. Tanzania -- Fiction 5. Human rights -- Fiction 6. Human skin color -- Fiction

ISBN 0399161120; 9780399161124

LC 2012043310

In this book, an albino boy named Habo does not fit in with his Tanzanian family, who shun him. "Only Habo's sister, Asu, protects and nurtures him. Poverty forces the family from their rural home near Arusha to Mwanza, hundreds of miles away, to stay with relatives. After their bus fare runs out, they hitch a ride across the Serengeti with an ivory poacher who sees opportunity in Habo. Forced to flee for his life, the boy eventually becomes an apprentice to Kweli, a wise, blind carver." (Kirkus)

Suma, Nova Ren

17 & gone; Nova Ren Suma. 1st ed. Dutton 2013 320 p. (hardcover) $17.99

Grades: 9 10 11 12 **Fic**

1. Occult fiction 2. Schizophrenia -- Fiction 3. Missing persons -- Fiction 4. Supernatural -- Fiction 5. Mental illness -- Fiction 6. Missing children -- Fiction 7. Psychiatric hospitals -- Fiction

ISBN 0525423400; 9780525423409

LC 2012029324

In this novel, by Nova Ren Suma, "seventeen-year-old Lauren is having visions of girls who have gone missing. And all these girls have just one thing in common--they are 17 and gone without a trace. As Lauren struggles to shake these waking nightmares, impossible questions demand urgent answers: Why are the girls speaking to Lauren? How can she help them? And . . . is she next?" (Publisher's note)

"Mature without being graphic, with a complex and intriguing plot, this novel should have no trouble finding readers." SLJ

Dani noir. Aladdin 2009 266p $15.99

Grades: 6 7 8 9 **Fic**

1. Mystery fiction 2. Divorce -- Fiction 3. Remarriage -- Fiction 4. Motion pictures -- Fiction 5. Mother-daughter relationship -- Fiction

ISBN 978-1-4169-7564-9; 1-4169-7564-0

LC 2009-22270

Imaginative thirteen-year-old Dani feels trapped in her small mountain town with only film noir at the local art theater and her depressed mother for company, but while trying to solve a real mystery she learns much about herself and life.

"Suma's watertight debut displays an expert balance of the realities of teenage life, humor and intrigue." Publ Wkly

Imaginary girls. Dutton 2011 348p $17.99

Grades: 9 10 11 12 **Fic**

1. Dead -- Fiction 2. Sisters -- Fiction 3. Supernatural -- Fiction 4. New York (State) -- Fiction

ISBN 978-0-525-42338-6; 0-525-42338-9

LC 2010-42758

Two years after sixteen-year-old Chloe discovered classmate London's dead body floating in a Hudson Valley reservoir, she returns home to be with her devoted older sister Ruby, a town favorite, and finds that London is alive and well, and that Ruby may somehow have brought her back to life and persuaded everyone that nothing is amiss.

The author "uses the story's supernatural, horror movie-ready elements in the best of ways; beneath all the strangeness lies beauty, along with a powerful statement about the devotion between sisters. Not your average paranormal novel." Publ Wkly

Summers, Courtney

Fall for anything. St. Martin's Griffin 2011 230p pa $9.99

Grades: 9 10 11 12 **Fic**

1. Mystery fiction 2. Suicide -- Fiction 3. Bereavement -- Fiction 4. Father-daughter relationship -- Fiction

ISBN 978-0-312-65673-7

LC 2010-37873

As she searches for clues that would explain the suicide of her successful photographer father, Eddie Reeves meets the strangely compelling Culler Evans who seems to know a great deal about her father and could hold the key to the mystery surrounding his death.

"Readers may find the book fascinating or mesmerizingly melancholy depending on their moods, but there is no denying that Summers has brought Eddie's intense experience into the world of her readers. An unusual, bold effort that deserves attention." Kirkus

Some girls are. St. Martin's Griffin 2010 245p pa $9.99

Grades: 9 10 11 12 **Fic**

1. School stories 2. Bullies -- Fiction

ISBN 978-0-312-57380-5

LC 2009-33859

Regina, a high school senior in the popular—and feared—crowd, suddenly falls out of favor and becomes the object of the same sort of vicious bullying that she used to inflict on others, until she finds solace with one of her former victims.

"Regina's every emotion is palpable, and it's impossible not to feel every punch—physical or emotional—she takes." Publ Wkly

This is not a test; Courtney Summers. St. Martin's Griffin 2012 336 p. $9.99; (pbk.) $9.99

Grades: 7 8 9 10 11 12 **Fic**

1. Adventure fiction 2. Zombies -- Fiction 3. Child abuse -- Fiction 4. Horror stories 5. Survival -- Fiction 6. High schools -- Fiction 7. Family problems -- Fiction

ISBN 0312656742; 9780312656744; 9781250011817

LC 2012004633

In this book, "six teens who barely know or like each other seek refuge in their high school while the undead hordes lurk outside. . . . The end of the world unfolds through the eyes of high school junior Sloane Price, who has been contemplating suicide since her older sister ran away six months earlier, leaving Sloane with their physically abusive father. But these worries are pushed aside as Sloane tries to keep her fellow students alive." (Publishers Weekly)

Sun, Amanda

Ink; Amanda Sun. Harlequin Books 2013 304 p. (paperback) $9.99

Grades: 7 8 9 10 11 12 **Fic**

1. Love stories 2. Fantasy fiction 3. Japan -- Fiction
ISBN 037321071X; 9780373210718

In this teen romance novel, by Amanda Sun, part of "The Paper Gods" series, "Katie Greene must move halfway across the world. Stuck with her aunt in Shizuoka, Japan, Katie feels lost. Alone. . . . When Katie meets aloof but gorgeous Tomohiro, the star of the school's kendo team, she is intrigued by him. . . . Somehow Tomo is connected to the kami, powerful ancient beings who once ruled Japan--and as feelings develop between Katie and Tomo, things begin to spiral out of control." (Publisher's note)

"Katie's tendency to jump to conclusions, cry, and act before she thinks is frustrating, but it leaves plenty of room for growth. The descriptions of life in Japan—particularly teen life—create a strong sense of place, and set a vivid backdrop for this intriguing series opener by a debut author." BookList

Supplee, Suzanne

Somebody everybody listens to. Dutton 2010 245p $16.99

Grades: 7 8 9 10 11 12 **Fic**

1. Singers -- Fiction 2. Country music -- Fiction 3. Nashville (Tenn.) -- Fiction
ISBN 978-0-525-42242-6; 0-525-42242-0

LC 2009-25089

Retta Lee Jones is blessed with a beautiful voice and has big dreams of leaving her tiny Tennessee hometown. With a beaten down car, a pocketful of hard-earned waitressing money, and stars in her eyes, Retta sets out to make it big in Nashville.

"While a must read for country music lovers, . . . [this book] will appeal to a wide audience, especially those who long to pursue a dream against the odds." Publ Wkly

Sutcliff, Rosemary

Sword song. Farrar, Straus & Giroux 1998 271p hardcover o.p. pa $6.95

Grades: 7 8 9 10 **Fic**

1. Vikings -- Fiction
ISBN 0-374-37363-9; 0-374-46984-9 pa

LC 98-16827

At sixteen, Bjarni is cast out of the Norse settlement in the Angles' Land for an act of oath-breaking and spends five years sailing the west coast of Scotland and witnessing the feuds of the clan chiefs living there

"This is a well-crafted story that will appeal to sophisticated readers." SLJ

★ The **Shining** Company. Farrar, Straus & Giroux 1990 295p hardcover o.p. pa $7.95

Grades: 9 10 11 12 **Fic**

1. Great Britain -- History -- 0-1066 -- Fiction
ISBN 0-374-36807-4; 0-374-46616-5 pa

LC 89-46142

"The realistic telling of the tale makes Sutcliff's story interesting. She creates a setting so genuine that readers will find themselves transposed into another time and place. Her language, reinforced by the Germanic influence of Old English, adds not only authenticity to the story but also a sense of poetry. This book will be cherished by the lover of history, the lover of literature, and the lover of adventure." Voice Youth Advocates

Sutton, Kelsey

Some quiet place; by Kelsey Sutton. 1st ed. Flux 2013 336 p. (paperback) $9.99

Grades: 7 8 9 10 **Fic**

1. Occult fiction 2. School stories 3. Fear -- Fiction 4. Emotions -- Fiction 5. Wisconsin -- Fiction 6. High schools -- Fiction 7. Supernatural -- Fiction 8. Family problems -- Fiction 9. Farm life -- Wisconsin -- Fiction
ISBN 0738736430; 9780738736433

LC 2013005021

In this book, "Elizabeth Caldwell's best friend is dying of cancer, one of the cutest boys in school loves her, and her alcoholic father beats her—but Elizabeth doesn't care about any of it. Her only meaningful interactions are with the Emotions, immortal personifications of the feelings she can't experience. With them, she does not have to pretend, as she must when she tries to muster believable social responses." The book explores the reasons behind Elizabeth's coldness. (Publishers Weekly)

"Haunting, chilling and achingly romantic, Sutton's debut novel for teens will keep readers up until the wee hours, unable to tear themselves away from this strange and beautifully crafted story. Elizabeth Caldwell can't feel emotions, yet she sees them everywhere, human in appearance, standing alongside their "summons."...Chills and goose bumps of the very best kind accompany this haunting, memorable achievement." (Kirkus)

Sweeney, Joyce

The **guardian**. Henry Holt and Co. 2009 177p $16.95

Grades: 7 8 9 10 **Fic**

1. School stories 2. Bullies -- Fiction 3. Siblings -- Fiction 4. Foster home care -- Fiction 5. Father-son relationship -- Fiction
ISBN 978-0-8050-8019-3; 0-8050-8019-8

LC 2008-40602

When thirteen-year-old Hunter, struggling to deal with a harsh, money-grubbing foster mother, three challenging foster sisters, and a school bully, returns to his childhood faith and prays to St. Gabriel, he instantly becomes aware that he does, indeed, have a guardian.

"Sweeney's prose is insightful and realistic, with cleverly delivered descriptions. The peripheral characters are believable, and the religious undercurrent supports the plot. Well-paced, and with a satisfying conclusion." SLJ

Tahmaseb, Charity

The **geek** girl's guide to cheerleading; [by] Charity Tahmaseb and Darcy Vance. Simon Pulse 2009 324p pa $8.99

Grades: 7 8 9 10 **Fic**

1. Friendship -- Fiction 2. Cheerleading -- Fiction 3. Dating (Social customs) -- Fiction

ISBN 978-1-4169-7834-3; 1-4169-7834-8

"Self-professed 'geek girl' Bethany has a crush on an unattainable jock, Jack. On a lark, she tries out for and makes the cheerleading squad and draws Jack's attention. But as her relationship with Jack blooms, complications arise that impact both her friendships and her romance. . . . The diverse characters and Bethany's introspective commentary on teen life creates an engaging and entertaining read." Booklist

Takoudes, Greg

When we wuz famous; Greg Takoudes. 1st ed. Christy Ottaviano Books 2013 320 p. (hardcover) $16.99

Grades: 9 10 11 12 **Fic**

1. School stories 2. Teenagers -- Fiction

ISBN 0805094520; 9780805094527

LC 2012027733

This novel "follows three teenagers in . . . Harlem, struggling to survive inside and outside the neighborhood. Francisco has been given the chance of a lifetime with a senior-year scholarship to a prestigious boarding school upstate. . . . While Francisco suffers bouts of homesickness, his cousin Vincent flounders back in N.Y.C. without Francisco to bail him out of trouble, and Francisco's girlfriend, Reignbow, has her hands full trying to take care of her wheelchair-bound mother." (Publishers Weekly)

Tal, Eve

Cursing Columbus. Cinco Puntos Press 2009 248p $17.95

Grades: 7 8 9 10 **Fic**

1. Jews -- Fiction 2. Immigrants -- Fiction 3. Family life -- Fiction 4. New York (N.Y.) -- Fiction 5. Russian Americans -- Fiction

ISBN 978-1-933693-59-0; 1-933693-59-2

LC 2009-15834

Sequel to: Double crossing (2005)

In 1907, fourteen-year-old Raizel, who has lived in New York City for three years, and her brother Lemmel, newly-arrived, respond very differently to the challenges of living as Ukrainian Jews in the Lower East Side as Raizel works toward fitting in and getting ahead, while Lemmel joins a gang and lives on the streets

"The story offers a realistic and poignant picture of a bygone time." SLJ

Double crossing. Cinco Puntos Press 2005 261p $16.95

Grades: 7 8 9 10 **Fic**

1. Jews -- Fiction 2. Immigrants -- Fiction

ISBN 0-938317-94-6

LC 2005-8188

In 1905, as life becomes increasingly difficult for Jews in Ukraine, eleven-year-old Raizel and her father flee to America in hopes of earning money to bring the rest of the family there, but her father's health and Orthodox faith become barriers.

"Tal's fictionalized account of her grandfather's journey to America is fast paced, full of suspense, and highly readable." SLJ

Followed by: Cursing Columbus (2009)

Tanner, Mike

★ **Resurrection** blues. Annick Press 2005 246p $19.95; pa $9.95

Grades: 9 10 11 12 **Fic**

1. Musicians -- Fiction 2. Rock music -- Fiction

ISBN 1-55037-897-X; 1-55037-896-1 pa

"In the middle of his senior year, 18-year-old Flynn Robinson drops out of high school to join a traveling bar band and chase his dream of being a professional musician like his uncle Ray. . . Flynn describes his six months on the road with the Sawyers band: the thrill of performing; his unease with his bandmates' adventures with drugs and sex; and ambivalence about his future, particularly his relationship with his high-school girlfriend. . . . Many readers, particularly teens who share his lyrically described musical passion, will easily connect with his questions, restlessness, and driving need for independence and expression." Booklist

Tashjian, Janet

The **gospel** according to Larry. Holt & Co. 2001 227p il $16.95; pa $5.99

Grades: 7 8 9 10 **Fic**

1. Fame 2. Web sites 3. Identity 4. Coming of age 5. Web sites -- Fiction

ISBN 0-8050-6378-1; 0-440-23792-0 pa

LC 2001-24568

Seventeen-year-old Josh, a loner-philosopher who wants to make a difference in the world, tries to maintain his secret identity as the author of a web site that is receiving national attention

"Tashjian fabricates a cleverly constructed scenario and expertly carries it out to the bittersweet end." Horn Book Guide

Other titles about Larry are:
Vote for Larry (2004)
Larry and the meaning of life (2008)

Taub, Melinda

Still star-crossed; by Melinda Taub. 1st ed. Random House Childrens Books 2013 352 p. (library) $19.99; (hardcover) $16.99

Grades: 7 8 9 10 11 12 **Fic**

1. Love stories 2. Historical fiction 3. Love -- Fiction 4. Families -- Fiction 5. Vendetta -- Fiction 6. Characters in literature -- Fiction 7. Italy -- History -- 1559-1789 -- Fiction 8. Verona (Italy) -- History -- 16th century -- Fiction

ISBN 0385743505; 9780375991189; 9780385743501

LC 2012032626

This young adult novel is a sequel to the events of the play "Romeo and Juliet." The "peace purchased with Romeo's and Juliet's deaths lasts two weeks before the Capulets and Montagues renew their fight in the streets of Verona. . . . Prince Escalus attempts to force the feuding families into concord by arranging a marriage between Rosaline and Benvolio." (Kirkus Reviews)

Tayleur, Karen

Chasing boys. Walker & Co. 2009 244p $16.99
Grades: 7 8 9 10 11 **Fic**

1. School stories 2. Fathers -- Fiction
ISBN 978-0-8027-9830-5; 0-8027-9830-6
LC 2008-23241

First published 2007 by Black Dog Books

With her father gone and her family dealing with financial problems, El transfers to a new school, where she falls for one of the popular boys and then must decide whether to remain true to herself or become like the girls she scorns.

"All the ingredients of El's life are blended seamlessly, never downplaying the audience's intelligence, as Tayleur captures the all-consuming nature of a teenage crush without making El ridiculous. Moody, poetic, and intimate, this book is billed as the 'romance for girls who don't like pink,' but is much more than that." Booklist

Taylor, Greg

Killer Pizza. Feiwel and Friends 2009 346p $16.99
Grades: 6 7 8 9 **Fic**

1. Horror fiction 2. Monsters -- Fiction
ISBN 978-0-312-37379-5; 0-312-37379-1
LC 2008028543

While working as summer employees in a local pizza parlor, three teenagers are recruited by an underground organization of monster hunters.

"Toby is an easygoing and relatable young adult, and young teens will enjoy the fun, slightly scary read." Voice Youth Advocates

Killer Pizza: the slice. Feiwel and Friends 2011 341p $16.99
Grades: 6 7 8 9 **Fic**

1. Horror fiction 2. Adventure fiction 3. Monsters -- Fiction
ISBN 978-0-312-58088-9; 0-312-58088-6
LC 2010048928

Having passed the tests to become Monster Combat Officers, teens Toby, Annabel, and Strobe are sent on a secret mission to deliver to the Monster Protection Program a beautiful fourteen-year-old monster who wants to defect, regardless of the considerable dangers this poses.

The **girl** who became a Beatle. Feiwel and Friends 2011 281p $16.99; pa $9.99
Grades: 6 7 8 9 **Fic**

1. Fame -- Fiction 2. Rock music -- Fiction 3. Space and time -- Fiction 4. Conduct of life -- Fiction
ISBN 978-0-312-65259-3; 0-312-65259-3; 978-0-312-60683-1 pa; 0-312-60683-4 pa
LC 2010-41450

Regina Bloomsbury, a sixteen-year-old, Beatles-obsessed rocker, takes a trip to an alternate reality where the Beatles never existed and her band, the Caverns, are the rock-and-roll superstars.

"Teens will likely skim over the fantasy's shaky logistical questions and enjoy the vicarious view of stardom's perks and pitfalls, which Taylor deepens with Regina's lingering, real-world sorrow over her parents' divorce." Booklist

Taylor, Laini

Blackbringer. G. P. Putnam's Sons 2007 437p (Faeries of Dreamdark) $17.99
Grades: 6 7 8 9 **Fic**

1. Fantasy fiction 2. Magic -- Fiction 3. Fairies -- Fiction
ISBN 978-0-399-24630-2; 0-399-24630-4
LC 2006026540

Magpie Windwitch, faerie, devil hunter, and granddaughter of the West Wind, must defeat an ancient evil creature, the Blackbringer, who has escaped from his bottle and threatens to unmake all of creation.

"Taylor drives the story forward by slowly teasing the reader with twists and turns in the plot. . . . Teen readers will identify with this faerie's humanness." Voice Youth Advocates

★ **Daughter** of smoke and bone. Little, Brown 2011 418p $18.99
Grades: 8 9 10 11 12 **Fic**

1. Love stories 2. Occult fiction 3. Fantasy fiction 4. School stories 5. Angels -- Fiction 6. Artists -- Fiction 7. Supernatural -- Fiction 8. Classical mythology -- Fiction
ISBN 978-0-316-13402-6; 0-316-13402-3; 9780316196192
LC 2010045802

Seventeen-year-old Karou, a lovely, enigmatic art student in a Prague boarding school, carries a sketchbook of hideous, frightening monsters—the chimaerae who form the only family she has ever known.

Taylor "again weaves a masterful mix of reality and fantasy with cross-genre appeal. Exquisitely written and beautifully paced." Publ Wkly

★ **Days** of blood & starlight; Laini Taylor. 1st ed. Little, Brown Books for Young Readers 2012 528 p. maps (Daughter of smoke and bone trilogy) (hardcover) $18.99
Grades: 9 10 11 12 **Fic**

1. Occult fiction 2. Fantasy fiction 3. Angels -- Fiction 4. Demonology -- Fiction 5. Supernatural -- Fiction 6. Czech Republic -- Fiction 7. Mythology, Greek -- Fiction 8. Prague (Czech Republic) -- Fiction 9. Chimera (Greek mythology) -- Fiction
ISBN 0316133973; 9780316133975
LC 2012028752

Sequel to: Daughter of smoke and bone

In this fantasy sequel to "Daughter of Smoke and Bone," "Karou . . . has taken up the resurrection work . . . under the direction of the dangerous chimaera leader, Thiago. . . . The angel army is menacing the countryside in an attempt to kill the remaining chimaera, so she is designing and resurrecting stronger, more effective winged warriors to protect her people." (Bulletin of the Center for Children's Books)

Dreams of gods & monsters; by Laini Taylor. Little, Brown and Co. 2014 624 p. (hardback) $19

Grades: 8 9 10 11 12 **Fic**

1. Angels -- Fiction 2. Supernatural -- Fiction 3. Good and evil -- Fiction 4. Greek mythology -- Fiction 5. Demonology -- Fiction 6. Chimera (Greek mythology) -- Fiction

ISBN 0316134074; 9780316134071

LC 2014003645

"Eliza Jones, a research fellow at Smithsonian's National Museum of Natural History, wakes from a recurring nightmare to the discovery that angels have appeared in the sky above Uzbekistan. Unbeknownst to Eliza, she is the linchpin upon which the salvation of worlds depends. The battle is well and truly on in this finale to the "Daughter of Smoke and Bone" trilogy (Little, Brown)... The conclusion promises resurrection, renewal, and long-postponed love happily resolved, and that should satisfy even the most meticulous fans." (School Library Journal(

Dreams of gods and monsters

Silksinger; illustrations by Jim Di Bartolo. G.P. Putnam's Sons 2009 449p il (Dreamdark) $18.99

Grades: 6 7 8 9 **Fic**

1. Fantasy fiction 2. Fairies -- Fiction 3. Mercenary soldiers -- Fiction 4. Good and evil -- Fiction

ISBN 978-0-399-24631-9; 0-399-24631-2

LC 2008047981

While journeying by dragonfly caravan over the Sayash Mountains, warrior-faerie Whisper Silksinger, hunted by devils, meets a young mercenary with an ancient scimitar and secrets of his own.

"With excellent world-building and deft pacing, this story is difficult to put down. The characters are well developed, and their close relationships and rapid-fire dialogue enhance the story." SLJ

Taylor, Mildred D.

★ The **land.** Phyllis Fogelman Bks. 2001 375p $17.99; pa $6.99

Grades: 7 8 9 10 **Fic**

1. Race relations -- Fiction 2. African Americans -- Fiction 3. Racially mixed people -- Fiction

ISBN 0-8037-1950-7; 0-14-250146-8 pa

LC 00-39329

Prequel to Roll of Thunder, Hear My Cry

Coretta Scott King Award for text

After the Civil War Paul-Edward Logan, the son of a white father and a black mother, finds himself caught between the two worlds of colored folks and white folks as he pursues his dream of owning land of his own.

"Taylor masterfully uses harsh historical realities to frame a powerful coming-of-age story that stands on its own merits." Horn Book Guide

Taylor, S. S.

The **Expeditioners** and the Treasure of Drowned Man's Canyon; and the Treasure of Drowned Man's Canyon. by S. S. Taylor; illustrated by Katherine Roy. Pgw 2012 320 p. $22

Grades: 5 6 7 8 **Fic**

1. Adventure fiction

ISBN 1938073061; 9781938073069

In this book by S. S. Taylor, illustrated by Katherine Roy, "computers have failed, electricity is extinct, and the race to discover new lands is underway! Brilliant explorer Alexander West has just died under mysterious circumstances, but not before smuggling half of a strange map to his intrepid children--Kit the brain, M.K. the tinkerer, and Zander the brave. Why are so many government agents trying to steal the half-map? (And where is the other half?)" (Publisher's note)

Teller, Janne

★ **Nothing**; translated from the Danish by Martin Aitken. Atheneum Books for Young Readers 2010 227p $16.99

Grades: 7 8 9 10 11 12 **Fic**

1. School stories 2. Meaning (Philosophy) -- Fiction

ISBN 978-1-4169-8579-2; 1-4169-8579-4

LC 2009-19784

Michael J. Printz honor book, 2011

When thirteen-year-old Pierre Anthon leaves school to sit in a plum tree and train for becoming part of nothing, his seventh grade classmates set out on a desperate quest for the meaning of life.

"Indelible, elusive, and timeless, this uncompromising novel has all the marks of a classic." Booklist

Templeman, McCormick

The **glass** casket; McCormick Templeman. Delacorte Press 2014 352 p. (hc) $17.99

Grades: 9 10 11 12 **Fic**

1. Villages -- Fiction 2. Young adult literature 3. Supernatural -- Fiction 4. Fairy tales 5. Love -- Fiction 6. Murder -- Fiction 7. Witches -- Fiction 8. Community life -- Fiction

ISBN 0385743459; 9780375991134; 9780385743457

LC 2013001970

In this young adult fantasy novel, by McCormick Templeman, "one bleak morning, . . . five horses and their riders thunder into [Rowan's] village and through the forest, disappearing into the hills. Days later, the riders' bodies are found. . . . Something has followed the path those riders made and has come down from the hills, through the forest, and into the village. Beast or man, it has brought death to Rowan's door." (Publisher's note)

"Templeman pulls a 180 from her incisive contemporary debut, The Little Woods (2012), with a fantasy involving witches, magic, and monsters...The story doesn't always fire, but, in fact, Templeman is at her best when leaving plot behind, as when one character's death acts as a sort of forbidden fruit leading to unleashed sexual passion—it's challenging, dizzying material. The legion of Maggie Stiefvater fans out there ought to look this way." (Booklist)

Terrill, Cristin

All our yesterdays; Cristin Terrill. Hyperion 2013 368 p. (hardback) $17.99

Grades: 7 8 9 10 11 12 **Fic**

1. Science fiction 2. Time travel -- Fiction 3. Love -- Fiction 4. Murder -- Fiction

ISBN 1423176375; 9781423176374

LC 2013008007

In this book, narrator "Em and her boyfriend, Finn, escape from their totalitarian future, time traveling back four years to commit a heart-wrenching assassination of a loved one in order to prevent time travel from being invented and the future from turning so wrong. . . . The other side of the storyline, taking place in the past that Em and Finn travel to and starring their past selves, is narrated by Marina" and talks about her best friend and crush, James. (Kirkus Reviews)

Terry, Chris L.

Zero fade; Chris L Terry. Curbside Splendor Publishing 2013 294 p. $12

Grades: 7 8 9 10 **Fic**

1. School stories 2. Bullies -- Fiction 3. Historical fiction

ISBN 0988480433; 9780988480438

LC 2013944486

This book focuses on Kevin Phifer, "a black seventh-grader in 1990s Richmond, Va." He "wants a fade, thinking the stylish haircut will bolster his shaky standing in the cut-throat world of middle school, where he's just one friend away from eating lunch alone. But his mother, a church secretary and solo parent studying for a nursing degree at night, won't even try. Expressing his frustration leads to a week's grounding. Tyrell and his entourage of bullies make Kevin's life miserable at school." (Kirkus Reviews)

"Original, hilarious, thought-provoking and wicked smart: not to be missed." (Kirkus)

Terry, Teri

Fractured; Teri Terry. Nancy Paulsen Books 2013 336 p. (Slated trilogy) $17.99

Grades: 7 8 9 10 **Fic**

1. Dystopian fiction 2. Memory -- Fiction 3. Science fiction 4. England -- Fiction 5. Identity -- Fiction 6. Terrorism -- Fiction 7. High schools -- Fiction 8. Identity (Psychology)

ISBN 0399161732; 9780399161735

LC 2012044317

Author Teri Terry presents the "second installment of the Slated trilogy . . . set in a future where violent teens have their memory erased as an alternative to jail. Kyla has been Slated--her personality wiped blank, her memories lost to her forever. Or so she thought. When a mysterious man from her past comes back into her life and wants her help, she thinks she's on her way to finding the truth." (Publisher's note)

"Kyla's memories, wiped by the government in Slated, are slowly returning; she's been found by an anti-government group that claims she's a member and wants her to complete one last mission. Kyla's struggles to uncover her identity and think through the consequences of her actions are realistic and add an emotional backbone to this fast-paced middle volume of the trilogy." (Horn Book)

Slated; Teri Terry. Nancy Paulsen Books 2013 346 p. (hardcover) $17.99

Grades: 7 8 9 10 **Fic**

1. Science fiction 2. Memory -- Fiction 3. Identity -- Fiction 4. High schools -- Fiction 5. Family life -- England -- Fiction

ISBN 0399161724; 9780399161728

LC 2012020873

In this novel, by Teri Terry, "Kyla has been Slated--her memory and personality erased as punishment for committing a crime she can't remember. The government has taught her how to walk and talk again, given her a new identity and a new family, and told her to be grateful for this second chance that she doesn't deserve. It's also her last chance--because they'll be watching to make sure she plays by their rules." (Publisher's note)

Testa, Dom

The **comet's** curse. Tor Teen 2009 236p (Galahad) $16.95

Grades: 7 8 9 10 11 12 **Fic**

1. Science fiction 2. Interplanetary voyages -- Fiction

ISBN 978-0-7653-2107-7; 0-7653-2107-6

LC 2008-35620

First published 2005 by Profound Impact Group

Desperate to save the human race after a comet's deadly particles devastate the adult population, scientists create a ship that will carry a crew of 251 teenagers to a home in a distant solar system.

This book is "both a mystery and an adventure, combining a solid cast of characters with humor, pathos, growing pains and just a hint of romance." Kirkus

Other titles in this series are:

The Cassini code (2010)

Cosmic storm (2011)

The dark zone (2011)

The web of Titan (2009)

Tharp, Tim

Badd. Alfred A. Knopf 2011 308p $16.99; lib bdg $19.99; ebook $10.99

Grades: 9 10 11 12 **Fic**

1. Siblings -- Fiction 2. Iraq War, 2003- -- Fiction 3. Post-traumatic stress disorder -- Fiction

ISBN 978-0-375-86444-5; 978-0-375-96444-2 lib bdg; 978-0-375-89579-1 ebook

LC 2010-12732

A teenaged girl's beloved brother returns home from the Iraq War completely unlike the person she remembers.

"With convincing three-dimensional characters, Tharp paints a sympathetic portrait of the constraints of small town life, the struggles of PTSD, and the challenges of faith." Publ Wkly

Knights of the hill country. Alfred A. Knopf 2006 233p hardcover o.p. pa $6.99

Grades: 8 9 10 11 12 **Fic**

1. School stories 2. Football -- Fiction 3. Oklahoma -- Fiction

ISBN 978-0-375-83653-4; 0-375-83653-5; 978-0-553-49513-3 pa; 0-553-49513-5 pa

LC 2005-33279

In his senior year, high school star linebacker Hampton Greene finally begins to think for himself and discovers that he might be interested in more than just football.

"Taut scenes on the football field and the dilemmas about choosing what feels right over what's expected are all made memorable by Hamp's unforgettable, colloquial voice." Booklist

Mojo; Tim Tharp. Knopf Books for Young Readers 2013 288 p. (hardcover) $16.99; (ebook) $50.97; (library) $19.99
Grades: 7 8 9 10 11 12 **Fic**

1. School stories 2. Mystery fiction 3. High schools -- Fiction 4. Missing children -- Fiction 5. Secret societies -- Fiction 6. Self-realization -- Fiction 7. Mystery and detective stories

ISBN 0375864458; 9780375864452; 9780375895807; 9780375964459

LC 2012023886

In this novel, by Tim Tharp, "all Dylan wants is mojo. What is mojo? . . . It's everything Dylan doesn't have. . . . So when Dylan hears about a missing rich girl from the other side of town, he jumps at the chance to dive into this mystery. . . . His investigation takes him into the world of an elite private high school and an underground club called Gangland." (Publisher's note)

★ The **spectacular** now. Alfred A. Knopf 2008 294p $16.99; lib bdg $19.99
Grades: 9 10 11 12 **Fic**

1. School stories 2. Oklahoma -- Fiction 3. Alcoholism -- Fiction 4. Stepfamilies -- Fiction 5. Dating (Social customs) -- Fiction

ISBN 978-0-375-85179-7; 0-375-85179-7; 978-0-375-95179-4 lib bdg; 0-375-95179-2 lib bdg

LC 2008-03544

In the last months of high school, charismatic eighteen-year-old Sutter Keely lives in the present, staying drunk or high most of the time, but that could change when he starts working to boost the self-confidence of a classmate, Aimee.

"Tharp offers a poignant, funny book about a teen who sees his life as livable only when his senses are dulled by drink . . . . Sutter is an authentic character [who] . . . will strike a chord with teen readers." Booklist

Thomas, Erin

Boarder patrol; written by Erin Thomas. Orca Book Publishers 2010 170p (Orca sports) pa $9.95
Grades: 6 7 8 9 **Fic**

1. Mystery fiction 2. Skiing -- Fiction 3. Cousins -- Fiction 4. Snowboarding -- Fiction

ISBN 978-1-55469-294-1 pa; 1-55469-294-6 pa

"Ryan, 16, works as a Junior Ski Patrol volunteer in order to earn a free lift pass. His dream is to pursue snowboarding professionally. His cousin, Kevin, who works at the lifts, starts acting strangely, especially when Ryan begins investigating the disappearance of some ski equipment, including his own, on the mountain. . . . The story includes vivid descriptions of snowboarding and mountain rescue, and the mystery is involving." SLJ

Thomas, Lex

Quarantine; the loners. Lex Thomas. EgmontUSA 2012 404 p. (Quarantine) (hardback) $17.99
Grades: 9 10 11 12 **Fic**

1. Horror fiction 2. Science fiction 3. Adventure fiction 4. Epidemics -- Fiction 5. Young adult literature 6. Gangs -- Fiction 7. Survival -- Fiction 8. High schools -- Fiction 9. Virus diseases -- Fiction 10. Interpersonal relations -- Fiction

ISBN 160684329X; 9781606843291; 9781606843307

LC 2011039460

This young adult horror-action novel by Lex Thomas presents "an apocalypse writ small: a sick teen infects a Colorado high school with a disease so deadly that half the building is blown up by the military and the rest is sealed inside a giant dome. Every two weeks the ceiling is split for an air drop of food and supplies, and it's during these drops that the 1,000 surviving kids split into warring cliques with names like the Nerds, the Sluts, and the Freaks "fight, steal, and even kill to make good. Because of a . . . feud with Sam, the leader of Varsity (the jocks' gang), David is forced to eke out a loner's existence. But while protecting his younger brother, Will . . . David becomes an underground hero which begins to infuriate Will, who also longs for the spotlight." (Booklist)

Thomas, Rob

Rats saw God. Simon & Schuster Bks. for Young Readers 1996 219p hardcover o.p. pa $6.99
Grades: 7 8 9 10 **Fic**

1. School stories 2. Father-son relationship -- Fiction

ISBN 0-689-80207-2; 1-4169-3897-4 pa

LC 95-43548

"High-school senior Steve York isn't doing well. The former straight-A student is flunking, and his new friends are dopers. . . . A counselor steps in and suggests Steve can write something to bring up his failing English grade. So Steve writes his story, and as the action flips between his former life in Texas and the present in California, readers will learn about Steve's cold war with his astronaut father, his dabbling with dadaism, and, most of all, his heavenly-hellish experience with first love." Booklist

"The sharp descriptions of cliques, clubs and annoying authority figures will strike a familiar chord. The dialogue is fresh and Steve's intelligent banter and introspective musings never sound wiser than his years." Publ Wkly

Thomas, Sherry

The **burning** sky; by Sherry Thomas. Balzer + Bray 2013 480 p. (hardcover bdg.) $17.99
Grades: 7 8 9 10 11 12 **Fic**

1. Fantasy fiction 2. Magic -- Fiction 3. Fantasy

ISBN 0062207296; 9780062207296

LC 2013014504

This book, by author Sherry Thomas presents "the story of a girl who fooled a thousand boys, a boy who fooled an entire country, a partnership that would change the fate of realms, and a power to challenge the greatest tyrant the world had ever known." (Publisher's note)

"When sixteen-year-old elemental mage Iolanthe summons a lightning bolt, she draws the unwelcome attention of the Inquisitor of Atlantis. She also draws the eye of resistance fighter Prince Titus, who rescues her and disguises her as a boy. Heightened action combined with Scarlet Pimpernel-esque cleverness will keep readers eagerly turning pages, while the romantic tension adds juiciness to the fantasy plot." (Horn Book)

Thompson, Holly

The **language** inside; Holly Thompson. 1st ed. Delacorte Press 2013 528 p. (hardcover) $17.99

Grades: 7 8 9 10 11 12 **Fic**

1. Novels in verse 2. Moving -- Fiction 3. Interpersonal relations -- Fiction 4. Japan -- Fiction 5. Cancer -- Fiction 6. Tsunamis -- Fiction 7. Massachusetts -- Fiction 8. Moving, Household -- Fiction 9. Family life -- Massachusetts -- Fiction

ISBN 0385739796; 9780375898358; 9780385739795; 9780385908078

LC 2012030596

In this novel in verse, by Holly Thompson, "Emma's family moves to a town outside Lowell, Massachusetts, to stay with Emma's grandmother while her mom undergoes treatment. Emma feels out of place in the United States. She begins to have migraines, and longs to be back in Japan. At her grandmother's urging, she volunteers in a long-term care center to help Zena, a patient with locked-in syndrome, write down her poems." (Publisher's note)

Orchards. Delacorte Press 2011 327p il $17.99; lib bdg $20.99

Grades: 7 8 9 10 **Fic**

1. Novels in verse 2. Japan -- Fiction 3. Suicide -- Fiction 4. Bereavement -- Fiction 5. Family life -- Fiction 6. Racially mixed people -- Fiction

ISBN 978-0-385-73977-1; 0-385-73977-X; 978-0-385-90806-1 lib bdg; 0-385-90806-7 lib bdg

LC 2010-23724

"After a classmate commits suicide, Kana, a half-Japanese, half-Jewish American eighth grader, is sent to her maternal grandmother's farm in rural Japan for personal reflection. Kana tells her story in poignantly straightforward verse directed at the deceased classmate as she struggles with blame and regret, wondering if she and her friends are responsible because they took part in ostracizing the girl. She struggles, too, with her biracial, bicultural identity, feeling isolated in her new surroundings." (School Library Journal)

"Kanako's urgent teen voice, written in rapid free verse and illustrated with occasional black-and-white sketches, will hold readers with its nonreverential family story." Booklist

Thompson, Kate

★ **Creature** of the night. Roaring Brook Press 2008 250p $17.95

Grades: 9 10 11 12 **Fic**

1. Ireland -- Fiction 2. Homicide -- Fiction 3. Juvenile delinquency -- Fiction

ISBN 978-1-59643-511-7; 1-59643-511-9

Bobby lives a reckless life smoking, drinking, and stealing cars in Dublin. So his mother moves the family to the country. But Bobby suspects their cottage might not be as quaint as it seems. And spooky details of the history of their little cottage gradually turn Bobby into a detective of night creatures real and imagined.

"A unique blend of subtlety and brashness, this is an honest coming-of-age novel in the guise of a gripping YA thriller." Booklist

★ The **new** policeman. Greenwillow Books 2007 442p hardcover o.p. pa $8.99

Grades: 7 8 9 10 **Fic**

1. Fantasy fiction 2. Music -- Fiction 3. Fairies -- Fiction 4. Ireland -- Fiction 5. Space and time -- Fiction

ISBN 978-0-06-117427-8; 0-06-117427-0; 978-0-06-117429-2 pa; 0-06-117429-7 pa

LC 2006-8246

First published 2005 in the United Kingdom

Irish teenager JJ Liddy discovers that time is leaking from his world into Tir na nOg, the land of the fairies, and when he attempts to stop the leak he finds out a lot about his family history, the music that he loves, and a crime his great-grandfather may or may not have committed.

"Mesmerizing and captivating, this book is guaranteed to charm fantasy fans." Voice Youth Advocates

Other titles in this series are:

The last of the High Kings (2008)

The white horse trick (2010)

Origins. Bloomsbury 2007 313p (Missing link trilogy) $17.95

Grades: 6 7 8 9 **Fic**

1. Science fiction 2. Animals -- Fiction 3. Future life -- Fiction 4. Genetic engineering -- Fiction 5. Young adult literature -- Works

ISBN 978-1-58234-652-6; 1-58234-652-6

LC 2007-06924

Christy 's souvenir stone from the yeti's cave proves to be fatal for many of the inhabitants of Fourth World leaving among the survivors a pair of genetically-altered twins whose eventual descendants face an uncertain future in a stone age world of nuclear devastation and disease.

This is "a post-apolcalyptic stunner. [It blends] weighty science fiction themes like genetic engineering and the future of human evolution with equally thought-provoking allegorical fable." Publ Wkly

Thompson, Ricki

City of cannibals. Front Street 2010 269p $18.95

Grades: 8 9 10 11 12 **Fic**

1. Monks -- Fiction 2. Persecution -- Fiction 3. Runaway teenagers -- Fiction 4. Great Britain -- History -- 1485-1603, Tudors -- Fiction

ISBN 978-1-59078-623-9; 1-59078-623-8

LC 2010-2105

In 1536 England, sixteen-year-old Dell runs away from her brutal father and life in a cave carrying only a handmade puppet to travel to London, where she learns truths about her mother's death and the conflict between King Henry VIII and the Catholic Church.

"Thompson's England is authentically vulgar, and her grasp of period slang—as well as Dell's burgeoning sexual desires—is expert. Packed with rich metaphor, this is a challenging but rewarding read." Booklist

Thomson, Jamie

Dark Lord, the early years; by Jamie Thomson. Walker & Co. 2012 290 p. (hardcover) $16.99

Grades: 6 7 8 9 **Fic**

1. School stories 2. Fantasy fiction 3. Fantasy 4.

Humorous stories 5. Magic -- Fiction 6. Identity -- Fiction
ISBN 0802728499; 9780802728494
LC 2012007152

In this book by Jamie Thomson, "the Dark Lord" renamed Dirk Lloyd by confused, puny Earthlings is taken to the Hospital Lockup and then to a House of Detention" after waking up in a parking lot "trapped in the body of a 12-year-old human." People think he's crazy, "but thankfully, Christopher, the child of his captors, agrees to be a minion, as does goth girl Sooz. Dirk must find a way back to his Darklands" before he loses his evil abilities. (Kirkus)

Thomson, Sarah L.

The **secret** of the Rose; 1st ed.; Greenwillow Books 2006 296p $16.99; lib bdg $17.89
Grades: 6 7 8 9 **Fic**
1. Authors 2. Dramatists 3. Theater -- Fiction 4. Sex role -- Fiction 5. Catholics -- Fiction
ISBN 978-0-06-087250-2; 0-06-087250-0; 978-0-06-087251-9 lib bdg; 0-06-087251-9 lib bdg
LC 2005-22177

When her father is imprisoned in 1592 England for being Catholic, fourteen-year-old Rosalind disguises herself as a boy and finds an ultimately dangerous job as servant to playwright Christopher Marlowe.

"Part historical mystery, part suspense, this fast-paced story is propelled by Rosalind's desire not just to survive but also to learn who she is." Voice Youth Advocates

Thurlo, Aimee

The **spirit** line; [by] Aimeé & David Thurlo. Viking 2004 216p $15.99
Grades: 6 7 8 9 **Fic**
1. Navajo Indians -- Fiction
ISBN 0-670-03645-5

When the special rug Crystal Manyfeathers is weaving for her kinaaldá, the traditional Navajo womanhood ceremony, is stolen from her loom, there are any number of suspects.

"Carefully combining humor and seriousness, this well-paced story contains accurate portrayals of Navajo customs, mostly believable teen dialogue, and a realistic depiction of the conflicts modern Native young people face." SLJ

Tibensky, Arlaina

And then things fall apart. Simon Pulse 2011 254p pa $9.99; ebook $9.99
Grades: 9 10 11 12 **Fic**
1. Poets 2. Authors 3. Novelists 4. Divorce -- Fiction 5. Chicago (Ill.) -- Fiction 6. Dating (Social customs) -- Fiction
ISBN 978-1-4424-1323-8 pa; 978-1-4424-1324-5 ebook
LC 2010044631

Devastated by her parents' decision to split up, pressured by her boyfriend to have sex, and saddled with a case of chicken pox, fifteen-year-old Keek finds consolation in her beloved, well-worn copy of Sylvia Plath's "The Bell Jar."

This "is a short, intoxicating, bouncy, lustful, stream-of-consciousness narrative. . . . Keek's poetry—not bad, either—punctuates the diary entries and offers more catnip to Plathians." Booklist

Tiernan, Cate

★ **Balefire.** Razorbill 2011 974p pa $8.99
Grades: 8 9 10 11 12 **Fic**
1. Twins -- Fiction 2. Sisters -- Fiction 3. Witchcraft -- Fiction 4. New Orleans (La.) -- Fiction
ISBN 978-1-59514-411-9

An omnibus edition of four titles previously published separately, the first three of which were first published 2005. The last, A necklace of water, was first published 2006

Separated since birth, seventeen-year-old twins Thais and Clio unexpectedly meet in New Orleans where they seem to be pursued by a coven of witches who want to harness the twins' magical powers for its own ends.

Immortal beloved. Little, Brown and Company 2010 407p $16.99
Grades: 8 9 10 11 12 **Fic**
1. Fantasy fiction 2. Magic -- Fiction 3. Immortality -- Fiction 4. Massachusetts -- Fiction 5. Conduct of life -- Fiction
ISBN 978-0-316-03592-7; 0-316-03592-0
LC 2010-06884

After seeing her best friend, a Dark Immortal called Incy, torture a human with magick, Nastasya, a spoiled party girl, enters a home for wayword immortals and finally begins to deal with life, even as she learns that someone wants her dead.

"Humor overlies serious issues of identity and personal responsibility explored within the story, and readers who enjoy character-driven works of romantic fantasy will flock to this book." Voice Youth Advocates

Tintera, Amy

Reboot; Amy Tintera. 1st ed. HarperTeen, an imprint of HarperCollinsPublishers 2013 384 p. (hardcover) $17.99
Grades: 9 10 11 12 **Fic**
1. Dead -- Fiction 2. Science fiction 3. Soldiers -- Fiction 4. Adventure and adventurers -- Fiction
ISBN 0062217070; 9780062217073
LC 2012051741

In this dystopian novel, by Any Tintera, "a seventeen-year-old girl rises from the dead as a Reboot and is trained as an elite crime-fighting soldier. . . . Wren 178 [is] the deadliest Reboot in the Republic of Texas. Callum 22, on the other hand, is practically still human. . . . When Callum fails to measure up to Reboot standards, Wren is told to eliminate him. Wren has never disobeyed before, but she'll do whatever it takes to save Callum's life." (Publisher's note)

Tocher, Timothy

Bill Pennant, Babe Ruth, and me. Cricket Books 2009 178p $16.95
Grades: 5 6 7 8 **Fic**
1. Baseball -- Fiction
ISBN 978-0-8126-2755-8; 0-8126-2755-5
LC 2008026829

In 1920, sixteen-year-old Hank finds his loyalties divided when he is assigned to care for the Giants' mascot, a wildcat named Bill Pennant, as well as keep an eye on Babe Ruth in Ruth's first season with the New York Yankees.

The author "seamlessly blends fact and fiction. He recreates the era with scrupulous attention to its syntax and slang, as well as details of daily life. Ruth, McGraw and the other historical figures come alive for readers, and the fictional Hank is a sympathetic, fully developed character." Kirkus

Chief Sunrise, John McGraw, and me; Timothy Tocher. 1st ed; Cricket Books 2004 154p $15.95

Grades: 5 6 7 8 **Fic**

1. Baseball -- Fiction 2. Race relations -- Fiction 3. Runaway teenagers -- Fiction

ISBN 0-8126-2711-3

LC 2003-23407

In 1919, fifteen-year-old Hank escapes an abusive father and goes looking for a chance to become a baseball player, accompanied by a man who calls himself Chief Sunrise and claims to be a full-blooded Seminole.

"The story is both entertaining and thought-provoking." Booklist

Todd, Pamela

The **blind** faith hotel; [by] Pamela Todd. Margaret K. McElderry Books 2008 312p $16.99; pa $8.99

Grades: 8 9 10 **Fic**

1. Nature -- Fiction 2. Prairies -- Fiction 3. Family life -- Fiction

ISBN 978-1-4169-5494-1; 1-4169-5494-5; 978-1-4169-9509-8 pa; 1-4169-9509-9 pa

LC 2007-43912

When her parents separate and she and her siblings move with their mother from the northwest coast to a midwest prairie farmhouse, fourteen-year-old Zoe, miserably unhappy to be away from the ocean and her father, begins to develop a deep attachment to her new surroundings, when, after a shoplifting episode, she is assigned to work at a nature preserve.

"This touching novel tackles many difficult issues; beautiful imagery and language keep the story vibrant." Horn Book Guide

Toliver, Wendy

Lifted. Simon Pulse 2010 309p pa $9.99

Grades: 7 8 9 10 **Fic**

1. School stories 2. Texas -- Fiction 3. Theft -- Fiction 4. Moving -- Fiction

ISBN 978-1-4169-9048-2; 1-4169-9048-8

"Poppy isn't happy with her single mother for moving her to Texas and enrolling the decidedly secular 16-year-old in a private Baptist high school. Soon, however, she becomes fascinated with the two most elite girls in class. . . . Her new friends, despite their pious attitudes, are shoplifters. Toliver does a good job of making clear the thefts are less about the desire for things like designer jeans than about the adrenaline rush of getting away with something. . . . Will appeal to all teens interested in wayward behavior." Booklist

Tomlinson, Heather

★ **Aurelie**; a faerie tale. Henry Holt 2008 184p $16.95

Grades: 7 8 9 10 **Fic**

1. Fantasy fiction 2. Music -- Fiction 3. Fairies -- Fiction 4. Princesses -- Fiction

ISBN 978-0-8050-8276-0; 0-8050-8276-X

LC 2007-41958

Heartsick at losing her two dearest companions, Princess Aurelie finds comfort in the glorious music of the faeries, but the duties of the court call her, as do the needs of her friends.

"Graceful prose leads the reader through a complex chronological narrative and a Shakespearean tangle of love stories." Booklist

Toads and diamonds. Henry Holt 2010 278p $16.99

Grades: 8 9 10 11 12 **Fic**

1. Fairy tales 2. India -- Fiction

ISBN 978-0-8050-8968-4; 0-8050-8968-3

LC 2009-23448

A retelling of the Perrault fairy tale set in pre-colonial India, in which two stepsisters receive gifts from a goddess and each walks her own path to find her gift's purpose, discovering romance along the way.

The author "creates a vivid setting. Lavish details starkly contrast the two girls' lives and personalities. . . . The complexities of the cultural backstory pose a challenge to readers, but this beautifully embroidered adventure is well worth the effort." Booklist

★ The **swan** maiden. Henry Holt 2007 292p $16.95

Grades: 6 7 8 9 **Fic**

1. Fairy tales 2. Magic -- Fiction

ISBN 978-0-8050-8275-3; 0-8050-8275-1

LC 2006-33774

Raised as a chastelaine-in-training unlike her sisters who are learning the arts of sorcery, Doucette discovers when she is sixteen years old that she too has magic in her blood, and she must brave her mother's wrath-and the loss of the man she loves-in order to follow her birthright.

"Layered, elegantly written, and filled with unexpected twists and turns, The Swan Maiden soars with grace and power." Booklist

Torres Sanchez, Jenny

Death, Dickinson, and the demented life of Frenchie Garcia; by Jenny Torres Sanchez. Running Press 2013 272 p. (paperback) $9.95

Grades: 9 10 11 12 **Fic**

1. Grief -- Fiction 2. Suicide -- Fiction

ISBN 0762446803; 9780762446803

LC 2013934992

In this book, "Frenchie is in the limbo of what-comes-next. She's finished high school but has been rejected by art school. She is sullen and anxious and can't seem to get her life moving. Gradually, what happened that night with Andy and its lingering impact on Frenchie are revealed. It was the same night that Andy ended his own life. No one even knows that she liked Andy, let alone about the time they spent together, so Frenchie keeps her guilt and confusion to herself." (Kirkus Reviews)

Townley, Roderick

Sky; a novel in three sets and an encore. by Roderick Townley. 1st ed; Atheneum Books for Young Readers 2004 265p $16.95

Grades: 7 8 9 10 **Fic**

1.. Jazz musicians -- Fiction 2. New York (N.Y.) -- History -- 20th century

ISBN 0-689-85712-8

LC 2003-11354

In New York City in 1959, fifteen-year-old Alec Schuyler, at odds with his widowed father over his love of music, finds a mentor and friend in a blind, black jazz musician.

"Townley presents a compassionate portrait of a young man who is battling for his own place in life and sets the story in the exciting time of the beat poets and the explosive development of jazz music." SLJ

Townsend, Wendy

★ **Lizard** love; [by] Wendy Townsend. Front Street 2008 196p $17.95

Grades: 6 7 8 9 **Fic**

1. Reptiles -- Fiction 2. Country life -- Fiction 3. City and town life -- Fiction

ISBN 978-1-932425-34-5; 1-932425-34-9

LC 2007017975

Grace, a teenager, and her mother have moved to Manhattan where she feels alienated and out of place, far from the ponds and farm where she grew up playing with bullfrogs and lizards, until she finds Fang & Claw, a reptile store, and meets the owner's son, Walter.

"Townsend displays a remarkable narrative gift. . . . Her sensitive herpetological descriptions are unflinching, evocative, and positively elegant. Even minor characterizations are full and complex." Booklist

Tracey, Scott

Darkbound; Scott Tracey. Flux 2014 360 p. (The legacy of Moonset) $9.99

Grades: 9 10 11 12 **Fic**

1. Magic -- Fiction 2. Orphans -- Fiction 3. Witches -- Fiction 4. Demonology -- Fiction

ISBN 073873649X; 9780738736495

LC 2013041665

"The children of a defeated terrorist witch coven called Moonset uncover more of their parents' legacy in this sequel to Moonset (2013)...Although the prose—plagued by awkward phrasing—could be smoother, the story is nicely built, and Malcolm is a sympathetic narrator. Moreover, despite Malcolm's tendency toward introspection, the plot doesn't flag. A solid sequel." (Karkus)

Moonset; Scott Tracey. Flux 2013 384 p. (The legacy of Moonset) (paperback) $9.99

Grades: 9 10 11 12 **Fic**

1. Occult fiction 2. Witchcraft -- Fiction 3. Magic -- Fiction 4. Orphans -- Fiction 5. Witches -- Fiction 6. Terrorism -- Fiction

ISBN 0738735299; 9780738735290

LC 2012033956

In this book, the "sins of the parents haunt 17-year-old Justin Daggett and four other children orphaned when the terrorist witch coven known as Moonset was destroyed 15 years ago. All their lives, the Moonset orphans have been guarded and scrutinized against the possibility of their accessing dark magic known as Maleficia, as their parents did before them. . . . The orphans learn that they are the target of both a warlock and Cullen Bridger, the last survivor of Moonset." (Publishers Weekly)

Tracy, Kristen

Sharks & boys. Hyperion 2011 272p $16.99

Grades: 6 7 8 9 **Fic**

1. Ships -- Fiction 2. Twins -- Fiction 3. Siblings -- Fiction 4. Survival after airplane accidents, shipwrecks, etc. -- Fiction

ISBN 978-1-4231-4354-3; 1-4231-4354-X

LC 2011-04803

Feeling betrayed, fifteen-year-old Enid follows her boyfriend, Wick, from Vermont to Maryland where he and six others they know from twin studies rent a yacht, but after she sneaks aboard a storm sets them adrift without food or water, fighting for survival.

"A page-turning thriller, . . . this emotionally complex novel makes everyone's worst beach nightmare palpable and provides a fascinating character study that explores what happens when instincts are pitted against relationships." Booklist

Tregay, Sarah

Love & leftovers; a novel in verse. Sarah Tregay. 1st ed. Katherine Tegen Books 2011 432 p. (hardcover) $17.99

Grades: 8 9 10 11 **Fic**

1. Love stories 2. Novels in verse 3. Teenagers -- Fiction 4. Children of gay parents -- Fiction 5. Iowa -- Fiction 6. Moving -- Fiction 7. Bisexuality -- Fiction 8. Family life -- Fiction 9. New Hampshire -- Fiction

ISBN 0062023586; 9780062023582

LC 2011019367

In this verse novel, "[s]ophomore Marcie Foster unwillingly moves from Idaho to her mother's childhood home in New Hampshire after her father leaves her mother for a male bartender. Marcie is resentful until she realizes the move could be a chance to remake herself." A heated relationship with "popular athlete J.D.," makes her question "her non-physical relationship with Linus," her boyfriend in Idaho. "Seven months later Marcie returns to Idaho, and things are more confusing than ever." (Publishers Weekly)

Treggiari, Jo

Ashes, ashes. Scholastic Press 2011 360p $17.99

Grades: 7 8 9 10 **Fic**

1. Science fiction 2. Dogs -- Fiction 3. Epidemics -- Fiction 4. New York (N.Y.) -- Fiction

ISBN 978-0-545-25563-9; 0-545-25563-5

LC 2010032398

In a future Manhattan devastated by environmental catastrophes and epidemics, sixteen-year-old Lucy survives alone until vicious hounds target her and force her to join Aidan and his band, but soon they learn that she is the target of Sweepers, who kidnap and infect people with plague.

"The tense plot, cinematic moments, and highly capable protagonists make this a fast, gripping read." Publ Wkly

Trevayne, Emma

Coda; Emma Trevayne. 1st ed. Running Press Teens 2013 320 p. (paperback) $9.95

Grades: 9 10 11 12 **Fic**

1. Science fiction 2. Music -- Fiction 3. Dystopian fiction

ISBN 0762447281; 9780762447282

LC 2012945893

In this book, society is controlled by the Corporation and "music is digitally enhanced so it acts like a drug. It's used to . . . control the citizenry and keep them dependent on the Corp." Eighteen-year-old Anthem is a conduit, "a person whose body is used to power the Corp's grid." He and his band make illegal music. "When it becomes clear that the Corp is . . . closing in on the renegade musicians, Anthem must risk everything to bring change to his society and free his beloved music." (School Library Journal)

Triana, Gaby

Riding the universe. HarperTeen 2009 267p $16.99

Grades: 9 10 11 12 **Fic**

1. Uncles -- Fiction 2. Adoption -- Fiction 3. Bereavement -- Fiction 4. Dating (Social customs) -- Fiction

ISBN 978-0-06-088570-0; 0-06-088570-X

LC 2008-31451

Seventeen-year-old Chloe, who inherited her uncle's beloved Harley after his death, spends the subsequent year trying to pass chemistry, wondering whether she should look for her birth parents, and beginning an unlikely relationship with her chemistry tutor, while also trying to figure out how she really feels about the boy who has been her best friend since they were children.

"Chloé's tough exterior, layered over her introspective inner voice, and the inclusion of such multidimensional topics as adoption and parent/teen relationships drive this text onto an open road that's filled with enough unexpected speed bumps to engage readers." Kirkus

Trigiani, Adriana

★ **Cruise** control; 1st ed; HarperTempest 2004 149p $15.99; lib bdg $16.89; pa $8.99

Grades: 7 8 9 10 **Fic**

1. Brothers -- Fiction 2. Basketball -- Fiction 3. People with disabilities 4. Cerebral palsy -- Fiction 5. Father-son relationship -- Fiction

ISBN 0-06-623960-5; 0-06-623961-3 lib bdg; 0-06-447377-5 pa

LC 2003-19822

A talented basketball player struggles to deal with the helplessness and anger that come with having a brother rendered completely dysfunctional by severe cerebral palsy and a father who deserted the family.

"This powerful tale is extremely well written and will give readers an understanding of what it's like to have a challenged sibling." SLJ

★ **Inside** out. HarperTempest 2003 117p hardcover o.p. pa $8.99

Grades: 7 8 9 10 **Fic**

1. Suicide -- Fiction 2. Hostages -- Fiction 3. Mentally ill -- Fiction 4. Schizophrenia -- Fiction 5. Juvenile delinquency -- Fiction

ISBN 0-06-623962-1; 0-06-447376-7 pa

LC 2002-151604

A sixteen-year-old with schizophrenia is caught up in the events surrounding an attempted robbery by two other teens who eventually hold him hostage.

"Trueman sometimes captures moments of heartbreaking truth, and his swift, suspenseful plot will have particular appeal to reluctant readers." Booklist

★ **Stuck** in neutral. HarperCollins Pubs. 2000 114p $14.95; lib bdg $16.89; pa $6.99

Grades: 7 8 9 10 **Fic**

1. Euthanasia -- Fiction 2. People with disabilities 3. Cerebral palsy -- Fiction 4. Father-son relationship -- Fiction

ISBN 0-06-028519-2; 0-06-028518-4 lib bdg; 0-06-447213-2 pa

LC 99-37098

Michael L. Printz Award honor book, 2001

Fourteen-year-old Shawn McDaniel, who suffers from severe cerebral palsy and cannot function, relates his perceptions of his life, his family, and his condition, especially as he believes his father is planning to kill him.

"Trueman has created a compelling novel that poses questions about ability and existence while fostering sympathy for people with severe physical limitations." Bull Cent Child Books

Viola in reel life. HarperTeen 2009 282p $16.99

Grades: 7 8 9 10 **Fic**

1. Ghost stories 2. School stories 3. Video recording -- Fiction 4. Dating (Social customs) -- Fiction

ISBN 978-0-06-145102-7; 0-06-145102-9

LC 2009-14269

When fourteen-year-old Viola is sent from her beloved Brooklyn to boarding school in Indiana for ninth grade, she overcomes her initial reservations as she makes friends with her roommates, goes on a real date, and uses the unsettling ghost she keeps seeing as the subject of a short film—her first.

This "is a sweet, character-driven story. Viola is very real, as are her feelings, hopes, desires, and dreams." SLJ

Viola in the spotlight. HarperTeen 2011 283p $16.99

Grades: 7 8 9 10 **Fic**

1. Theater -- Fiction 2. Family life -- Fiction 3. Dating (Social customs) -- Fiction

ISBN 978-0-06-145105-8; 0-06-145105-3

LC 2010045553

Back home in Brooklyn, fifteen-year-old Viola has big summer plans but with one best friend going to camp and the other not only working but experiencing her first crush, Viola is glad to be overworked as an unpaid lighting intern when her grandmother's play goes to Broadway.

"An equally enjoyable follow-up to Viola in Reel Life." Booklist

Trottier, Maxine

Three songs for courage. Tundra Books 2006 324p $16.95

Grades: 9 10 11 12 **Fic**

1. Canada -- Fiction 2. Bullies -- Fiction 3. Brothers -- Fiction 4. Homicide -- Fiction

ISBN 978-0-88776-745-6; 0-88776-745-1

LC 2005-927011

"From native wisdom to flatulence humor and from sexual assault to pigs in dresses, Trottier handles the serious with poignancy and lighter moments with flair. . . . This coming-of-age novel is rich, readable, and substantive." Voice Youth Advocates

Trueman, Terry

7 days at the hot corner. HarperTempest 2007 160p $15.99

Grades: 7 8 9 10 **Fic**

1. Baseball -- Fiction 2. Friendship -- Fiction 3. Homosexuality -- Fiction

ISBN 978-0-06-057494-9; 0-06-057494-1

LC 2006-03706

Varsity baseball player Scott Latimer struggles with his own prejudices and those of others when his best friend reveals that he is gay.

This "suspenseful story is enhanced by some late-inning surprises, the gay subplot is treated with honesty and integrity, and Scott and Travis are believable, sympathetic characters." Booklist

Life happens next; a novel. Terry Trueman. HarperTeen 2012 132 p. (trade bdg.) $17.99

Grades: 7 8 9 10 **Fic**

1. Love stories 2. Down syndrome -- Fiction 3. Cerebral palsy -- Fiction 4. Dogs -- Fiction 5. Communication -- Fiction 6. Seattle (Wash.) -- Fiction 7. Special education -- Fiction 8. People with disabilities -- Fiction 9. Family life -- Washington (State) -- Seattle -- Fiction

ISBN 0062028030; 9780062028037; 9780062028051

LC 2011044627

Sequel to: Stuck in neutral

This book is the sequel to author Terry Trueman's "Stuck in Neutral." Here, Shawn McDaniel, who has cerebral palsy, "fantasizes about his sister's best friend, Ally, and what it would be like if he ever got up the courage to tell her how he felt about her." He is also dealing with "Debi, [who] moves in with them. . . . Debi has Down's syndrome and is often disruptive, but . . . she becomes the first person to connect with Shawn on more than a surface level." (Voice of Youth Advocates)

Trumble, J. H.

Don't let me go; J.H. Trumble. Kensington Books 2012 344 p. (paperback) $15

Grades: 9 10 11 12 **Fic**

1. Love stories 2. Gay teenagers -- Fiction 3. Gays -- Fiction

ISBN 0758269277; 9780758269270

LC 2011275890

In this book, "Nate and Adam are smalltown adolescents whose relationship is threatened when Adam moves to New York. Nate recalls the first moments of their romance and its development even as it's threatened by the arrival of Luke, a closeted younger teen who's attracted to Nate. Told . . . from Nate's point of view, the novel explores issues like coming out, parental acceptance (and its lack), antigay violence, and the attitudes of faculty and fellow students." (Publishers Weekly)

Tubb, Kristin O'Donnell

The **13th** sign; Kristin O'Donnell Tubb. Feiwel and Friends 2013 272 p. $16.99

Grades: 6 7 8 9 **Fic**

1. Astrology -- Fiction 2. Occult fiction 3. Zodiac -- Fiction 4. Supernatural -- Fiction 5. Books and reading -- Fiction 6. New Orleans (La.) -- Fiction 7. Adventure and adventurers -- Fiction

ISBN 0312583524; 9780312583521

LC 2012034058

In this juvenile astrology-themed fantasy novel, by Kristin O'Donnell Tubb, "when a teen accidentally unlocks the lost 13th zodiac sign, everyone's personality shifts, and she must confront 12 Keepers of the zodiac to restore global order. . . . Unless she can find and restore Ophiuchus to the heavens within 23 hours, all personality changes will be permanent. To do this, Jalen must destroy 12 Keepers who protect Ophiuchus." (Kirkus Reviews)

★ **Selling** hope. Feiwel and Friends 2010 215p $16.99

Grades: 6 7 8 **Fic**

1. Comets -- Fiction 2. Mothers -- Fiction 3. Magic tricks -- Fiction 4. Single parent family -- Fiction

ISBN 978-0-312-61122-4; 0-312-61122-6

LC 2010-12571

In 1910, just before the earth passes through the tail of Halley's Comet, thirteen-year-old Hope McDaniels, whose father is a magician in a traveling vaudeville show, tries to earn enough money to quit the circuit by selling "anti-comet pills," with the help of fellow-performer Buster Keaton.

"Tubb deftly ingrains a thoughtful ethical question into the story . . . but never overdoes it in this bouncy tale populated by a terrific cast of characters." Booklist

Tucholke, April Genevieve

Between the devil and the deep blue sea; by April Genevieve Tucholke. Dial Books 2013 368 p. (hardcover) $17.99

Grades: 9 10 11 **Fic**

1. Horror fiction 2. Mystery fiction

ISBN 0803738897; 9780803738898

LC 2012035586

In this horror novel, "Violet White and her 17-year-old twin brother are living in the dilapidated glory of their family's coastal estate while their parents traipse Europe. To help pay the bills, Violet places an ad for a boarder for their guesthouse; it's quickly answered by River West, a mysterious boy who cannily avoids giving straight answers about his past. Violet doesn't typically pay boys much mind, but she's soon spending the night with River, both drawn to and wary of him." (Publishers Weekly)

"It's no coincidence that when the alluring River West shows up to rent the guesthouse of Violet's dilapidated seaside mansion, eerie and brutal things begin to happen in town. Yet love-struck Violet finds herself powerless to act, or really care. A highly atmospheric and unreliable narrative wends its way between scenes alternately homey and macabre to a twisty ending." (Horn Book)

Tullson, Diane

Riley Park. Orca Book Publishers 2009 102p (Orca soundings) $16.95; pa $9.95

Grades: 7 8 9 10 **Fic**

1. Homicide -- Fiction 2. Friendship -- Fiction 3. Bereavement -- Fiction 4. Brain -- Wounds and injuries -- Fiction

ISBN 978-1-55469-124-1; 1-55469-124-9; 978-1-55469-123-4 pa; 1-55469-123-0 pa

After Corbin and his best friend Darius are attacked in Riley Park, Corbin must cope with the loss of his friend, his physical impairments, and finding the culprit.

This is "a suspenseful, tightly plotted story that manages . . . to create both a memorable protagonist and a thought-provoking, emotionally involving story." Booklist

Tunnell, Michael O.

Wishing moon. Dutton Children's Books 2004 272p hardcover o.p. pa $9.99

Grades: 6 7 8 9 **Fic**

1. Magic -- Fiction 2. Orphans -- Fiction

ISBN 0-525-47193-6; 978-1-460-93919-2 pa; 1-460-93919-0 pa

LC 2003-62486

After a fourteen-year-old orphan named Aminah comes to possess a magic lamp, the wishes granted her by the genie inside it allow her to alter her life by choosing prosperity, purpose, and romance.

"Aminah strives to do good with her magic, and yet the tale skips preachiness and goes for rich characterizations and a strong, suspenseful plot worthy of the Arabian Nights." Booklist

Another title about Aminah is:

Moon without magic (2007)

Turner, Ann Warren

Father of lies; [by] Ann Turner. HarperTeen 2011 247p $16.99

Grades: 7 8 9 10 **Fic**

1. Witchcraft -- Fiction 2. Salem (Mass.) -- Fiction 3. Manic-depressive illness -- Fiction

ISBN 978-0-06-137085-4; 0-06-137085-1

LC 2010-15224

In 1692 when a plague of accusations descends on Salem Village in Massachusetts and "witch fever" erupts, fourteen-year-old Lidda, who has begun to experience visions and hear voices, tries to expose the lies of the witch trials without being hanged as a witch herself. Includes author's notes about the Salem Witch Trials and bipolar disease.

"Turner perfectly captures the nightmare nature of Salem's witchcraft period and of some of the outside forces that may have fueled it. . . . Yet the town's issues play a secondary role in Lidda's own believable struggles with encrouching insanity—or an otherworldly paranormal force: an appraisal left for engaged readers to make." Kirkus

Includes bibliographical references

Hard hit; [by] Ann Turner. Scholastic Press 2006 167p $16.99

Grades: 7 8 9 10 **Fic**

1. Novels in verse 2. Death -- Fiction 3. Cancer -- Fiction 4. Baseball -- Fiction 5. Father-son relationship -- Fiction

ISBN 0-439-29680-3

LC 2005-49906

A rising high school baseball star faces his most difficult challenge when his father is diagnosed with pancreatic cancer.

This is a "novel in verse that speaks volumes long after the book is closed." Voice Youth Advocates

Turner, Max

End of days. St. Martin's Griffin 2010 296p (Night runner) pa $9.99

Grades: 7 8 9 10 **Fic**

1. Vampires -- Fiction 2. Supernatural -- Fiction

ISBN 978-0-312-59252-3; 0-312-59252-3

LC 2010-30191

Sequel to: Night runner (2009)

While Charlie struggles with his vampirism, he, Zack, and their friends are pulled into a conflict with the mysterious Mr. Hyde, a creature who hunts vampires.

"The well-developed characters add dimension to the story line, and Zack's witty and sarcastic humor makes this a truly enjoyable read." SLJ

Night runner. St. Martin's Griffin 2009 261p pa $9.99

Grades: 7 8 9 10 **Fic**

1. Vampires -- Fiction

ISBN 978-0-312-59228-8; 0-312-59228-0

LC 2009-16672

Fifteen-year-old Zach is quite content living in a mental ward because of his unusual allergies until dark secrets about his past, his parents, and his strange sickness slowly surface, placing him in great danger

"This fast-paced vampire story featuring a likable character with a strong voice will appeal to a broad teen audience." Booklist

Followed by: End of days (2010)

Turner, Megan Whalen

★ The **thief.** Greenwillow Bks. 1996 219p $17.99; pa $6.99

Grades: 7 8 9 10 **Fic**

1. Adventure fiction 2. Thieves -- Fiction

ISBN 0-688-14627-9; 0-06-082497-2 pa

LC 95-41040

A Newbery Medal honor book, 1997

"A tantalizing, suspenseful, exceptionally clever novel. . . . The author's characterization of Gen is simply superb." Horn Book

Other titles in this series are:

A conspiracy of kings (2010)

The King of Attolia (2006)

The Queen of Attolia (2000)

Twomey, Cathleen

Beachmont letters. Boyds Mills Press 2003 223p $16.95
Grades: 7 8 9 10 **Fic**
1. Fires -- Fiction 2. Burns and scalds -- Fiction
ISBN 1-59078-050-7
LC 2002-111301

Scarred by a fire that killed her father, a seventeen-year-old girl begins a correspondence with a young soldier in 1944

This "has plenty of atmosphere and an appealing, courageous heroine who gradually realizes her own strength. This unusual survivor/love story is certain to be a three-hanky read." Booklist

Uchida, Yoshiko

★ **Journey** to Topaz; a story of the Japanese-American evacuation. illustrated by Donald Carrick. Heyday Books 2005 149p il pa $9.95
Grades: 5 6 7 8 **Fic**
1. World War, 1939-1945 -- Fiction 2. Japanese Americans -- Evacuation and relocation, 1942-1945 -- Fiction
ISBN 978-1-890771-91-1 pa; 1-890771-91-0 pa
LC 2004-16537

First published 1971 by Scribner

After the Pearl Harbor attack an eleven-year-old Japanese-American girl and her family are forced to go to an aliens camp in Utah

★ A **jar** of dreams. Atheneum Pubs. 1981 131p hardcover o.p. pa $4.99
Grades: 5 6 7 8 **Fic**
1. Prejudices -- Fiction 2. Family life -- Fiction 3. Japanese Americans -- Fiction
ISBN 0-689-50210-9; 0-689-71672-9 pa
LC 81-3480

A young girl grows up in a closely-knit Japanese American family in California during the 1930's, a time of great prejudice

"Rinko in her guilelessness is genuine and refreshing, and her worries and concerns seem wholly natural, honest, and convincing." Horn Book

Other titles about Rinko Tsujimura and her family are:
The best bad thing (1983)
The happiest ending (1985)

Uehashi, Nahoko

★ **Moribito**; Guardian of the Spirit. [by] Nahoko Uehashi; translated by Cathy Hirano; illustrated by Yuko Shimizu. Arthur A. Levine Books 2008 248p il $17.99
Grades: 6 7 8 9 **Fic**
1. Fantasy fiction 2. Martial arts -- Fiction
ISBN 978-0-5450-0542-5; 0-5450-0542-6

The wandering warrior Balsa is hired to protect Prince Chagum from both a mysterious monster and the prince's father, the Mikado.

"This book is first in a series of ten that have garnered literary and popular success in Japan. . . . Balsa and Chagum's story is brought to America with a strong translation. . . . Readers who are fans of action manga, especially with strong female characters, will enjoy the ninja-like fighting scenes. . . . The exciting premise, combined with an attractive cover, should insure that this title will circulate well." Voice Youth Advocates

Moribito II; Guardian of the Darkness. by Nahoko Uehashi; translated by Cathy Hirano; illustrated by Yuko Shimizu. Arthur A. Levine Books 2009 245p il $17.99
Grades: 6 7 8 9 **Fic**
1. Fantasy fiction
ISBN 978-0-545-10295-7; 0-545-10295-2
LC 2008-37444

ALA ALSC Batchelder Award Honor Book (2010)

The wandering female bodyguard Balsa returns to her native country of Kanbal, where she uncovers a conspiracy to frame her mentor and herself.

"Once again, Uehashi immerses readers in the culture, traditions, mythology–even diet–of the populace, creating a full, captivating world. . . . This growing series has something for everyone." Publ Wkly

Umansky, Kaye

Solomon Snow and the stolen jewel. Candlewick Press 2007 245p $12.99
Grades: 5 6 7 8 **Fic**
1. Orphans -- Fiction
ISBN 978-0-7636-2793-5; 0-7636-2793-3
LC 2006-47331

While trying to rescue Prudence's father from prison, Solomon, Prudence, the Infant Prodigy, and Mr. Skippy the rabbit find themselves caught up in the mad plans of the villainous Dr. Calimari to steal a fabulous and cursed ruby.

"Fans of Lemony Snicket will enjoy this fast-paced read. . . . Reluctant readers might find the short chapters, silly comedy, and simple characters attractive." SLJ

Under the moons of Mars; new adventures on Barsoom. edited by John Joseph Adams. Simon & Schuster Books for Young Readers 2012 xv, 352 p.p (hardcover) $16.99
Grades: 6 7 8 9 10 11 12 **Fic**
1. Science fiction 2. Adventure fiction 3. Short stories -- Collections 4. Short stories, American 5. Mars (Planet) -- Fiction 6. Science fiction, American 7. Carter, John (Fictitious character)
ISBN 9781442420304; 1442420294; 9781442420298; 9781442420311
LC 2011034391

This anthology, edited by John Joseph Adams, features several science fiction stories set in the world of Edgar Rice Burroughs' Barsoom series. "Fans of all ages have marveled at the adventures of John Carter, an Earthman who suddenly finds himself in a strange new world. A century later, readers can enjoy this compilation of brand-new stories starring John Carter of Mars." (Publisher's note)

Unsworth, Tania

The **one** safe place: a novel; by Tania Unsworth. Algonquin Young Readers. 2014 304p $15.95

Grades: 6 7 8 9 10 **Fic**

1. Abandoned children — Fiction; 2. Orphans — Fiction; 3. Science fiction; 4. Survival — Fiction; 5. Dystopian fiction

ISBN: 1616203293; 9781616203290

LC 2013043145

"Orphaned twelve-year-old Devin is invited to live at the paradisaical Home for Childhood, but something terrifying is happening to thechildren there. Devin's synesthesia, which makes him interesting to the Home's sinister Administrator, may provide the key to their escape. Set in a world of post climate change desperation, Unsworth's story thoughtfully explores the theme of adults' nostalgia for childhood." Horn Book

Updale, Eleanor

★ **Montmorency**; thief, liar, gentleman? Orchard Books 2004 232p $16.95

Grades: 6 7 8 9 10 **Fic**

1. Thieves -- Fiction 2. London (England) -- Fiction 3. Great Britain -- History -- 19th century -- Fiction

ISBN 0-439-58035-8

LC 2003-56345

First published 2003 in the United Kingdom

In Victorian London, after his life is saved by a young physician, a thief utilizes the knowledge he gains in prison and from the scientific lectures he attends as the physician's case study exhibit to create a new, highly successful, double life for himself.

"Updale adroitly works the tradition of devilish schemes and narrow escapes, and the plot moves as nimbly as the master thief himself." Bull Cent Child Books

Montmorency and the assassins. Orchard Books 2006 404p lib bdg $16.99

Grades: 6 7 8 9 **Fic**

1. Thieves -- Fiction 2. Great Britain -- Fiction 3. London (England) -- Fiction

ISBN 0-439-68343-2 lib bdg

LC 2005-11980

After twenty years as a gentleman, Montmorency is glad to be free of Scarper, his wretched alter-ego, but when a young friend is caught in the middle of a murderous political plot, Montmorency may have no choice but to call upon Scarper for help.

Montmorency on the rocks; doctor, aristocrat, murderer? Orchard Books 2005 362p $16.95; pa $6.99

Grades: 6 7 8 9 10 **Fic**

1. Thieves -- Fiction 2. London (England) -- Fiction 3. Great Britain -- History -- 19th century -- Fiction

ISBN 0-439-60676-4; 978-0-439-60676-9; 0-439-60677-2 pa; 978-0-439-60677-6 pa

LC 2004-15368

Sequel to Montmorency and the assassins (2006)

First published 2004 in the United Kingdom

In Victorian London, when Montmorency and his alter ego, Scarper, reunite with Dr. Farcett, the two cooperate to capture a bomber and become involved in solving the mystery of the poisoning of a village of Scottish children.

Montmorency's revenge. Orchard Books 2007 289p $16.99

Grades: 6 7 8 9 **Fic**

1. Criminals -- Fiction 2. London (England) -- Fiction 3. Great Britain -- History -- 19th century -- Fiction

ISBN 0-439-81373-5; 978-0-439-81373-0

LC 2006-09745

As Queen Victoria lies dying and with her family in danger, a group of friends races to track down the anarchists responsible for George's death, even as Montmorency seeks to teach a new generation to forgive.

"With all the fast-forward energy and finely detailed settings . . . of his earlier adventures, this one is as easy to fall into, and it ends with a breath-catching cliffhanger." Voice Youth Advocates

Upjohn, Rebecca

The **secret** of the village fool; by Rebecca Upjohn ; illustrated by Renne Benoit. Second Story Press 2012 32 p. $18.95

Grades: 5 6 7 8 **Fic**

1. World War, 1939-1945 -- Jews -- fiction 2. World War, 1939-1945 -- Poland -- fiction

ISBN 1926920759; 9781926920757

In this children's book by Rebecca Upjohn, illustrated by Renne Benoit, "Milek and his brother Munio live in a sleepy village in Poland. . . . They reluctantly do as their mother asks when she asks them to visit their neighbor Anton, knowing that the rest of the village laughs at him because of his strange habits of speaking to animals and only eating vegetables. Things change quickly when war comes to their town in the form of Nazi soldiers searching for Jewish families like that of Milek and Munio." (Publisher's note)

Vacco, Corina

My chemical mountain; by Corina Vacco. Delacorte Press 2013 185 p. (ebook) $50.97; (library) $19.99; (hardcover) $16.99

Grades: 9 10 11 12 **Fic**

1. School stories 2. Pollution -- Fiction 3. Vigilantes -- Fiction

ISBN 0385742428; 9780307975041; 9780375990571; 9780385742429

LC 2012030550

In this novel, Jason is about to enter high school with his two best friends, . . . Charlie Pellitero and . . . sickly William 'Cornpup' Schumacher. They live in a town all but owned by the overarching and ominous company Mareno Chem . . . . When a town meeting gives Cornpup the chance to show off the cysts covering his back and a forum to speak out against Mareno Chem for poisoning his family and friends, a shift occurs among the three boys." (School Library Journal)

Vail, Rachel

Kiss me again; Rachel Vail. HarperTeen 2013 256 p. (hardcover) $17.99

Grades: 7 8 9 10 **Fic**

1. Love stories 2. Kissing -- Fiction 3. Teenagers -- Sexual behavior -- Fiction 4. Dating (Social customs) -- Fiction 5. Interpersonal relations -- Fiction

ISBN 0061947172; 9780061947179

LC 2012011521

In this book, "ninth-grader Charlie Collins has lived with her mother, a divorced Harvard professor, for many years. Now Mom's new husband, Joe, has moved into the spacious house, along with his sweet 9-year-old daughter, Samantha, and his notoriously flirtatious ninth-grade son, Kevin. . . . Charlie copes with a mutual crush on Kevin; an increasingly tenuous relationship with her best friend, Tess; her first paying job; and other trials and triumphs of growing up." (Kirkus)

Lucky. HarperTeen 2008 233p $16.99; lib bdg $17.89

Grades: 7 8 9 10 **Fic**

1. School stories 2. Wealth -- Fiction 3. Friendship -- Fiction

ISBN 978-0-06-089043-8; 978-0-06-089044-5 lib bdg

As Phoebe and her clique of privileged girlfriends get ready to graduate from eighth grade, a financial scandal threatens her family's security—as well as Phoebe's social status—but ultimately it teaches her the real meaning of friendship.

"Vail's insightful characterizations of teen girls and their shifting loyalties is right on target." Booklist

Other titles in this series are:

Gorgeous (2009)

Brilliant (2010)

Valentine, Allyson

How (not) to find a boyfriend; by Allyson Valentine. Philomel Books 2013 304 p. (hardcover) $16.99

Grades: 7 8 9 10 **Fic**

1. School stories 2. Popularity -- Fiction 3. Genius -- Fiction 4. Cheerleading -- Fiction 5. High schools -- Fiction 6. Dating (Social customs) -- Fiction

ISBN 0399257713; 9780399257711

LC 2012019316

In this book, former nerd Nora Fulbright has worked hard to shed her geeky image since starting high school. "As sophomore year begins, she's made the cheerleading squad, and it looks like the handsome fullback is taking notice of her. . . . Worried that the cheer captain will mock her for taking AP classes, she switches her schedule, then has to switch it back so she'll have classes with Adam, the brainy and adorable new boy in school." (Publishers Weekly)

Valentine, Jenny

Broken soup. HarperTeen 2009 216p $16.99

Grades: 7 8 9 10 **Fic**

1. Bereavement -- Fiction 2. Family life -- Fiction 3. London (England) -- Fiction

ISBN 978-0-06-085071-5; 0-06-085071-X

LC 2008-11719

A photographic negative and two surprising new friends become the catalyst for healing as fifteen-year-old Rowan struggles to keep her family and her life together after her brother's death.

"The mystery Valentine sets in motion is quickly paced and packed with revelations. . . . The main appeal of the book, however, is her beautifully modulated tone. . . . Insightful details abound." Booklist

Double; Jenny Valentine. Disney-Hyperion 2012 246 p. (alk. paper) $16.99

Grades: 7 8 9 10 11 12 **Fic**

1. Mystery fiction 2. Identity -- Fiction 3. Homeless persons -- Fiction 4. London (England) -- Fiction 5. Missing children -- Fiction 6. England -- Fiction 7. Impersonation -- Fiction

ISBN 1423147146; 9781423147145

LC 2011010027

In this book, "[w]hat starts as a case of mistaken identity turns into a . . . mystery. . . . Homeless, 16-year-old Chap is . . . presented with . . . [the]opportunity of a lifetime: if he pretends to be Cassiel Roadnight, a teen who has been missing for two years and who looks just like Chap, Chap can have the life and family he's always dreamed of. As he tries to pass in his new identity . . . Chap begins to suspect that there's more to Cassiel's disappearance than meets the eye." (Publishers Weekly)

★ **Me**, the missing, and the dead. HarperTeen 2008 201p $16.99; lib bdg $17.89

Grades: 8 9 10 11 **Fic**

1. Death -- Fiction 2. Fathers -- Fiction 3. Missing persons -- Fiction 4. London (England) -- Fiction 5. Single parent family -- Fiction

ISBN 978-0-06-085068-5; 0-06-085068-X; 978-0-06-085069-2 lib bdg; 0-06-085069-8 lib bdg

LC 2007-14476

First published 2007 in the United Kingdom with title: Finding Violet Park

ALA YALSA Morris Award finalist, 2009

When a series of chance events leaves him in possession of an urn with ashes, sixteen-year-old Londoner Lucas Swain becomes convinced that its occupant, Violet Park, is communicating with him, initiating a voyage of self-discovery that forces him to finally confront the events surrounding his father's sudden disappearance.

"Part mystery, part magical realism, part story of personal growth, and in large part simply about a funny teenager making light of his and his family's pain, this short novel is engaging from start to finish." SLJ

Van Beirs, Pat

A **sword** in her hand; by Jean-Claude Van Rijckeghem and Pat Van Beirs; translated by John Nieuwenhuizen. Annick 2011 276p $21.95

Grades: 5 6 7 8 **Fic**

1. Plague -- Fiction 2. Princesses -- Fiction 3. Middle Ages -- Fiction 4. Father-daughter relationship -- Fiction

ISBN 978-1-55451-291-1; 1-55451-291-3

The Count of Flanders flies in a rage when his newborn child is not the expected male heir but a girl. Marguerite growing up under the disapproving eye of her heartless father learns to survive in the violent male world of the Middle Ages. Will she be able to resist the combined presure of politics, power and a foreign prince?

"The deft characterization of Marguerite and the sumptuous details woven throughout this captivating novel will engage readers." SLJ

Van de Ruit, John

Spud. Razorbill 2007 331p hardcover o.p. pa $9.99

Grades: 6 7 8 9 10 **Fic**

1. School stories 2. South Africa -- Fiction

ISBN 978-1-59514-170-5; 0-14-302484-1; 978-1-59514-187-3 pa; 1-59514-187-1 pa

LC 2007-6065

In 1990, thirteen-year-old John "Spud" Milton, a prepubescent choirboy, keeps a diary of his first year at an elite, boys-only boarding school in South Africa.

"This raucous autobiographical novel about a scholarship boy in an elite boys' boarding school in 1990 is mainly farce but also part coming-of-age tale." Booklist

Followed by Spud the madness continues... (2008)

Van Diepen, Allison

Takedown; Allison van Diepen. Simon Pulse 2013 288 p. (hardcover edition : alk. paper) $16.99

Grades: 9 10 11 12 **Fic**

1. Hostages 2. Adventure fiction 3. Vendetta -- Fiction 4. Drug traffic -- Fiction 5. African Americans -- Fiction 6. Criminal investigation -- Fiction

ISBN 1442463112; 9781442463110; 9781442463127

LC 2012039237

In this book, "Joe is hosting a party in honor of his favorite weekly wrestling show when a college student-turned-murderer crashes the get-together and holds the 13-year-olds hostage. As the terrifying ordeal continues, Joe thinks back about how he met each friend, their history together, and problems they are facing in their lives." (School Library Journal)

Van Draanen, Wendelin

Flipped. Knopf 2001 212p $14.95

Grades: 6 7 8 9 **Fic**

1. Family life 2. Conduct of life 3. Self-perception 4. Interpersonal relations

ISBN 9780375811746; 0-375-81174-5; 0-375-82544-4 pa

LC 2001-29238

In alternating chapters, two teenagers describe how their feelings about themselves, each other, and their families have changed over the years.

"There"s lots of laugh-out-loud egg puns and humor in this novel. There"s also, however, a substantial amount of serious social commentary woven in, as well as an exploration of the importance of perspective in relationships." SLJ

The **running** dream. Alfred A. Knopf 2011 336p $16.99; lib bdg $19.99

Grades: 7 8 9 10 11 12 **Fic**

1. School stories 2. Running -- Fiction 3. Amputees -- Fiction 4. People with disabilities -- Fiction

ISBN 978-0-375-86667-8; 0-375-86667-1; 978-0-375-96667-5 lib bdg; 0-375-96667-6 lib bdg

LC 2010-07072

When a school bus accident leaves sixteen-year-old Jessica an amputee, she returns to school with a prosthetic limb and her track team finds a wonderful way to help rekindle her dream of running again

"It's a classic problem novel in a lot of ways. . . . Overall, though, this is a tremendously upbeat book. . . . Van Draanen's extensive research into both running and amputees pays dividends." Booklist

Van Etten, David

Likely story. Alfred A. Knopf 2008 230p il $15.99; lib bdg $18.99

Grades: 7 8 9 10 **Fic**

1. Television -- Fiction 2. Mother-daughter relationship -- Fiction

ISBN 978-0-375-84676-2; 0-375-84676-X; 978-0-375-94676-9 lib bdg; 0-375-94676-4 lib bdg

LC 2007-22724

Sixteen-year-old Mallory, daughter of the star of a long-running but faltering soap opera, writes her own soap opera script and becomes deeply involved in the day-to-day life of a Hollywood player, while trying to hold on to some shaky personal relationships.

"Strong-willed, quick-witted Mallory is a sympathetic heroine, and Van Etten engagingly weds melodrama to the more mundane, universal dramas of teenage life." Horn Book Guide

Other titles in this series are:

All that glitters (2008)

Red carpet riot (2009)

Van Tol, Alex

Knifepoint; written by Alex Van Tol. Orca Book Publishers 2010 113p (Orca soundings) $16.95; pa $9.95

Grades: 7 8 9 10 **Fic**

1. Kidnapping -- Fiction

ISBN 978-1-55469-306-1; 1-55469-06-3; 978-1-55469-305-4 pa; 1-55469-305-5 pa

Jill is enduring a brutal job on a mountain ranch, guiding wannabe-cowboys on trail rides. On a solo ride with a handsome stranger she ends up in a fight for her life with no one to help her.

"The suspense is palpable. Both reluctant and avid readers who enjoy nail-biting tension will race through." Booklist

Vande Velde, Vivian

★ The **book** of Mordred; [illustrations by Justin Gerard] Houghton Mifflin 2005 342p hardcover o.p. pa $8.99

Grades: 8 9 10 11 12 **Fic**

1. Kings 2. Knights and knighthood -- Fiction 3. Mordred (Legendary character) -- Fiction 4. Great Britain -- History -- 0-1066 -- Fiction

ISBN 0-618-50754-X; 0-618-80916-3 pa

LC 2004-28223

As the peaceful King Arthur reigns, the five-year-old daughter of Lady Alayna, newly widowed of the village-wizard Toland, is abducted by knights who leave their barn burning and their only servant dead.

"All of the characters are well developed and have a strong presence throughout. . . . [This] provides an intriguing counterpoint to anyone who is interested in Arthurian legend." SLJ

Heir apparent. Harcourt 2002 315p $17; pa $6.95
Grades: 6 7 8 9 **Fic**
1. Science fiction 2. Virtual reality -- Fiction
ISBN 0-15-204560-0; 0-15-205125-2 pa
LC 2002-2441

While playing a total immersion virtual reality game of kings and intrigue, fourteen-year-old Giannine learns that demonstrators have damaged the equipment to which she is connected, and she must win the game quickly or be damaged herself

"This adventure includes a cast of intriguing characters and personalities. The feisty heroine has a funny, sarcastic sense of humor and succeeds because of her ingenuity and determination." SLJ

Magic can be murder. Harcourt 2000 197p hardcover o.p. pa $6.99
Grades: 6 7 8 9 **Fic**
1. Witchcraft 2. Mystery fiction 3. Murder
ISBN 0-15-202665-7; 0-547-25872-0 pa
LC 00-8595

Nola and her mother have unusual abilities that have always set them apart from others, but when Nola sees a murder using her power to call up images using water and a person's hair, she finds herself in the worst danger ever

"The well-developed characters provide entertaining reading." SLJ

Remembering Raquel. Harcourt 2007 160p $16
Grades: 8 9 10 11 **Fic**
1. School stories 2. Death -- Fiction 3. Obesity -- Fiction
ISBN 978-0-15-205976-7
LC 2006-35769

Various people recall aspects of the life of Raquel Falcone, an unpopular, overweight freshman at Quail Run High School, including classmates, her parents, and the driver who struck and killed her as she was walking home from an animated film festival.

"Easily booktalked and deeper than it initially seems, this will be popular with reluctant readers." Booklist

Vanhee, Jason

Engines of the broken world; Jason Vanhee. Henry Holt and Company 2013 272 p. (hardcover) $16.99
Grades: 8 9 10 11 12 **Fic**
1. Supernatural -- Fiction 2. Brothers and sisters -- Fiction 3. Science fiction
ISBN 0805096299; 9780805096293
LC 2013026768

"For siblings Merciful and Gospel Truth, it's the end of the world as they know it. But it's hardly fine when their recently deceased mother refuses to stay dead, and their "minister" (present in the form of an unsettling feline) can't be trusted. The real problem in this apocalyptic debut novel, however, is the fog devouring the world. Unlike most action-packed dystopias, the story's slower pace (almost too slow in some parts) allows readers to feel the fog encroaching on Merciful and Gospel's rustic home, and hear every scratch of their dead mother's awkward movements upon the cellar stairs." (Booklist)

Varrato, Tony

Fakie; written by Tony Varrato. Lobster Press 2008 142p pa $7.95
Grades: 6 7 8 9 10 **Fic**
1. Virginia -- Fiction 2. Witnesses -- Fiction 3. Skateboarding -- Fiction
ISBN 978-1-897073-79-7; 1-897073-79-8

"Fifteen-year-old Danny Torbert and his mom are on the run again, assuming yet another identity. Four years ago, Danny was the sole witness when Steve, his father's surveillance business partner, killed his father and severely wounded Danny. Awaiting appeal, Steve directs the search for Danny and his mother from prison, vowing to silence them forever. Now in the Witness Protection Program, Danny and his mom have had to flee their home several times, and Steve's men are getting close." Booklist

"This is an excellent novel for male teen readers. It is short, action packed, and full of activities that they can relate to." Voice Youth Advocates

Vasey, Paul

A **troublesome** boy; by Paul Vasey. Groundwood Books/House of Anansi Press 2012 225 p.
Grades: 9 10 11 12 **Fic**
1. Priests -- Fiction 2. Friendship -- Fiction 3. Private schools -- Fiction
ISBN 1554981549; 9781554981540

In this novel, "14-year-old Teddy's . . . despised stepfather sends him off to St. Ignatius Academy for Boys, an isolated Roman Catholic boarding school. St. Iggy's is run by priests who ruthlessly enforce discipline through intimidation and abuse. . . .The boys use their wits and humor to cope, but the endless beatings and humiliations take their toll, especially on the fragile Cooper. He reaches his breaking point when he becomes the victim of Father Prince, a pedophile." (Kirkus Reviews)

Vaughn, Carrie

Steel. HarperTeen 2011 294p $16.99; lib bdg $17.89
Grades: 7 8 9 10 **Fic**
1. Fencing -- Fiction 2. Pirates -- Fiction 3. Time travel -- Fiction
ISBN 978-0-06-154791-1; 0-06-154791-3; 978-0-06-195648-5 lib bdg; 0-06-195648-1 lib bdg
LC 2010012631

When Jill, a competitive high school fencer, goes with her family on vacation to the Bahamas, she is magically transported to an early-eighteenth-century pirate ship in the middle of the ocean.

This is "thoroughly enjoyable. . . . Through her assertive, appealing protagonist and a satisfying plot that sheds light on lesser-known aspects of pirate life, Vaughn introduces readers to an intriguing sport with an ancient pedigree." Kirkus

Voices of dragons. HarperTeen 2010 309p $16.99

Grades: 7 8 9 10 **Fic**

1. Fantasy fiction 2. Dragons -- Fiction

ISBN 978-0-06-179894-8; 0-06-179894-0

LC 2009-11604

In a parallel world where humans and dragons live in a state of cold war, seventeen-year-old Kay and her dragon friend, Artegal, struggle to find a way to show that dragons and humans can coexist.

"Vaughn's story is charming and fast paced with a strong, likable heroine." Publ Wkly

Vaught, Susan

★ **Big** fat manifesto. Bloomsbury 2008 308p $16.95

Grades: 9 10 11 12 **Fic**

1. School stories 2. Obesity -- Fiction 3. Prejudices -- Fiction

ISBN 978-1-59990-206-7; 1-59990-206-0

LC 2007-23550

Overweight, self-assured, high school senior Jamie Carcaterra writes in the school newspaper about her own attitude to being fat, her boyfriend's bariatric surgery, and her struggles to be taken seriously in a very thin world

"Jamie's forcefully articulated perspectives about body image and her well-justified anger provoke soul-searching at every turn. . . . Readers will not only be challenged but also changed by meeting Jamie." Bull Cent Child Books

Freaks like us; by Susan Vaught. Bloomsbury 2012 240 p. (hardcover) $16.99

Grades: 7 8 9 10 11 12 **Fic**

1. Friendship -- Fiction 2. Schizophrenia -- Fiction 3. Mental illness -- Fiction 4. Missing persons -- Fiction 5. Love -- Fiction 6. Missing children -- Fiction 7. Mystery and detective stories

ISBN 1599908727; 9781599908724

LC 2012004227

This is the story of Jason, whose selectively mute friend Sunshine has "vanished, and Jason, whose schizophrenia has shaped his life, is a suspect in her disappearance. Seniors Jason, Drip and Sunshine have ridden the short bus and gone through school labeled SED--that's 'Severely Emotionally Disturbed.' Bullying at the hands of kids with behavioral disabilities goes unreported and unpunished, but the trio's alliance made life bearable in their catchall special ed program . . . . As the FBI investigates, Jason's always-shaky world threatens to come apart. Not taking "fuzzy pills" keeps his brain sharp, but the voices plaguing him grow louder. Jason carries Sunshine's secrets--should he break his promise not to tell?" (Kirkus)

★ **Trigger**. Bloomsbury Children's Books 2006 292p $16.95

Grades: 9 10 11 12 **Fic**

1. Suicide -- Fiction 2. Brain -- Wounds and injuries -- Fiction

ISBN 978-1-58234-920-6; 1-58234-920-7

LC 2005-32249

Teenager Jersey Hatch must work through his extensive brain damage to figure out why he decided to shoot himself.

"Though teen suicide is a oft-chosen theme in young adult realism, Jersey's fresh voice, combined with the mystery elements fueled by his damaged memory, make this addition to the subgenre a compelling one." Bull Cent Child Books

Vaupel, Robin

My contract with Henry. Holiday House 2003 244p $16.95

Grades: 6 7 8 9 **Fic**

1. Friendship -- Fiction

ISBN 0-8234-1701-8

LC 2002-27471

A mission that begins as an eighth-grade project on Henry David Thoreau's experimental living at Walden Pond becomes a life-changing experience for a group of outsider students who become budding philosophers, environmental activists, and loyal friends

"Vaupel creates a painfully accurate portrayal of middle-school social dynamics." Booklist

Veciana-Suarez, Ana

The **flight** to freedom. Orchard Bks. 2002 215p (First person fiction) $16.95; pa $6.99

Grades: 6 7 8 9 **Fic**

1. Immigrants -- Fiction 2. Cuban Americans -- Fiction

ISBN 0-439-38199-1; 0-439-38200-9 pa

LC 2001-58783

Writing in the diary which her father gave her, thirteen-year-old Yara describes life with her family in Havana, Cuba, in 1967 as well as her experiences in Miami, Florida, after immigrating there to be reunited with some relatives while leaving others behind

"The story and characters ring true in their portrayal of loss, longing, and the hope of starting a new life." SLJ

Vega, Denise

Fact of life #31. Alfred A. Knopf 2008 375p $16.99; lib bdg $19.99

Grades: 7 8 9 10 11 12 **Fic**

1. Midwives -- Fiction 2. Pregnancy -- Fiction 3. Childbirth -- Fiction 4. Mother-daughter relationship -- Fiction

ISBN 978-0-375-84819-3; 0-375-84819-3; 978-0-375-94819-0 lib bdg; 0-375-94819-8 lib bdg

LC 2007-49654

Sixteen-year-old Kat, whose mother is a home-birth midwife, feels betrayed when a popular, beautiful classmate gets pregnant and forms a bond with Kat's mother that Kat herself never had.

"Graphic birthing details will startle some readers and fascinate others. . . . Athletic, artsy, oddball Kat is an unusual protagonist who doesn't easily fit into type, and many readers will welcome her strong individuality and believable growth." Booklist

Venkatraman, Padma

★ **Climbing** the stairs. G.P. Putnam's Sons 2008 247p $16.99

Grades: 6 7 8 9 10 **Fic**

1. Prejudices -- Fiction 2. Family life -- Fiction 3. Brain -- Wounds and injuries -- Fiction 4. India --

History -- 1765-1947, British occupation -- Fiction
ISBN 978-0-399-24746-0; 0-399-24746-7
LC 2007-21757

In India, in 1941, when her father becomes brain-damaged in a non-violent protest march, fifteen-year-old Vidya and her family are forced to move in with her father's extended family and become accustomed to a totally different way of life.

"Venkatraman paints an intricate and convincing backdrop of a conservative Brahmin home in a time of change. . . . The striking cover art . . . will draw readers to this vividly told story." Booklist

★ **Island's** end. G.P. Putnam's Sons 2011 240p $16.99
Grades: 5 6 7 8 9 **Fic**
1. Islands -- Fiction 2. Apprentices -- Fiction
ISBN 978-0-399-25099-6; 0-399-25099-9
LC 2010036298

"Uido's clear, intelligent, present-tense voice consistently engrosses as she pushes through doubt and loss to find the right path. The beach, jungle and cliff settings are palpable. . . . There is very little information known about Andaman Islanders, making it hard to gauge the authenticity of this portrayal; the author's note indicates a respectful and diligent approach to her subject. . . . Refreshingly hopeful and beautifully written." Kirku

★ A **time** to dance. Padma Venkatraman. Nancy Paulsen Books, an imprint of Penguin Group (USA) Inc. 2014 320p $17.99
Grades: 8 9 10 11 12 **Fic**
1. Amputees — Fiction; 2. Dance — Fiction; 3. Novels in verse; 4. People with disabilities — Fiction; 5. India — Fiction
ISBN: 0399257101; 9780399257100
LC 2013024244
Booklist Editor's Choice: Books for Youth (2014)
Kirkus Best Books: Teen (2014)
YALSA Best Fiction For Young Adults (2014)

"This free-verse novel set in contemporary India stars Veda, a teenage Bharatanatyam dancer. After a tragic accident, one of Veda's legs must be amputated below the knee. Veda tries a series of customized prosthetic legs, determined to return to dancing as soon as possible. Brief lines, powerful images, and motifs of sound communicate Veda's struggle to accept her changed body." Horn Book

Verday, Jessica

The **Hollow**. Simon Pulse 2009 515p $17.99
Grades: 7 8 9 10 11 12 **Fic**
1. Ghost stories 2. School stories 3. Bereavement -- Fiction 4. Supernatural -- Fiction
ISBN 1-4169-7893-3; 978-1-4169-7893-0
LC 2008042817

High-school junior Abbey struggles with the loss of her best friend Kristen, who vanished on a legendary bridge, but her grief is eased by Caspian, an attractive and mysterious stranger she meets in the Sleepy Hollow cemetery.

"Abbey's narration is heartfelt and authentically written." SLJ

Vernick, Shirley Reva

The **blood** lie; a novel. Cinco Puntos Press 2011 141p $15.95
Grades: 5 6 7 8 **Fic**
1. Love -- Fiction 2. Prejudices -- Fiction 3. Antisemitism -- Fiction 4. Jews -- United States -- Fiction
ISBN 978-1-933693-84-2; 1-933693-84-3
LC 2011011429

"Based on an actual incident in Massena in 1928, the slim novel effectively mines layers of ignorance, fear, intolerance and manipulation, and it connects the incident to Henry Ford's anti-Semitic writing and to the lynching of Jewish businessman Leo Frank in 1915." Kirkus

Vigan, Delphine de

No and me; translated by George Miller. Bloomsbury Children's Books 2010 244p $16.99
Grades: 9 10 11 12 **Fic**
1. Family life -- Fiction 2. Paris (France) -- Fiction 3. Gifted children -- Fiction 4. Homeless persons -- Fiction
ISBN 978-1-59990-479-5
LC 2009-36897
Original French edition, 2007

Precocious thirteen-year-old Lou meets a homeless eighteen-year-old girl on the streets of Paris and Lou's life is forever changed.

"Subtle, authentic details; memorable characters . . . and realistic ambiguities in each scene ground the story's weighty themes, and teens will easily recognize Lou's fragile shifts between heartbreak, bitter disillusionment, and quiet, miraculous hope." Booklist

Vigilante, Danette

Trouble with half a moon. G. P. Putnam's Sons 2011 181p $16.99
Grades: 5 6 7 8 **Fic**
1. Faith -- Fiction 2. Friendship -- Fiction 3. Bereavement -- Fiction 4. Child abuse -- Fiction 5. Puerto Ricans -- Fiction 6. City and town life -- Fiction 7. Jamaican Americans -- Fiction
ISBN 978-0-399-25159-7; 0-399-25159-6
LC 2010-07377

Overwhelmed by grief and guilt over her brother's death and its impact on her mother, and at odds with her best friend, thirteen-year-old Dellie reaches out to a neglected boy in her building in the projects and learns from a new neighbor to have faith in herself and others.

"The story is told with considerable appeal and accessibility, and kids won't have to lead the same life as Dellie to recognize her travails." Bull Cent Child Books

Villareal, Ray

Body slammed! by Ray Villareal. Piñata Books 2012 194 p. (alk. paper) $11.95
Grades: 7 8 9 10 **Fic**
1. Wrestling -- Fiction 2. Young adult literature 3. Father-son relationship 4. Choice -- Fiction 5. High schools -- Fiction 6. Fathers and sons -- Fiction 7. Mexican Americans -- Fiction 8. San Antonio (Tex.)

-- Fiction
ISBN 1558857494; 9781558857490
LC 2012003181

Sequel to: My father, the Angel of Death

This novel, by Ray Villareal, follows "[s]ixteen-year-old Jesse Baron . . . [who] is fed up with being cut down and dismissed, whether by the coach or his friends. . . . But it's through his dad that Jesse meets TJ Masters, a brash, new wrestling talent who's over 21, . . . TJ makes Jesse feel tough and confident. . . . But will Jesse listen to his family and friends when they warn him about hanging out with someone who's often reckless and irresponsible?" (Publisher's note)

Vincent, Zu

The **lucky** place. Front Street 2008 230p $17.95

Grades: 7 8 9 10 **Fic**

1. Death -- Fiction 2. Cancer -- Fiction 3. Alcoholism -- Fiction 4. Stepfathers -- Fiction 5. Father-daughter relationship -- Fiction
ISBN 978-1-932425-70-3; 1-932425-70-5
LC 2007-18357

"Readers meet Cassie when she is three years old and her inebriated father leaves her behind at the racetrack. . . . She is returned home by the police and their mother eventually realizes that this man is not a competent father. . . . Mom brings home Ellis, New Daddy, and Cassie can't help but feel his strength. . . . Cassie's voice changes as she grows into a 12-year-old who comes to know that inside herself is the real lucky place that she can truly count on. . . . Taking place in California in the late 1950s and early '60s . . . Vincent's novel ably creates a world that makes promises it can't keep. . . . A stunning fiction debut." SLJ

Violi, Jen

Putting makeup on dead people. Hyperion 2011 326p il $16.99

Grades: 8 9 10 11 12 **Fic**

1. School stories 2. Bereavement -- Fiction 3. Risk-taking (Psychology) -- Fiction
ISBN 978-1-4231-3481-7; 1-4231-3481-8

Donna's discovery, that she wants to be a mortician, helps her come into her own and finally understand that moving forward doesn't mean forgetting someone you love.

This book "grabs the reader in the first few pages and does not let go. Donna transforms from a girl going through the motions in life to figuring out her dreams and to finally standing up for her future. . . . It discusses her sexual experimentation, the same that many women her age experience. . . . This is a great read for teens searching to find themselves." Voice Youth Advocates

Vivian, Siobhan

The **list**; Siobhan Vivian. Scholastic 2012 333 p. (hardcover : alk. paper) $17.99

Grades: 7 8 9 10 11 12 **Fic**

1. Female friendship 2. Self-perception -- Fiction 3. Personal appearance -- Fiction 4. High school students -- Fiction 5. Identity (Psychology) -- Fiction 6. Friendship -- Fiction 7. Self-esteem -- Fiction 8. High schools -- Fiction
ISBN 0545169178; 9780545169172
LC 2012004248

This young adult novel presents an "exploration of physical appearance and the status it confers. . . . Every year during homecoming week, a list is posted anonymously at Mount Washington High naming the prettiest and ugliest girls in each class. . . . The list confers instant status, transforming formerly homeschooled sophomore Lauren from geeky to hot while consigning her counterpart . . . Candace, to pariah. But what the label mainly confers is anxiety. Prettiest junior Bridget despairs that she'll ever be thin enough to merit her title. . . . Jennifer, four-time 'ugliest' winner, tries to relish the notoriety. . . . Whether clued in or clueless to the intricate social complexities, boyfriends reinforce the status quo, while moms carry scars of their own past physical insecurities." (Kirkus)

A **little** friendly advice. Scholastic/Push 2008 248p $16.99

Grades: 7 8 9 10 11 12 **Fic**

1. Ohio -- Fiction 2. Divorce -- Fiction 3. Friendship -- Fiction 4. Father-daughter relationship -- Fiction
ISBN 978-0-545-00404-6; 0-545-00404-7
LC 2007-9905

When Ruby's divorced father shows up unexpectedly on her sixteenth birthday, the week that follows is full of confusing surprises, including discovering that her best friend has been keeping secrets from her, her mother has not been truthful about the past, and life is often complicated.

"Readers will find themselves and their relationships reflected in Ruby's story—for better and worse." Publ Wkly

Not that kind of girl. PUSH/Scholastic 2010 322p $17.99

Grades: 9 10 11 12 **Fic**

1. School stories 2. Dating (Social customs) -- Fiction
ISBN 978-0-545-16915-8; 0-545-16915-1
LC 2010-13806

High school senior and student body president, Natalie likes to have everything under control, but when she becomes attracted to one of the senior boys and her best friend starts keeping secrets from her, Natalie does not know how to act.

The author "challenges the assumptions about sex being rampant in high school and sends a positive message about acceptance, forgiveness, and love." Booklist

Vizzini, Ned, 1981-2013

★ **It's** kind of a funny story. Miramax Books/Hyperion Books For Children 2006 444p hardcover o.p. pa $9.99

Grades: 9 10 11 12 **Fic**

1. New York (N.Y.) -- Fiction 2. Psychiatric hospitals -- Fiction 3. Depression (Psychology) -- Fiction
ISBN 0-7868-5196-1; 1-4231-4191-1 pa
LC 2005-52670

A humorous account of a New York City teenager's battle with depression and his time spent in a psychiatric hospital.

"What's terrific about the book is Craig's voice—intimate, real, funny, ironic, and one kids will come closer to hear." Booklist

Vlahos, Len

The **Scar** Boys: a novel. Len Vlahos. Egmont USA. 2014 256p $17.99

Grades: 9 10 11 12 **Fic**

1. Bands (Music) — Fiction; 2. Disfigured persons — Fiction; 3. Family life — Fiction; 4. Friendship — Fiction; 5. Near-death experiences — Fiction; 6. New York (State) — Fiction; 7. Bullies — Fiction

ISBN: 9781606844397; 1606844393

LC 2013018265

William C. Morris Finalist (2015)

In this book, by Len Vlahos, "Harry is used to making people squirm. When others see his badly scarred face, there is an inevitable reaction that ranges from forced kindness to primal cruelty. In this first-person tale written as an extended college entrance essay, . . . he recounts the trauma of his young life spent recuperating from the act of childhood bullying that left him a burn victim. In middle school, he meets Johnny McKenna, the first person to seem to offer him genuine friendship." (Kirkus Reviews)

"Harry's obsession with punk music will appeal to music lovers, while his journey to accept himself for who he is--scarred face and all--is one that will likely resonate with any teen trying to find his way in the world." Booklist

Voigt, Cynthia

★ **Homecoming**. Atheneum Pubs. 1981 312p $18.95; pa $6.99

Grades: 6 7 8 9 **Fic**

1. Siblings -- Fiction 2. Abandoned children -- Fiction

ISBN 0-689-30833-7; 0-689-86361-6 pa

LC 80-36723

ALA YALSA Margaret A. Edwards Award (1995)

Abandoned by their mother, four children begin a search for a home and an identity.

"The characterizations of the children are original and intriguing, and there are a number of interesting minor characters encountered in their travels." SLJ

Other books about the Tillermans are:

Dicey's Song

A Solitary Blue

The Runner

Come a Stranger

Sons from Afar

Seventeen Against the Dealer

★ **Izzy,** willy-nilly; Rev. format ed.; Atheneum Books for Young Readers 2005 327p $17.95; pa $6.99

Grades: 7 8 9 10 **Fic**

1. Amputees -- Fiction 2. Friendship -- Fiction 3. Drunk driving -- Fiction

ISBN 978-1-4169-0340-6; 1-4169-0340-2; 978-1-4169-0339-0 pa; 1-4169-0339-9 pa

LC 2005299062

A reissue of the title first published 1986

ALA YALSA Margaret A. Edwards Award (1995)

A car accident causes fifteen-year-old Izzy to lose one leg and face the need to start building a new life as an amputee.

"Voigt shows unusual insight into the workings of a 15-year-old girl's mind. . . . Just as Voigt's perceptive empathy brings Izzy to life, other characterizations are memorable, whether of Izzy's shallow former friends or of her egocentric 10-year-old sister." Pub Wkly [review of 1986 edition]

Volponi, Paul

Black and white. Viking 2005 185p $15.99; pa $6.99

Grades: 7 8 9 10 **Fic**

1. Basketball -- Fiction 2. Race relations -- Fiction 3. African Americans -- Fiction

ISBN 0-670-06006-2; 0-14-240692-9 pa

LC 2004-24543

Two star high school basketball players, one black and one white, experience the justice system differently after committing a crime together and getting caught.

"These complex characters share a mutual respect and struggle with issues of loyalty, honesty, and courage. Social conflicts, basketball fervor, and tough personal choices make this title a gripping story." SLJ

The **Final** Four; by Paul Volponi. Viking 2012 244 p.

Grades: 9 10 11 12 **Fic**

1. Athletes -- Conduct of life 2. College basketball -- Fiction 3. Sports tournaments -- Fiction 4. African American youth -- Fiction 5. Immigrants -- United States -- Fiction 6. Conduct of life -- Fiction

ISBN 9780670012640

LC 2011011587

In this book by Paul "Volponi, . . . basketball's March Madness draws down toward the championship game with a match-up between the Michigan State Spartans and the Troy University (Alabama) Trojans, to see who will take on Duke or North Carolina for the national title. Spartans are led by Malcolm McBride, a . . . freshman who's headed directly to the NBA and is more than willing to spout his views to sports reporters concerning the inequity of unpaid college athletics. The Trojans boast Roko Bacic, a towering immigrant from war-torn Croatia who treasures his opportunity to play the game he loves and get a free college education into the bargain." (Bulletin of the Center for Children's Books)

★ The **hand** you're dealt. Atheneum Books for Young Readers 2008 176p $16.99

Grades: 8 9 10 11 **Fic**

1. School stories 2. Poker -- Fiction 3. Teachers -- Fiction

ISBN 978-1-4169-3989-4; 1-4169-3989-X

LC 2007-22988

When seventeen-year-old Huck's vindictive math teacher wins the town poker tournament and takes the winner's watch away from Huck's father while he is in a coma, Huck vows to get even with him no matter what it takes.

"The varied characters are unique and add to the book's interest quotient." Voice Youth Advocates

★ **Homestretch.** Atheneum Books for Young Readers 2009 151p $16.99

Grades: 6 7 8 9 10 **Fic**

1. Death -- Fiction 2. Prejudices -- Fiction 3. Horse racing -- Fiction 4. Mexican Americans -- Fiction 5.

Father-son relationship -- Fiction
ISBN 978-1-4169-3987-0; 1-4169-3987-3
LC 2008-30024

Five months after losing his mother, seventeen-year-old Gas runs away from an abusive father and gets a job working at an Arkansas race track, surrounded by the illegal Mexican immigrants that he and his father blame for her death.

"Volponi continues his streak of well-written novels in this simply written, coming-of-age story." Voice Youth Advocates

★ **Hurricane** song; a novel of New Orleans. Viking Childrens Books 2008 144p $15.99
Grades: 7 8 9 10 11 12 **Fic**
1. Jazz music -- Fiction 2. New Orleans (La.) -- Fiction 3. Father-son relationship -- Fiction 4. Hurricane Katrina, 2005 -- Fiction
ISBN 978-0-670-06160-0; 0-670-06160-3
LC 2007-38215

Twelve-year-old Miles Shaw goes to live with his father, a jazz musician, in New Orleans, and together they survive the horrors of Hurricane Katrina in the Superdome, learning about each other and growing closer through their painful experiences.

"A brilliant blend of reality and fiction, this novel hits every chord just right." Voice Youth Advocates

Rikers High. Viking 2010 216p $16.99
Grades: 8 9 10 11 12 **Fic**
1. Prisoners -- Fiction 2. African Americans -- Fiction 3. Juvenile delinquency -- Fiction
ISBN 978-0-670-01107-0; 0-670-01107-X
LC 2009-22471

Based on the adult novel, Rikers, published in 2002 by Black Heron Press

Arrested on a minor offense, a New York City teenager attends high school in the jail facility on Rikers Island, as he waits for his case to go to court.

"The author draws authentic situations and characters from his six years of teaching at Rikers. . . . An absorbing portrait of life in the stir. . . . Rare is the reader who won't find his narrative sobering." Booklist

★ **Rooftop**. Viking 2006 199p $15.99; pa $6.99
Grades: 9 10 11 12 **Fic**
1. Death -- Fiction 2. Race relations -- Fiction 3. New York (N.Y.) -- Fiction 4. African Americans -- Fiction
ISBN 0-670-06069-0; 0-14-240844-1 pa
LC 2005-22811

Still reeling from seeing police shoot his unarmed cousin to death on the roof of a New York City housing project, seventeen-year-old Clay is dragged into the whirlwind of political manipulation that follows.

"This thoughtfully crafted, deceptively simple story knits together a high-interest plot, a readable narrative crackling with street slang, and complex personal and societal issues that will engage teen readers." Booklist

★ **Rucker** Park setup. Viking 2007 149p $15.99
Grades: 7 8 9 10 11 12 **Fic**
1. Mystery fiction 2. Homicide -- Fiction 3. Basketball -- Fiction 4. African Americans -- Fiction
ISBN 978-0-670-06130-3; 0-670-06130-1
LC 2006-28463

While playing in a crucial basketball game on the very court where his best friend was murdered, Mackey tries to come to terms with his own part in that murder and decide whether to maintain his silence or tell J.R.'s father and the police what really happened.

The author's "description of playing pickup ball on one of the toughest courts in the world feels wholly authentic. The characters also feel real." Voice Youth Advocates

Voorhees, Coert

★ The **brothers** Torres. Hyperion Books for Children 2008 316p hardcover o.p. pa $8.99
Grades: 9 10 11 12 **Fic**
1. School stories 2. Gangs -- Fiction 3. Brothers -- Fiction 4. Racially mixed people -- Fiction 5. Dating (Social customs) -- Fiction
ISBN 978-1-4231-0304-2; 1-4231-0304-1; 978-1-4231-0306-6 pa; 1-4231-0306-8 pa
LC 2007-15152

Sophomore Frankie finally finds the courage to ask his long-term friend, Julianne, to the Homecoming dance, which ultimately leads to a face-off between a tough senior whose family owns most of their small, New Mexico town, and Frankie's soccer-star older brother and his gang-member friends.

This "novel is solidly plotted and exceptionally well paced; escalating tension keeps the pages flying, while narrator Frankie's self-deprecating humor prevents the action from devolving into Southwestside Story melodrama." Bull Cent Child Books

Lucky fools; Coert Voorhees. Hyperion Books 2012 293 p. $16.99
Grades: 8 9 10 11 12 **Fic**
1. College choice 2. Theater -- Fiction 3. Dating (Social customs) -- Fiction 4. Schools -- Fiction 5. College choice -- Fiction 6. Palo Alto (Calif.) -- Fiction 7. Preparatory schools -- Fiction
ISBN 1423123980; 9781423123989
LC 2011026252

Author Coert Voorhees presents a story about an aspiring high school actor. "For the seniors at prestigious Oak Fields Prep, the pressure is on to get into an Ivy League school. . . . But David Ellison, star of the school play . . . wants to go to Juilliard instead. As David's Juilliard audition and the play's opening night approach, he is plagued with doubts about his acting ability and his relationships with two girls." (Publishers Weekly)

Vrettos, Adrienne Maria

Burnout. Margaret K. McElderry Books 2011 193p $16.99
Grades: 7 8 9 10 **Fic**
1. Alcoholism -- Fiction 2. Drug abuse -- Fiction 3. New York (N.Y.) -- Fiction
ISBN 978-1-4169-9469-5; 1-4169-9469-6
LC 2010051617

Months after coming out of alcohol and drug rehab, high school student Nan wakes up on the subway the day after Halloween wearing a torn Halloween costume, her long hair cut, and "HELP ME" scrawled across her chest, feeling sick and having no idea how she got there.

"The gritty and biting story, coupled with its detective novel underpinnings, also has the potential to draw new fans, perhaps even some reluctant readers." Voice Youth Advocates

★ **Sight**; [by] Adrienne Maria Vrettos. Margaret K. McElderry Books 2007 254p $16.99

Grades: 7 8 9 10 **Fic**

1. School stories 2. Parapsychology -- Fiction 3. Missing persons -- Fiction 4. Criminal investigation -- Fiction

ISBN 978-1-4169-0657-5; 1-4169-0657-6

LC 2006-35999

Sixteen-year-old Dylan uses her psychic abilities to help police solve crimes against children, but keeps her extracurricular activities secret from her friends at school.

"Vrettos has created a creepy scenario with a taut plot and a gripping climax. . . . She has crafted a believable setting and characters." Bull Cent Books

★ **Skin**. Margaret K. McElderry Books 2006 227p $16.95

Grades: 7 8 9 10 **Fic**

1. Siblings -- Fiction 2. Anorexia nervosa -- Fiction

ISBN 1-4169-0655-X

LC 2005001119

When his parents decide to separate, eighth-grader Donnie watches with horror as the physical condition of his sixteen-year old sister, Karen, deteriorates due to an eating disorder.

"The overwhelming alienation Donnie endures will speak to many teens, while his honest perspective will be welcomed by boys." Booklist

Wakefield, Vikki

Friday never leaving; Vikki Wakefield. Simon & Schuster Books for Young Readers 2013 336 p. (hardcover) $16.99

Grades: 9 10 11 12 **Fic**

1. Runaway teenagers -- Fiction 2. Teenagers -- Conduct of life 3. Australia -- Fiction 4. Coming of age -- Fiction

ISBN 144248652X; 9781442486522; 9781442486539

LC 2012036386

This book by Vikki Wakefield follows "Friday Brown, [who] has never had a home. She and her mother live on the road, running away from the past. . . . So when her mom succumbs to cancer, the only thing Friday can do is keep moving. Her journey takes her to an abandoned house where a bunch of street kids are squatting, and an intimidating girl named Arden holds court. Friday gets initiated into the group, but her relationship with Arden is precarious." (Publisher's note)

Waldorf, Heather

Tripping. Red Deer Press 2008 342p pa $12.95

Grades: 8 9 10 11 12 **Fic**

1. Canada -- Fiction 2. Amputees -- Fiction 3. Voyages and travels -- Fiction 4. Wilderness survival -- Fiction

ISBN 978-0-88995-426-7; 0-88995-426-7

"Rainey and five other teens begin an eight-week school-sponsored educational/survival trek across Canada. . . . Rainey's challenge is heightened because she has an artificial leg and she learns that her mother, who abandoned her as a baby, lives near one of their stops and wants to meet her. As the trip progresses, the individuals bond and become part of a team. . . . Waldorf has written a unique story in which six very different young people are united in a common cause. Told with wit and humor, this fast-paced novel has character development that is extraordinary." SLJ

Walker, Brian F.

Black boy/white school; Brian F. Walker. HarperTeen 2012 246p (trade bdg.) $17.99

Grades: 9 10 11 12 **Fic**

1. Scholarships 2. Private schools -- Fiction 3. High school students -- Fiction 4. Maine -- Fiction 5. Schools -- Fiction 6. Identity -- Fiction 7. Race relations -- Fiction 8. African Americans -- Fiction 9. Preparatory schools -- Fiction

ISBN 9780061914836; 9780061914843

LC 2011016608

This book tells the story of "Anthony 'Ant' Jones [who] has never been outside his rough East Cleveland neighborhood when he's given a scholarship to Belton Academy, an elite prep school in Maine. But at Belton things are far from perfect. Everyone calls him 'Tony,' assumes he's from Brooklyn, expects him to play basketball, and yet acts shocked when he fights back. As Anthony tries to adapt to a world that will never fully accept him, he's in for a rude awakening: Home is becoming a place where he no longer belongs." (Publisher's note)

Walker, Kristin

7 clues to winning you; Kristin Walker. Razorbill 2012 317 p. (glb) $18.99; (trade pbk) $9.99

Grades: 8 9 10 11 **Fic**

1. Love stories 2. High school students -- Fiction 3. Treasure hunt (Game) -- Fiction

ISBN 9781451759150; 1595144145; 9781595144140

LC 2011279962

In this young adult romance novel, "[w]hen a humiliating picture of Blythe goes viral, she's instantly the target of ridicule at her new school. To salvage her reputation, Blythe teams up with Luke to win the Senior Scramble scavenger hunt. . . . Perhaps it's his Shakespearean witticisms that reel Blythe in despite her better judgment. . . . But as the hunt progresses, their relationship heats up. Soon their madcap mischief spirals out of control." (Publisher's note)

Wallace, Jason

Out of shadows. Holiday House 2011 282p $17.95

Grades: 7 8 9 10 11 12 **Fic**

1. School stories 2. Bullies -- Fiction 3. Zimbabwe

-- Fiction 4. Race relations -- Fiction
ISBN 978-0-8234-2342-2; 0-8234-2342-5
LC 2010-24372

In 1983, at an elite boys' boarding school in Zimbabwe, thirteen-year-old English lad Robert Jacklin finds himself torn between his black roommate and the white bullies still bitter over losing power through the recent civil war.

"This thought-provoking narrative offers teens a window into a distinctive time and place in history that is likely to be unfamiliar to most of them. A first purchase for high schools, especially those with a strong world cultures curriculum." SLJ

Wallace, Rich

One good punch. Alfred A. Knopf 2007 114p $15.99

Grades: 7 8 9 10 11 12 **Fic**

1. School stories 2. Journalism -- Fiction 3. Pennsylvania -- Fiction 4. Track athletics -- Fiction
ISBN 978-0-375-81352-8; 0-375-81352-7
LC 2006-33270

Eighteen-year-old Michael Kerrigan, writer of obituaries for the Scranton Observer and captain of the track team, is ready for the most important season of his life—until the police find four joints in his school locker, and he is faced with a choice that could change everything.

"This novel's success is in creating a multidimensional male character in a format that will appeal to all readers. The moral dilemma . . . makes this novel ripe for ethical discussions." Voice Youth Advocates

Perpetual check. Alfred A. Knopf 2009 112p $15.99; lib bdg $18.99

Grades: 8 9 10 11 **Fic**

1. Chess -- Fiction 2. Brothers -- Fiction 3. Father-son relationship -- Fiction
ISBN 978-0-375-84058-6; 0-375-84058-3; 978-0-375-94058-3 lib bdg; 0-375-94058-8 lib bdg
LC 2008-04159

Brothers Zeke and Randy participate in an important chess tournament, playing against each other while also trying to deal with their father's intensely competitive tendencies.

"Wallace cleverly positions Randy and Zeke for a win-win conclusion in this satisfying, engaging, and deceptively simple story." SLJ

War and watermelon. Viking 2011 184p $15.99

Grades: 6 7 8 9 **Fic**

1. School stories 2. Brothers -- Fiction 3. Football -- Fiction 4. Family life -- Fiction
ISBN 978-0-670-01152-0; 0-670-01152-5
LC 2010-41043

As the summer of 1969 turns to fall in their New Jersey town, twelve-year-old Brody plays football in his first year at junior high while his older brother's protest of the war in Vietnam causes tension with their father.

"Sixties culture and events . . . are well integrated into the story, and humorous vignettes . . . help lighten the mood." Booklist

★ **Wrestling** Sturbridge. Knopf 1996 135p hardcover o.p. pa $4.99

Grades: 7 8 9 10 **Fic**

1. Wrestling -- Fiction 2. Friendship -- Fiction
ISBN 0-679-87803-3; 0-679-88555-2 pa
LC 95-20468

Stuck in a small town where no one ever leaves and relegated by his wrestling coach to sit on the bench while his best friend becomes state champion, Ben decides he can't let his last high school wrestling season slip by without challenging his friend and the future.

"The wresting scenes are thrilling. . . . Like Ben, whose voice is so strong and clear here, Wallace weighs his words carefully, making every one count in this excellent, understated first novel." Booklist

Wallace, Sandra Neil

Muckers; Sandra Neil Wallace. Alfred A. Knopf 2013 288 p. (hardback) $16.99

Grades: 7 8 9 10 **Fic**

1. Football 2. Historical fiction 3. Grief -- Fiction 4. Schools -- Fiction 5. Football -- Fiction 6. High schools -- Fiction 7. Race relations -- Fiction 8. Mexican Americans -- Fiction 9. Copper mines and mining -- Fiction 10. Arizona -- History -- 20th century -- Fiction
ISBN 0375867546; 9780375867545; 9780375967542
LC 2013003537

In this book, "Felix 'Red' O'Sullivan is the best hope to lead his team to a statewide football championship. Unlike other teams in 1950 in Arizona, whites and Latinos play together on the Hartley Muckers. Nevertheless, both groups are aware of the dividing lines." Red must also deal with an alcoholic father and a mother grieving for Red's older brother, killed in World War II. "For Red, this season will be his last chance to return glory to 'Bobby's school.'" (Kirkus Reviews)

Wallenfels, Stephen

POD. Namelos 2009 212p $18.95; pa $9.95

Grades: 7 8 9 10 **Fic**

1. Science fiction 2. Extraterrestrial beings -- Fiction
ISBN 978-1-60898-011-6; 1-60898-011-1; 978-1-60898-010-9 pa; 1-60898-010-3 pa
LC 2008-29721

As alien spacecrafts fill the sky and zap up any human being who dares to go outside, fifteen-year-old Josh and twelve-year-old Megs, living in different cities, describe what could be their last days on Earth.

"The dire circumstances don't negate the humor, the hormones, or the humanity found in the young narrators. This is solid, straightforward sci-fi." Booklist

Waller, Sharon Biggs

A **mad**, wicked folly. Sharon Biggs Waller. Viking, published by the Penguin Group. 2014 448p $17.99

Grades: 8 9 10 11 12 **Fic**

1. Artists -- Fiction; 2. Love -- Fiction; 3. Sex role --Fiction; 4. Great Britain -- History -- Edward VII, 1901-1910 -- Fiction; 5. London (England)
ISBN: 0670014680; 9780670014682
LC 2013029858

A novel "about a young English woman who is talented, beautiful, passionate, and wealthy. Despite these advantages, Victoria Darling struggles with the harsh limitations imposed upon women prior to and during the Edwardian era of 1901-1910, which curtail her attempts to attend art school. While Victoria does not initially associate with the Suffragette Movement, she ultimately discovers that her fate is intertwined with the cause." (SLJ)

"Victoria's dream of becoming an artist leads her naively into scandals, tempts her into a convenient marriage, and drives her to join the Women's Social and Political Union. Persistence eventually triumphs, and friendships, love, and art lessons are her rewards. Sound historical research provides the backbone for this warm novel about the development of women's opportunities in Edwardian London." Horn Book

Walsh, Alice

A **Long** Way from Home. Orca Book Pub 2012 232 p. (paperback) $11.95

Grades: 7 8 9 10 **Fic**

1. Immigrants -- Fiction 2. Prejudices -- Fiction 3. September 11 terrorist attacks, 2001 -- Fiction

ISBN 1926920791; 9781926920795

In this book by Alice Walsh, "thirteen-year-old Rabia, along with her mother and younger brother, flees Afghanistan. . . . They take part in a program that is relocating refugee widows and orphans to America. . . . After the terrorist attack on the World Trade Center in New York City, their plane is diverted to Gander, Newfoundland. Also on the plane is a boy named Colin, who struggles with his prejudices against Rabia and her family." (Publisher's note)

Walsh, Pat

★ The **Crowfield** curse. Chicken House 2010 326p il $16.99

Grades: 5 6 7 8 **Fic**

1. Magic -- Fiction 2. Orphans -- Fiction 3. Monasteries -- Fiction

ISBN 0-545-22922-7; 978-0-545-22922-7

LC 2009-51483

In 1347, when fourteen-year-old orphan William Paynel, an impoverished servant at Crowfield Abbey, goes into the forest to gather wood and finds a magical creature caught in a trap, he discovers he has the ability to see fays and becomes embroiled in a strange mystery involving Old Magic, a bitter feud, and ancient secrets.

"This suspenseful and spooky story will thrill readers. . . . With fascinating attention to detail and an edgy battle between evil and good, Walsh sweeps readers almost effortlessly into another time and place." SLJ

The **Crowfield** demon; Pat Walsh. Scholastic 2012 360 p. $16.99

Grades: 5 6 7 8 **Fic**

1. Fantasy fiction 2. Adventure fiction 3. Children's stories 4. Demonology -- Fiction 5. Magic -- Fiction 6. Orphans -- Fiction 7. Identity -- Fiction 8. Monasteries -- Fiction 9. Blessing and cursing -- Fiction

ISBN 054531769X; 9780545317696; 9780545373500

LC 2011029246

This juvenile historical fantasy novel by Pat Walsh is the sequel to his earlier story "The Crowfield Curse." "In "The Crowfield Curse," young monks' apprentice Will learned he was gifted with the Sight: able to see beyond this mortal coil into the spirit realms of Old Magic. Protected by the warrior fay Shadlok -- and befriended by the wry, wary hobgoblin called Brother Walter -- the boy is just coming into his strange powers. But now, from its very foundations, Crowfield Abbey has begun to crumble. As Will slaves to salvage the chapel, he discovers something truly terrifying. A heathen creature from a pagan past is creeping up through the rubble -- avowed to unleash havoc on holy ground!" (Publisher's note)

Walters, Eric

In a flash. Orca 2008 108p (Orca currents) $16.95; pa $9.95

Grades: 7 8 9 10 **Fic**

1. School stories

ISBN 978-1-55469-035-0; 1-55469-035-8; 978-1-55469-034-3 pa; 1-55469-034-X pa

"The first flash mob Ian puts together himself is a sixty-plus person, four-minute pillow fight in a department store. His friend Oswald is thrilled with the event, but Julia, the one Ian really wants to impress, is still convinced that flash mobs are stupid. While Ian tries to prove Julia wrong by initiating flash mobs with political impact, Julia is busy waging war with the strict new principal at school. When Julia goes too far and gets herself suspended, Ian sees an opportunity for a relevant and persuasive flash mob." Publisher's note

"Snappy, realistic dialogue; multidimensional characters; and an unpredictable plot (not to mention a hip, contemporary phenomenon) will have both reluctant and struggling readers madly flipping the pages." SLJ

Sketches; by Eric Walters. Viking 2008 232p $15.99

Grades: 7 8 9 10 **Fic**

1. Artists -- Fiction 2. Homeless persons -- Fiction 3. Runaway teenagers -- Fiction

ISBN 978-0-670-06294-2; 0-670-06294-4

LC 2007-23123

After running away from home, fifteen-year-old Dana finds friends on the Toronto streets, and, eventually, a way to come to terms with what has happened to her.

"The characters' well-portrayed camaraderie, resourcefulness, and resiliency carry the tale, which ends on a note of promise." SLJ

Special Edward. Orca Book Publishers 2009 108p (Orca currents) $16.95; pa $9.95

Grades: 7 8 9 10 **Fic**

1. School stories 2. Learning disabilities -- Fiction

ISBN 978-1-55469-096-1; 1-55469-096-X; 978-1-55469-092-3 pa; 1-55469-092-7 pa

In an attempt to gain lower expectations and extra time for tests, Edward tries to fake a special education designation.

"Walters has a good ear for teen talk, and Edward is as charming to read about as he is in the classroom. The author deftly weaves subtle clues into Edward's character that will leave readers nodding in agreement with his true condition. . . . A refreshing read." SLJ

Splat! written by Eric Walters. Orca Book Publishers 2008 112p $16.95; pa $9.95
Grades: 7 8 9 10 **Fic**

1. Canada -- Fiction 2. Tomatoes -- Fiction 3. Friendship -- Fiction
ISBN 978-1-55143-988-4; 1-55143-988-3; 978-1-55143-986-0 pa; 1-55143-986-7 pa

"Keegan and Alex are the only kids in Leamington who haven't volunteered to help out with the town's annual tomato festival. In an attempt to teach them a sense of responsibility, their fathers put them in charge of the tomato toss. The boys decide it's their responsibility to add a little excitement to the event. They exchange the traditional wooden targets for human targets and, before they know it, they are running the most popular event at the fair. The excitement may be too much for the sleepy town and soon the tomato toss is taken to the streets." Publisher's note

"The relationship between Keegan and narrator Alex, with their relentless and often quite funny smartassed exhanges, is the core of this speedy and readable novel." Bull Cent Child Books

Walton, K. M.

Empty; K.M. Walton. Simon Pulse 2013 256 p. (hardcover) $16.99
Grades: 9 10 11 12 **Fic**

1. Bullies -- Fiction 2. Overweight teenagers -- Fiction 3. Rape -- Fiction 4. Obesity -- Fiction 5. Self-esteem -- Fiction 6. High schools -- Fiction 7. Family problems -- Fiction 8. Emotional problems -- Fiction
ISBN 1442453591; 9781442453593
LC 2012011562

In this book, "seventeen-year-old Dell is overweight, and she eats to deal with a series of letdowns, beginning when her father left the family. . . . She hides behind her weight and self-deprecating jokes. Her classmates" bully her. "The bullying turns vicious at a party; she drinks too much and is raped by one of the bullies, on whom she happens to have had a crush. She has no one to turn to, and rumors start that she attacked him." (School Library Journal)

Walton, Leslye

The **Strange** and beautiful sorrows of Ava Lavender; Leslye Walton. Candlewick Press 2014 320 p. $17.99
Grades: 9 10 11 12 **Fic**

1. Love stories 2. Teenagers -- Fiction 3. Supernatural -- Fiction
ISBN 0763665665; 9780763665661
LC 2013946615

In this book, by Leslye Walton, "Ava -- in all other ways a normal girl -- is born with the wings of a bird. . . . sixteen-year old Ava ventures into the wider world, ill-prepared for what she might discover and naive to the twisted motives of others. Others like the pious Nathaniel Sorrows, who mistakes Ava for an angel and whose obsession with her grows until the night of the summer solstice celebration." (Publisher's note)

"Ava Lavender, a typical girl in every respect except for the fact that she was born with wings, sits upon a family tree of doomed lovers...here are many sorrows in Walton's debut, and most of them are Ava's through inheritance. Readers should prepare themselves for a tale where myth and reality, lust and love, the corporal and the ghostly, are interchangeable and surprising." (Booklist)

Ward, David

★ **Escape** the mask. Amulet Books 2008 195p (The grassland trilogy) $15.95
Grades: 7 8 9 10 **Fic**

1. Science fiction 2. Slavery -- Fiction
ISBN 978-0-8109-9477-5; 0-8109-9477-1
LC 2007028212

Six young friends, tortured by the Spears and forced to work as slaves in the harsh fields of Grassland, vow to escape to find the freedom that was stolen from them long ago, and their opportunity arises when Outsiders come and wage war against the Spears.

"Ward's novel bursts with action and is laden with tense scenes. His excellent descriptive writing allows the reader to visualize the action. In addition, Ward's fantasy world is so believable that the text almost reads as historical fiction." Voice Youth Advocates

Other titles in this series are:
Beneath the mask (2008)
Beyond the mask (2010)

Ward, Rachel

The **Chaos.** Chicken House 2011 339p $17.99
Grades: 8 9 10 11 12 **Fic**

1. Science fiction 2. Death -- Fiction 3. Orphans -- Fiction 4. London (England) -- Fiction 5. Blacks -- Great Britain -- Fiction 7. Extrasensory perception -- Fiction
ISBN 978-0-545-24269-1; 0-545-24269-X
Sequel to: Numbers (2010)

When rising flood waters force him and his grandmother to evacuate their coastal home and return to London, sixteen-year-old Adam, who has inherited his mother's curse of being able to see the day that someone will die when he looks into their eyes, becomes disturbed when he begins to see January 1, 2027, a date six months into the future, in nearly everyone around him.

"In this sequel to Numbers a fascinating premise is again worked out through gripping episodes and a lightly handled metaphysical dilemma." Horn Book

Infinity; Rachel Ward. Chicken House/Scholastic 2012 249 p. (Numbers) $17.99
Grades: 8 9 10 11 12 **Fic**

1. Death -- Fiction 2. England -- Fiction 3. Psychic ability -- Fiction 4. London (England) -- Fiction 5. Interpersonal relations -- Fiction 6. Blacks -- England -- London -- Fiction
ISBN 0545350921; 9780545350921; 9780545381918
LC 2011032709

This novel, by Rachel Ward, is the conclusion to the "Numbers" trilogy. "Sarah loves Adam, but can't bear the thought that every time he looks in her eyes, he can see her dying; can see her last day. It's 2029. Two years since the Chaos. . . . Little Mia was supposed to die that New Year's Day. The numbers don't lie. But somehow she changed her date. Mia's just a baby, oblivious to her special power. But ruthless people are hunting her down, determined to steal her secret." (Publisher's note)

Num8ers. Chicken House/Scholastic 2010 325p $17.99
Grades: 8 9 10 11 12 **Fic**

1. Science fiction 2. Death -- Fiction 3. Runaway teenagers -- Fiction 4. Blacks -- Great Britain -- Fiction 5. Extrasensory perception -- Fiction
ISBN 978-0-545-14299-1; 0-545-14299-7
LC 2008-55440

Fifteen-year-old Jem knows when she looks at someone the exact date they will die, so she avoids relationships and tries to keep out of the way, but when she meets a boy named Spider and they plan a day out together, they become more involved than either of them had planned.

"Ward's debut novel is gritty, bold, and utterly unique. Jem's isolation and pain, hidden beneath a veneer of toughness, are palpable, and the ending is a real shocker." SLJ

Followed by: The Chaos (2011)

Warman, Jessica

Between. Walker 2011 454p $17.99
Grades: 10 11 12 **Fic**

1. Dead -- Fiction 2. Family life -- Fiction 3. Future life -- Fiction
ISBN 978-0-8027-2182-2
LC 2010-40986

"Liz runs the gamut of strong emotion throughout this compelling backtrack of a short life punctuated by early grief, parental failings, and honest, flawed love; her journey offers insight into the effects all of these things can have on an ordinary life." Bull Cent Child Books

★ **Breathless**. Walker 2009 311p $16.99
Grades: 9 10 11 12 **Fic**

1. School stories 2. Siblings -- Fiction 3. Swimming -- Fiction 4. Schizophrenia -- Fiction 5. Mental illness -- Fiction
ISBN 978-0-8027-9849-7; 0-8027-9849-7
LC 2008-42555

At boarding school, Katie tries to focus on swimming and becoming popular instead of the painful memories of her institutionalized schizophrenic older brother.

"Warman draws out Katie's emotions and her complex life and family with immediacy. Readers who dive in will surface with more awareness of the devastating effects of mental illness." Kirkus

Where the truth lies. Walker & Co. 2010 308p $16.99
Grades: 9 10 11 12 **Fic**

1. School stories 2. Dreams -- Fiction 3. Memory -- Fiction 4. Connecticut -- Fiction 5. Family life -- Fiction 6. Dating (Social customs) -- Fiction
ISBN 978-0-8027-2078-8; 0-8027-2078-1
LC 2010-00782

Emily, whose father is headmaster of a Connecticut boarding school, suffers from nightmares, and when she meets and falls in love with the handsome Del Sugar, pieces of her traumatic past start falling into place.

"Emily's unflinching, multilayered narration and realistic dialogue capture the wishes and fears that drive teens. A page-turner to the bittersweet ending." Kirkus

Wasserman, Robin

★ **Awakening**. Scholastic 2007 207p (Chasing yesterday) pa $5.99
Grades: 6 7 8 9 **Fic**

1. Amnesia -- Fiction
ISBN 978-0-439-93338-4

"A teenager wakes up just yards away from a mysterious industrial accident. . . . Although she is seriously injured and has amnesia, she should be dead. . . . As Jane Doe, or J.D., she receives national news attention. Then a woman shows up, claiming to be her mother, and J.D. goes 'home' to a house she cannot remember and begins psychiatric treatment with an old family friend, who unnervingly looks exactly like the monstrous doctor of her nightmares. . . . [Wasserman's] characters are well developed and believable, her plot is suspenseful, and her backgrounds . . . are nicely detailed." Voice Youth Advocates

Another title in this series is:
Betrayal (2007)

The **book** of blood and shadow; by Robin Wasserman. Alfred A. Knopf 2012 352p. $17.99
Grades: 7 8 9 **Fic**

1. Mystery fiction 2. Suspense fiction 3. Homicide -- Fiction 4. Prague (Czech Republic) -- Fiction
ISBN 9780375868764; 9780375872778; 9780375899614; 9780375968761
LC 2011003920

In this book, "Nora . . . help[s] an eccentric professor translate a sixteenth-century book by a notable alchemist (and the letters left by his daughter, Elizabeth), . . . spending more time with her best friend, Chris, and his roommate, Max, who are also working on the project. Just as quickly as Nora becomes invested in Elizabeth"s life, Max transforms from a slightly creepy tagalong to a sweet, solicitous boyfriend. Then Chris is brutally murdered, his girlfriend Adriane is left without memory of the night, and Max (the main suspect in the crime) disappears. . . . Nora . . . continu[es] her translation of the secrets encrypted in Elizabeth"s . . . communications and uncovering conspiracies . . . in which she herself is . . . a key figure." (Bulletin of the Center for Children"s Books)

Hacking Harvard; a novel. Simon Pulse 2007 320p pa $8.99
Grades: 9 10 11 12 **Fic**

1. School stories 2. Computer crimes -- Fiction 3. Harvard University -- Fiction
ISBN 978-1-4169-3633-6; 1-4169-3633-5

When three brilliant nerds—Max Kim, Eric Roth, and Isaac "The Professor" Schwarzbaum—bet $20,000 that they can get anyone into Harvard, they take on the Ivy League in their quest for popularity, money, and the love of a beauty queen valedictorian.

"There is enough action, computers, electronics, and shenanigans to entice girls and boys, geeks and nongeeks to this thought-provoking, enjoyable read." Voice Youth Advocates

Skinned. Simon Pulse 2008 361p $15.99; pa $9.99

Grades: 9 10 11 12 **Fic**

1. Science fiction 2. Bioethics -- Fiction

ISBN 978-1-4169-3634-3; 1-4169-3634-3; 978-1-4169-7449-9 pa; 1-4169-7449-0 pa

LC 2008-15306

To save her from dying in a horrible accident, Lia's wealthy parents transplant her brain into a mechanical body.

"This is a captivating story that brings up many questions for teens, including how they fit in with their peers and what is their role in larger society. There are underlying themes as well such as suicide, free will, and what makes someone human." Libr Media Connect

Other titles in this series are:
Crashed (2009)
Wired (2010)

The **waking** dark; Robin Wasserman. Alfred A. Knopf 2013 464 p. $17.99

Grades: 9 10 11 12 **Fic**

1. Horror fiction 2. Homicide -- Fiction 3. Science fiction 4. Death -- Fiction 5. Kansas -- Fiction 6. Murder -- Fiction 7. City and town life -- Kansas -- Fiction

ISBN 0375868771; 9780375868771; 9780375968778

LC 2012032802

In this horror novel set in a small Kansas town, "five people suddenly go on murder sprees, with four of them committing suicide. A year later, five survivors are united when a storm (and later, soldiers) isolate the town: loner Daniel, closeted jock West, newly evangelical Ellie, outcast Jule, and Cassie—the one remaining murderer, who has no recollection of what she did or why. As the days pass, the five grow increasingly aware that everyone else in Oleander is starting to act strange." (Publishers Weekly)

Waters, Daniel, 1969-

Break my heart 1,000 times; Daniel Waters. Hyperion 2012 342 p. (hardback) $16.99

Grades: 7 8 9 10 11 12 **Fic**

1. Homicide -- Fiction 2. Teenagers -- Fiction 3. Friendship -- Fiction 4. Supernatural -- Fiction 5. Ghosts -- Fiction 6. Schools -- Fiction 7. Teachers -- Fiction 8. High schools -- Fiction 9. Serial murders -- Fiction

ISBN 1423121988; 9781423121985

LC 2012009395

Author Daniel Waters presents a "supernatural thriller. Six years after the Event . . . ghosts . . . continue to inundate Jewell City. Teen Veronica Calder, born on leap day, sees many of these ghosts. . . . Hoping to capture Veronica's attention, classmate Kirk begins an independent study on the city's ghosts. Also vying for her attention is serial killer and . . . teacher August Bittner, whose daughter died on leap day" and who "plans to kill Veronica in an effort to bring back his daughter's spirit." (Kirkus Reviews)

Generation dead. Hyperion 2008 382p $16.99

Grades: 7 8 9 10 **Fic**

1. School stories 2. Death -- Fiction 3. Zombies -- Fiction 4. Prejudices -- Fiction

ISBN 978-1-4231-0921-1; 1-4231-0921-X

LC 2007-36361

When dead teenagers who have come back to life start showing up at her high school, Phoebe, a goth girl, becomes interested in the phenomenon, and when she starts dating a "living impaired" boy, they encounter prejudice, fear, and hatred.

This "is a classic desegregation story that also skewers adult attempts to make teenagers play nice. . . . Motivational speakers, politically correct speech and encounter groups come in for special ridicule." N Y Times Book Rev

Followed by: Kiss of life (2009)

Waters, Zack C.

Blood moon rider; [by] Zack C. Waters. Pineapple Press 2006 126p $13.95

Grades: 5 6 7 8 **Fic**

1. Ranch life -- Fiction 2. Grandfathers -- Fiction 3. World War, 1939-1945 -- Fiction

ISBN 978-1-56164-350-9; 1-56164-350-5

LC 2005030749

After his father's death in World War II, fourteen-year-old Harley Wallace tries to join the Marines but is, instead, sent to live with his grandfather in Peru Landing, Florida, where he soon joins a covert effort to stop Nazis from destroying a secret airbase on Tampa Bay

This is "an adventure filled with unexpected kindnesses and the irrepressibility of family ties, as well as a brush with espionage and a couple of suspenseful shoot'em-up scenes. A colorful cast of characters and a nod to teenage romance help make this a good choice for middle school boys." SLJ

Watkins, Steve

★ **Down** Sand Mountain. Candlewick Press 2008 327p $16.99

Grades: 7 8 9 10 **Fic**

1. School stories 2. Bullies -- Fiction 3. Family life -- Fiction 4. Race relations -- Fiction

ISBN 978-0-7636-3839-9; 0-7636-3839-0

LC 2007-52159

In a small Florida mining town in 1966, twelve-year-old Dewey faces one worst-day-ever after another, but comes to know that the issues he faces about bullies, girls, race, and identity are part of the adult world, as well.

"The simple, beautiful prose remains totally true to the child's bewildered viewpoint. . . . Readers will be haunted by the disturbing drama of harsh secrets close to home." Booklist

Juvie; by Steve Watkins. Candlewick Press 2013 320 p. $17.99

Grades: 9 10 11 12 **Fic**

1. Sisters -- Fiction 2. Juvenile delinquency

ISBN 0763655090; 9780763655099

LC 2012955219

This book, by Steve Watkins, "tells the story of two sisters grappling with accountability [and] sacrifice. Sadie Windas has always been the responsible one . . . not like her older sister, Carla, who leaves her three-year-old daughter,

Lulu, with Aunt Sadie while she parties and gets high. But when both sisters are caught up in a drug deal—wrong place, wrong time—it falls to Sadie to confess to a crime she didn't commit to keep Carla out of jail and Lulu out of foster care." (Publisher's note)

"When seventeen-year-old Sadie and her sister, Carla, are caught participating (unintentionally) in a drug deal, Sadie takes the blame to protect her family; her punishment is a six-month sentence in a juvenile corrections facility. The novel is bleak and brutal--which, of course, is the point--making Sadie's loyalty to Carla and resolve to survive all the more powerful." (Horn Book)

What comes after. Candlewick Press 2011 334p $16.99

Grades: 8 9 10 11 12 **Fic**

1. Moving -- Fiction 2. Farm life -- Fiction 3. Bereavement -- Fiction 4. Child abuse -- Fiction 5. North Carolina -- Fiction 6. Domestic animals -- Fiction

ISBN 0-7636-4250-9; 978-0-7636-4250-1

LC 2010-38711

When her veterinarian father dies, sixteen-year-old Iris Wight must move from Maine to North Carolina where her Aunt Sue spends Iris's small inheritance while abusing her physically and emotionally, but the hardest to take is her mistreatment of the farm animals.

"This is the kind of book where readers will likely literally sigh with relief when Iris finally catches a break—while there is no rainbows-and-clouds-parting happy ending for a life this hard, it is enough that she is, for the moment, loved by a few fiercely loyal allies, beginning to face her demons, and wielding a bit more control over her own life." Bull Cent Child Books

Watkins, Yoko Kawashima

★ **My** brother, my sister, and I. Bradbury Press 1994 275p hardcover o.p. pa $5.99

Grades: 6 7 8 9 **Fic**

1. World War, 1939-1945 -- Fiction

ISBN 0-02-792526-9; 0-689-80656-6 pa

LC 93-23535

Living as refugees in Japan in 1947 while trying to locate their missing father, thirteen-year-old Yoko and her older brother and sister must endure a bad fire, injury, and false charges of arson, theft, and murder.

"Watkins's first-person narrative is beautifully direct and emotionally honest." Publ Wkly

★ **So** far from the bamboo grove. Lothrop, Lee & Shepard Bks. 1986 183p map hardcover o.p. pa $5.99

Grades: 6 7 8 9 **Fic**

1. World War, 1939-1945 -- Fiction

ISBN 0-688-13115-8 pa

LC 85-15939

A fictionalized autobiography in which eight-year-old Yoko escapes from Korea to Japan with her mother and sister at the end of World War II

"An admirably told and absorbing novel." Horn Book

Watson, Cristy

Benched. Orca Book Publishers 2011 123p (Orca currents) pa $9.95

Grades: 6 7 8 9 **Fic**

1. Gangs -- Fiction 2. Brothers -- Fiction

ISBN 1-55469-408-6; 978-1-55469-408-2

Cody and his friends get caught up in gang activity when they steal a park bench.

"Reluctant readers, especially, will be hooked as the tension builds, and the realistic story, which avoids a slick resolution, will spark discussion." Booklist

Watts, Irene N.

★ **No** moon. Tundra Books 2010 234p pa $12.95

Grades: 6 7 8 9 **Fic**

1. Shipwrecks -- Fiction 2. Household employees -- Fiction

ISBN 978-0-88776-971-9; 0-88776-971-3

Louisa Gardener is the fourteen-year-old nursemaid to the young daughters of a wealthy, titled family living in London, England, in 1912. The family decides to sail to New York aboard the Titanic. An accident to the children's nanny, only days prior to the sailing, means that Louisa must go in her stead.

"Watts provides a fascinating account of what the great unsinkable ship was like. The catastrophe is rendered in a heartbreakingly graceful style. . . . [This is a] uniquely engaging and satisfying coming-of-age historical adventure." Booklist

Weatherford, Carole Boston

★ **Becoming** Billie Holiday; art by Floyd Cooper. Wordsong 2008 116p il $19.95

Grades: 7 8 9 10 **Fic**

1. Novels in verse 2. Singers -- Fiction 3. Jazz music -- Fiction 4. African Americans -- Fiction

ISBN 978-1-59078-507-2; 1-59078-507-X

LC 2007-51214

Coretta Scott King honor book for text, 2009

Jazz vocalist Billie Holiday looks back on her early years in this fictional memoir written in verse.

"This captivating title places readers solidly into Holiday's world, and is suitable for independent reading as well as a variety of classroom uses." SLJ

Includes bibliographical references

Weatherly, Lee

Angel burn; [by] L.A. Weatherly. Candlewick Press 2011 449p $17.99

Grades: 8 9 10 11 12 **Fic**

1. Love -- Fiction 2. Angels -- Fiction 3. Supernatural -- Fiction

ISBN 978-0-7636-5652-2; 0-7636-5652-6

LC 2010-44819

In a world where angels are fierce stalkers whose irresistible force allows them to feed off humans and drain them of their vitality, a ruthless teenaged assassin of angels falls in love with a half-angel half-human girl, with devastating consequences.

"Weatherly's plot and writing are first-rate, adrenaline-fueled while still taking the time to thoughtfully develop the characters and build the romance. This elevated twist on the angel genre deserves to be spread far and wide." Publ Wkly

Kat got your tongue. David Fickling Books 2007 195p $15.99; lib bdg $18.99
Grades: 7 8 9 10 **Fic**
1. Amnesia -- Fiction
ISBN 978-0-385-75117-9; 0-385-75117-6; 978-0-385-75122-3 lib bdg; 0-385-75122-2 lib bdg
LC 2006-24408

After being hit by a car, thirteen-year-old Kat wakes up in the hospital with no memory of her previous life.

"Weatherby writes with fluid grace and makes this story line compelling, sprinkling bits of humor into Kat's journey toward recovery." Booklist

Weaver, Will

Defect. Farrar, Straus and Giroux 2007 199p $16
Grades: 7 8 9 10 11 12 **Fic**
1. School stories 2. Minnesota -- Fiction 3. Birth defects -- Fiction 4. Foster home care -- Fiction
ISBN 0-374-31725-9; 978-0-374-31725-6
LC 2006-49152

After spending most of his life in Minnesota foster homes hiding a bizarre physical abnormality, fifteen-year-old David is offered a chance at normalcy, but must decide if giving up what makes him special is the right thing to do.

The author "skillfully interweaves the improbable with twenty-first-century realities in this provocative novel of the ultimate cost of being so, so different." Voice Youth Advocates

Full service. Farrar, Straus & Giroux 2005 231p hardcover o.p. pa $8.99
Grades: 7 8 9 10 **Fic**
1. Farm life -- Fiction 2. Minnesota -- Fiction 3. Service stations -- Fiction
ISBN 0-374-32485-9; 0-374-40022-9 pa
LC 2004-57671

In the summer of 1965, teenager Paul Sutton, a northern Minnesota farm boy, takes a job at a gas station in town, where his strict religious upbringing is challenged by new people and experiences.

"Weaver is a wonderful stylist and his beautifully chosen words put such a shine on his deeply felt story that most teens will be able to find their own faces reflected in its pages." Booklist

Saturday night dirt. Farrar, Straus and Giroux 2008 163p $14.95; pa $7.99
Grades: 8 9 10 11 **Fic**
1. Minnesota -- Fiction 2. Automobile racing -- Fiction
ISBN 978-0-374-35060-4; 0-374-35060-4; 978-0-312-56131-4 pa; 0-312-56131-8 pa
LC 2007-6988

In a small town in northern Minnesota, the much-anticipated Saturday night dirt-track race at the old-fashioned, barely viable, Headwaters Speedway becomes, in many ways, an important life-changing event for all the participants on and off the track.

"Weaver presents compelling character studies. . . . Young racing fans . . . will find much that rings true here." Booklist

Other titles in this series are:
Checkered flag cheater (2010)
Super stock rookie (2009)

The **survivors**; Will Weaver. 1st ed. Harper 2012 307p.
Grades: 7 8 9 10 **Fic**
1. Dystopian fiction 2. Amnesia -- Fiction 3. Wilderness survival -- Fiction
ISBN 9780060094768; 9780060094775
LC 2011002087

Sequel to: Memory boy

This book takes place after "[t]he volcanoes had erupted. . . . For Miles and his sister, Sarah, the real disaster started in the violent aftermath--when they were forced to leave their cushy suburban home and flee to the north woods for safety. Miles got them to a cabin, but now winter is setting in. All they have to get them through is the milk from Sarah's prized possession--her goat--and Miles's memory of wilderness survival skills. . . . And when a horrific twist of fate robs Miles of his memory, he discovers the heart of his true identity. They knew the volcanoes would change the world. Now, in order to survive, they must change with it." (Publisher's note)

Webb, Philip

Six days. Chicken House 2011 336p $17.99
Grades: 5 6 7 8 **Fic**
1. Science fiction 2. Siblings -- Fiction 3. Space and time -- Fiction
ISBN 978-0-545-31767-2; 0-545-31767-3
LC 2010054233

Cass and her brother Wilbur scavenge in the ruins of a future London seeking an artifact for their Russian masters, but the search takes on a new urgency after the arrival of Erin and Peyto, strangers from afar who claim to hold the key to locating the mysterious object.

Webb "has created a complex and intriguing dystopia filled with devastation, clever devices . . . and lots of local color. . . . The novel's rapid pacing will hook readers and keep them turning pages." Booklist

Weber, Lori

If you live like me. Lobster Press 2009 331p pa $14.95
Grades: 7 8 9 10 **Fic**
1. Family life -- Fiction 2. Newfoundland -- Fiction
ISBN 978-1-897550-12-0; 1-897550-12-X

Cheryl's unhappiness builds with each move as her family travels across Canada while her father does research for a book, and by the time they reach Newfoundland, she is planning her escape, but events cause her to re-examine her feelings

"Weber's depiction of Cheryl is true to life, an accurate account of an independent and intelligent teenager struggling with loneliness, acceptance of change, and her own approaching adulthood." SLJ

Wein, Elizabeth

★ **Code** name Verity; Elizabeth Wein. Hyperion Books 2012 343 p.
Grades: 9 10 11 12 Adult **Fic**

1. Historical fiction 2. Prisoners of war -- Fiction 3. Women air pilots -- Fiction 4. Female friendship -- Fiction 5. France -- History -- 1940-1945, German occupation -- Fiction 6. Nazis -- Fiction 7. Espionage -- Fiction 8. Air pilots -- Fiction 9. Friendship -- Fiction 10. Insurgency -- Fiction 11. World War, 1939-1945 -- Fiction 12. Great Britain -- History -- 1936-1945 -- Fiction

ISBN 1423152190; 9781423152194

LC 2011024857

Michael L. Printz Honor Book (2013)

This young adult historical fiction novel presents a "tale of friendship during World War II. In a cell in Nazi-occupied France, a young woman writes. Like Scheherezade, to whom she is compared by the SS officer in charge of her case, she dribbles out information . . . in exchange for time and a reprieve from torture. . . . [S]he describes her friendship with Maddie, the pilot who flew them to France. . . . She also describes . . . her unbearable current situation." (Kirkus Reviews)

The **empty** kingdom. Viking 2008 217p (Mark of Solomon) $16.99
Grades: 7 8 9 10 **Fic**

1. Princes -- Fiction

ISBN 978-0-670-06273-7; 0-670-06273-1

LC 2007-29082

Telemakos, imprisoned on the upper levels of Abreha's, ruler of Himyar, twelve-story palace and lacking any way to communicate his predicament to his family in faraway Aksum, tries to find a subtle and effective way to regain his freedom.

"Wein deftly balances the political with the personal. . . . A unique, epic journey into adulthood." Horn Book

★ The **lion** hunter. Viking 2007 223p (Mark of Solomon) $16.99
Grades: 7 8 9 10 **Fic**

1. Kings 2. Princes -- Fiction

ISBN 978-0-670-06163-1; 0-670-03638-2

Still recovering from his ordeal as a government spy, twelve-year-old Telemakos, the half-Ethiopian grandson of King Artos of Britain, is sent with his sister to live with Abreha, the ruler of Himyar. His Aunt Goewin warns him that Abreha is a dangerous man, but just how dangerous remains to be seen.

"The vividly evoked setting provides a lush backdrop for the story's seemingly casual permutations, and readers' sympathies toward the embattled, wounded hero will draw them on willingly while Wein weaves her web of loyalty and intrigue." Horn Book

★ **Rose** under fire; by Elizabeth Wein. 1st ed. Hyperion 2013 368 p. (hardcover) $17.99
Grades: 9 10 11 12 **Fic**

1. Historical fiction 2. World War, 1939-1945 -- Fiction 3. Diaries -- Fiction 4. Air pilots -- Fiction 5. Prisoners of war -- Fiction 6. Ravensbruck (Concentration camp) -- Fiction 7. World War, 1939-1945 -- Prisoners and prisons, German -- Fiction

ISBN 1423183096; 9781423183099

LC 2013010337

Schneider Family Book Award: Teen (2014)

Boston Globe-Horn Book Honor: Fiction (2014)

This historical novel chronicles the experiences of American pilot Rose in a Polish concentration camp. "After being brutally punished for her refusal to make fuses for flying bombs . . . , Rose is befriended by Polish 'Rabbits,' victims of horrific medical experimentation. She uses 'counting-out rhymes' to preserve her sanity and as a way to memorize the names of the Rabbits. Rose's poetry . . . is at the heart of the story, revealing her growing understanding of what's happening around her." (Kirkus Reviews)

"Wein excels at weaving research seamlessly into narrative and has crafted another indelible story about friendship borne out of unimaginable adversity." (Pub Wkly)

Weingarten, Lynn

Wherever Nina lies. Point 2009 316p $16.99
Grades: 8 9 10 11 12 **Fic**

1. Sisters -- Fiction 2. Missing persons -- Fiction

ISBN 978-0-545-06631-0; 0-545-06631-X

LC 2008-21527

"Sixteen-year-old Ellie Wrigley is desperate to find her unconventional, beloved older sister, Nina, who disappeared two years ago, seemingly without a trace. When Ellie uncovers a clue in a local secondhand shop . . . she is determined to investigate. . . . Ellie sets off on a cross-country chase with her new crush, Sean, who has also lost a sibling. . . . Weingarten's fast-paced, chatty style will keep readers tuned in." Publ Wkly

Wells, Dan

Fragments; Dan Wells. Balzer + Bray 2013 576 p. (hardcover bdg.) $17.99
Grades: 9 10 11 12 **Fic**

1. Survival skills -- Fiction 2. Genetic engineering -- Fiction 3. Identity (Psychology) -- Fiction 4. Science fiction 5. Robots -- Fiction 6. Identity -- Fiction 7. Survival -- Fiction 8. Medical care -- Fiction

ISBN 0062071076; 9780062071071

LC 2012038107

"In this second book in the saga, set in a postapocalyptic U.S. in 2076, Kira is struggling to accept the fact that she is a genetically enhanced human known as a Partial. She makes her way on foot from East Meadow, New York, to the company headquarters of ParaGen in Manhattan in search of a way to cure the RM virus that kills newborns and to stop the expiration of Partials at age 20. Kira allies herself with the last human in Manhattan . . . who may be able to help her." (School Library Journal)

Partials; Dan Wells. 1st ed. Balzer + Bray 2012 470 p. (paperback) $9.99; (hbk : trade bdg.) $17.99
Grades: 9 10 11 12 **Fic**

1. Science fiction 2. Genetic engineering -- Fiction 3. Communicable diseases -- Fiction 4. Robots -- Fiction 5. Diseases -- Fiction 6. Survival -- Fiction 7. Medical

care -- Fiction 8. Medicine -- Research -- Fiction
ISBN 9780062071057; 0062071041; 9780062071040; 9780062135698

LC 2011042146

In this work of speculative fiction by Dan Wells, "after a virus released by the Partials (genetically engineered supersoldiers) . . . topples human civilization . . . [the] government . . . mandates pregnancy for every woman older than eighteen. . . . Kira Walker . . . has an alternative plan: since the Partials were immune to the virus, why not leave the safety of the island, capture a Partial, and bring it back to be studied?" (Bulletin of the Center for Children's Books)

Ruins; Dan Wells; [edited by] Jordan Brown. Balzer + Bray 2014 464 p. (hardcover) $17.99
Grades: 9 10 11 12 **Fic**

1. Science fiction 2. Robots -- Fiction 3. Apocalyptic fiction
ISBN 0062071106; 9780062071101

LC 2013953788

The conclusion of the author's Partial sequence trilogy. "As the clock ticks closer and closer to the final Partial expiration date, humans and Partials stand on the brink of war. Caught in the middle . . . are Samm and Kira: Samm, who is trapped on the far side of the continent beyond the vast toxic wasteland of the American Midwest; and Kira, now in the hands of Dr. Morgan, who is hell-bent on saving what's left of the Partials." (Publisher's note)

"Wells concludes his post-apocalyptic, action-packed trilogy with a literal bang and a lot of blood. Believable characters face tough moral choices, and though the end is tidy, the twists and treachery that get readers there are all the fun. It's enjoyable alone but best read after the first two. Science (fiction) at the end of the world done right." (Kirkus)

Wells, Martha

Emilie & the hollow world; by Martha Wells. Strange Chemistry 2013 301 p. (paperback) $9.99
Grades: 9 10 11 12 **Fic**

1. Fantasy fiction 2. Runaway teenagers -- Fiction 3. Missing persons -- Fiction 4. Runaway children -- Fiction
ISBN 1908844493; 9781908844491

LC 2012277394

In this book, Emilie is trying to run away. "After spending too much on snacks, [she] can't afford the ferry ticket to reach her cousin's home. There's only one logical thing to do: jump off the docks, swim to the nearest boat and hope for the best. After boarding what she hopes is the right ship, she witnesses a pirate attack, saves a scaled man and watches as a merging of magic and science transports the ship to a legendary world within a world." (Kirkus Reviews)

Wells, Robison E.

Feedback; Robison Wells. HarperTeen 2012 312 p. (hardback) $17.99
Grades: 7 8 9 10 **Fic**

1. Private schools -- Fiction 2. School stories 3. Mystery fiction 4. Science fiction 5. Robots -- Fiction 6. Survival -- Fiction
ISBN 0062026100; 9780062026101; 9780062228307

LC 2012004296

Sequel to: Variant

In author Robison Wells' story, "Benson Fisher escaped from Maxfield Academy's deadly rules and brutal gangs. The worst was over. Or so he thought. But now he's trapped on the other side of the wall, in a different kind of prison. . . . [His friends] are all pawns in the school's twisted experiment, held captive and controlled by an unseen force. And while Benson struggles to figure out who, if anyone, can be trusted, he discovers that Maxfield Academy's plans are darker than anything he imagined--and they may be impossible to stop." (Publisher's note)

Variant. HarperTeen 2011 376p $17.99
Grades: 7 8 9 10 **Fic**

1. School stories 2. Science fiction
ISBN 978-0-06-202608-8; 0-06-202608-9

LC 2010042661

After years in foster homes, seventeen-year-old Benson Fisher applies to New Mexico's Maxfield Academy in hopes of securing a brighter future, but instead he finds that the school is a prison and no one is what he or she seems.

"Hard to put down from the very first page, this fast-paced novel with Stepford overtones answers only some of the questions it poses, holding some of the most tantalizing open for the next installment in a series that is anything but ordinary." Kirkus

Wells, Rosemary

★ **Red** moon at Sharpsburg. Viking 2007 236p $16.99; pa $7.99
Grades: 6 7 8 9 10 **Fic**

1. United States -- History -- 1861-1865, Civil War -- Fiction
ISBN 0-670-03638-2; 978-0-670-03638-7; 0-14-241205-8 pa; 978-0-14-241205-3 pa

As the Civil War breaks out, India, a young Southern girl, summons her sharp intelligence and the courage she didn't know she had to survive the war that threatens to destroy her family, her Virginia home and the only life she has ever known.

"This powerful novel is unflinching in its depiction of war and the devastation it causes, yet shows the resilience and hope that can follow such a tragedy. India is a memorable, thoroughly believable character." SLJ

Wemmlinger, Raymond

Booth's daughter. Calkins Creek 2007 210p $17.95
Grades: 7 8 9 10 **Fic**

1. Actors 2. Actors -- Fiction 3. New York (N.Y.) -- Fiction 4. Father-daughter relationship -- Fiction
ISBN 978-1-932425-86-4; 1-932425-86-1

LC 2006-12073

In nineteenth-century New York City, Edwina, daughter of the famous actor Edwin Booth and niece of John Wilkes Booth, finds it difficult to escape the family tragedy and to meet the needs of a demanding father while maintaining her independence.

"Elements reminiscent of an Edith Wharton novel—the mannered social interactions, Gilded Age settings, and matrimony-bound momentum—will draw many romantically inclined readers." Booklist

Wendig, Chuck

Under the Empyrean Sky. Amazon Childrens Pub 2013 368 p. $17.99

Grades: 7 8 9 10 **Fic**

1. Science fiction 2. Apocalyptic fiction

ISBN 1477817204; 9781477817209

In this first book in Chuck Wendig's Heartland Trilogy, "the haves hover above ruined Earth in luxurious flotillas and the have-nots toil below in the Heartland, [are] told whom to marry and what to grow. . . . When Cael and his friends discover a trail of precious, prohibited vegetables growing deep in the corn, they stumble on a secret that may save them—or get them killed." (Kirkus Reviews)

Werlin, Nancy

★ **Double** helix. Dial Books 2004 252p hardcover o.p. pa $6.99

Grades: 7 8 9 10 **Fic**

1. Science fiction 2. Bioethics -- Fiction 3. Genetic engineering -- Fiction

ISBN 0-8037-2606-6; 0-14-240327-X pa

LC 2003-12269

Eighteen-year-old Eli discovers a shocking secret about his life and his family while working for a Nobel Prizewinning scientist whose specialty is genetic engineering.

"Werlin clearly and dramatically raises fundamental bioethical issues for teens to ponder. She also creates a riveting story with sharply etched characters and complex relationships that will stick with readers long after the book is closed." SLJ

★ **Extraordinary**. Dial Books for Young Readers 2010 393p il $17.99

Grades: 8 9 10 11 12 **Fic**

1. Fantasy fiction 2. Jews -- Fiction 3. Fairies -- Fiction 4. Friendship -- Fiction

ISBN 978-0-8037-3372-5; 0-8037-3372-0

LC 2010-2086

Phoebe, a member of the wealthy Rothschilds family, befriends Mallory, an awkward new girl in school, and the two become as close as sisters, but Phoebe does not know that Mallory is a faerie, sent to the human world to trap the ordinary human girl into fulfilling a promise made by her ancestor Mayer to the queen of the faeries.

"The carefully nuanced, often sensual prose delivers a highly effective narrative. Characterizations are arresting and complex." SLJ

Impossible; a novel. Dial Books 2008 376p $17.99

Grades: 7 8 9 10 **Fic**

1. Magic -- Fiction 2. Pregnancy -- Fiction 3. Teenage mothers -- Fiction

ISBN 978-0-8037-3002-1; 0-8037-3002-0

LC 2008-06633

When seventeen-year-old Lucy discovers her family is under an ancient curse by an evil Elfin Knight, she realizes to break the curse she must perform three impossible tasks before her daughter is born in order to save them both.

"Werlin earns high marks for the tale's graceful interplay between wild magic and contemporary reality." Booklist

★ The **killer's** cousin; [by] Nancy Werlin. Dial Books 2009 227p $16.99; pa $7.99

Grades: 7 8 9 10 **Fic**

1. Cousins -- Fiction 2. Homicide -- Fiction

ISBN 978-0-8037-3370-1; 0-8037-3370-4; 978-0-14-241373-9 pa; 0-14-241373-9 pa

LC 2008-24294

A reissue of the title first published 1998 by Delacorte

After being acquitted of murder, seventeen-year-old David goes to stay with relatives in Cambridge, Massachusetts, where he finds himself forced to face his past as he learns more about his strange young cousin Lily.

"Teens will find this tautly plotted thriller, rich in complex, finely drawn characters, an absolute page-turner." Booklist

★ The **rules** of survival. Dial Books 2006 259p $16.99

Grades: 8 9 10 11 12 **Fic**

1. Siblings -- Fiction 2. Child abuse -- Fiction

ISBN 0-8037-3001-2

LC 2006-1675

Seventeen-year-old Matthew recounts his attempts, starting at a young age, to free himself and his sisters from the grip of their emotionally and physically abusive mother.

The author "tackles the topic of child abuse with grace and insight. . . . Teens will empathize with these siblings and the secrets they keep in this psychological horror story." SLJ

Wesselhoeft, Conrad

Adios, nirvana. Houghton Mifflin Harcourt 2010 235p $16

Grades: 10 11 12 **Fic**

1. School stories 2. Death -- Fiction 3. Musicians -- Fiction 4. Friendship -- Fiction 5. Bereavement -- Fiction 6. Seattle (Wash.) -- Fiction

ISBN 978-0-547-36895-5; 0-547-36895-X

LC 2010-06759

As Seattle sixteen-year-old Jonathan helps a dying man come to terms with a tragic event he experienced during World War II, Jonathan begins facing his own demons, especially the death of his twin brother, helped by an assortment of friends, old and new.

"The author gives the reader a wonderful blend of contemporary, historical, and literary fiction. His use of figurative language makes each page dance with images of raw realism. Wesselhoeft guides the reader down an open portal of teen suicide and grief issues. This is a poignant piece for older teens." Voice Youth Advocates

West, Kasie

Pivot point; Kasie West. HarperTeen 2013 352 p. (hardback) $17.99

Grades: 7 8 9 10 **Fic**

1. Love stories 2. Occult fiction 3. Divorce -- Fiction 4. Love -- Fiction 5. Schools -- Fiction 6. High schools -- Fiction 7. Choice (Psychology) -- Fiction

ISBN 0062117378; 9780062117373

LC 2012019089

This book tells the story of Addie Coleman, who has the ability to see into the future and choose between the better of two options. "She is a Searcher living in the Compound, the southern Texas home of the most gifted individuals in the county. When her parents decide to divorce, with her mother staying in the Compound, and her father opting to live in the normal world, she decides to use her ability to help her chose with whom to live." (Booklist)

Split second; Kasie West. HarperTeen, an imprint of HarperCollinsPublishers 2014 368 p. (hardcover bdg.) $17.99
Grades: 7 8 9 10 **Fic**

1. Love stories 2. Memory -- Fiction 3. Psychics -- Fiction 4. Love -- Fiction 5. Schools -- Fiction 6. Family life -- Fiction 7. High schools -- Fiction 8. Psychic ability -- Fiction 9. Choice (Psychology) -- Fiction

ISBN 0062117386; 9780062117380

LC 2013008053

"In this follow-up to Pivot Point (HarperCollins, 2013), Addie leaves the Compound after a bad breakup. As a Searcher, Addie can see two possible futures, and she finds it hard to believe this is the one she chose, the one in which she is betrayed by her best friend and her boyfriend... In this fast-paced fantasy, the plot is slow to begin but takes off after the first few chapters. Recommended for readers who love dystopian stories with a bit of romance." (School Library Journal)

Westerfeld, Scott

Afterworlds; by Scott Westerfeld. Simon Pulse. 2014 608p $19.99
Grades: 9 10 11 12 **Fic**

1. Dead — Fiction; 2. East Indian Americans — Fiction; 3. Ghosts — Fiction; 4. Lesbians — Fiction; 5. Love — Fiction; 6. New York (N.Y.) — Fiction;) 7. Authors -- Fiction

LC 2014006852

Rainbow List (2015)

"Eighteen-year-old Darcy drops her college plans and moves to New York to revise her soon-to-be-published novel and start the second one. Meanwhile, in chapters that alternate with Darcy's NYC adventures, her fictional protagonist, Lizzie, survives a near-death experience to find she has become a psychopomp, responsible for guiding souls to the afterlife." Booklist

"Readers who pay attention will see how Darcy's learning curve plays out and how she incorporates and transmutes her real-world experiences into her novel.Watching Darcy's story play off Darcy's novel will fascinate readers as well as writers." Kirkus

Blue noon; [by] Scott Westerfeld. 1st ed.; Eos 2006 378p (Midnighters) $15.99; lib bdg $16.89
Grades: 7 8 9 10 **Fic**

1. Science fiction

ISBN 0-06-051957-6; 0-06-051958-4 lib bdg

LC 2005017597

The five midnighters from Bixby discover that the secret hour is starting to invade the daylight world, and if they cannot stop it, the darklings will soon be free to hunt again.

"The plot maintains an exciting pace. . . . This is fun recreational reading." SLJ

Extras. Simon Pulse 2011 399p $17.99; pa $9.99
Grades: 7 8 9 10 **Fic**

1. Science fiction

ISBN 978-1-4424-3007-5; 978-1-4424-1978-0 pa

Sequel to Specials (2006)

First published 2007

Aya is "an 'extra' (face rank stuck in the mid-400,000s) in a city run on a 'reputation economy.' If Aya can win fame as a 'kicker,' reporting with her trusty hovercam on a story that captures the city's imagination, her face rank will soar. . . . Westerfeld shows he has a finger on the pulse of our reputation economy, alchemizing the cult of celebrity, advertising's constant competition for consumer attention." Horn Book

★ **Leviathan**; written by Scott Westerfeld; illustrated by Keith Thompson. Simon Pulse 2009 440p il map $19.99; pa $9.99
Grades: 7 8 9 10 **Fic**

1. War stories 2. Science fiction 3. Princes -- Fiction 4. Mythical animals -- Fiction 5. Genetic engineering -- Fiction

ISBN 978-1-4169-7173-3; 1-4169-7173-4; 978-1-4169-7174-0 pa; 1-4169-7174-2 pa

LC 2009-881

In an alternate 1914 Europe, fifteen-year-old Austrian Prince Alek, on the run from the Clanker Powers who are attempting to take over the globe using mechanical machinery, forms an uneasy alliance with Deryn who, disguised as a boy to join the British Air Service, is learning to fly genetically-engineered beasts.

"The protagonists' stories are equally gripping and keep the story moving, and Thompson's detail-rich panels bring Westerfeld's unusual creations to life." Publ Wkly

Other titles in this series are:
Behemoth (2010)
Goliath (2011)

★ **Peeps**. Razorbill 2005 312p hardcover o.p. pa $8.99
Grades: 9 10 11 12 **Fic**

1. Vampires -- Fiction

ISBN 1-59514-031-X; 1-59514-083-2 pa

LC 2005-8151

Cal Thompson is a carrier of a parasite that causes vampirism, and must hunt down all of the girlfriends he has unknowingly infected.

"This innovative and original vampire story, full of engaging characters and just enough horror without any gore, will appeal to a wide audience." SLJ

Followed by The last days (2006)

Pretties. Simon Pulse 2011 348p $17.99; pa $9.99
Grades: 7 8 9 10 **Fic**

1. Science fiction

ISBN 978-1-4169-3639-8; 978-1-4424-1980-3 pa

Sequel to Uglies

First published 2005

Tally's transformation to perfect and popular including her totally hot boyfriend is everything she always wanted. But beneath the fun and freedom something is wrong and now Tally has to fight for her life because what she knows has put her in danger with the authorities.

"Riveting and compulsively readable, this action-packed sequel does not disappoint." Booklist

Followed by Specials

★ **So** yesterday; a novel. Razorbill 2004 225p $16.99; pa $7.99
Grades: 7 8 9 10 **Fic**

1. Mystery fiction 2. Missing persons -- Fiction
ISBN 1-59514-000-X; 1-59514-032-8 pa
LC 2004-2302

Hunter Braque, a New York City teenager who is paid by corporations to spot what is "cool," combines his analytical skills with girlfriend Jen's creative talents to find a missing person and thwart a conspiracy directed at the heart of consumer culture

"This hip, fascinating thriller aggressively questions consumer culture. . . . Teens will inhale this wholly entertaining, thought-provoking look at a system fueled by their purchasing power. " Booklist

Specials. Simon Pulse 2011 350p $17.99; pa $9.99
Grades: 7 8 9 10 **Fic**

1. Science fiction
ISBN 978-1-4424-3008-2; 978-1-4424-1979-7 pa
Sequel to Pretties
First published 2006

Tally has been transformed from a repellent ugly to supermodel pretty. Now she's a super-amped fighting machine. Her mission is to keep the uglies down and the pretties stupid. But Tally's never been good at playing by the rules.

"Readers who enjoyed Uglies and Pretties . . . will not want to miss Specials. . . . Westerfeld's themes include vanity, environmental conservation, Utopian idealism, fascism, violence, and love." SLJ

Followed by Extras

Uglies. Simon Pulse 2005 425p rpt $17.99
Grades: 7 8 9 10 **Fic**

1. Science fiction
ISBN 9781416936381

"Tally is an ugly, waiting eagerly for her sixteenth birthday, when surgery will make her into a Pretty and she can join her old friend Peris in the life of the beautiful in New Pretty Town. In the meantime, she revels in hoverboarding and pulling tricks with her rebellious friend, Shay, who doesn't share Tally's anticipation for joining the Pretty world. When Shay runs away to join dissidents outside the city, Tally is blackmailed by the city's Special Circumstances unit into following Shay and uncovering the location of the anti-establishment rebels, a task that becomes more difficult when Tally's sympathies begin to skew toward the rebels, especially their charismatic leader, David. . . . Grades six to ten." (Bull Cent Child Books)

"Fifteen-year-old Tally's eerily harmonious, postapocalyptic society gives extreme makeovers to teens on their sixteenth birthdays. . . . When a top-secret agency threatens to leave Tally ugly forever unless she spies on runaway teens, she agrees to infiltrate the Smoke, a shadowy colony of refugees from the 'tyranny of physical perfection.'" Booklist

Weston, Robert Paul

Dust city; a novel. by Robert Weston. Razorbill 2010 299p $16.99
Grades: 7 8 9 10 **Fic**

1. Magic -- Fiction 2. Wolves -- Fiction 3. Fairies -- Fiction 4. Father-son relationship -- Fiction
ISBN 978-1-59514-296-2; 1-59514-296-7
LC 2010-36067

Henry Whelp, son of the Big Bad Wolf, investigates what happened to the fairies that used to protect humans and animalia, and what role the corporation that manufactures synthetic fairy dust played in his father's crime.

"The premise is fractured fairy tale, but the play is pure noir. . . . The clever setup and gutting of fairy-tale tropes will garner plenty of enthusiasm." Booklist

Weyn, Suzanne

Distant waves; a novel of the Titanic. Scholastic Press 2009 330p $17.99
Grades: 8 9 10 11 **Fic**

1. Inventors 2. Journalists 3. Financiers 4. Fur traders 5. Sisters -- Fiction 6. Electrical engineers 7. Inventors -- Fiction 8. Spiritualism -- Fiction 9. Titanic (Steamship) -- Fiction 10. Mother-daughter relationship -- Fiction
ISBN 978-0-545-08572-4; 0-545-08572-1
LC 2008-40708

In the early twentieth century, four sisters and their widowed mother, a famed spiritualist, travel from New York to London, and as the Titanic conveys them and their acquaintances, journalist W.T. Stead, scientist Nikola Tesla, and industrialist John Jacob Astor, home, Tesla's inventions will either doom or save them all.

"The interplay of science, spirituality, history and romance will satisfy." Publ Wkly

Dr. Frankenstein's daughters; by Suzanne Weyn. Scholastic Press 2013 320 p. (hardcover) $17.99
Grades: 9 10 11 **Fic**

1. Gothic novels 2. Horror stories 3. Twins -- Fiction 4. Diaries -- Fiction 5. Sisters -- Fiction 6. Monsters -- Fiction 7. Orkney (Scotland) -- Fiction 8. Human experimentation in medicine -- Fiction 9. Frankenstein, Victor (Fictitious character)
ISBN 0545425336; 9780545425339
LC 2012033039

In this book, "twin teen sisters Giselle and Ingrid discover that they've inherited a castle in the Orkneys from their father, Victor. For giddy Giselle, it's a . . . chance to throw a huge party. . . . For the more studious Ingrid, her father's old journals . . . provide not only exciting insights into her father's work, but also the tools with which to outfit Walter, the moody and disabled ex-soldier to whom she's given her heart, with a new arm and leg." (Kirkus Reviews)

"Seventeen-year-old twins tell their story in alternating diary entries as they journey to claim an inherited castle and learn about their father, Dr. Victor Frankenstein. Giselle longs for social grace; Ingrid strives for education. But both are haunted by strange dangers and a series of murders. This curious takeoff on Shelley's classic is ornamented with absorbing gothic elements and a brooding romance." (Horn Book)

Empty. Scholastic Press 2010 183p $17.99
Grades: 7 8 9 10 **Fic**

1. Science fiction 2. Ecology -- Fiction 3. Hurricanes -- Fiction 4. Energy resources -- Fiction 5. Environmental degradation -- Fiction
ISBN 978-0-545-17278-3; 0-545-17278-0
LC 2010-16743

When, just ten years in the future, oil supplies run out and global warming leads to devastating storms, senior high school classmates Tom, Niki, Gwen, Hector, and Brock realize that the world as they know it is ending and lead the way to a more environmentally-friendly society.

"The realistic and thought-provoking scenario is packaged into a speedy read, and given the popularity of dystopian fiction, it should find an audience." Booklist

Recruited. Darby Creek 2011 104p (Surviving Southside) lib bdg $27.93
Grades: 7 8 9 10 **Fic**

1. School stories 2. Football -- Fiction 3. African Americans -- Fiction
ISBN 978-0-7613-6153-4; 0-7613-6153-7
LC 2010023662

"Kadeem is ecstatic when scouts shower him with gifts, dinners, and parties and he realizes that his dream of playing college football may be coming true. His happiness quickly turns to dread, though, as he learns that the incentives offered to him are violations of recruitment policy. . . . [This] well-written [story reinforces] the importance of family, friends, values, and thoughtful decision-making. . . . [An] excellent [purchase, this book] will attract and engage reluctant readers." SLJ

Reincarnation; [by] Suzanne Weyn. Scholastic Press 2008 293p $17.99
Grades: 7 8 9 10 **Fic**

1. Love stories 2. Reincarnation -- Fiction 3. Space and time -- Fiction
ISBN 978-0-545-01323-9; 0-545-01323-2
LC 2007-08743

When a young couple dies in prehistoric times, their love—and link to various green stones—endures through the ages as they are reborn into new bodies and somehow find a way to connect.

"Readers with a romantic bent will be drawn to this story, which pushes the notion of eternal love to its limits: two spirits find each other again and again, at different moments in history." Publ Wkly

Whaley, John Corey

Noggin; by John Corey Whaley. Atheneum Books for Young Readers 2014 352 p. (hardback) $17.99
Grades: 9 10 11 12 **Fic**

1. Cryonics 2. Medical novels 3. Teenagers -- Fiction 4. Science fiction 5. Death -- Fiction 6. Identity -- Fiction 7. Interpersonal relations -- Fiction 8. Family life -- Missouri -- Kansas City -- Fiction 9. Transplantation of organs, tissues, etc. -- Fiction
ISBN 1442458720; 9781442458727; 9781442458734
LC 2013020137

"Losing his battle to terminal cancer, sixteen-year-old Travis opts to have his head surgically removed, stored cryogenically, and restored to life at some point in the distant future when medical technology is able to attach it to a new body...Readers will find it easy to become invested in Travis's second coming-of age -- brimming with humor, pathos, and angst -- and root for him to make peace with his new life." (Horn Book)

★ **Where** things come back. Atheneum Books for Young Readers 2011 228p. $16.99
Grades: 9 10 11 12 **Fic**

1. Birds -- Fiction 2. Arkansas -- Fiction 3. Friendship -- Fiction 4. Family life -- Fiction 5. Missing persons -- Fiction
ISBN 978-1-4424-1333-7; 1-4424-1333-6
LC 201024836

Michael L. Printz Award (2012)
William C. Morris YA Debut Award (2012)

Seventeen-year-old Cullen's summer in Lily, Arkansas, is marked by his cousin's death by overdose, an alleged spotting of a woodpecker thought to be extinct, failed romances, and his younger brother's sudden disappearance.

"The realistic characters and fascinating mix of mundane with life changing and tragic events create a memorable story most young adult readers will connect to." Libr Media Connect

Wharton, Thomas

The **shadow** of Malabron. Candlewick Press 2009 382p (The perilous realm) $16.99
Grades: 5 6 7 8 **Fic**

1. Fantasy fiction
ISBN 978-0-7636-3911-2; 0-7636-3911-7
LC 2009-7768

When Will, a rebellious teen, stumbles from the present into the realm where stories come from, he learns he has a mission concerning the evil Malabron and, aided by some of the story folk, he faces a host of perils while seeking the gateless gate that will take him home.

"Lush descriptive prose, cleverly sustained suspense, a sprinkling of humor and an exciting climax will keep readers riveted to the story, while those who know their folklore will be delighted by Wharton's twisting of the tropes and tales of myth and legend." Kirkus

Whelan, Gloria

After the train. HarperCollins 2009 152p $15.99; lib bdg $16.89
Grades: 6 7 8 9 **Fic**

1. Antisemitism -- Fiction 2. Jews -- Germany -- Fiction
ISBN 978-0-06-029596-7; 0-06-029596-1; 978-0-06-029597-4 lib bdg; 0-06-029597-X lib bdg
LC 2008-10185

Ten years after the end of the Second World War, the town of Rolfen, West Germany, looks just as peaceful and beautiful as ever, until young Peter Liebig discovers a secret about his past that leads him to question everything, including the town's calm facade and his own sense of comfort and belonging.

"The story offers effective suspense in the mystery of Peter's situation and a dramatic climax. . . . Fans of Whelan's middle-school-aimed historical fiction . . . will definitely want to get their hands on this title." Bull Cent Child Books

All my noble dreams and then what happens; Gloria Whelan. 1st ed. Simon & Schuster Books for Young Readers 2013 272 p. (hardcover) $15.99
Grades: 6 7 8 9 10 **Fic**

1. India -- History 2. Historical fiction 3. Aunts -- Fiction 4. Insurgency -- Fiction 5. Family life -- India -- Fiction 6. Great Britain -- History -- George V, 1910-1936 -- Fiction 7. India -- History -- British occupation, 1765-1947 -- Fiction 8. India -- History -- British occupation, 1765-1947

ISBN 1442449764; 9781442449763; 9781442449770

LC 2012018599

Sequel to: Small acts of amazing courage

This novel is a sequel to Gloria Whelan's "Small Acts of Amazing Courage." Set "in India in the year 1921," here British-born protagonist Rosy has returned to "India, the land she considers home, after an extended stay in England. The household . . . is bustling with preparations for a visit by the Prince of Wales. Rosy has promised to deliver a letter written by Mahatma Gandhi, an appeal to Great Britain to give India its freedom." (Publishers Weekly)

Burying the sun. HarperCollins Publishers 2004 205p $15.99; lib bdg $16.89 **Fic**
Grades: 56 7 8 **Fic**

1. Famines 2. Survival 3. World War, 1939-1945 -- Fiction 4. Saint Petersburg (Russia) -- Siege, 1941-1944 -- Fiction

ISBN 0-06-054112-1; 0-06-054113-X lib bdg

LC 2003-12487

In Leningrad in 1941, when Russia and Germany are at war, fourteen-year-old Georgi vows to help his family and his city during the terrible siege.

"Haunting images and elegant prose make this companion to The Impossible Journey . . . and Angel on the Square . . . memorable. . . .The lilting writing style and simple dignity of the characters help construct an honest portrait of everyday life in extraordinary circumstances." SLJ

Includes bibliographical references

Chu Ju's house. HarperCollins 2004 227p $15.99; lib bdg $16.89
Grades: 5 6 7 8 **Fic**

1. Gender role 2. Runaways 3. Sex role 4. Sex role -- Fiction 5. Runaway teenagers -- Fiction 6. China -- History -- 1976- -- Fiction

ISBN 0-06-050724-1; 0-06-050725-X lib bdg

LC 2003-6979

In order to save her baby sister, fourteen-year-old Chu Ju leaves her rural home in modern China and earns food and shelter by working on a sampan, tending silk worms, and planting rice seedlings, while wondering if she will ever see her family again.

"Whelan tells a compelling adventure story, filled with rich cultural detail, about a smart, likable teenage girl who overcomes society's gender restrictions." Booklist

The **Disappeared.** Dial Books 2008 136p $16.99; pa $6.99
Grades: 8 9 10 11 12 **Fic**

1. Siblings -- Fiction 2. Argentina -- Fiction

ISBN 978-0-8037-3275-9; 0-8037-3275-9; 978-0-14-241540-5 pa; 0-14-241540-5 pa

LC 2007-43750

Teenaged Silvia tries to save her brother, Eduardo, after he is captured by the military government in 1970s Argentina

"The deftly handled voices of Silvia and Eduardo follow the well-intentioned, but often grievous, mistakes of youth. Their compelling tale is a chilling account of the manipulative power of corruption." SLJ

Includes bibliographical references

★ **Homeless** bird. HarperCollins Pubs. 2000 216p hardcover o.p. pa $5.99
Grades: 6 7 8 9 10 **Fic**

1. India -- Fiction 2. Women -- India -- Fiction

ISBN 0-06-028454-4; 0-06-440819-1 pa

LC 99-33241

When thirteen-year-old Koly enters into an ill-fated arranged marriage, she must either suffer a destiny dictated by India's tradition or find the courage to oppose it.

"This beautifully told, inspiring story takes readers on a fascinating journey through modern India and the universal intricacies of a young woman's heart." Booklist

★ **Listening** for lions. HarperCollins 2005 194p $15.99; lib bdg $16.89; pa $5.99
Grades: 5 6 7 8 **Fic**

1. Orphans -- Fiction 2. Physicians -- Fiction

ISBN 0-06-058174-3; 0-06-058175-1 lib bdg; 0-06-058176-X pa

Left an orphan after the influenza epidemic in British East Africa in 1918, thirteen-year-old Rachel is tricked into assuming a deceased neighbor's identity to travel to England, where her only dream is to return to Africa and rebuild her parents' mission hospital.

"In a straightforward, sympathetic voice, Rachel tells an involving, episodic story." Booklist

See what I see. HarperTeen 2011 199p $16.99
Grades: 7 8 9 10 11 12 **Fic**

1. Sick -- Fiction 2. Artists -- Fiction 3. Detroit (Mich.) -- Fiction 4. Father-daughter relationship -- Fiction

ISBN 978-0-06-125545-8; 0-06-125545-9

LC 2010-03094

When eighteen-year-old Kate arrives on the Detroit doorstep of her long-estranged father, a famous painter, she is shocked to learn that he is dying and does not want to support her efforts to attend the local art school.

"With elegant prose, Whelan portrays a gradually developing and complex relationship built on guilt, curiosity, love, and a passion for art." Booklist

Small acts of amazing courage. Simon & Schuster Books for Young Readers 2011 217p $15.99

Grades: 6 7 8 9 10 **Fic**

1. Aunts -- Fiction 2. Bereavement -- Fiction
ISBN 978-1-4424-0931-6; 1-4424-0931-2
LC 2010-13164

In 1919, independent-minded fifteen-year-old Rosalind lives in India with her English parents, and when they fear she has fallen in with some rebellious types who believe in Indian self-government, she is sent "home" to London, where she has never been before and where her older brother died, to stay with her two aunts.

"Whelan balances the facts with distinctive, sometimes comical characterizations and vibrant, original sensory descriptions. . . . Whelan's vibrant, episodic story explores the tension between doing what's right, rather than what's expected, and the infinite complexities of colonialism." Booklist

Whipple, Natalie

House of ivy & sorrow. Natalie Whipple. HarperTeen 2014 362p $9.99

Grades: 8 9 10 11 12 **Fic**

1. Curses — Fiction; 2. Dating (Social customs) — Fiction; 3. Father-daughter relationship— Fiction; 4. Friendship — Fiction; 5. Grandmothers — Fiction; 6. Witchcraft — Fiction; 7. Fantasy fiction
ISBN: 0062120182; 9780062120182
LC 2013008052

"Josephine, 17, lives with her grandmother in a house under the interstate where it's rumored that an old witch can make someone love you if you're willing to give her your pinkie finger. Jo knows that the rumors are true, because her grandmother is that witch...This is a fast-paced fantasy, with just the right amount of romance and realism. Readers will relate to Jo's relationships with her family, crush, and two best friends. Despite the current glut of supernatural and urban fantasy, this tale will stand out." SLJ

Whitaker, Alecia

The **queen** of Kentucky. Little, Brown 2011 375p $17.99

Grades: 7 8 9 10 **Fic**

1. School stories 2. Farm life -- Fiction 3. Friendship -- Fiction 4. Popularity -- Fiction 5. Dating (Social customs) -- Fiction
ISBN 978-0-316-12506-2; 0-316-12506-7
LC 2010045840

In this book, "Ricki Jo is determined to give herself an extreme makeover as she enters high school, . . . expanding her horizons beyond her life as a hard-working farm girl. Another new girl, Mackenzie, becomes her ally, and . . . they join up with an established group of friends who are . . . in the cool crowd. Ricki Jo, now Ericka, becomes a cheerleader, develops a crush on a much sought after boy who teases her mercilessly, experiments with alcohol, and reinvents her sense of style through magazines. Her transformation doesn"t always go smoothly, and her best friend, Luke, tries his best to keep her grounded, but Ericka is determined to transform from her old self to what she considers her new and improved self." (Bulletin of the Center for Children"s Books)

"This is familiar territory, but Whitaker's setting is fresh, and readers from rural areas will recognize the class differences. . . . Ericka's first-person voice is sassy and quite believable as she tries to figure out who she is—and who everybody else is, too." Booklist

Whitcomb, Laura

A **certain** slant of light. Graphia 2005 282p $8.99

Grades: 9 10 11 12 **Fic**

1. Ghost stories 2. Future life -- Fiction
ISBN 0-618-58532-X pa
LC 2004-27208

After benignly haunting a series of people for 130 years, Helen meets a teenage boy who can see her and together they unlock the mysteries of their pasts.

The author "creatively pulls together a dramatic and compelling plot that cleverly grants rebellious teen romance a timeless grandeur." Bull Cent Child Books

The **Fetch**; a novel. Houghton Mifflin Harcourt 2009 379p il $17

Grades: 9 10 11 12 **Fic**

1. Monks 2. Princes 3. Princesses 4. Courtiers 5. Death -- Fiction 6. Soviet Union -- History -- 1917-1921, Revolution -- Fiction
ISBN 978-0-618-89131-3; 0-618-89131-5
LC 2008-13307

After 350 years as a Fetch, or death escort, Calder breaks his vows and enters the body of Rasputin, whose spirit causes rebellion in the Land of Lost Souls while Calder struggles to convey Ana and Alexis, orphaned in the Russian Revolution, to Heaven.

"The rich descriptions, particularly of the exquisitely imagined afterlife, are exceptionally drawn, as are the sympathetic characters and the unusual premise. A challenging book with an intriguing conclusion, this will lead thoughtful readers to spirited discussions." Booklist

White, Amy Brecount

Forget -her-nots. Greenwillow Books 2010 374p $16.99; lib bdg $17.89

Grades: 7 8 9 10 **Fic**

1. School stories 2. Magic -- Fiction 3. Flowers -- Fiction 4. Mother-daughter relationship -- Fiction
ISBN 978-0-06-167298-9; 0-06-167298-X; 978-0-06-167299-6 lib bdg; 0-06-167299-8 lib bdg
LC 2009-7105

At a Charlottesville, Virginia, boarding school, fourteen-year-old Laurel realizes that she shares her deceased mother's connection with flowers, but as she begins to learn their ancient language and share it with other students, she discovers powers that are beyond her control.

"A delicate sense of magical possibility and reverence for the natural world help elevate White's story from a typical prep-school drama into something more memorable." Publ Wkly

White, Andrea

Surviving Antarctica; reality TV 2083. HarperCollins Publishers 2005 327p hardcover o.p. pa $6.99

Grades: 7 8 9 10 **Fic**

1. Science fiction 2. Antarctica -- Fiction

ISBN 0-06-055454-1; 0-06-055456-8 pa

LC 2004-6249

In the year 2083, five fourteen-year-olds who were deprived by chance of the opportunity to continue their educations reenact Scott's 1910-1913 expedition to the South Pole as contestants on a reality television show, secretly aided by a Department of Entertainment employee

"A real page-turner, this novel will give readers pause as they ponder the ethics of teens risking their lives in adult-contrived situations for the entertainment of the masses." Booklist

Window boy. Bright Sky Press 2008 255p $17.95

Grades: 6 7 8 9 **Fic**

1. School stories 2. Cerebral palsy -- Fiction 3. Imaginary playmates -- Fiction

ISBN 978-1-933979-14-4; 1-933979-14-3

LC 2008-492

After his mother finally convinces the principal of Greenfield Junior High to admit him, twelve-year-old Sam arrives for his first day of school, along with his imaginary friend Winston Churchill, who encourages him to persevere with his cerebral palsy.

"Strong character development is combined with an accurate representation of the lack of educational opportunities for those who were physically and mentally disabled pre-IDEA." SLJ

Windows on the world. Namelos 2011 $18.95; pa $9.95

Grades: 6 7 8 9 **Fic**

1. School stories 2. Science fiction 3. Birds -- Fiction 4. Orphans -- Fiction 5. Time travel -- Fiction

ISBN 978-1-60898-105-2; 1-60898-105-3; 978-1-60898-106-9 pa; 1-60898-106-1 pa

LC 2011003678

In 2083, orphan Shama Katooee, who has just stolen an expensive pet bird, is mysteriously selected to attend the elite Chronos Academy to be trained in the practice of Time-Watch, although she has no idea how or why she has been given this honor.

"The third-person narrative focuses mainly on Shama, with intermittent chapters on Maye Jones in NYC in 2001 and Lt. Bazel. White . . . subtly poses other questions surrounding advancements in technology and capitalism in this well-imagined and disturbing future." Kirkus

White, Ellen Emerson

Long may she reign. Feiwel and Friends 2007 708p $15.95

Grades: 6 7 8 9 10 **Fic**

1. School stories 2. Presidents -- Fiction 3. Post-traumatic stress disorder -- Fiction

ISBN 978-0-312-36767-1; 0-312-36767-8

LC 2007-32635

Meg Powers, daughter of the president of the United States, is recovering from a brutal kidnapping, and in an effort to deal with her horrific experience and her anger at her mother—the president—for not negotiating for her release, Meg decides to go away for her second semester of college, where she encounters even more challenges.

"The hip dialogue will hook teens. . . . Beneath its chick-lit veneer, this book is a thought-provoking read." Voice Youth Advocates

The **President's** daughter. Feiwel and Friends 2008 304p pa $9.99

Grades: 7 8 9 10 **Fic**

1. Moving -- Fiction 2. Politics -- Fiction 3. Washington (D.C.) -- Fiction 4. Mother-daughter relationship -- Fiction

ISBN 0-312-37488-7; 978-0-312-37488-4

LC 2008-6888

First published 1984

Sixteen-year-old Meghan Powers' happy life in Massachusetts changes drastically when her mother, one of the most prestigious senators in the country, becomes the front-runner in the race for United States President.

"Besides offering a solid look at the political system, this [book] has very strong characterizations." Booklist

Other titles about Meg are:
White House autumn (2008)
Long live the queen (2008)
Long may she reign (2007)

White, Kiersten

Paranormalcy. HarperTeen 2010 335p $16.99

Grades: 7 8 9 10 11 12 **Fic**

1. Police -- Fiction 2. Fairies -- Fiction 3. Prophecies -- Fiction 4. Supernatural -- Fiction

ISBN 978-0-06-198584-3; 0-06-198584-3

LC 2010-07027

When a dark prophecy begins to come true, sixteen-year-old Evie of the International Paranormal Containment Agency must not only try to stop it, she must also uncover its connection to herself and the alluring shapeshifter, Lend.

"White shows the technique and polish of a pro in this absorbing romance, which comes closer than most to hitting the Buffy mark. . . . The action is fast; fun and fear are in abundance; and Lend's father is actually a cool grownup." Publ Wkly

Perfect lies; Kiersten White. HarperTeen, an imprint of HarperCollinsPublishers 2014 240 p. (Mind games) (hardcover bdg.) $17.99

Grades: 8 9 10 11 12 **Fic**

1. Sisters -- Fiction 2. Young adult literature 3. Psychic ability -- Fiction

ISBN 0062135848; 9780062135841

LC 2013008056

Written by Kiersten White, this novel is a "sequel to "Mind Games'," describing how "For years, Annie and Fia have been in an endless battle for survival against the Keane Foundation. Now the sisters have found allies who can help them escape. But Annie's visions of the future and Fia's flawless instincts can't always tell them who to trust." (Publisher's note)

"Fia and Annie, sisters with paranormal powers, plot to take down the ruthless Keane Foundation that has controlled them in this breathless sequel to Mind Games (2013)...Suspenseful and smart, this ties up the main story lines while leaving the greater world-building details to the imagination." (Booklist)

Supernaturally. HarperTeen 2011 342p $17.99
Grades: 7 8 9 10 **Fic**

1. Fairies -- Fiction 2. Prophecies -- Fiction 3. Supernatural -- Fiction
ISBN 978-0-06-198586-7; 0-06-198586-4
LC 2010040426

Sixteen-year-old Evie thinks she has left the International Paranormal Containment Agency, and her own paranormal activities, behind her when she is recruited to help at the Agency, where she discovers more about the dark faerie prophecy that threatens her future.

"Evie's voice is the best part of the story, as she balances her supernatural abilities against typical teen concerns and obsessions." Kirkus

White, Ruth

Memories of Summer. Farrar, Straus & Giroux 2000 135p $16
Grades: 7 8 9 10 **Fic**

1. Sisters 2. Mental illness 3. Sisters -- Fiction 4. Mentally ill -- Fiction
ISBN 0-374-34945-2
LC 99-54793

In 1955, thirteen-year-old Lyric finds her whole life changing when her family moves from the hills of Virginia to a town in Michigan and her older sister Summer begins descending into mental illness

"A marvelous recreation of time and place and a poignant story that has much to say about compassion." SLJ

★ A **month** of Sundays. Margaret Ferguson Books/Farrar Straus Giroux 2011 168p $16.99
Grades: 6 7 8 9 **Fic**

1. Sick -- Fiction 2. Family life -- Fiction 3. Country life -- Fiction 4. Christian life -- Fiction
ISBN 978-0-374-39912-2; 0-374-39912-3
LC 2010036311

In the summer of 1956 while her mother is in Florida searching for a job, fourteen-year-old April Garnet Rose, who has never met her father, stays with her terminally ill aunt in Virginia and accompanies her as she visits different churches, looking for God.

"White captures life in small-town America. . . . This heartwarming story has more than a touch of wonder. Expanding one's emotional life . . . is beautifully captured here." Booklist

Whitley, David

The **children** of the lost. Roaring Brook Press 2011 357p $16.99
Grades: 7 8 9 10 **Fic**

1. Fantasy fiction
ISBN 978-1-59643-614-5; 1-59643-614-X
LC 2010-28112

Sequel to: Midnight charter (2009)

Banished from Agora, the ancient city-state where absolutely everything must be bartered, Mark and Lily are happy to find the apparently perfect land of Giseth except that the inhabitants seem fearful, something strange lurks in the surrounding forest, and a mysterious woman keeps appearing in their dreams urging them to find the children of the lost.

This "explores tantalizing new territory and solidifies the Agora Trilogy as one of the more literary ambitious and complex fantasies going." Booklist

Midnight charter. Roaring Brook Press 2009 319p $17.99
Grades: 7 8 9 10 **Fic**

1. Science fiction
ISBN 978-1-59643-381-6; 1-59643-381-7

"Deft world-building and crafty plotting combine for a zinger of an ending that will leave readers poised for book two. Surprisingly sophisticated upper-middle-grade fare, with enough meat to satisfy older readers as well." Kirkus

Followed by: The children of the lost (2011)

Whitman, Emily

Wildwing. Greenwillow Books 2010 359p $16.99
Grades: 7 8 9 10 **Fic**

1. Falcons -- Fiction 2. Time travel -- Fiction 3. Social classes -- Fiction 4. Great Britain -- History -- 1066-1154, Norman period -- Fiction
ISBN 978-0-06-172452-7; 0-06-172452-1
LC 2009-44189

In 1913 London, fifteen-year-old Addy is a lowly servant, but when she gets inside an elevator car in her employer's study, she is suddenly transported to a castle in 1240 and discovers that she is mistaken for the lord's intended bride.

"Whitman populates both of her worlds with vivid, believable characters. . . . This historical novel with a time-travel twist of sci-fi will find an avid readership." SLJ

Whitman, Sylvia

The **milk** of birds; by Sylvia Whitman. 1st ed. Atheneum Books for Young Readers 2013 384 p. (hardcover) $16.99; (paperback) $9.99
Grades: 9 10 11 12 **Fic**

1. Pen pals -- Fiction 2. Friendship -- Fiction 3. Sudan -- History -- Darfur conflict, 2003- -- Fiction 4. Sudan -- Fiction 5. Letters -- Fiction 6. Genocide -- Fiction 7. Refugees -- Fiction 8. Darfur (Sudan) -- Fiction
ISBN 144244682X; 9781442446823; 9781442446830; 9781442446847
LC 2012005594

In this book, "an American teen from Richmond, Va., and a Sudanese teen in Darfur exchange letters. . . . Fourteen-year-old Nawra has been raped, her family murdered and her village burned in Darfur's genocidal war. . . . Nonprofit Save the Girls matches Nawra with American pen pal K.C. Cannelli, an unconventional 14-year-old with an undiagnosed learning disability. . . . As K.C. discovers everything Nawra has endured, she becomes an advocate and fundraiser for Darfur's refugees." (Kirkus Reviews)

Whitney, Daisy

The **Mockingbirds**. Little, Brown 2010 339p $16.99
Grades: 10 11 12 **Fic**

1. School stories 2. Rape -- Fiction 3. Sisters -- Fiction

4. Secret societies -- Fiction
ISBN 978-0-316-09053-7; 0-316-09053-0
LC 2009-51257

When Alex, a junior at an elite preparatory school, realizes that she may have been the victim of date rape, she confides in her roommates and sister who convince her to seek help from a secret society, the Mockingbirds.

"Authentic and illuminating, this strong . . . [title] explores vital teen topics of sex and violence; crime and punishment; ineffectual authority; and the immeasurable, healing influence of friendship and love." Booklist

The **rivals**; by Daisy Whitney. Little, Brown and Co. 2012 346 p. $17.99
Grades: 9 10 11 12 **Fic**

1. Private schools -- Fiction 2. Medication abuse -- Fiction 3. Secret societies -- Fiction 4. Cheating (Education) -- Fiction 5. Teenagers -- Conduct of life -- Fiction 6. Schools -- Fiction 7. Cheating -- Fiction 8. Conduct of life -- Fiction 9. Boarding schools -- Fiction
ISBN 9780316090575
LC 2011019227

This book provides a sequel to Daisy Whitney's 2010 book "The Mockingbirds." Here, "Alex is now the leader of the underground student-run justice system at Themis Academy, a boarding school where adults ignore bullying and reputation is more important than ethics. Themes of truth, power, leadership, and personal responsibility are echoed in the students' reading assignments . . . as the Mockingbirds investigate the source of illegal ADHD drugs on campus, and Alex finds a caring relationship." (Booklist)

When you were here; by Daisy Whitney. Little, Brown and Co. 2013 272 p. $18
Grades: 7 8 9 10 **Fic**

1. Cancer -- Fiction 2. Tokyo (Japan) -- Fiction 3. Mother-son relationship -- Fiction 4. Grief -- Fiction 5. Japan -- Fiction
ISBN 0316209740; 9780316209748
LC 2012031409

"Danny's mother has recently died from cancer, his father died years ago, his estranged sister lives in China, and he and Holland, the love of his life, have broken up. A trip to Japan is enlightening and helps him handle a shocking secret he learns about Holland. The extent of Danny's problems stretches credulity, but readers will be caught up in the drama." (Horn Book)

Whitney, Kim Ablon

The **other** half of life; a novel based on the true story of the MS St. Louis. Alfred A. Knopf 2009 237p $16.99; lib bdg $19.99
Grades: 6 7 8 9 10 **Fic**

1. Jews -- Germany -- Fiction 2. Holocaust, 1933-1945 -- Fiction
ISBN 978-0-375-85219-0; 0-375-85219-0; 978-0-375-95219-7 lib bdg; 0-375-95219-5 lib bdg
LC 2008-38949

In 1939, fifteen-year-old Thomas sails on a German ship bound for Cuba with more than nine hundred German Jews expecting to be granted safe haven in Cuba.

"The characters are intriguing enough, but it's the real-life history that provides the novel's energy." Horn Book Guide

Includes bibliographical references

The **perfect** distance. Knopf 2005 256p hardcover o.p. pa $5.99
Grades: 9 10 11 12 **Fic**

1. Horsemanship -- Fiction 2. Mexican Americans -- Fiction
ISBN 0-375-83243-2; 0-553-49467-8 pa
LC 2005-40726

While competing in the three junior national equitation championships, seventeen-year-old Francie Martinez learns to believe in herself and makes some decisions about the type of person she wants to be

The author "inhabits Francie's character wholly and convincingly and gets the universals of serious competition just right—any athlete will recognize the imperious, unfeeling coach; the snotty front-runner; and the unparalleled thrill of hitting the zone." Booklist

Whittenberg, Allison

Life is fine. Delacorte Press 2008 181p $15.99; lib bdg $18.99
Grades: 8 9 10 11 12 **Fic**

1. Child abuse -- Fiction 2. African Americans -- Fiction 3. Mother-daughter relationship -- Fiction
ISBN 978-0-385-73480-6; 978-0-385-90478-0 lib bdg
LC 2007-27604

With a neglectful mother who has an abusive, live-in boyfriend, life for fifteen-year-old Samara is not fine, but when a substitute teacher walks into class one day and introduces her to poetry, she starts to view life from a different perspective.

"Samara's voice is sharp and convincing." Publ Wkly

Sweet Thang. Delacorte Press 2006 149p $15.95
Grades: 5 6 7 8 **Fic**

1. School stories 2. Family life -- Fiction 3. African Americans -- Fiction
ISBN 0-385-73292-9
LC 2005-03809

In 1975, life is not fair for fourteen-year-old Charmaine Upshaw, who shares a room with her brother, tries to impress a handsome classmate, and acts as caretaker for a rambunctious six-year-old cousin who has taken over the family.

"Whittenberg has created a refreshing cast and a good read." SLJ

Another title about the Upshaw family is:
Hollywood & Maine (2009)

Whyman, Matt

Goldstrike; a thriller. Atheneum Books for Young Readers 2010 262p $16.99
Grades: 7 8 9 10 **Fic**

1. Computer crimes -- Fiction 2. London (England) -- Fiction 3. United States -- Central Intelligence Agency -- Fiction
ISBN 978-1-4169-9510-4; 1-4169-9510-2
LC 2009-17830

Sequel to: Icecore (2007)

After escaping Camp Twilight, eighteen-year-old Carl Hobbes and Beth, his girlfriend, begin a new life in London, England, where he attempts to program Sphynx Cargo's highly intelligent supercomputer to help protect them from the CIA and assassins.

"The action sequences are believable and often realistically brutal, and the climactic battle is intense and entertaining." Publ Wkly

Icecore; a Carl Hobbes thriller. Atheneum Books for Young Readers 2007 307p $16.99; pa $8.99
Grades: 7 8 9 10 **Fic**

1. Torture -- Fiction 2. Prisoners -- Fiction 3. Arctic regions -- Fiction 4. Military bases -- Fiction 5. Computer crimes -- Fiction

ISBN 978-1-4169-4907-7; 1-4169-4907-0; 978-1-4169-8960-8 pa; 1-4169-8960-9 pa

LC 2007-02674

Seventeen-year-old Englishman Carl Hobbes meant no harm when he hacked into Fort Knox's security system, but at Camp Twilight in the Arctic Circle, known as the Guantanamo Bay of the north, he is tortured to reveal information about a conspiracy of which he was never a part.

"Powered by a fast-paced narrative, this exploration of numerous timely themes . . . gives the eminently readable adventure a degree of depth." Publ Wkly

Followed by: Goldstrike (2010)

Wiggins, Bethany

Cured. by Bethany Wiggins. Bloomsbury/Walker. 2014 320p $17.99
Grades: 7 8 9 10 11 12 **Fic**

1. Brothers and sisters — Fiction; 2. Science fiction; 3. Survival — Fiction; 4. Twins — Fiction; 5. Voyages and travels — Fiction

ISBN: 0802734200; 9780802734204

LC 2013024935

This sequel to Stung is a "reimagining of our world after an environmental catastrophe. . . . Now that Fiona Tarsis and her twin brother, Jonah, are no longer beasts, they set out to find their mother. . . . Heading for a safe settlement rumored to be in Wyoming . . . they are attacked by raiders. Luckily, they find a new ally in Kevin, who saves them and leads them to safety in his underground shelter. But the more they get to know Kevin, the more they suspect he has ties to the raiders." (Publisher's note)

"While the Mad Max–esque raiders and zombielike beasts (children transformed into murderous monsters by their vaccines against the bee flu) seem to be standard post-apocalyptic fare, Wiggins poignantly raises issues of transformation and redemption." Kirkus

Stung; Bethany Wiggins. Walker & Company 2013 304 p. (hardcover) $17.99
Grades: 7 8 9 10 11 12 **Fic**

1. Science fiction 2. Epidemics -- Fiction 3. Survival -- Fiction

ISBN 0802734189; 9780802734181

LC 2012027183

In this novel, by Bethany Wiggins, "a worldwide pandemic occurred and the government tried to bio-engineer a cure. Only the solution was deadlier than the original problem-the vaccination turned people into ferocious, deadly beasts who were branded as a warning to un-vaccinated survivors. Key people needed to rebuild society are protected from disease and beasts inside a fortress-like wall. But Fiona has awakened branded, alone-and on the wrong side of the wall." (Publisher's note)

"Wiggins. . . muses on the dangers of science and medicine and deftly maps out the chain of events that has led to catastrophe, creating a violent world vastly different from ours but still recognizable. With a stirring conclusion and space for a sequel, it's an altogether captivating story." Kirkus

Wignall, K. J.

Blood; [by] K. J. Wignall. Egmont USA 2011 264p (Mercian triology) $16.99; ebook $16.99
Grades: 7 8 9 10 11 12 **Fic**

1. Vampires -- Fiction 2. Good and evil -- Fiction

ISBN 978-1-60684-220-1; 1-60684-220-X; 978-1-60684-258-4 ebook; 1-60684-258-7 ebook

LC 2011005899

A centuries-old vampire wakes up in the modern day to find he is being hunted by an unknown enemy, and begins to uncover the secrets of his origin and the path of his destiny.

Wignall "develops what could have been yet another vampire story into a promising series opener with a sophisticated plot and elegant prose." Booklist

Wild, K.

Fight game; [by] Kate Wild. Chicken House/Scholastic 2007 279p $16.99
Grades: 7 8 9 10 **Fic**

1. Science fiction 2. Spies -- Fiction 3. Martial arts -- Fiction 4. Genetic engineering -- Fiction

ISBN 978-0-439-87175-4; 0-439-87175-1

LC 2006-32889

Fifteen-year-old Freedom Smith is a fighter, just like all of his relatives who have the "Hercules gene," which leads him to a choice between being jailed for attempted murder or working with a covert law enforcement agency to break up a mysterious, illegal fight ring.

"Intriguing supporting characters pepper Wild's debut novel and bolster an already strong portagonist. . . . Wild's story pulsates with raw energy." Voice Youth Advocates

Wilhelm, Doug

Falling. Farrar, Straus and Giroux 2007 241p $17
Grades: 8 9 10 11 12 **Fic**

1. School stories 2. Vermont -- Fiction 3. Basketball -- Fiction 4. Drug abuse -- Fiction 5. Family life -- Fiction

ISBN 978-0-374-32251-9; 0-374-32251-1

LC 2006-45293

Fifteen-year-old Matt's life has been turned upside-down, first when the brother he idolizes turns to drugs, then when a visit to a chat room leads him to a classmate, Katie, who he likes very much but cannot trust with his family secret.

"The addiction scenes are stark, and the story holds surprises to the end." Booklist

Wilkins, Ebony Joy

Sellout. Scholastic Press 2010 267p $17.99
Grades: 7 8 9 10 **Fic**

1. Social classes -- Fiction 2. African Americans -- Fiction
ISBN 978-0-545-10928-4; 0-545-10928-0

NaTasha loves her life of affluence in Park Adams, but her grandmother fears she has lost touch with her roots and whisks her off to Harlem, where NaTasha meets rough, streetwise girls at a crisis center and finds the courage to hold her own against them.

"Some elements of the story tie up too easily—NaTasha's greatest tormentors warm up to her a bit too quickly to be believed—but the message of staying true to oneself shines through." SLJ

Wilkinson, Lili

Pink. HarperTeen 2011 310p $16.99
Grades: 7 8 9 10 11 12 **Fic**

1. School stories 2. Theater -- Fiction 3. Australia -- Fiction 4. Homosexuality -- Fiction 5. Identity (Psychology) -- Fiction
ISBN 978-0-06-192653-2; 0-06-192653-1
LC 2010-9389

Sixteen-year-old Ava does not know who she is or where she belongs, but when she tries out a new personality—and sexual orientation—at a different school, her edgy girlfriend, potential boyfriend, and others are hurt by her lack of honesty.

"The novel is in turn laugh-out-loud funny, endearing, and heartbreaking as Ava repeatedly steps into teenage social land mines—with unexpected results. Because Wilkinson doesn't rely on stereotypes, the characters are well-developed, and interactions between them feel genuine." Voice Youth Advocates

Wilks, Mike

Mirrorscape. Egmont USA 2009 340p $16.99; lib bdg $19.99
Grades: 6 7 8 9 **Fic**

1. Fantasy fiction 2. Adventure fiction 3. Art -- Fiction 4. Artists -- Fiction 5. Apprentices -- Fiction
ISBN 978-1-60684-008-5; 1-60684-008-8; 978-1-60684-040-5 lib bdg; 1-60684-040-1 lib bdg
LC 2009-16245

In a world where all pleasures are severely restricted, Melkin Womper is apprenticed to a master painter where he discovers the Mirrorscape, a world inside paintings, and becomes entangled in a war between the restrictive Fifth Mystery and the rebels fighting to stop them

"In this innovative debut, readers will find an imaginative fantasy devoid of typical wizardry." Booklist

Willey, Margaret

Beetle Boy; by Margaret Willey. Carolrhoda Lab. 2014 208p $17.95
Grades: 8 9 10 11 **Fic**

1. Dating (Social customs) — Fiction; 2. Emotional problems — Fiction; 3. Family problems — Fiction; 4. Father-son relationship — Fiction; 5. Child authors — Fiction
ISBN: 1467726397; 9781467726399
LC 2013036853

Charlie Porter "didn't intend to become famous, but at age seven, Charlie began telling a story about a talking beetle in order to stop his father from crying. Soon the story becomes a book, which becomes a long series of events, festivals, and marketing campaigns. . . . Now 18, Charlie is forced to reconcile his traumatic past and forge ahead building normal relationships." SLJ

"Willey takes readers along on Charlie's painful journey back to physical and emotional health via a meandering timeline of flashbacks, dreams and wrenching conversations, skillfully weaving together the bits and pieces of his life. Innovative use of type brings an immediacy to Charlie's struggles as he slowly looks the truth--and his brother--squarely in the face." Kirkus

A **summer** of silk moths. Flux 2009 246p il map pa $9.95
Grades: 7 8 9 10 **Fic**

1. Moths -- Fiction 2. Uncles -- Fiction 3. Fathers -- Fiction 4. Michigan -- Fiction
ISBN 978-0-73871-540-7; 0-73871-540-9
LC 2009-19681

A seventeen-year-old boy and girl learn long-held secrets about their pasts as they overcome their initial antipathy toward one another on a Michigan nature preserve dedicated to her dead father.

"A thoughtful, complex and moving story about loss and discovery of identity, love and the ability to change and the restorative powers of nature. . . . The believable characters and the insights into their awakening emotional lives will carry readers along." Kirkus

Williams, Alex

The **deep** freeze of Bartholomew Tullock. Philomel Books 2008 298p $16.99
Grades: 6 7 8 9 **Fic**

1. Adventure fiction 2. Dogs -- Fiction 3. Weather -- Fiction 4. Inventions -- Fiction
ISBN 978-0-399-25185-6; 0-399-25185-5
LC 2008-02663

Published in the United Kingdom with title: The storm maker

In a land of never-ending snow, Rufus Breeze and his mother must protect the family home from being seized by tyrant Bartholomew Tullock, while sister Madeline and her father, an inventor of fans that are now useless, join forces with a ne'er-do-well adventurer and his blue-haired terrier, hoping to make some money.

This offers "originality of setting, a full complement of truly heinous villains, insurmountable dangers cleverly surmounted, ingenious contraptions, and plucky, appealing underdogs. . . . William handles his material with fizz and verve." Bull Cent Child Books

Williams, Carol Lynch

The **chosen** one. St. Martin's Griffin 2009 213p $16.95
Grades: 7 8 9 10 **Fic**

1. Cults -- Fiction 2. Polygamy -- Fiction 3. Family

life -- Fiction
ISBN 978-0-312-55511-5; 0-312-55511-3
LC 2009-4800

In a polygamous cult in the desert, Kyra, not yet fourteen, sees being chosen to be the seventh wife of her uncle as just punishment for having read books and kissed a boy, in violation of Prophet Childs' teachings, and is torn between facing her fate and running away from all that she knows and loves.

"This book is a highly emotional, terrifying read. It is not measured or objective. Physical abuse, fear, and even murder are constants. It is a girl-in-peril story, and as such, it is impossible to put down and holds tremendous teen appeal." Voice Youth Advocates

Glimpse. Simon & Schuster Books for Young Readers 2010 484p $16.99
Grades: 7 8 9 10 **Fic**

1. Novels in verse 2. Sisters -- Fiction 3. Suicide -- Fiction 4. Child sexual abuse -- Fiction 5. Mother-daughter relationship -- Fiction
ISBN 978-1-4169-9730-6; 1-4169-9730-X
LC 2009-41147

Living with their mother who earns money as a prostitute, two sisters take care of each other and when the older one attempts suicide, the younger one tries to uncover the reason.

"Williams leans hard on her free-verse line breaks for drama . . . and it works. A page-turner for Ellen Hopkins fans." Kirkus

Miles from ordinary; a novel. St. Martin's Press 2011 197p $16.99
Grades: 7 8 9 10 **Fic**

1. Family life -- Fiction 2. Mental illness -- Fiction 3. Mother-daughter relationship -- Fiction
ISBN 978-0-312-55512-2; 0-312-55512-1
LC 2010-40324

As her mother's mental illness spins terrifyingly out of control, thirteen-year-old Lacey must face the truth of what life with her mother means for both of them.

"The author has crafted both a riveting, unusual suspense tale and an absolutely convincing character in Lacey. The book truly is miles from ordinary, in the very best way. Outstanding." Kirkus

Waiting; Carol Lynch Williams. Simon and Schuster Books For Young Readers 2012 335 p.
Grades: 9 10 11 12 **Fic**

1. Young adult literature 2. Siblings 3. Bereavement 4. Grief -- Fiction 5. Family problems -- Fiction 6. Brothers and sisters -- Fiction
ISBN 1442443537; 9781442443532; 9781442443556
LC 2011043898

This young adult novel by Carol Lynch Williams portrays "a teen [who] struggles to rediscover love and find redemption . . . [a]fter her brother's death. . . . Growing up, London and Zach were as close as could be. And then Zach dies, and the family is gutted. London's father is distant. Her mother won't speak. The days are filled with what-ifs and whispers: Was it London's fault? Alone and adrift, London finds herself torn between her brother's best friend and the handsome new boy in town as she struggles to find herself—and ultimately redemption." (Publisher's note)

Williams, Gabrielle

★ **Beatle** meets Destiny. Marshall Cavendish 2010 342p $17.99
Grades: 8 9 10 11 12 **Fic**

1. Love stories 2. Twins -- Fiction 3. Siblings -- Fiction 4. Australia -- Fiction 5. Family life -- Fiction 6. Dating (Social customs) -- Fiction
ISBN 978-0-7614-5723-7

When superstitious eighteen-year-old John "Beatle" Lennon, who is dating the best friend of his twin sister, meets Destiny McCartney, their instant rapport and shared quirkiness make it seem that their fate is written in the stars.

"Clever, amusing, yet surprisingly thoughtful, the book will appeal to readers looking for something a little different." Publ Wkly

Williams, Kathryn

Pizza, love, and other stuff that made me famous; Kathryn Williams. Henry Holt 2012 231 p. (hc) $16.99
Grades: 7 8 9 10 **Fic**

1. Cooking -- Fiction 2. Reality television programs -- Fiction 3. Restaurants -- Fiction 4. Interpersonal relations -- Fiction 5. Competition (Psychology) -- Fiction 6. Television -- Production and direction -- Fiction
ISBN 0805092854; 9780805092851
LC 2011034053

In this young adult novel by Kathryn Williams "Sixteen-year-old Sophie Nicolaides . . . audition[s] for a new reality show, 'Teen Test Kitchen.'. . . [T]he prize includes a full scholarship to one of America's finest culinary schools and a summer in Napa, California, not to mention fame. Once on set, Sophie immediately finds herself in the thick of the drama -- including a secret burn book, cutthroat celebrity judges, and a very cute French chef." (Publisher's note)

Williams, Katie

Absent; by Katie Williams. Chronicle Books 2013 288 p. (hardcover) $16.99
Grades: 9 10 11 12 **Fic**

1. Ghost stories 2. Suicide -- Fiction 3. High school students -- Fiction 4. Drug abuse -- Fiction 5. High schools -- Fiction
ISBN 0811871509; 9780811871501
LC 2012033600

In this novel, by Katie Williams, "when seventeen-year-old Paige dies in a freak fall from the roof . . . , her spirit is bound to the grounds of her high school. . . . But when Paige hears the rumor that her death wasn't an accident--that she supposedly jumped on purpose--she can't bear it. Then Paige discovers . . . she can possess living people when they think of her. . . . Maybe . . . she can get to the most popular girl in school and stop the rumors once and for all." (Publisher's note)

"The mystery is solid, but it is complicated; funny Paige herself sets the story apart." Booklist

The **space** between trees. Chronicle Books 2010 274p $17.99
Grades: 8 9 10 11 12 **Fic**

1. School stories 2. Homicide -- Fiction
ISBN 978-0-8118-7175-4; 0-8118-7175-4
LC 2009-48561

When the body of a classmate is discovered in the woods, sixteen-year-old Evie's lies wind up involving her with the girl's best friend, trying to track down the killer.

"Evie's raw honesty and the choices she makes make for difficult reading, but also a darkly beautiful, emotionally honest story of personal growth." Publ Wkly

Williams, Laura E.

Slant; [by] Laura E. Williams. Milkweed Editions 2008 149p $16.95; pa $6.95
Grades: 5 6 7 8 9 **Fic**

1. Mothers -- Fiction 2. Adoption -- Fiction 3. Friendship -- Fiction 4. Prejudices -- Fiction 5. Plastic surgery -- Fiction 6. Korean Americans -- Fiction
ISBN 978-1-57131-681-3; 1-57131-681-7; 978-1-57131-682-0 pa; 1-57131-682-5 pa
LC 2008007093

Thirteen-year-old Lauren, a Korean-American adoptee, is tired of being called "slant" and "gook," and longs to have plastic surgery on her eyes, but when her father finds out about her wish—and a long-kept secret about her mother's death is revealed—Lauren starts to question some of her own assumptions

"The characters are exceptionally well drawn, and the friendship between Julie and Lauren is not only believable, featuring humor, conflict, and true wit, but also captures both girls' gains in maturity." SLJ

Williams, Lori Aurelia

★ **When** Kambia Elaine flew in from Neptune. Simon & Schuster 2000 246p hardcover o.p. pa $10
Grades: 7 8 9 10 **Fic**

1. Houston (Tex.) -- Fiction 2. African Americans -- Fiction
ISBN 0-689-82468-8; 0-689-84593-6 pa
LC 99-65154

"Shayla Dubois lives in a Houston neighborhood known as the Bottom, where life is colorful but never easy. She wants only two things out of life: to become a writer and to have a nice, peaceful home. Instead, her life has been turned upside down. Shayla's mama kicked her sister, Tia, out of the house for messing around with an older guy, and months later Tia still hasn't come home. Shayla's father, Mr. Anderson Fox, has rolled back into town and has been spending a lot of time at the house with Mama. And Shayla still doesn't know what to make of her strange new neighbor, Kambia Elaine." Publisher's note

"This is a strong and disturbing novel, told in beautiful language. Teens will find it engrossing." SLJ

Williams, Michael

Now is the time for running. Little, Brown 2011 233p $17.99
Grades: 6 7 8 9 10 **Fic**

1. Soccer -- Fiction 2. Brothers -- Fiction 3. Refugees -- Fiction 4. Zimbabwe -- Fiction 5. Homeless persons -- Fiction 6. People with mental disabilites -- Fiction
ISBN 978-0-316-07790-3; 0-316-07790-9
LC 2010043460

"There is plenty of material to captivate readers: fast-paced soccer matches every bit as tough as the players; the determination of Deo and his fellow refugees to survive unthinkably harsh conditions; and raw depictions of violence. . . . But it's the tender relationship between Deo and Innocent, along with some heartbreaking twists of fate, that will endure in readers' minds." Publ Wkly

Williams, Sarah DeFord

★ **Palace** beautiful. G.P. Putnam's Sons 2010 232p $16.99
Grades: 6 7 8 9 **Fic**

1. Moving -- Fiction 2. Diaries -- Fiction 3. Influenza -- Fiction 4. Family life -- Fiction
ISBN 978-0-399-25298-3; 0-399-25298-3
LC 2009-03213

After her move in 1985 to Salt Lake City, thirteen-year-old Sadie finds a journal in a hidey-hole in the attic, and along with her sister and new friend she reads about the influenza epidemic of 1918.

"Williams does a super job with the characters in this beautifully written book, and it is satisfying to see how they develop." SLJ

Williams, Sean

Twinmaker; by Sean Williams. HarperCollins 2013 352 p. (hardcover bdg.) $17.99
Grades: 9 10 11 12 **Fic**

1. Fantasy fiction 2. Conspiracies -- Fiction 3. Teleportation -- Fiction 4. Science fiction 5. Friendship -- Fiction 6. Best friends -- Fiction 7. Space and time -- Fiction
ISBN 0062203215; 9780062203212
LC 2012043498

In this book, "thanks to D-mat technology, teen Clair" and her friends "can jump around the globe in a matter of minutes simply by entering a booth. . . . They initially dismiss Improvement, a way to transform yourself through a series of jumps, but then Libby uses Improvement to remove her permanent birthmark, and as the disturbing consequences roll out, Clair digs for answers." (Booklist)

Williams, Susan

Wind rider. HarperCollins 2006 309p $16.99
Grades: 7 8 9 10 **Fic**

1. Horses -- Fiction 2. Sex role -- Fiction 3. Prehistoric peoples -- Fiction
ISBN 978-0-06-087236-6; 0-06-087236-5; 978-0-06-087237-3 lib bdg; 0-06-087237-3 lib bdg
LC 2005028595

Fern, a teenager living in 4000 B.C., defies the expectations of her people by displaying a unique and new ability to tame horses and by also questioning many of the traditional activities of women.

"Fern aggressively strains against her mother's expectations and her society's traditional gender roles, and it is these timeless struggles, narrated in Fern's poetic voice, that transform Williams' impressively researched details into a vividly imagined, wholly captivating world." Booklist

Williams, Suzanne

Bull rider; [by] Suzanne Morgan Williams. Margaret K. McElderry Books 2009 241p $16.99

Grades: 7 8 9 10 **Fic**

1. Brothers -- Fiction 2. Veterans -- Fiction 3. Bull riding -- Fiction 4. Wounds and injuries -- Fiction

ISBN 978-1-4169-6130-7; 1-4169-6130-5

LC 2007-52518

When his older brother, a bull-riding champion, returns from the Iraq War partially paralyzed, fourteen-year-old Cam takes a break from skateboarding to enter a bull-riding contest, in hopes of winning the $15,000 prize and motivating his depressed brother to continue with his rehabilitation.

"The mix of wild macho action with family anguish and tenderness will grab teens. . . . [This is a] powerful contemporary story of family, community, and work." Booklist

Williams-Garcia, Rita

★ **Jumped**. HarperTeen 2009 169p $16.99; lib bdg $17.89

Grades: 8 9 10 11 12 **Fic**

1. School stories 2. Bullies -- Fiction

ISBN 978-0-06-076091-5; 0-06-076091-5; 978-0-06-076092-2 lib bdg; 0-06-076092-3 lib bdg

LC 2008-22381

The lives of Leticia, Dominique, and Trina are irrevocably intertwined through the course of one day in an urban high school after Leticia overhears Dominique's plans to beat up Trina and must decide whether or not to get involved.

"In alternating chapters narrated by Leticia, Trina, and Dominique, Williams-Garcia has given her characters strong, individual voices that ring true to teenage speech, and she lets them make their choices without judgment or moralizing." SLJ

★ **Like** sisters on the homefront. Lodestar Bks. 1995 165p hardcover o.p. pa $5.99

Grades: 7 8 9 10 **Fic**

1. Family life -- Fiction 2. Teenage mothers -- Fiction 3. African Americans -- Fiction

ISBN 0-525-67465-9; 0-14-038561-4 pa

LC 95-3690

"It's bad enough that 14-year-old Gayle has one baby, but when she becomes pregnant again by another boy, Mama's had enough. She takes Gayle for an abortion and then ships her and her baby south to stay with religious relatives. . . . With the help of her dying great-grandmother, who leaves Gayle the family's African-American oral tradition, she begins to mature and understand her place in the family and her future." Child Book Rev Serv

"Beautifully written, the text captures the cadence and rhythm of New York street talk and the dilemma of being poor, black, and uneducated. This is a gritty, realistic, well-told story." SLJ

No laughter here. HarperCollins 2004 133p $15.99; lib bdg $16.89

Grades: 7 8 9 10 **Fic**

1. Friendship -- Fiction 2. African Americans -- Fiction 3. Female circumcision -- Fiction

ISBN 0-688-16247-9; 0-688-16248-7 lib bdg

LC 2003-9331

In Queens, New York, ten-year-old Akilah is determined to find out why her closest friend, Victoria, is silent and withdrawn after returning from a trip to her homeland, Nigeria.

This is a "disturbing and poignant coming-of-age novel. . . . This contemporary tale about the ancient rite of female circumcision will no doubt leave an indelible mark on preteens." Publ Wkly

Williamson, Jill

By darkness hid. Marcher Lord Press 2009 490p map (Blood of kings) $14.99

Grades: 7 8 9 10 **Fic**

1. Fantasy fiction 2. Gifted children -- Fiction 3. Knights and knighthood -- Fiction

ISBN 978-0-9821049-5-8; 0-9821049-5-2

"With no family, Achan Cham is marked as a stray and lives the brutal life of a slave. When he is lucky enough to be chosen to begin training as a Kingsguard Knight, his life changes completely, but he is left to wonder if it is for the better. . . . Wonderfully written with a superb plot, this book is a sure-fire hit with almost any reader. . . . The novel is a solid choice for any collection." Voice Youth Advocates

Captives. Zondervan 2013 415 p. $9.99

Grades: 9 10 11 12 **Fic**

1. Dystopian fiction 2. Kidnapping -- Fiction

ISBN 0310724228; 1480604100; 9780310724223; 9781480604100

In this dystopian novel, a pandemic decades earlier in the Safe Lands "has made reproduction problematic. Consequently, the state abducts uninfected young outsiders for breeding purposes." One such kidnapped is Jem, fiancée of eighteen-year-old Levi, who plans to risk everything to rescue her. (Booklist)

"Well-observed details skewer today's materialistic and superficial values. ...The biblical references can be too explicit, but that's not a knock on the message, which is important and worth discussing. Ultimately, the multilayered, futuristic narrative should intrigue fans of sf." Booklist

To darkness fled. Marcher Lord Press 2010 680p map (Blood of kings) pa $17.99

Grades: 7 8 9 10 **Fic**

1. Fantasy fiction 2. Knights and knighthood -- Fiction

ISBN 978-0-9825987-0-2; 0-9825987-0-X

"Achan, Vrell, and the Kingsguard Knights have fled into Darkness to escape the wrath of the former prince. They head for Ice Island to rescue two of Sir Gavin's colleagues who were falsely imprisoned years ago. Darkness is growing and only one man can push it back. Achan wanted freedom, not a crown. His true identity has bound him more than ever." Publisher's note

"Once again the superb writing enhances the thought-provoking story, making this a package too good to miss. . . . Reading this will certainly leave the reader anxiously awaiting the next installment." Voice Youth Advocates

Willis, Cynthia Chapman

Buck fever. Feiwel and Friends 2009 228p $16.99

Grades: 7 8 9 10 **Fic**

1. Artists -- Fiction 2. Hunting -- Fiction 3. Siblings -- Fiction 4. Family life -- Fiction 5. Father-son relationship -- Fiction

ISBN 978-0-312-38297-1; 0-312-38297-9

LC 2008034748

Twelve-year-old Joey and his fifteen-year-old sister Philly relate their experiences trying to cope in a family already strained by the mother's extended travel, and pushed further apart by the father's disappointment that Joey is more interested in drawing deer than hunting them.

"The quietness of nature and small-town life is wonderfully reflected in Willis' patient and artful prose, and every hunting detail feels authentic. . . . An unusually sensitive and reflective boy-centric book." Booklist

Wilson, Diane L.

Black storm comin' Margaret K. McElderry Books 2005 295p $17.99

Grades: 7 8 9 10 **Fic**

1. Pony express -- Fiction 2. Racially mixed people -- Fiction 3. Frontier and pioneer life -- Fiction

ISBN 0-689-87137-6; 0-689-87138-2

LC 2004-9438

Twelve-year-old Colton, son of a black mother and a white father, takes a job with the Pony Express in 1860 after his father abandons the family on their California-bound wagon train, and risks his life to deliver an important letter that may affect the growing conflict between the North and South.

"Wilson masterfully creates a multidimensional character in Colton. . . . Readers will absorb greater lessons as they become engrossed in the excitement, beauty, and terror of Colton's journey to California and manhood." Booklist

Firehorse. Margaret K. McElderry Books 2006 325p $16.95

Grades: 7 8 9 10 **Fic**

1. Arson -- Fiction 2. Horses -- Fiction 3. Sex role -- Fiction 4. Family life -- Fiction 5. Boston (Mass.) -- Fiction 6. Veterinary medicine -- Fiction

ISBN 1-4169-1551-6; 978-1-4169-1551-5

LC 2005-30785

Spirited fifteen-year-old horse lover Rachel Selby determines to become a veterinarian, despite the opposition of her rigid father, her proper mother, and the norms of Boston in 1872, while that city faces a serial arsonist and an epidemic spreading through its firehorse population.

"Wilson paces the story well, with tension building. . . . The novel's finest achievement, though, is the convincing depiction of family dynamics in an era when men ruled the household and and women, who had few opportunities, folded their dreams and put them away with the linens they embroidered." Booklist

Wilson, Jacqueline

Kiss. Roaring Brook Press 2010 248p $16.99

Grades: 7 8 9 10 **Fic**

1. Friendship -- Fiction

ISBN 978-1-59643-242-0; 1-59643-242-X

"Sylvie, 14, has always assumed she would marry her best friend, Carl, but lately he has been distant and doesn't even seem interested in their secret fantasy, Glassworld. When a game of spin the bottle results in Carl kissing Sylvie's new friend, Miranda, and refusing to kiss her, Sylvie begins to doubt her attractiveness. But when Carl suddenly insists on including his new friend, Paul, on all their outings, especially his birthday party, Sylvie is even more confused. . . . With sharply drawn characters, Wilson handles the confusion and angst of teen love and sexuality with careful sensitivity." SLJ

Wilson, John

And in the morning. Kids Can Press 2003 198p $16.95

Grades: 7 8 9 10 **Fic**

1. World War, 1914-1918 -- Fiction

ISBN 1-55337-400-2

"Jim Hay, 16, is caught up in the patriotic fervor sweeping across Scotland as the British troops prepare to enter World War I. . . . His father is killed in action and 10 days later his mother dies from shock and grief. Within weeks, Jim has signed up and is soon in the trenches. . . . A compelling, fascinating, and ultimately disturbing book that is not to be missed." SLJ

Ghost moon. Orca 2011 (Desert legends trilogy) 172p pa $12.95

Grades: 6 7 8 9 **Fic**

1. Outlaws 2. Frontier and pioneer life -- Fiction

ISBN 978-1-55469-879-0; 1-55469-879-0

"A young wanderer lands in the middle of New Mexico's Lincoln County War. . . . 16-year-old James Doolen falls in with Bill Bonney (not yet known as 'Billy the Kid') a charming but decidedly mercurial teenager who hares off on a vicious killing spree after their new boss, John Tunstall, is murdered by a rival merchant's gang of hired gunmen. . . . Action fans will thrill to the gunplay and other dangers. James' conflicting feelings about his archetypically dangerous friend . . . introduce thought provoking elements. A tale of the Old West with a sturdy historical base and nary a dull moment." Kirkus

Victorio's war; John Wilson. Orca Book Publishers 2012 157p (paperback) $12.95

Grades: 6 7 8 9 **Fic**

1. Western stories 2. Historical fiction 3. Biographical fiction

ISBN 9781554698820 pa; 9781554698837 (pdf); 9781554698844 (epub)

LC 2011942580

In this historical novel, by John Wilson, after "taking up a new job scouting for a troop of Buffalo Soldiers, Jim Doolen finds himself caught between friends in the military and friends riding with the Apaches they are chasing. . . . He is saved by his mystic old mentor Too-ah-yay-say from being killed . . . and held captive until a final massacre by Mexican soldiers." (Kirkus)

Wilson, Martin

★ **What** they always tell us. Delacorte Press 2008 293p $15.99; lib bdg $18.99

Grades: 9 10 11 12 **Fic**

1. School stories 2. Alabama -- Fiction 3. Brothers -- Fiction 4. Homosexuality -- Fiction

ISBN 978-0-385-73507-0; 0-385-73507-3; 978-0-385-90500-8 lib bdg; 0-385-90500-9 lib bdg

LC 2007-30269

Sixteen-year-old Alex feels so disconnected from his friends that he starts his junior year at a Tuscaloosa, Alabama, high school by attempting suicide, but soon, a friend of his older brother draws him into cross-country running and a new understanding of himself.

This "novel does an excellent job of showing the tension with which siblings deal on a daily basis. He also does a great job of exploring controversial issues, such as suicide and homosexuality. . . . Public and school libraries should seriously consider adding this book to their shelves." Voice Youth Advocates

Wilson, N. D.

★ The **dragon's** tooth; [by] N. D. Wilson. Random House 2011 485p (Ashtown burials) $16.99; lib bdg $19.99; e-book $16.99

Grades: 5 6 7 8 **Fic**

1. Fantasy fiction 2. Magic -- Fiction 3. Siblings -- Fiction 4. Secret societies -- Fiction

ISBN 978-0-375-86439-1; 0-375-86439-3; 978-0-375-96439-8 lib bdg; 0-375-96439-8 lib bdg; 978-0-375-89572-2 e-book

LC 2009038651

When their parents' seedy old motel burns down on the same night they are visited by a strange man covered in skeleton tattoos, Cyrus, Antigone, and their brother Daniel are introduced to an ancient secret society, and discover that they have an important role in keeping it alive.

"This fast-paced fantasy quickly draws readers in to its alternate reality. . . . Allusions to mythology and complex character development . . . make Wilson's first in a proposed series a gem." Booklist

Wilson, Nancy Hope

Mountain pose. Farrar, Straus & Giroux 2001 233p $17

Grades: 5 6 7 8 **Fic**

1. Wills 2. Diaries -- Fiction 3. Grandmothers -- Fiction

ISBN 0-374-35078-7

LC 00-57269

When twelve-year-old Ellie inherits an old Vermont farm from her cruel and heartless grandmother Aurelia, she reads a set of diaries written by an ancestor and discovers secrets from the past

"Beautifully written and suspenseful, this novel explores the many emotions associated with the tragedy of spousal and child abuse." Voice Youth Advocates

Winston, Sherri

The **Kayla** chronicles; a novel. Little, Brown 2007 188p hardcover o.p. pa $7.99

Grades: 6 7 8 9 10 **Fic**

1. School stories 2. Dancers -- Fiction 3. Journalism -- Fiction 4. African Americans -- Fiction

ISBN 978-0-316-11430-1; 0-316-11430-8; 978-0-316-11431-8 pa; 0-316-11431-6 pa

LC 2006-933219

Kayla transforms herself from mild-mannered journalist to hot-trotting dance diva in order to properly investigate her high school's dance team, and has a hard time remaining true to her real self while in the role.

"Few recent novels for younger YAs mesh levity and substance this successfully." Booklist

Winters, Cat

★ **In** the shadow of blackbirds; Cat Winters. Amulet Books 2013 400 p. $16.95

Grades: 8 9 10 11 12 **Fic**

1. Occult fiction 2. Historical fiction 3. Ghosts -- Fiction 4. Spiritualism -- Fiction 5. World War, 1914-1918 -- Fiction 6. Influenza Epidemic, 1918-1919 -- Fiction 7. San Diego (Calif.) -- History -- 20th century -- Fiction

ISBN 141970530X; 9781419705304

LC 2012039262

William C. Morris Honor Book (2014)

In this book, sixteen-year-old Mary Shelley Black lives in 1918. "With WWI raging on and Mary's father on trial for treason, she goes to live with her Aunt Eva in San Diego, Calif. . . . Grieving for her childhood beau Stephen, who died while fighting overseas with the Army, Mary goes outside during a thunderstorm and is struck dead by lightning—for a few minutes. When Mary comes to, she discovers she can communicate with the dead, including Stephen." (Publishers Weekly)

"Winters strikes just the right balance between history and ghost story . . . . Vintage photographs contribute to the authenticity of the atmospheric and nicely paced storytelling." Kirkus

Wise, Tama

Street dreams. Bold Strokes Books 2012 264 p. $13.95

Grades: 9 10 11 12 **Fic**

1. Hip-hop culture -- Fiction 2. Gay men -- Fiction 3. Street life -- Fiction 4. Graffiti -- Fiction

ISBN 1602826501; 9781602826502

LC 2011279902

In this novel by Tama Wise "Tyson Rua has more than his fair share of problems growing up in South Auckland. . . . Now Tyson's fallen in love at first sight. Only thing is, it's another guy. Living life on the sidelines of the local hip-hop scene, Tyson finds that to succeed in becoming a local graffiti artist or in getting the man of his dreams, he's going to have to get a whole lot more involved. And that means more problems." (Publisher's note)

Wiseman, Eva

Puppet; a novel. Tundra Books 2009 243p $17.95

Grades: 7 8 9 10 11 12 **Fic**

1. Prejudices -- Fiction 2. Jews -- Hungary -- Fiction

ISBN 978-0-88776-828-6; 0-88776-828-8

"Times are hard in Julie Vamosi's Hungarian village in the late nineteenth-century, and the townspeople . . . blame the Jews. After Julie's best friend, Esther, . . . disappears, the rumor spreads that the Jews cut her throat and drained her blood to drink with their Passover matzos. . . . Based on the records of a trial in 1883, this searing novel dramatizes virulent anti-Semitism from the viewpoint of a Christian child. . . . The climax is electrifying." Booklist

Wiseman, Rosalind

Boys, girls, and other hazardous materials. Putnam 2010 282p $17.99
Grades: 8 9 10 11 12 **Fic**

1. School stories
ISBN 978-0-399-247965; 0-399-24796-3
LC 2009-18446

Transferring to a new high school, freshman Charlotte "Charlie" Healey faces tough choices as she tries to shed her "mean girl" image.

Wiseman "succeeds in delivering realistic, likable characters whose challenges and mistakes are all too relatable." Bull Cent Child Books

Wisler, G. Clifton

Caleb's choice. Lodestar Bks. 1996 154p hardcover o.p. pa $4.99 **Fic**
Grades: 5 6 7 8 **Fic**

1. Slavery -- Fiction 2. Underground railroad -- Fiction
ISBN 0-14-038256-9 pa
LC 96-2339

While living in Texas in 1858, fourteen-year-old Caleb faces a dilemma in deciding whether or not to assist fugitive slaves in their run for freedom

"This fast-paced, easy-to-read novel proves that history can be intriguing and exciting, Wisler draws readers into this masterful, and often humorous tale." ALAN

Withers, Pam

First descent. Tundra Books 2011 265p $17.95
Grades: 7 8 9 10 **Fic**

1. Colombia -- Fiction 2. Kayaks and kayaking -- Fiction
ISBN 978-1-77049-257-8; 1-77049-257-7

"Seventeen-year-old champion slalom kayaker Rex Scruggs is determined to kayak Colombia's Furioso River, when he meets a young woman, an Andean indigena, who both aids Rex in his quest and puts him in the crosshairs of Colombia's battling guerrillas and paramilitaries. . . . Withers flings the reader from one perilous adventure to another." Booklist

Wittlinger, Ellen

Hard love. Simon & Schuster Bks. for Young Readers 1999 224p hardcover o.p. pa $8.99
Grades: 7 8 9 10 **Fic**

1. Lesbians -- Fiction 2. Authorship -- Fiction
ISBN 0-689-82134-4; 0-689-84154-X pa
LC 98-6668

Michael L. Printz Award honor book, 2000

"John, cynical yet vulnerable, thinks he's immune to emotion until he meets bright, brittle Marisol, the author of his favorite zine. He falls in love, but Marisol, a lesbian, just wants to be friends. A love story of a different sort—funny, poignant, and thoughtful." Booklist

Followed by: Love & lies: Marisol's story (2008)

Love & lies; Marisol's story. Simon & Schuster Books for Young Readers 2008 245p $16.99
Grades: 7 8 9 10 **Fic**

1. Lesbians -- Fiction 2. Authorship -- Fiction 3. Massachusetts -- Fiction
ISBN 978-1-4169-1623-9; 1-4169-1623-7
LC 2007-18330

When Marisol, a self-confident eighteen-year-old lesbian, moves to Cambridge, Massachusetts to work and try to write a novel, she falls under the spell of her beautiful but deceitful writing teacher, while also befriending a shy, vulnerable girl from Indiana.

"The emotional morass of Marisol's life . . . is complex and realistic; it will draw in both fans of the earlier novel . . . and realistic-fiction readers seeking a love story with depth." Bull Cent Child Books

★ **Parrotfish.** Simon & Schuster Books for Young Readers 2007 294p $16.99
Grades: 7 8 9 10 **Fic**

1. School stories 2. Family life -- Fiction 3. Transgender people -- Fiction
ISBN 978-1-4169-1622-2; 1-4169-1622-9
LC 2006-9689

Grady, a transgender high school student, yearns for acceptance by his classmates and family as he struggles to adjust to his new identity as a male.

"The author demonstrates well the complexity faced by transgendered people and makes the teen's frustration with having to fit into a category fully apparent." Publ Wkly

★ **Sandpiper.** Simon & Schuster Books for Young Readers 2005 227p hardcover o.p. pa $6.99
Grades: 9 10 11 12 **Fic**

1. Dating (Social customs) -- Fiction
ISBN 0-689-86802-2; 1-4169-3651-3 pa
LC 2004-7576

When The Walker, a mysterious boy who walks constantly, intervenes in an argument between Sandpiper and a boy she used to see, their lives become entwined in ways that change them both.

"While heavy on message and mature in subject matter, the novel is notable for the bold look it takes at relationships and at the myth that oral sex is not really sex." SLJ

Zigzag. Simon & Schuster Bks. for Young Readers 2003 267p $16.95
Grades: 7 8 9 10 **Fic**

1. Cousins -- Fiction 2. Automobile travel -- Fiction
ISBN 0-689-84996-6
LC 2002-2145

A high-school junior makes a trip with her aunt and two cousins, discovering places she did not know existed and strengths she did not know she had

"Teens will easily hear themselves in Robin's hilarious, sharp observations and feel her excitement as she travels through new country and discovers her own strength." Booklist

Wizner, Jake

Spanking Shakespeare. Random House Children's Books 2007 287p $15.99; lib bdg $18.99
Grades: 8 9 10 **Fic**

1. School stories 2. Authorship -- Fiction
ISBN 978-0-375-84085-2; 978-0-375-94085-9 lib bdg
LC 2006-27035

Shakespeare Shapiro navigates a senior year fraught with feelings of insecurity while writing the memoir of his embarrassing life, worrying about his younger brother being cooler than he is, and having no prospects of ever getting a girlfriend.

"Raw, sexual, cynical, and honest, this book belongs on library shelves and gift lists." Voice Youth Advocates

Wolf, Allan

New found land; Lewis and Clark's voyage of discovery: a novel. Candlewick Press 2004 500p map $18.99
Grades: 7 8 9 10 **Fic**

1. Lewis and Clark Expedition (1804-1806) -- Fiction
ISBN 0-7636-2113-7
LC 2003-65254

The letters and thoughts of Thomas Jefferson, members of the Corps of Discovery, their guide Sacagawea, and Captain Lewis's Newfoundland dog, all tell of the historic exploratory expedition to seek a water route to the Pacific Ocean.

"This is an extraordinary, engrossing book that would appeal most to serious readers, but it should definitely be added to any collection." SLJ

Includes glossary and bibliographical references

★ The **watch** that ends the night; voices from the Titanic. Candlewick Press 2011 466p $21.99
Grades: 7 8 9 10 **Fic**

1. Novels in verse 2. Shipwrecks -- Fiction 3. Titanic (Steamship) -- Fiction
ISBN 978-0-7636-3703-3
LC 2010040150

Recreates the 1912 sinking of the Titanic as observed by millionaire John Jacob Astor, a beautiful young Lebanese refugee finding first love, "Unsinkable" Molly Brown, Captain Smith, and others including the iceberg itself.

"A lyrical, monumental work of fact and imagination that reads like an oral history revved up by the drama of the event." Kirkus

Zane's trace. Candlewick Press 2007 177p $16.99
Grades: 7 8 9 10 11 12 **Fic**

1. Novels in verse 2. Death -- Fiction 3. Orphans -- Fiction 4. Epilepsy -- Fiction 5. Automobile travel -- Fiction 6. Racially mixed people -- Fiction
ISBN 978-0-7636-2858-1; 0-7636-2858-1
LC 2007-24187

Believing he has killed his grandfather, Zane Guesswind heads for his mother's Zanesville, Ohio, grave to kill himself, driving the 1969 Plymouth Barracuda his long-gone father left behind, and meeting along the way assorted characters who help him discover who he really is.

"This novel manages to be suspenseful, funny, and deeply moving at the same time." Voice Youth Advocates

Wolf, Jennifer Shaw

Breaking beautiful; Jennifer Shaw Wolf. Walker 2012 356 p. (hardcover) $16.99
Grades: 9 10 11 12 **Fic**

1. Siblings -- Fiction 2. Date rape -- Fiction 3. Young adult literature 4. Traffic accidents -- Fiction 5. Twins -- Fiction 6. Memory -- Fiction 7. Dating violence -- Fiction 8. Mystery and detective stories 9. Brothers and sisters -- Fiction 10. Dating (Social customs) -- Fiction
ISBN 0802723527; 9780802723529
LC 2011010944

This novel, by Jennifer Shaw Wolf, follows "Allie[, who] lost everything the night her boyfriend, Trip, died in a horrible car accident—including her memory of the event. As their small town mourns his death, Allie is afraid to remember because doing so means delving into what she's kept hidden for so long: the horrible reality of their abusive relationship. . . . Can she reach deep enough to remember that night so she can finally break free?" (Publisher's note)

Wolff, Tobias

Old school; a novel. Knopf 2003 195p $22; pa $12
Grades: 9 10 11 12 **Fic**

1. School stories 2. Authors -- Fiction 3. New England -- Fiction
ISBN 0-375-40146-6; 0-375-70149-4 pa
LC 2003-52930

"The unnamed narrator of this coming-of-age story set in 1960 is a scholarship student at a prestigious New England prep school that has a tradition of inviting literary stars to the campus. Prior to the visit, the seniors are requested to write a piece to be 'judged' by the guest. The winner is given a private meeting with the literary luminary and the story is published in the school paper. . . . In his fervent desire to be chosen, the narrator 'borrows' an idea and reveals a secret about his heritage that he has carefully hidden. He wins, but the results of his story's publication are disastrous and his life is forever changed. The events and ideas in this thoughtful and thought-provoking novel remain with readers after the story is over and could provide meat for discussion." SLJ

Wolff, Virginia Euwer

★ **Make** lemonade. Holt & Co. 1993 200p $17.95; pa $7.95
Grades: 8 9 10 11 12 **Fic**

1. Novels in verse 2. Poverty -- Fiction 3. Babysitters -- Fiction 4. Teenage mothers -- Fiction
ISBN 978-0-8050-2228-5; 0-8050-2228-7; 978-0-8050-8070-4 pa; 0-8050-8070-8 pa
LC 92-41182

"Fourteen-year-old LaVaughn accepts the job of babysitting Jolly's two small children but quickly realizes that the young woman, a seventeen-year-old single mother, needs as much help and nurturing as her two neglected children. The four become something akin to a temporary family, and through their relationship each makes progress toward a better life. Sixty-six brief chapters, with words arranged on the page like poetry, perfectly echo the patterns of teenage speech." Horn Book Guide

Other titles in this trilogy are:
This full house (2009)
True believer (2001)

★ **Probably** still Nick Swansen. Holt & Co. 1988 144p hardcover o.p. pa $7.99
Grades: 7 8 9 10 **Fic**

1. Learning disabilities -- Fiction
ISBN 0-8050-0701-6; 0-689-85226-6 pa
LC 88-13175

Sixteen-year-old learning-disabled Nick struggles to endure a life in which the other kids make fun of him, he has to take special classes, his date for the prom makes an excuse not to go with him, and he is haunted by the memory of his older sister who drowned while he was watching

"It is a poignant, gentle, utterly believable narrative." Booklist

Wolfson, Jill

Cold hands, warm heart. Henry Holt and Co. 2009 245p
Grades: 7 8 9 10 **Fic**

1. Death -- Fiction 2. Siblings -- Fiction 3. Hospitals -- Fiction 4. Jews -- United States -- Fiction 6. Transplantation of organs, tissues, etc. -- Fiction
ISBN 0-8050-8282-4; 978-0-8050-8282-1
LC 2008040594

After sixteen-year-old Tyler convinces his parents to donate the organs of his fourteen-year-old sister, who died during a gymnastics meet, he writes letters to the recipients, including Dani, who finally has a chance at normalcy after living fifteen years with a congenital heart defect.

"Detailed, accurate descriptions of medical procedures are leavened with humor and sincerity, providing a powerful, multifaceted exploration of ethics, love and the celebration." Kirkus

★ **Furious**; by Jill Wolfson. 1st ed. Henry Holt and Co. 2013 336 p. (hardcover) $17.99
Grades: 9 10 11 12 **Fic**

1. Revenge -- Fiction 2. Erinyes (Greek mythology) -- Fiction 3. High schools -- Fiction 4. Erinyes (Greek mythology)
ISBN 0805082832; 9780805082838
LC 2012027653

This book presents "a cautionary tale of bullying and retribution, featuring three righteously angry 10th-grade girls. Meg, a neglected and abused foster kid . . . Alix . . . [who] has a soft spot for her developmentally disabled big brother; and Stephanie . . . an environmental activist. . . . After each girl comes undone by her rage, cool, popular classmate Ambrosia explains to them that they are 'Furies' and then manipulates them into . . . embrac[ing] a vindictive twisted justice." (School Library Journal)

"For readers moving beyond Percy Jackson into the more complex realm of teen angst, this is an enthralling and chilling tale that uses Greek mythology to create a timely fable." Kirkus

Wolitzer, Meg

★ **Belzhar**; a novel; Meg Wolitzer. Dutton Books for Young Readers. 2014 272p $17.99
Grades: 9 10 11 12 **Fic**

1. Boarding schools — Fiction; 2. Dating (Social customs) — Fiction; 3. Emotional problems — Fiction; 4. Friendship — Fiction; 5. Schools — Fiction
ISBN: 0525423052; 9780525423058
LC 2014010747

"When Jam suffers a terrible trauma and feels isolated by grief, her parents send her to the Wooden Barn, a boarding school for "highly intelligent, emotionally fragile" teens. Once there she is enrolled in a class with only five specially selected students where they exclusively read Sylvia Plath... While the conclusion is a touch heavy-handed, older teen readers, especially rabid Plath fans, will relish Wolitzer's deeply respectful treatment of Jam's realistic emotional struggle." Booklist

Wollman, Jessica

Switched. Delacorte Press 2007 249p $15.99
Grades: 6 7 8 9 **Fic**

1. School stories 2. Social classes -- Fiction 3. Household employees -- Fiction 4. Mother-daughter relationship -- Fiction
ISBN 978-0-385-73396-0

Laura and Willa, born the same night seventeen years ago on opposite sides of Darien, Connecticut, are both unhappy with their lives and when they discover they look remarkably alike, they decide to try out one another's lives for four months.

"Wollman turns a potentially clichéd premise . . . into an entertaining and thoughtful novel. . . . Wollman creates credible characters who should endear themselves to readers." Publ Wkly

Wood, Maggie L.

Captured. Lobster Press 2011 284p (The Divided Realms) $12.95
Grades: 6 7 8 9 **Fic**

1. Fantasy fiction 2. Young adult literature -- Works
ISBN 978-1-77080-071-7 pa; 1-77080-071-9 pa

"Willow was brought up believing she was just a normal girl with a grandmother that had a penchant for telling fantastic stories about another realm where she was a princess and magic and fairies were everyday occurrences. . . . Or, at least that is what Willow thought until the day her Nana died and she was transported to the home she never knew to save a family she never knew she had. . . Wood's characters must think outside the game to save their world. Sometimes it takes an outsider to see things that those on the inside cannot. This is a wonderful book—well written and likely to fly off the shelves while fantasy is still the hot genre." Voice Youth Advocates

The **darkening.** Lobster Press 2011 283p (The Divided Realms) pa $12.95
Grades: 6 7 8 9 **Fic**

1. Fantasy fiction 2. Fairies -- Fiction
ISBN 978-1-77080-072-4 pa; 1-77080-072-7 pa

"Willow travels to the faery realm, but when Brand breaks the all-important rules by stowing away in the magical transport spell, the faeries turn the pair over to the dark lord Jarlath Thornheart, who throws them into the terrifying goblin's gauntlet. . . . This story remains entertaining." Kirkus

Wood, Maryrose

My life the musical; by Maryrose Wood. 1st ed.; Delacorte Press 2008 228p $15.99; lib bdg $18.99
Grades: 7 8 9 10 **Fic**

1. School stories 2. Theater -- Fiction 3. Musicals -- Fiction
ISBN 978-0-385-73278-9; 0-385-73278-3; 978-0-385-90297-7 lib bdg; 0-385-90297-2 lib bdg
LC 2007015034

Sixteen-year-old Emily Pearl's obsession with Broadway shows, and one musical in particular, lands her in trouble in school and at home, but it might also allow her and her best friend, Phillip, to find a dramatic solution to the problems.

"Teens will enjoy the fast pace and humor in this uplifting novel." SLJ

The **poison** diaries; based on a concept by the Duchess of Northumberland. Balzer + Bray 2010 278p $16.99
Grades: 8 9 10 11 **Fic**

1. Plants -- Fiction 2. Supernatural -- Fiction 3. Great Britain -- Fiction 4. Poisons and poisoning -- Fiction 5. Father-daughter relationship -- Fiction
ISBN 978-0-06-180236-2; 0-06-180236-0
LC 2009-54427

In late eighteenth-century Northumberland, England, sixteen-year-old Jessamine Luxton and the mysterious Weed uncover the horrible secrets of poisons growing in Thomas Luxton's apothecary garden.

"This intriguing fantasy has many tendrils to wrap around teen hearts. . . . The haunting ending will leave readers wanting to talk about the themes of cruelty, honesty, and loyalty." Booklist

Another title in this series is:
Nightshade (2011)

Wooding, Chris

The **haunting** of Alaizabel Cray. Orchard Bks. 2004 292p $16.95; pa $7.99
Grades: 7 8 9 10 **Fic**

1. Horror fiction 2. Supernatural -- Fiction 3. London (England) -- Fiction
ISBN 0-439-54656-7; 0-439-59851-6 pa
LC 2003-69108

First published 2001 in the United Kingdom

In a world similar to Victorian London, Thaniel, a seventeen-year-old hunter of deadly, demonic creatures called the wych-kin, takes in a lost, possessed girl, and becomes embroiled in a plot to unleash evil on the world

"Eerie and exhilarating. . . . [The author] fuses together his best storytelling skills . . . to create a fabulously horrific and ultimately timeless underworld." SLJ

Havoc; illustrated by Dan Chernett. Scholastic Press 2010 396p il $16.99
Grades: 6 7 8 9 **Fic**

1. Magic -- Fiction 2. Good and evil -- Fiction 3. Comic books, strips, etc. -- Fiction
ISBN 978-0-545-16045-2; 0-545-16045-6

"As Seth makes his way back into Malice with the talismanic Shard and joins the effort to mount an attack on the dread Deadhouse, a new ally, Alicia, nervously tracks the House's sinister master Tall Jake to the decrepit English psychiatric hospital where Grendel—the mad, disturbed, misshapen graphic artist (and maybe god?) who has created both the comic and the world it depicts—is imprisoned. . . . This features expertly meshed multiple plotlines, colorful supporting characters . . . frequent eerie skitterings and sudden feelings of dread plus nonstop action that breaks, occasionally, from prose into graphic-novel–style panels festooned with noisy sound effects." Kirkus

★ **Malice**; illustrated by Dan Chernett. Scholastic Press 2009 377p il $14.99; pa $8.99
Grades: 6 7 8 9 10 **Fic**

1. Horror fiction 2. Comic books, strips, etc. -- Fiction
ISBN 978-0-545-16043-8; 0-545-16043-X; 978-0-545-16044-5 pa; 0-545-16044-8 pa

Everyone's heard the rumors. Call on Tall Jake and he'll take you to Malice, a world that exists inside a horrifying comic book. A place most kids never leave. Seth and Kady think it's all a silly myth. But then their friend disappears.

"This nail-biter will keep readers glued to the story until the very last page is turned. . . . Seth and Kady are strong and exciting characters." SLJ

Poison. Orchard Bks. 2005 273p $16.99; pa $7.99
Grades: 7 8 9 10 **Fic**

1. Fantasy fiction 2. Fairies -- Fiction 3. Storytelling -- Fiction
ISBN 0-439-75570-0; 0-439-75571-9 pa
LC 2005-02174

First published 2003 in the United Kingdom

When Poison leaves her home in the marshes of Gull to retrieve the infant sister who was snatched by the fairies, she and a group of unusual friends survive encounters with the inhabitants of various Realms, and Poison herself confronts a surprising destiny.

"Poison's story should please crowds of horror fans who like their books fast-paced, darkly atmospheric, and melodramatic." SLJ

Silver; Chris Wooding. Scholastic Press 2014 320 p. (hc) $17.99
Grades: 7 8 9 10 11 12 **Fic**

1. Horror fiction 2. School stories 3. Survival -- Fiction 4. Boarding schools -- Fiction 5. Communicable diseases -- Fiction
ISBN 0545603927; 9780545603928
LC 2013014037

In this young adult science fiction horror novel, by Chris Wooding, "without warning, a horrifying infection will spread across the school grounds [of Mortingham Boarding Academy], and a group of students with little in common will find themselves barricaded in a classroom, fighting for their lives. Some will live. Some will die. And then it will get even worse." (Publisher's note)

"When strange insects assault a remote boarding school in England, the kids try to save the day in this tense page-turner...Skillfully managed subplots keep the pages flying. It looks like the end of the world is nigh.... It's just all kinds of white-knuckle fun." (Kirkus)

The **storm** thief. Orchard Books 2006 310p $16.99
Grades: 6 7 8 9 10 **Fic**
1. Science fiction
ISBN 0-439-86513-1
LC 2005-35993

With the help of a golem, two teenaged thieves try to survive on the city island of Orokos, where unpredictable probability storms continually change both the landscape and the inhabitants.

The author "delivers memorable characters, such as Vago, whose plight—Who am I and where do I belong in the world?—will be understood by many teens. Wooding also creates a unique world for his characters to explore, and the setting serves as an excellent backdrop for the author to develop his theme of order versus chaos and the need for balance between the two." Voice Youth Advocates

Woodruff, Elvira

★ **From** the notebooks of Melanin Sun. G.P. Putnam's Sons 2010 126p $17.99; pa $7.99
Grades: 7 8 9 10 **Fic**
1. Lesbians -- Fiction 2. African Americans -- Fiction 3. Mother-son relationship -- Fiction
ISBN 978-0-399-25280-8; 0-399-25280-0; 978-0-14-241641-9 pa; 0-14-241641-X pa
LC 2009011314

A reissue of the title first published 1995 by Blue Sky Press

A Coretta Scott King honor book, 1996

Almost-fourteen-year-old Melanin Sun's comfortable, quiet life is shattered when his mother reveals she has fallen in love with a woman

"Offering no easy answers, Woodson teaches the reader that love can lead to acceptance of all manner of differences." Publ Wkly

Lena; by Jacqueline Woodson. 1st G.P. Putnam's Sons ed.; G. P. Putnam's Sons 2006 135p $17.99
Grades: 6 7 8 9 **Fic**
1. Sisters -- Fiction 2. Runaway teenagers -- Fiction
ISBN 0-399-24469-7
LC 2005032666

A reissue of the title first published 1999 by Delacorte Press

ALA YALSA Margaret A. Edwards Award (2006)

Thirteen-year-old Lena and her younger sister Dion mourn the death of their mother as they hitchhike from Ohio to Kentucky while running away from their abusive father.

"Soulful, wise and sometimes wrenching, this taut story never loses its grip on the reader." Publ Wkly

Woods, Brenda

Emako Blue. G. P. Putnam's Sons 2004 124p $15.99
Grades: 7 8 9 10 **Fic**
1. African Americans -- Fiction
ISBN 0-399-24006-3
LC 2003-16647

Monterey, Savannah, Jamal, and Eddie have never had much to do with each other until Emako Blue shows up at chorus practice, but just as the lives of the five Los Angeles high school students become intertwined, tragedy tears them apart.

"This short, succinct, and poignant story of friendship, family, and overwhelming sadness will leave some readers in tears." SLJ

A **star** on the Hollywood Walk of Fame. G. P. Putnam's Sons 2010 164p il $16.99
Grades: 6 7 8 9 10 11 12 **Fic**
1. School stories 2. Authorship -- Fiction
ISBN 978-0-399-24683-8; 0-399-24683-5
LC 2009-08750

Nine Los Angeles high school students use a creative writing class assignment to shed light on their own lives.

"Woods is such a master of pace and voice that her storytelling will rivet even reluctant readers to the page. Her use of dialect is flawless, and her quick transitions from one character's perspective to the next keep things lively." Bull Cent Child Books

Woods, Elizabeth Emma

Choker; [by] Elizabeth Woods. Simon & Schuster Books for Young Readers 2011 233p $16.99
Grades: 9 10 11 12 **Fic**
1. School stories 2. Friendship -- Fiction 3. Mental illness -- Fiction
ISBN 978-1-4424-1233-0
LC 2010-34672

Teenaged Cara, solitary and bullied in high school, is delighted to reconnect with her childhood best friend Zoe whose support and friendship help Cara gain self-confidence, even as her classmates start dying.

"Terrific pacing and mounting suspense lead to a resolution that may not surprise savvy readers but is nonetheless chilling." Booklist

Woods, Ron

The **hero**. Knopf 2002 215p hardcover o.p. pa $4.99
Grades: 5 6 7 8 **Fic**
1. Death -- Fiction 2. Rafting (Sports) -- Fiction
ISBN 0-375-80612-1; 0-440-22978-2 pa
LC 00-54460

In the summer of 1957 in Idaho, when 14 year old Jamie and his older cousin Jerry reluctantly include outsider Dennis in their rafting adventure, Dennis drowns and Jamie lies that Dennis made a heroic sacrifice

"The author deftly handles a convincing adventure with emotional depth and tenderness toward his characters." SLJ

Woodson, Jacqueline

★ **After** Tupac and D Foster. G.P. Putnam's Sons 2008 153p $15.99
Grades: 7 8 9 10 **Fic**
1. Poets 2. Actors 3. Rap musicians 4. Friendship

-- Fiction 5. African Americans -- Fiction
ISBN 978-0-399-24654-8
LC 2007-23725

A Newbery honor book, 2009

In the New York City borough of Queens in 1996, three girls bond over their shared love of Tupac Shakur's music, as together they try to make sense of the unpredictable world in which they live.

"The subtlety and depth with which the author conveys the girls' relationships lend this novel exceptional vividness and staying power." Publ Wkly

Behind you. Putnam 2004 118p $15.99; pa $7.99

Grades: 7 8 9 10 **Fic**

1. Death -- Fiction 2. New York (N.Y.) -- Fiction 3. African Americans -- Fiction
ISBN 978-0-399-23988-5; 0-399-23988-X; 978-0-14-241554-2 pa; 0-14-241554-5 pa

Sequel to: If you come softly

After fifteen-year-old Jeremiah is mistakenly shot by police, the people who love him struggle to cope with their loss as they recall his life and death, unaware that 'Miah is watching over them.

"Woodson writes with impressive poetry about race, love, death, and what grief feels like—the things that 'snap the heart' and her characters' open strength and wary optimism will resonate with many teens." Booklist

★ **Beneath** a meth moon; Jacqueline Woodson. Nancy Paulsen Books 2012 181p

Grades: 9 10 11 12 **Fic**

1. Teenagers -- Drug use -- Fiction 2. Hurricane Katrina, 2005 -- Fiction 3. Iowa -- Fiction 4. Grief -- Fiction 5. Runaways -- Fiction 6. Drug abuse -- Fiction 7. Methamphetamine -- Fiction 8. Pass Christian (Miss.) -- Fiction
ISBN 9780399252501
LC 2011046799

In this novel, "Laurel, her father, and her little brother are reeling from the deaths of her mother and grandmother, who refused to leave their home in Pass Christian, Mississippi, during Hurricane Katrina. As they try to start life over in a new town, things look better for Laurel: she meets a sympathetic new friend named Kaylee, becomes a cheerleader, and starts dating T-Boom. Their first night together, though, T-Boom introduces her to meth, and she becomes instantly addicted. Her addiction progresses quickly, and when Kaylee confronts her and her father finds her stash, she runs away and lives on the streets, begging for money and trying desperately to stay high." (Bulletin of the Center for Children's Books)

If you come softly. Putnam 1998 181p $15.99; pa $5.99

Grades: 7 8 9 10 **Fic**

1. Race relations -- Fiction 2. New York (N.Y.) -- Fiction 3. African Americans -- Fiction
ISBN 0-399-23112-9; 0-698-11862-6 pa
LC 97-32212

ALA YALSA Margaret A. Edwards Award (2006)

After meeting at their private school in New York, fifteen-year-old Jeremiah, who is black and whose parents are separated, and Ellie, who is white and whose mother has twice abandoned her, fall in love and then try to cope with people's reactions

"The gentle and melancholy tone of this book makes it ideal for thoughtful readers and fans of romance." Voice Youth Advocates

Another title about Jeremiah is:
Behind you (2004)

Miracle's boys. Putnam 2000 133p $15.99; pa $5.99

Grades: 9 10 11 12 **Fic**

1. Orphans -- Fiction 2. Brothers -- Fiction 3. New York (N.Y.) -- Fiction 4. African Americans -- Fiction
ISBN 0-399-23113-7; 0-698-11916-9 pa
LC 99-40050

ALA YALSA Margaret A. Edwards Award (2006)

Twelve-year-old Lafayette's close relationship with his older brother Charlie changes after Charlie is released from a detention home and blames Lafayette for the death of their mother

"The fast-paced narrative is physically immediate, and the dialogue is alive with anger and heartbreak." Booklist

Woodworth, Chris

Double -click for trouble. Farrar, Straus and Giroux 2008 162p $16

Grades: 6 7 8 9 **Fic**

1. Uncles -- Fiction 2. Country life -- Fiction
ISBN 978-0-374-30987-9; 0-374-30987-6
LC 2006-38351

After he is caught viewing inappropriate websites on the Internet, a fatherless, thirteen-year-old Chicago boy is sent to rural Indiana to spend school break with his eccentric great-uncle.

"Woodworth perfectly captures an eighth-grade boy on the cusp of adolescence, struggling with his identity as he learns about himself, his family, and what is really important in relationships." SLJ

When Ratboy lived next door. Farrar, Straus and Giroux 2005 181p $16

Grades: 6 7 8 9 **Fic**

1. Raccoons -- Fiction 2. Friendship -- Fiction
ISBN 0-374-34677-1
LC 2004-50634

When his strange family moves into her quiet southern Indiana town, sixth-grader Lydia Carson initially despises her new neighbor and classmate, who seems as wild as the raccoon that is his closest companion.

"There are serious issues present, including poverty, alcoholism, abuse, learning disabilities, and bullying. The conflicts of the plot are effectively tied up, though not too neatly to lose believability. . . . An outstanding offering." SLJ

Woolston, Blythe

★ **Black** helicopters; Blythe Woolston. Candlewick Press 2013 176 p. $15.99

Grades: 9 10 11 12 **Fic**

1. Dystopias 2. Adventure fiction 3. Survivalism --

Fiction
ISBN 0763661465; 9780763661465
LC 2012942619

This young adult suspense novel, by Blythe Woolston, follows "a teenage girl. A survivalist childhood. And now a bomb strapped to her chest. . . . With Da unexpectedly gone and no home to return to, [the] teenage . . . Valkyrie . . . and her big brother must bring their message to the outside world--a not-so-smart place where little boys wear their names on their backpacks and young men don't pat down strangers before offering a lift." (Publisher's note)

Catch & release; Blythe Woolston. Carolrhoda Lab 2012 210 p.
Grades: 9 10 11 12 **Fic**

1. Fishing -- Fiction 2. Friendship -- Fiction 3. Automobile travel -- Fiction 4. Communicable diseases -- Fiction 5. People with disabilities -- Fiction 6. Trout -- Fiction 7. West (U.S.) -- Fiction 8. Disfigured persons -- Fiction
ISBN 0761377557; 9780761377559
LC 2011009630

In this book, "[e]ighteen-year-old Polly recounts her road trip with Odd, a fellow survivor of the disease that killed five others from their small town, in D'Elegance, his Gramma's old baby-blue Cadillac. Fishing is ostensibly the purpose of their outing, and it symbolically charts the way the two teens process their disabilities. . . . Polly once had a boyfriend and a sense of a normal future. . . . Odd Estes lost a foot as well as some football buddies, and although the two barely knew each other before, they both now struggle to accommodate their good fortune in surviving and their misfortune of disability. . . . Odd and Polly move from isolation to a mutual connection that helps them deal with their pain." (Kirkus)

★ The **Freak** Observer. Carolrhoda Lab 2010 202p $16.95
Grades: 8 9 10 11 12 **Fic**

1. Post-traumatic stress disorder -- Fiction
ISBN 978-0-7613-6212-8; 0-7613-6212-6
LC 2010-989

Suffering from a crippling case of post-traumatic stress disorder, sixteen-year-old Loa Lindgren tries to use her problem solving skills, sharpened in physics and computer programming, to cure herself.

"Woolston's talent for dialogue and her unique approach to scenes make what sounds standard about this story feel fresh and vital. . . . A strong . . . [novel] about learning to see yourself apart from the reflection you cast off others." Booklist

Woon, Yvonne

Dead beautiful. Disney/Hyperion 2010 456p $16.99; pa $9.99
Grades: 7 8 9 10 11 12 **Fic**

1. School stories 2. Immortality -- Fiction 3. Supernatural -- Fiction
ISBN 978-1-4231-1956-2; 1-4231-1956-8; 978-1-4231-1961-6 pa; 1-4231-1961-4 pa
LC 2009-42850

After her parents die under mysterious circumstances, sixteen-year-old Renee Winters is sent from California to an old-fashioned boarding school in Maine, where she meets a fellow student to whom she seems strangely connected.

"This hefty novel takes a new and unconventional look at the undead, focusing on story and interesting characters and leaving gore and mayhem hidden in the background. . . . Well written, intriguing and, above all, different." Kirkus

Life eternal; a Dead beautiful novel. Yvonne Woon. 1st ed. Hyperion 2012 393 p. (paperback) $9.99; (hardcover) $16.99
Grades: 9 10 11 12 **Fic**

1. Love stories 2. Suspense fiction 3. Supernatural -- Fiction 4. Canada -- Fiction 5. Immortality -- Fiction 6. Boarding schools -- Fiction 7. Montreal (Quebec) -- Fiction
ISBN 9781423137627; 1423119576; 9781423119579
LC 2011018257

This book is a sequel to "Dead Beautiful." Having "been saved by [her Undead soul mate] Dante . . . Renée is left to wonder whether she too is now one of the Undead." She is transferred to a new school, away from Dante. "Knowing that Dante only has five more years of animation before he will need to either take a life or die a second time, Renée searches the school's library and mystical texts for a solution." (Kirkus)

Wrede, Patricia C., 1953-

Across the Great Barrier; Patricia C. Wrede. Scholastic Press 2011 339p (Frontier magic) $16.99
Grades: 7 8 9 10 11 12 **Fic**

1. Fantasy 2. Magic -- Fiction 3. Twins -- Fiction 4. Brothers and sisters -- Fiction 5. Frontier and pioneer life -- Fiction
ISBN 978-0-545-03343-5; 0-545-03343-8; 9780545033435
LC 2011032260

Eff is an unlucky thirteenth child. Her twin brother, Lan, is a powerful seventh son of a seventh son. And yet, Eff is the one who saved the day for the settlements west of the Great Barrier. Her unique ways of doing magic and seeing the world, and her fascination with the magical creatures and land in the Great Plains push Eff to work toward joining an expedition heading west. But things are changing on the frontier.

"Splendid worldbuilding and deliciously complex characterization continue to be the hallmarks of this standout fantasy." Kirkus

The **Far** West; Patricia C. Wrede. Scholastic Press 2012 378 p. $17.99
Grades: 7 8 9 10 11 12 **Fic**

1. Steampunk fiction 2. Fantasy fiction 3. Fantasy 4. Magic -- Fiction 5. Twins -- Fiction 6. Friendship -- Fiction 7. Magic 8. Friendship
ISBN 0545033446; 9780545033442
LC 2012288790

This young adult speampunk novel, by Patricia C. Wrede, concludes the "Frontier Magic" trilogy. "Eff is an unlucky thirteenth child . . . but also the seventh daughter in her family. Her twin brother, Lan, is a powerful double seventh son. Her life at the edge of the Great Barrier Spell is different from anyone else's that she knows. . . . With Lan, William, Professor Torgeson, Wash, and Professor Ochiba, Eff finds that nothing on the wild frontier is as they expected." (Publisher's note)

Sorcery and Cecelia, or, The enchanted chocolate pot; being the correspondence of two young ladies of quality regarding various magical scandals in London and the country. [by] Patricia C. Wrede and Caroline Stevermer. Harcourt 2003 316p $17; pa $6.95

Grades: 7 8 9 10 **Fic**

1. Cousins -- Fiction 2. Supernatural -- Fiction

ISBN 0-15-204615-1; 0-15-205300-X pa

LC 2002-38706

In 1817 in England, two young cousins, Cecilia living in the country and Kate in London, write letters to keep each other informed of their exploits, which take a sinister turn when they find themselves confronted by evil wizards

"This is a fun story that quickly draws in the reader." Voice Youth Advocates

Other titles about Kate and Cecilia are:

The grand tour (2004)

The mislaid magician (2006)

The **thirteenth** child. Scholastic Press 2009 344p (Frontier magic) $16.99

Grades: 7 8 9 10 11 12 **Fic**

1. School stories 2. Fantasy fiction 3. Magic -- Fiction 4. Twins -- Fiction 5. Frontier and pioneer life -- Fiction

ISBN 978-0-545-03342-8; 0-545-03342-X

LC 2008-34048

Eighteen-year-old Eff must finally get over believing she is bad luck and accept that her special training in Aphrikan magic, and being the twin of the seventh son of a seventh son, give her extraordinary power to combat magical creatures that threaten settlements on the western frontier.

Wrede "creates a rich world where steam dragons seem as normal as bears, and a sympathetic character in Eff." Publ Wkly

Followed by Across the Great Barrier (2011)

Wright, Barbara

Crow; Barbara Wright. 1st ed. Random House 2012 297 p. (hardcover) $16.99; (lib. bdg.) $19.99; (ebook) $16.99

Grades: 9 10 11 12 **Fic**

1. Racism 2. African Americans -- Fiction 3. Historical fiction 4. Friendship -- Fiction 5. Family life -- Fiction 6. North Carolina -- Fiction 7. Race relations -- Fiction

ISBN 037586928X; 0375969284; 9780375869280; 9780375969287; 9780375982705

LC 2011014892

This historical novel by author Barbara Wright is set in the nineteenth century, when "Moses Thomas['s] . . . father, a reporter for an expanding African-American newspaper in Wilmington, NC, sets high expectations for . . . the general prosperity of his middle-class black community . . . An inflammatory article on the perceived threat to white womanhood provokes an equally incendiary response from Mr. Thomas' editor, and the issue becomes a flashpoint upon which the Wilmington election turns." (Bulletin of the Center for Children's Books)

Wright, Bil

Putting makeup on the fat boy. Simon & Schuster Books for Young Readers 2011 219p $16.99

Grades: 7 8 9 10 11 12 **Fic**

1. School stories 2. Cosmetics -- Fiction 3. Homosexuality -- Fiction 4. Hispanic Americans -- Fiction 5. Single parent family -- Fiction

ISBN 978-1-4169-3996-2; 1-4169-3996-2

LC 2010032450

"Carlos, 16 and fabulous, just knows he's going to be famous. Cocky but playful—'I had just the slightest touch of color in my cheeks. I'd given myself a manicure. I looked beyond excellent!'—Carlos strides purposefully toward his goal: Makeup artist to the stars. Zipping around Manhattan, he obtains employment with a hip, prestigious cosmetics company in Macy's and nabs a position working for the star of a Saturday Night Live equivalent." Kirkus

"Obviously, there's a whole lot going on in Wright's novel, but it's handled deftly and, for the most part, believably. Best of all, Carlos is not completely defined by his homosexuality." Booklist

When the black girl sings; [by] Bil Wright. Simon & Schuster Books for Young Readers 2007 266p $16.99; pa $5.99

Grades: 6 7 8 9 10 **Fic**

1. Divorce -- Fiction 2. Adoption -- Fiction 3. African Americans -- Fiction

ISBN 978-1-4169-3995-5; 1-4169-3995-4; 978-1-4169-4003-6 pa; 1-4169-4003-0 pa

LC 2006030837

Adopted by white parents and sent to an exclusive Connecticut girls' school where she is the only black student, fourteen-year-old Lahni Schuler feels like an outcast, particularly when her parents separate, but after attending a local church where she hears gospel music for the first time, she finds her voice.

"Readers will enjoy the distinctive characters, lively dialogue, and palette of adolescent and racial insecurities in this contemporary, upbeat story." SLJ

Wright, Denis

Violence 101; a novel. G. P. Putnam's Sons 2010 213p $16.99

Grades: 8 9 10 **Fic**

1. Genius -- Fiction 2. Violence -- Fiction 3. New Zealand -- Fiction 4. Reformatories -- Fiction 5. Race relations -- Fiction

ISBN 978-0-399-25493-2; 0-399-25493-5

LC 2010-02851

First published 2007 in New Zealand

In a New Zealand reformatory, Hamish Graham, an extremely intelligent fourteen-year-old who believes in the compulsory study of violence, learns that it is not always the answer.

"Wright's novel is clever and biting, a tragedy of society's failure to deal with kids like Hamish and a satire of society's winking condemnations of violence. Hamish's actions can be revolting, despite his justifications, but he still draws empathy as a product of the environment at large. Hardly a comfortable book to read, but a gripping one." Publ Wkly

Wulffson, Don L.

Soldier X. Viking 2001 226p $15.99; pa $6.99
Grades: 7 8 9 10 **Fic**

1. World War, 1939-1945 -- Fiction 2. World War, 1939-1945 -- Campaigns -- Soviet Union
ISBN 0-670-88863-X; 0-14-250073-9 pa
LC 99-49418

In 1943 sixteen-year-old Erik experiences the horrors of war when he is drafted into the German army and sent to fight on the Russian front

"Erik's first-person narrative records battlefield sequences with an unflinching—and occasionally numbing—brutality, in a story notable for its unusual perspective." Horn Book Guide

Wunder, Wendy

★ The **museum** of intangible things. Wendy Wunder. Razorbill 2014 295p $17.99
Grades: 8 9 10 11 12 **Fic**

1. Automobile travel — Fiction; 2. Best friends — Fiction; 3. Female Friendship — Fiction; 4. Manic-depressive illness — Fiction; 5. Runaways — Fiction
ISBN: 1595145141; 9781595145147
LC 2013030169

"As Hannah and best friend Zoe (diagnosed bipolar) embark on a cross-country road trip, Zoe gives Hannah "intangible lessons" (e.g., Hannah learns insouciance when they overnight in an IKEA). When Zoe's irrationality gets scary, Hannah learns betrayal and, later, forgiveness. With each lesson, Hannah becomes more confident, building her own distinct identity. Meanwhile, Zoe is a complex character--intelligent, loyal, and funny." Horn Book

★ The **probability** of miracles. Razorbill 2011 360p $17.99
Grades: 8 9 10 11 12 **Fic**

1. Death -- Fiction 2. Maine -- Fiction 3. Cancer -- Fiction 4. Miracles -- Fiction
ISBN 978-1-59514-368-6; 1-59514-368-8

"Faced with death, one teen discovers life in this bittersweet debut. . . . Cynical and loner Campbell Cooper (an Italian-Samoan-American) gave up on magic after her parents divorced, her father died and she developed neuroblastoma. . . . Having exhausted Western medicine, her single mother suggests spending the summer after Cam's graduation in Promise, Maine, a hidden town . . . known to have mysterious healing powers. . . . Exploring both sides of Cam's heritage, the story unfolds through narration as beautiful as the sun's daily 'everlasting gobstopper descent behind the lighthouse.' Irreverent humor, quirky small-town charm and surprises along the way help readers brace themselves for the tearjerker ending." Kirkus

Wyatt, Melissa

Funny how things change. Farrar, Straus & Giroux 2009 196p $16.95
Grades: 9 10 11 12 **Fic**

1. Artists -- Fiction 2. Mountains -- Fiction 3. Country life -- Fiction 4. West Virginia -- Fiction
ISBN 978-0-374-30233-7; 0-374-30233-2
LC 2008-16190

Remy, a talented, seventeen-year-old auto mechanic, questions his decision to join his girlfriend when she starts college in Pennsylvania after a visiting artist helps him to realize what his family's home in a dying West Virginia mountain town means to him.

"Laconic but full of heart, smart, thoughtful and proudly working-class, Remy makes a fresh and immensely appealing hero." Kirkus

Wylie, Sarah

All these lives; Sarah Wylie. 1st ed. Margaret Ferguson Books/Farrar Straus Giroux 2012 248 p. (hardcover) $17.99
Grades: 9 10 11 12 **Fic**

1. Sisters -- Fiction 2. Leukemia -- Fiction 3. Teenagers -- Suicide -- Fiction 4. Sick -- Fiction 5. Twins -- Fiction 6. Cancer -- Fiction 7. Family life -- Fiction 8. Near-death experiences -- Fiction
ISBN 0374302081; 9780374302085; 9781429954952
LC 2011030779

This book tells the story of Dani. Ever "since surviving a car crash and a chest infection as a child, 16-year-old Dani has been told that she's a miracle" which she "interprets . . . as evidence that she literally has nine lives. But Dani's twin, Jena, is dying from leukemia, and Dani thinks her parents are acting disturbingly normal under the circumstances. . . . She persuades herself that by ridding herself of her extra 'lives,' she can transfer them to her sister." (Publishers Weekly)

Wynne-Jones, Tim

★ **Blink** & Caution. Candlewick Press 2011 342p $16.99
Grades: 9 10 11 12 **Fic**

1. Crime -- Fiction 2. Guilt -- Fiction 3. Canada -- Fiction 4. Runaway teenagers -- Fiction
ISBN 978-0-7636-3983-9; 0-7636-3983-4
LC 2010-13563

Two teenagers who are living on the streets and barely getting by become involved in a complicated criminal plot, and make an unexpected connection with each other

"The short, punchy sentences Wynne-Jones fires like buckshot; the joy, fear, and doubt that punctuate the teens' every action. This is gritty, sure, but more than that, it's smart, and earns every drop of its hopeful finish." Booklist

The **boy** in the burning house. Farrar, Straus & Giroux 2001 213p hardcover o.p. pa $5.95
Grades: 6 7 8 9 **Fic**

1. Mystery fiction
ISBN 0-374-30930-2; 0-374-40887-4 pa
LC 99-89534

First published 2000 in Canada

Trying to solve the mystery of his father's disappearance from their rural Canadian community, fourteen-year-old Jim gets help from the disturbed Ruth Rose, who suspects her stepfather, a local pastor

"A gripping, fast-moving plot offers the pure adrenaline rush of a thriller." Horn Book Guide

The **uninvited**. Candlewick Press 2009 351p $16.99
Grades: 10 11 12 **Fic**
1. Canada -- Fiction 2. Vacations -- Fiction 3. Father-daughter relationship -- Fiction
ISBN 978-0-7636-3984-6; 0-7636-3984-2
LC 2009-7520

After a disturbing freshman year at New York University, Mimi is happy to get away to her father's remote Canadian cottage only to discover a stranger living there who has never heard of her or her father and who is convinced that Mimi is responsible for leaving sinister tokens around the property.

"This suspenseful and deftly crafted family drama will appeal to older teens who are exploring their options beyond high school." Voice Youth Advocates

Yancey, Richard

★ The **5th** Wave; Rick Yancey. G.P. Putnam's Sons, an imprint of Penguin Group (USA) Inc. 2013 480 p. (hardcover) $18.99
Grades: 9 10 11 12 **Fic**
1. Science fiction 2. Extraterrestrial beings -- Fiction 3. War -- Fiction 4. Survival -- Fiction
ISBN 0399162410; 9780399162411
LC 2012047622

In this post-apocalyptic novel, by Rick Yancey, "on a lonely stretch of highway, Cassie runs from Them. The beings who only look human, who roam the countryside killing anyone they see. Who have scattered Earth's last survivors. To stay alone is to stay alive, Cassie believes, until she meets Evan Walker. Beguiling and mysterious, Evan Walker may be Cassie's only hope for rescuing her brother--or even saving herself." (Publisher's note)

"Yancey makes a dramatic 180 from the intellectual horror of his Monstrumologist books to open a gripping SF trilogy about an Earth decimated by an alien invasion. The author fully embraces the genre, while resisting its more sensational tendencies... It's a book that targets a broad commercial audience, and Yancey's aim is every bit as good as Cassie's." Pub Wkly

The **extraordinary** adventures of Alfred Kropp; by Rick Yancey. Bloomsbury Pub. 2005 339p $16.95; pa $7.95
Grades: 7 8 9 10 **Fic**
1. Adventure fiction 2. Kings 3. Orphans -- Fiction
ISBN 1-58234-693-3; 1-59990-044-0 pa
LC 2005-13044

Through a series of dangerous and violent misadventures, teenage loser Alfred Kropp rescues King Arthur's legendary sword Excalibur from the forces of evil.

"True to its action-adventure genre, the story is lighthearted, entertaining, occasionally half-witted, but by and large fun." SLJ

Other titles about Alfred Kropp are:
Alfred Kropp: the seal of Solomon (2007)
Alfred Kropp: the thirteenth skull (2008)

The **final** descent; Rick Yancey. Simon & Schuster Books for Young Readers 2013 320 p. (Monstrumologist) (hardback) $18.99
Grades: 9 10 11 12 **Fic**
1. Monsters -- Fiction 2. Apprentices -- Fiction 3. Horror stories 4. Orphans -- Fiction 5. Supernatural -- Fiction
ISBN 144245153X; 9781442451537
LC 2013015811

In this final installment of Rick Yancey's Monstrumologist series, "Will Henry, now 16, often drunk and colder than ever, helps Monstrumologist Pellinore Warthrop track down the T. cerrejonensis, a giant, snakelike critter that poisons its human prey then swallows them whole. At the same time, the novel also fast-forwards decades later to 1911, when Will returns to care for an elderly Warthrop and then reverts back to when he was first taken in by his employer." (Kirkus Reviews)

★ The **monstrumologist**; [by] William James Henry; edited by Rick Yancey. Simon & Schuster Books for Young Readers 2009 454p il $17.99; pa $9.99
Grades: 9 10 11 12 **Fic**
1. Orphans -- Fiction 2. Monsters -- Fiction 3. Apprentices -- Fiction 4. Supernatural -- Fiction
ISBN 978-1-4169-8448-1; 1-4169-8448-8; 978-1-4169-8449-8 pa; 1-4169-8449-6 pa
LC 2009-4562

ALA YALSA Printz Award Honor Book (2010)

In 1888, twelve-year-old Will Henry chronicles his apprenticeship with Dr. Warthrop, a scientist who hunts and studies real-life monsters, as they discover and attempt to destroy a pod of Anthropophagi.

"As the action moves from the dissecting table to the cemetery to an asylum to underground catacombs, Yancey keeps the shocks frequent and shrouded in a splattery miasma of blood, bone, pus, and maggots. . . . Yancey's prose is stentorian and wordy, but it weaves a world that possesses a Lovecraftian logic and hints at its own deeply satisfying mythos. . . . 'Snap to!' is Warthrop's continued demand of Will, but readers will need no such needling." Booklist

Other titles in this series include:
The curse of the wendigo (2010)
The Isle of Blood (2011)

Yang, Dori Jones

Daughter of Xanadu. Delacorte Press 2011 336p map $17.99
Grades: 7 8 9 10 11 12 **Fic**
1. Travelers 2. Love stories 3. Kings 4. Travel writers 5. Sex role -- Fiction 6. Soldiers -- Fiction
ISBN 0385739230; 0385907788; 9780385739238; 9780385907781
LC 2009-53652

Emmajin, the sixteen-year-old granddaughter of Khublai Khan, becomes a warrior and falls in love with explorer Marco Polo in thirteenth-century China.

"Daughter of Xanadu offers rich descriptions and vivid depictions of fictional characters and historical figures, making them charming and believable. A colorful and compelling read." SLJ

Yansky, Brian

Alien invasion and other inconveniences. Candlewick Press 2010 227p $15.99

Grades: 9 10 11 12 **Fic**

1. Science fiction 2. Telepathy -- Fiction 3. Extraterrestrial beings -- Fiction

ISBN 978-0-7636-4384-3

LC 2009-49103

When a race of aliens quickly takes over the earth, leaving most people dead, high-schooler Jesse finds himself a slave to an inept alien leader—a situation that brightens as Jesse develops telepathic powers and attracts the attention of two beautiful girls.

"The story is action-packed, provocative, profound, and wickedly funny. Yansky takes on questions philosophical, ecological, religious, moral, and social, and the satire is right on target." Horn Book Guide

Homicidal aliens and other disappointments; Brian Yansky. Candlewick Press 2013 336 p. $16.99

Grades: 9 10 11 12 **Fic**

1. Teenagers -- Fiction 2. Extraterrestrial beings -- Fiction

ISBN 0763659622; 9780763659622

LC 2013931461

"Narrator Jesse (Alien Invasion and Other Inconveniences) continues to battle the lethal aliens who have taken control of Earth as thirty-million Sanginian colonists are about to arrive. Jesse finds that in addition to his telepathic abilities, he's now able to see glimpses of possible futures. The fast-paced action, realistically developed relationships, and dry, self-deprecating voice drive this readable and thought-provoking sequel." (Horn Book)

Yee, Lisa

Absolutely Maybe. Arthur A. Levine Books 2009 274p $16.99

Grades: 8 9 10 11 12 **Fic**

1. Fathers -- Fiction 2. Runaway teenagers -- Fiction 3. Los Angeles (Calif.) -- Fiction 4. Mother-daughter relationship -- Fiction

ISBN 978-0-439-83844-3; 0-439-83844-4

LC 2008-17787

When living with her mother, an alcoholic ex-beauty queen, becomes unbearable, almost seventeen-year-old Maybelline "Maybe" Chestnut runs away to California, where she finds work on a taco truck and tries to track down her birth father.

"The characters are complex and their friendships layered—they sweep readers up in their path." Publ Wkly

Warp speed. Arthur A. Levine Books 2011 310p $16.99

Grades: 5 6 7 8 **Fic**

1. School stories 2. Bullies -- Fiction 3. Popularity -- Fiction 4. Family life -- Fiction

ISBN 978-0-545-12276-4; 0-545-12276-7

LC 2010-24228

Marley Sandelski has always felt invisible at school when he is not facing bullies, but a series of unexpected events gives him a taste of popularity and insights into some classmates, well-liked or greatly-feared

"Yee's combination of humor and sympathy works a charm here, giving Marley a life of his own and a chance at success in this solid addition to her prismatic look at middle school." Kirkus

Yee, Paul

Learning to fly; [by] Paul Yee. Orca Book Pub. 2008 108p (Orca soundings) $16.95

Grades: 7 8 9 10 **Fic**

1. Chinese -- Fiction 2. Drug abuse -- Fiction 3. Friendship -- Fiction 4. Immigrants -- Fiction 5. Prejudices -- Fiction 6. Native Americans -- Fiction

ISBN 978-1-55143-955-6; 1-55143-955-7

"Jason Chen, 17, wants to leave his small town in Canada and return to China. . . . His white high-school teachers do not know how smart he is, and his classmates jeer at him. Driven to join the crowd of potheads, he bonds especially with his Native American classmate, Charles ('Chief'). Narrated in Jason's wry, first-person, present-tense narrative, Yee's slim novel packs in a lot. . . . The clipped dialogue perfectly echoes the contemporary scene, the harsh prejudice felt by the new immigrant and the Native American, and their gripping friendship story." Booklist

Yeomans, Ellen

Rubber houses; a novel. Little, Brown and Company 2007 152p $15.99

Grades: 7 8 9 10 **Fic**

1. Novels in verse 2. Death -- Fiction 3. Siblings -- Fiction 4. Bereavement -- Fiction

ISBN 978-0-316-10647-4; 0-316-10647-X

LC 2005-37297

A novel in verse that relates seventeen-year-old Kit's experiences as her younger brother is diagnosed with and dies of cancer and as she withdraws into and gradually emerges from her grief.

"This slim work speaks volumes about the grieving process. Yeomans has very precisely selected her words to convey the fear and the grief that Kit feels." SLJ

Yep, Laurence, 1948-

★ **Dragon** road; Golden Mountain chronicles: 1939. HarperCollins 2008 291p $16.99; lib bdg $17.89

Grades: 6 7 8 9 **Fic**

1. Basketball -- Fiction 2. Chinese Americans -- Fiction 3. Great Depression, 1929-1939 -- Fiction

ISBN 978-0-06-027520-4; 0-06-027520-0; 978-0-06-027521-1 lib bdg; 0-06-027521-9 lib bdg

LC 2008-00784

In 1939, unable to find regular jobs because of the Great Depression, long-time friends Cal Chin and Barney Young tour the country as members of a Chinese American basketball team.

"As always, Yep's history is impeccable; now he's written an episode with appeal to basketball fans as well." Booklist

Includes bibliographical references

★ **Dragon's** gate; Golden Mountain chronicles: 1867. HarperCollins Pubs. 1993 273p $16.99; pa $6.99

Grades: 6 7 8 9 **Fic**

1. Railroads -- Fiction 2. Young adult literature -- Works 3. Chinese -- United States -- Fiction

ISBN 0-06-022971-3; 0-06-440489-7 pa

LC 92-43649

A Newbery Medal honor book, 1994

When he accidentally kills a Manchu, a fifteen-year-old Chinese boy is sent to America to join his father, an uncle, and other Chinese working to build a tunnel for the transcontinental railroad through the Sierra Nevada mountains in 1867

"Yep has succeeded in realizing the primary characters and the irrepressibly dramatic story. . . . The carefully researched details will move students to thought and discussion." Bull Cent Child Books

Dragons of silk. Harper 2011 339p $15.99

Grades: 6 7 8 9 **Fic**

1. Silkworms -- Fiction 2. Chinese Americans -- Fiction

ISBN 978-0-06-027518-1; 0-06-027518-9

LC 2011016553

Four generations of Chinese and Chinese-American girls, beginning in 1835, are tied together by the tradition of raising silkworms and the legacy of the legendary Weaving Maid.

"Yep doesn't shy away from some harsh historical truths: the pervasiveness of opium addiction, bloody battles erupting between silk-factory owners and independent weavers and severe exclusion laws. The earlier chapters, while slowly paced, are more interesting, as Yep deftly conjures the culture and spirit of long-ago China. . . . Overall, however, the author captures the world of women well, and lush silk is a prominent backdrop." Kirkus

★ **Dragonwings**; Golden Mountain chronicles: 1903. Harper & Row 1975 248p lib bdg $16.89; pa $6.99

Grades: 6 7 8 9 **Fic**

1. Chinese Americans -- Fiction

ISBN 0-06-026738-0 lib bdg; 0-06-440085-9 pa

A Newbery Medal honor book, 1976

"In 1903 Moon Shadow, eight years old, leaves China for the 'Land of the Golden Mountains,' San Francisco, to be with his father, Windrider, a father he has never seen. There, beset by the trials experienced by most foreigners in America, Moonrider shares his father's dream—to fly. This dream enables Windrider to endure the mockery of the other Chinese, the poverty he suffers in this hostile place—the land of the white demons—and his loneliness for his wife and his own country." Shapiro. Fic for Youth. 3d edition

★ The **traitor**; Golden Mountain chronicles, 1885. HarperCollins Pubs. 2003 310p hardcover o.p. pa $6.99

Grades: 5 6 7 8 **Fic**

1. Friendship -- Fiction 2. Illegitimate children 3. Prejudices -- Fiction 4. Chinese Americans -- Fiction 5. Rock Springs Massacre, Rock Springs, Wyo., 1885

ISBN 0-06-027522-7; 0-06-000831-8 pa

LC 2002-22534

In 1885, a lonely illegitimate American boy and a lonely Chinese American boy develop an unlikely friendship in the midst of prejudices and racial tension in their coal mining town of Rock Springs, Wyoming

"The short chapters read quickly, and readers will become involved through the first-person voices that capture each boy's feelings of being an outsider and a traitor." Booklist

Yolen, Jane

Curse of the Thirteenth Fey; the True Tale of Sleeping Beauty. Jane Yolen. Philomel Books 2012 290 p. $16.99

Grades: 6 7 8 9 10 **Fic**

1. Curses -- Fiction 2. Princesses 3. Family life 4. Fairy tales 5. Elves -- Fiction 6. Magic -- Fiction 7. Fairies -- Fiction 8. Prophecies -- Fiction 9. Family life -- Fiction

ISBN 0399256644; 9780399256646

LC 2011038847

In author Jane Yolen's book, "Gorse is the thirteenth . . . in a family of fairies tied to the evil king's land and made to do his bidding. . . . When accident-prone Gorse falls ill just as the family is bid to bless the new princess . . . [she] races to the castle with the last piece of magic the family has left. . . . But that is when accident, mayhem, and magic combine to drive Gorse's story into the unthinkable, threatening the baby, the kingdom, and all." (Publisher's note)

Dragon's blood. Harcourt 2004 303p (Pit dragon chronicles) pa $6.95

Grades: 6 7 8 9 **Fic**

1. Fantasy fiction 2. Dragons -- Fiction

ISBN 0-15-205126-0

LC 2003-56661

A reissue of the title first published 1982 by Delacorte Press

Jakkin, a bond boy who works as a Keeper in a dragon nursery on the planet Austar IV, secretly trains a fighting pit dragon of his own in hopes of winning his freedom

"An original and engrossing fantasy." Horn Book

Other titles in this series are:

Heart's blood (2004)

Sending of dragons (2004)

Dragon's heart (2009)

Girl in a cage; [by] Jane Yolen & Robert J. Harris. Philomel Bks. 2002 234p hardcover o.p. pa $6.99

Grades: 7 8 9 10 **Fic**

1. Kings 2. Scotland -- History -- Robert I, 1306-1329

ISBN 0-399-23627-9; 0-14-240132-3 pa

LC 2001-55978

As English armies invade Scotland in 1306, eleven-year-old Princess Marjorie, daughter of the newly crowned Scottish king, Robert the Bruce, is captured by England's King Edward Longshanks and held in a cage on public display

"Marjorie's first-person narration of her captivity and the events leading up to it is exciting and moving, and her strategies for coping with a hideous imprisonment are models of ingenuity and staying true to oneself." SLJ

Pay the piper; [by] Jane Yolen and Adam Stemple. Tor/Starscape 2005 175p $16.95

Grades: 6 7 8 9 **Fic**

1. Fantasy fiction 2. Rock music -- Fiction
ISBN 0-7653-1158-5

When Callie interviews the band, Brass Rat, for her school newspaper, her feelings are ambivalent, but when all the children of Northampton begin to disappear on Halloween, she knows where the dangerous search must begin.

The authors "have produced a rollicking good riff on the Pied Piper. . . . The authors keep the action moving. . . . An entertaining as well as meaty read." Booklist

★ The **Rogues**; [by] Jane Yolen & Robert J. Harris. Philomel Books 2007 277p $18.99

Grades: 7 8 9 10 **Fic**

1. Adventure fiction
ISBN 978-0-399-23898-7

LC 2006-26434

After his family is evicted from their Scottish farm, fifteen-year-old Roddy forms an unlikely friendship with a notorious rogue who helps him outwit a tyrant landlord in order to find a family treasure and make his way to America.

"The suspense mounts and the plot races along flawlessly in this excellent historical adventure." Booklist

Troll Bridge; a rock 'n' roll fairy tale. [by] Jane Yolen and Adam Stemple. 1st ed.; Starscape 2006 240p $16.95; pa $5.99

Grades: 7 8 9 10 **Fic**

1. Fairy tales 2. Musicians -- Fiction
ISBN 0-7653-1426-6; 0-7653-5284-2 pa

LC 2005034517

Sixteen-year-old harpist prodigy Moira is transported to a strange and mystical wilderness, where she finds herself in the middle of a deadly struggle between a magical fox and a monstrous troll.

"The story ends with a grand twist that is totally satisfying. The writing is filled with humor and straightforward prose, and the song lyrics are so well written that one can almost hear the music that accompanies them." SLJ

Yoo, Paula

Good enough. HarperTeen 2008 322p $16.99; lib bdg $17.89

Grades: 7 8 9 10 **Fic**

1. Violinists -- Fiction 2. Korean Americans -- Fiction
ISBN 978-0-06-079085-1; 978-0-06-079086-8 lib bdg

LC 2007-02985

A Korean American teenager tries to please her parents by getting into an Ivy League college, but a new guy in school and her love of the violin tempt her in new directions.

"The frequent lists, . . . SAT questions, and even spam recipes are, like Patti's convincing narration, filled with laugh-out-loud lines, but it's the deeper questions about growing up with immigrant parents, confronting racism, and how best to find success and happiness that will stay with readers." Booklist

Young, E. L.

STORM : The Infinity Code. Dial 2008 311p il $16.99

Grades: 6 7 8 9 **Fic**

1. Adventure fiction 2. Spies -- Fiction
ISBN 978-0-8037-3265-0

In London, the teenaged geniuses of STORM, a secret organization dedicated to eliminating the world's misery through science and technology, uncover plans for a deadly weapon and race to find and dismantle it, then confront the corrupt scientist behind the scheme.

"Young's debut novel is full of unusual scientific creations—all based on real inventions. The novel is plot-driven and packed with unlikely escapes and improbable plot twists—exactly what many middle school and junior high readers crave." Voice Youth Advocates

Other titles in this series are:
STORM: The ghost machine (2008)
STORM: The black sphere (2009)

Young, Moira

Blood red road. Margaret K. McElderry Books 2011 512p (Dustlands trilogy) $17.99

Grades: 6 7 8 9 10 **Fic**

1. Science fiction 2. Twins -- Fiction 3. Orphans -- Fiction 4. Siblings -- Fiction 5. Kidnapping -- Fiction
ISBN 978-1-4424-2998-7; 1-4424-2998-4

LC 2011-03423

"When 18-year-old Saba's father is killed and her twin brother, Lugh, is kidnapped, she sets out to rescue him, along with their younger sister, Emmi, and Saba's intelligent raven, Nero. Their travels across the desert wasteland bring them to a violent city in which Saba is forced to fight for her life in an arena. When she escapes with the help of a group of women warriors, she and her new allies (including a handsome and infuriating male warrior named Jack) try to prevent Lugh from being sacrificed. Readers will . . . be riveted by the book's fast-paced mix of action and romance. It's a natural for Hunger Games fans." Publ Wkly

Young, Suzanne

A **need** so beautiful. Balzer + Bray 2011 267p $16.99; ebook $9.99

Grades: 8 9 10 11 12 **Fic**

1. Supernatural -- Fiction 2. Good and evil -- Fiction 3. Portland (Or.) -- Fiction
ISBN 978-0-06-200824-4; 0-06-200824-2; 978-0-06-208454-5 ebook; 0-06-208454-2 ebook

LC 2010040810

A compelling Need that Charlotte has felt all her life is growing stronger, forcing her to connect with people in crisis, but at the same time other changes are taking place and she is terrified by what Monroe, a doctor and family friend, says must happen next.

"Charlotte is an exceptionally likable character who demonstrates an extraordinary amount of personal growth as she learns to accept her fate. . . . A unique take on the age-old struggle of good vs. evil." SLJ

Yovanoff, Brenna

★ The **replacement.** Razorbill 2010 343p $17.99

Grades: 9 10 11 12 **Fic**

1. Fantasy fiction 2. Death -- Fiction 3. Siblings -- Fiction 4. Supernatural -- Fiction 5. Missing children

-- Fiction
ISBN 978-1-59514-337-2; 1-59514-337-8
LC 2010-36066

Sixteen-year-old Mackie Doyle knows that he replaced a human child when he was just an infant, and when a friend's sister disappears he goes against his family's and town's deliberate denial of the problem to confront the beings that dwell under the town, tampering with human lives.

"Yovanoff's spare but haunting prose creates an atmosphere shrouded in gloom and secrecy so that readers, like Mackie, must attempt to make sense of a situation ruled by chaos and fear. The ethical complications of the town's deal with the creatures of Mayhem are clearly presented but never overwrought, while Mackie's problematic relationship to the townspeople as both an outsider and a savior is poignantly explored." Bull Cent Child Books

Zadoff, Allen

★ **Boy** Nobody; a novel by Allen Zadoff. 1st ed. Little, Brown, and Co. 2013 352 p. (hardcover) $18
Grades: 9 10 11 12 **Fic**

1. Assassins -- Fiction 2. Undercover operations -- Fiction 3. Teenagers -- Conduct of life -- Fiction 4. Schools -- Fiction 5. High schools -- Fiction 6. Conduct of life -- Fiction 7. Interpersonal relations -- Fiction
ISBN 0316199680; 9780316199681
LC 2012029484

In this book by Allen Zadoff, the "unnamed 16-year-old protagonist lost his identity when he was kidnapped and his parents murdered. Forced into a grueling training program, the teen now gets sent on undercover missions, befriending the children of powerful targets, getting invited to their houses, and killing their parents. He never questions his orders or actions until he's given five days to infiltrate a ritzy private school and kill the mayor of New York City." (Publishers Weekly)

Food, girls, and other things I can't have. Egmont USA 2009 311p $16.99; lib bdg $19.99
Grades: 7 8 9 10 **Fic**

1. School stories 2. Obesity -- Fiction 3. Football -- Fiction 4. Popularity -- Fiction
ISBN 978-1-60684-004-7; 1-60684-004-5; 978-1-60684-051-1 lib bdg; 1-60684-051-7 lib bdg
LC 2009-16242

Fifteen-year-old Andrew Zansky, the second fattest student at his high school, joins the varsity football team to get the attention of a new girl on whom he has a crush.

"The author does not lead Andy down the expected path. When forced to make a decision, his choice is unique and the conclusion satisfying. . . . The possibly offensive locker room language is typical and lends credibility. More importantly, Andy's character is thoughtful and refreshing." SLJ

My life, the theater, and other tragedies; a novel. Egmont USA 2011 282p $16.99
Grades: 7 8 9 10 **Fic**

1. School stories 2. Theater -- Fiction 3. Bereavement -- Fiction
ISBN 978-1-60684-036-8; 1-60684-036-3
LC 2010043619

While working backstage on a high school production of 'A Midsummer Night's Dream,' sixteen-year-old Adam develops feelings for a beautiful actress—which violates an unwritten code—and begins to overcome the grief that has controlled him since his father's death nearly two years earlier.

"Zadoff captures the confusion, torn loyalties, and overwrought drama of teenage life—not to mention student theater." Publ Wkly

Zail, Suzy

Playing for the commandant; Suzy Zail . Candlewick Press. 2014 245p $16.99
Grades: 7 8 9 10 11 12 **Fic**

1. Concentration camps -- Fiction; 2. Historical fiction; 3. Birkenau (Concentration camp) -- Fiction 4. Pianists — Fiction; 5. Holocaust, 1933-1945 —Fiction
ISBN: 0763664030; 9780763664039
LC 2013955694

"Hanna, 15, is a talented pianist living in Hungary in 1944, until the SS storms the ghetto and takes her and her family to Birkenau. The camp is a horror, but Hanna and her sister manage to survive. When word gets out that Hanna is a gifted musician, she is selected to play piano daily in the commandant's drawing room...Zail's story is as gut-wrenching as any Holocaust tale, particularly when, upon their liberation by Russian troops, Hanna discovers that her own dehumanizing experiences in the labor camp were nothing compared to the barbarity that occurred in the extermination camps. The haunting, matter-of-fact tone of Hanna's story will likely resonate with teens learning about the Holocaust." Booklist

Zalben, Jane Breskin

Four seasons. Alfred A. Knopf 2011 322p $15.99; lib bdg $18.99
Grades: 6 7 8 9 **Fic**

1. Music -- Fiction 2. Pianists -- Fiction
ISBN 978-0-375-86222-9; 0-375-86222-6; 978-0-375-96222-6 lib bdg; 0-375-96222-0 lib bdg
LC 2010-12731

Over the course of a year, thirteen-year-old Allegra Katz, a student at the demanding Julliard School and the daughter of two musicians, tries to decide whether she wants to continue to pursue a career as a concert pianist or to do something else with her life.

"The warm, complicated relationships and respectful treatment of Ally's depression animate an involving, perceptive, and reassuring novel that will hit readers where they live." Bull Cent Child Books

Zarr, Sara

★ **How** to save a life; Sara Zarr. Little, Brown 2011 341 p. $17.99
Grades: 6 7 8 9 10 11 12 **Fic**

1. Adoption -- Fiction 2. Bereavement -- Fiction 3. Mother-daughter relationship -- Fiction 4. Colorado -- Fiction 5. Pregnancy -- Fiction 6. Family life -- Fiction
ISBN 9780316036061
LC 2010045832

Told from their own viewpoints, seventeen-year-old Jill, in grief over the loss of her father, and Mandy, nearly nineteen, are thrown together when Jill's mother agrees to adopt Mandy's unborn child but nothing turns out as they had anticipated.

"Filled with so many frustrations, so many dilemmas needing reasonable solutions, and so much hope and faith in the midst of sadness, Zarr's novel is a rich tapestry of love and survival that will resonate with even the most cynical readers." Booklist

★ The **Lucy** variations; by Sara Zarr. 1st ed. Little, Brown and Co. 2013 320 p. (hardcover) $17.99

Grades: 7 8 9 10 11 12 **Fic**

1. Pianists -- Fiction 2. Brothers and sisters -- Fiction 3. Ability -- Fiction 4. San Francisco (Calif.) -- Fiction 5. Family life -- California -- Fiction 6. Self-actualization (Psychology) -- Fiction

ISBN 031620501X; 9780316205016

LC 2012029852

In this novel, by Sara Zarr, "Lucy Beck-Moreau once had a promising future as a concert pianist. . . . Now, at sixteen, it's over. A death, and a betrayal, led her to walk away. That leaves her talented ten-year-old brother, Gus, to shoulder the full weight of the Beck-Moreau family expectations. Then Gus gets a new piano teacher who is young, kind, and interested in helping Lucy rekindle her love of piano--on her own terms." (Publisher's note)

"The third-person narration focuses entirely on Lucy but allows readers enough distance to help them understand her behavior in ways Lucy cannot. Occasional flashbacks fill out the back story. The combination of sympathetic main character and unusual social and cultural world makes this satisfying coming-of-age story stand out." Kirkus

★ **Once** was lost. Little, Brown 2009 217p $16.99

Grades: 7 8 9 10 **Fic**

1. Clergy -- Fiction 2. Alcoholism -- Fiction 3. Kidnapping -- Fiction 4. Christian life -- Fiction

ISBN 978-0-316-03604-7; 0-316-03604-8

LC 2009-25187

As the tragedy of a missing girl unfolds in her small town, fifteen-year-old Samara, who feels emotionally abandoned by her parents, begins to question her faith.

"This multilayered exploration of the intersection of the spiritual life and imperfect people features suspense and packs an emotional wallop." SLJ

Roomies; Sara Zarr and Tara Altebrando. Little, Brown and Company 2014 288 p. $18

Grades: 9 10 11 12 **Fic**

1. Roommates -- Fiction 2. Teenage girls -- Fiction 3. Email -- Fiction 4. Friendship -- Fiction 5. Dating (Social customs) -- Fiction 6. Family life -- California -- Fiction 7. Family life -- New Jersey -- Fiction

ISBN 0316217492; 9780316217491

LC 2012048431

"Jersey girl Elizabeth (EB) and San Franciscan Lauren, soon to be college roommates, correspond throughout the summer; chapters with alternating perspectives unwrap each girl's backstory, personality, and coming-to-terms with changes looming on the horizon. The premise will have mass appeal with teens who fantasize about their post-high-school futures, and the authors succeed in presenting two distinct and relatable narrative voices." (Horn Book)

★ **Story** of a girl; a novel. Little, Brown 2006 192p $16.99

Grades: 10 11 12 **Fic**

1. California -- Fiction 2. Family life -- Fiction

ISBN 978-0-316-01453-3; 0-316-01453-2

LC 2005-28467

In the three years since her father caught her in the back seat of a car with an older boy, sixteen-year-old Deanna's life at home and school has been a nightmare, but while dreaming of escaping with her brother and his family, she discovers the power of forgiveness.

"This highly recommended novel will find a niche with older, more mature readers because of frank references to sex and some x-rated language." Voice Youth Advocates

★ **Sweethearts**. Little, Brown and Co. 2008 217p $16.99

Grades: 8 9 10 11 12 **Fic**

1. Love stories 2. School stories 3. Utah -- Fiction 4. Weight loss -- Fiction

ISBN 978-0-316-01455-7; 0-316-01455-9

LC 2007-41099

After losing her soul mate, Cameron, when they were nine, Jennifer, now seventeen, transformed herself from the unpopular fat girl into the beautiful and popular Jenna, but Cameron's unexpected return dredges up memories that cause both social and emotional turmoil.

"Zarr's writing is remarkable. . . . She conveys great delicacy of feeling and shades of meaning, and the realistic, moving ending will inspire excellent discussion." Booklist

Zeises, Lara M.

The **sweet** life of Stella Madison; [by] Lara Zeises. Delacorte Press 2009 230p $16.99; lib bdg $19.99

Grades: 9 10 11 12 **Fic**

1. Food -- Fiction 2. Journalism -- Fiction 3. Family life -- Fiction 4. Dating (Social customs) -- Fiction

ISBN 978-0-385-73146-1; 0-385-73146-9; 978-0-385-90178-9 lib bdg; 0-385-90178-X lib bdg

LC 2008-32024

Seventeen-year-old Stella struggles with the separation of her renowned chef parents, writing a food column for the local paper even though she is a junk food addict, and having a boyfriend but being attracted to another.

The author "has created a refreshing protagonist sure to captivate readers, who will enjoy following along as she learns about romance through food, and vice versa." SLJ

Zeitlin, Meredith

Freshman year & other unnatural disasters; Meredith Zeitlin. G.P. Putnam's Sons 2012 282 p. (hardcover) $16.99

Grades: 8 9 10 11 12 **Fic**

1. Humorous fiction 2. High school students -- Fiction 3. Schools -- Fiction 4. Friendship -- Fiction 5. High schools -- Fiction 6. New York (N.Y.) -- Fiction 7. Self-perception -- Fiction 8. Family life -- New York

(State) -- New York -- Fiction
ISBN 0399254234; 9780399254239
LC 2011005690

This young adult novel, by Meredith Zeitlin, follows "Kelsey Finkelstein--fourteen and frustrated. Every time she tries to live up to her awesome potential, her plans are foiled. Kelsey wants to rebrand herself for high school to make the kind of mark she knows is her destiny. But just because Kelsey has a plan for greatness . . . it doesn't mean the rest of the world is in on it." (Publisher's note)

Zemser, Amy Bronwen

Dear Julia. Greenwillow Books 2008 327p $16.99; lib bdg $17.89

Grades: 7 8 9 10 **Fic**

1. Cooking -- Fiction 2. Contests -- Fiction 3. Feminism -- Fiction 4. Mother-daughter relationship -- Fiction
ISBN 978-0-06-029458-8; 0-06-029458-2; 978-0-06-029459-5 lib bdg; 0-06-029459-0 lib bdg
LC 2008-3824

Shy sixteen-year-old Elaine has long dreamed of being the next Julia Child, to the dismay of her feminist mother, but when her first friend, the outrageous Lucida Sans, convinces Elaine to enter a cooking contest, anything could happen.

"Readers will laugh throughout, but Zemser never loses sight of Elaine's frailties and hopes." Publ Wkly

Zenatti, Valerie

A **bottle** in the Gaza Sea; translated by Adriana Hunter. Bloomsbury Children's Books 2008 149p il $16.95

Grades: 7 8 9 10 11 12 **Fic**

1. Letters -- Fiction 2. Israel-Arab conflicts -- Fiction
ISBN 978-1-59990-200-5; 1-59990-200-1
LC 2007-42361

Original French edition, 2005

Seventeen-year-old Tal Levine of Jerusalem, despondent over the ongoing Arab-Israeli conflict, puts her hopes for peace in a bottle and asks her brother, a military nurse in the Gaza Strip, to toss it into the sea, leading ultimately to friendship and understanding between her and an 'enemy.'

"Zenatti uses short, riveting chapters, . . . to pack a punch with readers reluctant to voracious. The overall effect is one of a haunting relationship that will help teens understand both sides of the Israeli-Palestinian conflict." Kirkus

Zephaniah, Benjamin

Face. Bloomsbury Pub. 2002 207p $15.95; pa $6.95

Grades: 7 8 9 10 **Fic**

1. Prejudices 2. Traffic accidents 3. Disfigured persons 4. Burns and scalds -- Fiction
ISBN 1-58234-774-3; 1-58234-921-5 pa
LC 2002-22758

First published 1999 in the United Kingdom

A teenage boy's face is disfigured in an automobile accident, and he must learn to deal with the changes in his life.

"This book will not only be enjoyed by teen readers for its entertaining story, but also for its statement about prejudice." Voice Youth Advocates

Zettel, Sarah

Bad luck girl; Sarah Zettel. Random House Inc. 2014 357p $17.99

Grades: 7 8 9 10 Fic

1. Fairies — Fiction; 2. Magic — Fiction; 3. Racially mixed people — Fiction; 4. Chicago (Ill.) — Fiction
ISBN: 0375869409; 9780375869402; 9780375969409
LC 2013013855

In this concluding volume to the author's American fairy trilogy, "half-fairy, half-human Callie . . . has reunited with her family, thus starting a war between the two fairy kingdoms. Fleeing Los Angeles for Chicago, Callie realizes that to end the war she must stand and fight. Zettel brings the street life, locales, and culture of jazz-age Chicago into the imagery of her fantasy, packing the story with incident and adventure." Horn Book

Dust girl; Sarah Zettel. Random House 2012 292 p. (trade : alk. paper) $17.99

Grades: 6 7 8 9 **Fic**

1. Fairies -- Fiction 2. Voyages and travels -- Fiction 3. Father-daughter relationship -- Fiction 4. Magic -- Fiction
ISBN 9780375869389; 9780375873812; 9780375969386; 9780375983184
LC 2011043310

In this book, "a mixed-race girl in Dust Bowl Kansas discovers her long-lost father isn't just a black man: He's a fairy. . . . [A] strange man . . . tells Callie secrets of her never-met father. Soon Callie's walking the dusty roads with Jack, a ragged white kid. . . . Callie and Jack dodge fairy politics and dangers, from grasshopper people to enchanted food to magic movie theaters--but the conventional dangers are no less threatening." (Kirkus Reviews)

Golden girl; by Sarah Zettel. 1st ed. Random House Inc. 2013 308 p. (The American fairy trilogy) (hardcover) $17.99; (library) $20.99

Grades: 7 8 9 10 **Fic**

1. Fantasy fiction 2. Voyages and travels 3. Magic -- Fiction 4. Fairies -- Fiction 5. Racially mixed people -- Fiction 6. Hollywood (Los Angeles, Calif.) -- History -- 20th century -- Fiction
ISBN 0375869395; 9780375869396; 9780375969393
LC 2013006238

In this book, it's 1935, and Callie LeRoux has journeyed to Hollywood from Slow Run, Kan., in search of her white human mother and black fairy father. A fairy kidnap attempt is foiled by none other than the famous Renaissance man Paul Robeson, a human who seems impervious to fairy magic. . . . Callie just wants to find her parents and get the heck out of Dodge, but with a prophecy hanging over her head, it won't be easy." (Kirkus Reviews)

Palace of Spies; being a true, accurate, and complete account of the scandalous and wholly remarkable adventures of Margaret Preston Fitzroy... by Sarah Zettel. Harcourt, Houghton Mifflin Harcourt 2013 368 p. (Palace of spies) $16.99

Grades: 8 9 10 **Fic**

1. Spies -- Fiction 2. London (England) -- Fiction

3. Great Britain -- History -- 1714-1837 -- Fiction 4. Love -- Fiction 5. Orphans -- Fiction 6. Courts and courtiers -- Fiction 7. London (England) -- History -- 18th century -- Fiction
ISBN 0544074114; 9780544074118
LC 2012046366

"In eighteenth-century London, destitute orphan Peggy Fitzroy agrees to impersonate the recently deceased spy Lady Francesca as maid of honor to Princess Caroline. With a war of succession, jilted love, and religious turmoil in the mix, Peggy must navigate intrigue and shady liaisons to uncover the truth behind her predecessor's death. The feisty narrator and lush period details will garner fans for this new series." (Horn Book)

Zevin, Gabrielle

All these things I've done. Farrar Straus Giroux 2011 354p $16.99
Grades: 8 9 10 11 12 **Fic**
1. Science fiction 2. Celebrities -- Fiction 3. Family life -- Fiction 4. New York (N.Y.) -- Fiction 5. Organized crime -- Fiction
ISBN 978-0-374-30210-8
LC 2010035873

In a future where chocolate and caffeine are contraband, teenage cellphone use is illegal, and water and paper are carefully rationed, sixteen-year-old Anya Balanchine finds herself thrust unwillingly into the spotlight as heir apparent to an important New York City crime family.

"Offering the excitement of a crime drama and the allure of forbidden romance, this introduction to a reluctant Godfather-in-the making will pique the interest of dystopia-hungry readers." Publ Wkly

Because it is my blood; Gabrielle Zevin. Farrar Straus Giroux 2012 350 p. $17.99
Grades: 7 8 9 10 **Fic**
1. Crime -- Fiction 2. Criminals -- Fiction 3. High school students -- Fiction 4. Science fiction 5. Mexico -- Fiction 6. Violence -- Fiction 7. Chocolate -- Fiction 8. Celebrities -- Fiction 9. New York (N.Y.) -- Fiction 10. Organized crime -- Fiction 11. Oaxaca de Juárez (Mexico) -- Fiction 12. Family life -- New York (State) -- New York -- Fiction
ISBN 0374380740; 9780374380748
LC 2011036991

In Gabrielle Zeven's book, "Anya Balanchine is determined to follow the straight and narrow . . . since her release from Liberty Children's Facility . . . Unfortunately, her criminal record is making it hard for her to do that. No high school wants her with a gun possession charge . . . But when old friends return demanding that certain debts be paid, Anya is thrown right back into the criminal world that she had been determined to escape." (Macmillan)

Elsewhere. Farrar, Straus & Giroux 2005 275p $16; pa $6.95
Grades: 7 8 9 10 **Fic**
1. Death -- Fiction 2. Future life -- Fiction
ISBN 0-374-32091-8; 0-312-36746-5 pa
LC 2004-56279

After fifteen-year-old Liz Hall is hit by a taxi and killed, she finds herself in a place that is both like and unlike Earth, where she must adjust to her new status and figure out how to "live."

"Zevin's third-person narrative calmly, but surely guides readers through the bumpy landscape of strongly delineated characters dealing with the most difficult issue that faces all of us. A quiet book that provides much to think about and discuss." SLJ

Memoirs of a teenage amnesiac. Farrar, Straus and Giroux 2007 271p $17; pa $8.99
Grades: 7 8 9 10 **Fic**
1. School stories 2. Amnesia -- Fiction 3. Friendship -- Fiction
ISBN 978-0-374-34946-2; 0-374-34946-0; 978-0-312-56128-4 pa; 0-312-56128-8 pa
LC 2006-35287

After a nasty fall, Naomi realizes that she has no memory of the last four years and finds herself reassessing every aspect of her life.

This is a "sensitive, joyful novel. . . . Pulled by the the heart-bruising love story, readers will pause to contemplate irresistible questions." Booklist

Zhang, Kat, 1991-

Once we were; the second book in the Hybrid chronicles. Kat Zhang. HarperTeen 2014 340 p. $17.99
Grades: 8 9 10 11 12 **Fic**
1. Science fiction 2. Sisters -- Fiction 3. Identity (Psychology) -- Fiction 4. Resistance to government -- Fiction 5. Identity -- Fiction 6. Government, Resistance to -- Fiction
ISBN 0062114905; 9780062114907; 9780062114914
LC 2013032811

In this sequel to "What's Left of Me," by Kat Zhang, "Eva and Addie struggle to share their body as they clash over romance and join the fight for hybrid freedom. . . . Addie and Eva escaped imprisonment at a horrific psychiatric hospital. Now they should be safe, living among an underground hybrid movement. But safety is starting to feel constricting. Faced with the possibility of being in hiding forever, the girls are eager to help bring about change—now." (Publisher's note)

"Because sisters Addie and Eva grew up hiding their hybrid nature, they're now learning-along with readers-some of the nuances of what it means for two souls to share one body...hang has a unique challenge: she must give each character two distinct personalities, which she skillfully manages. While this book lacks some of the freshness of What's Left of Me (HarperCollins, 2012), simply by virtue of being a sequel, the lovely, atmospheric storytelling is still very much present. Zhang has envisioned a complex, unique world and deftly brings it to life." (School Library Journal)

What's left of me. Harper 2012 343 p. $17.99
Grades: 8 9 10 11 12 **Fic**
1. Twins 2. Dystopian fiction 3. Science fiction
ISBN 0062114875; 9780062114877
LC 2012289047

This novel, by Kat Zhang, is the first book of the young adult science fiction "Hybrid Chronicles." "Eva and Addie started out the same way as everyone else--two souls woven together in one body, taking turns controlling their movements. . . . Finally Addie was pronounced healthy and Eva was declared gone. Except, she wasn't. . . . For the past three years, Eva has clung to the remnants of her life, . . . for a chance to smile, to twirl, to speak, Eva will do anything." (Publisher's note)

Ziegler, Jennifer

How not to be popular. Delacorte Press 2008 339p $15.99; lib bdg $18.99

Grades: 7 8 9 10 11 12 **Fic**

1. School stories 2. Texas -- Fiction 3. Hippies -- Fiction 4. Popularity -- Fiction

ISBN 978-0-385-73465-3; 0-385-73465-4; 978-0-385-90463-6 lib bdg; 0-385-90463-0 lib bdg

LC 2007-27603

Seventeen-year-old Sugar Magnolia Dempsey is tired of leaving friends behind every time her hippie parents decide to move, but her plan to be unpopular at her new school backfires when other students join her on the path to "supreme dorkdom."

This "balances laugh-out-loud, sardonic commentary with earnest reflections that will directly connect with teens." Booklist

Zielin, Lara

Donut days. G.P. Putnam's Sons 2009 246p $16.99

Grades: 7 8 9 10 **Fic**

1. Clergy -- Fiction 2. Sex role -- Fiction 3. Minnesota -- Fiction 4. Journalism -- Fiction 5. Christian life -- Fiction

ISBN 978-0-399-25066-8; 0-399-25066-2

LC 2008-26138

During a camp-out promoting the opening of a donut shop in a small Minnesota town, sixteen-year-old Emma, an aspiring journalist, begins to connect an ongoing pollution investigation with the turmoil in the evangelical Christian church where her parents are pastors.

This is a "sweet, satisfying treat. . . . Teens will enjoy this lighter look at some serious issues of faith and family." SLJ

Zimmer, Tracie Vaughn

Reaching for sun. Bloomsbury Children's Books 2007 192p $14.95

Grades: 7 8 9 10 **Fic**

1. Novels in verse 2. Friendship -- Fiction 3. Cerebral palsy -- Fiction

ISBN 1-59990-037-8

LC 2006-13197

Josie, who lives with her mother and grandmother and has cerebral palsy, befriends a boy who moves into one of the rich houses behind her old farmhouse.

"Written in verse, this quick-reading, appealing story will capture readers' hearts with its winsome heroine and affecting situations." Booklist

Zindel, Paul

★ The **Pigman**; a novel. Harper & Row 1968 182p hardcover o.p. pa $6.99

Grades: 7 8 9 10 **Fic**

ISBN 0-06-026828-X; 0-06-0757353-3 pa

ALA YALSA Margaret A. Edwards Award (2002)

"John Conlan and Lorraine Jensen, high school sophomores, are both troubled young people who have problems at home. They become friendly with an elderly widower, Mr. Pignati, who welcomes them into his home and shares with them his simple pleasures, including his collection of ceramic pigs, of which he is proud. When the Pigman, as the young people call him, goes to the hospital after a heart attack, they take advantage of his house for a party that becomes destructive. The consequences are tragic and propel the two young friends into more responsible behavior." Shapiro. Fic for Youth. 3d edition

Another title about the Pigman is:

The Pigman's legacy (1980)

Zink, Michelle

Guardian of the Gate. Little, Brown 2010 340p $17.99

Grades: 7 8 9 10 **Fic**

1. Magic -- Fiction 2. Twins -- Fiction 3. Sisters -- Fiction 4. Supernatural -- Fiction 5. Good and evil -- Fiction

ISBN 978-0-316-03447-0; 0-316-03447-9

Sequel to: Prophecy of the sisters (2009)

In 1891 London, sixteen-year-old orphan Lia Milthorpe continues her quest to end an ancient prophecy requiring her to search for missing pages and human "keys" and develop her powers for an inevitable final confrontation with her twin sister Alice.

"An intense and captivating story that gives a whole new meaning to sibling rivalry." Voice Youth Advocates

Prophecy of the sisters. Little, Brown 2009 343p $17.99

Grades: 7 8 9 10 **Fic**

1. Twins -- Fiction 2. Sisters -- Fiction 3. Supernatural -- Fiction 4. Good and evil -- Fiction

ISBN 978-0-316-02742-7; 0-316-02742-1

LC 2008-45290

In late nineteenth-century New York state, wealthy sixteen-year-old twin sisters Lia and Alice Milthorpe find that they are on opposite sides of an ancient prophecy that has destroyed their parents and seeks to do even more harm.

"This arresting story takes readers to other planes of existence." Booklist

Followed by: Guardian of the gate (2010)

Zinn, Bridget

Poison; by Bridget Zinn. 1st ed. Disney/Hyperion Books 2013 276 p. (hardcover) $16.99

Grades: 7 8 9 10 11 12 **Fic**

1. Occult fiction 2. Fantasy fiction 3. Fantasy 4. Magic -- Fiction 5. Heroes -- Fiction 6. Princesses -- Fiction 7. Impersonation -- Fiction 8. Fugitives from justice -- Fiction

ISBN 1423139933; 9781423139935

LC 2012008693

In this novel, sixteen-year-old "Kyra is on the run. She may be one of the Kingdom of Mohr's most highly skilled potions masters, but she has also just tried—and failed—to poison Princess Ariana. And Kyra is determined to finish her mission even if it means killing her best friend. . . . In order to save her kingdom from a nefarious plot, Kyra will have to come to terms with all the gifts she possesses." (School Library Journal)

Zuckerman, Linda

A **taste** for rabbit. Arthur A. Levine Books 2007 310p $16.99

Grades: 7 8 9 10 **Fic**

1. Foxes -- Fiction 2. Animals -- Fiction 3. Rabbits -- Fiction 4. Resistance to government -- Fiction

ISBN 0-439-86977-3; 978-0-439-86977-5

LC 2007-7787

Quentin, a rabbit who lives in a walled compound run by a militaristic government, must join forces with Harry, a fox, to stop the sinister disappearances of outspoken and rebellious rabbit citizens.

"The blend of adventure, mystery and morality in this heroic tale of honor and friendship will appeal to middle-school fantasy fans." Publ Wkly

Zulkey, Claire

An **off** year. Dutton 2009 213p $17.99

Grades: 9 10 11 12 **Fic**

1. Family life -- Fiction 2. Chicago (Ill.) -- Fiction 3. Colleges and universities -- Fiction

ISBN 978-0-525-42159-7; 0-525-42159-9

LC 2008-48968

Upon arriving at her dorm room, eighteen-year-old Cecily decides to postpone her freshman year of college and return to her Chicago home, where she spends a year pondering what went wrong while forging new relationships with family and friends.

"Teens who have doubted the high-school-college-life progression for even a moment will recognize themselves in Cecily, perhaps to their parents' dismay." Kirkus

Zusak, Markus, 1975-

★ The **book** thief. Knopf 2006 552p il $16.95; lib bdg $18.99

Grades: 8 9 10 11 12 **Fic**

1. Death -- Fiction 2. Jews -- Germany -- Fiction 3. Books and reading -- Fiction 4. Holocaust, 1933-1945 -- Fiction 5. World War, 1939-1945 -- Fiction

ISBN 0-375-83100-2; 0-375-93100-7 lib bdg

LC 2005-08942

Michael L. Printz Award honor book, 2007

Trying to make sense of the horrors of World War II, Death relates the story of Liesel—a young German girl whose book-stealing and storytelling talents help sustain her family and the Jewish man they are hiding, as well as their neighbors.

"This hefty volume is an achievement—a challenging book in both length and subject, and best suited to sophisticated older readers." Publ Wkly

★ **I** am the messenger. Knopf 2005 357p hardcover o.p. pa $8.95

Grades: 9 10 11 12 **Fic**

1. Mystery fiction

ISBN 0-375-83099-5; 0-375-83667-5 pa

LC 2003-27388

Michael L. Printz Award honor book, 2006

After capturing a bank robber, nineteen-year-old cab driver Ed Kennedy begins receiving mysterious messages that direct him to addresses where people need help, and he begins getting over his lifelong feeling of worthlessness

"Zusak's characters, styling, and conversations are believably unpretentious, well conceived, and appropriately raw. Together, these key elements fuse into an enigmatically dark, almost film-noir atmosphere where unknowingly lost Ed Kennedy stumbles onto a mystery—or series of mysteries—that could very well make or break his life." SLJ

Zweig, Eric

Fever season. Dundurn Press 2009 254p $10

Grades: 7 8 9 10 **Fic**

1. Hockey -- Fiction 2. Orphans -- Fiction 3. Influenza -- Fiction

ISBN 978-1-55488-432-2; 1-55488-432-2

When David is orphaned by the Spanish influenza outbreak in 1919 Montreal, he needs to find his long-lost uncle if he wants to avoid the orphanage, and he gets his chance when he gets a job with the Montreal Canadiens.

"Zweig tells a good story while he weaves a vibrant tapestry of life in the early 1900's. . . . Dramatic descriptions of war nightmares and flu sick-rooms hung with bleach-dipped sheets make history come alive. Interesting tidbits about hockey and its stars such as Bad Joe Hall, coupled with play-by-play action and French Canadian expressions, give the story true hockey flavor." Voice Youth Advocates

AUTHOR, TITLE, AND SUBJECT INDEX

This index to the books in the collection includes author, title, and subject entries; added entries for publishers' series, illustrators, joint authors, and editors of works entered under title; and name and subject cross-references; all arranged in one alphabet.

The **10** p.m. question. De Goldi, K.
100 sideways miles. Smith, A.
13 little blue envelopes. Johnson, M.
The **13th** sign. Tubb, K. O.
17 & gone. Suma, N. R.
172 hours on the moon.
3 willows; the sisterhood grows. Brashares, A.
37 things I love (in no particular order) Magoon, K.
The **5th** Wave. Yancey, R.
50 Cent (Musician), 1975-
Playground
7 days at the hot corner. Trueman, T.
7 clues to winning you. Walker, K.

A

ABANDONED CHILDREN -- FICTION
Gagnon, M. Don't Look Now
Jocelyn, M. Folly
Murdoch, E. If you find me
ABANDONED TOWNS *See* Extinct cities; Ghost towns
Abbott, Ellen Jensen
Watersmeet
ABBREVIATIONS
See also Writing
Abdel-Fattah, Randa
Does my head look big in this?
Ten things I hate about me
ABDOMINAL EXERCISES
See also Exercise
ABDUCTION *See* Kidnapping
Abhorsen. Nix, G.
ABILITY -- FICTION
Ashby, A. Fairy bad day
Bardugo, L. Shadow and bone
Cole, K. Poison princess
Jacobs, J. H. The twelve-fingered boy
Sales, L. Mostly good girls
Zarr, S. The Lucy variations
ABNORMALITIES, HUMAN -- FICTION
McQuerry, M. D. The Peculiars
ABOLITION OF CAPITAL PUNISHMENT
See Capital punishment
ABOLITIONISTS -- FICTION
Engle, M. The Lightning Dreamer
ABORIGINAL AUSTRALIAN ART
See also Art
ABORIGINAL AUSTRALIANS
See also Australians; Indigenous peoples
ABORIGINES *See* Indigenous peoples
ABORTION -- ETHICAL ASPECTS
See also Ethics
ABORTION -- FICTION
Levine, E. In trouble
Above. Bobet, L.
Abrahams, Peter
Bullet point
Reality check
Abrams, Amir
Hollywood High
Absent. Williams, K.
ABSENT MOTHERS -- FICTION
Howard, J. J. That time I joined the circus
ABSENTEEISM (LABOR)
See also Hours of labor; Personnel management
Absolute brightness. Lecesne, J.
Absolutely Maybe. Yee, L.
The **absolutely** true diary of a part-time Indian. Alexie, S.
ABSTINENCE, SEXUAL
See Sexual abstinence
An **abundance** of Katherines. Green, J.
ABUSED CHILDREN -- FICTION
Murdoch, E. If you find me
The **abused** werewolf rescue group. Jinks, C.
ABUSED WOMEN -- FICTION
Brown, J. Bitter end
Hubbard, A. But I love him
Peters, J. A. Rage
Acampora, Paul
Defining Dulcie
Acceleration. McNamee, G.
Accidental love. Soto, G. 1952-
ACCIDENTS -- FICTION
Griffin, P. Burning blue
McKinnon, H. R. The properties of water
Perez, M. Dead is a killer tune

Accidents of nature. Johnson, H. M.
ACCLIMATIZATION *See* Adaptation (Biology); Environmental influence on humans
Accomplice. Corrigan, E.
According to Kit. Doyle, E. F.
Ackley, Amy
Sign language
Acosta, Marta
Dark companion
Across a star-swept sea. Peterfreund, D.
Across a war-tossed sea. Elliott, L.
Across the Great Barrier. Wrede, P. C.
Across the universe. Revis, B.
ACTING -- FICTION
Hand. E. Illyria
Rennison, L. Withering tights
Acting up. Staunton, T.
ACTORS -- FICTION
Myers, A. Assassin
Woodson, J. After Tupac and D Foster
ACTORS -- FICTION
Collins, Y. Now starring Vivien Leigh Reid: Diva in training
Collins, Y. The new and improved Vivien Leigh Reid; diva in control
Lockhart, E. Dramarama
Selfors, S. Saving Juliet
ACTORS AND ACTRESSES -- FICTION
Bass, R. Lucid
Forman, G. Just one day
Shukert, R. Starstruck
Shukert, R. Love me
Smith, J. E. This is what happy looks like
ACTRESSES -- FICTION
Rennison, L. The taming of the tights
Shukert, R. Starstruck
Ada, Alma Flor, 1938-
Yes! we are Latinos
ADAGES *See* Proverbs
Adams, John Joseph
(ed) Under the moons of Mars
Adams, John Quincy, 1767-1848
About
Pesci, D. Amistad
Adams, Richard
Watership Down
Adaptation. Lo, M.
Adios, nirvana. Wesselhoeft, C.
ADIRONDACK MOUNTAINS (N.Y.) -- FICTION
McGhee, A. All rivers flow to the sea
Adler, David
Dont talk to me about the war
Adler, Emily
Sweet 15
Adlington, L. J.
Cherry Heaven
The diary of Pelly D
ADOLESCENCE -- FICTION
Mason, B. A. In country
Min, K. Secondhand world
Mitchell, D. Black swan green
Strykowski, M. Call Me Amy
ADOLESCENCE -- FICTION
Calame, D. Swim the fly
Grossman, N. A world away
ADOLESCENTS *See* Teenagers
ADOPTION -- FICTION
Burg, Ann E. All the broken pieces
Cooney, C. B. Three black swans
Johnson, A. Heaven
Kephart, B. Small damages
McKay, H. Saffy's angel
Sheinmel, A. B. The lucky kind
Williams, L. E. Slant
Wright, B. When the black girl sings
Zarr, S. How to save a life
The **adoration** of Jenna Fox. Pearson, M.
ADULT CHILD ABUSE VICTIMS -- FICTION
Kraus, D. Scowler
ADULTERY -- FICTION
Mankell, H. Shadow of the leopard
ADULTS ABUSED AS CHILDREN *See* Adult child abuse victims
ADVENTURE AND ADVENTURERS -- FICTION *See* Adventure fiction
ADVENTURE FICTION
Bacigalupi, P. Adventure fiction
Benway, R. Also known as
Block, F. L. The island of excess love
Bobet, L. Above
Cadnum, M. Peril on the sea
Carson, R. The crown of embers
Charbonneau, J. Graduation day
Charbonneau, J. Independent study
Coben, H. Seconds away
Cole, S. Thieves like us
Cole, S. Thieves till we die
Colfer, E. Airman
Crockett, S. D. After the snow
Crossan, S. Breathe
Dagg, C. E. The year we were famous
Doctorow, C. Homeland
Durst, S. B. Vessel
Elliott, P. The Pale Assassin
Elliott, P. The traitor's smile
Falkner, B. The project
Frazier, A. The Eternal Sea
Frazier, A. Everlasting
Friesner, E. M. Nobody's princess
Friesner, E. M. Nobody's prize

Funke, C. Fearless
Funke, C. Reckless
Gardner, S. The red necklace
Gardner, S. The Silver Blade
Gill, D. M. Invisible sun
Gilman, D. Blood sun
Gilman, D. The devil's breath
Gilman, D. Ice claw
Golden, C. The sea wolves
Golden, C. The wild
Grant, K. M. How the hangman lost his heart
Heath, J. The Lab
Heath, J. Money run
Heath, J. Remote control
Henderson, J. The Triumph of Death
Hill, W. The rising
Higgins, J. Sure fire
Horowitz, A. Stormbreaker
Jansen, H. Over a thousand hills I walk with you
Johnston, E. K. Prairie fire
Johnston, E.K. The story of Owen
Kearney, M. The girl in the mirror
Kittredge, C. The nightmare garden
Lake, N. Hostage Three
Lowitz, L. Jet Black and the ninja wind
Lupica, M. Hero
MacHale, D. J. Raven rise
MacHale, D. J. The pilgrims of Rayne
MacHale, D. J. SYLO
Malaghan, M. Greek ransom
Mancusi, M. Scorched
Marillier, J. Shadowfell
Mary-Todd, J. Shot down
McCaughrean, G. The death -defying Pepper Roux
McDonald, I. Empress of the sun
McQuerry, M. D. The Peculiars
Meehan, K. Hannah's winter
Meloy, M. The apprentices
Meloy, C. Under Wildwood
Meyer, L. A. Bloody Jack
Meyer, L. A. My bonny light horseman
Meyer, L. A. Rapture of the deep
Meyer, L. A. Viva Jacquelina!
Miéville, C. Railsea
Molloy, M. Peter Raven under fire
Monaghan, A. A girl named Digit
Moore, P. V is for villian
Moran, K. Bloodline
Morgan, N. The highwayman's footsteps
Mourlevat Winter's end
Mowll, J. Operation Red Jericho
Mowll, J. Operation Storm City
Mowll, J. Operation typhoon shore
Mussi, S. The door of no return
Nix, G. A confusion of princes
O'Brien, J. Day of the assassins
Park, L. S. Click
Pauley, K. Cat Girl's day off
Perkins, L. R. As easy as falling off the face of the earth
Pratchett, T. Dodger
Preus, M. Shadow on the mountain
Rees, C. The fool's girl
Rees, C. Pirates!
Schreiber, J. Au revoir, crazy European chick
Schreiber, J. Perry's killer playlist
Somper, J. Demons of the ocean
Stevenson, R. H. Dead in the water
Stroud, J. Heroes of the valley
Summers, C. This is not a test
Taylor, S. S. The Expeditioners and the Treasure of Drowned Man's Canyon
Thomas, L. Quarantine
Tintera, A. Reboot
Tubb, K. O. The 13th sign
Turner, M. W. A conspiracy of kings
Turner, M. W. The King of Attolia
Turner, M. W. The Queen of Attolia
Turner, M. W. The thief
Under the moons of Mars
Van Diepen, A. Takedown
Walsh, P. The Crowfield demon
Wilks, M. Mirrorscape
Williams, A. The deep freeze of Bartholomew Tullock
Woolston, B. Black helicopters
Yancey, R. The extraordinary adventures of Alfred Kropp
Yolen, J. The Rogues
Young, E. L. STORM : The Infinity Code

ADVENTURE FICTION
See also fiction
ADVENTURE FILMS
See also Motion pictures
ADVENTURE FICTION
Schrefer, E. Threatened
ADVENTURE STORIES
See Adventure fiction
ADVENTURE TELEVISION PROGRAMS
See also Television programs
ADVENTURE TRAVEL
See also Travel; Voyages and travels
ADVICE COLUMNS -- FICTION
Bjorkman, L. Miss Fortune Cookie
ADVOCACY (POLITICAL SCIENCE)
See also Political science
AESTHETICS -- FICTION
Headley, J. C. North of beautiful
AFFECTION *See* Friendship; Love

AFGHAN WAR, 2001- -- FICTION
Massey, D. Torn
AFGHANISTAN -- FICTION
Doller, T. Something like normal
Massey, D. Torn
McKay, S. E. Thunder over Kandahar
Staples, S. F. Under the Persimmon tree
AFRICA -- FICTION
Kinch, M. The fires of New SUN
Kinch, M. The rebels of New SUN
AFRICAN AMERICAN WOMEN
See also Black women; Women
AFRICAN AMERICAN YOUTH -- FICTION
Blythe, C. Revenge of a not-so-pretty girl
Volponi, P. The Final Four
AFRICAN AMERICANS -- FICTION
Nelson, Vaunda Micheaux. No crystal stair
Taylor, M. D. The land
Woodson, J. If you come softly
AFRICAN AMERICANS -- CIVIL RIGHTS -- FICTION
Magoon, K. Fire in the streets
McMullan, M. Sources of light
AFRICAN AMERICANS -- FICTION
Anderson, M. T. The astonishing life of Octavian Nothing, traitor to the nation
Flake, S. G. Pinned
Grimes, N. Jazmin's notebook
Johnson, A. Heaven
Johnson, A. Sweet, hereafter
Johnson, A.Toning the sweep
Jones, T. L. Finding my place
Jones, T. L. Standing against the wind
Lyons, M. E. Letters from a slave boy
Lyons, M. E. Letters from a slave girl
Magoon, K. How it went down
Maldonado, T. Secret Saturdays
Moses, S. P. Joseph
Moses, S. P. The legend of Buddy Bush
Mosley, W. 47
Myers, W. D. All the right stuff
Myers, W. D. Harlem summer
Myers, W. D. Hoops
Myers, W. D. Riot
Myers, W. D. Scorpions
Myers, W. D. Slam!
Myers, W. D. Street love
Nolan, H. A summer of Kings
Paulsen, G. Nightjohn
Rabin, S. Black powder
Volponi, P. Black and white
Volponi, P. Rikers High
Volponi, P. Rucker Park setup
Weatherford, C. B. Becoming Billie Holiday
Weyn, S. Recruited
Whittenberg, A. Life is fine
Whittenberg, A. Sweet Thang
Williams-Garcia, R. No laughter here
Woods, B. Emako Blue
Woodson, J. After Tupac and D Foster
Woodson, J. From the notebooks of Melanin Sun
Wright, B. Crow
Wright, B. When the black girl sings
AFRICAN AMERICANS -- INTELLECTUAL LIFE *See also* Blacks -- Intellectual life; Intellectual life
AFRICAN AMERICANS -- MISSISSIPPI
AFRICANS -- FICTION
Park, L. S. A long walk to water
AFRICANS -- UNITED STATES -- FICTION
Cooney, C. B. Diamonds in the shadow
Griffin, P. The Orange Houses
Afrika. Craig, C.
AFRO-AMERICAN ART
See African American art
AFRO-AMERICAN ARTISTS
See African American artists
AFRO-AMERICAN ATHLETES
See African American athletes
AFRO-AMERICAN AUTHORS
See African American authors
AFRO-AMERICAN BUSINESSPEOPLE
See African American businesspeople
AFRO-AMERICAN CHILDREN
See African American children
AFRO-AMERICAN MUSICIANS
See African American musicians
AFRO-AMERICAN WOMEN
See African American women
After. Efaw, A.
After Eli. Rupp, R.
After ever after. Sonnenblick, J.
After hello. Mangum, L.
After. Prose, F.
After the first death. Cormier, R.
After the rain. Mazer, N. F.
After the kiss. McVoy, T. E.
After the moment. Freymann-Weyr, G.
After the snow. Crockett, S. D.
After the train. Whelan, G.
After the war. Matas, C.
After Tupac and D Foster. Woodson, J.,
AFTERLIFE *See* Future life
Aftershocks. Lavender, W.
Afterworlds. Westerfeld, S.
Agard, John
The young inferno
Age 14. Spillebeen, G.
Agell, Charlotte
Shift
The Agency [series]

Lee, Y. S. The body at the tower
Lee, Y. S. A spy in the house
AGENT ORANGE -- FICTION
Lynch, C. Casualties of war
AGORAPHOBIA -- FICTION
De Goldi, K. The 10 p.m. question
Aguirre, Ann
Enclave
Horde
Outpost
AIDS (DISEASE) -- FICTION
Minchin, A. The beat goes on
Stratton, A. Chanda's secrets
AIR PILOTS -- FICTION
Smith, S. L. Flygirl
Wein, E. Code name Verity
Wein, E. Rose under fire
AIR TRAVEL -- FICTION
Smith, J. E. The statistical probability of love at first sight
AIR WARFARE *See* Military aeronautics; Military airplanes
AIRCRAFT ACCIDENTS -- FICTION
Scott, E. Miracle
Airborn. Oppel, K.
Airman. Colfer, E.
AIRCRAFT CARRIERS
See also Military aeronautics; Warships
Airhead. Cabot, M.
AIRMEN -- FICTION
Lynch, C. Casualties of war
AIRPLANES -- FICTION
Colfer, E. Airman
AIRSHIPS -- FICTION
McDonald, I. Empress of the sun
Oppel, K. Airborn
Oppel, K. Skybreaker
Oppel, K. Starclimber
Ryan, A. K. Flame
Akata witch. Okorafor, N.
ALASKA -- FICTION
Bell, H. Traitor's son
Hobbs, W. Leaving Protection
Smelcer, J. E. The trap
ALASKA -- GOLD DISCOVERIES -- FICTION
Sedgwick, M. Revolver
Albatross. Bloss, J.
ALBIGENSES -- FICTION
Grant, K. M. Paradise red
Alban, Andrea
Anya's War
Albin, Gennifer
Crewel
ALBINOS AND ALBINISM -- FICTION
Laban, E. The Tragedy Paper
Okorafor, N. Akata witch
Sullivan, T. Golden boy
ALCHEMY
See also Chemistry; Occultism
ALCHEMY -- FICTION
Mahoney, K. The iron witch
Meloy, M. The apothecary
Meloy, M. The apprentices
Scott, M. The enchantress
The **alchemist's** dream. Wilson, J.
The **alchemyst.** Scott, M.
ALCOHOLISM -- FICTION
Hyde, C. R. The year of my miraculous reappearance
Luedeke, L. Smashed
Sanchez, A. Rainbow boys
Alegria, Malin
Estrella's quinceanera
Alekse Nikolaevich, Czarevitch, son of Nicholas II, Emperor of Russia, 1904-1918 FICTION
Whitcomb, L. The Fetch
Alender, Katie
Bad girls don't die
Alexander, Jill S.
The sweetheart of Prosper County
Paradise
Alexander, Kwame
The crossover
He said, she said
Alexie, Sherman
Alexie, S. The absolutely true diary of a part-time Indian
Alice in April. Naylor, P. R.
Alice in rapture, sort of. Naylor, P. R.
Alien invasion and other inconveniences. Yansky, B.
ALIEN PESTS *See* Nonindigenous pests
ALIENATION (SOCIAL PSYCHOLOGY)
See also Social psychology
ALIENATION (SOCIAL PSYCHOLOGY) -- FICTION
Lewis, S. Beautiful decay
Alis. Rich, N.
All good children. Austen, C.
All my noble dreams and then what happens. Whelan, G.
All our pretty songs. McCarry, S.
All our yesterdays. Terrill, C.
All rivers flow to the sea. McGhee, A.
All the broken pieces. Burg, Ann E.,
All the right stuff. Myers, W. D.
All the truth that's in me. Berry, J.
All these lives. Wylie, S.
All these things I've done. Zevin, G.
All unquiet things. Jarzab, A.
All we know of heaven. Mitchard, J.

All we know of love. Baskin, N. R.
All you desire; can you trust your heart? Miller, K.,
All you never wanted. Griffin, A.
All-American girl. Cabot, M.
All-in. Hautman, P.
Allegiant. Roth, V.
ALLEGORIES
Adams, R. Watership Down
Allegra. Hrdlitschka, S.
ALLERGY -- FICTION
Moskowitz, H. Break
Alliance. Frost, M.
Alligator bayou. Napoli, D. J.,
Almond, David
Clay
The fire-eaters
Kit's wilderness
Skellig
The true tale of the monster Billy Dean
Almost perfect. Katcher, B.
Along for the ride. Dessen, S.
Alonzo, Sandra
Riding invisible
Alphabet of dreams. Fletcher, S.
Alpine, Rachele
Canary
Also known as. Benway, R.
Alt ed. Atkins, C.
Altebrando, Tara
The best night of your (pathetic) life
Dreamland social club
(jt. auth) Zarr, S. Roomies
Altered. Rush, J.
ALTERNATIVE ENERGY RESOURCES
See Renewable energy resources
ALTERNATIVE HISTORIES
Cameron, S. The dark unwinding
Gardner, S. Maggot moon
Hesse, K. Safekeeping
Moore, K. Neverwas
Rutkoski, M. The shadow society
Alvarez, Julia
Before we were free
Finding miracles
Always a witch. MacCullough, C.
Always upbeat / All that. Moore, D.
Always watching. Collins, B.
Amateau, Gigi
A certain strain of peculiar.
Amato, Joseph Anthony
The **amazing** Maurice and his educated rodents. Pratchett, T.
Amato, Mary
Invisible lines
AMAZONS -- FICTION
Hoffman, A. The foretelling
Amber House. Moore, K.
Amber House trilogy [series]
Moore, K. Neverwas
The **amber** spyglass. Pullman, P.
Amelia Anne is dead and gone. Rosenfield, K.
America. Frank, E. R.
AMERICA -- DISCOVERY AND EXPLORATION -- SPANISH -- FICTION
Mlawski, S. Hammer of witches
AMERICA -- EXPLORATION -- FICTION
Mlawski, S. Hammer of witches
The American fairy trilogy [series]
Zettel, S. Golden girl
AMERICAN SIGN LANGUAGE -- FICTION
Ferris, J. Of sound mind
AMERICAN STUDENTS -- SOVIET UNION -- FICTION
Standiford, N. The boy on the bridge
AMERICANS -- ITALY -- FICTION
Beyer, K. The demon catchers of Milan
AMHERST (MASS.) -- FICTION
Hubbard, J. And we stay
MacColl, M. Nobody's secret
Amigas [series]
Chambers, V. Fifteen candles
Amin, Idi, 1925-2003
Nanji, S. Child of dandelions
Amiri & Odette; a love story. Myers, W. D., 1937-
AMISH -- FICTION
Bickle, L. The outside
Grossman, N. A world away
Amistad. Pesci, D.
AMISTAD (SCHOONER) -- FICTION
Pesci, D. Amistad
AMNESIA -- FICTION
Armistead, C. Being Henry David
Lerangis, P. Somebody, please tell me who I am
Lowry, L. Son
Wasserman, R. Awakening
Weaver, W. The survivors
AMPUTEES -- FICTION
Baratz-Logsted, L. Crazy beautiful
Bingham, K. Shark girl
Mankell, H. Shadow of the leopard
Rorby, G. The outside of a horse
Van Draanen, W. The running dream
Volponi, P. Izzy, willy-nilly
Waldorf, H. Tripping
The **Amulet** of Samarkand. Stroud, J.
AMUSEMENT PARKS -- FICTION
Strohmeyer, S. How Zoe made her dreams (mostly) come true
Amy & Roger's epic detour. Matson, M.

ANARCHISTS -- FICTION
Burgess, M. Smack
Anastasia Nikolaevna, Grand Duchess, daughter of Nicholas II, Emperor of Russia, 1901-1918 FICTION *See* Amin, Idi
Whitcomb, L. The Fetch
ANATOMY -- FICTION
Quick, B. A golden web
The **anatomy** of wings. Foxlee, K.
ANATOMY, ARTISTIC *See* Artistic anatomy
ANATOMY, COMPARATIVE
See Comparative anatomy
Ancient, strange, and lovely. Fletcher, S.
And in the morning. Wilson, J.
And then things fall apart. Tibensky, A.
And we stay. Hubbard, J.
Anderson, Jessica Lee
Border crossing
Anderson, Katie D.
Kiss & Make Up
Anderson, Laurie Halse, 1961-
Anderson, L. H. Chains
Anderson, L. H. Wintergirls
Chains
Fever, 1793
Forge
The impossible knife of memory
Prom
Speak
Twisted
Wintergirls
Anderson, M. T., 1968-
The astonishing life of Octavian Nothing, traitor to the nation
Burger Wuss
Anderson, R. J.
Ultraviolet
Spell Hunter
Andreu, M. E.
The secret side of empty
Andrews, Jesse
Me & Earl & the dying girl
Andromeda Klein. Portman, F.
ANEXORIA NERVOSA -- FICTION
Letting Ana go
Angel. McNish, C.
Angel burn. Weatherly, L.,
Angel Isle. Dickinson, P.
Angelfire. Moulton, C. A.
ANGELS -- FICTION
Brockenbrough, M. Devine intervention
De la Cruz, M. Gates of Paradise
Shirvington, J. Embrace
Shirvington, J. Entice
Taylor, L. Dreams of gods & monsters
Weatherly, L. Angel burn
ANGER -- FICTION
Galante, C. The summer of May
McMullan, M. Cashay
ANGLICAN AND EPISCOPAL CLERGY -- FICTION
Paton, A. Cry, the beloved country
Angry young man. Lynch, C.
Angus, thongs and full-frontal snogging. Rennison, L.
ANIMAL ABUSE *See* Animal welfare
ANIMAL RESCUE -- FICTION
Schrefer, E. Threatened
ANIMAL SANCTUARIES -- FICTION
Schrefer, E. Endangered
ANIMAL SEXUAL BEHAVIOR
See Sexual behavior in animals
ANIMAL SHELTERS
See also Animal welfare
ANIMAL SIGNS *See* Animal tracks
ANIMALS -- ANATOMY
See also Anatomy; Zoology
ANIMALS -- BEHAVIOR *See* Animal behavior
ANIMALS -- COLOR
See also Color
ANIMALS -- DISEASES
See also Diseases
ANIMALS -- FICTION
Meloy, C. Under Wildwood
Meloy, C. Wildwood
Zuckerman, L. A taste for rabbit
ANIMALS -- FOLKLORE
See also Folklore
ANIMALS -- FOOD
See also Animal behavior; Food
ANIMISM
See also Religion
Anna and the French kiss. Perkins, S.
Anna begins. Davenport, J.
Anna's world. Coleman, W.
Anne Boleyn, Queen, consort of Henry VIII, King of England, 1507-1536 About
Longshore, K. Tarnish
Annexed. Dogar, S.
ANOREXIA NERVOSA -- FICTION
Burton, R. Leaving Jetty Road
Letting Ana go
Metzger, L. A trick of the light
Another Faust. Nayeri, D.
Another kind of cowboy. Juby, S.
Another Pan. Nayeri, D.
ANTARCTICA -- FICTION
McCaughrean, G. The white darkness
White, A. Surviving Antarctica
Anthem for Jackson Dawes. Bryce, C.
Anthony, Joelle
Restoring Harmony

Anthony, Piers
Jumper cable
A spell for chameleon
ANTHROPOLOGY
See also Social sciences
ANTHROPOLOGY -- FICTION
Pearson, J. The rites & wrongs of Janice Wills
ANTI-APARTHEID MOVEMENT
See also Civil rights; Social movements; South Africa -- Race relations
The **anti-prom.** McDonald, A.
ANTI-UTOPIAS *See* Dystopias
ANTI-WAR POETRY *See* War poetry
ANTI-WAR STORIES *See* War stories
ANTIABORTION MOVEMENT
See Pro-life movement
ANTIBIOTIC RESISTANCE IN MICROORGANISMS
See Drug resistance in microorganisms
Antieau, Kim
Broken moon
Ruby's Imagine
ANTISEMITISM -- FICTION
Whelan, G. After the train
ANTIETAM (MD.), BATTLE OF, 1862
See also Battles; United States -- History -- 1861-1865, Civil War -- Campaigns
ANTISEMITISM -- FICTION
Sanders, S. Rachel's secret
Antonius, Marcus, ca. 83-30 B.C. About
Shecter, V. A. Cleopatra's moon
Antsy does time. Shusterman, N.
Anya's war. Alban, A
APARTMENT HOUSES -- FICTION
Hyde, C. R. Jumpstart the world
APES *See also* Primates
APES -- FICTION
Schrefer, E. Endangered
APOCALYPTIC FICTION
Aguirre, A. Enclave
Bacigalupi, P. The drowned cities
Block, F. L. Love in the time of global warming
Coutts, A. Tumble & fall
Falls, K. Inhuman
Kessler, J. Loss
Kizer, A. A matter of days
Mary-Todd, J. Shot down
Peterfreund, D. For darkness shows the stars
Roberts, J. Rage within
Rossi, V. Under the never sky
Roth, V. Insurgent
Ruins
Shards and Ashes
Smith, A. Grasshopper jungle
Wendig, C. Under the Empyrean Sky
APOCALYPTIC FICTION
See also fiction
APOCALYPTIC FILMS
See also Motion pictures
APOLLO (GREEK DEITY)
See also Gods and goddesses
Apollo's outcasts. Steele, A.
Gormley, B. Poisoned honey
The **apothecary.** Meloy, M.
APPALACHIAN REGION -- FICTION
Marshall, C. Christy
Applegate, Katherine
Eve & Adam
The **apprentices.** Meloy, M.
APPRENTICES -- FICTION
Fisher, C. The dark city
Fisher, C. The hidden Coronet
Fisher, C. The lost heiress
Fisher, C. The Margrave
Oliver, J. G. The demon trapper's daughter
Wilks, M. Mirrorscape
Yancey, R. The final descent
ARAB-ISRAELI CONFLICT -- FICTION
Miklowitz, G. D. The enemy has a face
Arbuthnott, Gill
The Keepers' tattoo
Archer, E.
Geek: fantasy novel
Archer, Jennifer
Through her eyes
ARCHEOLOGY -- FICTION
Peterson, W. Triskellion 2: The burning
ARCHERY -- FICTION
Lloyd, A. Year of the tiger
ARCHITECTURE -- FICTION
Chen, J. Return to me
Arclight. McQuein, J. L.
Arcos, Carrie
Out of reach
ARCTIC REGIONS -- FICTION
Soonchild
Are these my basoomas I see before me? Rennison, L.
Are you there God? Blume, J.,
ARENA THEATER
See also Theater
ARGENTINA -- FICTION
Whelan, G. The Disappeared
ARGENTINE AMERICANS -- FICTION
Ockler, S. The Book of Broken Hearts
ARISTOCRACY -- FICTION
Doyle, M. Courtship and curses
Aristotle and Dante discover the secrets of

the universe. Sáenz, B. A.
ARIZONA -- FICTION
King, A. S. Everybody sees the ants
Wallace, S. N. Muckers
ARKANSAS -- FICTION
Whaley, J. C. Where things come back
ARMENIAN MASSACRES, 1915-1923 -- FICTION
Skrypuch, M. F. Daughter of war
Armistead, Cal
Being Henry David
Armstrong, Kelley
The awakening
The reckoning
Armstrong, William Howard
Sounder
ARMY OFFICERS -- FICTION
Spillebeen, G. Kipling's choice
Arnett, M.
Avalon
Arnold, Tedd
Rat life
Arntson, Steven
The wrap-up list
AROMATIC PLANTS
See also Plants
Aronson, Sarah
Head case
Around the worl in 100 days. Blackwood, G.
ARSON -- FICTION
Ehrenberg, P. Tillmon County fire
Wilson, D. L. Firehorse
ART -- FICTION
Gallagher, L. The opposite of invisible
Kephart, B. Nothing but ghosts
Wilks, M. Mirrorscape
ART THEFTS -- FICTION
Renn, D. Tokyo heist
Arthur, King
About
Crossley-Holland, K. Crossing to Paradise
McKenzie, N. Guinevere's gamble
Reeve, P. Here lies Arthur
Spinner, S. Damosel
Springer, N. I am Mordred
Springer, N. I am Morgan le Fay
Vande Velde, V. The book of Mordred
ARTHURIAN ROMANCES
See also Romances
Article 5. Simmons, K.
ARTISTS -- FICTION
Beaufrand, M. J. Primavera
Bingham, K. Formerly shark girl
Bryant, J. Pieces of Georgia
Cullen, L. I am Rembrandt's daughter
Johnson, A. D. The summer prince
Kamata, S. Gadget Girl
Napoli, D. J. The smile
Pearce, J. As you wish
Walters, E. Sketches
Wilks, M. Mirrorscape
Willis, C. C. Buck fever
ARUBA -- FICTION
Haas, A. Dangerous girls
As easy as falling off the face of the earth. Perkins, L. R.
As you wish. Pearce, J.
The **ascension.** Carroll, M. O.
Ash. Lo, M.
ASHANTI (AFRICAN PEOPLE)
See also Africans; Indigenous peoples
Ashby, Amanda
Fairy bad day
Zombie queen of Newbury High
Asher, Jay
The future of us
Thirteen reasons why
Ashes. Lasky, K.
Ashes. Bick, I. J.
Ashes, ashes. Treggiari, J.
Ashfall. Mullin, M.
Ashton, Brodi
Everbound
Everneath
ASIA -- CIVILIZATION
ASIAN AMERICANS -- FICTION
Budhos, M. Ask me no questions
The **Ask** and the Answer. Ness, P.
Ask me no questions. Budhos, M.
Ask the passengers. King, A. S.
ASPERGER'S SYNDROME -- FICTION
Brenna, B. Waiting for no one
Franklin, E. The half life of planets
Kelly, T. Harmonic feedback
Miller, A. E. Colin Fischer
Roy, J. R. Mindblind
Stork, F. X. Marcelo in the real world
Assassin. Myers, A.
ASSASSINATION -- FICTION
Lu, M. Prodigy
ASSASSINS -- FICTION
Carriger, G. Etiquette & espionage
Heath, J. Money run
LaFevers, R. Dark triumph
Maas, S. J. Crown of midnight
Maas, S. J. Throne of glass
Schreiber, J. Perry's killer playlist
Zadoff, A. Boy Nobody
ASSERTIVENESS (PSYCHOLOGY) -- FICTION
Myracle, L. The infinite moment of us
ASTEROIDS -- COLLISIONS WITH

EARTH -- FICTION
Coutts, A. Tumble & fall
The **astonishing** adventures of Fanboy & Goth Girl. Lyga, B.
The **astonishing** life of Octavian Nothing, traitor to the nation. Anderson, M. T.
Astor, John Jacob, 1763-1848
About
Weyn, S. Distant waves
Astra. Platt, C.
ASTROLOGERS -- FICTION
Wilson, J. The alchemist's dream
ASTROLOGY -- FICTION
Tubb, K. O. Selling hope
Tubb, K. O. The 13th sign
ASTRONAUTS -- FICTION
172 hours on the moon
ASTRONOMY -- FICTION
At the firefly gate. Newbery, L.
At Yellow Lake. McLoughlin, J.
ATHLETES -- CONDUCT OF LIFE
Volponi, P. The Final Four
Atkins, Catherine
The file on Angelyn Stark
ATLANTA (GA.) -- FICTION
McVoy, T. E. After the kiss
Myracle, L. The infinite moment of us
Myracle, L. Bliss
Myracle, L. Peace, love, and baby ducks
Oliver, J. G. The demon trapper's daughter
Oliver, J. Soul thief
ATLANTIS -- FICTION
Scott, M. The enchantress
Atwater-Rhodes, Amelia
Persistence of memory
Snakecharm
Au revoir, crazy European chick. Schreiber, J.
Auch, Mary Jane
Ashes of roses
Guitar boy
X-isle
Augarde, Steve
X-Isle
Augustus, Emperor of Rome, 63 B.C.-14 A.D.
About
Dray, S. Lily of the Nile
AUNTS -- FICTION
Archer, E. Geek: fantasy novel
Baratz-Logsted, L. Twin's daughter
Bauer, J. Hope was here
Fusco, K. N. Tending to Grace
Grossman, N. A world away
Johnson, M. 13 little blue envelopes
Les Becquets, D. Love, Cajun style
Mackler, C. Vegan virgin Valentine
Mulder, M. Out of the box
Weeks, S. Jumping the scratch
Whelan, G. All my noble dreams and then what happens
Whelan, G. Small acts of amazing courage,
Aurelia. Osterlund, A.
The **Auslander.** Dowswell, P.
Aurelie; a faerie tale. Tomlinson, H.
Austen, Catherine
All good children
Austen, Jane, 1775-1817
About
Harrison, C. I was Jane Austen's best friend
AUSTRALIA -- FICTION
Abdel-Fattah, R. Does my head look big in this?
Abdel-Fattah, R. Ten things I hate about me
Boyd, M. Will
Buzo, L. Love and other perishable items
Clarke, J. One whole and perfect day
Clarke, J. The winds of heaven
Crowley, C. A little wanting song
Foxlee, K. The anatomy of wings
Foxlee, K. The midnight dress
Frazier, A. Everlasting
Hartnett, S. Butterfly
Hartnett, S. Thursday's child
Healey, K. When we wake
Herrick, S. By the river
Herrick, S. Cold skin
Herrick, S. The wolf
James, R. Beautiful malice
Jinks, C. Evil genius
Jinks, C. Genius squad
Jinks, C. The genius wars
Larbalestier, J. Magic lessons
Larbalestier, J. Magic or madness
Marchetta, M. Jellicoe Road
Marchetta, M. The piper's son
Marchetta, M. Saving Francesca
Marsden, J. Tomorrow, when the war began
Marsden, J. Incurable
Marsden, J. The other side of dawn
Marsden, J. While I live
McCarthy, M. Rose by any other name
Meyer, L. A. The wake of the Lorelei Lee
Moriarty, J. The ghosts of Ashbury High
Moriarty, J. The year of secret assignments
Murray, M. How to make a bird
Russon, P. Breathe
Silvey, C. Jasper Jones
Slade, A. G. Empire of ruins
Wakefield, V. Friday never leaving
Wilkinson, L. Pink
Williams, G. Beatle meets Destiny
AUTHORS -- FICTION
Chambers, A. Dying to know you

Pennington, K. Brief candle
Poblocki, D. The random child
Scieszka, J. Who done it?
Smith, A. 100 sideways miles
Thomson, S. L. The secret of the Rose
AUTHORSHIP -- FICTION
Arnold, T. Rat life
Cooney, C. B. Janie face to face
Cornwell, A. Carpe diem
Davenport, J. Anna begins
Freitas, D. This gorgeous game
Grimes, N. Jazmin's notebook
Hemphill, S. Hideous love
Johnson, M. Suite Scarlett
Lubar, D. Sleeping freshmen never lie
Mitchell, D. Black swan green
Myers, W. D. Darius & Twig
Nance, A. Daemon Hall
Nance, A. Return to Daemon Hall: evil roots
Sales, L. Mostly good girls
Scieszka, J. Who done it?
Selfors, S. Mad love
Wittlinger, E. Hard love
Wittlinger, E. Love & lies
Wizner, J. Spanking Shakespeare
Woods, B. A star on the Hollywood Walk of Fame
AUTISM -- FICTION
Coker, R. Chasing Jupiter
Kehoe, S. W. The sound of letting go
Myers, W. D. A star is born
AUTOBIOGRAPHICAL STORIES
Peck, R. N. A day no pigs would die
AUTOMOBILE TRAVEL -- FICTION
Wittlinger, E. Zigzag
Woolston, B. Catch & release
AUTOMOBILES -- FICTION
Moloney, J. Black taxi
Monninger, J. Finding somewhere
Avalon. Arnett, M.
Avasthi, Swati
Chasing Shadows
Split
Avi, 1937-
City of orphans
Crispin: the cross of lead
Nothing but the truth
Traitor's gate
The **awakening.** Armstrong, K.
Awakening. Wasserman, R.
Away. Hall, T.
Awkward. Bates, M.
Ayarbe, Heidi
Compromised
Compulsion
Ayres, Katherine
North by night

B

BABIES -- FICTION
Scott, K. This is so not happening
Babylonne. Jinks, C.
BABYSITTERS -- FICTION
McClymer, K. Must love black
Prose, F. The turning
Bacigalupi, Paolo
The drowned cities
Ship Breaker
Back before dark. Shoemaker, T.
Back when you were easier to love. Smith, E. W.
Backes, M. Molly
The princesses of Iowa
Bad apple. Ruby, L.
A **bad** boy can be good for a girl. Stone, T. L.
Bad girls don't die. Alender, K.
Bad Island. Zweig, E.
Bad kitty. Jaffe, M.
Bad taste in boys. Harris, C.
Badd. Tharp, T.
Badoe, Adwoa
Between sisters
Baer, Marianna
Frost
BAHAMAS -- FICTION
Stevenson, R. A thousand shades of blue
Bailey, Em
Shift
Bailey, Kristin
Legacy of the clockwork key
Bait. Sanchez, A.
BAKING -- FICTION
Hepler, H. The cupcake queen
Balefire. Tiernan, C.
Ball don't lie. De la Pena, M.
Ballad. Stiefvater, M.
Ballard, J. G., 1930-2009
Empire of the Sun
BALLET -- FICTION
Castellucci, C. Rose sees red
Doyle, E. F. According to Kit
Flack, S. Bunheads
Padian, M. Jersey tomatoes are the best
BALLET DANCERS -- FICTION
Draper, S. M. Panic
Balog, Cyn
Sleepless
BALTIMORE (MD.) -- FICTION
Hahn, M. D. Mister Death's blue-eyed girls
Mitchell, S. The vespertine
Smith-Ready, J. Shade
Smith-Ready, J. Shift
Standiford, N. Confessions of the

Sullivan sisters
Standiford, N. How to say goodbye in Robot
Bancks, Tristan
Mac Slater hunts the cool
Mac Slater vs. the city
Banks, Kate
Walk softly, Rachel
BANDS (MUSIC) -- FICTION
Beaudoin, S. Wise Young Fool
Briant, E. I am (not) the walrus
Hannan, P. My big mouth
LaCour, N. The Disenchantments
Perez, M. Dead is a killer tune
Raskin, J. My misadventures as a teenage rock star,
Bang! Flake, S. G.
BAR MITZVAH -- FICTION
Rubens, M. Sons of the 613
Baratz-Logsted, Lauren
Crazy beautiful
Twin's daughter
Bardugo, Leigh
Ruin and rising
Shadow and bone
Siege and storm
Barkley, Brad
Dream factory
Jars of glass
Scrambled eggs at midnight
Barlowe, Wayne Douglas
God's demon
Barnes, Jennifer Lynn
The Squad: perfect cover
Barnes, John
Losers in space
Tales of the Madman Underground
Barnhouse, Rebecca
The book of the maidservant
Barratt, Mark
Joe Rat
The wild man
Barrett, Tracy
Dark of the moon
King of Ithaka
Barron, T. A.
The lost years of Merlin
Merlin's dragon
Barry, Max
Lexicon
Bartimaeus trilogy [series]
Stroud, J. The Amulet of Samarkand
Stroud, J. The golem's eye
Stroud, J. Ptolemy's gate
Bartoletti, Susan Campbell
The boy who dared
BASEBALL -- FICTION
Deuker, C. Painting the black
Fitzmaurice, K. A diamond in the desert
Gratz, A. Samurai shortstop
Lupica, M. The batboy
Lupica, M. The big field
McCormick, P. My brother's keeper
Murphy, C. R. Free radical
Smith, J. E. The comeback season
Tocher, T. Bill Pennant, Babe Ruth, and me
Tocher, T. Chief Sunrise, John McGraw, and me
Trueman, T. 7 days at the hot corner
Turner, A. W. Hard hit
BASKETBALL -- FICTION
Alexander, K. The crossover
Coy, J. Box out
Deuker, C. Night hoops
Deuker, C. Swagger
Lupica, M. Miracle on 49th Street
Lupica, M. Summer ball
Mackel, K. Boost
Myers, W. D. Hoops
Myers, W. D. Slam!
Parker, R. B. The Edenville Owls
Quick, M. Boy21
Volponi, P. Black and white
Volponi, P. Rucker Park setup
Yep, L. Dragon road; Golden Mountain chronicles: 1939
BASKETBALL PLAYERS -- FICTION
Simone, N. Upgrade U
Baskin, Nora Raleigh
All we know of love
Bass, Karen
Graffiti knight
Summer of fire
Bass, Ron
Lucid
Bassoff, L.
Lost girl found
Bastedo, Jamie
On thin ice
The **batboy.** Lupica, M.
Bates, Marni
Awkward
BATH (ENGLAND) -- FICTION
Pitcher, A. Ketchup clouds
Battle dress. Efaw, A.
The **Battle** of Jericho. Draper, S. M.
Bauer, Joan
Hope was here
Peeled
Squashed
Bauman, Beth Ann
Rosie & Skate
Be my enemy. McDonald, I.

BEACHES -- FICTION
Bancks, T. Mac Slater hunts the cool
Dessen, S. The moon and more
Han, J. It's not summer without you
Han, J. The summer I turned pretty
Han, J. We'll always have summer
Kirby, J. Moonglass
Nelson, B. They came from below
Beachmont letters. Twomey, C.
Beacon Hill boys. Mochizuki, K.
BEAGLE EXPEDITION (1831-1836) -- FICTION
Meyer, C. The true adventures of Charley Darwin
Beam, Cris
I am J
Beard, Philip
Dear Zoe
Beardance. Hobbs, W.
BEARS -- FICTION
Hobbs, W. Beardance
Mikaelsen, B. Touching Spirit Bear
Pattou, E. East
Bearstone. Hobbs, W.
Beast. Napoli, D. J.
The **beast** of Noor. Carey, J. L.
Beastly. Flinn, A.
The **beat** goes on. Minchin, A.
Beat the band. Calame, D.
Beating heart. Jenkins, A. M.
Beatle meets Destiny. Williams, G.
Beaudoin, Sean
Wise Young Fool
You killed Wesley Payne
Beaufrand, Mary Jane
Primavera
The river
The **beautiful** and the cursed. Morgan, P.
Beautiful creatures. Garcia, K.
Beautiful darkness. Garcia, K.
Beautiful decay. Lewis, S.
A **beautiful** lie. Master, I.
Beautiful malice. James, R.
Beautiful Music for Ugly Children. Cronn-Mills, K.
Beauty. McKinley, R.
BEAUTY CONTESTS -- FICTION
Eulberg, E. Revenge of the Girl With the Great Personality
Beauty queens. Bray, L.
BEAUTY, PERSONAL -- FICTION
Friend, N. My life in black and white
Griffin, P. Burning blue
Rainfield, C. Stained
Ross, E. Belle epoque
Rudnick, P. Gorgeous
Westerfeld, S. Uglies
Beauty shop for rent; --fully equipped, inquire within. Bowers, L.
BEAUTY SHOPS -- FICTION
Bowers, L. Beauty shop for rent; -- fully equipped, inquire within
BEAVERS
See also Furbearing animals; Mammals
Because I am furniture. Chaltas, T.
Because it is my blood. Zevin, G.
Bechard, Margaret
Hanging on to Max
Beck, Ian
Pastworld
Becker, Tom
Darkside
Lifeblood
Becoming Billie Holiday. Weatherford, C. B.
Becoming Chloe. Hyde, C. R.
Bedford, Martyn
Flip
Never ending
BEES -- FICTION
Koja, K. Kissing the bee
McKinley, R. Chalice
Beetle boy. Willey, M..
Before I die. Downham, J.
Before I fall. Oliver, L.
Before we were free. Alvarez, J.
Before wings. Goobie, B.,
Before, after, and somebody in between. Garsee, J.
The **beginner's** guide to living. Hills, L.
The **beginning** of everything. Schneider, R.
BEHAVIOR
See Animal behavior; Human behavior
BEHAVIOR -- FICTION
FitzGerald, H. Deviant
Behemoth.
Behind the masks. Patron, S.
Behind you. Woodson, J.
Beige. Castellucci, C.
Being. Brooks, K.
Being Henry David. Armistead, C.
Being Nikki. Cabot, M.
Beitia, Sara
The last good place of Lily Odilon
Beka Cooper [series]
Pierce, T. Bloodhound
Pierce, T. Mastiff
Pierce, T. Terrier
BELGIUM -- HISTORY -- 1814-1830 -- FICTION
Doyle, M. Courtship and curses
Bell, Cathleen Davitt
Slipping
Bell, Hilari

Fall of a kingdom
Forging the sword
The Goblin Wood
The last knight
Rise of a hero
Shield of stars
Traitor's son
Trickster's girl
Bell, Joanne
Juggling fire
Belladonna. Finn, M.
Belle epoque. Ross, E.
Belzhar. Wolitzer, M.
Bemis, John Claude
The White City
The Wolf Tree
Benched. Watson, C.
Beneath a meth moon. Woodson, J.
Beneath my mother's feet. Qamar, A.
Benito runs. Fontes, J.
Bennett Wealer, Sara
Rival
Bennett, Holly
Shapeshifter
Benoit, Charles
You
Benway, Robin
Also known as
Audrey, wait!
The extraordinary secrets of April, May and June
BEREAVEMENT -- FICTION
Berk, J. Guy Langman, crime scene procrastinator
Bryant, J. Pieces of Georgia
Frank, E. R. Wrecked
Friend, N. Perfect
Johnson, J. J. The theory of everything
Kittle, K. Reasons to be happy
Knowles, J. *See* you at Harry's
Lynch, C. Pieces
McMullan, M. Cashay
McNamee, G. Bonechiller
Michaels, R. The reminder
Newbery, L. Flightsend
O'Connell, M. The sharp time
Plum, A. Die for me
Polisner, G. The pull of gravity
Smith, H. T. Wild awake
Whelan, G. Small acts of amazing courage,
Williams, C. L. Waiting
Yeomans, E. Rubber houses
Zadoff, A. My life, the theater, and other tragedies,
Zarr, S. How to save a life
Berk, Ari
Death watch
Mistle child
Berk, Josh
The dark days of Hamburger Halpin
Guy Langman, crime scene procrastinator
BERLIN (GERMANY) -- FICTION
Dowswell, P. The Auslander
Sharenow, R. The Berlin Boxing Club
The **Berlin** Boxing Club. Sharenow, R.
Bernard, Romily
Find me
Bernobich, Beth
Fox & Phoenix
Berry, Julie
All the truth that's in me
The Amaranth enchantment
Bertagna, Julie
Exodus
Zenith
The **best** bad luck I ever had. Levine, K.
BEST FRIENDS -- FICTION
Derting, K. The last echo
Farizan, S. If you could be mine
Flake, S. G. Pinned
Griffin, N. The whole stupid way we are
Haas, A. Dangerous girls
Howard, J. J. That time I joined the circus
Howland, L. Nantucket blue
Johnson, J. J. The theory of everything
LaCour, N. The Disenchantments
May, K. Kiki
McCarry, S. All our pretty songs
Moore, C. The stalker chronicles
Myers, W. D. Darius & Twig
Oliver, L. Requiem
Scheibe, L. Riptide
Shoemaker, T. Back before dark
Singleton, L. J. Dead girl dancing
Singleton, L. J. Dead girl in love
Skuse, C. J. Rockoholic
Strohmeyer, S. Smart girls get what they want
Vacco, C. My chemical mountain
Williams, S. Twinmaker
Best friends forever; a World War II scrapbook. Patt, B.
The **best** night of your (pathetic) life. Altebrando, T.
BEST-BOOK LISTS *See* Best books
Beta. Cohn, R.
The **betrayal** of Maggie Blair. Laird, E.
The **betrayal** of Natalie Hargrove. Kate, L.
Between. Warman, J.
Between here and forever. Scott, E.
Between shades of gray. Sepetys, R.
Between sisters. Badoe, A.

Between the devil and the deep blue sea. Tucholke, A. G.
Between two worlds. Kirkpatrick, K.
Betraying season. Doyle, M.
Between Mom and Jo. Peters, J. A., 1952-
Between us Baxters. Hegedus, B.
BEVERLY HILLS (CALIF.) -- FICTION
Block, F. L. Teen spirit
Beware, Princess Elizabeth. Meyer, C.
Bewitching season. Doyle, M.
Beyer, Kat
The demon catchers of Milan
Beyond. McNamee, G.
Beyond repair. Peterson, L. J.
Beyond the chocolate war. Cormier, R.
Bi-Normal. Higgins, M. G.
BIBLE -- HISTORY OF BIBLICAL EVENTS -- FICTION
Gormley, B. Poisoned honey
Bick, Ilsa J.
Ashes
Draw the dark
The Sin eater's confession
Bickle, Laura
The hallowed ones
The outside
BICYCLES -- FICTION
Milford, K. The Boneshaker
Biederman, Lynn
Teenage waistland
Bifocal. Ellis, D.
The **Big** Burn. Ingold, J.
The **big** crunch. Hautman, P.
Big fat disaster. Fehlbaum, B.
Big fat manifesto. Vaught, S.
The **big** field. Lupica, M.
The **Big** Game of Everything. Lynch, C.
Big Mouth & Ugly Girl. Oates, J. C.
The **big** nothing. Fogelin, A.
Bigelow, Lisa Jenn
Starting from here
BIGOTRY *See* Prejudices; Toleration
BILDUNGSROMANS
Danforth, E. M. The miseducation of Cameron Post
Dessen, S. The moon and more
Grossman, N. A world away
Johnson, A. A certain October
Johnson, L. Muchacho
Joseph, L. Flowers in the sky
LaCour, N. The Disenchantments
Lynch, J. N. My beautiful hippie
Marsh, K. Jepp, who defied the stars
Myers, W. D. All the right stuff
Powell, W. C. Expiration day
Rupp, R. After Eli
Sáenz, B. A. Aristotle and Dante discover the secrets of the universe
Skilton, S. Bruised
Bilen, Tracy
What she left behind
Bill Pennant, Babe Ruth, and me. Tocher, T.
Billerbeck, Kristin
Perfectly dateless
Billie Standish was here. Crocker, N.
Billingsley, Franny
Chime
BILLS OF FARE *See* Menus
Bingham, Kelly
Formerly shark girl
Shark girl
BIOETHICS -- FICTION
Pearson, M. E. Fox forever
Pearson, M. The adoration of Jenna Fox
Pearson, M. The Fox Inheritance
Wasserman, R. Crashed
Wasserman, R. Skinned
Wasserman, R. Wired
Werlin, N. Double helix
Quick, B. A golden web
BIOMEDICAL ENGINEERING -- FICTION
Applegate, K. Eve & Adam
BIOTECHNOLOGY -- FICTION
Pearson, M. E. Fox forever
BIOTERRORISM -- FICTION
Bell, H. Traitor's son
BIRDS -- FICTION
Whaley, J. C. Where things come back
White, A. B. Windows on the world
BIRMINGHAM (ALA.) -- FICTION
Green, J. Looking for Alaska
Naslund, S. J. Four spirits
BIRTH DEFECTS -- FICTION
Rosen, R. Every crooked pot
Smith, A. Stick
Weaver, W. Defect
Birthmarked. O'Brien, C. M.
BIRTHMARKS -- FICTION
Rainfield, C. Stained
BISEXUALITY -- FICTION
Ryan, S. Empress of the world
BISEXUALITY -- FICTION
Peters, J. A. It's our prom (so deal with it)
Tregay, S. Love & leftovers
Bitter end. Brown, J.
The **bitter** kingdom. Carson, R.
Bitter melon. Chow, C.
Bitterblue. Cashore, K.
Bjorkman, Lauren
Miss Fortune Cookie
My invented life
Black, Bekka

iDrakula
Black and white. Volponi, P.
Black box. Schumacher, J.
Black boy/white school. Walker, B. F.
Black heart. Black, H.
Black helicopters. Woolston, B.
Black hole sun. Gill, D. M.
Black Hole Sun Trilogy [series]
Gill, D. M. Invisible sun
Gill, D. M. Shadow on the sun
Black ice. Lane, A.
BLACK MUSLIMS -- FICTION
Nolan, H. A summer of Kings
BLACK NATIONALISM -- FICTION
Magoon, K. Fire in the streets
BLACK PANTHER PARTY -- FICTION
Magoon, K. Fire in the streets
Magoon, K. The rock and the river
Black powder. Rabin, S.
Black Rabbit summer. Brooks, K.
Black radishes. Meyer, S.
BLACK SEPARATISM *See* Black nationalism
Black spring. Croggon, A.
Black storm comin'. Wilson, D. L.
Black swan green. Mitchell, D.
Black taxi. Moloney, J.
Black, Holly
Black heart
The coldest girl in Coldtown
Red glove
The white cat
Blackbringer. Taylor, L.
Blacker, Terence
Boy2girl
Black, white, other. Lester, J. S.
BLACKS -- CONGO (DEMOCRATIC REPUBLIC) -- FICTION
Schrefer, E. Endangered
BLACKS -- ENGLAND -- LONDON -- FICTION
Ward, R. Infinity
BLACKS -- FICTION
Cardenas, T. Letters to my mother
Mussi, S. The door of no return
BLACKS -- FOLKLORE
See also Folklore
BLACKS -- GREAT BRITAIN -- FICTION
Ward, R. The Chaos
Ward, R. Numbers
BLACKS IN MOTION PICTURES
See also Minorities in moFICTION pictures; Motion pictures
Blade: out of the shadows. Bowler, T.
Blade: playing dead. Bowler, T.
Blagden, Scott
Dear Life, You Suck
Blair, Jamie
Leap of Faith
Blake, Kendare
Anna Dressed in Blood
Blank confession. Hautman, P.
Blankman, Anne
Prisoner of night and fog
The **blending** time. Kinch, M. P.
Blending time [series]
Kinch, M. The fires of New SUN
Kinch, M. The rebels of New SUN
Blessed. Smith, C. L.
BLESSING AND CURSING -- FICTION
Funke, C. Fearless
Walsh, P. The Crowfield demon
Blessing's bead. Edwardson, D. D.
BLIND -- FICTION
Cadnum, M. Flash
Clements, A. Things not seen
Clements, A. Things that are
Cummings, P. Blindsided
Ellen, L. Blind spot
Miller, S. Miss Spitfire
Sedgwick, M. She is not invisible
The blind faith hotel. Todd, P.
Blind spot. Ellen, L.
Blindsided. Cummings, P.
Blink & Caution. Wynne-Jones, T.
Bliss. Myracle, L.
BLIZZARDS -- FICTION
Northrop, M. Trapped
Sorrells, W. Whiteout
Block, Francesca Lia
Dangerous angels
The frenzy
The island of excess love
Love in the time of global warming
Missing Angel Juan
Necklace of kisses
Pretty dead
Teen spirit
Weetzie Bat
Blood. Wignall, K. J.
BLOOD -- FICTION
Knutsson, C. Shadows cast by stars
Blood and chocolate. Klause, A. C.
The **blood** keeper. Gratton, T.
Blood ninja II: the revenge of Lord Oda. Lake, N.
The **blood lie.** Vernick, S. R.
Blood of Eden [series]
Kagawa, J. The immortal rules
Blood moon rider. Waters, Z. C.
Blood red road. Young, M.
Blood red horse. Grant, K.
Blood sun. Gilman, D.
Blood wounds. Pfeffer, S. B.

Bloodhound. Pierce, T.
Bloodline. Moran, K.
Bloodline. Cary, K.
Bloodline [series]
Cary, K. Bloodline: reckoning
Bloodline rising. Moran, K.
Bloodline: reckoning. Cary, K.
Bloody Jack. Meyer, L. A.
Bloor, Edward
A plague year
Taken
Bloss, Josie
Albatross
Blubaugh, Penny
Serendipity Market
Blue lily, lily blue. Stiefvater, M.
Blue bloods. De la Cruz, M.
Blue Bloods [series]
De la Cruz, M. The Van Alen legacy
A Blue Bloods novel [series]
De la Cruz, M. Misguided angel
Blue flame. Grant, K. M.
The **blue** girl. De Lint, C.
Blue plate special. Kwasney, M. D.
A **blue** so dark. Schindler, H.
The **blue** sword. McKinley, R.
Blue thread. Feldman, R. T.
Blue noon. Westerfeld, S.
BLUES MUSICIANS -- FICTION
Weatherford, C. B. Becoming Billie Holiday
Blume, Judy
Are you there God?.
Forever
Here's to you, Rachel Robinson
Tiger eyes
Blume, Lesley M. M.
Tennyson
Blumenthal, D.
Mafia girl
Blundell, Judy
Strings attached
What I saw and how I lied
Blythe, Carolita
Revenge of a not-so-pretty girl
Boarder patrol. Thomas, E.
BOARDING SCHOOLS -- FICTION
Acosta, M. Dark companion
Carriger, G. Curtsies & conspiracies
Carriger, G. Etiquette & espionage
Daugherty, C. J. Night School
Halpin, B. A really awesome mess
Hubbard, J. And we stay
Johnson, M. The madness underneath
Laban, E. The Tragedy Paper
Maizel, R. Stolen nights
Miranda, M. Hysteria
Whitney, D. The rivals
Winger. Smith, A.
Wolitzer, M. Belzhar
Wooding, C. Silver
Woon, Y. Life eternal
BOATS AND BOATING -- FICTION
Fletcher, R. The one o'clock chop
Bobet, Leah
Above
Bock, Caroline
LIE
Bodeen, S. A.
The Compound
The gardener
The raft
The **body** at the tower. Lee, Y. S.
The **body** finder. Derting, K.
BODY IMAGE -- FICTION
Rainfield, C. Stained
Body slammed! Villareal, R.
Bog child. Dowd, S.
The **Boggart.** Cooper, S.
Boll, Rosemarie
The second trial.
Bonechiller. McNamee, G.
Bones of Faerie. Simner, J. L.
The **Boneshaker.** Milford, K.
BONOBO -- FICTION
Schrefer, E. Endangered
Book of a thousand days. Hale, S.
The **Book** of Broken Hearts. Ockler, S.
The **book** of dreams. Melling, O. R.\
The **book** of maidservant. Barnhouse, R.
The **book** of Mordred. Vande Velde, V.
The **Book** of Lies. Moloney, J.,
The **book** of the Lion. Cadnum, M.
The **book** thief. Zusak, M.
BOOKS AND READING -- FICTION
Brody, J. My life undecided
Mantchev, L. Eyes like stars
Mantchev, L. So silver bright
Mont, E. M. A breath of Eyre
North, P. The boy from Ilysies
North, P. Libyrinth
Petrucha, S. The Rule of Won
Poblocki, D. The random child
Portman, F. Andromeda Klein
Tubb, K. O. The 13th sign
Zusak, M. The book thief
BOOKSELLERS AND BOOKSELLING -- FICTION
Nelson, V. M. No crystal stair
BOOKSTORES -- NEW YORK (STATE) -- NEW YORK
Nelson, V. M. No crystal stair
Booraem, Ellen

The unnameables
Boost. Mackel, K.
Boot camp. Strasser, T.
Booth's daughter. Wemmlinger, R.
Booth, Coe
Bronxwood
Kendra
Tyrell
Booth, Edwin, 1833-1893
About
Wemmlinger, R. Booth's daughter
Border crossing. Anderson, J. L.
Borderline. Stratton, A.
Born confused. Desai Hidier, T.
Borris, Albert
Crash into me
BORZOI -- FICTION
O'Brien, A. Lara's gift
BOSTON (MASS.) -- FICTION
Kluger, S. My most excellent year
Meyer, L. A. Curse of the blue tattoo
Reinhardt, D. The things a brother knows
Shea, J. A kid from Southie
Smith, S. The other side of dark
Sones, S. What my girlfriend doesn't know
Wilson, D. L. Firehorse
Bosworth, Jennifer
Struck
Botticelli, Sandro, 1444 or 5-1510
About
Beaufrand, M. J. Primavera
A **bottle** in the Gaza Sea. Zenatti, V.
Bounce. Friend, N.
Bound. Napoli, D. J.
Bow, Erin
Plain Kate
Sorrow's knot
Bowers, Laura
Beauty shop for rent; --fully equipped, inquire within
Bowler, Tim
Blade: out of the shadows
Blade: playing dead
Frozen fire
Box out. Coy, J.
The **boxer** and the spy. Parker, R. B.
BOXING -- FICTION
Dixon, J. Phoenix Island
Friend, N. My life in black and white
Lipsyte, R. The contender
Parker, R. B. The boxer and the spy
Sharenow, R. The Berlin Boxing Club
Shea, J. A kid from Southie
A **boy** at war; a novel of Pearl Harbor. Mazer, H.
The **boy** book. Lockhart, E.
A **boy** called Twister. Schraff, A. E.
The **boy** from Ilysies. North, P.
Boy2girl. Blacker, T.
Boy Nobody. Zadoff, A.
Boy O'Boy. Doyle, B.
The **boy** on the bridge. Standiford, N.
Boy proof. Castellucci, C.
The boy Sherlock Holmes [series]
Peacock, S. Death in the air
Peacock, S. The dragon turn
Peacock, S. Eye of the crow
Peacock, S. The secret fiend
Peacock, S. Vanishing girl
Boy toy. Lyga, B.
Boy vs. girl. Robert, N. B.
The **boy** who dared. Bartoletti, S.C.
Boy21. Quick, M.
Boyd, Maria
Will
The **boyfriend** list. Lockhart, E.
BOYS -- FICTION
Ballard, J. G. Empire of the Sun
Harper, H. Letters to a young brother 170
Mitchell, D. Black swan green
BOYS -- FICTION
Herbach, G. Stupid fast
Ness, P. The knife of never letting go
BOYS -- FICTION
Quick, M. Boy21
Boys, bears, and a serious pair of hiking boots. McDonald, A.
Boys, girls, and other hazardous materials. Wiseman, R.
Bradbury, Jennifer
Shift
Wrapped,
Bradley, Alex
24 girls in 7 days
The **braid.** Frost, H.
BRAIDS (HAIRSTYLING)
See also Hair
BRAILLE
See also Writing
BRAIN -- WOUNDS AND INJURIES -- FICTION
McCormick, P. Purple Heart
Tullson, D. Riley Park
Vaught, S. Trigger
Venkatraman, P. Climbing the stairs.
Brain Jack. Falkner, B.
BRAINWASHING -- FICTION
Cashore, K. Bitterblue
Price, L. Enders
Brand new Emily. Rue, G.
Brande, Robin
Evolution, me, & other freaks of nature

Fat Cat
Brashares, Ann
Forever in blue
Girls in pants
The here and now
The second summer of the sisterhood
The sisterhood of the traveling pants
3 willows; the sisterhood grows
Bray, Libba
Beauty queens
The diviners
Going bovine
A great and terrible beauty
Rebel angels
The sweet far thing
BRAZIL -- FICTION
De la Cruz, M. Revelations
Johnson, A. D. The summer prince
Break. Moskowitz, H.
Break my heart 1,000 times. Waters, D.
Breakfast served anytime. Combs, S.
Breaking beautiful. Wolf, J. S.
Breaking dawn. Meyer, S.
Breaking point. Flinn, A.
Breaking through. Jimenez, F.
BREAKING UP (INTERPERSONAL RELATIONS) -- FICTION
Handler, D. Why we broke up
BREAKTHROUGHS, SCIENTIFIC
See Discoveries in science
Breath. Kessler, J. M.
A **breath** of Eyre. Mont, E. M.
Breathe. Crossan, S.
Breathe. Russon, P.
Breathe my name. Nelson, R. A.
Breathing underwater. Flinn, A.
Breathless. McDaniel, L.
Breathless. Warman, J.
Bremer, Fredrika, 1801-1865
About
Engle, M. Firefly letters
Brenna, Beverly
Waiting for no one
Brennan, Caitlin
House of the star
Brennan, Herbie
The Doomsday Box: a Shadow Project adventure
The Shadow Project
Brennan, Sarah Rees
The demon's covenant
The demon's lexicon
Team Human
Unspoken
Brett McCarthy. Padian, M.
Brewer, Heather
First kill
Brewster, Alicia Wright
Echo
Brezenoff, Steve
Brooklyn, burning
Guy in real life
Briant, Ed
Choppy socky blues
I am (not) the walrus
The **brides** of Rollrock Island. Lanagan, M.
BRIDGE (GAME) -- FICTION
Sachar, L. The cardturner
A **bridge** to the stars. Mankell, H.
BRIDGES -- FICTION
Milford, K. The Broken Lands
Bridges, Robin
The gathering storm
Brief candle. Pennington, K.
A **brief** chapter in my impossible life. Reinhardt, D.
Brisingr. Paolini, C.
BRITISH COLUMBIA -- FICTION
Juby, S. Another kind of cowboy
Razzell, M. Snow apples
BRITTANY (FRANCE) -- HISTORY -- 1341-1532 -- FICTION
LaFevers, R. Dark triumph
LaFevers, R. Grave mercy
Brockenbrough, Martha
Devine intervention
Brody, Jessica
My life undecided
The **Broken** Lands. Milford, K.
Broken memory. Combres, E.
Broken moon. Antieau, K.
Broken soup. Valentine, J.
Brontë family
About
Dunkle, C. The house of dead maids
BRONX (NEW YORK, N.Y.) -- FICTION
Booth, C. Bronxwood
Booth, C. Tyrell
Griffin, P. The Orange Houses
Grimes, N. Bronx masquerade
McGuigan, M. A. Morning in a different place
Quintero, S. Efrain's secret
Rice-Gonzalez, C. Chulito
Bronx masquerade. Grimes, N.
Bronxwood. Booth, C.
Brooke, Rupert, 1887-1915
About
Poets of World War I: Rupert Brooke & Siegfried Sassoon **821**
BROOKLYN (NEW YORK, N.Y.) -- FICTION
Bayoumi, M. How does it feel to

be a problem? 305.8
BROOKLYN (NEW YORK, N.Y.) -- FICTION
Blythe, C. Revenge of a not-so-pretty girl
Brezenoff, S. Brooklyn, burning
Chayil, E. Hush
Frank, E. R. Life is funny
Grant, C. Teenie
McDonald, J. Off-color
When I was the greatest
BROOKLYN (NEW YORK, N.Y.) -- FICTION
Kiem, E. Dancer, daughter, traitor, spy
Brooklyn, burning. Brezenoff, S.
Brooks, Kevin
Being
Black Rabbit summer
Candy
Dawn
iBoy
Kissing the rain
Lucas
The road of the dead
Brooks, Martha
Mistik Lake
Queen of hearts
Brooks, Terry
The elves of Cintra
The gypsy morph
BROTHERS -- FICTION
Mosley, W. Fortunate son
Woodson, J. Miracle's boys
BROTHERS -- FICTION
Alexander, K. The crossover
Black, H. Black heart
Bowler, T. Frozen fire
Elliott, L. Across a war-tossed sea
Funke, C. Fearless
Funke, C. Reckless.
Graff, L. Lost in the sun
Harmon, M. Under the bridge
Lynch, C. Pieces
Martin, T. M. The end games
McCormick, P. My brother's keeper
Michaels, R. Genesis Alpha
Nuzum, K. A. A small white scar
Philbrick, W. R. The mostly true adventures of Homer P. Figg
Rubens, M. Sons of the 613
Sternberg, L. The case against my brother
Trueman, T. Cruise control
Wallace, R. War and watermelon
Watson, C. Benched
Williams, S. Bull rider
BROTHERS AND SISTERS -- FICTION
Freymann-Weyr, G. My heartbeat
Lawson, M. Crow Lake
Peters, J. A. Luna
BROTHERS AND SISTERS – FICTION
Coker, R. Chasing Jupiter
Joseph, L. Flowers in the sky
Kuehn, S. Complicit
Morgan, P. The beautiful and the cursed
Sedgwick, M. She is not invisible
Wrede, P. C. Across the Great Barrier
Vanhee, J. Engines of the broken world
Zarr, S. The Lucy variations
The **brothers** story. Sturtevant, K.
The **brothers** Torres. Voorhees, C.
Brothers, Meagan
Debbie Harry sings in French
Supergirl mixtapes
Brouwer, Sigmund
Devil's pass
Brown, Jennifer
Bitter end
Hate list
Perfect escape
Brown, Jordan
(ed) Ruins
Brown, P.
Red rising
Brown, Skila
Caminar
Bruchac, Joseph, 1942-
Code talker
Sacajawea
Wolf mark
Bruised. Skilton, S.
Bruiser. Shusterman, N.
Brushing Mom's hair. Cheng, A.
BRUSSELS (BELGIUM) -- HISTORY -- FICTION
Doyle, M. Courtship and curses
Brutal. Harmon, M. B.
Bryant, Jennifer
Pieces of Georgia
Ringside, 1925
Bryce, Celia
Anthem for Jackson Dawes
Buck fever. Willis, C. C.
Buckhanon, Kalisha
Upstate
Buddha boy. Koja, K.
BUDDHISM -- FICTION
Koja, K. Buddha boy
Budhos, Marina Tamar
Tell us we're home
Ask me no questions
Buffie, Margaret
Winter shadows
Bug boy. Luper, E.
BUILDING -- FICTION
Reinhardt, D. How to build a house

BULIMIA -- FICTION
Friedman, R. Nothing
Friend, N. Perfect
Kittle, K. Reasons to be happy
Bull rider. Williams, S.
BULL RIDING -- FICTION
Williams, S. Bull rider
Bullen, Alexandra
Wish
Bullet point. Abrahams, P.
BULLIES
Nielsen, S. The reluctant journal of Henry K. Larsen
BULLIES -- FICTION
Altebrando, T. The best night of your (pathetic) life
Davis, L. I swear
Gale, E. K. The Bully Book
Garden, N. Endgame
Hannan, P. My big mouth
Harrington, H. Speechless
Kessler, J. Loss
Koss, A. G. Poison Ivy
Lange, E. J. Dead ends
Love, D. A. Defying the diva
MacLean, J. The nine lives of Travis Keating
Maciel, A.. Tease.
Medina, M. Yaqui Delgado wants to kick your ass
Mikaelsen, B. Ghost of Spirit Bear
Preller, J. Bystander
Rowell, R. Eleanor & Park
Sales, L. This song will save your life
Terry, C. L. Zero fade
Walton, K. M. Empty
Watkins, S. Down Sand Mountain,
Yang, D. J. Warp speed
Zweig, E. Cornered
The **Bully** Book. Gale, E. K.,
Bumped. McCafferty, M.
Bunce, Elizabeth C.
A curse dark as gold
Liar's moon
Star crossed
Bunheads. Flack, S.
Bunker 10. Henderson, J.-A.
Bunting, Eve
The pirate captain's daughter
Burd, Nick
The vast fields of ordinary
Burg, Ann E.
All the broken pieces
Burger Wuss. Anderson, M. T.
Burgess, Melvin
The hit
Nicholas Dane
Smack
Buried. MacCready, R. M.
Buried onions. Soto, G.
BURIED TREASURE -- FICTION
Hobbs, W. Leaving Protection
Lowitz, L. Jet Black and the ninja wind
Meyer, L. A. Rapture of the deep
Mussi, S. The door of no return
Burn. Phillips, S.
Burn mark. Powell, L.
Burn my heart. Naidoo, B.
Burned. Hopkins, E.
Burning blue. Griffin, P.
The **burning** sky. Thomas, S.
Burnout. Vrettos, A. M.
BURNS AND SCALDS -- FICTION
Katcher, B. Playing with matches
Zephaniah, B. Face
Burns, Laura J.
Crave
Burtenshaw, Jenna
Shadowcry
Burton, Rebecca
Leaving Jetty Road
Burying the sun. Whelan, G.
BUSINESS ENTERPRISES -- FICTION
Chambers, V. Fifteen candles
Jennings, R. W. Ghost town
But I love him. Hubbard, A.
Butcher, Kristin
Cheat
Butter. Lange, E. J.
Butterfly. Hartnett, S.
The **butterfly** clues. Ellison, K.
Buzo, Laura
Love and other perishable items
By darkness hid. Williamson, J.
By the river. Herrick, S.
By the time you read this, I'll be dead. Peters, J. A.
By these ten bones. Dunkle, C. B.
Bystander. Preller, J.

C

CABALA -- FICTION
Goelman, A. The path of names
Cabot, Meg
Airhead
All-American girl
Being Nikki
The princess diaries
Runaway
Cadnum, Michael
The book of the Lion
Flash

Peril on the sea
Caine, R.
Prince of shadows
Calame, Don
Beat the band
Call the shots
Swim the fly
Caleb's choice. Wisler, G. C.
Caleb's wars. Dudley, D. L.
Caletti, Deb
The fortunes of Indigo Skye
The last forever
The secret life of Prince Charming
The six rules of maybe
Stay
CALIFORNIA -- FICTION
Castan, M. Fighting for Dontae
De la Peña, M. Mexican whiteboy
De la Pena, M. We were here
Harmon, M. B. Brutal
Hernandez, D. No more us for you
Hurwin, D. Freaks and revelations
Jarzab, A. All unquiet things
Jimenez, F. Reaching out
Kirby, J. Moonglass
Korman, G. Son of the mob: Hollywood hustle
Leavitt, L. Going vintage
Lester, J. S. Black, white, other
Madigan, L. K. The mermaid's mirror
McNeal, L. Dark water
Murray, Y. M. The good girl's guide to getting kidnapped
Nichols, J. Messed up
Ockler, S. Twenty boy summer
Otsuka, J. When the emperor was divine
Price, C. Desert Angel
Prinz, Y. The Vinyl Princess
Schneider, R. The beginning of everything
Seigel, A. Like the red panda
Stevenson, S. J. The Latte Rebellion
Stone, M. H. Invisible girl
Zarr, S. Story of a girl
CALIFORNIA -- HISTORY -- FICTION
Patron, S. Behind the masks
CALIFORNIA, SOUTHERN -- FICTION
Arcos, C. Out of reach
Call Me Amy. Strykowski, M.
Call me Maria. Ortiz Cofer, J.
The **call** of the wild. London, J.
Call the shots. Calame, D.
CAMBODIA -- HISTORY -- 1975- -- FICTION
McCormick, P. Never fall down
CAMBODIAN AMERICANS -- FICTION
Schmidt, G. D. Trouble
CAMBODIAN REFUGEES -- FICTION
McCormick, P. Never fall down
CAMBRIDGE (ENGLAND) -- FICTION
Moriarty, J. A corner of white
Moriarty, J. The cracks in the kingdom
Cameron, Peter
Someday this pain will be useful to you
Cameron, Sharon
The dark unwinding
Caminar. Brown, S.
Camo girl. Magoon, K.,
CAMPING -- FICTION
Cummings, P. The journey back
Campoy, F. Isabel
(jt. auth) Ada, A. F. Yes! we are Latinos
CAMPS (MILITARY) *See* Military camps
CAMPS -- FICTION
Cole, B. The goats,
Connelly, N. O. The miracle stealer
Davis, H. Never cry werewolf
De Gramont, N. Every little thing in the world
Friesen, G. The Isabel factor
Frost, H. Hidden
Goelman, A. The path of names
Goobie, B. Before wings
Howell, S. Everything beautiful
Johnson, H. M. Accidents of nature
Lupica, M. Summer ball
Nixon, J. L. Nightmare
Padian, M. Jersey tomatoes are the best
Paley, S. Huge
Rennison, L. Withering tights
CANADA -- FICTION
Brouwer, S. Devil's pass
Frost, H. The braid
Hopkinson, N. The Chaos
Huser, G. Stitches
Ibbitson, J. The Landing
Lawson, M. Crow Lake
Martin, C. K. K. I know it's over
McBay, B. Waiting for Sarah
McDonald, A. Boys, bears, and a serious pair of hiking boots
McNamee, G. Acceleration
McPhee, P. New blood
Melling, O. R. The book of dreams
Oppel, K. Half brother
Pignat, C. Wild geese
Staunton, T. Acting up
Trottier, M. Three songs for courage
Waldorf, H. Tripping
Walters, E. Splat!
Woon, Y. Life eternal
Wynne-Jones, T. Blink & Caution
Wynne-Jones, T. The uninvited
CANADA -- HISTORY -- FICTION
Martin, C. K. K. Yesterday
Canales, Viola

The tequila worm
Canary. Alpine, R.
CANCER -- FICTION
Bauer, J. Hope was here
CANCER -- FICTION
Cheng, A. Brushing Mom's hair
Gurtler, J. I'm not her
Koss, A. G. Side effects
Matson, M. Second chance summer
Mccall, G. G. Under the mesquite
McDaniel, L. Breathless
Padian, M. Brett McCarthy: work in progress
Seamon, H. Somebody up there hates you
Whitney, D. When you were here
CANCER -- PATIENTS -- FICTION
Bryce, C. Anthem for Jackson Dawes
Green, J. The fault in our stars
Candy. Brooks, K.
Cann, Kate
Consumed
Possessed
CANNIBALISM -- FICTION
O Guilin, P. The inferior
Rossi, V. Under the never sky
CANOL HERITAGE TRAIL (N.W.T.) — FICTION
Brouwer, S. Devil's pass
Can't get there from here. Strasser, T.
A **canticle** for Leibowitz. Miller, W. M.
Cantor, Jillian
The life of glass
The September sisters
CAPITAL PUNISHMENT -- FICTION
Shan, D. The thin executioner
Captives. Williamson, J.
Captured. Wood, M. L.
Carbone, Elisa Lynn
Jump
Card, Orson Scott
Children of the mind
Ender in exile
Ender's game
Pathfinder
Ruins
Shadow of the giant
Shadow of the Hegemon
Shadow puppets
Speaker for the Dead
Xenocide
Cardenas, Teresa
Letters to my mother
Old dog
Cardi, A.
The chance you won't return
The **cardturner.** Sachar, L.
Carey, E.
Heap house
Carey, Janet Lee
The beast of Noor
Dragons of Noor
Dragonswood
Carleson, J. C.
The tyrant's daughter
Carlson, Melody
Premiere
Carmen; an urban adaptation of the opera. Myers, W. D., 1937-
CARNIVALS
Barnaby, H. Wonder show
CAROLS
Carpe diem. Cornwell, A.
Carriger, Gail
Curtsies & conspiracies
Etiquette & espionage
Carroll, Michael Owen, 1966-
The ascension
Super human
Carrying Mason. Magnin, J.
Carson, Rae
The bitter kingdom
The crown of embers
The girl of fire and thorns
Carter [series]
Crawford, B. Carter's unfocused, one-track mind
Carter's big break. Crawford, B.
Carter's unfocused, one-track mind. Crawford, B.
Carter, Ally
Heist Society
Perfect scoundrels
Carter, Caela
Me, him, them, and it
Carter finally gets it. Crawford, B.
CARTER, JOHN (FICTITIOUS CHARACTER)
Under the moons of Mars
CARTOONS AND CARICATURES -- FICTION
Lyga, B. The astonishing adventures of Fanboy & Goth Girl
Smibert, A. Memento Nora
CARTOONS AND COMICS -- FICTION
Kamata, S. Gadget Girl
Carvell, Marlene
Sweetgrass basket
Who will tell my brother?
Cary, Kate
Bloodline
Bloodline: reckoning
Casanova, Mary
Frozen
The **case** against my brother. Sternberg, L.

The **case** of the deadly desperados.
Lawrence, C.
The **case** of the missing marquess.
Springer, N.
Casella, Jody
Thin space
Cashay. McMullan, M.
Cashore, Kristin
Bitterblue
Fire
Graceling
The **Cassini** code. Testa, D.
Castan, Mike
Fighting for Dontae
The price of loyalty
Castellucci, Cecil
Beige
Boy proof
First day on Earth
The queen of cool
Rose sees red
Castle, Jennifer
You look different in real life
CASTLES -- FICTION
Kindl, P. Keeping the castle
Castor, H. M.
VIII
Castro, Fidel, 1926-
Casualties of war. Lynch, C.
Cat Girl's day off. Pauley, K.
The **catastrophic** history of you & me.
Rothenberg, J.
Catch. Leitch, W.
Catch & release. Woolston, B.
Catch rider. Lyne, J. H.
Catching fire. Collins, S.
Cate of the Lost Colony. Klein, L. M.
Catharine Howard, Queen, consort of Henry VIII, King of England, d. 1542
About
Libby, A. M. The king's rose
Longshore, K. Gilt
CATHOLIC CHURCH -- CLERGY -- FICTION
Erdrich, L. The last report on the miracles at Little No Horse
CATHOLIC SCHOOLS -- FICTION
Blagden, S. Dear Life, You Suck
Blythe, C. Revenge of a not-so-pretty girl
CATHOLICS -- FICTION
Freitas, D. The possibilities of sainthood
CATS -- FICTION
Bow, E. Plain Kate
Deedy, C. A. The Cheshire Cheese cat
MacLean, J. The nine lives of Travis Keating
Pauley, K. Cat Girl's day off
Rossetti, R. The girl with borrowed wings
Caveney, Philip
Sebastian Darke: Prince of Fools
CAVES -- FICTION
Muller, R. D. Squeeze
CELEBRITIES -- FICTION
Castle, J. You look different in real life
Strasser, T. Famous
Zevin, G. All these things I've done
Zevin, G. Because it is my blood
Cellular. Schwartz, E.
CELLULAR TELEPHONES -- FICTION
Brooks, K. iBoy
CELTIC MYTHOLOGY -- FICTION
McBride, R. The fire opal
CENTENNIAL EXHIBITION (1876: PHILADELPHIA, PA.) -- FICTION
Kephart, B. Dangerous neighbors
The **center** of everything. Moriarty, L.
The **center** of the universe. Liberty, A.
CENTRAL AMERICA -- FICTION
Hubbard, K. Wanderlove
CEREBRAL PALSY -- FICTION
Kamata, S. Gadget Girl
Koertge, R. Stoner & Spaz
Trueman, T. Life happens next
White, A. B. Window boy
Zimmer, T. V. Reaching for sun
Cerrito, Angela
The end of the line
A **certain** October. Johnson, A.
A **certain** slant of light. Whitcomb, L.
A **certain** strain of peculiar. Amateau, G.
Chadda, Sarwat
The devil's kiss
Chains. Anderson, L. H.
Chalice. McKinley, R.
Chaltas, Thalia
Because I am furniture
Chambers, Aidan
Dying to know you
Chambers, Veronica
Fifteen candles
Champion. Lu, M.
Chan, Gillian
A foreign field
Chandler, Kristen
Girls don't fly
CHANCE -- FICTION
Perkins, L. R. As easy as falling off the face of the earth
The **chance** you won't return. Cardi, A.
Chanda's secrets. Stratton, A.
Chanda's wars. Stratton, A.
Chandler, Kristen
Wolves, boys, & other things that might kill me

Changers. Cooper, T.
The **Chaos.** Ward, R.
The **Chaos.** Hopkinson, N.
Chaos walking [series]
Ness, P. The Ask and the Answer
Ness, P. The knife of never letting go
Ness, P. Monsters of men
Chapman, Fern Schumer
Is it night or day?
Chapman, Lara
Flawless
CHARACTERS AND CHARACTERISTICS IN LITERATURE -- FICTION
Rowell, R. Fangirl
CHARACTERS IN LITERATURE -- FICTION
Cross, S. Kill me softly
Lies, knives and girls in red dresses
Reese, J. The strange case of Doctor Jekyll and Mademoiselle Odile
Shepherd, M. The madman's daughter
Taub, M. Still star-crossed
Charbonneau, Joelle
Graduation day
Independent study
The Testing
Charlton-Trujillo, e. E.
Fat Angie
Charm & strange. Kuehn, S.
CHARMS -- FICTION
Cremer, A. Invisibility
Chasing AllieCat. Davis, R. F.
Chasing boys. Tayleur, K.
Chasing Brooklyn. Schroeder, L.,
Chasing Jupiter. Coker, R.
Chasing Orion. Lasky, K.
Chasing Shadows. Avasthi, S.
Chasing tail lights. Jones, P.
Chasing the bear. Parker, R. B.
Chayil, Eishes
Hush
Chbosky, Stephen
The perks of being a wallflower
Cheat. Butcher, K.
CHEATING (EDUCATION) -- FICTION
Brown, J. Perfect escape
Butcher, K. Cheat
Whitney, D. The rivals
Checkered flag cheater. Weaver, W.
CHEERLEADING -- FICTION
Moore, D. Always upbeat / All that
Perez, M. Dead is the new black
The Chemical Garden trilogy [series]
DeStefano, L. Fever
DeStefano, L. Sever
DeStefano, L. Wither
Chen, Justina
Return to me
Cheng, Andrea
Brushing Mom's hair
CHEROKEE INDIANS-- FICTION
Mckinney-Whitaker, C. The last sister
CHEROKEE NATIONAL FEMALE SEMINARY -- FICTION
Gensler, S. The revenant
Cherry Heaven. Adlington, L. J.
The **Cheshire** Cheese cat; a Dickens of a tale. Deedy, C. A.
CHESS -- FICTION
Wallace, R. Perpetual check
Cheva, Cherry
DupliKate
CHICAGO (ILL.) -- FICTION
Goeglein, T. M. Cold fury
CHICAGO (ILL.) -- FICTION
Magoon, K. Fire in the streets
Chief **Sunrise,** John McGraw, and me. Tocher, T.
CHILD ABUSE -- FICTION
Crocker, N. Billie Standish was here
Summers, C. This is not a test
Whittenberg, A. Life is fine
Child of dandelions. Nanji, S.
Child of the prophecy. Marillier, J.
CHILD SEXUAL ABUSE -- FICTION
Atkins, C. The file on Angelyn Stark
Deuker, C. Swagger
Doyle, B. Boy O'Boy
Kiely, B. The gospel of winter
Rainfield, C. Scars
Scott, M. Live through this
Weeks, S. Jumping the scratch,
CHILDBIRTH -- FICTION
Vega, D. Fact of life #31
CHILDREN -- FICTION
Crowe, C. Mississippi trial, 1955
Dogar, S. Annexed
CHILDREN -- FICTION
Hubbard, K. Wanderlove
CHILDREN AND WAR -- FICTION
Almond, D. The true tale of the monster Billy Dean
Crockett, S. D. After the snow
CHILDREN OF ALCOHOLICS -- FICTION
Castellucci, C. First day on Earth
Palmer, R. The Corner of Bitter and Sweet
CHILDREN OF DIVORCED PARENTS -- FICTION
Howland, L. Nantucket blue
Schrefer, E. Endangered
CHILDREN OF DRUG ADDICTS -- FICTION
Blair, J. Leap of Faith
Murdoch, E. If you find me

CHILDREN OF GAY PARENTS -- FICTION
Kenneally, M. Stealing Parker
Tregay, S. Love & leftovers
CHILDREN OF PROMINENT PERSONS -- FICTION
Spillebeen, G. Kipling's choice
The **children** of the lost. Whitley, D.
Children of the mind. Card, O. S.
CHILDREN WITH DISABILITIES -- ABUSE OF -- FICTION
Edwards, J. Earth girl
Edwards, J. Earth star
CHILDREN WITH DISABILITIES -- FICTION
Castan, M. Fighting for Dontae
CHILDREN WITH DISABILITIES -- INSTITUTIONAL CARE -- FICTION
Nussbaum, S. Good kings bad kings
CHILDREN WITH PHYSICAL DISABILITIES -- FICTION
Friesner, E. Spirit's princess
CHILDREN'S SECRETS -- FICTION
Jarzab, A. The opposite of hallelujah
Pitcher, A. Ketchup clouds
Childs, Tera Lynn
Oh. My. Gods
Sweet venom
CHILE -- FICTION
Miller-Lachmann, L. Gringolandia
Chill wind. McDonald, J.
Chima, Cinda Williams
The Crimson Crown
The Demon King
The enchanter heir
The exiled queen
The Gray Wolf Throne
The warrior heir
The wizard heir
Chime. Billingsley, F.
CHIMERA (GREEK MYTHOLOGY) -- FICTION
Taylor, L. Days of blood & starlight
Taylor, L. Dreams of gods & monsters
CHIMPANZEES -- FICTION
Dickinson, P. Eva
Oppel, K. Half brother
Schrefer, E. Threatened
CHINA -- FICTION
Whelan, G. Chu Ju's house
CHINA -- FICTION
Holland, L. T. The counterfeit family tree of Vee Crawford-Wong
Mowll, J. Operation Storm City
Mowll, J. Operation typhoon shore
Napoli, D. J. Bound
Pon, C. Fury of the phoenix
Pon, C. Silver phoenix
Yee, P. Learning to fly
CHINA -- HISTORY -- YÜAN DYNASTY, 1260-1368
McCaughrean, G. The kite rider
CHINATOWN (SAN FRANCISCO, CALIF.) -- FICTION
Bjorkman, L. Miss Fortune Cookie
CHINESE -- FICTION
Murray, K. The secret life of Maeve Lee Kwong
CHINESE -- UNITED STATES -- FICTION
Namioka, L. An ocean apart, a world away
Yep, L. Dragon's gate; Golden Mountain chronicles: 1867
CHINESE AMERICANS -- FICTION
Halpin, B. A really awesome mess
Namioka, L. Mismatch
Yep, L. Dragon road; Golden Mountain chronicles: 1939
Yep, L. Dragons of silk
Yep, L. Dragonwings; Golden Mountain chronicles: 1903.
Yep, L. The traitor; Golden Mountain chronicles, 1885
Chinese Cinderella and the Secret Dragon Society. Mah, A. Y.
CHIPPEWA INDIANS -- FICTION
Erdrich, L. The last report on the miracles at Little No Horse
CHIVALRY -- ROMANCES *See* Romances
CHOCOLATE -- FICTION
Selfors, S. The sweetest spell
Zevin, G. Because it is my blood
The **chocolate** war. Cormier, R.
Choi, Sook Nyul
Year of impossible goodbyes
CHOICE (PSYCHOLOGY) -- FICTION
Kirby, J. Golden
Villareal, R. Body slammed!
West, K. Pivot point
West, K. Split second
Choker. Woods, E. E.
Choppy socky blues. Briant, E.
Chopsticks. Anthony, J.
The **chosen** one. Williams, C. L.
Chotjewitz, David
Daniel half human
Chow, Cara
Bitter melon
CHRISTIAN FUNDAMENTALISM -- FICTION
Danforth, E. M. The miseducation of Cameron Post
Nader, E. Escape from Eden
CHRISTIAN LIFE -- FICTION
Galante, C. The patron saint of butterflies
Kirkpatrick, J. A flickering light

Nelson, R. A. Days of Little Texas
White, R. A month of Sundays
The **Christopher** killer. Ferguson, A.
Christopher, Lucy
The killing woods
Christy. Marshall, C.
Chronicles of Faerie [series]
Melling, O. R. The book of dreams
Melling, O. R. The Hunter's Moon
Melling, O. R. The Light-Bearer's daughter
Melling, O. R. The Summer King
The Chronicles of Kazam [series]
Fforde, J. The last Dragonslayer
Fforde, J. The song of the Quarkbeast
The Chrysalis Queen quartet [series]
McKenzie, N. Guinevere's gamble
McKenzie, N. Guinevere's gift
Chu Ju's house. Whelan, G.
Chulito. Rice-Gonzalez, C.
CHURCH SCHOOLS -- FICTION
Blagden, S. Dear Life, You Suck
Cinder. Meyer, M.
The **circle** of blood. Ferguson, A.
Circle of secrets. Little, K. G.
The **circuit :** stories from the life of a migrant child. Jimenez, F.
CIRCUS -- FICTION
Howard, J. J. That time I joined the circus
Lam, L. Pantomime
Cisneros, Sandra
The house on Mango Street
CITY AND TOWN LIFE -- FICTION
Oliver, L. Panic
Jones, T. L. Standing against the wind
CITY AND TOWN LIFE -- KANSAS -- FICTION
Wasserman, R. The waking dark
City boy. Michael, J.
The **City** in the Lake. Neumeier, R.
City of a Thousand Dolls. Forster, M.
City of ashes. Clare, C.
City of bones. Clare, C.
City of cannibals. Thompson, R.
City of fallen angels. Clare, C.
City of Glass. Clare, C.
City of lost souls. Clare, C.
City of orphans. Avi, 1937.
The **city's** son. Pollock, T.
CIVIL RIGHTS -- FICTION
Doctorow, C. Homeland
Doctorow, C. Little brother
CIVIL RIGHTS MOVEMENTS -- FICTION
Magoon, K. Fire in the streets
CLAIRVOYANCE -- FICTION
King, A. S. Glory O'Brien's history of the future
Mitchard, J. The midnight twins
Clare, Cassandra
City of ashes
City of bones
City of fallen angels
City of Glass
City of lost souls
Clockwork angel
Clockwork prince
Clockwork princess
(ed) The Shadowhunter's codex
Clariel. Nix, G.
Clark, Kathy
Guardian angel house
Clark, Kristin Elizabeth
Freakboy
Clark, William, 1770-1838
About
Clarke, Judith
One whole and perfect day
The winds of heaven
CLASSICAL MYTHOLOGY -- FICTION
Barrett, T. Dark of the moon
Barrett, T. King of Ithaka
Childs, T. L. Oh. My. Gods
Childs, T. L. Sweet venom
Friesner, E. M. Nobody's princess
Geras, A. Ithaka
Halam, A. Snakehead
Marsh, K. The night tourist
Napoli, D. J. The great god Pan
Taylor, L. Daughter of smoke and bone
Clay. Almond, D.
Clement-Davies, David
Fell
The sight
Clement-Moore, Rosemary
Hell Week
Highway to hell
Prom dates from Hell
The splendor falls
Texas gothic
Clements, Andrew, 1949-
Things not seen
Things that are
Cleopatra confesses Elizabeth. Meyer, C.
Cleopatra Selene, Queen, Consort of Juba II, King of Mauretania, b. 40 B.C. About
Shecter, V. A. Cleopatra's moon
Cleopatra's moon. Shecter, V. A.
Cleopatra, Queen of Egypt, d. 30 B.C.About
Dray, S. Lily of the Nile
Meyer, C. Cleopatra confesses
Shecter, V. A. Cleopatra's moon
CLERGY -- FICTION
Erdrich, L. The last report on the miracles at Little No Horse

Johnson, V. Saving Maddie
Marsden, C. Sahwira
Zarr, S. Once was lost
Zielin, L. Donut days
CLEVELAND (OHIO) -- FICTION
Ellison, K. The butterfly clues
Click. Park, L. S.
Climbing the stairs. Venkatraman, P.
Clinton, Cathryn
A stone in my hand
Cloaked. Flinn, A.
Clockwork angel. Clare, C.
The clockwork dark [series]
Bemis, J. C. The White City
Bemis, J. C. The Wolf Tree
Clockwork prince. Clare, C.
Clockwork princess. Clare, C.
The **clockwork** scarab. Gleason, C.
CLONING -- FICTION
Cohn, R. Beta
Farmer, N. The house of the scorpion
Farmer, N. The lord of Opium
Patrick, C. The Originals
CLOTHING AND DRESS -- FICTION
Foxlee, K. The midnight dress
CLOWNS -- FICTION
Perez, M. Dead is just a dream
CLUBS -- FICTION
Berk, J. Guy Langman, crime scene procrastinator
May, K. Kiki
Petrucha, S. The Rule of Won
Coakley, Lena
Witchlanders
COAL MINES AND MINING -- FICTION
Almond, D. Kit's wilderness
Bloor, E. A plague year
Coates, Jan L.
A hare in the elephant's trunk
Coats, Jillian Anderson
The wicked and the just
Coben, Harlan, 1962-
Seconds away
Shelter
Coda. Trevayne, E.
Code name Verity. Wein, E.
Code of silence. Shoemaker, T.
Code orange. Cooney, C. B.
Code talker. Bruchac, J.
Coffeehouse angel. Selfors, S.
Cohen, Joshua C.
Leverage
Cohen, Tish
Little black lies
Cohn, Rachel
Beta
Cupcake
Dash & Lily's book of dares
Gingerbread
Naomi and Ely's no kiss list
Nick & Norah's infinite playlist
Shrimp
You know where to find me
Cokal, Susann
The Kingdom of little wounds
Coker, Rachel, 1997-
Chasing Jupiter
Colasanti, Susane
So much closer
Something like fate
Cold case. Leonard, J. P.
Cold fury. Goeglein, T. M.
Cold hands, warm heart. Wolfson, J.
Cold kiss. Garvey, A.
Cold skin. Herrick, S.
COLD WAR -- FICTION
Brennan, H. The Doomsday Box: a Shadow Project adventure
Meloy, M. The apothecary
The **coldest** girl in Coldtown. Black, H.
Cole, Brock
The goats
Cole, Kresley
Poison princess
Cole, Stephen
Thieves like us
Thieves till we die
Z. Raptor
Z. Rex
Coleman, Wim
Anna's world
Colfer, Eoin, 1965-
Airman
Colin Fischer. Miller, A. E.
COLLEGE BASKETBALL -- FICTION
Feinstein, J. Foul trouble
Simone Upgrade U
Volponi, P. The Final Four
COLLEGE CHOICE
See also Colleges and universities; School choice
COLLEGE CHOICE -- FICTION
Voorhees, C. Lucky fools
COLLEGE STUDENTS -- FICTION
Charbonneau, J. Independent study
Simone Upgrade U
COLLEGES AND UNIVERSITIES -- FICTION
Freitas, D. This gorgeous game
Houck, C. Tiger's quest
Zulkey, C. An off year
Collins, Amberly
Collins, B. Always watching

Collins, Brandilyn
Always watching
Collins, Pat Lowery
Hidden voices
Collins, P. J. Sarah
What happened to Serenity?
Collins, Suzanne, 1962-
Catching fire
The Hunger Games
Mockingjay
Collins, Yvonne
The new and improved Vivien Leigh Reid; diva in control
Now starring Vivien Leigh Reid: Diva in training
Collomore, Anna
The ruining
COLOMBIA -- FICTION
Withers, P. First descent
COLOR -- FICTION
Moriarty, J. A corner of white
Moriarty, J. The cracks in the kingdom
COLORADO -- FICTION
Kizer, A. Meridian
Mills, T. Heartbreak river
Peters, J. A. She loves you, she loves you not--
Zarr, S. How to save a life
The **colors of Madeleine** [series]
Moriarty, J. The cracks in the kingdom
Colors of Madeleine trilogy [series]
Moriarty, J. A corner of white
Columbus, Christopher
About
Mlawski, S. Hammer of witches
COMA -- FICTION
Forman, G. If I stay
Jocelyn, M. Would you
Little, K. G. The healing spell
Magoon, K. 37 things I love (in no particular order)
Mass, W. Heaven looks a lot like the mall
Scott, E. Between here and forever
COMBAT -- FICTION
Silver, E. Rush
Combres, Elisabeth
Broken memory
Combs, S.
Breakfast served anytime
Come Juneteenth; a story of the Boston Massacre. Rinaldi, A.
Come up [series]
LeFlore, L. The world is mine
The **comeback** season. Smith, J. E.
The **comet's** curse. Testa, D.
COMETS -- FICTION
McDevitt, J. Moonfall
COMIC BOOKS, STRIPS, ETC. -- FICTION
Wooding, C. Havoc
Wooding, C. Malice
COMING OF AGE -- FICTION
Bickle, L. The hallowed ones
Bickle, L. The outside
Cummings, P. The journey back
Dessen, S. The moon and more
Hahn, M. D. Mister Death's blue-eyed girls
Joseph, L. Flowers in the sky
Kamata, S. Gadget Girl
Lynch, J. N. My beautiful hippie
Myers, W. D. All the right stuff
Powell, W. C. Expiration day
Rosoff, M. Picture me gone
Rubens, M. Sons of the 613
Sáenz, B. A. Aristotle and Dante discover the secrets of the universe
Simner, J. L. Faerie after
Wakefield, V. Friday never leaving
COMING OUT (SEXUAL ORIENTATION) -- FICTION
Sanchez, A. Rainbow boys
COMING OUT (SEXUAL ORIENTATION) -- FICTION
Lennon, T. When love comes to town
Rice-Gonzalez, C. Chulito
COMMUNAL LIVING -- FICTION
Reed, A. Over you
COMMUNICABLE DISEASES -- FICTION
Wells, D. Partials
Wooding, C. Silver
Woolston, B. Catch & release
COMMUNICATION -- FICTION
Trueman, T. Life happens next
COMMUNISM -- FICTION
Mackall, D. D. Eva underground
COMMUNIST COUNTRIES -- FICTION
Bass, K. Graffiti knight
Marsden, C. My Own Revolution
COMMUNITY LIFE -- FICTION
Berry, J. All the truth that's in me
COMPETITION (PSYCHOLOGY) -- FICTION
Williams, K. Pizza, love, and other stuff that made me famous
Complicit. Kuehn, S.
COMPOSERS -- FICTION
Collins, P. L. Hidden voices
Dunlap, S. E. The musician's daughter
The **Compound.** Bodeen, S. A.
Compromised. Ayarbe, H.
Compulsion. Ayarbe, H.
COMPULSIVE BEHAVIOR -- FICTION
Ellison, K. The butterfly clues
COMPULSIVE EATING -- FICTION

Fehlbaum, B. Big fat disaster
Vacco, C. My chemical mountain
COMPUTER CRIMES -- FICTION
Wasserman, R. Hacking Harvard
Whyman, M. Goldstrike
Whyman, M. Icecore
COMPUTER GAMES -- FICTION
Cheva, C. DupliKate
COMPUTER HACKERS -- FICTION
Gagnon, M. Don't Look Now
Gagnon, M. Don't turn around
COMPUTER PROGRAMS -- FICTION
Lancaster, M. A. The future we left behind
COMPUTERS -- FICTION
Asher, J. The future of us
Barnes, J. L. The Squad: perfect cover
Doctorow, C. Little brother
Falkner, B. Brain Jack **Fi**
Fisher, C. Sapphique **Fi**
Lancaster, M. A. Human.4
Petrucha, S. Split **Fi**
Plum-Ucci, C. Streams of Babel
CONCENTRATION CAMPS -- FICTION
Otsuka, J. When the emperor was divine
Zail, S. Playing for the commandant
CONCORD (MASS.) -- FICTION
Armistead, C. Being Henry David
Condie, Allyson Braithwaite.
Crossed
Matched
CONDORS -- FICTION
Hobbs, W. The maze
CONDUCT OF LIFE -- FICTION
Brashares, A. The sisterhood of the traveling pants
Mass, W. Jeremy Fink and the meaning of life
Wolff, V. E. True believer
CONDUCT OF LIFE -- FICTION
Arntson, S. The wrap-up list
Bick, I. J. The Sin eater's confession
Casanova, M. Frozen
CONEY ISLAND (NEW YORK, N.Y.) -- FICTION
Altebrando, T. Dreamland social club
CONEY ISLAND (NEW YORK, N.Y.) -- FICTION
Milford, K. The Broken Lands
Confessions. Minato, K.
Confessions of a Hater. Crane, C.
Confessions of a Hollywood star. Sheldon, D.
Confessions of the Sullivan sisters. Standiford, N.
CONFORMITY -- FICTION
Anderson, M. T. Burger Wuss
CONGO (DEMOCRATIC REPUBLIC) -- FICTION
Schrefer, E. Endangered
CONNECTICUT -- FICTION
Cooney, C. B. Diamonds in the shadow
Cooney, C. B. If the witness lied
Mlynowski, S. Ten things we did (and probably shouldn't have)
Warman, J. Where the truth lies
Connelly, Neil O.
The miracle stealer
Connor, Leslie
Dead on town line
CONSERVATION OF NATURAL RESOURCES -- FICTION
Lloyd, S. The carbon diaries 2015
Lloyd, S. The carbon diaries 2017
CONSPIRACIES -- FICTION
Carriger, G. Curtsies & conspiracies
Cashore, K. Bitterblue
Gagnon, M. Don't turn around
Giles, L. Fake ID
O'Neal, E. The false princess
Prose, F. After
Williams, S. Twinmaker
A **conspiracy** of kings. Turner, M. W.
Constable, Kate
The singer of all songs
Consumed. Cann, K.
Contaminated. Garner, E.
The **contender.** Lipsyte, R.
CONTESTS -- FICTION
Chandler, K. Girls don't fly
Maas, S. J. Throne of glass
Weissman, E. B. The trouble with Mark Hopper
CONVENTS -- FICTION
Strauss, V. Passion blue
Conversion. Howe, K.
Cook, Eileen
The education of Hailey Kendrick
Cook, Trish
(jt. auth) Halpin, B. A really awesome mess
Notes from the blender
COOKING -- FICTION
Lewis, S. The secret ingredient
Williams, K. Pizza, love, and other stuff that made me famous
COOKS -- FICTION
Ryan, T. Way to go
Cooney, Caroline B., 1947-
Code orange
Diamonds in the shadow
The face on the milk carton
If the witness lied
Janie face to face
Three black swans
The voice on the radio

What Janie found
Whatever happened to Janie?
Cooper, Michelle
A brief history of Montmaray
The FitzOsbornes at war
The FitzOsbornes in exile
COPPER MINES AND MINING -- FICTION
Wallace, S. N. Muckers
Copper sun. Draper, S. M.
Cooper, Susan
The Boggart
Over sea, under stone
Cooper, T.
Changers
COPYRIGHT
Doctorow, C. Pirate cinema
Cormier, Robert
After the first death
Beyond the chocolate war
The chocolate war
I am the cheese
The **Corner** of Bitter and Sweet. Palmer, R.
A **corner** of white. Moriarty, J.
Cornered. Zweig, E.
Cornish, D. M.
Factotum
Foundling
Cornwell, Autumn
Carpe diem
Cornwell, Betsy
Tides
Corral, Rodrigo
(jt. auth) Anthony, J. Chopsticks
Corrigan, Eireann
Accomplice
Ordinary ghosts
COSMETICS -- FICTION
Wright, B. Putting makeup on the fat boy
Cosmic storm. Testa, D.
COSTUME -- FICTION
Perkins, S. Lola and the boy next door
COUNTERCULTURE -- FICTION
Doctorow, C. Homeland
The **counterfeit** family tree of Vee Crawford-Wong. Holland, L. T.
COUNTERFEITS AND COUNTERFEITING -- FICTION
Pierce, T. Bloodhound
COUNTRY LIFE -- FICTION
Friedman, A. The year my sister got lucky
Herrick, S. Cold skin
Magnin, J. Carrying Mason
Michael, J. City boy
Napoli, D. J. Alligator bayou
Sanders, S. L. Gray baby
Sanders, S. L. The Hanging Woods
Slayton, F. C. When the whistle blows
Woodworth, C. Double -click for trouble,
Wyatt, M. Funny how things change
COUNTRY MUSIC -- FICTION
Supplee, S. Somebody everybody listens to
COUPS D'ÉTAT -- FICTION
Steele, A. Apollo's outcasts
COURAGE -- FICTION
Bartoletti, S. C. The boy who dared
Roth, V. Allegiant
Roth, V. Insurgent
COURTS AND COURTIERS--FICTION
Whitcomb, L. The Fetch
COURTS AND COURTIERS -- FICTION
Bridges, R. The gathering storm
Hartman, R. Seraphina
LaFevers, R. Grave mercy
Longshore, K. Gilt
Maas, S. J. Crown of midnight
Maas, S. J. Throne of glass
Marsh, K. Jepp, who defied the stars
Murdock, C. G. Princess Ben
Zettel, S. Palace of Spies
COURTSHIP -- FICTION
Kindl, P. Keeping the castle
Courtship and curses. Doyle, M.
COUSINS -- FICTION
Archer, E. Geek: fantasy novel
Blacker, T. Boy2girl
Clarke, J. The winds of heaven
Clement-Moore, R. The splendor falls
Cohn, R. You know where to find me
Cooney, C. B. Three black swans
De la Peña, M. Mexican whiteboy
Draper, S. M. The Battle of Jericho
Elliott, P. The traitor's smile
Fletcher, R. The one o'clock chop
Hahn, M. D. The ghost of Crutchfield Hall
Hand, E. Illyria
Harrison, C. I was Jane Austen's best friendlein, r
Howells, A. The summer of skinny dipping
Lecesne, J. Absolute brightness
Levitin, S. Strange relations
McKenzie, N. Guinevere's gift
Meyerhoff, J. Queen of secrets
Minchin, A. The beat goes on
Paulsen, G. Harris and me; a summer remembered
Perera, A. Guantanamo boy
Schwartz, V. F. Send one angel down
Seigel, A. The kid table
Strohmeyer, S. How Zoe made her dreams (mostly) come true
Werlin, N. The killer's cousin
Wittlinger, E. Zigzag
Wrede, P. C. Sorcery and Cecelia, or, The en-

chanted chocolate pot
Coutts, Alexandra
Tumble & fall
Coventry, Susan
The queen's daughter
Cowan, Jennifer
Earthgirl
COWHANDS -- FICTION
Nuzum, K. A. A small white scar
Cox, Suzy
The Dead Girls Detective Agency
Coy, John
Box out
Crackback
Crackback. Coy, J.
The **cracks** in the kingdom. Moriarty, J.
Craig, Colleen
Afrika
Crane, Caprice
Confessions of a Hater
Crane, Dede
Poster boy
Crane, E. M.
Skin deep
Crap kingdom. Pierson, D. C.
Crash and Burn. Hassan, M.
Crash into me. Borris, A.
Crash. Spinelli, J.
Crashed. Wasserman, R.
Crave. Burns, L. J.
Crawford, Brent
Carter's big break
Carter finally gets it
Carter's unfocused, one-track mind
Crazy. Nolan, H.
Crazy. Reed, A.
Crazy beautiful. Baratz-Logsted, L.
The **crazy** things girls do for love. Sheldon, D.,
CREATION (LITERARY, ARTISTIC, ETC.) -- FICTION
Hand, E. Radiant days
CREATIVE WRITING
See also Authorship; Creation (Literary, artistic, etc.); Language arts
A **creature** of moonlight. Hahn, R.
Creature of the night. Thompson, K.
Cremer, Andrea
Invisibility
Cress. Meyer, M.
CREUTZFELDT-JAKOB DISEASE -- FICTION
Bray, L. Going bovine
Crewe, Megan
Give up the ghost
The lives we lost
The way we fall
Crewel. Albin, G.
CRIME -- FICTION
Carter, A. Perfect scoundrels
Ellison, K. The butterfly clues
Fredericks, M. The girl in the park
Heath, J. Money run
Zevin, G. Because it is my blood
CRIMINAL INVESTIGATION -- FICTION
Vrettos, A. M. Sight
CRIMINALS -- FICTION
Grant, V. Res judicata
Kerr, M. E. Gentlehands
Miller, K. How to lead a life of crime
Newton, R. Runner
Stewart, A. Dragonwood
Zevin, G. Because it is my blood
The **Crimson** Crown. Chima, C. W.
Crispin: the cross of lead. Avi, 1937.
Criss cross. Perkins, L. R.
Croak. Damico, G.
Crocker, Nancy
Billie Standish was here
Crockett, S. D.
After the snow
One Crow Alone
Croggon, Alison
Black spring
The Crow
The Naming
The Riddle
The Singing
Cronn-Mills, Kirstin
Beautiful Music for Ugly Children
Cross my heart. Gould, S.
Cross, Gillian, 1945-
Where I belong
Cross, Julie
Tempest
Cross, Sarah
Dull boy
Kill me softly
Crossan, Sarah
Breathe
Crossed. Condie, A. B.
Crossing stones. Frost, H.
Crossing the tracks. Stuber, B.
Crossing the wire. Hobbs, W.,
Crossing to Paradise. Crossley-Holland, K.
Crossley-Holland, Kevin
Crossing to Paradise
The **crossover.** Alexander, K.
Crow. Wright, B.
The **Crow.** Croggon, A.
Crow Lake. Lawson, M.
Crowe, Chris
Mississippi trial, 1955

The **Crowfield** curse. Walsh, P.
The **Crowfield** demon. Walsh, P.
Crowley, Cath
A little wanting song
Crowley, Suzanne
The stolen one
The **crown** of embers. Carson, R.
Crown of midnight. Maas, S. J.
Cruel Beauty. Hodge, R.
Cruise control. Trueman, T.
CRUISE SHIPS -- FICTION
De la Peña, M. The living
Cruisers [series]
Myers, W. D. A star is born
The **Cruisers.** Myers, W. D., 1937-
Crunch time. Fredericks, M.
Crusade. Holder, N.
CRUSADES -- FICTION
Cadnum, M. The book of the Lion
Grant, K. M. Blood red horse
Crush; the theory, practice, and destructive properties of love. Paulsen, G.
CRUSHES -- FICTION
Paulsen, G. Crush; the theory, practice, and destructive properties of love
Crutcher, Chris
Deadline
Ironman
Whale talk
Period 8
Running loose
Staying fat for Sarah Byrnes
Stotan!
Cry of the giraffe. Oron, J.
Cry, the beloved country. Paton, A.
Cryer's Cross. McMann, L.
CRYONICS -- FICTION
Whaley, J. C. Noggin
CRYPTOGRAPHY -- FICTION
Monaghan, A. A girl named Digit
Crystal bones. Hall, C. A.
CUBA -- FICTION
Cardenas, T. Old dog
Engle, M. Firefly letters
CUBA -- FICTION
Engle, M. The Lightning Dreamer
Cuba 15. Osa, N.
CUBAN AMERICANS -- FICTION
Chambers, V. Fifteen candles
Dole, M. L. Down to the bone
Hijuelos, O. Dark Dude
Osa, N. Cuba 15
Culbertson, Kim
Instructions for a broken heart
I am Rembrandt's daughter
The **culling.** Dos Santos, S.
CULTS -- FICTION
Bosworth, J. Struck
Galante, C. The patron saint of butterflies
Lancaster, M. A. The future we left behind
Mills, S. The viper within
Nader, E. Escape from Eden
Parker, A. C. Gated
Smith-Ready, J. This side of salvation
CULTURE CONFLICT
Power, S. The grass dancer
CULTURE CONFLICT -- FICTION
Kerbel, D. Mackenzie, lost and found
Ostlere, C. Karma
Cummings, Priscilla
Red kayak
Cupcake. Cohn, R.
The **cupcake** queen. Hepler, H.
CURẠCAO -- FICTION
Patterson, V. O. The other side of blue
A **curse** dark as gold. Bunce, E. C.
Curse of the blue tattoo. Meyer, L. A.
Curse of the Thirteenth Fey. Yolen, J.
The **curse** of the Wendigo. Yancey, R.
The curse workers [series]
Black, H. Black heart
Black, H. Red glove
Black, H. The white cat
CURSES -- FICTION
Yolen, J. Curse of the Thirteenth Fey
Cursing Columbus. Tal, E.
Curtsies & conspiracies. Carriger, G.
Cut. McCormick, P.
CUTTING (SELF-MUTILATION) -- FICTION
Oates, J. C. Two or three things I forgot to tell you
Rainfield, C. Scars
Cybele's secret. Marillier, J.
CYBERBULLYING -- FICTION
Davis, L. I swear
CYBORGS -- FICTION
Meyer, M. Scarlet
CYCLING -- FICTION
Bradbury, J. Shift
The **Cydonian** pyramid. Hautman, P.
Cypess, Leah
Death sworn
Mistwood
Nightspell
Cyrano. McCaughrean, G.
Cyrano de Bergerac, 1619-1655
About
McCaughrean, G. Cyrano
CYSTIC FIBROSIS -- FICTION
Monninger, J. Wish
Moskowitz, H. Teeth
CZECH AMERICANS -- FICTION

Myers, W. D. Game
CZECH REPUBLIC -- FICTION
Taylor, L. Days of blood & starlight
CZECHOSLOVAKIA -- FICTION
Marsden, C. My Own Revolution

D

Daemon Hall. Nance, A.
Dagg, Carole Estby
The year we were famous
Dairy Queen. Murdock, C. G.
The dairy queen trilogy [series]
Murdock, C. G. Front and center
DAKOTA INDIANS -- FICTION
Power, S. The grass dancer
Damico, Gina
Croak
Rogue
Scorch
Damned. Holder, N.
Damosel. Spinner, S.
Dana, Barbara
A voice of her own
DANCE -- FICTION
Blundell, J. Strings attached
Dixon, H. Entwined
Draper, S. M. (. M. Panic
Leap
Dancer, daughter, traitor, spy. Kiem, E.
DANCERS -- FICTION
Clement-Moore, R. The splendor falls
Fletcher, C. Ten cents a dance
Kephart, B. House of Dance
Winston, S. The Kayla chronicles
Danforth, Emily M.
The miseducation of Cameron Post
Danger zone [series]
Gilman, D. Blood sun
Gilman, D. The devil's breath
Gilman, D. Ice claw
Dangerous angels. Block, F. L.
Dangerous girls. Haas, A.
Dangerous neighbors. Kephart, B.
Dangerous skies. Staples, S. F.
Dani noir. Suma, N. R.
Daniel half human. Chotjewitz, D.
Dare You to. McGarry, K.
DARFUR (SUDAN) -- FICTION
Whitman, S. The milk of birds
Darius & Twig. Myers, W. D.
DARK AGES *See* Middle Ages
The **dark** and hollow places. Ryan, C.
The dark city. Fisher, C.
Dark companion. Acosta, M.
The **dark** days of Hamburger Halpin. Berk, J.
The **dark** deeps. Slade, A. G.
The **dark** Divine. Despain, B.
Dark Dude. Hijuelos, O.
Dark hours. Pausewang, G.
Dark inside. Roberts, J.
Dark Lord, the early years. Thomson, J.
Dark of the moon. Barrett, T.
Dark reflections [series]
Meyer, K. The glass word
Meyer, K. The stone light
Dark song. Giles, G.
Dark sons. Grimes, N.
Dark triumph. LaFevers, R.
The **dark** unwinding. Cameron, S.
Dark water. McNeal, L.
The **dark** zone. Testa, D.
Darkbound. Tracey, S.
The darkening. Wood, M. L.
Darkest mercy. Marr, M.
Darkest powers [series]
Armstrong, K. The awakening
Armstrong, K. The reckoning
Armstrong, K. The summoning
Darkside. Becker, T.
Darkside [series]
Becker, T. Darkside
Becker, T. Lifeblood
Darksolstice. Llewellyn, S.
Darkwater. Fisher, C.
Darwin, Charles, 1809-1882 About
Meyer, C. The true adventures of Charley Darwin
Dash & Lily's book of dares. Cohn, R.
Dashner, James
The kill order
The maze runner
The scorch trials
Daswani, Kavita
Indie girl
DATE RAPE -- FICTION
Wolf, J. S. Breaking beautiful
DATING (SOCIAL CUSTOMS) -- FICTION
Sones, S. What my mother doesn't know
DATING (SOCIAL CUSTOMS) -- FICTION
Bradley, A. 24 girls in 7 days
Chandler, K. Girls don't fly
Crawford, B. Carter's unfocused, one-track mind
Dessen, S. The moon and more
Fredericks, M. Head games
Goldblatt, S. Stray
Hautman, P. The big crunch
Hautman, P. What boys really want?
Kerr, M. E. If I love you, am I trapped forever?
Leavitt, L. Going vintage
Matson, M. Since you've been gone
Namioka, L. Mismatch

Naylor, P. R. Incredibly Alice
Patrick, C. Forgotten
Patrick, C. The Originals
Paulsen, G. Crush; the theory, practice, and destructive properties of love
Scheidt, E. L. Uses for boys
Scott, K. This is so not happening
Smith, H. T. Wild awake
Voorhees, C. Lucky fools
Whitaker, A. The queen of Kentucky
DATING VIOLENCE -- FICTION
Jayne, H. Truly, madly, deadly
Rosenfield, K. Amelia Anne is dead and gone
Wolf, J. S. Breaking beautiful
Daugherty, C. J.
Night School
Daughter of smoke and bone. Taylor, L.
Daughter of smoke and bone trilogy [series]
Taylor, L. Days of blood & starlight
Daughter of the forest. Marillier, J.
Daughter of war. Skrypuch, M. F.
Daughter of Xanadu. Yang, D. J.,
DAUGHTERS -- FICTION
Coats, J. A. The wicked and the just
The **daughters.** Philbin, J.
Davenport, Jennifer
Anna begins
David, Keren
Lia's guide to winning the lottery
When I was Joe
Davidson, Jenny
The Explosionist
Davies, Anna
Identity Theft
Davies, Jacqueline
Lost
Davies, Stephen
Hacking Timbuktu
Outlaw
Davis, Lane
I swear
Davis, Heather
Never cry werewolf
Davis, Rebecca Fjelland
Chasing AllieCat
Davis, Tanita S.
Happy families
A la carte
Mare's war
Dawn and dusk. Mead, A.
Dawn. Brooks, K.
A **day** no pigs would die. Peck, R. N.
Day of tears. Lester, J.
Day of the assassins. O'Brien, J.
Day of the predator. Scarrow, A.
The **daykeeper's** grimoire. Raedeke, C.
Days of blood & starlight. Taylor, L.
Days of Little Texas. Nelson, R. A.
De Goldi, Kate
The 10 p.m. question
De Gramont, Nina
Every little thing in the world
De la Cruz, Melissa
Blue bloods
Gates of Paradise
Lost in time
Masquerade
Misguided angel
Revelations
The Van Alen legacy
De la Peña, Matt
Ball don't lie
De la Peña, M. Mexican whiteboy
The living
Mexican whiteboy
We were here
De Lint, Charles
The blue girl
Dingo
Little (grrl) lost
De Quidt, Jeremy
The toymaker
The **dead.** Higson, C.
DEAD -- FICTION
Bow, E. Sorrow's knot
Burtenshaw, J. Shadowcry
Noel, A. Radiance
Plum, A. Die for me
Tintera, A. Reboot
Dead beautiful. Woon, Y.
Dead connection. Price, C.
Dead ends. Lange, E. J.
Dead girl dancing. Singleton, L. J.
Dead girl in love. Singleton, L. J.
Dead girl walking. Singleton, L. J.
The **Dead** Girls Detective Agency. Cox, S.
Dead in the water. Stevenson, R. H.
Dead is [series]
Perez, M. Dead is just a dream
Dead is a battlefield. Perez, M.
Dead is a killer tune. Perez, M.
Dead is just a dream. Perez, M.
Dead is the new black. Perez, M.
Dead on town line. Connor, L.
Dead reckoning; a pirate voyage with Captain Drake. Lawlor, L.
Dead rules. Russell, R.
The **dead-tossed** waves. Ryan, C.
Deadline. Crutcher, C.
Deadly. Chibbaro, J.
The **deadly** sister. Schrefer, E.
DEAF -- FICTION

Berk, J. The dark days of Hamburger Halpin
Ferris, J. Of sound mind
John, A. Five flavors of dumb
LeZotte, A. C. T4
Miller, S. Miss Spitfire
Na, A. Wait for me
Portman, F. Andromeda Klein
Dear Julia. Zemser, A. B.
Dear Life, You Suck. Blagden, S.
Dear Zoe. Beard, P.
DEATH -- FICTION
Arntson, S. The wrap-up list
Avasthi, S. Chasing Shadows
Blume, J. Tiger eyes
Burgess, M. The hit
Caletti, D. The last forever
Crane, E. M. Skin deep
Crutcher, C. Deadline
Cummings, P. Red kayak
Damico, G. Croak
Damico, G. Scorch
Dellaira, A. Love letters to the dead
Goobie, B. Before wings
Harness, C. Just for you to know
Hegamin, T. M +O 4evr
Johnson, A. A certain October
Johnson, A. Toning the sweep
Kessler, J. M. Breath
LaFevers, R. Dark triumph
Lupica, M. Hero
MacCullough, C. Drawing the ocean
Marsh, K. The night tourist
Mazer, N. F. After the rain
Moore, K. Amber House
Nelson, J. I'll give you the sun
Ness, P. More than this
Oppel, K. Such wicked intent
Scrimger, R. Me & death
Smith, C. L. Rain is not my Indian name
Volponi, P. Homestretch
Woods, R. The hero
Yeomans, E. Rubber houses
Zusak, M. The book thief,
Death benefits. Harvey, S. N.
The **death** -defying Pepper Roux. McCaughrean, G.
Death in the air. Peacock, S.
Death mountain. Shahan, S.
Death sentence. Smith, A. G.
Death sworn. Cypess, L.
Death, Dickinson, and the demented life of Frenchie Garcia. Torres Sanchez, J.
A **death-struck** year. Lucier, M.
DEBATES AND DEBATING -- FICTION
Schneider, R. The beginning of everything
Debbie Harry sings in French. Brothers, M.
DEER -- FICTION
Rawlings, M. K. The yearling
DECEPTION -- FICTION
Master, I. A beautiful lie
Shoemaker, T. Code of silence
DECISION MAKING -- FICTION
Brody, J. My life undecided
DECLAMATIONS *See* Monologues; Recitations
The **Declaration.** Malley, G.
The **decoding** of Lana Morris. McNeal, L.
Dee, John, 1527-1608 About
Scott, M. The enchantress
Deebs, Tracy
Tempest rising
Deedy, Carmen Agra
The Cheshire Cheese cat; a Dickens of a tale
The **deep** freeze of Bartholomew Tullock. Williams, A.
Defect. Weaver, W.
Define normal. Peters, J. A., 1952-
Defining Dulcie. Acampora, P.
Defy the dark. Defoe, D.
Defying the diva. Love, D. A.
Delirium. Oliver, L.
Dellaira, A.
Love letters to the dead
Delsol, Wendy
Flock
Frost
Stork
Demetrios, Heather
Something real
The **demon** catchers of Milan. Beyer, K.
Demon catchers of Milan trilogy [series]
Beyer, K. The demon catchers of Milan
Demon chick. Kaye, M.
The **Demon** King. Chima, C. W.
The **demon** trapper's daughter. Oliver, J. G.
A demon trappers novel [series]
Oliver, J. Soul thief
The **demon's** covenant. Brennan, S. R.
The **demon's** lexicon. Brennan, S. R.
The demon's lexicon trilogy [series]
Brennan, S. R. The demon's covenant
Demonglass. Hawkins, R.
DEMONIAC POSSESSION -- FICTION
Beyer, K. The demon catchers of Milan
DEMONOLOGY -- FICTION
Clare, C. Clockwork angel
Clare, C. Clockwork prince
Oliver, J. G. The demon trapper's daughter
The Shadowhunter's codex
Tracey, S. Darkbound
Walsh, P. The Crowfield demon
Demons of the ocean. Somper, J.
Deng, Jacob About

Coates, J. L. A hare in the elephant's trunk
DENMARK -- FICTION
Marsden, J. Hamlet: a novel
Dennard, Susan
Something strange and deadly
Department 19. Hill, W.
DEPRESSION (PSYCHOLOGY) -- FICTION
Kessler, J. M. Breath
Roskos, E. Dr. Bird's advice for sad poets
DEPRESSION, MENTAL -- FICTION
Barnaby, H. Wonder show
Roskos, E. Dr. Bird's advice for sad poets
Deriso, Christine Hurley
Then I met my sister
Derting, Kimberly
The body finder
Desires of the dead
The last echo
The taking
DES MOINES (WASH.) -- FICTION
Flores-Scott, P. Jumped in
Desai Hidier, Tanuja
Born confused
Desert Angel. Price, C.
DESERTS -- FICTION
Durst, S. B. Vessel
Kinch, M. The fires of New SUN
Kinch, M. The rebels of New SUN
Mason, P. Camel rider
DESIGNER DRUGS -- FICTION
Burgess, M. The hit
Desires of the dead. Derting, K.
Despain, Bree
The dark Divine
Desperate journey. Murphy, J.
DESPOTISM -- FICTION
Mourlevat Winter's end
Scott, E. Grace
Dessen, Sarah
Along for the ride
Just listen
Lock and key
The moon and more
That summer
The truth about forever
What happened to goodbye
DeStefano, Lauren
Fever
Perfect ruin
Sever
Wither
Destiny's path. Jones, A. F.
Destroy all cars. Nelson, B.
DETECTIVE AND MYSTERY STORIES
Carter, A. Perfect scoundrels
Gleason, C. The clockwork scarab
DETECTIVES -- FICTION
Whelan, G. *See* what I see
Deuker, Carl
Gym candy
High heat
Night hoops
Painting the black
Payback time
Runner
Swagger
DEVELOPMENTAL PSYCHOLOGY
See also Psychology
Deviant. FitzGerald, H.
DEVIL -- FICTION
Clare, C. City of ashes
Clare, C. City of bones
Clare, C. City of Glass
Clement-Moore, R. Prom dates from Hell
Gill, D. M. Soul enchilada
Jenkins, A. M. Repossessed
Napoli, D. J. The wager
Nayeri, D. Another Faust
DeVillers, Julia
Lynn Visible
The **devil's** breath. Gilman, D.
The **devil's** kiss. Chadda, S.
The **devil's** paintbox. McKernan, V.
Devil's pass. Brouwer, S.
Devine intervention. Brockenbrough, M.
DIABETES -- FICTION
Hautman, P. Sweetblood
A **diamond** in the desert; Kathryn Fitzmaurice. Fitzmaurice, K.
Diamonds in the shadow. Cooney, C. B.
DIARIES -- FICTION
Patterson, J. Homeroom diaries
Rennison, L. Angus, thongs and full-frontal snogging
DIARIES -- FICTION
Chibbaro, J. Deadly
Cooper, M. The FitzOsbornes at war
Kirby, J. Golden
May, K. Kiki
Nielsen, S. The reluctant journal of Henry K. Larsen
Patron, S. Behind the masks
Powell, W. C. Expiration day
Williams, S. D. Palace beautiful
Wilson, N. H. Mountain pose
DIARISTS -- FICTION
Dogar, S. Annexed
The **diary** of Pelly D. Adlington, L. J.
DiCamillo, Kate, 1964-
Flora and Ulysses
Pratchett, T. Dodger
Dickerson, Melanie

The merchant's daughter
The ropemaker
Dickinson, Emily, 1830-1886
About
Dana, B. A voice of her own
MacColl, M. Nobody's secret
Dickinson, Peter
Angel Isle
Eva
DICTATORS -- FICTION
Carleson, J. C. The tyrant's daughter
Revis, B. Across the universe
DIDACTIC FICTION
See also fiction
Die for me. Plum, A.
DIET -- FICTION
Letting Ana go
The **difference** between you and me. George, M.
The **difference** between you and me. George, M.
Dingo. De Lint, C.
DINOSAURS -- FICTION
Cole, S. Z. Raptor
Cole, S. Z. Rex
Dirty little secrets. Omololu, C. J.
DISABILITIES
Flake, S. G. Pinned
The **Disappeared.** Whelan, G.
DISASTERS
McDevitt, J. Moonfall
DISC JOCKEYS -- FICTION
Cronn-Mills, K. Beautiful Music for Ugly Children
Sales, L. This song will save your life
Discordia. Salmon, D. K.
DISEASES -- FICTION
Kagawa, J. The immortal rules
Kessler, J. M. Loss
Thomas, L. Quarantine
The **Disenchantments.** LaCour, N.
DISFIGURED PERSONS -- FICTION
Griffin, P. Burning blue
Vlahos, L. The scar boys
Woolston, B. Catch & release
Zephaniah, B. Face
The **disreputable** history of Frankie Landau-Banks. Lockhart, E.
DISSENTERS -- FICTION
Standiford, N. The boy on the bridge
Distant waves. Weyn, S.
Divergent. Roth, V.
The **diviners.** Bray, L.
DIVORCE -- FICTION
Colasanti, S. So much closer
Gant, G. The Thunder in His Head
Mills, S. The viper within
Moore, C. The stalker chronicles
Preller, J. Bystander
West, K. Pivot point
Wright, B. When the black girl sings
Dixon, Heather
Entwined
Dixon, John
Phoenix Island
Dobkin, Bonnie
Neptune's children
Doctorow, Cory
For the win
Homeland
Little brother
Pirate cinema
DOCUMENTARY FILMS -- PRODUCTION AND DIRECTION -- FICTION
Castle, J. You look different in real life
Dessen, S. The moon and more
Dodger. Pratchett, T.
Does my head look big in this? Abdel-Fattah, R.
DOG RACING -- FICTION
Doyle, R. A greyhound of a girl
Dogar, Sharon
Annexed
DOGS -- FICTION
Bigelow, L. J. Starting from here
Crane, E. M. Skin deep
Goldblatt, S. Stray
Griffin, P. Stay with me
Hartnett, S. Surrender
London, J. The call of the wild
London, J. White Fang
O'Brien, A. Lara's gift
Sherlock, P. Letters from Wolfie
Treggiari, J. Ashes, ashes
Trueman, T. Life happens next
Williams, A. The deep freeze of Bartholomew Tullock
Doktorski, Jennifer Salvato
Famous last words
Dolamore, Jaclyn
Magic under glass
Dole, Mayra L.
Down to the bone
Doller, Trish
Something like normal
DOLLS -- FICTION
Golds, C. The museum of Mary Child
Domenic's war; a story of the Battle of Monte Cassino. Parkinson, C.
DOMESTIC ANIMALS -- FICTION
Watkins, S. What comes after
DOMESTIC RELATIONS -- FICTION
King, A. S. Everybody sees the ants

DOMESTIC VIOLENCE -- FICTION
Bilen, T. What she left behind
Boll, R. The second trial
DOMESTICS
Chibbaro, J. Deadly
DOMINICAN REPUBLIC -- FICTION
Joseph, L. Flowers in the sky
Dominy, Amy Fellner
OyMG
Don't even think about it. Mlynowski, S.
Don't let go. Gagnon, M.
Don't let me go. Trumble, J. H.
Don't Look Now. Gagnon, M.
Don't turn around. Gagnon, M.
Donaldson, Julia
Running on the cracks
DONATION OF ORGANS, TISSUES, ETC. -- FICTION
Lynch, C. Pieces
Donnelly, Jennifer
A northern light
Revolution
Donovan, John
I'll get there, it better be worth the trip
Donut days. Zielin, L.
Dooley, Sarah
Livvie Owen lived here
The **Doomsday** Box: a Shadow Project adventure. Brennan, H.
The **door** of no return. Mussi, S.
Dope sick. Myers, W. D.
Doppelganger. Stahler, D.
Dos Santos, Steven
The culling
Double. Valentine, J.
Double crossing. Tal, E.
Double helix. Werlin, N.
Dough Boy. Marino, P.
Dowd, Siobhan
Bog child
Solace of the road
A swift pure cry
Dowell, Frances O' Roark
Ten miles past normal
Down Sand Mountain. Watkins, S.
DOWN SYNDROME -- FICTION
Hyde, C. R. The year of my miraculous reappearance
Lange, E. J. Dead ends
Trueman, T. Life happens next
Down to the bone. Dole, M. L.
Downham, Jenny
Before I die
You against me
Downriver. Hobbs, W.
Downsiders. Shusterman, N.
Dowswell, Paul
The Auslander
Doyle, Brian
Boy O'Boy
Pure Spring
Doyle, Eugenie F.
According to Kit
Doyle, Marissa
Betraying season
Bewitching season
Courtship and curses
Doyle, Roddy
A greyhound of a girl
Wilderness
Dr. Bird's advice for sad poets. Roskos, E.
Dr. Frankenstein's daughters. Weyn, S.
Dr. Franklin's island. Halam, A.
Dr. Radway's Sarsaparilla Resolvent. Kephart, B.
Draanen, Wendelin van
Runaway
DRACULA, COUNT (FICTIONAL CHARACTER)
Hill, W. The rising
Drago, Ty
The dragon's lair
DRAFTERS -- FICTION
Cullen, L. I am Rembrandt's daughter
Dragon road; Golden Mountain chronicles: 1939. Yep, L.
The **dragon** turn. Peacock, S.
Dragon's Keep. Carey, J. L.
Dragon's kin. McCaffrey, A.
Dragonflight. McCaffrey, A.\
Dragongirl. McCaffrey, T. J.
Dragonhaven. McKinley, R.
Dragonriders of Pern [series]
McCaffrey, A. Dragonflight
McCaffrey, T. J. Dragongirl
DRAGONS -- FICTION
McCaffrey, A. Dragonflight
DRAGONS -- FICTION
Carey, J. L. Dragons of Noor
Carey, J. L. Dragonswood
Fforde, J. The last Dragonslayer
Fletcher, S. Ancient, strange, and lovely
Fletcher, S. Dragon's milk
Hahn, R. A creature of moonlight
Hartman, R. Seraphina
Hill, C. J. Slayers
McKinley, R. Dragonhaven
O'Hearn, K. Kira
Yolen, J. Dragon's blood
Dragon's blood. Yolen, J.
Dragon's gate; Golden Mountain chronicles: 1867. Yep, L.

The **dragon's** lair. Drago, T.
Dragon's milk. Fletcher, S.
The **dragons** of darkness. Michaelis, A.
Dragons of Noor. Carey, J. L.
Dragons of silk. Yep, L.
The **dragon's** tooth. Wilson, N. D.
Dragonswood. Carey, J. L.
Dragonwings; Golden Mountain chronicles: 1903. Yep, L.
Dragonwood. Stewart, A.
The Drake chronicles [series]
Harvey, A. Hearts at stake
Drama! [series]
Ruditis, P. The four Dorothys
Dramarama. Lockhart, E.
Draper, Sharon M. (Sharon Mills), 1948-
The Battle of Jericho
Copper sun
Double Dutch
Fire from the rock
Just another hero
November blues
Panic
Tears of a tiger
Draw the dark. Bick, I. J.
DRAWING -- FICTION
McNeal, L. The decoding of Lana Morris
Drawing the ocean. MacCullough, C.
Dray, Stephanie
Lily of the Nile
Dream factory. Barkley, B.
The **dream** thieves. Stiefvater, M.
Dreamhunter. Knox, E.
Dreamhunter duet [series]
Knox, E. Dreamhunter
Knox, E. Dreamquake
Dreamland social club. Altebrando, T.
Dreamquake. Knox, E.
DREAMS -- FICTION
Bass, R. Lucid
MacDonald, A. L. Seeing red
Stiefvater, M. The dream thieves
Dreams of gods & monsters. Taylor, L.
Dreams of significant girls. García, C.
Dreams of the dead. Randall, T.
Drop. Papademetriou, L.
The **drop.** Ross, J.
DROPOUTS -- FICTION
O'Connell, M. The sharp time
The **drowned** cities. Bacigalupi, P.
DRUG ABUSE -- FICTION
Burgess, M. Smack
Koertge, R. Stoner & Spaz
DRUG ABUSE -- FICTION
Arcos, C. Out of reach
Cohn, R. You know where to find me
Brothers, M. Supergirl mixtapes
McCormick, P. My brother's keeper
Moses, S. P. Joseph
Rapp, A. The children and the wolves
Saenz, B. A. He forgot to say good-bye
Yee, P. Learning to fly
Zailckas, K. Mother, mother
DRUG ADDICTS -- REHABILITATION -- FICTION
Nelson, B. Recovery Road
DRUG DEALERS -- FICTION
Goodman, S. Kindness for weakness
Harmon, M. Under the bridge
DRUG TRAFFIC -- FICTION
Farmer, N. The lord of Opium
DRUGS -- FICTION
Burgess, M. The hit
Patrick, C. Revived
Drums, girls, & dangerous pie. Sonnenblick, J.
DRUNK DRIVING -- FICTION
Aronson, S. Head case
Duble, Kathleen Benner
Hearts of iron
Phantoms in the snow
Quest
DUBLIN (IRELAND) -- FICTION
Doyle, R. A greyhound of a girl
Dubosarsky, Ursula
The golden day
Duchessina. Meyer, C.
Dudley, David L.
Caleb's wars
Duey, Kathleen
Sacred scars
Skin hunger
Dull boy. Cross, S.
Duncan, Lois
I know what you did last summer
Killing Mr. Griffin
Locked in time
Stranger with my face
DUNGEONS & DRAGONS (GAME) -- FICTION
Halpern, J. Into the wild nerd yonder
Dunkle, Clare B.
By these ten bones
The house of dead maids
Dunlap, Susanne
In the shadow of the lamp
Dunlap, Susanne Emily
The musician's daughter
Dunmore, Helen
Ingo
The duplicate. Sleator, W.
DupliKate. Cheva, C.
Durst, Sarah Beth

Ice
Vessel
Dust & decay. Maberry, J.
Dust city. Weston, R. P.
Dust girl. Zettel, S.
Dustlands trilogy [series]
Young, M. Blood red road
Dut, Salva
About
Park, L. S. A long walk to water
DWARFS -- FICTION
Marsh, K. Jepp, who defied the stars
DWELLINGS -- FICTION
Moore, K. Neverwas
The **dying** breath. Ferguson, A.
Dying to know you. Chambers, A.
DYSFUNCTIONAL FAMILIES -- FICTION
Carter, C. Me, him, them, and it
Elston, A. The rules for disappearing
Griffin, N. The whole stupid way we are
Herbach, G. Nothing special
McGarry, K. Dare You to
Zailckas, K. Mother, mother
DYSLEXIA -- FICTION
Chambers, A. Dying to know you
DYSTOPIAN FICTION
Aguirre, A. Enclave
Aguirre, A. Horde
Almond, D. The true tale of the monster Billy Dean
Barry, M. Lexicon
Brown, P. Red Rising
Charbonneau, J. Graduation day
Crossan, S. Breathe
DeStefano, L. Fever
Dos Santos, S. The culling
Falls, K. Inhuman
Gagnon, M. Don't let go
Gagnon, M. Don't turn around
Gardner, S. Maggot moon
Garner, E. Contaminated
Healey, K. When we wake
Howard, J. L. Katya's World
Kinch, M. The fires of New SUN
Kinch, M. The rebels of New SUN
London, A. Guardian
Lowry, L. Son
Lu, M. Champion
Lu, M. Prodigy
MacHale, D. J. SYLO
MacHale, D. J. Storm
McCafferty, M. Thumped
Ness, P. More than this
Ness, P. The knife of never letting go
Pearson, M. E. Fox forever
Reeve, P. Scrivener's moon
Roth, V. Allegiant
Simmons, K. Article 5
Terry, T. Fractured
Trevayne, E. Coda
Unsworth, T. The one safe place
Weaver, W. The survivors
Williamson, J. Captives
Zhang, K. What's left of me
DYSTOPIAN FICTION
Woolston, B. Black helicopters

E

The Ear. Farmer, N.
Earth girl. Edwards, J.
Earth girl trilogy [series]
Edwards, J. Earth girl
The **earth,** my butt, and other big, round things.Mackler, C.
Earthbound. Pike, A.
Earthgirl. Cowan, J.
An **earthly** knight. McNaughton, J.
EARTHQUAKES -- FICTION
Lake, N. In darkness
EAST HARLEM (NEW YORK, N.Y.) -- HISTORY -- 20TH CENTURY -- FICTION
Manzano, S. The revolution of Evelyn Serrano
EAST INDIAN AMERICANS -- FICTION
Desai Hidier, T. Born confused
Meminger, N. Shine, coconut moon
EAST INDIANS -- FICTION
Nanji, S. Child of dandelions
East. Pattou, E.
EATING DISORDERS -- FICTION
Fehlbaum, B. Big fat disaster
Price, N. Zoe letting go
EATING HABITS -- FICTION
Lange, E. J. Butter
ECCENTRICS AND ECCENTRICITIES -- FICTION
Cameron, S. The dark unwinding
Echo. Brewster, A. W.
Echo. Morgenroth, K.
Eclipse. Meyer, S.
ECOLOGY -- FICTION
Nelson, B. Destroy all cars
Weyn, S. Empty
ECUADOR -- FICTION
Farinango, M. V. The Queen of Water
Resau, L. The indigo notebook
Edda. Kostick, C.
The **Edenville** Owls. Parker, R. B.
Edwards, Janet
Earth girl
Earth star
Edwardson, Debby Dahl

Blessing's bead
My name is not easy
Efaw, Amy
After
Battle dress
Efrain's secret. Quintero, S.
Egan, Laury A.
The Outcast Oracle
Egg & spoon. Maguire, G.
An **egg** on three sticks. Fischer, J.
EGGS -- FICTION
Mancusi, M. Scorched
Egloff, Z.
Leap
EGYPT -- FICTION
De la Cruz, M. Lost in time
Frazier, A. The Eternal Sea
Shecter, V. A. Cleopatra's moon
EGYPT -- HISTORY -- FICTION
Friesner, E. M. Sphinx's princess
Friesner, E. M. Sphinx's queen
Ehrenberg, Pamela
Ethan, suspended
Tillmon County fire
Ehrenhaft, Daniel
Friend is not a verb
8th grade superzero. Rhuday-Perkovich, O.
ELDERLY MEN -- FICTION
Chambers, A. Dying to know you
Eldest. Paolini, C.
Eleanor & Park. Rowell, R.
ELECTRICAL ENGINEERS -- FICTION
Weyn, S. Distant waves
ELEMENTARY SCHOOLS -- FICTION
May, K. Kiki
An **elephant** in the garden. Morpurgo, M.
Elephant run. Smith, R.
ELEPHANTS -- FICTION
Morpurgo, M. An elephant in the garden
The **eleventh** plague. Hirsch, J.
Elizabeth I, Queen of England, 1533-1603 About
Klein, L. M. Cate of the Lost Colony
Meyer, C. Beware
Elkeles, Simone
How to ruin a summer vacation
How to ruin my teenage life
How to ruin your boyfriend's reputation
Perfect chemistry
Rules of attraction
Ella enchanted. Levine, G. C.
Ellen, Laura
Blind spot
The Ellie chronicles [series]
Marsden, J. Incurable
Marsden, J. While I live
Elliot Allagash. Rich, S.
Elliott, L.
Across a war-tossed sea
Elliott, Patricia
The Pale Assassin
The traitor's smile
Ellis, Ann Dee
Everything is fine
This is what I did
Ellis, Deborah
Bifocal
My name is Parvana
No safe place
Ellison, Kate
The butterfly clues
Ellsworth, Loretta
Unforgettable
Elsewhere. Zevin, G.
Elston, Ashley
The rules for disappearing
ELVES -- FICTION
Stewart, A. Dragonwood
The **elves** of Cintra. Brooks, T.
EMAIL -- FICTION
Reed, A. Crazy
Zarr, S. Roomies
Emako Blue. Woods, B.
Embers & echoes. Knight, K.
Emblaze. Shirvington, J.
Embrace. Shirvington, J.
Emerald green.
EMIGRATION AND IMMIGRATION -- FICTION
Ada, A. F. Yes! we are Latinos
Andreu, M. E. The secret side of empty
Auch, M. J. Ashes of roses
Emilie & the hollow world. Wells, M.
Emily Goldberg learns to salsa. Ostow, M.
Emily the Strange: the lost days. Reger, R.
Emond, Stephen
Happyface
Winter town
EMOTIONAL PROBLEMS -- FICTION
Blagden, S. Dear Life, You Suck
Carter, C. Me, him, them, and it
Collomore, A. The ruining
Ellison, K. The butterfly clues
Halpin, B. A really awesome mess
Hassan, M. Crash and Burn
Hopkins, E. Smoke
King, A. S. Reality Boy
Luedeke, L. Smashed
Mesrobian, C. Sex and violence
Price, N. Zoe letting go
Rainfield, C. Scars
Reed, A. Crazy

Singleton, L. J. Dead girl dancing
Walton, K. M. Empty
EMOTIONALLY DISTURBED CHILDREN -- FICTION
Halpin, B. A really awesome mess
EMOTIONS -- FICTION
Sutton, K. Some quiet place
EMPERORS -- FICTION
Dray, S. Lily of the Nile
Miller, S. The lost crown
Empire of ruins. Slade, A. G.
Empire of the Sun. Ballard, J. G.
EMPLOYMENT AGENCIES -- FICTION
Fforde, J. The last Dragonslayer
Empress of the sun. McDonald, I.
Empress of the world. Ryan, S.
Empty. Walton, K. M.
Empty. Weyn, S.
Empty Coffin [series]
Olsen, G. Envy
The **empty** kingdom. Wein, E. E.
Enchanted. Kontis, A.
The **enchanter** heir. Chima, C. W.
The **enchantress.** Scott, M.
Enchantress from the stars. Engdahl, S. L.
Enclave. Aguirre, A.
Endgame. Garden, N.
The **end** games. Martin, T. M.
End of days. Turner, M.
The **end** of the line. Cerrito, A.
Endangered. Schrefer, E.
ENDANGERED SPECIES -- FICTION
Gilmore, K. The exchange student
Ender in exile. Card, O. S.
Ender's game. Card, O. S.
Ender's Game [series]
Card, O. S. Children of the mind
Card, O. S. Xenocide
Ender's Saga [series]
Card, O. S. Speaker for the Dead
Enders. Price, L.
Endymion Spring. Skelton, M.
The **enemy.** Higson, C.
The **enemy** has a face. Miklowitz, G. D.
Enemy territory. McKay, S. E.
ENERGY CONSERVATION -- FICTION
Weyn, S. Empty
Engdahl, Sylvia Louise
Enchantress from the stars
Engines of the broken world. Vanhee, J.
ENGLAND -- FICTION
Brennan, S. R. Unspoken
Doctorow, C. Pirate cinema
Emerald green
Fisher, C. Darkwater
Green, S. Half bad
Johnson, M. The madness underneath
Lancaster, M. A. The future we left behind
Mitchell, D. Black swan green
Moriarty, J. A corner of white
Moriarty, J. The cracks in the kingdom
Pitcher, A. Ketchup clouds
Pitcher, A. My sister lives on the mantelpiece
Powell, L. Burn mark
Powell, L. The Master of Misrule
Powell, W. C. Expiration day
Reeve, P. Scrivener's moon
Rennison, L. The taming of the tights
Sapphire blue
Smith, J. E. The statistical probability of love at first sight
Terry, T. Fractured
Valentine, J. Double
Ward, R. Infinity
ENGLAND -- FICTION
Kindl, P. Keeping the castle
Engle, Margarita
Firefly letters
Hurricane dancers
The Lightning Dreamer
Silver people
Tropical secrets
Enthusiasm. Shulman, P.
Entice. Shirvington, J.
The **entomological** tales of Augustus T. Percival. Low, D.
Entwined. Dixon, H.
ENVIRONMENTAL MOVEMENT -- FICTION
Henry, A. Torched
ENVIRONMENTAL DEGRADATION -- FICTION
Bell, H. Traitor's son
ENVIRONMENTAL PROTECTION -- FICTION
Gilman, D. Blood sun
Gilman, D. The devil's breath
Golding, J. Secret of the sirens
McDonald, A. Boys, bears, and a serious pair of hiking boots
Scarrow, A. TimeRiders
Vacco, C. My chemical mountain
Envy. Olsen, G.
Eon: Dragoneye reborn. Goodman, A.
Eona: the last Dragoneye. Goodman, A.
Ephron, Delia
Frannie in pieces
The girl with the mermaid hair
Epic. Kostick, C.
EPIDEMICS -- FICTION
Anderson, L. H. Fever, 1793
Crewe, M. The lives we lost
Crewe, M. The way we fall

Howe, K. Conversion
Kagawa, J. The Eternity Cure
Lucier, M. A death-struck year
Thomas, L. Quarantine
Wiggins, B. Stung
EPIDEMIOLOGY -- FICTION
Chibbaro, J. Deadly
EPILEPSY -- FICTION
Philbrick, W. R. The last book in the universe
Wolf, A. Zane's trace
EPISTOLARY FICTION
Moriarty, J. A corner of white
Epstein, Robin
God is in the pancakes
Eragon. Paolini, C.
Erasing time. Hill, C. J.
Erdrich, Louise
The last report on the miracles at Little No Horse
ERINYES (GREEK MYTHOLOGY) -- FICTION
Wolfson, J. Furious
EROS (GREEK DEITY) -- FICTION
Selfors, S. Mad love
Erskine, Kathryn
Quaking
Escape from Eden. Nader, E.
Escape from Furnace [series]
Smith, A. G. Death sentence
Smith, A. G. Lockdown
Smith, A. G. Solitary
Escape the mask. Ward, D.
Escape velocity. Stevenson, R. H.
ESCAPES -- FICTION
DeStefano, L. Fever
Nader, E. Escape from Eden
Escaping the tiger. Manivong, L.
Esckilsen, Erik E.
The last mall rat
ESKIMOS -- FICTION
Kirkpatrick, K. Between two worlds
Soonchild
ESPIONAGE -- FICTION
Carriger, G. Curtsies & conspiracies
Estrella's quinceanera. Alegria, M.
ETCHERS -- FICTION
Cullen, L. I am Rembrandt's daughter
ETCHING
See also Art; Pictures
Eternal. Smith, C. L.
The **eternal** ones. Miller, K.
The **Eternal** Sea. Frazier, A.
The **Eternity** Cure. Kagawa, J.
Ethan, suspended. Ehrenberg, P.
Etiquette & espionage. Carriger, G.
ETIQUETTE -- FICTION
Carriger, G. Curtsies & conspiracies
Carriger, G. Etiquette & espionage
Rumley, C. Never sit down in a hoopskirt and other things I learned in Southern belle hell
Eulberg, Elizabeth
Revenge of the Girl With the Great Personality
EUROPE -- FICTION
Schreiber, J. Perry's killer playlist
EUROPE -- HISTORY -- 16TH CENTURY -- FICTION
Marsh, K. Jepp, who defied the stars
EUROPE -- HISTORY -- 1789-1815 -- FICTION
Meyer, L. A. Viva Jacquelina!
EUROPE -- HISTORY -- 1918-1945 -- FICTION
Ruiz Zafon, C. The Prince of Mist
EUTHANASIA -- FICTION
Epstein, R. God is in the pancakes
LeZotte, A. C. T4
Trueman, T. Stuck in neutral
Eva. Dickinson, P.
Eva underground. Mackall, D. D.
EVACUATION OF CIVILIANS -- FICTION
Crockett, S. D. One Crow Alone
EVANGELISTIC WORK -- FICTION
Nelson, R. A. Days of Little Texas
Eve & Adam. Applegate, K.
Ever. Levine, G. C.
The **everafter.** Huntley, A.
Everbound. Ashton, B.
Everlasting. Frazier, A.
Everlost. Shusterman, N.
Everneath. Ashton, B.
Everneath [series]
Ashton, B. Everbound
Everness [series]
McDonald, I. Empress of the sun
Evernight. Gray, C.
Evernight [series]
Gray, C. Evernight
Everwild. Shusterman, N.
Every crooked pot. Rosen, R.
Every day. Levithan, D.
Every little thing in the world. De Gramont, N.
Every you, every me.
Everybody sees the ants. King, A. S.
Everything beautiful. Howell, S.
Everything beautiful in the world. Levchuk, L.
Everything is fine. Ellis, A. D.
Everything leads to you. LaCour, N.
Evil genius. Jinks, C.
EVOLUTION -- FICTION
Card, O. S. Ruins
EVOLUTION -- FICTION
Bryant, J. Ringside, 1925
The **evolution** of Mara Dyer. Hodkin, M.
Evolution, me, & other freaks of nature.

Brande, R.
EX-NUNS -- FICTION
Jarzab, A. The opposite of hallelujah
EXAMINATIONS -- FICTION
Charbonneau, J. The Testing
The **exchange.** Joyce, G.
The **exchange** student. Gilmore, K.
EXECUTIONS AND EXECUTIONERS -- FICTION
LaFevers, R. Grave mercy
Exile. Osterlund, A.
The **exiled** queen. Chima, C. W.
EXILES -- FICTION
Cooper, M. The FitzOsbornes at war
Marchetta, M. Froi of the exiles
Exit strategy. Potter, R.
Exodus. Bertagna, J.
The **Expeditioners** and the Treasure of Drowned Man's Canyon. Taylor, S. S.
EXPERIMENTS -- FICTION
Gagnon, M. Don't Look Now
Gagnon, M. Don't turn around
Expiration day. Powell, W. C.
EXPLORERS -- FICTION
Bruchac, J. Sacajawea
Mlawski, S. Hammer of witches
Wilson, J. The alchemist's dream
The **Explosionist.** Davidson, J.
Exposed. Marcus, K.
The **extraordinary** adventures of Alfred Kropp. Yancey, R.
The **extraordinary** secrets of April, May and June. Benway, R.
Extraordinary. Werlin, N.
Extras. Westerfeld, S.
EXTRASENSORY PERCEPTION -- FICTION
Clement-Davies, D. The sight
EXTRASENSORY PERCEPTION -- FICTION
Brennan, H. The Doomsday Box: a Shadow Project adventure
Derting, K. The body finder
Derting, K. Desires of the dead
Garcia, K. Beautiful creatures
Garcia, K. Beautiful darkness
Gee, M. Salt
Le Guin, U. K. The left hand of darkness
Lubar, D. Hidden talents
Lubar, D. True talents
MacDonald, A. L. Seeing red
Mlynowski, S. Don't even think about it
Perez, M. Dead is the new black
St. Crow, L. Strange angels
Ward, R. The Chaos
Ward, R. Numbers
EXTRATERRESTRIAL BEINGS -- FICTION
Castellucci, C. First day on Earth
Gilmore, K. The exchange student
Palma, F. J. The map of the sky
Silver, E. Rush
Yancey, R. The 5th Wave
Yansky, B. Homicidal aliens and other disappointments
Eye of the crow. Peacock, S.
The **Eyeball** Collector. Higgins, F. E.
Eyes like stars. Mantchev, L.
Eyes of the emperor. Salisbury, G.
EYRE, JANE (FICTIONAL CHARACTER)
Mont, E. M. A breath of Eyre

F

A **face** in every window. Nolan, H.
The **face** on the milk carton. Cooney, C. B.
Face. Zephaniah, B.
Fact of life #31. Vega, D.
FACTORIES -- FICTION
Bunce, E. C. A curse dark as gold
Davies, J. Lost
Factotum. Cornish, D. M.
Fade. McMann, L.
Faerie after. Simner, J. L.
The **faerie** ring. Hamilton, K.
Faerie winter. Simner, J. L.
Fahy, Thomas Richard
The unspoken
FAIRIES -- FICTION
Carey, J. L. Dragonswood
Hall, C. A. Crystal bones
Long, R. F. The treachery of beautiful things
Malchow, A. The Sword of Darrow
Simner, J. L. Faerie after
Springer, N. I am Morgan le Fay
Werlin, N. Extraordinary
White, K. Paranormalcy
White, K. Supernaturally
Wood, M. L. The darkening
Zettel, S. Dust girl
Zettel, S. Golden girl
FAIRS -- FICTION
Barkley, B. Scrambled eggs at midnight
Dennard, S. Something strange and deadly
Fairy bad day. Ashby, A.
FAIRY TALES
Anderson, J. L. Tiger Lily
Blubaugh, P. Serendipity Market
Cross, S. Kill me softly
Durst, S. B. Ice
Flinn, A. Cloaked
George, J. D. Princess of glass
George, J. D. Princess of the midnight ball
George, J. D. Sun and moon, ice and snow
Hale, S. The Goose girl
Levine, G. C. Ella enchanted

Levine, G. C. Fairest
Lies, knives and girls in red dresses
Lo, M. Ash
Lo, M. Huntress
Martin, R. Birdwing
McKinley, R. Rose daughter
McKinley, R. Beauty
Meyer, M. Cinder
Moss, J. Shadow
Murdock, C. G. Princess Ben
Murdock, C. G. Wisdom's kiss
Myers, E. Storyteller
Napoli, D. J. Beast
Napoli, D. J. The magic circle
Napoli, D. J. The wager
Pattou, E. East
Tomlinson, H. The swan maiden
Tomlinson, H. Toads and diamonds
Yolen, J. Troll Bridge; a rock 'n' roll fairy tale
Faith, hope, and Ivy June. Naylor, P. R.
FAITH -- FICTION
Coker, R. Chasing Jupiter
Vigilante, D. Trouble with half a moon
Fake ID. Giles, L.
Fakie. Varrato, T.
The **falconer's** knot. Hoffman, M.
FALCONS -- FICTION
Whitman, E. Wildwing
Falkner, Brian
Brain Jack
The project
Fall for anything. Summers, C.
Fallen angels. Myers, W. D.
Fallen Grace. Hooper, M.
The fallen world [series]
Crewe, M. The lives we lost
Falling. Wilhelm, D.
Fallout. Krisher, T.
Falls, Kat
Inhuman
FALSE ACCUSATION -- FICTION
Fombelle, T. Vango
Grace, A. In too deep
False memory. Krokos, D.
The **false** princess. O'Neal, E.
Fama, Elizabeth
Overboard
FAME -- FICTION
Barnes, J. Losers in space
Bates, M. Awkward
Harmel, K. When you wish
Rudnick, P. Gorgeous
Shukert, R. Starstruck
Taylor, G. The girl who became a Beatle
FAMILIES -- FICTION
Berk, A. Mistle child
Block, F. L. Love in the time of global warming
Burgess, M. The hit
Casanova, M. Frozen
FitzGerald, H. Deviant
Friesner, E. M. Spirit's princess
Hemphill, S. Sisters of glass
Holland, L. T. The counterfeit family tree of Vee Crawford-Wong
LaCour, N. Everything leads to you
Lockhart, E. We were liars
Pitcher, A. Ketchup clouds
Roth, V. Allegiant
Roth, V. Insurgent
Sáenz, B. A. Aristotle and Dante discover the secrets of the universe
Taub, M. Still star-crossed
FAMILIES OF DRUG ADDICTS -- FICTION
Arcos, C. Out of reach
FAMILY -- FICTION
David, K. Lia's guide to winning the lottery
Davis, T. S. Happy families
Demetrios, H. Something real
Friesner, E. Spirit's princess
King, A. S. Everybody sees the ants
Lerangis, P. Somebody, please tell me who I am
Matson, M. Second chance summer
FAMILY LIFE -- FICTION
Bass, K. Graffiti knight
Freymann-Weyr, G. My heartbeat
Keplinger, K. A midsummer's nightmare
Lockhart, E. We were liars
Magoon, K. 37 things I love (in no particular order)
Mason, B. A. In country
Mitchell, D. Black swan green
Na, A. A step from heaven
Otsuka, J. When the emperor was divine
Van Draanen, W. Flipped
Yolen, J. Curse of the Thirteenth Fey
FAMILY LIFE -- CALIFORNIA -- FICTION
Leavitt, L. Going vintage
Lynch, J. N. My beautiful hippie
Schneider, R. The beginning of everything
Zarr, S. The Lucy variations
Zarr, S. Roomies
FAMILY LIFE -- CANADA -- FICTION
Hopkinson, N. The Chaos
Martin, C. K. K. Yesterday
FAMILY LIFE -- ENGLAND -- FICTION
Burgess, M. The hit
Cooper, M. The FitzOsbornes at war
Green, S. Half bad
Lancaster, M. A. The future we left behind

Pitcher, A. Ketchup clouds
Terry, T. Slated
FAMILY LIFE -- ENGLAND -- LONDON -- FICTION
Emerald green
Sapphire blue
FAMILY LIFE -- FICTION
Andrews, J. Me & Earl & the dying girl
Blume, Lesley M. M., Tennyson.
Boll, R. The second trial.
Brooks, M. Mistik Lake
Chandler, K. Girls don't fly
Chen, J. Return to me
Clarke, J. One whole and perfect day
Cooney, C. B. Janie face to face
Díaz, J. The brief wondrous life of Oscar Wao
Doyle, R. A greyhound of a girl
Fehlbaum, B. Big fat disaster
Fitzpatrick, H. My life next door
Fogelin, A. The big nothing
Garden, N. Endgame
Harness, C. Just for you to know
Harper, S. The secret life of Sparrow Delaney
Hautman, P. How to steal a car
Hegamin, T. M +O 4evr
Hepler, H. The cupcake queen
Hesser, T. S. Kissing doorknobs
Hodkin, M. The unbecoming of Mara Dyer
Ingold, J. Mountain solo
Jimenez, F. The circuit : stories from the life of a migrant child
Johnson, A.Toning the sweep
Kade, S. Queen of the dead
Laskas, G. M. The miner's daughter
Lottridge, C. B. Semiprecious
Lupica, M. Hero
Madden, K. Gentle's Holler
Magnin, J. Carrying Mason
Manivong, L. Escaping the tiger
Martin, A. M. Here today
Mayall, B. Mermaid Park
McKay, H. Saffy's angel
Metzger, L. A trick of the light
Murphy, J. Desperate journey
Murphy, R. Looking for Lucy Buick
Naylor, P. R. Alice in April
Naylor, P. R. Alice in rapture, sort of
Naylor, P. R. Incredibly Alice
Naylor, P. R. Reluctantly Alice
Ockler, S. The Book of Broken Hearts
Ortiz Cofer, J. If I could fly
Ostow, M. Emily Goldberg learns to salsa
Padian, M. Brett McCarthy: work in progress
Patrick, C. Forgotten
Peck, R. N. A day no pigs would die
Polisner, G. The pull of gravity
Preller, J. Bystander
Wallace, R. War and watermelon
Watkins, S. Down Sand Mountain
White, R. A month of Sundays
Whittenberg, A. Sweet Thang
Williams, S. D. Palace beautiful
Willis, C. C. Buck fever
Yang, D. J. Warp speed
FAMILY LIFE -- GEORGIA -- FICTION
Coker, R. Chasing Jupiter
Myracle, L. The infinite moment of us
FAMILY LIFE -- ILLINOIS -- CHICAGO -- FICTION
Pauley, K. Cat Girl's day off
FAMILY LIFE -- ILLINOIS -- FICTION
Stone, T. I. Time between us
FAMILY LIFE -- INDIA -- FICTION
Whelan, G. All my noble dreams and then what happens
FAMILY LIFE -- IOWA -- FICTION
Kraus, D. Scowler
Smith, A. Grasshopper jungle
FAMILY LIFE -- ITALY -- FICTION
Beyer, K. The demon catchers of Milan
FAMILY LIFE -- JAPAN -- FICTION
Lowitz, L. Jet Black and the ninja wind
FAMILY LIFE -- LOUISIANA -- FICTION
Elston, A. The rules for disappearing
FAMILY LIFE -- MARYLAND -- FICTION
Moore, K. Neverwas
FAMILY LIFE -- MASSACHUSETTS -- FICTION
Thompson, H. The language inside
FAMILY LIFE -- MINNESOTA -- FICTION
Rubens, M. Sons of the 613
FAMILY LIFE -- MISSOURI -- KANSAS CITY -- FICTION
Whaley, J. C. Noggin
FAMILY LIFE -- NEW JERSEY -- FICTION
Scott, K. This is so not happening
Zarr, S. Roomies
FAMILY LIFE -- NEW YORK (STATE) -- BROOKLYN -- FICTION
When I was the greatest
FAMILY LIFE -- NEW YORK (STATE) -- FICTION
Castle, J. You look different in real life
Johnson, J. J. The theory of everything
Moore, C. The stalker chronicles
FAMILY LIFE -- NEW YORK (STATE) -- HARLEM -- FICTION
Manzano, S. The revolution of Evelyn Serrano
FAMILY LIFE -- NEW YORK (STATE) -- NEW YORK -- FICTION
Zeitlin, M. Freshman year & other unnatural disasters

Zevin, G. Because it is my blood
FAMILY LIFE -- NORTH CAROLINA
Moses, S. P. The legend of Buddy Bush
FAMILY LIFE -- PENNSYLVANIA -- FICTION
Andrews, J. Me & Earl & the dying girl
Matson, M. Second chance summer
FAMILY LIFE -- PENNSYLVANIA -- HERSHEY -- FICTION
Finneyfrock, K. The sweet revenge of Celia Door
FAMILY LIFE -- RHODE ISLAND -- FICTION
Gray, C. Spellcaster
Gray, C. Steadfast
FAMILY LIFE -- RUSSIA -- FICTION
O'Brien, A. Lara's gift
FAMILY LIFE -- TEXAS -- FICTION
Fehlbaum, B. Big fat disaster
FAMILY LIFE -- VIRGINIA -- FICTION
Lyne, J. H. Catch rider
FAMILY LIFE -- WASHINGTON (STATE) -- FICTION
Flores-Scott, P. Jumped in
Scott, M. Live through this
FAMILY LIFE -- WASHINGTON (STATE) -- SEATTLE -- FICTION
Trueman, T. Life happens next
FAMILY PROBLEMS -- FICTION
Bedford, M. Never ending
Ferris, J. Of sound mind
Fischer, J. An egg on three sticks
Hopkins, E. Rumble
McCormick, P. Cut
Nolan, H. A face in every window
Peters, J. A. Luna
Woodson, J. Miracle's boys
FAMILY PROBLEMS -- FICTION
Anderson, L. H. The impossible knife of memory
Armistead, C. Being Henry David
Blythe, C. Revenge of a not-so-pretty girl
Brothers, M. Supergirl mixtapes
Carter, C. Me, him, them, and it
Castan, M. Fighting for Dontae
Chen, J. Return to me
Cremer, A. Invisibility
Doller, T. Something like normal
Fehlbaum, B. Big fat disaster
Griffin, N. The whole stupid way we are
Jaden, D. Never enough
Keplinger, K. A midsummer's nightmare
King, A. S. Ask the passengers
King, A. S. Reality Boy
Kirby, J. Golden
Knowles, J. *See* you at Harry's
Letting Ana go
Metzger, L. A trick of the light
Peterfreund, D. For darkness shows the stars
Peters, J. A. It's our prom (so deal with it)
Pitcher, A. My sister lives on the mantelpiece
Pollock, T. The city's son
Reed, A. Over you
Roskos, E. Dr. Bird's advice for sad poets
Summers, C. This is not a test
Sutton, K. Some quiet place
Walton, K. M. Empty
Williams, C. L. Waiting
FAMILY SECRETS -- FICTION
Carey, E. Heap house
Egloff, Z. Leap
Lowitz, L. Jet Black and the ninja wind
Moore, K. Amber House
Scott, M. Live through this
FAMILY VIOLENCE -- FICTION
Bilen, T. What she left behind
FAMILY-OWNED BUSINESS ENTERPRISES -- FICTION
Dessen, S. The moon and more
FAMINES -- FICTION
Pignat, C. Greener grass
Whelan, G. Burying the sun
Famous. Strasser, T.
Famous last words. Doktorski, J. S.
FAN FICTION -- FICTION
Rowell, R. Fangirl
Fangirl. Rowell, R.
Fantaskey, Beth
Buzz kill
Jessica's guide to dating on the dark side
FANTASY FICTION
Abbott, E. J. Watersmeet
Aguirre, A. Enclave
Almond, D. Skellig
Anderson, R. J. Spell Hunter
Anthony, P. Jumper cable
Anthony, P. A spell for chameleon
Archer, E. Geek: fantasy novel
Arntson, S. The wrap-up list
Ashby, A. Fairy bad day
Ashton, B. Everneath
Bardugo, L. Ruin and rising
Bardugo, L. Shadow and bone
Bardugo, L. Siege and storm
Barron, T. A. The lost years of Merlin
Barron, T. A. Merlin's dragon
Bass, R. Lucid
Bell, H. Fall of a kingdom
Bell, H. Forging the sword
Bell, H. The Goblin Wood
Bell, H. The last knight
Bell, H. Rise of a hero
Bell, H. Shield of stars
Bell, H. Trickster's girl

Bemis, J. C. The White City
Bemis, J. C. The Wolf Tree
Bennett, H. Shapeshifter
Berk, A. Death watch
Bernobich, B. Fox & Phoenix
Berry, J. The Amaranth enchantment
Black, H. The poison eaters and other stories
Bobet, L. Above
Booraem, E. The unnameables
Bow, E. Plain Kate
Brennan, C. House of the star
Brennan, S. R. Unspoken
Bridges, R. The gathering storm
Brooks, T. The elves of Cintra
Brooks, T. The gypsy morph
Bullen, A. Wish
Bunce, E. C. Liar's moon
Bunce, E. C. Star crossed
Burtenshaw, J. Shadowcry
Cameron, S. The dark unwinding
Carey, J. L. Dragons of Noor
Carey, J. L. Dragon's Keep
Carey, J. L. Dragonswood
Carey, J. L. Stealing death
Carey, J. L. The beast of Noor
Carson, R. The bitter kingdom
Carson, R. The crown of embers
Carson, R. The girl of fire and thorns
Casella, J. Thin space
Cashore, K. Bitterblue
Cashore, K. Fire
Cashore, K. Graceling
Caveney, P. Sebastian Darke: Prince of Fools
Chima, C. W. The Crimson Crown
Chima, C. W. The Demon King
Chima, C. W. The exiled queen
Chima, C. W. The Gray Wolf Throne
Chima, C. W. The warrior heir
Chima, C. W. The wizard heir
Clare, C. City of lost souls
Clare, C. Clockwork angel
Clare, C. Clockwork princess
Clement-Davies, D. Fell
Clement-Davies, D. The sight
Coakley, L. Witchlanders
Condie, A. B. Crossed
Condie, A. B. Matched
Constable, K. The singer of all songs
Cooper, S. Over sea, under stone
Cornish, D. M. Factotum
Cornish, D. M. Foundling
Croggon, A. The Crow
Croggon, A. The Naming
Croggon, A. The Riddle
Croggon, A. The Singing
Cypess, L. Death sworn
Cypess, L. Mistwood
Damico, G. Scorch
De la Cruz, M. Gates of Paradise
De la Cruz, M. Lost in time
De Lint, C. Little (grrl) lost
Dickinson, P. Angel Isle
Dixon, H. Entwined
Dolamore, J. Magic under glass
Drago, T. The dragon's lair
Duey, K. Sacred scars
Duey, K. Skin hunger
Durst, S. B. Vessel
Farmer, N. The lord of Opium
Fisher, C. Incarceron
Fisher, C. The dark city
Fisher, C. The hidden Coronet
Fisher, C. The lost heiress
Fisher, C. The Margrave
Fisher, C. The oracle betrayed
Fisher, C. The obsidian mirror
Fisher, C. Sapphique
Fletcher, S. Ancient, strange, and lovely
Fletcher, S. Dragon's milk
Flinn, A. Beastly
Forster, M. City of a Thousand Dolls
Frost, G. Lord Tophet
Frost, G. Shadowbridge
Funke, C. Fearless
Funke, C. Reckless
Gee, M. Gool
Gee, M. The Limping Man
Gee, M. Salt
George, J. D. Sun and moon, ice and snow
Goodman, A. Eon: Dragoneye reborn
Goodman, A. Eona: the last Dragoneye
Goto, H. Half World
Grant, K. M. Paradise red
Grove, S. E. The glass sentence
Hahn, R. A creature of moonlight
Hale, S. Book of a thousand days
Hall, C. A. Crystal bones
Hamilton, K. R. Tyger tyger
Hamilton, K. The faerie ring
Hardy, J. The shifter
Harland, R. Worldshaker
Harris, J. Runemarks
Harry Potter and the deathly hallows
Hartman, R. Seraphina
Hocking, A. Wake
Hubbard, A. Ripple
Humphreys, C. The hunt of the unicorn
Jacobs, J. H. The twelve-fingered boy
Kessler, J. Loss
Kessler, J. M. Loss
Kittredge, C. The Iron Thorn
Kittredge, C. The nightmare garden

Knox, E. Dreamhunter
Knox, E. Dreamquake
Knox, E. Mortal fire
Kontis, A. Enchanted
Kostick, C. Epic
Kostick, C. Saga
Lackey, M. To light a candle
Lackey, M. When darkness falls
LaFevers, R. Dark triumph
Lam, L. Pantomime
Lanagan, M. The brides of Rollrock Island
Lanagan, M. Tender morsels
Langrish, K. The shadow hunt
Le Guin, U. K. Gifts
Le Guin, U. K. Powers
Le Guin, U. K. The farthest shore
Le Guin, U. K. Voices
L'Engle, M. A wrinkle in time
Lindskold, J. M. Thirteen orphans
Llewellyn, S. Darksolstice
Long, R. F. The treachery of beautiful things
Maas, S. J. Throne of glass
MacHale, D. J. Raven rise
MacHale, D. J. The pilgrims of Rayne
Mahy, M. The Magician of Hoad
Malchow, A. The Sword of Darrow
Mancusi, M. Scorched
Marchetta, M. Finnikin of the rock
Marchetta, M. Froi of the exiles
Marchetta, M. Quintana of Charyn
Marillier, J. Child of the prophecy
Marillier, J. Daughter of the forest
Marillier, J. Raven flight
Marillier, J. Shadowfell
Marillier, J. Son of the shadows
Marr, M. Darkest mercy
Marr, M. Fragile eternity
Marr, M. Ink exchange
Marr, M. Radiant shadows
Marr, M. Wicked lovely
Marriott, Z. The swan kingdom
Masson, S. Snow, fire, sword
McCaffrey, A. Dragonflight
McCaffrey, A. Dragon's kin
McCaffrey, T. J. Dragongirl
McKinley, R. Chalice
McKinley, R. Dragonhaven
McKinley, R. The blue sword
McKinley, R. The hero and the crown
McKinley, R. Pegasus
McNamee, E. The Navigator
McNaughton, J. An earthly knight
McNeal, T. Far far away
McQuein, J. L. Arclight
McQuerry, M. D. The Peculiars
Meloy, C. Under Wildwood
Meloy, C. Wildwood
Michaelis, A. The dragons of darkness
Mieville, C. Un Lun Dun
Miller, W. M. A canticle for Leibowitz
Mlawski, S. Hammer of witches
Moloney, J. The Book of Lies
Mont, E. M. A breath of Eyre
Moriarty, J. A corner of white
Moriarty, J. The cracks in the kingdom
Moskowitz, H. Teeth
Mourlevat Winter's end
Nayeri, D. Another Pan
Neumeier, R. The City in the Lake
Nicholson, W. Jango
Nicholson, W. Noman
Nicholson, W. Seeker
Nix, G. Abhorsen
Nix, G. Clariel
Nix, G. Lirael, daughter of the Clayr
Nix, G. Mister Monday; Keys to the kingdom
Nix, G. Sabriel
North, P. The boy from Ilysies
North, P. Libyrinth
O'Hearn, K. Kira
Okorafor, N. The shadow speaker
Okorafor, N. Akata witch
Oppel, K. Airborn
Oppel, K. Skybreaker
Oppel, K. Starclimber
Owen, J. A. Here, there be dragons
Paolini, C. Brisingr
Paolini, C. Eldest
Paolini, C. Eragon
Perez, M. Dead is just a dream
Pierce, T. Bloodhound
Pierce, T. Mastiff
Pierce, T. Terrier
Pierce, T. The will of the empress
Pierson, D. C. Crap kingdom
Pike, A. Illusions
Pike, A. Spells
Pike, A. Wings
Pratchett, T. The amazing Maurice and his educated rodents
Pratchett, T. I shall wear midnight
Pratchett, T. The Wee Free Men
Pullman, P. The amber spyglass
Pullman, P. The golden compass
Pullman, P. Once upon a time in the North
Pullman, P. The subtle knife
Reese, J. The strange case of Doctor Jekyll and Mademoiselle Odile
Rowling, J. K. Harry Potter and the Chamber of Secrets
Rowling, J. K. Harry Potter and the Goblet of Fire

Rowling, J. K. Harry Potter and the Half-blood Prince
Rowling, J. K. Harry Potter and the Order of the Phoenix
Rowling, J. K. Harry Potter and the prisoner of Azkaban
Rowling, J. K. Harry Potter and the Sorcerer's Stone
Salmon, D. K. Discordia
Sanderson, B. The Rithmatist
Sapphire blue
Scott, E. Grace
Selfors, S. The sweetest spell
The Shadowhunter's codex
Shirvington, J. Emblaze
Shirvington, J. Embrace
Simner, J. L. Bones of Faerie
Simner, J. L. Faerie after
Simner, J. L. Thief eyes
Singleton, L. J. Dead girl dancing
Singleton, L. J. Dead girl in love
Smith, A. Passenger
Smith, C. L. Feral curse
Stewart, A. Dragonwood
Stiefvater, M. The dream thieves
Stiefvater, M. The Scorpio Races
Stoffels, K. Heartsinger
Stroud, J. The Amulet of Samarkand
Stroud, J. The golem's eye
Stroud, J. Ptolemy's gate
Stroud, J. The ring of Solomon
Sullivan, L. L. Guardian of the Green Hill
Sullivan, L. L. Under the green hill
Sun, A. Ink
Taylor, L. Blackbringer
Taylor, L. Silksinger
Taylor, L. Daughter of smoke and bone
Taylor, L. Days of blood & starlight
Thomas, S. The burning sky
Thompson, K. The last of the High Kings
Thompson, K. The new policeman
Thompson, K. The white horse trick
Tiernan, C. Immortal beloved
Tomlinson, H. Aurelie; a faerie tale
Turner, M. W. The Queen of Attolia
Uehashi, N. Moribito; Guardian of the Spirit
Uehashi, N. Moribito II; Guardian of the Darkness
Vaughn, C. Voices of dragons
Walsh, P. The Crowfield demon
Wells, M. Emilie & the hollow world
Werlin, N. Extraordinary
Wharton, T. The shadow of Malabron
Whipple, N. House of ivy and sorrow
Whitley, D. The children of the lost
Wilks, M. Mirrorscape
Williams, S. Twinmaker
Williamson, J. By darkness hid
Williamson, J. To darkness fled
Wilson, N. D. The dragon's tooth
Wood, M. L. Captured
Wood, M. L. The darkening
Wooding, C. Poison
Wrede, P. C. Across the Great Barrier
Wrede, P. C. The Far West
Wrede, P. C. The thirteenth child
Yolen, J. Dragon's blood
Yolen, J. Pay the piper
Yovanoff, B. The replacement
Zettel, S. Golden girl
Zinn, B. Poison

Far far away. McNeal, T.
Far from you. Schroeder, L.
The **Far** West. Wrede, P. C.

Farinango, Maria Virginia
The Queen of Water

Farish, Terry
The good braider

Farizan, Sara
If you could be mine

FARM LIFE -- FICTION
Bauer, J. Peeled
Clement-Moore, R. Texas gothic
Donnelly, J. A northern light
Doyle, E. F. According to Kit
Hartnett, S. Thursday's child
Lawson, M. Crow Lake
Markandaya, K. Nectar in a sieve
Murdock, C. G. Dairy Queen
Murdock, C. G. Front and center
Murdock, C. G. The off season
Paulsen, G. Harris and me; a summer remembered
Watkins, S. What comes after
Weaver, W. Full service
Whitaker, A. The queen of Kentucky

FARM LIFE -- GEORGIA -- FICTION
Coker, R. Chasing Jupiter

FARM LIFE -- IOWA -- FICTION
Kraus, D. Scowler

FARM LIFE -- KANSAS -- FICTION

FARM LIFE -- NEBRASKA -- FICTION
Reed, A. Over you

FARM LIFE -- WISCONSIN -- FICTION
Bick, I. J. The Sin eater's confession
Sutton, K. Some quiet place

Farmer, Nancy
The Ear
The Ear, the Eye, and the Arm
A girl named Disaster
The house of the scorpion
The lord of Opium

FARMERS -- FICTION
Peterfreund, D. For darkness shows the stars
Farrey, Brian
With or without you
Farsala trilogy [series]
Bell, H. Forging the sword
Bell, H. Rise of a hero
The **farthest** shore. Le Guin, U. K.
FASHION -- FICTION
Carlson, M. Premiere
Daswani, K. Indie girl
May, K. Kiki
FASHION DESIGN -- FICTION
May, K. Kiki
FASHION DESIGNERS -- FICTION
Cross, G. Where I belong
FASHION MODELS -- FICTION
Cabot, M. Airhead
Cabot, M. Being Nikki
Cabot, M. Runaway
FAST FOOD RESTAURANTS -- FICTION
Anderson, M. T. Burger Wuss
Fat Angie. Charlton-Trujillo, e. E.
Fat Cat. Brande, R.
Fat kid rules the world. Going, K. L.
Fat vampire. Rex, A.
FATE AND FATALISM -- FICTION
Bow, E. Sorrow's knot
Childs, T. L. Sweet venom
Durst, S. B. Vessel
Jones, A. F. Destiny's path
McCaughrean, G. The death-defying Pepper Roux
Miller, K. All you desire
Miller, K. The eternal ones
Nadol, J. The mark
Nadol, J. The vision
Smith, J. E. The statistical probability of love at first sight
FATHER AND CHILD -- FICTION
Soonchild
Father of lies. Turner, A. W.
FATHER-DAUGHTER RELATIONSHIP -- FICTION
Alpine, R. Canary
Anderson, L. H. The impossible knife of memory
Bigelow, L. J. Starting from here
Bunting, E. The pirate captain's daughter
Cabot, M. The princess diaries
Caletti, D. The last forever
Dessen, S. The moon and more
Falls, K. Inhuman
Fitzmaurice, K. A diamond in the desert
Friesner, E. M. Spirit's princess
Friesner, E. Spirit's princess
Harmel, K. When you wish
Kade, S. The rules
Keplinger, K. A midsummer's nightmare
Lake, N. Hostage Three
Lupica, M. Miracle on 49th Street
McQuerry, M. D. The Peculiars
North, P. Starglass
O'Brien, A. Lara's gift
Oates, J. C. Freaky green eyes
Oliver, J. G. The demon trapper's daughter
Platt, C. Astra
Renn, D. Tokyo heist
Rosoff, M. Picture me gone
Rossetti, R. The girl with borrowed wings
Rush, J. Altered
Shepherd, M. Her Dark Curiosity
Shepherd, M. The madman's daughter
Zettel, S. Dust girl
FATHER-SON RELATIONSHIP--FICTION
Alexander, K. The crossover
Berk, J. Guy Langman, crime scene procrastinator
Bruchac, J. Wolf mark
Cole, S. Z. Raptor
Cole, S. Z. Rex
Crutcher, C. Ironman; a novel
Crowe, C. Mississippi trial, 1955
Fitzmaurice, K. A diamond in the desert
Fogelin, A. The real question
Green, S. Half bad
Johnson, P. What happened
Kerr, M. E. If I love you, am I trapped forever?
Lawlor, L. He will go fearless
Lupica, M. Hero
Lupica, M. The big field
Lyga, B. I hunt killers
Malloy, B. The year of ice
Mankell, H. A bridge to the stars
Mass, W. Jeremy Fink and the meaning of life
Master, I. A beautiful lie
McDonald, I. Be my enemy
Villareal, R. Body slammed!
Volponi, P. Homestretch
Wallace, S. N. Muckers
Willey, M. Beetle boy
Willis, C. C. Buck fever
FATHERS -- FICTION
Barratt, M. The wild man
Bilen, T. What she left behind
Bodeen, S. A., The gardener
Fontes, J. Benito runs
Higgins, J. Sure fire
Paquette, A.-J. Nowhere girl
Resau, L. The jade notebook
Vanderpool, C. Moon over Manifest

Wilson, J. Written in blood
The **fault** in our stars. Green, J.
FEAR -- FICTION
Scaletta, K. Mamba Point
Sutton, K. Some quiet place
Fearless. Funke, C.
Feedback. Wells, R.
Fehlbaum, Beth
Big fat disaster
Hope in Patience
Fehler, Gene
Beanball
Feinstein, John
Foul trouble
Last shot
Feldman, Ruth Tenzer
Blue thread
Felin, M. Sindy
Touching snow
Fell. Clement-Davies, D.
FEMALE CIRCUMCISION -- FICTION
Williams-Garcia, R. No laughter here
FEMALE FRIENDSHIP -- FICTION
Bailey, E. Shift
Bjorkman, L. Miss Fortune Cookie
Brennan, S. R. Team Human
Foxlee, K. The midnight dress
Haas, A. Dangerous girls
Howland, L. Nantucket blue
Longshore, K. Gilt
Perez, M. Dead is a battlefield
Reed, A. Over you
Ross, E. Belle epoque
Singleton, L. J. Dead girl in love
Strohmeyer, S. Smart girls get what they want
Vivian, S. The list
Wein, E. Code name Verity
Wunder, W. The museum of intangible things
FEMALE IMPERSONATORS -- FICTION
St. James, J. Freak show
FEMINISM -- FICTION
Lessing, D. M. The sweetest dream
Lynch, J. N. My beautiful hippie
Zemser, A. B. Dear Julia
FEMINISTS -- FICTION
Engle, M. The Lightning Dreamer
FENCING -- FICTION
Vaughn, C. Steel
Feral curse Smith, C. L.
Feral nights. Smith, C. L.
Fergus, Maureen
Recipe for disaster
Ferguson, Alane
The Christopher killer
The circle of blood
The dying breath
Ferraiolo, Jack D.
Sidekicks
Ferris, Jean
Of sound mind
The **Fetch.** Whitcomb, L.
Fever. DeStefano, L.
Fever Crumb. Reeve, P.
Fever Crumb series
Reeve, P. Scrivener's moon
Fever, 1793. Anderson, L. H.
Fever season. Zweig, E.
Fforde, Jasper
The last Dragonslayer
The song of the Quarkbeast
FIANCES -- FICTION
Palma, F. J. The map of the sky
Fichera, Liz
Hooked
Fiedler, Lisa
Romeo's ex
FIELD HOCKEY PLAYERS -- FICTION
Luedeke, L. Smashed
Fienberg, Anna
Number 8
Fifteen candles. Chambers, V.
The **fifth** of March; a story of the Boston Massacre. Rinaldi, A.
Fifty degrees below. Robinson, K. S.
Fight game. Wild, K.
Fighting for Dontae. Castan, M.
The **file** on Angelyn Stark. Atkins, C.
The **final** descent. Yancey, R.
The **Final** Four. Volponi, P.
FINANCIERS -- FICTION
Weyn, S. Distant waves
FINANCIERS *See* Capitalists and financiers
Find me. Bernard, R.
Finding miracles. Alvarez, J.
Finding my place. Jones, T. L.
Finishing school [series]
Carriger, G. Curtsies & conspiracies
Finding somewhere. Monninger, J.
Fink, Mark
The summer I got a life
FINN MACCOOL -- FICTION
Hamilton, K. When the stars threw down their spears
Finn, Mary
Belladonna
Finneyfrock, Karen
The sweet revenge of Celia Door
Finnikin of the rock. Marchetta, M.
Fire. Cashore, K.
The **fire**-eaters. Almond, D.
FIRE FIGHTERS -- FICTION

Lynch, C. Hothouse
Fire from the rock. Draper, S. M. (Sharon Mills)
Fire in the streets. Magoon, K.
The **fire** opal. McBride, R.
Fire will fall. Plum-Ucci, C.
Firefly letters. Engle, M.
Firehorse. Wilson, D. L.
FIRES -- FICTION
Friesner, E. M. Threads and flames
Haddix, M. P. Uprising
Min, K. Secondhand world
McNeal, L. Dark water
Twomey, C. Beachmont letters
The **fires** of New SUN. Kinch, M.
Firestarter. King, S.
Firestorm. Klass, D.
First day on Earth. Castellucci, C.
First descent. Withers, P.
First kill. Brewer, H.
First test. Pierce, T.
First shot. Sorrells, W.
Fischer, Jackie
An egg on three sticks
Fisher, Catherine
The dark city
Darkwater
The hidden Coronet
Incarceron
The lost heiress
The Margrave
The obsidian mirror
The oracle betrayed
Sapphique
FISHING -- FICTION
Rocco, J. Swim that rock
Salisbury, G. Lord of the deep
Woolston, B. Catch & release
FitzGerald, Helen
Deviant
Fitzmaurice, Kathryn
A diamond in the desert; Kathryn Fitzmaurice
The **FitzOsbornes** at war. Cooper, M.
The **FitzOsbornes** in exile. Cooper, M.
Fitzpatrick, Huntley
My life next door
Five flavors of dumb. John, A.
Fixing Delilah. Ockler, S.
Flack, Sophie
Bunheads
Flake, Sharon G.
Bang!
Pinned
Flame. Ryan, A. K.
Flamel, Nicolas, d. 1418
About
Scott, M. The enchantress
FLAMEL, NICOLAS, D. 1418
About
Scott, M. The enchantress
Flash. Cadnum, M.
Flash burnout. Madigan, L. K.
Flawless. Chapman, L.
Fleischman, Paul
Seek
Fletcher, Christine
Ten cents a dance
Fletcher, Ralph
The one o'clock chop
Fletcher, Susan
Alphabet of dreams
Ancient, strange, and lovely
Dragon's milk
A **flickering** light. Kirkpatrick, J.
FLIGHT -- FICTION
Reeve, P. A Web of Air
The **flight** to freedom. Veciana-Suarez, A.
Flightsend. Newbery, L.
Flinn, Alex
Beastly
Breaking point
Breathing underwater
Cloaked
A kiss in time
Flip. Bedford, M.
Flipped. Van Draanen, W.
Flock. Delsol, W.
FLOODS -- FICTION
Bertagna, J. Exodus
Bertagna, J. Zenith
Richards, J. Three rivers rising
Flora and Ulysses. DiCamillo, K.
Flores-Scott, Patrick
Jumped in
FLORIDA -- FICTION
Blundell, J. What I saw and how I lied
Green, J. Paper towns
Hodkin, M. The evolution of Mara Dyer
Howard, J. J. That time I joined the circus
McCarthy, S. C. True fires
St. James, J. Freak show
FLOWERS -- FICTION
Hahn, R. A creature of moonlight
White, A. B. Forget -her-nots
Flowers in the sky. Joseph, L.
Flygirl. Smith, S. L.
FLYING -- FICTION
Rossetti, R. The girl with borrowed wings
Fogelin, Adrian
The big nothing
The real question
FOLKLORE -- FICTION

Bardugo, L. Shadow and bone
Folly. Jocelyn, M.
Fombelle, T.
Vango
Fontes, Justine
Benito runs
FOOD HABITS -- FICTION
Letting Ana go
Food, **girls,** and other things I can't have. Zadoff, A.
The **fool's** girl. Rees, C.
FOOLS AND JESTERS -- FICTION
Caveney, P. Sebastian Darke: Prince of Fools
Spinner, S. Damosel
FOOTBALL -- FICTION
Cohen, J. C. Leverage
Coy, J. Crackback
Deuker, C. Gym candy
Harris, C. Bad taste in boys
Herbach, G. Stupid fast
Lipsyte, R. Raiders night
Lynch, C. Inexcusable
McKissack, F. Shooting star
Murdock, C. G. Dairy Queen
Murdock, C. G. The off season
Powell, R. Three clams and an oyster
Spinelli, J. Crash
Tharp, T. Knights of the hill country
Wallace, S. N. Muckers
Wallace, R. War and watermelon
Weyn, S. Recruited
Zadoff, A. Food, girls, and other things I can't have
FOOTBALL PLAYERS -- FICTION
Moore, D. Always upbeat / All that
For darkness shows the stars. Peterfreund, D.
For keeps. Friend, N.
For the win. Doctorow, C.
Ford, John C.
The morgue and me
Ford, Michael
The poisoned house
Ford, Michael Thomas
Suicide notes
Z
A **foreign** field. Chan, G.
FOREIGN STUDY -- FICTION
Perkins, S. Anna and the French kiss
Standiford, N. The boy on the bridge
FOREST FIRES -- FICTION
Ingold, J. The Big Burn
The **Forest** of Hands and Teeth. Ryan, C.
FORESTS AND FORESTRY -- FICTION
Long, R. F. The treachery of beautiful things
The **foretelling.** Hoffman, A.
Forever. Stiefvater, M.
Forever. Blume, J.
Forever in blue. Brashares, A.
Forge. Anderson, L. H.
Forget -her-nots. White, A. B.
Forgive me, Leonard Peacock. Quick, M.
FORGIVENESS -- FICTION
Kwasney, M. D. Blue plate special
Forgotten. Patrick, C.
Forman, Gayle
I was here
If I stay
Just one day
Where she went
Formerly shark girl. Bingham, K.
Forster, Miriam
City of a Thousand Dolls
Fortunate son. Mosley, W.
The **fortunes** of Indigo Skye. Caletti, D.
47. Mosley, W.
Forty signs of rain. Robinson, K. S.
FOSTER CHILDREN -- FICTION
Bernard, R. Find me
Myracle, L. The infinite moment of us
FOSTER HOME CARE -- FICTION
Ayarbe, H. Compromised
Bernard, R. Find me
Booth, C. Bronxwood
De la Pena, M. Ball don't lie
Dowd, S. Solace of the road
Frank, E. R. America
Gagnon, M. Don't Look Now
Gagnon, M. Don't turn around
Koertge, R. Strays
McNeal, L. The decoding of Lana Morris
Murray, Y. M. The good girl's guide to getting kidnapped
Rutkoski, M. The shadow society
Shaw, L. Fostergirls
Sweeney, J. The guardian
Weaver, W. Defect
Fostergirls. Shaw, L.
Foul trouble. Feinstein, J.
Foundling. Cornish, D. M.
FOUNDLING HOSPITAL (LONDON, ENGLAND) -- FICTION
Jocelyn, M. Folly
FOUNDLINGS -- FICTION
Murdoch, E. If you find me
The **four** Dorothys. Ruditis, P.
FOUR HORSEMEN OF THE APOCALYPSE -- FICTION
Kessler, J. M. Breath
Kessler, J. M. Loss
Four seasons. Zalben, J. B.
Four spirits. Naslund, S. J.

FOURTH DIMENSION
Fox forever. Pearson, M. E.
The **Fox** Inheritance. Pearson, M.
Fox, Margaret, 1833-1893
About
Salerni, D. K. We hear the dead
Fox & Phoenix Bernobich, B
FOXES -- FICTION
Zuckerman, L. A taste for rabbit
Foxlee, Karen
The anatomy of wings
The midnight dress
Fractured. Terry, T.
FRACTURED FAIRY TALES
Kontis, A. Enchanted
Meyer, M. Scarlet
FRACTURES -- FICTION
Moskowitz, H. Break
Fragile eternity. Marr, M.
Fragments. Wells, D.
FRANCE -- FICTION
Ellis, D. No safe place
Kamata, S. Gadget Girl
Perkins, S. Anna and the French kiss
Resau, L. The ruby notebook
Simmons, M. The rise of Lubchenko
Spillebeen, G. Kipling's choice
FRANCE -- HISTORY -- 0-1328 -- FICTION
Grant, K. M. Blue flame
Grant, K. M. White heat
FRANCE -- HISTORY -- 1589-1789, BOURBONS -- FICTION
McCaughrean, G. Cyrano
FRANCE -- HISTORY -- 1789-1799, REVOLUTION -- FICTION
Donnelly, J. Revolution
Elliott, P. The Pale Assassin
Elliott, P. The traitor's smile
Gardner, S. The red necklace
Gardner, S. The Silver Blade
Rees, C. Sovay
FRANCE -- HISTORY -- 1799-1815 -- FICTION
Holub, J. An innocent soldier
Meyer, L. A. My bonny light horseman
FRANCE -- HISTORY -- 20TH CENTURY -- FICTION
Myers, W. D. Invasion!
FRANCE -- HISTORY -- CHARLES VIII, 1483-1498 -- FICTION
LaFevers, R. Dark triumph
LaFevers, R. Grave mercy
FRANCE -- HISTORY -- GERMAN OCCUPATION, 1940-1945 -- FICTION
Macdonald, M. Odette's secrets
Wein, E. Code name Verity
FRANCE -- HISTORY -- LOUIS IX, 1226-1270 -- FICTION
Grant, K. M. Paradise red
FRANCE -- HISTORY -- OCCUPATION AND EVACUATION, 1871-1873 -- FICTION
Reese, J. The strange case of Doctor Jekyll and Mademoiselle Odile
FRANCE -- HISTORY -- REVOLUTION, 1789-1799 -- FICTION
FRANCE -- HISTORY -- THIRD REPUBLIC, 1870-1940 -- FICTION
Morgan, P. The beautiful and the cursed
Ross, E. Belle epoque
Frank, Anne, 1929-1945
About
Dogar, S. Annexed
Frank, E. R.
America
Life is funny
Wrecked
Frank, Hillary
Better than running at night
The view from the top
FRANKENSTEIN'S MONSTER (FICTIONAL CHARACTER)
Priestly, C. Mister Creecher
FRANKENSTEIN, VICTOR (FICTITIOUS CHARACTER)
Weyn, S. Dr. Frankenstein's daughters
Franklin, Emily
The half life of planets
The other half of me
Frannie in pieces. Ephron, D.
FRAUD -- FICTION
Egan, L. A. The Outcast Oracle
Frazier, Angie
The Eternal Sea
Everlasting
The **Freak** Observer. Woolston, B.
Freak show. St. James, J.
Freakboy. Clark, K. E.
Freaks and revelations. Hurwin, D.
Freaks like us. Vaught, S.
Freaky green eyes. Oates, J. C.
Fredericks, Mariah
Crunch time
The girl in the park
Head games
Free radical. Murphy, C. R.
FREEDOM -- FICTION
Anderson, M. T. The astonishing life of Octavian Nothing, traitor to the nation
The **freedom** maze. Sherman, D.
Freefall. Scott, M.
Freitas, Donna
The possibilities of sainthood
The Survival Kit

This gorgeous game
The **frenzy.** Block, F. L.
Freshman year & other unnatural disasters. Zeitlin, M.
Freymann-Weyr, Garret
After the moment
My heartbeat
Stay with me
Friday never leaving. Wakefield, V.
Friedman, Aimee
The year my sister got lucky
Friedman, Robin
Nothing
Friend is not a verb. Ehrenhaft, D.
Friend, Natasha
Bounce
Perfect
For keeps
Lush
My life in black and white
FRIENDSHIP -- FICTION
Andrews, J. Me & Earl & the dying girl
Blume, J. Here's to you, Rachel Robinson
Booraem, E. The unnameables,
Brashares, A. The sisterhood of the traveling pants
Brashares, A. 3 willows; the sisterhood grows
Burton, R. Leaving Jetty Road
Buzo, L. Love and other perishable items
Calame, D. Call the shots
Chambers, A. Dying to know you
Chapman, L. Flawless
Colasanti, S. Something like fate
Cole, B. The goats
Crane, E. M. Skin deep
Crocker, N. Billie Standish was here
Crossan, S. Breathe
Cummings, P. Red kayak
David, K. Lia's guide to winning the lottery
Dubosarsky, U. The golden day
Elston, A. The rules for disappearing
Ferris, J. Of sound mind
Flores-Scott, P. Jumped in
Forman, G. I was here
Friesen, G. The Isabel factor
Giles, G. Girls like us
Griffin, N. The whole stupid way we are
Halpin, B. Shutout
Hartinger, B. Project Sweet Life
Hautman, P. What boys really want?
Hegamin, T. M +O 4evr
Hegedus, B. Between us Baxters
Herbach, G. Nothing special
Hesser, T. S. Kissing doorknobs
Hubbard, J. R. Try not to breathe
Jones, T. L. Finding my place,
LaCour, N. The Disenchantments
Lubar, D. True talents
Magoon, K. Camo girl
Mangum, L. After hello
Marcus, K. Exposed
Marsden, C. Sahwira
May, K. Kiki
McDaniel, L. Breathless
McKay, S. E. Enemy territory
Moore, K. Amber House
Morrison, T. Sula
Myers, W. D. Darius & Twig
Myers, W. D. Invasion!
Nowlin, L. If he had been with me
Oates, J. C. Big Mouth & Ugly Girl
Oates, J. C. Two or three things I forgot to tell you
O'Connell, T. True love, the sphinx, and other unsolvable riddles; a comedy in four voices
O'Neal, E. Torn
Oppel, K. Such wicked intent
Padian, M. Brett McCarthy: work in progress
Paley, S. Huge
Papademetriou, L. M or F?
Parker, R. B. The Edenville Owls
Patt, B. Best friends forever; a World War II scrapbook
Paulsen, G. The Schernoff discoveries
Powell, R. Three clams and an oyster
Quick, M. Boy21
Ryan, A. K. Spark
Sáenz, B. A. Aristotle and Dante discover the secrets of the universe
Shimko, B. The private thoughts of Amelia E. Rye
Simone Upgrade U
Staples, S. F. Dangerous skies
Vasey, P. A troublesome boy
Vaught, S. Freaks like us
Vaupel, R. My contract with Henry
Waters, D. Break my heart 1,000 times
Werlin, N. Extraordinary
Whitaker, A. The queen of Kentucky
Whitman, S. The milk of birds
Williams, L. E. Slant
Williams-Garcia, R. No laughter here
Wilson, J. Kiss
Woodson, J. After Tupac and D Foster
Woolston, B. Catch & release
Yee, P. Learning to fly
Yep, L. The traitor; Golden Mountain chronicles, 1885
Zimmer, T. V. Reaching for sun
Friesen, Gayle
The Isabel factor

Friesner, Esther M.
Nobody's princess
Nobody's prize
Spirit's princess
Sphinx's princess
Sphinx's queen
Spirit's princess
Threads and flames
FROGS -- FICTION
Kontis, A. Enchanted
Froi of the exiles. Marchetta, M.
From Somalia with love. Robert, N.
From the notebooks of Melanin Sun. Woodson, J.
Front and center. Murdock, C. G.
FRONTIER AND PIONEER LIFE -- CALIFORNIA -- FICTION
Patron, S. Behind the masks
FRONTIER AND PIONEER LIFE -- FICTION
Larson, K. Hattie Big Sky
McKernan, V. The devil's paintbox
Nelson, J. On the volcano
Wilson, D. L. Black storm comin'
Wilson, J. Ghost moon
Wilson, J. Written in blood
Wood, F. When Molly was a Harvey Girl
Wrede, P. C. Across the Great Barrier
Wrede, P. C. The thirteenth child
Frontier magic [series]
Wrede, P. C. The thirteenth child
Frost. Baer, M.
Frost. Delsol, W.
Frost, Gregory
Lord Tophet
Shadowbridge
Frost, Helen
The braid
Crossing stones
Hidden
Keesha's house
Frost, Mark
Alliance
Frozen. Casanova, M.
Frozen fire. Bowler, T.
FUGITIVE SLAVES -- FICTION
Ayres, K. North by night
FUGITIVES FROM JUSTICE -- FICTION
Cummings, P. The journey back
Lu, M. Prodigy
Meyer, M. Cress
Fukuda, Andrew
The Prey
Full ride. Haddix, M. P.
Full service. Weaver, W.
Full tilt. Shusterman, N.
FUNERAL RITES AND CEREMONIES -- FICTION
Hooper, M. Fallen Grace
Smith, J. E. The statistical probability of love at first sight
Funke, Cornelia, 1958-
Fearless
Reckless
FUNNIES *See* Comic books, strips, etc.
Funny how things change. Wyatt, M.
Weyn, S. Distant waves
Furious. Wolfson, J.
Fury of the phoenix. Pon, C.
Fusco, Kimberly Newton
Tending to Grace
FUTURE -- FICTION
Miller, W. M. A canticle for Leibowitz
FUTURE LIFE -- FICTION
Cox, S. The Dead Girls Detective Agency
Hill, C. J. Erasing time
FUTURE LIFE -- FICTION
Ashton, B. Everbound
Brockenbrough, M. Devine intervention
Damico, G. Croak
Damico, G. Rogue
Noel, A. Radiance
Rothenberg, J. The catastrophic history of you & me
The **future** of us. Asher, J.
The **future** we left behind. Lancaster, M. A.

G

Gabi, a girl in pieces. Quintero, I.
GABON -- FICTION
Schrefer, E. Threatened
Gadget Girl. Kamata, S.
Gagnon, Michelle
Don't let go
Don't Look Now
Don't turn around
Strangelets
Gaiman, Neil
Interworld
Galahad [series]
Testa, D. The Cassini code
Testa, D. The comet's curse
Testa, D. Cosmic storm
Testa, D. The dark zone
Testa, D. The web of Titan
Galante, Cecilia
The patron saint of butterflies
The summer of May
The sweetness of salt
Willowood
Gale, Eric Kahn
The Bully Book
Gallagher, Liz

The opposite of invisible
Games. Gorman, C.
GAMBLING -- FICTION
Abrahams, P. Reality check
Hautman, P. All-in
Luper, E. Bug boy
Papademetriou, L. Drop
Game. Myers, W. D.
The game [series]
Silver, E. Rush
Game. Lyga, B.
The **game** of triumphs. Powell, L.
GAMES -- FICTION
Gorman, C. Games
Powell, L. The Master of Misrule
Gandhi, Mahatma, 1869-1948
About
Sheth, K. Keeping corner
GANGS -- FICTION
Castan, M. Fighting for Dontae
Castan, M. The price of loyalty
Flores-Scott, P. Jumped in
Goodman, S. Kindness for weakness
Strasser, T. If I grow up
Thomas, L. Quarantine
Watson, C. Benched
Gant, Gene
The Thunder in His Head
García, Cristina, 1958-
Dreams of significant girls
Garcia, Kami
Beautiful creatures
Beautiful darkness
Garden, Nancy
Endgame
The **gardener.** Bodeen, S. A.
GARDENING -- FICTION
Hoffman, A. Green angel
Hoffman, A. Green witch
Kephart, B. Nothing but ghosts
Gardner, Sally
Maggot moon
The red necklace
The Silver Blade
GARGOYLES -- FICTION
Morgan, P. The beautiful and the cursed
Garner, Em
Contaminated
Garsee, Jeannine
Before, after, and somebody in between
Say the word
Garvey, Amy
Cold kiss
Glass Heart
Gated. Parker, A. C.
Gates of Paradise. De la Cruz, M.
Gateway. Shinn, S.
Gathering blue. Lowry, L.
The **gathering** storm. Bridges, R.
GAWAIN (LEGENDARY CHARACTER) -- FICTION
Morris, G. The squire's tale
GAY TEENAGERS -- FICTION
Gant, G. The Thunder in His Head
Higgins, M. G. Bi-Normal
Knowles, J. *See* you at Harry's
Konigsberg, B. Openly straight
Lennon, T. When love comes to town
Levithan, D. Two boys kissing
Rice-Gonzalez, C. Chulito
Ryan, T. Way to go
Sáenz, B. A. Aristotle and Dante discover the secrets of the universe
Trumble, J. H. Don't let me go
GAYS -- FICTION
Danforth, E. M. The miseducation of Cameron Post
Finneyfrock, K. The sweet revenge of Celia Door
Lennon, T. When love comes to town
Leslea, N. October mourning
Levithan, D. Two boys kissing
Trumble, J. H. Don't let me go
Gee, Maurice
Gool
The Limping Man
Salt
Geek charming. Palmer, R.
The **geek** girl's guide to cheerleading. Tahmaseb, C.
Geek magnet. Scott, K.
Geek: fantasy novel. Archer, E.
Geekspeak. Tattersall, G.
Gelbwasser, Margie
Inconvenient
Gem X. Singer, N.
Gemini bites. Ryan, P.
GENDER IDENTITY -- FICTION
Smith, A. Grasshopper jungle
GENDER ROLE -- FICTION
Clark, K. E. Freakboy
Whelan, G. Chu Ju's house
GENERALS -- FICTION
Nanji, S. Child of dandelions
Shecter, V. A. Cleopatra's moon
Generation dead. Waters, D.
Genesis Alpha. Michaels, R.
The genesis of Shannara [series]
Brooks, T. The elves of Cintra
Brooks, T. The gypsy morph
GENETIC ENGINEERING -- FICTION
Halam, A. Dr. Franklin's island

GENETIC ENGINEERING -- FICTION
Bodeen, S. A., The gardener
DeStefano, L. Fever
DeStefano, L. Sever
Henderson, J. Bunker 10
Michaels, R. Genesis Alpha
Patterson, J. Maximum Ride: the angel experiment
Wells, D. Fragments
Wells, D. Partials
Wild, K. Fight game
GENETIC TRANSFORMATION -- FICTION
Krokos, D. False memory
GENEVA (REPUBLIC) -- HISTORY -- 18TH CENTURY -- FICTION
Oppel, K. Such wicked intent
GENIUS -- FICTION
Jinks, C. Evil genius
Jinks, C. Genius squad
Jinks, C. The genius wars
Roy, J. R. Mindblind
Valentine, A. How (not) to find a boyfriend
Wright, D. Violence 101
Genius squad. Jinks, C.
The **genius** wars. Jinks, C.
GENOCIDE -- FICTION
McCormick, P. Never fall down
Gensler, Sonia
The revenant
Gentlehands. Kerr, M. E.
Gentle's Holler. Madden, K.
Gentlemen. Northrop, M.
George, Jessica Day
Princess of glass
Princess of the midnight ball
Sun and moon, ice and snow
George, Madeleine
The difference between you and me
Looks
GEORGIA -- FICTION
Dudley, D. L. Caleb's wars
GEORGIA -- FICTION
Coker, R. Chasing Jupiter
Geras, Adele
Ithaka
Troy
GERMANS -- FICTION
Dudley, D. L. Caleb's wars
GERMANY -- FICTION
Bass, K. Summer of fire
Lasky, K. Ashes
Pausewang, G. Traitor
Schröder, M. My brother's shadow
GERMANY -- HISTORY -- 1918-1933 -- FICTION
Blankman, A. Prisoner of night and fog
GERMANY -- HISTORY -- 1933-1945 -- FICTION
Dowswell, P. The Auslander
LeZotte, A. C. T4
Sharenow, R. The Berlin Boxing Club
Get well soon. Halpern, J.
Getting it. Sanchez, A.
Getting the girl; a guide to private investigation surveillance, and cookery. Juby, S.
GHANA -- FICTION
Badoe, A. Between sisters
Mussi, S. The door of no return
The **ghost** and the goth. Kade, S.
Ghost medicine. Smith, A.
Ghost moon, Wilson, J.
The **ghost** of Crutchfield Hall. Hahn, M. D.
Ghost of Spirit Bear. Mikaelsen, B.
GHOST STORIES
Almond, D. Kit's wilderness
Armstrong, K. The awakening
Armstrong, K. The reckoning
Armstrong, K. The summoning
Bauer, J. Peeled
Bell, C. D. Slipping
Berk, A. Mistle child
Blake, K. Anna Dressed in Blood
Block, F. L. Missing Angel Juan
Clement-Moore, R. Texas gothic
Connor, L. Dead on town line
Cox, S. The Dead Girls Detective Agency
Crewe, M. Give up the ghost
Cypess, L. Nightspell
Damico, G. Rogue
Doyle, R. A greyhound of a girl
De Lint, C. The blue girl
Dennard, S. Something strange and deadly
Ford, M. The poisoned house
Gensler, S. The revenant
Goelman, A. The path of names
Griffin, A. Tighter
Hahn, M. D. The ghost of Crutchfield Hall
Harvey, A. Haunting Violet
Hartnett, S. The ghost's child
Hawkins, R. Demonglass
Hoffman, N. K. A stir of bones
The house of dead maids
Hudson, T. Hereafter
Hurley, T. Ghostgirl
Jenkins, A. M. Beating heart
Johnson, M. The madness underneath
Johnson, M. The name of the star
Kade, S. Queen of the dead
Kade, S. The ghost and the goth
Levithan, D. Marly's ghost
MacCullough, C. Drawing the ocean
McNamee, G. Beyond

McNeal, T. Far far away
Miller, K. How to lead a life of crime
Morris, P. Ruined
Nelson, R. A. Days of Little Texas
Nixon, J. L. The haunting
Noel, A. Radiance
Peck, R. Three-quarters dead
Pratchett, T. I shall wear midnight
Price, C. Dead connection
Prose, F. The turning
Smith, S. The other side of dark
Smith-Ready, J. Shade
Smith-Ready, J. Shift
Trigiani, A. Viola in reel life
Verday, J. The Hollow
Waters, D. Break my heart 1,000 times
Winters, C. In the shadow of blackbirds
Westerfeld, S. Afterworlds
Whitcomb, L. A certain slant of light
Williams, K. Absent
The **ghost's** child. Hartnett, S.
Ghostgirl. Hurley, T.
Ghost town. Jennings, R. W.
GHOST TOWNS -- FICTION
Jennings, R. W. Ghost town
GHOST STORIES
The **ghosts** of Ashbury High. Moriarty, J.
Gier, Kerstin
Emerald green
Ruby red
Sapphire blue
The **gift** moves. Lyon, S.
GIFTED CHILDREN -- FICTION
Blume, J. Here's to you, Rachel Robinson
Combs, S. Breakfast served anytime
Myers, W. D. A star is born
Williamson, J. By darkness hid
Gifts. Le Guin, U. K.
Giles, Gail
Dark song
Girls like us
Playing in traffic
Right behind you
Shattering Glass
What happened to Cass McBride?
Giles, Lamar
Fake ID
Giliani, Alessandra, 1307-1326
About
Quick, B. A golden web
Gill, David Macinnis
Black hole sun
Invisible sun
Shadow on the sun
Soul enchilada
Gilman, Charles
Professor Gargoyle
Gilman, David
Blood sun
The devil's breath
Ice claw
Gilt. Longshore, K.
Gilmore, Kate
The exchange student
Gimme a call. Mlynowski, S.
Gingerbread. Cohn, R.
Girl in a cage. Yolen, J.
Girl in blue. Rinaldi, A.
The **girl** in the mirror. Kearney, M.
The **girl** in the park. Fredericks, M.
The **girl** is murder. Haines, K. M.
The **girl** is trouble. Haines, K. M.
A **girl** named Digit. Monaghan, A.
A **girl** named Disaster. Farmer, N.
A **girl** named Mister. Grimes, N.
The **girl** of fire and thorns. Carson, R.
The **girl** who became a Beatle. Taylor, G.
The **girl** with a baby. Olsen, S.
The **girl** with borrowed wings. Rossetti, R.
The **girl** with the mermaid hair. Ephron, D.
Girlhearts. Mazer, N. F.
GIRLS -- FICTION
Cisneros, S. The house on Mango Street
Lawson, M. Crow Lake
Magoon, K. 37 things I love (in no particular order)
Moriarty, L. The center of everything
Girls don't fly. Chandler, K.
GIRLS -- FICTION
Fredericks, M. The girl in the park
Girls in pants. Brashares, A.
Girls like us. Giles, G.
Give a boy a gun. Strasser, T.
Give up the ghost. Crewe, M.
The **giver.** Lowry, L.
GLASS BLOWING AND WORKING -- FICTION
Hemphill, S. Sisters of glass
The **glass** casket. Templeman, M.
The **glass** sentence. Grove, S. E.
Glass Heart. Garvey, A.
Gleason, Colleen
The clockwork scarab
Glimpse. Williams, C. L.
The **glorious** adventures of the Sunshine Queen. McCaughrean, G.
Glory O'Brien's history of the future. King, A. S.
The **glory** wind. Sherrard, V.
Glow. Ryan, A. K.
The **goats.** Cole, B.
Gods of Manhattan. Mebus, S.
Going going. Nye, N. S.

Gómez de Avellaneda y Arteaga, Gertrudis, 1814-1873
About
Engle, M. The Lightning Dreamer
Goblin wars [series]
Hamilton, K. R. Tyger tyger
The **goblin** wood Bell, C.D.
GOBLINS -- FICTION
Hamilton, K. When the stars threw down their spears
God is in the pancakes. Epstein, R.
GODDESSES -- FICTION
Durst, S. B. Vessel
Knight, K. Embers & echoes
Godless. Hautman, P.
GODS AND GODDESSES--FICTION
Durst, S. B. Vessel
Halam, A. Snakehead
Knight, K. Embers & echoes
LaFevers, R. Dark triumph
LaFevers, R. Grave mercy
Goeglein, T. M.
Cold fury
Goelman, Ari
The path of names
Gogh, Vincent van, 1853-1890
About
Renn, D. Tokyo heist
Going bovine. Bray, L.
Going over. Kephart, B.
Going vintage. Leavitt, L.
Going, K. L.
Fat kid rules the world
King of the screwups
Saint Iggy
GOLD MINES AND MINING -- FICTION
Patron, S. Behind the masks
Goldblatt, Stacey
Stray
Golden. Kirby, J.
Golden boy. Sullivan, T.
The **golden** compass. Pullman, P.
The **golden** day. Dubosarsky, U.
Golden girl. Zettel, S.
A **golden** web. Quick, B.
Golden, Christopher
The sea wolves
Golden, Christopher
The wild
Golding, Julia
Secret of the sirens
Goldman, Steven
Two parties, one tux, and a very short film about the Grapes of Wrath
Golds, Cassandra
The museum of Mary Child
Goldstrike. Whyman, M.
The **golem's** eye. Stroud, J.
GOLF -- FICTION
Fichera, L. Hooked
Goliath. Westerfeld, S.
Gone. Grant, M.
Gonzalez, Julie
Imaginary enemy
Goobie, Beth
Before wings
GOOD AND EVIL -- FICTION
Carroll, M. O. Super human
Cooper, S. Over sea, under stone
Grant, M. Gone
MacCullough, C. Always a witch
Mebus, S. Gods of Manhattan
Nelson, R. A. Days of Little Texas
Taylor, L. Dreams of gods & monsters
Wooding, C. Havoc
The **good** braider. Farish, T.
Good enough. Yoo, P.
The **good** girl's guide to getting kidnapped. Murray, Y. M.
Good kings bad kings. Nussbaum, S.
A **good** long way. Saldana, R.
The **goodbye** season. Hale, M.
Goodman, Alison
Eon: Dragoneye reborn
Eona: the last Dragoneye
Singing the Dogstar blues
Goodman, Shawn
Kindness for weakness
Something like hope
Gool. Gee, M.
The **Goose** girl. Hale, S.
Gordimer, Nadine
The house gun
My son's story
Gorgeous. Rudnick, P.
Gorman, Carol
Games
Gormley, Beatrice
Poisoned honey
The **gospel** of winter. Kiely, B.
GOSSIP -- FICTION
Harrington, H. Speechless
Goth girl rising. Lyga, B.
Gothic Lolita. Lane, D.
GOTHIC NOVELS
Brennan, S. R. Unspoken
Weyn, S. Dr. Frankenstein's daughters
Goto, Hiromi
Half World
Gould, Sasha
Cross my heart
GOVERNMENT, RESISTANCE TO -- FICTION

Brown, P. Red Rising
Charbonneau, J. Graduation day
Charbonneau, J. Independent study
Dos Santos, S. The culling
Hill, C. J. Erasing time
Johnson, A. D. The summer prince
Lu, M. Prodigy
Oliver, L. Requiem
Pearson, M. E. Fox forever
Peterfreund, D. Across a star-swept sea
Simmons, K. Article 5
Zhang, K. Once we were
Grace. Scott, E.
Grace, Amanda
In too deep
Graceling. Cashore, K.
GRADING AND MARKING (EDUCATION) -- FICTION
Strohmeyer, S. Smart girls get what they want
GRADUATION (SCHOOL) -- FICTION
Charbonneau, J. The Testing
Graduation day. Charbonneau, J.
Graff, Lisa
Lost in the sun
GRAFFITI -- FICTION
Bass, K. Graffiti knight
Hand, E. Radiant days
Graffiti knight. Bass, K.
Grail prince. McKenzie, N.
GRANDFATHERS -- FICTION
Brouwer, S. Devil's pass
Clarke, J. One whole and perfect day
Crowe, C. Mississippi trial, 1955
Egan, L. A. The Outcast Oracle
Harvey, S. N. Death benefits
Kerr, M. E. Gentlehands
Morpurgo, M. Half a man
Waters, Z. C. Blood moon rider
GRANDMOTHERS -- FICTION
Johnson, A.Toning the sweep
Manzano, S. The revolution of Evelyn Serrano
Moore, K. Amber House
Padian, M. Brett McCarthy: work in progress
Wilson, N. H. Mountain pose
GRANDPARENT-GRANDCHILD RELATIONSHIP--FICTION
Block, F. L. Teen spirit
Brouwer, S. Devil's pass
Manzano, S. The revolution of Evelyn Serrano
GRANDPARENTS -- FICTION
McDonnell, M. Torn to pieces
Meyerhoff, J. Queen of secrets
Grandpre, Mary
(il) Harry Potter and the deathly hallows
Rowling, J. K. Harry Potter and the Chamber of Secrets
Rowling, J. K. Harry Potter and the Goblet of Fire
Rowling, J. K. Harry Potter and the Half-blood Prince
Rowling, J. K. Harry Potter and the Order of the Phoenix
Rowling, J. K. Harry Potter and the prisoner of Azkaban
Rowling, J. K. Harry Potter and the Sorcerer's Stone
Grant, Christopher
Teenie
Grant, K. M.
Blood red horse
Blue flame
How the hangman lost his heart
Paradise red
White heat
Grant, Michael
Gone
(jt. auth) Applegate, K. Eve & Adam
Grant, Vicki
Quid pro quo
Res judicata
The **grass** dancer. Power, S.
Grasshopper jungle. Smith, A.
Gratton, Tessa
The blood keeper
Gratz, Alan
Samurai shortstop
Something rotten
Grave mercy. LaFevers, R.
The **grave** robber's secret. Myers, A.
GRAVE ROBBING -- FICTION
Kraus, D. Rotters
Gray baby. Sanders, S. L.
The **Gray** Wolf Throne. Chima, C. W.
Gray, Claudia
Evernight
Spellcaster
Steadfast
Gray, Keith
Ostrich boys
GREAT BRITAIN -- HISTORY -- 0-1066 -- FICTION
McKenzie, N. Grail prince
McKenzie, N. Guinevere's gamble
McKenzie, N. Guinevere's gift
Moran, K. Bloodline
Moran, K. Bloodline rising
Reeve, P. Here lies Arthur
Sandell, L. A. Song of the sparrow
Spinner, S. Damosel
Springer, N. I am Mordred
Springer, N. I am Morgan le Fay

Sutcliff, R. The Shining Company
Vande Velde, V. The book of Mordred
GREAT BRITAIN -- HISTORY -- 1066-1154, NORMAN PERIOD -- FICTION
Carey, J. L. Dragon's Keep
Whitman, E. Wildwing
GREAT BRITAIN -- HISTORY -- 1485-1603, TUDORS -- FICTION
Castor, H. M. VIII
GREAT BRITAIN -- HISTORY -- 1485-1603, TUDORS -- FICTION
Castor, H. M. VIII
Longshore, K. Gilt
Longshore, K. Tarnish
GREAT BRITAIN -- HISTORY -- 1642-1660, CIVIL WAR AND COMMONWEALTH -- FICTION
Hearn, J. The minister's daughter
GREAT BRITAIN -- HISTORY -- 1714-1837 -- FICTION
Zettel, S. Palace of Spies
GREAT BRITAIN -- HISTORY -- 1789-1820 -- FICTION
Kindl, P. Keeping the castle
GREAT BRITAIN -- HISTORY -- 1800-1837 -- FICTION
Doyle, M. Courtship and curses
GREAT BRITAIN -- HISTORY -- 1837-1901 -- FICTION
Bailey, K. Legacy of the clockwork key
Cameron, S. The dark unwinding
Carriger, G. Curtsies & conspiracies
Carriger, G. Etiquette & espionage
Cooper, M. The FitzOsbornes at war
Clare, C. Clockwork princess
Gleason, C. The clockwork scarab
Hooper, M. Velvet
Pratchett, T. Dodger
GREAT BRITAIN -- HISTORY -- 1936-1945 -- FICTION
Wein, E. Code name Verity
GREAT BRITAIN -- HISTORY -- 19TH CENTURY -- FICTION
Baratz-Logsted, L. Twin's daughter
Ford, M. The poisoned house
Hamilton, K. The faerie ring
Hearn, J. Ivy
Hooper, M. Fallen Grace
Jocelyn, M. Folly
Lee, Y. S. The body at the tower
Lee, Y. S. A spy in the house
MacColl, M. Prisoners in the palace
Peacock, S. The dragon turn
Peacock, S. Eye of the crow
Peacock, S. The secret fiend
Peacock, S. Vanishing girl
Slade, A. G. The dark deeps
Slade, A. The hunchback assignments
Updale, E. Montmorency
Updale, E. Montmorency on the rocks
Updale, E. Montmorency's revenge
GREAT BRITAIN -- HISTORY -- EDWARD VII, 1901-1910 -- FICTION
Fisher, C. Darkwater
GREAT BRITAIN -- HISTORY -- FICTION
Emerald green
Sapphire blue
GREAT BRITAIN -- HISTORY -- GEORGE III, 1760-1820 -- FICTION
Meyer, L. A. Viva Jacquelina!
GREAT BRITAIN -- HISTORY -- GEORGE V, 1910-1936 -- FICTION
Whelan, G. All my noble dreams and then what happens
GREAT BRITAIN -- HISTORY -- HENRY VII, 1485-1509 -- FICTION
Castor, H. M. VIII
GREAT DEPRESSION, 1929-1939 -- FICTION
Ingold, J. Hitch
Yep, L. Dragon road; Golden Mountain chronicles: 1939
The **great** god Pan. Napoli, D. J.
The **great** wide sea. Herlong, M.
GREEK MYTHOLOGY -- FICTION
Taylor, L. Days of blood & starlight
Taylor, L. Dreams of gods & monsters
Wolfson, J. Furious
Greek ransom. Malaghan, M.
Green witch. Hoffman, A.
Green, John
An abundance of Katherines
The fault in our stars
Looking for Alaska
Paper towns
Will Grayson, Will Grayson
Green, Sally
Half bad
Green angel. Hoffman, A.
Greenberg, Joanne
I never promised you a rose garden
Greener grass. Pignat, C.
GREENHOUSE EFFECT -- FICTION
Bastedo, J. On thin ice
Bertagna, J. Exodus
Bertagna, J. Zenith
A **greyhound** of a girl. Doyle, R.
GRIEF -- FICTION
Caletti, D. The last forever
Ellison, K. The butterfly clues
Kearney, M. The girl in the mirror
Kephart, B. Dr. Radway's Sarsaparilla

Resolvent
Magoon, K. 37 things I love (in no particular order)
Nielsen, S. The reluctant journal of Henry K. Larsen
Pitcher, A. Ketchup clouds
Rothenberg, J. The catastrophic history of you & me
Torres Sanchez, J. Death, Dickinson, and the demented life of Frenchie Garcia
Griffin, Adele
All you never wanted
The Julian game
Tighter
Where I want to be
Griffin, Claire J.
Nowhere to run
Griffin, N.
The whole stupid way we are
Griffin, Paul
Burning blue
The Orange Houses
Stay with me
Ten Mile River
GRIM REAPER (SYMBOLIC CHARACTER)
Damico, G. Rogue
Grimes, Nikki
Bronx masquerade
Dark sons
A girl named Mister
Jazmin's notebook
Grimm, Jacob, 1785-1863
About
McNeal, T. Far far away
Gringolandia. Miller-Lachmann, L.
Grisha trilogy [series]
Bardugo, L. Shadow and bone
Bardugo, L. Siege and storm
Grossman, Nancy
A world away
Grove, S. E.
The glass sentence
GUANTANAMO BAY NAVAL BASE (CUBA) -- DETENTION CAMP -- FICTION
Perera, A. Guantanamo boy
Guantanamo boy. Perera, A.
Guardian. Lester, J.
Guardian. London, A.
Guardian of the Green Hill. Sullivan, L. L.
The **guardian.** Sweeney, J.
Guardian angel house. Clark, K.
GUARDIAN ANGELS -- FICTION
Brockenbrough, M. Devine intervention
Guardian of the dead. Healey, K.
Guardian of the Gate. Zink, M.
GUATEMALA -- FICTION
Brown, S. Caminar
Guibord, Maurissa
Warped
GUIDES (PERSONS) -- FICTION
Bruchac, J. Sacajawea
The Guild of Specialists [series]
Mowll, J. Operation Red Jericho
Mowll, J. Operation Storm City
Mowll, J. Operation typhoon shore
GUILT -- FICTION
Cerrito, A. The end of the line
Colasanti, S. Something like fate
Fitzmaurice, K. A diamond in the desert
Jarzab, A. The opposite of hallelujah
Johnson, A. A certain October
Knowles, J. Living with Jackie Chan
Little, K. G. Circle of secrets
Marcus, K. Exposed
Min, K. Secondhand world
Pitcher, A. Ketchup clouds
GUINEVERE (LEGENDARY CHARACTER)
McKenzie, N. Guinevere's gamble
McKenzie, N. Guinevere's gift
Guinevere's gamble. McKenzie, N.
Guinevere's gift. McKenzie, N.
GUITARS -- FICTION
Auch, M. J. Guitar boy
Guitar girl. Manning, S.
Gurtler, Janet
I'm not her
Guy in real life. Brezenoff, S.
Guy Langman, crime scene procrastinator. Berk, J.
Guyaholic. Mackler, C.
Gym candy. Deuker, C.
GYMNASTICS -- FICTION
Cohen, J. C. Leverage
GYPSIES -- FICTION
Brooks, K. The road of the dead
Dunlap, S. E. The musician's daughter
Gardner, S. The red necklace
Sedgwick, M. My swordhand is singing
The **gypsy** morph. Brooks, T.

H

Haas, Abigail
Dangerous girls
Habibi. Nye, N. S.
Hacking Harvard. Wasserman, R.
Hacking Timbuktu. Davies, S.
HACKTIVISM -- FICTION
Doctorow, C. Homeland
Haddix, Margaret Peterson
Full ride
Just Ella

Leaving Fishers
Uprising
Hahn, Mary Downing, 1937-
The ghost of Crutchfield Hall
Mister Death's blue-eyed girls
Hahn, Rebecca
A creature of moonlight
HAIKU
Mecum, R. Zombie haiku
Haines, Kathryn Miller
The girl is murder
The girl is trouble
HAITI -- FICTION
Lake, N. In darkness
HAITIAN AMERICANS -- FICTION
Felin, M. S. Touching snow
Halam, Ann
Dr. Franklin's island
Snakehead
Hale, Marian
The goodbye season
Hale, Shannon
Book of a thousand days
The Goose girl
Half a man. Morpurgo, M.
Half bad. Green, S.
Half brother. Oppel, K.
The **half** life of planets. Franklin, E.
Half World. Goto, H.
Hall, C. Aubrey
Crystal bones
Hall, Teri
Away
The Line
The **hallowed** ones. Bickle, L.
Halpern, Julie
Get well soon
Have a nice day
Into the wild nerd yonder
Halpin, Brendan
A really awesome mess
Shutout
Halpin, Brendan
Cook, T. Notes from the blender
Franklin, E. The half life of planets
Hamilton, K. R.
Tyger tyger
Hamilton, Kersten
When the stars threw down their spears
Hamilton, Kiki
The faerie ring
Hamlet: a novel. Marsden, J.
Hamley, Dennis
Without warning
Hammer of witches. Mlawski, S.
Han, Jenny
It's not summer without you
The summer I turned pretty
We'll always have summer
The **hand** you're dealt. Volponi, P.
Hand, Elizabeth
Illyria
Radiant days
Handler, Daniel, 1970-
Why we broke up
Hanging on to Max. Bechard, M.
The **Hanging** Woods. Sanders, S. L.
Hannah's winter. Meehan, K.
Hannan, Peter
My big mouth
Happy families. Davis, T. S.
Happyface. Emond, S.
Hard hit. Turner, A. W.
Hard love. Wittlinger, E.
Hardy, Janice
The shifter
A **hare** in the elephant's trunk. Coates, J. L.
Harland, Richard
Liberator
Worldshaker
HARLEM (NEW YORK, N.Y.) -- FICTION
Myers, W. D. Darius & Twig
Nelson, Vaunda Micheaux. No crystal stair
Harlem Hustle. McDonald, J.
HARLEM RENAISSANCE -- FICTION
Myers, W. D. Harlem summer
Harlem summer. Myers, W. D., 1937-
Harmel, Kristin
When you wish
Harmless. Reinhardt, D.
Harmon, Michael
Under the bridge
Harmon, Michael B.
Brutal
The last exit to normal
Shea, J. A kid from Southie
Harmonic feedback. Kelly, T.
Harness, Cheryl
Just for you to know
Harper, Suzanne
The Juliet club
The secret life of Sparrow Delaney
Harrington, Hannah
Speechless
Harris and me; a summer remembered. Paulsen, G.
Harris, Carrie
Bad taste in boys
Harris, Joanne
Runemarks
Harrison, Cora
I was Jane Austen's best friend

Harry Potter and the Chamber of Secrets. Rowling, J. K.
Harry Potter and the deathly hallows.
Harry Potter and the Goblet of Fire. Rowling, J. K.
Harry Potter and the Half-blood Prince. Rowling, J. K.
Harry Potter and the Order of the Phoenix. Rowling, J. K.
Harry Potter and the prisoner of Azkaban. Rowling, J. K.
Harry Potter and the Sorcerer's Stone. Rowling, J. K.
Harstad, Johan
172 hours on the moon
Hartinger, Brent
Geography Club
Project Sweet Life
Hartman, Rachel
Seraphina
Hartnett, Sonya
Hartnett, S. Butterfly
The ghost's child
Surrender
Thursday's child
What the birds see
HARVARD UNIVERSITY -- FICTION
Wasserman, R. Hacking Harvard
Harvey, Alyxandra
Haunting Violet
Hearts at stake
Harvey, Sarah N.
Death benefits
Plastic
Hassan, Michael
Crash and Burn
HATE CRIMES -- FICTION
Bick, I. J. The Sin eater's confession
Harrington, H. Speechless
Hate list. Brown, J.
Hattemer, K.
The vigilante poets of the Selwyn Academy
Hattie Big Sky. Larson, K.
Hattie ever after. Larson, K.
Haugen, David
HAUNTED HOUSES -- FICTION
Moore, K. Amber House
Nixon, J. L. The haunting
The **haunting** of Alaizabel Cray. Wooding, C.
The haunting. Nixon, J. L.
Haunting Violet. Harvey, A.
Hausman, Gerald
Thoreau
Hautman, Pete
All-in
The big crunch
Blank confession
The Cydonian pyramid
Godless
Hole in the sky
How to steal a car
Invisible
The klaatu terminus
The obsidian blade
Snatched
Sweetblood
What boys really want?
Have a nice day. Halpern, J.
Haveli. Staples, S. F.
Havoc. Wooding, C.
HAWAII -- FICTION
Levitin, S. Strange relations
Salisbury, G. Under the blood-red sun
Hawk, Tony, 1968-
About
Hornby, N. Slam
Hawkins, Rachel
Demonglass
Hex Hall
School spirits
Hawksmaid. Lasky, K.
Haydn, Joseph, 1732-1809
About
Dunlap, S. E. The musician's daughter
Haydu, Corey Ann
OCD love story
Hayes, Rosemary
Payback
Hazel. Hearn, J.
He forgot to say good-bye. Saenz, B. A.
He said, she said. Alexander, K.
He will go fearless. Lawlor, L.
Head case. Aronson, S.
Head games. Fredericks, M.
Headley, Justina Chen
North of beautiful
Headlong. Koja, K.
Healey, Karen
Guardian of the dead
The shattering
When we wake
While we run
The **healing** spell. Little, K. G.
Heap house. Carey, E.
Hearn, Julie
Hazel
Ivy
The minister's daughter
The **heart** is not a size. Kephart, B.
Hearts at stake. Harvey, A.
Hearts of iron. Duble, K. B.
Heartsinger. Stoffels, K.

Heath, Jack
The Lab
Money run
Remote control
HEAVEN -- FICTION
Brockenbrough, M. Devine intervention
Heaven. Johnson, A.
Heaven looks a lot like the mall. Mass, W.
Heavy metal and you. Krovatin, C.
Hegamin, Tonya
M +O 4evr
Hegedus, Bethany
Between us Baxters
Heir apparent. Vande Velde, V.
The heir chronicles [series]
Chima, C. W. The enchanter heir
Heist Society. Carter, A.
HELEN OF TROY (LEGENDARY CHARACTER)
Friesner, E. M. Nobody's princess
Friesner, E. M. Nobody's prize
McLaren, C. Inside the walls of Troy
Helena, Saint, ca. 255-329
About
HELL -- FICTION
Agard, J. The young inferno
Ashton, B. Everbound
Kaye, M. Demon chick
Hell Week. Clement-Moore, R.
Hemphill, Stephanie
Hideous love
Sisters of glass
Wicked girls
Henderson, Jan-Andrew
Bunker 10
Henderson, Jason
The Triumph of Death
Vampire rising
Heneghan, James
McBay, B. Waiting for Sarah
Henry, April
Torched
Henry VIII, King of England, 1491-1547
About
Castor, H. M. VIII
Libby, A. M. The king's rose
Longshore, K. Gilt
Hepler, Heather
The cupcake queen
Her Dark Curiosity. Shepherd, M.
Herbach, Geoff
Stupid fast
Here, there be dragons. Owen, J. A.
The **here** and now. Brashares, A.
Here lies Arthur. Reeve, P.
Here today. Martin, A. M.
Here's to you, Rachel Robinson. Blume, J.
Hereafter. Hudson, T.
Herlong, Madaline
The great wide sea
Hernandez, Daniel, 1990-
No more us for you
Suckerpunch
The **hero** and the crown. McKinley, R.
Hero. Lupica, M.
Hero. Moore, P.
The **hero.** Woods, R.
Hero-type. Lyga, B.
HEROES AND HEROINES -- FICTION
Lyga, B. Hero-type
Pierson, D. C. Crap kingdom
Zinn, B. Poison
Heroes of the valley. Stroud, J.
HEROIN
Burgess, M. Smack
Herrick, Steven
By the river
Cold skin
The wolf
HERSHEY (PA.) -- FICTION
Finneyfrock, K. The sweet revenge of Celia Door
Hesse, Karen
Safekeeping
Hesser, Terry Spencer
Kissing doorknobs
Hex Hall. Hawkins, R.
Hiaasen, C.
Skink
Hidden. Frost, H.
HIDDEN CHILDREN (HOLOCAUST) -- FICTION
Macdonald, M. Odette's secrets
The **hidden** Coronet. Fisher, C.
Hidden talents. Lubar, D.
Hidden voices. Collins, P. L.
Hideous love. Hemphill, S.
Higgins, F. E.
The Eyeball Collector
Higgins, Jack
Sure fire
Higgins, M. G.
Bi-Normal
High dive. Stein, T.
High heat. Deuker, C.
HIGH SCHOOL STUDENTS -- FICTION
Alexander, K. He said, she said
Andrews, J. Me & Earl & the dying girl
Bailey, E. Shift
Brockenbrough, M. Devine intervention
Crawford, B. Carter's unfocused, one-track mind

Feinstein, J. Foul trouble
George, M. The difference between you and me
Grace, A. In too deep
Hautman, P. What boys really want?
Hubbard, J. And we stay
Jaden, D. Never enough
Moore, D. Always upbeat / All that
Pauley, K. Cat Girl's day off
Paulsen, G. Crush; the theory, practice, and destructive properties of love
Perez, M. Dead is a battlefield
Peters, J. A. It's our prom (so deal with it)
Quick, M. Boy21
Reed, J. Living violet
Strohmeyer, S. Smart girls get what they want
Vivian, S. The list
Walker, B. F. Black boy/white school
Walker, K. 7clues to winning you
Williams, K. Absent
Zeitlin, M. Freshman year & other unnatural disasters
Zevin, G. Because it is my blood

HIGH SCHOOLS -- FICTION
Altebrando, T. The best night of your (pathetic) life
Coben, H. Seconds away
Crane, C. Confessions of a Hater
Cronn-Mills, K. Beautiful Music for Ugly Children
Kessler, J. M. Loss
Klass, D. You don't know me
Koertge, R. Stoner & Spaz
Mackler, C. Vegan virgin Valentine
Oates, J. C. Big Mouth & Ugly Girl
Thomas, L. Quarantine
Sanchez, A. Rainbow boys

Highway to hell. Clement-Moore, R.

The **highwayman's** footsteps. Morgan, N.

Higson, Charles
The dead
The enemy

Hijuelos, Oscar
Dark Dude

Hill, C. J.
Erasing time
Slayers

Hill, Will
Department 19
The rising

Hills, Lia
The beginner's guide to living

Hinton, S. E.
The outsiders

Hinwood, Christine
The returning

Hippie chick. Monninger, J.

HIPPIES -- FICTION
Lynch, J. N. My beautiful hippie

Hirsch, Jeff
The eleventh plague

His fair assassin [series]
LaFevers, R. Dark triumph

HISPANIC AMERICANS--FICTION
Arntson, S. The wrap-up list
Fontes, J. Benito runs
Hernandez, D. Suckerpunch
Nichols, J. Messed up
Quintero, S. Efrain's secret
Wright, B. Putting makeup on the fat boy

HISPANIC AMERICANS -- POETRY
Ada, A. F. Yes! we are Latinos

HISTORIC BUILDINGS -- FICTION
Cann, K. Consumed
Cann, K. Possessed

HISTORICAL FICTION
Bray, L. The diviners
Cooper, M. The FitzOsbornes at war
Engle, M. The Lightning Dreamer\
Feldman, R. T. Blue thread
Gleason, C. The clockwork scarab
Gould, S. Cross my heart
Hahn, M. D. The girl is trouble
Hahn, M. D. Mister Death's blue-eyed girls
Hemphill, S. Hideous love
Hemphill, S. Sisters of glass
Hooper, M. Velvet
Kirkpatrick, J. A flickering light
LaFevers, R. Grave mercy
Larson, K. Hattie ever after
Lennon, T. When love comes to town
Longshore, K. Gilt
Longshore, K. Tarnish
Lynch, J. N. My beautiful hippie
MacColl, M. Nobody's secret
Magoon, K. Fire in the streets
Manzano, S. The revolution of Evelyn Serrano
Marsh, K. Jepp, who defied the stars
Meyer, L. A. Viva Jacquelina!
Moore, K. Neverwas
O'Brien, A. Lara's gift
Palma, F. J. The map of time
Pratchett, T. Dodger
Preus, M. Shadow on the mountain
Reese, J. The strange case of Doctor Jekyll and Mademoiselle Odile
Ross, E. Belle epoque
Sanders, S. Rachel's secret
Sepetys, R. Out of the Easy
Strauss, V. Passion blue
Taub, M. Still star-crossed
Terry, C. L. Zero fade

Wallace, S. N. Muckers
Wein, E. Code name Verity
Wein, E. Rose under fire
Whelan, G. All my noble dreams and then what happens
Wilson, J. Victorio's war
Winters, C. In the shadow of blackbirds
Wright, B. Crow
The **hit.** Burgess, M.
Hit and run. McDaniel, L.
Hitch. Ingold, J.
Hitler, Adolf, 1889-1945
About
Blankman, A. Prisoner of night and fog
Hoban, Julia
Willow
Hoban, Russell, 1925-2011
Soonchild
Hobbs, Valerie
Sonny's war
Hobbs, Will
Beardance
Bearstone
Crossing the wire
Downriver
Leaving Protection
The maze
Wild Man Island
HOCKEY -- FICTION
Zweig, E. Fever season
Hocking, Amanda
Wake
Hodge, Rosamund
Cruel Beauty
Hodkin, Michelle
The evolution of Mara Dyer
The unbecoming of Mara Dyer
Hoffman, Alice
The foretelling
Green angel
Green witch
Incantation
Hoffman, Mary
The falconer's knot
Hoffman, Nina Kiriki
A stir of bones
Hokenson, Terry
The winter road
Hold me closer, necromancer. McBride, L.
Hold still. LaCour, N.
Holder, Nancy
Crusade
Damned
Hole in the sky. Hautman, P.
Holiday, Billie, 1915-1959
About
Weatherford, C. B. Becoming Billie Holiday
Holland, L. Tam
The counterfeit family tree of Vee Crawford-Wong
Holliday, John Henry, 1851-1887
About
The **Hollow.** Verday, J.
HOLLYWOOD (CALIF.) -- FICTION
Strasser, T. Famous
Shukert, R. Starstruck
Zettel, S. Golden girl
Hollywood High. Abrams, A.
HOLMES, SHERLOCK (FICTIONAL CHARACTER)
Lane, A. Black ice
Holocaust remembrance book for young readers [series]
Clark, K. Guardian angel house
HOLOCAUST, 1933-1945 -- FICTION
Chapman, F. S. Is it night or day?
Clark, K. Guardian angel house
Dogar, S. Annexed
Lieberman, L. Lauren Yanofsky hates the holocaust
Macdonald, M. Odette's secrets
Matas, C. After the war
Meyer, S. Black radishes
Polak, M. What world is left
Sax, A. The war within these walls
Sharenow, R. The Berlin Boxing Club
Whitney, K. A. The other half of life
Zusak, M. The book thief
HOUSES -- FICTION
Frost, H. Keesha's house
Homecoming. Voigt, C.
HOME SCHOOLING -- FICTION
Doyle, E. F. According to Kit
Kephart, B. You are my only
HOME-BASED EDUCATION
See Home schooling
Homeland. Doctorow, C.
Homeless bird. Whelan, G.
HOMELESS PERSONS -- FICTION
Griffin, P. Ten Mile River
Millard, G. A small free kiss in the dark
Strasser, T. Can't get there from here
Strasser, T. No place
Valentine, J. Double
Walters, E. Sketches
Homeroom diaries. Patterson, J.
Homestretch. Volponi, P.
Homicidal aliens and other disappointments. Yansky, B.
HOMICIDE -- FICTION
Connor, L. Dead on town line
Ellen, L. Blind spot

Giles, L. Fake ID
Haas, A. Dangerous girls
Hahn, M. D. Mister Death's blue-eyed girls
Hopkins, E. Smoke
Mackall, D. D. The silence of murder
Michaels, R. Genesis Alpha
Miranda, M. Hysteria
Myers, A. The grave robber's secret
Nixon, J. L. Nightmare
O'Neal, E. Torn
Perez, M. Dead is just a dream
Revis, B. A million suns
Rosenfield, K. Amelia Anne is dead and gone
Volponi, P. Rucker Park setup
Wasserman, R. The waking dark
Waters, D. Break my heart 1,000 times
Werlin, N. The killer's cousin
HOMOSEXUALITY -- FICTION
Bick, I. J. The Sin eater's confession
Dos Santos, S. The culling
Ford, M. T. Suicide notes
Freymann-Weyr, G. My heartbeat
Konigsberg, B. Openly straight
Moore, P. Hero
Papademetriou, L. M or F?
Pearce, J. As you wish
Ryan, S. Empress of the world
Sanchez, A. Rainbow boys
Wright, B. Putting makeup on the fat boy
HONESTY -- FICTION
Grace, A. In too deep
Honey Bea. Siegelson, K. L.
Hooked. Fichera, L.
Hooper, Mary
Fallen Grace
Velvet
Hoops. Myers, W. D., 1937-
Hope in Patience. Fehlbaum, B.
Hope was here. Bauer, J.
Hopkins, Ellen
Burned
Identical
Rumble
Smoke
Tricks
Hopkinson, Nalo
The Chaos
Horde. Aguirre, A.
Hornby, Nick, 1957-
Slam
Horner, Emily
A love story starring my dead best friend
Horowitz, Anthony
Raven's gate
Stormbreaker
HORROR FICTION
172 hours on the moon
Aguirre, A. Enclave
Almond, D. Clay
Becker, T. Darkside
Becker, T. Lifeblood
Bickle, L. The hallowed ones
Bickle, L. The outside
Black, B. iDrakula
Blake, K. Anna Dressed in Blood
Brennan, S. R. Unspoken
Bickle, L. The hallowed ones
Brewer, H. First kill
Cary, K. Bloodline
Cary, K. Bloodline: reckoning
Clare, C. City of ashes
Clare, C. City of bones
Clare, C. City of Glass
Clare, C. City of lost souls
Clement-Moore, R. Hell Week
Clement-Moore, R. Highway to hell
Clement-Moore, R. Prom dates from Hell
Dennard, S. Something strange and deadly
Dunkle, C. B. By these ten bones
Fahy, T. R. The unspoken
Fukuda, A. The Prey
Gagnon, M. Strangelets
Garner, E. Contaminated
Garvey, A. Glass Heart
Gilman, C. Professor Gargoyle
Gray, C. Evernight
Gray, C. Spellcaster
Gray, C. Steadfast
Henderson, J. Vampire rising
Higgins, F. E.The Eyeball Collector
Harris, C. Bad taste in boys
Henderson, J. The Triumph of Death
Higson, C. The dead
Higson, C. The enemy
Hill, W. Department 19
Holder, N. Crusade
Holder, N. Damned
Jenkins, A. M. Night road
King, S. Firestarter
Klause, A. C. Blood and chocolate
Kraus, D. Scowler
Maberry, J. Dust & decay
Maberry, J. Rot & ruin
Moulton, C. A. Angelfire
Myracle, L. Bliss
Nance, A. Daemon Hall
Nance, A. Return to Daemon Hall: evil roots
Oppel, K. This dark endeavor
Oppel, K. Such wicked intent
Peck, R. Three-quarters dead
Priestly, C. Mister Creecher
Prose, F. The turning

Randall, T. Spirits of the Noh
Ryan, C. The dark and hollow places
Ryan, C. The dead-tossed waves
Ryan, C. The Forest of Hands and Teeth
Sedgwick, M. My swordhand is singing
Sedgwick, M. White crow
Smith, A. G. Death sentence
Smith, A. G. Solitary
Smith, A. The Marbury lens
Smith, A. Passenger
Stahler, D. Doppelganger
Summers, C. This is not a test
Taylor, G. Killer Pizza
Taylor, G. Killer Pizza: the slice
Thomas, L. Quarantine
Tucholke, A. G. Between the devil and the deep blue sea
Wasserman, R. The waking dark
Weyn, S. Dr. Frankenstein's daughters
Wooding, C. The haunting of Alaizabel Cray
Wooding, C. Malice
Wooding, C. Silver
Yancey, R. The curse of the Wendigo
Yancey, R. The final descent
HORSE RACING -- FICTION
Luper, E. Bug boy
Volponi, P. Homestretch
HORSE SHOWS -- FICTION
Lyne, J. H. Catch rider
HORSEMANSHIP -- FICTION
Kenneally, M. Racing Savannah
HORSES -- FICTION
Brennan, C. House of the star
Kenneally, M. Racing Savannah
Grant, K. M. Blood red horse
Lyne, J. H. Catch rider
Monninger, J. Finding somewhere
Platt, C. Astra
Williams, S. Wind rider
HOSPICES (TERMINAL CARE) -- FICTION
Seamon, H. Somebody up there hates you
HOSPITALS -- FICTION
Bryce, C. Anthem for Jackson Dawes
Ford, M. T. Suicide notes
Hostage Three. Lake, N.
HOSTAGES -- FICTION
Lake, N. Hostage Three
Van Diepen, A. Takedown
HOTELS AND MOTELS -- FICTION
Beaufrand, M. J. The river
Johnson, M. Scarlett fever
Johnson, M. Suite Scarlett
Hothouse. Lynch, C.
Houck, Colleen
Tiger's curse
Tiger's quest
The hound of Rowan. Neff, H. H.
Hourglass. McEntire, M.
The **house** gun. Gordimer, N.
House of Dance. Kephart, B.
The **house** of dead maids.
The **house** of djinn. Staples, S. F.
House of ivy and snow. Whipple, N.
The **house** of the scorpion. Farmer, N.
House of the red fish. Salisbury, G.
House of the star. Brennan, C.
The **house** on Mango Street. Cisneros, S.
HOUSEHOLD EMPLOYEES -- FICTION
Coats, J. A. The wicked and the just
Jocelyn, M. Folly
Stuber, B. Crossing the tracks
Watts, I. N. No moon
Wollman, J. Switched
HOUSES -- FICTION
Baer, M. Frost
HOUSTON (TEX.) -- FICTION
Williams, L. A. When Kambia Elaine flew in from Neptune
How it went down. Magoon, K.
How (not) to find a boyfriend. Valentine, A.
How not to be popular. Ziegler, J.
How the hangman lost his heart. Grant, K. M.
How to be bad. Lockhart, E.
How to build a house. Reinhardt, D.
How to ditch your fairy. Larbalestier, J.
How to get suspended and influence people. Selzer, A.
How to lead a life of crime. Miller, K.
How to make a bird. Murray, M.
How to ruin a summer vacation. Elkeles, S.
How to ruin my teenage life. Elkeles, S.
How to ruin your boyfriend's reputation. Elkeles, S.
How to save a life. Zarr, S.
How to say goodbye in Robot. Standiford, N.
How to steal a car. Hautman, P.
How to take the ex out of ex-boyfriend. Rallison, J.
How Zoe made her dreams (mostly) come true. Strohmeyer, S.
Howard, J. J.
That time I joined the circus
Howard, Jonathan L.
Katya's World
Howe, K.
Conversion
Howell, Simmone
Everything beautiful
Howells, Amanda
The summer of skinny dipping
Howland, Leila
Nantucket blue

Hrdlitschka, Shelley
Allegra
Sister wife
Hubbard, Amanda
But I love him
Ripple
Hubbard, Jennifer R.
Try not to breathe
Hubbard, Jenny
And we stay
Paper covers rock
Hubbard, Kirsten
Like Mandarin
Wanderlove
Hübener, Helmuth, 1925-1942
About
Bartoletti, S. C. The boy who dared
Hudson, Tara
Hereafter
Huge. Paley, S.
Hughes, Dean
Search and destroy
HUMAN BEHAVIOR -- FICTION
Bailey, E. Shift
HUMAN CLONING -- FICTION
Cohn, R. Beta
Patrick, C. The Originals
HUMAN EXPERIMENTATION IN MEDICINE -- FICTION
Weyn, S. Dr. Frankenstein's daughters
Human.4. Lancaster, M. A.
HUMAN RIGHTS -- FICTION
McCormick, P. Never fall down
HUMAN SKIN COLOR -- FICTION
Sullivan, T. Golden boy
HUMAN TRAFFICKING -- FICTION
Purcell, K. Trafficked
HUMAN-ALIEN ENCOUNTERS -- FICTION
Lo, M. Inheritance
McDonald, I. Empress of the sun
Meyer, M. Cress
HUMAN-ANIMAL COMMUNICATION -- FICTION
Pauley, K. Cat Girl's day off
HUMAN-ANIMAL RELATIONSHIPS -- FICTION
Clement-Davies, D. The sight
HUMOROUS FICTION
Calame, D. Beat the band
Pierson, D. C. Crap kingdom
Paulsen, G. Crush; the theory, practice, and destructive properties of love
Scieszka, J. Who done it?
Zeitlin, M. Freshman year & other unnatural disasters
HUMOROUS STORIES
Andrews, J. Me & Earl & the dying girl
Berk, J. Guy Langman, crime scene procrastinator
Damico, G. Rogue
Damico, G. Scorch
Paulsen, G. Crush; the theory, practice, and destructive properties of love
Powell, R. Three clams and an oyster
Pratchett, T. Dodger
Rennison, L. The taming of the tights
Scieszka, J. Who done it?
Smith, A. Grasshopper jungle
Humphreys, Chris
The hunt of the unicorn
The **hunchback** assignments. Slade, A.
The hunchback assignments [series]
Slade, A. G. The dark deeps
Slade, A. G. Empire of ruins
The **Hunger** Games. Collins, S.
Hunger Games [series]
Collins, S. Mockingjay
The **hunt** of the unicorn. Humphreys, C.
Hunted [series]
Sorrells, W. Whiteout
The **Hunter's** Moon. Melling, O. R.
HUNTING -- FICTION
Mary-Todd, J. Shot down
O Guilin, P. The inferior
Willis, C. C. Buck fever
Huntley, Amy
The everafter
Huntress. Lo, M.
Hurley, Tonya
Ghostgirl
Hurricane dancers. Engle, M.
HURRICANE KATRINA, 2005 -- FICTION
Woodson, J. Beneath a meth moon
Hurricane song. Volponi, P.
HURRICANES -- FICTION
Weyn, S. Empty
Hurwin, Davida
Freaks and revelations
Huser, Glen
Stitches
Hush. Chayil, E.
Hush. Napoli, D. J.
HUTU (AFRICAN PEOPLE) -- FICTION
Combres, E. Broken memory
Hyde, Catherine Ryan
Becoming Chloe
Jumpstart the world
The year of my miraculous reappearance
HYPOCHONDRIA -- FICTION
Raf, M. The symptoms of my insanity
Hysteria. Miranda, M.

I

I am (not) the walrus. Briant, E.
I am J. Beam, C.
I am Mordred. Springer, N.
I am Morgan le Fay. Springer, N.
I am Rembrandt's daughter. Cullen, L.
I am the cheese. Cormier, R.
I am the messenger. Zusak, M.
I hunt killers. Lyga, B.
I kissed a zombie, and I liked it. Selzer, A.
I know it's over. Martin, C. K. K.
I know what you did last summer. Duncan, L.
I never promised you a rose garden. Greenberg, J.
I now pronounce you someone else. McCahan, E.
I shall wear midnight. Pratchett, T.
I swear. Davis, L.
I was here. Foreman, G.
I was Jane Austen's best friend. Harrison, C.
Ibbitson, John
The Landing
iBoy. Brooks, K.
Ice. Durst, S. B.
Ice claw. Gilman, D.
Icecore. Whyman, M.
ICELAND -- FICTION
Simner, J. L. Thief eyes
Identical. Hopkins, E.
IDENTITY -- FICTION
Ortiz Cofer, J. Call me Maria
IDENTITY -- FICTION
Hartman, R. Seraphina
IDENTITY (PHILOSOPHICAL CONCEPT) -- FICTION
Bow, E. Sorrow's knot
Roth, V. Allegiant
IDENTITY (PSYCHOLOGY) -- FICTION
Clark, K. E. Freakboy
Gurtler, J. I'm not her
Kearney, M. The girl in the mirror
King, A. S. Ask the passengers
Lowry, L. Son
Shusterman, N. UnWholly
Terry, T. Slated
Valentine, J. Double
Vivian, S. The list
Walsh, P. The Crowfield demon
Wells, D. Fragments
Zhang, K. Once we were
Identity Theft. Davies, A.
IDENTITY THEFT -- FICTION
Davies, A. Identity Theft
iDrakula. Black, B.
If he had been with me. Nowlin, L.
If I could fly. Ortiz Cofer, J.
If I grow up. Strasser, T.
If I love you, am I trapped forever? Kerr, M. E.
I'll be there. Sloan, H. G.
I'll get there, it better be worth the trip. Donovan, J.
I'll give you the sun. Nelson, J.
If I stay. Forman, G.
If the witness lied. Cooney, C. B.
If you come softly. Woodson, J.
If you could be mine. Farizan, S.
If you find me. Murdoch, E.
If you live like me. Weber, L.
Illegal. Restrepo, B.
ILLEGAL ALIENS -- FICTION
Griffin, P. The Orange Houses
Hobbs, W. Crossing the wire
McNeal, L. Dark water
Price, C. Desert Angel
Restrepo, B. Illegal
ILLEGITIMATE CHILDREN -- FICTION
Yep, L. The traitor; Golden Mountain chronicles, 1885
ILLINOIS -- FICTION
Keplinger, K. A midsummer's nightmare
Leitch, W. Catch
Nadol, J. The vision
Rapp, A. Under the wolf, under the dog
Rutkoski, M. The shadow society
Stone, T. I. Time between us
Illusions. Pike, A.
Illyria. Hand, E.
I'm not her. Gurtler, J.
IMAGINARY CREATURES -- FICTION
Hamilton, K. When the stars threw down their spears
Oppel, K. Airborn
Imaginary enemy. Gonzalez, J.
Imaginary girls. Suma, N. R.
IMAGINARY PLACES
DeStefano, L. Perfect ruin
Gray, C. Steadfast
Hodge, R. Cruel Beauty
IMAGINARY PLACES -- FICTION
Miéville, C. Railsea
IMAGINARY PLAYMATES -- FICTION
Gonzalez, J. Imaginary enemy
Jennings, R. W. Ghost town
White, A. B. Window boy
IMMIGRANTS -- FICTION
Jaramillo, A. La linea
Joseph, L. Flowers in the sky
Matas, C. The whirlwind
Mead, A. Swimming to America
Veciana-Suarez, A. The flight to freedom
Walsh, A. A Long Way from Home
Walsh, A. A Long Way from Home

IMMIGRANTS -- NEW YORK (N.Y.) -- FICTION
Auch, M. J. Ashes of roses
IMMIGRANTS -- UNITED STATES -- FICTION
Purcell, K. Trafficked
Volponi, P. The Final Four
Immortal beloved. Tiernan, C.
The **immortal** rules. Kagawa, J.
IMMORTALITY -- FICTION
Khoury, J. Origin
Woon, Y. Dead beautiful
IMPERSONATION -- FICTION
Valentine, J. Double
Zinn, B. Poison
IMPOSTORS AND IMPOSTURE -- FICTION
Barratt, M. The wild man
Cooney, C. B. Three black swans
Impossible. Werlin, N.
The **impossible** knife of memory. Anderson, L. H.
In a flash. Walters, E.
In country. Mason, B. A.
In darkness. Lake, N.
In Mike we trust. Ryan, P.
In the belly of The Bloodhound. Meyer, L. A.
In the name of God. Jolin, P.
In the shadow of blackbirds. Winters, C.
In the shadow of the ark. Provoost, A.
In the shadow of the lamp. Dunlap, S.
In too deep. Grace, A.
In trouble. Levine, E.
Incantation. Hoffman, A.
Incarceron. Fisher, C.
INCEST -- FICTION
Brooks, K. Dawn
Hand, E. Illyria
Jones, P. Chasing tail lights
Scott, M. Live through this
Inconvenient. Gelbwasser, M.
Incredibly Alice. Naylor, P. R.
Incurable. Marsden, J.
Independent study. Charbonneau, J.
INDIA -- FICTION
Houck, C. Tiger's curse
Houck, C. Tiger's quest
Markandaya, K. Nectar in a sieve
Ostlere, C. Karma
Perkins, M. Secret keeper
Sheth, K. Keeping corner
Tiger moon
Tomlinson, H. Toads and diamonds
Whelan, G. Homeless bird
INDIA -- HISTORY -- 1765-1947, BRITISH OCCUPATION -- FICTION
Venkatraman, P. Climbing the stairs
INDIA -- HISTORY -- BRITISH OCCUPATION, 1765-1947 -- FICTION
Whelan, G. All my noble dreams and then what happens
INDIA -- HISTORY -- FICTION
Master, I. A beautiful lie
INDIAN LANGUAGES
See also Language and languages
INDIAN LEADERS
Black Elk Black Elk speaks
Brave Bird, M. Lakota woman
Eagle, A. F. Pipestone
Jones, V. G. Pocahontas
Menchu, R. I, Rigoberta Menchu
Woodward, G. S. Pocahontas
INDIANS OF NORTH AMERICA -- ALASKA -- FICTION
Bell, H. Traitor's son
Mikaelsen, B. Touching Spirit Bear
INDIANS OF NORTH AMERICA -- FICTION
Knutsson, C. Shadows cast by stars
Indie girl. Daswani, K.
The **indigo** notebook. Resau, L.
INDIGENOUS PEOPLES -- FICTION
Khoury, J. Origin
INDIVIDUALISM -- FICTION
Austen, C. All good children
INDIVIDUALITY -- FICTION
Patrick, C. The Originals
INDONESIA -- FICTION
Fama, E. Overboard
Inexcusable. Lynch, C.
INFANTICIDE -- FICTION
Millard, G. A small free kiss in the dark
INFANTS -- FICTION
Delsol, W. Flock
The **inferior.** O Guilin, P.
The infernal devices [series]
Clare, C. Clockwork angel
Clare, C. Clockwork prince
Clare, C. Clockwork princess
INFERTILITY -- FICTION
McCafferty, M. Thumped
Infiltration. Rodman, S.
Infinite days. Maizel, R.
The **infinite** moment of us. Myracle, L.
Infinity. Ward, R.
INFLUENZA EPIDEMIC, 1918-1919 -- FICTION
Lucier, M. A death-struck year
Winters, C. In the shadow of blackbirds
INFLUENZA -- FICTION
Williams, S. D. Palace beautiful
Zweig, E. Fever season
Ingo. Dunmore, H.
Ingold, Jeanette
The Big Burn
Hitch

INSECTS -- FICTION
Low, D. The entomological tales of Augustus T. Percival
Mountain solo
Inheritance. Lo, M.
Inheritance [series]
Paolini, C. Brisingr
Paolini, C. Eldest
Paolini, C. Eragon
INHERITANCE AND SUCCESSION -- FICTION
Nix, G. A confusion of princes
Inhuman. Falls, K.
Ink. Sun, A.
Ink exchange. Marr, M.
INQUISITION -- FICTION
Grant, K. M. White heat
Hoffman, A. Incantation
INSECTS -- FICTION
Smith, A. Grasshopper jungle
Inside out. Trueman, T.
Inside the walls of Troy. McLaren, C.
INSPIRATIONAL WRITERS -- FICTION
Miller, S. Miss Spitfire
INSTITUTIONAL CARE -- EMPLOYEES -- FICTION
Nussbaum, S. Good kings bad kings
Instructions for a broken heart. Culbertson, K.
INSURGENCY -- FICTION
Crossan, S. Breathe
Dowswell, P. The Auslander
Marillier, J. Raven flight
Marillier, J. Shadowfell
North, P. Starglass
Scott, E. Grace
Wein, E. Code name Verity
Whelan, G. All my noble dreams and then what happens
Insurgent. Roth, V.
INTELLIGENCE SERVICE -- FICTION
Cormier, R. I am the cheese
The **intelligencer.** Silbert, L.
Intensely Alice. Naylor, P. R.
INTERGENERATIONAL RELATIONS -- FICTION
Price, L. Starters
The Internment chronicles [series]
DeStefano, L. Perfect ruin
INTERNSHIP PROGRAMS -- FICTION
Cornwell, B. Tides
Doktorski, J. S. Famous last words
Strohmeyer, S. How Zoe made her dreams (mostly) come true
INTERPERSONAL RELATIONS -- FICTION
Clare, C. City of lost souls
Cohn, R. Gingerbread
Freymann-Weyr, G. My heartbeat
Hautman, P. What boys really want?
Hobbs, W. Leaving Protection
Howland, L. Nantucket blue
Johnson, J. J. The theory of everything
Klass, D. You don't know me
Lewis, S. The secret ingredient
Martin, C. K. K. Yesterday
Moore, C. The stalker chronicles
O'Rourke, E. Tangled
Paulsen, G. Crush; the theory, practice, and destructive properties of love
Peters, J. A. It's our prom (so deal with it)
Reed, A. Crazy
Sanchez, A. Rainbow boys
Scott, E. Miracle
Thompson, H. The language inside
INTERPLANETARY VOYAGES -- FICTION
Barnes, J. Losers in space
North, P. Starglass
Revis, B. A million suns
INTERPLANETARY WARS -- FICTION
Card, O. S. Ender's game
Card, O. S. Xenocide
INTERPRETERS -- FICTION
Bruchac, J. Sacajawea
Preus, M. Heart of a samurai
INTERRACIAL RELATIONS *See* Race relations
The **interrogation** of Gabriel James. Price, C.
Interstellar pig. Sleator, W.
Intertwined. Showalter, G.
Interworld. Gaiman, N.
Into the wild nerd yonder. Halpern, J.
INUIT -- FICTION
Bastedo, J. On thin ice
Orenstein, D. G. Unseen companion
Polak, M. The middle of everywhere
Soonchild
Invasion! Myers, W. D.
INVENTIONS -- FICTION
Bailey, K. Legacy of the clockwork key
Bancks, T. Mac Slater vs. the city
Cameron, S. The dark unwinding
Williams, A. The deep freeze of Bartholomew Tullock
INVENTORS -- FICTION
Colfer, E. Airman
Skelton, M. Endymion Spring
Weyn, S. Distant waves
Invisibility. Cremer, A.
INVISIBILITY -- FICTION
Cremer, A. Invisibility
Invisible. Hautman, P.
Invisible girl. Stone, M. H.
Invisible lines. Amato, M.
Invisible sun. Gill, D. M.
IOWA -- FICTION

Backes, M. M. The princesses of Iowa
Burd, N. The vast fields of ordinary
Kraus, D. Rotters
Kraus, D. Scowler
Smith, A. Grasshopper jungle
Tregay, S. Love & leftovers
Woodson, J. Beneath a meth moon
IRAN -- FICTION
Farizan, S. If you could be mine
Fletcher, S. Alphabet of dreams
Napoli, D. J. Beast
IRAN-IRAQ WAR, 1980-1988 -- FICTION
Mead, A. Dawn and dusk
IRAQ -- FICTION
Ellis, D. No safe place
IRAQ WAR, 2003-2011 -- FICTION
Cerrito, A. The end of the line
Johnson, A. Sweet, hereafter
McCormick, P. Purple Heart
Myers, W. D. Sunrise over Fallujah
Schreck, K. While he was away
Tharp, T. Badd
IRAQ WAR, 2003-2011 -- VETERANS -- DRAMA
Anderson, L. H. The impossible knife of memory
IRELAND -- FICTION
Dowd, S. A swift pure cry
Doyle, R. A greyhound of a girl
Lennon, T. When love comes to town
McBride, R. The fire opal
Melling, O. R. The Hunter's Moon
Melling, O. R. The Light-Bearer's daughter
Melling, O. R. The Summer King
Napoli, D. J. Hush
Parkinson, S. Long story short
Pignat, C. Greener grass
Thompson, K. Creature of the night
Thompson, K. The last of the High Kings
Thompson, K. The new policeman
Thompson, K. The white horse trick
IRISH -- FICTION
Pignat, C. Wild geese
IRISH AMERICANS -- FICTION
Auch, M. J. Ashes of roses
Hamilton, K. R. Tyger tyger
Hamilton, K. When the stars threw down their spears
Myers, W. D. Riot
Iron Codex [series]
Kittredge, C. The Iron Thorn
The **iron codex** [series]
Kittredge, C. The nightmare garden
Ironman; a novel. Crutcher, C.
The **Iron** Thorn. Kittredge, C.
The **iron** witch. Mahoney, K.
Is it night or day? Chapman, F. S.
The **Isabel** factor. Friesen, G.
ISLAMIC FUNDAMENTALISM -- FICTION
Jolin, P. In the name of God
The **island** of excess love. Block, F. L.
The **island.** Paulsen, G.
ISLANDS -- FICTION
Augarde, S. X-Isle
Brooks, K. Lucas
Caletti, D. Stay
Cohn, R. Beta
Cole, S. Z. Raptor
Cooper, M. A brief history of Montmaray
Crewe, M. The way we fall
Halam, A. Dr. Franklin's island
Lanagan, M. The brides of Rollrock Island
Medina, M. Milagros
Moskowitz, H. Teeth
Paulsen, G. The island
Pratchett, T. Nation
Venkatraman, P. Island's end
Island's end. Venkatraman, P.
ISLANDS OF THE ATLANTIC -- FICTION
Coutts, A. Tumble & fall
ISLANDS OF THE PACIFIC -- FICTION
Knox, E. Mortal fire
ISLES OF SHOALS (ME. AND N.H.) -- FICTION
Cornwell, B. Tides
ISRAEL -- FICTION
Elkeles, S. How to ruin a summer vacation
Elkeles, S. How to ruin your boyfriend's reputation
ISRAEL-ARAB CONFLICTS -- FICTION
McKay, S. E. Enemy territory
Zenatti, V. A bottle in the Gaza Sea
ISRAELIS -- FICTION
Elkeles, S. How to ruin my teenage life
It's kind of a funny story. Vizzini, N.
It's not summer without you. Han, J.
It's our prom (so deal with it) Peters, J. A.
ITALIAN AMERICANS -- FICTION
Blundell, J. Strings attached
Freitas, D. The possibilities of sainthood
Napoli, D. J. Alligator bayou
ITALY -- FICTION
Beyer, K. The demon catchers of Milan
ITALY -- HISTORY -- 1559-1789 -- FICTION
Taub, M. Still star-crossed
ITALY -- HISTORY -- 15TH CENTURY -- FICTION
Strauss, V. Passion blue
ITALY -- HISTORY -- 16TH CENTURY -- FICTION
Gould, S. Cross my heart
Ithaka. Geras, A.
Ivy. Hearn, J.
Izzy, willy-nilly. Volponi, P.

J

Jacobs, Harriet A., 1813-1897
Lyons, M. E. Letters from a slave girl
Jacobs, John Hornor
The shibboleth
The twelve-fingered boy
Jacobs, Joseph
Lyons, M. E. Letters from a slave boy
Jacobson, Jennifer, 1958-
The complete history of why I hate her
The **jade** notebook. Resau, L.
Jaden, Denise
Losing Faith
Never enough
Jaffe, Michele
Bad kitty
Rosebush
JAMAICA -- FICTION
Rees, C. Pirates!
James, Rebecca
Beautiful malice
Jango. Nicholson, W.
Janie face to face. Cooney, C. B.
Janie Johnson [series]
Cooney, C. B. Janie face to face
JANITORS -- FICTION
Cohen, T. Little black lies
Jansen, Hanna
Over a thousand hills I walk with you
JAPAN -- FICTION
Sun, A. Ink
JAPAN -- HISTORY -- TO 645 -- FICTION
Friesner, E. Spirit's princess
JAPANESE -- UNITED STATES -- FICTION
Preus, M. Heart of a samurai
JAPANESE AMERICANS -- EVACUATION AND RELOCATION, 1942-1945 -- FICTION
Fitzmaurice, K. A diamond in the desert
Otsuka, J. When the emperor was divine
Patneaude, D. Thin wood walls
Patt, B. Best friends forever; a World War II scrapbook
JAPANESE AMERICANS -- FICTION
Mochizuki, K. Beacon Hill boys
Namioka, L. Mismatch
Salisbury, G. Eyes of the emperor
Salisbury, G. House of the red fish
Salisbury, G. Under the blood-red sun
Jaramillo, Ann
La linea
A **jar** of dreams. Uchida, Y.
Jars of glass. Barkley, B.
Jarzab, Anna
All unquiet things
The opposite of hallelujah
JASON (GREEK MYTHOLOGY) -- FICTION
Friesner, E. M. Nobody's prize
Jazmin's notebook. Grimes, N.
Jasper Jones. Silvey, C.
Jayne, Hannah
Truly, madly, deadly
JAZZ MUSIC -- FICTION
Volponi, P. Hurricane song
Weatherford, C. B. Becoming Billie Holiday
JAZZ MUSICIANS -- FICTION
Townley, R. Sky
JEALOUSY -- FICTION
Anderson, J. L. Tiger Lily
Hautman, P. What boys really want?
JEANS (CLOTHING) -- FICTION
Brashares, A. The sisterhood of the traveling pants
Jellicoe Road. Marchetta, M.
Jenkins, A. M.
Beating heart
Night road
Repossessed
Jennings, Richard W.
Ghost town
Jepp, who defied the stars. Marsh, K.
Jeremy Fink and the meaning of life. Mass, W.
Jersey tomatoes are the best. Padian, M.
JERUSALEM -- FICTION
Gormley, B. Poisoned honey
Kerbel, D. Mackenzie, lost and found
Stroud, J. The ring of Solomon
Jeschonek, Robert T.
My favorite band does not exist
Jessica's guide to dating on the dark side. Fantaskey, B.
Jesus Christ
About
Fletcher, S. Alphabet of dreams
Gormley, B. Poisoned honey
Jet Black and the ninja wind. Lowitz, L.
JEWISH GHETTOS -- FICTION
Sax, A. The war within these walls
JEWISH REFUGEES -- FICTION
Chapman, F. S. Is it night or day?
JEWISH-ARAB RELATIONS -- FICTION
Nye, N. S. Habibi
JEWISH WOMEN -- FICTION
Feldman, R. T. Blue thread
JEWISH-ARAB RELATIONS -- FICTION
Clinton, C. A stone in my hand
JEWS -- ETHIOPIA -- FICTION
Oron, J. Cry of the giraffe
JEWS -- FICTION
Chotjewitz, D. Daniel half human
Kositsky, L. The thought of high windows
Lieberman, L. Lauren Yanofsky hates the

holocaust
North, P. Starglass
Matas, C. After the war
Matas, C. The whirlwind
Ostow, M. Emily Goldberg learns to salsa
Werlin, N. Extraordinary
JEWS -- FRANCE -- FICTION
Meyer, S. Black radishes
Macdonald, M. Odette's secrets
JEWS -- GERMANY -- FICTION
Blankman, A. Prisoner of night and fog
Chapman, F. S. Is it night or day?
Sharenow, R. The Berlin Boxing Club
Whelan, G. After the train
Whitney, K. A. The other half of life
Zusak, M. The book thief
JEWS -- HUNGARY -- FICTION
Clark, K. Guardian angel house
Wiseman, E. Puppet
JEWS -- NETHERLANDS -- FICTION
Polak, M. What world is left
JEWS -- NEW YORK (N.Y.) -- FICTION
Chayil, E. Hush
JEWS -- PERSECUTIONS -- FICTION
Hoffman, A. Incantation
Oron, J. Cry of the giraffe
JEWS -- POLAND -- FICTION
Sax, A. The war within these walls
JEWS -- UNITED STATES -- FICTION
Andrews, J. Me & Earl & the dying girl
Chapman, F. S. Is it night or day?
Gelbwasser, M. Inconvenient
Goelman, A. The path of names
Miklowitz, G. D. The enemy has a face
Meyerhoff, J. Queen of secrets
Ostow, M. So punk rock (and other ways to disappoint your mother)
Pixley, M. Without Tess
Reinhardt, D. The things a brother knows
Rubens, M. Sons of the 613
Wolfson, J. Cold hands, warm heart
Jimenez, Francisco
Breaking through
The circuit : stories from the life of a migrant child
Reaching out
Jinks, Catherine
The abused werewolf rescue group
Babylonne
Evil genius
Genius squad
The genius wars
Living hell
The reformed vampire support group
Joan, of England, 1165-1199
About
Coventry, S. The queen's daughter
Jocelyn, Marthe
Folly
Would you
Joe rat. Barratt, M.
John, Antony
Five flavors of dumb
Johnson, Alaya Dawn
The summer prince
Johnson, Angela
A certain October
Heaven
Sweet, hereafter
Toning the sweep
Johnson, Christine
Claire de Lune
Nocturne
Johnson, Harriet McBryde
Accidents of nature
Johnson, J. J.
The theory of everything
Johnson, Lindsay Lee
Worlds apart
Johnson, LouAnne
Muchacho
Johnson, Maureen
13 little blue envelopes
The madness underneath
The name of the star
Scarlett fever
Suite Scarlett
Johnson, Peter
What happened
Johnson, Varian
Saving Maddie
Johnston, E. K.
Prairie fire
The story of Owen
Jolin, Paula
In the name of God
Jolted; Newton Starker's rules for survival. Slade, A. G.
Jones, Allan Frewin
Destiny's path
Jones, Patrick
Chasing tail lights
The tear collector
Jones, Traci L.
Finding my place
Standing against the wind
Joseph, Lynn
Flowers in the sky
Joseph. Moses, S. P.
JOURNALISM -- FICTION
Bauer, J. Peeled
Clement-Moore, R. Hell Week

Clement-Moore, R. Highway to hell
Doktorski, J. S. Famous last words
Schröder, M. My brother's shadow
Wallace, R. One good punch
Winston, S. The Kayla chronicles
Zeises, L. M. The sweet life of Stella Madison
Zielin, L. Donut days
JOURNALISTS -- FICTION
Ford, J. C. The morgue and me
Myers, W. D. Oh, Snap!
The **journey** back. Cummings, P.
Journey to Topaz; a story of the Japanese-American evacuation. Uchida, Y.
Joyce, Graham, 1954-
The exchange
Juby, Susan
Another kind of cowboy
Getting the girl; a guide to private investigation, surveillance, and cookery
JUDAISM -- FICTION
Chayil, E. Hush
JUDAISM -- RELATIONS -- CHRISTIANITY -- FICTION
Sanders, S. Rachel's secret
Juggling fire. Bell, J.
The **Julian** game. Griffin, A.
The **Juliet** club. Harper, S.
Jump. Carbone, E.
Jumped. Williams-Garcia, R.
Jumped in. Flores-Scott, P.
Jumper cable. Anthony, P.
Jumping off swings. Knowles, J.
Jumping the scratch. Weeks, S.
Jumpstart the world. Hyde, C. R.
JUNIOR HIGH SCHOOLS -- FICTION
Rubens, M. Sons of the 613
Just another hero. Draper, S. M.
Just Ella. Haddix, M. P.
Just for you to know. Harness, C.
Just listen. Dessen, S.
Just one day. Forman, G.
Just one wish. Rallison, J.
JUSTICE -- FICTION
Damico, G. Croak
JUVENILE DELINQUENCY -- FICTION
Beaudoin, S. Wise Young Fool
Dixon, J. Phoenix Island
Goodman, S. Kindness for weakness
Griffin, C. J. Nowhere to run
Griffin, P. Ten Mile River
Mikaelsen, B. Touching Spirit Bear
Volponi, P. Rikers High
Watkins, S. Juvie
JUVENILE DETENTION HOMES -- FICTION
Beaudoin, S. Wise Young Fool
Cummings, P. The journey back
Jacobs, J. H. The twelve-fingered boy
Perez, A. H. The knife and the butterfly
JUVENILE PROSTITUTION -- FICTION
Leavitt, M. My book of life by Angel
Purcell, K. Trafficked
Juvie. Watkins, S.
The **Juvie** three. Korman, G.

K

Kade, Stacey
The ghost and the goth
Queen of the dead
The rules
Kagawa, Julie
The Eternity Cure
The immortal rules
Kamata, Suzanne
Gadget Girl
KANSAS -- FICTION
Moriarty, L. The center of everything
Nadol, J. The mark
Peck, D. Sprout
Wasserman, R. The waking dark
KARATE -- FICTION
Briant, E. Choppy socky blues
Karim, Sheba
Skunk girl
Karma. Ostlere, C.
Karp, Jesse
Those that wake
Kaslik, Ibolya
Skinny
Katcher, Brian
Almost perfect
Playing with matches
Kat got your tongue. Weatherly, L.
Kate, Lauren
The betrayal of Natalie Hargrove
Katerina trilogy [series]
Bridges, R. The gathering storm
Katya's World. Howard, J. L.
KAYAKS AND KAYAKING -- FICTION
Withers, P. First descent
Kaye, Marilyn
Demon chick
The **Kayla** chronicles. Winston, S.
Kearney, Meg
The girl in the mirror
Keeper of the Grail. Spradlin, M. P.
The **Keepers'** tattoo. Arbuthnott, G.
Keeping corner. Sheth, K.
Keeping the castle. Kindl, P.
Keesha's house. Frost, H.
Kehoe, S. W.

The sound of letting go
Keller, Helen, 1880-1968
About
Miller, S. Miss Spitfire
Kelly, Tara
Harmonic feedback
Kempe, Margery, b. ca. 1373
About
Barnhouse, R. The book of the maidservant
Kempe, Margery, b. ca. 1373 -- FICTION
About
Barnhouse, R. The book of the maidservant
Kendra. Booth, C.
Kenneally, Miranda
Racing Savannah
Stealing Parker
KENTUCKY -- FICTION
Mary-Todd, J. Shot down
Mason, B. A. In country
KENYA -- FICTION
Naidoo, B. Burn my heart
Kephart, Beth
Dangerous neighbors
Dr. Radway's Sarsaparilla Resolvent
Going over
The heart is not a size
House of Dance
Nothing but ghosts
Small damages
Undercover
You are my only
Keplinger, Kody
A midsummer's nightmare
Kerbel, Deborah
Mackenzie, lost and found
Kerr, M. E.
Gentlehands
If I love you, am I trapped forever?
Kessler, Jackie Morse
Breath
(jt. auth) Kessler, J. Loss
Loss; Jackie Morse Kessler
Ketchup clouds. Pitcher, A.
Khoury, Jessica
Origin
Kick. Myers, W. D.
A **kid** from Southie. Shea, J.
The **kid** table. Seigel, A.
KIDNAPPING -- FICTION
Berry, J. All the truth that's in me
Blair, J. Leap of Faith
Cooney, C. B. Janie face to face
Cooney, C. B. What Janie found
Cooney, C. B. Whatever happened to Janie?
Draper, S. M. (. M. Panic
Hautman, P. Snatched
Lubar, D. True talents
McDonald, I. Be my enemy
Mahoney, K. The iron witch
Malaghan, M. Greek ransom
Mills, S. The viper within
Rapp, A. The children and the wolves
Rainfield, C. Stained
Skuse, C. J. Rockoholic
Smith, A. Passenger
Williamson, J. Captives
Kiely, Brendan
The gospel of winter
Kiem, Elizabeth
Dancer, daughter, traitor, spy
Kiki. May, K.
Kill me softly. Cross, S.
The **kill** order. Dashner, J.
Killer Pizza. Taylor, G.
Killer Pizza: the slice. Taylor, G.
The **killer's** cousin. Werlin, N.
Killing Mr. Griffin. Duncan, L.
The **killing** woods. Christopher, L.
Kinch, Michael
The fires of New SUN
The rebels of New SUN
Kinch, Michael P.
The blending time
Kincy, Karen
Other
Kindl, Patrice
Keeping the castle
Kindness for weakness. Goodman, S.
Kindred. Stein, T.
King Dork. Portman, F.
The **King** of Attolia. Turner, M. W.
King of Ithaka. Barrett, T.
King of the screwups. Going, K. L.
The **king's** rose. Libby, A. M.
King, A. S.
Ask the passengers
Everybody sees the ants
Glory O'Brien's history of the future
Please ignore Vera Dietz
Reality Boy
King, Anita
King, Stephen, 1947-
Firestarter
The **Kingdom** of little wounds. Cokal, S.
KINGS -- FICTION
Carleson, J. C. The tyrant's daughter
Carson, R. The bitter kingdom
Carson, R. The crown of embers
Castor, H. M. VIII
Chima, C. W. The Crimson Crown
Crossley-Holland, K. Crossing to Paradise
Hartman, R. Seraphina

Johnson, A. D. The summer prince
Klein, L. M. Lady Macbeth's daughter
Libby, A. M. The king's rose
Long, R. F. The treachery of beautiful things
Longshore, K. Gilt
Longshore, K. Tarnish
Maas, S. J. Crown of midnight
McKenzie, N. Guinevere's gamble
Moss, J. Shadow
Reeve, P. Here lies Arthur
Spinner, S. Damosel
Springer, N. I am Mordred
Springer, N. I am Morgan le Fay
Stroud, J. The ring of Solomon
Vande Velde, V. The book of Mordred
Wein, E. E. The lion hunter
Yancey, R. The extraordinary adventures of Alfred Kropp
Yang, D. J. Daughter of Xanadu
Yolen, J. Girl in a cage
Kipling's choice. Spillebeen, G.
Kipling, John, 1897-1915
About
Spillebeen, G. Kipling's choice
Kira. O'Hearn, K.
Kirby, Jessi
Golden
Moonglass
Kirkpatrick, Jane
A flickering light
Kirkpatrick, K.
Between two worlds
Kiss & Make Up. Anderson, K. D.
A **kiss** in time. Flinn, A.
Kiss me again. Vail, R.
Kiss. Wilson, J.
Kissing doorknobs. Hesser, T. S.
KISSING -- FICTION
Vail, R. Kiss me again
Kissing the bee. Koja, K.
Kissing the rain. Brooks, K.
Kit's wilderness. Almond, D.
The **kite** rider. McCaughrean, G.
KITES -- FICTION
McCaughrean, G. The kite rider
Kittle, Katrina
Reasons to be happy
Kittredge, Caitlin
The Iron Thorn
The nightmare garden
Kizer, Amber
A matter of days
Meridian
Wildcat fireflies
The Klaatu Diskos [series]
Hautman, P. The Cydonian pyramid
Hautman, P. The obsidian blade
Hautman, P. The klaatu terminus
Klass, David
Firestorm
You don't know me
Klass, Sheila Solomon
Soldier's secret
Klause, Annette Curtis
Blood and chocolate
The silver kiss
Klein, Lisa M.
Cate of the Lost Colony
Lady Macbeth's daughter
Ophelia
Kluger, Steve
My most excellent year
The **knife** and the butterfly. Perez, A. H.
The **knife** of never letting go. Ness, P.
The **knife** that killed me. McGowan, A.
Knifepoint. Van Tol, A.
Knight, Karsten
Embers & echoes
KNIGHTS AND KNIGHTHOOD
Bell, H. The last knight
Springer, N. I am Morgan le Fay
KNIGHTS AND KNIGHTHOOD -- FICTION
Cadnum, M. The book of the Lion
Grant, K. M. Blue flame
Grant, K. M. Paradise red
Grant, K. M. White heat
Morris, G. The squire's tale
Pierce, T. First test
Sandell, L. A. Song of the sparrow
Vande Velde, V. The book of Mordred
Williamson, J. By darkness hid
Williamson, J. To darkness fled
Knights of the hill country. Tharp, T.
KNOTS AND SPLICES -- FICTION
Bow, E. Sorrow's knot
Knowles, Jo
Jumping off swings
Living with Jackie Chan
See you at Harry's
Knox, Elizabeth
Dreamhunter
Dreamquake
Mortal fire
Knutsson, Catherine
Shadows cast by stars
Koertge, Ronald
Lies, knives and girls in red dresses
Margaux with an X
Now playing
Shakespeare makes the playoffs
Stoner & Spaz
Strays
Koja, Kathe
Buddha boy

Headlong
Kissing the bee
Konigsberg, Bill
Openly straight
Konigsburg, E. L.
Silent to the bone
Kontis, Alethea
Enchanted
Kooistra, Alison
(ed) Leap
KOREA -- FICTION
Choi, S. N. Year of impossible goodbyes
KOREAN AMERICANS -- FICTION
Min, K. Secondhand world
Na, A. A step from heaven
Na, A. Wait for me
Williams, L. E. Slant
Yoo, P. Good enough
Korman, Gordon
The Juvie three
Son of the mob
Son of the mob: Hollywood hustle
Kositsky, Lynne
The thought of high windows
Kostick, Conor
Edda
Epic
Saga
Koss, Amy Goldman
Poison Ivy
Side effects
Kraus, Daniel
Rotters
Scowler
Krisher, Trudy
Fallout
Krokos, Dan
False memory
Krovatin, Christopher
Heavy metal and you
Kuehn, Stephanie
Charm & strange
Complicit
Kwasney, Michelle D.
Blue plate special

L

L'Engle, Madeleine
A wrinkle in time
A **la** carte. Davis, T. S.
The **Lab.** Heath, J.
La linea. Jaramillo, A.
Laban, Elizabeth
The Tragedy Paper
LABYRINTHS -- FICTION
Goelman, A. The path of names
Lackey, Mercedes
To light a candle
When darkness falls
LaCour, Nina
The Disenchantments
Everything leads to you
Hold still
Lady Macbeth's daughter. Klein, L. M.
LaFaye, A.
Stella stands alone
LaFevers, Robin
Dark triumph
Grave mercy
Mortal hearts
Laird, Elizabeth
The betrayal of Maggie Blair
A little piece of ground
Lake, Nick
Blood ninja II: the revenge of Lord Oda
Hostage Three
In darkness
Lake of secrets. Littke, L.
LAKES -- FICTION
Les Becquets, D. Season of ice
Lam, Laura
Pantomime
Lanagan, Margo
The brides of Rollrock Island
Tender morsels
Lancaster, Mike A.
The future we left behind
Human.4
The **land.** Taylor, M. D.
The **Landing.** Ibbitson, J.
Lane, Andrew
Black ice
Rebel fire
Langdon Prep novel [series]
Reid, K. My own worst frenemy
Lange, Erin Jade
Butter
Langrish, Katherine
The shadow hunt
The **language** inside. Thompson, H.
LANGUAGES -- VOCABULARY
See Vocabulary
LANGUEDOC (FRANCE) -- HISTORY -- 13TH CENTURY -- FICTION
Grant, K. M. Paradise red
Lara's gift. O'Brien, A.
LARAMIE (WYO.) -- FICTION
Leslea, N. October mourning
Larbalestier, Justine
(jt. auth) Brennan, S. R. Team Human
How to ditch your fairy
Liar
Magic lessons

Magic or madness
Lark. Porter, T.
Larson, Kirby
Hattie Big Sky
Hattie ever after
LAS VEGAS (NEV.) -- FICTION
Hautman, P. All-in
Jaffe, M. Bad kitty
Laskas, Gretchen Moran
The miner's daughter
Lasky, Kathryn
Ashes
Chasing Orion
Hawksmaid
Lone wolf
The **last** book in the universe. Philbrick, W. R.
Last chance for Paris. McNicoll, S.
Last Child. Spooner, M.
The **last** Dragonslayer. Fforde, J.
The **last** echo. Derting, K.
The **last** exit to normal. Harmon, M. B.
The **last** forever. Caletti, D.
The **last** good place of Lily Odilon. Beitia, S.
The **last** knight. Bell, H.
The **last** mall rat. Esckilsen, E. E.
The **last** mission. Mazer, H.
Last night I sang to the monster. Sáenz, B. A.
The **last** of the High Kings. Thompson, K.
The **last** report on the miracles at Little No Horse. Erdrich, L.
The **last** sister. McKinney-Whitaker, C.
Last shot. Feinstein, J.
The **last** summer of the death warriors. Stork, F. X.
The **latent** powers of Dylan Fontaine. Lurie, A.
The **lathe** of heaven. Le Guin, U. K.
LATIN AMERICANS -- NEW YORK (STATE) -- NEW YORK -- FICTION
Rice-Gonzalez, C. Chulito
LATIN AMERICANS -- UNITED STATES -- FICTION
Ada, A. F. Yes! we are Latinos
The **Latte** Rebellion. Stevenson, S. J.
Lauren Yanofsky hates the holocaust. Lieberman, L.
Lavender, William
Aftershocks
Lawrence, Caroline
The case of the deadly desperados
Lawlor, Laurie
Dead reckoning; a pirate voyage with Captain Drake
He will go fearless
The two loves of Will Shakespeare
Lawson, Mary
Crow Lake
LAWYERS -- FICTION
Grant, V. Quid pro quo
Grant, V. Res judicata
Patron, S. Behind the masks
Le Guin, Ursula K.
The farthest shore
Gifts
The lathe of heaven
The left hand of darkness
Powers
Voices
A wizard of Earthsea
Leap. Egloff, Z.
Leap.
Leap of Faith. Blair, J.
LEARNING DISABILITIES -- FICTION
Flake, S. G. Pinned
Walters, E. Special Edward
Wolff, V. E. Probably still Nick Swansen
Learning to fly. Yee, P.
Leaving Fishers. Haddix, M. P.
Leaving Jetty Road. Burton, R.
Leaving Protection. Hobbs, W.
Leavitt, Lindsey
Going vintage
Leavitt, Lindsey
Sean Griswold's head
Leavitt, Martine
My book of life by Angel
LEBANESE -- FICTION
Abdel-Fattah, R. Ten things I hate about me
Lebbon, Tim
Golden, C. The wild
Lecesne, James
Absolute brightness
Lee, Harper, 1926-
To kill a mockingbird
Lee, Tanith
Piratica
Piratica II: return to Parrot Island
Lee, Ying S.
The body at the tower
A spy in the house
LeFlore, Lyah
The world is mine
The **left** hand of darkness. Le Guin, U. K.
The legacy of Moonset [series]
Tracey, S. Darkbound
Tracey, S. Moonset
Legacy of the clockwork key. Bailey, K.
Legend. Lu, M.
Legend [series]
Lu, M. Prodigy
Leitch, Will
Catch
Lena. Woodson, J.

Leonard, Julia Platt
Cold case
Lennon, Tom
When love comes to town
Leroux, Gaston
The phantom of the opera
Les Becquets, Diane
Love, Cajun style
Season of ice
LESBIANS -- FICTION
Bigelow, L. J. Starting from here
Charlton-Trujillo, E. E. Fat Angie
Danforth, E. M. The miseducation of Cameron Post
George, M. The difference between you and me
Hegamin, T. M +O 4evr
Lo, M. Adaptation
Peters, J. A. It's our prom (so deal with it)
Rainfield, C. Scars
Ryan, S. Empress of the world
Woodson, J. From the notebooks of Melanin Sun
Leslea, Newman
October mourning
Lessing, Doris May
The sweetest dream
Lester, Joan Steinau
Black, white, other
Lester, Julius
Day of tears
Guardian
Time's memory
LETTERS -- FICTION
Beard, P. Dear Zoe
Buckhanon, K. Upstate
Chbosky, S. The perks of being a wallflower
Handler, D. Why we broke up
Harper, S. The Juliet club
Lyons, M. E. Letters from a slave boy,
Lyons, M. E. Letters from a slave girl,
Pitcher, A. Ketchup clouds **Fi**
Price, N. Zoe letting go **Fi**
Whitman, S. The milk of birds
Zenatti, V. A bottle in the Gaza Sea
Letters from a slave boy; the story of Joseph Jacobs. Lyons, M. E.
Letters from a slave girl; the story of Harriet Jacobs. Lyons, M. E.
Letters from Wolfie. Sherlock, P.
Letters to my mother. Cardenas, T.
Letting Ana go.
LEUKEMIA -- FICTION
Andrews, J. Me & Earl & the dying girl
Schwartz, E. Cellular
Wylie, S. All these lives
Levchuk, Lisa
Everything beautiful in the world
Leverage. Cohen, J. C.
Levine, Ellen, 1939-2012
In trouble
Levine, Gail Carson, 1947-
Ella enchanted
Ever
Fairest
Levithan, David
(jt. auth) Cohn, R. Dash & Lily's book of dares
(jt. auth). Naomi and Ely's no kiss list
(jt. auth) Nick & Norah's infinite playlist
(jt. auth) Cremer, A. Invisibility
Every you, every me
Every day
Green, J. Will Grayson, Will Grayson
Love is the higher law
Marly's ghost
Two boys kissing
Levitin, Sonia
Strange relations
LEWIS AND CLARK EXPEDITION (1804-1806) -- FICTION
Bruchac, J. Sacajawea
Wolf, A. New found land; Lewis and Clark's voyage of discovery
Lewis, Joshua
(ed) The Shadowhunter's codex
Lewis, Stewart
The secret ingredient
Lewis, Sylvia
Beautiful decay
Lexicon. Barry, M.
LeZotte, Ann Clare
T4
Lia's guide to winning the lottery. David, K.
Liar. Larbalestier, J.
The **Liar** Society. Roecker, L.
The **Liar** Society [series]
Roecker, L. The lies that bind
Liar's moon. Bunce, E. C.
Libby, Alisa M.
The king's rose
Liberator. Harland, R.
Liberty, Anita
The center of the universe
LIBRARIES -- FICTION
Portman, F. Andromeda Klein
Libyrinth. North, P.
LIE. Bock, C.
Lieberman, Leanne
Lauren Yanofsky hates the holocaust
The **lies** that bind. Roecker, L.
Lies, knives and girls in red dresses.
Life. Peet, M.

Life, after. Littman, S.
LIFE -- FICTION
Life as we knew it. Pfeffer, S. B.
LIFE CHANGE EVENTS -- FICTION
Egloff, Z. Leap
Life eternal. Woon, Y.
Life happens next. Trueman, T.
Life is fine. Whittenberg, A.
Life is funny. Frank, E. R.
The **life** of glass. Cantor, J.
LIFE ON OTHER PLANETS -- FICTION
McCaffrey, A. Dragonflight
Revis, B. Shades of Earth
Lifeblood. Becker, T.
LIFESAVING -- FICTION
Pratchett, T. Dodger
Lifted. Toliver, W.
LIGHT -- FICTION
Defy the dark
The **light** in the forest. Richter, C.
Light years. Stein, T.
The **Light-Bearer's** daughter. Melling, O. R.
The **lighter** side of life and death. Martin, C. K. K.
LIGHTNING -- FICTION
Bosworth, J. Struck
The **Lightning** Dreamer. Engle, M.
Like Mandarin. Hubbard, K.
Like sisters on the homefront. Williams-Garcia, R.
Like the red panda. Seigel, A.
Lily of the Nile. Dray, S.
The **Limping** Man. Gee, M.
Likely story. Van Etten, D.
Lindskold, Jane M.
Thirteen orphans
The **Line.** Hall, T.
Linger. Stiefvater, M.
LINGUISTS -- FICTION
Barry, M. Lexicon
The **lion** hunter. Wein, E. E.
The **lions** of Little Rock. Levine, K.
Lipsyte, Robert
The contender
One fat summer
Raiders night
Lirael, daughter of the Clayr. Nix, G.
The **list.** Vivian, S.
Lisle, Holly
The Ruby Key
Listening for lions. Whelan, G.
LISTS -- FICTION
Leavitt, L. Going vintage
LITERACY -- FICTION
Crossley-Holland, K. Crossing to Paradise
LITHUANIA -- FICTION
Sepetys, R. Between shades of gray
LITIGATION -- FICTION
Davis, L. I swear
LITTERING *See* Refuse and refuse disposal
Littke, Lael
Lake of secrets
Little, Kimberley Griffiths
Circle of secrets
The healing spell
Little (grrl) lost. De Lint, C.
Little black lies. Cohen, T.
Little brother. Doctorow, C.
A **little** friendly advice. Vivian, S.
A **little** piece of ground. Laird, E.
A **little** wanting song. Crowley, C.
Little, Brown & Co. Inc.
Littman, Sarah
Life, after
Live through this. Scott, M.
The **lives** we lost. Crewe, M.
The **living.** De la Peña, M.
Living dead girl. Scott, E.
Living hell. Jinks, C.
Living violet. Reed, J.
Living with Jackie Chan. Knowles, J.
Livvie Owen lived here. Dooley, S.
Lizard love. Townsend, W.
Lizzie Bright and the Buckminster boy. Schmidt, G. D.
Llewellyn, Sam
Darksolstice
The well between the worlds
Lloyd, Alison
Year of the tiger
Lloyd, Saci
The carbon diaries 2015
The carbon diaries 2017
Lo, Malinda
Adaptation
Ash
Huntress
Inheritance
LOBSTERS -- FICTION
Lock and key. Dessen, S.
Lockdown. Myers, W. D.
Lockdown. Smith, A. G.
Locked in time. Duncan, L.
Lockhart, E.
The boy book
The boyfriend list
The disreputable history of Frankie Landau-Banks
Dramarama
How to be bad
Real live boyfriends
The treasure map of boys

We were liars
Logue, Mary
Hautman, P. Snatched
Lola and the boy next door. Perkins, S.
LONDON (ENGLAND) -- FICTION
Clare, C. Clockwork prince
Pollock, T. The city's son
Reeve, P. Scrivener's moon
Smith, A. Passenger
Valentine, J. Double
Zettel, S. Palace of Spies
LONDON (ENGLAND) -- HISTORY -- 18TH CENTURY -- FICTION
Zettel, S. Palace of Spies
LONDON (ENGLAND) -- HISTORY -- 19TH CENTURY -- FICTION
Bailey, K. Legacy of the clockwork key
Clare, C. Clockwork angel
Clare, C. Clockwork prince
Clare, C. Clockwork princess
Gleason, C. The clockwork scarab
Hooper, M. Velvet
Pratchett, T. Dodger
London, A.
Guardian
London, Jack, 1876-1916
About
Golden, C. The sea wolves
Golden, C. The wild
The call of the wild
White Fang
LONELINESS -- FICTION
Schreck, K. While he was away
Lone wolf. Lasky, K.
Long may she reign. White, E. E.
Long story short. Parkinson, S.
A **long** walk to water. Park, L. S.
A **Long** Way from Home. Walsh, A.
Long, Ruth Frances
The treachery of beautiful things
Longshore, Katherine
Gilt
Tarnish
Looking for Alaska. Green, J.
Looks. George, M.
The **lord** of Opium. Farmer, N.
Lord Tophet. Frost, G.
Looking for Lucy Buick. Murphy, R.
Lord Loss. Shan, D.
Lord of the deep. Salisbury, G.
LOS ANGELES (CALIF.) -- FICTION
Block, F. L. Dangerous angels
Block, F. L. Love in the time of global warming
Bosworth, J. Struck
Castellucci, C. Beige
Castellucci, C. Boy proof
De la Pena, M. Ball don't lie
Lewis, S. The secret ingredient
Purcell, K. Trafficked
Yee, L. Absolutely Maybe
Losers in space. Barnes, J.
Losing Faith. Jaden, D.
Loss. Kessler, J.
LOSS (PSYCHOLOGY) -- FICTION
Baskin, N. R. All we know of love
Brooks, K. Lucas
Galante, C. The summer of May
Johnson, J. J. The theory of everything
Kephart, B. Nothing but ghosts
A monster calls
Schindler, H. Playing hurt
Stein, T. High dive
The **lost** art. Morden, S.
Lost girl found. Bassoff, L.
Lost. Davies, J.
The **lost** years of Merlin. Barron, T. A.
LOST AND FOUND POSSESSIONS -- FICTION
Huntley, A. The everafter
The **lost** crown. Miller, S.
Lost in the river of grass. Rorby, G.
Lost in the sun. Graff, L.
Lost in time. De la Cruz, M.
Lost voices. Porter, S.
LOTTERY WINNERS -- FICTION
David, K. Lia's guide to winning the lottery
Louis XVII, of France, 1785-1795
About
Donnelly, J. Revolution
LOUISIANA -- FICTION
Les Becquets, D. Love, Cajun style
LOVE -- FICTION
Clement-Davies, D. The sight
Sones, S. What my mother doesn't know
Love, D. Anne
Semiprecious
Love & leftovers. Tregay, S.
Love letters to the dead. Dellaira, A.
Love & lies. Wittlinger, E.
Love me. Shukert, R.
LOVE -- FICTION
Buzo, L. Love and other perishable items
Caletti, D. The last forever
Charbonneau, J. Independent study
Cremer, A. Invisibility
Dickerson, M. The merchant's daughter
Joseph, L. Flowers in the sky
Kenneally, M. Racing Savannah
LaCour, N. Everything leads to you
Lockhart, E. We were liars
Lu, M. Champion
Maizel, R. Stolen nights
Myers, W. D. Carmen

Myers, W. D. Street love
Paulsen, G. Crush; the theory, practice, and destructive properties of love
Vernick, S. R. The blood lie
Weatherly, L. Angel burn
LOVE AFFAIRS -- FICTION
Gordimer, N. My son's story
Love and other perishable items. Buzo, L.
Love in the time of global warming. Block, F. L.
Love is the higher law. Levithan, D.
LOVE STORIES
Anderson, J. L. Tiger Lily
Ashton, B. Everbound
Ashton, B. Everneath
Balog, C. Sleepless
Barkley, B. Dream factory
Barkley, B. Scrambled eggs at midnight
Black, H. Black heart
Blankman, A. Prisoner of night and fog
Block, F. L. The frenzy
Bosworth, J. Struck
Brennan, S. R. Team Human
Briant, E. I am (not) the walrus
Carey, J. L. Dragonswood
Chan, G. A foreign field
Chapman, L. Flawless
Clare, C. Clockwork princess
Cohn, R. Beta
Cohn, R. Dash & Lily's book of dares
Colasanti, S. Something like fate
Cole, K. Poison princess
Cooney, C. B. Janie face to face
Cornwell, B. Tides
Coutts, A. Tumble & fall
Cross, J. Tempest
Derting, K. The last echo
DeStefano, L. Sever
Doller, T. Something like normal
Fichera, L. Hooked
Fiedler, L. Romeo's ex
Fink, M. The summer I got a life
Fitzpatrick, H. My life next door
Forman, G. Just one day
Garcia, K. Beautiful creatures
Garcia, K. Beautiful darkness
Gier, K. Emerald green
Grant, K. M. Paradise red
Gratton, T. The blood keeper
Gray, C. Spellcaster
Green, J. The fault in our stars
Griffin, P. Burning blue
Hale, S. Book of a thousand days
Hamilton, K. When the stars threw down their spears
Han, J. We'll always have summer
Haydu, C. A. OCD love story
Hemphill, S. Sisters of glass
Hodge, R. Cruel Beauty
Hoffman, M. The falconer's knot
Horner, E. A love story starring my dead best friend
Howells, A. The summer of skinny dipping
Hubbard, A. Ripple
Kagawa, J. The immortal rules
Kehoe, S. W. The sound of letting go
Kindl, P. Keeping the castle
King, A. S. Ask the passengers
Kirby, J. Golden
Koja, K. Kissing the bee
Laban, E. The Tragedy Paper
LaFevers, R. Grave mercy
Lam, L. Pantomime
Larbalestier, J. Team Human
Levithan, D. Every day
Lo, M. Ash
Lo, M. Huntress
Lo, M. Inheritance
Madison, B. September Girls
Martin, C. K. K. I know it's over
McCaughrean, G. Cyrano
McGarry, K. Dare You to
McGarry, K. Pushing the limits
Miller, K. All you desire
Miller, K. The eternal ones
Mont, E. M. A breath of Eyre
Morgan, P. The beautiful and the cursed
Myers, W. D. Amiri & Odette
Myracle, L. The infinite moment of us
Nowlin, L. If he had been with me
O'Connell, T. True love, the sphinx, and other unsolvable riddles; a comedy in four voices
Ockler, S. The Book of Broken Hearts
Oppel, K. Such wicked intent
Parker, A. C. Gated
Plum, A. Die for me
Pratchett, T. Dodger
Reed, A. Crazy
Reed, J. Living violet
Rennison, L. The taming of the tights
Ross, E. Belle epoque
Roth, V. Allegiant
Rothenberg, J. The catastrophic history of you & me
Rowell, R. Eleanor & Park
Scheidt, E. L. Uses for boys
Schindler, H. Playing hurt
Schreck, K. While he was away
Scott, K. This is so not happening
Selfors, S. Mad love
Selfors, S. The sweetest spell
Shirvington, J. Entice
Simone Upgrade U

Smith, E. W. Back when you were easier to love
Smith, J. E. The statistical probability of love at first sight
Smith, J. E. This is what happy looks like
Soto, G. Accidental love
Standiford, N. The boy on the bridge
Stiefvater, M. Forever
Stiefvater, M. The Scorpio Races
Stone, T. I. Time between us
Sun, A. Ink
Taub, M. Still star-crossed
Taylor, L. Daughter of smoke and bone
Tregay, S. Love & leftovers
Trueman, T. Life happens next
Trumble, J. H. Don't let me go
Vail, R. Kiss me again
Walker, K. 7clues to winning you
Walton, L. The Strange and beautiful sorrows of Ava Lavender
West, K. Pivot point
West, K. Split second
Weyn, S. Reincarnation
Williams, G. Beatle meets Destiny
Woon, Y. Life eternal
Yang, D. J. Daughter of Xanadu
Zarr, S. Sweethearts

A **love** story starring my dead best friend. Horner, E.
Love you hate you miss you. Scott, E.
Love, Cajun style. Les Becquets, D.
Love, D. Anne
Defying the diva
The lovely shoes. Shreve, S.
Low, Dene
The entomological tales of Augustus T. Percival
LOWER EAST SIDE (NEW YORK, N.Y.) -- FICTION
Brothers, M. Supergirl mixtapes
Lowitz, Leza
Jet Black and the ninja wind
Lowry, Lois
Gathering blue
The giver
Son
LOYALTY -- FICTION
Charbonneau, J. Graduation day
Roth, V. Allegiant
Lu, Marie
Champion
Legend
Prodigy
Lubar, David
Hidden talents
Sleeping freshmen never lie
True talents
Lucas. Brooks, K.
Lucid. Bass, R.
Lucier, Makiia
A death-struck year
Lucky fools. Voorhees, C.
The **lucky** place. Vincent, Z.
The **Lucy** variations. Zarr, S.
The **lucky** kind. Sheinmel, A. B.
Lucky. Vail, R.
Luddy, Karon
Spelldown
Luedeke, Lisa
Smashed
Lulu Dark and the summer of the Fox; a mystery. Madison, B.
Lumatere chronicles [series]
Marchetta, M. Quintana of Charyn
LUMBEE INDIANS -- FICTION
Klein, L. M. Cate of the Lost Colony
Luna. Peters, J. A.
Lunch-box dream. Abbott, T.
Lundgren, Jodi
Leap
Luper, Eric
Bug boy
Seth Baumgartner's love manifesto
Lupica, Mike
The batboy
The big field
Hero
Miracle on 49th Street
Summer ball
Lurie, April
The latent powers of Dylan Fontaine
Lush. Friend, N.
Lyga, Barry
The astonishing adventures of Fanboy & Goth Girl
Boy toy
Game
Goth girl rising
Hero-type
I hunt killers
The **lying** game. Shepard, S.
The Lynburn legacy [series]
Brennan, S. R. Unspoken
Lynch, Chris, 1962-
Angry young man
The Big Game of Everything
Casualties of war
Hothouse
Inexcusable
Pieces
Lynch, Janet Nichols
My beautiful hippie
LYNCHING -- FICTION
Lester, J. Guardian
Lyne, Jennifer H.

Catch rider
Lynn Visible. DeVillers, J.
Lyon, Steve
The gift moves
Lyons, Mary E.
Letters from a slave boy; the story of Joseph Jacobs
Letters from a slave girl; the story of Harriet Jacobs

M

M +O 4evr. Hegamin, T.
M or F? Papademetriou, L.
Maas, Sarah J.
Crown of midnight
Throne of glass
Maberry, Jonathan
Dust & decay
Rot & ruin
Mac Slater hunts the cool Bancks, T.
Mac Slater vs. the city Bancks, T.
Macbeth, King of Scotland, d. 1057
About
Klein, L. M. Lady Macbeth's daughter
MacColl, Michaela
Nobody's secret
Prisoners in the palace
Promise the night
MacCready, Robin Merrow
Buried
MacCullough, Carolyn
Always a witch
Drawing the ocean
Once a witch
Stealing Henry
MacDonald, Anne Louise
Seeing red
Macdonald, Maryann
Odette's secrets
MacHale, D. J.
The pilgrims of Rayne
Raven rise
Storm
SYLO
Maciel, A.
Tease
Mackall, Dandi Daley
Eva underground
The silence of murder
Mackel, Kathy
Boost
Mackenzie, lost and found. Kerbel, D.
Mackey, Weezie Kerr
Throwing like a girl
Mackler, Carolyn
(jt. auth) Asher, J. The future of us
The earth, my butt, and other big, round things
Guyaholic
Tangled
Vegan virgin Valentine
MacLean, Jill
Nix Minus One
The nine lives of Travis Keating
Mad love. Selfors, S.
A **Mad**, wicked folly. Waller, S. B..
Madapple. Meldrum, C.
Madden, Kerry
Gentle's Holler
Madigan, L. K.
Flash burnout
The mermaid's mirror
Madison, Bennett
Lulu Dark and the summer of the Fox; a mystery
September Girls
The **madman** of Venice. Masson, S.
The **madman's** daughter. Shepherd, M.
The **madness** underneath. Johnson, M.
MAFIA -- FICTION
Blumenthal, D. Mafia girl
Goeglein, T. M. Cold fury
Mafia girl. Blumenthal, D.
Maggot moon. Gardner, S.
MAGIC -- FICTION
Bardugo, L. Shadow and bone
Bell, H. Traitor's son
Bow, E. Plain Kate
Bow, E. Sorrow's knot
Brennan, C. House of the star
Bunce, E. C. A curse dark as gold
Carson, R. The bitter kingdom
Carson, R. The crown of embers
Chima, C. W. The enchanter heir
Constable, K. The singer of all songs
Dennard, S. Something strange and deadly
Doyle, M. Courtship and curses
Fforde, J. The last Dragonslayer
Fforde, J. The song of the Quarkbeast
Flinn, A. Cloaked
Foxlee, K. The midnight dress
Friesner, E. M. Spirit's princess
Frost, G. Lord Tophet
Funke, C. Reckless
Garvey, A. Glass Heart
Gratton, T. The blood keeper
Gray, C. Steadfast
Hamilton, K. When the stars threw down their spears
Harris, J. Runemarks
Hodge, R. Cruel Beauty
Kontis, A. Enchanted
Lam, L. Pantomime

Lanagan, M. The brides of Rollrock Island
Larbalestier, J. How to ditch your fairy
Mahoney, K. The iron witch
Malchow, A. The Sword of Darrow
Marillier, J. Shadowfell
Masson, S. Snow, fire, sword
Medina, M. Milagros
Meloy, M. The apprentices
Moloney, J. The Book of Lies
Morris, G. The squire's tale
Mosley, W. 47
Neff, H. H. The hound of Rowan
O'Neal, E. The false princess
O'Neal, E. Torn
O'Rourke, E. Tangled
Pollock, T. The city's son
Rudnick, P. Gorgeous
Sanderson, B. The Rithmatist
The Shadowhunter's codex
Siegelson, K. L. Honey Bea
Stiefvater, M. The raven boys
Thomas, S. The burning sky
Tracey, S. Darkbound
Tunnell, M. O. Wishing moon
Vande Velde, V. Stolen
Walsh, P. The Crowfield curse
Walsh, P. The Crowfield demon
White, A. B. Forget -her-nots
Wilson, N. D. The dragon's tooth
Wooding, C. Havoc
Wrede, P. C. Across the Great Barrier
Magic. Zettle, S.
Magic can be murder. Vande Velde, V.
The **magic** circle. Napoli, D. J.
Magic lessons. Larbalestier, J.
Magic of Xanth [series]
Anthony, P. A spell for chameleon
Magic or madness. Larbalestier, J.
MAGIC TRICKS -- FICTION
Goelman, A. The path of names
Magic under glass. Dolamore, J.
The **Magician** of Hoad. Mahy, M.
MAGICIANS -- FICTION
Chima, C. W. The Crimson Crown
Wilson, J. The alchemist's dream
Magnin, Joyce
Carrying Mason
Magoon, Kekla
37 things I love (in no particular order)
Camo girl
Fire in the streets
How it went down
The rock and the river
Maguire, Gregory
Egg & Spoon
Mah, Adeline Yen
Chinese Cinderella and the Secret Dragon Society
Mahoney, Karen
The iron witch,
Mahy, Margaret
The Magician of Hoad
MAINE -- FICTION
Blagden, S. Dear Life, You Suck
Brennan, S. R. Team Human
Frank, H. The view from the top
Griffin, N. The whole stupid way we are
Jacobson, J. The complete history of why I hate her
Les Becquets, D. Season of ice
Oliver, L. Delirium
Oliver, L. Requiem
Smith, J. E. This is what happy looks like
Walker, B. F. Black boy/white school
Wunder, W. The probability of miracles
Maizel, Rebecca
Infinite days
Stolen nights
Make lemonade. Wolff, V. E.
Malaghan, Michael
Greek ransom
Malchow, Alex
The Sword of Darrow
Maldonado, Torrey
Secret Saturdays
Malley, Gemma
The Declaration
The resistance
Malice. Wooding, C.
Mallory, James
Lackey, M. To light a candle
Lackey, M. When darkness falls
Malloy, Brian
The year of ice
Mamba Point. Scaletta, K.
MANATEES -- FICTION
Monninger, J. Hippie chick
MAN-WOMAN RELATIONSHIP -- FICTION
Alexander, K. He said, she said
Calame, D. Call the shots
Handler, D. Why we broke up
Mangum, L. After hello
McGarry, K. Dare You to
Peterfreund, D. For darkness shows the stars
Rossi, V. Under the never sky
MANCHESTER (ENGLAND) -- FICTION
Burgess, M. The hit
Mancusi, Mari
Scorched
Manga touch. Pearce, J.
A **mango** -shaped space. Mass, W.
Mangum, Lisa

After hello
MANIC-DEPRESSIVE ILLNESS -- FICTION
Michaels, R. Nobel genes
Selfors, S. Mad love
Turner, A. W. Father of lies
MANITOBA -- FICTION
Brooks, M. Queen of hearts
Buffie, M. Winter shadows
Manivong, Laura
Escaping the tiger
Mankell, Henning
A bridge to the stars
Shadow of the leopard
Manning, Sarra
Guitar girl
Mantchev, Lisa
Eyes like stars
Perchance to dream
So silver bright
Manzano, Sonia
The revolution of Evelyn Serrano
MAORIS -- FICTION
Healey, K. Guardian of the dead
The **map** of the sky. Palma, F. J.
The **Marbury** lens. Smith, A.
Marcelo in the real world. Stork, F. X.
Marchetta, Melina
Finnikin of the rock
Froi of the exiles
Jellicoe Road
The piper's son
Quintana of Charyn
Saving Francesca
Mare's war. Davis, T. S.
Margaux with an X. Koertge, R.
The **Margrave.** Fisher, C.
Marillier, Juliet
Child of the prophecy
Cybele's secret
Daughter of the forest
Raven flight
Shadowfell
Son of the shadows
Wildwood dancing
MARIN COUNTY (CALIF.) -- FICTION
Collomore, A. The ruining
Marina. Ruiz Zafon, C.
MARINE POLLUTION -- FICTION
Nelson, B. They came from below
Marino, Peter
Dough Boy
Mariz, Rae
The Unidentified
The **mark.** Nadol, J.
The **mark** of the golden dragon. Meyer, L. A.
Markandaya, Kamala
Nectar in a sieve
Marcus, Kimberly
Exposed
Marlowe, Christopher, 1564-1593
About
Silbert, L. The intelligencer
Marly's ghost. Levithan, D.
Marr, Melissa
Darkest mercy
Fragile eternity
Ink exchange
Radiant shadows
Wicked lovely
MARRIAGE -- FICTION
Kindl, P. Keeping the castle
MARRIAGE PROBLEMS -- FICTION
Min, K. Secondhand world
Marriott, Zoe
The swan kingdom
MARS (PLANET) -- FICTION
Gill, D. M. Invisible sun
Gill, D. M. Shadow on the sun
Under the moons of Mars
Marsden, Carolyn, 1950-
My Own Revolution
Sahwira; an African friendship
Marsden, John
Marsden, J. Tomorrow, when the war began
Hamlet: a novel
Incurable
The other side of dawn
While I live
Marsh, Katherine
Jepp, who defied the stars
The night tourist
Marshall, Catherine
Christy
MARTIAL ARTS -- FICTION
Skilton, S. Bruised
Mah, A. Y. Chinese Cinderella and the Secret Dragon Society
Wild, K. Fight game
Martin, Ann M., 1955-
Here today
Martin, C. K. Kelly
I know it's over
The lighter side of life and death
Yesterday
Martin, T. Michael
The end games
Martinez, Jessica
Virtuosity
Martinez, Victor
Parrot in the oven
Martino, Alfred C.
Over the end line

Mary Magdalene, Saint
About
Gormley, B. Poisoned honey
Mary, Blessed Virgin, Saint
About
Grimes, N. A girl named Mister
Mary-Todd, Jonathan
Shot down
MARYLAND -- FICTION
Cummings, P. Blindsided
Cummings, P. The journey back
LeFlore, L. The world is mine
Lyga, B. Hero-type
Moore, K. Amber House
Moore, K. Neverwas
Naylor, P. R. Intensely Alice
MASCULINITY -- FICTION
Rubens, M. Sons of the 613
Masked. McClintock, N.
Mason, Bobbie Ann
In country
Masquerade. De la Cruz, M.
Mass, Wendy
Heaven looks a lot like the mall
Jeremy Fink and the meaning of life
A mango -shaped space
MASSACHUSETTS -- FICTION
Dana, B. A voice of her own
Friend, N. For keeps
Konigsberg, B. Openly straight
Reinhardt, D. A brief chapter in my impossible life
Sales, L. Mostly good girls
Thompson, H. The language inside
Tiernan, C. Immortal beloved
Wittlinger, E. Love & lies
MASSACRES -- FICTION
Chima, C. W. The enchanter heir
Massey, David
Torn
Masson, Sophie
The madman of Venice
Snow, fire, sword
The **Master** of Misrule. Powell, L.
Master, Irfan
A beautiful lie
Mastiff. Pierce, T.
Matched. Condie, A. B.
Matas, Carol
After the war
The whirlwind
MATHEMATICIANS -- FICTION
Wilson, J. The alchemist's dream
MATHEMATICS -- FICTION
Green, J. An abundance of Katherines
Moranville, S. B. A higher geometry
Matson, Morgan
Amy & Roger's epic detour
Second chance summer
Since you've been gone
A **matter** of days. Kizer, A.
A **matter** of souls. Patrick, D.L.
Matthew, the Apostle, Saint
About
Gormley, B. Poisoned honey
Matthews, Andrew
The way of the warrior
Matthews, L. S.
The outcasts
Mattison, Booker T.
Unsigned hype
MATURATION (PSYCHOLOGY) -- FICTION
Buzo, L. Love and other perishable items
Maximum Ride: the angel experiment. Patterson, J.
May, Kyla
Kiki
Mayall, Beth
Mermaid Park,
MAYAS -- FICTION
Raedeke, C. The daykeeper's grimoire
The **maze.** Hobbs, W.
The **maze** runner. Dashner, J.
Mazer, Harry
A boy at war; a novel of Pearl Harbor
The last mission
Snow bound
Mazer, Norma Fox
After the rain
Girlhearts
MAZUNTE (MEXICO) -- FICTION
Resau, L. The jade notebook
McBay, Bruce
Waiting for Sarah
McBride, Lish
Hold me closer, necromancer
McBride, Regina
The fire opal
McCafferty, Megan
Bumped
Thumped
McCaffrey, Anne
Dragonflight
Dragon's kin
McCaffrey, Todd J.
McCaffrey, A. Dragon's kin
Dragongirl
McCahan, Erin
I now pronounce you someone else
Mccall, Guadalupe Garcia
Under the mesquite
McCarry, Sarah

All our pretty songs
McCarthy, Maureen
Rose by any other name
McCarthy, Susan Carol
True fires
McCaughrean, Geraldine
Cyrano
The death -defying Pepper Roux
The glorious adventures of the Sunshine Queen
The kite rider
Not the end of the world
The white darkness
McClintock, Norah
Masked
Taken
McClymer, Kelly
Must love black
McCormick, Patricia
Cut
My brother's keeper
Never fall down
Purple Heart
Sold
McDaniel, Lurlene
Breathless
Hit and run
McDevitt, Jack
Moonfall
McDonald, Abby
The anti-prom
Boys, bears, and a serious pair of hiking boots
McDonald, Ian
Be my enemy
Empress of the sun
Planesrunner
McDonald, Janet
Chill wind
Harlem Hustle
Off-color
McDonnell, Margot
Torn to pieces
McEntire, Myra
Hourglass
McGarry, Katie
Dare You to
Pushing the limits
McGhee, Alison
All rivers flow to the sea
McGowan, Anthony
The knife that killed me
McGowan, Keith
The witch's guide to cooking with children
McGuigan, Mary Ann
Morning in a different place
McKay, Hilary
Saffy's angel
McKay, Sharon E.
Enemy territory
Thunder over Kandahar
McKenzie, Nancy
Grail prince
Guinevere's gamble
Guinevere's gift
McKernan, Victoria
The devil's paintbox
Shackleton's stowaway
McKinley, Robin
Beauty
The blue sword
Chalice
Dragonhaven
The hero and the crown
Pegasus
Rose daughter
McKinney-Whitaker, C.
The last sister
McKinnon, Hannah Roberts
The properties of water
McKissack, Fredrick
Shooting star
McLaren, Clemence
Inside the walls of Troy
McLaughlin, Lauren
Scored
McLoughlin, Jane
At Yellow Lake
McMann, Lisa
Cryer's Cross
Fade
Wake
McMullan, Margaret
Cashay
Sources of light
McNamee, Eoin
The Navigator
McNamee, Graham
Acceleration
Beyond
Bonechiller
McNaughton, Janet
An earthly knight
McNeal, Laura
Dark water
The decoding of Lana Morris
Zipped
McNeal, Tom
Far far away
McNeal, L. The decoding of Lana Morris
McNeal, L. Zipped
McNicoll, Sylvia
Last chance for Paris
McNish, Cliff

Angel
McPhee, Peter
New blood
McQuein, Josin L.
Arclight
McQuerry, Maureen Doyle
The Peculiars
McVoy, Terra Elan
After the kiss
Pure
McWilliams, Kelly
Doormat
Me & death. Scrimger, R.
Me & Earl & the dying girl. Andrews, J.
Me, him, them, and it. Carter, C.
Me, the missing, and the dead. Valentine, J.
Mead, Alice
Dawn and dusk
Swimming to America
MEANING (PHILOSOPHY) -- FICTION
Nothing
Mebus, Scott
Gods of Manhattan
Mecum, Ryan
Zombie haiku
MEDICAL CARE -- FICTION
Bryce, C. Anthem for Jackson Dawes
Forman, G. If I stay
Jocelyn, M. Would you
Massey, D. Torn
Wells, D. Fragments
Wells, D. Partials
MEDICAL ETHICS -- FICTION
Pearson, M. E. Fox forever
MEDICAL GENETICS -- FICTION
Applegate, K. Eve & Adam
MEDICAL NOVELS
Whaley, J. C. Noggin
MEDICATION ABUSE -- FICTION
Whitney, D. The rivals
MEDICINE -- RESEARCH -- FICTION
Wells, D. Partials
Medina, Meg
Milagros; girl from Away
Yaqui Delgado wants to kick your ass
MEDIUMS
Salerni, D. K. We hear the dead
MEDUSA (GREEK MYTHOLOGY)
Childs, T. L. Sweet venom
Halam, A. Snakehead
Meehan, Kierin
Hannah's winter
Meehl, Brian
You don't know about me
Meehl, Brian
Suck it up
You don't know about me
Meldrum, Christina
Madapple
Melling, O. R.
The book of dreams
The Hunter's Moon
The Light-Bearer's daughter
The Summer King
Meloy, Colin
Wildwood
Under Wildwood
Meloy, Maile
The apothecary
The apprentices
Melting stones. Pierce, T.
Memento Nora. Smibert, A.
Meminger, Neesha
Shine, coconut moon
Memories of Summer. White, R.
Memoirs of a teenage amnesiac. Zevin, G.
MEMORY -- FICTION
Miranda, M. Hysteria
Patrick, C. Forgotten
Rainfield, C. Scars
Richards, N. D. Six months later
Terry, T. Fractured
Terry, T. Slated
Weeks, S. Jumping the scratch
West, K. Split second
MENTAL ILLNESS -- FICTION
Fischer, J. An egg on three sticks
White, R. Memories of Summer
MENTAL ILLNESS -- FICTION
Anthony, J. Chopsticks
Cardi, A. The chance you won't return
Collomore, A. The ruining
Halpern, J. Have a nice day
Hesser, T. S. Kissing doorknobs
Kuehn, S. Complicit
Reed, A. Crazy
Shepherd, M. The madman's daughter
Vaught, S. Freaks like us
MENTALLY ILL -- FICTION
White, R. Memories of Summer
MENTALLY ILL -- INSTITUTIONAL CARE -- FICTION
Hubbard, J. R. Try not to breathe
MENTORING -- FICTION
McMullan, M. Cashay
Myers, W. D. All the right stuff
MERCENARY TROOPS -- FICTION
Dixon, J. Phoenix Island
The **merchant's** daughter. Dickerson, M.
Mercian triology [series]
Wignall, K. J. Blood
Meridian. Kizer, A.

MERLIN (LEGENDARY CHARACTER)
Barron, T. A. The lost years of Merlin
McKenzie, N. Guinevere's gamble
Mermaid Park. Mayall, B.
The **mermaid's** mirror. Madigan, L. K.
MERMAIDS AND MERMEN -- FICTION
Dunmore, H. Ingo
Madison, B. September Girls
Moskowitz, H. Teeth
Porter, S. Lost voices
Merlin's dragon. Barron, T. A.
Mesrobian, Carrie
Sex and violence
Messed up. Nichols, J.
METAPHYSICS -- FICTION
Kittredge, C. The nightmare garden
METEORITES -- FICTION
Kraus, D. Scowler
METHAMPHETAMINE -- FICTION
Arcos, C. Out of reach
Woodson, J. Beneath a meth moon
Metz, Melinda
Burns, L. J. Crave
Metzger, Lois
A trick of the light
The **museum** of intangible things. Wunder, W.
Mexican whiteboy. de la Peña, M.
MEXICAN AMERICANS -- FICTION
Castan, M. The price of loyalty
Johnson, L. Muchacho
Volponi, P. Homestretch
Sáenz, B. A. Aristotle and Dante discover the secrets of the universe
Quintero, I. Gabi, a girl in pieces
MEXICAN-AMERICANS -- FICTION
Jimenez, F. Breaking through
Jimenez, F. The circuit : stories from the life of a migrant child
Mccall, G. G. Under the mesquite
Sáenz, B. A. Aristotle and Dante discover the secrets of the universe
MEXICANS -- FICTION
Hobbs, W. Crossing the wire
Jaramillo, A. La linea
Restrepo, B. Illegal
MEXICO -- FICTION
Resau, L. The jade notebook
Meyer, Carolyn
Duchessina
The true adventures of Charley Darwin
Meyer, L. A.
Bloody Jack
Curse of the blue tattoo
In the belly of The Bloodhound
The mark of the golden dragon
Mississippi Jack
My bonny light horseman
Rapture of the deep
Under the Jolly Roger
Viva Jacquelina!
The wake of the Lorelei Lee
Meyer, Carolyn
Beware, Princess Elizabeth
Cleopatra confesses
Duchessina; a novel of Catherine de' Medici
Meyer, Marissa, 1984-
Cinder
Cress
Scarlet
Meyer, Stephenie
Breaking dawn
Eclipse
New moon
Twilight
Meyer, Susan
Black radishes
Meyerhoff, Jenny
Queen of secrets
Meyers, Odette
About
Macdonald, M. Odette's secrets
MIAMI (FLA.) -- FICTION
Knight, K. Embers & echoes
Michael, Jan
City boy
Michaelis, Antonia
The dragons of darkness
Tiger moon
Michaels, Rune
Genesis Alpha
Nobel genes
The reminder
Michaux, Lewis H., 1885-1976
About
Nelson, Vaunda Michaux. No crystal stair
MICHIGAN -- FICTION
Ford, J. C. The morgue and me
Jones, P. Chasing tail lights
Jones, P. The tear collector
McCahan, E. I now pronounce you someone else
Potter, R. Exit strategy
Willey, M. A summer of silk moths
MIDDLE AGES -- FICTION
Cadnum, M. The book of the Lion
Clement-Davies, D. The sight
Grant, K. M. Blood red horse
Jinks, C. Babylonne
MIDDLE AGES -- FICTION
Coats, J. A. The wicked and the just
MIDDLE EAST -- FICTION
Carleson, J. C. The tyrant's daughter

MIDDLE EAST -- POLITICS AND GOVERNMENT -- FICTION
Carleson, J. C. The tyrant's daughter
The **middle** of everywhere. Polak, M.
MIDDLE SCHOOLS -- FICTION
Castan, M. Fighting for Dontae
Gilman, C. Professor Gargoyle
Myers, W. D. A star is born
Midnight charter. Whitley, D.
The **midnight** dress. Foxlee, K.
A **midsummer's** nightmare. Keplinger, K.
The **Midnight** Palace. Ruiz Zafon, C. 1964-
The **midnight** twins. Mitchard, J.
MIDWIVES -- FICTION
O'Brien, C. M. Birthmarked
Vega, D. Fact of life #31
Miéville, China, 1972-
Railsea
Un Lun Dun
MIGRANT LABOR -- FICTION
Jimenez, F. Breaking through
Jimenez, F. The circuit : stories from the life of a migrant child
Mikaelsen, Ben
Ghost of Spirit Bear
Touching Spirit Bear
Miklowitz, Gloria D.
The enemy has a face
Milagros; girl from Away. Medina, M.
MILAN (ITALY) -- FICTION
Beyer, K. The demon catchers of Milan
The **miles** between. Pearson, M.
Miles from ordinary. Williams, C. L.
Milford, Kate
The Boneshaker
The Broken Lands
MILITARY BASES -- FICTION
Elkeles, S. How to ruin your boyfriend's reputation
Whyman, M. Icecore
MILITARY EDUCATION -- FICTION
Efaw, A. Battle dress
MILITARY PERSONNEL -- UNITED STATES -- FICTION
Doller, T. Something like normal
The **milk** of birds. Whitman, S.
Millard, Glenda
A small free kiss in the dark
Miller, Ashley Edward
Colin Fischer
Miller, Kirsten
All you desire; can you trust your heart?
The eternal ones
How to lead a life of crime
Miller, Sarah
The lost crown
Miss Spitfire
Miller, Walter M.
A canticle for Leibowitz
Miller-Lachmann, Lyn
Gringolandia
A **million** suns. Revis, B.
Mills, Sam
The viper within
Mills, Tricia
Heartbreak river
Minato, K.
Confessions
Min, Katherine
Secondhand world
Minchin, Adele
The beat goes on
Mind games [series]
White, K. Perfect lies
Mindblind. Roy, J. R.
MINERS -- FICTION
Gill, D. M. Black hole sun
The **minister's** daughter. Hearn, J.
MINNESOTA -- FICTION
Casanova, M. Frozen
Delsol, W. Stork
Malloy, B. The year of ice
Rubens, M. Sons of the 613
Schindler, H. Playing hurt
Sorrells, W. Whiteout
Weaver, W. Checkered flag cheater
Weaver, W. Defect
Weaver, W. Full service
Weaver, W. Saturday night dirt
Weaver, W. Super stock rookie
Zielin, L. Donut days
Miracle on 49th Street. Lupica, M.
Miracle. Scott, E.
The **miracle** stealer. Connelly, N. O.
Miracle's boys. Woodson, J.
MIRACLES -- FICTION
Connelly, N. O. The miracle stealer
Erdrich, L. The last report on the miracles at Little No Horse
Meldrum, C. Madapple
Wunder, W. The probability of miracles
Miranda, Megan
Hysteria
Mirrorscape. Wilks, M.
The **miseducation** of Cameron Post. Danforth, E. M.
Misfit. Skovron, J.
Misguided angel. De la Cruz, M.
Mismatch. Namioka, L.
Miss Fortune Cookie. Bjorkman, L.
Miss Peregrine's home for peculiar children. Riggs, R.

Miss Spitfire. Miller, S.
Missing Angel Juan. Block, F. L.
MISSING CHILDREN -- FICTION
Anthony, J. Chopsticks
Bowler, T. Frozen fire
Hartnett, S. What the birds see
Massey, D. Torn
Valentine, J. Double
The **missing** girl. Mazer, N. F.
MISSING PERSONS -- FICTION
Bilen, T. What she left behind
Collins, P. J. S. What happened to Serenity?
Crockett, S. D. After the snow
Crutcher, C. Period 8
Dubosarsky, U. The golden day
Flinn, A. Cloaked
Goeglein, T. M. Cold fury
Grant, V. Quid pro quo
Hautman, P. The obsidian blade
Low, D. The entomological tales of Augustus T. Percival
Masson, S. The madman of Venice
McMann, L. Cryer's Cross
Meloy, C. Wildwood
Miklowitz, G. D. The enemy has a face
Moriarty, J. The cracks in the kingdom
Resau, L. The jade notebook
Roecker, L. The lies that bind
Rosoff, M. Picture me gone
Sedgwick, M. She is not invisible
Suma, N. R. 17 & gone
Vaught, S. Freaks like us
Vrettos, A. M. Sight
Westerfeld, S. So yesterday
MISSISSIPPI -- RACE RELATIONS
Crowe, C. Mississippi trial, 1955
Mississippi Jack. Meyer, L. A.
MISSISSIPPI RIVER -- FICTION
Meyer, L. A. Mississippi Jack
Mississippi trial, 1955. Crowe, C.
MISSOURI -- FICTION
Katcher, B. Almost perfect
Katcher, B. Playing with matches
Milford, K. The Boneshaker
MISTAKEN IDENTITY -- FICTION
Maguire, G. Egg & spoon
Mister Creecher. Priestly, C.
Mister Death's blue-eyed girls. Hahn, M. D.
Mister Monday; Keys to the kingdom. Nix, G.
Mistik Lake. Brooks, M.
Mistle child. Berk, A.
Mistwood. Cypess, L.
Mitchard, Jacquelyn
All we know of heaven
The midnight twins
Mitchell, David
Black swan green
Mitchell, Saundra
(ed) Defy the dark
The vespertine
Mitchell, Todd
The secret to lying
Mlawski, Shana
Hammer of witches
Mlynowski, Sarah
Don't even think about it
Lockhart, E. How to be bad
Gimme a call
Ten things we did (and probably shouldn't have)
Mochizuki, Ken
Beacon Hill boys
The **Mockingbirds.** Whitney, D.
Mockingjay. Collins, S.
MOHAWK INDIANS -- FICTION
Carvell, M. Sweetgrass basket
Carvell, M. Who will tell my brother?
MOLDOVANS -- UNITED STATES -- FICTION
Purcell, K. Trafficked
Molloy, Michael
Peter Raven under fire
Moloney, James
Black taxi
The Book of Lies
Monaghan, Annabel
A girl named Digit
MONASTERIES -- FICTION
Walsh, P. The Crowfield curse
Walsh, P. The Crowfield demon
MONASTICISM AND RELIGIOUS ORDERS -- FICTION
Miller, W. M. A canticle for Leibowitz
MONEY -- FICTION
Rich, S. Elliot Allagash
Money run. Heath, J.
MONEYMAKING PROJECTS -- FICTION
Coker, R. Chasing Jupiter
MONKS -- FICTION
Thompson, R. City of cannibals
Whitcomb, L. The Fetch
Monninger, Joseph
Finding somewhere
Hippie chick
Wish
Monster. Myers, W. D.
Monster blood tattoo [series]
Cornish, D. M. Factotum
Cornish, D. M. Foundling
A **monster** calls.
MONSTERS -- FICTION
Aguirre, A. Horde
Aguirre, A. Outpost

Bardugo, L. Shadow and bone
Bardugo, L. Siege and storm
Cornish, D. M. Factotum
Gilman, C. Professor Gargoyle
Golden, C. The sea wolves
Hawkins, R. School spirits
McNamee, G. Bonechiller
Poblocki, D. The random child
Scott, M. The enchantress
Smith, C. L. Feral nights
Yancey, R. The final descent
Monsters of men. Ness, P.
The **monstrumologist.** Yancey, R.
Monstrumologist [series]
Yancey, R. The curse of the Wendigo
Yancey, R. The final descent
Mont, Eve Marie
A breath of Eyre
MONTANA -- FICTION
Danforth, E. M. The miseducation of Cameron Post
Harmon, M. B. The last exit to normal
Ingold, J. Hitch
Larson, K. Hattie Big Sky
Price, C. The interrogation of Gabriel James
Montmorency. Updale, E.
Montmorency and the assassins. Updale, E.
Montmorency on the rocks. Updale, E.
Montmorency's revenge. Updale, E.
MONTREAL (QUEBEC) -- FICTION
Woon, Y. Life eternal
MONTSÉGUR (FRANCE) -- HISTORY -- 13TH CENTURY -- FICTION
Grant, K. M. Paradise red
The **moon** and more. Dessen, S.
Moon over Manifest. Vanderpool, C.
Moonfall. McDevitt, J.
Moonglass. Kirby, J.
Moonset. Tracey, S.
Moonshine express; with a history of moonshine today and yesterday. Norville, R.
MOONSHINING -- FICTION
Norville, R. Moonshine express; with a history of moonshine today and yesterday
Moore, Carley
The stalker chronicles
Moore, Derrick
Always upbeat / All that
Moore, Kelley
Amber House
Neverwas
Moore, Perry
Hero
Moore, Peter
Red moon rising
V is for villian
Moore, Stephanie Perry
(jt. auth) Moore, D. Always upbeat / All that
Moran, Katy
Bloodline
Bloodline rising
Moranville, Sharelle Byars
A higher geometry
Morden, Simon
The lost art
MORDRED (LEGENDARY CHARACTER)
Springer, N. I am Mordred
Vande Velde, V. The book of Mordred
More than this. Ness, P.
Morel, Alex
Survive
MORGAN LE FAY (LEGENDARY CHARACTER)
McKenzie, N. Guinevere's gamble
Springer, N. I am Morgan le Fay
Morgan, Nicola
The highwayman's footsteps
Morgan, Page
The beautiful and the cursed
Morgenroth, Kate
Echo
The **morgue** and me. Ford, J. C.
Moriarty, Jaclyn
A corner of white
The cracks in the kingdom
The ghosts of Ashbury High
The year of secret assignments
Moriarty, Laura
The center of everything
Moribito; Guardian of the Spirit. Uehashi, N.
Moribito II; Guardian of the Darkness. Uehashi, N.
MORMONS -- FICTION
Hopkins, E. Burned
Hopkins, E. Smoke
Smith, E. W. Back when you were easier to love
Morning in a different place. McGuigan, M. A.
Morpurgo, Michael
An elephant in the garden
Half a man
Private Peaceful
Morris, Gerald
The squire's tale
Morris, Paula
Ruined
Morrison, Toni
Sula
Mortal fire. Knox, E.

Mortal hearts. LaFevers, R.
The mortal instruments [series]
Clare, C. City of ashes
Clare, C. City of bones
Clare, C. City of Glass
Clare, C. City of lost souls
Morton-Shaw, Christine
The riddles of Epsilon
Moskowitz, Hannah
Break
Teeth
Moses, Shelia P.
Joseph
The legend of Buddy Bush
Mosley, Walter
Fortunate son
47
Moss, Jenny
Shadow
Mostly good girls. Sales, L.
Mother, mother. Zailckas, K.
MOTHER-CHILD RELATIONSHIP -- FICTION
Lowry, L. Son
Zailckas, K. Mother, mother
MOTHER-DAUGHTER RELATIONSHIP -- FICTION
Applegate, K. Eve & Adam
Blythe, C. Revenge of a not-so-pretty girl
Bosworth, J. Struck
Bowers, L. Beauty shop for rent; --fully equipped, inquire within
Brothers, M. Supergirl mixtapes
Casanova, M. Frozen
Cheng, A. Brushing Mom's hair
Cohn, R. Gingerbread
Collins, Y. The new and improved Vivien Leigh Reid; diva in control
Collins, Y. Now starring Vivien Leigh Reid: Diva in training
Crockett, S. D. One Crow Alone
Doyle, R. A greyhound of a girl
Farish, T. The good braider
Fischer, J. An egg on three sticks
Galante, C. The summer of May
Goldblatt, S. Stray
Goto, H. Half World
Haddix, M. P. Full ride
Harmel, K. When you wish
Kamata, S. Gadget Girl
Kirby, J. Golden
Lessing, D. M. The sweetest dream
Mazer, N. F. After the rain
Medina, M. Milagros
Min, K. Secondhand world
Moriarty, L. The center of everything
Oates, J. C. Freaky green eyes
Palmer, R. The Corner of Bitter and Sweet
Reed, A. Over you
Resau, L. The jade notebook
Sepetys, R. Out of the Easy
Simmons, K. Article 5
Singleton, L. J. Dead girl in love
Stevenson, R. H. Escape velocity
White, A. B. Forget -her-nots
Whittenberg, A. Life is fine
Wollman, J. Switched
Zailckas, K. Mother, mother
Zarr, S. How to save a life
MOTHER-SON RELATIONSHIP -- FICTION
Grant, V. Quid pro quo
Grant, V. Res judicata
Lupica, M. The batboy
Moses, S. P. Joseph
Whitney, D. When you were here
Woodson, J. From the notebooks of Melanin Sun
MOTHERS
Fusco, K. N. Tending to Grace
MOTHERS -- FICTION
Brooks, M. Mistik Lake
Doyle, R. Wilderness
Lewis, S. The secret ingredient
Lowry, L. Son
Martin, A. M. Here today
Michaels, R. The reminder
Williams, L. E. Slant
MOTHS -- FICTION
Willey, M. A summer of silk moths
MOFICTION PICTURES -- FICTION
Castellucci, C. Boy proof
MOTION PICTURES -- PRODUCTION AND DIRECTION -- FICTION
Crawford, B. Carter's big break
Doctorow, C. Pirate cinema
Pauley, K. Cat Girl's day off
Moulton, Courtney Allison
Angelfire
Mountain pose. Wilson, N. H.
Mountain solo. Ingold, J.
MOUNTAINEERING -- FICTION
Smith, R. Peak
MOUNTAINS -- FICTION
Wyatt, M. Funny how things change
Mourlevat, Jean-Claude
Winter's end
The **mourning** wars. Steinmetz, K.
MOVING -- FICTION
Chen, J. Return to me
Colasanti, S. So much closer
Elston, A. The rules for disappearing
Fehlbaum, B. Big fat disaster

Friend, N. Bounce
Hepler, H. The cupcake queen
Jones, T. L. Finding my place
King, A. S. Ask the passengers
Newbery, L. Flightsend
Patrick, C. Revived
Preller, J. Bystander
Schraff, A. E. A boy called Twister
Stanley, G. E. Night fires
Thompson, H. The language inside
Williams, S. D. Palace beautiful
Mowll, Joshua
Operation Red Jericho
Operation Storm City
Operation typhoon shore
MOZAMBIQUE -- FICTION
Mankell, H. Shadow of the leopard
Muchacho. Johnson, L.
Muckers. Wallace, S. N.
Mulder, Michelle
Out of the box
Muller, Rachel Dunstan
Squeeze
Mulligan, Andy
Trash
Mullin, Mike
Ashfall
Sunrise
MULTIPLE SCLEROSIS -- FICTION
Leavitt, L. Sean Griswold's head
MUMMIES -- FICTION
Dowd, S. Bog child
MUNICH (GERMANY) -- HISTORY -- 20TH CENTURY -- FICTION
Blankman, A. Prisoner of night and fog
HOMICIDE -- FICTION
Shepherd, M. Her Dark Curiosity
HOMICIDE VICTIMS
Crowe, C. Mississippi trial, 1955
Murdoch, Emily
If you find me
Murdock, Catherine Gilbert
Dairy Queen
Front and center
The off season
Princess Ben
Wisdom's kiss
Murphy, Claire Rudolf
Free radical
Murphy, Jim
Desperate journey
Murphy, Rita
Looking for Lucy Buick
Murray, Martine
How to make a bird
Murray, Yxta Maya
The good girl's guide to getting kidnapped
MUSEUMS -- FICTION
Golds, C. The museum of Mary Child
MUSIC -- FICTION
Hartman, R. Seraphina
McCarry, S. All our pretty songs
Trevayne, E. Coda
Zalben, J. B. Four seasons
MUSIC INDUSTRY -- FICTION
LeFlore, L. The world is mine
MUSICALS -- FICTION
Boyd, M. Will
Ruditis, P. The four Dorothys
Wood, M. My life the musical
The **musician's** daughter. Dunlap, S. E.
MUSICIANS -- FICTION
Anthony, J. Chopsticks
McCormick, P. Never fall down
Yolen, J. Troll Bridge; a rock 'n' roll fairy tale
MUSLIMS -- FICTION
Clinton, C. A stone in my hand
Fama, E. Overboard
Hayes, R. Payback
Mussi, Sarah
The door of no return
Must love black. McClymer, K.
MUTATION (BIOLOGY) -- FICTION
Reeve, P. Scrivener's moon
My beautiful hippie. Lynch, J. N.
My big mouth. Hannan, P.
My bonny light horseman. Meyer, L. A.
My book of life by Angel. Leavitt, M.
My brother, my sister, and I. Watkins, Y. K.
My brother's keeper. McCormick, P.
My brother's shadow. Schröder, M.
My chemical mountain. Vacco, C.
My contract with Henry. Vaupel, R.
My favorite band does not exist. Jeschonek, R. T.
My heartbeat. Freymann-Weyr, G.
My invented life. Bjorkman, L.
My life in black and white. Friend, N.
My life the musical. Wood, M.
My life, the theater, and other tragedies. Zadoff, A.
My life next door. Fitzpatrick, H.
My life undecided. Brody, J.
My misadventures as a teenage rock star. Raskin, J.
My most excellent year. Kluger, S.
My mother the cheerleader. Sharenow, R.
My name is not easy. Edwardson, D. D.
My name is Parvana. Ellis, D.
My Own Revolution. Marsden, C.
My own worst frenemy. Reid, K.
My perfect life. Sheldon, D.

My sister lives on the mantelpiece. Pitcher, A.
My son's story. Gordimer, N.
My swordhand is singing. Sedgwick, M.
Myers, Anna
Assassin
The grave robber's secret
Spy!
Tulsa burning
Myers, Edward
Storyteller
Myers, Walter Dean
Amiri & Odette; a love story
A star is born
All the right stuff
Carmen; an urban adaptation of the opera
The Cruisers
Darius & Twig
Dope sick
Fallen angels
Game
Harlem summer
Hoops
Invasion!
Kick
Lockdown
Monster
Oh, Snap!
Riot
Scorpions
Slam!
Street love
Sunrise over Fallujah
Myracle, Lauren
Lockhart, E. How to be bad
Myracle, L. Shine
Bliss
The infinite moment of us
Peace, love, and baby ducks
Shine
TTYL
MYSTERY FICTION
Anthony, J. Chopsticks
Archer, J. Through her eyes
Armistead, C. Being Henry David
Arnold, T. Rat life
Avi City of orphans
Baratz-Logsted, L. Twin's daughter
Beaudoin, S. You killed Wesley Payne
Beaufrand, M. J. The river
Beitia, S. The last good place of Lily Odilon
Berk, J. Guy Langman, crime scene procrastinator
Bernard, R. Find me
Blundell, J. What I saw and how I lied
Bradbury, J. Wrapped
Bray, L. The diviners
Bray, L. A great and terrible beauty
Bray, L. Rebel angels
Bray, L. The sweet far thing
Brennan, S. R. Unspoken
Brooks, K. Black Rabbit summer
Bunce, E. C. Liar's moon
Coben, H. Seconds away
Coben, H. Shelter
Collins, B. Always watching
Cox, S. The Dead Girls Detective Agency
Crutcher, C. Period 8
Damico, G. Croak
Daugherty, C. J. Night School
Davies, A. Identity Theft
Derting, K. The body finder
Doyle, M. Courtship and curses
Dubosarsky, U. The golden day
Dunlap, S. E. The musician's daughter
Ellen, L. Blind spot
Ellison, K. The butterfly clues
Fantaskey, B. Buzz kill
Feinstein, J. Last shot
Ferguson, A. The Christopher killer
Ferguson, A. The circle of blood
Ferguson, A. The dying breath
FitzGerald, H. Deviant
Ford, J. C. The morgue and me
Forster, M. City of a Thousand Dolls
Foxlee, K. The midnight dress
Fredericks, M. The girl in the park
Gagnon, M. Strangelets
Giles, L. Fake ID
Gilman, D. Blood sun
Gilman, D. Ice claw
Gleason, C. The clockwork scarab
Goeglein, T. M. Cold fury
Goelman, A. The path of names
Gould, S. Cross my heart
Grant, V. Quid pro quo
Grant, V. Res judicata
Gratz, A. Something rotten
Green, J. Paper towns
Griffin, P. Burning blue
Haas, A. Dangerous girls
Hahn, M. D. The girl is trouble
Hahn, M. D. Mister Death's blue-eyed girls
Haines, K. M. The girl is murder
Harvey, A. Haunting Violet
Hautman, P. Snatched
Healey, K. The shattering
Herrick, S. Cold skin
Hiaasen, C. Skink
Higgins, F. E.The Eyeball Collector
Jinks, C. The abused werewolf rescue group
Jaffe, M. Bad kitty
Jaffe, M. Rosebush

Jarzab, A. All unquiet things
Jinks, C. The reformed vampire support group
Johnson, M. The madness underneath
Juby, S. Getting the girl
Kirby, J. Golden
Kuehn, S. Charm & strange
Lawrence, C. P.K. Pinkerton and the petrified man
Lee, Y. S. The body at the tower
Lee, Y. S. A spy in the house
Lo, M. Adaptation
Lyga, B. Game
Lyga, B. I hunt killers
MacColl, M. Nobody's secret
Mackall, D. D. The silence of murder
Madison, B. Lulu Dark and the summer of the Fox
Martin, C. K. K. Yesterday
McClintock, N. Masked
McLoughlin, J. At Yellow Lake
McMann, L. Cryer's Cross
McNamee, G. Acceleration
Miller, A. E. Colin Fischer
Moloney, J. Black taxi
Moore, K. Amber House
Mulligan, A. Trash
Nixon, J. L. Nightmare
Osterlund, A. Aurelia
Parker, R. B. The boxer and the spy
Parker, R. B. The Edenville Owls
Patron, S. Behind the masks
Pauley, K. Cat Girl's day off
Peacock, S. Death in the air
Peacock, S. The dragon turn
Peacock, S. Eye of the crow
Peacock, S. The secret fiend
Peacock, S. Vanishing girl
Perez, M. Dead is a killer tune
Poblocki, D. The nightmarys
Reichs, K. J. Virals
Reid, K. My own worst frenemy
Renn, D. Tokyo heist
Roecker, L. The Liar Society
Rosenfield, K. Amelia Anne is dead and gone
Rosoff, M. Picture me gone
Ruiz Zafon, C. Marina
Ryan, A. K. Spark
Samms, O. Sketchy
Schrefer, E. The deadly sister
Scieszka, J. Who done it?
Sedgwick, M. She is not invisible
Sepetys, R. Out of the Easy
Shepard, S. The lying game
Shoemaker, T. Back before dark
Silbert, L. The intelligencer
Silvey, C. Jasper Jones
Sorrells, W. First shot
Sorrells, W. Whiteout
Stewart, A. Dragonwood
Suma, N. R. Dani noir
Summers, C. Fall for anything
Tharp, T. Mojo
Thomas, E. Boarder patrol
Tucholke, A. G. Between the devil and the deep blue sea
Valentine, J. Double
Vaught, S. Freaks like us
Volponi, P. Rucker Park setup
Wells, R. Feedback
Westerfeld, S. So yesterday
Weyn, S. Dr. Frankenstein's daughters
Wolf, J. S. Breaking beautiful
Zusak, M. I am the messenger
The **mystery** of the third Lucretia. Runholt, S.
MYTHICAL ANIMALS -- FICTION
Behemoth
Golding, J. Secret of the sirens
Leviathan
Thompson, K. The last of the High Kings
Westerfeld, S. Goliath

N

Na, An
A step from heaven
Wait for me
Nader, Elisa
Escape from Eden
Nadin, Joanna
Wonderland
Nadol, Jen
The mark
The vision
Naidoo, Beverley
Burn my heart
Nakahama, Manjiro, 1827-1898
About
Preus, M. Heart of a samurai
The **name** of the star. Johnson, M.
NAMIBIA -- FICTION
Gilman, D. The devil's breath
The **Naming.** Croggon, A.
Namioka, Lensey
Mismatch
An ocean apart, a world away
Nance, Andrew
Daemon Hall
Return to Daemon Hall: evil roots
Nanji, Shenaaz
Child of dandelions
NANNIES -- FICTION
Collomore, A. The ruining

Nantucket blue. Howland, L.
NANTUCKET ISLAND (MASS.) -- FICTION
Howland, L. Nantucket blue
Naomi and Ely's no kiss list. Cohn, R.
Napoli, Donna Jo
Alligator bayou
Beast
Bound
The great god Pan
Hush
The magic circle
The smile
Storm
The wager
NARCISSISTS -- FAMILY RELATIONSHIPS -- FICTION
Zailckas, K. Mother, mother
NASHVILLE (TENN.) -- FICTION
Supplee, S. Somebody everybody listens to
Naslund, Sena Jeter
Four spirits
NATCHITOCHES (LA.) -- FICTION
Elston, A. The rules for disappearing
Nation. Pratchett, T.
NATIONAL SOCIALISM -- FICTION
Bartoletti, S. C. The boy who dared
Chotjewitz, D. Daniel half human
Dowswell, P. The Auslander
Falkner, B. The project
Lasky, K. Ashes
Sharenow, R. The Berlin Boxing Club
NATIONAL SOCIALISM -- FICTION
Blankman, A. Prisoner of night and fog
NATIVE AMERICANS -- ALASKA -- FICTION
Bell, H. Traitor's son
NATIVE AMERICANS -- FICTION
Bruchac, J. Wolf mark
McLoughlin, J. At Yellow Lake
Olsen, S. The girl with a baby
Yee, P. Learning to fly
NATIVE AMERICANS -- WEST INDIES -- FICTION
Engle, M. Hurricane dancers
NATURAL DISASTERS -- FICTION
Dashner, J. The kill order
De la Peña, M. The living
NATURAL HISTORY -- FICTION
Meyer, C. The true adventures of Charley Darwin
NATURE -- FICTION
Todd, P. The blind faith hotel
NAVAJO INDIANS -- FICTION
Bruchac, J. Code talker
Thurlo, A. The spirit line
NAVIGATION -- FICTION
Wilson, J. The alchemist's dream
The Navigator. **McNamee, E.**
Nayeri, Daniel
Another Faust
Another Pan
Nayeri, Dina
Nayeri, D. Another Faust
Nayeri, D. Another Pan
Naylor, Phyllis Reynolds
Alice in April
Alice in rapture, sort of
Faith, hope, and Ivy June
Incredibly Alice
Intensely Alice
Reluctantly Alice
NAZIS -- FICTION
Blankman, A. Prisoner of night and fog
Wein, E. Code name Verity
NEAR-DEATH EXPERIENCES -- FICTION
McNamee, G. Beyond
NEBRASKA -- FICTION
McNeal, L. The decoding of Lana Morris
Reed, A. Over you
Necklace of kisses. Block, F. L.
Nectar in a sieve. Markandaya, K.
A **need** so beautiful. Young, S.
Neely, Cynthia
Unearthly
Nefertiti, Queen, consort of Akhenaton, King of Egypt, 14th cent. B.C.
About
Friesner, E. M. Sphinx's princess
Friesner, E. M. Sphinx's queen
Neff, Henry H.
The hound of Rowan
NEIGHBORHOODS -- FICTION
When I was the greatest
Nelson, Blake
They came from below
Destroy all cars
Recovery Road
Rock star, superstar
Nelson, James
On the volcano
Nelson, Jandy
I'll give you the sun
The sky is everywhere
Nelson, R. A.
Breathe my name
Days of Little Texas
NEPAL -- FICTION
McCormick, P. Sold
Michaelis, A. The dragons of darkness
Neptune's children. Dobkin, B.
Ness, Patrick
A monster calls
The Ask and the Answer

The knife of never letting go
Monsters of men
More than this
NETHERLANDS -- FICTION
Cullen, L. I am Rembrandt's daughter
Dogar, S. Annexed
Peet, M. Tamar
NETHERLANDS -- HISTORY -- 1940-1945, GERMAN OCCUPATION -- FICTION
Polak, M. What world is left
Neumeier, Rachel
The City in the Lake
Never cry werewolf.. Davis, H.
Never ending. Bedford, M.
Never enough. Jaden, D.
Never fall down. McCormick, P.
Never sit down in a hoopskirt and other things I learned in Southern belle hell. Rumley, C.
Neverwas. Moore, K.
New blood. McPhee, P.
NEW ENGLAND -- FICTION
Sales, L. Past perfect
Wolff, T. Old school
New found land; Lewis and Clark's voyage of discovery. Wolf, A.
NEW HAMPSHIRE -- FICTION
Tregay, S. Love & leftovers
NEW MEXICO -- FICTION
Johnson, L. Muchacho
Saenz, B. A. Sammy and Juliana in Hollywood
Stork, F. X. The last summer of the death warriors
New moon. Meyer, S.
NEW ORLEANS (LA.) -- FICTION
Sepetys, R. Out of the Easy
Smith, S. L. Orleans
The **new** policeman. Thompson, K.
NEW YORK (N.Y.) -- FICTION
Brothers, M. Supergirl mixtapes
Fredericks, M. The girl in the park
Joseph, L. Flowers in the sky
Milford, K. The Broken Lands
Shusterman, N. Downsiders
Woodson, J. If you come softly
NEW YORK (N.Y.) -- HISTORY -- 1865-1898 -- FICTION
Milford, K. The Broken Lands
NEW YORK (N.Y.) -- HISTORY -- 1898-1951 -- FICTION
Bray, L. The diviners
Chibbaro, J. Deadly
NEW YORK (N.Y.) -- FICTION
Manzano, S. The revolution of Evelyn Serrano
NEW YORK (STATE) -- FICTION
Altebrando, T. Dreamland social club
Bauer, J. Peeled
Castle, J. You look different in real life
Friedman, A. The year my sister got lucky
Johnson, J. J. The theory of everything
Karim, S. Skunk girl
Levine, E. In trouble
Luper, E. Bug boy
Mackler, C. Tangled
Mazer, N. F. The missing girl
Moore, C. The stalker chronicles
Runyon, B. Surface tension
Salerni, D. K. We hear the dead
Strasser, T. Wish you were dead
Suma, N. R. Imaginary girls
NEW ZEALAND -- FICTION
De Goldi, K. The 10 p.m. question
Healey, K. Guardian of the dead
Healey, K. The shattering
Wright, D. Violence 101
Newbery, Linda
At the firefly gate
Flightsend
NEWFOUNDLAND -- FICTION
Weber, L. If you live like me
Newman, Lesléa
October mourning
NEWSPAPERS -- FICTION
Doktorski, J. S. Famous last words
Kerr, M. E. If I love you, am I trapped forever?
Newton, Robert
Runner
Nicholas Dane. Burgess, M.
Nicholas II, Emperor of Russia, 1868-1918
About
Miller, S. The lost crown
Nicholas, Lynn H.
Nichols, Janet
Messed up
Nicholson, William
Jango
Noman
Seeker
Nick & Norah's infinite playlist. Cohn, R.
Nielsen, Susin
The reluctant journal of Henry K. Larsen
Night road. Jenkins, A. M.
Night runner. Turner, M.
Night fires. Stanley, G. E.
Night hoops. Deuker, C.
Night runner [series]
Turner, M. End of days
Night School. Daugherty, C. J.
The **nightmare** garden. Kittredge, C.
The **night** tourist. Marsh, K.
Nightjohn. Paulsen, G.
Nightmare. Nixon, J. L.
NIGHTMARES -- FICTION

Perez, M. Dead is just a dream
The **nightmarys.** Poblocki, D.
Nightspell. Cypess, L.
Nilsson, Per
You & you & you
NINJA -- FICTION
Lowitz, L. Jet Black and the ninja wind
Nix Minus One. MacLean, J.
Nix, Garth
Abhorsen
Clairel
A confusion of princes
Lirael, daughter of the Clayr
Mister Monday; Keys to the kingdom
Sabriel
Shade's children
Nix Minus One. MacLean, J.
Nixon, Joan Lowery
The haunting
Nightmare
No and me. Vigan, D. d.
No crystal stair.
No laughter here, Williams-Garcia, R.
No moon. Watts, I. N.
No more us for you. Hernandez, D.
No place. Strasser, T.
No safe place. Ellis, D.
NOAH'S ARK -- FICTION
McCaughrean, G. Not the end of the world
Napoli, D. J. Storm
Provoost, A. In the shadow of the ark
Nobel genes. Michaels, R.
Noble warriors [series]
Nicholson, W. Jango
Nicholson, W. Noman
Nicholson, W. Seeker
Nobody's princess. Friesner, E. M.
Nobody's prize. Friesner, E. M.
Nobody's secret. MacColl, M.
Nocturne. Johnson, C.
Noggin. Whaley, J. C.
Noel, Alyson
Radiance
Nolan, Han
A face in every window
Crazy
A summer of Kings
Noman. Nicholson, W.
NORMANDY (FRANCE), ATTACK ON, 1944 -- FICTION
Myers, W. D. Invasion!
NORSE MYTHOLOGY -- FICTION
Harris, J. Runemarks
North by night Ayres, K.
NORTH CAROLINA -- FICTION
Hubbard, J. Paper covers rock
Myracle, L. Shine
Pearson, J. The rites & wrongs of Janice Wills
Watkins, S. What comes after
Wright, B. Crow
NORTH DAKOTA -- FICTION
Erdrich, L. The last report on the miracles at Little No Horse
North of beautiful. Headley, J. C.
North, Pearl
The boy from Ilysies
Libyrinth
North, Phoebe
Starglass
NORTHERN IRELAND -- FICTION
Dowd, S. Bog child
A **northern** light. Donnelly, J.
Northrop, Michael
Gentlemen
Trapped
NORTHWEST, PACIFIC -- FICTION
LaCour, N. The Disenchantments
Norville, Rod
Moonshine express; with a history of moonshine today and yesterday
NORWAY -- HISTORY -- GERMAN OCCUPATION, 1940-1945 -- FICTION
Preus, M. Shadow on the mountain
Not the end of the world. McCaughrean, G.
Not that kind of girl. Vivian, S.
Notes from the blender. Cook, T.
Notes from the midnight driver. Sonnenblick, J.
Nothing. Friedman, R.
Nothing but ghosts. Kephart, B.
Nothing special. Herbach, G.
Nothing but the truth. Avi, 1937.
NOVELISTS
Pennington, K. Brief candle
NOVELS IN VERSE
Agard, J. The young inferno
Bingham, K. Shark girl
Bryant, J. Ringside, 1925
Burg, Ann E. All the broken pieces
Chaltas, T. Because I am furniture
Cheng, A. Brushing Mom's hair
Engle, M. Firefly letters
Engle, M. Hurricane dancers
Engle, M. Silver people
Engle, M. Tropical secrets
Friedman, R. Nothing
Frost, H. The braid
Frost, H. Crossing stones
Frost, H. Hidden
Grimes, N. Dark sons
Grimes, N. A girl named Mister
Hemphill, S. Hideous love
Hemphill, S. Sisters of glass

Hemphill, S. Wicked girls
Herrick, S. Cold skin
Herrick, S. The wolf
Hopkins, E. Burned
Hopkins, E. Identical
Hopkins, E. Tricks
Kearney, M. The girl in the mirror
Leavitt, M. My book of life by Angel
LeZotte, A. C. T4
Macdonald, M. Odette's secrets
MacLean, J. Nix Minus One
Marcus, K. Exposed
McVoy, T. E. After the kiss
Myers, W. D. Street love
Ostlere, C. Karma
Phillips, W. Fishtailing
Richards, J. Three rivers rising
Schroeder, L. Chasing Brooklyn
Schroeder, L. Far from you
Sones, S. What my mother doesn't know
Thompson, H. The language inside
Thompson, H. Orchards
Tregay, S. Love & leftovers
Turner, A. W. Hard hit
Weatherford, C. B. Becoming Billie Holiday
Williams, C. L. Glimpse
Wolf, A. The watch that ends the night
Wolf, A. Zane's trace
Wolff, V. E. Make lemonade
Wolff, V. E. This full house
Wolff, V. E. True believer
Yeomans, E. Rubber houses
Zimmer, T. V. Reaching for sun

November blues. Draper, S. M.
Now is the time for running. Williams, M.
Now playing. Koertge, R.
Now starring Vivien Leigh Reid: Diva in training. Collins, Y.
Nowhere girl. Paquette, A.-J.
Nowhere to run. Griffin, C. J.
Nowlin, Laura
If he had been with me
Number 8. Fienberg, A.
Numbers. Ward, R.
Numbers [series]
Ward, R. Infinity
NUNS -- FICTION
Blagden, S. Dear Life, You Suck
Clark, K. Guardian angel house
Jarzab, A. The opposite of hallelujah
LaFevers, R. Mortal heart
Strauss, V. Passion blue
NURSES -- FICTION
Lucier, M. A death-struck year
Nussbaum, Susan
Good kings bad kings
Nuzum, K. A.
A small white scar
Nye, Naomi Shihab
Going going
Habibi
Nyembezi, C. L. Sibusiso
The rich man of Pietermaritzburg

O

O Guilin, Peadar
The inferior
O'Brien, Annemarie
Lara's gift
O'Brien, Caragh M.
Birthmarked
O'Brien, Johnny
Day of the assassins
O'Brien, Robert C.
Z for Zachariah
O'Connell, Tyne
True love, the sphinx, and other unsolvable riddles
O'Hearn, Kate
Kira
O'Neal, Eilis
The false princess
O'Neill, Molly
(ed) Allegiant
O'Rourke, Erica
Tangled
Torn
Oaks, J. Adams
Why I fight
Oates, Joyce Carol
Big Mouth & Ugly Girl
Freaky green eyes
Two or three things I forgot to tell you
OAXACA DE JUÁREZ (MEXICO) -- FICTION
Zevin, G. Because it is my blood
OBESITY -- FICTION
Charlton-Trujillo, e. E. Fat Angie
Cohn, R. You know where to find me
Going, K. L. Fat kid rules the world
Paley, S. Huge
OBSESSIVE-COMPULSIVE DISORDER -- FICTION
Brown, J. Perfect escape
Haydu, C. A. OCD love story
Hesser, T. S. Kissing doorknobs
McMann, L. Cryer's Cross
The **obsidian** blade. Hautman, P.
The **obsidian** mirror. Fisher, C.
Obsidian trilogy [series]
Lackey, M. To light a candle
Lackey, M. When darkness falls
OCCULT FICTION
Anderson, K. D. Kiss & Make Up

Ashton, B. Everbound
Ashton, B. Everneath
Barry, M. Lexicon
Berk, A. Mistle child
Beyer, K. The demon catchers of Milan
Bickle, L. The outside
Black, H. The coldest girl in Coldtown
Bray, L. The diviners
Carey, J. L. Dragonswood
Casella, J. Thin space
Cole, K. Poison princess
De la Cruz, M. Gates of Paradise
De la Cruz, M. Lost in time
Delsol, W. Flock
Frost, G. Lord Tophet
Fukuda, A. The Prey
Gray, C. Spellcaster
Hawkins, R. School spirits
Henderson, J. The Triumph of Death
Hoban, R. Soonchild
Hocking, A. Wake
Johnson, M. The madness underneath
Knight, K. Embers & echoes
Knox, E. Mortal fire
Levithan, D. Every day
Maas, S. J. Crown of midnight
Mancusi, M. Scorched
Marillier, J. Raven flight
Martin, C. K. K. Yesterday
McNeal, T. Far far away
O'Rourke, E. Tangled
Pike, A. Earthbound
Powell, L. Burn mark
Reese, J. The strange case of Doctor Jekyll and Mademoiselle Odile
Samms, O. Sketchy
Shirvington, J. Emblaze
Simner, J. L. Faerie after
Smith, A. Passenger
Smith, C. L. Feral nights
Stiefvater, M. The dream thieves
Suma, N. R. 17 & gone
Sutton, K. Some quiet place
Taylor, L. Daughter of smoke and bone
Taylor, L. Days of blood & starlight
Tracey, S. Moonset
Tubb, K. O. The 13th sign
West, K. Pivot point
Winters, C. In the shadow of blackbirds
Zinn, B. Poison

OCCULT FICTION
King, S. Firestarter

OCD love story. Haydu, C. A.

An **ocean** apart, a world away. Namioka, L.

OCEAN -- FICTION
Howells, A. The summer of skinny dipping

Ockler, Sarah
The Book of Broken Hearts
Fixing Delilah
Twenty boy summer

October mourning. Leslea, N.

Odette's secrets. Macdonald, M.

ODYSSEUS (GREEK MYTHOLOGY) -- FICTION
Barrett, T. King of Ithaka
Geras, A. Ithaka

Of sound mind. Ferris, J.

The **off** season. Murdock, C. G.

An **off** year. Zulkey, C.

Off-color. McDonald, J.

Offermann, Andrea
Milford, K. The Boneshaker

Oh. My. Gods. Childs, T. L.

Oh, Snap! Myers, W. D.

OHIO -- FICTION
Anderson, L. H. Twisted
Barnes, J. Tales of the Madman Underground
Garsee, J. Say the word
Haddix, M. P. Full ride
Morrison, T. Sula
Vivian, S. A little friendly advice

OJIBWA INDIANS -- FICTION
Erdrich, L. The last report on the miracles at Little No Horse

Oketani, Shogo, 1958-
(jt. auth) Lowitz, L. Jet Black and the ninja wind

OKLAHOMA -- FICTION
Gensler, S. The revenant
Hudson, T. Hereafter
Tharp, T. Knights of the hill country
Tharp, T. The spectacular now

Okorafor, Nnedi
Akata witch

Okorafor, Nnedimma
The shadow speaker

OLD AGE -- FICTION
Blythe, C. Revenge of a not-so-pretty girl
Epstein, R. God is in the pancakes
Harvey, S. N. Death benefits
Myers, W. D. Lockdown
Sonnenblick, J. Notes from the midnight driver

Old dog. Cardenas, T.

Old school. Wolff, T.

Oliver, Jana G.
The demon trapper's daughter
Oliver, J. Soul thief

Oliver, Lauren
Before I fall
Delirium
Pandemonium
Panic

Requiem
Olsen, Gregg
Envy
Olsen, Sylvia
The girl with a baby
White girl
Omololu, Cynthia Jaynes
Dirty little secrets
On the runway [series]
Carlson, M. Premiere
On the volcano. Nelson, J.
On thin ice. Bastedo, J.
Once a witch. MacCullough, C.
Once upon a time in the North. Pullman, P.
Once was lost. Zarr, S.
Once we were. Zhang, K.
One Crow Alone. Crockett, S. D.
One fat summer. Lipsyte, R.
One good punch. Wallace, R.
One of the survivors. Shaw, S.
One of those hideous books where the mother dies. Sones, S.
The **one** safe place, Unsworth, T.
One whole and perfect day. Clarke, J.
ONLINE DATING -- FICTION
Smith, J. E. This is what happy looks like
Only you can save mankind. Pratchett, T.
Openly straight. Konigsberg, B.
Operation Red Jericho. Mowll, J.
Operation Storm City. Mowll, J.
Operation typhoon shore. Mowll, J.
Ophelia. Klein, L. M.
Oppel, Kenneth
Airborn
Half brother
This dark endeavor
Skybreaker
Starclimber
Such wicked intent
The **opposite** of hallelujah. Jarzab, A.
The **opposite** of invisible. Gallagher, L.
The **oracle** betrayed. Fisher, C.
The **Orange** Houses. Griffin, P.
ORATORS
Shecter, V. A. Cleopatra's moon
Orca currents [series]
Walters, E. In a flash
Orca soundings [series]
Harvey, S. N. Plastic
McClintock, N. Masked
Tullson, D. Riley Park
Van Tol, A. Knifepoint
Orchards. Thompson, H.
Ordinary ghosts. Corrigan, E.
OREGON -- FICTION
Beaufrand, M. J. The river
Caletti, D. The six rules of maybe
Forman, G. If I stay
Houck, C. Tiger's quest
Orenstein, Denise Gosliner
Unseen companion
ORGANIZED CRIME -- FICTION
Black, H. Black heart
Korman, G. Son of the mob
Origin. Khoury, J.
The **Originals.** Patrick, C.
Origins. Thompson, K.
ORKNEY (SCOTLAND) -- FICTION
Weyn, S. Dr. Frankenstein's daughters
Orleans. Smith, S. L.
Oron, Judie
Cry of the giraffe
ORPHANAGES -- FICTION
Barnaby, H. Wonder show
ORPHANS -- FICTION
Acosta, M. Dark companion
Blagden, S. Dear Life, You Suck
Bow, E. Plain Kate
Bunce, E. C. A curse dark as gold
Clare, C. Clockwork angel
Clare, C. Clockwork prince
Cornish, D. M. Factotum
Crowley, S. The stolen one
Curtis, C. P. Bud, not Buddy
Donaldson, J. Running on the cracks
Egan, L. A. The Outcast Oracle
FitzGerald, H. Deviant
Hahn, M. D. The ghost of Crutchfield Hall
Hall, C. A. Crystal bones
Hardy, J. The shifter
Hooper, M. Fallen Grace
Hooper, M. Velvet
Horowitz, A.Stormbreaker
Jinks, C. Babylonne
Kuehn, S. Complicit
LaFaye, A. Stella stands alone
Larson, K. Hattie ever after
Lawlor, L. Dead reckoning
Lawson, M. Crow Lake
Lies, knives and girls in red dresses
Mahoney, K. The iron witch
Mazer, N. F. After the rain
McQuein, J. L. Arclight
Meyer, C. Duchessina
Michael, J. City boy
Moloney, J. The Book of Lies
O'Connell, M. The sharp time
Price, L. Starters
Schrefer, E. Threatened
Tracey, S. Darkbound
Umansky, K. Solomon Snow and the stolen jewel

Walsh, P. The Crowfield curse
Walsh, P. The Crowfield demon
Whelan, G. Listening for lions
White, A. B. Windows on the world
Woodson, J. Miracle's boys
Yancey, R. The extraordinary adventures of Alfred Kropp
Zweig, E. Fever season
Ortiz Cofer, Judith
Call me Maria
If I could fly
Osa, Nancy
Cuba 15
Osterlund, Anne
Academy 7
Aurelia
Exile
Ostlere, Cathy
Karma
Ostow, Micol
So punk rock (and other ways to disappoint your mother)
Ostrich boys. Gray, K.
Other. Kincy, K.
The **other** half of life. Whitney, K. A.
The **other** half of me. Franklin, E.
The **other** side of blue. Patterson, V. O.
The **other** side of dark. Smith, S.
The **other** side of dawn. Marsden, J.
Ostow, Micol
Emily Goldberg learns to salsa
Otsuka, Julie
When the emperor was divine
Out of order. Stevenson, R. H.
Out of reach. Arcos, C.
Out of shadows. Wallace, J.
Out of the blue. Rottman, S. L.
Out of the box. Mulder, M.
Out of the Easy. Sepetys, R.
The **Outcast** Oracle. Egan, L. A.
The **outcasts.** Matthews, L. S.
OUTER SPACE -- EXPLORATION -- FICTION
Oppel, K. Starclimber
Outlaw. Davies, S.
OUTLAWS
Wilson, J. Ghost moon
Outpost. Aguirre, A.
The **outside.** Bickle, L.
The **outside** of a horse. Rorby, G.
The **outsiders.** Hinton, S. E.
Over a thousand hills I walk with you. Jansen, H.
Over sea, under stone. Cooper, S.
Over the end line. Martino, A. C.
Over you. Reed, A.
Overboard. Fama, E.
Owen, James A.
Here, there be dragons
OVERLAND JOURNEYS TO THE PACIFIC -- FICTION
McKernan, V. The devil's paintbox
OVERWEIGHT TEENAGERS -- FICTION
Fehlbaum, B. Big fat disaster
Walton, K. M. Empty
OyMG. Dominy, A. F.

P

PACIFIC NORTHWEST -- FICTION
LaCour, N. The Disenchantments
PACIFISTS -- FICTION
Sheth, K. Keeping corner
Padian, Maria
Brett McCarthy
Jersey tomatoes are the best
PAINTERS -- FICTION
Cullen, L. I am Rembrandt's daughter
Painting the black. Deuker, C.
PAKISTAN -- FICTION
Antieau, K. Broken moon
Master, I. A beautiful lie
Qamar, A. Beneath my mother's feet
Staples, S. F. Haveli
Staples, S. F. The house of djinn
Staples, S. F. Shabanu
PAKISTANI AMERICANS -- FICTION
Karim, S. Skunk girl
PAKISTANIS -- GREAT BRITAIN -- FICTION
Robert, N. B. Boy vs. girl
Palace beautiful. Williams, S. D.
Palace of Spies. Zettel, S.
Palace of spies [series]
Zettel, S. Palace of Spies
The Paladin Prophecy [series]
Frost, M. Alliance
The **Pale** Assassin. Elliott, P.
PALESTINIAN ARABS -- FICTION
Clinton, C. A stone in my hand
Miklowitz, G. D. The enemy has a face
Paley, Sasha
Huge
Palma, Felix J.
The map of the sky
The map of time
Palmer, Robin
The Corner of Bitter and Sweet
Geek charming
PALO ALTO (CALIF.) -- FICTION
Voorhees, C. Lucky fools
Pandemonium. Oliver, L.
PAN (GREEK DEITY)
Napoli, D. J. The great god Pan

Panic. Oliver, L.
Panic. Draper, S. M.
Paolini, Christopher
Brisingr
Eldest
Eragon
Papademetriou, Lisa
Drop
M or F?
Paper covers rock. Hubbard, J.
Paper towns. Green, J.
Paquette, Ammi-Joan
Nowhere girl
Paradise. Alexander, J.
Paradise red. Grant, K. M.
Paranormalcy. White, K.
PARANORMAL FICTION
Reed, J. Living violet
Stiefvater, M. The dream thieves
Stiefvater, M. The raven boys
PARAPSYCHOLOGY -- FICTION
Derting, K. The last echo
Pauley, K. Cat Girl's day off
Vrettos, A. M. Sight
A **parcel** of patterns. Paton Walsh, J.
PARENT-CHILD RELATIONSHIP -- FICTION
Almond, D. The true tale of the monster Billy Dean
Boll, R. The second trial.
Cooney, C. B. What Janie found
Halpern, J. Have a nice day
Jaden, D. Never enough
Rosoff, M. Picture me gone
Ryan, A. K. Spark
PARENTING -- FICTION
Blair, J. Leap of Faith
PARIS (FRANCE) -- FICTION
Donnelly, J. Revolution
Kamata, S. Gadget Girl
Leroux, G. The phantom of the opera
Perkins, S. Anna and the French kiss
Vigan, D. d. No and me
PARIS (FRANCE) -- HISTORY -- 1870–1940 -- FICTION
Morgan, P. The beautiful and the cursed
Reese, J. The strange case of Doctor Jekyll and Mademoiselle Odile
Ross, E. Belle epoque
Park, Linda Sue
Park, L. S. A long walk to water
Click
Parker, Amy Christine
Gated
Parker, Robert B.
The boxer and the spy
Chasing the bear
The Edenville Owls
Parkinson, Curtis
Domenic's war; a story of the Battle of Monte Cassino
Parkinson, Siobhán
Long story short
Parrot in the oven. Martinez, V.
Parrotfish. Wittlinger, E.
Partials. Wells, D.
PARTIES -- FICTION
Seamon, H. Somebody up there hates you
PARTY OF DEMOCRATIC KAMPUCHEA -- FICTION
McCormick, P. Never fall down
PASS CHRISTIAN (MISS.) -- FICTION
Woodson, J. Beneath a meth moon
Passenger. Smith, A.
Passion blue. Strauss, V.
Past perfect. Sales, L.
Pastworld. Beck, I.
The **path** of names. Goelman, A.
Pathfinder. Card, O. S.
Patneaude, David
Thin wood walls
Paton, Alan
Cry, the beloved country
Paton Walsh, Jill
A parcel of patterns
Patrick, Cat
Forgotten
The Originals
Revived
Patrick, D. L.
A matter of souls
PATRIOTISM -- FICTION
Lyga, B. Hero-type
The **patron** saint of butterflies. Galante, C.
Patron, Susan
Behind the masks
Patt, Beverly
Best friends forever; a World War II scrapbook
Patterson, James
Homeroom diaries
Maximum Ride: the angel experiment
Patterson, Valerie O.
The other side of blue
Pattou, Edith
East
Pauley, Kimberly
Cat Girl's day off
Paulsen, Gary
Crush; the theory, practice, and destructive properties of love
Harris and me; a summer remembered
The island
Nightjohn

The Schernoff discoveries
Soldier's heart
Pausewang, Gudrun
Dark hours
Traitor
Pay the piper. Yolen, J.
Payback. Hayes, R.
Payback time. Deuker, C.
Pazer, Lisa S.
Biederman, L. Teenage waistland
Peace, love, and baby ducks. Myracle, L.
Peacock, Shane
Death in the air
The dragon turn
Eye of the crow
The secret fiend
Vanishing girl
Peak. Smith, R.
Pearce, Jackson
As you wish
Sisters red
Pearce, Jacqueline
Manga touch
PEARL HARBOR (OAHU, HAWAII), ATTACK ON, 1941 -- FICTION
Mazer, H. A boy at war
Salisbury, G. Under the blood-red sun
Pearson, Joanna
The rites & wrongs of Janice Wills
Pearson, Mary
The adoration of Jenna Fox
Fox forever
The Fox Inheritance
The miles between
A room on Lorelei Street
Peck, Dale
Sprout
Peck, Richard
The river between us
Three-quarters dead
Peck, Robert Newton
A day no pigs would die
The **Peculiars.** McQuerry, M. D.
Peeled. Bauer, J.
Peeps. Westerfeld, S.
PEER PRESSURE -- FICTION
Friend, N. My life in black and white
Peet, Mal
Life
Tamar
Pegasus. McKinley, R.
PEGASUS (GREEK MYTHOLOGY)
McKinley, R. Pegasus
Pellinor [series]
Croggon, A. The Crow
Croggon, A. The Naming
Croggon, A. The Riddle
Croggon, A. The Singing
PEN PALS -- FICTION
Whitman, S. The milk of birds
Pennington, Kate
Brief candle
PENNSYLVANIA -- FICTION
Anderson, L. H. Forge
Anderson, L. H. Prom
Bloor, E. A plague year
Connelly, N. O. The miracle stealer
Leavitt, L. Sean Griswold's head
Quick, M. Boy21
Richards, J. Three rivers rising
Wallace, R. One good punch
PEOPLE WITH DISABILITIES -- FICTION
Aronson, S. Head case
Clements, A. Things not seen
Edwards, J. Earth girl
Fink, M. The summer I got a life
Flake, S. G. Pinned
Giles, G. Girls like us
Griffin, P. The Orange Houses
Johnson, H. M. Accidents of nature
McNeal, L. The decoding of Lana Morris
Nussbaum, S. Good kings bad kings
Portman, F. Andromeda Klein
Steele, A. Apollo's outcasts
Van Draanen, W. The running dream
Venkatraman, P. A time to dance
Woolston, B. Catch & release
PEOPLE WITH MENTAL DISABILITIES -- FICTION
Castan, M. Fighting for Dontae
Hamilton, K. When the stars threw down their spears
Lange, E. J. Dead ends
Nolan, H. A face in every window
PEOPLE WITH PHYSICAL DISABILITIES -- FICTION
Baratz-Logsted, L. Crazy beautiful
Friesner, E. M. Spirit's princess
Howell, S. Everything beautiful
Klein, L. M. Lady Macbeth's daughter
McBay, B. Waiting for Sarah
Selfors, S. The sweetest spell
Slade, A. G. The dark deeps
Slade, A. G. Empire of ruins
Slade, A. The hunchback assignments
Perchance to dream. Mantchev, L.
Perera, Anna
Guantanamo boy
Perez, Ashley Hope
The knife and the butterfly
What can(t) wait
Perez, Marlene

Dead is a battlefield
Dead is a killer tune
Dead is just a dream
Dead is the new black
Perfect chemistry. Elkeles, S.
The **perfect** distance. Whitney, K. A.
Perfect escape. Brown, J.
Perfect you. Scott, E.
Perfect fire trilogy [series]
Grant, K. M. Blue flame
Grant, K. M. White heat
Perfect. Friend, N.
Perfect lies. White, K.
Perfect ruin. DeStefano, L.
Perfect scoundrels. Carter, A.
Perfectly dateless. Billerbeck, K.
PERFORMING ARTS -- FICTION
Rennison, L. The taming of the tights
PERFORMING ARTS HIGH SCHOOLS -- TON
Hrdlitschka, S. Allegra
PERFUMES -- FICTION
Perez, M. Dead is a battlefield
Peril on the sea. Cadnum, M.
Period 8. Crutcher, C.
Perkins, Lynne Rae
As easy as falling off the face of the earth
Criss cross
Perkins, Mitali
Secret keeper
Perkins, Stephanie
Anna and the French kiss
Lola and the boy next door
The **perks** of being a wallflower. Chbosky, S.
Perl, Erica S.
Vintage Veronica
Perpetual check. Wallace, R.
Perrin, Pat
Coleman, W. Anna's world
Perry's killer playlist. Schreiber, J.
PERSECUTION -- FICTION
Thompson, R. City of cannibals
PERSEUS (GREEK MYTHOLOGY)
Halam, A. Snakehead
PERSIAN MYTHOLOGY -- FICTION
Bell, H. Fall of a kingdom
Persistence of memory. Atwater-Rhodes, A.
PERSONAL APPEARANCE -- FICTION
Chapman, L. Flawless
Griffin, A. All you never wanted
Jaden, D. Never enough
Kittle, K. Reasons to be happy
Vivian, S. The list
PERSONALITY -- FICTION
Roth, V. Insurgent
PERSONALITY DISORDERS -- FICTION
Alonzo, S. Riding invisible
Jacobson, J. The complete history of why I hate her
PERSUASION (PSYCHOLOGY) -- FICTION
Barry, M. Lexicon
Pesci, David
Amistad
PETER PAN (FICTIONAL CHARACTER)
Anderson, J. L. Tiger Lily
Nayeri, D. Another Pan
Peter Raven under fire. Molloy, M.
Peterfreund, Diana
Across a star-swept sea
For darkness shows the stars
Peters, Julie Anne, 1952-
Between Mom and Jo
By the time you read this, I'll be dead
Define normal
It's our prom (so deal with it)
Luna
Rage
She loves you, she loves you not--
Peterson, Lois J.
Beyond repair
Silver rain
Peterson, Will
Triskellion
Triskellion 2: The burning
Petrucha, Stefan
The Rule of Won
Split
Teen, Inc.
PETS
Pfeffer, Susan Beth
Blood wounds
Life as we knew it
The **phantom** of the opera. Leroux, G.
Phantoms in the snow. Duble, K. B.
PHILADELPHIA (PA.) -- FICTION
Anderson, L. H. Fever, 1793
Dennard, S. Something strange and deadly
Kephart, B. Dangerous neighbors
Philbin, Joanna
The daughters
Philbrick, W. R.
The last book in the universe
Phillips, Suzanne
Burn
Phoenix Island. Dixon, J.
PHOTOGRAPHERS -- FICTION
Kirkpatrick, J. A flickering light
Mangum, L. After hello
Marcus, K. Exposed
McMullan, M. Sources of light
PHOTOGRAPHY -- FICTION
Bick, I. J. The Sin eater's confession
Jaden, D. Never enough

PHOTOJOURNALISM -- FICTION
Park, L. S. Click
PHYSICIANS -- FICTION
Whelan, G. Listening for lions.
PIANISTS -- FICTION
Fogelin, A. The big nothing
Zalben, J. B. Four seasons
Zarr, S. The Lucy variations
PIANO MUSIC -- FICTION
Anthony, J. Chopsticks
Picture me gone. Rosoff, M.
Pieces of Georgia. Bryant, J.
Pieces. Lynch, C.
Pierce, Tamora
Bloodhound
First test
Mastiff
Melting stones
Sandry's book
Terrier
Trickster's choice
The will of the empress
Pierson, D. C.
Crap kingdom
PIGEONS -- FICTION
Ortiz Cofer, J. If I could fly
The **Pigman**. Zindel, P.
Pignat, Caroline
Greener grass
Wild geese
PIGS -- FICTION
Peck, R. N. A day no pigs would die
Pike, Aprilynne
Earthbound
Illusions
Spells
Wings
PILGRIMS AND PILGRIMAGES -- FICTION
Barnhouse, R. The book of the maidservant
Crossley-Holland, K. Crossing to Paradise
The **pilgrims** of Rayne. MacHale, D. J.
Pink. Wilkinson, L.
Pinned. Flake, S. G.
The **piper's** son. Marchetta, M.
Pirate cinema. Doctorow, C.
The **pirate** captain's daughter. Bunting, E.
PIRATES -- FICTION
Bunting, E. The pirate captain's daughter
Lake, N. Hostage Three
Lee, T. Piratica
Pirates! Rees, C.
Piratica II: return to Parrot Island. Lee, T.
Piratica. Lee, T.
Pitcher, Annabel
Ketchup clouds
My sister lives on the mantelpiece
PITTSBURGH (PA.) -- FICTION
Andrews, J. Me & Earl & the dying girl
Pivot point. West, K.
Pixley, Marcella
Without Tess
Pizza, love, and other stuff that made me famous. Williams, K.
PLAGIARISM -- FICTION
Hautman, P. What boys really want?
PLAGUE -- FICTION
Brennan, H. The Doomsday Box: a Shadow Project adventure
Kessler, J. Loss
Knutsson, C. Shadows cast by stars
Lu, M. Champion
Van Beirs, P. A sword in her hand
A **plague** year. Bloor, E.
Plain Kate. Bow, E.
Planesrunner. McDonald, I.
PLANTS -- FICTION
Pike, A. Wings
Wood, M. The poison diaries
Plastic. Harvey, S. N.
PLASTIC SURGERY -- FICTION
Harvey, S. N. Plastic
Williams, L. E. Slant
Plath, Sylvia
About
Tibensky, A. And then things fall apart
Platt, Chris
Astra
Playing for the commandant. Zail, S.
Playing hurt. Schindler, H.
Playing in traffic. Giles, G.
Playing with matches. Katcher, B.
Playground. 50 Cent (Musician)
Please ignore Vera Dietz. King, A. S.
The **pledge.** Derting, K.
Plum, Amy
Die for me
Plum-Ucci, Carol
Fire will fall
Streams of Babel
POACHING -- FICTION
Fletcher, S. Ancient, strange, and lovely
Poblocki, Dan
The nightmarys
POCASSET INDIANS -- FICTION
Smith, P. C. Weetamoo, heart of the Pocassets
POCONO MOUNTAINS (PA.) -- FICTION
Matson, M. Second chance summer
POD. Wallenfels, S.
POETRY -- FICTION
Leslea, N. October mourning
Mecum, R. Zombie haiku
Roskos, E. Dr. Bird's advice for sad poets

POETS -- FICTION
Dana, B. A voice of her own
MacColl, M. Nobody's secret
Owen, J. A. Here, there be dragons
Pennington, K. Brief candle
Schmidt, G. D. The Wednesday wars
Woodson, J. After Tupac and D Foster
Poison. Zinn, B.
Poison. Wooding, C.
The **poison** diaries. Wood, M.
Poison Ivy. Koss, A. G.
Poison princess. Cole, K.
Poisoned honey. Gormley, B.
The **poisoned** house. Ford, M.
POISONS AND POISONING -- FICTION
Wood, M. The poison diaries
POKER -- FICTION
Hautman, P. All-in
Volponi, P. The hand you're dealt
Polak, Monique
The middle of everywhere
What world is left
POLAND -- FICTION
Mackall, D. D. Eva underground
POLAND -- HISTORY -- OCCUPATION, 1939-1945 -- FICTION
Sax, A. The war within these walls
POLAR BEAR -- FICTION
Bastedo, J. On thin ice
Durst, S. B. Ice
POLICE -- FICTION
Myers, W. D. Kick
Pierce, T. Bloodhound
Pierce, T. Mastiff
Pierce, T. Terrier
White, K. Paranormalcy
POLICE BRUTALITY -- FICTION
Kephart, B. Dr. Radway's Sarsaparilla Resolvent
POLISH AMERICANS -- FICTION
Friesner, E. M. Threads and flames
Polisner, Gae
The pull of gravity
POLITICAL ACTIVISTS -- FICTION
Miller-Lachmann, L. Gringolandia
Nye, N. S. Going going
Schröder, M. My brother's shadow
POLITICAL LEADERS -- FICTION
Sheth, K. Keeping corner
POLITICS -- FICTION
Kaye, M. Demon chick
Lupica, M. Hero
Rallison, J. How to take the ex out of ex-boyfriend
White, E. E. The President's daughter
POLITICS, PRACTICAL -- FICTION
Doctorow, C. Homeland
Fitzpatrick, H. My life next door
Pollock, Tom
The city's son
POLLUTION -- FICTION
Vacco, C. My chemical mountain
POLYGAMY -- FICTION
Hrdlitschka, S. Sister wife
Williams, C. L. The chosen one
Pon, Cindy
Fury of the phoenix
Silver phoenix
PONY EXPRESS -- FICTION
Wilson, D. L. Black storm comin'
POOR -- FICTION
Lyne, J. H. Catch rider
Wolff, V. E. True believer
POPULARITY -- FICTION
Crane, C. Confessions of a Hater
Calame, D. Beat the band
Griffin, A. All you never wanted
Griffin, P. Burning blue
Juby, S. Getting the girl
Kittle, K. Reasons to be happy
Pearce, J. As you wish
Raskin, J. My misadventures as a teenage rock star
Schneider, R. The beginning of everything
Valentine, A. How (not) to find a boyfriend
Whitaker, A. The queen of Kentucky
Yang, D. J. Warp speed
The **porcupine** year. Erdrich, L.
Porter, Sarah
Lost voices
Porter, Tracey
Lark
PORTLAND (ME.) -- FICTION
Farish, T. The good braider
PORTLAND (OR.) -- FICTION
Lucier, M. A death-struck year
Portman, Frank
Andromeda Klein
King Dork
Possessed. Cann, K.
The **possibilities** of sainthood. Freitas, D.
POST-TRAUMATIC STRESS DISORDER -- FICTION
Anderson, L. H. The impossible knife of memory
Fontes, J. Benito runs
Hodkin, M. The evolution of Mara Dyer
Hodkin, M. The unbecoming of Mara Dyer
Scott, E. Miracle
Poster boy. Crane, D.
Potter, Ryan
Exit strategy

POVERTY -- FICTION
Avi Traitor's gate
Cullen, L. I am Rembrandt's daughter
Fletcher, C. Ten cents a dance
Hartnett, S. Thursday's child
Hooper, M. Fallen Grace
Lawson, M. Crow Lake
Madden, K. Gentle's Holler
Morrison, T. Sula
Mulligan, A. Trash
Newton, R. Runner
Qamar, A. Beneath my mother's feet
Shulman, M. Scrawl
Strasser, T. No place
Wolff, V. E. Make lemonade
Wolff, V. E. True believer
Powell, Laura
Burn mark
The game of triumphs
The Master of Misrule
Powell, Randy
Swiss mist
Three clams and an oyster
Powell, William Campbell
Expiration day
Power, Susan
The grass dancer
Powers. Le Guin, U. K.
Powers, J. L.
This thing called the future
PRAGUE (CZECH REPUBLIC) -- FICTION
Taylor, L. Days of blood & starlight
Prairie fire. Johnston, E. K.
Pratchett, Terry
The amazing Maurice and his educated rodents
Dodger
I shall wear midnight
Nation
Only you can save mankind
The Wee Free Men
PRAYER -- FICTION
Coy, J. Box out
PRAYING MANTIS -- FICTION
Smith, A. Grasshopper jungle
PREGNANCY -- FICTION
Caletti, D. The six rules of maybe
Carter, C. Me, him, them, and it
Chandler, K. Girls don't fly
De Gramont, N. Every little thing in the world
Dowd, S. A swift pure cry
Draper, S. M. November blues
Efaw, A. After
Grimes, N. A girl named Mister
Kephart, B. Small damages
Knowles, J. Jumping off swings
Levine, E. In trouble
Martin, C. K. K. I know it's over
McCafferty, M. Bumped
McCafferty, M. Thumped
McWilliams, K. Doormat
Razzell, M. Snow apples
Soonchild
Vega, D. Fact of life #31
Werlin, N. Impossible
Zarr, S. How to save a life
PREHISTORIC PEOPLES -- FICTION
Williams, S. Wind rider
PREJUDICES -- FICTION
Brooks, K. Lucas
Coats, J. A. The wicked and the just
Jones, T. L. Finding my place,
Krisher, T. Fallout
Levine, K. The best bad luck I ever had
Magoon, K. Camo girl
Namioka, L. Mismatch
Napoli, D. J. Alligator bayou
Sherrard, V. The glory wind
Taylor, M. D. The land
Uchida, Y. A jar of dreams
Volponi, P. Homestretch
Walsh, A. A Long Way from Home
Williams, L. E. Slant
Yee, P. Learning to fly
Yep, L. The traitor; Golden Mountain chronicles, 1885
Zephaniah, B. Face
Preller, James
Bystander
Premiere. Carlson, M.
PREPARATORY SCHOOLS -- FICTION
Konigsberg, B. Openly straight
Oates, J. C. Two or three things I forgot to tell you
Voorhees, C. Lucky fools
Walker, B. F. Black boy/white school
The **President's** daughter. White, E. E.
PRESIDENTS -- FICTION
Cabot, M. All-American girl
Nanji, S. Child of dandelions
Pesci, D. Amistad
White, E. E. Long may she reign
Pretties. Westerfeld, S.
Pretty dead. Block, F. L.
Preus, Margi
Heart of a samurai
Shadow on the mountain
The **Prey.** Fukuda, A.
Price, Charlie
Dead connection
Desert Angel
The interrogation of Gabriel James
Price, Lissa

Enders
Starters
The **price** of loyalty. Castan, M.
Price, Nora
Zoe letting go
PRIDE AND VANITY
See also Conduct of life; Sin
Priestly, Chris
Mister Creecher
PRIESTS -- FICTION
Kiely, B. The gospel of winter
Vasey, P. A troublesome boy
Primavera. Beaufrand, M. J.
Prince of shadows. Caine, R.
PRINCES -- FICTION
Donnelly, J. Revolution
O'Brien, J. Day of the assassins
Whitcomb, L. The Fetch
PRINCES -- FICTION
Behemoth
Klein, L. M. Ophelia
Kontis, A. Enchanted
Leviathan
Maas, S. J. Throne of glass
Marsden, J. Hamlet: a novel
Nix, G. A confusion of princes
Rudnick, P. Gorgeous
Turner, M. W. A conspiracy of kings
Wein, E. E. The empty kingdom
Wein, E. E. The lion hunter
Westerfeld, S. Goliath
Princess Ben. Murdock, C. G.
The **princess** diaries. Cabot, M.
Princess of glass. George, J. D.
Princess of the midnight ball. George, J. D.
PRINCESSES -- FICTION
Brennan, C. House of the star
Cabot, M. The princess diaries
Caveney, P. Sebastian Darke: Prince of Fools
Cokal, S. The Kingdom of little wounds
Flinn, A. A kiss in time
Flinn, A. Cloaked
George, J. D. Princess of glass
Haddix, M. P. Just Ella
Hahn, R. A creature of moonlight
Hale, S. The Goose girl
Lies, knives and girls in red dresses
Malchow, A. The Sword of Darrow
Meyer, C. Cleopatra confesses
Moriarty, J. The cracks in the kingdom
O'Neal, E. The false princess
Whitcomb, L. The Fetch
Yolen, J. Curse of the Thirteenth Fey
The **princesses** of Iowa. Backes, M. M.
Prinz, Yvonne
The Vinyl Princess
Prisoner of night and fog. Blankman, A.
PRISONERS -- FICTION
Abrahams, P. Bullet point
Buckhanon, K. Upstate
Colfer, E. Airman
Dowd, S. Bog child
Fisher, C. Incarceron
Fisher, C. Sapphique
Green, S. Half bad
Maas, S. J. Throne of glass
Meyer, L. A. The wake of the Lorelei Lee
O'Hearn, K. Kira
Perera, A. Guantanamo boy
Smith, A. G. Death sentence
Smith, A. G. Lockdown
Smith, A. G. Solitary
Volponi, P. Rikers High
Whyman, M. Icecore
Prisoners in the palace. MacColl, M.
PRISONERS OF WAR -- FICTION
Wein, E. Code name Verity
Private Peaceful. Morpurgo, M.
PRIVATE SCHOOLS -- FICTION
Acosta, M. Dark companion
Fisher, C. Darkwater
Halpin, B. A really awesome mess
Kuehn, S. Complicit
Stiefvater, M. The raven boys
Vasey, P. A troublesome boy
Walker, B. F. Black boy/white school
Wells, R. Feedback
Whitney, D. The rivals
The **private** thoughts of Amelia E. Rye. Shimko, B.
The **probability** of miracles. Wunder, W.
Probably still Nick Swansen. Wolff, V. E.
Prodigy. Lu, M.
Professor Gargoyle. Gilman, C.
The **project.** Falkner, B.
Project X. Shepard, J.
Prom. Anderson, L. H.
Prom dates from Hell. Clement-Moore, R.
Proimos, James
12 things to do before you crash and burn
Project Sweet Life. Hartinger, B.
Promise the night. MacColl, M.
PROMS -- FICTION
Peters, J. A. It's our prom (so deal with it)
The **properties** of water. McKinnon, H. R.
PROPHECIES -- FICTION
Carson, R. The bitter kingdom
Carson, R. The crown of embers
Carson, R. The girl of fire and thorns
Cole, K. Poison princess
Raedeke, C. The daykeeper's grimoire
White, K. Paranormalcy

White, K. Supernaturally
Yolen, J. Curse of the Thirteenth Fey
Prophecy of days [series]
Raedeke, C. The daykeeper's grimoire
Prophecy of the sisters. Zink, M.
Prose, Francine
After
Touch
The turning
PROSTITITION -- FICTION
Burgess, M. Smack
Sepetys, R. Out of the Easy
PROTEST MOVEMENTS -- NEW YORK (STATE) -- NEW YORK
Manzano, S. The revolution of Evelyn Serrano
Provoost, Anne
In the shadow of the ark
PSYCHIATRIC HOSPITALS -- FICTION
Ford, M. T. Suicide notes
Halpern, J. Get well soon
Jacobs, J. H. The shibboleth
Johnson, L. L. Worlds apart
McCormick, P. Cut
Suma, N. R. 17 & gone
Vizzini, N. It's kind of a funny story
PSYCHIC ABILITY -- FICTION
Bray, L. The diviners
Derting, K. The last echo
Garvey, A. Glass Heart
Moore, K. Amber House
Moore, K. Neverwas
Perez, M. Dead is just a dream
Ward, R. Infinity
West, K. Split second
White, K. Perfect lies
PSYCHICS -- FICTION
Albin, G. Crewel
Garvey, A. Glass Heart
Ness, P. The knife of never letting go
West, K. Split second
PSYCHOKINESIS -- FICTION
King, S. Firestarter
PSYCHOLOGICAL ABUSE -- FICTION
Kuehn, S. Charm & strange
PSYCHOLOGICAL FICTION
Rapp, A. The children and the wolves
PSYCHOLOGICAL NOVELS
Mosley, W. Fortunate son
PSYCHOPATHS -- FICTION
Barnes, J. Losers in space
Collomore, A. The ruining
Lyga, B. Game
Lyga, B. I hunt killers
Rainfield, C. Stained
PSYCHOTHERAPY -- FICTION
Giles, G. Right behind you
Greenberg, J. I never promised you a rose garden
Halpin, B. A really awesome mess
Haydu, C. A. OCD love story
Lyga, B. Goth girl rising
Mesrobian, C. Sex and violence
Sáenz, B. A. Last night I sang to the monster
Ptolemy's gate. Stroud, J.
PUBERTY -- FICTION
Raf, M. The symptoms of my insanity
PUERTO RICANS -- FICTION
Manzano, S. The revolution of Evelyn Serrano
Ortiz Cofer, J. Call me Maria
Ortiz Cofer, J. If I could fly
Ostow, M. Emily Goldberg learns to salsa
The **pull** of gravity. Polisner, G.
Pullman, Philip, 1946-
The amber spyglass
The golden compass
Once upon a time in the North
The subtle knife
PUNK ROCK MUSIC -- FICTION
Castellucci, C. Beige
Punkzilla. Rapp, A.
Puppet. Wiseman, E.
PUPPETEERS -- FICTION
Frost, G. Lord Tophet
PUPPETS AND PUPPET PLAYS -- FICTION
Huser, G. Stitches
Purcell, Kim
Trafficked
Pure. McVoy, T. E.
Pure Spring. Doyle, B.
Purple Heart. McCormick, P.
Pushing the limits. McGarry, K.
Putting makeup on dead people. Violi, J.
Putting makeup on the fat boy. Wright, B.
PUZZLES -- FICTION
Ephron, D. Frannie in pieces

Q

Qamar, Amjed
Beneath my mother's feet
Quaking. Erskine, K.
Quarantine. Thomas, L.
QUARANTINE -- FICTION
Falls, K. Inhuman
QUÉBEC (PROVINCE) -- FICTION
Polak, M. The middle of everywhere
The **Queen** of Attolia. Turner, M. W.
The **queen** of cool. Castellucci, C.
The **queen** of Kentucky. Whitaker, A.
Queen of the dead. Kade, S.
Queen of hearts. Brooks, M.
Queen of secrets. Meyerhoff, J.

The **Queen** of Water. Farinango, M. V.
The **queen's** daughter. Coventry, S.
QUEENS -- FICTION
Carson, R. The bitter kingdom
Carson, R. The crown of embers
Cashore, K. Bitterblue
Chima, C. W. The Crimson Crown
Cokal, S. The Kingdom of little wounds
Coventry, S. The queen's daughter
Dray, S. Lily of the Nile
Friesner, E. M. Sphinx's princess
Friesner, E. M. Sphinx's queen
Klein, L. M. Cate of the Lost Colony
Libby, A. M. The king's rose
MacColl, M. Prisoners in the palace
Meyer, C. Cleopatra confesses
Meyer, C. Duchessina
Shecter, V. A. Cleopatra's moon
Quest. Duble, K. B.
Quick, Barbara
A golden web
Quick, Matthew
Boy21
Forgive me, Leonard Peacock
Sorta like a rockstar
Quicksilver. Spinner, S.
Quid pro quo. Grant, V.
QUINCEAÑERA (SOCIAL CUSTOM) -- FICTION
Alegria, M. Estrella's quinceanera
Chambers, V. Fifteen candles
Quintana of Charyn. Marchetta, M.
Quintero, I.
Gabi, a girl in pieces
Quintero, Sofia
Efrain's secret
Quiver. Spinner, S.

R

RABBITS -- FICTION
Adams, R. Watership Down
Zuckerman, L. A taste for rabbit
Rabin, Staton
Black powder
RACE RELATIONS -- FICTION
Cardenas, T. Letters to my mother
Hegedus, B. Between us Baxters
Jones, T. L. Finding my place
Marsden, C. Sahwira
McMullan, M. Sources of light
Moses, S. P. The legend of Buddy Bush
Myers, W. D. Riot
Nolan, H. A summer of Kings
Paton, A. Cry, the beloved country
Quick, M. Boy21
Schmidt, G. D. Lizzie Bright and the Buckminster boy
Taylor, M. D. The land
Volponi, P. Black and white
Watkins, S. Down Sand Mountain
Rachel's secret. Sanders, S.
RACIALLY MIXED PEOPLE -- FICTION
Crutcher, C. Whale talk
Frank, E. R. America
Hearn, J. Hazel
Hopkinson, N. The Chaos
Magoon, K. Camo girl
Maldonado, T. Secret Saturdays
McMullan, M. Cashay
Myers, W. D. Riot
Ostow, M. Emily Goldberg learns to salsa
Taylor, M. D. The land
Wilson, D. L. Black storm comin'
Woodson, J. Miracle's boys
RACING -- FICTION
Stiefvater, M. The Scorpio Races
Racing Savannah. Kenneally, M.
RACISM -- FICTION
Crowe, C. Mississippi trial, 1955
Magoon, K. Fire in the streets
Wright, B. Crow
Radiance. Noel, A.
Radiant days. Hand, E.
Radiant shadows. Marr, M.
RADIO -- FICTION
Fleischman, P. Seek
RADIO PROGRAMS -- FICTION
Cooney, C. B. The voice on the radio
Raedeke, Christy
The daykeeper's grimoire
The serpent's coil
Raf, Mindy
The symptoms of my insanity
The **raft.** Bodeen, S. A.
RAFTING (SPORTS) -- FICTION
Mills, T. Heartbreak river
Woods, R. The hero
Rage. Peters, J. A.
Rage within. Roberts, J.
Raiders night. Lipsyte, R.
RAILROADS -- FICTION
Miéville, C. Railsea
Railsea. Miéville, C.
RAIN FORESTS -- FICTION
Gilman, D. Blood sun
Khoury, J. Origin
Yep, L. Dragon's gate; Golden Mountain chronicles: 1867
Rain is not my Indian name. Smith, C. L.
Rainbow boys. Sanchez, A.
Rainbow High. Sanchez, A.

Rainbow road. Sanchez, A.
Rainfield, Cheryl
Scars
Stained
Raleigh, Walter Sir, 1552?-1618
About
Klein, L. M. Cate of the Lost Colony
Rallison, Janette
How to take the ex out of ex-boyfriend
Just one wish
RAMADAN -- FICTION
Robert, N. B. Boy vs. girl
RANCH LIFE -- FICTION
Brennan, C. House of the star
Smith, A. Ghost medicine
Waters, Z. C. Blood moon rider
RANCH LIFE -- SPAIN -- FICTION
Kephart, B. Small damages
Randall, Thomas
Dreams of the dead
Spirits of the Noh
RAP MUSIC -- FICTION
Alexander, K. The crossover
Mattison, B. T. Unsigned hype
McDonald, J. Harlem Hustle
RAP MUSICIANS -- FICTION
Woodson, J. After Tupac and D Foster
RAPE -- FICTION
Crocker, N. Billie Standish was here
Grace, A. In too deep
Hopkins, E. Smoke
Marcus, K. Exposed
RAPE VICTIMS -- FICTION
Alpine, R. Canary
Rapp, Adam
The children and the wolves
Punkzilla
Under the wolf, under the dog
Rapture of the deep. Meyer, L. A.
Raskin, Joyce
My misadventures as a teenage rock star
Rasputin, Grigori Efimovich, 1871-1916
About
Whitcomb, L. The Fetch
Rat life. Arnold, T.
RATS -- FICTION
Pratchett, T. The amazing Maurice and his educated rodents
Rats saw God. Thomas, R.
Ravel, Edeet
The saver
The **raven** boys. Stiefvater, M.
Raven cycle [series]
Stiefvater, M. The dream thieves
The Raven duet [series]
Bell, H. Traitor's son
Bell, H. Trickster's girl
Raven flight. Marillier, J.
Raven rise. MacHale, D. J.
RAVENS -- FICTION
Raven's gate. Horowitz, A.
RAVENSBRUCK (CONCENTRATION CAMP) -- FICTION
Wein, E. Rose under fire
Rawlings, Marjorie Kinnan
The yearling
Rayne Tour [series]
Collins, B. Always watching
RAYS (FISHES) -- FICTION
Medina, M. Milagros
Razzell, Mary
Snow apples
Reaching for sun. Zimmer, T. V.
Reaching out. Jimenez, F.
READING -- FICTION
Castan, M. Fighting for Dontae
Paulsen, G. Nightjohn
Real live boyfriends. Lockhart, E.
The **real** quesFICTION. Fogelin, A.
Reality Boy. King, A. S.
Reality check. Abrahams, P.
REALITY TELEVISION PROGRAMS -- FICTION
Demetrios, H. Something real
Hattemer, K. The vigilante poets of the Selwyn Academy
King, A. S. Reality Boy
Williams, K. Pizza, love, and other stuff that made me famous
A **really** awesome mess. Halpin, B.
Reasons to be happy. Kittle, K.
Reaves, Michael
Gaiman, N. Interworld
The **redheaded** princess. Rinaldi, A.
Rebel angels. Bray, L.
Rebel fire. Lane, A.
The **rebels** of New SUN. Kinch, M.
Reboot. Tintera, A.
Recipe for disaster. Fergus, M.
Reckless. Funke, C.
The **reckoning.** Armstrong, K.
Recruited. Weyn, S.
RECONSTRUCTION (U.S. HISTORY, 1865-1877) -- FICTION
Recovery Road. Nelson, B.
RECYCLING -- FICTION
Bacigalupi, P. Ship Breaker
Red glass. Resau, L.
Red glove. Black, H.
Red kayak. Cummings, P.
Red moon rising. Moore, P.
Red moon at Sharpsburg. Wells, R.

The **red** necklace. Gardner, S.
The **redheaded** princess. Rinaldi, A.
Reed, Amy
Crazy
Over you
Reed, Jaime
Living violet
Reed, Larkin
(jt. auth) Moore, K. Amber House
(jt. auth) Moore, K. Neverwas
Reedy, Trent
Words in the dust
Reed, Tucker
(jt. auth) Moore, K. Amber House
(jt. auth) Moore, K. Neverwas
Rees, Celia
The fool's girl
Pirates!
Sovay
Rees, D.
Vampire High: sophomore year
Rees, Douglas C.
Vampire High
Reese, James
The strange case of Doctor Jekyll and Mademoiselle Odile
Reeve, Philip, 1966-
Fever Crumb
Here lies Arthur
Scrivener's moon
A Web of Air
Reeves, Dia
Slice of cherry
REFORMATORIES -- FICTION
Cerrito, A. The end of the line
Wright, D. Violence 101
The **reformed** vampire support group. Jinks, C.
REFUGEES -- FICTION
Bacigalupi, P. The drowned cities
Bassoff, L. Lost girl found
Coates, J. L. A hare in the elephant's trunk
Farish, T. The good braider
Manivong, L. Escaping the tiger
Millard, G. A small free kiss in the dark
Park, L. S. A long walk to water
Pausewang, G. Dark hours
REFUSE AND REFUSE DISPOSAL -- FICTION
Mulligan, A. Trash
REGENCY NOVELS -- FICTION
Doyle, M. Courtship and curses
Kindl, P. Keeping the castle
REGENTS -- FICTION
Meyer, C. Duchessina
Reger, Rob
Emily the Strange: the lost days
REGRESSION (CIVILIZATION) -- FICTION
Steele, A. Apollo's outcasts
REHABILITATION -- FICTION
Price, N. Zoe letting go
Reichs, Kathleen J.
Seizure
Virals
Reid, Kimberly
My own worst frenemy
Reign check. Rowen, M.
Reign or shine. Rowen, M.
REINCARNATION -- FICTION
Littke, L. Lake of secrets
Miller, K. All you desire
Weyn, S. Reincarnation
Reincarnation. Weyn, S.
Reinhardt, Dana
A brief chapter in my impossible life
Harmless
How to build a house
The things a brother knows
We are the goldens
RELIEF WORKERS -- FICTION
Park, L. S. A long walk to water
RELIGION -- FICTION
Blume, J. Are you there God?
Bunce, E. C. Star crossed
Epstein, R. God is in the pancakes
Hautman, P. The obsidian blade
Hautman, P. Godless
Johnson, V. Saving Maddie
Levitin, S. Strange relations
Mills, S. The viper within
Rich, N. Alis
RELIGION AND SCIENCE -- FICTION
Morden, S. The lost art
RELIGIOUS LEADERS -- FICTION
Parker, A. C. Gated
RELIGIOUS LIFE -- FICTION
Barnhouse, R. The book of the maidservant
Hoffman, M. The falconer's knot
Howell, S. Everything beautiful
The **reluctant** journal of Henry K. Larsen. Nielsen, S.
Reluctantly Alice. Naylor, P. R.
REMARRIAGE -- FICTION
Collins, Y. The new and improved Vivien Leigh Reid; diva in control
Friend, N. Bounce
Keplinger, K. A midsummer's nightmare
Martin, C. K. K. The lighter side of life and death
Smith, J. E. The statistical probability of love at first sight
Rembrandt Harmenszoon van Rijn, 1606-1669
About

Cullen, L. I am Rembrandt's daughter
Remembering Raquel. Vande Velde, V.
The **reminder.** Michaels, R.
Remote control. Heath, J.
RENAISSANCE -- FICTION
Beaufrand, M. J. Primavera
Hoffman, M. The falconer's knot
Marsh, K. Jepp, who defied the stars
Napoli, D. J. The smile
Renn, Diana
Tokyo heist
Rennison, Louise
Angus, thongs and full-frontal snogging
Are these my basoomas I *see* before me?
Stop in the name of pants!
The taming of the tights
Withering tights
The **replacement.** Yovanoff, B.
REPORTERS AND REPORTING -- FICTION
Larson, K. Hattie ever after
REPTILES -- FICTION
Townsend, W. Lizard love
Repossessed. Jenkins, A. M.
Requiem. Oliver, L.
Res judicata. Grant, V.
Resau, Laura
(jt. auth) Farinango, M. V. The Queen of Water
The indigo notebook
Red glass
The ruby notebook
What the moon saw
RESEARCH -- FICTION
Oppel, K. Half brother
The **resistance.** Malley, G.
GOVERNMENT, RESISTANCE TO--FICTION
Bass, K. Graffiti knight
Charbonneau, J. Independent study
Dos Santos, S. The culling
Hall, T. Away
Hill, C. J. Erasing time
Johnson, A. D. The summer prince
Lu, M. Prodigy
Marsden, C. My Own Revolution
Oliver, L. Requiem
Zhang, K. Once we were
RESORTS -- FICTION
Cohn, R. Beta
Dessen, S. The moon and more
Jacobson, J. The complete history of why I hate her
Schindler, H. Playing hurt
RESTAURANTS -- FICTION
Knowles, J. See you at Harry's
Wood, F. When Molly was a Harvey Girl
Restoring harmony. Anthony, J.
Restrepo, Bettina
Illegal
Resurrection blues. Tanner, M.
Resurrection of magic [series]
Duey, K. Skin hunger
Resurrection of magic [series]
Duey, K. Sacred scars
Return to Daemon Hall: evil roots. Nance, A.
Return to me. Chen, J.
The **returning.** Hinwood, C.
Revelations. De la Cruz, M.
The **revenant.** Gensler, S.
REVENGE -- FICTION
Croggon, A. Black spring
Finneyfrock, K. The sweet revenge of Celia Door
Minato, K.. Confessions.
Wolfson, J. Furious
Revenge of a not-so-pretty girl. Blythe, C.
Revenge of the Girl With the Great Personality. Eulberg, E.
Revis, Beth
Across the universe
A million suns
Shades of Earth
Revived. Patrick, C.
Revolution. Donnelly, J.
The **revolution** of Evelyn Serrano. Manzano, S.
REVOLUTIONARIES -- FICTION
Shusterman, N. UnSouled
Shusterman, N. UnWholly
REVOLUTIONS -- FICTION
Harland, R. Liberator
Hesse, K. Safekeeping
Revolver. Sedgwick, M.
Rex, Adam
Fat vampire
Reynolds, Jason
When I was the greatest
Reynolds, Marilyn
Shut up!
RHODE ISLAND -- FICTION
Freitas, D. The possibilities of sainthood
Gray, C. Spellcaster
Gray, C. Steadfast
Griffin, A. Tighter
Griffin, A. Where I want to be
Rhuday-Perkovich, Olugbemisola
8th grade superzero
Rice-Gonzalez, Charles
Chulito
The **rich** man of Pietermaritzburg. Nyembezi, C. L. S.
Rich, Naomi
Alis
Rich, Simon
Elliot Allagash

Richards, Jame
Three rivers rising
Richards, Natalie D.
Six months later
Richter, Conrad
The light in the forest
The **Riddle.** Croggon, A.
The **riddles** of Epsilon. Morton-Shaw, C.
Riding invisible. Alonzo, S.
Riding the universe. Triana, G.
Right behind you. Giles, G.
Riley Park. Tullson, D.
Riggs, Ransom
Miss Peregrine's home for peculiar children
Rikers High. Volponi, P.
Rimbaud, Arthur
About
Hand, E. Radiant days
Rinaldi, Ann
Come Juneteenth
The fifth of March; a story of the Boston Massacre
Girl in blue
The redheaded princess
An unlikely friendship
The **ring** of Solomon. Stroud, J.
Ringo, John, 1844-1882
About
Ringside, 1925. Bryant, J.
Riordan, James
The sniper
Riot. Myers, W. D., 1937-
RIOTS -- FICTION
Myers, A. Tulsa burning.
Myers, W. D. Riot
Ripple. Hubbard, A.
Riptide. Scheibe, L.
The **rise** of a hero. Bell, H.
The **rise** of Lubchenko. Simmons, M.
The **rising.** Hill, W.
RISK-TAKING (PSYCHOLOGY) -- FICTION
Oliver, L. Panic
Violi, J. Putting makeup on dead people
The **rites** & wrongs of Janice Wills. Pearson, J.
The **Rithmatist.** Sanderson, B.
Rival. Bennett Wealer, S.
The **rivals.** Whitney, D.
The **river.** Beaufrand, M. J.
The **river** between us. Peck, R.
RIVERS -- FICTION
Mills, T. Heartbreak river
The **road** of the dead. Brooks, K.
ROANOKE ISLAND (N.C.) -- HISTORY -- FICTION
Klein, L. M. Cate of the Lost Colony
ROBBERS AND OUTLAWS -- FICTION
Heath, J. Money run
Patron, S. Behind the masks
Shoemaker, T. Code of silence
Updale, E. Montmorency
Robert, Na'ima B.
Boy vs. girl
From Somalia with love
Roberts, Jeyn
Dark inside
Rage within
Robinson, A. M.
Vampire crush
Robinson, Kim Stanley
Fifty degrees below
Forty signs of rain
ROBOTS -- FICTION
Meyer, M. Cinder
Michaels, R. The reminder
Powell, W. C. Expiration day
Ruins
The **rock** and the river. Magoon, K.
Rocco, John
Swim that rock
ROCK MUSIC -- FICTION
Briant, E. I am (not) the walrus
Calame, D. Beat the band
Hannan, P. My big mouth
Raskin, J. My misadventures as a teenage rock star
Yolen, J. Pay the piper
ROCK MUSICIANS -- FICTION
Skuse, C. J. Rockoholic
Rock star, superstar. Nelson, B.
Rockoholic. Skuse, C. J.
ROCK SPRINGS MASSACRE, ROCK SPRINGS, WYO., 1885 -- FICTION
Yep, L. The traitor; Golden Mountain chronicles, 1885
ROCKS
Roecker, Lisa
The Liar Society
The lies that bind
Rodman, Sean
Infiltration
Rogue. Damico, G.
The **Rogues**. Yolen, J.
ROLE PLAYING -- FICTION
Brezenoff, S. Guy in real life
Powell, L. The Master of Misrule
ROME -- HISTORY -- FICTION
Dray, S. Lily of the Nile
Shecter, V. A. Cleopatra's moon
Romeo's ex. Fiedler, L.
Rooftop. Volponi, P.
A **room** on Lorelei Street. Pearson, M.
Roomies. Zarr, S.

ROOMMATES -- FICTION
Giles, G. Girls like us
Zarr, S. Roomies
The ropemaker. Dickerson, M.
Rorby, Ginny
Lost in the river of grass
The outside of a horse
Rose by any other name. McCarthy, M.
Rose daughter. McKinley, R.
Rose sees red. Castellucci, C.
Rose under fire. Wein, E.
Rosebush. Jaffe, M.
Rosen, Renee
Every crooked pot
Rosenfield, Kat
Amelia Anne is dead and gone
Rosie & Skate. Bauman, B. A.
Roskos, Evan
Dr. Bird's advice for sad poets
Rosoff, Meg
Picture me gone
There is no dog
Ross, Elizabeth
Belle epoque
Ross, Jeff
The drop
Rossetti, Rinsai
The girl with borrowed wings
Rossi, Veronica
Under the never sky
Rot & ruin. Maberry, J.
Roth, Veronica
Allegiant
Divergent
Insurgent
Rothenberg, Jess
The catastrophic history of you & me
Rotters. Kraus, D.
Rottman, S. L.
Out of the blue
Rowell, Rainbow
Eleanor & Park
Fangirl
Rowen, Michelle
Reign check
Reign or shine
Rowling, J. K.
Harry Potter and the deathly hallows
Harry Potter and the Chamber of Secrets
Harry Potter and the Goblet of Fire
Harry Potter and the Half-blood Prince
Harry Potter and the Order of the Phoenix
Harry Potter and the prisoner of Azkaban
Harry Potter and the Sorcerer's Stone
Roy, Jennifer Rozines
Mindblind
Rubber houses. Yeomans, E.
Rubens, Michael
Sons of the 613
The Ruby Key. Lisle, H.
The **ruby** notebook. Resau, L.
Ruby red. Gier, K.
Ruby, Laura
Bad apple
Ruby, Lois
The secret of Laurel Oaks
Shanghai shadows
Ruby's imagine. Antieau, K.
Rucker Park setup. Volponi, P.
Ruditis, Paul
The four Dorothys
Rudnick, Paul, 1957-
Gorgeous
Rue, Ginger
Brand new Emily
RUGBY FOOTBALL -- FICTION
Winger . Smith, A.
Ruin and rising. Bardugo, L.
Ruined. Morris, P.
The **ruining.** Collomore, A.
Ruins. Card, O. S.
Ruiz Zafon, Carlos
Marina
The Midnight Palace
The Prince of Mist
The **Rule** of Won. Petrucha, S.
The **rules.** Kade, S.
The **rules** for disappearing. Elston, A.
Rules of attraction. Elkeles, S.
The **rules** of survival. Werlin, N.
Rumble. Hopkins, E.
Rumley, Crickett
Never sit down in a hoopskirt and other things I learned in Southern belle hell
RUMOR -- FICTION
Grace, A. In too deep
Runaway. Cabot, M.
RUNAWAY CHILDREN -- FICTION
Barnaby, H. Wonder show
Mazer, H. Snow bound
Parkinson, S. Long story short
Wells, M. Emilie & the hollow world
Runaway. Draanen, W. V.
RUNAWAY TEENAGERS -- FICTION
Barnes, J. Losers in space
Cross, S. Kill me softly
Doctorow, C. Pirate cinema
Griffin, P. Ten Mile River
Leavitt, M. My book of life by Angel
Rush, J. Altered
Walters, E. Sketches
Wakefield, V. Friday never leaving

Whelan, G. Chu Ju's house
Woodson, J. Lena
Wells, M. Emilie & the hollow world
RUNAWAYS -- FICTION
Arcos, C. Out of reach
Armistead, C. Being Henry David
Barnaby, H. Wonder show
Blair, J. Leap of Faith
Hopkins, E. Smoke
Lam, L. Pantomime
Leavitt, M. My book of life by Angel
Ross, E. Belle epoque
Rush, J. Altered
Woodson, J. Beneath a meth moon
Runemarks. Harris, J.
Runholt, Susan
The mystery of the third Lucretia
Runner. Deuker, C.
Runner. Newton, R.
RUNNING -- FICTION
Childs, T. L. Oh. My. Gods
Myers, W. D. Darius & Twig
Newton, R. Runner
Van Draanen, W. The running dream
Running on the cracks. Donaldson, J.
The **running** dream. Van Draanen, W.
Running loose. Crutcher, C.
Runyon, Brent
Surface tension
Rupp, Rebecca
After Eli
Rush. Silver, E.
Rush, Jennifer
Altered
Russell, Randy
Dead rules
RUSSIA -- FICTION
Bardugo, L. Siege and storm
RUSSIA -- FICTION
Bridges, R. The gathering storm
RUSSIA -- HISTORY -- 1904-1914 -- FICTION
O'Brien, A. Lara's gift
RUSSIA -- HISTORY -- 1905, REVOLUTION -- FICTION
Miller, S. The lost crown
RUSSIAN AMERICANS -- FICTION
Kiem, E. Dancer, daughter, traitor, spy
RUSSIANS -- FICTION
Castellucci, C. Rose sees red
Russon, Penni
Breathe
Rutkoski, Marie
The shadow society
RWANDA -- FICTION
Combres, E. Broken memory
Jansen, H. Over a thousand hills I walk with you
Ryan, Amy Kathleen
Flame
Glow
Spark
Zen & Xander undone
Ryan, Carrie
The dark and hollow places
The dead-tossed waves
The Forest of Hands and Teeth
Ryan, Patrick
Gemini bites
In Mike we trust
Ryan, Sara
Empress of the world
Ryan, Tom
Way to go

S

Sabriel. Nix, G.
Sacagawea, b. 1786
About
Bruchac, J. Sacajawea
Sacajawea. Bruchac, J.
The cardturner
Sacred scars. Duey, K.
Saenz, Benjamin Alire
Sáenz, B. A. Last night I sang to the monster
Aristotle and Dante discover the secrets of the universe
He forgot to say good-bye
Last night I sang to the monster
Sammy and Juliana in Hollywood
Safe. Shaw, S.
Safekeeping. Hesse, K.
Saga. Kostick, C.
Saffy's angel. McKay, H.
SAHARA DESERT -- FICTION
Okorafor, N. The shadow speaker
Sahwira; an African friendship. Marsden, C.
SAILING – FICTION
Herlong, M. The great wide sea
Stevenson, R. A thousand shades of blue
Saint Iggy. Going, K. L.
SAINT PETERSBURG (RUSSIA) -- HISTORY -- 20TH CENTURY -- FICTION
Standiford, N. The boy on the bridge
SAINT PETERSBURG (RUSSIA) -- SIEGE, 1941-1944 -- FICTION
Whelan, G. Burying the sun
SAINTS -- FICTION
Gormley, B. Poisoned honey
Grimes, N. A girl named Mister
SAINTS -- FICTION

Freitas, D. The possibilities of sainthood
Gormley, B. Poisoned honey
Saldaña, René
A good long way
SALEM (MASS.) -- FICTION
Hearn, J. The minister's daughter
Hemphill, S. Wicked girls
Turner, A. W. Father of lies
Salerni, Dianne K.
We hear the dead
Sales, Leila
Mostly good girls
Past perfect
This song will save your life
Salisbury, Graham
Eyes of the emperor
House of the red fish
Lord of the deep
Under the blood-red sun
Salmon, Dena K.
Discordia
Salt. Gee, M.
The Salt trilogy [series]
Gee, M. Gool
Gee, M. The Limping Man
Gee, M. Salt
Salter, Sydney
Swoon at your own risk
SALVADORAN AMERICANS -- FICTION
Perez, A. H. The knife and the butterfly
T**Samms, Olivia**
Sketchy
Sammy and Juliana in Hollywood. Saenz, B. A.
Sampson, Deborah, 1760-1827
About
Klass, S. S. Soldier's secret
SAMURAI -- FICTION
Matthews, A. The way of the warrior
Samurai shortstop. Gratz, A.
SAN ANTONIO (TEX.) -- FICTION
Villareal, R. Body slammed!
SAN DIEGO (CALIF.) -- FICTION
Scheibe, L. Riptide
Winters, C. In the shadow of blackbirds
SAN FRANCISCO (CALIF.) -- FICTION
Bjorkman, L. Miss Fortune Cookie
Bullen, A. Wish
Cadnum, M. Flash
Childs, T. L. Sweet venom
Doctorow, C. Homeland
Doctorow, C. Little brother
Fischer, J. An egg on three sticks
Lavender, W. Aftershocks
Perkins, S. Lola and the boy next door
Zarr, S. The Lucy variations
SAN FRANCISCO (CALIF.) -- HISTORY --
20TH CENTURY -- FICTION
Larson, K. Hattie ever after
Lynch, J. N. My beautiful hippie
Sanchez, Alex
Bait
Getting it
Rainbow boys
Rainbow High
Rainbow road
So hard to say
Sandell, Lisa Ann
Song of the sparrow
Sanders, Scott Loring
Gray baby
The Hanging Woods
Sanders, Shelly
Rachel's secret
Sanderson, Brandon
The Rithmatist
Sandler, Karen
Tankborn
Sandpiper. Wittlinger, E.
Sapphique. Fisher, C.
Sapphire blue.
Sandry's book. Pierce, T.
Saturday night dirt. Weaver, W.
SAVANTS (SAVANT SYNDROME) -- FICTION
The **saver.** Ravel, E.
Saving Francesca. Marchetta, M.
Saving Maddie. Johnson, V.
Saving Juliet. Selfors, S.
Sax, Aline
The war within these walls
Say the word. Garsee, J.
Scaletta, Kurtis
Mamba Point
SCARABS -- FICTION
Gleason, C. The clockwork scarab
Scarlet. Meyer, M.
Scarlett fever. Johnson, M.
Scarrow, Alex
Day of the predator
TimeRiders
The **scar** boys. Vlahos, L
Scars. Rainfield, C.
Scheibe, Lindsey
Riptide
Scheidt, Erica Lorraine
Uses for boys
The **Schernoff** discoveries. Paulsen, G.
Schindler, Holly
A blue so dark
Playing hurt
SCHIZOPHRENIA -- FICTION
Suma, N. R. 17 & gone
Vaught, S. Freaks like us

Schmeling, Max, 1905-2005
About
Sharenow, R. The Berlin Boxing Club
Schmidt, Gary D.
Lizzie Bright and the Buckminster boy
Trouble
The Wednesday wars
Schneider, Robyn
The beginning of everything
SCHOLARSHIPS -FICTION
Walker, B. F. Black boy/white school
SCHOLARSHIPS -- FICTION
Haddix, M. P. Full ride
SCHOOL INTEGRATION -- FICTION
Levine, K. The lions of Little Rock
Sharenow, R. My mother the cheerleader
SCHOOL SHOOTINGS -- FICTION
Hassan, M. Crash and Burn
Quick, M. Forgive me, Leonard Peacock
School spirits. Hawkins, R.
SCHOOL SPORTS -- FICTION
Fichera, L. Hooked
SCHOOL STORIES
Abdel-Fattah, R. Does my head look big in this?
Abdel-Fattah, R. Ten things I hate about me
Abrahams, P. Reality check
Abrams, A. Hollywood High
Acosta, M. Dark companion
Alender, K. Bad girls don't die
Alexie, S. The absolutely true diary of a part-time Indian
Altebrando, T. Dreamland social club
Alvarez, J. Finding miracles
Anderson, K. D. Kiss & Make Up
Anderson, L. H. Prom
Anderson, L. H. Speak
Anderson, L. H. Twisted
Archer, J. Through her eyes
Ashby, A. Fairy bad day
Ashby, A. Zombie queen of Newbury High
Asher, J. The future of us
Asher, J. Thirteen reasons why
Atkins, C. Alt ed
Avi Nothing but the truth
Ayarbe, H. Compulsion
Badoe, A. Between sisters
Baer, M. Frost
Bancks, T. Mac Slater hunts the cool
Baratz-Logsted, L. Crazy beautiful
Barnes, J. L. The Squad: perfect cover
Barnes, J. Tales of the Madman Underground
Bates, M. Awkward
Bauer, J. Peeled
Beaudoin, S. You killed Wesley Payne
Bennett Wealer, S. Rival
Benoit, C. You
Benway, R. Also known as
Benway, R. The extraordinary secrets of April, May and June
Berk, J. The dark days of Hamburger Halpin
Bigelow, L. J. Starting from here
Billerbeck, K. Perfectly dateless
Bjorkman, L. Miss Fortune Cookie
Bjorkman, L. My invented life
Bloor, E. A plague year
Bloss, J. Albatross
Boyd, M. Will
Brande, R. Evolution, me, & other freaks of nature
Brande, R. Fat Cat
Brennan, S. R. Team Human
Brody, J. My life undecided
Brown, J. Hate list
Budhos, M. Ask me no questions
Burton, R. Leaving Jetty Road
Butcher, K. Cheat
Calame, D. Beat the band
Carriger, G. Etiquette & espionage
Castan, M. The price of loyalty
Castellucci, C. The queen of cool
Castellucci, C. Rose sees red
Castle, J. You look different in real life
Carvell, M. Sweetgrass basket
Carvell, M. Who will tell my brother?
Chaltas, T. Because I am furniture
Chapman, L. Flawless
Charlton-Trujillo, e. E. Fat Angie
Chbosky, S. The perks of being a wallflower
Cheva, C. DupliKate
Childs, T. L. Oh. My. Gods
Chow, C. Bitter melon
Clement-Moore, R. Hell Week
Clement-Moore, R. Prom dates from Hell
Coben, H. Shelter
Cohen, J. C. Leverage
Cohen, T. Little black lies
Cohn, R. Shrimp
Colasanti, S. So much closer
Colasanti, S. Something like fate
Cook, E. The education of Hailey Kendrick
Cooney, C. B. Code orange
Cormier, R. Beyond the chocolate war
Cormier, R. The chocolate war
Corrigan, E. Accomplice
Corrigan, E. Ordinary ghosts
Coy, J. Box out
Coy, J. Crackback
Crawford, B. Carter finally gets it
Crawford, B. Carter's unfocused, one-track mind
Crewe, M. Give up the ghost

Crutcher, C. Deadline
Crutcher, C. Ironman
Crutcher, C. Ironman; a novel
Crutcher, C. Period 8
Crutcher, C. Running loose
Crutcher, C. Whale talk
Cummings, P. Blindsided
Daugherty, C. J. Night School
David, K. Lia's guide to winning the lottery
Davidson, J. The Explosionist
De Goldi, K. The 10 p.m. question
De Lint, C. The blue girl
Delsol, W. Frost
Delsol, W. Stork
Derting, K. Desires of the dead
Despain, B. The dark Divine
Dessen, S. 1. What happened to goodbye
Dessen, S. Just listen
Deuker, C. Gym candy
Deuker, C. Painting the black
DeVillers, J. Lynn Visible
Dooley, S. Livvie Owen lived here
Draper, S. M. The Battle of Jericho
Draper, S. M. Just another hero
Draper, S. M. November blues
Duey, K. Sacred scars
Duncan, L. Killing Mr. Griffin
Efaw, A. After
Elkeles, S. Perfect chemistry
Elkeles, S. Rules of attraction
Ellis, D. Bifocal
Emond, S. Happyface
Every you, every me
Fehlbaum, B. Hope in Patience
Fehler, G. Beanball
Finneyfrock, K. The sweet revenge of Celia Door
Flinn, A. Breaking point
Frank, H. Better than running at night
Fredericks, M. Crunch time
Fredericks, M. Head games
Freitas, D. The possibilities of sainthood
Friend, N. For keeps
García, C. Dreams of significant girls
Garcia, K. Beautiful creatures
Garden, N. Endgame
Garsee, J. Before, after, and somebody in between
Garvey, A. Cold kiss
Gelbwasser, M. Inconvenient
Gensler, S. The revenant
George, M. Looks
Giles, G. Playing in traffic
Giles, G. Shattering Glass
Gilman, C. Professor Gargoyle
Goldman, S. Two parties, one tux, and a very short film about the Grapes of Wrath
Gorman, C. Games
Grant, C. Teenie
Gratz, A. Samurai shortstop
Gray, C. Evernight
Green, J. Looking for Alaska
Griffin, A. The Julian game
Griffin, C. J. Nowhere to run
Grimes, N. Bronx masquerade
Halpern, J. Into the wild nerd yonder
Hannan, P. My big mouth
Harris, C. Bad taste in boys
Hartinger, B. Geography Club
Hassan, M. Crash and Burn
Hautman, P. The big crunch
Hautman, P. Blank confession
Hawkins, R. Hex Hall
Hawkins, R. School spirits
Healey, K. Guardian of the dead
Henderson, J. Vampire rising
Hernandez, D. No more us for you
Higgins, M. G. Bi-Normal
Hills, L. The beginner's guide to living
Hodkin, M. The unbecoming of Mara Dyer
Holland, L. T. The counterfeit family tree of Vee Crawford-Wong
Horner, E. A love story starring my dead best friend
Hrdlitschka, S. Allegra
Hubbard, A. But I love him
Hubbard, J. Paper covers rock
Hubbard, K. Like Mandarin
Hurley, T. Ghostgirl
Hyde, C. R. Jumpstart the world
Jaden, D. Losing Faith
Jarzab, A. All unquiet things
Jayne, H. Truly, madly, deadly
Jenkins, A. M. Repossessed
Jinks, C. Evil genius
Johnson, C. Nocturne
Johnson, M. The name of the star
Johnson, M. Scarlett fever
Jones, P. The tear collector
Jones, T. L. Finding my place
Jones, T. L. Standing against the wind
Juby, S. Getting the girl
Kade, S. The ghost and the goth
Karim, S. Skunk girl
Katcher, B. Almost perfect
Katcher, B. Playing with matches
Kate, L. The betrayal of Natalie Hargrove
Kenneally, M. Stealing Parker
Kephart, B. Undercover
Kerr, M. E. If I love you, am I trapped forever?
Kittle, K. Reasons to be happy
Klass, D. You don't know me

Koertge, R. Now playing
Koertge, R. Stoner & Spaz
Koja, K. Buddha boy
Koja, K. Headlong
Koja, K. Kissing the bee
Konigsberg, B. Openly straight
Kraus, D. Rotters
Krovatin, C. Heavy metal and you
Kuehn, S. Charm & strange
Laban, E. The Tragedy Paper
Leavitt, L. Going vintage
Leavitt, L. Sean Griswold's head
LeFlore, L. The world is mine
Levchuk, L. Everything beautiful in the world
Levithan, D. Two boys kissing
Liberty, A. The center of the universe
Lockhart, E. The boy book
Lockhart, E. The boyfriend list
Lockhart, E. The disreputable history of Frankie Landau-Banks
Lockhart, E. Real live boyfriends
Lockhart, E. The treasure map of boys
Love, D. A. Defying the diva
Lubar, D. Hidden talents
Lubar, D. Sleeping freshmen never lie
Luddy, K. Spelldown
Lyga, B. The astonishing adventures of Fanboy & Goth Girl
Lyga, B. Boy toy
Lyga, B. Goth girl rising
Lyga, B. Hero-type
Lynch, C. Inexcusable
Mackler, C. The earth, my butt, and other big, round things
Mackler, C. Vegan virgin Valentine
Mackey, W. K. Throwing like a girl
MacLean, J. Nix Minus One
Madigan, L. K. Flash burnout
Maizel, R. Infinite days
Maldonado, T. Secret Saturdays
Marchetta, M. Jellicoe Road
Marchetta, M. Saving Francesca
Marcus, K. Exposed
Marino, P. Dough Boy
Mariz, R. The Unidentified
Martin, C. K. K. I know it's over
Martin, C. K. K. The lighter side of life and death
Mass, W. A mango -shaped space
Mass, W. Heaven looks a lot like the mall
Matthews, L. S. The outcasts
McDaniel, L. Hit and run
McDonald, A. The anti-prom
McGowan, A. The knife that killed me
McKissack, F. Shooting star
McMann, L. Fade
McMann, L. Wake
McNish, C. Angel
McPhee, P. New blood
McVoy, T. E. After the kiss
Medina, M. Yaqui Delgado wants to kick your ass
Meminger, N. Shine, coconut moon
Mesrobian, C. Sex and violence
Meyer, S. Eclipse
Meyer, S. New moon
Meyer, S. Twilight
Meyerhoff, J. Queen of secrets
Myers, W. D. Slam!
Miller, K. How to lead a life of crime
Miranda, M. Hysteria
Mitchell, T. The secret to lying
Mlynowski, S. Gimme a call
Monaghan, A. A girl named Digit
A monster calls
Moore, C. The stalker chronicles
Moranville, S. B. A higher geometry
Moriarty, J. The ghosts of Ashbury High
Moriarty, J. The year of secret assignments
Myers, W. D. Game
Myers, W. D. A star is born
Myracle, L. Bliss
Nayeri, D. Another Faust
Naylor, P. R. Alice in April
Naylor, P. R. Faith, hope, and Ivy June
Naylor, P. R. Incredibly Alice
Naylor, P. R. Reluctantly Alice
Neely, C. Unearthly
Neff, H. H. The hound of Rowan
Nelson, B. Destroy all cars
Nelson, R. A. Breathe my name
Nichols, J. Messed up
Nolan, H. Crazy
Northrop, M. Gentlemen
Northrop, M. Trapped
Nothing
Oates, J. C. Two or three things I forgot to tell you
Oates, J. C. Big Mouth & Ugly Girl
O'Connell, T. True love, the sphinx, and other unsolvable riddles; a comedy in four voices
Oliver, L. Before I fall
Omololu, C. J. Dirty little secrets
Osterlund, A. Academy 7
Ostow, M. So punk rock (and other ways to disappoint your mother)
Padian, M. Brett McCarthy: work in progress
Palmer, R. Geek charming
Patrick, C. Forgotten
Paulsen, G. The Schernoff discoveries
Pausewang, G. Dark hours
Pearson, J. The rites & wrongs of

Janice Wills
Pearson, M. The miles between
Perkins, S. Anna and the French kiss
Phillips, S. Burn
Pike, A. Illusions
Portman, F. King Dork
Preller, J. Bystander
Prose, F. After
Prose, F. Touch
Quick, M. Forgive me, Leonard Peacock
Quick, M. Sorta like a rockstar
Quintero, S. Efrain's secret
Raf, M. The symptoms of my insanity
Rallison, J. How to take the ex out of ex-boyfriend
Randall, T. Dreams of the dead
Randall, T. Spirits of the Noh
Rees, D. Vampire High: sophomore year
Reid, K. My own worst frenemy
Rennison, L. The taming of the tights
Rex, A. Fat vampire
Rice-Gonzalez, C. Chulito
Rich, S. Elliot Allagash
Richards, N. D. Six months later
Roecker, L. The Liar Society
Roecker, L. The lies that bind
Rowell, R. Eleanor & Park
Rowell, R. Fangirl
Ruby, L. Bad apple
Ruditis, P. The four Dorothys
Russell, R. Dead rules
Saldana, R. A good long way
Sales, L. Mostly good girls
Sanchez, A. Getting it
Sanchez, A. Rainbow boys
Sanchez, A. Rainbow High
Schindler, H. A blue so dark
Schneider, R. The beginning of everything
Schumacher, J. Black box
Scott, E. Love you hate you miss you
Scott, K. Geek magnet
Scott, K. She's so dead to us
Seigel, A. Like the red panda
Shepard, J. Project X
Shulman, M. Scrawl
Shulman, P. Enthusiasm
Shusterman, N. Antsy does time
Siddell, T. Gunnerkrigg Court 3
Simon, C. Plan B
Skovron, J. Misfit
Sones, S. What my girlfriend doesn't know
Spinelli, J. Stargirl
Spinelli, J. There's a girl in my hammerlock
Stahler, D. Spinning out
St. James, J. Freak show
Standiford, N. The boy on the bridge
Staunton, T. Acting up
Stevenson, R. H. Out of order
Stevenson, S. J. The Latte Rebellion
Stiefvater, M. Ballad
Stone, T. L. A bad boy can be good for a girl
Strasser, T. Give a boy a gun
Strasser, T. Wish you were dead
Summers, C. Some girls are
Sutton, K. Some quiet place
Sweeney, J. The guardian
Takoudes, G. When we wuz famous
Tayleur, K. Chasing boys
Terry, C. L. Zero fade
Tharp, T. Knights of the hill country
Tharp, T. Mojo
Tharp, T. The spectacular now
Thomas, R. Rats saw God
Toliver, W. Lifted
Vacco, C. My chemical mountain
Valentine, A. How (not) to find a boyfriend
Vail, R. Lucky
Van de Ruit, J. Spud
Van Draanen, W. The running dream
Vande Velde, V. Remembering Raquel
Vaught, S. Big fat manifesto
Violi, J. Putting makeup on dead people
Vivian, S. Not that kind of girl
Volponi, P. Bad girls in love
Volponi, P. The hand you're dealt
Voorhees, C. The brothers Torres
Vrettos, A. M. Sight
Wallace, J. Out of shadows
Wallace, R. One good punch
Wallace, R. War and watermelon
Walters, E. In a flash
Walters, E. Special Edward
Warman, J. Breathless
Warman, J. Where the truth lies
Wasserman, R. Hacking Harvard
Waters, D. Generation dead
Watkins, S. Down Sand Mountain
Weaver, W. Defect
Weissman, E. B. The trouble with Mark Hopper
Wells, R. Feedback
Wells, R. E. Variant
Wesselhoeft, C. Adios, nirvana
Weyn, S. Recruited
Whitaker, A. The queen of Kentucky
White, A. B. Forget -her-nots
White, A. B. Window boy
White, A. B. Windows on the world
White, E. E. Long may she reign
Whitney, D. The Mockingbirds
Whittenberg, A. Sweet Thang
Wilhelm, D. Falling

Wilkinson, L. Pink
Williams, K. The space between trees
Williams-Garcia, R. Jumped
Wilson, M. What they always tell us
Winger . Smith, A.
Winston, S. The Kayla chronicles
Wiseman, R. Boys, girls, and other hazardous materials
Wittlinger, E. Parrotfish
Wizner, J. Spanking Shakespeare
Wolff, T. Old school
Wolff, V. E. This full house
Wollman, J. Switched
Wood, M. My life the musical
Wooding, C. Silver
Woods, B. A star on the Hollywood Walk of Fame
Woods, E. E. Choker
Woon, Y. Dead beautiful
Wrede, P. C. The thirteenth child
Wright, B. Putting makeup on the fat boy
Yang, D. J. Warp speed
Zadoff, A. Food, girls, and other things I can't have
Zadoff, A. My life, the theater, and other tragedies
Zarr, S. Sweethearts
Zevin, G. Memoirs of a teenage amnesiac
Ziegler, J. How not to be popular
Zweig, E. Cornered,

SCHOOL VIOLENCE -- FICTION
Prose, F. After

SCHOOLS -- FICTION
Kessler, J. M. Loss
Klass, D. You don't know me
Koertge, R. Stoner & Spaz
Mackler, C. Vegan virgin Valentine
Myers, W. D. The Cruisers
Oates, J. C. Big Mouth & Ugly Girl
Ryan, S. Empress of the world
Sanchez, A. Rainbow boys

Schraff, Anne E.
A boy called Twister

Schreck, Karen
While he was away

Schrefer, Eliot
The deadly sister
Endangered
Threatened

Schreiber, Ellen
Vampire kisses

Schreiber, Joe
Au revoir, crazy European chick
Perry's killer playlist

Schröder, Monika
My brother's shadow

Schroeder, Lisa
Chasing Brooklyn
Far from you

Schumacher, Julie
Black box

The **Schwa** was here. Shusterman, N.

Schwartz, Ellen
Cellular

Schwartz, Virginia Frances
Send one angel down

SCIENCE -- EXPERIMENTS -- FICTION
Khoury, J. Origin
Patrick, C. Revived
Price, L. Enders
Shepherd, M. The madman's daughter

SCIENCE FICTION
Adlington, L. J. Cherry Heaven.
Adlington, L. J. The diary of Pelly D
Aguirre, A. Horde
Aguirre, A. Outpost
Albin, G. Crewel
Anderson, R. J. Ultraviolet
Arnett, M. Avalon
Augarde, S. X Isle
Bacigalupi, P. Ship Breaker
Bacigalupi, P. The drowned cities
Bailey, K. Legacy of the clockwork key
Barnes, J. Losers in space
Beck, I. Pastworld
Bell, H. Traitor's son
Bick, I. J. Ashes
Black, H. Black heart
Black, H. Red glove
Black, H. The white cat
Block, F. L. Love in the time of global warming
Bloor, E. Taken
Bodeen, S. A. The gardener
Brooks, K. Being
Brooks, K. IBoy
Card, O. S. Children of the mind
Card, O. S. Ender in exile
Card, O. S. Ender's game
Card, O. S. Pathfinder
Card, O. S. Ruins
Card, O. S. Shadow of the giant
Card, O. S. Shadow of the Hegemon
Card, O. S. Shadow puppets
Card, O. S. Speaker for the Dead
Card, O. S. Xenocide
Carriger, G. Curtsies & conspiracies
Carriger, G. Etiquette & espionage
Clements, A. Things not seen
Clements, A. Things that are
Cohn, R. Beta
Cole, S. Z. Raptor

Cole, S. Z. Rex
Collins, P. J. S. What happened to Serenity?
Collins, S. Catching fire
Collins, S. Mockingjay
Collins, S. The Hunger Games
Cooper, T. Changers
Coutts, A. Tumble & fall
Crewe, M. The lives we lost
Crewe, M. The way we fall
Crockett, S. D. After the snow
Cross, J. Tempest
Cross, S. Dull boy
Crossan, S. Breathe
Dashner, J. The kill order
Dashner, J. The maze runner
Dashner, J. The scorch trials
DeStefano, L. Fever
DeStefano, L. Perfect ruin
DeStefano, L. Sever
DeStefano, L. Wither
Dickinson, P. Eva
Dixon, J. Phoenix Island
Doctorow, C. For the win
Doctorow, C. Pirate cinema
Dos Santos, S. The culling
Edwards, J. Earth girl
Engdahl, S. L. Enchantress from the stars
Falkner, B. Brain Jack
Falls, K. Inhuman
Farmer, N. The Ear, the Eye, and the Arm
Farmer, N. The house of the scorpion
Farmer, N. The lord of Opium
Fisher, C. The obsidian mirror
FitzGerald, H. Deviant
Ford, M. T. Z
Gagnon, M. Strangelets
Gaiman, N. Interworld
Garner, E. Contaminated
Gill, D. M. Black hole sun
Gill, D. M. Invisible sun
Gill, D. M. Shadow on the sun
Gilmore, K. The exchange student
Goodman, A. Singing the Dogstar blues
Halam, A. Dr. Franklin's island
Hall, T. Away
Hall, T. The Line
Harstad, J. 172 hours on the moon
Hautman, P. The Cydonian pyramid
Hautman, P. Hole in the sky
Hautman, P. The obsidian blade
Healey, K. When we wake
Healey, K. While we run
Heath, J. Remote control
Heath, J. The Lab
Hill, C. J. Erasing time
Hirsch, J. The eleventh plague
Hopkinson, N. The Chaos
Howard, J. L. Katya's World
Jinks, C. Living hell
Jinks, C. The genius wars
Johnson, A. D. The summer prince
Kade, S. The rules
Kagawa, J. The Eternity Cure
Karp, J. Those that wake
Khoury, J. Origin
Kinch, M. The blending time
Kinch, M. The fires of New SUN
Kinch, M. The rebels of New SUN
Kizer, A. A matter of days
Klass, D. Firestorm
Knutsson, C. Shadows cast by stars
Kostick, C. Edda
Krokos, D. False memory
Lancaster, M. A. The future we left behind
Le Guin, U. K. The lathe of heaven
Le Guin, U. K. The left hand of darkness
Lloyd, S. The carbon diaries 2015
Lloyd, S. The carbon diaries 2017
Lo, M. Adaptation
Lo, M. Inheritance
Lowry, L. Gathering blue
Lowry, L. Son
Lowry, L. The giver
Lu, M. Champion
Lu, M. Legend
Lu, M. Prodigy
Lyon, S. The gift moves
Malley, G. The Declaration
Malley, G. The resistance
Mariz, R. The Unidentified
Martin, C. K. Kelly Yesterday
Martin, T. M. The end games
Mary-Todd, J. Shot down
McCafferty, M. Thumped
McCaffrey, A. Dragonflight
McDevitt, J. Moonfall
McDonald, I. Be my enemy
McDonald, I. Empress of the sun
McDonald, I. Planesrunner
McEntire, M. Hourglass
McLaughlin, L. Scored
McQuein, J. L. Arclight
Meyer, M. Cinder
Meyer, M. Scarlet
Miller, W. M. A canticle for Leibowitz
Molina-Gavilan, Y. Cosmos latinos
Moore, P. Hero
Morden, S. The lost art
Mullin, M. Ashfall
Mullin, M. Sunrise
Ness, P. Monsters of men
Ness, P. The Ask and the Answer

Ness, P. The knife of never letting go
Nix, G. Shade's children
Nix, G. A confusion of princes
North, P. Starglass
O Guilin, P. The inferior
O'Brien, C. M. Birthmarked
O'Brien, J. Day of the assassins
O'Brien, J. Z for Zachariah
Okorafor, N. The shadow speaker
Oliver, L. Delirium
Oliver, L. Pandemonium
Oliver, L. Requiem
Osterlund, A. Academy 7
Palma, F. J. The map of time
Patterson, J. Maximum Ride: the angel experiment
Pearson, M. Fox forever
Pearson, M. The adoration of Jenna Fox
Pearson, M. The Fox Inheritance
Peterfreund, D. Across a star-swept sea
Peterfreund, D. For darkness shows the stars
Pfeffer, S. B. Life as we knew it
Philbrick, W. R. The last book in the universe
Pike, A. Earthbound
Powell, W. C. Expiration day
Price, L. Enders
Price, L. Starters
Rabin, S. Black powder
Reeve, P. A Web of Air
Reeve, P. Fever Crumb
Reeve, P. Scrivener's moon
Revis, B. A million suns
Revis, B. Across the universe
Revis, B. Shades of Earth
Roberts, J. Dark inside
Roberts, J. Rage within
Robinson, K. M. Fifty degrees below
Robinson, K. M. Forty signs of rain
Rossi, V. Under the never sky
Roth, V. Allegiant
Roth, V. Divergent
Roth, V. Insurgent
Rush, J. Altered
Rutkoski, M. The shadow society
Ryan, A. K. Flame
Ryan, A. K. Glow
Ryan, A. K. Spark
Salmon, D. K. Discordia
Sandler, K. Tankborn
Scalzi, J.Fuzzy nation
Scarrow, A. Day of the predator
Scarrow, A. TimeRiders
Shepherd, M. The madman's daughter
Shusterman, N. UnSouled
Shusterman, N. UnWholly
Shusterman, N. Unwind
Silver, E. Rush
Simmons, K. Article 5
Simmons, K. Three
Slade, A. Empire of ruins
Slade, A. The dark deeps
Slade, A. The hunchback assignments
Sleator, W. Singularity
Smibert, A. Memento Nora
Smith, A. G. Death sentence.
Smith, A. G. Lockdown
Smith, A. G. Solitary
Smith, A. Grasshopper jungle
Smith, S. L. Orleans
Steele, A. Apollo's outcasts
Terrill, C. All our yesterdays
Terry, T. Fractured
Terry, T. Slated
Testa, D. Cosmic storm
Testa, D. The Cassini code
Testa, D. The comet's curse
Testa, D. The dark zone
Testa, D. The web of Titan.
Thomas, L. Quarantine
Thompson, K. Origins
Tintera, A. Reboot
Treggiari, J. Ashes, ashes
Trevayne, E. Coda
Umansky, K. Under the moons of Mars; new adventures on Barsoom
Under the moons of Mars
Vande Velde, V. Heir apparent
Vanhee, J. Engines of the broken world
Wallenfels, S. POD
Walton, K. M. Empty
Ward, D. Escape the mask
Ward, R. Numbers
Ward, R. The Chaos
Wasserman, R. Crashed
Wasserman, R. Skinned
Wasserman, R. The waking dark
Wasserman, R. Wired
Webb, P. Six days
Wells, D. Fragments
Wells, D. Partials
Wells, D. Ruins
Wells, R. Feedback
Wells, R. Variant
Wendig, C. Under the Empyrean Sky
Werlin, N. Double helix
Westerfeld, S. Behemoth
Westerfeld, S. Blue noon
Westerfeld, S. Extras
Westerfeld, S. Goliath
Westerfeld, S. Leviathan
Westerfeld, S. Pretties
Westerfeld, S. Specials

Westerfeld, S. Uglies
Whaley, J. C. Noggin
White, A. Surviving Antarctica
White, A. B. Windows on the world
Whitley, D. Midnight charter
Wiggins, B. Stung
Wild, K. Fight game
Williams, S. Twinmaker
Wooding, C. The storm thief
Yancey, R. The 5th Wave
Yansky, B. Alien invasion and other inconveniences
Young, M. Blood red road
Zevin, G. All these things I've done
Zevin, G. Because it is my blood
Zhang, K. Once we were
Zhang, K. What's left of me
SCIENTISTS -- FICTION
Durst, S. B. Ice
Robinson, K. S. Forty signs of rain
Scieszka, Jon
Who done it?
Scopes, John Thomas
About
Bryant, J. Ringside, 1925
Scorch. Damico, G.
The **scorch** trials. Dashner, J.
Scorched. Mancusi, M.
Scored. McLaughlin, L.
The **Scorpio** Races. Stiefvater, M.
Scorpions. Myers, W. D., 1937-
SCOTLAND -- FICTION
Davidson, J. The Explosionist
Dunkle, C. B. By these ten bones
Frost, H. The braid
Gray, K. Ostrich boys
Klein, L. M. Lady Macbeth's daughter
Raedeke, C. The daykeeper's grimoire
SCOTLAND -- HISTORY -- ROBERT I, 1306-1329 -- FICTION
Yolen, J. Girl in a cage
SCOTLAND -- HISTORY -- 17TH CENTURY -- FICTION
Laird, E. The betrayal of Maggie Blair
Scott, Elizabeth
Between here and forever
Grace
Living dead girl
Love you hate you miss you
Miracle
Perfect you
Stealing Heaven
Scott, Kieran
Geek magnet
She's so dead to us
This is so not happening
Scott, Michael
The alchemyst, The enchantress
Scott, Mindi
Freefall
Live through this
Scowler. Kraus, D.
Scrambled eggs at midnight Barkley B.
Scrivener's moon. Reeve, P.
Scrimger, Richard
Me & death
SEA STORIES
Golden, C. The sea wolves
Meyer, L. A. The wake of the Lorelei Lee
Molloy, M. Peter Raven under fire
Rees, C. Pirates!
The **sea** wolves. Golden, C.
SEAFARING LIFE -- FICTION
Bunting, E. The pirate captain's daughter
Frazier, A. Everlasting
Meyer, L. A. Bloody Jack
Meyer, L. A. In the belly of The Bloodhound
Meyer, L. A. The mark of the golden dragon
Meyer, L. A. Rapture of the deep
Meyer, L. A. Under the Jolly Roger
Meyer, L. A. Viva Jacquelina!
Meyer, L. A. The wake of the Lorelei Lee
Pignat, C. Wild geese
Seamon, Hollis
Somebody up there hates you
Sean Griswold's head. Leavitt, L.
Search and destroy. Hughes, D.
SEASIDE RESORTS -- FICTION
Hocking, A. Wake
Season of ice. Les Becquets, D.
Sebastian Darke: Prince of Fools. Caveney, P.
SEATTLE (WASH.) -- FICTION
Gallagher, L. The opposite of invisible
John, A. Five flavors of dumb
Lockhart, E. Real live boyfriends
Lockhart, E. The treasure map of boys
McBride, L. Hold me closer, necromancer
Renn, D. Tokyo heist
Skovron, J. Misfit
Trueman, T. Life happens next
Wesselhoeft, C. Adios, nirvana
Second chance summer. Matson, M.
The **second** summer of the sisterhood. Brashares, A.
The **second** trial. Boll, R.
Secondhand world. Min, K.
Seconds away. Coben, H.
SECRECY -- FICTION
Albin, G. Crewel
Alpine, R. Canary
George, M. The difference between you and me

Hill, C. J. Erasing time
Krokos, D. False memory
Lo, M. Adaptation
Lowry, L. Son
Oates, J. C. Two or three things I forgot to tell you
O'Rourke, E. Tangled
Patrick, C. Revived
Shoemaker, T. Code of silence
The **secret** fiend. Peacock, S.
The **secret** ingredient. Lewis, S.
The secret journeys of Jack London [series]
Golden, C. The wild
Secret keeper. Perkins, M.
The **secret** life of Prince Charming. Caletti, D.
The **secret** of Laurel Oaks. Ruby, L.
The **secret** of the Rose. Thomson, S. L.
Secret of the sirens. Golding, J.
The **secret** life of Sparrow Delaney. Harper, S.
The **secret** of the village fool. Upjohn, R.
Secret Saturdays. Maldonado, T.
SECRET SOCIETIES -- FICTION
Bailey, K. Legacy of the clockwork key
Clare, C. Clockwork angel
Clare, C. Clockwork prince
Emerald green
Frost, M. Alliance
Gould, S. Cross my heart
Kade, S. Queen of the dead
Roecker, L. The lies that bind
Sapphire blue
Whitney, D. The rivals
Wilson, N. D. The dragon's tooth
The secret side of empty. Andreu, M. E.
The **secret** story of Sonia Rodriguez. Sitomer, A. L.
The **secret** to lying. Mitchell, T.
SECRETS -- FICTION
Hartman, R. Seraphina
Jarzab, A. The opposite of hallelujah
LaCour, N. Everything leads to you
Pitcher, A. Ketchup clouds
Richards, N. D. Six months later
Siddell, T. Gunnerkrigg Court 3
Sedgwick, Marcus
My swordhand is singing
Revolver
She is not invisible
White crow
See what I see. Whelan, G.
See you at Harry's. Knowles, J.
Seeds of America [series]
Anderson, L. H. Forge
Seeing red. MacDonald, A. L.
Seek. Fleischman, P.
Seeker. Nicholson, W.
SEGREGATION -- FICTION
Myers, W. D. Invasion!
SEGREGATION IN EDUCATION -- FICTION
McCarthy, S. C. True fires
Seigel, Andrea
The kid table
Like the red panda
Seizure. Reichs, K. J.
Sekret. Smith, L.
SELECTIVE MUTISM -- FICTION
Berry, J. All the truth that's in me
Casanova, M. Frozen
SELF PERCEPTION -- FICTION
Chambers, A. Dying to know you
Koertge, R. Stoner & Spaz
SELF-ACCEPTANCE -- FICTION
Doyle, M. Courtship and curses
Friend, N. My life in black and white
Kincy, K. Other
Koertge, R. Now playing
SELF-ACTUALIZATION (PSYCHOLOGY) -- FICTION
Chen, J. Return to me
Forman, G. Just one day
Hartman, R. Seraphina
King, A. S. Reality Boy
Magoon, K. 37 things I love (in no particular order)
Zarr, S. The Lucy variations
SELF-CONSCIOUSNESS -- FICTION
Friend, N. My life in black and white
SELF-DESTRUCTIVE BEHAVIOR
Griffin, A. All you never wanted
SELF-ESTEEM -- FICTION
Goodman, S. Kindness for weakness
Kessler, J. Loss
Oates, J. C. Two or three things I forgot to tell you
Singleton, L. J. Dead girl dancing
Vivian, S. The list
Walton, K. M. Empty
SELF-MUTILATION -- FICTION
McCormick, P. Cut
Rainfield, C. Scars
SELF-PERCEPTION -- FICTION
Chambers, A. Dying to know you
Friend, N. My life in black and white
Halpern, J. Have a nice day
Klass, D. You don't know me
Vivian, S. The list
SELF-REALIZATION -- FICTION
Bigelow, L. J. Starting from here
Strauss, V. Passion blue
SELF-RELIANCE -- FICTION
Larson, K. Hattie ever after

Selfors, Suzanne
Coffeehouse angel
Mad love
Saving Juliet
The sweetest spell
SELKIES -- FICTION
Cornwell, B. Tides
Lanagan, M. The brides of Rollrock Island
Selling hope. Tubb, K. O.
Sellout. Wilkins, E. J.
Selzer, Adam
How to get suspended and influence people
I kissed a zombie, and I liked it
Semiprecious. Love, D. A.
SENATORS
Pesci, D. Amistad
Send one angel down. Schwartz, V. F.
SEPARATION (PSYCHOLOGY) -- FICTION
Lowry, L. Son
Sepetys, Ruta
Between shades of gray
Out of the Easy
SEPTEMBER 11 TERRORIST ATTACKS, 2001 -- FICTION
Walsh, A. A Long Way from Home
September Girls. Madison, B.
The **September** sisters. Cantor, J.
Seraphina. Hartman, R.
Serendipity Market. Blubaugh, P.
Seraphina. Hartman, R.
SERIAL KILLERS -- FICTION
Derting, K. The last echo
Lyga, B. Game
Lyga, B. I hunt killers
Waters, D. Break my heart 1,000 times
The **serpent's** coil. Raedeke, C.
Service, Pamela F.
Tomorrow's magic
Yesterday's magic
SERVICE STATIONS -- FICTION
Weaver, W. Full service
SET DESIGNERS -- FICTION
LaCour, N. Everything leads to you
Seth Baumgartner's love manifesto. Luper, E.
Seven Realms [series]
Chima, C. W. The Demon King
Chima, C. W. The exiled queen
Chima, C. W. The Gray Wolf Throne
Sevenwaters trilogy [series]
Marillier, J. Child of the prophecy
Marillier, J. Daughter of the forest
Marillier, J. Son of the shadows
Sever. DeStefano, L.
SEWING -- FICTION
Foxlee, K. The midnight dress
SEX -- FICTION
Mesrobian, C. Sex and violence
Sex and violence. Mesrobian, C.
SEX REASSIGNMENT SURGERY -- FICTION
Farizan, S. If you could be mine
SEX ROLE
Whelan, G. Chu Ju's house
SEX ROLE -- FICTION
Bunting, E. The pirate captain's daughter
Brothers, M. Debbie Harry sings in French
Chibbaro, J. Deadly
Engle, M. Firefly letters
Friesner, E. M. Nobody's princess
Friesner, E. M. Nobody's prize
Friesner, E. Spirit's princess
Goodman, A. Eon: Dragoneye reborn
Gould, S. Cross my heart
Haddix, M. P. Just Ella
Hoffman, A. The foretelling
Hopkins, E. Burned
Huser, G. Stitches
Lavender, W. Aftershocks
Longshore, K. Tarnish
Meyer, L. A. Bloody Jack
Meyer, L. A. Curse of the blue tattoo
Meyer, L. A. Under the Jolly Roger
Meyer, L. A. Viva Jacquelina!
Meyer, L. A. The wake of the Lorelei Lee
Moranville, S. B. A higher geometry
Napoli, D. J. Bound
O'Brien, A. Lara's gift
Pierce, T. First test
Qamar, A. Beneath my mother's feet
Quick, B. A golden web
Rees, C. Sovay
Reeve, P. Fever Crumb
Staples, S. F. Haveli
Staples, S. F. The house of djinn
Staples, S. F. Shabanu
Whelan, G. Chu Ju's house
Williams, S. Wind rider
Wilson, D. L. Firehorse
Yang, D. J. Daughter of Xanadu,
Zielin, L. Donut days
SEXUAL ABUSE -- FICTION
Crutcher, C. Period 8
Deuker, C. Swagger
Draper, S. M. (. M. Panic
Kuehn, S. Charm & strange
Rainfield, C. Stained
Reinhardt, D. We are the Goldens
Scott, M. Live through this
SEXUAL HARASSMENT -- FICTION
Freitas, D. This gorgeous game
SEXUAL ORIENTATION -- FICTION
Clark, K. E. Freakboy
Lo, M. Adaptation

Lo, M. Inheritance
Shabanu. Staples, S. F.
Shade. Smith-Ready, J.
Shackleton, Ernest Henry Sir, 1874-1922
About
McKernan, V. Shackleton's stowaway
Shackleton's stowaway. McKernan, V.
SHADES AND SHADOWS -- FICTION
Defy the dark
McNamee, G. Beyond
Shade's children. Nix, G.
Shades of Earth. Revis, B.
Shades of London [series]
Johnson, M. The madness underneath
Shadow and bone. Bardugo, L.
Shadow of the giant. Card, O. S.
Shadow of the Hegemon. Card, O. S.
Shadow of the leopard. Mankell, H.
Shadow on the mountain. Preus, M.
Shadow on the sun. Gill, D. M.
Shadow puppets. Card, O. S.
The **shadow** society. Rutkoski, M.
The **shadow** speaker. Okorafor, N.
Shadowbridge. Frost, G.
Shadowfell. Marillier, J.
The **Shadowhunter's** codex.
Shadows cast by stars. Knutsson, C.
Shadow. Moss, J.
The **shadow** hunt. Langrish, K.
The **shadow** of Malabron. Wharton, T.
The **Shadow** Project. Brennan, H.
Shadowcry. Burtenshaw, J.
The **Shadowing:** Hunted. Slater, A.
Shahan, Sherry
Death mountain
SHAKERS -- FICTION
Coleman, W. Anna's world
Peck, R. N. A day no pigs would die
Shakespeare, William, 1564-1616
About
Bjorkman, L. My invented life
Fiedler, L. Romeo's ex
Gratz, A. Something rotten
Hand, E. Illyria
Harper, S. The Juliet club
Klein, L. M. Lady Macbeth's daughter
Klein, L. M. Ophelia
Lawlor, L. The two loves of Will Shakespeare
Marsden, J. Hamlet: a novel
Rees, C. The fool's girl
Shakespeare makes the playoffs. Koertge, R.
SHAMANS -- FICTION
Friesner, E. M. Spirit's princess
Soonchild
Shan, Darren
Lord Loss
The thin executioner
Shanahan, Lisa
The sweet, terrible, glorious year I truly, completely lost it
SHANGHAI (CHINA) -- FICTION
Ballard, J. G. Empire of the Sun
Shanghai shadows. Ruby, L.
Shapeshifter. Bennett, H.
SHAPESHIFTING -- FICTION
Bell, H. Traitor's son
Reese, J. The strange case of Doctor Jekyll and Mademoiselle Odile
Rossetti, R. The girl with borrowed wings
Sharenow, Rob
Sharenow, R. The Berlin Boxing Club
My mother the cheerleader
SHARK ATTACKS -- FICTION
Bingham, K. Formerly shark girl
Shark girl. Bingham, K.
SHARKS -- FICTION
Monninger, J. Wish
Sharks & boys. Tracy, K.
The **sharp** time. O'Connell, M.
The **shattering.** Healey, K.
Shattering Glass. Giles, G.
Shaw, Liane
Fostergirls
Shaw, Susan
One of the survivors
Safe
Tunnel vision
She is not invisible. Sedgwick, M.
She loves you, she loves you not-- Peters, J. A.
She's so dead to us. Scott, K.
Shea, John
A kid from Southie
Shecter, Vicky Alvear
Cleopatra's moon
Sheinmel, Alyssa B.
The lucky kind
Sheldon, Dyan
Confessions of a Hollywood star
The crazy things girls do for love
My perfect life
Shelley, Percy Bysshe, 1792-1822
About
Hemphill, S. Hideous love
Shelter. Coben, H.
Shepard, Jim
Project X
Shepard, Matthew, d. 1998
About
Leslea, N. October mourning
Shepard, Sara
The lying game
Shepherd, Megan

Her Dark Curiosity
The madman's daughter
Sherlock, Patti
Letters from Wolfie
Sherman, Delia
The freedom maze
Sherrard, Valerie
The glory wind
Sheth, Kashmira
Keeping corner
The **shibboleth.** Jacobs, J. H.
Shield of stars. Bell, H.
Shift. Agell, C.
Shift. Bradbury, J.
Shift. Smith-Ready, J.
Shift. Bailey, E.
The **shifter.** Hardy, J.
Shine. Myracle, L.
Shine, coconut moon. Meminger, N.
The **Shining** Company. Sutcliff, R.
Shimko, Bonnie
The private thoughts of Amelia E. Rye
Shimura Takako
Wandering son
Shinn, Sharon
Gateway
Ship Breaker. Bacigalupi, P.
SHIPS -- FICTION
Mowll, J. Operation typhoon shore
Tracy, K. Sharks & boys
SHIPWRECKS -- FICTION
Fama, E. Overboard
Monninger, J. Hippie chick
Watts, I. N. No moon
Shirvington, Jessica
Emblaze
Embrace
Entice
Shiver. Stiefvater, M.
Shoemaker, Tim
Back before dark
Code of silence
SHOEMAKERS -- FICTION
Shreve, S. The lovely shoes
SHOES -- FICTION
Flinn, A. Cloaked
Shooting star. McKissack, F.
SHOPPING CENTERS AND MALLS -- FICTION
Esckilsen, E. E. The last mall rat
Mass, W. Heaven looks a lot like the mall
SHORT STORIES
Cornered
A matter of souls. Patrick, D. L.
Under the moons of Mars
SHOSHONI INDIANS
Bruchac, J. Sacajawea
Shot down. Mary-Todd, J.
Shrimp. Cohn, R.
Showalter, Gena
Intertwined
Shreve, Susan
The lovely shoes
Shukert, Rachel, 1980-
Love me
Starstruck
Shulman, Mark
Scrawl
Shulman, Polly
Enthusiasm
Shusterman, Neal
Antsy does time
Bruiser
Downsiders
Everlost
Everwild
Full tilt
The Schwa was here
Shusterman, N. Unwind
UnSouled
UnWholly
Unwind
Shut up! Reynolds, M.
Shutout. Halpin, B.
SHYNESS -- FICTION
Crowley, C. A little wanting song
SIBLING RIVALRY -- FICTION
Griffin, A. All you never wanted
SIBLINGS -- FICTION
Arcos, C. Out of reach
Blume, J. Here's to you, Rachel Robinson
Brown, J. Perfect escape
Clare, C. City of lost souls
Hopkinson, N. The Chaos
Hyde, C. R. The year of my miraculous reappearance
Jaramillo, A. La linea
Knowles, J. *See* you at Harry's
Konigsburg, E. L. Silent to the bone
Lisle, H. The Ruby Key
MacCullough, C. Drawing the ocean
Mackall, D. D. The silence of murder
Malaghan, M. Greek ransom
McDaniel, L. Breathless
McGowan, K. The witch's guide to cooking with children
McNicoll, S. Last chance for Paris
Meloy, C. Wildwood
Myers, W. D. A star is born
Peterson, W. Triskellion
Peterson, W. Triskellion 2: The burning
Roskos, E. Dr. Bird's advice for sad poets

Volponi, P. Homecoming
Webb, P. Six days
Williams, C. L. Waiting
Willis, C. C. Buck fever
Wilson, N. D. The dragon's tooth
Wolf, J. S. Breaking beautiful
Yeomans, E. Rubber houses
SICILY (ITALY) -- FICTION
Coventry, S. The queen's daughter
SICK - FICTION
Cheng, A. Brushing Mom's hair
Chibbaro, J. Deadly
White, R. A month of Sundays
Side effects. Koss, A. G.
Sidekicks. Ferraiolo, J. D.
SIDESHOWS -- FICTION
Barnaby, H. Wonder show
Siege and storm. Bardugo, L.
Siegelson, Kim L.
Honey Bea
SIERRA LEONE -- HISTORY -- CIVIL WAR, 1991- -- FICTION
Sight. Vrettos, A. M.
The **sight.** Clement-Davies, D.
Sign Language. Ackley, A.
Silbert, Leslie
The intelligencer
The **silence** of murder. Mackall, D. D.
Silent to the bone. Konigsburg, E. L.
Silksinger. Taylor, L.
SILKWORMS -- FICTION
Yep, L. Dragons of silk
Silver rain. Peterson, L. J.
Silver. Wooding, C.
The **Silver** Blade. Gardner, S.
The **silver** kiss. Klause, A. C.
Silver people. Engle, M.
Silver phoenix. Pon, C.
Silver, Eve
Rush
Silvey, Craig
Jasper Jones
Simmons, Kristen
Article 5
Three
Simmons, Michael
The rise of Lubchenko
Simner, Janni Lee
Bones of Faerie
Faerie after
Thief eyes
Faerie winter
Simon, Charnan
Plan B
Simone, Ni-Ni
(jt. auth) Abrams, A. Hollywood High
Upgrade U
SIN - FICTION
Fisher, C. Darkwater
The **Sin** eater's confession. Bick, I. J.
Since you've been gone
The **Singing.** Croggon, A.
Singer, Nicky
Gem X
The **singer** of all songs. Constable, K.
SINGERS -- FICTION
Harmel, K. When you wish
Ortiz Cofer, J. If I could fly
Weatherford, C. B. Becoming Billie Holiday
SINGING -- FICTION
Bennett Wealer, S. Rival
Crossley-Holland, K. Crossing to Paradise
Levine, G. C. Fairest
Porter, S. Lost voices
Singing the Dogstar blues. Goodman, A.
SINGLE-PARENT FAMILIES -- FICTION
Block, F. L. Teen spirit
Brothers, M. Supergirl mixtapes
Bodeen, S. A. The gardener
Caletti, D. The fortunes of Indigo Skye
Clarke, J. The winds of heaven
Collins, B. Always watching
Foxlee, K. The midnight dress
Herrick, S. By the river
Howard, J. J. That time I joined the circus
Joyce, G. The exchange
Katcher, B. Almost perfect
Kamata, S. Gadget Girl
Lange, E. J. Dead ends
Lynch, C. Angry young man
Lyne, J. H. Catch rider
Maldonado, T. Secret Saturdays
McDonald, J. Off-color
Moriarty, L. The center of everything
Ockler, S. Fixing Delilah
Patrick, C. The Originals
Rapp, A. The children and the wolves
Resau, L. The indigo notebook
Resau, L. The ruby notebook
Resau, L. The jade notebook
Sanders, S. L. Gray baby
Skovron, J. Misfit
Stein, T. High dive
Valentine, J. Me, the missing, and the dead
Wolff, V. E. True believer
Wright, B. Putting makeup on the fat boy
Singleton, Linda Joy
Dead girl dancing
Dead girl in love
Dead girl walking
Singularity. Sleator, W.
SIRENS (MYTHOLOGY)

Hocking, A. Wake
Hubbard, A. Ripple
Sister wife. Hrdlitschka, S.
The **sisterhood** of the traveling pants. Brashares, A.
SISTERS -- FICTION
Bunce, E. C. A curse dark as gold
Carvell, M. Sweetgrass basket
Cooney, C. B. Three black swans
Delsol, W. Flock
Eulberg, E. Revenge of the Girl With the Great Personality
Friend, N. My life in black and white
Gurtler, J. I'm not her
Hooper, M. Fallen Grace
Jarzab, A. The opposite of hallelujah
Knight, K. Embers & echoes
Leavitt, L. Going vintage
McClymer, K. Must love black
McKinnon, H. R. The properties of water
Meyer, C. Beware
Patrick, C. The Originals
Plum, A. Die for me
Sones, S. Stop pretending; what happened when my big sister went crazy
Watkins, S. Juvie
Weyn, S. Dr. Frankenstein's daughters
White, K. Perfect lies
White, R. Memories of Summer
Wood, F. When Molly was a Harvey Girl
Woodson, J. Lena
Wylie, S. All these lives
Zhang, K. Once we were
Sisters of glass. Hemphill, S.
Sisters red. Pearce, J.
Sitomer, Alan Lawrence
The secret story of Sonia Rodriguez
Six days. Webb, P.
Six months later. Richards, N. D.
The **six** rules of maybe. Caletti, D.
SIZE -- FICTION
De Lint, C. Little (grrl) lost
SKATEBOARDERS -- FICTION
Hornby, N. Slam
SKATEBOARDING -- FICTION
Harmon, M. Under the bridge
Skellig. Almond, D.
Sketchy. Samms, O.
Skelton, Matthew
Endymion Spring
Sketches. Walters, E.
Skilton, Sarah
Bruised
Skin deep. Crane, E. M.
SKIN -- DISEASES -- FICTION
Skin. Vrettos, A. M.
Skin hunger. Duey, K.
The Skinjacker trilogy [series]
Shusterman, N. Everlost
Shusterman, N. Everwild
Skink. Hiaasen, C.
Skinned. Wasserman, R.
Skinny. Kaslik, I.
Skovron, Jon
Misfit
Skrypuch, Marsha Forchuk
Daughter of war
Skunk girl. Karim, S.
Skurzynski, Gloria
The Virtual War
Skuse, C. J.
Rockoholic
Sky chasers [series]
Ryan, A. K. Glow
Sky Chasers [series]
Ryan, A. K. Flame
Sky. Townley, R.
The **sky** is everywhere. Nelson, J.
Skybreaker. Oppel, K.
Slade, Arthur
The hunchback assignments
Slade, Arthur G.
The dark deeps
Empire of ruins
Jolted; Newton Starker's rules for survival
Slade, A. The hunchback assignments
Slam. Hornby, N.
Slam!. Myers, W. D., 1937-
SLAM POETRY - FICTION
Flores-Scott, P. Jumped in
Slant. Williams, L. E.
Slated. Terry, T.
Slated trilogy [series]
Terry, T. Fractured
Slater, Adam
The Shadowing : Hunted
Pesci, D. Amistad
SLAVERY -- FICTION
Anderson, M. T. The astonishing life of Octavian Nothing, traitor to the nation
Ayres, K. North by night
Hearn, J. Hazel
Hegamin, T. M +O 4evr
Lyons, M. E. Letters from a slave boy
Lyons, M. E. Letters from a slave girl
Moran, K. Bloodline rising
Mosley, W. 47
Nelson, R. A. Days of Little Texas
Paulsen, G. Nightjohn
Purcell, K. Trafficked
Ward, D. Escape the mask
Wisler, G. C. Caleb's choice

SLAVIC MYTHOLOGY
Bardugo, L. Shadow and bone
Slayers. Hill, C. J.
Slayton, Fran Cannon
When the whistle blows
Sleator, William
The duplicate
Interstellar pig
Singularity
SLEEP DISORDERS -- FICTION
Sleeper code. Sniegoski, T.
Sleeping freshmen never lie. Lubar, D.
Sleepless. Balog, C.
Slice of cherry. Reeves, D.
Slipping. Bell, C. D.
Sloan, Brian
A tale of two summers
Sloan, Holly Goldberg
I'll be there
Smack. Burgess, M.
Small acts of amazing courage. Whelan, G.
SMALL BUSINESS -- FICTION
Nye, N. S. Going going
Small damages. Kephart, B.
A **small** free kiss in the dark. Millard, G.
SMALL TOWN LIFE -- FICTION
Lee, H. To kill a mockingbird
Mason, B. A. In country
A **small** white scar. Nuzum, K. A.
SMALLPOX -- FICTION
Cooney, C. B. Code orange
Simmons, M. The rise of Lubchenko
Spooner, M. Last Child
Smart girls get what they want. Strohmeyer, S.
Smashed. Luedeke, L.
Smelcer, John E.
The Great Death
The trap
Smibert, Angie
Memento Nora
The **smile.** Napoli, D. J.
Smiles to go. Spinelli, J.
Smith, Alexander Gordon
Death sentence
Lockdown
Solitary
Smith, Andrew
Passenger
Ghost medicine
Grasshopper jungle
The Marbury lens
100 sideways miles
Stick
Winger
Smith, Cynthia Leitich
Blessed
Eternal
Feral curse
Feral nights
Tantalize
Rain is not my Indian name
Smith, Emily Wing
Back when you were easier to love
The way he lived
Smith, Hilary T.
Wild awake
Smith, Jennifer E.
The comeback season
The georgraphy of you and me
The statistical probability of love at first sight
This is what happy looks like
Smith, Lindsay
Sekret
Smith, Patricia Clark
Weetamoo, heart of the Pocassets
Smith, Roland
Elephant run
Peak
Tentacles
Smith, Sarah
The other side of dark
Smith, Sherri L.
Flygirl
Orleans
Smith-Ready, Jeri
Shade
Shift
This side of salvation
Smoke. Hopkins, E.
SMUGGLING -- FICTION
Deuker, C. Runner
Snap. Snow, C.
Snatched. Hautman, P.
Snakecharm. Atwater-Rhodes, A.
Snakehead. Halam, A.
The **sniper.** Riordan, J.
Sniegoski, Tom
Sleeper code
SNOW -- FICTION
Delsol, W. Frost
Schroeder, L. Far from you
Snow apples. Razzell, M.
Snow, Carol
Snap
Switch
Snow bound. Mazer, H.
Snow, fire, sword. Masson, S.
So far from the bamboo grove. Watkins, Y. K.
So hard to say. Sanchez, Alex
So much closer. Colasanti, S.
So punk rock (and other ways to disappoint your mother) Ostow, M.

So silver bright. Mantchev, L.
So yesterday. Westerfeld, S.
SOCCER -- FICTION
Ayarbe, H. Compulsion
Halpin, B. Shutout
Martino, A. C. Over the end line
Myers, W. D. Kick
Williams, M. Now is the time for running
SOCIAL ACTION -- FICTION
McDonald, A. Boys, bears, and a serious pair of hiking boots
Nelson, B. Destroy all cars
SOCIAL CHANGE -- FICTION
Levithan, D. Two boys kissing
SOCIAL CLASSES -- FICTION
Barratt, M. The wild man
Croggon, A. Black spring
Harvey, A. Haunting Violet
Hearn, J. Hazel
Kerr, M. E. Gentlehands
Roth, V. Allegiant
Roth, V. Insurgent
Wollman, J. Switched
SOCIAL CONFLICT -- FICTION
Harland, R. Liberator
Myers, W. D. All the right stuff
SOCIAL PROBLEMS -- FICTION
Morrison, T. Sula
SOCIAL PROBLEMS -- FICTION
Ness, P. The Ask and the Answer
Ness, P. Monsters of men
SOCIAL WELFARE LEADERS -- FICTION
Miller, S. Miss Spitfire
SOCIALITES -- NEW YORK (STATE) -- NEW YORK -- FICTION
Palma, F. J. The map of the sky
SOFTBALL -- FICTION
Mackey, W. K. Throwing like a girl`
Solace of the road. Dowd, S.
Sold. McCormick, P.
Soldier's heart. Paulsen, G.
Soldier's secret. Klass, S. S.
Soldier X. Wulffson, D. L.
SOLDIERS -- FICTION
Klass, S. S. Soldier's secret
Lynch, C. Casualties of war
McCaughrean, G. Cyrano
Tintera, A. Reboot
Yang, D. J. Daughter of Xanadu
Solitary. Smith, A. G.
Solomon, King of Israel
About
Stroud, J. The ring of Solomon
Solomon Snow and the stolen jewel. Umansky, K.
SOMALIA -- FICTION
Cross, G. Where I belong
Some girls are. Summers, C.
Some quiet place. Sutton, K.
Somebody everybody listens to. Supplee, S.
Somebody up there hates you. Seamon, H.
Somebody, please tell me who I am. Lerangis, P.
Someday this pain will be useful to you. Cameron, P.
Something like fate. Colasanti, S.
Something like hope. Goodman, S.
Something like normal. Doller, T.
Something real. Demetrios, H.
Something rotten. Gratz, A.
Something strange and deadly. Dennard, S.
Son. Lowry, L.
Son of the mob. Korman, G.
Son of the mob: Hollywood hustle. Korman, G.
Son of the shadows. Marillier, J.
Something like fate. Colasanti, S.
Somper, Justin
Demons of the ocean
Sones, Sonya
One of those hideous books where the mother dies
Stop pretending; what happened when my big sister went crazy
What my girlfriend doesn't know
What my mother doesn't know
The **song** of the Quarkbeast. Fforde, J.
Song of the sparrow. Sandell, L. A.
Sonnenblick, Jordan
After ever after
Drums, girls, & dangerous pie
Notes from the midnight driver
Zen and the art of faking it
Sonny's war. Hobbs, V.
Sons of the 613. Rubens, M.
Soonchild.
Sorcery and Cecelia, or, The enchanted chocolate pot. Wrede, P. C.
Sorrells, Walter
First shot
Whiteout
Sorrow's knot. Bow, E.
Sorta like a rockstar. Quick, M.
Soto, Gary
Accidental love
Buried onions
Taking sides
SOUL -- FICTION
Brockenbrough, M. Devine intervention
Damico, G. Croak
Soul enchilada. Gill, D. M.
Soul thief. Oliver, J.
SOULS -- FICTION
Moulton, C. A. Angelfire

Sounder. Armstrong, W. H.
The **sound** of letting go. Kehoe, S. W.
SOUND RECORDINGS -- FICTION
Prinz, Y. The Vinyl Princess
SOUP KITCHENS -- FICTION
Myers, W. D. All the right stuff
Sources of light. McMullan, M.
SOUTH AFRICA -- FICTION
Craig, C. Afrika
Gordimer, N. The house gun
Gordimer, N. My son's story
Lessing, D. M. The sweetest dream
Nyembezi, C. L. S. The rich man of Pietermaritzburg
Powers, J. L. This thing called the future
Van de Ruit, J. Spud
SOUTH CAROLINA -- FICTION
Garcia, K. Beautiful creatures
Garcia, K. Beautiful darkness
Johnson, V. Saving Maddie
Kate, L. The betrayal of Natalie Hargrove
SOUTHEAST ASIA -- FICTION
Cornwell, A. Carpe diem
SOUTHEAST ASIA -- FICTION
Meloy, M. The apprentices
SOUTHERN STATES -- FICTION
Lester, J. Guardian
O'Connor, F. Collected works
Sovay. Rees, C.
SOVIET UNION -- FICTION
Sepetys, R. Between shades of gray
SOVIET UNION -- HISTORY -- 1917-1921, REVOLUTION -- FICTION
Whitcomb, L. The Fetch
SOVIET UNION -- HISTORY -- 1953-1985 -- FICTION
Standiford, N. The boy on the bridge
SOVIET UNION -- RELATIONS -- UNITED STATES -- FICTION
Kiem, E. Dancer, daughter, traitor, spy
SPACE AND TIME -- FICTION
De Lint, C. Dingo
Gaiman, N. Interworld
Hautman, P. The obsidian blade
Larbalestier, J. Magic lessons
Larbalestier, J. Magic or madness
McEntire, M. Hourglass
Mebus, S. Gods of Manhattan
Petrucha, S. Split
Powell, L. The game of triumphs
Powell, L. The Master of Misrule
Shinn, S. Gateway
Stone, T. I. Time between us
Thompson, K. The new policeman
Webb, P. Six days
Weyn, S. Reincarnation
Williams, S. Twinmaker
The **space** between trees. Williams, K.
SPACE COLONIES -- FICTION
Card, O. S. Ruins
McDevitt, J. Moonfall
Revis, B. Shades of Earth
SPACE FLIGHT -- FICTION
Revis, B. A million suns
SPACE FLIGHT TO THE MOON -- FICTION
172 hours on the moon
SPACE VEHICLES -- FICTION
Barnes, J. Losers in space
SPAIN -- FICTION
Kephart, B. Small damages
SPAIN -- HISTORY -- FICTION
Meyer, L. A. Viva Jacquelina!
SPANISH-AMERICAN WAR, 1898
See also Spain -- History; United States -- History -- 1865-1898; United States -- History -- 1898-1919
Spanking Shakespeare. Wizner, J.
Spark. Ryan, A. K.
Speak. Anderson, J. D.
Speak. Anderson, L. H.
Speaker for the Dead. Card, O. S.
Sparrow, Rebecca
The year Nick McGowan came to stay
Speare, Elizabeth George
The witch of Blackbird Pond
SPECIAL EDUCATION -- FICTION
King, A. S. Reality Boy
Special Edward. Walters, E.
Specials. Westerfeld, S.
The **spectacular** now. Tharp, T.
SPEECH DISORDERS -- FICTION
Fusco, K. N. Tending to Grace
Mitchell, D. Black swan green
Speechless. Harrington, H.
SPELEOLOGY *See* Caves
A **spell** for chameleon. Anthony, P.
Spellcaster. Gray, C.
SPELLING BEES -- FICTION
Luddy, K. Spelldown
Spells. Pike, A.
Sphinx's princess. Friesner, E. M.
Sphinx's queen. Friesner, E. M.
Spelldown. Luddy, K.
SPIES -- FICTION
Avi Traitor's gate
Barnes, J. L. The Squad: perfect cover
Bradbury, J. Wrapped
Brennan, H. The Doomsday Box: a Shadow Project adventure
Brennan, H. The Shadow Project
Bruchac, J. Wolf mark
Higgins, J. Sure fire

Horowitz, A.Stormbreaker
Leonard, J. P. Cold case
McNab, A. Traitor
Myers, A. Spy!
Meyer, L. A. Viva Jacquelina!
Preus, M. Shadow on the mountain
Smith, L. Sekret
Wild, K. Fight game
Young, E. L. STORM : The Infinity Code
Zettel, S. Palace of Spies
Spillebeen, Geert
Age 14
Kipling's choice
Spinelli, Jerry
Crash
Smiles to go
Stargirl
There's a girl in my hammerlock
Spinner, Stephanie
Damosel
Quicksilver
Quiver
Spinning out. Stahler, D.
The **spirit** line. Thurlo, A.
Spirit's princess. Friesner, E.
SPIRITS -- FICTION
Block, F. L. Teen spirit
Friesner, E. M. Spirit's princess
Spirits of the Noh. Randall, T.
SPIRITUAL GIFTS -- FICTION
Albin, G. Crewel
SPIRITUALISM -- FICTION
Harper, S. The secret life of Sparrow Delaney
Harvey, A. Haunting Violet
Salerni, D. K. We hear the dead
Weyn, S. Distant waves
Winters, C. In the shadow of blackbirds
SPIRITUALISTS -- FICTION
Hooper, M. Velvet
Splat! Walters, E.
The **splendor** falls. Clement-Moore, R.
Split. Avasthi, S.
Split. Petrucha, S.
Split second. West, K.
SPOKANE (WASH.) -- FICTION
Harmon, M. Under the bridge
Spooner, Michael
Last Child
SPORTS TOURNAMENTS -- FICTION
Volponi, P. The Final Four
Spradlin, Michael P.
Keeper of the Grail
Springer, Nancy
I am Mordred
I am Morgan le Fay
The case of the missing marquess
Sprout. Peck, D.
Spud. Van de Ruit, J.
A **spy** in the house. Lee, Y. S.
Spy!. Myers, A.
SPY STORIES
Benway, R. Also known as
Carriger, G. Etiquette & espionage
Peterfreund, D. Across a star-swept sea
The **squad**: perfect cover. Barnes, J.L.
Squashed. Bauer, J.
Squeeze. Muller, R. D.
The **squire's** tale. Morris, G.
St. Crow, Lili
Strange angels
St. James, James
Freak show
Stahler, David
Doppelganger
Spinning out
Stained. Rainfield, C.
STALINGRAD, BATTLE OF, 1942-1943 -- FICTION
Riordan, J. The sniper
The **stalker** chronicles. Moore, C.
STALKERS -- FICTION
Hodkin, M. The evolution of Mara Dyer
Jayne, H. Truly, madly, deadly
Singleton, L. J. Dead girl dancing
Standiford, Natalie
The boy on the bridge
Confessions of the Sullivan sisters
How to say goodbye in Robot
Standing against the wind. Jones, T. L.
Stanley, George Edward
Night fires
Staples, Suzanne Fisher
Dangerous skies
Haveli
The house of djinn
Shabanu
Under the Persimmon tree
Star crossed. Bunce, E. C.
A **star** is born. Myers, W. D.
A **star** on the Hollywood Walk of Fame. Woods, B.
Starglass. North, P.
Starstruck. Shukert, R.
Starters. Price, L.
Starting from here. Bigelow, L. J.
Starclimber. Oppel, K.
Stargirl. Spinelli, J.
Staunton, Ted
Acting up
Stay. Caletti, D.
Stay with me. Griffin, P.
Stay with me. Freymann-Weyr, G.

Staying fat for Sarah Byrnes. Crutcher, C.
Stead, William Thomas, 1849-1912
About
Weyn, S. Distant waves
Steadfast. Gray, C.
STEALING -- FICTION
Heath, J. Money run
Stealing death. Carey, J. L.
Stealing Heaven. Scott, E.
Stealing Henry. MacCullough, C.
Stealing Parker. Kenneally, M.
STEAMPUNK FICTION
Carriger, G. Curtsies & conspiracies
Clare, C. Clockwork angel
Harland, R. Liberator
Kittredge, C. The nightmare garden
Miéville, C. Railsea
Reeve, P. Scrivener's moon
Wrede, P. C. The Far West
Steel. Vaughn, C.
Steele, Allen
Apollo's outcasts
Stein, Tammar
High dive
Kindred
Light years
Steinmetz, Karen
The mourning wars
Stella stands alone. LaFaye, A.
Stentz, Zack
(jt. auth) Miller, A. E. Colin Fischer
A **step** from heaven. Na, A.
STEPBROTHERS -- FICTION
Knox, E. Mortal fire
STEPFAMILIES -- FICTION
Childs, T. L. Oh. My. Gods
Cohn, R. Gingerbread
Friend, N. Bounce
Keplinger, K. A midsummer's nightmare
Scott, M. Live through this
STEPFATHERS -- FICTION
Beitia, S. The last good place of Lily Odilon
Felin, M. S. Touching snow
McCahan, E. I now pronounce you someone else
Sanchez, A. Bait
Vincent, Z. The lucky place
STEPMOTHERS -- FICTION
Billingsley, F. Chime
Buffie, M. Winter shadows
Prose, F. Touch
Sternberg, Libby
The case against my brother
STEROIDS -- FICTION
Deuker, C. Gym candy
Harris, C. Bad taste in boys
Mackel, K. Boost
McKissack, F. Shooting star
Potter, R. Exit strategy
Stevenson, Robin H
Dead in the water
Escape velocity
Out of order
A thousand shades of blue
Stevenson, Sarah Jamila
The Latte Rebellion
Stewart, Alex
Dragonwood
Stick. Smith, A.
Stiefvater, Maggie
Ballad
The dream thieves
Forever
Linger
The raven boys
The Scorpio Races
Shiver
Still star-crossed. Taub, M.
Stitches. Huser, G.
A **stir** of bones. Hoffman, N. K.
Stoffels, Karlijn
Heartsinger
Stohl, Margaret
(jt. auth) Garcia, K. Beautiful creatures
(jt. auth) Garcia, K. Beautiful darkness
Stoker & Holmes [series]
Gleason, C. The clockwork scarab
Stolen nights. Maizel, R.
Stolen. Vande Velde, V.
The **stolen** one. Crowley, S.
Stoltz, Adrienne
(jt. auth) Bass, R. Lucid
A **stone** in my hand. Clinton, C.
Stone, Mary Hanlon
Invisible girl
Stone, Tamara Ireland
Time between us
Stone, Tanya Lee
A bad boy can be good for a girl
Stoner & Spaz. Koertge, R.
Stop in the name of pants! Rennison, L.
Stork. Delsol, W.
Stop pretending; what happened when my big sister went crazy. Sones, S.
Stork, Francisco X.
The last summer of the death warriors
Marcelo in the real world
Storm. MacHale, D. J.
Storm. Napoli, D. J.
STORM : The Infinity Code. Young, E. L.
The **storm** thief. Wooding, C.
Stormbreaker. Horowitz, A.

The **Story** of Owen. Johnston, E. K.
Storyteller. Myers, E.
STORYTELLING -- FICTION
Bobet, L. Above
Mlawski, S. Hammer of witches
Stotan! Crutcher, C.
STOWAWAYS -- FICTION
Barnes, J. Losers in space
The **Strange** and beautiful sorrows of Ava Lavender. Walton, L.
Strange angels. St. Crow, L.
The **strange** case of Doctor Jekyll and Mademoiselle Odile. Reese, J.
Strange relations. Levitin, S.
Strangelets. Gagnon, M.
Stranger with my face. Duncan, L.
Strasser, Todd
Boot camp
Can't get there from here
Famous
Give a boy a gun
If I grow up
No place
Wish you were dead
Stratton, Allan
Borderline
Chanda's secrets
Chanda's wars
Strauss, Victoria
Passion blue
Stray. Goldblatt, S.
Strays. Koertge, R.
Streams of Babel. Plum-Ucci, C.
STREET CHILDREN -- FICTION
Armistead, C. Being Henry David
Street dreams. Wise, T.
STREET LIFE -- FICTION
When I was the greatest
Street love. Myers, W. D., 1937-
STREET MUSICIANS -- FICTION
Brouwer, S. Devil's pass
STRIKES -- FICTION
Haddix, M. P. Uprising
Strings attached. Blundell, J.
Strohmeyer, Sarah
How Zoe made her dreams (mostly) come true
Smart girls get what they want
Stroud, Jonathan
The Amulet of Samarkand
The golem's eye
Heroes of the valley
Ptolemy's gate
The ring of Solomon
Struck. Bosworth, J.
Strykowski, Marcia
Call Me Amy
Stuber, Barbara
Crossing the tracks
Stuck in neutral. Trueman, T.
STUDENTS, FOREIGN -- FICTION
Delsol, W. Flock
Stung. Wiggins, B.
The **subtle** knife. Pullman, P.
Stupid fast. Herbach, G.
Sturtevant, Katherine
A true and faithful narrative
The brothers story
SUBWAYS -- FICTION
Shusterman, N. Downsiders
Such wicked intent. Oppel, K.
Suck it up. Meehl, B.
Suckerpunch. Hernandez, D.
SUDAN -- HISTORY -- CIVIL WAR, 1983-2005 -- FICTION
Coates, J. L. A hare in the elephant's trunk
Farish, T. The good braider
Park, L. S. A long walk to water
SUDAN -- HISTORY -- DARFUR CONFLICT, 2003- -- FICTION
Whitman, S. The milk of birds
SUDANESE AMERICANS -- FICTION
Farish, T. The good braider
SUICIDE -- FICTION
Cohn, R. You know where to find me
Davis, L. I swear
Ford, M. T. Suicide notes
Lange, E. J. Butter
McDaniel, L. Breathless
Morel, A. Survive
Quick, M. Forgive me, Leonard Peacock
Torres Sanchez, J. Death, Dickinson, and the demented life of Frenchie Garcia
Trueman, T. Inside out
Williams, K. Absent
Suicide notes. Ford, M. T.
Suite Scarlett. Johnson, M.
Sula. Morrison, T.
Sullivan, Anne, 1866-1936
About
Miller, S. Miss Spitfire
Sullivan, Laura L.
Under the green hill
Guardian of the Green Hill
Sullivan, Tara
Golden boy
Suma, Nova Ren
17 & gone
Dani noir
Imaginary girls
SUMATRA (INDONESIA) -- FICTION
Fama, E. Overboard
SUMMER -- FICTION

Egloff, Z. Leap
Galante, C. The summer of May
Howland, L. Nantucket blue
LaCour, N. Everything leads to you
Lockhart, E. We were liars
Madison, B. September Girls
Summer ball. Lupica, M.
SUMMER EMPLOYMENT -- FICTION
Hartinger, B. Project Sweet Life
Mayall, B. Mermaid Park
Strohmeyer, S. How Zoe made her dreams (mostly) come true
The **summer** I got a life. Fink, M.
The **summer** I turned pretty. Han, J.
The **Summer** King. Melling, O. R.
Summer of fire. Bass, K.
A **summer** of Kings. Nolan, H.,
The **summer** of May. Galante, C.
A **summer** of silk moths. Willey, M.
The **summer** of skinny dipping. Howells, A.
The **summer** prince. Johnson, A. D.
SUMMER RESORTS -- FICTION
Rosenfield, K. Amelia Anne is dead and gone
Summers, Courtney
Fall for anything
Some girls are
This is not a test
The **summoning.** Armstrong, K.
Sun, Amanda
Ink
Sun and moon, ice and snow. George, J. D.
Sunrise. Mullin, M.
Sunrise over Fallujah. Myers, W. D.
Super stock rookie. Weaver, W.
Supergirl mixtapes. Brothers, M.
Super human. Carroll, M. O.
SUPERHEROES -- FICTION
Carroll, M. O. Super human
Carroll, M. O. The ascension
Ferraiolo, J. D. Sidekicks
Lupica, M. Hero
Moore, P. Hero
SUPERMARKETS -- FICTION
Bloor, E. A plague year
SUPERNATURAL -- FICTION
Acosta, M. Dark companion
Bowler, T. Frozen fire
Bradbury, J. Wrapped
Brennan, H. The Shadow Project
Bridges, R. The gathering storm
Bruchac, J. Wolf mark
Clare, C. City of fallen angels
Clare, C. Clockwork prince
Cooper, S. The Boggart
Frost, M. Alliance
Golden, C. The sea wolves
Golding, J. Secret of the sirens
Grant, M. Gone
Hautman, P. The obsidian blade
Henderson, J. Vampire rising
Hill, W. The rising
Hodkin, M. The evolution of Mara Dyer
Hodkin, M. The unbecoming of Mara Dyer
Holder, N. Damned
Hopkinson, N. The Chaos
Horowitz, A. Raven's gate
Lewis, S. Beautiful decay
Maizel, R. Stolen nights
Matthews, L. S. The outcasts
McCarry, S. All our pretty songs
McMann, L. Cryer's Cross
McNamee, G. Beyond
McNamee, G. Bonechiller
Milford, K. The Broken Lands
Mont, E. M. A breath of Eyre
Morton-Shaw, C. The riddles of Epsilon
Nelson, B. They came from below
Nelson, R. A. Days of Little Texas
Newbery, L. At the firefly gate
Oliver, J. G. The demon trapper's daughter
Perez, M. Dead is a battlefield
Perez, M. Dead is the new black
Peterson, W. Triskellion
Peterson, W. Triskellion 2: The burning
Petrucha, S. The Rule of Won
Poblocki, D. The nightmarys
Poblocki, D. The random child
Pollock, T. The city's son
Porter, S. Lost voices
Powell, L. Burn mark
Powell, L. The Master of Misrule
Reed, J. Living violet
Rutkoski, M. The shadow society
Shirvington, J. Entice
Singleton, L. J. Dead girl dancing
Singleton, L. J. Dead girl in love
Stiefvater, M. The raven boys
Taylor, L. Dreams of gods & monsters
Templeman, M. The glass casket
Vanhee, J. Engines of the broken world
Walton, L. The Strange and beautiful sorrows of Ava Lavender
Waters, D. Break my heart 1,000 times
Weatherly, L. Angel burn
White, K. Paranormalcy
White, K. Supernaturally
Woon, Y. Dead beautiful
Woon, Y. Life eternal
Wrede, P. C. Sorcery and Cecelia, or, The enchanted chocolate pot
Supernaturally. White, K.
Supplee, Suzanne

Somebody everybody listens to
Sure fire. Higgins, J.
Surface tension. Runyon, B.
SURFING -- FICTION
Scheibe, L. Riptide
Surrender. Hartnett, S.
SURVIVAL -- FICTION
Falls, K. Inhuman
Smith, A. Passenger
Wooding, C. Silver
Whelan, G. Burying the sun
SURVIVAL AFTER AIRPLANE ACCIDENTS, SHIPWRECKS, ETC. -- FICTION
Bodeen, S. A. The raft
De la Peña, M. The living
Fama, E. Overboard
Hokenson, T. The winter road
Mary-Todd, J. Shot down
McKernan, V. Shackleton's stowaway
Monninger, J. Hippie chick
Morel, A. Survive
The **Survival** Kit. Freitas, D.
SURVIVAL SKILLS -- FICTION
Aguirre, A. Outpost
Bodeen, S. A. The raft
Charbonneau, J. The Testing
Crewe, M. The lives we lost
Crewe, M. The way we fall
Dashner, J. The kill order
Fukuda, A. The Prey
Mary-Todd, J. Shot down
Rainfield, C. Stained
Shusterman, N. UnWholly
Wells, D. Fragments
SURVIVALISM -- FICTION
Woolston, B. Black helicopters
Survive. Morel, A.
Surviving Antarctica. White, A.
The **survivors.** Weaver, W.
SUSPENSE FICTION
Cross, J. Tempest
Derting, K. The taking
Woon, Y. Life eternal
Sutcliff, Rosemary
The Shining Company
Sword song
Sutton, Kelsey
Some quiet place
Swagger. Deuker, C.
The **swan** kingdom. Marriott, Z.
The **swan** maiden. Tomlinson, H.
SWEDEN -- FICTION
Nilsson, P. You & you & you
Sweeney, Joyce
The guardian
The **sweet** far thing. Bray, L.
Sweet, hereafter. Johnson, A.
The **sweet,** terrible, glorious year I truly, completely lost it. Shanahan, L.
The **sweet** life of Stella Madison. Zeises, L. M.
The **sweet** revenge of Celia Door. Finneyfrock, K.
Sweet Thang. Whittenberg, A.
Sweetblood. Hautman, P.
Sweetgrass basket. Carvell, M.
Sweet 15. Adler, E.
Sweet venom. Childs, T. L.
Sweet, hereafter. Johnson, A.
The **sweetest** dream. Lessing, D. M.
The **sweetest** spell. Selfors, S.
The **sweetheart** of Prosper County. Alexander, J. S.
Sweethearts. Zarr, S.
A **swift** pure cry. Dowd, S.
Swim that rock. Rocco, J.
Swim the fly. Calame, D.
SWIMMING -- FICTION
Calame, D. Swim the fly
Crutcher, C. Whale talk
Mayall, B. Mermaid Park
Swimming to America. Mead, A.
SWINDLERS AND SWINDLING -- FICTION
Black, H. Red glove
Black, H. The white cat
Carter, A. Perfect scoundrels
Hooper, M. Fallen Grace
Lee, Y. S. A spy in the house
Luper, E. Bug boy
Nyembezi, C. L. S. The rich man of Pietermaritzburg
Ryan, P. In Mike we trust
Swiss mist. Powell, R.
Switch. Snow, C.
Switched. Wollman, J.
SWITZERLAND -- FICTION
García, C. Dreams of significant girls
Swoon at your own risk. Salter, S.
A **sword** in her hand. Van Beirs, P.
The **Sword** of Darrow. Malchow, A.
Sword song. Sutcliff, R.
SYLO. MacHale, D. J.
SYMBOLISM
Min, K. Secondhand world
The **symptoms** of my insanity. Raf, M.
SYNESTHESIA -- FICTION
Anderson, R. J. Ultraviolet
Mass, W. A mango -shaped space
SYRIA -- FICTION
Jolin, P. In the name of God

T

T4. LeZotte, A. C.

TAE KWON DO -- FICTION
Skilton, S. Bruised
Tahmaseb, Charity
The geek girl's guide to cheerleading
Takedown. Van Diepen, A.
Taken. McClintock, N.
Taken. Bloor, E.
Takoudes, Greg
When we wuz famous
Tal, Eve
Cursing Columbus
Double crossing
A **tale** of two summers. Sloan, B.
Tales of the Madman Underground. Barnes, J.
TALISMANS -- FICTION
Strauss, V. Passion blue
The **taking**. Derting, K.
Tamar. Peet, M.
The **taming** of the tights. Rennison, L.
Tangled. O'Rourke, E.
Tangled. Mackler, C.
Tankborn. Sandler, K.
Tanner, Mike
Resurrection blues
Tantalize. Smith, C. L.
TANZANIA -- FICTION
Sullivan, T. Golden boy
TAPESTRY -- FICTION
Guibord, M. Warped
Tarnish. Longshore, K.
TAROT -- FICTION
Powell, L. The Master of Misrule
A **taste** for rabbit. Zuckerman, L.
TATTOOING -- FICTION
Arbuthnott, G. The Keepers' tattoo
Cornish, D. M. Factotum
Joyce, G. The exchange
Marr, M. Ink exchange
Taub, Melinda
Still star-crossed
Tayleur, Karen
Chasing boys
Taylor, Laini
Blackbringer
Daughter of smoke and bone
Days of blood & starlight
Dreams of gods & monsters
Silksinger
Taylor, Mildred D.
The land
Taylor, S. S.
The Expeditioners and the Treasure of Drowned Man's Canyon
TEACHER-STUDENT RELATIONSHIP -- FICTION
Atkins, C. The file on Angelyn Stark
Hrdlitschka, S. Allegra
O'Connell, M. The sharp time
TEACHERS -- FICTION
Galante, C. The summer of May
Gilman, C. Professor Gargoyle
Gordimer, N. My son's story
Marshall, C. Christy
Parker, R. B. The Edenville Owls
TEACHERS OF THE BLIND -- FICTION
Miller, S. Miss Spitfire
TEACHERS OF THE DEAF -- FICTION
Miller, S. Miss Spitfire
Team Human. Brennan, S. R.
The **tear** collector. Jones, P.
Tears of a tiger. Draper, S. M.
Tease. Maciel, A.
TECHNOLOGICAL INNOVATIONS -- FICTION
Lancaster, M. A. The future we left behind
TECHNOLOGY -- FICTION
McDonald, I. Be my enemy
Reeve, P. Scrivener's moon
Teen, Inc. Petrucha, S.
TEENAGE BOYS -- FICTION
Mitchell, D. Black swan green
TEENAGE FATHERS
Knowles, J. Living with Jackie Chan
TEENAGE FATHERS -- FICTION
Bechard, M. Hanging on to Max
Hornby, N. Slam
Scott, K. This is so not happening
TEENAGE GIRLS -- FICTION
Aguirre, A. Outpost
Avasthi, S. Chasing Shadows
Raf, M. The symptoms of my insanity
Scheibe, L. Riptide
Smith, J. E. This is what happy looks like
Zarr, S. Roomies
TEENAGE MOTHERS -- FICTION
McCafferty, M. Thumped
Olsen, S. The girl with a baby
TEENAGE PARENTS -- FICTION
Scott, K. This is so not happening
TEENAGE PREGNANCY -- FICTION
Abrams, A. Hollywood High
Carter, C. Me, him, them, and it
Kephart, B. Small damages
McCafferty, M. Thumped
Teenage waistland. Biederman, L.
TEENAGERS -- ALCOHOL USE -- FICTION
Luedeke, L. Smashed
TEENAGERS -- CONDUCT OF LIFE -- FICTION
Wakefield, V. Friday never leaving
TEENAGERS -- CONDUCT OF LIFE -- FICTION

Blagden, S. Dear Life, You Suck
Blythe, C. Revenge of a not-so-pretty girl
Grace, A. In too deep
Haas, A. Dangerous girls
Herbach, G. Nothing special
Lyga, B. I hunt killers
Scheidt, E. L. Uses for boys
Whitney, D. The rivals
Zadoff, A. Boy Nobody
TEENAGERS -- DRUG USE -- FICTION
Burgess, M. The hit
Woodson, J. Beneath a meth moon
TEENAGERS -- FICTION
Aguirre, A. Outpost
Anderson, M. T. Burger Wuss
Beaudoin, S. Wise Young Fool
Berk, J. Guy Langman, crime scene procrastinator
Burgess, M. The hit
Calame, D. Call the shots
Carleson, J. C. The tyrant's daughter
Egloff, Z. Leap
Ellen, L. Blind spot
Finneyfrock, K. The sweet revenge of Celia Door
Fisher, C. Darkwater
Fitzpatrick, H. My life next door
Gagnon, M. Don't turn around
Hill, C. J. Slayers
Jacobs, J. H. The twelve-fingered boy
Johnson, A. A certain October
Johnson, L. Muchacho
King, A. S. Everybody sees the ants
Knight, K. Embers & echoes
Krokos, D. False memory
LaCour, N. The Disenchantments
Lange, E. J. Butter
Levithan, D. Every day
Lo, M. Inheritance
McLoughlin, J. At Yellow Lake
Price, L. Enders
Rennison, L. The taming of the tights
Shirvington, J. Embrace
Skuse, C. J. Rockoholic
Takoudes, G. When we wuz famous
Tregay, S. Love & leftovers
Walton, L. The Strange and beautiful sorrows of Ava Lavender
Waters, D. Break my heart 1,000 times
Whaley, J. C. Noggin
When I was the greatest
Yansky, B. Homicidal aliens and other disappointments
TEENAGERS -- SEXUAL BEHAVIOR -- FICTION
Clark, K. E. Freakboy
Vail, R. Kiss me again
TEENAGERS -- SUICIDE -- FICTION
Bernard, R. Find me
Hubbard, J. R. Try not to breathe
Hubbard, J. And we stay
Oates, J. C. Two or three things I forgot to tell you
Wylie, S. All these lives
Teenie. Grant, C.
Teeth. Moskowitz, H.
TELEPATHY -- FICTION
Mitchard, J. The midnight twins
Ness, P. The Ask and the Answer
Ness, P. The knife of never letting go
Ness, P. Monsters of men
Yansky, B. Alien invasion and other inconveniences
TELEPORTATION -- FICTION
Williams, S. Twinmaker
TELEVISION -- FICTION
Van Etten, D. Likely story
TELEVISION -- PRODUCTION AND DIRECTION -- FICTION
Williams, K. Pizza, love, and other stuff that made me famous
TELEVISION PERSONALITIES -- FICTION
Palmer, R. The Corner of Bitter and Sweet
TELEVISION PROGRAMS -- FICTION
Carlson, M. Premiere
Rex, A. Fat vampire
Tell us we're home. Budhos, M. T.
Teller, Janne
Nothing
Tempest. Cross, J.
Tempest rising. Deebs, T.
TEMPLARS -- FICTION
Chadda, S. The devil's kiss
Templeman, McCormick
The glass casket
Ten cents a dance. Fletcher, C.
Ten things I hate about me. Abdel-Fattah, R.
Ten things we did (and probably shouldn't have) Mlynowski, S.
Tender morsels. Lanagan, M.
Tending to Grace. Fusco, K. N.
Ten Mile River. Griffin, P.
Ten miles past normal. Dowell, F. O.
TENNESSEE -- FICTION
Bryant, J. Ringside, 1925
Gratz, A. Something rotten
Kenneally, M. Racing Savannah
Miller, K. The eternal ones
Reinhardt, D. How to build a house
TENNIS -- FICTION
Padian, M. Jersey tomatoes are the best
Tennyson, Blume, L. M. M.

Tentacles. Smith, R.
The **tequila** worm. Canales, V.
TERMINALLY ILL -- FICTION
Downham, J. Before I die
Green, J. The fault in our stars
Master, I. A beautiful lie
Matson, M. Second chance summer
Seamon, H. Somebody up there hates you
TERMINALLY ILL CHILDREN -- FICTION
Green, J. The fault in our stars
Seamon, H. Somebody up there hates you
Terrier. Pierce, T.
Terrill, Cristin
All our yesterdays
TERRITORIAL GOVERNORS -- FICTION
Bruchac, J. Sacajawea
TERRORISM -- FICTION
Dobkin, B. Neptune's children
Henry, A. Torched
Horowitz, A.Stormbreaker
Littman, S. Life, after
Monaghan, A. A girl named Digit
Terry, T. Fractured
Terry, Chris L.
Zero fade
Terry, Teri
Fractured
Slated
Tesla, Nikola, 1856-1943
About
Weyn, S. Distant waves
Testa, Dom
The Cassini code
The comet's curse
Cosmic storm
The dark zone
The web of Titan
The **Testing.** Charbonneau, J.
The testing [series]
Charbonneau, J. Independent study
TEXAS -- FICTION
Alexander, J. S. The sweetheart of Prosper County
Archer, J. Through her eyes
Canales, V. The tequila worm
Clement-Moore, R. Highway to hell
Clement-Moore, R. Texas gothic
Fehlbaum, B. Big fat disaster
Fehlbaum, B. Hope in Patience
Hale, M. The goodbye season
Mccall, G. G. Under the mesquite
Pearson, M. A room on Lorelei Street
Reeves, D. Slice of cherry
Restrepo, B. Illegal
Saldana, R. A good long way
Smith, C. L. Blessed
Smith, C. L. Tantalize
Toliver, W. Lifted
Ziegler, J. How not to be popular
Texas gothic. Clement-Moore, R.
Tharp, Tim
Badd
Knights of the hill country
Mojo
The spectacular now
That summer. Dessen, S.
That time I joined the circus. Howard, J. J.
The **gospel** according to Larry. Tashjian, J.
The **Great** Death. Smelcer, J. E.
THEATER -- FICTION
McCaughrean, G. The glorious adventures of the Sunshine Queen
McWilliams, K. Doormat
Naylor, P. R. Incredibly Alice
Trigiani, A. Viola in the spotlight
Voorhees, C. Lucky fools
Wood, M. My life the musical
Zadoff, A. My life, the theater, and other tragedies
THEFT -- FICTION
Carter, A. Perfect scoundrels
Hautman, P. How to steal a car
Myers, W. D. Oh, Snap!
Then I met my sister. Deriso, C. H.
The **theory** of everything. Johnson, J. J.
There is no dog. Rosoff, M.
There's a girl in my hammerlock. Spinelli, J.
THESEUS (GREEK MYTHOLOGY)
Barrett, T. Dark of the moon
They came from below. Nelson, B.
The **thief.** Turner, M. W.
Thief eyes. Simner, J. L.
THIEVES -- FICTION
Carter, A. Heist Society
Heath, J. Money run
Patron, S. Behind the masks
Thieves like us. Cole, S.
Thieves till we die. Cole, S.
The **thin** executioner. Shan, D.
Thin space. Casella, J.
The **things** a brother knows. Reinhardt, D.
Thirteen orphans. Lindskold, J. M.
Thirteen reasons why. Asher, J.
The **thirteenth** child. Wrede, P. C.
This dark endeavor. Oppel, K.
This full house. Wolff, V. E.
This gorgeous game. Freitas, D.
This is not a test. Summers, C.
This is so not happening. Scott, K.
This is what happy looks like. Smith, J. E.
This side of salvation. Smith-Ready, J.
This song will save your life. Sales, L.

This thing called the future. Powers, J. L.
Thin wood walls. Patneaude, D.
Things not seen. Clements, A.
Things that are. Clements, A.
This is what I did. Ellis, A. D.
Thomas, Erin
Boarder patrol
Thomas, Rob
Rats saw God
Thomas, Sherry
The burning sky
Thompson, Holly
The language inside
Orchards
Thompson, Kate
Creature of the night
The last of the High Kings
The new policeman
The white horse trick
Origins
Thompson, Ricki
City of cannibals
Thomson, Jamie
Dark Lord, the early years
Thomson, Sarah L.
The secret of the Rose
Thoreau, Henry David
About
Armistead, C. Being Henry David
Those that wake. Karp, J.
The **thought** of high windows. Kositsky, L.
A **thousand** shades of blue. Stevenson, R.
Threads and flames. Friesner, E. M.
Threatened. Schrefer, E.
Three. Simmons, K
Three clams and an oyster. Powell, R.
Three rivers rising. Richards, J.
Three songs for courage. Trottier, M.
Three-quarters dead. Peck, R.
Throne of glass. Maas, S. J.
Through her eyes. Archer, J.
Thumped. McCafferty, M.
The **Thunder** in His Head. Gant, G.
Thunder over Kandahar. McKay, S. E.
Three black swans. Cooney, C. B.
Throwing like a girl. Mackey, W. K.
THUNDERSTORMS -- FICTION
Bosworth, J. Struck
Thurlo, Aimee
The spirit line
Thursday's child. Hartnett, S.
Tibensky, Arlaina
And then things fall apart
Tides. Cornwell, B.
Tiernan, Cate
Balefire
Immortal beloved
Tiger eyes. Blume, J.
Tiger Lily. Anderson, J. L.
Tiger moon.
Tiger's curse. Houck, C.
Tiger's quest. Houck, C.
TIGERS -- FICTION
Houck, C. Tiger's curse
Houck, C. Tiger's quest
Tiger moon
Tighter. Griffin, A.
Till, Emmett, 1941-1955
About
Crowe, C. Mississippi trial, 1955
Tillmon County fire. Ehrenberg, P.
TIME -- FICTION
McNamee, E. The Navigator
Time between us. Stone, T. I.
A **time** to dance, Venkatraman, P
TIME TRAVEL -- FICTION
Brashares, A. The here and now
Brennan, H. The Doomsday Box: a Shadow Project adventure
Card, O. S. Ruins
Cross, J. Tempest
Emerald green
Gleason, C. The clockwork scarab
Goodman, A. Singing the Dogstar blues
Hand, E. Radiant days
Hautman, P. The Cydonian pyramid
Hautman, P. The klaatu terminus
Hautman, P. The obsidian blade
Kessler, J. M. Loss
MacCullough, C. Always a witch
O'Brien, J. Day of the assassins
Palma, F. J. The map of the sky
Palma, F. J. The map of time
Sapphire blue
Scott, M. The enchantress
Stone, T. I. Time between us
Terrill, C. All our yesterdays
White, A. B. Windows on the world
Time's memory. Lester, J.
TimeRiders. Scarrow, A.
TimeRiders [series]
Scarrow, A. Day of the predator
Tintera, Amy
Reboot
TITANIC (STEAMSHIP) -- FICTION
Weyn, S. Distant waves
Wolf, A. The watch that ends the night
To darkness fled. Williamson, J.
To kill a mockingbird. Lee, H.
To light a candle. Lackey, M.
Toads and diamonds. Tomlinson, H.
Tocher, Timothy

Bill Pennant, Babe Ruth, and me
Chief Sunrise, John McGraw, and me
Todd, Pamela
The blind faith hotel
TODD, SWEENEY (LEGENDARY CHARACTER)
Pratchett, T. Dodger
TOKYO (JAPAN) -- FICTION
Renn, D. Tokyo heist
Whitney, D. When you were here
Tokyo heist. Renn, D.
TOLERATION -- FICTION
McKay, S. E. Enemy territory
Toliver, Wendy
Lifted
TOMATOES -- FICTION
Walters, E. Splat!
Tomlinson, Heather
Aurelie; a faerie tale
The swan maiden
Toads and diamonds
Tomorrow, when the war began. Marsden, J.
Tomorrow's magic. Service, P. F.
Toning the sweep. Johnson, A.
The torch keeper [series]
Dos Santos, S. The culling
Torched. Henry, A.
Torn. Massey, D.
Torn to pieces. McDonnell, M.
Torn. O'Rourke, E.
TORONTO (ONT.) -- FICTION
Hopkinson, N. The Chaos
Torres Sanchez, Jenny
Death, Dickinson, and the demented life of Frenchie Garcia
TORTURE -- FICTION
Perera, A. Guantanamo boy
Strasser, T. Boot camp
Whyman, M. Icecore
TOTALITARIANISM -- FICTION
Austen, C. All good children
Touch. Prose, F.
Touching snow. Felin, M. S.
Touching Spirit Bear. Mikaelsen, B.
Toussaint Louverture, 1743-1803
About
Lake, N. In darkness
Townley, Roderick
Sky
Townsend, Wendy
Lizard love
The **toymaker.** De Quidt, J.
TOYS -- FICTION
Cameron, S. The dark unwinding
Tracey, Scott
Darkbound
Moonset
TRACK ATHLETICS -- FICTION
Wallace, R. One good punch
Tracy, Kristen
Sharks & boys
TRAFFIC ACCIDENTS -- FICTION
Shusterman, N. UnSouled
Zephaniah, B. Face
TRAFFIC ACCIDENTS -- FICTION
Frank, E. R. Wrecked
Johnson, P. What happened
McDaniel, L. Hit and run
Wolf, J. S. Breaking beautiful
Trafficked. Purcell, K.
The **Tragedy** Paper. Laban, E.
Traitor. Pausewang, G.
Traitors gate. Avi, 1937.
Traitors son. Bell, H.
The **traitor;** Golden Mountain chronicles, 1885. Yep, L.
Traitor. McNab, A.
The **traitor's** smile. Elliott, P.
Traitor's son. Bell, H.
TRANSGENDER PARENTS -- FICTION
Davis, T. S. Happy families
TRANSGENDER PEOPLE -- FICTION
Beam, C. I am J
Clark, K. E. Freakboy
Cronn-Mills, K. Beautiful Music for Ugly Children
Davis, T. S. Happy families
Hyde, C. R. Jumpstart the world
Katcher, B. Almost perfect
Peters, J. A. Luna
Wittlinger, E. Parrotfish
TRANSPLANTATION OF ORGANS, TISSUES, ETC. -- FICTION
Cabot, M. Airhead
Cabot, M. Being Nikki
Cabot, M. Runaway
Whaley, J. C. Noggin
Wolfson, J. Cold hands, warm heart
TRANSVESTITES -- FICTION
Brothers, M. Debbie Harry sings in French
Erdrich, L. The last report on the miracles at Little No Horse
The **trap.** Smelcer, J. E.
Trapped. Northrop, M.
Trash. Mulligan, A.
TRAVEL -- FICTION
Hubbard, K. Wanderlove
Pearce, J. Manga touch
Shusterman, N. UnSouled
TRAVEL WRITERS -- FICTION
Yang, D. J. Daughter of Xanadu
TRAVELERS -- FICTION

Yang, D. J. Daughter of Xanadu
The **treachery** of beautiful things. Long, R. F.
TREASURE HUNT (GAME) -- FICTION
Altebrando, T. The best night of your (pathetic) life
Walker, K. 7clues to winning you
The **treasure** map of boys. Lockhart, E.
Tregay, Sarah
Love & leftovers
Treggiari, Jo
Ashes, ashes
Trevayne, Emma
Coda
TRIALS
Pesci, D. Amistad
TRIALS (MURDER) -- FICTION
Haas, A. Dangerous girls
TRIALS -- FICTION
Hemphill, S. Wicked girls
Meldrum, C. Madapple
Myers, W. D. Monster
Pesci, D. Amistad
Smith-Ready, J. Shade
Triana, Gaby
Riding the universe
TRIANGLE SHIRTWAIST COMPANY, INC. -- FICTION
Davies, J. Lost
Friesner, E. M. Threads and flames
Haddix, M. P. Uprising
TRIANGLES (INTERPERSONAL RELATIONS) -- FICTION
Doller, T. Something like normal
McCarry, S. All our pretty songs
TRIATHLON -- FICTION
Crutcher, C. Ironman; a novel
A **trick** of the light. Metzger, L.
Tricks. Hopkins, E.
Trickster's girl. Bell, H.
Trickster's choice. Pierce, T.
TRICKSTERS -- FICTION
Knight, K. Embers & echoes
Trigiani, Adriana
Viola in reel life
Viola in the spotlight
Trigger. Vaught, S.
Tripping. Waldorf, H.
The **Triumph** of Death. Henderson, J.
TRIPLETS -- FICTION
Cooney, C. B. Three black swans
Triskellion 2: The burning. Peterson, W.
Triskellion. Peterson, W.
TROJAN WAR -- FICTION
Geras, A. Troy
Troll Bridge; a rock 'n' roll fairy tale. Yolen, J.
TROLLS -- FICTION
Pike, A. Illusions
Pike, A. Spells
Pike, A. Wings
Tropical secrets. Engle, M.
Trottier, Maxine
Three songs for courage
Trouble. Schmidt, G. D.
A **troublesome** boy. Vasey, P.
Trouble with half a moon. Vigilante, D.
TROUT -- FICTION
Woolston, B. Catch & release
Troy. Geras, A.
The **true** adventures of Charley Darwin. Meyer, C.
A **true** and faithful narrative. Sturtevant, K.
True believer. Wolff, V. E.
True fires. McCarthy, S. C.
The **true** tale of the monster Billy Dean. Almond, D.
True love, the sphinx, and other unsolvable riddles. O'Connell, T.
True-to-life series from Hamilton High [series]
Reynolds, M. Shut up!
True talents. Lubar, D.
Trueman, Terry
Cruise control
Inside out
7 days at the hot corner
Life happens next
Stuck in neutral
Truly, madly, deadly. Jayne, H.
Trumble, J. H.
Don't let me go
TRUST -- FICTION
Mangum, L. After hello
TRUTH -- FICTION
Berry, J. All the truth that's in me
The **truth** about forever. Dessen, S.
TRUTHFULNESS AND FALSEHOOD -- FICTION
Holland, L. T. The counterfeit family tree of Vee Crawford-Wong
Try not to breathe. Hubbard, J. R.
TSUNAMIS -- FICTION
Pratchett, T. Nation
Thompson, H. The language inside
Tubb, Kristin O'Donnell
Selling hope
The 13th sign
TUBERCULOSIS -- FICTION
Brooks, M. Queen of hearts
Tucholke, April Genevieve
Between the devil and the deep blue sea
Tucker, Reed
(jt. auth) Moore, K. Amber House

Tullson, Diane
Riley Park
Tulsa burning. Myers, A.
Tumble & fall. Coutts, A.
Tunnel vision. Shaw, S.
Tunnell, Michael O.
Wishing moon
TURKEY -- FICTION
Marillier, J. Cybele's secret
Skrypuch, M. F. Daughter of war
Turner, Ann Warren
Father of lies
Hard hit
Turner, Max
End of days
Night runner
Turner, Megan Whalen
A conspiracy of kings
The King of Attolia
The Queen of Attolia
The thief
The **turning.** Prose, F.
TUTSI (AFRICAN PEOPLE) -- FICTION
Combres, E. Broken memory
The **twelve-fingered** boy. Jacobs, J. H.
12 things to do before you crash and burn. Proimos, J.
The Twelve-Fingered Boy Trilogy [series]
Jacobs, J. H. The twelve-fingered boy
Twenty boy summer. Ockler, S.
Twilight. Meyer, S.
Twin's daughter. Baratz-Logsted, L.
Twinmaker. Williams, S.
24 girls in 7 days. Bradley, A.
TWINS -- FICTION
Davis, T. S. Happy families
Higgins, J. Sure fire
MacCullough, C. Drawing the ocean
McClymer, K. Must love black
McNicoll, S. Last chance for Paris
Mitchard, J. The midnight twins
Nuzum, K. A. A small white scar
Peterson, W. Triskellion
Stein, T. Kindred
Sturtevant, K. The brothers story
Wrede, P. C. Across the Great Barrier
Wrede, P. C. The Far West
Zhang, K. What's left of me
Twisted. Anderson, L. H.
Two boys kissing. Levithan, D.
The **two** loves of Will Shakespeare. Lawlor, L.
Two or three things I forgot to tell you. Oates, J. C.
Two parties, one tux, and a very short film about the Grapes of Wrath. Goldman, S.
Tyger tyger. Hamilton, K. R.
Twomey, Cathleen
Beachmont letters
TYPHOID FEVER -- FICTION
Chibbaro, J. Deadly
Typhoid Mary, d. 1938
About
Chibbaro, J. Deadly
The **tyrant's** daughter. Carleson, J. C.
Tyrell. Booth, C.

U

Uchida, Yoshiko
A jar of dreams
Journey to Topaz; a story of the Japanese-American evacuation
Uehashi, Nahoko
Moribito; Guardian of the Spirit
Moribito II; Guardian of the Darkness
UGANDA -- FICTION
Nanji, S. Child of dandelions
Uglies. Westerfeld, S.
Ultraviolet. Anderson, R. J.
Umansky, Kaye
Under the moons of Mars; new adventures on Barsoom
Solomon Snow and the stolen jewel
Umubyeyi, Jeanne d'Arc, 1986-
About
Jansen, H. Over a thousand hills I walk with you
Un Lun Dun. Mieville, C.
The **unbecoming** of Mara Dyer. Hodkin, M.
UNCLES -- FICTION
Bunce, E. C. A curse dark as gold
Cerrito, A. The end of the line
Hautman, P. The obsidian blade
Knowles, J. Living with Jackie Chan
Low, D. The entomological tales of Augustus T. Percival
Napoli, D. J. Alligator bayou
Proimos, J. 12 things to do before you crash and burn
Woodworth, C. Double -click for trouble
Under the blood-red sun. Salisbury, G.
Under the bridge. Harmon, M.
Under the Empyrean Sky. Wendig, C.
Under the Jolly Roger. Meyer, L. A.
Under the mesquite. Mccall, G. G.
Under the moons of Mars.
Under the never sky. Rossi, V.
Under the wolf, under the dog. Rapp, A.
Undercover. Kephart, B.
Under the green hill. Sullivan, L. L.
Under the mesquite. Mccall, G. G.
Under the moons of Mars; new adventures on Barsoom. Umansky, K.

Under the Persimmon tree. Staples, S. F.
Under Wildwood. Meloy, C.
UNDERCOVER OPERATIONS -- FICTION
Zadoff, A. Boy Nobody
UNDERGROUND LEADERS -- FICTION
Bartoletti, S. C. The boy who dared
UNDERGROUND MOVEMENTS -- FICTION
North, P. Starglass
UNDERGROUND RAILROAD -- FICTION
Ayres, K. North by night
Wisler, G. C. Caleb's choice
The Undertaken trilogy [series]
Berk, A. Death watch
Berk, A. Mistle child
UNDERTAKERS AND UNDERTAKING -- FICTION
Berk, A. Mistle child
Nadol, J. The vision
Unearthly. Neely, C.
Unforgettable. Ellsworth, L.
UNICORNS -- FICTION
Humphreys, C. The hunt of the unicorn
The **Unidentified.** Mariz, R.
The **uninvited.** Wynne-Jones, T.
UNITED STATES -- ARMED FORCES -- AFRICAN AMERICANS -- HISTORY -- 20TH CENTURY -- FICTION
Myers, W. D. Invasion!
UNITED STATES. ARMY--WOMEN'S ARMY CORPS--FICTION
Davis, T. S. Mare's war
UNITED STATES -- FEDERAL BUREAU OF INVESTIGATION -- FICTION
Derting, K. Desires of the dead
UNITED STATES -- FICTION
Steele, A. Apollo's outcasts
UNITED STATES -- HISTORY -- 1702-1713, QUEEN ANNE'S WAR -- FICTION
Steinmetz, K. The mourning wars
UNITED STATES -- HISTORY -- 1775-1783, REVOLUTION -- FICTION
Anderson, M. T. The astonishing life of Octavian Nothing, traitor to the nation
UNITED STATES -- HISTORY -- REVOLUTION, 1775-1783 --NAVAL OPERATIONS, BRITISH -- FICTION
Anderson, M. T. The astonishing life of Octavian Nothing, traitor to the nation
UNITED STATES -- HISTORY -- 1861-1865, CIVIL WAR -- FICTION
Garcia, K. Beautiful creatures
Paulsen, G. Soldier's heart
Peck, R. The river between us
Wells, R. Red moon at Sharpsburg
UNITED STATES -- HISTORY -- 20TH CENTURY -- FICTION
Magoon, K. Fire in the streets
UNITED STATES -- RACE RELATIONS -- FICTION
Lee, H. To kill a mockingbird
Mosley, W. Fortunate son
UNITED STATES -- RELATIONS -- SOVIET UNION -- FICTION
Kiem, E. Dancer, daughter, traitor, spy
UNITED STATES. AIR FORCE -- FICTION
Lynch, C. Casualties of war
UNITED STATES. CENTRAL INTELLIGENCE AGENCY -- FICTION
Cross, J. Tempest
Whyman, M. Goldstrike
UNITED STATES. DEPT. OF HOMELAND SECURITY -- FICTION
Doctorow, C. Homeland
Doctorow, C. Little brother
UNITED STATES. MARINE CORPS -- FICTION
Doller, T. Something like normal
UNITED STATES. NATIONAL AERONAUTICS AND SPACE ADMINISTRATION -- FICTION
172 hours on the moon
UNIVERSITIES AND COLLEGES -- FICTION
Charbonneau, J. Independent study
Charbonneau, J. The Testing
Cooney, C. B. Janie face to face
An **unlikely** friendship. Rinaldi, A.
The **unnameables.** Booraem, E.
Unseen companion. Orenstein, D. G.
Unsigned hype. Mattison, B. T.
UnSouled. Shusterman, N.
Unspoken. Brennan, S. R.
The **unspoken.** Fahy, T. R.
Unsworth, Tania
The one safe place
UnWholly. Shusterman, N.
Unwind. Shusterman, N.
Unwind trilogy [series]
Shusterman, N. UnSouled
Updale, Eleanor
Montmorency
Montmorency and the assassins
Montmorency on the rocks
Montmorency's revenge
Upgrade U. Simone
Uprising. Haddix, M. P.
Upstate. Buckhanon, K.
Upjohn, Rebecca
The secret of the village fool
URBAN FICTION
Harmon, M. Under the bridge
Uses for boys. Scheidt, E. L.
UTAH -- FICTION

Zarr, S. Sweethearts
UTE INDIANS -- FICTION
Hobbs, W. Beardance
UTOPIAS -- FICTION
Booraem, E. The unnameables
DeStefano, L. Perfect ruin
Parker, A. C. Gated

V

V is for villian. Moore, P.
VACATIONS -- FICTION
Matson, M. Second chance summer
Vacco, Corina
My chemical mountain
Vail, Rachel
Kiss me again
Lucky
VALENTINE'S DAY -- FICTION
Levithan, D. Marly's ghost
Valentine, Allyson
How (not) to find a boyfriend
Valentine, Jenny
Broken soup
Double
Me, the missing, and the dead
Vampire crush. Robinson, A. M.
Vampire High. Rees, D. C.
Vampire High: sophomore year. Rees, D.
Vampire kisses. Schreiber, E.
Vampire queen [series]
Maizel, R. Infinite days
Vampire rising. Henderson, J.
VAMPIRES -- FICTION
Bickle, L. The outside
Black, H. The coldest girl in Coldtown
Brennan, S. R. Team Human
Brewer, H. First kill
Clare, C. City of fallen angels
Henderson, J. Vampire rising
Henderson, J. The Triumph of Death
Hill, W. The rising
Holder, N. Damned
Kagawa, J. The Eternity Cure
Kagawa, J. The immortal rules
Maizel, R. Stolen nights
Moore, P. Red moon rising
Rees, D. Vampire High: sophomore year
Schreiber, E. Vampire kisses
Showalter, G. Intertwined
The **Van** Alen legacy. De la Cruz, M.
Van Beirs, Pat
A sword in her hand
Van de Ruit, John
Spud
Van Diepen, Allison
Takedown
Van Draanen, Wendelin
The running dream
Flipped
Van Etten, David
Likely story
Van Tol, Alex
Knifepoint
Vance, Darcy
Tahmaseb, C. The geek girl's guide to cheerleading
VANCOUVER (B.C.) -- FICTION
Leavitt, M. My book of life by Angel
Vande Velde, Vivian
The book of Mordred
Heir apparent
Magic can be murder
Remembering Raquel
Stolen
Vanderpool, Clare
Moon over Manifest
Vango. Fombelle, T.
Vanhee, Jason
Engines of the broken world
Vanishing girl. Peacock, S.
Variant. Wells, R. E.
Varrato, Tony
Fakie
Vasey, Paul
A troublesome boy
The **vast** fields of ordinary. Burd, N.
Vaughn, Carrie
Steel
Voices of dragons
Vaught, Susan
Big fat manifesto
Freaks like us
Trigger
Vaupel, Robin
My contract with Henry
Veciana-Suarez, Ana
The flight to freedom
Vega, Denise
Fact of life #31
Vegan virgin Valentine. Mackler, C.
Velvet. Hooper, M.
VENDETTA -- FICTION
Caine, R. Prince of shadows
Taub, M. Still star-crossed
Van Diepen, A. Takedown
VENICE (ITALY) -- FICTION
Collins, P. L. Hidden voices
Hemphill, S. Sisters of glass
VENICE (ITALY) -- HISTORY -- 16TH CENTURY -- FICTION
Gould, S. Cross my heart

Venkatraman, Padma
Climbing the stairs
Island's end
A time to dance
Verday, Jessica
The Hollow
VERMONT -- FICTION
Doyle, E. F. According to Kit
Galante, C. The sweetness of salt
Ockler, S. Fixing Delilah
Wilhelm, D. Falling
Vernick, Shirley Reva
The blood lie
VERONA (ITALY) -- FICTION
Taub, M. Still star-crossed
The **vespertine.** Mitchell, S.
Vessel. Durst, S. B.
VETERANS -- FICTION
Williams, S. Bull rider
VETERINARY MEDICINE -- FICTION
Wilson, D. L. Firehorse
Victoria, Queen of Great Britain, 1819-1901 About
MacColl, M. Prisoners in the palace
Victorio's war. Wilson, J.
VIDEO GAMES -- FICTION
Kostick, C. Edda
Kostick, C. Epic
Kostick, C. Saga
Michaels, R. Genesis Alpha
VIDEO RECORDINGS -- FICTION
Bancks, T. Mac Slater hunts the cool
Koertge, R. Stoner & Spaz
VIENNA (AUSTRIA) -- FICTION
Dunlap, S. E. The musician's daughter
VIETNAM WAR, 1961-1975 -- FICTION
Burg, Ann E. All the broken pieces
Lynch, C. Casualties of war
Myers, W. D. Fallen angels
VIETNAMESE AMERICANS -- FICTION
Burg, Ann E. All the broken pieces
The **view** from the top. Frank, H.
Vigan, Delphine de
No and me
Vigilante, Danette
Trouble with half a moon
The vigilante poets of the Selwyn Academy. Hattemer, K.
VIGILANTES -- FICTION
Vacco, C. My chemical mountain
Viguie, Debbie
Holder, N. Damned
VIKINGS -- FICTION
Sutcliff, R. Sword song
Viguie, Debbie
Holder, N. Crusade
VIII. Castor, H. M.
VILLAGES -- FICTION
Templeman, M. The glass casket
Villareal, Ray
Body slammed!
Vincent, Zu
The lucky place
VINTAGE CLOTHING -- FICTION
O'Connell, M. The sharp time
Vintage Veronica. Perl, E. S.
The **Vinyl** Princess. Prinz, Y.
Viola in reel life. Trigiani, A.
Viola in the spotlight. Trigiani, A.
VIOLENCE -- FICTION
Davis, R. F. Chasing AllieCat
Garden, N. Endgame
Mesrobian, C. Sex and violence
Nelson, J. On the volcano
Silver, E. Rush
Violence 101. Wright, D.
Violi, Jen
Putting makeup on dead people
VIOLINISTS -- FICTION
Collins, P. L. Hidden voices
VIOLINISTS -- FICTION
Ibbitson, J. The Landing
Ingold, J. Mountain solo
Martinez, J. Virtuosity
Yoo, P. Good enough
VIOLONCELLOS -- FICTION
Forman, G. Where she went
The **viper** within. Mills, S.
Virals. Reichs, K. J.
VIRGINIA --HISTORY -- REVOLUTION, 1775-1783 -- FICTION
Anderson, M. T. The astonishing life of Octavian Nothing, traitor to the nation
VIRTUAL REALITY -- FICTION
Cheva, C. DupliKate
Cole, S. Z. Raptor
Cole, S. Z. Rex
Henderson, J. Bunker 10
The **Virtual** War. Skurzynski, G.
Virtuosity. Martinez, J.
VIRUSES--FICTION
Dashner, J. The kill order
DeStefano, L. Fever
Falls, K. Inhuman
Smith, S. L. Orleans
The **vision.** Nadol, J.
VISIONS -- FICTION
Moore, K. Amber House
Moore, K. Neverwas
O'Brien, A. Lara's gift
Viva Jacquelina! Meyer, L. A.
Vivaldi, Antonio, 1678-1741

About
Collins, P. L. Hidden voices
Vivian, Siobhan
The list
A little friendly advice
Not that kind of girl
Vizzini, Ned, 1981-2013
It's kind of a funny story
Vlahos, Len
The scar boys
VOICE -- FICTION
Casanova, M. Frozen
A **voice** of her own. Dana, B.
The **voice** on the radio. Cooney, C. B.
Voices. Le Guin, U. K.
Voices of dragons. Vaughn, C.
Voigt, Cynthia
Homecoming
VOLCANOES -- FICTION
Mullin, M. Ashfall
Nelson, J. On the volcano
Volponi, Paul
Black and white
The Final Four
The hand you're dealt
Homestretch
Hurricane song
Izzy, willy-nilly
Rikers High
Rooftop
Rucker Park setup
VOLUNTEER WORK -- FICTION
Reinhardt, D. How to build a house
Voorhees, Coert
The brothers Torres
Lucky fools
VOYAGES AND TRAVELS -- FICTION
Block, F. L. Love in the time of global warming
Brouwer, S. Devil's pass
Brown, J. Perfect escape
Cummings, P. The journey back
Forman, G. Just one day
Hesse, K. Safekeeping
Kittredge, C. The nightmare garden
Kizer, A. A matter of days
McQuerry, M. D. The Peculiars
Meloy, M. The apprentices
Paquette, A.-J. Nowhere girl
Rossetti, R. The girl with borrowed wings
Smith, J. E. The geography of you and me
Sullivan, T. Golden boy
Wilson, J. Written in blood
Zettel, S. Dust girl
Zettel, S. Golden girl
VOYAGES AROUND THE WORLD -- FICTION
Meyer, C. The true adventures of Charley Darwin
Vrettos, Adrienne Maria
Burnout
Skin
Sight

W

The **wager.** Napoli, D. J.
Wait for me. Na, A.
WAITERS AND WAITRESSES -- FICTION
Caletti, D. The fortunes of Indigo Skye
Waiting. Williams, C. L.
Waiting for no one. Brenna, B.
Waiting for Sarah. McBay, B.
Wake. Hocking, A.
Wake. McMann, L.
The **wake** of the Lorelei Lee. Meyer, L. A.
Wakefield, Vikki
Friday never leaving
The waking [series]
Randall, T. Dreams of the dead
Randall, T. Spirits of the Noh
Wakling backward. Austen, C.
The **waking** dark. Wasserman, R.
Waldorf, Heather
Tripping
WALES -- FICTION
Jones, A. F. Destiny's path
Skuse, C. J. Rockoholic
WALES -- HISTORY -- 1284-1536 -- FICTION
Coats, J. A. The wicked and the just
Walk softly, rachel. Banks, K.
Walker, Brian F.
Black boy/white school
Walker, Kristin
7clues to winning you
Wallace, Jason
Out of shadows
Wallace, Rich
One good punch
Perpetual check
Wrestling Sturbridge
War and watermelon
Wallace, Sandra Neil
Muckers
Wallenfels, Stephen
POD
Waller, S. B.
A mad, wicked folly
Walsh, Alice
A Long Way from Home
Walsh, Pat
The Crowfield curse
The Crowfield demon

Walters, Eric
In a flash
Splat!
Sketches
Special Edward
Walton, Leslye
The Strange and beautiful sorrows of Ava Lavender
Wanderlove. Hubbard, K.
Wandering son. Shimura Takako
War and watermelon. Wallace, R.
WAR STORIES
Bacigalupi, P. The drowned cities
Behemoth
Berry, J. All the truth that's in me
Brown, S. Caminar
Coakley, L. Witchlanders
Cooper, M. The FitzOsbornes at war
Deebs, T. Tempest rising
Frost, H. Crossing stones
Hardy, J. The shifter
Hinwood, C. The returning
Holub, J. An innocent soldier
Jinks, C. Babylonne
Jones, A. F. Destiny's path
Kostick, C. Edda
Leviathan
Lu, M. Legend
Lu, M. Prodigy
Lynch, C. Casualties of war
Marchetta, M. Froi of the exiles
Marchetta, M. Quintana of Charyn
Marsden, J. Tomorrow, when the war began
Marsden, J. Incurable
Marsden, J. The other side of dawn
Marsden, J. While I live
Mason, P. Camel rider
Massey, D. Torn
McDonald, I. Empress of the sun
Millard, G. A small free kiss in the dark
Moran, K. Bloodline
Myers, W. D. Invasion!
Ness, P. Monsters of men
Peet, M. Life
Riordan, J. The sniper
Ryan, A. K. Flame
Sandell, L. A. Song of the sparrow
Stratton, A. Chanda's wars
Westerfeld, S. Goliath
Yancey, R. The 5th Wave
The **war** within these walls. Sax, A.
Ward, David
Escape the mask
Ward, Rachel
The Chaos
Infinity
Numbers
Warman, Jessica
Between
Breathless
Where the truth lies
Warp speed. Yang, D. J.
Warped. Guibord, M.
The **warrior** heir. Chima, C. W.
WARSAW (POLAND) -- HISTORY -- WARSAW GHETTO UPRISING, 1943 -- FICTION
Sax, A. The war within these walls
WASHINGTON (D.C.) -- FICTION
Hand, E. Radiant days
Robinson, K. S. Fifty degrees below
Robinson, K. S. Forty signs of rain
White, E. E. The President's daughter
WASHINGTON (STATE) -- FICTION
Caletti, D. The fortunes of Indigo Skye
Caletti, D. Stay
Derting, K. Desires of the dead
Derting, K. The last echo
Deuker, C. Gym candy
Hubbard, A. But I love him
Kelly, T. Harmonic feedback
Kincy, K. Other
Lockhart, E. The boyfriend list
Meyer, S. Eclipse
Meyer, S. New moon
Meyer, S. Twilight
Olsen, G. Envy
Reed, A. Crazy
Wasserman, Robin
Awakening
Crashed
Hacking Harvard
Skinned
The waking dark
Wired
WATER -- FICTION
Park, L. S. A long walk to water
Waters, Dan
Generation dead
Waters, Daniel
Break my heart 1,000 times
Waters, Zack C.
Blood moon rider
Watership Down. Adams, R.
Watersmeet. Abbott, E. J.
Watkins, Steve
Down Sand Mountain
Juvie
What comes after
Watkins, Yoko Kawashima
My brother, my sister, and I
So far from the bamboo grove
Watson, Cristy

Benched
Watts, Irene N.
No moon
The **way** he lived. Smith, E. W.
The **way** of the warrior. Matthews, A.
Way to go. Ryan, T.
The **way** we fall. Crewe, M.
We are the Goldens. Reinhardt, D.
We hear the dead. Salerni, D. K.
We were here. De la Pena, M.
We were liars. Lockhart, E.
We'll always have summer. Han, J.
WEALTH -- FICTION
Lockhart, E. We were liars
WEATHER -- FICTION
Williams, A. The deep freeze of Bartholomew Tullock
Weatherford, Carole Boston
Becoming Billie Holiday
Weatherly, Lee
Angel burn
Kat got your tongue
Weaver, Will
Checkered flag cheater
Defect
Full service
Saturday night dirt
Super stock rookie
The survivors
A **Web** of Air. Reeve, P.
The **web** of Titan. Testa, D.
Webb, Philip
Six days
Weber, Lori
If you live like me
WEBLOGS -- FICTION
Bancks, T. Mac Slater hunts the cool
Brody, J. My life undecided
Cowan, J. Earthgirl
Lane, D. Gothic Lolita
Prinz, Y. The Vinyl Princess
Strasser, T. Wish you were dead
WEB SITES -- FICTION
Bancks, T. Mac Slater vs. the city
WEDDINGS -- FICTION
Smith, J. E. The statistical probability of love at first sight
The **Wednesday** wars. Schmidt, G. D.
The **Wee** Free Men. Pratchett, T.
Weetzie Bat. Block, F. L.
Weeks, Sarah
Jumping the scratch
Weetamoo, heart of the Pocassets. Smith, P. C.
WEIGHT LOSS -- FICTION
Lipsyte, R. One fat summer
Zarr, S. Sweethearts
Wein, Elizabeth
Code name Verity
The empty kingdom
The lion hunter
Rose under fire
Weingarten, Lynn
Wherever Nina lies
The **well** between the worlds. Llewellyn, S.
Wells, Dan
Ruins
Fragments
Partials
Wells, H. G. (Herbert George), 1866-1946
About
Palma, F. J. The map of the sky
Wells, Martha
Emilie & the hollow world
Wells, Robison
Feedback
Variant
Wells, Rosemary
Red moon at Sharpsburg
Wemmlinger, Raymond
Booth's daughter
Wendig, Chuck
Under the Empyrean Sky
WEREWOLVES -- FICTION
Armstrong, K. The reckoning
Block, F. L. The frenzy
Dunkle, C. B. By these ten bones
Jinks, C. The abused werewolf rescue group
Johnson, C. Claire de Lune
Johnson, C. Nocturne
Klause, A. C. Blood and chocolate
Larbalestier, J. Liar
McBride, L. Hold me closer, necromancer
Meyer, S. Breaking dawn
Meyer, S. Eclipse
Moore, P. Red moon rising
Pearce, J. Sisters red
Smith, C. L. Blessed
Smith, C. L. Tantalize
St. Crow, L. Strange angels
Stiefvater, M. Forever
Stiefvater, M. Linger
Stiefvater, M. Shiver
Werlin, Nancy
Double helix
Extraordinary
Impossible
The killer's cousin
The rules of survival
Wesselhoeft, Conrad
Adios, nirvana
WEST (U.S.) -- FICTION
Smith, A. Ghost medicine

Woolston, B. Catch & release
WEST AFRICA -- FICTION
Okorafor, N. The shadow speaker
WEST VIRGINIA -- FICTION
Ehrenberg, P. Tillmon County fire
Martin, T. M. The end games
Slayton, F. C. When the whistle blows
Wyatt, M. Funny how things change
West, Kasie
Pivot point
Split second
Westerfeld, Scott
Afterworlds
Behemoth
Leviathan
WESTERN STORIES
Westerfeld, S. Blue noon
Westerfeld, S. Extras
Wilson, J. Victorio's war
Westerfeld, S. So yesterday
Weston, Robert Paul
Dust city
Weyn, Suzanne
Distant waves
Dr. Frankenstein's daughters
Empty
Recruited
Reincarnation
Whale talk. Crutcher, C.
Whaley, John Corey
Noggin
Where things come back
Wharton, Thomas
The shadow of Malabron
What boys really want? Hautman, P.
What can(t) wait. Perez, A. H.
What comes after. Watkins, S.
What happened to Cass McBride? Giles, G.
What happened to goodbye. Dessen, S. 1.
What happened. Johnson, P.
What happened to Serenity? Collins, P. J. S.
What I saw and how I lied. Blundell, J.
What Janie found. Cooney, C. B.
What my girlfriend doesn't know. Sones, S.
What my mother doesn't know. Sones, S.
What she left behind. Bilen, T.
What the birds see. Hartnett, S.
What the moon saw. Resau, L.
What they always tell us. Wilson, M.
What world is left. Polak, M.
Whatever happened to Janie? Cooney, C. B.
What's left of me. Zhang, K.
Whelan, Gloria
After the train
All my noble dreams and then what happens
Burying the sun
Chu Ju's house
The Disappeared
Homeless bird
Listening for lions
See what I see
Small acts of amazing courage
When darkness falls. Lackey, M.
When the emperor was divine. Otsuka, J
When I was Joe. David, K.
When I was the greatest.
When Kambia Elaine flew in from Neptune. Williams, L. A.
When love comes to town. Lennon, T
When Molly was a Harvey Girl. Wood, F.
When the black girl sings. Wright, B.
When the stars threw down their spears. Hamilton, K
When the whistle blows. Slayton, F. C
When we wake. Healey, K
When we wuz famous. Takoudes, G
When you were here. Whitney, D
When you wish. Harmel, K.
Where I belong. Cross, G
Where I want to be. Griffin, A
Where she went. Forman, G
Where the truth lies. Warman, J
Where things come back. Whaley, J. C
Wherever Nina lies. Weingarten, L
While he was away. Schreck, K
While I live. Marsden, J
While we run. Healey, K.
Whipple, Natalie
House of ivy and sorrow
The **whirlwind**. Matas, C.
Whitaker, Alecia
The queen of Kentucky
Whitcomb, Laura
A certain slant of light
The Fetch
White, Amy Brecount
Forget -her-nots
Window boy
Windows on the world
The **white** cat. Black, H.
White crow. Sedgwick, M.
The **white** darkness. McCaughrean, G.
White girl. Olsen, S.
White heat. Grant, K. M.
The **white** horse trick. Thompson, K.
White, Andrea
Surviving Antarctica
White, Ellen Emerson
Long may she reign
The President's daughter
White, Kiersten
Paranormalcy

Perfect lies
Supernaturally
White, Ruth
A month of Sundays
Memories of Summer
White Fang. London, J.
Whiteout. Sorrells, W.
WHITE-WATER CANOEING -- FICTION
Hobbs, W. Downriver
Whitley, David
The children of the lost
Midnight charter
Whitman, Emily
Wildwing
Whitman, Sylvia
The milk of birds
Whitney, Daisy
The Mockingbirds
The rivals
When you were here
Whitney, Kim Ablon
The other half of life
The perfect distance
Whittenberg, Allison
Life is fine
Sweet Thang
Who done it? Scieszka, J.
Who will tell my brother? Carvell, M.
The **whole** stupid way we are. Griffin, N.
Why I fight. Oaks, J. A.
Why we broke up. Handler, D.
Whyman, Matt
Goldstrike
Icecore
The **wicked** and the just. Coats, J. A.
Wicked girls. Hemphill, S.
Wicked lovely. Marr, M.
WIDOWS -- FICTION
Sheth, K. Keeping corner
WIFE ABUSE -- FICTION
Boll, R. The second trial.
Hoffman, N. K. A stir of bones
Wiggins, Bethany
Stung
Wignall, K. J.
Blood
The **wild.** Golden, C. Fi
Wild awake. Smith, H. T.
The **wild** man. Barratt, M.
WILD DOGS -- FICTION
De Lint, C. Dingo
Wild geese. Pignat, C.
Wild, K.
Fight game
Wild Man Island. Hobbs, W.
Wildcat fireflies. Kizer, A.
WILDERNESS AREAS -- FICTION
De Gramont, N. Every little thing in the world
McDonald, A. Boys, bears, and a serious pair of hiking boots
Morel, A. Survive
Nelson, J. On the volcano
Wilderness. Doyle, R.
WILDERNESS SURVIVAL -- FICTION
Bodeen, S. A. The raft
Hobbs, W. Wild Man Island
Mason, P. Camel rider
Mazer, H. Snow bound
Mikaelsen, B. Touching Spirit Bear
Morel, A. Survive
Weaver, W. The survivors
WILDLIFE CONSERVATION -- FICTION
Gilmore, K. The exchange student
Schrefer, E. Endangered
WILDLIFE RESCUE -- FICTION
Schrefer, E. Endangered
Schrefer, E. Threatened
Wildwing. Whitman, E.
Wildwood dancing. Marillier, J.
Wildwood. Meloy, C.
Wilhelm, Doug
Falling
Wilkins, Ebony Joy
Sellout
Wilkinson, Lili
Pink
Wilks, Mike
Mirrorscape
Will. Boyd, M.
Will Grayson, Will Grayson. Green, J.
The **will** of the empress. Pierce, T.
Willey, Margaret
Beetle boy
A summer of silk moths
Williams, Alex
The deep freeze of Bartholomew Tullock
Williams, Carol Lynch
The chosen one
Glimpse
Miles from ordinary
Waiting
Williams, Gabrielle
Beatle meets Destiny
Williams, Kathryn
Pizza, love, and other stuff that made me famous
Williams, Katie
Absent
The space between trees
Williams, Laura E.
Slant
Williams, Lori Aurelia

When Kambia Elaine flew in from Neptune
Williams, Michael
Now is the time for running
Williams, Sarah DeFord
Palace beautiful
Williams, Sean
Twinmaker
Williams, Susan
Wind rider
Williams, Suzanne
Bull rider
Williams-Garcia, Rita
Jumped
Like sisters on the homefront
No laughter here
Williamson, Jill
Captives
To darkness fled
By darkness hid
Willis, Cynthia Chapman
Buck fever
Willow. Hoban, J.
Willowood. Galante, C.
WILLS -- FICTION
Wilson, N. H. Mountain pose
Wilson, Diane L.
Firehorse
Black storm comin'
Wilson, Jacqueline
Kiss
Wilson, John
The alchemist's dream
Ghost moon
And in the morning
Victorio's war
Written in blood
Wilson, Martin
What they always tell us
Wilson, N. D.
The dragon's tooth
Wilson, Nancy Hope
Mountain pose
Wind rider. Williams, S.
Window boy. White, A. B.
Windows on the world. White, A. B.
The **winds** of heaven. Clarke, J.
Windsor, Edward, Duke of, 1894-1972
About
Whelan, G. All my noble dreams and then what happens
Winger. Smith, A.
Wings. Pike, A.
Winston, Sherri
The Kayla chronicles
WINTER -- FICTION
Crockett, S. D. After the snow
The **winter** road. Hokenson, T.
Winter shadows. Buffie, M.
Winter town. Emond, S.
Winter's end. Mourlevat
Wintergirls. Anderson, J. D.
Winters, Cat
In the shadow of blackbirds
Wired. Wasserman, R.
WISCONSIN -- FICTION
Bauer, J. Hope was here
Bick, I. J. Draw the dark
Bick, I. J. The Sin eater's confession
Farrey, B. With or without you
Fink, M. The summer I got a life
Hijuelos, O. Dark Dude
Miller-Lachmann, L. Gringolandia
Sutton, K. Some quiet place
Wisdom's kiss. Murdock, C. G.
Wise Young Fool. Beaudoin, S.
Wise, Tama
Street dreams
Wiseman, Eva
Puppet
Wiseman, Rosalind
Boys, girls, and other hazardous materials
Wish. Monninger, J.
Wish. Bullen, A.
Wish you were dead. Strasser, T.
WISHES -- FICTION
Archer, E. Geek: fantasy novel
Bullen, A. Wish
Monninger, J. Wish
Pearce, J. As you wish
Wishing moon. Tunnell, M. O.
Wisler, G. Clifton
Caleb's choice
WITCHCRAFT -- FICTION
Bow, E. Plain Kate
Horowitz, A. Raven's gate
Okorafor, N. Akata witch
O'Neal, E. The false princess
Reese, J. The strange case of Doctor Jekyll and Mademoiselle Odile
Tracey, S. Moonset
Vande Velde, V. Magic can be murder
WITCHES -- FICTION
Coakley, L. Witchlanders
Croggon, A. Black spring
Flinn, A. A kiss in time
Gray, C. Spellcaster
Green, S. Half bad
MacCullough, C. Always a witch
McGowan, K. The witch's guide to cooking with children
Powell, L. Burn mark
Tracey, S. Darkbound

Witchlanders. Coakley, L.
The **witch's** guide to cooking with children. McGowan, K.
With or without you. Farrey, B.
Wither. DeStefano, L.
Withering tights. Rennison, L.
Withers, Pam
First descent
Without Tess. Pixley, M.
Without warning. Hamley, D.
WITNESS PROTECTION PROGRAMS -- FICTION
Elston, A. The rules for disappearing
Giles, L. Fake ID
WITNESSES -- FICTION
Elston, A. The rules for disappearing
Giles, L. Fake ID
Shoemaker, T. Code of silence
Wittlinger, Ellen
Hard love
Love & lies
Parrotfish
Sandpiper
Zigzag
The **wizard** heir. Chima, C. W.
A **wizard** of Earthsea. Le Guin, U. K.
WIZARDS -- FICTION
Chima, C. W. The enchanter heir
Wizner, Jake
Spanking Shakespeare
The **wolf.** Herrick, S.
Wolf, Allan
New found land; Lewis and Clark's voyage of discovery
The watch that ends the night
Zane's trace
Wolf, Jennifer Shaw
Breaking beautiful
Wolf mark. Bruchac, J.
Wolff, Tobias
Old school
Wolff, Virginia Euwer
Make lemonade
Probably still Nick Swansen
This full house
True believer
Wolfson, Jill
Cold hands, warm heart
Furious
Wolitzer, Meg
Belzhar
Wollman, Jessica
Switched
WOLVES -- FICTION
Chandler, K. Wolves, boys, & other things that might kill me
Clement-Davies, D. Fell
Clement-Davies, D. The sight
Golden, C. The wild
McNicoll, S. Last chance for Paris
Weston, R. P. Dust city
Wolves, boys, & other things that might kill me. Chandler, K.
WOMEN -- INDIA -- FICTION
Whelan, G. Homeless bird
WOMEN -- IRELAND -- FICTION
Doyle, R. A greyhound of a girl
WOMEN -- SOCIAL CONDITIONS
Frost, H. Crossing stones
WOMEN AIR PILOTS -- FICTION
MacColl, M. Promise the night
Wein, E. Code name Verity
WOMEN DETECTIVES -- FICTION
Hahn, M. D. The girl is trouble
WOMEN ART STUDENTS -- FICTION
Hand, E. Radiant days
WOMEN ARTISTS -- FICTION
Hand, E. Radiant days
Strauss, V. Passion blue
WOMEN JOURNALISTS -- FICTION
Doktorski, J. S. Famous last words
WOMEN PHOTOGRAPHERS -- FICTION
Kirkpatrick, J. A flickering light
WOMEN PHYSICIANS -- FICTION
Lessing, D. M. The sweetest dream
Obreht, T. The tiger's wife
WOMEN POETS--FICTION
MacColl, M. Nobody's secret
WOMEN STORYTELLERS -- FICTION
Frost, G. Lord Tophet
WOMEN'S RIGHTS -- FICTION
Feldman, R. T. Blue thread
Wonder show. Barnaby, H.
Wonderland. Nadin, J.
Wood, Frances
When Molly was a Harvey Girl
Wood, Maggie L.
Captured
The darkening
Wood, Maryrose
The poison diaries
My life the musical
WOOD CARVING -- FICTION
Bow, E. Plain Kate
Wooding, Chris
The haunting of Alaizabel Cray
Havoc
Malice
Poison
Silver
The storm thief
Woods, Brenda

A star on the Hollywood Walk of Fame
Emako Blue
Woods, Elizabeth Emma
Choker
Woods, Ron
The hero
Woodson, Jacqueline
After Tupac and D Foster
Behind you
Beneath a meth moon
If you come softly
Lena
Miracle's boys
From the notebooks of Melanin Sun
Woodworth, Chris
Double -click for trouble
Woolston, Blythe
Black helicopters
Catch & release
The Freak Observer
Woon, Yvonne
Dead beautiful
Life eternal
WORK -- FICTION
Buzo, L. Love and other perishable items
Workman, Ross
(jt. auth) Myers, W. D. Kick
A **world** away. Grossman, N.
The **world** is mine. LeFlore, L.
Words in the dust. Reedy, T.
WORLD WAR, 1914-1918 -- FICTION
Cary, K. Bloodline
Cary, K. Bloodline: reckoning
Frost, H. Crossing stones
Larson, K. Hattie Big Sky
Miller, S. The lost crown
Morpurgo, M. Private Peaceful
O'Brien, J. Day of the assassins
Schröder, M. My brother's shadow
Spillebeen, G. Age 14
Spillebeen, G. Kipling's choice
Wilson, J. And in the morning
Winters, C. In the shadow of blackbirds
WORLD WAR, 1939-1945 -- CAMPAIGNS -- FRANCE -- NORMANDY -- FICTION
Myers, W. D. Invasion!
WORLD WAR, 1939-1945 -- CAMPAIGNS -- SOVIET UNION
Wulffson, D. L. Soldier X
WORLD WAR, 1939-1945 -- ENGLAND -- FICTION
Cooper, M. The FitzOsbornes at war
WORLD WAR, 1939-1945 -- FICTION
Bruchac, J. Code talker
Chan, G. A foreign field
Chapman, F. S. Is it night or day?
Cooper, M. The FitzOsbornes at war
Hamley, D. Without warning
Mah, A. Y. Chinese Cinderella and the Secret Dragon Society
Matas, C. The whirlwind
Morpurgo, M. An elephant in the garden
Newbery, L. At the firefly gate
Parkinson, C. Domenic's war; a story of the Battle of Monte Cassino
Patneaude, D. Thin wood walls
Patt, B. Best friends forever; a World War II scrapbook
Pausewang, G. Dark hours
Preus, M. Shadow on the mountain
Sax, A. The war within these walls
Uchida, Y. Journey to Topaz; a story of the Japanese-American evacuation
Waters, Z. C. Blood moon rider
Watkins, Y. K. My brother, my sister, and I
Watkins, Y. K. So far from the bamboo grove
Wein, E. Rose under fire
Whelan, G. Burying the sun
Wulffson, D. L. Soldier X
Zusak, M. The book thief
WORLD WAR, 1939-1945 -- FRANCE -- FICTION
Macdonald, M. Odette's secrets
WORLD WAR, 1939-1945 -- JEWS -- FICTION
Upjohn, R. The secret of the village fool
WORLD WAR, 1939-1945 -- NETHERLANDS -- FICTION
Polak, M. What world is left
WORLD WAR, 1939-1945 -- PARTICIPATION, AFRICAN AMERICAN -- FICTION
Myers, W. D. Invasion!
WORLD WAR, 1939-1945 -- PRISONERS AND PRISONS -- FICTION
Ballard, J. G. Empire of the Sun
WORLD WAR, 1939-1945 -- PRISONERS AND PRISONS, GERMAN -- FICTION
Wein, E. Rose under fire
WORLD WAR, 1939-1945 -- UNDERGROUND MOVEMENTS -- NORWAY -- FICTION
Preus, M. Shadow on the mountain
WORLD WAR, 1939-1945 -- UNITED STATES -- FICTION
Fitzmaurice, K. A diamond in the desert
Worlds apart. Johnson, L. L.
Worldshaker. Harland, R.
WORRY -- FICTION
De Goldi, K. The 10 p.m. question
Would you. Jocelyn, M.
The **wrap-up** list. Arntson, S.
WOUNDS AND INJURIES -- FICTION
Williams, S. Bull rider
Wrapped. Bradbury, J.

Wrecked. **Frank, E. R.**
Wrede, Patricia C. , 1953-
Across the Great Barrier
The Far West
Sorcery and Cecelia, or, The enchanted chocolate pot
The thirteenth child
WRESTLING -- FICTION
Villareal, R. Body slammed!
Wrestling Sturbridge. Wallace, R.
Wright, Barbara
Crow
Wright, Bil
Putting makeup on the fat boy
When the black girl sings
Wright, Denis
Violence 101
A **wrinkle** in time. L'Engle, M.
Written in blood. Wilson, J.
Wulffson, Don L.
Soldier X
Wunder, Wendy
The museum of intangible things
The probability of miracles
Wyatt, Melissa
Funny how things change
Wylie, Sarah
All these lives
Wynne-Jones, Tim
Blink & Caution
The uninvited

X

X-Isle. Auch, M.J.
X-Isle. Augarde, S.
The Xanth series
Anthony, P. Jumper cable
Xenocide. Card, O. S.

Y

YACHTS -- FICTION
Lake, N. Hostage Three
Yancey, Richard
The curse of the Wendigo
The extraordinary adventures of Alfred Kropp
The monstrumologist
Yancey, Rick
The 5th Wave
The final descent
Yang, Dori Jones
Daughter of Xanadu
Warp speed
Yansky, Brian
Alien invasion and other inconveniences
Homicidal aliens and other disappointments
Yaqui Delgado wants to kick your ass. Medina, M.
The **year** my sister got lucky. Friedman, A.
The **year** of ice. Malloy, B.
The **year** of my miraculous reappearance. Hyde, C. R.
The **year** of secret assignments. Moriarty, J.
The **year** we were famous. Dagg, C. E.
The **year** Nick McGowan came to stay. Sparrow, R.
Year of impossible goodbyes. Choi, S. N.
Year of the tiger. Lloyd, A.
The **yearling**. Rawlings, M. K.
Yee, Lisa
Absolutely Maybe
Yee, Paul
Learning to fly
YELLOW FEVER -- FICTION
Anderson, L. H. Fever, 1793
YELLOWSTONE NATIONAL PARK -- FICTION
Chandler, K. Wolves, boys, & other things that might kill me
Yeomans, Ellen
Rubber houses
Yep, Laurence
Dragon road; Golden Mountain chronicles: 1939
Dragon's gate; Golden Mountain chronicles: 1867
Dragons of silk
Dragonwings; Golden Mountain chronicles: 1903
The traitor; Golden Mountain chronicles, 1885
Yes! we are Latinos. Ada, A. F.
Yesterday. Martin, C. K. K.
Yesterday's magic. Service, P. F.
Yolen, Jane
Curse of the Thirteenth Fey
Dragon's blood
Girl in a cage
Pay the piper
The Rogues
Troll Bridge; a rock 'n' roll fairy tale
Yoo, Paula
Good enough
YORKSHIRE (ENGLAND) -- FICTION
Rennison, L. The taming of the tights
You. Benoit, C.
You & you & you. Nilsson, P.
You against me. Downham, J.
You are my only. Kephart, B.
You don't know about me. Meehl, B.
You don't know me. Klass, D.
You killed Wesley Payne. Beaudoin, S.
You know where to find me

You know where to find me. Cohn, R.
You look different in real life. Castle, J.
Young, E. L.
STORM : The Infinity Code
The **young** inferno. Agard, J.
YOUNG MEN -- FICTION
Chbosky, S. The perks of being a wallflower
Cross, J. Tempest
Young royals [series]
Meyer, C. Beware
Meyer, C. Duchessina
YOUNG WOMEN -- FICTION
Atkins, C. The file on Angelyn Stark
Cross, S. Kill me softly
Rosenfield, K. Amelia Anne is dead and gone
Young, Moira
Blood red road
Young, Suzanne
A need so beautiful
YOUTH -- FICTION
Shoemaker, T. Code of silence
YOUTH WITH DISABILITIES -- FICTION
Nussbaum, S. Good kings bad kings
Yovanoff, Brenna
The replacement
YUKON RIVER VALLEY (YUKON AND ALASKA) -- FICTION
Golden, C. The wild

Z

Z for Zachariah. O'Brien, R. C.
Z. Ford, M. T.
Z. Raptor. Cole, S.
Z. Rex. Cole, S.
Zadoff, Allen
Boy Nobody
Food, girls, and other things I can't have
My life, the theater, and other tragedies
Zail, Suzy
Playing for the commandant
Zailckas, Koren
Mother, mother
Zalben, Jane Breskin
Four seasons
Zane's trace. Wolf, A.
Zarr, Sara
How to save a life
The Lucy variations
Once was lost
Roomies
Story of a girl
Sweethearts
Zeises, Lara M.
The sweet life of Stella Madison
Zeitlin, Meredith
Freshman year & other unnatural disasters
Zemser, Amy Bronwen
Dear Julia
Zen and the art of faking it. Sonnenblick, J.
Zen & Xander undone. Ryan, A. K.
Zenith. Bertagna, J.
Zero fade. Terry, C. L.
Zenatti, Valerie
A bottle in the Gaza Sea
Zephaniah, Benjamin
Face
Zettel, Sarah
Dust girl
Golden girl
Magic
Palace of Spies
Zevin, Gabrielle
All these things I've done
Because it is my blood
Elsewhere
Memoirs of a teenage amnesiac
Zhang, Kat
Once we were
What's left of me
Ziegler, Jennifer
How not to be popular
Zielin, Lara
Donut days
Zigzag. Wittlinger, E.
ZIMBABWE -- FICTION
Farmer, N. The Ear, the Eye, and the Arm
Wallace, J. Out of shadows
Williams, M. Now is the time for running
Zimmer, Tracie Vaughn
Reaching for sun
Zindel, Paul
The Pigman
ZINES -- FICTION
Prinz, Y. The Vinyl Princess
Zink, Michelle
Guardian of the Gate
Prophecy of the sisters
Zinn, Bridget
Poison
Zipped. McNeal, L.
ZODIAC -- FICTION
Tubb, K. O. The 13th sign
Zoe letting go. Price, N.
Zombie haiku. Mecum, R.
Zombie queen of Newbury High. Ashby, A.
ZOMBIES -- FICTION
Dennard, S. Something strange and deadly
Martin, T. M. The end games
Mecum, R. Zombie haiku
Perez, M. Dead is a battlefield
Summers, C. This is not a test
ZOMBIES -- FICTION

Mecum, R. Zombie haiku
ZOOLOGISTS -- FICTION
Lawson, M. Crow Lake
ZOOS -- FICTION
Castellucci, C. The queen of cool
Hamilton, K. When the stars threw down their spears
Morpurgo, M. An elephant in the garden
ZOROASTRIANISM -- FICTION
Fletcher, S. Alphabet of dreams
Zuckerman, Linda
A taste for rabbit
Zulkey, Claire
An off year
ZULUS (AFRICAN PEOPLE) -- FICTION
Paton, A. Cry, the beloved country
Zusak, Markus
Zusak, M. The book thief
I am the messenger
The book thief
Zweig, Eric
Bad Island
Cornered
Fever season